中国向西开放的桥头堡

阿拉山口口岸

阿拉山口口岸党委书记、综合保税区第一副主任　赵德智

阿拉山口口岸党委副书记、管委会主任、综合保税区副主任　居来提·阿不都克里木

阿拉山口口岸位于博州东北角，东邻塔城地区托里县，南依艾比湖，西接州府博乐市，北与哈萨克斯坦共和国毗邻，海拔在190–340米之间，平均宽约20公里，由西北向东南倾斜，是我国西北地区最宽、最平坦的口岸，距哈国多斯特克口岸12公里，距博乐市79公里，距乌鲁木齐市477公里(铁路)，是第二条亚欧大陆桥国内段的西桥头堡。口岸行政管理区面积155平方公里，设市规划面积1204平方公里，第二轮修编规划建设面积42.5平方公里，建成区面积12平方公里。辖区常住人口3万余人。目前，阿拉山口口岸已发展成为我国唯一的铁路、公路、管道三种运输方式为一体的国家一类陆路口岸，成为向西开放的陆桥经济带和国际贸易大通道的最前沿，成为国家进口能源资源的陆路安全大通道。

优良的通关环境，使阿拉山口自1991年通关以来(当年过货15.8万吨)，口岸过货量以年均25%的速度增长。2011年，完成进出口货运量2631万吨、对外贸易进出口总额173.93亿美元、海关税收141.58亿元，分别同比增长4.23%、90.52%和36.6%。目前，口岸已累计实现过货1.82亿吨，完成进出口贸易额756亿美元，上缴海关税收618亿元。

经过20多年的建设和发展，口岸基础设施日臻完善，城市功能逐步齐全，各项社会事业健康发展，口岸管理和检验机构健全，社会服务机构、设施完备，投资环境不断得到改善，呈现出人口聚集、工贸兴旺的景象，一座具有现代化品味的边境口岸城市正在快速崛起。

铁路站场

清洁能源

风口第一哨

世界石油城克拉玛依

全国文明城市

克石化500万吨原油装置

东湖公园规划图

克拉玛依市地处新疆准噶尔盆地西北缘，1958年批准建市，现为新疆维吾尔自治区设区的地级市，下辖克拉玛依、独山子、白碱滩、乌尔禾四个行政区，总面积7733平方公里，居住着汉、维吾尔、哈萨克等38个民族，人口40余万人。

建市50多年来，在石油工业快速发展的有力推动下，克拉玛依市的经济和社会各项事业得到了长足的发展，城市综合实力显著提升，城市面貌发生了翻天覆地的变化，已成为一座以石油石化工业为主、经济快速发展、城市功能完善、显示着蓬勃生命力的现代化新型石油城市。2011年，全市实现地区生产总值800亿元，地方财政收入57亿元，经济总量继续位居自治区各地州市前列。随着经济的快速发展，人民生活水平有了较大提高，2011年，城镇居民人均可支配收入19768元，年末城镇居民储蓄余额214.3亿元。今天的克拉玛依，已初步进入小康社会。2011年12月20日，克拉玛依市喜获“全国文明城市”荣誉称号。

克拉玛依拥有丰富的油气资源和雄厚的工业基础，具备广阔的发展前景。预计到2015年前后，克拉玛依油田将年产油气当量2000万吨，实现由大油田向大油气田转变的历史性跨越，并初步建成智能化油田。面对国家支持新疆跨越式发展和长治久安的历史机遇，克拉玛依市确定了打造“世界石油城”的奋斗目标。依托克拉玛依雄厚的工业基础优势、石油技术人才聚集优势、位于中亚油气富集区中心的区位优势和“克拉玛依”的城市品牌优势，着力建设油气生产、炼油化工、技术服务、机械制造、石油储备、工程教育六大基地，加快发展金融、信息、旅游三大新兴产业，努力打造一流的教育、一流的医疗服务、一流的城市管理、发达的通讯网络、秀美宜居的环境，把克拉玛依建成高品质的城市和最安全的城市，实现由“单一资源型城市”逐步向“综合型城市”迈进，由“工业型经济”逐步向“服务型经济”迈进，从而推动克拉玛依的城市转型和可持续发展。

新疆维吾尔自治区统计局·编
Compiled by Statistics Bureau of Xinjiang Uygur Autonomous Region

2012

新疆统计年鉴

XINJIANG STATISTICAL YEARBOOK

中国统计出版社
China Statistics Press

图书在版编目(CIP)数据

新疆统计年鉴. 2012 : 汉英对照 / 新疆维吾尔自治区统计局编. -- 北京 : 中国统计出版社, 2012.9
ISBN 978-7-5037-6687-9

Ⅰ. ①新... Ⅱ. ①新... Ⅲ. ①统计资料－新疆－2012－年鉴－汉、英 Ⅳ. ①C832.45-54

中国版本图书馆CIP数据核字(2012)第211683号

新疆统计年鉴—2012

作　　者/新疆维吾尔自治区统计局
责任编辑/佘竞雄　王立群
执行编辑/仲　玲
封面设计/王红刚
出版发行/中国统计出版社
通信地址/北京市西城区月坛南街75号　邮政编码/100826
办公地址/北京市丰台区西三环南路甲6号　邮政编码/100073
电　　话/邮购（010）63376909　书店（010）68783171
网　　址/http://csp.stats.gov.cn
印　　刷/新疆统计印刷厂
经　　销/新华书店
开　　本/890mm×1240mm　1/16
字　　数/1900 千字
印　　张/50.5
版　　别/2012年9月第1版
版　　次/2012年9月第1次印刷
定　　价/460.00元（含光盘）

本书附同版本CD-ROM一张，光盘内容以书面文字为准。
如有印装差错，由本社发行部调换。

《新疆统计年鉴——2012》编辑委员会

XINJIANG STATISTICAL YEARBOOK-2012

NAME LIST OF EDITORIAL BOARD

编者说明

一、《新疆统计年鉴—2012》，是一部全面反映新疆维吾尔自治区经济和社会发展情况的资料性年刊，本书收录了全区和各地、县（市）2011 年以及重要历史年份的经济和社会各方面大量的统计数据，并收录了全国及各省市区 2011 年的主要统计数据。

二、全书内容分为：特载（新疆维吾尔自治区 2011 年国民经济和社会发展统计公报）；综合；国民经济核算；人口与就业；固定资产投资；对外经济贸易和旅游；能源生产和消费；财政、金融和保险；物价指数；人民生活和社会保障；城市概况；自然资源和环境保护；农业；工业；建筑业；运输和邮电；批发和零售、住宿和餐饮业；教育、科技和文化；体育、卫生及其他；各地、州、市主要经济指标排序；附录（各省、市、区主要经济指标排序）等，各篇前有简要说明，篇末附有《主要统计指标解释》。

三、本年鉴的资料来源，大部分来自年度报表，部分来自抽样调查资料。

四、资料中所使用的度量衡单位均采用国家法定计量单位。

五、本《年鉴》总量指标计算所采用的价格均为现行价格。

六、本《年鉴》伊犁哈萨克自治州的数据包括伊犁州直属县（市）、塔城地区和阿勒泰地区。

七、本《年鉴》使用符号说明：“#”表示其中项；“…”表示不足小数位的数据；“空”表示没有或未掌握该指标数据。

八、本《年鉴》在编辑过程中得到自治区内外许多单位和同志们的大力支持，在此深表谢意。限于我们的水平，加之时间仓促，不足之处，敬请各级领导、各界人士和统计战线的同仁批评指正。

Editor's Explanatory Notes

Ⅰ.Xinjiang Statistical Yearbook-2012 is an annual statistic publication of comprehensive information with highly density. The yearbook covers very comprehensive data in 2011 and some selected data series in important years and the data since reform and opening of Xinjiang, reflects various aspects of Xinjiang's social and economic development and included the whole nation and provinces 2011 main statistical data.

Ⅱ.The yearbook comprises such sections as: Special Article (Statistical Communique on National Economy and Social Development of Xinjiang Uygur Autonomous Region in the year 2011); general survey; national accounts; population and employment; investment in fixed assets; government finance, financial intermediation and insurance; price indices; people's livelihood and social security; general survey of cities; natural resources and environment protection; agriculture; industry; construction; transport, post and telecommunication services; wholesale & retail trades, hotels and catering services; production and consumption of energy; foreign trade & economic cooperation and tourism; education, science & technology and culture; sports, public health and others; ranking of main economic indicators by region of Xinjiang; appendix (ranking of main economic indicators by region),etc. Each section is equipped with Explanatory Notes on Main Statistical Indicators at the end.

Ⅲ. The Yearbook of sources are mostly from the annual financial statements, in part from the sample survey data.

Ⅳ.The units of measurement used in this yearbook are internationally standard measurement units.

Ⅴ.The computation of all the indicators in the yearbook is equipped with current prices.

Ⅵ.The data about Ili Kazak Autonomous Prefecture in the present Xinjiang Statistical Yearbook covers counties (cities) direct under Ili Prefecture, Tacheng Prefecture and Altay Prefecture.

Ⅶ.Description of signs or symbols in the yearbook:

"#"stands for interim item; "…" for data with insufficient decimal place; "blank" for absence of data indicators or ignorance of them.

Ⅷ.In the course of complication, the yearbook has received great support from many units and comrades in and out of Autonomous Region, we acknowledge their help to the book. Mistakes and faults are inevitable to take place for inadequate proficiency and limited time. Leaders, personnel from all walks of life and colleagues from statistical sector are welcome to make their critical comments and suggestions.

目 录 CONTENTS

第一篇 综 合

CHAPTER 1 GENERAL SURVEY

1-1 行政区划 3
Divisions of Administrative Areas in Xinjiang Uygur Autonomous Region
1-2 县级以上行政区划 4
Divisions of Administrative Areas at and above County Level
1-3 主要年份平均每天主要社会经济活动 5
Selected Indicators on Average Daily Social and Economic Activities in Main Years
1-4 主要年份国民经济和社会发展总量与速度指标 6
Principal Aggregate Indicators on National Economic and Social Development and Growth Rates in Main Years
1-5 主要年份国民经济和社会发展结构指标 14
Composition Indicators on National Economic and Social Development in Main Years
1-6 主要年份国民经济和社会发展比例和效益指标 17
Indicators on Proportions and Efficiency in National Economic and Social Development in Main Years
1-7 主要年份人均主要工农业产品产量 20
Per capita Output of Major Industrial and Agricultural Products in Main Years
1-8 主要年份人均国民经济主要指标 21
Per Capita Main Indicators on National Economy in Main Years
1-9 新疆建区以来主要年份国民经济主要指标 22
Main Indicators of National Economic since Xinjing Established in Main Years
1-10 各时期社会经济主要指标 26
Major Social and Economic Indicators of Each Period
1-11 各时期社会经济主要指标平均增长率 27
Growth Rate of Major Social and Economic Indicators of Each Period
1-12 天山北坡经济带主要经济指标 28
Main Economic Indicators for Economic Belt on the Northern Slope of the Tianshan Mountains

1-13 法人单位数和产业活动单位数 36
Number of Legal Entities and Establishment Entities
1-14 按三次产业分的法人单位数及构成 37
Number of Legal Entities by Three Strata of Industry and Its Composition
1-15 按登记注册、机构类型分的法人单位数和产业活动单位数 39
Number of Legal Entities and Establishment Entities by Status of Registration and Institutions
1-16 按行业分的法人单位数和产业活动单位数 40
Number of Legal Entities and Establishment Entities by Sector
1-17 各地区按机构类型分法人单位数 43
Number of Legal Entities by Type of Institutions and Region
1-18 按地区和营业状态分企业法人单位数 44
Number of Business Entities by Region and Operation Status
1-19 各地区非公有制企业法人单位数 45
Number of Business Entities by Region
1-20 服务业法人单位数和从业人员数 46
Number of Services to Legal Entities and Employed Persons
1-21 服务业分行业法人单位数及从业人员数 46
Number of Services to Legal Entities and Employed Persons by Industry
1-22 各地区服务业法人单位数 47
Number of Services to Legal Entities by Region
1-23 企业家信心指数 50
Entrepreneur Confidence Index
1-24 企业景气指数 52
Prosperity Index on Enterprises
主要统计指标解释 54
Explanatory Notes on Main Statistical Indicators

第 二 篇 国民经济核算

CHAPTER 2 NATIONAL ACCOUNTS

2-1 1978-2011 年历年新疆生产总值 61
Gross Domestic Product in Xinjiang(1978-2011)
2-2 1978-2011 年历年新疆生产总值构成 62
Composition of Gross Domestic Product in Xinjiang(1978-2011)
2-3 1978-2011 年历年新疆生产总值指数(上年＝100) 63
Indices of Gross Domestic Product in Xinjiang(1978-2011)(preceding year=100)
2-4 1978-2011 年历年新疆生产总值指数(1978 年＝100) 64
Indices of Gross Domestic Product in Xinjiang(1978-2011)(1978=100)
2-5 分行业新疆生产总值 65
Gross Domestic Product by Sector in Xinjiang

2-6 新疆生产总值项目结构 66
Components of Gross Domestic Product in Xinjiang
2-7 主要年份支出法新疆生产总值 67
Gross Domestic Product by Expenditure Approach in Xinjiang in Main Years
2-8 主要年份资本形成总额及其构成 68
Gross Capital Formation and Its Composition in Main Years
2-9 主要年份最终消费及其构成 69
Final Consumption Expenditure and Its Composition in Main Years
2-10 各地、州、市、县(市)地区生产总值 70
Gross Regional Product by Prefecture, Autonomous Prefecture, City and County
2-11 各地、州、市、县(市)地区生产总值构成 76
Composition of Gross Domestic Product by Prefecture, Autonomous Prefecture, City and County
2-12 各地、州、市、县(市)地区生产总值指数(上年＝100) 82
Indices of Gross Domestic Product by Prefecture, Autonomous Prefecture, City and County(preceding year=100)
2-13 主要年份居民消费水平及指数 88
Household Consumption Expenditure and Its Indices in Main Years
2-14 居民消费支出 89
Household Consumption Expenditure
主要统计指标解释 90
Explanatory Notes on Main Statistical Indicators

第 三 篇 人口与就业

CHAPTER 3 POPULATION AND EMPLOYMENT

3-1 主要年份人口数及构成 95
Population and Its Composition in Main Years
3-2 主要年份人口出生率、死亡率、自然增长率 95
Birth Rate,Death Rate and Natural Growth Rate of Population in Main Years
3-3 新疆人口普查基本情况 96
Basic Statistics on National Population Census in Xinjiang
3-4 主要年份婚姻登记情况 96
Number of Marriages Registry in Main Years
3-5 各地、州、市、县(市)户数、人口数、土地面积 97
Household, Population, Land Area by Prefecture, Autonomous Prefecture,City and County
3-6 各地、州、市、县(市)人口自然变动情况 101
Statistics on Population Natural Changes by Prefecture, Autonomous Prefecture, City and County
3-7 各地、州、市、县(市)分民族人口数 104
Population of Major Major Nationalities by Prefecture,Autonomous Prefecture,City and County
3-8 主要年份分民族人口数 110
Population by Nationality in Main Years
3-9 各地、州、市、县(市)按城镇、乡村和农业、非农业分人口数 111
Population of Urban and Rural, Agriculture and Non-Agriculture by Prefecture,Autonomous Prefecture,City and County

3-10 各地、州、市采取各种避孕措施情况 114
Condition of Adopting Various Contraceptions by Prefecture, Autonomous Prefecture, City and County

3-11 各地、州、市计划生育及领证情况 115
Family Planning and Certificate Receiving by Prefecture, Autonomous Prefecture and City

3-12 主要年份新疆生产建设兵团人口情况 115
Population of Xinjiang Production and Construction Group in Main Years

3-13 按县、市分列的团场户数、人口数 116
Household and Population of Regiment Farms by City and County

3-14 主要年份从业人员(年末数) 119
Number of Employed Person at Year-end

3-15 分行业、分地区从业人员(年末数) 120
Number of Employed Persons at Year-end by Sector and Region

3-16 主要年份城镇登记失业人数及失业率 121
Number of Registered Unemployed Persons in Urban Areas and Unemployment Rate in Main Years

3-17 各地、州、市城镇登记失业率 121
Registered Unemployment Rate in Urban Area by Prefecture, Autonomous Prefecture and City

3-18 各地区按行业分城镇单位就业人员(年末数) 122
Number of Employed Persons in Urban Units at Year-end by Sectors and Region

3-19 各地区年底单位在岗职工人数 123
Number of Staff and Workers at Year-end by Region

3-20 分行业年底单位在岗职工(含劳务派遣工)人数 124
Number of Staff and Workers at Year-end by Sectors(including the dispatched workers)

3-21 各地、州、市分行业年底单位在岗职工(含劳务派遣工)人数 127
Number of Staff and Workers at Year-end by Sector and Prefecture, Autonomous Prefecture and City(including the dispatched workers)

3-22 分行业城镇单位年底女性就业人员 129
Number of Female Employed in Urban Units at Year-end by Sectors

3-23 单位在岗职工工资总额及构成 130
Total Wages of Staff and Workers and Its Composition

3-24 主要年份在岗职工工资总额指数 131
Indices of Total Wages of Staff and Workers in Main Years

3-25 主要年份在岗职工工资情况 131
Wages of Full-Employed Staff and Workers in Main Years

3-26 主要年份在岗职工平均货币工资 132
Average Money Wage of Staff and Workers in Main Years

3-27 主要年份在岗职工平均工资指数 132
Indices of Average Wage of Staff and Workers in Main Years

3-28 各地、州、市分行业单位在岗职工(含劳务派遣工)平均货币工资 133
Average Money Wage of Staff and Workers by Sector and by Prefecture, Autonomous Prefecture and City(including the dispatched workers)

3-29 各地、州、市、县(市)在岗职工(含劳务派遣工)平均货币工资 135
Average Wages of Fully Employed Staff and Workers by Prefecture, Autonomous Prefecture, City and County

主要统计指标解释 138
Explanatory Notes on Main Statistical Indicators

第 四 篇 固定资产投资

CHAPTER 4 INVESTMENT IN FIXED ASSETS

4-1 1978-2011 年历年全社会固定资产投资 143
Total Investment in Fixed Assets in the Whole Country by Period(1978-2011)

4-2 全社会固定资产投资 144
Total Investment in Fixed Assets in the Whole Country

4-3 按构成分全社会固定资产投资 148
Structure of Total Investment in Fixed Assets in the whole Country

4-4 全社会固定资产投资资金来源情况 149
Sources of Funds of Total Investment in Fixed Assets in the Whole Country

4-5 按行业分全社会固定资产投资 150
Total Investment in Fixed Assets in the Whole Country by Sector

4-6 全社会房屋施工面积、竣工面积 153
Floor Space of Buildings under Construction and Completed in Whole Country

4-7 按构成及建设性质分城镇固定资产投资 154
Investment in Fixed Assets in Urban Area by Composition of Funds and Type of Construction

4-8 分行业城镇固定资产投资主要指标 156
Main Indicators of Investment in Fixed Assets in Urban Area by Sector

4-9 分行业城镇固定资产投资资金来源情况 160
Sources of Funds of Investment in Fixed Assets in Urban Area by Sector

4-10 各地、州、市、县(市)城镇固定资产投资和新增固定资产 168
Total Investment and Newly Increased Fixed Assets in Urban Area
by Prefecture, Autonomous Prefecture, City and County

4-11 各地、州、市分行业城镇固定资产投资 172
Investment in Fixed Assets in Urban Area by Sectors in Prefecture, Autonomous Prefecture and City

4-12 城镇固定资产投资效果指标 174
Investment Result of Urban Investment

4-13 主要年份房地产开发企业基本情况 175
Basic Condition of Enterprises for Real Estate Development in Main Years

4-14 主要年份房地产投资主要指标 176
Main Indicators of Real Estate Investment in Main Years

4-15 按用途分房地产开发企业（单位）投资完成额 177
Investment Actually Completed by Enterprises for Real Estate Development by Use

4-16 房地产开发企业（单位）资金来源 179
Sources of Funds of Enterprises for Real Estate Development

4-17 房地产开发企业（单位）施工、销售和待售情况 180
Condition of Under Construction, Sale and Idle of Enterprises for Real Estate Development

4-18 新增主要产品生产能力 183
Newly Increased Production Capacity of Major Products
4-19 农村非农户固定资产投资情况 185
Investment in Fixed Assets of Non-Rural Households in Rural Areas
4-20 农户固定资产投资情况 186
Investment in Fixed Assets of Rural Households in Rural Areas
主要统计指标解释 187
Explanatory Notes on Main Statistical Indicators

第 五 篇 对外经济贸易和旅游

CHAPTER 5 FOREIGN TRADE & ECONOMIC COOPERATION AND TOURISM

5-1 进出口贸易总额 195
Total Value of Imports and Exports
5-2 主要进出口商品数量和金额 196
Main Imports and Exports in Volume and Value
5-3 新疆同各国(地区)海关进出口总额 197
Value of Xinjiang's Imports and Exports by Countries(Region) of Destination
5-4 按贸易方式和登记注册类型分的海关进出口额 201
Total Volue of Imports and Exports by Customs Regime and Registration (Customs Statiatics)
5-5 主要年份人民币对主要外币年平均汇价(中间价) 201
Average Exchange Rate of RMB Yuan Against Main Convertible Currences in Main Years (Medium Rate)
5-6 对外承包工程和劳务合作 202
Contracted Projects in Foreign Countries or Territories
5-7 外商直接投资 202
Direct Foreign Investments
5-8 外国和港澳台地区在华直接投资情况 203
Basic Conditions of Direct Investment in China
by Foreign Countries and Compatriots from Hongkong, Macao and Taiwan
5-9 各地、州、市利用外商直接投资情况 204
Conditions of Foreign Direct Investment Used by Prefecture, Autonomous Prefecture and City
5-10 新疆在外国和港澳台地区直接投资 204
Direct Investment in Foreign Countries and Hong Kong, Macao and Taiwan Made by Xinjiang Partner
5-11 主要年份旅游事业发展情况 205
Development of Tourism in Main Years
5-12 各地、州、市旅行社及旅游宾馆(酒店)基本情况 206
Accommodation of Travel Agencies and Tourist Hotels by Prefecture, Autonomous Prefecture and City
5-13 各地、州、市旅游收入情况 207
Income of Tourism by Prefecture, Autonomous Prefecture and City
5-14 入境旅游收入及构成 208
Foreign Exchange Earnings from International Tourism and Composition
5-15 接待外国旅游人数(按国别分) 208
Number of Foreign Tourists Received by Country

主要统计指标解释 209
Explanatory Notes on Main Statistical Indicators

第 六 篇　能源生产和消费

CHAPTER 6 PRODUCTION AND CONSUMPTION OF ENERGY

6-1 主要年份能源生产总量及构成 213
Total Production of Energy and Its Composition in Main Years
6-2 主要年份能源消费总量及构成 213
Total Consumption of Energy and Its Composition in Main Years
6-3 主要年份综合能源平衡表 214
Overall Energy Balance Sheet in Main Years
6-4 主要年份石油平衡表 215
Petroleum Balance Sheet in Main Years
6-5 主要年份煤炭平衡表 216
Coal Balance Sheet in Main Years
6-6 主要年份电力平衡表 217
Electricity Balance Sheet in Main Years
6-7 分行业能源消费总量和主要能源消费量 218
Consumption of Total Energy and Its Main Varieties by Sector
6-8 主要年份能源生产弹性系数 222
Elasticity Ration of Energy Production in Main Years
6-9 主要年份能源消费弹性系数 222
Elasticity Ration of Energy Consumption in Main Years
6-10 主要年份能源加工转换效率 223
Efficiency of Energy Procession and Conversion in Main Years
6-11 主要年份平均每天各种能源消费量 223
Average Daily Energy Consumption by Type of Energy in Main Years
6-12 主要年份分品种生活能源年消费总量 224
Average Annual Energy Consumption for Household by Variety in Main Years
6-13 主要年份每人年平均生活用能源 224
Annual Per-Capital Energy Consumption of Households in Main Years
6-14 各地、州、市规模以上工业企业能源消费量 225
Energy Consumption of Industry above Designated Size by Prefecture, Autonomous Prefecture and City
主要统计指标解释 227
Explanatory Notes on Main Statistical Indicators

第 七 篇　财政、金融、保险

CHAPTER 7 GOVERNMENT FINANCE, FINANCIAL INTERMEDIATION AND INSURANCE

7-1 主要年份地方财政一般预算收支及增长速度 231
The General Budgetary Revenue & Expenses and Growth Rate of Local Finance in Main Years

7-2 主要年份地方财政一般预算收入占新疆生产总值的比重 231
Ration of the General Budgetary Revenue in Local Finance to GDP of Xinjiang in Main Years

7-3 地方财政收支情况 232
Statistics on Total Government Revenue and Expenditures in Local Finance

7-4 各地、州、市、县(市)地方财政一般预算收支 233
Government Revenue and Expenditures by Prefecture, Autonomous Prefecture, City and County

7-5 1978-2011 年历年金融机构各项存款和各项贷款余额 236
Banlance of Deposits and Loans of National Banking System (1978-2011)

7-6 金融机构和人员数 237
Number of Financial Institutions and Staff

7-7 金融机构人民币信贷资金平衡表 239
Credit Funds Balance Sheet of Financial Institutions by Sources

7-8 各地区金融机构存贷款年底余额 240
Deposits and Loans of Financial Institution by Region

7-9 个人消费贷款情况 240
Basic Conditons of Personal Consumption Loan

7-10 主要年份国内保险业务情况 241
Conditions of Domestic Insurance Service in Main Years

7-11 保险业务经济技术指标 241
Economic and Technical Indicators of Insurance Company

7-12 新疆辖区保险机构 242
Number of Insurance Institutions in Xinjiang

7-13 新疆辖区保险事业发展情况 244
Statistics on Development of Insurance in Xinjiang

7-14 各地区保险业务情况 245
Conditions of Insurance Service by Region

7-15 新疆辖区证券、期货经营机构和人员数 246
Operators and Staff of Securities and Futures in Xinjiang

7-16 上市公司基本情况表 247
Basic Condition of Listed Companies

主要统计指标解释 248
Explanatory Notes on Main Statistical Indicators

第 八 篇 物价指数

CHAPTER 8 PRICE INDICES

8-1 主要年份各种物价指数 251
Price Indices in Main Years

8-2 居民消费价格分类指数 252
Consumer Price Indices by Category

8-3 各市县居民消费价格分类指数 254
Consumer Price Indices by Category in Cities and Counties

8-4 商品零售价格分类指数 258
Retail Price Indices by Category
8-5 各市县商品零售价格分类指数 260
Retail Price Indices by Category in Cities and Counties
8-6 主要年份农业生产资料价格分类指数 264
Price Indices for Means of Agricultural Production by Category in Main Years
8-7 各市县农业生产资料价格指数 264
Price Indices for Means of Agricultural Production in Cities and Counties
8-8 主要年份工业生产者出厂价格分类指数 265
Producer Price Indices for Manufactured Goods by Category in Main Years
8-9 主要年份工业生产者购进价格分类指数 266
Purchasing Prices Indices for Raw Material, Fuels and Power by Category in Main Years
8-10 主要年份固定资产投资价格指数 266
Price Indices for Investment in Fixed Assets in Main Years
主要统计指标解释 267
Explanatory Notes on Main Statistical Indicators

第 九 篇　人民生活和社会保障

CHAPTER 9 PEOPLE'S LIVELIHOOD AND SOCIAL SECURITY

9-1 主要年份人民物质文化生活情况 271
People's Material and Cultural Living Conditions in Main Years
9-2 主要年份城乡居民储蓄存款年底余额和年增加额 273
Savings Deposit of Urban and Rural Households at Year-end in Main Years
9-3 主要年份城乡居民家庭人均收入及指数 273
Per Capita Annual Income of Urban and Rural Households and the Related Index in Main Years
9-4 主要年份城镇居民家庭生活基本情况 274
Basic Living Conditions of Urban Households in Main Years
9-5 城镇居民家庭基本情况 275
Basic Conditions of Urban Households
9-6 城镇居民家庭平均每人全年消费性支出 276
Per Capita Annual Living Expenditure of Urban Households
9-7 城镇居民家庭平均每人全年消费性支出构成 277
Composition of Per Capita Living Expenditure of Urban Households
9-8 主要年份城镇居民家庭年人均购买的主要商品数量 278
Per Capita Annual Purchases of Major Commodities of Urban Households in Main Years
9-9 主要年份城镇居民家庭平均每百户年底耐用消费品拥有量 278
Number of Major Durable Consumer Goods Owned Per-100 Urban Households at Year-end in Main Years
9-10 按收入等级分城镇居民家庭平均每人全年购买商品数量 279
Per Capita Annual Purchases of Major Commodities of Urban Households by Level of Income
9-11 按收入等级分城镇居民家庭平均每百户年底耐用消费品拥有量 281
Ownership of Durable Consumer Goods Per100 Urban Households at Year-end by Level of Income

9-12 按收入等级分城镇居民家庭年末住房情况 282
Living Conditions of Urban Households by level of Income at Year-end
9-13 城镇居民家庭就业情况 284
Employment Conditions of Urban households
9-14 主要年份农村居民家庭基本情况 285
Basic Conditions of Rural Households in Main Years
9-15 农村居民家庭人均年总收入、纯收入和构成 286
Per Capita Annual Gross and Net Income and Its Composition of Rural Households
9-16 主要年份农村居民家庭平均每人总收入和纯收入 286
Per Capita Annual Gross and Net Income of Rural Households in Main Years
9-17 主要年份农村居民家庭人均主要消费品消费量 287
Per Capita Consumption of Major Consumer Goods of Rural Households in Main Years
9-18 主要年份农村居民家庭平均每百户耐用消费品拥有量 287
Number of Durable Consumer Goods Owned by Per100 Rural Households in Main Years
9-19 农村居民人均生活消费支出及构成 288
Composition of Per Capita Living Expendture of Rural Households
9-20 农村居民家庭平均每百户耐用消费品拥有量 288
Number of Durable Consumer Goods Owned by Per100 Rural Households
9-21 农村居民家庭人均商品性和自给性生活消费品支出 289
Per Capita Self-Sufficiency and Consumption on Commodity Goods of Living Expenditure in Rural Households
9-22 分地区农村居民家庭人均总收入和纯收入 290
Per Capita Annual Gross and Net Income of Rural Households by Region
9-23 分地区农村居民家庭平均每人总支出 292
Per Capita Total Expenditure of Rural Household by Region
9-24 分地区农村居民家庭人均现金收支 294
Per Capita Income and Expenditure in Cash of Rural Household by Region
9-25 农村居民家庭人均纯收入分组 298
Rural Households Grouped by Per Capita Annual Net Income
9-26 主要年份农村居民家庭房屋使用情况 299
Housing Conditions of Rural Households in Main Years
9-27 主要年份城乡新建住宅面积和居民住房情况 299
Floor Space of Newly Built Residential Buildings and Housing Conditions of Urban and Rural Residents in Main Years
9-28 分地区农村居民家庭平均每人粮食收支平衡表 300
Per Capita Grain Banlance of Debit and Credit by Region
9-29 主要年份农村居民家庭平均每户饲养畜禽、其他小动物生产情况 301
Output of Livestock, Poultry and Other Small Animals Per Rural Households in Main Years
9-30 主要年份农村居民家庭平均每户饲养畜禽、其他小动物出售量 301
Quantities of Livestock, Poultry and Other Small Animals Sold Per Rural Households in Main Years
9-31 社会保险基本情况 302
Basic Conditions on Social Insurance
9-32 各地、州、市社会保险年末参保人数 303
Number of Social Insured Persons at the Year-end by Prefecture, Autonomous Prefecture and City

主要统计指标解释 305
Explanatory Notes on Main Statistical Indicators

第 十 篇 城市概况

CHAPTER 10 GENERAL SURVEY OF CITIES

10-1 城市公用事业基本情况 311
Basic Statistics on City Public Utilities
10-2 各城市主要经济指标 312
Major Economic Indicators by Cities
10-3 各城市市区设施水平 314
Level of Urban Public Facilities in Cities
10-4 主要年份城市自来水情况 314
Basic Statistics on Tap Water Supply in Cities in Main Years
10-5 主要年份城市市政建设情况 315
Statistics on City Construction in Cities in Main Years
10-6 主要年份城市园林绿化情况 315
Basic Statistics on Parks and Green Areas in Cities in Main Years
10-7 主要年份城市环境卫生情况 315
Basic Statistics on Urban Environment in Cities in Main Years
10-8 主要年份城市煤气、液化石油气、天然气情况 316
Basic Statistics on Supply of Gas, Liquefied Petroleum Gas and Natural Gas in Cities in Main Years
10-9 主要年份城市集中供热情况 316
Basic Statistics on Heating in Cities in Main Years
主要统计指标解释 317
Explanatory Notes on Main Statistical Indicators

第 十一 篇 自然资源和环境保护

CHAPTER 11 NATURAL RESOURCES AND ENVIRONMENT PROTECTION

11-1 自然资源 321
Natural Resources
11-2 主要城市平均气温 323
Monthly Average Temperature of Major Cities
11-3 主要城市降水量 324
Monthly Precipitation of Major Cities
11-4 主要城市日照时数 325
Monthly Sunshine Hours of Major Cities
11-5 环境保护基本情况 326
Basic Statistics on Environmental Protection

11-6 水资源情况 329
Water Resource
11-7 供水和用水情况 330
Water Supply and Water Used
11-8 主要年份环保系统机构、人员数 331
Number of Environmental Protection Agencies and Persons Engaged in Main Years
11-9 工业按行业重点调查工业企业废气及污染物排放情况 331
Emission and Treatment of Waste Water and Pollutant in Industrial Enterprises by Sector
11-10 工业按行业重点调查工业企业废水及污染物排放情况 332
Emission and Treatment of Waste Water and Pollutant in Industrial Enterprises by Sector
11-11 工业按行业重点调查一般工业企业固体废物产生量及处理利用情况 332
Productian and Treatment of Waste Solid in Industrial Enterprises by Region
11-12 环境污染治理投资 333
Investment in the Treatment of Environment Pollution
11-13 主要年份工业污染治理投资完成情况 333
Investment Completed in the Treatment of Industrial Pollution in Main Years
11-14 工业污染治理投资来源 334
Source of Investment in the Treatment of Industrial Pollution
11-15 主要城市空气质量指标 334
Ambient Air Quality in Main Cities
11-16 主要城市道路交通噪声监测情况 335
Monitoring of Urban Road Traffic Noise in Major Cities
11-17 主要城市区域环境噪声监测情况 335
Monitoring of Urban Environment Noise in Major Cities under National Control Programme
11-18 主要年份自然保护区基本情况 336
Basic Situation of Natural Protection in Main Years
11-19 各地区城市生活垃圾清运和处理情况 336
Collection, Transport and Disposal of Consumption Wastes in Cities by Region
11-20 各地区土地利用情况 337
Land Use by Region
11-21 造 林 面 积 338
Area of Afforestation
11-22 林业重点工程造林面积 339
Area of Key Afforestation Projects
11-23 各地区天然湿地面积 340
Area of Wetlands by Region
11-24 森林火灾情况 341
Forest Fires
11-25 森林病虫害防治情况 342
Prevention of Forest Diseases and Pests
11-26 地震灾害情况 343
Earthquake Disasters

11-27 林业系统营林固定资产投资完成情况 345
Completed Investment in Fixed Assets for Afforestation in Forest System
主要统计指标解释 346
Explanatory Notes on Main Statistical Indicators

第十二篇 农 业

CHAPTER 12 AGRICULTURE

12-1 主要年份农村基层组织情况 355
Basic Conditions of Rural Grass-roots Unit in Main Years
12-2 国有农林牧渔场基本情况 355
Basic Conditions of State Agriculture, Forestry, Animal Husbandry and Fishery
12-3 各地、州、市、县(市)农村基层组织情况 356
Basic Conditions of Rural Grass-roots Units by Prefecture, Autonomous Prefecture, City and County
12-4 各地、州、市、县(市)耕地面积 360
Area of Cultivated land by Prefecture, Autonomous Prefecture, City and County
12-5 农、林、牧、渔业总产值 362
Gross Output Value of Agriculture, Forestry, Animal Husbandry and Fishery
12-6 主要年份农、林、牧、渔业总产值指数 363
Indices of Gross Output Value of Agriculture, Forestry, Animal Husbandry and Fishery in Main Years
12-7 各地、州、市、县(市)农林牧渔业总产值 364
Gross Output Value of Agriculture, Forestry, Animal Husbandry and Fishery
by Prefecture, Autonomous Prefecture, City and County
12-8 各地、州、市、县(市)农业机械拥有量 367
Agricultural Machinery by Prefecture, Autonomous Prefecture, City and County
12-9 各地、州、市、县(市)农村电气化和农田水利情况 371
Statistics on Water Conservancy and Electrification in Rural Areas
by Prefecture, Autonomous Prefecture, City and County
12-10 灌溉、水库和除涝、治水情况 375
Irrigation, Reservoirs, Flood Prevention, Water and Soil Conservation
12-11 各地、州、市水利设施和除涝面积 376
Water Conservancy Facilities and Area with Flood Prevention Measures
by Prefecture, Autonomous Prefecture and City
12-12 各地、州、市农村饮水安全情况 376
Basic Statistics on Security of Drinking Water in Rural Area by Prefecture, Autonomous Prefecture and City
12-13 主要年份农作物播种面积 377
Total Sown Areas of Farm Crops in Main Years
12-14 各地、州、市、县(市)农作物播种面积 378
Sown Areas of Farm Crops by Prefecture, Autonomous Prefecture, City and County
12-15 主要年份农作物种植结构 382
Planting Structure of Major Farm Crops in Main Years

12-16 主要年份农作物产品产量 383
Output of Major Farm Crops in Main Years
12-17 各地、州、市、县(市)主要农产品产量 384
Output of Major Farm Crops by Prefecture, Autonomous Prefecture, City and County
12-18 各地、州、市、县(市)农作物单位面积产量 388
Output of Major Farm Products Per Hectare by Prefecture, Autonomous Prefecture, City and County
12-19 各地、州、市、县(市)特色农作物播种面积 390
Soun Areas of Characteristic Farm Crops by Prefecture,Autonomous Prefecture ,City and County
12-20 各地、州、市、县(市)特色农作物产量 393
Output of Characteristic Farm Crops by Prefecture,Autonomous Prefectura,City and County
12-21 各地、州、市林业生产情况 396
Condition on Forest Products by Prefecture, Autonomous Prefecture, City
12-22 各地、州、市水果种植面积 397
Planted Area of Fruits by Prefecture, Autonomous Prefecture, City
12-23 各地、州、市水果产量 398
Output of Fruits by Prefecture, Autonomous Prefecture, City
12-24 主要年份牲畜饲养情况 399
Number of Livestock in Main Years
12-25 各地、州、市、县(市)牲畜年底头数 400
Number of Livestock at the Year-end by Prefecture, Autonomous Prefecture, City and County
12-26 主要年份畜产品产量 402
Output of Livestock Products in Main Years
12-27 各地、州、市、县(市)总产肉量 403
Total Output of Meat by Prefecture, Autonomous Prefecture, City and County
12-28 水产品产量和养殖面积 406
Output of Aquatic Products and Cultured Area
12-29 乡镇企业主要指标 407
Main Indicators of Township Enterprises
主要统计指标解释 409
Explanatory Notes on Main Statistical Indicators

第十三篇 工 业

CHAPTER 13 INDUSTRY

13-1 主要年份工业总产值 415
Gross Industrial Output Value in Main Years
13-2 主要年份工业总产值指数 415
Indices of Gross Industrial Output Value in Main Years
13-3 规模以上工业企业分行业、地区增加值(GB/T4754-2011) 416
Value-added of Industrial Enterprises above Designated Size by Sector and Region (GB/T4754-2011)

13-4 规模以上工业企业分行业、地区增加值(GB/T4754-2002) 418
Value-added of Industrial Enterprises above Designated Size by Sector and Region (GB/T4754-2002)

13-5 规模以上工业企业主要经济指标 420
Main Economic Indicators of Industrial Enterprises above Designated Size

13-6 按行业分规模以上工业企业主要经济指标(GB/T4754-2011) 424
Main Economic Indicators of Industrial Enterprises above Designated Size by Sectors (GB/T4754-2011)

13-7 按行业分规模以上工业企业主要经济指标(GB/T4754-2002) 428
Main Economic Indicators of Industrial Enterprises above Designated Size by Sectors (GB/T4754-2002)

13-8 各地、州、市、县(市)规模以上工业企业主要经济指标 432
Main Economic Indicators of Industrial Enterprises above Designated Size
by Prefecture,Autonomous Prefecture, City and County

13-9 规模以上工业企业主要经济效益指标 444
Main Indicators on Economic Efficiency of Industrial Enterprises above Designated Size

13-10 分行业规模以上工业企业主要经济效益指标(GB/T4754-2011) 446
Main Indicators on Economic Efficiency of Industrial Enterprises above Designated Size
by Sectors(GB/T4754-2011)

13-11 分行业规模以上工业企业主要经济效益指标(GB/T4754-2002) 448
Main Indicators on Economic Efficiency of Industrial Enterprises above Designated Size
by Sectors(GB/T4754-2002)

13-12 各地、州、市、县(市)规模以上工业企业主要经济效益指标 450
Main Indicators on Economic Benefit of Industrial Enterprises above Designated Size
by Prefecture, Autonomous Prefecture, City and County

13-13 国有控股工业企业主要经济指标 456
Main Economic Indicators Efficiency of State-holding Industrial Enterprises

13-14 分行业国有控股工业企业主要经济指标(GB/T4754-2011) 460
Main Economic Indicators of State-holding Industrial Enterprises by Sectors (GB/T4754-2011)

13-15 分行业国有控股工业企业主要经济指标(GB/T4754-2002) 464
Main Economic Indicators of State-holding Industrial Enterprises by Sectors (GB/T4754-2002)

13-16 各地、州、市、县(市)国有控股工业企业主要经济指标 468
Main Economic Indicators of State-holding Industrial Enterprises
by Prefecture, Autonomous Prefecture, City and County

13-17 国有控股工业企业主要经济效益指标 480
Main Indicators on Economic Efficiency of State-holding Industrial Enterprises

13-18 分行业国有控股工业企业主要经济效益指标(GB/T4754-2011) 482
Main Indicators on Economic Efficiency of State-holding Industrial Enterprises by Sectors(GB/T4754-2011)

13-19 分行业国有控股工业企业主要经济效益指标(GB/T4754-2002) 484
Main Indicators on Economic Efficiency of State-holding Industrial Enterprises by Sectors(GB/T4754-2002)

13-20 各地、州、市、县(市)国有控股工业企业主要经济效益指标 486
Main Indicators on Economic Efficiency of State-holding Industrial Enterprises
by Prefecture, Autonomous Prefecture, City and County

13-21 分行业大中型工业企业主要经济指标(GB/T4754-2011) 492
Main Indicators of Large-scale and Medium-scale Industrial Enterprises by Sectors(GB/T4754-2011)

13-22 分行业大中型工业企业主要经济指标(GB/T4754-2002) 496
Main Indicators of Large-scale and Medium-scale Industrial Enterprises by Sectors(GB/T4754-2002)
13-23 分行业大中型工业企业主要经济效益指标(GB/T4754-2011) 500
Main Indicators on Economic Efficiency of Large-scale and Medium-scale Industrial Enterprises by Sectors(GB/T4754-2011)
13-24 分行业大中型工业企业主要经济效益指标(GB/T4754-2002) 502
Main Indicators on Economic Efficiency of Large-scale and Medium-scale Industrial Enterprises by Sectors(GB/T4754-2002)
13-25 主要工业产品产量 504
Output of Major Industrial Products
13-26 各地、州、市主要工业产品产量 508
Output of Major Industrial Products by Prefecture, Autonomous Prefecture and City
13-27 国有控股企业主要指标占全区规模以上工业比重 512
Percentage of Main Indicators in State-holding Enterprises to Enterprises above Designated Size
13-28 重点行业主要指标占全区规模以上工业比重(GB/T4754-2011) 513
Percentage of Main Indicators in Key Industrial Sectors to Xinjiang's Industry above Designated Size(GB/T4754-2011)
13-29 重点行业主要指标占全区规模以上工业比重(GB/T4754-2002) 515
Percentage of Main Indicators in Key Industrial Sectors to Xinjiang's Industry above Designated Size(GB/T4754-2002)
13-30 规模以上工业主要产品生产能力 517
Production Capacity of Major Industrial Products above Designated Size
主要统计指标解释 518
Explanatory Notes on Main Statistical Indicators

第 十四 篇 建筑业

CHAPTER 14 CONSTRUCTION

14-1 建筑企业概况 527
Main Indicators on Construction Enterprises
14-2 按登记注册类型分建筑企业总产值 528
Total Output Value of Construction Enterprises by Registration Status
14-3 按构成分建筑企业总产值 529
Total Output Value of Construction Enterprises by Composition
14-4 按行业和登记注册类型分建筑企业总产值 530
Total Output Value of Construction Enterprises by Registration Status and Sectors
14-5 建筑企业增加值 531
Value-added of Construction Enterprises
14-6 建筑企业利税总额 532
Total Pre-tax Profits of Construction Enterprises
14-7 建筑企业劳动生产率 533
Labor Productivity of Construction Enterprises

14-8 建筑企业技术装备情况 534
Number and Power of Machinery and Equipment Owned by Construction Enterprises
14-9 按登记注册类型分建筑企业技术装备情况 535
Number and Power of Machinery and Equipment Owned by Registration Status
14-10 建筑企业签订合同情况 536
Contracts Signed by Construction Enterprises
14-11 建筑企业承包工程完成情况 537
Completion of Contracted Projects by Construction Enterprises
14-12 建筑企业资产及资本金 538
Assets and Capital Principal of Construction Enterprises
14-13 建筑企业负债及所有者权益 539
Liabilities and Owner's Equity of Construction Enterprises
14-14 建筑企业总收入 540
Total Income of Construction Enterprises
14-15 建筑企业亏损额及从业人数 541
Losses and Employed Persons of Construction Enterprises
14-16 建筑企业工程施工情况 542
Condition of Building Works by Construction Enterprise
14-17 按登记注册类型分建筑企业工程施工情况 543
Condition of Building Works by Construction Enterprise by Registration Status
14-18 按登记注册类型分建筑企业竣工房屋建筑面积 544
Floor Space of Buildings Constructed of Construction Enterprises by Registration Status
主要统计指标解释 546
Explanatory Notes on Main Statistical Indicators

第 十五 篇 运输和邮电

CHAPTER 15 TRANSPORT, POSTAL AND TELECOMMUNICATION SERVICES

15-1 主要年份运输业基本情况 551
Basic Conditions of Transport in Main Years
15-2 主要年份运输线路长度 552
Length of Transport Routes in Main Years
15-3 主要年份运输线路质量 552
Quality of Transport Routes in Main Years
15-4 主要年份客运量及周转量 553
Passenger Traffic and Passenger kilometers in Main Years
15-5 主要年份货运量及货物周转量 554
Freight Traffic and Ton-kilometers in Main Years
15-6 主要年份货物运输平均运距 555
Average Transport Distance of Freight in Main Years

15-7 主要年份铁路运输主要财务指标 555
Main Financial Indicators of Railway Transport in Main Years

15-8 铁路运输技术经济主要指标 556
Main Technical and Economic Indicators of Railway Transport

15-9 民用车辆拥有量 556
Number of Civil Vehicles

15-10 主要年份邮电事业情况 557
Basic Conditions of Postal and Telecommunication Services in Main Years

15-11 主要年份邮电业务情况 558
Conditions of Postal and Telecommunication Services in Main Years

主要统计指标解释 560
Explanatory Notes on Main Statistical Indicators

第 十六 篇　批发和零售业、住宿和餐饮业

CHAPTER 16 WHOLESALE & RETAIL TRADES, HOTELS AND CATERING SERVICES

16-1 主要年份国内贸易基本情况 565
Basic Conditions of Domestic Trade in Main Years

16-2 主要年份社会消费品零售总额 566
Total Retail Sales of Consumer Goods in Main Years

16-3 分类型、分地区限额以上批发和零售业、住宿和餐饮业基本情况 567
Basic Conditions of Enterprises above Designated Size in Wholesale and Retail Trades,
Hotels and Catering Services by Category and Region

16-4 分行业、分地区限额以上批发零售业商品销售额 569
Total Sales Values of Enterprises above Designated Size of Wholesale and Retail Trades by Sector and Region

16-5 限额以上餐饮企业经营情况 572
Operations of Enterprises above Designated Size of Catering Services

16-6 限额以上住宿企业经营情况 573
Operation of Enterprises above Designated Size in Hotels Services

16-7 各地、州、市、县(市)社会消费品零售总额 575
Total Retail Sales of Consumer Goods by Prefecture, Autonomous Prefecture, City and County

16-8 各地、州、市、县(市)社会消费品零售总额(按行业分) 577
Total Retail Sales of Consumer Goods by Sector and Prefecture, Autonomous Prefecture, City and County

16-9 限额以上批发企业资产及负债情况 579
Assets and Liabilities of Enterprises above Designated Size of Wholesale Trades

16-10 限额以上零售企业资产及负债情况 581
Assets and Liabilities of Enterprises above Designated Size of Retail Trades

16-11 限额以上餐饮企业资产及负债情况 583
Assets and Liabilities of Enterprises above Designated Size of Catering Services

16-12 限额以上住宿企业资产及负债情况 584
Assets and Liabilities of Enterprises above Designated Size of Accommodation Services

16-13 限额以上批发企业主要财务指标 585
Main Financial Indicators of Wholesale Enterprises above Designated Size

16-14 限额以上零售企业主要财务指标 587
Main Financial Indicators of Retail Enterprises above Designated Size

16-15 限额以上餐饮企业主要财务指标 589
Main Financial Indicators of Catering Enterprises above Designated Size

16-16 限额以上住宿企业主要财务指标 590
Main Financial Indicators of Hotels Enterprises above Designated

16-17 限额以上批发和零售业商品销售类值 591
Total Sales of Enterprises above Designated Size in Wholesale and Retail Trades by Category of Commodities

16-18 亿元以上商品交易市场总体情况 592
Statistics on Commodity Exchange Markets of Transaction Value over 100 Million Yuan

16-19 商品交易市场成交情况(按摊位分)........ 594
Basic Statistics on Commodity Exchange Markets (by Booths)

16-20 各地区商品交易市场总体情况 595
Basic Statistics on Commodity Exchange Markets by Region

16-21 连锁零售企业总体情况 596
Total Conditions of Chain Retail Enterprises

16-22 连锁零售企业基本情况 597
Basic Condition of Chain Retail Enterprises

16-23 连锁餐饮企业总体情况 602
Total Conditions of Chain Catering Enterprises

16-24 连锁餐饮企业基本情况 603
Basic Condition of Chain Catering Enterprises

主要统计指标解释 605
Explanatory Notes on Main Statistical Indicators

第 十七 篇　教育、科技和文化

CHAPTER 17 EDUCATION, SCIENCE & TECHNOLOGY AND CULTURE

17-1 主要年份各级各类学校数 611
Number of Schools by Level and Type in Main Years

17-2 主要年份各级各类学校教师数 611
Number of Teachers by Level and Type of School in Main Years

17-3 主要年份各级各类学校在校学生数 612
Number of Students Enrollment by Level and Type of School in Main Years

17-4 主要年份各级各类学校招生数 612
Number of New Students Enrollment by Level and Type of School in Main Years

17-5 主要年份各级各类学校毕业生数 613
Number of Graduates by Level and Type of School in Main Years
17-6 主要年份研究生数 614
Number of Postgraduates in Main Years
17-7 高等学校基本情况 614
Basic Statistics on Institutions of Higher Education
17-8 中等专业学校基本情况 615
Basic Statistics on Specialized Secondary Schools
17-9 普通中学和其他学校基本情况 615
Basic Statistics on Regular Secondary Schools and Other Schools
17-10 各类成人教育情况 616
Basic Statistics on Adult Education by Type
17-11 主要年份教育发展水平 616
Development Level of Education in Main Years
17-12 主要年份各级学校教师负担学生数 617
Student-teacher Ratio by Level of School in Main Years
17-13 主要年份各级学校女学生和女教师数 617
Number of Female Students and Teachers by Level of School in Main Years
17-14 主要年份初中毕业生和小学生升学率及小学学龄儿童入学率 618
Percentage of Graduates of Junior Secondary Schools and Primary Schools Entering Higher Level Schools, Enrollment Rate of School-age Children in Main Years
17-15 主要年份各级各类学校少数民族在校学生数 618
Number of Students Enrollment of Minority Nationalities by Level and Type of School in Main Years
17-16 各地、州、市各级各类学校数 619
Number of Schools by Level, Type and by Prefecture, Autonomous Prefecture and City
17-17 各地、州、市各级各类学校教职工数 620
Number of Teachers and Staff by Level and Type of School and by Prefecture, Autonomous Prefecture and City
17-18 各地、州、市各级各类学校教师数 621
Number of Teachers by Level and Type of School and by Prefecture, Autonomous Prefecture and City
17-19 各地、州、市各级各类学校在校学生数 622
Number of Students Enrollment by Level and Type of School and by Prefecture, Autonomous Prefecture and City
17-20 各地、州、市各级各类学校招生数 623
Number of New Students Enrollment by Level and Type of School and by Prefecture, Autonomous Prefecture and City
17-21 各地、州、市各级各类学校毕业生数 624
Number of Graduates by Level and Type of School and by Prefecture, Autonomous Prefecture and City
17-22 各类学校教育经费情况 625
Educational Funds in Various Schools
17-23 科技活动基本情况 626
Basic Statistics on Scientific and Technological Activities

17-24 县级以上政府部门属研究与开发机构及科技信息与文献机构数、人员数 626
State-owned Research and Development Institutions and Information and Literature Institutions at and above County Level and Persons Engaged

17-25 重大科学技术研究成果及奖励数 627
Number of Major Achievements in Scientific and Technological Research and Awarded Prizes

17-26 专利申请和批准数 627
Number of Patent Applications Examined and Approved

17-27 高等学校科技活动情况 628
Basic Statistics on Higher Education for Scientific and Technological Activities

17-28 主要年份企事业单位主要专业技术人员数 629
Number of Main Scientific and Technical Personnel in Enterprises and Institutions in Main Years

17-29 主要年份企事业单位主要专业技术人员比重 629
Proportion of Scientific and Technical Personnel in Enterprises and Institutions in Main Years

17-30 大中型工业企业科技活动情况 630
Statistics on Technical Activities of Large and Medium-sized Industrial Enterprises

17-31 各类技术合同签定及执行情况 634
Statistics on Signing and Implementing Technical Contracts by Type

17-32 各级技术计划项目进入技术市场情况 634
Statistics on Projects for Technical Plan Entering Technical Market by Level

17-33 技术流向地域情况 635
Statistics on Location of Technical Contract

17-34 技术经济合同成交情况 636
Statistics on Transaction in Technical and Economic Contract

17-35 主要年份文化产业基本情况 636
Basic Statistics on Culture in Main Years

17-36 文化艺术、文物事业机构和人员情况 637
Number of Institutions and Personnel in Culture, Art and Cultural Relics

17-37 电影、电视、广播事业基本情况 638
Basic Statistics on Feature Film, Television and Broadcasting

主要统计指标解释 639
Explanatory Notes on Main Statistical Indicators

第十八篇 体育、卫生及其他

CHAPTER 18 SPORTS, PUBLIC HEALTH AND OTHERS

18-1 体育局系统从业人员数 645
Statistics on Staff and Workers in Physical Education System

18-2 按项目分等级裁判员发展人数 646
Number of Referees in Levels by Type of Sports

18-3 按项目分等级运动员发展人数 647
Number of Athletes at Levels by Type of Sports
18-4 各地、州、市体育局系统机构数 648
Number of Institutions in Sports Committees by Prefecture,Autonomous Prefecture and City
18-5 各地、州、市体育局系统机构从业人员数 649
Number of Staff and Workers in Sports Bureau by Region
18-6 卫生机构、床位、人员数 650
Number of Health Institutions, Beds and Persons Engaged by Type of Institutons
18-7 主要年份卫生机构数(不含村卫生室) 654
Number of Health Institutions in Main Years(Excluding Village Clinics)
18-8 主要年份卫生人员数(不含村卫生室) 654
Number of Persons Engaged in Health Institutions in Main Years(Excluding Village Clinics)
18-9 主要年份卫生机构床位数 655
Number of Sick-Beds in Health Institutions in Main Years
18-10 医疗机构病床使用情况 656
Utilization of Beds in Medical Institutions
18-11 各地、州、市卫生机构、床位和人员数 658
Number of Health Institutions, Beds and Personnel by Prefecture, Autonomous Prefecture and City
18-12 各地、州、市卫生技术人员数 660
Number of Medical Technical Personnel by Prefecture, Autonomous Prefecture and City
18-13 医疗机构、诊疗人次及入院出院人数 662
Number of Visits and Inpatients in Medical Institutions
18-14 2000-2011 年历年分市县医院床位和专业卫生技术人员数 663
Hospital Beds and Medical Technical Personnel by City and County Areas(2000-2011)
18-15 2000-2011 年历年分市县卫生院床位和专业卫生技术人员数 663
Hospital Beds and Medical Technical Personnel by City and County Areas(2000-2011)
18-16 社区卫生服务中心（站）工作量 664
Medical Services in Health Service Centers for Community
18-17 乡村卫生室基本情况 664
Basic Conditions of Country Health Room
18-18 新型农牧区合作医疗基本情况 665
Basic Statistics on New Cooperative Health Care in Agricultural and Pastoral Areas
18-19 法定报告传染病发病及死亡情况 666
Confirmed Incidence and Death from Infectious Diseases
18-20 城市前十位疾病死亡原因及构成 667
Death Causes and Percentage of 10 Major Diseases in Urban Areas
18-21 安全生产情况 667
Basic Statistics on Work Safety

18-22 社会福利事业单位基本情况 668
Basic Statistics on Social Welfare Institutions
18-23 社会福利事业、企业单位数和工作人员数 668
Number of Social Welfare Institutions and Enterprises and Persons Engaged
18-24 社会救济情况 669
Basic Statistics on Social Relief Funds
18-25 主要年份工会组织情况 669
Basic Statistics on Trades Unions in Main Years
18-26 残疾人事业基本情况 670
Basic Information of People with Disabilities
18-27 历届全区人民代表大会代表人数 672
Number of Deputies to all the Previous People's Congresses of Xinjiang
18-28 历届全区政治协商会议委员人数 672
Number of Deputies to all the Previous People's Political Consultative Conferences of Xinjiang
18-29 主要年份律师、公证、调解工作基本情况 673
Basic Statistics on Lawyers, Notarization and Mediation in Main Years
18-30 调解民间纠纷分类 674
Number of Civil Disputes Mediated by Type
18-31 火灾事故发生情况 674
Basic Statistics on Fire Accidents
18-32 2009-2011 年历年交通事故发生情况 674
Basic Statistics on Traffic Accidents(2009-2011)
18-33 公安机关受理查处治安案件情况 675
Offense Cases Against Public Order Handled by Public Security Organs
18-34 2007-2011 年历年刑事案件中青少年犯罪情况 675
Juvenile Delinquency Among Criminal Cases(2007-2011)
主要统计指标解释 676
Explanatory Notes on Main Statistical Indicators

第 十九 篇 各地州市主要经济指标排序

CHAPTER 19 RANKING OF MAIN ECONOMIC INDICATORS BY REGION OF XINJIANG

19-1 各地、州、市生产总值 683
Gross Regional Product by Prefecture, Autonomous Prefecture and City
19-2 各地、州、市人口状况 684
Population Status by Prefecture, Autonomous Prefecture and City
19-3 各地、州、市全社会固定资产投资 685
Total Investment in Fixed Assets by Prefecture, Autonomous Prefecture and City

19-4 各地、州、市农林牧渔业总产值 686
Gross Output Value of Farming, Forestry, Animal Husbandry
and Fishery by Prefecture, Autonomous Prefecture and City
19-5 各地、州、市主要农产品产量 687
Yield of Major Farm Crops by Prefecture, Autonomous Prefecture and City
19-6 各地、州、市规模以上工业企业主要经济指标 688
Main Indicators on Economic of Industrial Enterprises above Designated Size
by Prefecture, Autonomous Prefecture and City
19-7 各地、州、市主要工业产品产量 690
Output of Major Industrial Products by Prefecture, Autonomous Prefecture and City
19-8 各地、州、市社会消费品零售总额 692
Total Retail Sales of Consumer Goods by Prefecture, Autonomous Prefecture and City
19-9 各地、州、市海关进出口总额 693
Total Value of Imports and Exports by Prefecture, Autonomous Prefecture and City
19-10 各地、州、市在岗职工工资总额和平均工资 693
Total Wages of Employed Staff and Workers and Average Wage
by Prefecture, Autonomous Prefecture and City
19-11 各地、州、市地方财政一般预算收支 694
The General Budgetary Revenue and Expenditures of Local Finance
by Prefecture, Autonomous Prefecture and City
19-12 分城镇居民消费价格指数和商品零售价格指数 694
General Retail Price and Consumer Price Index by City/County
19-13 各地、州、市各类学校在校学生数 695
Number of Students Enrollment by Type of School and by Prefecture, Autonomous Prefecture and City
19-14 各地、州、市每万人口医院床位数和医生数 696
Number of Doctors and Hospital Beds Per 10 000 Population by Prefecture, Autonomous Prefecture and City
19-15 各地、州、市卫生技术人员和医生数 696
Medical Technical Personnel and Doctors by Prefecture, Autonomous Prefecture and City

附录： 各省市区主要经济指标排序

APPENDIX: RANKING OF MAIN ECONOMIC INDICATORS BY REGION

各省市区主要经济指标排序 699
Ranking of Main Economic Indicators by Region

2012

新疆统计年鉴

XINJIANG STATISTICAL YEARBOOK

特载

Special Article

新疆统计年鉴

XINJIANG STATISTICAL YEARBOOK

2012

新疆维吾尔自治区 2011年国民经济和社会发展 统计公报

2011年，面对复杂多变的国际国内形势，全区各族人民在自治区党委、人民政府的正确领导下，认真贯彻落实中央新疆工作座谈会、自治区党委七届九次、十次全委（扩大）会议和八次党代会精神，以科学发展为主题，以转变经济发展方式为主线，弘扬新疆精神，践行新疆效率，在变化变革中求新创新，民生建设年取得新成效，经济发展取得新成就，实现“十二五”良好开局。

一、综　合

初步核算，全年实现生产总值（GDP）6610.05亿元，比上年增加1172.58亿元，突破6000亿元大关。按可比价格计算，比上年增长12.0%。其中，第一产业增加值1139.03亿元，增长6.5%；第二产业增加值3225.90亿元，增长12.0%；第三产业增加值2145.12亿元，增长15.2%。三次产业比例为17.2∶48.8∶34.0。

人均生产总值30087元，按可比价格计算，增长10.7%，以当年平均汇率折算，人均4658美元。

居民消费价格比上年上涨5.9%，其中，食品价格上涨12.6%，居住价格上涨5.4%。服务项目价格上涨4.0%。

表1　2011年居民消费价格比上年涨跌幅度

指　　标	涨跌幅度（%）
居民消费价格	5.9
城　市	5.5
农　村	6.8
食　品	12.6
#粮　食	8.7
肉禽及其制品	20.1
油　脂	12.6
蛋　类	12.2
水产品	10.7
菜　类	4.6
烟酒及用品	3.3
衣　着	1.1
家庭设备用品及服务	2.4
医疗保健和个人用品	4.3
交通和通信	0.5
娱乐教育文化用品及服务	1.1
居　住	5.4
水、电、燃料	3.7
自有住房	6.6
建房及装饰材料	4.8

工业生产者出厂价格上涨14.8%，其中，轻工业上涨10.1%，重工业上涨15.6%。工业生产者购进价格上涨17.8%。农业生产资料价格上涨6.6%。固定资产投资价格上涨7.1%。

二、农　业

农林牧渔业总产值1955.39亿元，按可比价格计算，比上年增长6.9%。其中，农业产值1437.89亿元，增长8.3%；林业产值38.08亿元，增长5.9%；畜牧业产值415亿元，增长2.0%；渔业产值14.17亿元，增长7.1%；农林牧渔服务业产值50.25亿元，增长4.1%。

农作物播种面积7475.21万亩，增长4.7%。其中，粮食播种面积3000.54万亩，增长0.4%；棉花播种面积2457.09万亩，增长12.2%；油料播种面积396.43万亩，下降3.3%；甜菜播种面积113.14万亩，增长0.2%；蔬菜播种面积483.91万亩，增长6.3%。

全年粮食产量1200.75万吨，增长4.4%。棉花产量289.77万吨，增长16.9%。油料产量66.76万吨，增长0.2%。甜菜产量518.95万吨，增长6.6%。蔬菜产量1866.15万吨，增长7.6%。水果（含果用瓜）产量1035.96万吨，增长0.7%，其中，园林水果601.65万吨，增长1.3%。

年末农业机械总动力1795.94万千瓦，增长9.3%。拥有大中型拖拉机29.52万台，增长16.3%。小型拖拉机34.91万台，下降3.4%。化肥施用量（折纯）183.79万吨，增长9.7%。农村用电量71.65亿千瓦时，增长11.5%。

三、工业和建筑业

全部工业增加值2700.20亿元，按可比价格计算，比上年增长11.4%。

规模以上工业增加值增长11.4%。其中，轻工业增长9.2%，重工业增长11.6%；石油工业增长5.3%，非石油工业增长17.9%；公有制经济增长10.1%，非公有制经济增长16.2%；地方工业增长16.3%；园区工业增长15.0%；中小型企业增长20.7 %。

在自治区重点监测的十大产业中，有色工业增长32.9%；电力工业增长31.2%；化学工业增长22.5%；煤炭工业增长17.7%；钢铁工业增长10.9%；农副食品加工工业增长2.1%；汽车工业增长1.8%；纺织工业下降0.8%；装备制造工业下降3.3%。

规模以上工业产品销售率98.0%，其中，轻工业94.7%，重工业98.4%。出口交货值70.47亿元，增长11.9%。实现利润总额963.74亿元，增长13.4%。

表2　2011年工业企业主要产品产量及增速

产品名称	单　位	产　量	比上年增长%
原　煤	万吨	11991.71	20.8
原　油	万吨	2615.63	2.2
天然气	亿立方米	235.38	-5.8
原油加工量	万吨	2388.41	9.0
乙　烯	万吨	103.99	-12.9
发电量	亿千瓦时	875.19	28.8
成品糖	万吨	46.11	2.2
卷　烟	亿支	160.01	6.7
罐　头	万吨	115.41	4.3
纱	万吨	39.91	-4.0
布	亿米	7302.77	-51.5
机制纸及纸板	万吨	42.29	14.0
化肥(折 100%)	万吨	233.56	46.8
十种有色金属	万吨	37.84	284.6
电解铝	万吨	29.41	346.0
粗　钢	万吨	892.98	8.2
钢　材	万吨	985.14	10.4
生　铁	万吨	1088.45	15.7
水　泥	万吨	3171.71	32.1
变压器	万千伏安	4855.01	35.5
塑料制品	万吨	104.22	25.5
铝　材	万吨	5.48	21.2
服　装	万件	1820.54	25.4
轻　革	万平方米	479.12	45.1

全社会建筑业增加值525.70亿元，按可比价格计算，比上年增长15.0%。具有资质等级的总承包和专业承包建筑企业总产值1274.47亿元，增长19.9%。

四、固定资产投资

全社会固定资产投资4712.77亿元，比上年增长33.1%。其中，城镇投资4204.50亿元，增长

32.2%；农村投资508.27亿元，增长41.9%。

按三次产业划分，第一产业投资237.78亿元，增长12.5%；第二产业投资2465.35亿元，增长47.9%；第三产业投资2009.64亿元，增长21.0%。在第二产业中，工业投资2378.70亿元，增长46.3%，其中，制造业投资1156.82亿元，增长86.5%。

在全社会固定资产投资中，地方投资3533.57亿元，增长45.3%；民间投资1900.02亿元，增长56.9%；安居富民、定居兴牧、保障性住房建设等民生类工程投资1009.08亿元，增长53.9%。

房地产开发投资516.39亿元，增长48.5%。房屋施工面积5481.44万平方米，增长37.7%；竣工面积1270.48万平方米，增长25.4%。商品房销售面积1728.23万平方米，增长10.4%；销售额613.31亿元，增长27.0%。

五、国内贸易

社会消费品零售总额1557.09亿元，比上年增长17.5%，扣除价格因素，实际增长11.8%。

按经营地划分，城镇零售额1411.01亿元，增长17.8%；乡村零售额146.08亿元，增长15.5%。

按行业划分，批发和零售业零售额1351.36亿元，增长16.8%；住宿和餐饮业零售额205.73亿元，增长22.6%。

限额以上批发零售贸易企业食品类零售额增长24.5%，服装、鞋帽、针纺织品类增长30.9%，金银珠宝类增长68.3%，家用电器和音像制品类增长36.9%，石油及制品类增长31.8%，家具类增长29.2%，汽车类增长23.7%。

六、对外经济

全年货物进出口总额228.22亿美元，比上年增长33.2%。其中，出口168.29亿美元，增长29.8%；进口59.93亿美元，增长44.0%。全区口岸过货量3468万吨，增长32.1%。

新批准设立外商直接投资企业50个，比上年下降2.0%。合同使用外商直接投资项目69个，增长17.0%；实际利用外商直接投资3.35亿美元，增长41.0%。

表 3　2011 年货物进出口总额及增速

单位：亿美元

指　标	绝对数	比上年增长（%）
货物进出口总额	**228.22**	**33.2**
货物出口额	168.29	29.8
其中：一般贸易	47.68	1.3 倍
加工贸易	2.35	-22.7
边境小额贸易	88.19	14.9
其中：机电产品	31.33	41.2
高新技术产品	1.98	82.0
货物进口额	59.93	44.0
其中：一般贸易	17.09	10.5
加工贸易	0.30	30.3
边境小额贸易	40.18	69.5
其中：机电产品	6.98	持平
高新技术产品	2.51	14.8

七、交通、邮电和旅游

铁路货运量6903.70万吨，比上年增长0.7%；公路货运量55965万吨，增长10.9%；民航货邮吞吐量11.60万吨，增长14.7%。铁路客运量2001.70万人，增长28.8%；公路客运量47927万人，增长8.1%；民航旅客吞吐量1423万人，增长21.6%。

年末铁路营业里程4480公里，增长12.5%；民航通航里程17.58万公里，增长0.6%；公路里程15.52万公里，增长1.6%，其中，高速公路1459

公里，增长28.3%。

年末民用汽车保有量169.79万辆（包括三轮车和低速货车），增长25.0%，其中，私人汽车113.19万辆，增长32.0%。

电信业务总量212.66亿元，增长18.5%；邮政业务总量13.84亿元，下降27.8%。固定电话用户540.80万户，下降1.2%，固定电话普及率每百人25部；移动电话用户1670.90万户，增长22.9%，移动电话普及率每百人77.4部；互联网用户208.80万户，增长29.6%。

全年接待国际旅游人数132.50万人次，比上年增长24.5%；国际旅游外汇收入4.65亿美元，增长26.3%。接待国内旅游人数3829万人次，增长26.0%；国内旅游收入411亿元，增长46.0%。

八、财政和金融

全口径财政收入1654.91亿元，增长38.9%。地方财政收入1040.42亿元，增长50.1%。地方财政一般预算收入720.43亿元，增长43.9%，其中，各项税收收入593.41亿元，增长42.6%。在税收收入中，国内增值税96.69亿元，增长28.4%；营业税209.84亿元，增长38.7%；企业所得税63.43亿元，增长58.5%；个人所得税38.34亿元，增长40.0%；资源税65.01亿元，增长1.0倍。

地方财政支出2599.67亿元，增长37.9%。地方财政一般预算支出2284.49亿元，增长34.5%。财政用于民生的支出1670.5亿元，占地方财政一般预算支出的73.2%。其中，交通运输支出206.83亿元，增长1.3倍；住房保障支出170.04亿元，增长88.9%；城乡社区事务支出140.10亿元，增长47.1%；教育支出399.80亿元，增长27.4%；医疗卫生支出132.43亿元，增长27.9%；社会保障和就业支出201.64亿元，增长21.2%。

年末金融机构（含外资）人民币各项存款余额10387亿元，比年初增加1506.11亿元，比上年增长17.1%。其中，单位存款余额5573.38亿元，比年初增加850.75亿元；个人存款余额4421.93亿元，比年初增加715.77亿元。

金融机构（含外资）人民币各项贷款余额6270.21亿元，比年初增加1297.05亿元，增长26.1%。其中，短期贷款2250.61亿元，增长21.9%；中长期贷款3757.93亿元，增长28.5%。个人消费贷款603.81亿元，增长31.9%。

年末共有上市公司37家，与上年持平。股票总股本231.77亿股，比上年增长12.8%；股票总市值2233.71亿元，减少39.7%。全年实现再融资156.77亿元。

全年保险公司各项保费收入203.62亿元，比上年增长13.9%。其中，寿险102.86亿元，增长5.2%；财产险78.51亿元，增长24.6%；健康险15.32亿元，增长17.6%；意外伤害险6.92亿元，增长40.5%。

各类保险赔款及给付支出57.48亿元，增长16.5%。其中，财产险赔款34.24亿元，增长17.2%；寿险给付15.50亿元，增长18.1%；健康险赔付6.24亿元，增长6.9%；意外伤害险赔付1.51亿元，增长30.2%。

九、教育和科学技术

年末共有普通高等学校32所。全年研究生教育招生4972人，比上年增长8.2%；在校研究生14099人，增长11.2%；毕业生3421人，增长1.8%。本专科招生7.44万人，下降0.3%；在校生25.87万人，增长3.0%；毕业生6.38万人，增长0.5%。

各类中等职业教育招生9.02万人，下降8.8%；在校生24.30万人，增长4.2%；毕业生6.45万人，下降2.8%。普通高中招生15.65万人，增长2.1%；在校生43.27万人，增长3.2%；毕业生12.95万人，下降4.6%。初中招生32.60万人，下降3.0%；在校生97.66万人，下降2.7%；毕业生

32.85万人，下降2.7%。小学招生32.24万人，增长3.4%；在校生191.95万人，下降0.8%；毕业生32.77万人，下降2.0%；幼儿园在园幼儿65.11万人，增长12.5%。

小学学龄儿童入学率99.7%，初中阶段适龄少年入学率99.5%。初中毕业升入普通高中（含技工）升学率83.9%。

全年安排自治区级科技计划项目1445项，承担国家级科技计划项目（课题）506项。获得省部级以上科技成果206项。拥有县以上部门属研究与技术开发机构118个。重点实验室28个。批准成立的工程技术研究中心19个，其中，国家级4个。组建期内的工程技术中心54个。自治区级科技成果转化基地50个。截至2011年底，拥有高新技术企业153个，国家级高新技术产业开发区2个，自治区级高新技术工业园区4个，国家大学科技园1个。生产力促进中心48家，其中，国家级示范中心9家。国家级创新型企业5个，国家级创新型试点企业5个。

受理专利申请4736项。其中，受理发明专利申请1273项，占26.9%；获得专利授权2642项，其中，获得发明专利授权302项，占11.4%。签订技术合同1473项，技术合同成交金额4.38亿元，其中，技术交易额4.30亿元。

十、文化、卫生和体育

年末拥有文化馆112个，公共图书馆103个，博物馆73个。拥有广播电台6座，中、短波广播发射台和转播台53个，广播综合人口覆盖率94.9%。电视台8座，电视人口综合覆盖率95.3%。有线电视用户208.02万户，增长8.3%，其中，有线数字电视用户188.45万户，增长43.9%。拍摄故事片1部，译制少数民族语故事片134部。

全区共有卫生机构17412个，拥有床位12.54万张，卫生技术人员13.06万人。其中，医院、卫生院1742个，床位11.88万张；疾病预防控制中心216个；妇幼保健机构90个。乡镇卫生院913个，床位2.13万张，卫生技术人员1.72万人。

在国内外重大比赛中取得58枚金牌，50枚银牌，48枚铜牌。在第九届全国少数民族传统体育运动会上夺得14个第一名、21个第二名、15个第三名。

十一、人民生活

年末总人口2208.71万人，比上年增长1.1%，其中，城镇人口961.67万人，乡村人口1247.04万人。城镇化率为43.5%。男性人口1128.75万人，女性人口1079.96万人，性别比为104.52。全年出生人口33.11万人，出生率14.99‰；死亡人口9.28万人，死亡率4.42‰。人口自然增长率10.57‰。

城镇居民人均可支配收入15514元，比上年增长13.7%，扣除价格因素，实际增长7.8%。其中，工资性收入12653元，增长11.7%。人均消费性支出11839元，增长16.1%，其中，人均食品支出4537元，增长22.8%。

农村居民人均纯收入5442元，增长17.2%，扣除价格因素，实际增长9.8%。其中，工资性收入805元，增长44.7%；家庭经营纯收入3887元，增长6.5%；转移性纯收入603元，增长94.6%；财产性纯收入147元，增长16.3%。人均生活消费支出4398元，增长27.2%，其中，人均食品支出1589元，增长14.0%。

十二、劳动就业和社会保障

年末就业人员1163.29万人。通过各种途径实现城镇就业再就业58.29万人，其中，就业困难人员实现就业6.75万人。全区累计消除“零就业”家庭4.2万户，帮助实现就业4.8万人。城镇登记失业率3.2%。

年末参加城镇失业保险196.72万人，领取失业保险金5.55万人。参加基本养老保险291.99万人，增加32.32万人，其中，参保职工214.66万人，增加21.59万人；参保离退休人员77.33万人，增加10.73万人。

城镇职工参加基本医疗保险322.73万人，增加26.01万人，其中，参保职工245.06万人，增加20.28万人；参保退休人员77.67万人，增加5.73万人。参加工伤保险208.18万人，增加24.05万人。参加生育保险206.14万人，增加17.91万人。

城镇居民中有84.82万人得到政府最低生活保障救济，比上年减少0.31万人。年末各类收养性社会福利单位拥有床位3.78万张，增长26.7%；收养各类人员2.91万人，增长12.0%。城镇各种社区服务设施1491个，增长20.6%。销售社会福利彩票22.54亿元，增长16.8%；筹集社会福利资金6.60亿元，增长16.6%。直接接受社会捐赠317万元。

开展新型农村合作医疗工作的县（市）89个，参加新农合的人口1050.93万人，参合率99.7%。

新型农村养老保险试点扩大到92个县（市），参保人员490.58万人，已领取养老保险待遇84.68万人。

十三、资源、环境和安全生产

已发现矿种138种。查明有资源储量的矿种96种，其中，能源矿产3种，金属矿产32种，非金属矿产61种。新发现大中型矿产地6处，其中，能源矿产地4处，金属矿产地1处，水气矿产地1处。新增查明资源储量23种，其中，煤炭储量297亿吨。

在监测的19个城市中，有12个城市空气质量达到国家Ⅱ级以上标准；城市空气质量好于Ⅱ级的优良天数占80.9%。首府乌鲁木齐市空气质量好于Ⅱ级的优良天数占75.6%，比上年提高2.7个百分点。

在监测的79条河流170个断面中，Ⅰ～Ⅲ类优良水质断面比例为93.5%，提高2.3个百分点；Ⅳ～Ⅴ类轻中度污染水质断面比例为3.6%，下降1.4个百分点；劣Ⅴ类重度污染水质断面比例为2.9%，下降0.9个百分点。

在监测的32座湖库中，Ⅰ～Ⅲ类优良水质湖库占62.5%；Ⅳ～Ⅴ类轻中度污染水质湖库占18.7%；劣Ⅴ类重度污染水质湖库占18.8%，与上年相比保持稳定。

各类国家和自治区级自然保护区28个，保护区总面积2096万公顷，占辖区面积比重的12.6%，其中，国家级自然保护区9个。

全年共发生各类安全生产事故10630起，比上年上升0.3%。死亡2396人，下降4.4%。亿元GDP安全生产事故死亡率0.36，下降28.0%；工矿商贸十万从业人员事故死亡率7.10，下降12.4%；道路交通万车死亡率6.47，下降14.6%；煤矿百万吨死亡率0.77，下降24.5%。

说　明：

1、地区生产总值（GDP）、农林牧渔业总产值、建筑业总产值及各产业增加值绝对数按现价计算，增长速度按可比价格计算。

2、规模以上工业指年销售收入2000万元以上的工业企业。

3、邮政业务和电信业务总量按2010年不变价格计算，2001年至2010年按照2000年不变价格计算，因此2011年邮政业务和电信业务总量绝对数与2010年不可比，但比上年增速是按可比口径计算的。

4、文化部调整指标，将群众艺术馆与文化馆合并统称为文化馆。

Statistical Communique on the 2011 National Economic & Social Development of the Xinjiang Uygur Autonomous Region

In 2011, under the correct leadership of the Autonomous Region Party Committee and the People's Government, facing the sophisticated and changable domestic and foreign situation, the people in different nationalities of the Autonomous Region fully implemented the view Scientific Developments Stratgy, fully implemented the spirit of the central committee of Xinjiang, the Autonomous Region Party Committee of the ninth and the tenth plenary session of the seventh committee of the Xinjiang autonomous region, changing the mode of economic development as the main line, carrying forward the spirit of Xinjiang, practicing Xinjiang Efficiency, innovating in transformationgs and reforms, the people's livelihood achieved new progress, and general economic strengh stood a new stage and got new achievement. Twelfith Five-Year Plan got a good start.

I. General Outlook

According to the Preliminary statistics, the gross domestic product (GDP) of Xinjiang was 661.005 billion yuan, breakthrough exceeding 600 billion yuan, an increase of 117.258 billion yuan over the previous year, up by 12% over the previous year, of which, the added value of the primary industry was 113.903 billion yuan,up by 6.5%; that of the secondary industry was 322.590 billion yuan,up by 12%; and that of the tertiary industry was 214.512 billion yuan,up by 15.2% over the previous year.The composition of three industries was 17.2:48.8:34.0.

The permanent-population-based per-capita GDP reached 30087 yuan, up by 10.7% over the previous year, equivalent to US$ 4658 at current exchange rate.

The total consumer price index of the year was up by 5.9% over the previous year, of which, the price of food was up by 12.6%.The price of housing was up by 5.4%, the price for service up by 4.0%.

Table 1: Span of rise and decrease on the consumer price indices

unit: %

Items	2011
Consumer price index	5.9
rural	5.5
urban	6.8
Food	12.6
# Grain	8.7
Meal poultry and processed products	20.1
Oil and Fat	12.6
Eggs	12.2
Aquatic products	10.7
Greengrocery	4.6
Tobacco,Liquor and Articles	3.3
Clothing	1.1
Household Facilities, Articles and Services	2.4
Health Care and Personal Articles	4.3
Transportation and Communication	0.5
Recreation, Education and Culture Articles	1.1
Residence	5.4
Water Electric and fuel	3.7
Renting	6.6
Building and building decoration materials	4.8

The ex-Factory price index of industrial product was up by 14.8%, of which, light industry was up by 10.1%, heavy industry was up by 15.6%. The purchasing price of industrial product was up by 17.8%. The production price of agriculture products increased up by 6.6%. The price of fixed asset investment was up by 7.1%.

II. Agriculture

Gross output value of agriculture, forestry, animal husbandry and fishery was 195.539 billion yuan,up by 6.9% over the previous year, of which, Gross output of agriculture was 143.789 billion yuan,up by 8.3%; Gross output of forestry was 3.808 billion yuan,up by 5.9%; Gross output of animal husbandry was 41.500 billion yuan, up by 2.0%; Gross output of fishery was 1.417 billion yuan, up by 7.1%; Gross output of services of agriculture, forestry, animal husbandry was 5.025 billion yuan, up by 4.1%.

The total sown areas of farm crops was 4.9835 million hectares，up by 1.0% over the previous year；of which, The sown area of grain crops was 2.0004 million hectares, up by 0.4%；The sown area of cotton crops was 1.6381 million hectares, up by 12.2%; The sown area of oil bearing crops was 26.43 ten thousand hectares，down by 3.3%；The sown area of sugar crops was 7.54 ten thousand acres, up by 0.2% over the previous year. The area of vegetable crops was 32.26 ten thousand hectares, up by 6.3% over the previous year.

The total output of grain was 1200.75 ten thousand tons，up by 4.4% over the previous year；The output of cotton was 289.77 ten thousand tons，up by 16.9% over the previous year；The output of oil-bearing crops was 66.76 ten thousand tons, an increase of 0.2%；The output of sugar was 518.95 ten thousand tons，up by 6.6%. The output of vegetable was 18.6615 million tons，an increase of 7.6% over the previous year; The output of fruit was 1035.96 ten thousand tons, up by 2.6%, of which, the output of garden fruit was 601.65 ten thousand, an increase of 1.3%.

The year-end total agricultural machinery power was 17.9594 million kilowatt，up by 9.3% over the previous year. There were 29.52 ten thousand large and medium-size tractors，up by 16.3%；and 34.91 ten thousand small-size tractors，down by 3.4%. The consumption of chemical fertilizer was 183.79ten thousand tons(100% equivalent)，up by 9.7%. Electricity consumed in rural areas was 7.165 billion kwh, up by 11.5%.

III. Industry and Construction

The total value-added of the industrial sector was 270.020 billion yuan，up by 11.4% over the previous year.

Table2: Output of Major Industrial Products 2011

Item	Unit	Output	Increase over 2010(%)
Coal	10 000 tons	11991.7	20.8
Crude oil	10 000 tons	2615.63	2.2
Natural gas	100 million cubic meters	235.38	-5.8
Processed oil	10 000 tons	2388.41	9.0
Ethylene	10 000 tons	103.99	-12.9
Electricity	100 million kilowatt-hours	875.19	28.8
Refind sugar	10 000 tons	46.11	2.2
Cigarettes	100 million pieces	160.01	6.7
Can	10 000 tons	115.41	4.3
Yarn	10 000 tons	39.91	-4.0
Cloth	10 000 meters	7302.77	-51.5
Machine-made paper and paperbord	10 000 tons	42.29	14.0
Chemical fertilizers (100% equivalent)	10 000 tons	233.56	46.8
Ten non-ferrous metals	10 000 tons	37.84	284.6
Electrolytic aluminium	10 000 tons	29.41	346.0
Crude steel	10 000 tons	892.98	8.2
Rolled steel	10 000 tons	985.14	10.4
Pig Iron	10 000 tons	1088.45	15.7
Cement	10 000 tons	3171.71	32.1
Transformer	10 000 kilovolt-ampere	4855.01	35.5
Plastics	10 000 tons	104.11	25.5
Aluminium	10 000 tons	5.48	21.2
Clothing	10 000 pieces	1820.54	25.4
Light leather	10 000 square meters	479.12	45.1

The added value of industrial enterprises above designated size was up by 11.4%. Of which, the added value of light industry was up by 9.2%; the added value of heavy industry was up by 11.6%; oil industry was up by 5.3%,;non-oil industry was up by 17.9%; public owned economy was up by 10.1; non-public owned economy was up by 16.2; local industry was up by 16.3%; industry park was up by 15.0%; medium and small-sized enterprises was up by 20.7% over the previous year.

Among the ten proportion of industrial enterprises above designated，Minging and processing of non-ferrous metal ores was up by 32.9%; Production of electric power was up by 31.2%; Manufacture of chemical products was up by 22.5%; Minging of coal was up by 17.7%; Processing of food from agriculture products was up by 2.1%; Manufacture of cars was up by 1.8%; Manufacture of textile was down by 0.8%; equipment manufactory industry was down 3.3%.

The proportion of products sold of above designated

size was 98.0%.Of which, the proportion of light industry of products sold was 94.7%; the proportion of heavy industry of products sold was 98.4%. The value of delivered exported goods creat by industrial enterprises above designated size was 7.047 billion yuan, up by 11.9%. The profits achieved to 96.374 billion yuan, up by 13.4%.

The added value of the construction sector was 52.570 billion yuan, up by 15.0% over the previous year, General contracting and special contracting construction enterprises with qualification grade reaped profits of 127.447 billion yuan, up by 19.9%.

IV. Investment in Fixed Asset

The completed investment in fixed assets was 471.227 billion yuan, up by 33.1% over the previous year. In terms of urban and rural areas, that in urban areas was 420.450 billion yuan, up by 32.2%; that in rural areas was 50.827 billion yuan, up by 41.9%.

In terms of three industries, the investment in the primary industry was 23.778 billion yuan, up by 12.5%; the investment in the secondary industry was 246.535 billion yuan, up by 47.9%, The tertiary industry investment was 200.964 billion yuan, up by 21%. Among the investment in the secondary industry, the investment in industry was 237.870 billion yuan,up by 46.3%, Of which ,the investment in manufature was 115.682 billion yuan ,up by 86.5%.

The investment in the total social fixed assets, local investment was 353.357 billion yuan, up by 45.3%; private investment was 190.002 billion yuan, up by 56.9%; the people's livelihood project investment, such as Home to Enrich People, Settle to Develop Animal Husbandry, and Affordable Housing Construction, was100.908 billion yuan, up by 53.9%.

The investment in real estate development was 51.639 billion yuan, up by 48.5% over the previous year. The floor space of buildings under construction was 54.8144 million square meters, up by 37.7%. The floor space of building completed was 12.7048 million square meters, up by 25.4%. The total sales area of commercial buildings for the whole year reached 17.2823 million square meters, up by 10.4%. The total sales of commercial building was 61.331 billion yuan, up by 27.0%.

V. Domestic Trade

The total retail sales of consumer goods reached 155.709 billion yuan, up by 17.5% over the previous year. Really up by 11.8%.

In terms of urban and rural areas, the retail sales of consumer goods in urban areas reached 141.101 billion yuan, up by17.8%; and the retail sales of consumer goods in rural areas reached 14.608 billion yuan, up by 15.5%.

In terms of different sectors, the sales of the wholesale and retail trade reached 205.73 billion yuan, up by 16.8%; the sales of the accommodation and catering service was 20.573 billion yuan, up by 22.6%.

In the enterprises of wholesale retailsale trade, the volume of food retail sales increased by 24.5%; the volume of clothing, BC and textiles, up by 30.9%; gold, silver and jewelry, up by 68.3%; household appliance and audiovisual products, up by 36.9%; petroleum product, up by 31.8%; furniture, up by 29.2%; automobiles, up by 23.7%.

VI. Foreign Trade

The total value of import and export reached US$ 22.822 billion, up by 33.2% over the previous year. Of which, the value of export was US$ 16.829 billion, up by 29.8%; and the value of import was US$ 5.993 billion, up by 44.0%.

The number of newly estabishied foeign directly investment enterprises was 50, down by 2.0% over the previous year. The number of using the projects invested directly by foreign business was 69. Foreign directly investment actually utilized this year stood at US$ 335 million, up by 41.0%.

Table3: Total Value of Imports and Exports and Growth Rates

unit: US$ 100 million

Item	2011	Increase over 2010(%)
Total value of imports and exports	228.22	33.2
Total exports	168.29	29.8
#Ordinary trade	47.68	128.2
Processing trade	2.35	-22.7
Frontier small trade	88.19	14.9
#mechanical and electrical products	31.33	41.2
New and high-tech products	1.98	82.0
Total imports	59.93	44.0
#Ordinary trade	17.09	10.5
Processing trade	0.30	30.3
Frontier small trade	40.18	69.5
#mechanical and electrical products	6.98	Equal
New and high-tech products	2.51	-14.8

VII. Transportation, Postal & Telecommunication and Tourism

The freight turnover by railways was 69.037 million tons, up by 7.0%; that by highways 559.65 million tons, up by 10.9%;that by civil aviation 11.60 ten thousands tons, up by 14.7%； Passenger traffic by railways was 20.017 million passengers,up by 28.8%；that by highways 47.927 million passengers，up by 8.1%；that by civil aviation 14.23 million passengers，up by 28.3%.

At the end of the year, railway in operation reached 4480 kilometers,up by 12.5%; Total civil aviation routes reached 17.58 ten thousand kilometers,up by 0.6%; Length of high- ways was 15.52 ten thousand kilometers,up by 1.6%, of which, the length of freeways was 1459 kilometers, up by 28.3%.

At the end of the year, there were 169.79 ten thousand civilian automobiles, up by 25%, of which, there were 113.19 ten thousand private automobiles, up by 32%.

The total volume of telecommunication was 21.266 billion yuan，up by 18.5% over the previous year. The total volume of post stood at 1.384 billion yuan，down by 27.8%. Number of fixed phone users 5.4080 million，down by 1.2%. Number of mobile phone users 16.7090 million, up by 22.9%. Year-end Internet customer 2.0880 million，up by 29.6%.

Tourists through customs to Xinjiang numbered 132.50 ten thousand, up by 24.5%. Forien exchange income from tourism amounted to US$ 465 million, up by 26.3%. In the year, Xinjiang recevied 3829 ten thousand forien tourists, increased by 26.0% over the previous year. Income from foreign tourists amounted 41.1 billion yuan, up by 46.0%.

VIII. Finance，Banking and Insurance

In the year, the total revenue was 165.491 billion yuan, up by 38.9%. The Local government revenue was 104.042 billion yuan， up by 50.1%. The general budgetary revenue was 72.043 billion yuan，up by 43.9%. Of which, total taxes were 41.623 billion yuan, up by 38.2% over the previous year.In categories of taxes, income of deed tax were 9.669 billion yuan,up by 28.4%; Income of business tax were 20.984 billion yuan, up by 38.7%; Income of business taxs was 6.343 billion yuan, up by 58.5%; Income of individual tax 3.834 billion yuan, up by 40%; Income of resource tax was 6.501 billion yuan ,up by 1times.

Local government expenditure reached 259.967 billion yuan，up by 37.9%, the general budgetary expenditure was 228.449 billion yuan，up by 34.5%.The expenditure for people's livelihood was 167.05 billion yuan, which occupied 73.2% of the general budgetary expenditure. Of which, expenditure of education were 39.980 billion yuan,up by 27.4%; expenditure of medical and health care were 13.243 billion yuan,up by 27.9%; expenditure of social safety and employment were 20.164 billion yuan, up by 21.2%.

By the end of 2011，savings deposits of all kinds in financial institutions reached 1038.7 billion yuan，increase by 150.611 billion yuan over the year of beginning, up by 17.1% over the previous year. Of which，enterprise savings deposits were 557.388 billion yuan，increase by 85.075 billion yuan; Personal savings deposits were 442.193 billion yuan, increase by 71.577 billion yuan over the year of beginning.

Loans of all kinds in financial institutions were 627.021 billion yuan, increase by 129.705 billion yuan over the beginning, up by 26.1%; of which, Loans of short-term were 225.061 billion yuan, up by 21.9%; loan of medium-and long-term were 375.793 billion yuan,up by 28.5%. Individual consumption loans were 60.381 billion yuan, up by 31.9%.

At the end of 2011, there were 37 listed companies, equal to the previous year; total volume issued were 23.177 billion shares, up by 12.8%; Total market capitalization were 223.371 billion yuan, down by 39.7%. In the year of 2011, the refinancing totaled 15.677 billion yuan.

The total premium of insurance companies reached 20.362 billion yuan，up by 13.9% over the previous year. of the total，life insurance premium was 10.286 billion yuan，up by 5.2%; Property insurance premium 7.851 billion yuan, up by 24.6%.; health and casualty insurance premium were 1.532 billion yuan，up by17.6%; that against health and accidental injury were 6.92 billion yuan, up by 40.5%.

Insurance companies paid an indemnity of 5.748 billion yuan as reparation for various property and life insurance programs, up by 16.5%, of which, and that against property was 3.424 billion yuan, up by 17.2%, the indemnity against life insurance was 1.550 billion yuan, down by 18.1%; that against health were 624 million yuan, up by 6.9%, and accidental injury were 151 million yuan, up by 30.2%.

IX. Education and Scientific Technology

By the end of 2011,there were totally 32 general colleges and universities.The enrollment of postgraduate students were 4972 new entrants，up by 8.2%; the enrollment of post- graduate students was 14099， up by 11.2%, graduates students were 3421, up by 1.8%. The enrollment of regular under-graduates and college student were 7.44 ten thousand, down by 0.3%; the enrollment of students was 25.87 ten thousand，up by 3.0%, graduates students were 6.38 ten thousand,up by 0.5%.

The enrollment of vocational secondary education was 9.02 ten thousand, down by 8.8%; enrollment were 24.30 ten thousand, up by 4.2%, graduates students were 6.45 ten thousand, down by 2.8%. The enrollment of general senior high schools were 156.5 thousand, up by 2.1%; enrollment were 432.7 thousand, up by 3.2%; with 129.5 thousand graduates, down by 4.6%. Students enrolled in junior secondary schools totaled 326.0 ten thousand, down by 3.0%; enrollment were 97.66 ten thousand, down by 2.7%; with 328.5 thousand graduates, down by 2.7%. Regular primary schools had an enrollment of 32.24 ten thousand，up by 3.4%; Enrollment were 1.9195 million, down by 0.8%, with 327.7 thousand graduates, down by 2.0%. There were 651.1 thousand pre-school children in kindergartens,up by 12.5%.

The enrollment rate of school-age children reached 99.7%. Enrollment rate of junior secondary school-age youth was 99.5%. Promotion rate from junior sendary school to senior secondary school was 83.9%.

In 2011, the autonomous region formulated 1445 sci-tech project plans, undertook 506 project plans of the national level, obtained 206 scientific and technological achievements of the provincial level or above, built 118 scientific research and technological development institutions above the county level and 28 key laboratories, founded 19 engineering and technological research centers, of which, 4 national level. 54 engineering and technological centers which are still at the forming stage, and 50 bases for the commercialization of research findings at the level of autonomous region were established. By the end of 2011, we had 153 high and new tech enterprises, 2 state-level hi-tech industrial development zones, 4 municipality-level hi-tech industrial parks, and one university national science park. 48 productivity promotion centers were founded, of which, there are 9 state-level demonstration centers, 5 national innovative enterprises and 5 national innovative enterprises under experiment.

There are totally 4736 patent applications, of which, there are 1273 for a patent for invention taking up 26.9%, and 2642 patent licenses, including 302 invention patent licenses accounting for 11.4%. 1473 technology contracts were signed, and the turnover reached 438 million yuan, of which, the volume of technology trade was 430 million yuan.

X. Culture, Public Health and Sports

At the end of 2011，there were 112 cutural centers, 103 public library, 73 museums; There were 6 radio broadcasting stations, radio broadcasting coverage rate was 94.9%; 8 television stations, television coverage rate was 95.3%. Number of users of cable television was 208.02 ten thousand, up by 8.3%, of which, number of Users of digital TV was 188.45 ten thousand, up by 43.9%. The Autonomous Region shot 1 feature movie，translated and edited 134 feature movies of minority language.

There were 17 412 institutions of public health in all,the total number of beds was 12.54 ten thousand, the medical technical personnel totaled 13.06 ten thousands, of which, there were 1712 hospitals and public health centers,the total number beds was 11.88 ten thousand; ,the medical technical personnel totaled 12.29 ten thousands. The total number of Centers for Disease Control and Prevention (CDC) was 216; the total number of maternal and child care service center was 90; the number of health clinics in town and townships was 913,and the number of beds was 21.3 thousand; the medical technical personnel totaled 1.72 ten thousands.

Athletes from the Autonomous Region in matches home and abroad won 58 gold medals, 50 silver medals, 48 bronze medals. In the 9th Ethnic Minority Traditional Sports, Athletes from the Autonomous Region won 14 gold medal, 21 silver medal, 15 bronze medal.

XI. Populatin and People's Life

By the end of 2011，the population of autonomous region was 22.0871 million, up by 1.1% compared with the previous year. Of which, the population in urban areas was 9.6167 million, rural areas 12.4704 million; the urbanization rate was 43.5%. There were 11.2875 million men and 10.7996 women, and the sex ratio was 104:52. The birth population was 33.11 ten thousand, and the birthrate was 14.99‰; the dead population was 9.28 ten thousand, and the deathrate was 4.42‰. The natural growth rate of population was 10.57‰.

The per capital disposable income of urban residents reached 15514 yuan，up by 13.7% over the previous year. Of which, income of salary and wage was 12653 yuan, up by 11.7%, per capital annual expenditure was 11839 yuan, up by 16.1%, of which,the per capital annual food expenditure was 4357 yuan, up by 22.8%.

The per capital auunal net income of rural households was 5442 yuan, up by 17.2%, of which, income of salaries and wages was 805 yuan, up by 44.7%; income from household operations was 3887 yuan, up by 6.5%; Income from transfers was 603 yuan, up by 94.6%; Income from properties was 147 yuan, up by 16.3%. Per capita consumption expenditure of rural households was 4398 yuan, up by 27.2% over the previous year, of which, the per capital annual food expenditure was 1589 yuan, up by 14.0%.

XII.Employment and Social Security

Number of employed person was 11.6329 million at year-end, of which, number of urban employed persons were 58.29 ten thousand, of which,the reemployment of zero-employment workers was 6.75 ten thousand. Registered unemployment rate in urban areas was 3.2%, equal to the previous year.

A total of 1.9672 million people participated in unemployment insurance programs, Receive unemployment insurance compensation was 5.55 ten thousand. 2.9199 million people participated in the basic retirement security programs, or an increase of 32.32 ten thousand people as compared with the previous year. Among them, 2.1466 million were employees, an increase of 21.59 ten thousand people; 77.33 ten thousand were retirees, an increase of 10.73 ten thousand people.

The population covered by basic medical insurance programs was 3.2273 million, an increase of 20.28 ten thousand people. Among them, 2.4506 million were employees, 77.67 ten thousand were retirees, an increase of 5.73 ten thousand people; 208.18 ten thousand people participated in the industrial injury insruance program, an increase of 24.05 ten thousand; 206.14 ten thousand people participated in the maternity insurance, an increase of 17.91 ten thousand people.

84.82 ten thousand people recevied basic welfare for urban residents, a decrease of 0.31 ten thousand over the previous year. Number of beds were 3.78 ten thousand in social welfare institutions at the end of year, up by 26.7%; Number of inmates were 2.91 ten thousand, up by 12.0%. The number of community service equipment was 1491, up by 20.6%. Revenue from social welfare lottery tickets were 2.254 billion yuan, up by 16.8%; Social welfare fund were 660 million yuan, up by 16.6%. 3.17 million yuan of donatioas were received from the general public.

There are 89 countries(cities) which participated in the new rural cooperative medical service, covered total rural population was 10.5093 million, the rate of participation was 99.7%.

XIII. Resources Environment and Safe production

138 mineral products were found, of which, 96 mineral products have resources. Of which, there were 3 energy minerals, 32 metal minerals, and 61 non-metal minerals. 6 large-medium orefield were discovered, of which, there were 4 energy resouses mines, 1 metal mine, and 1 vapor mine.

Reduction of pollutant emissions of sulphur dioxide were 2.10ten thousand tons and pollutant emissions of waste water were 1.62ten thousand tons.

In the 19 monitored cities, 12 cities had their air quality reach national standard Grade II. In the Autonomous Region about 80.9% of the year the air quality was better than Grade II. And 75.6% of the year in Urmqi the air quality was better than Grade II, up by 2.7% over the previous year.

Monitoring of water quality on 170 sections of the 79 rivers showed that good quality water of standard Grade I~III accounted for 93.5%, up by 2.3%. Quality water of standard GradeIV~V accounted for 3.6%, down by 1.4%, Quality water of standard Grade V accounted for 2.9%, down by 0.9%.

Monitoring of water quality of 32 lakes and reservoirs showed that good quality water of standard Grade I～III accounted for 62.5%. Quality water of standard Grade IV～V accounted for 18.7%. Quality water of standard Grade V accounted for 18.8%, equal to the previous year.

There were 28 national and regional nature reserves. Area of nature reserves were 2096 ten thousand sqkm, proportion of nature reserves in total area of territory was 12.6%, of which, there were 9 national nature reserves.

There were 10630 safety accidents occurred, up by 0.3%, with 2396 person died, decrease of 4.4%. The 100-million-GDP-based death rate in production safety accidents was 0.36, down by 28% over the previous year; among every 100 000 employees in trade sectors, 7.10 persons died, down by 12.4%; for every 10 000 vehicles, 6.47 persons died, down by 14.6%; for every one million tons output of coal mines, 0.77 persons died, down by 24.5%.

Notes to the Communique:

1. Regional gross domestic product,GDP, gross output value of farming, forestry, animal husbandry and fishery, the construction industry output value and value-added quoted in the Communique are at current prices, whereas growth rates are calculated at comparable prices.

2. Industrial enterprises above designated size refer to industrial enterprises of more than 20 million yuan in annual sales revenue.

3. The value of business transactions of postal and telecommunication services was calculated at the constant prices of 2010, and from 2001 to 2010 in accordance with the 2000 constant prices. So In 2011, postal services and telecommunications business volume in absolute terms compared with the 2010 are not available, but growth rates are calculated over the previous year.

4. The Ministry of Culture adjusted targets, and mass art center merged with culture center.They are collectively referred to as culture center.

2012

新疆统计年鉴

XINJIANG STATISTICAL YEARBOOK

第一篇 综 合

CHAPTER 1 General Suevey

简要说明
Brief Introduction

本篇资料的主要内容及来源

综合篇资料包括行政区划、国民经济和社会发展综合资料、基本单位资料及企业景气指数四部分。

行政区划划分资料由新疆维吾尔自治区民政厅根据国务院批准的、截止到2011年末全区行政区划变更情况汇总整理并提供；国民经济和社会发展综合资料由新疆维吾尔自治区统计局国民经济综合统计处根据各篇主要指标加工整理而成；基本单位统计资料由新疆维吾尔自治区统计局普查中心依据基本单位年报整理提供；企业景气指数由国家统计局新疆调查总队统计监测处提供。

Main Content and Source of Data

This chapter mainly covers: the data of division of administrative areas, grass-roots units and summary data on the national economy and social development,basic units and enterprises business climate index.

Data on division of administrative areas are provided and prepared by the Bureau of Civil Affairs of Xinjiang Uygur Autonomous Region on the basis of the changes in the divisions of administrative areas as approved by the state council at the year end of the previous year.Data on grass-roots units and the national economy and social development are compiled and processed by the Department of Comprehensive statistics of the Xinjiang Bureau of Statistics using relevant.enterprises business climate index are provided by the Department of Monitoring Statistics , NBS Survey Office in Xinjiang.

1-1 行 政 区 划

Divisions of Administrative Areas in Xinjiang Uygur Autonomous Region

单位：个 (2011 年) (unit)

区划名称	Region	地级区划数 Number of Regions at Prefecture Level	地级市 Cities at Prefecture Level	地区 Administrative Offices	自治州 Autonomous Prefectures	县级区划数 Number of Regions at County level	自治区直辖市 Cities under the Autonomous Region	地州辖市 Cities under the Prefectures
总　计	**Total**	**14**	**2**	**7**	**5**	**99**	**5**	**15**
乌鲁木齐市	Urumqi City	1	1			8		
克拉玛依市	Karamay City	1	1			4		
吐鲁番地区	Turpan Administrative Offices	1		1		3		1
哈密地区	Hami [Kumul] Administrative Offices	1		1		3		1
昌吉回族自治州	Changji Hui Autonomous Prefecture	1			1	7		2
伊犁哈萨克自治州	Ili Kazak Autonomous Prefecture	3		2	1	24		5
伊犁州直属县(市)	Counties (Cities) Direct Under Ili Prefecture	1			1	10		2
塔城地区	Tacheng [Tarbagatai] Administrative Offices	1		1		7		2
阿勒泰地区	Altay Administrative Offices	1		1		7		1
博尔塔拉自治州	Bortala Mongol Autonomous Prefecture	1			1	3		1
巴音郭楞自治州	Bayangol Mongol Autonomous Prefecture	1			1	9		1
阿克苏地区	Aksu Administrative Offices	1		1		9		1
克孜勒苏自治州	Kizilsu Kirgiz Autonomous Prefecture	1			1	4		1
喀什地区	Kashgar [Kaxgar] Administrative Offices	1		1		12		1
和田地区	Hotan Administrative Offices	1		1		8		1
石河子市	Shihezi City					1	1	
阿拉尔市	Aral City					1	1	
图木舒克市	Tumxuk City					1	1	
五家渠市	Wujiaqu City					1	1	
北屯市	Beitun City					1	1	

区划名称	Region	县级区划数 Number of Counties			乡镇级区划数 Number of Regions at Town-ships Level	#镇 Town	#乡 Township	#民族乡 National Township	#街道办事处 Street Communities
		市辖区 Districts under the Jurisdiction of Cities	县 Counties	#自治县 Autonomous Counties					
总　计	**Total**	**11**	**68**	**6**	**1020**	**242**	**615**	**42**	**162**
乌鲁木齐市	Urumqi City	7	1		87	8	14	1	65
克拉玛依市	Karamay City	4			14		2		12
吐鲁番地区	Turpan Administrative Offices		2		30	11	16	1	3
哈密地区	Hami [Kumul] Administrative Offices		2	1	42	12	25	3	5
昌吉回族自治州	Changji Hui Autonomous Prefecture		5	1	79	38	32	11	9
伊犁哈萨克自治州	Ili Kazak Autonomous Prefecture		19	2	241	62	155	17	24
伊犁州直属县(市)	Counties (Cities) Direct Under Ili Prefecture		8	1	110	21	76	10	13
塔城地区	Tacheng [Tarbagatai] Administrative Offices		5	1	74	27	39	5	8
阿勒泰地区	Altay Administrative Offices		6		57	14	40	2	3
博尔塔拉自治州	Bortala Mongol Autonomous Prefecture		2		20	7	9		4
巴音郭楞自治州	Bayangol Mongol Autonomous Prefecture		8	1	90	25	60	1	5
阿克苏地区	Aksu Administrative Offices		8		94	30	54	2	10
克孜勒苏自治州	Kizilsu Kirgiz Autonomous Prefecture		3		39	6	31	1	2
喀什地区	Kashgar [Kaxgar] Administrative Offices		11	1	173	30	138	3	4
和田地区	Hotan Administrative Offices		7		93	12	77	2	4
石河子市	Shihezi City				7	1	1		5
阿拉尔市	Aral City				5		1		4
图木舒克市	Tumxuk City				3				3
五家渠市	Wujiaqu City				3				3
北屯市	Beitun City								

1-2 县级以上行政区划

Divisions of Administrative Areas at and above County Level

(2011 年)

地、州、市名称 Name of Administrative Offices, Autonomous Prefectures, Cities		市、县(市辖区)名称 Names of Cities and Counties (Districts under Cities)
乌鲁木齐市 Urumqi City		天山区、沙依巴克区、新市区、水磨沟区、头屯河区、达坂城区、米东区、乌鲁木齐县 Tianshan District, Shayibak District, Xinshi District, Shui Mogou District, Tou Tunhe District, Da Bancheng District, Midong District, Urumqi County
克拉玛依市 Karamay City		克拉玛依区、独山子区、白碱滩区、乌尔禾区 Karamay District, Dushanzi District, Bai Jiantan District, Urhe District
吐鲁番地区 Turpan Administrative Offices		吐鲁番市、鄯善县、托克逊县 Turpan City, Shanshan [Piqan] County, Toksun County
哈密地区 Hami [Kumul] Administrative Offices		哈密市、巴里坤哈萨克自治县、伊吾县 Hami [Kumul] City, Barkol Kazak Autonomous County, Yiwu[Araturuk] County
昌吉回族自治州 Changji Hui Autonomous Prefecture		昌吉市、阜康市、呼图壁县、玛纳斯县、奇台县、吉木萨尔县、木垒哈萨克自治县 Changji City, Fukang City, Hutubi County, Manas County, Qitai County, Jimsar County, Mori Kazak Autonomous County
伊犁哈萨克自治州 Ili Kazak Autonomous Prefecture	伊犁州直属县(市) Counties (Cities) Direct Under Ili Prefecture	伊宁市、奎屯市、伊宁县、察布查尔锡伯自治县、霍城县、巩留县、新源县、昭苏县、特克斯县、尼勒克县 Yining [Gulja] City, Kuytun City , Yining [Gulja] County, Qapqal Xibe AutonomousCounty, Huocheng [Korgas] County, Gongliu [Tokkuzlara] County, Xinyuan [Kunes] County, Zhaosu [Mongolkure] County, Tekes County, Nilka County
	塔城地区 Tacheng [Tarbagatai] Administrative Offices	塔城市、乌苏市、额敏县、沙湾县、托里县、裕民县、和布克赛尔蒙古自治县 Tacheng [Qoqek] City, Usu City, Emin [Dorbiljin] County, Shawan County, Toli County, Yumin [Qagantokay] County, Hoboksar Mongol Autonomous County
	阿勒泰地区 Altay Administrative Offices	阿勒泰市、布尔津县、富蕴县、福海县、哈巴河县、青河县、吉木乃县 Altay City, Burqin County, Fuyun [Koktokay] County, Fuhai [Burultokay] County, Habahe [Kaba] County, Qinghe [Qinggil] County, Jeminay county
博尔塔拉蒙古自治州 Bortala Mongol Autonomous Prefecture		博乐市、精河县、温泉县 Bole [Bortala] City, Jinghe [Jing] County, Wenquan [Arxang] County
巴音郭楞蒙古自治州 Bayangol Mongol Autonomous Prefecture		库尔勒市、轮台县、尉犁县、若羌县、且末县、焉耆回族自治县、和静县、和硕县、博湖县 Korla City, Luntai [Bugur] County, Yuli [Lopnur] County, Ruoqiang [Qarkilik] County, Qiemo [Qarqan] County, Yanqi Hui Autonomous County, Hejing County, Bohu [Bagrax] County
阿克苏地区 Aksu Administrative Offices		阿克苏市、温宿县、库车县、沙雅县、新和县、拜城县、乌什县、阿瓦提县、柯坪县 Aksu City, Wensu [Onsu] County, Kuqa County, Xayar County, Xinhe [Toksu] County, Baicheng [Bay] County, Wushi [Uqturpan] County, Awat County, Kalpin County
克孜勒苏柯尔克孜自治州 Kizilsu Kirgiz Autonomous Prefecture		阿图什市、阿克陶县、阿合奇县、乌恰县 Artux City, Akto County, Akqi County, Wuqia [Ulugqat] County
喀什地区 Kashgar [Kaxgar] Administrative Offices		喀什市、疏附县、疏勒县、英吉沙县、泽普县、莎车县、叶城县、麦盖提县、岳普湖县、伽师县、巴楚县、塔什库尔干塔吉克自治县 Kashgar [Kaxgar] City, Shufu County, Shule County, Yengisar County, Zepu [Poskam] County, Shache [Yarkant] County, Yecheng [Kagilik] County, Makit County, Yopurga County, Jiashi [Payzawat] County, Bachu [Maralbexi] County, Taxkorgan Tajik Aotonomous County
和田地区 Hotan Administrative Offices		和田市、和田县、墨玉县、皮山县、洛浦县、策勒县、于田县、民丰县 Hotan City, Hotan County, Moyu [Karakax] County, Pishan [Guma] County, Lop County, Qira County, Yutian [Keriya] County, Minfeng [niya] County
自治区直辖县级市 Municpality Country-Level City directly under the Central Government	石河子市 Shihezi City	
	阿拉尔市 Aral City	
	图木舒克市 Tumxuk City	
	五家渠市 Wujiaqu City	
	北屯市 Beitun City	

1-3 主要年份平均每天主要社会经济活动

Selected Indicators on Average Daily Social and Economic Activities in Main Years

指　　标	Item	1978	1990	2000	2010	2011
每天创造的财富	**Daily Production**					
新疆生产总值(万元)	Gross Domestic Product (10 000 yuan)	1070.4	7162.7	37357.8	148971.8	181097.3
第一产业	Primary Industry	382.7	2851.8	7895.3	29551.5	31206.3
第二产业	Secondary Industry	502.7	2278.9	14728.2	71017.8	88380.8
工　业	Industry	396.7	1958.9	11469.3	59216.2	73978.1
建筑业	Construction	106.0	320.0	3258.9	11801.6	14402.7
第三产业	Tertiary Industry	184.9	2032.0	14734.3	48402.5	61510.1
＃交通运输仓储和邮政业	Transport, Storage and Post	32.6	400.8	4072.1	6095.1	7033.4
批发和零售业	Wholesale and Retail Trades	56.7	561.1	3016.4	7569.3	10189.0
地方财政一般预算收入(万元)	General Budgetary Revenue in Local Finance (10 000 yuan)	195.6	596.7	2166.4	13714.4	19737.8
地方财政一般预算支出(万元)	General Budgetary Expenditure in Local Finance (10 000 yuan)	466.3	1304.7	5231.6	46545.6	62588.8
粮食(吨)	Grain (ton)	10137.3	18544.9	22153.4	31512.3	32897.3
棉花(吨)	Cotton (ton)	150.7	1284.4	4109.6	6791.8	7938.9
油料(吨)	Oil-bearing Crops (ton)	283.0	1067.4	1647.7	1825.2	1829.0
肉类(吨)	Meat (ton)	264.4	834.5	2465.8	3335.3	3288.8
水产品(吨)	Aquatic Products (ton)	15.6	63.6	164.6	277.0	320.3
布(万米)	Cloth (10 000 m)	76.7	82.2	76.9	41.4	20.0
原煤(吨)	Coal (ton)	29561.9	57534.3	76682.1	271965.2	328540.0
发电量(万千瓦小时)	Electricity (10 000 kwh)	580.0	1912.1	5013.2	18611.5	23977.8
原油(吨)	Crude Oil (ton)	9672.6	19041.1	50641.9	70086.6	71661.1
粗钢(吨)	Crude Steel (ton)	231.8	999.7	3005.4	22617.5	24465.2
钢材(吨)	Steel Products (ton)	187.1	780.3	3596.1	24430.1	26990.1
水泥(吨)	Cement (ton)	2141.1	7808.2	24538.9	65780.8	86896.2
每天消费量	**Daily National Consumption**					
最终消费(万元)	Final Consumption Expenditure (10 000 yuan)	757.2	4569.1	20827.4	78508.6	96406.0
居民消费	Resident Consumption	619.3	3318.4	13488.1	43258.4	53543.3
农村居民	Rural Household	330.9	1251.1	4382.8	12501.7	15350.7
城镇居民	Urban Household	288.4	2067.3	9105.3	30756.7	38192.6
政府消费	Government Consumption Expenditure	137.9	1250.7	7339.3	35250.2	42862.7
能源消费量(万吨标准煤)	Energy Consumption (10 000 tons of SCE)		5.4	9.1	22.7	
社会消费品零售总额(万元)	Total Retail Sales of Consumer Goods (10 000 yuan)	599.7	2857.7	10260.3	36287.1	42660.0
每天其他经济活动	**Other Daily Economic Activities**					
资本形成总额(万元)	Gross Capital Formation (10 000 yuan)	504.9	3867.6	16934.9	92362.1	114036.2
固定资产形成	Fixed Capital Formation	363.0	2506.7	17756.8	88575.3	108188.2
存货增加	Increase in Stock	141.9	1360.9	-821.9	3786.9	5847.9
全社会固定资产投资总额	Total investment in Fixed Assets	35.6	2432.3	16722.7	96977.8	129117.0
城　镇	Urban	35.6	2168.8	15256.2	87166.6	115191.8
农　村	Rural		263.6	1466.6	98112.6	13925.2
能源生产总量(万吨标准煤)	Total Energy Production	3.9	7.7	14.8	41.1	
货运量(万吨)	Freight Traffic (10 000 tons)	16.6	38.1	90.7	177.0	192.8
客运量(万人)	Passenger Traffic (10 000 persons)	2.6	26.3	63.5	127.0	138.3
邮政业务总量(亿元)	Business Volume of Postal Services		22.5	162.7	454.2	379.2
电信业务总量(亿元)	Business Volume of Telecommunication Services		22.7	1133.2	15492.3	5826.3
进出口总额(万美元)	Total Value of Imports and Exports (USD 10 000)	6.4	112.4	620.3	4692.7	6252.7
出口额	Exports	2.6	91.9	329.9	3479.4	4610.7
进口额	Imports	3.8	20.5	290.4	1139.3	1642.0
实际利用外资额(万美元)	Foreign Capital Actually Used (USD 10 000)		20.9	5.3	65.0	91.7
入境旅游收入(万美元)	Foreign Exchange Earnings from International Tourism	…	3.3	26.0	100.9	127.5
国际旅游外汇收入(万美元)	Number of Tourists from Abroad (person)					
每天婚姻变动	**Daily Marriages Changes**					
结　婚(对)	Marriages (couple)		434	445	723	774
离　婚(对)	Divorces (couple)		155	162	268	272

1-4 主要年份国民经济和社会发展总量与速度指标

指　　标	Item	1978
人口与就业	**Population and Employment**	
人口(万人)	**Population (10 000 persons)**	
年末总人口	Population at the Year-end	1233.01
男　性	Male	630.18
女　性	Female	602.83
就业(万人)	**Employment (10 000 persons)**	
就业人员数	Employment	491.25
#在岗职工人数	Staff and Workers	226.69
城镇登记失业人数	Urban Registeration Unemployment	
宏观经济	**Macro Economy**	
国民经济核算(亿元)	**National Accounting (100 million yuan)**	
新疆生产总值	Gross Domestic Product	39.07
第一产业	Primary Industry	13.97
第二产业	Secondary Industry	18.35
第三产业	Tertiary Industry	6.75
支出法新疆生产总值	Gross Domestic Product by Expenditure Approach	
#最终消费	Final Consumption Expenditure	27.64
居民消费	Houshold Consumption Expenditure	22.61
政府消费	Government Consumption Expenditure	5.03
资本形成总额	Gross Capital Formation	18.43
固定资本形成	Gross Fixed Capital Formation	13.25
存货增加	Changes in Inventories	5.18
货物和服务净出口	Net Export of Goods and Services	-7.00
固定资产投资(亿元)	**Investment in Fixed Assets (100 million yuan)**	
全社会固定资产投资总额	Total Investment in Fixed Assets	13.00
城　镇	Urban	13.00
#房地产	Real Estate Development	
农　村	Rural	
全社会施工房屋建筑面积（万平方米）	Floor Space of Buildings under Construction (10 000 sq.m)	
全社会竣工房屋建筑面积（万平方米）	Floor Space of Building Completed (10 000 sq.m)	
消　费	Consumption	
社会消费品零售总额(亿元)	Total Retail Sales of Consumer Goods (100 million yuan)	21.89
对外贸易	Foreign Trade	
进出口总额(万美元)	Total Value of Imports and Exports	2346
出口额	Exports	937
进口额	Imports	1409
利用外资(万美元)	**Utilization of Foreign Capital (USD 10 000)**	
签订利用外资协议额	Amount of Foreign Capital for Utilization through Signed Contracts or Agreements	
实际利用外资额	Amount of Foreign Capital Actually Utilized	
财政(亿元)	**Public Finance (100 million yuan)**	
地方财政一般预算收入	Local Financial Governments Intrabudgetary Ordinary Revenue	7.14
#税收收入	Various Taxes	4.34

Principal Aggregate Indicators on National Economic and Social Development and Growth Rates in Main Years

总量指标 Aggregate Data				速度指标(%) Indices and Growth Rates						
				指数(2011 年比以下各年) Index (2011 as percentuage of the following years)				平均增长速度 Average Annual Growth Rate		
1990	2000	2010	2011	1978	1990	2000	2010	1979-2011	1991-2011	2001-2011
1529.16	1849.41	2181.58	2208.71	179.1	144.4	119.4	101.3	1.8	1.8	1.6
785.06	957.07	1127.01	1128.75	179.1	143.8	117.9	100.2	1.8	1.7	1.5
744.10	892.34	1054.57	1079.96	179.1	145.1	121.0	102.4	1.8	1.8	1.7
617.70	672.50	894.65	953.34	194.1	154.3	141.8	106.6	2.0	2.1	3.2
300.53	255.75	245.48	270.77	119.4	90.1	105.9	110.3	0.5	-0.5	0.5
9.60	11.00	10.99	11.12		115.8	101.1	101.2		0.7	0.1
261.44	1363.56	5437.47	6610.05	2623.3	755.0	298.8	112.0	10.4	10.1	10.5
104.09	288.18	1078.63	1139.03	1056.9	337.2	184.2	106.5	7.4	6.0	5.7
83.18	537.58	2592.15	3225.90	2408.7	892.4	330.0	112.0	10.1	11.0	11.5
74.17	537.80	1766.69	2245.12	7524.1	1196.9	363.4	111.4	13.7	12.5	11.7
166.77	760.20	2865.56	3518.82							
121.12	492.32	1578.93	1954.33							
45.65	267.88	1286.63	1564.49							
141.17	618.12	3371.22	4162.32							
91.50	648.12	3233.00	3948.87							
49.67	-30.00	138.22	213.45							
-46.50	-14.76	-799.31	-1071.09							
88.78	610.38	3539.69	4712.77	36252.1	5308.4	772.1	133.1	19.6	20.8	20.4
79.16	556.85	3181.58	4204.50	32342.3	5311.4	755.1	132.2	19.1	20.8	20.1
0.95	57.43	347.72	516.39		54356.8	899.2	148.5		35.0	22.1
9.62	53.53	358.11	508.27		5283.5	949.5	141.9		20.8	22.7
1740.94	4485.77	11361.96	16804.88		965.3	374.6	147.9		11.4	12.8
1337.06	2633.23	4649.89	5899.06		441.2	224.0	126.9		7.3	7.6
104.30	374.50	1324.48	1557.09	7113.2	1492.9	415.8	117.6	13.8	13.7	13.8
41025	226399	1712834	2282225	97281.5	5563.0	1008.1	133.2	23.2	21.1	23.4
33530	120408	1296981	1682886	179603.6	5019.0	1397.7	129.8	25.5	20.5	27.1
7495	105991	415853	599339	42536.5	7996.5	565.5	144.1	20.1	23.2	17.1
4463	9212	30091	55834		1251.0	606.1	185.6		12.8	17.8
7629	1923	23742	33485		438.9	1741.3	141.0		7.3	29.7
21.78	79.07	500.58	720.43	10090.1	3307.8	911.1	143.9	15.0	18.1	22.2
20.45	64.53	416.23	593.41	13673.0	2901.8	919.6	142.6	16.1	17.4	22.3

1-4 续表 1

指　　标	Item	1978
地方财政一般预算支出	Local Financial Governments Intrabudgetary Ordinary Expenditures	17.02
＃一般公共服务	General Common Service	
教育与科学技术	Operating Expenses for Education and Operating Expenses for Science and Technology	
社会保障和就业	Operating Expenses for Medical Treatment and Sanitation	
节能环保	Energy Saving and Environmental Protection	
城乡社区事务	Expenses of Community	
农林水事务	Expenses of Agriculture, Forest and Irrigation	
物价总指数(上年=100)	**Price Indices (preceding year=100)**	
居民消费价格总指数	Consumer Price Index	101.2
商品零售价格总指数	Retail Price Index	101.4
工业品出厂价格指数	Producer Price Indices for Manufacture Goods	
工业品购进价格指数	Purchasing Price Indices of Industrial Products	
固定资产投资价格指数	Investment in Fixed Assets Price Indices	
能源生产与消费(万吨标准煤)	**Production and Consumption of Energy (10 000 tons of SCE)**	
能源生产总量	Total Energy Production	1410.75
能源消费总量	Total Energy Consumption	979.27
产　业	**Industry**	
农　业	**Agriculture**	
农林牧渔业总产值(亿元)	Gross Output Value of Farming, Forestry, Animal Husbandry and Fishery (100 million yuan)	19.12
主要农产品产量(万吨)	Output of Major Farm Products (10 000 tons)	
粮　食	Grain	370.01
棉　花	Cotton	5.50
油　料	Oil-bearing Crops	10.33
甜　菜	Beet Roots	16.37
水　果	Fruits	13.98
肉　类	Meat	9.65
奶　类	Milk	5.25
水产品	Aquatic Products	0.57
工　业	**Industry**	
主要工业产品产量	Output of Major Industrial Products	
纱(万吨)	Yarn (10 000 tons)	2.80
布(亿米)	Cloth (100 million meter)	1.56
绒线(吨)	Knitting Wool (ton)	1239
呢绒(万米)	Woolen Goods (10 000 meter)	189
原盐(万吨)	Crude Salt (10 000 tons)	51.71
机制纸及纸板(万吨)	Machine-Made Paper and Paperboards (10 000 tons)	1.99
成品糖(万吨)	Refined Sugar (10 000 tons)	2.08
原煤(万吨)	Natural Crude Petroleum Coal (10 000 tons)	1079.01
原油(万吨)	Crude Oil (10 000 tons)	353.05
天然气(亿立方米)	Natural Gas (100 million cu.m)	2.51
发电量(亿千瓦小时)	ElectriCity (100 million kwh)	21.17

Continued

总量指标 Aggregate Data				速度指标(%) Indices and Growth Rates						
				指数(2011 年比以下各年) Index (2011 as percentuage of the following years)				平均增长速度 Average Annual Growth Rate		
1990	2000	2010	2011	1978	1990	2000	2010	1979-2011	1991-2011	2001-2011
47.62	190.95	1698.91	2284.49	13422.4	4797.3	1196.4	134.5	16.0	20.2	25.3
		195.57	245.36				125.5			
		334.02	426.24				127.6			
		166.40	201.64				121.2			
		51.02	53.67				105.2			
		95.28	140.10				147.0			
		220.50	297.59				135.0			
105.0	99.4	104.3	105.9							
104.1	98.3	104.6	105.1							
	129.4	125.3	114.8							
	115.2	123.9	117.8							
	103.6	104.6	107.1							
2801.57	5419.77	15000.47								
1924.38	3316.03	8290.20								
144.65	487.20	1846.18	1955.39	1145.6	377.2	195.4	106.9	7.7	6.5	6.3
676.89	808.60	1150.20	1200.75	324.5	177.4	148.5	104.4	3.6	2.8	3.7
46.88	150.00	247.90	289.77	5268.5	618.1	193.2	116.9	12.8	9.1	6.2
38.96	60.14	66.62	66.76	646.3	171.4	111.0	100.2	5.8	2.6	1.0
224.37	292.65	486.97	518.95	3170.1	231.3	177.3	106.6	11.0	4.1	5.3
79.88	151.87	593.85	601.65	4303.6	753.2	396.2	101.3	12.1	10.1	13.3
30.46	90.00	121.74	120.04	1243.9	394.1	133.4	98.6	7.9	6.7	2.7
35.64	78.23	132.82	133.91	2550.7	375.7	171.2	100.8	10.3	6.5	5.0
2.32	6.01	10.11	11.69	2050.9	503.9	194.5	115.6	9.6	8.0	6.2
10.19	33.43	41.58	39.91	1425.4	391.7	119.4	96.0	8.4	6.7	1.6
3.00	2.81	1.51	0.73	46.8	24.3	26.0	48.3	-2.3	-6.5	-11.5
2179	1184	741	444	35.8	20.4	37.5	59.9	-3.1	-7.3	-8.5
1230	754	326	383	202.6	31.1	50.8	117.5	2.2	-5.4	-6.0
159.00	31.78	174.67	258.05	499.0	162.3	812.0	147.7	5.0	2.3	21.0
9.09	17.65	37.10	42.29	2125.1	465.2	239.6	114.0	9.7	7.6	8.3
16.84	30.76	45.10	46.11	2216.8	273.8	149.9	102.2	9.8	4.9	3.7
2100.00	2798.90	9926.72	11991.71	1111.4	571.0	428.4	120.8	7.6	8.7	14.1
695.00	1848.43	2558.16	2615.63	740.9	376.3	141.5	102.2	6.3	6.5	3.2
5.02	35.39	249.91	235.38	9377.7	4688.8	665.1	94.2	14.7	20.1	18.8
69.79	182.98	679.33	875.19	4134.1	1254.0	478.3	128.8	11.9	12.8	15.3

1-4 续表 2

指　　标	Item	1978
粗钢(万吨)	Crude Steel (10 000 tons)	8.46
钢材(万吨)	Steel Products (10 000 tons)	6.83
水泥(万吨)	Cement (10 000 tons)	78.15
全部工业总产值(亿元)	Gross industrial Output Value (100 million yuan)	33.91
规模以上工业企业主要经济指标	Principal Financial Indicators of Industrial Enterprises Above Designated Size	
工业总产值	Gross Industrial Output Value	28.43
资产总计	Orignінal Value of fixed Assets	
主营业务收入	Revenue from Principal Business	
利润总额(亿元)	Profits (100 million yuan)	4.28
建筑业	**Construction**	
建筑业企业从业人员(万人)	Number of Employed Persons (10 000 persons)	
建筑业企业总产值(亿元)	Gross Output Value (100 million yuan)	
施工房屋面积(万平方米)	Floor Space of Buildings under Construction (10 000 sq.m)	
竣工房屋面积(万平方米)	Floor Space of Buildings Completed (10 000 sq.m)	
交通运输	**Transportation**	
货运量(万吨)	Freight Traffic (10 000 tons)	6064
铁　路	Railways	923
公　路	Highways	4843
管　道	Pipelines	298
航　空	Civil Aviation	0.12
客运量(万人)	Passenger Traffic Volume (10 000 persons)	941
铁　路	Railways	148
公　路	Highways	786
航　空	Civil Aviation	7
邮电通信业	**Postal and Telecommunication Services**	
邮政业务总量(亿元)	Business Volume of Postal Services (100 million yuan)	
电信业务总量(亿元)	Business Volume of Telecommunication Services (100 million yuan)	
函　件(万件)	Number of Letters Delivered (10 000 pieces)	4843
报刊期发数(万份)	Number of Newspapers and Magazines Distributed (10 000 copies)	224
局用交换机容量(万门)	CapaCity of Office Telephone Exchanges (10 000 lines)	
固定电话年末用户(万部)	Local Telephone Subscribers at Year-end (10 000 subscribers)	2.90
移动电话用户(万户)	Number of Mobile Telephone Subscribers (10 000 subscribers)	
旅　游	**Tourism**	
入境旅游过夜者人数(万人)	Number of Tourists (10 000 person-times)	0.01
入境旅游收入(万美元)	Foreign Exchange Eearnings from International Tourism (100 million yuan)	5
金　融	**Finance and Insurance**	
金融机构各项存款(亿元)	Deposits of National Banking System (100 million yuan)	32.07
金融机构各项贷款(亿元)	Loans of National Banking System (100 million yuan)	18.26
教育、科技、文化	**Education, Science & Technology and Culture**	
教　育	**Education**	
专任教师数(人)	Full-time Teachers (person)	
普通高等学校	Regular Institutions of Higher Education	2458

Continued

总量指标 Aggregate Data				速度指标(%) Indices and Growth Rates						
				指数(2011 年比以下各年) Index (2011 as percentuage of the following years)				平均增长速度 Average Annual Growth Rate		
1990	2000	2010	2011	1978	1990	2000	2010	1979-2011	1991-2011	2001-2011
36.49	109.70	825.54	892.98	10555.3	2447.2	814.0	108.2	15.2	16.4	21.0
28.48	131.26	891.70	985.14	14423.7	3459.1	750.5	110.5	16.3	18.4	20.1
285.00	895.67	2400.96	3171.71	4058.5	1112.9	354.1	132.1	11.9	12.2	12.2
219.92	1061.29	5766.51	7105.31	3721.3	978.5	372.0	111.7	11.6	11.5	12.7
174.24	852.01	5341.90	6720.85							
	1708.81	7911.97	9304.95			544.5	117.6			16.7
139.05	821.26	5492.61	6782.25		4877.6	825.8	123.5		20.3	21.2
3.13	90.49	852.43	963.74	22517.3	30790.4	1065.0	113.1	17.8	31.4	24.0
22.86	26.16	56.48	52.73		230.7	201.6	93.4		4.1	6.6
27.39	234.95	969.47	1327.83		4847.9	565.2	137.0		20.3	17.1
578.05	2241.48	6620.14	8947.71		1547.9	399.2	135.2		13.9	13.4
282.88	1261.42	2891.44	3465.49		1225.1	274.7	119.9		12.7	9.6
13920	33091	64597	70362	1160.1	505.5	212.6	108.9	7.7	8.0	7.1
1691	4199	6853	6904	748.0	408.3	164.4	100.7	6.3	6.9	4.6
11551	27048	50448	55965	1155.6	484.5	206.9	110.9	7.7	7.8	6.8
677	1840	7292	7489	2513.1	1106.2	407.0	102.7	10.3	12.1	13.6
0.87	3.50	3.70	3.90	3250.0	448.3	111.4	105.4	11.1	7.4	1.0
9602	23191	46346	50461	5362.5	525.5	217.6	108.9	12.8	8.2	7.3
388	1147	1523	2002	1352.7	516.0	174.5	131.5	8.2	8.1	5.2
9161	21877	44333	47927	6097.6	523.2	219.1	108.1	13.3	8.2	7.4
53	167	490	532	7600.0	1003.8	318.6	108.6	14.0	11.6	11.1
0.82	5.94	16.58	13.84		1687.8	233.0	83.5		14.4	8.0
0.83	41.36	565.47	212.66		25621.7	514.2	37.6		30.2	16.1
7381	7148	2926	3202	66.1	43.4	44.8	109.4	-1.2	-3.9	-7.0
806	535	307	296	132.1	36.7	55.3	96.4	0.8	-4.7	-5.2
	241.67	928.20	915.10			378.7	98.6			12.9
8.94	191.03	547.50	540.80	18648.3	6049.2	283.1	98.8	17.2	21.6	9.9
	78.00	1359.80	1670.90			2142.2	122.9			32.1
7.98	25.61	101.03	132.50	1325000.0	1660.4	517.4	131.1	33.3	14.3	16.1
1212	9494	36844	46519	930380.0	3838.2	490.0	126.3	31.9	19.0	15.5
221.80	1863.48	8870.72	10387.00	32388.5	4683.0	557.4	117.1	19.1	20.1	16.9
233.72	1403.13	4973.16	6270.21	34338.5	2682.8	446.9	126.1	19.4	17.0	14.6
7002	7924	16506	17256	702.0	246.4	217.8	104.5	6.1	4.4	7.3

1-4 续表 3

指　　标	Item	1978
中等学校	Regular Secondary Schools	44417
小　学	Regular Primary Schools	82616
在校学生数(万人)	Students Enrollment (10 000 persons)	
普通高等学校	Regular Institutions of Higher Education	1.02
中等学校	Regular Secondary Schools	83.86
小　学	Regular Primary Schools	202.88
科　技	**Science and Technology**	
研究与发展经费支出(万元)	Expenditures on Research and Development (10 000 yuan)	
技术市场交易额(万元)	Volume of Transaction in Technical Markets (10 000 yuan)	
文　化	**Culture**	
电视节目制作时间(小时)	Time for TV Programs Production (hour)	
家庭、生活、环境	**Family, People's Livelihood and Environment**	
家　庭	**Family**	
家庭总户数(万户)	Total Number of Households (10 000 households)	
婚　姻	**Marriages and Divorces**	
结婚数(万对)	Number of Marriages (10 000 couples)	
离婚数(万对)	Number of Divorces (10 000 couples)	
居　住	**Housing**	
城镇居民人均住房建筑面积(平方米)	Per capita Gross Floor Space of Urban Residents (sq.m)	
农村居民人均住房面积(平方米)	Per capita Net Floor Space of Rural Residents (sq.m)	
生　活	**People's Livelihood**	
城镇居民人均可支配收入(元)	Per Capita Annual Disposable Income of Urban Households (yuan)	319
农村居民人均纯收入(元)	Per Capita Net Income of Rural Residents (yuan)	119
城乡居民储蓄存款余额(亿元)	Outstanding Amount of Saving Deposits in Urban and Rural Areas (100 million yuan)	6.42
卫　生	**Health Care**	
医院、卫生院(个)	Number of Hospitals (unit)	806
医生(人)	Number of Doctors (person)	16898
医院、卫生院床位数(张)	Number of Hospital Beds (unit)	39179
市政建设	**Municipal Works**	
自来水供应量(亿立方米)	Volume of Tapping Water Supply(100 million cu.m)	
下水道长度(公里)	Length of Sewer Pipelines (km)	
铺装道路长度(公里)	Length of Paved Roads (km)	
环境、灾害	**Environment and Disaster**	
化学需氧量排放量(万吨)	COD Discharge (10 000 tons)	
二氧化硫排放量(万吨)	Sulphur Dioxide Emission (10 000 tons)	
火灾发生数(起)	Number of Fire Disasters (times)	
火灾损失(万元)	Fire Loss (10 000 yuan)	
交通事故发生数(起)	Number of Traffic Accidents (times)	
交通事故损失(万元)	Loss of Traffic Accidents (10 000 yuan)	

Continued

总量指标 Aggregate Data				速度指标(%) Indices and Growth Rates						
				指数(2011 年比以下各年) Index (2011 as percentuage of the following years)				平均增长速度 Average Annual Growth Rate		
1990	2000	2010	2011	1978	1990	2000	2010	1979-2011	1991-2011	2001-2011
78596	89211	128306	132748	298.9	168.9	148.8	103.5	3.4	2.5	3.7
95060	131259	133963	135182	163.6	142.2	103.0	100.9	1.5	1.7	0.3
3.13	7.41	26.38	27.28	2674.5	871.6	368.2	103.4	10.5	10.9	12.6
101.52	131.18	168.40	167.52	199.8	165.0	127.7	99.5	2.1	2.4	2.2
185.72	247.74	193.58	191.95	94.[illegible]	103.4	77.5	99.2	-0.2	0.2	-2.3
	32381	266545								
	66168	43146	43045			65.1	99.8			-3.8
3699	29261	76467	85002		2298.0	290.5	111.2		16.1	10.2
356.67	481.91	639.86	663.70		186.1	137.7	103.7		3.0	3.0
15.84	16.25	26.40	28.23		178.2	173.7	106.9		2.8	5.1
5.65	5.90	9.78	9.94		175.9	168.5	101.6		2.7	4.9
18.07	26.75	27.25	28.92		160.0	108.1	106.1		2.3	0.7
14.04	17.25	24.00	26.14		186.2	151.5	108.9		3.0	3.9
1314	5645	13644	15514	4863.3	1180.7	274.8	113.7	12.5	12.5	9.6
684	1618	4643	5442	4573.1	795.6	336.3	117.2	12.3	10.4	11.7
114.13	908.55	3713.47	4421.93	68877.4	3874.5	486.7	119.1	21.9	19.0	15.5
1049	1352	1712	1742	216.1	166.1	128.8	101.8	2.4	2.4	2.3
33683	45402	48166	48618	287.7	144.3	107.1	100.9	3.3	1.8	0.6
60707	65916	109851	118781	303.2	195.7	180.2	108.1	3.4	3.2	5.5
1.57	5.00	7.73	8.09		515.3	161.8	104.7		8.1	4.5
533	2008	4372	4592		861.5	228.7	105.0		10.8	7.8
970	2809	5178	5476		564.5	194.9	105.8		8.6	6.3
		29.60	67.29				227.3			
15.70	31.10	58.85	76.31		486.1	245.4	129.7		7.8	8.5
	3050	5209	5093			167.0	97.8			4.8
	2329	3041	5179			222.4	170.3			7.5
	10048	4949	5182			51.6	104.7			-5.8
	4443	864	1036			23.3	119.9			-12.4

1-5 主要年份国民经济和社会发展结构指标
Composition Indicators on National Economic and Social Development in Main Years

单位：% (%)

指　标	Item	1978	1990	2000	2010	2011
人口与就业	**Population and Employment**					
人　口	**Population**					
性别结构	Sexual Composition					
男	Male	51.1	51.3	51.8	51.3	51.1
女	Female	48.9	48.7	48.2	48.7	48.9
就　业	**Employment**					
产业结构	Industrial Composition					
第一产业	Primary Industry	72.1	61.3	57.7	49.0	48.7
第二产业	Secondary Industry	14.3	17.4	13.8	14.8	15.6
第三产业	Tertiary Industry	13.6	21.3	28.5	36.2	35.7
宏观经济	**Macro Economy**					
国民核算	**National Accounting**					
新疆生产总值产业结构	Industrial Composition					
第一产业	Primary Industry	35.8	39.8	21.1	19.8	17.1
第二产业	Secondary Industry	47.0	31.8	39.4	47.7	48.5
#工　业	Industry	37.1	27.3	30.7	39.8	40.6
第三产业	Tertiary Industry	17.2	28.4	39.5	32.5	34.4
固定资产投资	**Investment**					
全社会固定资产投资结构	Composition of Total Investment in Fixed Assets					
城　镇	Urban	100	89.2	91.2	89.9	89.2
#房地产	Real Estate Development		1.2	10.3	9.8	11.0
农　村	Rural		10.8	8.8	10.1	10.8
资金来源结构	Composition of Funded Sources					
国家预算内资金	State Budgetary Appropriation	79.0	11.9	8.3	16.8	12.2
国内贷款	Domestic Loans		33.2	22.1	15.2	13.0
利用外资	Foreign Investment		4.6	1.6	0.3	0.3
自筹和其他投资	Fundraising and Other Investment	21.0	50.3	68.0	67.7	74.5
对外经济贸易	**Foreign Economic Trade**					
进出口总额结构	Composition of total Value of Exports and Imports					
出口额	Exports	39.9	81.7	53.2	75.7	73.7
进口额	Imports	60.1	18.3	46.8	24.3	26.3
财　政	**Government Finance**					
地方财政一般预算收入结构	Composition of Government Revenue					
税收收入	Various Taxes	60.8	93.9	81.6	83.2	82.4
非税收入	Nontax Revenues	39.2	6.1	18.4	16.8	17.6
地方财政一般预算支出结构	Composition of Government Expenditures					
一般公共服务	General Common Service				11.5	10.7
教育与科学技术	Operating Expenses for Education and Operating Expenses for Science and Technology				19.7	18.7
社会保障和就业	Operating Expenses for Medical Treatment and Sanitation				9.8	8.8
环境保护	Operating Expenses for Environmental Conservation				3.0	2.3
城乡社区事务	Expenses of Community				5.6	6.1
农林水事务	Expenses of Agriculture, Forest and Irrigation				13.0	13.0
其他各项支出	Other Expense				37.4	40.4
能源生产与消费	**Energy Production and Consumption**					
能源生产总量结构	Composition of Total Energy Production					
原　煤	Coal	60.0	58.8	40.6	50.3	
原　油	Petroleum Crude Oil	35.8	35.8	48.7	24.4	
天然气	Natural Gas	2.4	2.4	7.9	22.2	
水风电	Water, Wind and Electricity	1.8	3.0	2.8	3.1	

1-5 续表 1 Continued

单位: % (%)

指 标	Item	1978	1990	2000	2010	2011
能源消费总量结构	Composition of Total Energy Consumption					
煤 炭	Coal	72.5	69.6	63.6	65.8	
石 油	Petroleum Oil	21.5	22.5	23.3	15.8	
天然气	Natural Gas	3.4	3.5	8.6	12.4	
水电、风电	Hydro-power, Wind Power	2.6	4.4	4.5	5.6	
产 业	**Industrial**					
农 业	**Agriculture**					
农林牧渔业产值结构	Composition of Gross Output Value of AgricultureForestry,Animal Husbandry, Fishery					
农 业	Farming	74.5	76.4	74.0	74.6	73.5
林 业	Forestry	1.8	2.6	1.7	1.9	2.0
牧 业	Animal Husbandry	23.5	20.4	23.5	20.4	21.2
渔 业	Fishery	0.2	0.6	0.8	0.7	0.7
农林牧渔服务业	Agricultural, Forestry, Animal Husbandry, Fishery and Their Services				2.4	2.6
工 业	**Industry**					
工业总产值规模结构	Composition of Gross Output Value of Industry					
大型企业	Large Enterprises		27.5	53.7	55.2	57.1
中型企业	Medium-sized Enterprises		17.4	10.1	24.4	24.4
小型企业	Small Enterprises		55.1	36.2	20.4	18.5
建筑业	**Construction**					
建筑业总产值结构	Composition of Gross Output Value of Construction Industry					
建筑工程	Construction Projects		88.2	88.3	87.2	89.3
安装工程	Installation Projects		10.3	9.1	11.4	9.2
其 他	Others		1.5	2.6	1.4	1.5
交通运输业	**Transportation**					
货运量结构按运输方式分	By Means of Transportation					
铁 路	Railways	15.2	12.1	12.7	10.6	9.8
公 路	Highways	79.9	83.0	81.7	78.1	79.5
民用航空	Civil Aviation	…	…	…	…	…
管道输油(气)	Pipelines	4.9	4.9	5.6	11.3	10.6
旅游业	**International Tourism**					
来华旅游人数结构	Composition of Tourists					
外国人	Foreigners	100.0	80.4	81.4	94.8	94.3
港澳台同胞	Compatriots form Hong Kong, Macao and Taiwan		19.6	18.6	5.2	5.7
金 融	**Finance**					
金融机构资金来源结构	Composition of Sources of Funds in State Banks					
各项存款	Various Deposits			122.8	110.1	105.3
应付及暂收款	Payable and Temporary Collection			…	1.5	1.6
所有者权益	Owner's Right and Interest			0.1	3.6	4.4
其 他	Others			-22.9	-15.3	-11.3
金融机构资金运用结构	Composition of Fund Uses in State Banks					
各项贷款	Loans			92.5	61.8	63.6
有价证券及投资	Securities and Investment			4.4	5.6	4.7
系统内资金往来	Funds Tranfer inward Banks			1.6	29.1	23.6
库存现金	Cash in Stock			1.1	0.7	0.8
其 他	Others			0.4	2.8	7.3
教育、科技	**Education and Science**					
教 育	**Education**					
在校学生结构	Composition of Student Enrollment					
大学生	College and University Students	0.4	1.1	2.0	6.8	7.0
中学生	Secondary School Students	29.1	31.4	30.8	43.4	43.4
小学生	Primary School Students	70.5	67.5	67.2	49.8	49.6

1-5 续表 2 Continued

单位: % (%)

指　标	Item	1978	1990	2000	2010	2011
专任教师结构	Full-time Teachers by Type					
大　学	Colleges and Universities	1.9	3.9	3.5	5.9	6.0
中　学	Secondary Schools	34.3	43.5	39.1	46.0	46.7
小　学	Primary Schools	63.8	52.6	57.4	48.1	47.3
科　技	**Science and Technology**					
科学研究与试验发展经费支出结构	Composition of Expenditure on Research and Development					
基础研究	Basic Research			4.7	5.4	
应用研究	Supplied Research			27.4	23.6	
实验发展	Experimental Development			67.9	71.0	
生活、环境	**People's Livelihood and Environment**					
生　活	**People's Livelihood**					
城镇居民消费结构	Consumption Composition of Urban Residents					
食品类	Food		47.8	36.4	36.2	38.3
衣着类	Clothing		15.6	13.1	14.8	14.5
家庭设备、用品及服务	Articles for Daily Use and Others		11.0	7.6	6.6	6.7
医疗保健	Health Care and Medical Services		2.5	7.5	6.9	7.7
交通通讯	Transport and Communication		1.6	7.5	12.3	11.6
教育文化娱乐服务	Education,Cultral and Recreation Services		11.2	15.1	9.9	9.5
居　住	Residence		4.6	9.4	8.8	7.5
杂项商品和服务	Miscellaneous Goods and Services		5.7	3.4	4.5	4.2
农村居民消费结构	Consumption Composition of Rural Residents					
食品类	Food		53.7	50.0	40.3	36.1
衣着类	Clothing		15.3	9.2	8.8	8.5
家庭设备、用品及服务	Articles for Daily Use and Others		17.4	3.7	4.0	4.5
医疗保健	Health Care and Medical Services		7.0	6.0	9.1	12.1
交通和通讯	Transport and Communication		1.1	4.9	11.1	5.2
文教娱乐用品及服务	Education,Cultural and Recreation Services		5.3	8.6	4.9	8.6
居　住	Residence		13.5	13.8	20.1	23.3
其他商品和服务	Other Goods and Services		0.7	3.8	1.7	1.7
卫　生	**Health Care**					
卫生技术人员结构	Doctors by Types					
执业医师(西医师)	(Doctors of Western Medicine)	14.4	31.3	76.9	32.0	30.8
执业助理医师(西医士)	(Paramedics of Western Medicine)	18.7	10.9	23.1	7.2	7.1
注册护士	Registered Nurses	21.1	29.3		36.0	37.3
药剂人员	Pharmacist		7.9		5.2	5.0
技师(士)	Laboratory Technician				6.3	5.9
其他	Others				13.3	13.9
环境、灾害	**Environment and Disasters**					
治理工业污染资金使用结构	Uses of Funds Inindustrial Pollution Treatment					
治理废水	Waste Water Treatment		55.3	38.2	29.5	18.2
治理废气	Waste Gas Treatment		32.4	40.9	69.3	81.6
治理固体废物	Solid Wastes Treatment		10.6	1.6	1.2	
治理噪声	Noise Abatement		0.9	18.4		
其　他	Others		0.8	0.9	…	0.2
火灾事故损失额结构	Composition of Fire Losses Converted into Cash					
特　大	Extraordinarily Serious Fires			15.7		
重　大	Serious Fires			14.3	...	
较　大	Big Fires				0.1	…
一　般	Ordinary Fires			70.0	99.9	100.0

1-6 主要年份国民经济和社会发展比例和效益指标

Indicators on Proportions and Efficiency in National Economic and Social Development in Main Years

指　　标	Item	1978	1990	2000	2010	2011
就　业	**Employment**					
城镇登记失业率(%)	Unemployment Rate in Urban Areas (%)		3.8	3.8	3.2	3.2
国民经济核算	**National Accounting**					
人均生产总值(元/人)	Per capita GDP (yuan/person)	313	1713	7372	25034	30087
固定资产投资	**Investment in Fixed Assets**					
全社会固定资产投资相当于新疆生产总值比例(%)	Proportion of Investment in Fixed Assets to GDP of Xinjiang (%)	33.3	34	44.8	65.1	71.3
全社会房屋建筑面积竣工率(%)	Rate of Total Floor Space of Buildings Completed in Construction (%)		76.8	58.7	40.9	35.1
消　费	**Consumption**					
人均社会消费品零售额(元)	Per Capita Retail Sales of Consumer Goods(yuan)	179	699	2066	6104	7094
对外贸易	**Foreign Trade**					
进出口总额相当于新疆生产总值比例(%)	Proportion of Total Value of Imports & Exports to GDP	1.01	7.52	13.74	21.32	22.30
财　政	**Finance**					
地方财政一般预算收入相当于新疆生产总值比例(%)	Proportion of Local Financial Revenue to GDP of Xinjiang (%)	18.3	8.3	5.8	9.2	10.9
地方财政一般预算支出相当于新疆生产总值比例(%)	Proportion of Local Financial Expenditure to GDP of Xinjiang (%)	43.6	18.2	14.0	31.2	34.6
利用外资	**Utilization of Foreign Capital**					
实际利用外资额相当于签订利用外资额比例(%)	Proportion of Actually Foreign Direct Investment for Foreign Direct Investment (%)		80.94	20.87	78.90	59.97
能　源	**Energy**					
能源生产弹性系数	Elasticity Ratio of Energy Production	1.20	0.50	0.40	1.02	
电力生产弹性系数	Elasticity Ratio of Electricety Production		0.92	0.99	2.02	
能源消费弹性系数	Elasticity Ratio of Energy Consumption	0.74	0.79	0.38	0.96	
电力消费弹性系数	Elasticity Ratio of Electricity Consumption		0.92	0.99	1.96	

1-6 续表 1 Continued

指　标	Item	1978	1990	2000	2010	2011
农　业	**Agriculture**					
每公顷播种面积农产品产量（公斤）	Output of Farm Crops per Hectare of Sown Area (kg)					
粮　食	Grain	1650	3705	5595	5771	6003
棉　花	Cotton	375	1080	1485	1697	1769
油　料	Oil-bearing Crops	510	1440	1935	2437	2526
工业（规模以上）	**Industry(Aboue Designated Size)**					
总资产贡献率（%）	Rate of Total Assets to Industrial Output Value (%)			11.2	18.2	18.4
资产负债率（%）	Assets-Liability Ratio (%)			62.7	50.8	53.8
成本费用利润率（%）	Rate of Profits to Industrial Cost (%)		2.6	12.8	19.3	17.5
流动资产周转次数（次/年）	Number of Times of Annual of Turnover Circulating Funds (times/year)		1.5	1.6	2.2	2.2
建筑业	**Construction**					
技术装备率（元/人）	Value of Machinery per Laborer (yuan/person)		2511	8582	7145	6812
动力装备率（千瓦/人）	Power of Machines Per Laborer (kw/person)		5	7	4	4
全员劳动生产率(按总产值计算)(元/人)	Overall Labor Productivity (yuan/person) (in terms of gross output value per employee)		12014	74994	176404	226848
交通运输业	**Transportation**					
铁路网密度（公里/万平方公里）	Railway Density (km/10 000 sq.km)	6.19	9.48	18.08	26.39	26.91
公路网密度（公里/万平方公里）	Highway Density (km/10 000 sq.km)	143	153	208	918	932
邮电通信业	**Post and Communications**					
固定电话普及率(部/百人)	PopularizationRate of Telephones (set/100 persons)		0.6	15.0	25.4	25.0
移动电话普及率(部/百人)	Popularization Rate of Mobile Telephone (set/100 persons)				63.0	77.4
国际旅游	**International Tourism**					
每一来华游客花费(美元)	Expenditure per International Tourist in China (USD)		152	371	346	351

1-6 续表 2 Continued

指　标	Item	1978	1990	2000	2010	2011
金　融	**Finance**					
金融机构存款相当于新疆生产总值比例(%)	Bank Deposits as Percentage of GDP in Xinjiang (%)	82.08	84.98	136.62	163.13	157.14
金融机构贷款相当于新疆生产总值比例(%)	Bank Loans as Percentage of GDP in Xinjiang (%)	46.74	89.55	102.87	91.46	94.86
教　育	**Education**					
学龄儿童入学率(%)	Rate of School-age Children Enrollment (%)	96.00	97.50	97.03	99.78	99.73
小学升学率(%)	Rate of Graduates of Primary Schools Entering Junior Secondary Schools (%)	88.67	82.17	92.01	100.53	99.47
初中升学率(%)	Rate of Graduates of Junior Secondary Schools Entering Senior Secondary Schools (%)	48.22	39.12	30.30	45.40	47.64
学校教师负担系数(%)	Student-teacher Ratio (in percentage) (%)					
高等学校	Colleges and Universities	4.16	4.47	9.34	15.22	14.99
普通中等	Secondary Schools	19.36	13.12	14.92	12.48	12.10
小学学校	Primary Schools	24.56	19.54	18.87	14.45	14.20
科　技	**Science and Technology**					
研究与开发经费支出相当于新疆生产总值比例(%)	R&D Expenditures as Percentage of GDP (%)			0.38	0.49	
文　化	**Culture**					
每百万人有艺术表演团体(个)	Number of Troupes per Million Persons(unit)	5.24	6.21	4.76	6.08	6.06
每百万人有公共图书馆(个)	Number of Public Libraries per Million Persons(unit)	0.41	4.05	4.33	4.75	4.69
每百万人有博物馆(个)	Number of Museums per Million Persons(unit)	0.08	0.52	1.24	3.27	3.32
卫　生	**Health Care**					
每万人医院、卫生院数(个)	Number of Hospitals and Health Centers per 10 000 Persons (unit)	0.66	0.69	0.73	0.79	0.79
每万人医生数(人)	Number of Doctors per 10 000 Persons (person)	13.70	22.03	24.55	22.25	22.49
每万人医院、卫生院床位数(张)	Number of Hospital and Health Centers Beds per 10 000 Persons (unit)	31.78	39.70	35. 64	50.36	53.93
医院病床使用率(%)	Utilization Rate of Hospital Beds (%)		77.20	66.31	89.19	92.50
市政建设	**City Construction**					
城市自来水普及率(%)	Percentage of Households with Access to Tap Water (%)	59.0	80.9	98.8	99.2	99.2
城市燃气普及率(%)	Percentage of Households with Access to Tap Gas (%)	11.0	49.8	92.8	95.8	96.2
建成区绿化覆盖率(%)	Green Covrage Rate in Completed Area(%)		26.0	29.1	36.4	36.6
灾　害	**Disasters**					
平均每起火灾损失(元)	Average Loss of per Fire Disaster (yuan)			7635	5422	12529
平均每起交通事故损失(元)	Average Loss of per Traffic Accident (yuan)			4775	1746	2000

1-7 主要年份人均主要工农业产品产量

Per capita Output of Major Industrial and Agricultural Products in Main Years

年 份 Year	粮 食 (公斤) Grain (kg)	棉 花 (公斤) Cotton (kg)	油 料 (公斤) Oil-bearing Crops (kg)	甜 菜 (公斤) Sugar Crops (kg)	水 果 (公斤) Fruits (kg)	猪牛羊肉 (公斤) Pork, Beef and Mutton (kg)	水产品 (公斤) Aquatic Products (kg)
1978	303.0	4.5	8.5	13.4	11.4	7.9	0.5
1980	304.1	6.2	13.9	30.3	12.3	9.4	0.5
1985	367.2	13.9	25.3	30.1	36.4	12.8	0.7
1990	453.8	31.4	26.1	150.4	53.6	18.6	1.6
1995	443.3	56.8	30.0	174.9	69.4	27.9	2.7
2000	446.2	82.8	33.2	161.5	83.8	42.4	3.3
2001	427.3	84.3	22.9	244.3	82.8	44.5	3.3
2002	463.3	79.3	23.5	246.9	104.8	46.9	3.4
2003	417.6	83.4	26.1	198.8	113.7	50.4	3.5
2004	425.2	89.9	22.9	176.7	135.6	55.2	3.8
2005	441.5	98.5	19.6	211.0	146.6	60.5	4.0
2006	441.0	131.8	16.2	273.6	169.0	66.5	4.1
2007	418.3	139.9	19.4	283.2	214.7	67.1	4.3
2008	430.2	142.7	26.9	207.7	213.4	47.4	4.4
2009	537.1	117.7	29.8	195.1	263.5	46.5	4.5
2010	530.1	114.2	30.7	224.4	275.1	48.6	4.7
2011	547.0	132.0	30.4	236.4	274.1	46.8	5.3

年 份 Year	布 (米) Cloth (m)	机制纸及纸板 (公斤) Machine-made Paper and Paperboard (kg)	纱 (公斤) Yarn (kg)	原 煤 (公斤) Coal (kg)	原 油 (公斤) Crude Oil (kg)	发电量 (千瓦小时) Electricity (kwh)	粗钢 (公斤) Steel (kg)	水 泥 (公斤) Cement (kg)
1978	13.0	1.6	2.3	884	289	173	7	64
1980	13.0	1.9	2.5	895	308	186	8	72
1985	16.0	3.1	2.9	1183	369	282	15	149
1990	20.0	6.1	6.8	1408	466	468	23	191
1995	18.0	11.0	14.9	1652	770	731	43	297
2000	15.0	9.7	18.5	1546	1021	1011	61	495
2001	14.0	10.4	16.3	1514	1045	1061	72	527
2002	11.0	12.0	16.7	1639	1077	1123	93	545
2003	8.0	12.2	15.3	1814	1116	1222	106	588
2004	7.0	13.5	15.0	1924	1156	1367	128	623
2005	7.0	14.6	17.2	1962	1212	1545	154	625
2006	8.0	14.5	17.6	2226	1219	1759	194	657
2007	8.0	12.2	19.7	2421	1257	2011	216	742
2008	7.2	14.3	18.8	3201	1285	2315	254	792
2009	7.1	16.6	18.0	4108	1171	2664	305	956
2010	7.0	17.1	19.2	4575	1179	3131	380	1106
2011	2.0	19.3	18.2	5463	1146	3987	407	1445

1-8 主要年份人均国民经济主要指标
Per Capita Main Indicators on National Economy in Main Years

指　　标	Item	1978	1990	2000	2010	2011
新疆生产总值(元)	Gross Domestic Product of Xinjiang (yuan)	313	1713	7372	25034	30087
工农业总产值(元)	Gross Output Value of Industry and Agriculture (yuan)	450	2444	8544	35082	41276
工业总产值	Gross Industrial Output Value	278	1474	5856	26574	32368
农林牧渔业总产值	Gross Output Value of Agriculture, Forestry, Animal Husbandry and Fishery	172	970	2688	8508	8908
固定资产投资总额(元)	Total Investment in Fixed Assets (yuan)	106	595	3368	16312	21470
地方财政一般预算收入(元)	General Budgetary Revenue in Local Finance (yuan)	58	146	436	2307	3282
地方财政一般预算支出(元)	General Budgetary Expenditure in Local Finance (yuan)	139	319	1054	7829	10408
主要工农业产品产量	Output of Major Industrial and Agriculturd Produts					
粮食(公斤)	Grain Yield (kg)	303.0	453.8	446.2	530.1	547.0
棉花(公斤)	Cotton Yield (kg)	4.5	31.4	82.8	114.2	132.0
油料(公斤)	Oil-bearing Crops Yield (kg)	8.5	26.1	33.2	30.7	30.4
甜菜(公斤)	Beet Roots Yield (kg)	13.4	150.4	161.5	224.4	236.4
猪牛羊肉(公斤)	Pork, Beef and Mutton Yield (kg)	7.9	18.6	42.4	48.6	46.8
水产品(公斤)	Aquatic Products Yield (kg)	0.5	1.6	3.3	4.7	5.3
水果(公斤)	Fruits Yield (kg)	11.4	53.6	83.8	275.1	274.1
果用瓜(公斤)	Fruit Melon Yield (kg)	36.1	62.6	83.3	200.5	197.9
布(米)	Cloth (m)	13.0	20.0	15.0	7.0	2.0
机制纸和纸板(公斤)	Machine-made Paper and Paperboard (kg)	1.6	6.1	9.7	17.1	19.3
纱(公斤)	Yarn (kg)	2.3	6.8	18.5	19.2	18.2
原煤(公斤)	Coal Output (kg)	884	1408	1546	4575	5463
原油(公斤)	Crude Oil Output (kg)	289	466	1021	1179	1146
发电量(千瓦小时)	Electric Power (kwh)	173	468	1011	3131	3987
水泥(公斤)	Cement (kg)	64	191	495	1106	1445
社会消费品零售总额(元)	Total Retail Sales of Consumer Goods (yuan)	179	699	2066	6104	7094
海关出口总额(美元)	Value of Exports (USD)	0.8	23.2	66.5	789.3	766.7
高等学校在校学生数(人/万人)	Students Enrollment in Institions of Higher Education (person/10 000 persons)	8.3	20.5	41.1	115.1	117.1
中等专业学校在校学生数(人/万人)	Students Enrollment in Specialized Secondary Schools (person/10 000 persons)	19.2	30.0	56.9	69.8	73.2
普通中学在校学生数(人/万人)	Students Enrollment in Regular Secondary Schools (person/10 000 persons)	654.0	564.0	638.0	652.1	638.1
医院、卫生院床位数(张/万人)	Beds of Medical and Health Centers (unit/10 000 persons)	31.8	39.7	35.6	50.4	53.9
卫生技术人员数(人/万人)	Medical Technical Personnel (person/10 000 persons)	41.4	52.2	53.0	56.3	59.5
#医　生	Doctors	13.7	22.0	24.6	22.3	22.5
城乡居民储蓄存款余额(元)	Urban and Rural Savings Deposits (yuan)	57	746	4913	17113	20145

1-9 新疆建区以来主要年份国民经济主要指标

年 份 Year	年末总人口（万人） Year-end Population (10 000 persons)	就业人员（万人） Employed Persons (10 000 persons)	新疆生产总值(亿元) Gross Domestic Product of Xinjiang (100 million yuan)	第一产业 Primary Industry	第二产业 Secondary Industry	#工 业 Industry	第三产业 Tertiary Industry	人均新疆生产总值(元) Per Capita GDP (yuan)
1955	511.78	254.58	12.31	6.69	3.22	2.10	2.40	241
1960	686.33	338.32	25.20	9.27	11.06	8.12	4.87	374
1965	789.10	350.25	24.20	12.48	7.32	5.03	4.40	312
1970	976.58	410.33	23.08	10.35	8.67	6.19	4.06	236
1975	1154.53	466.43	28.12	11.21	12.20	8.86	4.71	240
1978	1233.01	491.25	39.07	13.97	18.35	14.48	6.75	313
1980	1283.24	506.35	53.24	21.53	21.44	17.48	10.27	410
1985	1361.14	565.81	112.24	42.89	40.50	32.14	28.85	820
1990	1529.16	617.70	261.44	104.09	83.18	71.50	74.17	1713
1991	1554.57	638.49	335.91	111.86	107.99	84.07	116.06	2101
1992	1580.63	646.94	402.31	114.50	147.64	106.29	140.17	2477
1993	1605.26	655.98	495.25	126.85	205.07	155.92	163.33	2964
1994	1632.70	657.54	662.32	187.69	249.11	190.00	225.52	3888
1995	1661.35	676.00	814.85	240.71	283.97	219.01	290.17	4701
1996	1689.29	684.00	900.93	249.31	313.70	239.07	337.92	5102
1997	1718.08	715.40	1039.85	279.73	385.37	302.50	374.75	5848
1998	1747.35	680.92	1106.95	291.05	395.75	298.53	420.15	6174
1999	1775.00	694.34	1163.17	268.51	420.48	315.86	474.18	6443
2000	1849.41	672.50	1363.56	288.18	537.58	418.63	537.80	7372
2001	1876.19	685.38	1491.60	288.12	573.91	445.60	629.57	7945
2002	1905.19	701.49	1612.65	305.00	603.15	463.59	704.50	8457
2003	1933.95	721.27	1886.35	412.90	719.54	563.57	753.91	9828
2004	1963.11	744.49	2209.09	446.13	914.47	734.10	848.49	11337
2005	2010.35	791.62	2604.14	510.00	1164.80	961.62	929.34	13108
2006	2050.00	811.75	3045.26	527.80	1459.30	1241.33	1058.16	15000
2007	2095.19	830.42	3523.16	628.72	1647.55	1405.11	1246.89	16999
2008	2130.81	847.58	4183.21	691.07	2070.76	1755.35	1421.38	19797
2009	2158.63	866.15	4277.05	759.74	1929.59	1555.84	1587.72	19942
2010	2181.58	894.65	5437.47	1078.63	2592.15	2161.39	1766.69	25034
2011	2208.71	953.34	6610.05	1139.03	3225.90	2700.20	2245.12	30087
			平均增长速度(%)					
1956-2011	2.6	2.3	8.3	5.8	9.3	9.7	9.6	5.3
1979-2011	1.8	2.0	10.4	7.4	10.1	10.1	13.7	8.5
2001-2011	1.6	3.2	10.5	5.7	11.5	11.7	11.7	8.8

Main Indicators of National Economic since Xinjing Established in Main Years

全社会固定资产投资总额(亿元) Total Investment in Fixed Assets (100 million yuan)	社会消费品零售总额(亿元) Total Retail Sales of Consumer Goods (100 million yuan)	地方财政一般预算收入(亿元) General Budgetary Revenue in Local Finance (100 million yuan)	地方财政一般预算支出(亿元) General Budgetary Expenditure in Local Finance (100 million yuan)	金融机构存款余额(亿元) Deposits of National Banking System (100 million yuan)	金融机构贷款余额(亿元) Loans of National Banking System (100 million yuan)	进出口 总额(亿美元) Total Imports And Exports (USD 100 million)	#出口额 Exports	农村居民人均纯收入(元) Annual Per capita Net Income of Rural Residents (yuan)	城镇居民人均可支配收入(元) Annual Per capita Disposable Income of Urban Residents (yuan)
2.62	6.14	1.73	1.83	2.72	3.41	0.51	0.20		
10.59	11.91	6.36	9.58	6.89	15.50	0.73	0.48		
4.03	11.30	4.53	4.89	11.52	9.70	0.14	0.13		
4.50	13.23	3.57	6.05	17.25	14.35	0.02	...		
6.11	16.85	1.01	8.85	26.88	14.71	0.09	0.04		
13.00	21.89	7.14	17.02	32.07	18.26	0.23	0.09	119	319
20.47	29.36	4.03	16.22	38.56	24.74	0.32	0.17	201	427
44.48	57.38	8.47	28.60	82.96	72.68	2.92	1.80	394	735
88.78	104.30	21.78	47.62	221.80	233.72	4.10	3.35	684	1314
124.93	121.52	26.47	50.34	282.21	299.59	4.59	3.63	703	1476
170.03	138.25	26.07	56.09	336.58	380.26	7.50	4.54	740	1952
248.44	168.37	35.13	64.71	397.39	467.81	9.22	4.95	778	2423
285.48	197.11	28.70	71.10	634.44	632.32	10.41	5.76	936	3170
333.34	253.65	38.28	96.40	838.42	843.38	14.28	7.69	1137	4163
387.85	295.36	48.31	114.88	1012.47	1016.20	14.04	5.50	1290	4650
446.81	310.42	54.52	123.35	1180.78	1215.39	14.47	6.65	1500	4845
519.77	327.52	65.39	145.99	1336.58	1318.41	15.32	8.08	1600	5001
534.65	347.40	71.31	166.28	1548.72	1386.78	17.65	10.27	1473	5320
610.38	374.50	79.07	190.95	1863.48	1403.13	22.64	12.04	1618	5645
706.00	406.35	95.09	263.32	1972.55	1584.73	17.71	6.68	1710	6215
813.02	442.88	116.47	361.17	2225.31	1801.15	26.92	13.08	1863	6551
1002.13	421.16	128.22	368.47	2661.65	2099.09	47.72	25.42	2106	7006
1161.52	563.41	155.70	421.04	2959.78	2214.66	56.36	30.47	2245	7503
1352.27	637.78	180.32	519.02	3427.48	2272.08	79.42	50.40	2482	7990
1567.05	727.59	219.46	678.47	4040.78	2412.69	91.03	71.39	2737	8871
1850.84	847.70	285.86	795.15	4614.62	2685.00	137.16	115.03	3183	10313
2259.97	1025.72	361.06	1059.36	5399.34	2826.53	222.17	192.99	3503	11432
2827.24	1177.53	388.78	1346.91	6845.07	3782.92	138.28	108.23	3883	12258
3539.69	1324.48	500.58	1698.91	8870.02	4973.16	171.28	129.70	4643	13644
4712.77	1557.09	720.43	2284.49	10387.00	6270.21	228.22	168.29	5442	15514
Average Annual Growth Rate (%)									
14.3	10.4	11.4	13.6	15.9	14.4	11.5	12.8		
19.6	13.8	15.0	16.0	19.1	19.4	23.3	25.6	12.3	12.5
20.4	13.8	22.2	25.3	16.9	14.6	23.4	27.1	11.7	9.6

1-9 续表

年 份 Year	主要农产品产量（万吨）Output of Major Farm(10 000 tons)					年末牲畜存栏数（万头（只））The Year-end Domesticated Animals in Stock (10 000 heads)	
	粮食 Grain	棉花 Cotton	油料 Oil-bearing Crops	甜菜 Beet	水果 Fruit		#羊 Sheep and Goats
1955	147.02	2.51	6.84	0.10	12.33	1640.07	1224.33
1960	197.98	3.19	5.88	7.09	16.10	1911.59	1529.89
1965	261.74	7.59	6.97	15.97	22.35	2697.53	2192.31
1970	303.21	6.46	6.84	21.06	13.70	2431.32	1949.67
1975	310.96	4.67	9.04	15.12	14.25	2436.08	1916.15
1978	370.01	5.50	10.33	16.37	13.98	2476.98	1927.54
1980	386.13	7.92	17.59	38.52	15.62	2672.60	2105.43
1985	496.65	18.78	34.25	40.69	49.25	3016.04	2431.91
1990	676.89	46.88	38.96	224.37	79.88	3496.40	2830.81
1991	672.52	63.95	40.49	256.85	81.10	3494.00	2830.65
1992	706.27	66.76	35.62	329.07	91.89	3495.41	2830.36
1993	720.37	68.00	37.02	236.91	99.82	3514.72	2842.83
1994	666.17	88.21	50.76	299.24	107.52	3599.01	2905.80
1995	730.16	93.50	49.41	288.14	114.43	3724.32	3009.02
1996	818.20	94.04	30.95	354.52	115.99	3863.80	3136.21
1997	825.34	115.00	29.95	388.71	123.67	4007.66	3261.81
1998	830.00	140.00	37.52	513.12	121.48	4223.99	3447.38
1999	838.78	140.75	60.46	354.24	136.42	4396.54	3592.29
2000	808.60	150.00	60.14	292.65	151.87	4524.67	3690.21
2001	796.00	157.00	42.64	455.12	154.25	4603.78	3764.88
2002	875.87	150.00	44.37	466.81	198.20	4781.77	3908.23
2003	801.64	160.00	50.13	381.65	218.34	5026.54	4104.30
2004	828.53	175.25	44.54	344.21	264.22	5206.37	4266.73
2005	877.21	195.70	38.94	419.12	291.26	5333.60	4355.50
2006	895.22	267.53	32.82	555.53	343.14	5339.71	4359.50
2007	867.04	290.00	40.30	586.93	411.98	5023.37	4083.44
2008	909.00	301.55	56.85	438.88	450.87	3746.11	3025.70
2009	1152.00	252.40	63.91	418.41	565.15	3844.75	3127.50
2010	1150.20	247.90	66.62	486.97	593.85	3722.15	3013.37
2011	1200.75	289.77	66.76	518.95	601.65	3697.60	3016.40
			平均增长速度(%)				
1956-2011	3.8	8.8	4.2	16.5	6.2	1.3	1.6
1979-2011	3.6	12.8	5.8	11.0	12.1	1.2	1.4
2001-2011	3.7	6.2	1.0	5.3	13.3	-1.8	-1.8

Continued

主要畜产品产量（万吨） Output of Major Livestock Products(10 000 tons)			水产品产量（万吨） Output of Aquatic Products (10 000 tons)	主要工业产品产量 Output of Major Industrial Products				
肉类 Meat	羊毛 Wool	奶类 Milk		原煤（万吨） Crude Coal (10 000 tons)	原油（万吨） Crude Oil (10 000 tons)	天然气（亿立方米） Natural Gas (100 million cu.m)	发电量（亿千瓦时） Volume of Electric Generation (100 million kwh)	钢材（万吨） Steel Rolled (10 000 tons)
6.69			0.07	64.55	3.29	0.01	0.55	0.66
6.08			0.57	473.85	166.23	0.06	3.44	3.63
9.17			0.46	387.00	97.31	0.01	4.46	3.94
8.84		8.53	0.65	558.82	153.60	0.66	7.95	4.21
9.16	3.16	6.35	0.50	716.25	300.19	3.76	13.23	2.20
9.65	3.08	5.25	0.57	1079.01	353.05	2.51	21.17	6.83
12.70	3.31	7.28	0.66	1136.84	390.58	3.53	23.58	8.59
18.37	7.07	19.70	0.90	1600.22	499.00	5.46	38.11	16.73
30.46	5.09	35.64	2.32	2100.00	695.00	5.02	69.79	28.48
32.94	5.19	37.49	2.52	2111.00	762.00	5.54	78.04	33.80
36.02	5.20	39.79	2.66	2204.46	831.66	6.75	86.80	40.30
38.30	5.28	40.85	2.88	2392.29	1065.50	8.43	95.78	45.98
42.81	5.46	44.83	3.53	2633.29	1156.62	9.06	106.17	57.71
52.38	5.66	49.81	4.44	2720.74	1267.83	11.48	120.43	66.55
60.31	5.99	54.22	4.79	2986.00	1457.10	14.06	136.03	86.70
64.40	6.25	58.78	5.24	3021.37	1629.25	21.30	150.58	99.89
75.19	6.48	65.02	5.34	2926.91	1628.38	23.78	157.76	116.19
81.36	6.76	70.43	5.58	2778.15	1739.65	31.06	169.30	117.30
90.00	6.98	78.23	6.01	2798.90	1848.43	35.39	182.98	131.25
97.00	7.30	87.85	6.09	2819.61	1946.95	41.74	197.62	134.42
105.44	7.78	100.71	6.39	3098.67	2036.19	48.52	212.24	173.07
115.00	8.21	119.21	6.73	3482.90	2141.40	50.29	234.62	203.10
128.13	8.91	139.73	7.33	3749.40	2253.02	57.48	266.30	238.52
141.46	9.38	157.84	7.93	3898.81	2408.32	106.64	306.92	326.96
158.21	9.62	185.41	8.45	4518.52	2474.74	164.21	357.15	411.45
160.58	9.34	201.77	8.89	5018.64	2604.31	210.33	416.87	470.94
114.74	9.03	137.40	9.26	6763.41	2715.13	235.89	489.17	576.62
115.31	7.60	125.15	9.70	8812.55	2512.86	245.39	571.31	690.81
121.74	8.69	132.82	10.11	9926.72	2558.16	249.91	679.32	891.70
120.04	9.01	133.91	11.69	11991.71	2615.63	235.38	875.19	985.14
Average Annual Growth Rate (%)								
5.3			9.6	9.8	12.7	19.7	14.1	13.9
7.9	3.3	10.3	9.6	7.6	6.3	14.7	11.9	16.3
2.7	2.3	5.0	6.2	14.1	3.2	18.7	15.3	20.1

1-10 各时期社会经济主要指标
Major Social and Economic Indicators of Each Period

时期	Period	新疆生产总值(亿元) Gross Domestic Product of Xinjiang (100 million yuan)	第一产业 Primary Industry	第二产业 Secondary Industry	#工业 Industry	第三产业 Tertiary Industry	全社会固定资产投资总额(亿元) Total Investment in Fixed Assets (100 million yuan)
"一五"时期	"First Five-year Plan" Period	60.35	33.86	15.54	8.82	10.95	
"二五"时期	"Second Five-year Plan" Period	102.65	43.27	39.48	28.37	19.90	31.42
	1963—1965	64.76	33.56	19.27	13.64	11.93	10.43
"三五"时期	"Third Five-year Plan" Period	111.94	53.53	38.02	27.84	20.39	18.82
"四五"时期	"Fourth Five-year Plan" Period	128.37	54.38	50.55	36.84	23.44	24.72
"五五"时期	"Fifth Five-year Plan" Period	205.39	77.27	91.75	72.34	36.37	69.12
"六五"时期	"Sixth Five-year Plan" Period	405.19	165.70	146.99	117.51	92.50	149.13
"七五"时期	"Seventh Five-year Plan" Period	948.99	356.55	318.96	263.20	273.48	331.97
"八五"时期	"Eighth Five-year Plan" Period	2710.64	781.61	993.78	755.30	935.25	1162.22
"九五"时期	"Ninth Five-year Plan" Period	5574.46	1376.78	2052.88	1574.58	2144.80	2499.46
"十五"时期	"Tenth Five-year Plan" Period	9803.83	1962.15	3975.87	3168.48	3865.81	5034.95
"十一五"时期	"Eleventh Five-year Plan " Period	20466.15	3685.96	9699.35	8119.02	7080.84	12044.80

时期	Period	住宅竣工建筑面积(万平方米) Floor Space of Building Completed (10 000 sq.m)	地方财政一般预算收入(亿元) General Budgetary Revenue in Local Finance (100 million yuan)	地方财政一般预算支出(亿元) General Budgetary Expenditure in Local Finance (100 million yuan)	进出口总额(万美元) Total Imports And Exports (USD 10 000)	#出口额 Exports	社会消费品零售总额(亿元) Total Retail Sales of Consumer Goods (100 million yuan)
"一五"时期	"First Five-year Plan" Period		8.65	9.50	20819	10945	31.38
"二五"时期	"Second Five-year Plan" Period		21.39	27.16	26197	17976	53.43
	1963—1965		12.20	11.61	4806	4632	31.92
"三五"时期	"Third Five-year Plan" Period		15.38	21.78	1243	633	63.75
"四五"时期	"Fourth Five-year Plan" Period		11.11	39.78	2922	1217	76.26
"五五"时期	"Fifth Five-year Plan" Period		18.24	54.80	10255	4310	113.51
"六五"时期	"Sixth Five-year Plan" Period	3279.57	27.35	100.30	81536	57445	215.35
"七五"时期	"Seventh Five-year Plan" Period	4175.39	75.48	197.04	190173	142124	323.14
"八五"时期	"Eighth Five-year Plan" Period	4928.74	155.63	338.64	460033	265704	878.89
"九五"时期	"Ninth Five-year Plan" Period	8341.78	318.60	741.45	841181	425462	1655.20
"十五"时期	"Tenth Five-year Plan" Period	12466.98	675.80	1933.02	2281284	1260601	2471.83
"十一五"时期	"Eleventh Five-year Plan " Period	19074.22	1755.75	5578.82	7599235	6173465	5134.21

1-11 各时期社会经济主要指标平均增长率

Growth Rate of Major Social and Economic Indicators of Each Period

单位：% (%)

时期	Period	新疆生产总值 Gross Domestic Product of Xinjiang	第一产业 Primary Industry	第二产业 Secondary Industry	#工业 Industry	第三产业 Tertiary Industry	全社会固定资产投资总额 Total Investment in Fixed Assets
"一五"时期	"First Five-year Plan" Period	9.0	5.1	12.6	8.8	18.8	
"二五"时期	"Second Five-year Plan" Period	4.5	2.8	11.0	24.5	-1.3	-14.8
	1963—1965	12.9	17.9	8.4	3.3	5.4	28.4
"三五"时期	"Third Five-year Plan" Period	0.3	-3.1	3.8	4.3	4.8	2.2
"四五"时期	"Fourth Five-year Plan" Period	2.9	…	7.2	7.3	-0.5	6.3
"五五"时期	"Fifth Five-year Plan" Period	10.5	7.4	11.6	14.3	14.5	34.1
"六五"时期	"Sixth Five-year Plan" Period	12.5	13.0	9.2	9.3	17.6	10.9
"七五"时期	"Seventh Five-year Plan" Period	9.8	7.9	8.2	9.2	14.7	14.8
"八五"时期	"Eighth Five-year Plan" Period	11.8	6.7	14.2	13.5	15.0	30.3
"九五"时期	"Ninth Five-year Plan" Period	7.7	5.8	6.8	5.9	10.3	12.9
"十五"时期	"Tenth Five-year Plan" Period	10.0	5.6	10.6	11.3	11.2	17.2
"十一五"时期	"Eleventh Five-year Plan " Period	10.6	5.6	11.8	12.1	11.4	21.2

时期	Period	住宅竣工建筑面积 Floor Space of Building Completed	地方财政一般预算收入 General Budgetary Revenue in Local Finance	地方财政一般预算支出 General Budgetary Expenditure in Local Finance	进出口总额 Total Imports And Exports	#出口额 Exports	社会消费品零售总额 Total Retail Sales of Consumer Goods
"一五"时期	"First Five-year Plan" Period		25.0	30.7	17.8	17.8	18.5
"二五"时期	"Second Five-year Plan" Period		4.7	-0.4	-12.5	-9.6	4.3
	1963—1965		16.8	30.5	-20.4	-13.8	2.3
"三五"时期	"Third Five-year Plan" Period		-4.7	4.3	-34.4	-50.3	3.2
"四五"时期	"Fourth Five-year Plan" Period		-22.3	7.9	40.6	58.0	5.0
"五五"时期	"Fifth Five-year Plan" Period		31.9	12.9	28.4	35.5	11.7
"六五"时期	"Sixth Five-year Plan" Period		16.0	12.0	56.0	60.2	14.3
"七五"时期	"Seventh Five-year Plan" Period	2.3	20.8	10.7	7.0	13.2	12.7
"八五"时期	"Eighth Five-year Plan" Period	3.1	11.9	15.1	28.3	18.1	19.4
"九五"时期	"Ninth Five-year Plan" Period	12.1	15.6	14.6	9.7	9.4	8.1
"十五"时期	"Tenth Five-year Plan" Period	14.0	17.9	22.1	28.5	33.2	11.2
"十一五"时期	"Eleventh Five-year Plan " Period	-1.9	22.7	26.8	16.6	20.8	15.7

1-12 天山北坡经济带主要经济指标

(2011 年)

指 标	Item	全区合计 Total of the whole region	北坡经济带合计 Total of the economic belt	北坡经济带占全区比重(%) ratio of the economic belt (%)	乌昌合计 Total of Urmqi and Changji	乌昌占全区比重(%) Pencentage of Urmqi and Changji to total(%)	乌鲁木齐市 Urumqi City
人 口	**Population**						
年末总人口	Total Population at Year-end	2208.71	857.68	38.8	388.81	17.6	249.35
#少数民族人口	Minority Nationalities Population	1358.24	309.73	22.8	105.19	7.7	68.20
城镇人口	Urban Population	961.67	702.72	73.1	357.78	37.2	242.24
乡村人口	Rural Population	1247.04	117.51	9.4	31.03	2.5	7.11
综 合	**General**						
新疆生产总值(亿元)	Gross Domestic Produc in Xinjiang (100 million yuan)	6610.05	4507.02	68.2	2392.97	36.2	1690.03
第一产业	First Industry	1139.03	482.69	42.4	212.39	18.6	22.05
第二产业	Second Industry	3225.90	2371.25	73.5	1090.17	33.8	759.06
#工 业	Industry	2700.20	2066.54	76.5	927.33	34.3	659.06
第三产业	Tertiary Industry	2245.12	1653.08	73.6	1090.41	48.6	908.92
新疆生产总值构成(%)	Composition of Gross Domestic Produc in Xinjiang (%)						
第一产业	First Industry	17.2	10.7		8.9		1.3
第二产业	Second Industry	48.8	52.6		45.6		44.9
#工 业	Industry	40.8	45.9		38.8		39.0
第三产业	Tertiary Industry	34.0	36.7		45.6		53.8
财政收入相当于新疆生产总值比重(%)	Ratio of GDP covered by financial Expenditure (%)	10.9	9.0		10.6		12.2
财政支出相当于新疆生产总值比重(%)	Ratio of GDP covered by financial Expenditure (%)	34.6	14.0		15.0		14.1
固定资产投资(亿元)	**Fixed Asset Investment (100 million yuan)**						
#城镇固定资产投资总额	Fixed Asset Value of the town	3688.11	1923.73	52.2	869.97	23.6	434.36
财政、金融(亿元)	**Finance and Public Money(100 million yuan)**						
地方财政一般预算收入	Local Financial Income	720.43	405.85	56.3	254.42	35.3	206.20
#各项税收	Various Tax Incomes	593.41	361.43	60.9	225.12	37.9	182.82
地方财政一般预算支出	Expenditure of Local Finance	2284.49	631.33	27.6	359.87	15.8	238.49
#一般公共服务	General Common Service	245.36	68.53	27.9	39.65	16.2	26.88
教 育	Operating Expenses for Education	399.80	123.67	30.9	62.22	15.6	40.85
社保和就业	Operating Expenses for Medical Treatment and Sanitation	201.64	50.00	24.8	28.80	14.3	21.89
金融机构年末存款余额	Year-end Loan Balance of Finance	10387.00	7230.36	69.6	4735.52	45.6	4080.50
金融机构年末贷款余额	Year-end Deposit Balance of Finance	6270.21	4051.18	64.6	2989.32	47.7	2553.98
物价(上年=100)	**Commodity Price (Preceding year=100)**						
商品零售价格指数	Index of Commodity Retail Price	105.1					104.1
居民消费价格指数	Index of Price for Residents' Consumption	105.9					104.5
人民生活	**People's life**						
在岗职工平均货币工资(元)	Average Staff's Money Wage (yuan)	38820					47747
农村居民家庭人均纯收入(元)	Annual Per capita Net Income of Rural Residents (yuan)	5442					8437
城乡居民储蓄存款余额(亿元)	Balance of Both Urban and Rural Deposit(100 million yuan)	4421.93	2929.38	66.2	1800.28	40.7	1470.34
建成区绿化覆盖率(%)	Ratio of Green Coverage in Completed Areas(%)	36.64					36.16

Main Economic Indicators for Economic Belt on the Northern Slope of the Tianshan Mountains

克拉玛依市 Karamay City	石河子市 Shihezi City	五家渠市 Wujiaqu City	哈密市 Hami [Kumul] City	吐鲁番市 Turpan City	鄯善县 Shanshan [Piqan] County	托克逊县 Toksun County	伊宁市 Yining [Gulja] City	奎屯市 Kuytun City	伊宁县 Yining [Gulja] County	察布查尔锡伯自治县 Qapqal Xibe Autonomous county	霍城县 Huocheng [Korgas] County	乌苏市 Usu City	沙湾县 Shawan County
28.23	62.44	9.10	45.79	28.35	22.95	11.89	50.39	30.75	42.68	19.30	40.42	22.77	21.61
7.10	3.84	0.33	13.31	22.61	16.60	10.01	32.28	1.61	35.42	12.72	23.25	8.23	6.97
28.23	62.44		45.79		14.75	2.43	50.39	30.75	8.82	6.50	21.26	22.77	18.45
					8.20	9.46			33.86	12.80	19.16		3.16
801.69	170.59	68.15	176.70	58.65	129.67	33.89	113.90	90.02	48.81	25.89	60.30	120.75	129.56
4.15	11.00	7.13	18.08	10.49	10.15	6.35	5.68	4.78	19.17	12.92	20.22	39.54	64.25
716.20	94.37	39.10	87.36	22.92	102.08	20.72	31.65	49.48	17.53	5.81	12.41	58.29	36.09
698.82	77.22	30.82	59.20	19.08	89.47	16.92	17.70	40.93	14.56	3.88	9.86	44.91	27.18
81.34	65.22	21.92	71.26	25.24	17.44	6.82	76.57	35.76	12.11	7.16	27.67	22.92	29.22
0.5	6.4		10.2	17.9	7.8	18.7	5.0	5.3	39.3	49.9	33.5	32.7	49.6
89.3	55.3		49.4	39.1	78.7	61.1	27.8	55.0	35.9	22.4	20.6	48.3	27.9
87.2	45.3		33.5	32.5	69.0	49.9	15.5	45.5	29.8	15.0	16.4	37.2	21.0
10.1	38.2		40.3	43.0	13.4	20.1	67.2	39.7	24.8	27.7	45.9	19.0	22.6
6.4	11.3	5.5	10.6	8.3	5.9	11.2	12.4	12.1	5.9	7.7	3.9	5.3	3.1
7.9	14.8	7.3	14.7	23.2	11.5	30.6	24.7	17.4	37.3	48.7	24.4	14.8	10.7
199.37	150.75	87.50	116.52	24.25	68.28	31.70	76.50	58.22	48.43	30.62	29.95	35.14	41.27
50.97	19.28	3.77	18.72	4.88	7.68	3.78	14.09	10.91	2.89	2.00	2.37	6.34	4.06
45.88	17.14	3.58	17.91	4.00	7.00	3.07	12.67	9.04	2.50	1.48	2.03	5.36	3.26
63.30	25.26	4.97	26.03	13.62	14.87	10.37	28.17	15.70	18.23	12.62	14.69	17.84	13.84
8.35	1.92	0.69	2.70	1.24	1.92	0.94	2.74	1.57	1.30	1.04	1.28	3.00	1.58
14.57	3.58	1.08	4.61	2.88	2.83	2.03	6.86	3.27	5.57	3.07	4.10	3.54	3.26
3.30	0.88	0.17	1.91	0.88	0.92	0.81	3.51	0.88	2.47	1.60	1.74	1.34	1.19
860.80	356.19	70.25	288.69	63.78	63.00	22.15	262.00	160.39	35.81	35.48	63.68	73.19	60.67
132.67	248.05	71.86	145.15	37.69	29.40	15.75	124.60	78.03	38.02	20.00	19.77	49.40	46.00
104.8	105.6		104.7	105.5			107.5	104.8				105.0	
105.8	105.4		105.3	105.7			106.7	105.2				105.3	
58657	38909	33570	39873	36909	54810	39985	33525	34397	23580	28759	26931	23119	32503
11735	10372	10311	7773	6311	6304	5570	8937	8370	7718	7406	8171	11620	13187
214.30	226.15	33.09	154.11	37.02	37.50	12.65	120.92	89.79	19.01	17.40	40.76	43.83	43.44
42.91	42.17	34.18	42.65	33.78	14.78	31.17	39.00	40.15	35.53	25.81	42.04	30.86	33.44

1-12 续表 1

指 标	Item	全区合计 Total of the whole region	北坡经济带合计 Total of the economic belt	北坡经济带占全区比重(%) ratio of the economic belt (%)	乌昌合计 Total of Urmqi and Changji	乌昌占全区比重(%) Pencent-age of Urmqi and Changji to total(%)	乌鲁木齐市 Urumqi City
农 业	**Agriculture**						
农林牧渔业总产值(亿元)	Value of Farm, Forestry, Herding and Fishery (100 million yuan)	1955.39	970.52	49.6	271.21	13.9	30.27
农 业	Farming	1437.89	619.90	43.1	121.59	8.5	13.68
林 业	Forestry	38.08	12.75	33.5	2.74	7.2	0.53
牧 业	Animal Husbandry	415.00	289.02	69.6	141.89	34.2	15.22
渔 业	Fishery	14.17	6.37	45.0	2.39	16.9	0.71
农林牧渔服务业	Services for Farming, Forestry, Animal Husbandary and Fishery	50.25	39.47	78.5	2.59	5.2	0.13
主要农产品产量(万吨)	Main Rural Products Output (10 000 tons)						
粮 食	Grain	1200.75	505.25	42.1	197.13	16.4	16.87
棉 花	Cotton	289.77	142.60	49.2	20.09	6.9	0.17
油 料	Oil-bearing Crops	66.76	27.34	41.0	9.12	13.7	0.89
甜 菜	Beet	518.95	257.57	49.6	56.87	11.0	0.50
水 果	Fruit	601.65	159.92	26.6	16.86	2.8	1.07
肉 类	Meat	120.04	110.13	91.7	55.77	46.5	5.74
工 业	**Industry**						
工业总产值(规模以上)(亿元)	Total Value of Industrial Products (100 million yuan)	6720.85	5167.94	76.9	2467.91	36.7	1992.58
轻工业	Light Industry	799.49	555.78	69.5	272.94	34.1	109.28
重工业	Heavy Industry	5921.36	4612.16	77.9	2194.97	37.1	1883.30
主要工业产品产量(全口径)	Output of Main Industrial Products						
纱(万吨)	Cotton Yarn (10 000 tons)	39.91	28.52	71.5	10.18	25.5	2.53
布(万米)	Cloth (10 000 m)	7302.77	5838.80	80.0	1007.22	13.8	444.25
绒线(吨)	Woolen knitting wool (ton)	444.22	261.22	58.8	260.00	58.5	260.00
呢绒(万米)	Woolen Goods (10 000 m)	383.11	383.11	100.0	156.30	40.8	
原盐(万吨)	Crude Salt (10 000 tons)	258.05	82.35	31.9	10.31	4.0	10.31
成品糖(万吨)	Sugar (10 000 tons)	46.11	21.10	45.8	5.00	10.9	
原煤(万吨)	Crude Coal (10 000 tons)	11991.71	8521.03	71.1	5816.52	48.5	1930.28
原油(万吨)	Crude Oil (10 000 tons)	2615.63	2038.01	77.9	725.00	27.7	725.00
发电量(亿千瓦小时)	Volume of Electric Generation (100 million kwh)	875.19	665.61	76.1	374.86	42.8	241.35
粗钢(万吨)	Grude steel (10 000 tons)	892.98	715.54	80.1	694.90	77.8	694.90
钢材(万吨)	Steel Rolled (10 000 tons)	985.14	806.77	81.9	792.65	80.5	791.99
水泥(万吨)	Cement (10 000 tons)	3171.71	1840.51	58.0	806.95	25.4	552.25
运输邮电业	**Traffic and Telecommunication Sector**						
公路客运量(万人)	Highway Passenger Volume (10 000 persons)	47927	17936	37.4	8858	18.5	2915
公路货运量(万吨)	Highway Cargo Volume (10 000 tons)	55965	35717	63.8	22158	39.6	14472
公路货物周转量(亿吨公里)	Turnover of Highway Cargo (100million tons-km)	852.17	389.45	45.7	312.91	36.7	203.93
邮电业务总量(亿元)	Volume of Postal-Telecommunication (100 million yuan)	226.50	89.92	39.7	61.48	27.1	51.34
国内商业	**Domestic Trades**						
社会消费品零售总额(亿元)	Retail Volume of Social Commodities (100 million yuan)	1557.09	1213.53	77.9	782.76	49.7	649.73
教育、卫生	**Education and Health**						
在校学生数(人)	Number of Registered Students (person)						
高等学校	Institutions of Higher Education	258719	227601	88.0	173317	67.0	152314
中等专业学校	Specialized Secondary School	243039	141940	58.4	91635	37.7	79024
普通中学	Ordinary Middle School	1409293	594779	42.2	230877	16.4	148896
小 学	Elementary School	1919457	680081	35.4	261823	13.6	181702
毕业生数(人)	Number of Graduates (person)						
高等学校	Institutions of Higher Education	63798	58382	91.5	42731	67.0	36726
中等专业学校	Specialized Secondary School	64508	45410	70.4	30275	46.9	26386
普通中学	Ordinary Middle School	457944	188085	41.1	73792	16.1	47614
小 学	Elementary School	327704	118531	36.2	44408	13.6	29473
医院、卫生院床位数(张)	Number of Sick Beds (unit)	118781	65431	55.1	35754	30.1	26530
卫生技术人员数(人)	Number of Hygiene Technicians (person)	130604	81206	62.2	42152	32.3	31762

Continued

克拉玛依市 Karamay City	石河子市 Shihezi City	五家渠市 Wujiaqu City	哈密市 Hami [Kumul] City	吐鲁番市 Turpan City	鄯善县 Shanshan [Piqan] County	托克逊县 Toksun County	伊宁市 Yining [Gulja] City	奎屯市 Kuytun City	伊宁县 Yining [Gulja] County	察布查尔锡伯自治县 Qapqal Xibe Autonomous county	霍城县 Huocheng [Korgas] County	乌苏市 Usu City	沙湾县 Shawan County
9.50	22.20	15.04	18.38	17.41	16.90	10.55	9.96	1.30	32.08	16.47	19.58	40.69	54.38
3.37	14.28	8.11	12.45	13.90	13.83	7.80	6.21	0.65	17.49	11.15	10.20	30.36	40.53
1.49	0.20	0.07	0.63	0.18	0.14	0.09	0.13	0.02	0.56	0.35	0.50	0.58	0.23
3.16	6.03	5.56	4.90	2.90	2.78	2.46	3.17	0.53	12.89	4.62	8.43	9.25	12.92
0.07	0.53	0.14	0.18	0.03	0.01	---	0.20		0.62	0.05	0.02	0.05	0.13
1.41	1.16	1.16	0.22	0.40	0.14	0.20	0.25	0.10	0.52	0.30	0.43	0.45	0.57
0.35	3.34	2.64	3.87	0.44	0.64	1.32	11.98	0.67	65.11	33.17	23.01	19.31	19.83
1.27	3.43	1.10	2.74	0.57	0.76	1.58		0.19	0.02	1.38	0.21	9.83	12.00
0.03	0.08	0.23	0.07			0.05	0.23	0.17	1.32	0.87	1.09	0.77	1.13
	0.08	0.29					3.13		19.78	4.32	50.94	5.03	4.71
	3.80	0.75	8.37	28.65	31.38	4.20	2.93		5.79	2.06	7.43	0.27	0.94
1.04	2.16	2.25	2.19	2.25	0.97	0.90	1.21	0.36	3.87	1.74	3.16	3.33	4.78
1639.04	289.34	90.45	114.67	43.86	144.07	34.12	35.60	92.77	40.03	10.87	17.28	62.53	52.27
2.54	78.51	24.33	8.62	3.43	0.31	0.85	16.41	48.53	11.66	6.71	12.18	18.55	34.25
1636.50	210.83	66.12	106.05	40.43	143.76	33.27	19.20	44.23	28.37	4.16	5.10	43.98	18.01
	10.76	0.79	1.20	0.39				1.80				1.13	0.67
	3778.08							159.00				91.50	688.00
	1.22												
	226.81												
0.09			17.41			48.60							
								1.90	3.91		7.73		
90.00	27.79	9.00	977.81	33.18	306.00	962.87	25.82	60.10	208.17	96.27	15.37	248.18	53.96
1090.01					155.00							68.00	
43.36	126.49		26.35	3.64	0.98	22.43	2.39	18.79	6.06	4.18	1.17	27.59	1.26
									1.17			11.89	7.58
0.03	2.86								1.10	0.05	1.43		8.68
	267.04		172.39	87.02	37.04	8.20			175.33	84.42	3.97	27.14	105.73
164	928	1663	334	1183			1380	692	471	212	455	1369	1105
2565	2278	2264	954	837			1530	475	151	150	290	396	1131
55.40	40.25	9.57	16.50	14.33			13.01	3.93	1.28	1.28	2.47	6.99	7.04
5.50	7.19	0.52	5.28	1.91	1.64	0.57	0.45	0.46	0.07	0.06	0.20	1.35	0.53
43.58	52.38	16.84	41.59	13.31	8.81	4.21	43.00	15.64	8.95	2.00	12.93	9.93	10.73
3851	5822	3421	1665				26237						
1013	1786	1682	2681	2441	323	426	8914	167					
25067	18692	12029	27608	14626	11917	6493	35400	14146	22145	9516	15214	14803	15714
23107	10745	7400	26210	22356	19509	8870	46298	9964	37885	13508	24387	17164	15208
1257	1185	920	467				6185						
347	310	468	499	646	112	168	2342	26	55				
7941	5912	2477	8159	4961	4076	2075	10840	4173	6993	3336	4816	4737	5461
4538	2074	1264	4890	3850	3036	1444	7374	1874	6363	2296	3808	2928	3400
1805	4055	795	2154	654	506	253	3448	764	376	180	621	1261	755
2695	5274	824	3035	1258	961	545	4620	1110	1183	652	1002	1168	873

1-12 续表 2

(2011 年)

指　　标	Item	昌吉市 Changji City	阜康市 Fukang City	呼图壁县 Hu Tubi County	玛纳斯县 Manas County	奇台县 Qitai County	吉木萨尔县 Jimsar County
人　口	**Population**						
年末总人口	Total Population at Year-end	36.32	16.76	21.81	17.61	23.97	14.06
#少数民族人口	Minority Nationalities Population	9.78	4.80	5.14	3.40	6.33	4.39
城镇人口	Urban Population	36.32	14.71	20.27	14.15	16.30	9.87
乡村人口	Rural Population		2.05	1.54	3.46	7.67	4.19
综　合	**General**						
新疆生产总值(亿元)	Gross Domestic Produc in Xinjiang (100 million yuan)	221.37	103.10	120.20	96.04	70.90	38.87
第一产业	First Industry	29.73	18.04	51.10	36.15	31.72	13.43
第二产业	Second Industry	103.63	65.06	45.14	36.01	22.63	15.48
#工　业	Industry	86.14	58.57	38.53	22.65	17.72	12.95
第三产业	Tertiary Industry	88.01	20.00	23.96	23.88	16.55	9.96
新疆生产总值构成(%)	Composition of Gross Domestic Produc in Xinjiang (%)						
第一产业	First Industry	13.4	17.5	42.5	37.6	44.7	34.6
第二产业	Second Industry	46.8	63.1	37.6	37.5	31.9	39.8
#工　业	Industry	38.9	56.8	32.1	23.6	25.0	33.3
第三产业	Tertiary Industry	39.8	19.4	19.9	24.9	23.3	25.6
财政收入相当于新疆生产总值比重(%)	Ratio of GDP covered by financial Expenditure (%)	7.3	8.3	3.3	4.5	6.6	12.2
财政支出相当于新疆生产总值比重(%)	Ratio of GDP covered by financial Expenditure (%)	11.2	15.4	9.7	11.4	23.5	31.6
固定资产投资(亿元)	**Fixed Asset Investment (100 million yuan)**						
#城镇固定资产投资总额	Fixed Asset Value of the town	71.41	77.65	46.33	58.81	61.53	117.30
财政、金融(亿元)	**Finance and Public Money(100 million yuan)**						
地方财政一般预算收入	Local Financial Income	16.18	8.60	3.95	4.33	4.70	4.75
#各项税收	Various Tax Incomes	15.13	7.84	3.49	3.93	4.36	4.16
地方财政一般预算支出	Expenditure of Local Finance	24.80	15.84	11.64	10.93	16.64	12.29
#一般公共服务	General Common Service	3.06	1.67	0.91	1.03	1.31	1.13
教　育	Operating Expenses for Education	4.05	2.37	2.63	2.24	3.26	1.79
社保和就业	Operating Expenses for Medical Treatment and Sanitation	1.08	0.78	0.62	0.55	0.77	1.05
金融机构年末存款余额	Year-end Loan Balance of Finance	286.30	67.96	64.87	57.64	56.06	34.12
金融机构年末贷款余额	Year-end Deposit Balance of Finance	184.10	54.20	37.54	38.68	28.83	13.09
物价(上年=100)	**Commodity Price (Preceding year=100)**						
商品零售价格指数	Index of Commodity Retail Price	105.8					
居民消费价格指数	Index of Price for Residents' Consumption	105.3					
人民生活	**People's life**						
在岗职工平均货币工资(元)	Average Staff"s Money Wage (yuan)	38685	36767	30592	36447	33451	40189
农村居民家庭人均纯收入(元)	Annual Per capita Net Income of Rural Residents (yuan)	10536	10666	11496	12868	9421	9232
城乡居民储蓄存款余额(亿元)	Balance of Both Urban and Rural Deposit(100 million yuan)	127.80	34.79	41.27	37.43	29.72	17.71
建成区绿化覆盖率(%)	Ratio of Green Coverage in Completed Areas(%)	35.67	38.55	37.37	26.84	37.67	34.25

Continued

博乐市 Bole [Bortala] City	精河县 Jinghe [Jing] County	农四师 XJPCC No.4 Division	农五师 XJPCC No.5 Division	农六师 XJPCC No.6 Division	农七师 XJPCC No.7 Division	农八师 XJPCC No.8 Division	建工师 XJPCC architectural engineer Division	农十二师 XJPCC No.12 Division	农十三师 XJPCC No.13 Division	兵团直属 Directly under XPCG
26.69	14.44									
8.85	4.56									
26.69	9.59									
	4.85									
99.91	38.03									
26.43	20.13									
23.29	6.94									
16.21	4.16									
50.19	10.96									
26.5	52.9									
23.3	18.2									
16.2	11.0									
50.2	28.8									
4.0	3.7									
12.0	24.2									
42.90	14.94									
4.01	1.39									
3.61	1.17									
11.98	9.21									
1.39	0.88									
2.74	2.49									
1.09	0.57									
130.80	36.03									
56.36	28.01									
106.4										
106.0										
31050	25445									
8526	8470									
57.06	23.29									
34.29	26.52									

1-12 续表 3

指标	Item	昌吉市 Changji City	阜康市 Fukang City	呼图壁县 Hu Tubi County	玛纳斯县 Manas County	奇台县 Qitai County	吉木萨尔县 Jimsar County
农业	**Agriculture**						
农林牧渔业总产值(亿元)	Value of Farm, Forestry, Herding and Fishery (100 million yuan)	36.52	27.52	42.61	46.08	50.82	20.12
农业	Farming	16.48	12.31	16.79	25.55	21.70	8.87
林业	Forestry	0.31	0.19	0.33	0.19	0.52	0.53
牧业	Animal Husbandry	18.42	14.86	21.12	19.34	28.57	10.50
渔业	Fishery	0.98	0.04	0.32	0.22		0.12
农林牧渔服务业	Services for Farming, Forestry, Animal Husbandary and Fishery	0.33	0.12	1.05	0.78	0.03	0.10
主要农产品产量(万吨)	Main Rural Products Output (10 000 tons)						
粮食	Grain	27.04	18.61	20.83	14.97	66.69	15.97
棉花	Cotton	5.42	0.05	6.39	8.06		
油料	Oil-bearing Crops	1.41	1.50	0.37	1.10	2.28	0.94
甜菜	Beet	5.76	3.52	6.06	1.76	35.72	2.55
水果	Fruit	4.16	1.44	0.78	7.51	0.09	1.52
肉类	Meat	8.77	6.81	8.16	6.57	11.38	5.01
工业	**Industry**						
工业总产值(规模以上)(亿元)	Total Value of Industrial Products (100 million yuan)	194.16	97.74	42.92	78.42	38.08	20.78
轻工业	Light Industry	74.01	1.57	18.79	48.12	15.3	5.88
重工业	Heavy Industry	120.16	96.17	24.13	30.30	22.78	14.90
主要工业产品产量(全口径)	Output of Main Industrial Products						
纱(万吨)	Cotton Yarn (10 000 tons)	4.67		2.29	0.69		
布(万米)	Cloth (10 000 m)			447.00	115.97		
绒线(吨)	Woolen knitting wool (ton)						
呢绒(万米)	Woolen Goods (10 000 m)	156.30					
原盐(万吨)	Crude Salt (10 000 tons)						
成品糖(万吨)	Sugar (10 000 tons)	1.49				3.52	
原煤(万吨)	Crude Coal (10 000 tons)	756.74	343.55	328.04	133.33	1114.94	799.63
原油(万吨)	Crude Oil (10 000 tons)						
发电量(亿千瓦小时)	Volume of Electric Generation (100 million kwh)	17.19	40.82		74.87	0.13	0.47
粗钢(万吨)	Grude steel (10 000 tons)						
钢材(万吨)	Steel Rolled (10 000 tons)	0.66					
水泥(万吨)	Cement (10 000 tons)	166.28	46.33			42.10	
运输邮电业	**Traffic and Telecommunication Sector**						
公路客运量(万人)	Highway Passenger Volume (10 000 persons)	2230	492	660	146	885	124
公路货运量(万吨)	Highway Cargo Volume (10 000 tons)	2862	3610	113		1103	
公路货物周转量(亿吨公里)	Turnover of Highway Cargo (100million tons-km)	0.29	0.55	1.07		11.56	
邮电业务总量(亿元)	Volume of Postal-Telecommunication (100 million yuan)	4.83	1.14	1.35	1.10	0.54	0.96
国内商业	**Domestic Trades**						
社会消费品零售总额(亿元)	Retail Volume of Social Commodities (100 million yuan)	55.26	18.36	15.61	17.16	15.02	7.22
教育、文化、卫生	**Education, Culture and Health**						
在校学生数(人)	Number of Registered Students (person)						
高等学校	Institutions of Higher Education	34291					
中等专业学校	Specialized Secondary School	6243	2400	632	697	1093	
普通中学	Ordinary Middle School	32900	11200	9373	5180	13108	6522
小学	Elementary School	28600	8200	11043	6620	11995	6819
毕业生数(人)	Number of Graduates (person)						
高等学校	Institutions of Higher Education	11642					
中等专业学校	Specialized Secondary School	1200	554	229	52	335	
普通中学	Ordinary Middle School	10500	2642	2936	1608	4433	2118
小学	Elementary School	5168	1540	2004	1291	2292	1376
医院床位数(张)	Number of Sick Beds (unit)	3769	550	950	585	882	512
卫生技术人员数(人)	Number of Hygiene Technicians (person)	4200	244	932	743	752	375

Continued

博尔市 Bole [Bortala] City	精河县 Jinghe [Jing] County	农四师 XJPCC No.4 Division	农五师 XJPCC No.5 Division	农六师 XJPCC No.6 Division	农七师 XJPCC No.7 Division	农八师 XJPCC No.8 Division	建工师 XJPCC architectural engineer Division	农十二师 XJPCC No.12 Division	农十三师 XJPCC No.13 Division	兵团直属 Directly under XPCG
23.93	26.47	47.66	31.73	78.94	60.93	129.01	0.05	11.61	19.08	2.73
18.26	22.38	29.08	26.43	53.90	44.85	97.10	0.05	7.15	12.73	2.26
0.20	0.32	0.31	0.18	0.61	0.53	2.43		0.22	0.17	0.01
4.51	2.52	15.45	2.89	18.64	11.75	17.90		3.60	3.98	0.15
0.02	0.12	0.47	0.06	0.25	0.24	0.56		0.18	0.02	0.03
0.94	1.13	2.36	2.17	5.55	3.56	11.02		0.45	2.17	0.27
23.31	2.74	39.02	8.74	36.77	13.45	9.44	0.03	1.14	2.89	1.06
5.70	7.89	2.16	9.29	13.06	11.44	35.25	0.01	0.02	2.52	0.09
0.18	0.01	7.06	0.72	1.89	1.99	0.30	0.02	0.13	0.04	0.47
8.61	0.44	44.23	10.26	9.12	39.60	0.08		1.02		0.06
0.06	0.17	12.51	2.72	4.24	2.44	8.12		6.05	8.87	1.60
0.86	0.57	5.90	1.20	7.23	3.57	5.89		0.92	1.30	0.04
29.89	6.47									
12.68	3.27									
17.21	3.20									
1.04	0.56									
115.00										
	5.94									
2.55										
5.11	0.98									
65.28										
527										
536										
2.93										
15.67	3.83	10.38	7.72	32.76	18.10	43.22	0.69	12.43	4.84	1.63
		2719	154	1682	574	2047	2650	438	301	21853
11056	6716	16791	12017	18897	11292	23742	5791	5257	5416	7255
13304	9377	20394	12653	21686	12472	29162	7167	6073	7664	2539
		169		468	261	1044	686	165		8888
3244	2252	5396	3762	6022	3608	8108	1670	1789	1942	2484
2248	1578	3620	2251	3624	2582	5952	1180	1236	1511	466
1102	508	1358	761	1744	1739	5023	80	210	960	541
1905	457	1512	1023	2383	1992	5262	165	314	1026	959

1-13 法人单位数和产业活动单位数
Number of Legal Entities and Establishment Entities

单位：个 (unit)

年份 Year	地区 Region	法人单位数 Number of Legal Entities	单产业法人 Single Sector	多产业法人 Multi-sector	产业活动单位数 Number of Establishments Entities	#多产业法人的活动单位 Establishments Entities of Multi-sector
	2000	53982	47574	6408		
	2001	66477	60857	5620	114912	54055
	2002	66186	60736	5450	114141	53405
	2003	68203	62895	5308	115782	52887
	2004	63429	58196	5233	112499	54303
	2005	69756	64157	5599	122055	57898
	2006	75447	69724	5723	128165	58441
	2007	79767	73984	5783	132750	58766
	2008	88115	82100	6015	139686	57586
	2009	93673	87408	6265	148845	61437
	2010	96727	90456	6271	151303	60847
	2011	101926	95614	6312	155890	60276
乌鲁木齐市	Urumqi City	27420	26626	794	30686	4061
克拉玛依市	Karamay City	3186	2931	255	4162	1231
吐鲁番地区	Turpan Administrative Offices	3262	3075	187	4307	1232
哈密地区	Hami [Kumul] Administrative Offices	5118	4767	351	6927	2160
昌吉回族自治州	Changji Hui Autonomous Prefecture	7664	7081	583	10753	3672
伊犁哈萨克自治州	Ili Kazak Autonomous Prefecture	15309	14195	1114	23621	9426
伊犁州直属县(市)	Counties (Cities) Direct Under Ili Prefecture	7145	6675	470	11373	4698
塔城地区	Tacheng [Tarbagatai] Administrative Offices	3856	3560	296	6177	2617
阿勒泰地区	Altay Administrative Offices	4308	3960	348	6071	2111
博尔塔拉蒙古自治州	Bortala Mongol Autonomous Prefecture	2942	2727	215	4269	1542
巴音郭楞蒙古自治州	Bayangol Mongol Autonomous Prefecture	8401	7660	741	12203	4543
阿克苏地区	Aksu Administrative Offices	7834	7197	637	15010	7813
克孜勒苏柯尔克孜自治州	Kizilsu Kirgiz Autonomous Prefecture	1937	1783	154	3992	2209
喀什地区	Kashgar [Kaxgar] Administrative Offices	7191	6550	641	22528	15978
和田地区	Hotan Administrative Offices	8346	7845	501	12550	4705
自治区直辖县级市	Municpality Country-level Gity Directly under the Central Government	3316	3177	139	4711	1534
石河子市	Shihezi City	2588	2505	83	3068	563
阿拉尔市	Aral City	231	211	20	593	382
图木舒克市	Tumxuk City	153	140	13	502	362
五家渠市	Wujiaqu City	344	321	23	548	227

注：2004 年数据不包括农、林、牧、渔业。
Note: Data in 2004 does not include statistics of agriculture,forestry,animal husbandry and fishery.

1-14 按三次产业分的法人单位数及构成

Number of Legal Entities by Three Strata of Industry and Its Composition

年份 Year	地区 Region	法人单位数 Number of Legal Entities	第一产业 Primary Industry	
			绝对数 Value	构成 (%) Composition (%)
	2000	53982		
	2001	66477	3439	5.17
	2002	66186	3421	5.17
	2003	68203	3195	4.68
	2004	63429		
	2005	69756	1449	2.08
	2006	75447	1524	2.02
	2007	79767	1715	2.15
	2008	88115	203	0.23
	2009	93673	2439	2.60
	2010	96727	2842	2.94
	2011	101926	3650	3.58
乌鲁木齐市	Urumqi City	27420	158	0.58
克拉玛依市	Karamay City	3186	67	2.10
吐鲁番地区	Turpan Administrative Offices	3262	81	2.48
哈密地区	Hami [Kumul] Administrative Offices	5118	241	4.71
昌吉回族自治州	Changji Hui Autonomous Prefecture	7664	452	5.90
伊犁哈萨克自治州	Ili Kazak Autonomous Prefecture	15309	710	4.64
伊犁州直属县(市)	Counties (Cities) Direct Under Ili Prefecture	7145	276	3.86
塔城地区	Tacheng [Tarbagatai] Administrative Offices	3856	114	2.96
阿勒泰地区	Altay Administrative Offices	4308	320	7.43
博尔塔拉蒙古自治州	Bortala Mongol Autonomous Prefecture	2942	143	4.86
巴音郭楞蒙古自治州	Bayangol Mongol Autonomous Prefecture	8401	665	7.92
阿克苏地区	Aksu Administrative Offices	7834	488	6.23
克孜勒苏柯尔克孜自治州	Kizilsu Kirgiz Autonomous Prefecture	1937	70	3.61
喀什地区	Kashgar [Kaxgar] Administrative Offices	7191	86	1.20
和田地区	Hotan Administrative Offices	8346	411	4.92
自治区直辖县级市	Municpality Country-level Gity Directly under the Central Government	3316	78	2.35
石河子市	Shihezi City	2588	53	2.05
阿拉尔市	Aral City	231	12	5.19
图木舒克市	Tumxuk City	153	8	5.23
五家渠市	Wujiaqu City	344	5	1.45

注：2004 年数据不包括农、林、牧、渔业。
Note: Data in 2004 does not include statistics of agriculture,forestry,animal husbandry and fishery.

1-14 续表 Continued

年 份 Year	地 区 Region	第二产业 Secondary Inclustry		第三产业 Tertiary Industry	
		绝对数 Value	构成(%) Composition	绝对数 Value	构成 (%) Composition (%)
	2000				
	2001	8446	12.71	54592	82.12
	2002	8360	12.63	54405	82.20
	2003	8529	12.51	56479	82.81
	2004	7824	12.34	55605	87.66
	2005	8713	12.49	59594	85.43
	2006	9425	12.49	64498	85.49
	2007	10226	12.82	67826	85.03
	2008	11276	12.80	76636	86.97
	2009	12034	12.85	79200	84.55
	2010	13005	13.45	80880	83.62
	2011	14595	14.32	83681	82.10
乌鲁木齐市	Urumqi City	3506	12.79	23756	86.64
克拉玛依市	Karamay City	454	14.25	2665	83.65
吐鲁番地区	Turpan Administrative Offices	538	16.49	2643	81.02
哈密地区	Hami [Kumul] Administrative Offices	1020	19.93	3857	75.36
昌吉回族自治州	Changji Hui Autonomous Prefecture	1697	22.14	5515	71.96
伊犁哈萨克自治州	Ili Kazak Autonomous Prefecture	2290	14.96	12309	80.40
伊犁州直属县(市)	Counties (Cities) Direct Under Ili Prefecture	1125	15.75	5744	80.39
塔城地区	Tacheng [Tarbagatai] Administrative Offices	617	16.00	3125	81.04
阿勒泰地区	Altay Administrative Offices	548	12.72	3440	79.85
博尔塔拉蒙古自治州	Bortala Mongol Autonomous Prefecture	341	11.59	2458	83.55
巴音郭楞蒙古自治州	Bayangol Mongol Autonomous Prefecture	1224	14.57	6512	77.51
阿克苏地区	Aksu Administrative Offices	1180	15.06	6166	78.71
克孜勒苏柯尔克孜自治州	Kizilsu Kirgiz Autonomous Prefecture	246	12.70	1621	83.69
喀什地区	Kashgar [Kaxgar] Administrative Offices	869	12.08	6236	86.72
和田地区	Hotan Administrative Offices	434	5.20	7501	89.88
自治区直辖县级市	Municpality Country-level Gity Directly under the Central Government	796	24.00	2442	73.64
石河子市	Shihezi City	572	22.10	1963	75.85
阿拉尔市	Aral City	101	43.72	118	51.08
图木舒克市	Tumxuk City	29	18.95	116	75.82
五家渠市	Wujiaqu City	94	27.33	245	71.22

1-15 按登记注册、机构类型分的法人单位数和产业活动单位数

Number of Legal Entities and Establishment Entities by Status of Registration and Institutions

单位：个 (2011 年) (unit)

类型		法人单位数 Number of Legal Entities	单产业法人 Single Sector	多产业法人 Multisector	产业活动单位数 Number of Establishments Entities	#多产业法人的活动单位 Establishments Entities of Multisector
总计	**Total**	**101926**	**95614**	**6312**	**155890**	**60276**
按登记注册类型分组	**By Status of Registration**					
内资	**Domestic Funded**	**101598**	**95311**	**6287**	**155186**	**59875**
国有	State-owned Enterprises	25728	21923	3805	50645	28722
集体	Collective-owned Enterprises	1174	975	199	2877	1902
股份合作	Cooperative Enterprises	168	154	14	352	198
联营	Joint Ownership Enterprises	121	117	4	212	95
国有联营	State Joint Ownership Enterprises	37	35	2	43	8
集体联营	Collective Joint Ownership Enterprises	41	40	1	47	7
国有与集体联营	Joint State-collective Enterprises	14	13	1	27	14
其他联营	Other Joint Ownership Enterprises	29	29		95	66
有限责任公司	Limited Liability Corporations	9110	8422	688	12074	3652
国有独资公司	State Sole Funded Corporations	429	358	71	715	357
其他有限责任公司	Other Limited Liability Corporations	8681	8064	617	11359	3295
股份有限公司	Share-holding Corporations Limited	675	462	213	2821	2359
私营	Private Enterprises	42916	41725	1191	46316	4591
私营独资	Private-funded Enterprises	6588	6494	94	6949	455
私营合伙	Private Partnership Enterprises	1060	1044	16	1107	63
私营有限责任公司	Private Limited Liability Corporations	34595	33534	1061	37512	3978
私营股份有限公司	Private Share-holding Corporations Ltd.	673	653	20	748	95
其他内资	Other Enterprises	21706	21533	173	39889	18356
港澳台商投资	**Enterprises with Funds from Hong Kong, Macao and Taiwan**	**134**	**123**	**11**	**283**	**160**
与港澳台商合资经营	Joint-venture Enterprises	59	58	1	80	22
与港澳台商合作经营	Cooperative Enterprises	4	4		6	2
港澳台商独资	Enterprises with Sole Investment	52	50	2	79	29
港澳台商投资股份有限公司	Enterprises with Sole Investment Share-holding Corporations Ltd.	17	9	8	116	107
其他港、澳、台商投资	Other	2	2		2	
外商投资	**Foreign Funded Enterprises**	**194**	**180**	**14**	**421**	**241**
中外合资经营	Joint-venture Enterprises	92	89	3	106	17
中外合作经营	Cooperation Enterprises	14	13	1	17	4
外资企业	Enterprises with Sole Funds	71	63	8	257	194
外商投资股份有限公司	Share-holding Corporations Ltd.	15	14	1	36	22
其他外商投资	Other	2	1	1	5	4
按机构类型分组	**by Status of Organization**					
企业	Enterprise	57559	54797	2762	73465	18668
事业单位	Institution	13694	12517	1177	26849	14332
机关	Organ	7762	5736	2026	11202	5466
社会团体	Social Organization	3845	3784	61	5079	1295
民办非企业单位	Private Non-enterprises Units	1436	1431	5	1431	
基金会	Foundation	14	14		15	1
居委会	Neighborhood Committee	1596	1588	8	1635	47
村委会	Village Commitlee	8795	8668	127	8913	245
其他组织机构	Other Units	7225	7079	146	27301	20222

1-16 按行业分的法人单位数和产业活动单位数

Number of Legal Entities and Establishment Entities by Sector

单位：个 (2011 年) (unit)

类 型		法人单位数 Number of Legal Entities	单产业法人 Single Sector	多产业法人 Multi-sector	产业活动单位数 Number of Establishments Entities	#多产业法人的活动单位 Establishments Entities of Multi-sector
总 计	**Total**	**101926**	**95614**	**6312**	**155890**	**60276**
农、林、牧、渔业	**Agriculture, Forestry, Animal Husbandry and Fishery**	**3650**	**3384**	**266**	**7889**	**4505**
农 业	Farming	1190	1021	169	3244	2223
林 业	Forestry	212	200	12	306	106
畜牧业	Animal Husbandry	835	799	36	979	180
渔 业	Fishery	47	44	3	65	21
农、林、牧、渔服务业	Services in Support of Agriculture	1366	1320	46	3295	1975
采矿业	**Mining Ores**	**2088**	**2038**	**50**	**2253**	**215**
煤炭开采和洗选业	Mining and Washing of Coal	398	384	14	429	45
石油和天然气开采业	Extraction of Petroleum and Natural Gas	98	87	11	137	50
黑色金属矿采选业	Mining and Processing of Ferrous Metal Ores	624	614	10	644	30
有色金属矿采选业	Mining and Processing of Non-Ferrous Metal Ores	343	340	3	357	17
非金属矿采选业	Mining and Processing of Nonmetal Ores	549	538	11	610	72
其他采矿业	Mining of Other Ores	76	75	1	76	1
制造业	**Manufacture**	**9649**	**9461**	**188**	**10495**	**1034**
农副食品加工业	Processing of Food from Agricultural Products	1030	1009	21	1208	199
食品制造业	Manufacture of Foods	439	423	16	471	48
饮料制造业	Manufacture of Beverages	378	370	8	408	38
烟草制品业	Manufacture of Tobacco	1	1		2	1
纺织业	Manufacture of Textile	361	350	11	387	37
纺织服装、鞋、帽制造业	Manufacture of Textile Wearing Apparel, Footware and Caps	125	125		135	10
皮革、毛皮、羽毛(绒)及其制品业	Manufacture of Leather, Fur, Feather and Related Products	72	70	2	76	6
木材加工及木、竹、藤、棕、草制品业	Processing of Timber, Manufacture of Wood, bamboo,rattan,palm,and straw products	199	197	2	211	14
家具制造业	Manufacture of Furniture	154	153	1	164	11
造纸及纸制品业	Manufacture of Paper and Paper Products	231	225	6	247	22
印刷业和记录媒介的复制	Printing,Reproduction of Recording Media	336	331	5	357	26
文教体育用品制造业	Manufacture of Articles For Culture, Education and Sport Activities	19	19		20	1
石油加工、炼焦及核燃料加工业	Processing of Petroleum, Coking, Processing of Nuclear Fuel	231	223	8	237	14
化学原料及化学制品制造业	Manufacture of Raw Chemical Materials and Chemical Products	786	765	21	852	87
医药制造业	Manufacture of Medicines	104	102	2	110	8
化学纤维制造业	Manufacture of Chemical Fibers	26	25	1	27	2
橡胶制品业	Manufacture of Rubber	54	53	1	57	4
塑料制品业	Manufacture of Plastics	873	866	7	931	65
非金属矿物制品业	Manufacture of Non-metallic Mineral Products	1979	1941	38	2194	253
黑色金属冶炼及压延加工业	Smelting and Pressing of Ferrous Metals	156	154	2	158	4
有色金属冶炼及压延加工业	Smelting and Pressing of Non-ferrous Metals	106	104	2	111	7
金属制品业	Manufacture of Metal Products	652	641	11	690	49
通用设备制造业	Manufacture of General Purpose Machinery	398	393	5	417	24

1-16 续表 1 Continued

单位：个 (unit)

类　型		法人单位数 Number of Legal Entities	单产业法人 Single Sector	多产业法人 Multi-sector	产业活动单位数 Number of Establishments Entities	#多产业法人的活动单位 Establishments Entities of Multi-sector
专用设备制造业	Manufacture of Special Purpose Machinery	323	318	5	356	38
交通运输设备制造业	Manufacture of Transport Equipment	174	169	5	208	39
电气机械及器材制造业	Manufacture of Electrical Machinery and Equipment	268	263	5	278	15
通信设备、计算机及其他电子设备制造业	Manufacture of Communication Equipment, Computers and Other Electronic Equipment	14	12	2	14	2
仪器仪表及文化、办公用机械制造业	Manufacture of Measuring Instruments and Machinery for Cultural Activity and Office Work	21	21		26	5
工艺品及其他制造业	Manufacture of Artwork and Other Manufacturing	108	107	1	108	1
废弃资源和废旧材料回收加工业	Recycling and Disposal of Waste	31	31		35	4
电力、燃气及水的生产和供应业	**Production and Supply of Electricity,Gas and Water**	**722**	**674**	**48**	**1061**	**387**
电力、热力的生产和供应业	Production and Supply of Electric Power and Heat Power	512	485	27	748	263
燃气生产和供应业	Production and Supply of Gas	69	61	8	93	32
水的生产和供应业	Production and Supply of Water	141	128	13	220	92
建筑业	**Construction**	**2136**	**1936**	**200**	**2935**	**999**
房屋和土木工程建筑业	Building and Civil Engineering	1004	845	159	1672	827
建筑安装业	Construction　Installation	408	382	26	481	99
建筑装饰业	Construction　Decoration	453	445	8	479	34
其他建筑业	Other Construction	271	264	7	303	39
交通运输、仓储和邮政业	**Transport,Storage and Postal**	**2636**	**2440**	**196**	**4241**	**1801**
铁路运输业	Railway　Transport	28	28		32	4
道路运输业	Road Transport	1365	1243	122	1767	524
城市公共交通业	Urban Public Transport	160	146	14	197	51
水上运输业	Water Transport	1	1		1	
航空运输业	Air Transport	27	25	2	41	16
管道运输业	Pipeline　Transport	5	3	2	13	10
装卸搬运和其他运输服务业	Loading,Unloading and Other	764	736	28	827	91
仓储业	Storage	224	219	5	316	97
邮政业	Posts	62	39	23	1047	1008
信息传输、计算机服务和软件业	**Information Transmission Computer Services and Software**	**2061**	**1965**	**96**	**3054**	**1089**
电信和其他信息传输服务业	Telecommunications and Other Information Services	522	442	80	1463	1021
计算机服务业	Computer Services	1353	1338	15	1393	55
软件业	Software industry	186	185	1	198	13
批发和零售业	**Wholesale and Retail Trades**	**21779**	**20735**	**1044**	**27690**	**6955**
批发业	Wholesalel Trade	14774	14124	650	18348	4224
零售业	Retail Trade	7005	6611	394	9342	2731
住宿和餐饮业	**Hotels and Catering Services**	**1061**	**992**	**69**	**1473**	**481**
住宿业	Hotels	756	707	49	1022	315
餐饮业	Catering Services	305	285	20	451	166
金融业	**Financial Intermediation**	**753**	**452**	**301**	**3861**	**3409**
银行业	Bank	266	75	191	2538	2463

1-16 续表 2 Continued

单位：个 (unit)

类　型		法　人单位数 Number of Legal Entities	单产业法　人 Single Sector	多产业法　人 Multi-sector	产业活动单位数 Number of Establishments Entities	#多产业法人的活动单位 Establishments Entities of Multi-sector
证券业	Securities	8	7	1	67	60
保险业	Insurance	185	89	96	860	771
其他金融活动	Other Services	294	281	13	396	115
房地产业	**Real Estate**	**3505**	**3305**	**200**	**3948**	**643**
房地产业	Real Estate	3505	3305	200	3948	643
租赁和商务服务业	**Leasing and Business Services**	**5493**	**5306**	**187**	**6477**	**1171**
租赁业	Leasing	400	393	7	442	49
商务服务业	Business Services	5093	4913	180	6035	1122
科学研究、技术服务和地质勘查业	**Scientific Research, Technical Services,and Geological Prospecting**	**3495**	**3333**	**162**	**4674**	**1341**
研究与试验发展	Research and Experimental Development	231	220	11	265	45
专业技术服务业	Technical service industry	1874	1794	80	2259	465
科技交流和推广服务业	Services of science and technology	991	929	62	1742	813
地质勘查业	Geological prospecting	399	390	9	408	18
水利、环境和公共设施管理业	**Management of Water Conservancy,Enviroment and Public Facilities**	**925**	**819**	**106**	**1902**	**1083**
水利管理业	Management of Water Conservancy	328	252	76	1069	817
环境管理业	Management of　Enviroment	242	228	14	380	152
公共设施管理业	Management of and Public Facilities	355	339	16	453	114
居民服务和其他服务业	**Services to Households and other services**	**1477**	**1439**	**38**	**1767**	**328**
居民服务业	Services to Households	565	544	21	759	215
其他服务业	Other services	912	895	17	1008	113
教　育	**Education**	5275	4871	404	8295	3424
教　育	Education	5275	4871	404	8295	3424
卫生、社会保障和社会福利业	**Health,Social Securities and Social Welfare**	**2676**	**2497**	**179**	**4436**	**1939**
卫　生	Public Health	2256	2090	166	3707	1617
社会保障业	Social Securities	160	152	8	344	192
社会福利业	Social Welfare	260	255	5	385	130
文化、体育和娱乐业	**Culture,Sports and Entertainment**	**1161**	**1114**	**47**	**2127**	**1013**
新闻出版业	Journalism and　Publishing Activities	119	116	3	129	13
广播、电视、电影和音像业	Broadcasting,Movies,Television and Audiovisual Activies	301	273	28	762	489
文化艺术业	Culture and Art Activities	509	499	10	945	446
体　育	Sports Activities	91	89	2	123	34
娱乐业	Entertainment	141	137	4	168	31
公共管理和社会组织	**Public Management and Social Organization**	**31384**	**28853**	**2531**	**57312**	**28459**
中国共产党机关	Communist Party of China	1032	925	107	1142	217
国家机构	Government Agencies	9991	7765	2226	17515	9750
人民政协和民主党派	People's Political Consultative Conference and Democratic Parties	132	130	2	133	3
群众团体、社会团体和宗教组织	Non-Government Organizations,Social Organizations and Religion Organizations	9838	9777	61	27974	18197
基层群众自治组织	Grass Roots Self-governing Organizations	10391	10256	135	10548	292

1-17 各地区按机构类型分法人单位数
Number of Legal Entities by Type of Institutions and Region

单位：个　　(2011 年)　　(unit)

地　区	Region	法人单位数 Number of Legal Entities	企业法人 Business Entity	事业法人 Institution Entity	机关法人 Governmint Entity	社会团体 Social Organization	其他 Others
总　计	**Total**	**101926**	**57559**	**13694**	**7762**	**3845**	**19066**
乌鲁木齐市	Urumqi City	27420	23172	1590	834	458	1366
克拉玛依市	Karamay City	3186	2393	193	235	159	206
吐鲁番地区	Turpan Administrative Offices	3262	1243	403	233	160	1223
哈密地区	Hami [Kumul] Administrative Offices	5118	3010	875	365	202	666
昌吉回族自治州	Changji Hui Autonomous Prefecture	7664	4002	1176	620	477	1389
伊犁哈萨克自治州	Ili Kazak Autonomous Prefecture	15309	6112	3578	1835	709	3075
伊犁州直属县(市)	Counties (Cities) Direct Under Ili Prefecture	7145	3394	1671	795	204	1081
塔城地区	Tacheng [Tarbagatai] Administrative Offices	3856	1136	901	512	149	1158
阿勒泰地区	Altay Administrative Offices	4308	1582	1006	528	356	836
博尔塔拉蒙古自治州	Bortala Mongol Autonomous Prefecture	2942	1614	459	277	188	404
巴音郭楞蒙古自治州	Bayangol Mongol Autonomous Prefecture	8401	5340	1009	654	236	1162
阿克苏地区	Aksu Administrative Offices	7834	3808	1583	667	353	1423
克孜勒苏柯尔克孜自治州	Kizilsu Kirgiz Autonomous Prefecture	1937	708	248	347	68	566
喀什地区	Kashgar [Kaxgar] Administrative Offices	7191	2248	1103	871	399	2570
和田地区	Hotan Administrative Offices	8346	1498	1121	628	322	4777
自治区直辖县级市	Municpality Country-level Gity Directly under the Central Government	3316	2411	356	196	114	239
石河子市	Shihezi City	2588	2044	160	75	95	214
阿拉尔市	Aral City	231	146	43	30	1	11
图木舒克市	Tumxuk City	153	45	57	44	2	5
五家渠市	Wujiaqu City	344	176	96	47	16	9

1-18 按地区和营业状态分企业法人单位数

Number of Business Entities by Region and Operation Status

单位：个 (2011 年) (unit)

地区	Region	企业单位数 Number of Business Entities	营业 In Business or Operating	停业(歇业) Closed	筹建 In Preparation	当年关闭 Closed in the Year	当年破产 Bankrupted in the Year	其他 Others
总计	**Total**	**57559**	**44889**	**4435**	**7044**	**573**	**82**	**536**
乌鲁木齐市	Urumqi City	23172	18234	2507	2045	244	20	122
克拉玛依市	Karamay City	2393	2122	154	110	2		5
吐鲁番地区	Turpan Administrative Offices	1243	1055	62	121	4		1
哈密地区	Hami [Kumul] Administrative Offices	3010	1795	150	986	38	2	39
昌吉回族自治州	Changji Hui Autonomous Prefecture	4002	3157	226	447	69	25	78
伊犁哈萨克自治州	Ili Kazak Autonomous Prefecture	6112	4974	352	675	66	4	41
伊犁州直属县(市)	Counties (Cities) Direct Under Ili Prefecture	3394	2917	188	195	59	3	32
塔城地区	Tacheng [Tarbagatai] Administrative Offices	1136	1025	63	38	3		7
阿勒泰地区	Altay Administrative Offices	1582	1032	101	442	4	1	2
博尔塔拉蒙古自治州	Bortala Mongol Autonomous Prefecture	1614	1258	142	180	6		28
巴音郭楞蒙古自治州	Bayangol Mongol Autonomous Prefecture	5340	4269	217	786	36	6	26
阿克苏地区	Aksu Administrative Offices	3808	2641	184	884	55	8	36
克孜勒苏柯尔克孜自治州	Kizilsu Kirgiz Autonomous Prefecture	708	472	102	127	5		2
喀什地区	Kashgar [Kaxgar] Administrative Offices	2248	1950	116	135	19	9	19
和田地区	Hotan Administrative Offices	1498	864	123	356	14	4	137
自治区直辖县级市	Municpality Country-level Gity Directly under the Central Government	2411	2098	100	192	15	4	2
石河子市	Shihezi City	2044	1789	82	170	3		
阿拉尔市	Aral City	146	115	12	17	2		
图木舒克市	Tumxuk City	45	43	1	1			
五家渠市	Wujiaqu City	176	151	5	4	10	4	2

1-19 各地区非公有制企业法人单位数
Number of Business Entities by Region

单位：个　　(2011 年)　　(unit)

地　区	Region	全部企业法人单位数 Number of total Enterprises	非公有制企业法人单位数 Number of Non-public Enterprises	非公有制占全部比例(%) As Percentage of Total Enterprises
总　计	**Total**	**57559**	**54133**	**94.05**
乌鲁木齐市	Urumqi City	23172	22158	95.62
克拉玛依市	Karamay City	2393	2316	96.78
吐鲁番地区	Turpan Administrative Offices	1243	1138	91.55
哈密地区	Hami [Kumul] Administrative Offices	3010	2806	93.22
昌吉回族自治州	Changji Hui Autonomous Prefecture	4002	3824	95.55
伊犁哈萨克自治州	Ili Kazak Autonomous Prefecture	6112	5543	90.69
伊犁州直属县(市)	Counties (Cities) Direct Under Ili Prefecture	3394	3108	91.57
塔城地区	Tacheng [Tarbagatai] Administrative Offices	1136	998	87.85
阿勒泰地区	Altay Administrative Offices	1582	1437	90.83
博尔塔拉蒙古自治州	Bortala Mongol Autonomous Prefecture	1614	1466	90.83
巴音郭楞蒙古自治州	Bayangol Mongol Autonomous Prefecture	5340	5027	94.14
阿克苏地区	Aksu Administrative Offices	3808	3606	94.70
克孜勒苏柯尔克孜自治州	Kizilsu Kirgiz Autonomous Prefecture	708	650	91.81
喀什地区	Kashgar [Kaxgar] Administrative Offices	2248	1962	87.28
和田地区	Hotan Administrative Offices	1498	1359	90.72
自治区直辖县级市	Municpality Country-level Gity Directly under the Central Government	2411	2278	94.48
石河子市	Shihezi City	2044	1944	95.11
阿拉尔市	Aral City	146	140	95.89
图木舒克市	Tumxuk City	45	34	75.56
五家渠市	Wujiaqu City	176	160	90.91

1-20 服务业法人单位数和从业人员数

Number of Services to Legal Entities and Employed Persons

年 份 Year	合 计 Total	企 业 Enterprises	行政事业 Administrative	社会团体及其他 Social Organizations and Others
单位数(个) Number of Enterprises				
2008	76636	34382	20543	21711
2009	79200	36738	20616	21846
2010	80880	38226	20636	22018
2011	83681	40854	20729	22098
从业人数(万人) Number of Employed Persons				
2008	172.11	63.22	93.92	14.96
2009	173.31	64.48	93.70	15.12
2010	178.72	68.24	95.05	15.43
2011	184.51	73.15	95.76	15.60

1-21 服务业分行业法人单位数及从业人员数

Number of Services to Legal Entities and Employed Persons by Industry

(2011 年)

行 业	Sector	法人单位数 Number of Legal Entities	从业人数(万人) Employed Persons
总 计	**Total**	**83681**	**184.51**
交通运输、仓储和邮政业	Transport,Storage and Post	2636	11.50
信息传输、计算机服务和软件业	Information Transmission,Comupter Services and Software	2061	3.06
批发和零售业	Wholesale and Retail Trades	21779	23.04
住宿和餐饮业	Hotels and Catering Services	1061	5.11
金融业	Financil Intermediation	753	8.05
房地产业	Real Estate	3505	7.30
租赁和商务服务业	Leasing and Business Services	5493	10.99
科学研究、技术服务和地质勘查业	Scientific Research,Technical Services and Geological Prospecting	3495	7.38
水利、环境和公共设施管理业	Mangement of Water Conservancy,Environment and Public Facilities	925	4.93
居民服务和其他服务业	Services to Households and other Services	1477	1.73
教 育	Education	5275	34.26
卫生、社会保障和社会福利业	Health,Social Securities and Social Welfare	2676	13.01
文化、体育和娱乐业	Culture,Sports and Entertainment	1161	2.70
公共管理和社会组织	Public Mangement and Social Organization	31384	51.45

1-22 各地区服务业法人单位数
Number of Services In Stitutional Unit by Region

单位：个　　(2011 年)　　(unit)

地区	Region	合计 Total	交通运输仓储及邮政业 Traffic, transport, storage and post	信息传输计算机服务和软件业 Information transmission, Computer, services and software	批发和零售业 Wholesale and retail trade	住宿和餐饮业 Accommodation and Restaurants
总　计	**Total**	**83681**	**2636**	**2061**	**21779**	**1061**
乌鲁木齐市	Urumqi City	23756	899	828	11327	336
克拉玛依市	Karamay City	2665	123	79	985	29
吐鲁番地区	Turpan Administrative Offices	2643	46	46	278	41
哈密地区	Hami [Kumul] Administrative Offices	3857	189	93	898	33
昌吉回族自治州	Changji Hui Autonomous Prefecture	5515	214	157	729	56
伊犁哈萨克自治州	Ili Kazak Autonomous Prefecture	12309	347	278	1480	183
伊犁州直属县(市)	Counties (Cities) Direct Under Ili Prefecture	5744	176	114	1032	101
塔城地区	Tacheng [Tarbagatai] Administrative Offices	3125	59	68	167	24
阿勒泰地区	Altay Administrative Offices	3440	112	96	281	58
博尔塔拉蒙古自治州	Bortala Mongol Autonomous Prefecture	2458	119	93	623	23
巴音郭楞蒙古自治州	Bayangol Mongol Autonomous Prefecture	6512	218	67	2196	125
阿克苏地区	Aksu Administrative Offices	6166	146	219	1091	60
克孜勒苏柯尔克孜自治州	Kizilsu Kirgiz Autonomous Prefecture	1621	59	13	218	12
喀什地区	Kashgar [Kaxgar] Administrative Offices	6236	95	60	646	79
和田地区	Hotan Administrative Offices	7501	73	24	512	29
自治区直辖县级市	Municpality Country-level Gity Directly under the Central Government	2442	108	104	796	55
石河子市	Shihezi City	1963	88	104	762	47
阿拉尔市	Aral City	118	5		14	1
图木舒克市	Tumxuk City	116	1		1	1
五家渠市	Wujiaqu City	245	14		19	6

1-22 续表 1 Continued

单位：个 (unit)

地　区	Region	金融业 Finance	房地产业 Real estate	租赁和商务服务业 Leasing and Business Services	科学研究技术服务和地质勘察业 Scientific research, technical service and geologic perambulation	水利、环境和公共设施管理业 Management of water conservancy, environment and public establishment
总　计	**Total**	**753**	**3505**	**5493**	**3495**	**925**
乌鲁木齐市	Urumqi City	207	1205	2844	1340	210
克拉玛依市	Karamay City	25	127	302	142	33
吐鲁番地区	Turpan Administrative Offices	19	59	90	55	18
哈密地区	Hami [Kumul] Administrative Offices	63	217	212	169	62
昌吉回族自治州	Changji Hui Autonomous Prefecture	47	249	285	322	103
伊犁哈萨克自治州	Ili Kazak Autonomous Prefecture	110	494	502	569	166
伊犁州直属县(市)	Counties (Cities) Direct Under Ili Prefecture	52	294	280	216	67
塔城地区	Tacheng [Tarbagatai] Administrative Offices	27	80	50	189	36
阿勒泰地区	Altay Administrative Offices	31	120	172	164	63
博尔塔拉蒙古自治州	Bortala Mongol Autonomous Prefecture	32	88	111	107	28
巴音郭楞蒙古自治州	Bayangol Mongol Autonomous Prefecture	62	299	468	187	60
阿克苏地区	Aksu Administrative Offices	54	300	268	233	78
克孜勒苏柯尔克孜自治州	Kizilsu Kirgiz Autonomous Prefecture	16	29	37	52	23
喀什地区	Kashgar [Kaxgar] Administrative Offices	43	190	129	98	49
和田地区	Hotan Administrative Offices	34	62	99	112	66
自治区直辖县级市	Municpality Country-level Gity Directly under the Central Government	41	186	146	109	29
石河子市	Shihezi City	35	132	136	91	13
阿拉尔市	Aral City		17	3	2	7
图木舒克市	Tumxuk City		8	3	4	2
五家渠市	Wujiaqu City	6	29	4	12	7

1-22 续表 2 Continued

单位：个 (unit)

地　　区	Region	居民服务和其他服务业 Resident services and other services	教育 Education	卫生、社会保障和社会福利业 Sanitation, social security and social welfare	文化、体育和娱乐业 Culture, Sports and entertainment	公共管理和社会组织 Public management and social organization
总　计	**Total**	**1477**	**5275**	**2676**	**1161**	**31384**
乌鲁木齐市	Urumqi City	620	845	331	270	2494
克拉玛依市	Karamay City	83	140	30	27	540
吐鲁番地区	Turpan Administrative Offices	50	191	69	22	1659
哈密地区	Hami [Kumul] Administrative Offices	55	253	126	58	1429
昌吉回族自治州	Changji Hui Autonomous Prefecture	84	428	305	86	2450
伊犁哈萨克自治州	Ili Kazak Autonomous Prefecture	105	1179	652	239	6005
伊犁州直属县(市)	Counties (Cities) Direct Under Ili Prefecture	56	699	311	120	2226
塔城地区	Tacheng [Tarbagatai] Administrative Offices	23	269	180	47	1906
阿勒泰地区	Altay Administrative Offices	26	211	161	72	1873
博尔塔拉蒙古自治州	Bortala Mongol Autonomous Prefecture	30	142	79	28	955
巴音郭楞蒙古自治州	Bayangol Mongol Autonomous Prefecture	197	373	237	99	1924
阿克苏地区	Aksu Administrative Offices	74	646	238	125	2634
克孜勒苏柯尔克孜自治州	Kizilsu Kirgiz Autonomous Prefecture	26	65	39	32	1000
喀什地区	Kashgar [Kaxgar] Administrative Offices	47	485	276	67	3972
和田地区	Hotan Administrative Offices	53	330	223	62	5822
自治区直辖县级市	Municpality Country-level Gity Directly under the Central Government	53	198	71	46	500
石河子市	Shihezi City	48	151	33	34	289
阿拉尔市	Aral City		15	12	2	40
图木舒克市	Tumxuk City	1	15	10	3	67
五家渠市	Wujiaqu City	4	17	16	7	104

1-23 企业家信心指数
Entrepreneur Confidence Index

(2011 年)

经济类型及行业	Ownership and Sector	一季度 First Quarter 本期实际 Index	一季度 First Quarter 比上年同期增减 as±of Last Same Period Index	二季度 Second Quarter 本期实际 Index	二季度 Second Quarter 比上年同期增减 as±of Last Same Period Index
企业家信心指数	**Entrepreneur Confidence Index**	**143.1**	**13.2**	**135.9**	**3.1**
按企业登记注册类型分	**Grouped by Status of Registration**				
国有企业	State-owned Enterprises	143.6	4.7	142.5	3.8
集体企业	Collective-owned Enterprises	112.4	11.4	84.1	-2.7
股份合作企业	Cooperative Enterprises	200.0		200.0	
有限责任公司	Limited-Liability Corporations	138.7	10.7	127.9	
股份有限公司	Share Holding Corporations Ltd.	157.7	11.5	155.2	9.0
私营企业	Private Enterprises	144.1	28.0	136.4	11.7
按行业分	**Grouped by Sector**				
工　业	Industry	142.9	16.1	139.2	5.8
建筑业	Construction	145.3	11.5	124.0	8.3
交通运输、仓储和邮政业	Transportation, Storage,Post and Telecommunications	131.7	7.2	130.1	5.4
批发和零售业	Wholesale and Retail Trades	150.1	10.1	133.3	0.7
房地产业	Real Estate	132.8	12.2	114.6	14.4
社会服务业	Social Services	131.4	18.6	159.1	30.9
信息传输、计算机服务和软件业	Information Transmission, Computer Servcie and Software Industries	170.6	5.4	169.8	6.2
住宿和餐饮业	Accommodation and Catering Services	136.4	23.7	132.7	14.5
按企业规模分	**Grouped by Size of Enterprises**				
大　型	Large	164.2	10.8	170.3	17.7
中　型	Medium	148.5	13.6	136.9	0.1
小　型	Small	135.6	11.0	131.1	5.8
按特殊群体分	**Grouped by Special Group**				
上市公司	Listed Companies	160.1	3.3	172.2	15.6
国有控股企业	State-owned and State-holding Enterprises	149.8	9.8	146.0	5.6

1-23 续表 Continued

经济类型及行业	Ownership and Sector	三季度 Third Quarter		四季度 Fourth Quarter	
		本期实际 Index	比上年同期增减 as±of Last Same Period Index	本期实际 Index	比上年同期增减 as±of Last Same Period Index
企业家信心指数	**Entrepreneur Confidence Index**	**136.8**	**1.6**	**129.1**	**6.8**
按企业登记注册类型分	**Grouped by Status of Registration**				
国有企业	State-owned Enterprises	150.5	11.4	142.7	4.6
集体企业	Collective-owned Enterprises	134.1	61.6	121.6	34.8
股份合作企业	Cooperative Enterprises	150.0	50.0	150.0	50.0
有限责任公司	Limited-Liability Corporations	127.9	10.9	116.1	19.0
股份有限公司	Share Holding Corporations Ltd.	149.2	1.9	137.3	15.5
私营企业	Private Enterprises	136.4	6.4	127.3	4.0
按行业分	**Grouped by Sector**				
工　业	Industry	135.3	2.1	130.1	4.1
建筑业	Construction	135.7	6.5	124.3	17.0
交通运输、仓储和邮政业	Transportation, Storage,Post and Telecommunications	140.0	11.6	135.8	15.0
批发和零售业	Wholesale and Retail Trades	140.6	3.0	132.2	14.5
房地产业	Real Estate	112.7	25.0	84.0	-49.1
社会服务业	Social Services	148.8	2.5	133.4	7.6
信息传输、计算机服务和软件业	Information Transmission, Computer Servcie and Software Industries	160.6	3.0	159.9	0.8
住宿和餐饮业	Accommodation and Catering Services	156.4	5.5	134.6	5.4
按企业规模分	**Grouped by Size of Enterprises**				
大　型	Large	161.1	10.4	155.2	0.2
中　型	Medium	139.7	2.3	126.4	14.9
小　型	Small	131.6	3.9	122.1	9.8
按特殊群体分	**Grouped by Special Group**				
上市公司	Listed Companies	145.8	12.2	146.2	13.3
国有控股企业	State-owned and State-holding Enterprises	146.4	1.2	140.2	5.5

1-24 企业景气指数
Prosperity Index on Enterprises

(2011 年)

经济类型及行业	Ownership and Sector	一季度 First Quarter		二季度 Second Quarter	
		本期实际 Index	比上年同期增减 as±of Last Same Period Index	本期实际 Index	比上年同期增减 as±of Last Same Period Index
企业景气指数	**Enterprises Business Climate Index**	**131.4**	**6.3**	**139.9**	**7.8**
按企业登记注册类型分	**Grouped by Status of Registration**				
国有企业	State-owned Enterprises	136.5	3.7	138.9	1.0
集体企业	Collective-owned Enterprises	83.8	9.1	96.6	4.4
股份合作企业	Cooperative Enterprises	100.0		150.0	50.0
有限责任公司	Limited-Liability Corporations	127.9	8.5	140.0	16.2
股份有限公司	Share Holding Corporations Ltd.	157.6	12.1	145.4	7.6
私营企业	Private Enterprises	120.2	11.5	138.6	22.5
按行业分	**Grouped by Sector**				
工　业	Industry	133.5	7.7	138.7	6.4
建筑业	Construction	115.4	11.7	134.1	5.3
交通运输、仓储和邮政业	Transportation, Storage, Posts and Telecommunications	121.5	-2.8	139.8	10.2
批发和零售业	Wholesale and Retail Trades	144.2	3.3	153.8	21.3
房地产业	Real Estate	133.5	1.4	140.7	9.7
社会服务业	Social Services	125.6	25.6	135.9	15.4
信息传输、计算机服务和软件业	Information Transmission, Computer Servcie and Software Industries	165.2	6.1	154.2	9.4
住宿和餐饮业	Accommodation and Catering Services	112.7	5.4	132.7	18.1
按企业规模分	**Grouped by Size of Enterprises**				
大　型	Large	173.3	5.7	167.8	0.3
中　型	Medium	138.5	6.2	146.4	6.6
小　型	Small	120.4	6.8	127.9	8.8
按特殊群体分	**Grouped by Special Group**				
上市公司	Listed Companies	168.3	6.5	162.6	4.5
国有控股企业	State-owned and State-holding Enterprises	144.1	6.1	145.4	4.0
按观察指标分	**Grouped by Indicator Observed**				
生产总量	Production (Operation)	104.2	11.0	136.2	6.2
盈利(亏损)变化	Changes of Profit(Loss)	98.2	3.3	119.2	0.9
流动资金	Liquid Capital	93.3	1.2	93.2	0.9
货款拖欠	Payment Arrears for Goods	113.7	1.1	100.6	3.4
劳动力需求	Demand on Labors	113.8	10.1	135.2	9.7
固定资产投资	Investment in Fixed Assets	108.1	6.9	127.2	3.4
产品订货	Ordering of Productions	107.7	7.7	127.4	5.0
企业融资	Financing of Enterprises	84.5	0.8	78.7	4.1

1-24 续表 Continued

经济类型及行业	Ownership and Sector	三季度 Third Quarter		四季度 Fourth Quarter	
		本期实际 Index	比上年同期增减 as±of Last Same Period Index	本期实际 Index	比上年同期增减 as±of Last Same Period Index
企业景气指数	**Enterprises Business Climate Index**	**139.3**	**0.5**	**130.4**	**5.2**
按企业登记注册类型分	**Grouped by Status of Registration**				
国有企业	State-owned Enterprises	143.6	3.1	141.6	6.7
集体企业	Collective-owned Enterprises	112.5	2.8	112.5	12.5
股份合作企业	Cooperative Enterprises	150.0	50.0	150.0	50.0
有限责任公司	Limited-Liability Corporations	137.0	1.1	120.1	14.1
股份有限公司	Share Holding Corporations Ltd.	152.4	3.2	134.9	14.0
私营企业	Private Enterprises	131.8	6.8	115.9	6.6
按行业分	**Grouped by Sector**				
工　业	Industry	136.5	1.3	126.9	8.3
建筑业	Construction	141.0	2.8	127.1	8.1
交通运输、仓储和邮政业	Transportation, Storage, Posts and Telecommunications	140.5	12.4	130.5	1.2
批发和零售业	Wholesale and Retail Trades	142.5	3.8	156.9	12.1
房地产业	Real Estate	135.3	3.2	108.4	-24.7
社会服务业	Social Services	148.2	0.5	125.2	3.0
信息传输、计算机服务和软件业	Information Transmission, Computer Servcie and Software Industries	165.5	1.9	170.5	14.4
住宿和餐饮业	Accommodation and Catering Services	149.1	10.9	120.0	持平
按企业规模分	**Grouped by Size of Enterprises**				
大　型	Large	162.0	6.6	151.7	9.1
中　型	Medium	146.9	3.4	136.5	7.4
小　型	Small	131.6	0.4	115.3	9.9
按特殊群体分	**Grouped by Special Group**				
上市公司	Listed Companies	170.3	2.5	140.6	14.6
国有控股企业	State-owned and State-holding Enterprises	146.9	0.6	139.0	5.6
按观察指标分	**Grouped by Indicator Observed**				
生产总量	Production (Operation)	138.6	3.6	105.0	5.6
盈利(亏损)变化	Changes of Profit(Loss)	128.9	6.7	106.8	12.7
流动资金	Liquid Capital	93.6	1.6	91.1	1.1
货款拖欠	Payment Arrears for Goods	98.8	-4.0	99.4	10.8
劳动力需求	Demand on Labors	137.3	9.8	101.2	4.4
固定资产投资	Investment in Fixed Assets	124.2	1.4	113.8	4.4
产品订货	Ordering of Productions	126.5	3.0	98.8	4.2
企业融资	Financing of Enterprises	77.2	5.1	77.9	8.3

主要统计指标解释

行政区划 指国家对行政区域的划分，根据宪法规定，我国的行政区域划分如下：(1)全国分为省、自治区、直辖市；(2)省、自治区分为自治州、县、自治县、市；(3)自治州分为县、自治县、市；(4)县、自治县分为乡、民族乡、镇；(5)直辖市和较大的市分为区、县；(6)国家在必要时设立的特别行政区。

平均增长速度 我国计算平均增长速度有两种方法：一种是习惯上经常使用的"水平法"，又称几何平均法，是以间隔期最后一年的水平同基期水平对比来计算平均每年增长(或下降)速度；另一种是"累计法"，又称代数平均法或方程法，是以间隔期内各年水平的总和同基期水平对比来计算平均每年增长(或下降)速度。在一般正常情况下，两种方法计算的平均每年增长速度比较接近；但在经济发展不平衡、出现大起大落时，两种方法计算的结果差别较大。

本《年鉴》内所列的平均增长速度，均用"水平法"计算。从某年到某年平均增长速度的年份，均不包括基期年在内。如建国四十三年的平均增长速度是以1949年为基期计算的，则写为1950-1992年平均增长速度，其余类推。

国民经济行业分类 自 2012 年定期报表开始使用新的《国民经济行业分类》(GB/T4754-2011)，该分类是由国家统计局组织修订，经国家检验检疫总局和国家标准化委员会批准，于 2011 年 4 月 29 日发布实施。这次修订是在 2002 年分类标准的基础上，参照联合国《全部经济活动的国际标准产业分类》(ISIC/Rev.4)进行的。修订后的《国民经济行业分类》(GB/T4754-2011)共有门类 20 个，大类 96 个，中类 432 个，小类 1094 个。行业门类的数目保持不变，部分门类的名称和顺序作了调整，大类增加 1 个，中类增加 36 个，小类增加 181 个。

企业(单位)登记注册类型 是以在工商行政管理机关登记注册的各类企业为划分对象，以工商行政管理部门对企业登记注册的类型为依据，将企业登记注册类型分为内资企业、港澳台商投资企业和外商投资企业三大类。内资企业包括国有企业、集体企业、股份合作企业、联营企业、有限责任公司、股份有限公司、私营公司和其他企业；港澳台商投资企业和外商投资企业分别包括合资经营企业、合作经营企业、独资经营企业和股份有限公司。对不在工商行政管理部门进行登记注册的行政机关、事业单位和社会团体，主要按其经费来源和管理方式进行划分。

国有企业 指企业全部资产归国家所有，并按《中华人民共和国企业法人登记管理条例》规定登记注册的非公司制的经济组织。不包括有限责任公司中的国有独资公司。

集体企业 指企业资产归集体所有，并按《中华人民共和国企业法人登记管理条例》规定登记注册的经济组织。

股份合作企业 指以合作制为基础，由企业职工共同出资入股，吸收一定比例的社会资产投资组建，实行自主经营，自负盈亏，共同劳动，民主管理，按劳分配与按股分红相结合的一种集体经济组织。

联营企业 指两个及两个以上相同或不同所有制性质的企业法人或事业单位法人，按自愿、平等、互利的原则，共同投资组成的经济组织。联营企业包括国有联营企业、集体联营企业、国有与集体联营企业和其他联营企业。

有限责任公司 指根据《中华人民共和国公司登记管理条例》规定登记注册，由两个以上、五十个以下的股东共同出资，每个股东以其所认缴的出资额对公司承担有限责任，公司以其全部资产对其债务承担责任的经济组织。有限责任公司包括国有独资公司以及其他有限责任公司。

股份有限公司 指根据《中华人民共和国公司登记管理条例》规定登记注册，其全部注册资本由等额股份构成并通过发行股票筹集资本，股东以其认购的股份对公司承担有限责任，公司以其全部资产对其债务承担责任的经济组织。

私营企业 指由自然人投资设立或由自然人控股，以雇佣劳动为基础的营利性经济组织。包括按照《公司法》、《合伙企业法》、《私营企业暂行条例》规定登记注册的私营有限责任公司、私营股份有限公司、私营合伙企业和个人独资企业。

其他企业 指上述企业之外的其他内资经济组织。

与港澳台商合资经营企业 指港澳台地区投资者与内地的企业依照《中华人民共和国中外合资经营企业法》及有关法律的规定，按合同规定的比例投资设立、分享利润和分担风险的企业。

与港澳台商合作经营企业 指港澳台地区投资者与内地企业依照《中华人民共和国中外合作经营企业法》及有关法律的规定，依照合作合同的约定进行投资或提供条件设立、分配利润和分担风险和亏损的企业。

港澳台商独资经营企业 指依照《中华人民共和国外资企业法》及有关法律的规定，在内地由港澳台地区投资者全额投资设立的企业。

港澳台商投资股份有限公司 指根据国家有关规定，经商务部批准设立，并且其中港、澳、台商的股本占公司注册资本的比例达 25% 以上的股份有限公司。凡其中港、澳、台商的股本占公司注册资本的比例小于 25%的，属于内资企业中的股份有限公司。

中外合资经营企业 指外国企业或外国人与中国内地企业依照《中华人民共和国中外合资经营企业法》及有关法律的规定，按合同规定的比例投资设立、分享利润和分担风险的企业。

中外合作经营企业 指外国企业或外国人与中国内地

企业依照《中华人民共和国中外合作经营企业法》及有关法律的规定，依照合作合同的约定进行投资或提供条件设立、分配利润和分担风险和亏损的企业。

外资企业 指依照《中华人民共和国外资企业法》及有关法律的规定，在中国内地由外国投资者全额投资设立的企业。

外商投资股份有限公司 指根据国家有关规定，经商务部批准设立，并且其中外资的股本占公司注册资本的比例达25% 以上的股份有限公司。凡其中外资股本占公司注册资本的比例小于25%的，属于内资中的股份有限公司。

行政机关、事业单位和社会团体 参照企业登记注册类型，主要按其经费来源和管理方式划分。具体规定如下：

(1)行政机关：包括国家机关和政党机关，原则上均列为“国有”。但有特殊规定的，如供销社等，则列为“集体”。

(2)事业单位：包括经国家机构编制部门和有关业务主管部门批准成立的各类事业单位，不包括实行企业化管理的事业单位。事业单位的划分办法如下：

①由国家财政预算拨款或列入财政预算外资金管理以及经费主要来源于国有主管部门或国有上级单位的事业单位，列为“国有”。

②经费主要来源于集体单位的事业单位，列为“集体”。

③公民个人(或个人合伙)开办的事业单位，列为“私营”。

④上述以外的其他事业单位，如果其经费来源不明确，按管理方式进行归类。

(3)社会团体：包括经民政部门批准成立以及未纳入社会团体管理条例范围的工会、妇联等各类社会团体。社会团体的划分办法如下：

①未纳入民政部社会团体管理条例范围的工会、妇联、共青团、青联、工商联、科协、侨联等社会团体，国家拨款设立的基金会或基金管理组织以及经费主要来源于国有业务主管部门或国有上级单位的社会团体，列为“国有”。

②经费主要来源于集体单位的社会团体，列为“集体”。

③公民个人(或个人合伙)开办的社会团体，划为“私营”。

④上述以外的其他社会团体，如果其经费来源不明确，改按管理方式进行归类。

各个计划时期 表内所用各个“时期”代表的年份如下：恢复时期为 1950 到 1952 年；第一个五年计划时期(简称“一五”时期)为 1953 到 1957 年；第二个五年计划时期(简称“二五”时期)为 1958 到 1962 年；第三个五年计划时期(简称“三五”时期)为 1966 到 1970 年；第四个五年计划时期(简称“四五”时期)为 1971 到 1975 年；第五个五年计划时期(简称“五五”时期)为 1976 到 1980 年；第六个五年计划时期(简称“六五”时期)为 1981 到 1985 年；第七个五年计划时期(简称“七五”时期)为 1986 到 1990 年；第八个五年计划时期(简称“八五”时期)为 1991 到 1995 年；第九个五年计划时期(简称“九五”时期)为 1996 到 2000 年；第十个五年计划时期(简称“十五”时期)为 2001 到 2005 年；第十一个五年计划时期(简称“十一五”时期)为 2006 到 2010 年。第十二个五年计划时期（简称“十二五”时期）为 2011 到 2015 年。

企业家信心指数 也称宏观经济景气指数，是根据企业家对企业外部市场经济环境与宏观政策的认识、看法、判断与预期而编制的指数，用以综合反映企业家对宏观经济环境的感受与信心。

企业景气指数 也称企业综合生产经营景气指数，是根据企业家对本企业综合生产经营情况的判断与预期而编制的指数，用以反映企业的综合生产经营状况。

法人单位 指具备：

(1)依法成立、有自己的名称、组织机构和场所、能够独立承担民事责任；

(2)独立拥有和使用（或授权使用）资产、承担负债、有权与其它单位签订合同；

(3)会计上独立核算、能够编制资产负债表。法人单位包括企业法人、事业单位法人、机关法人、社会团体法人和其他法人。

单产业法人 指只在一个地点，主要从事一种生产经营活动的法人单位。

多产业法人 指坐落于两个及两个以上地点、或主要从事两种及两种以上生产经营活动的，按照单位划分规定可以划分为两个或两个以上产业活动单位的法人单位。

产业活动单位 是法人单位的附属单位。产业活动单位应具备下列条件：

(1)在一个场所从事一种或主要从事一种社会经济活动；

(2)相对独立组织生产经营和业务活动；

(3)能够掌握收入和支出等业务核算资料。

服务业 指生产和销售产品的生产部门和企业的集合。在国民经济核算中，将服务业视同为第三产业，即除农业、工业、建筑业以外的其它所有产业部门。

Explanatory Notes on Main Statistical Indicators

Administrative Division refers to the division of administrative areas by the state. The Constitution of the People's Republic of China stipulates that the administrative areas in China are divided as: 1) The whole Country is divided into provinces, autonomous regions and municipalities directly under the central government; 2) Provinces and autonomous regions are divided into autonomous prefectures, counties, autonomous counties and cities; 3) Autonomous prefectures are divided into counties, autonomous counties and cities; 4) Counties and autonomous counties are divided into townships, nationality townships and towns; 5) Municipalities and large cities are divided into districts and counties, 6) The state shall, when necessary, establish special administrative regions.

Average Annual Growth Rate Two methods for calculating average annual growth rate are applied in China,one is often called level approachor the method of calculating geometric average,which is derived by comparing the level of the last year of the interval with that of the beginning year;the other is calledaccumulative approach or algebraic average or equation method,which is derived by the summation of the actual figure of each year in the interval divided by the figure in the base year.Usually the results calculated by the two methods are.

fairly close, but they differed sharply when uneven economic development occurred with striking fluctuations in growth.

The average annual growth rates listed in this statistical yearbook are calculated by level approach except for the growth rate of investment in fixed assets. The base years are not listed when the years are listed for average annual growth rates. For instance,the average annual growth rate of 43 years since 1949 is listed as average annual growth rate of 1950-1992 without listing the base year 1949.And the analogy of this is also the same for the rest of the years.

Industrial Classification of the National Economy The new Industrial Classification of the National Economy (GB/T 4754-2011) is introduced starting from the compilation of 2012annual statistics. The new revision was based on the 2002 classification and organized by the National Bureau of Statistics taking into consideration of the International Standards of the Industrial Classification of All Economic Activities (ISIC/Rev.4) of the United Nations, and the new Classification was promulgated by the National Administration of Quality Supervision, Inspection and Quarantine on April 29, 2011. The revised version of the Industrial Classification of the National Economy (GB/T 4754-2011) is composed of 20 major divisions, 96 divisions, 432 major groups and 1094 groups, including 1 new divisions, 36 major groups and 181 groups.

Registration Status of Enterprises Enterprises are classified into 3 categories, namely domestic-funded enterprises, enterprises with investment from Hong Kong, Macao and Taiwan, and enterprises with foreign investment, in the light of the registration status of an enterprise in industrial and commercial administration agencies. Domestic-funded enterprises include state-owned enterprises, collective-owned enterprises, cooperative enterprises, joint ownership enterprises, limited liability corporations, share-holding corporations Ltd., private enterprises and other enterprises. Included in the enterprises with investment from Hong Kong, Macao and Taiwan and enterprises with foreign investment are joint-venture enterprises, cooperative enterprises, sole investment enterprises and share-holding corporations Ltd. For government agencies, institutions and social organizations which are not requested to be registered in industrial and commercial administration agencies, they are classified mainly by their sources of funds and way of management.

State-owned Enterprises refer to non-corporation economic units where the entire assets are owned by the state and which have registered in accordance with the Regulation of the People's Republic of China on the Management of Registration of Corporate Enterprises. Excluded from this category are sole state-funded corporations in the limited liability corporations.

Collective-owned Enterprises refer to economic units where the assets are owned collectively and which have registered in accordance with the Regulation of the People's Republic of China on the Management of Registration of Corporate Enterprises.

Cooperative Enterprises refer to a form of collective economic units (enterprises) where capitals come mainly from employees as their shares, with certain proportion of capital from the outside, where production is organized on the basis of independent operation, independent accounting for profits and losses, joint work, democratic management, and a distribution system that integrates remuneration according to work with dividend according to capital share.

Joint Ownership Enterprises refer to economic units established by two or more corporate enterprises or corporate institutions of the same or different ownership, through joint investment on the basis of equality, voluntary participation and mutual benefits. They include state joint ownership enterprises, collective joint ownership enterprises, joint state-collective enterprises, other joint ownership enterprises.

Limited Liability Corporations refer to economic units established with investment from 2-50 investors and registered in accordance with the Regulation of the People's Republic of China on the Management of Registration of Corporations, each investor bearing limited liability to the corporation depending on its share of investment, and the corporation bearing liability to its debt to the maximum of its total assets. Limited liability corporations include exclusive state-funded limited liability corporations and other limited liability corporations.

Share-holding Corporations Ltd. refer to economic units registered in accordance with the Regulation of the People's Republic of China on the Management of Registration of Corporations, with total registered capitals divided into equal shares and raised through issuing stocks. Each investor bears limited liability to the corporation depending on the holding of shares, and the corporation bears liability to its debt to the maximum of its total assets.

Private Enterprises refer to profit-making economic units invested and established by natural persons, or controlled by natural persons using employed labour. Included in this category are private limited liability corporations, private share-holding corporations Ltd., private partnership enterprises and private-funded enterprises registered in accordance with the Corporation Law, Partnership Enterprises Law and Interim Regulations on Private Enterprises.

Other Domestic-funded Enterprises refer to domesticfunded economic units other than those mentioned above.

Joint-venture Enterprises with Funds from Hong Kong, Macao and Taiwan refer to enterprises jointly established by investors from Hong Kong, Macao and Taiwan with enterprises in the mainland of China in accordance with the Law of the People's Republic of China on Sino-foreign Joint Venture Enterprises and other relevant laws, where the share of investment, profits and risks is stipulated in the contract.

Cooperative Enterprises with Funds from Hong Kong Macao and Taiwan established by investors from Hong Kong, Macao and Taiwan with enterprises in the mainland of China in accordance with the Law of the People's Republic of China on Sino-foreign Cooperative Enterprises and other relevant laws, where the investment or provision of facilities, and the share of profits and risks is stipulated in the cooperative contract.

Enterprises with Sole (exclusive) Investment from Hong Kong, Macao and Taiwan refer to enterprises established in the mainland of China with exclusive investment from investors from Hong Kong, Macao and Taiwan in accordance with the Law of the People's Republic of China on Foreign-Funded Enterprises and other relevant laws.

Share-holding Corporations Ltd. with Investment from Hong Kong, Macao and Taiwan refer to share-holding corporations Ltd. established with the approval from the Ministry of Foreign Trades and Economic Relations in line with relevant state regulations, where the share of investment from Hong Kong, Macao or Taiwan businessmen exceeds 25% of the total registered capital of the corporation. In case the share of investment from Hong Kong, Macao or Taiwan is less than 25% of the total registered capital, the enterprise is to be classified as domestic-funded share-holding corporation Ltd.

Joint-venture Enterprises with Foreign Investment refer to enterprises jointly established by foreign enterprises or foreigners with enterprises in the mainland of China in accordance with the Law of the People's Republic of China on Sino-foreign Joint Venture Enterprises and other relevant laws, where the share of investment, profits and risks is stipulated in the contract.

Cooperation Enterprises with Foreign Investment refer to enterprises jointly established by foreign enterprises or foreigners with enterprises in the mainland of China in accordance with the Law of the People's Republic of China on Sino-foreign Cooperative Enterprises and other relevant laws, where the investment or provision of facilities, and the share of profits and risks is stipulated in the cooperative contract.

Enterprises with Sole (exclusive) Foreign Investment refer to enterprises established in the mainland of China with exclusive investment from foreign investors in accordance with the Law of the People's Republic of China on Foreign-Funded Enterprises and other relevant laws.

Shareholding Corporations Ltd. with Foreign Investment refer to share-holding corporations Ltd. established with the approval from the Ministry of Foreign Trades and Economic Relations in line with relevant state regulations, where the share of investment from foreign investors exceeds 25% of the total registered capital of the corporation. In case the share of foreign investment is less than 25% of the total registered capital, the enterprise is to be classified as domestic-funded share-holding corporation Ltd.

Government Agencies, Institutions and Social Organizations are classified into following categories by source of funds and way of management taking reference of the re- gistration status of enterprises:

(1) Government agencies: include state and party agencies, classified in principle as "state-owned". There are exceptions, such as supply and marketing cooperatives which are classified as "collective".

(2) Institutions: include institutions of various types established with the approval by organization and staffing departments of the government, but exclude institutions where enterprise management system is introduced. Institutions are further classified as follows:

(a) Institutions whose main budget is listed in the government budget appropriations or extra-budget funds, or allocated from the budget of their competent government agencies. Such institutions are classified as "state-owned".

(b) Institutions whose budget mainly comes from collective units. Such institutions are classified as "collective".

(c) Institutions other than those mentioned above whose source of budget is not clear. Such institutions are classified by way of management.

(3) Social organizations: include social organizations established with the approval from the Ministry of Civil Affairs, and organizations that are not covered by social organization management regulations such as Trades unions, women's federations etc. Social organizations are further classified as follows:

(a) Social organizations that are not covered by social organization management regulations of the Ministry of Civil Affairs such as Trades unions, women's federations, communist youth leagues, youth associations, industrial and commerce associations, scientists associations, overseas Chinese associations, etc.foundations and fund management organizations established with funds from the state, and social organizations whose funds mainly come from the budget of their competent government agencies. Such institutions are classified as "state-owned".

(b) Social organizations whose budget mainly comes from collective units. Such institutions are classified as "collective".

(c) Social organizations established by individual or a group of citizens, which are classified as "private".

(d) Social organizations other than those mentioned above whose source of budget is not clear. Such organizations are classified by way of management.

Each Plan Period recovery period refer to 1950-1952;the first five-year plan refer to 1953-1957;the second five-year plan refer to 1958-1962;the third five-year plan refer to 1966-1970;the fourth five-year plan refer to 1971-1975;the fifth five-yaer plan refer to 1976-1980;the sixth five-year plan refer to 1980-1985;the seventh five-yaer plan refer to 1986-1990;the eighth five-yaer plan refer to 1991-1995;the ninth five-year plan refer to 1996-2000;the tenth five-year plan refer to 2001-2005;the eleventh five-year plan refer to 2006-2010the twelvth five-yaer plan refer to 2011-2015.

Entrepreneur confidence index also called as the macro-economy climate index. It is a index based on entrepreneur's recognition, opinion, judgement and forecast to the market circumstances and macro-policies, It is a comprehensive desc-

ryption of the entrepreneur's impression and confidents of the macro-economy circumstances .

Business climate index also called as the comprehensive production and management climate index of enterprises. It is compiled basing on entrepreneur's judgement on production situation of their own expectation for the future performance. It is the description of the comprehensive production and management situation of the enterprises

Artificial person refer to unit that have following condition:

(1) legally Estabilished,have own name,organization,location and can

undertake a civil case responsibility independently by law.

(2) independently own and use (or authorizable usage)a property,undertake

liabilities and can make a bargain with other units.

(3) can independently account and workout balance sheet.artificial person unit

Includes business artificial person,artifial person organization,artifial person,meeting group artificial person and other.

Single sector artificial person Refer to the unit that have only one location and be engaged in one kind of production mangement activity.

Multi-sector artificial person Refer to the unit that have 2 or above 2 locations,or mainly be engaged in 2 kinds or above 2 kinds of production management activity,and who can be diviede 2 or above 2 establishment units.

Establishments unit:Refer to the subsidiary unit of artificial person unit.it should have following conditions:

(1) Be engaged in only one kind of social economic activities in excusive conditon.

(2) Opposite independtly organize management and business activity.

(3) Predominate data of business,such as income and expenditure ect.

Service refer to the enterprises and prodution department for production and selling the products.In the national economy accounting,services for the third industry,other said that refers to all sectors except agriculture,industry and construction.

2012

新疆统计年鉴

XINJIANG STATISTICAL YEARBOOK

第二篇
国民经济核算

CHAPTER 2
National Accounts

简要说明
Brief Introduction

本篇资料的主要内容及来源

国民经济核算篇资料主要包括新疆维吾尔自治区主要年份生产总值的绝对值、构成和指数，居民消费水平，各地、州、市、县生产总值、构成和指数等资料。以上资料是由新疆维吾尔自治区统计局国民经济核算处根据不同产业部门、不同支出构成的特点和资料来源，严格按照国家国民经济核算制度计算的。

关于数据使用的说明。本篇表2－1、表2－4中三次产业数据使用的是国家1994年国民经济行业分类标准；2－5、2－6表使用的是国家2002年国民经济行业分类标准。若做历史数据分析比较请使用表2－1表中公布的数据资料；若只使用当年数据，请用表2－5表或2－6表中公布的数据。

本章所列分地、州（市）、县的数据来自各地、州（市）、县统计局的国民经济核算资料。由于采用分级核算，各地区数据相加不等于全疆总计，地区所辖县、市数据相加不等于地区合计。

Main Content and Source of Data

Statistics on national accounts include mainly gross domestic product of Xinjiang Bureau of Statistics, it's composition and indices of gross domestic product, household consumption level, composition and indices of gross domestic product by prefecture, autonomous prefecture, city and county. Data on GDP are calculated by the Department of National Accounts Statistics of the Xinjiang Bureau of Statistics with various approaches in the light of the features of various sectors, various expenditure structures and the data sources and National Accounts system.

Data on the table 2-1 and 2-4 use the Industrial Classification of National Economy of 1994;The table 2-5 and 2-6 use the Industrial Classification of National Economy of 2002.If analyze the historical data ,you could use the data of table 2-1.If use the present data, you use the data of 2-5 or 2-6.

Regional data in this Yearbook are prepared from the national accounts data provided by the statistical bureau of the prefecture,autonomous prefecture and city.The sum of the regional data is not equal to the national total due to the decentralized accounting approach.

2-1 1978-2011 年历年新疆生产总值
Gross Domestic Product in Xinjiang(1978-2011)

单位：亿元 (100 million yuan)

年 份 Year	新疆生产总值 Gross Domestic Product	第一产业 Primary Industry	第二产业 Secondary Industry	工 业 Industry	建筑业 Construction	第三产业 Tertiary Industry	#交通运输仓储和邮政业 Transport, Storage and Post	#批发和零售业 Wholesale, and Retail Trades	人均新疆生产总值(元) Per Capita GDP (yuan)
1978	39.07	13.97	18.35	14.48	3.87	6.75	1.19	2.07	313
1979	45.63	16.32	21.43	17.16	4.27	7.88	1.52	2.34	359
1980	53.24	21.53	21.44	17.48	3.96	10.27	1.91	2.91	410
1981	59.41	25.18	22.39	17.93	4.46	11.84	2.25	3.41	450
1982	65.24	28.11	23.35	18.66	4.69	13.78	2.53	3.84	488
1983	78.55	32.84	29.10	23.33	5.77	16.61	3.01	4.75	583
1984	89.75	36.68	31.65	25.45	6.20	21.42	4.01	6.29	661
1985	112.24	42.89	40.50	32.14	8.36	28.85	4.59	8.97	820
1986	129.04	46.00	45.63	36.79	8.84	37.41	5.98	10.48	924
1987	148.50	56.18	50.30	41.16	9.14	42.02	7.73	12.45	1053
1988	192.72	72.27	66.02	53.53	12.49	54.43	11.60	16.11	1347
1989	217.29	78.01	73.83	60.21	13.62	65.45	12.90	17.59	1493
1990	261.44	104.09	83.18	71.50	11.68	74.17	14.63	20.48	1713
1991	335.91	111.86	107.99	84.07	23.92	116.06	22.63	36.88	2101
1992	402.31	114.50	147.64	106.29	41.35	140.17	28.32	39.85	2477
1993	495.25	126.85	205.07	155.92	49.15	163.33	32.58	43.46	2964
1994	662.32	187.69	249.11	190.00	59.11	225.52	44.40	57.67	3888
1995	814.85	240.71	283.97	219.01	64.96	290.17	59.63	73.78	4701
1996	900.93	249.31	313.70	239.07	74.63	337.92	73.74	87.25	5102
1997	1039.85	279.73	385.37	302.50	82.87	374.75	85.70	94.23	5848
1998	1106.95	291.05	395.75	298.53	97.22	420.15	106.87	98.06	6174
1999	1163.17	268.51	420.48	315.86	104.62	474.18	129.60	102.26	6443
2000	1363.56	288.18	537.58	418.63	118.95	537.80	148.63	110.10	7372
2001	1491.60	288.12	573.91	445.60	128.31	629.57	148.38	118.45	7945
2002	1612.65	305.00	603.15	463.59	139.56	704.50	168.58	123.88	8457
2003	1886.35	412.90	719.54	563.57	155.97	753.91	159.43	141.32	9828
2004	2209.09	446.13	914.47	734.10	180.37	848.49	186.70	160.30	11337
2005	2604.14	510.00	1164.80	961.62	203.18	929.34	149.61	145.10	13108
2006	3045.26	527.80	1459.30	1241.33	217.97	1058.16	165.60	163.15	15000
2007	3523.16	628.72	1647.55	1405.11	242.44	1246.89	177.28	187.10	16999
2008	4183.21	691.07	2070.76	1755.35	315.41	1421.38	191.84	222.74	19797
2009	4277.05	759.74	1929.59	1555.84	373.75	1587.72	209.10	253.60	19942
2010	5437.47	1078.63	2592.15	2161.39	430.76	1766.69	222.47	276.28	25034
2011	6610.05	1139.03	3225.90	2700.20	525.70	2245.12	256.72	371.90	30087

注：根据自治区第三次全国人口普查结果,对 2010 年人均新疆生产总值数据进行了调整。
Note: According to the results of the third national census of 2010,per capita GDP of Xinjiang data were adjusted.

2-2 1978-2011 年历年新疆生产总值构成

Composition of Gross Domestic Product in Xinjiang(1978-2011)

单位：% (%)

年 份 Year	新疆生产总值构成 Composition of Gross Domestic Product	第一产业 Primary Industry	第二产业 Secondary Industry	工 业 Industry	建筑业 Construction	第三产业 Tertiary Industry	#交通运输仓储和邮政业 Transport, Storage and Post	#批发和零售业 Wholesale, and Retail Trades
1978	100	35.8	47.0	37.1	9.9	17.2	3.0	5.3
1979	100	35.7	47.0	37.6	9.4	17.3	3.3	5.1
1980	100	40.4	40.3	32.9	7.4	19.3	3.6	5.5
1981	100	42.4	37.7	30.2	7.5	19.9	3.8	5.7
1982	100	43.1	35.8	28.6	7.2	21.1	3.9	5.9
1983	100	41.8	37.1	29.8	7.3	21.1	3.8	6.0
1984	100	40.9	35.2	28.3	6.9	23.9	4.5	7.0
1985	100	38.2	36.1	28.7	7.4	25.7	4.1	8.0
1986	100	35.6	35.4	28.5	6.9	29.0	4.6	8.1
1987	100	37.8	33.9	27.7	6.2	28.3	5.2	8.4
1988	100	37.5	34.3	27.8	6.5	28.2	6.0	8.4
1989	100	35.9	34.0	27.7	6.3	30.1	5.9	8.1
1990	100	39.8	31.8	27.3	4.5	28.4	5.6	7.8
1991	100	33.3	32.1	25.0	7.1	34.6	6.7	11.0
1992	100	28.5	36.7	26.4	10.3	34.8	7.0	9.9
1993	100	25.6	41.4	31.5	9.9	33.0	6.6	8.8
1994	100	28.3	37.6	28.7	8.9	34.1	6.7	8.7
1995	100	29.5	34.9	26.9	8.0	35.6	7.3	9.1
1996	100	27.7	34.8	26.5	8.3	37.5	8.2	9.7
1997	100	26.9	37.1	29.1	8.0	36.0	8.2	9.1
1998	100	26.3	35.7	27.0	8.7	38.0	9.7	8.9
1999	100	23.1	36.1	27.1	9.0	40.8	11.1	8.8
2000	100	21.1	39.4	30.7	8.7	39.5	10.9	8.1
2001	100	19.3	38.5	29.9	8.6	42.2	9.9	7.9
2002	100	18.9	37.4	28.7	8.7	43.7	10.5	7.7
2003	100	21.9	38.1	29.8	8.3	40.0	8.5	7.5
2004	100	20.2	41.4	33.2	8.2	38.4	8.5	7.3
2005	100	19.6	44.7	36.9	7.8	35.7	5.7	5.6
2006	100	17.3	47.9	40.7	7.2	34.8	5.4	5.4
2007	100	17.8	46.8	39.9	6.9	35.4	5.0	5.3
2008	100	16.5	49.5	42.0	7.5	34.0	4.6	5.3
2009	100	17.8	45.1	36.4	8.7	37.1	4.9	5.9
2010	100	19.8	47.7	39.8	7.9	32.5	4.1	5.1
2011	100	17.2	48.8	40.8	8.0	34.0	3.9	5.6

注：本表按当年价格计算。
Note: Data in value terms in this table are calculated at current prices.

2-3　1978-2011 年历年新疆生产总值指数
Indices of Gross Domestic Product in Xinjiang(1978-2011)

(上年=100)　　(preceding year=100)

年　份 Year	新疆生产总值 Gross Domestic Product	第一产业 Primary Industry	第二产业 Secondary Industry	工　业 Industry	建筑业 Construction	第三产业 Tertiary Industry	#交通运输仓储和邮政业 Transport, Storage and Post	#批发和零售业 Wholesale, and Retail Trades	人均新疆生产总值 Per Capita GDP
1978	109.8	110.2	110.3	112.8	101.8	107.2	102.1	109.3	106.9
1979	112.4	109.8	111.5	111.2	112.6	120.8	121.6	117.5	110.2
1980	107.3	106.0	105.2	108.5	93.1	116.6	115.6	125.5	105.0
1981	108.5	115.2	99.3	99.1	100.3	113.4	119.4	117.9	106.6
1982	109.9	111.2	104.3	104.6	102.8	117.1	118.9	119.8	108.5
1983	113.5	112.1	111.9	112.4	109.8	118.7	113.3	108.8	112.5
1984	114.1	113.6	114.7	115.1	112.9	114.0	100.0	109.2	113.2
1985	116.9	112.9	116.6	116.1	119.0	125.0	100.3	126.6	115.9
1986	111.7	108.3	109.5	111.0	102.5	120.7	124.7	110.0	109.2
1987	110.0	110.7	105.6	108.5	91.4	114.7	119.3	111.0	108.7
1988	109.6	103.3	114.6	113.6	120.2	112.9	118.8	114.7	108.0
1989	106.1	101.8	105.0	106.9	94.5	113.5	112.7	107.5	104.1
1990	111.7	116.0	106.7	106.4	108.6	112.0	106.7	104.5	106.8
1991	114.4	111.2	117.0	113.1	140.6	115.7	128.8	101.6	109.0
1992	113.1	105.5	119.4	112.6	152.8	115.7	124.6	112.6	111.3
1993	110.2	101.1	113.3	111.4	120.3	117.7	118.3	121.3	106.9
1994	112.1	111.2	110.2	111.3	106.3	115.3	109.7	105.6	110.2
1995	109.1	104.9	111.5	113.3	105.0	110.9	119.5	108.9	107.4
1996	106.5	103.5	107.8	107.4	109.5	108.0	113.0	109.6	104.5
1997	108.4	110.8	105.2	103.4	112.0	109.7	119.6	105.8	107.6
1998	107.5	107.2	105.7	103.0	115.0	109.6	117.5	104.9	106.6
1999	107.4	102.7	106.8	106.5	107.7	112.3	114.7	107.9	106.6
2000	108.7	104.8	108.6	109.1	107.3	112.1	114.4	109.6	106.2
2001	108.6	102.8	108.1	107.8	109.0	112.1	109.5	105.0	107.0
2002	108.2	105.0	107.4	107.7	106.3	110.4	114.3	110.3	106.5
2003	111.2	108.2	111.6	111.2	112.8	112.3	115.1	110.9	110.5
2004	111.4	105.7	114.0	114.5	112.2	111.5	115.1	112.6	109.7
2005	110.9	106.5	114.4	115.7	109.7	109.4	109.0	111.9	108.8
2006	111.0	105.7	111.2	112.5	105.0	113.6	107.2	110.5	108.7
2007	112.2	107.1	112.7	114.1	105.4	114.3	106.1	109.1	109.9
2008	111.0	106.4	114.3	114.3	114.1	109.2	108.7	110.3	108.9
2009	108.1	104.5	108.5	106.2	120.9	109.2	107.0	113.4	106.5
2010	110.6	104.5	112.6	113.5	108.3	110.8	107.9	108.3	109.3
2011	112.0	106.5	112.0	111.4	115.0	115.2	117.3	116.6	110.7

注：本表按可比价计算。
Note: Data in this table are calculated at constant prices.

2-4 1978-2011 年历年新疆生产总值指数
Indices of Gross Domestic Product in Xinjiang(1978-2011)

(1978 年=100)

年 份 Year	新疆生产总值 Gross Domestic Product	第一产业 Primary Industry	第二产业 Secondary Industry	工 业 Industry	建筑业 Construction	第三产业 Tertiary Industry	#交通运输仓储和邮政业 Transport, Storage and Post	#批发和零售业 Wholesale, and Retail Trades	人均新疆生产总值 Per Capita GDP
1978	100	100	100	100	100	100	100	100	100
1979	112.4	109.8	111.5	111.2	112.6	120.8	121.6	117.5	110.2
1980	120.6	116.4	117.3	120.7	104.8	140.9	140.6	147.5	115.7
1981	130.9	134.1	116.5	119.6	105.1	159.8	167.9	173.9	123.3
1982	143.9	149.1	121.5	125.1	108.0	187.1	199.6	208.3	133.8
1983	163.3	167.1	136.0	140.6	118.6	222.1	226.1	226.6	150.6
1984	186.3	189.8	156.0	161.8	133.9	253.2	226.1	247.4	170.4
1985	217.8	214.3	181.9	187.8	159.3	316.5	226.8	313.2	197.5
1986	243.3	232.1	199.2	208.5	163.3	382.0	282.8	344.5	215.7
1987	267.6	256.9	210.4	226.2	149.3	438.2	337.4	382.4	234.5
1988	293.3	265.4	241.1	257.0	179.5	494.7	400.8	438.6	253.2
1989	311.2	270.2	253.2	274.7	169.6	561.5	451.7	471.5	263.6
1990	347.6	313.4	270.2	292.3	184.2	628.9	482.0	492.7	281.5
1991	397.7	348.5	316.1	330.6	259.0	727.6	620.8	500.6	306.9
1992	449.8	367.7	377.4	372.3	395.8	841.8	773.5	563.7	341.6
1993	495.7	371.7	427.6	414.7	476.1	990.8	915.1	683.8	365.1
1994	555.7	413.3	471.2	461.6	506.1	1142.4	1003.9	722.1	402.4
1995	606.3	433.6	525.4	523.0	531.4	1266.9	1199.7	786.4	432.1
1996	645.7	448.8	566.4	561.7	581.9	1368.3	1355.7	861.9	451.6
1997	699.9	497.3	595.9	580.8	651.7	1501.0	1621.4	911.9	485.9
1998	752.4	533.1	629.9	598.2	749.5	1645.1	1905.1	956.6	518.0
1999	808.1	547.5	672.7	637.1	807.2	1847.4	2185.1	1032.2	552.2
2000	878.4	573.8	730.6	695.1	866.1	2070.9	2499.8	1131.3	586.4
2001	953.9	589.9	789.8	749.3	944.0	2321.5	2737.3	1187.9	627.4
2002	1032.1	619.4	848.2	807.0	1003.5	2562.9	3128.7	1310.3	668.2
2003	1147.7	670.2	946.6	897.4	1131.9	2878.1	3601.1	1453.1	738.4
2004	1278.5	708.4	1079.1	1027.5	1270.0	3209.1	4144.9	1636.2	810.0
2005	1417.9	754.4	1234.5	1188.8	1393.2	3510.8	4517.9	1830.9	881.3
2006	1573.9	797.4	1372.8	1337.4	1462.9	3988.3	4843.2	2023.1	958.0
2007	1765.9	854.0	1547.1	1526.0	1541.9	4558.6	5138.6	2207.2	1052.8
2008	1960.1	908.7	1768.3	1744.2	1759.3	4978.0	5585.7	2434.5	1146.5
2009	2118.9	949.5	1918.6	1852.4	2127.0	5436.0	5976.7	2760.8	1221.0
2010	2343.5	992.2	2160.3	2102.5	2303.5	6023.1	6448.9	2989.9	1334.6
2011	2624.7	1056.7	2419.5	2342.2	2649.0	6938.6	7564.6	3486.2	1477.4

注：本表按可比价计算。
Note: Data in this table are calculated at constant prices.

2-5 分行业新疆生产总值

Gross Domestic Product by Sector in Xinjiang

指　　标	Item	增加值(亿元) Added Value (100 million yuan)		构　成(%) Composition (%)		指数(上年=100) Indices (preceding year=100)	
		2010	2011	2010	2011	2010	2011
新疆生产总值	**Gross Domestic Product**	**5437.47**	**6610.05**	**100**	**100**	**110.6**	**112.0**
第一产业	Primary Industry	1078.63	1139.03	19.8	17.2	104.5	106.5
第二产业	Secondary Industry	2592.15	3225.90	47.7	48.8	112.6	112.0
工　业	Industry	2161.39	2700.20	39.8	40.8	113.5	111.4
建筑业	Construction	430.76	525.70	7.9	8.0	108.3	115.0
第三产业	Tertiary Industry	1766.69	2245.12	32.5	34.0	110.8	115.2
交通运输、仓储和邮政业	Transport, storage and Post	222.47	256.72	4.1	3.9	107.9	117.3
批发和零售业	Wholesale and Retail Trades	276.28	371.90	5.1	5.6	108.3	116.6
住宿和餐饮业	Hotels and Catering Services	68.06	77.87	1.3	1.2	105.8	109.0
金融业	Financial Intermediation	225.20	288.77	4.1	4.4	113.6	112.8
房地产业	Real Estate	143.44	176.22	2.6	2.7	119.0	109.1
其他服务业	Others	831.24	1073.64	15.3	16.2	110.9	116.4

注：本表按当年价格计算，采用 GB/T4754-2002 国民经济行业分类标准。
Note: Data in value terms in this table are calculated at current prices and adopted the new Industrial Classification of National Economy (GB/T4754-2002).

2-6 新疆生产总值项目结构

Components of Gross Domestic Product in Xinjiang

(2011 年)

指　　标	Item	新疆生产总值 Gross Domestic Product	劳动者报酬 Compensation of Employees	生产税净额 Net Taxes on Production	固定资产折旧 Depreciation of Fixed Assets	营业盈余 Operating Surplus
新疆生产总值(亿元)	**Gross Domestic Product (100 million yuan)**	**6610.05**	**3345.03**	**1084.37**	**884.74**	**1295.91**
第一产业	Primary Industry	1139.03	1066.26		72.77	
第二产业	Secondary Industry	3225.90	907.69	811.99	487.25	1018.97
工　业	Industry	2700.20	577.84	692.97	443.43	985.96
建筑业	Construction	525.70	329.85	119.02	43.82	33.01
第三产业	Tertiary Industry	2245.12	1371.08	272.38	324.72	276.94
交通运输、仓储和邮政业	Transport, storage and Post	256.72	165.31	20.93	67.54	2.94
信息传输、计算机服务和软件业	Information Transmission, Computer Service and Software	99.79	27.92	7.34	44.25	20.28
批发和零售业	Wholesale and Retail Trades	371.90	138.32	157.15	24.95	51.48
住宿和餐饮业	Hotels and Catering Services	77.87	66.73	6.57	5.32	-0.75
金融业	Financial Intermediation	288.77	89.57	26.77	13.40	159.03
房地产业	Real Estate	176.22	20.48	36.01	84.90	34.83
租赁和商务服务业	Leasing and Business Service	51.69	33.90	5.63	8.72	3.44
科学研究、技术服务和地质勘查业	Scientific Research, Technology Service and Geological Prospecting	58.32	42.47	3.73	5.13	6.99
水利、环境和公共设施管理业	Water Conservancy, Environment and Public Facility Management	33.57	20.54	0.93	11.92	0.18
居民服务和其他服务业	Community Service and Other Services	57.51	50.80	4.66	1.52	0.53
教　育	Education	219.02	203.76	0.58	16.81	-2.13
卫生、社会保障和社会福利业	Health, Social Security and Social Welfare	107.12	92.69	0.76	12.42	1.25
文化、体育和娱乐业	Culture, Sports and Entertainment	24.05	20.64	1.08	3.03	-0.7
公共管理和社会组织	Public Management and Social Organizations	422.57	397.95	0.24	24.81	-0.43

注：本表按当年价格计算。
Note: Data in value terms in this table are calculated at current prices.

2-7 主要年份支出法新疆生产总值

Gross Domestic Product by Expenditure Approach in Xinjiang in Main Years

单位：亿元 (100 million yuan)

年 份 Year	支出法新疆生产总值 Gross Domestic Product by Expenditure	最终消费 Final Consumption Expenditures	资本形成总额 Gross Capital Formation	货物和服务净出口 Net Export of Goods and Services	最终消费率（消费率）(%) Final Consumption Rate (%)	资本形成率（投资率）(%) Capital Formation Rate (%)
1978	39.07	27.64	18.43	-7.00	70.7	47.2
1980	53.24	39.82	23.15	-9.73	74.8	43.5
1985	112.24	78.04	58.43	-24.23	69.5	52.1
1986	129.04	92.38	60.26	-23.60	71.6	46.7
1987	148.51	103.77	69.94	-25.20	69.9	47.1
1988	192.72	126.09	98.31	-31.67	65.4	51
1989	217.29	137.50	117.84	-38.05	63.3	54.2
1990	261.44	166.77	141.17	-46.50	63.8	54
1991	335.91	196.58	169.15	-29.81	58.5	50.4
1992	402.31	221.57	249.26	-68.52	55.1	61.9
1993	495.25	269.92	356.16	-130.83	54.5	71.9
1994	662.32	336.94	487.55	-162.17	50.9	73.6
1995	814.85	444.62	473.71	-103.48	54.6	58.1
1996	900.93	553.90	456.96	-109.93	61.5	50.7
1997	1039.85	611.81	564.92	-136.89	58.8	54.3
1998	1106.95	642.48	685.85	-221.37	58	62
1999	1163.17	690.57	581.59	-108.99	59.4	50
2000	1363.56	760.20	618.12	-14.76	55.8	45.3
2001	1491.60	859.00	771.42	-138.82	57.6	51.7
2002	1612.65	963.71	864.27	-215.33	59.8	53.6
2003	1886.35	1027.22	1119.21	-260.08	54.5	59.3
2004	2209.09	1125.11	1350.47	-266.50	50.9	61.1
2005	2604.14	1266.52	1505.97	-168.35	48.6	57.8
2006	3045.26	1464.53	1654.70	-73.97	48.1	54.3
2007	3513.16	1740.56	1970.06	-197.46	49.5	56.1
2008	4183.21	2073.05	2301.50	-191.34	49.6	55
2009	4277.05	2266.20	2549.75	-538.90	53	59.6
2010	5437.47	2865.56	3371.22	-799.31	52.7	62
2011	6610.05	3518.82	4162.32	-1071.09	53.2	63.0

注：2005 年以后数据依据 2008 年经济普查资料已修订。
Note: Since 2005 the data has adjusted according to the economic census in 2008.

2-8 主要年份资本形成总额及其构成

Gross Capital Formation and Its Composition in Main Years

年 份	Year	资本形成总额(亿元) Gross Capital Formation (100 million yuan)	固定资本形成 Gross Fixed Capital Formation	存货增加 Change in Inventories	以资本形成总额为100 Gross Capital Formation=100 固定资本形成(%) Gross Fixed Capital Formation (%)	存货增加(%) Change in Inventories (%)
	1978	18.43	13.25	5.18	71.9	28.1
	1980	23.15	18.14	5.01	78.3	21.7
	1985	58.43	46.78	11.65	80.1	19.9
	1990	141.17	91.50	49.67	64.8	35.2
	1991	169.15	124.77	44.38	73.8	26.2
	1992	249.26	181.17	68.09	72.7	27.3
	1993	356.16	264.90	91.26	74.4	25.6
	1994	487.55	376.95	110.60	77.3	22.7
	1995	473.71	377.91	95.80	79.8	20.2
	1996	456.96	422.87	34.09	92.5	7.5
	1997	564.92	461.41	103.51	81.7	18.3
	1998	685.85	543.78	142.06	79.3	20.7
	1999	581.59	551.72	29.87	94.9	5.1
	2000	618.12	648.12	-30.00	104.9	-4.9
	2001	771.42	720.12	51.30	93.3	6.7
	2002	864.27	856.70	7.57	99.1	0.9
	2003	1119.21	1079.24	39.98	96.4	3.6
	2004	1350.47	1239.50	110.97	91.8	8.2
	2005	1505.97	1384.33	121.63	91.9	8.1
	2006	1654.70	1596.16	58.54	96.5	3.5
	2007	1970.06	1885.24	84.83	95.7	4.3
	2008	2301.50	2285.60	15.90	99.3	0.7
	2009	2549.75	2473.24	76.51	97	3
	2010	3371.22	3233.00	138.22	95.9	4.1
	2011	4162.32	3948.87	213.45	94.9	5.1
“一五” 时期	"First Five-year Plan" Period	16.26	14.33	1.94	88.1	11.9
“二五” 时期	"Second Five-year Plan" Period	36.39	26.69	9.70	73.3	26.7
	1963—1965	19.40	14.34	5.06	73.9	26.1
“三五” 时期	"Third Five-year Plan" Period	30.65	20.96	9.68	68.4	31.6
“四五” 时期	"Fourth Five-year Plan" Period	51.70	32.13	19.57	62.1	37.9
“五五” 时期	"Fifth Five-year Plan" Period	87.76	62.50	25.26	71.2	28.8
“六五” 时期	"Sixth Five-year Plan" Period	191.38	158.48	32.91	82.8	17.2
“七五” 时期	"Seventh Five-year Plan" Period	487.52	361.64	125.88	74.2	25.8
“八五” 时期	"Eighth Five-year Plan" Period	1735.83	1325.70	410.12	76.4	23.6
“九五” 时期	"Ninth Five-year Plan" Period	2907.43	2627.90	279.53	90.4	9.6
“十五” 时期	"Tenth Five-year Plan" Period	5611.34	5279.89	331.45	94.1	5.9
“十一五”时期	"Eleventh Five-year Plan " Period	11847.23	11473.23	374.00	96.8	3.2

注：本表按当年价格计算。
Note: Data in value terms in this table are calculated at current prices.

2-9 主要年份最终消费及其构成

Final Consumption Expenditure and Its Composition in Main Years

单位：%　　　　(%)

年份	Year	最终消费(亿元) Final Consumption Expenditures (100 million yuan)	居民消费 Household Consumption	农村居民 Rural Household	城镇居民 Urban Household	政府消费 Government Consumption	最终消费=100 Final Consumption Expenditure=100: 居民消费 Household Consumption	政府消费 Government Consumption	居民消费=100 Houshold Consumption=100: 农村居民 Rural Household	城镇居民 Urban Household
	1978	27.64	22.61	12.08	10.53	5.03	81.8	18.2	53.4	46.6
	1980	39.82	32.78	16.20	16.58	7.04	82.3	17.7	49.4	50.6
	1985	78.04	58.51	26.41	32.10	19.53	75.0	25.0	45.1	54.9
	1990	166.77	121.12	45.67	75.46	45.65	72.6	27.4	37.7	62.3
	1991	196.58	145.55	52.30	93.26	51.02	74.0	26.0	35.9	64.1
	1992	221.57	159.20	55.18	104.02	62.37	71.9	28.1	34.7	65.3
	1993	269.92	197.78	63.96	133.82	72.14	73.3	26.7	32.3	67.7
	1994	336.94	242.79	83.04	159.75	94.15	72.1	27.9	34.2	65.8
	1995	444.62	320.70	108.43	212.27	123.93	72.1	27.9	33.8	66.2
	1996	553.90	397.61	156.07	241.54	156.29	71.8	28.2	39.3	60.7
	1997	611.81	436.67	164.84	271.84	175.14	71.4	28.6	37.7	62.3
	1998	642.48	457.38	175.72	281.66	185.10	71.2	28.8	38.4	61.6
	1999	690.57	475.74	158.98	316.76	214.83	68.9	31.1	33.4	66.6
	2000	760.20	492.32	159.97	332.34	267.88	64.8	35.2	32.5	67.5
	2001	859.00	545.49	176.00	369.49	313.51	63.5	36.5	32.3	67.7
	2002	963.71	615.47	190.85	424.62	348.25	63.9	36.1	31.0	69.0
	2003	1027.22	623.61	202.67	420.94	403.61	60.7	39.3	32.5	67.5
	2004	1125.11	671.28	209.99	461.29	453.84	59.7	40.3	31.3	68.7
	2005	1266.52	764.26	238.98	525.28	502.26	60.3	39.7	31.3	68.7
	2006	1464.53	853.88	253.58	600.31	610.65	58.3	41.7	29.7	70.3
	2007	1740.56	1013.48	295.52	717.96	727.09	58.2	41.8	29.2	70.8
	2008	2073.05	1171.05	340.69	830.36	902.00	56.5	43.5	29.1	70.9
	2009	2266.20	1284.66	385.66	898.99	981.54	56.7	43.3	30.0	70.0
	2010	2865.56	1578.93	456.31	1122.62	1286.63	55.1	44.9	28.9	71.1
	2011	3518.82	1954.33	560.30	1394.03	1564.49	55.5	44.5	28.7	71.3
"一五" 时期	"First Five-year Plan" Period	42.97	38.62	23.89	14.73	4.35	89.9	10.1	61.9	38.1
"二五" 时期	"Second Five-year Plan" Period	71.40	64.02	39.30	24.72	7.38	89.7	10.3	61.4	38.6
	1963—1965	47.00	42.42	30.93	11.49	4.58	90.3	9.7	72.9	27.1
"三五" 时期	"Third Five-year Plan" Period	80.09	72.97	49.13	23.84	7.12	91.1	8.9	67.3	32.7
"四五" 时期	"Forth Five-year Plan" Period	97.46	83.75	51.78	31.97	13.71	85.9	14.1	61.8	38.2
"五五" 时期	"Fifth Five-year Plan" Period	149.77	123.11	65.02	58.09	26.66	82.2	17.8	52.8	47.2
"六五" 时期	"Sixth Five-year Plan" Period	289.27	227.00	107.93	119.06	62.28	78.5	21.5	47.5	52.5
"七五" 时期	"Seventh Five-year Plan" Period	626.51	464.17	186.47	277.70	162.34	74.1	25.9	40.2	59.8
"八五" 时期	"Eighth Five-year Plan" Period	1469.63	1066.03	362.91	703.12	403.60	72.5	27.5	34.0	66.0
"九五" 时期	"Ninth Five-year Plan" Period	3258.96	2259.72	815.58	1444.14	999.24	69.3	30.7	36.1	63.9
"十五" 时期	"Tenth Five-year Plan" Period	5241.57	3220.11	1018.50	2201.61	2021.46	61.4	38.6	31.6	68.4
"十一五"时期	"Eleventh Five-year Plan " Period	10409.90	5902.00	1731.76	4170.24	4507.90	56.7	43.3	29.3	70.7

注：本表按当年价格计算。
Note: Data in value terms in this table are calculated at current prices.

2-10 各地、州、市、县(市)地区生产总值

单位：万元 (2011 年) (10 000 Yuan)

地　　区	Region	地区生产总值 Gross Regional Product	第一产业 Primary Industry
乌鲁木齐市	**Urumqi City**	**16900347**	**220550**
＃乌鲁木齐县	Urumqi County	145675	48092
克拉玛依市	**Karamay City**	**8016856**	**41509**
石河子市	**Shihezi City**	**1705948**	**110015**
吐鲁番地区	**Turpan Administrative Offices**	**2214322**	**269967**
吐鲁番市	Turpan City	586534	104968
鄯善县	Shanshan [Piqan] County	1296737	101485
托克逊县	Toksun County	338855	63515
哈密地区	**Hami [Kumul] Administrative Offices**	**2209185**	**290925**
哈密市	Hami [Kumul] City	1766951	180746
巴里坤哈萨克自治县	Barkol Kazak Autonomous County	290160	76226
伊吾县	Yiwu [Araturuk] County	151810	33954
昌吉回族自治州	**Changji Hui Autonomous Prefecture**	**7029369**	**1903414**
昌吉市	Changji City	2213651	297309
阜康市	Fukang City	1031019	180386
呼图壁县	Hutubi County	1202032	510996
玛纳斯县	Manas County	960404	361511
奇台县	Qitai County	709042	317235
吉木萨尔县	Jimsar County	388704	134301
木垒哈萨克自治县	Mori Kazak Autonomous County	182429	90658
伊犁哈萨克自治州	**Ili Kazak Autonomous Prefecture**	**10785471**	**2957942**
伊犁州直属县(市)	**Counties (Cities) Direct Under Ili Prefecture**	**4951624**	**1155822**
伊宁市	Yining [Gulja] City	1139000	56838
奎屯市	Kuytun City	900159	47806
伊宁县	Yining [Gulja] County	488069	191680
察布查尔锡伯自治县	Qapqal Xibe Autonomous County	258915	129197
霍城县	Huocheng [Korgas] County	603016	202191
巩留县	Gongliu [Tokkuztara] County	225704	88182
新源县	Xinyuan [Kunes] County	641735	175860
昭苏县	Zhaosu [Mongolkure] County	252568	114251
特克斯县	Tekes County	153375	68571
尼勒克县	Nilka County	286801	81246

Gross Regional Product by Prefecture, Autonomous Prefecture, City and County

(10 000 yuan)

第二产业 Secondary Industry	工 业 Industry	建筑业 Construction	第三产业 Tertiary Industry	#交通运输、仓储和邮政业 Transport,storage And Post	#批发和零售业 Wholesale, and Retail Trades	人均地区生产总值(元) Per Capita GDP (yuan)
7590607	**6590607**	**1000000**	**9089191**	**1759876**	**1590219**	**52649**
49521	46083	3438	48062	4088	5593	25738
7162011	**6988211**	**173800**	**813335**	**130882**	**106308**	**129105**
943672	**772178**	**171494**	**652261**	**61303**	**69830**	**54037**
1454538	**1251938**	**202600**	**489816**	**152370**	**33103**	**35629**
229202	190803	38400	252364	72200	20197	21267
1020871	894670	126201	174381	69393	7556	56825
207188	169188	38000	68152	8765	4430	28658
1088357	**748357**	**340000**	**829903**	**216556**	**124264**	**38231**
873590	592020	281570	712615	197229	110284	39060
135012	106020	28992	78922	10687	10200	28206
78225	48786	29439	39631	6509	4020	67143
3311095	**2682748**	**628347**	**1814859**	**274193**	**280188**	**44456**
1036261	861414	174847	880081	158608	91286	46118
650619	585724	64895	200013	27874	36325	62373
451394	385288	66106	239643	24129	47206	46196
360113	226488	133625	238780	34595	64421	43398
226330	177170	49160	165477	18735	34693	33342
154842	129494	25348	99562	6432	14000	30016
29167	19617	9550	62604	2998	8507	20498
4142546	**3126594**	**1015952**	**3684983**	**386738**	**673544**	**23354**
1801656	**1361956**	**439700**	**1994146**	**199369**	**293728**	**18528**
316484	177047	139437	765678	62888	136422	23615
494798	409330	85468	357555	59114	34115	59066
175267	145636	29631	121122	12990	5697	11633
58078	38800	19278	71640	4369	4715	13853
124106	98618	25488	276719	26750	97084	15064
70601	44691	25910	66921	5769	963	11658
332169	275794	56375	133706	15668	6706	20876
52621	38124	14497	85696	5304	4979	13885
25852	16923	8929	58952	3646	1299	9223
148254	113567	34687	57301	2042	3506	15698

2-10 续表 1

单位：万元

地　　区	Region	地区生产总值 Gross Regional Product	第一产业 Primary Industry
塔城地区	**Tacheng [Tarbagatai] Administrative Offices**	**4196156**	**1473326**
塔城市	Tacheng [Qoqek] City	501824	119919
乌苏市	Usu City	1207499	395426
额敏县	Emin [Dorbiljin] County	502452	170990
沙湾县	Shawan County	1295603	642567
托里县	Toli County	299512	35785
裕民县	Yumin [Qagantokay] County	104869	42905
和布克赛尔蒙古自治县	Hoboksar Mongol Autonomous County	273790	51071
阿勒泰地区	**Altay Administrative Offices**	**1637691**	**328794**
阿勒泰市	Altay City	403595	65967
布尔津县	Burqin County	126799	27094
富蕴县	Fuyun [Koktokay] County	411166	57867
福海县	Fuhai [Burultokay] County	227481	89580
哈巴河县	Habahe [Kaba] County	347397	54249
青河县	Qinghe [Qinggil] County	123005	26849
吉木乃县	Jeminay County	47010	15241
博尔塔拉蒙古自治州	**Bortala Mongolian Autonomous Prefecture**	**1513225**	**524493**
博乐市	Bole [Bortala] City	999142	264366
精河县	Jinghe [Jing] County	380251	201289
温泉县	Wenquan [Araxang] County	125258	57632
巴音郭楞蒙古自治州	**Bayangol Mongol ian Autonomous Prefecture**	**7998671**	**1301123**
库尔勒市	Korla City	5582944	318190
轮台县	Luntai [Bugur] County	398509	134103
尉犁县	Yuli [Lopnur] County	342675	191259
若羌县	Ruoqiang [Qarkilik] County	454795	99802
且末县	Qiemo [Qarqan] County	140122	66191
焉耆回族自治县	Yanqi Hui Autonomous County	393844	115206
和静县	Hejing County	540655	148427
和硕县	Hoxud County	173867	100554
博湖县	Bohu [Bagrax] County	147989	66831
阿克苏地区	**Aksu Administrative Offices**	**5061427**	**1613602**
阿克苏市	Aksu City	1429142	263367
温宿县	Wensu [Onsu] County	387105	184988
库车县	Kuqa County	1037407	159555

Continued

(10 000 yuan)

第二产业 Secondary Industry	工　业 Industry	建筑业 Construction	第三产业 Tertiary Industry	#交通运输、仓储和邮政业 Transport,storage And Post	#批发和零售业 Wholesale, and Retail Trades	人均地区生产总值(元) Per Capita GDP (yuan)
1557170	**1155318**	**401852**	**1165660**	**119520**	**329525**	**31373**
135273	78518	56755	246632	31946	71721	29442
582910	449050	133860	229163	28780	61999	35778
164470	120633	43837	166992	16847	38327	23056
360873	271786	89087	292163	37440	77572	33357
204437	169374	35063	59290	8903	7877	29891
25567	6287	19280	36397	1588	3433	17744
154834	103782	51052	67885	7085	8412	42780
783720	**609320**	**174400**	**525177**	**67849**	**50291**	**26927**
84311	51611	32700	253317	24841	33079	21456
43880	22780	21100	55825	4845	5460	18869
290054	256054	34000	63245	18302	6133	45940
68119	41919	26200	69782	8301	7632	29543
241492	211692	29800	51656	10382	3747	41407
56767	41667	15100	39389	2197	3921	19012
13636	5336	8300	18133	1036	1264	12570
321491	**209691**	**111800**	**667241**	**119160**	**162156**	**31204**
232897	162105	70792	501879	88473	153577	37661
69349	41649	27700	109613	23694	13964	26425
22794	10198	12596	44832	2964	2505	16525
5279183	**4669183**	**610000**	**1418365**	**211810**	**168454**	**57636**
4497423	4021762	475661	767331	94816	120341	99094
145886	130841	15045	118520	23576	12200	34354
73868	52604	21264	77548	8759	10947	29928
321106	313122	7984	33887	4550	1270	81798
19756	8636	11120	54175	3000	326	18935
126006	87635	38371	152632	27323	14199	27522
238054	212499	25555	154174	53033	5610	27941
29357	18500	10857	43956	6269	4609	23090
29959	16662	13297	51199	5100	6209	24260
1680934	**1234342**	**446592**	**1766891**	**205109**	**238623**	**20145**
485573	372478	113096	680201	79685	117955	29714
96852	48428	48424	105265	4885	13342	15939
590340	459794	130546	287512	70935	35273	21991

2-10 续表 2

单位：万元

地　　区	Region	地区生产总值 Gross Regional Product	第一产业 Primary Industry
沙雅县	Xayar County	325785	114612
新和县	Xinhe [Toksu] County	206783	89539
拜城县	Baicheng [Bay] County	353465	72697
乌什县	Wushi [Uxturpan] County	173208	71750
阿瓦提县	Awat County	351199	182615
柯坪县	Kalpin County	53903	13901
克孜勒苏柯尔克孜自治州	**Kizilsu Kirgiz Autonomous Prefecture**	**480250**	**90412**
阿图什市	Artux City	232925	39711
阿克陶县	Akto County	120898	36891
阿合奇县	Akqi County	82647	7569
乌恰县	Wuqia [Ulugqat] County	42900	6816
喀什地区	**Kashgar [Kaxgar] Administrative Offices**	**4201512**	**1506655**
喀什市	Kashgar [Kaxgar] City	1075965	46000
疏附县	Shufu County	253459	150659
疏勒县	Shule County	403037	148000
英吉沙县	Yengisar County	173981	83904
泽普县	Zepu [Poskam] County	241393	89622
莎车县	Shache [Yarkant] County	480233	266775
叶城县	Yecheng [Kagilik] County	409921	229518
麦盖提县	Makit County	203042	109058
岳普湖县	Yopurga County	163000	55500
伽师县	Jiashi [Payzawat] County	355337	174433
巴楚县	Bachu [Maralbexi] County	391000	144786
塔什库尔干塔吉克自治县	Taxkorgan Tajik Autonomous County	51144	8400
和田地区	**Hotan Administrative Offices**	**1269941**	**408264**
和田市	Hotan City	351173	33574
和田县	Hotan County	162187	64663
墨玉县	Moyu [Karakax] County	217387	95352
皮山县	Pishan [Guma] County	126515	61147
洛浦县	Lop County	130321	41823
策勒县	Qira County	94916	40128
于田县	Yutian [Keriya] County	135923	50332
民丰县	Minfeng [Niya] County	50459	11857

Continued

(10 000 yuan)

第二产业 Secondary Industry	工业 Industry	建筑业 Construction	第三产业 Tertiary Industry	#交通运输、仓储和邮政业 Transport,storage And Post	#批发和零售业 Wholesale, and Retail Trades	人均地区生产总值(元) Per Capita GDP (yuan)
66574	42710	23865	144598	8724	25031	13455
37960	26487	11473	79285	11389	10158	12540
179337	154431	24907	101431	15327	5814	15422
22360	12446	9914	79098	2674	1915	8346
48592	23773	24819	119992	5488	11392	14588
11500	5442	6058	28503	2201	90	11230
121615	**64628**	**56987**	**268223**	**21951**	**14462**	**8664**
52396	33940	18456	140818	16255	7827	9284
33261	15653	17608	50746	1699	1385	5947
31106	16854	14252	43972	2869	2417	14324
7640	336	7304	28444	1410	1173	10047
1072198	**588632**	**483566**	**1622659**	**130161**	**482477**	**10558**
369500	264500	105000	660465	73054	260034	19962
30800	7800	23000	72000	3365	5025	7577
182012	90012	92000	73025	3063	6121	12158
36177	8268	27909	53900	2251	6191	6382
46836	26598	20238	104935	5564	36609	11555
63446	30246	33200	150012	4997	14515	5936
67857	34157	33700	112546	6885	15769	9081
37485	17431	20054	56499	2838	14956	9184
55000	15200	39800	52500	3408	6516	10457
93700	60300	33400	87204	15792	18053	9203
65550	26402	39148	180664	8252	97230	11783
23835	7718	16117	18909	692	1458	13459
245083	**101683**	**143400**	**616594**	**26717**	**43131**	**6172**
122552	45688	76864	195047	14109	19799	5954
35552	14065	21487	61972	939	613	5974
22672	6557	16115	99363	3354	9065	4138
16514	8109	8405	48854	983	1516	4823
23268	5597	17671	65230	1585	2474	5417
13958	952	13006	40830	978	1394	6143
15054	1602	13452	70537	2438	2666	5379
8982	3108	5874	29620	951	606	13431

2-11 各地、州、市、县(市)地区生产总值构成

单位：%　　(2011 年)

地　　区	Region	地区生产总值 Gross Regional Product	第一产业 Primary Industry
乌鲁木齐市	**Urumqi City**	**100.0**	**1.3**
#乌鲁木齐县	Urumqi County	100.0	33.0
克拉玛依市	**Karamay City**	**100.0**	**0.5**
石河子市	**Shihezi City**	**100.0**	**6.4**
吐鲁番地区	**Turpan Administrative Offices**	**100.0**	**12.2**
吐鲁番市	Turpan City	100.0	17.9
鄯善县	Shanshan [Piqan] County	100.0	7.8
托克逊县	Toksun County	100.0	18.7
哈密地区	**Hami [Kumul] Administrative Offices**	**100.0**	**13.2**
哈密市	Hami [Kumul] City	100.0	10.2
巴里坤哈萨克自治县	Barkol Kazak Autonomous County	100.0	26.3
伊吾县	Yiwu [Araturuk] County	100.0	22.4
昌吉回族自治州	**Changji Hui Autonomous Prefecture**	**100.0**	**27.1**
昌吉市	Changji City	100.0	13.4
阜康市	Fukang City	100.0	17.5
呼图壁县	Hutubi County	100.0	42.5
玛纳斯县	Manas County	100.0	37.6
奇台县	Qitai County	100.0	44.7
吉木萨尔县	Jimsar County	100.0	34.6
木垒哈萨克自治县	Mori Kazak Autonomous County	100.0	49.7
伊犁哈萨克自治州	**Ili Kazak Autonomous Prefecture**	**100.0**	**27.4**
伊犁州直属县(市)	**Counties (Cities) Direct Under Ili Prefecture**	**100.0**	**23.4**
伊宁市	Yining [Gulja] City	100.0	5.0
奎屯市	Kuytun City	100.0	5.3
伊宁县	Yining [Gulja] County	100.0	39.3
察布查尔锡伯自治县	Qapqal Xibe Autonomous County	100.0	49.9
霍城县	Huocheng [Korgas] County	100.0	33.5
巩留县	Gongliu [Tokkuztara] County	100.0	39.1
新源县	Xinyuan [Kunes] County	100.0	27.4
昭苏县	Zhaosu [Mongolkure] County	100.0	45.2
特克斯县	Tekes County	100.0	44.7
尼勒克县	Nilka County	100.0	28.3

Composition of Gross Domestic Product by Prefecture, Autonomous Prefecture, City and County

(%)

第二产业 Secondary Industry	工 业 Industry	建筑业 Construction	第三产业 Tertiary Industry	#交通运输、仓储和邮政业 Transport,storage And Post	#批发和零售业 Wholesale, and Retail Trades
44.9	**39.0**	**5.9**	**53.8**	**10.4**	**9.4**
34.0	31.6	2.4	33.0	2.8	3.8
89.3	**87.2**	**2.2**	**10.1**	**1.6**	**1.3**
55.3	**45.3**	**10.1**	**38.2**	**3.6**	**4.1**
65.7	**56.5**	**9.1**	**22.1**	**6.9**	**1.5**
39.1	32.5	6.5	43.0	12.3	3.4
78.7	69.0	9.7	13.4	5.4	0.6
61.1	49.9	11.2	20.1	2.6	1.3
49.3	**33.9**	**15.4**	**37.6**	**9.8**	**5.6**
49.4	33.5	15.9	40.3	11.2	6.2
46.5	36.5	10.0	27.2	3.7	3.5
51.5	32.1	19.4	26.1	4.3	2.6
47.1	**38.2**	**8.9**	**25.8**	**3.9**	**4.0**
46.8	38.9	7.9	39.8	7.2	4.1
63.1	56.8	6.3	19.4	2.7	3.5
37.6	32.1	5.5	19.9	2.0	3.9
37.5	23.6	13.9	24.9	3.6	6.7
31.9	25.0	6.9	23.3	2.6	4.9
39.8	33.3	6.5	25.6	1.7	3.6
16.0	10.8	5.2	34.3	1.6	4.7
38.4	**29.0**	**9.4**	**34.2**	**3.6**	**6.2**
36.3	**27.4**	**8.9**	**40.3**	**4.0**	**6.0**
27.8	15.5	12.2	67.2	5.5	12.0
55.0	45.5	9.5	39.7	6.6	3.8
35.9	29.8	6.1	24.8	2.7	1.2
22.4	15.0	7.4	27.7	1.7	1.8
20.6	16.4	4.2	45.9	4.4	16.1
31.3	19.8	11.5	29.6	2.6	0.4
51.8	43.0	8.8	20.8	2.4	1.0
20.8	15.1	5.7	33.9	2.1	2.0
16.9	11.0	5.8	38.4	2.4	0.8
51.7	39.6	12.1	20.0	0.7	1.2

2-11 续表 1

单位：%

地　　区	Region	地区生产总值 Gross Regional Product	第一产业 Primary Industry
塔城地区	**Tacheng [Tarbagatai] Administrative Offices**	**100.0**	**35.1**
塔城市	Tacheng [Qoqek] City	100.0	23.9
乌苏市	Usu City	100.0	32.7
额敏县	Emin [Dorbiljin] County	100.0	34.0
沙湾县	Shawan County	100.0	49.6
托里县	Toli County	100.0	11.9
裕民县	Yumin [Qagantokay] County	100.0	40.9
和布克赛尔蒙古自治县	Hoboksar Mongol Autonomous County	100.0	18.7
阿勒泰地区	**Altay Administrative Offices**	**100.0**	**20.1**
阿勒泰市	Altay City	100.0	16.3
布尔津县	Burqin County	100.0	21.4
富蕴县	Fuyun [Koktokay] County	100.0	14.1
福海县	Fuhai [Burultokay] County	100.0	39.4
哈巴河县	Habahe [Kaba] County	100.0	15.6
青河县	Qinghe [Qinggil] County	100.0	21.8
吉木乃县	Jeminay County	100.0	32.4
博尔塔拉蒙古自治州	**Bortala Mongolian Autonomous Prefecture**	**100.0**	**34.7**
博乐市	Bole [Bortala] City	100.0	26.5
精河县	Jinghe [Jing] County	100.0	52.9
温泉县	Wenquan [Araxang] County	100.0	46.0
巴音郭楞蒙古自治州	**Bayangol Mongol ian Autonomous Prefecture**	**100.0**	**16.3**
库尔勒市	Korla City	100.0	5.7
轮台县	Luntai [Bugur] County	100.0	33.7
尉犁县	Yuli [Lopnur] County	100.0	55.8
若羌县	Ruoqiang [Qarkilik] County	100.0	21.9
且末县	Qiemo [Qarqan] County	100.0	47.2
焉耆回族自治县	Yanqi Hui Autonomous County	100.0	29.3
和静县	Hejing County	100.0	27.5
和硕县	Hoxud County	100.0	57.8
博湖县	Bohu [Bagrax] County	100.0	45.2
阿克苏地区	**Aksu Administrative Offices**	**100.0**	**31.9**
阿克苏市	Aksu City	100.0	20.8
温宿县	Wensu [Onsu] County	100.0	55.4
库车县	Kuqa County	100.0	17.1

Continued

(%)

第二产业 Secondary Industry	工业 Industry	建筑业 Construction	第三产业 Tertiary Industry	#交通运输、仓储和邮政业 Transport,storage And Post	#批发和零售业 Wholesale, and Retail Trades
37.1	**27.5**	**9.6**	**27.8**	**2.8**	**7.9**
27.0	15.6	11.3	49.1	6.4	14.3
48.3	37.2	11.1	19.0	2.4	5.1
32.7	24.0	8.7	33.2	3.4	7.6
27.9	21.0	6.9	22.6	2.9	6.0
68.3	56.5	11.7	19.8	3.0	2.6
24.4	6.0	18.4	34.7	1.5	3.3
56.6	37.9	18.6	24.8	2.6	3.1
47.9	**37.2**	**10.6**	**32.1**	**4.1**	**3.1**
20.9	12.8	8.1	62.8	6.2	8.2
34.6	18.0	16.6	44.0	3.8	4.3
70.5	62.3	8.3	15.4	4.5	1.5
29.9	18.4	11.5	30.7	3.6	3.4
69.5	60.9	8.6	14.9	3.0	1.1
46.2	33.9	12.3	32.0	1.8	3.2
29.0	11.4	17.7	38.6	2.2	2.7
21.2	**13.9**	**7.4**	**44.1**	**7.9**	**10.7**
23.3	16.2	7.1	50.2	8.9	15.4
18.2	11.0	7.3	28.8	6.2	3.7
18.2	8.1	10.1	35.8	2.4	2.0
66.0	**58.4**	**7.6**	**17.7**	**2.6**	**2.1**
80.6	72.0	8.5	13.7	1.7	2.2
36.6	32.8	3.8	29.7	5.9	3.1
21.6	15.4	6.2	22.6	2.6	3.2
70.6	68.8	1.8	7.5	1.0	0.3
14.1	6.2	7.9	38.7	2.1	0.2
32.0	22.3	9.7	38.8	6.9	3.6
44.0	39.3	4.7	28.5	9.8	1.0
16.9	10.6	6.2	25.3	3.6	2.7
20.2	11.3	9.0	34.6	3.4	4.2
33.2	**24.4**	**8.8**	**34.9**	**4.1**	**4.7**
29.4	19.7	9.7	49.8	5.9	9.1
21.4	11.5	9.9	23.2	0.9	2.8
56.4	43.6	12.9	26.4	7.3	2.9

2-11 续表 2

单位：%

地　　区	Region	地区生产总值 Gross Regional Product	第一产业 Primary Industry
沙雅县	Xayar County	100.0	38.4
新和县	Xinhe [Toksu] County	100.0	48.3
拜城县	Baicheng [Bay] County	100.0	24.4
乌什县	Wushi [Uxturpan] County	100.0	45.1
阿瓦提县	Awat County	100.0	55.7
柯坪县	Kalpin County	100.0	29.7
克孜勒苏柯尔克孜自治州	**Kizilsu Kirgiz Autonomous Prefecture**	**100.0**	**18.8**
阿图什市	Artux City	100.0	17.0
阿克陶县	Akto County	100.0	30.5
阿合奇县	Akqi County	100.0	9.2
乌恰县	Wuqia [Ulugqat] County	100.0	15.9
喀什地区	**Kashgar [Kaxgar] Administrative Offices**	**100.0**	**35.9**
喀什市	Kashgar [Kaxgar] City	100.0	4.3
疏附县	Shufu County	100.0	59.4
疏勒县	Shule County	100.0	36.7
英吉沙县	Yengisar County	100.0	48.2
泽普县	Zepu [Poskam] County	100.0	37.1
莎车县	Shache [Yarkant] County	100.0	55.6
叶城县	Yecheng [Kagilik] County	100.0	56.0
麦盖提县	Makit County	100.0	53.7
岳普湖县	Yopurga County	100.0	34.0
伽师县	Jiashi [Payzawat] County	100.0	49.1
巴楚县	Bachu [Maralbexi] County	100.0	37.0
塔什库尔干县	Taxkorgan Tajik Autonomous County	100.0	16.4
和田地区	**Hotan Administrative Offices**	**100.0**	**32.1**
和田市	Hotan City	100.0	9.6
和田县	Hotan County	100.0	39.9
墨玉县	Moyu [Karakax] County	100.0	43.9
皮山县	Pishan [Guma] County	100.0	48.3
洛浦县	Lop County	100.0	32.1
策勒县	Qira County	100.0	42.3
于田县	Yutian [Keriya] County	100.0	37.0
民丰县	Minfeng [Niya] County	100.0	23.5

Continued

(%)

第二产业 Secondary Industry	工　业 Industry	建筑业 Construction	第三产业 Tertiary Industry	#交通运输、仓储和邮政业 Transport,storage And Post	#批发和零售业 Wholesale, and Retail Trades
17.6	10.3	7.3	44.0	2.9	8.1
16.8	11.7	5.1	34.9	5.9	4.8
45.4	37.8	7.6	30.2	4.7	1.9
9.8	4.1	5.7	45.1	1.5	3.3
12.6	5.6	6.9	31.8	1.6	2.4
15.9	3.2	12.7	54.3	4.5	0.2
25.3	**13.5**	**11.9**	**55.9**	**4.6**	**3.0**
22.5	14.6	7.9	60.5	7.0	3.4
27.5	12.9	14.6	42.0	1.4	1.1
37.6	20.4	17.2	53.2	3.5	2.9
17.8	0.8	17.0	66.3	3.3	2.7
25.5	**14.0**	**11.5**	**38.6**	**3.1**	**11.5**
34.3	24.6	9.8	61.4	6.8	24.2
12.2	3.1	9.1	28.4	1.3	2.0
45.2	22.3	22.8	18.1	0.8	1.5
20.8	4.8	16.0	31.0	1.3	3.6
19.4	11.0	8.4	43.5	2.3	15.2
13.2	6.3	6.9	31.2	1.0	3.0
16.6	8.3	8.2	27.5	1.7	3.8
18.5	8.6	9.9	27.8	1.4	7.4
33.7	9.3	24.4	32.2	2.1	4.0
26.4	17.0	9.4	24.5	4.4	5.1
16.8	6.8	10.0	46.2	2.1	24.9
46.6	15.1	31.5	37.0	1.4	2.9
19.3	**8.0**	**11.3**	**48.6**	**2.1**	**3.4**
34.9	13.0	21.9	55.5	4.0	5.6
21.9	8.7	13.2	38.2	0.6	0.4
10.4	3.0	7.4	45.7	1.5	4.2
13.1	6.4	6.6	38.6	0.8	1.2
17.9	4.3	13.6	50.1	1.2	1.9
14.7	1.0	13.7	43.0	1.0	1.5
11.1	1.2	9.9	51.9	1.8	2.0
17.8	6.2	11.6	58.7	1.9	1.2

2-12 各地、州、市、县(市)地区生产总值指数

(上年=100) (2011 年)

地　　区	Region	地区生产总值 Gross Regional Product	第一产业 Primary Industry
乌鲁木齐市	**Urumqi City**	**115.3**	**105.8**
#乌鲁木齐县	Urumqi County	113.8	111.0
克拉玛依市	**Karamay City**	**102.9**	**105.2**
石河子市	**Shihezi City**	**117.6**	**114.4**
吐鲁番地区	**Turpan Administrative Offices**	**105.4**	**96.1**
吐鲁番市	Turpan City	106.6	97.3
鄯善县	Shanshan [Piqan] County	101.2	87.7
托克逊县	Toksun County	111.8	108.5
哈密地区	**Hami [Kumul] Administrative Offices**	**122.0**	**108.1**
哈密市	Hami [Kumul] City	122.2	107.0
巴里坤哈萨克自治县	Barkol Kazak Autonomous County	121.7	108.9
伊吾县	Yiwu [Araturuk] County	116.9	110.9
昌吉回族自治州	**Changji Hui Autonomous Prefecture**	**116.6**	**106.0**
昌吉市	Changji City	116.8	107.0
阜康市	Fukang City	118.9	107.0
呼图壁县	Hutubi County	116.0	106.4
玛纳斯县	Manas County	111.9	105.2
奇台县	Qitai County	117.2	105.5
吉木萨尔县	Jimsar County	120.0	106.3
木垒哈萨克自治县	Mori Kazak Autonomous County	117.4	106.8
伊犁哈萨克自治州	**Ili Kazak Autonomous Prefecture**	**115.0**	**106.5**
伊犁州直属县(市)	**Counties (Cities) Direct Under Ili Prefecture**	**115.0**	**106.5**
伊宁市	Yining [Gulja] City	115.4	104.2
奎屯市	Kuytun City	118.1	104.1
伊宁县	Yining [Gulja] County	114.0	106.5
察布查尔锡伯自治县	Qapqal Xibe Autonomous County	113.5	106.6
霍城县	Huocheng [Korgas] County	112.4	106.4
巩留县	Gongliu [Tokkuztara] County	112.8	107.8
新源县	Xinyuan [Kunes] County	116.6	105.3
昭苏县	Zhaosu [Mongolkure] County	112.0	108.3
特克斯县	Tekes County	110.7	106.9
尼勒克县	Nilka County	116.3	108.4

Indices of Gross Domestic Product by Prefecture, Autonomous Prefecture, City and County

(preceding year=100)

第二产业 Secondary Industry	工业 Industry	建筑业 Construction	第三产业 Tertiary Industry	#交通运输、仓储和邮政业 Transport,storage And Post	#批发和零售业 Wholesale, and Retail Trades
110.0	**110.7**	**105.9**	**120.0**	**122.0**	**120.2**
113.8	114.5	105.7	116.4	110.0	118.0
102.4	**102.2**	**106.3**	**107.5**	**100.9**	**100.6**
125.1	**127.6**	**115.0**	**109.2**	**101.9**	**110.9**
106.2	**105.7**	**109.3**	**108.8**	**110.6**	**116.0**
109.9	111.2	102.9	107.7	107.8	122.8
101.8	100.9	107.8	105.8	108.9	86.3
114.8	115.9	109.4	106.0	108.9	107.7
131.0	**129.0**	**135.7**	**116.9**	**115.6**	**133.1**
130.8	129.7	133.4	117.1	114.5	130.0
134.4	131.8	144.9	116.0	118.0	150.9
120.4	105.3	151.8	116.1	122.0	226.7
127.5	**129.4**	**120.0**	**111.7**	**113.8**	**110.7**
125.4	127.6	115.5	111.1	106.9	109.9
122.8	122.7	124.5	117.0	127.0	118.8
129.9	136.3	100.0	114.9	108.6	115.6
119.4	122.3	114.8	112.9	111.2	120.9
141.6	153.8	108.3	114.3	114.7	113.2
139.1	148.2	103.5	114.2	107.5	113.4
144.7	155.6	125.4	121.1	109.0	117.2
121.4	**124.3**	**112.5**	**114.3**	**113.2**	**113.6**
122.2	**125.3**	**112.5**	**113.8**	**112.0**	**114.0**
118.9	120.7	116.0	114.8	114.1	113.0
122.2	124.0	113.1	114.6	109.7	114.2
123.3	126.5	107.8	113.2	114.6	110.9
132.2	145.3	107.9	111.4	114.1	118.1
119.0	119.8	115.6	114.0	110.8	115.8
117.9	122.5	109.4	113.9	112.3	120.4
126.6	130.2	111.6	111.0	112.3	109.7
119.0	120.8	113.0	112.2	111.3	114.0
118.9	123.1	109.4	111.3	113.0	103.0
122.9	128.5	106.6	111.5	111.4	110.1

2-12 续表 1

(上年=100)

地　　区	Region	地区生产总值 Gross Regional Product	第一产业 Primary Industry
塔城地区	**Tacheng [Tarbagatai] Administrative Offices**	**114.1**	**108.8**
塔城市	Tacheng [Qoqek] City	113.0	109.0
乌苏市	Usu City	114.0	106.9
额敏县	Emin [Dorbiljin] County	109.7	112.8
沙湾县	Shawan County	114.5	109.9
托里县	Toli County	117.0	107.0
裕民县	Yumin [Qagantokay] County	113.1	108.6
和布克赛尔蒙古自治县	Hoboksar Mongol Autonomous County	115.0	111.9
阿勒泰地区	**Altay Administrative Offices**	**111.8**	**105.0**
阿勒泰市	Altay City	111.3	103.8
布尔津县	Burqin County	107.9	105.0
富蕴县	Fuyun [Koktokay] County	108.8	98.1
福海县	Fuhai [Burultokay] County	107.5	109.3
哈巴河县	Habahe [Kaba] County	108.5	103.6
青河县	Qinghe [Qinggil] County	105.6	95.4
吉木乃县	Jeminay County	109.8	100.1
博尔塔拉蒙古自治州	**Bortala Mongolian Autonomous Prefecture**	**112.1**	**107.9**
博乐市	Bole [Bortala] City	112.5	106.6
精河县	Jinghe [Jing] County	111.7	111.8
温泉县	Wenquan [Araxang] County	108.8	100.4
巴音郭楞蒙古自治州	**Bayangol Mongol ian Autonomous Prefecture**	**107.2**	**105.8**
库尔勒市	Korla City	105.5	99.6
轮台县	Luntai [Bugur] County	113.2	117.1
尉犁县	Yuli [Lopnur] County	108.8	107.6
若羌县	Ruoqiang [Qarkilik] County	151.7	123.8
且末县	Qiemo [Qarqan] County	114.5	115.5
焉耆回族自治县	Yanqi Hui Autonomous County	112.8	108.8
和静县	Hejing County	118.1	100.5
和硕县	Hoxud County	113.2	112.9
博湖县	Bohu [Bagrax] County	114.5	109.4
阿克苏地区	**Aksu Administrative Offices**	**119.1**	**109.8**
阿克苏市	Aksu City	119.4	106.5
温宿县	Wensu [Onsu] County	119.1	107.8
库车县	Kuqa County	118.0	107.9

Continued

(preceding year=100)

第二产业 Secondary Industry	工　业 Industry	建筑业 Construction	第三产业 Tertiary Industry	#交通运输、仓储和邮政业 Transport,storage And Post	#批发和零售业 Wholesale, and Retail Trades
120.8	**124.7**	**110.7**	**112.8**	**107.3**	**110.2**
111.3	109.9	113.3	115.9	110.2	121.7
119.2	129.6	97.6	115.7	110.1	118.6
104.8	111.4	89.9	111.7	115.0	116.7
120.6	121.0	119.7	118.2	113.2	114.6
122.1	122.9	118.5	107.7	115.9	110.4
125.4	91.0	141.7	111.0	108.0	111.8
116.0	114.0	119.9	115.3	106.0	108.4
117.1	**121.0**	**105.6**	**109.4**	**111.0**	**111.1**
120.4	110.8	142.2	110.6	102.3	120.2
106.9	125.8	93.3	110.2	105.9	111.4
112.3	114.0	103.0	106.3	107.2	106.9
103.3	146.6	69.7	109.5	107.2	101.6
110.3	107.2	133.7	106.8	104.8	103.0
108.8	112.6	99.9	103.8	131.7	98.6
133.7	180.2	119.2	106.3	116.0	96.9
116.5	**124.5**	**103.4**	**113.7**	**110.2**	**115.3**
113.8	125.7	93.5	115.4	110.3	120.2
117.2	109.3	132.4	108.4	109.2	99.2
125.3	127.8	123.2	113.1	98.4	83.7
105.8	**105.9**	**104.8**	**113.4**	**109.2**	**121.5**
104.5	104.0	108.4	113.3	109.1	113.1
107.4	107.0	110.9	116.4	110.1	110.4
102.9	101.2	107.1	118.3	114.4	116.5
170.0	172.8	111.5	112.7	135.0	110.6
110.9	108.8	112.7	114.4	101.3	104.9
110.7	107.4	119.5	117.5	115.6	127.7
134.1	137.0	112.9	116.1	118.9	109.6
114.7	113.7	116.9	113.0	125.0	110.2
118.4	120.6	115.7	119.9	112.4	122.4
128.4	**133.7**	**115.1**	**120.1**	**113.9**	**115.0**
135.9	155.6	95.5	115.0	113.9	114.9
132.1	122.1	143.8	134.1	168.5	148.0
119.1	120.8	113.5	122.2	111.4	141.0

2-12 续表 2

(上年=100)

地　　区	Region	地区生产总值 Gross Regional Product	第一产业 Primary Industry
沙雅县	Xayar County	118.3	111.1
新和县	Xinhe [Toksu] County	118.6	108.5
拜城县	Baicheng [Bay] County	127.1	107.9
乌什县	Wushi [Uxturpan] County	118.1	109.1
阿瓦提县	Awat County	117.3	111.5
柯坪县	Kalpin County	124.2	112.3
克孜勒苏柯尔克孜自治州	**Kizilsu Kirgiz Autonomous Prefecture**	**113.2**	**106.4**
阿图什市	Artux City	119.0	108.2
阿克陶县	Akto County	111.0	103.5
阿合奇县	Akqi County	119.5	105.7
乌恰县	Wuqia [Ulugqat] County	116.3	107.8
喀什地区	**Kashgar [Kaxgar] Administrative Offices**	**115.6**	**105.6**
喀什市	Kashgar [Kaxgar] City	110.9	106.3
疏附县	Shufu County	116.1	113.3
疏勒县	Shule County	117.4	104.9
英吉沙县	Yengisar County	125.2	121.4
泽普县	Zepu [Poskam] County	114.2	110.3
莎车县	Shache [Yarkant] County	109.4	104.1
叶城县	Yecheng [Kagilik] County	115.4	105.6
麦盖提县	Makit County	109.3	102.5
岳普湖县	Yopurga County	110.3	97.9
伽师县	Jiashi [Payzawat] County	114.6	103.9
巴楚县	Bachu [Maralbexi] County	113.1	106.0
塔什库尔干县	Taxkorgan Tajik Autonomous County	121.2	97.3
和田地区	**Hotan Administrative Offices**	**114.6**	**105.6**
和田市	Hotan City	122.8	100.8
和田县	Hotan County	112.3	104.7
墨玉县	Moyu [Karakax] County	112.7	108.4
皮山县	Pishan [Guma] County	113.7	109.5
洛浦县	Lop County	110.7	99.6
策勒县	Qira County	112.7	107.4
于田县	Yutian [Keriya] County	111.4	105.0
民丰县	Minfeng [Niya] County	111.4	104.0

Continued

(preceding year=100)

第二产业 Secondary Industry	工 业 Industry	建筑业 Construction	第三产业 Tertiary Industry	#交通运输、仓储和邮政业 Transport,storage And Post	#批发和零售业 Wholesale, and Retail Trades
126.7	134.4	115.8	121.2	111.8	114.3
127.7	131.1	120.0	128.0	109.5	118.3
145.2	151.9	112.0	115.5	112.0	108.5
132.0	157.6	113.7	124.2	122.6	117.8
120.7	124.8	117.4	126.2	113.9	161.7
172.2	429.4	108.3	116.6	115.0	113.9
111.7	**109.4**	**114.1**	**116.3**	**111.7**	**110.4**
130.5	147.2	113.4	119.2	111.9	109.8
119.8	133.4	111.2	112.0	113.0	103.6
125.1	116.2	137.5	118.7	111.3	110.9
110.9	110.5	110.9	120.1	106.8	104.0
133.1	**135.8**	**130.5**	**117.5**	**115.2**	**116.0**
112.4	114.0	121.7	115.1	109.3	137.0
145.5	111.0	162.9	112.6	108.5	109.5
144.1	136.6	149.0	114.0	125.8	123.2
163.2	122.0	181.3	111.3	156.8	110.1
120.4	139.2	102.8	115.1	119.1	114.2
118.7	128.7	111.5	116.6	124.9	118.8
109.8	165.9	138.7	112.1	103.8	86.8
120.8	125.7	116.4	118.0	99.5	112.2
181.5	187.9	191.4	103.2	121.8	113.7
157.0	158.8	127.7	113.4	127.4	123.5
126.2	111.3	139.2	117.6	142.1	120.7
138.0	231.1	116.6	116.7	157.8	109.3
124.2	**148.1**	**112.0**	**117.7**	**110.1**	**121.9**
137.0	132.7	139.7	119.7	112.1	119.7
114.0	117.0	112.1	120.7	108.7	112.2
118.4	108.5	122.9	115.8	136.6	113.5
128.5	143.7	118.6	115.3	110.2	112.2
134.5	123.9	138.1	111.9	107.7	114.1
129.3	112.0	130.7	113.4	127.2	110.8
120.6	108.5	122.2	114.8	110.5	109.9
119.1	109.4	124.5	112.9	111.7	165.2

2-13 主要年份居民消费水平及指数

Household Consumption Expenditure and Its Indices in Main Years

年份 Year	居民消费水平(元) Household Consumption (yuan)	农村居民 Rural Households	城镇居民 Urban Households	居民消费水平指数(1952年=100) Index of Residents' Consumption Level (1952=100)	农村居民 Rural Households	城镇居民 Urban Households	居民消费水平指数(上年=100) Index of Residents' Consumption Level (preceding year=100)	农村居民 Rural Households	城镇居民 Urban Households
1978	181	131	323	140.5	144.5	99	104.7	102.3	102.8
1980	252	180	417	182.4	184.4	119.3	111.9	107.6	113.1
1985	428	280	755	267	252.3	183.8	110.5	105.9	114.6
1990	796	447	1508	299.5	236.3	226.4	103.8	98.8	105
1995	1852	977	3414	344.1	246.5	257.4	109	102.3	112.3
1996	2266	1387	3836	377.1	312.6	260.7	109.6	126.8	101.3
1997	2455	1445	4261	384.6	313.9	268.5	102	100.4	103
1998	2539	1520	4364	396.1	339.3	268.5	103	108.1	100
1999	2606	1358	4841	413.1	319.3	297.8	104.3	94.1	110.9
2000	2662	1308	5131	415.2	299.2	315.7	100.5	93.7	106
2001	2905	1427	5743	434.3	307.6	338.7	104.6	102.8	107.3
2002	3228	1525	6483	484.7	325.4	386.8	111.6	105.8	114.2
2003	3249	1603	6427	488.6	338.1	386.8	100.8	103.9	100
2004	3445	1652	6808	502.3	339.8	396.1	102.8	100.5	102.4
2005	3814	1884	7221	556.0	385.7	421.1	110.7	113.5	106.3
2006	4151	2000	7728	596.2	400.6	445.3	107.2	103.9	105.7
2007	4831	2320	8833	661.4	432.7	489.7	110.9	108.0	110.0
2008	5521	2686	9882	700.1	452.7	512.3	105.9	104.6	104.6
2009	5945	3029	10366	753.6	503.9	540.7	107.6	111.3	105.5
2010	7400	3674	12665	894.8	587.6	627.2	118.7	116.6	116.0
2011	8895	4495	14663	991.5	644.6	676.7	110.8	109.7	107.9

2-14 居民消费支出
Household Consumption Expenditure

单位：亿元 (100 million yuan)

项目	Item	2010	2011
居民消费支出	**Household Consumption Expenditure**	**1607.25**	**1954.33**
食品类支出	Foods	526.77	629.5
衣着类支出	Clothes	179.75	209.52
居住类支出	Residence	108	113.97
家庭设备、用品及服务类支出	Family Facilities and Servises	81.06	101.71
医疗保健类支出	Medical and Hygiencic Expenditure	171.4	212.38
交通和通信类支出	Traffic and Telecommunications	167.89	197.82
文教娱乐用品及服务类支出	Teathing, Entertainment and Services	115.8	135.31
金融中介服务虚拟支出	Imaginary Expenditure of Middle Finance Services	95.52	116.7
自由住房服务虚拟支出	Imaginary Expenditure of Freeform Resident Services	67.2	135.42
实物消费支出	Reality Consumption	21.48	19.24
其他商品和服务类支出	Other Goods and Services	72.38	82.76
按城乡分	**By Residence**		
农村居民支出	Agricaltural Households Expenditure	467.37	560.30
食品类支出	Foods	187.72	198.11
衣着类支出	Clothes	40.87	46.38
居住类支出	Residence	40.3	41.32
家庭设备、用品及服务类支出	Family Facilities and Servises	19.59	26.47
医疗保健类支出	Medical and Hygiencic Expenditure	50.78	57.80
交通和通信类支出	Traffic and Telecommunications	52.65	66.84
文教娱乐用品及服务类支出	Teathing, Entertainment and Services	22.9	28.62
金融中介服务虚拟支出	Imaginary Expenditure of Middle Finance Services	23.63	34.34
自由住房服务虚拟支出	Imaginary Expenditure of Freeform Resident Services	18.42	48.39
其他商品和服务类支出	Other Goods and Services	10.51	12.03
城镇居民支出	Non-agricaltural Households Expenditure	1139.88	1394.03
食品类支出	Foods	339.05	431.39
衣着类支出	Clothes	138.88	163.14
居住类支出	Residence	67.7	72.65
家庭设备、用品及服务类支出	Family Facilities and Servises	61.47	75.24
医疗保健类支出	Medical and Hygiencic Expenditure	120.62	154.58
交通和通信类支出	Traffic and Telecommunications	115.24	130.98
文教娱乐用品及服务类支出	Teathing, Entertainment and Services	92.9	106.69
金融中介服务虚拟支出	Imaginary Expenditure of Middle Finance Services	71.89	82.36
自由住房服务虚拟支出	Imaginary Expenditure of Freeform Resident Services	48.78	87.03
实物消费支出	Reality Consumption	21.48	19.24
其他商品和服务类支出	Other Goods and Services	61.87	70.73

主要统计指标解释

国内生产总值(GDP) 指按市场价格计算的一个国家(或地区)所有常住单位在一定时期内生产活动的最终成果。国内生产总值有三种表现形态，即价值形态、收入形态和产品形态。从价值形态看，它是所有常住单位在一定时期内生产的全部货物和服务价值超过同期投入的全部非固定资产货物和服务价值的差额，即所有常住单位的增加值之和；从收入形态看，它是所有常住单位在一定时期内创造并分配给常住单位和非常住单位的初次收入之和；从产品形态看，它是所有常住单位在一定时期内最终使用的货物和服务价值减去货物和服务进口价值。在实际核算中，国内生产总值有三种计算方法，即生产法、收入法和支出法。三种方法分别从不同的方面反映国内生产总值及其构成。

对于一个地区来说，称为地区生产总值或地区GDP.

三次产业 三产业的划分是世界上较为常用的产业结构分类，但各国的划分不尽一致。我国的三次产业划分是：

第一产业是指农、林、牧、渔业和农林牧渔服务业。。

第二产业是指采矿业，制造业，电力、煤气及水的生产和供应业，建筑业。

第三产业是指除第一、二产业以外的其他行业。

劳动者报酬 指劳动者因从事生产活动所获得的全部报酬。包括劳动者获得的各种形式的工资、奖金和津贴，既包括货币形式的，也包括实物形式的，还包括劳动者所享受的公费医疗和医药卫生费、上下班交通补贴、单位支付的社会保险费、住房公积金等。对于个体经济来说，其所有者所获得的劳动报酬和经营利润不易区分，这两部分统一作为劳动者报酬处理。

生产税净额 指生产税减生产补贴后的余额。生产税指政府对生产单位从事生产、销售和经营活动以及因从事生产活动使用某些生产要素(如固定资产、土地、劳动力)所征收的各种税、附加费和规费。生产补贴与生产税相反，指政府对生产单位的单方面转移支出，因此视为负生产税，包括政策亏损补贴、价格补贴等。

固定资产折旧 指一定时期内为弥补固定资产损耗按照规定的固定资产折旧率提取的固定资产折旧，或按国民经济核算统一规定的折旧率虚拟计算的固定资产折旧。它反映了固定资产在当期生产中的转移价值。各类企业和企业化管理的事业单位的固定资产折旧是指实际计提的折旧费；不计提折旧的政府机关、非企业化管理的事业单位和居民住房的固定资产折旧是按照统一规定的折旧率和固定资产原值计算的虚拟折旧。原则上，固定资产折旧应按固定资产当期的重置价值计算，但是目前我国尚不具备对全社会固定资产进行重估价的基础，所以暂时只能采用上述办法。

营业盈余 指常住单位创造的增加值扣除劳动者报酬、生产税净额和固定资产折旧后的余额。它相当于企业的营业利润加上生产补贴，但要扣除从利润中开支的工资和福利等。

支出法国内生产总值 是从最终使用的角度反映一个国家(或地区)一定时期内生产活动最终成果的一种方法，包括最终消费支出、资本形成总额及货物和服务净出口三部分。计算公式为：

支出法国内生产总值=最终消费支出+资本形成总额+货物和服务净出口

最终消费支出 指常住单位为满足物质、文化和精神生活的需要，从本国经济领土和国外购买的货物和服务的支出。它不包括非常住单位在本国经济领土内的消费支出。最终消费分为居民消费和政府消费。

居民消费支出 指常住住户在一定时期内对于货物和服务的全部最终消费支出。居民消费除了直接以货币形式购买的货物和服务的消费支出外，还包括以其他方式获得的货物和服务的消费支出，即所谓的虚拟消费支出。居民虚拟消费支出包括如下几种类型：单位以实物报酬及实物转移的形式提供给劳动者的货物和服务；住户生产并由本住户消费了的货物和服务，其中的服务仅指住户的自有住房服务和付酬的家庭雇员提供的家庭和个人服务；金融机构提供的金融媒介服务；保险公司提供的保险服务。

政府消费支出 指政府部门为全社会提供的公共服务的消费支出和免费或以较低的价格向居民住户提供的货物和服务的净支出，前者等于政府服务的产出价值减去政府单位所获得的经营收入的价值，后者等于政府部门免费或以较低价格向居民住户提供的货物和服务的市场价值减去向住户收取的价值。

资本形成总额 指常住单位在一定时期内获得减去处置的固定资产和存货的净额，包括固定资本形成总额和存货增加两部分。

固定资本形成总额 指生产者在一定时期内获得的固定资产减处置的固定资产的价值总额。固定资产是通过生产活动生产出来的，且其使用年限在一年以上、单位价值在规定标准以上的资产，不包括自然资产。可分为有形固定资本形成总额和无形固定资本形成总额。有形固定资本形成总额包括一定时期内完成的建筑工程、安装工程和设备工器具购置(减处置)价值，以及土地改良、新增役、种、奶、毛、娱乐用牲畜和新增经济林木价值。无形固定资本形成总额包括矿藏的勘探、计算机软件等获得减处置。

存货增加 指常住单位在一定时期内存货实物量变动的市场价值，即期末价值减期初价值的差额，再扣除当期由于价格变动而产生的持有收益。存货增加可以是正值，也可以是负值，正值表示存货上升，负值表示存货下降。存货包括生产单位购进的原材料、燃料和储备物资等存货，以及生产单位生产的产成品、在制品和半成品等存货。

货物和服务净出口 指货物和服务出口减货物和服务进口的差额。出口包括常住单位向非常住单位出售或无偿转让的各种货物和服务的价值；进口包括常住单位从非常住单位购买或无偿得到的各种货物和服务的价值。由于服务活动的提供与使用同时发生，一般把常住单位从非常住单位得到的服务作为进口，非常住单位从常住单位得到的服务作为出口。货物的出口和进口都按离岸价格计算。

Explanatory Notes on Main Statistical Indicators

Gross Domestic Product (GDP) refers to the final products at market prices produced by all resident units in a country (or a region) during a certain period of time. Gross domestic product is expressed in three different forms, i.e. value, income, and products respectively. GDP in its value form refers to the total value of all goods and services produced by all resident units during a certain period of time, minus the total value of input of goods and services of the nature of non-fixed assets; in other term, it is the sum of the value-added of all resident units. GDP in the form of income includes the income created by all resident units and distributed to resident and non-resident units. GDP in the form of products refers to the value of all goods and services for final consumption by all resident units minus the net exports of goods and services during a given period of time. In the practice of national accounting, gross domestic product is calculated with three approaches, i.e. production approach, income approach and expenditure approach, which reflect gross domestic product and its composition from different aspects.

Three Industries Classification of economic activities into three branches of industries is a common practice in the world, although the grouping varies to some extent form country to country. In China economic activities are categorized into following industries:

Primary industry: refers to agriculture, forestry, animal husbandry and fishery.

Secondary industry: refers to mining and quarrying, manufacturing, production and supply of electricity, water and gas, and construction.

Tertiary industry: refers to all other economic activities not included in primary or secondary industry.

Labourers Remuneration refers to the whole payment of various forms earned by the labourers from the productive activities they are engaged in. It includes wages, bonuses and allowances the labourers earned in monetary form and in kind. It also includes the free medical services provided to the labourers and the medicine expenses, traffic subsidies and social insurance, housing fund paid by the employers. As the individual economy is concerned, since the labourers remuneration is not easily distinguished from the operating profit, both are treated as labourers remuneration.

Net Taxes on Production refers to the difference of the taxes on production minus the subsidies on production. The taxes on production refers to the various taxes, extra charges and fees levied on the production units on their production, sale and business activities as well as on the use of some factors of production, such as fixed assets, land and labour force in the production activities they are engaged in. In contrast to the taxes on production, the subsidies on production refer to the unilateral government transfer to the production units and are therefore regarded as negative taxes on production. They include subsidies on the loss due to implementation of government policies, price subsidies, etc.

Depreciation of Fixed Assets refers to the depreciation of fixed assets of a given period, drawn in accordance with the stipulated depreciation rate for the purpose of compensating the wear loss of the fixed assets or the depreciation of fixed assets calculated in a fictitious way in accordance with the stipulated unified depreciation rate in the national economic accounting system. It reflects the value of transfer of the fixed assets in the production of the current period. The depreciation of fixed assets in various enterprises and institutions managed as enterprises refers to the depreciation expenses actually drawn. In government agencies and institutions not managed as enterprises which do not draw the depreciation expenses, as well as for the houses of residents, the depreciation of fixed assets is the imputed depreciation, which is calculated in accordance with the stipulated unified depreciation rate. In principle, the depreciation of fixed assets should be calculated on the basis of the re-purchased value of the fixed assets. However, there is no actual condition to re-evaluate all the fixed assets in China. Therefore, the above-mentioned methods are temporarily adopted at present.

Operating Surplus refers to the balance of the value added created by the resident units deducting the labourers remuneration, net taxes on production and the depreciation of fixed assets. It is equivalent to the business profit of the enterprises plus subsidies on production, but the wages and welfare expenses paid from the profits should be deducted.

GDP by Expenditure Approach refers to the method of measuring the final results of production activities of a country (region) during a given period from the perspective of final use. It includes final consumption, total capital formation and net export of goods and services, i.e:

GDP by expenditure approach = final consumption + total capital formation + net export of goods and services

Final Consumption refers to the total expenditure of resident units for purchases of goods and services from domestic economic territory and abroad to meet the requirements of material, cultural and spiritual life. It excludes the expenditure of non-resident units on consumption in the economic territory of the country. The final consumption is broken down into household consumption and government consumption.

Households Consumption refers to the total expenditure of resident households on the final consumption of goods and services. In addition to the consumption of goods and services bought by the households directly with money, the households consumption also includes expenditure on goods and services obtained by the households in other ways, i.e. the so-called imputed consumption expenditure, which includes the following: (a) the goods and services provided to the households by the employer in the form of payment in kind and transfer in kind; (b) goods and services produced and consumed by the households themselves, in which the services refer only to the owner-occupied housing and domestic and individual services provided by the paid household workers; (c) financial intermediate services provided by financial institutions; (d) insurance services provided by insurance companies.

Government Consumption refers to the expenditure on the consumption of the public services provided by the government to the whole society and the net expenditure on the goods and services provided by the government to the households free of charge or at low prices. The former equals to the output value of the government services minus the value of operating income obtained by the government departments. The latter equals to the market value of the goods and services provided by the government free of charge or at low prices to the households minus the value received by the government from the households.

Total Capital Formation refers to the fixed assets acquired minus those disposed of and the net value of inventory, including the total fixed capital formation and the increase in inventory.

Total Fixed Capital Formation refers to the value of fixed assets acquired minus those disposed of during a given period. Fixed assets are the assets produced through production activities with specified unit value which could be used for over one year, excluding natural assets. Total fixed capital formation can be categorized into total tangible capital formation and total intangible capital formation. The total tangible capital formation include the value of the construction projects, installation projects completed and the equipment, apparatus and instruments purchased as well as the value of land improved, the value of draught animals, breeding stock, animals for milk, wool and for recreational purpose, and the newly increased forest with economic value during a given period. The total intangible capital formation includes the prospecting of minerals, the acquisition of computer software minus the disposal of them.

Increase in Inventory refers to the market value of the change in inventory of resident units during a given period, i.e. the difference of value between the beginning and the end of the period minus the current gains due to the change in prices. The increase in inventory can be positive or negative. A positive value indicates the increase in inventory while a negative value indicates the decrease in stock. The inventory includes the raw materials, fuels and reserve materials purchased by the production units as well as the inventory of finished products, semi-finished products, work-in-progress, etc.

Net Export of Goods and Services refers to the difference of the exports of goods and services minus the imports of goods and services. The imports include the value of various goods and services sold or gratuitously transferred by the resident units to the non-resident units. The imports include the value of various goods and services purchased or gratuitously acquired by the resident units from the non-resident units. Because the provision of services and the use of them happen simultaneously, the acquisition of services by the resident units from abroad is usually treated as import while the acquisition of services by non-resident units in this country is usually treated as export. The export and import of goods are Valued at free on board(f.o.b) prices.

2012

新疆统计年鉴

XINJIANG STATISTICAL YEARBOOK

第三篇
人口与就业

CHAPTER 3
Population and Employment

简要说明
Brief Introduction

本篇资料的主要内容及来源

本篇内容主要包括人口、计划生育、就业、工资等资料。人口资料包括全区、各地、州、市、县及兵团人口情况。

分地区人口数据为户籍人口，由新疆维吾尔自治区公安厅提供；计划生育资料由新疆维吾尔自治区计划生育委员会提供；失业资料由新疆维吾尔自治区人力资源和社会保障厅提供；全区人口为常住人口由新疆维吾尔自治区统计局人口与就业统计处根据2011年人口变动情况抽样调查数据推算；就业和工资资料由新疆维吾尔自治区统计局人口与就业统计处提供。

Main Content and Source of Data

Data in this chapter show the basic condition of population, employment, wages of staff and workers, family planning. Data of population mainly include the condition of population by whole region, prefecture, autonomous prefecture, city, country and Xinjiang Production and Construction Group.

The data on household registered population are provided by Municipal Bureau of Public Security of Xinjiang Uygur Autonomous Region; Data on family planning come from Municipal Family Planning Commission. Data on unemployment are provided by Bureau of Labor and Social Security. Total region population are estimated by the Department of Population and Social Science Technology Statistics of the Xinjiang Bureau of Statistics in accordance with the annual national sample survey on population changes in 2011; The data of population census, employment and wages are provided by the Department of Population and Social Science and Technology Statistic of the Xinjiang Bureau of Statistics.

3-1 主要年份人口数及构成
Population and Its Composition in Main Years

单位：万人、%　　(10 000 persons,%)

年份 Year	年末总人口 Total Population (Year-end)	按性别分 By Sex				按城乡分 By Residence			
		男 Male		女 Female		城镇人口 Urban		乡村人口 Rural	
		人口数 Population	比重 Proportion	人口数 Population	比重 Proportion	人口数 Population	比重 Proportion	人口数 Population	比重 Proportion
1978	1233.01	630.18	51.11	602.83	48.89	321.40	26.07	911.61	73.93
1980	1283.24	654.90	51.03	628.34	48.97	372.74	29.05	910.50	70.95
1985	1361.14	696.81	51.19	664.33	48.81	582.24	42.78	778.90	57.22
1990	1529.16	785.06	51.34	744.10	48.66	685.96	44.86	843.20	55.14
1995	1661.35	848.12	51.05	813.23	48.95	822.53	49.51	838.82	50.49
1996	1689.29	869.59	51.48	819.70	48.52	846.17	50.09	843.12	49.91
1997	1718.08	883.03	51.40	835.05	48.60	860.76	50.10	857.32	49.90
1998	1747.35	897.90	51.39	849.45	48.61	875.42	50.10	871.93	49.90
1999	1775.00	910.98	51.32	864.02	48.68	929.00	52.34	846.00	47.66
2000	1849.41	957.07	51.75	892.34	48.25	624.18	33.75	1225.23	66.25
2001	1876.19	954.23	50.86	921.96	49.14	633.21	33.75	1242.98	66.25
2002	1905.19	975.46	51.20	929.73	48.80	644.72	33.84	1260.47	66.16
2003	1933.95	994.24	51.41	939.71	48.59	665.11	34.39	1268.84	65.61
2004	1963.11	1008.02	51.30	955.09	48.70	690.11	35.15	1273.00	64.85
2005	2010.35	1029.70	51.22	980.65	48.78	746.85	37.15	1263.50	62.85
2006	2050.00	1050.01	51.22	999.99	48.78	777.77	37.94	1272.23	62.06
2007	2095.19	1072.53	51.19	1022.66	48.81	820.27	39.15	1274.92	60.85
2008	2130.81	1083.94	50.87	1046.87	49.13	844.65	39.64	1286.16	60.36
2009	2158.63	1098.31	50.88	1060.32	49.12	860.21	39.85	1298.42	60.15
2010	2181.58	1127.01	51.66	1054.57	48.34	933.58	42.79	1248.01	57.21
2011	2208.71	1128.75	51.10	1079.96	48.90	961.67	43.54	1247.04	56.46

3-2 主要年份人口出生率、死亡率、自然增长率
Birth Rate,Death Rate and Natural Growth Rate of Population in Main Years

单位：‰　　(‰)

年份 Year	出生率 Birth Rate	死亡率 Death Rate	自然增长率 Natural Growth Rate	年份 Year	出生率 Birth Rate	死亡率 Death Rate	自然增长率 Natural Growth Rate
1978	22.55	7.69	14.86	1998	19.74	6.93	12.81
1980	21.28	7.62	13.66	1999	18.76	6.96	11.80
1985	19.80	6.39	13.41	2000	17.57	5.40	12.17
1986	20.54	6.13	14.41	2001	16.82	5.69	11.13
1987	21.03	5.96	15.07	2002	16.30	5.43	10.87
1988	19.72	5.99	13.73	2003	16.01	5.23	10.78
1989	21.15	5.77	15.38	2004	16.00	5.09	10.91
1990	26.41	7.81	18.60	2005	16.42	5.04	11.38
1991	24.45	7.86	16.59	2006	15.97	5.03	10.94
1992	22.80	7.84	14.96	2007	16.79	5.01	11.78
1993	21.53	7.68	13.85	2008	16.05	4.88	11.17
1994	20.82	7.43	13.39	2009	15.99	5.43	10.56
1995	18.90	6.45	12.45	2010	14.85	4.14	10.71
1996	19.45	6.60	12.85	2011	14.99	4.42	10.57
1997	19.66	6.55	13.11				

3-3 新疆人口普查基本情况

Basic Statistics on National Population Census in Xinjiang

单位：万人 (10 000 persons)

指标	Items	第二次普查(1964年) 1964 Census	第三次普查(1982年) 1982 Census	第四次普查(1990年) 1990 Census	第五次普查(2000年) 2000 Census	第六次普查(2010年) 2010 Census
总人口	**Total Population**	**727.01**	**1308.15**	**1515.69**	**1845.95**	**2181.58**
男	Male	389.47	673.22	782.32	955.22	1127.01
女	Female	337.54	634.93	733.37	890.73	1054.57
总户数(万户)	**Total Household (10 000 household)**	**178.00**	**293.79**	**337.41**	**491.66**	**690.29**
家庭户	Family Households		292.70	334.89	479.38	670.56
集体户	Collective Households		1.09	2.52	12.28	19.73
各年龄组人口	Population by Age Group					
0-5 岁	Age 0-5	121.86	186.70	218.85	165.12	185.03
6-14 岁	Age 6-14	146.77	330.85	282.12	338.18	261.15
15-64 岁	Age 15-64	428.73	742.42	955.49	1256.40	1593.99
65 岁及以上	Aged 65 and Over	29.65	48.18	59.23	86.25	141.41
民族人口	**Nationality Population**					
汉族	Han Nationality	232.12	528.40	569.54	748.99	882.99
少数民族	Minority Nationalities	494.89	779.75	946.15	1096.96	1298.59
各种文化程度人口	**Population by Educational Level**					
大专及以上	College and Above	4.10	8.37	27.98	94.65	231.53
高中和中专	Senior Secondary School and Specialized Secondary School	15.51	84.28	157.42	224.79	254.56
初中	Junior Secondary School	50.37	228.63	313.51	508.59	790.62
小学	Primary School	197.34	442.57	552.55	699.78	656.32
不识字或识字很少	Illiterate and Semi-iliterate	249.03	265.39	198.11	103.68	63.52

注：不识字或识字很少除 1964 年包含 12-14 岁人口外，其他均为 15 岁及以上人口。
Note：Illiterate or semi-illiterate population refers to the population aged above 15 except for the population aged between 12 and 14 in 1964.

3-4 主要年份婚姻登记情况

Number of Marriages Registry in Main Years

单位：万人

指标	Item	2005	2010	2011
登记结婚(对)	**Registered Marriages (couple)**	**184714**	**264013**	**282346**
初婚(人)	First Marriage (person)	275752	389342	419328
再婚(人)	Remarriage (person)	93676	138684	145364
＃男	Male	42576	73863	70997
＃再婚中恢复结婚(对)	Resumed Marriages (couple)	6815	11108	12403
登记离婚(对)	**Registered Divorces (couple)**	**74342**	**97817**	**99414**
民政部门批准	Approved by the Civil Administration	47917	69137	73927
法院调判	Mediated by the court	26425	28680	25487
涉外及华侨港澳台居民婚姻	**Marital status of OverseasChinese ,Foreigner and Hong Kong, Macao and Taiwan Compatriots**			
登记结婚(对)	Registered Marriages (couple)	223	235	261
国内公民(人)	Citizen (person)	223	235	255
港澳台居民(人)	Compatriots of Hong Kong, Macao and Taiwan (person)	57	31	20
华侨(人)	Overseas Chinese (person)	12	13	6
外国人(人)	Foreigner (person)	154	191	241
登记离婚(对)	Registered Divorces (couple)	6	26	43

3-5 各地、州、市、县(市)户数、人口数、土地面积

Household, Population, Land Area by Prefecture, Autonomous Prefecture,City and County

(2011 年)

地区	Region	户数(万户) Number of Households (10 000 households)	年末人口(万人) Population at Year-end (10 000 persons)	#男 Male	平均每户人口(人) Average Persons Per Household (person)	土地面积(平方公里) Land Area (sq.km)
总 计	**Total**	**663.70**	**2208.71**	**1128.75**	**3.32**	**1664897.17**
乌鲁木齐市	**Urumqi City**	**84.59**	**249.35**	**128.95**	**2.95**	**14875.50**
天山区	Tianshan District	17.84	55.79	28.11	3.13	47.31
沙依巴克区	Shayibak District	17.93	52.74	27.26	2.94	38.60
新市区	Xinshi District	17.48	52.88	27.49	3.03	57.07
水磨沟区	Shui Mogou Distric	10.06	28.20	14.81	2.80	10.76
头屯河区	Tou Tunhe District	8.14	21.95	11.63	2.70	20.11
达坂城区	Da Bancheng District	1.51	4.44	2.40	2.94	1111.85
米东区	Midong District	9.68	27.57	14.35	2.85	3789.22
乌鲁木齐县	Urumqi County	1.95	5.78	2.90	2.96	9800.58
克拉玛依市	**Karamay City**	**10.56**	**28.23**	**14.39**	**2.67**	**8654.08**
独山子区	Dushanzi District	2.08	5.60	2.91	2.69	379.11
克拉玛依区	Karamay District	6.88	18.26	9.22	2.65	4231.56
乌尔河区	Urhe District	0.08	0.23	0.12	2.88	1424.65
白碱滩区	Bai Jiantan District	1.52	4.14	2.14	2.72	2618.76
吐鲁番地区	**Turpan Administrative Offices**	**18.66**	**63.19**	**31.84**	**3.39**	**67562.91**
吐鲁番市	Turpan City	7.86	28.35	14.34	3.61	13589.22
鄯善县	Shanshan [Piqan] County	7.23	22.95	11.48	3.17	38281.46
托克逊县	Toksun County	3.57	11.89	6.02	3.33	15692.23
哈密地区	**Hami [Kumul] Administrative Offices**	**20.77**	**58.39**	**29.91**	**2.81**	**142094.88**
哈密市	Hami [Kumul] City	16.25	45.79	23.51	2.82	85587.23
巴里坤哈萨克自治县	Barkol Kazak Autonomous County	3.72	10.32	5.23	2.77	36988.55
伊吾县	Yiwu [Araturuk] County	0.80	2.28	1.17	2.85	19519.10

注：1.全区年末人口数依据 1%人口抽样调查数推算，各地、州、市、县、区人口数据为 2011 年公安年报数据。
2.全疆各地州市土地面积为国土资源厅 2008 年数据。

Note：a) The data of population by prefecture,antonomous prefecture,city and county come from the annual data of public security.
b) The land area of different prefectures and cities come from the Burean of State Land.

3-5 续表 1 Continued

地　　区	Region	户 数 (万户) Number of Households (10 000 households)	年末人口 (万人) Population at Year-end (10 000 persons)	#男 Male	平均每户人口 (人) Average Persons Per Household (person)	土地面积 (平方公里) Land Area (sq.km)
昌吉回族自治州	**Changji Hui Autonomous Prefecture**	**46.93**	**139.46**	**70.94**	**2.97**	**73139.75**
昌吉市	Changji City	12.14	36.32	18.38	2.99	7505.12
阜康市	Fukang City	5.65	16.76	8.56	2.97	8534.97
呼图壁县	Hutubi County	7.75	21.81	11.08	2.81	9421.03
玛纳斯县	Manas County	6.23	17.61	8.88	2.83	9597.27
奇台县	Qitai County	7.51	23.97	12.22	3.19	16635.92
吉木萨尔县	Jimsar County	4.79	14.06	7.22	2.94	8144.58
木垒哈萨克自治县	Mori Kazak Autonomous County	2.86	8.93	4.60	3.12	13300.86
伊犁哈萨克自治州	**Ili Kazak Autonomous Prefecture**	**148.39**	**459.84**	**233.34**	**3.10**	**268778.72**
伊犁州直属县(市)	**Counties (Cities) Direct Under Ili Prefecture**	**92.18**	**288.47**	**146.63**	**3.13**	**56381.53**
伊宁市	Yining [Gulja] City	16.14	50.39	25.05	3.12	524.94
奎屯市	Kuytun City	11.06	30.75	15.50	2.78	1109.89
伊宁县	Yining [Gulja] County	11.48	42.68	21.83	3.72	4681.90
察布查尔锡伯自治县	Qapqal Xibe Autonomous County	6.40	19.30	9.85	3.02	4471.95
霍城县	Huocheng [Korgas] County	13.98	40.42	20.79	2.89	5429.83
巩留县	Gongliu [Tokkuztara] County	6.24	20.10	10.30	3.22	4326.90
新源县	Xinyuan [Kunes] County	9.83	31.16	15.91	3.17	6813.74
昭苏县	Zhaosu [Mongolkure] County	6.25	18.46	9.42	2.95	11127.91
特克斯县	Tekes County	5.45	16.78	8.56	3.08	7764.10
尼勒克县	Nilka County	5.35	18.43	9.42	3.44	10130.37
塔城地区	**Tacheng [Tarbagatai] Administrative Offices**	**35.06**	**104.48**	**52.90**	**2.98**	**94698.18**
塔城市	Tacheng [Qoqek] City	5.69	17.05	8.58	3.00	3991.25
乌苏市	Usu City	7.32	22.77	11.65	3.11	14299.86
额敏县	Emin [Dorbiljin] County	7.88	21.79	11.02	2.77	9448.37
沙湾县	Shawan County	7.21	21.61	10.91	3.00	12676.58
托里县	Toli County	2.96	10.01	5.04	3.38	28192.65
裕民县	Yumin [Qagantokay] County	2.04	5.91	3.00	2.90	6112.13
和布克赛尔蒙古自治县	Hoboksar Mongol Autonomous County	1.96	5.34	2.70	2.72	19977.34

3-5 续表 2 Continued

地　　区	Region	户 数 (万户) Number of Households (10 000 households)	年末人口 (万人) Year-end Population (10 000 persons)	#男 Male	平均每户人口 (人) Average Persons Per Household (person)	土地面积 (平方公里) Land Area (sq.km)
阿勒泰地区	**Altay Administrative Offices**	**21.15**	**66.89**	**33.81**	**3.16**	**117699.01**
阿勒泰市	Altay City	7.52	23.48	11.89	3.12	10829.06
布尔津县	Burqin County	2.39	7.22	3.63	3.02	10357.35
富蕴县	Fuyun [Koktokay] County	2.76	9.53	4.81	3.45	32186.11
福海县	Fuhai [Burultokay] County	2.35	7.54	3.85	3.21	33250.74
哈巴河县	Habahe [Kaba] County	2.79	8.75	4.43	3.14	8166.58
青河县	Qinghe [Qinggil] County	1.88	6.43	3.23	3.42	15756.87
吉木乃县	Jemnay County	1.46	3.94	1.97	2.70	7152.30
博尔塔拉蒙古自治州	**Bortala Mongol Autonomous Prefecture**	**17.33**	**48.73**	**24.96**	**2.81**	**24934.33**
博乐市	Bole [Bortala] City	9.52	26.69	13.68	2.80	7877.34
精河县	Jinghe [Jing] County	4.98	14.44	7.40	2.90	11175.25
温泉县	Wenquan [Araxang] County	2.83	7.60	3.88	2.69	5881.74
巴音郭楞蒙古自治州	**Bayangol Mongol Autonomous Prefecture**	**43.31**	**136.60**	**70.31**	**3.15**	**470954.25**
库尔勒市	Korla City	17.90	54.20	27.88	3.03	7215.90
轮台县	Luntai [Bugur] County	3.28	11.61	5.87	3.54	14156.61
尉犁县	Yuli [Lopnur] County	3.80	10.97	5.62	2.89	59234.48
若羌县	Ruoqiang [Qarkilik] County	1.09	3.36	1.72	3.08	198793.52
且末县	Qiemo [Qarqan] County	1.79	6.54	3.36	3.65	137831.05
焉耆回族自治县	Yanji Hui Autonomous County	4.35	16.87	8.74	3.88	2440.73
和静县	Hejing County	6.65	19.42	10.06	2.92	34886.74
和硕县	Hoxud County	2.55	7.53	3.93	2.95	12816.49
博湖县	Bohu [Bagrax] County	1.90	6.10	3.13	3.21	3578.73
阿克苏地区	**Aksu Administrative Offices**	**63.13**	**238.97**	**121.92**	**3.79**	**127144.91**
阿克苏市	Aksu City	14.63	49.62	25.24	3.39	13987.61
温宿县	Wensu [Onsu] County	6.68	24.57	12.61	3.68	14202.46
库车县	Kuqa County	11.20	46.93	24.17	4.19	14602.95
沙雅县	Xayar County	6.83	25.86	12.93	3.79	31955.15
新和县	Xinhe [Toksu] County	4.77	16.96	8.56	3.56	5817.82
拜城县	Baicheng [Bay] County	6.57	23.09	11.87	3.51	15553.70
乌什县	Wushi [Uxturpan] County	5.44	21.75	11.12	4.00	9082.00
阿瓦提县	Awat County	5.85	25.27	12.90	4.32	13233.57
柯坪县	Kalpin County	1.16	4.92	2.52	4.24	8709.65

3-5 续表 3 Continued

地　　区	Region	户 数 (万户) Number of Households (10 000 households)	年末人口 (万人) Year-end Population (10 000 persons)	#男 Male	平均每户人口 (人) Average Persons Per Household (person)	土地面积 (平方公里) Land Area (sq.km)
克孜勒苏柯尔克孜自治州	**Kizilsu Kirgiz Autonomous Prefecture**	**14.04**	**55.43**	**28.16**	**3.95**	**72468.08**
阿图什市	Artux City	5.93	25.09	12.76	4.23	16151.17
阿克陶县	Akto County	5.13	20.23	10.29	3.94	24539.86
阿合奇县	Akqi County	1.15	4.27	2.14	3.71	12737.09
乌恰县	Wuqia [Ulugqat] County	1.83	5.84	2.97	3.19	19039.96
喀什地区	**Kashgar [Kaxgar] Administrative Offices**	**101.40**	**410.20**	**206.63**	**4.05**	**137578.51**
喀什市	Kashgar [Kaxgar] City	13.79	48.02	23.84	3.48	199.38
疏附县	Shufu County	8.12	33.58	17.20	4.14	3323.12
疏勒县	Shule County	8.59	34.33	17.35	4.00	2485.31
英吉沙县	Yengisar County	6.43	27.39	13.94	4.26	3223.87
泽普县	Zepu [Poskam] County	6.32	20.89	10.48	3.31	826.90
莎车县	Shache [Yarkant] County	17.42	81.38	40.77	4.67	9066.86
叶城县	Yecheng [Kagilik] County	10.98	45.71	23.02	4.16	29359.29
麦盖提县	Makit County	6.49	25.61	12.95	3.95	10276.57
岳普湖县	Yopurga County	4.22	16.00	8.13	3.79	2700.48
伽师县	Jiashi [Payzawat] County	9.51	39.86	20.15	4.19	6668.59
巴楚县	Bachu [Maralbexi] County	8.40	33.62	16.87	4.00	18903.70
塔什库尔干塔吉克自治县	Taxkorgan Tajik Autonomous County	1.13	3.81	1.93	3.37	50544.44
和田地区	**Hotan Administrative Offices**	**55.78**	**207.58**	**105.66**	**3.72**	**249146.59**
和田市	Hotan City	8.72	32.14	16.21	3.69	495.84
和田县	Hotan County	6.30	27.15	13.83	4.31	40876.80
墨玉县	Moyu [Karakax] County	13.64	53.11	27.12	3.89	25624.02
皮山县	Pishan [Guma] County	7.18	26.56	13.57	3.70	39819.75
洛浦县	Lop County	6.25	24.07	12.25	3.85	14286.97
策勒县	Qira County	4.99	15.52	7.89	3.11	31342.58
于田县	Yutian [Keriya] County	7.45	25.27	12.88	3.39	39126.14
民丰县	Minfeng [Niya] County	1.25	3.76	1.91	3.01	57574.49
自治区直辖县级市	**Municpality Country-LevelCity directly under the Central Govern-ment**	**38.82**	**106.69**	**54.75**	**2.75**	**7267.04**
石河子市	Shihezi City	23.14	62.44	31.72	2.70	459.94
阿拉尔市	Aral City	7.46	19.10	10.11	2.56	4196.00
图木舒克市	Tumxuk City	4.64	16.05	8.32	3.46	1901.10
五家渠市	Wujiaqu City	3.58	9.10	4.60	2.54	710.00

3-6 各地、州、市、县(市)人口自然变动情况

Statistics on Population Natural Changes by Prefecture, Autonomous Prefecture, City and County

单位：‰ (2011 年) (‰)

地　区	Region	出生率 Birth Rate	#少数民族 Minority Nationalities	死亡率 Death Rate	#少数民族 Minority Nationalities	自然增长率 Natural Growth Rate	#少数民族 Minority Nationalities
乌鲁木齐市	**Urumqi City**	**8.54**	**13.95**	**2.66**	**2.92**	**5.88**	**11.03**
天山区	Tianshan District	7.91	12.26	2.78	2.99	5.13	9.27
沙依巴克区	Shayibak District	8.00	12.13	3.32	3.77	4.68	8.36
新市区	Xinshi District	8.71	13.23	2.07	1.82	6.64	11.41
水磨沟区	Shui Mogou Distric	7.90	19.26	2.24	4.06	5.66	15.20
头屯河区	Tou Tunhe District	7.70	13.85	3.46	4.67	4.24	9.18
达坂城区	Da Bancheng District	10.75	16.56	2.47	3.06	8.28	13.50
米东区	Midong District	10.04	15.70	2.29	1.81	7.75	13.89
乌鲁木齐县	Urumqi County	15.51	19.13	1.68	1.84	13.83	17.29
克拉玛依市	**Karamay City**	**9.15**	**15.88**	**4.01**	**4.97**	**5.14**	**10.91**
独山子区	Dushanzi District	12.46	18.27	2.99	3.63	9.47	14.64
克拉玛依区	Karamay District	8.80	15.96	4.50	5.72	4.30	10.24
乌尔河区	Urhe District	8.94	15.54	1.79	1.94	7.15	13.60
白碱滩区	Bai Jiantan District	6.31	12.61	3.39	4.12	2.92	8.49
吐鲁番地区	**Turpan Administrative Offices**	**18.30**	**21.70**	**3.38**	**3.48**	**14.92**	**18.22**
吐鲁番市	Turpan City	19.62	22.89	3.34	3.16	16.28	19.73
鄯善县	Shanshan [Piqan] County	18.22	22.79	3.38	3.88	14.84	18.91
托克逊县	Toksun County	15.32	17.21	3.48	3.56	11.84	13.65
哈密地区	**Hami [Kumul] Administrative Offices**	**10.16**	**19.00**	**4.35**	**5.39**	**5.81**	**13.61**
哈密市	Hami [Kumul] City	9.65	18.82	4.15	5.69	5.50	13.13
巴里坤哈萨克自治县	Barkol Kazak Autonomous County	12.12	21.21	5.09	4.30	7.03	16.91
伊吾县	Yiwu [Araturuk] County	11.37	14.73	4.87	5.56	6.50	9.17
昌吉回族自治州	**Changji Hui Autonomous Prefecture**	**10.28**	**19.09**	**3.44**	**3.80**	**6.84**	**15.29**
昌吉市	Changji City	9.95	17.14	2.99	3.89	6.96	13.25
阜康市	Fukang City	10.48	18.10	3.91	3.77	6.57	14.33
呼图壁县	Hutubi County	9.98	19.91	3.87	2.63	6.11	17.28
玛纳斯县	Manas County	8.78	17.92	3.26	3.67	5.52	14.25
奇台县	Qitai County	11.51	22.79	3.78	4.54	7.73	18.25
吉木萨尔县	Jimsar County	9.91	16.62	2.99	3.38	6.92	13.24
木垒哈萨克自治县	Mori Kazak Autonomous County	12.32	22.68	3.47	4.66	8.85	18.02

3-6 续表 1 Continued

单位：‰ (‰)

地　区	Region	出生率 Birth Rate	#少数民族 Minority Nationalities	死亡率 Death Rate	#少数民族 Minority Nationalities	自然增长率 Natural Growth Rate	#少数民族 Minority Nationalities
伊犁哈萨克自治州	**Ili Kazak Autonomous Prefecture**	**17.41**	**24.37**	**4.47**	**4.75**	**12.94**	**19.62**
伊犁州直属县(市)	**Counties (Cities) Direct Under Ili Prefecture**	**19.92**	**26.79**	**4.48**	**4.58**	**15.44**	**22.21**
伊宁市	Yining [Gulja] City	21.84	29.74	3.87	4.11	17.97	25.63
奎屯市	Kuytun City	5.46	10.81	4.93	3.69	0.53	7.12
伊宁县	Yining [Gulja] County	20.08	21.61	3.02	2.92	17.06	18.69
察布查尔锡伯自治县	Qapqal Xibe Autonomous County	23.25	29.51	5.02	4.93	18.23	24.58
霍城县	Huocheng [Korgas] County	19.04	25.22	4.45	4.47	14.59	20.75
巩留县	Gongliu [Tokkuztara] County	21.02	24.95	3.24	2.92	17.78	22.03
新源县	Xinyuan [Kunes] County	22.79	31.03	3.12	3.20	19.67	27.83
昭苏县	Zhaosu [Mongolkure] County	24.23	28.62	3.94	3.99	20.29	24.63
特克斯县	Tekes County	20.68	24.24	2.98	3.21	17.70	21.03
尼勒克县	Nilka County	26.20	31.84	13.72	15.52	12.48	16.32
塔城地区	**Tacheng [Tarbagatai] Administrative Offices**	**12.73**	**19.81**	**4.57**	**5.47**	**8.16**	**14.34**
塔城市	Tacheng [Qoqek] City	11.11	16.29	4.82	6.19	6.29	10.10
乌苏市	Usu City	12.19	19.42	5.96	7.29	6.23	12.13
额敏县	Emin [Dorbiljin] County	11.73	18.61	4.11	5.06	7.62	13.55
沙湾县	Shawan County	11.19	21.08	3.36	3.72	7.83	17.36
托里县	Toli County	19.10	23.01	5.19	5.45	13.91	17.56
裕民县	Yumin [Qagantokay] County	15.66	25.52	3.70	4.96	11.96	20.56
和布克赛尔蒙古自治县	Hoboksar Mongol Autonomous County	15.30	17.31	4.40	4.87	10.90	12.44
阿勒泰地区	**Altay Administrative Offices**	**13.94**	**18.56**	**4.29**	**4.76**	**9.65**	**13.80**
阿勒泰市	Altay City	10.07	16.22	3.83	4.17	6.24	12.05
布尔津县	Burqin County	17.20	20.71	6.58	7.44	10.62	13.27
富蕴县	Fuyun [Koktokay] County	17.39	19.63	5.27	5.61	12.12	14.02
福海县	Fuhai [Burultokay] County	15.24	24.39	3.22	3.77	12.02	20.62
哈巴河县	Habahe [Kaba] County	17.00	20.23	4.07	3.88	12.93	16.35
青河县	Qinghe [Qinggil] County	16.47	17.79	3.25	3.22	13.22	14.57
吉木乃县	Jemnay County	9.37	9.94	4.71	5.77	4.66	4.17
博尔塔拉蒙古自治州	**Bortala Mongol Autonomous Prefecture**	**11.44**	**19.95**	**3.75**	**4.74**	**7.69**	**15.21**
博乐市	Bole [Bortala] City	10.65	18.13	3.26	3.78	7.39	14.35
精河县	Jinghe [Jing] County	12.63	25.03	4.09	5.39	8.54	19.64
温泉县	Wenquan [Araxang] County	11.98	17.80	4.86	6.46	7.12	11.34
巴音郭楞蒙古自治州	**Bayangol Mongol Autonomous Prefecture**	**13.26**	**20.75**	**5.01**	**6.33**	**8.25**	**14.42**
库尔勒市	Korla City	10.46	19.40	4.66	7.51	5.80	11.89
轮台县	Luntai [Bugur] County	21.80	24.25	6.59	7.69	15.21	16.56
尉犁县	Yuli [Lopnur] County	11.93	22.27	5.48	7.94	6.45	14.33
若羌县	Ruoqiang [Qarkilik] County	16.38	24.26	4.18	5.71	12.20	18.55
且末县	Qiemo [Qarqan] County	20.12	23.51	4.55	5.30	15.57	18.21
焉耆回族自治县	Yanji Hui Autonomous County	13.76	17.89	3.96	3.86	9.80	14.03
和静县	Hejing County	14.03	21.08	5.64	5.56	8.39	15.52
和硕县	Hoxud County	11.71	18.03	4.77	4.89	6.94	13.14
博湖县	Bohu [Bagrax] County	13.20	19.37	6.21	7.37	6.99	12.00

3-6 续表 2 Continued

单位：‰ (‰)

地　区	Region	出生率 Birth Rate	#少数民族 Minority Nationalities	死亡率 Death Rate	#少数民族 Minority Nationalities	自然增长率 Natural Growth Rate	#少数民族 Minority Nationalities
阿克苏地区	**Aksu Administrative Offices**	**17.11**	**18.28**	**5.37**	**5.85**	**11.74**	**12.43**
阿克苏市	Aksu City	16.45	20.32	4.69	6.23	11.76	14.09
温宿县	Wensu [Onsu] County	16.52	19.31	5.59	5.79	10.93	13.52
库车县	Kuqa County	18.92	18.94	7.34	7.86	11.58	11.08
沙雅县	Xayar County	18.53	18.39	5.62	5.76	12.91	12.63
新和县	Xinhe [Toksu] County	17.40	17.98	3.06	3.16	14.34	14.82
拜城县	Baicheng [Bay] County	16.19	17.31	3.74	3.86	12.45	13.45
乌什县	Wushi [Uxturpan] County	15.04	15.30	4.77	4.64	10.27	10.66
阿瓦提县	Awat County	17.11	18.30	6.51	7.27	10.60	11.03
柯坪县	Kalpin County	14.08	14.41	3.42	3.48	10.66	10.93
克孜勒苏柯尔克孜自治州	**Kizilsu Kirgiz Autonomous Prefecture**	**23.74**	**24.79**	**3.56**	**3.55**	**20.18**	**21.24**
阿图什市	Artux City	22.01	23.26	3.23	3.03	18.78	20.23
阿克陶县	Akto County	26.80	27.45	3.19	3.26	23.61	24.19
阿合奇县	Akqi County	21.91	23.24	3.71	4.01	18.20	19.23
乌恰县	Wuqia [Ulugqat] County	21.90	22.53	6.96	7.47	14.94	15.06
喀什地区	**Kashgar [Kaxgar] Administrative Offices**	**24.80**	**25.64**	**5.71**	**5.84**	**19.09**	**19.80**
喀什市	Kashgar [Kaxgar] City	20.72	22.86	5.26	5.38	15.46	17.48
疏附县	Shufu County	22.54	22.76	14.71	14.87	7.83	7.89
疏勒县	Shule County	22.69	23.70	4.42	4.55	18.27	19.15
英吉沙县	Yengisar County	34.14	33.46	3.71	3.71	30.43	29.75
泽普县	Zepu [Poskam] County	37.33	42.28	4.16	4.36	33.17	37.92
莎车县	Shache [Yarkant] County	23.45	23.89	6.48	6.60	16.97	17.29
叶城县	Yecheng [Kagilik] County	27.30	28.32	3.86	3.91	23.44	24.41
麦盖提县	Makit County	18.69	17.43	7.68	8.03	11.01	9.40
岳普湖县	Yopurga County	15.18	15.79	5.16	5.33	10.02	10.46
伽师县	Jiashi [Payzawat] County	24.78	25.08	2.47	2.48	22.31	22.60
巴楚县	Bachu [Maralbexi] County	29.90	30.89	4.67	4.75	25.23	26.14
塔什库尔干塔吉克自治县	Taxkorgan Tajik Autonomous County	16.40	16.04	3.36	3.49	13.04	12.55
和田地区	**Hotan Administrative Offices**	**19.16**	**19.66**	**5.69**	**5.79**	**13.47**	**13.87**
和田市	Hotan City	17.88	19.93	4.23	4.69	13.65	15.24
和田县	Hotan County	18.04	18.13	2.52	2.51	15.52	15.62
墨玉县	Moyu [Karakax] County	13.77	13.88	4.43	4.49	9.34	9.39
皮山县	Pishan [Guma] County	20.02	20.23	6.15	6.22	13.87	14.01
洛浦县	Lop County	27.05	27.42	6.16	6.23	20.89	21.19
策勒县	Qira County	21.71	21.88	11.41	11.54	10.30	10.34
于田县	Yutian [Keriya] County	23.38	23.68	9.05	8.72	14.33	14.96
民丰县	Minfeng [Niya] County	18.67	19.63	6.64	7.05	12.03	12.58
自治区直辖县级市	**Municpality Country-LevelCity dire-ctlyunder the Central overn-ment**						
石河子市	Shihezi City	4.51	10.74	4.91	2.93	-0.40	7.81
阿拉尔市	Aral City	6.45	7.49	3.38	5.57	3.07	1.92
图木舒克市	Tumxuk City	8.25	12.15	2.84	1.53	5.41	10.62
五家渠市	Wujiaqu City	5.16	8.90	6.28	3.00	-1.12	5.90

3-7 各地、州、市、县(市)分民族人口数

Population of Major Major Nationalities by Prefecture,Autonomous Prefecture,City and County

单位：人 (2011 年)

地 区	Region	合 计 Total	#少数民族 Minority Nationalities	维吾尔族 Uygur	汉 族 Han	哈萨克族 Kazak
乌鲁木齐市	**Urumqi City**	**2493517**	**682026**	**314987**	**1811491**	**69581**
天山区	Tianshan District	557883	205583	138788	352300	12999
沙依巴克区	Shayibak District	527404	121449	62989	405955	9053
新市区	Xinshi District	528815	108674	47186	420141	8029
水磨沟区	Shui Mogou Distric	281956	44185	27853	237771	2950
头屯河区	Tou Tunhe District	219538	48491	24152	171047	1962
达坂城区	Da Bancheng District	44377	23411	2593	20966	6680
米东区	Midong District	275727	91743	10580	183984	4551
乌鲁木齐县	Urumqi County	57817	38490	846	19327	23357
克拉玛依市	**Karamay City**	**282267**	**71004**	**44035**	**211263**	**11553**
独山子区	Dushanzi District	56038	14735	9063	41303	2513
克拉玛依区	Karamay District	182602	43837	26904	138765	7243
乌尔河区	Urhe District	2260	1036	356	1224	75
白碱滩区	Bai Jiantan District	41367	11396	7712	29971	1722
吐鲁番地区	**Turpan Administrative Offices**	**631883**	**492162**	**451484**	**139721**	**297**
吐鲁番市	Turpan City	283536	226126	205213	57410	26
鄯善县	Shanshan [Piqan] County	229467	165969	154286	63498	38
托克逊县	Toksun County	118880	100067	91985	18813	233
哈密地区	**Hami [Kumul] Administrative Offices**	**583861**	**186370**	**107779**	**397491**	**54418**
哈密市	Hami [Kumul] City	457903	133069	98142	324834	13724
巴里坤哈萨克自治县	Barkol Kazak Autonomous County	103179	38692	157	64487	36466
伊吾县	Yiwu [Araturuk] County	22779	14609	9480	8170	4228
昌吉回族自治州	**Changji Hui Autonomous Prefecture**	**1394568**	**369918**	**64747**	**1024650**	**140948**
昌吉市	Changji City	363270	97780	10910	265490	19349
阜康市	Fukang City	167560	47968	10274	119592	14460
呼图壁县	Hutubi County	218054	51406	6265	166648	25837
玛纳斯县	Manas County	176047	34008	5937	142039	19129
奇台县	Qitai County	239696	63296	18862	176400	26331
吉木萨尔县	Jimsar County	140627	43857	7537	96770	11563
木垒哈萨克自治县	Mori Kazak Autonomous County	89314	31603	4962	57711	24279

Population of Major Nationalities by Prefecture, Autonomous Prefecture, City and County

(person)

回 族 Hui	柯尔克孜族 Kirgiz	蒙古族 Mongolian	锡伯族 Xibo	俄罗斯族 Russion	塔吉克族 Tajik	乌孜别克族 Uzbek	塔塔尔族 Tatar	满 族 Manchu	达斡尔族 Daur	其 它 Others
253371	**1902**	**9883**	**5422**	**3626**	**290**	**1999**	**999**	**10555**	**598**	**8813**
41304	764	2747	1666	1208	109	1127	548	2447	189	1687
38457	471	2685	1333	991	42	414	175	2630	147	2062
43472	442	2165	1330	737	103	258	135	2800	155	1862
9678	95	933	475	296	17	85	34	995	41	733
19204	39	585	483	176	12	43	11	930	29	865
13790	13	25	2	12	1	1	4	94	2	194
73584	44	615	124	205	6	14	22	652	31	1315
13882	34	128	9	1		57	70	7	4	95
6819	**138**	**2530**	**906**	**616**	**29**	**296**	**89**	**1173**	**132**	**2688**
1562	8	466	151	156	3	72	8	258	21	454
4396	87	1231	636	407	22	189	52	750	98	1822
17	2	577	5				1			3
844	41	256	114	53	4	35	28	165	13	409
38663	**3**	**227**	**30**	**56**	**1**	**20**	**5**	**321**	**5**	**1050**
19885		136	20	42	1	5	2	157	5	634
11086	2	77	5	14		15	3	120		323
7692	1	14	5					44		93
17604	**21**	**2621**	**173**	**105**		**10**	**30**	**1791**	**9**	**1809**
16473	17	1078	166	87		7	3	1736	9	1627
311	4	1536	7	18		1	27	49		116
820		7				2		6		66
141054	**172**	**6761**	**613**	**716**	**8**	**2398**	**920**	**3239**	**61**	**8281**
60979	101	1547	381	304	3	152	100	1345	27	2582
20855	20	415	66	105	5	37	62	222	13	1434
16786	2	319	38	99		4	31	170	3	1852
7596	33	119	29	107		21	8	172	13	844
13242	8	1773	68	70		645	449	1157	4	687
20682	5	2560	22	19		496	177	123	1	672
914	3	28	9	12		1043	93	50		210

3-7 续表 1

单位：人

地　　区	Region	合　计 Total	#少数民族 Minority Nationalities	维吾尔族 Uygur	汉　族 Han	哈萨克族 Kazak
伊犁哈萨克自治州	**Ili Kazak Autonomous Prefecture**	**4598423**	**2632623**	**767523**	**1965800**	**1210533**
伊犁州直属县(市)	**Counties (Cities) Direct Under Ili Prefecture**	**2884689**	**1793521**	**715883**	**1091168**	**599881**
伊宁市	Yining [Gulja] City	503944	322828	243232	181116	24033
奎屯市	Kuytun City	307457	16131	1003	291326	5217
伊宁县	Yining [Gulja] County	426834	354233	195546	72601	52331
察布查尔锡伯自治县	Qapqal Xibe Autonomous County	192961	127244	54126	65717	39191
霍城县	Huocheng [Korgas] County	404156	232506	87840	171650	35601
巩留县	Gongliu [Tokkuztara] County	201062	142505	44688	58557	58203
新源县	Xinyuan [Kunes] County	311569	198237	31266	113332	141171
昭苏县	Zhaosu [Mongolkure] County	184616	133004	18018	51612	89164
特克斯县	Tekes County	167824	131643	19044	36181	71683
尼勒克县	Nilka County	184266	135190	21120	49076	83287
塔城地区	**Tacheng [Tarbagatai] Administrative Offices**	**1044843**	**445798**	**41878**	**599045**	**264421**
塔城市	Tacheng [Qoqek] City	170441	62684	5122	107757	26723
乌苏市	Usu City	227711	82345	16877	145366	22614
额敏县	Emin [Dorbiljin] County	217925	99997	8084	117928	74823
沙湾县	Shawan County	216086	69720	9299	146366	36709
托里县	Toli County	100179	73655	1268	26524	70376
裕民县	Yumin [Qagantokay] County	59121	23753	181	35368	18365
和布克赛尔蒙古自治县	Hoboksar Mongol Autonomous County	53380	33644	1047	19736	14811
阿勒泰地区	**Altay Administrative Offices**	**668891**	**393304**	**9762**	**275587**	**346231**
阿勒泰市	Altay City	234845	95487	5067	139358	78368
布尔津县	Burqin County	72157	50495	1032	21662	41498
富蕴县	Fuyun [Koktokay] County	95307	74134	1982	21173	69304
福海县	Fuhai [Burultokay] County	75436	34009	536	41427	30078
哈巴河县	Habahe [Kaba] County	87470	61093	370	26377	53228
青河县	Qinghe [Qinggil] County	64273	52351	573	11922	49143
吉木乃县	Jemnay County	39403	25735	202	13668	24612
博尔塔拉蒙古自治州	**Bortala Mongol Autonomous Prefecture**	**487304**	**166207**	**65349**	**321097**	**48143**
博乐市	Bole [Bortala] City	266887	88504	43072	178383	20103
精河县	Jinghe [Jing] County	144423	45612	18773	98811	13802
温泉县	Wenquan [Araxang] County	75994	32091	3504	43903	14238
巴音郭楞蒙古自治州	**Bayangol Mongol Autonomous Prefecture**	**1366011**	**579585**	**449781**	**786426**	**1321**
库尔勒市	Korla City	541951	160112	139731	381839	106
轮台县	Luntai [Bugur] County	116082	88201	87597	27881	8
尉犁县	Yuli [Lopnur] County	109744	35354	34279	74390	18
若羌县	Ruoqiang [Qarkilik] County	33565	14437	12838	19128	5
且末县	Qiemo [Qarqan] County	65448	48470	48153	16978	3
焉耆回族自治县	Yanji Hui Autonomous County	168663	95279	55330	73384	43
和静县	Hejing County	194212	90876	50146	103336	1087
和硕县	Hoxud County	75292	25123	11724	50169	33
博湖县	Bohu [Bagrax] County	61054	21733	9983	39321	18

Continued

(person)

回族 Hui	柯尔克孜族 Kirgiz	蒙古族 Mongolian	锡伯族 Xibo	俄罗斯族 Russion	塔吉克族 Tajik	乌孜别克族 Uzbek	塔塔尔族 Tatar	满族 Manchu	达斡尔族 Daur	其它 Others
412519	**20907**	**74958**	**34363**	**5503**	**174**	**7625**	**2769**	**5017**	**5978**	**84754**
308571	**18694**	**34144**	**32282**	**1564**	**168**	**7035**	**1252**	**3847**	**610**	**69590**
36836	635	1891	4847	779	86	4277	507	1974	165	3566
6744	25	1098	273	99	2	17	5	452	39	1157
71444	344	290	268	25	5	690	60	363	6	32861
10327	308	176	20576	102		136	12	95	16	2179
83780	296	756	3263	244	4	209	118	327	331	19737
30839	466	2284	1617	99		148	108	292	6	3755
21801	444	174	429	108	7	661	147	143	5	1881
5168	5286	13889	82	49	9	383	270	35	1	650
23078	10215	4561	230	5	14	262	20	77	2	2452
18554	675	9025	697	54	41	252	5	89	39	1352
80077	**2151**	**34406**	**1990**	**3506**	**5**	**405**	**505**	**814**	**5350**	**10290**
13201	1789	1824	1520	2379	1	161	257	236	5167	4304
32795	4	8308	161	136	1	56	32	121	33	1207
7339	304	6194	91	585		119	64	153	60	2181
21424	11	478	40	117	2	23	19	187	22	1389
1102	18	528	63	19	1	23	43	51	9	154
3704	5	146	59	236			10	29	37	981
512	20	16928	56	34		23	80	37	22	74
23871	**62**	**6408**	**91**	**433**	**1**	**185**	**1012**	**356**	**18**	**4874**
6861	36	2820	44	197	1	127	302	189	5	1470
4526	6	1736	13	143		3	325	45	3	1165
1920	13	299	9	43		15	88	43	5	413
2558		202	8	32			51	33	3	508
6029	4	439	6			9	47	8		953
1259		874	9	12		30	189	10		252
718	3	38	2	6		1	10	28	2	113
19455	**89**	**28565**	**408**	**189**	**4**	**173**	**19**	**367**	**31**	**3415**
10287	31	12926	286	145	4	101	14	278	13	1244
6076	24	5232	65	41		42	4	59		1494
3092	34	10407	57	3		30	1	30	18	677
68927	**275**	**49788**	**206**	**257**	**4**	**132**	**1**	**1343**	**41**	**7509**
11078	10	4993	179	221	4	78	1	1067	15	2629
387	3	50	7	3		6		18		122
570		31	2	9		15		32	6	392
1076	1	20	1					9		487
193		17	2			8		6		88
35331	95	3503	1	3		19		86	18	850
7014	148	30783	11	13		6		89	2	1577
6656	6	5924	2	8				11		759
6622	12	4467	1					25		605

3-7 续表 2

单位：人

地　区	Region	合　计 Total	#少数民族 Minority Nationalities	维吾尔族 Uygur	汉　族 Han	哈萨克族 Kazak
阿克苏地区	**Aksu Administrative Offices**	**2389717**	**1906553**	**1873808**	**483164**	**158**
阿克苏市	Aksu City	496184	261187	252653	234997	39
温宿县	Wensu [Onsu] County	245676	191737	185651	53939	9
库车县	Kuqa County	469339	414633	411453	54706	52
沙雅县	Xayar County	258613	217389	214680	41224	6
新和县	Xinhe [Toksu] County	169647	159050	158503	10597	12
拜城县	Baicheng [Bay] County	230948	203387	201146	27561	17
乌什县	Wushi [Uxturpan] County	217456	204984	197692	12472	13
阿瓦提县	Awat County	252689	206474	204394	46215	10
柯坪县	Kalpin County	49165	47712	47636	1453	
克孜勒苏柯尔克孜自治州	**Kizilsu Kirgiz Autonomous Prefecture**	**554281**	**512812**	**354522**	**41469**	**141**
阿图什市	Artux City	250882	228157	198217	22725	60
阿克陶县	Akto County	202329	194478	145463	7851	15
阿合奇县	Akqi County	58409	51661	9644	6748	32
乌恰县	Wuqia [Ulugqat] County	42661	38516	1198	4145	34
喀什地区	**Kashgar [Kaxgar] Administrative Offices**	**4102044**	**3817994**	**3756475**	**284050**	**246**
喀什市	Kashgar [Kaxgar] City	480202	398321	393791	81881	137
疏附县	Shufu County	335781	330192	329376	5589	7
疏勒县	Shule County	343262	319949	319036	23313	
英吉沙县	Yengisar County	273987	269244	268472	4743	8
泽普县	Zepu [Poskam] County	208863	172711	166714	36152	13
莎车县	Shache [Yarkant] County	813782	786389	779251	27393	11
叶城县	Yecheng [Kagilik] County	457122	434437	428886	22685	30
麦盖提县	Makit County	256055	205835	204723	50220	9
岳普湖县	Yopurga County	160048	149521	149299	10527	1
伽师县	Jiashi [Payzawat] County	398622	390223	389925	8399	11
巴楚县	Bachu [Maralbexi] County	336195	325604	324967	10591	8
塔什库尔干塔吉克自治县	Taxkorgan Tajik Autonomous County	38125	35568	2035	2557	11
和田地区	**Hotan Administrative Offices**	**2075811**	**2003345**	**1998831**	**72466**	**80**
和田市	Hotan City	321366	284779	283426	36587	21
和田县	Hotan County	271541	269733	269410	1808	2
墨玉县	Moyu [Karakax] County	531124	516387	516190	14737	4
皮山县	Pishan [Guma] County	265564	261821	259756	3743	2
洛浦县	Lop County	240649	236315	236187	4334	32
策勒县	Qira County	155281	152567	152464	2714	2
于田县	Yutian [Keriya] County	252716	247744	247458	4972	16
民丰县	Minfeng [Niya] County	37570	33999	33940	3571	1
自治区直辖县级市	**Municpality Country-LevelCity directly under the Central Govern-ment**					
石河子市	Shihezi City	624435	38372	8525	586063	4539
阿拉尔市	Aral City	190978	17496	10947	173482	501
图木舒克市	Tumxuk City	160512	102718	101531	57794	1
五家渠市	Wujiaqu City	91018	3260	92	87758	107

Continued

(person)

回 族 Hui	柯尔克孜族 Kirgiz	蒙古族 Mongolian	锡伯族 Xibo	俄罗斯族 Russion	塔吉克族 Tajik	乌孜别克族 Uzbek	塔塔尔族 Tatar	满 族 Manchu	达斡尔族 Daur	其 它 Others
14453	**11231**	**864**	**136**	**125**	**7**	**159**	**13**	**586**		**5013**
4915	213	615	73	62	1	43	1	350		2222
814	4186	41	3		3		4	12		1014
2471	148	73	29	26	2	16		98		265
2171	11	19	7	19		6		26		444
346	4	10	3	13				41		118
903	1139	32	11		1	14	3	24		97
1496	5485	13	7			69	4	6		199
1320	17	57	3	5		11	1	29		627
17	28	4								27
706	**151034**	**85**	**34**	**5**	**5615**	**166**	**27**	**101**		**376**
282	29186	52	16	5	24	18	1	83		213
211	43012	22	6		5555	97	26	1		70
121	41679	9	10		35	51		14		66
92	37157	2	2		1			3		27
6334	**7014**	**672**	**145**	**96**	**40096**	**4358**	**68**	**522**	**15**	**1953**
1607	358	160	73	58	165	1262	24	257	10	419
79	614	4	2			9		3	1	97
325	346	99	3	3	1	13		32		91
63	607	14	3	5	16	22	3	25	2	4
989	547	125	10	11	3761	81	1	51		408
987	1187	105	29	7	2801	1780	30	32	1	168
960	1123	47	6	8	2083	1068	1	42		183
647	4	34	2	1	2	40	7	32		334
102		49	2		2			2		64
56	37	23	5			64	1	31		70
494	4	5	4	2	1	19	1	8	1	90
25	2187	7	6	1	31264			7		25
1617	**901**	**178**	**46**	**8**	**998**	**33**	**9**	**93**		**551**
831	15	87	20	8	7	25	5	59		275
319		1								1
106	1	10	7					8		61
95	882	16	4		987	5				74
41		20	2					6		27
50		8	3		1	1		2		36
151	2	26	10		3			17		61
24	1	10				2	4	1		16
17894	62	879	163	242	20	18	1	931	12	5086
1554	309	317	19	21	8	1		108		3711
578		57	2	6		32		37		474
1857	4	472	20	50		1		180	2	475

3-8 主要年份分民族人口数

Population by Nationality in Main Years

单位：万人 (10 000 persons)

年 份 Year	维吾尔族 Uygur	汉 族 Han	哈萨克族 Kazak	回 族 Hui	柯尔克孜族 Kirgiz	蒙古族 Mongolian	锡伯族 Xibo
1978	555.53	512.90	82.10	53.12	10.40	10.74	2.55
1980	576.46	531.03	87.68	56.56	10.89	11.32	2.59
1985	629.44	534.92	98.72	59.96	12.35	12.33	2.93
1990	724.95	574.66	113.92	68.89	14.44	14.28	3.42
1995	780.00	631.81	123.77	74.76	15.78	15.28	3.82
1996	791.60	643.28	125.70	76.02	16.05	15.54	3.89
1997	802.00	660.13	127.08	77.06	16.27	15.75	3.90
1998	813.95	674.11	128.70	78.20	16.41	15.91	3.95
1999	825.03	687.15	130.45	79.26	16.64	16.13	4.00
2000	852.33	725.08	131.87	83.93	16.47	16.20	4.05
2001	860.56	742.20	131.92	84.42	17.01	16.19	4.13
2002	869.23	759.57	133.35	85.46	17.13	16.38	4.10
2003	882.35	771.10	135.21	86.67	17.37	16.69	4.03
2004	897.67	780.25	138.16	87.63	17.12	16.96	4.08
2005	923.50	795.66	141.39	89.35	17.15	17.17	4.15
2006	941.38	812.16	143.50	90.96	17.59	17.46	4.19
2007	965.06	823.93	148.39	94.30	18.19	17.71	4.24
2008	983.18	836.33	151.05	95.30	18.64	18.10	4.32
2009	1001.98	841.69	151.48	98.04	18.93	17.96	4.28
2010	1017.15	832.29	151.16	98.40	18.92	17.74	4.23
2011	1037.04	844.42	154.26	100.34	19.40	17.89	4.27

年 份 Year	俄罗斯族 Russian	塔吉克族 Tajik	乌孜别克族 Uzbek	塔塔尔族 Tatar	满 族 Manchu	达斡尔族 Daur	其他民族 Others
1978	0.06	2.28	0.77	0.31	0.42	0.41	1.42
1980	0.06	2.41	0.79	0.31	0.50	0.40	2.24
1985	0.43	2.89	0.93	0.33	0.95	0.48	4.49
1990	0.75	3.44	1.14	0.40	1.66	0.56	6.65
1995	0.90	3.82	1.33	0.47	1.99	0.62	7.00
1996	0.92	3.89	1.35	0.47	2.05	0.63	7.90
1997	0.92	3.90	1.35	0.46	2.06	0.63	6.56
1998	0.93	3.96	1.37	0.47	2.09	0.64	6.66
1999	0.94	4.01	1.39	0.48	2.12	0.65	6.75
2000	1.09	4.09	1.36	0.48	2.31	0.66	9.48
2001	1.08	4.12	1.37	0.47	2.30	0.67	9.75
2002	1.12	4.07	1.39	0.48	2.35	0.67	9.89
2003	1.11	4.09	1.46	0.49	2.39	0.67	10.32
2004	1.13	4.35	1.42	0.47	2.41	0.67	10.79
2005	1.12	4.40	1.51	0.47	2.46	0.65	11.37
2006	1.14	4.47	1.60	0.47	2.52	0.66	11.91
2007	1.16	4.48	1.61	0.47	2.56	0.67	12.42
2008	1.16	4.54	1.69	0.49	2.59	0.68	12.74
2009	1.17	4.72	1.67	0.49	2.62	0.69	12.91
2010	1.16	4.69	1.70	0.49	2.61	0.67	13.23
2011	1.16	4.73	1.74	0.49	2.64	0.69	13.59

3-9 各地、州、市、县(市)按城镇、乡村和农业、非农业分人口数

Population of Urban and Rural, Agriculture and Non-Agriculture by Prefecture, Autonomous Prefecture, City and County

单位：万人　　(2011 年)　　(10 000 persons)

地区	Region	城镇人口 Urban Population	#非农业人口 Non-agri-cultural Population	乡村人口 Rural Population	农业人口 Agricul-tural Population	非农业人口 Non-agri-cultural Population
乌鲁木齐市	**Urumqi City**	**242.24**	**182.42**	**7.11**	**66.05**	**183.30**
天山区	Tianshan District	55.79	46.63		9.16	46.63
沙依巴克区	Shayibak District	52.74	45.04		7.70	45.04
新市区	Xinshi District	52.88	37.16		15.72	37.16
水磨沟区	Shui Mogou Distric	28.20	19.01		9.19	19.01
头屯河区	Tou Tunhe District	21.95	17.56		4.39	17.56
达坂城区	Da Bancheng District	3.43	1.77	1.01	2.56	1.88
米东区	Midong District	25.91	14.78	1.66	12.58	14.99
乌鲁木齐县	Urumqi County	1.34	0.47	4.44	4.75	1.03
克拉玛依市	**Karamay City**	**28.23**	**27.84**		**0.39**	**27.84**
独山子区	Dushanzi District	5.60	5.60			5.60
克拉玛依区	Karamay District	18.26	18.06		0.20	18.06
乌尔河区	Urhe District	0.23	0.07		0.16	0.07
白碱滩区	Bai Jiantan District	4.14	4.11		0.03	4.11
吐鲁番地区	**Turpan Administrative Offices**	**45.53**	**15.93**	**17.66**	**45.13**	**18.06**
吐鲁番市	Turpan City	28.35	8.60		19.75	8.60
鄯善县	Shanshan [Piqan] County	14.75	5.14	8.20	16.94	6.01
托克逊县	Toksun County	2.43	2.19	9.46	8.44	3.45
哈密地区	**Hami [Kumul] Administrative Offices**	**51.58**	**32.02**	**6.81**	**24.42**	**33.97**
哈密市	Hami [Kumul] City	45.79	29.78		16.01	29.78
巴里坤哈萨克自治县	Barkol Kazak Autonomous County	4.73	1.58	5.59	7.03	3.29
伊吾县	Yiwu [Araturuk] County	1.06	0.66	1.22	1.38	0.90
昌吉回族自治州	**Changji Hui Autonomous Prefecture**	**115.54**	**67.03**	**23.92**	**70.11**	**69.35**
昌吉市	Changji City	36.32	23.43		12.89	23.43
阜康市	Fukang City	14.71	9.24	2.05	7.16	9.60
呼图壁县	Hutubi County	20.27	11.99	1.54	9.12	12.69
玛纳斯县	Manas County	14.15	7.31	3.46	9.96	7.65
奇台县	Qitai County	16.30	8.60	7.67	15.03	8.94
吉木萨尔县	Jimsar County	9.87	4.58	4.19	9.32	4.74
木垒哈萨克自治县	Mori Kazak Autonomous County	3.92	1.88	5.01	6.63	2.30

注：1.各地、州、市城镇人口、乡村人口为 2011 年公安年报按行政建制划分的人口数。
2.各地、州、市农业人口数均含未落常住户口人员。

Note: a) Population of urban and rural by prefecture,Autonomous prefecture,city and county come from Annual Report on Public Security in 2011.
b) Population of agriculture by Prefecture,Autonomous prefecture,city and county included population of without habitual residence.

3-9 续表 1 Continued

单位：万人 (10 000 persons)

地　　区	Region	城镇人口 Urban Population	#非农业人口 Non-agri-cultural Population	乡村人口 Rural Population	农业人口 Agricul-tural Population	非农业人口 Non-agri-cultural Population
伊犁哈萨克自治州	**Ili Kazak Autonomous Prefecture**	**269.89**	**173.08**	**189.95**	**251.37**	**208.47**
伊犁州直属县(市)	**Counties (Cities) Direct Under Ili Prefecture**	**156.30**	**98.22**	**132.17**	**168.37**	**120.10**
伊宁市	Yining [Gulja] City	50.39	33.61		16.78	33.61
奎屯市	Kuytun City	30.75	27.73		3.02	27.73
伊宁县	Yining [Gulja] County	8.82	4.74	33.86	35.62	7.06
察布查尔锡伯自治县	Qapqal Xibe Autonomous County	6.50	4.81	12.80	12.87	6.43
霍城县	Huocheng [Korgas] County	21.26	5.74	19.16	25.17	15.25
巩留县	Gongliu [Tokkuztara] County	3.92	3.05	16.18	15.79	4.31
新源县	Xinyuan [Kunes] County	20.73	7.27	10.43	22.33	8.83
昭苏县	Zhaosu [Mongolkure] County	5.74	4.93	12.72	11.36	7.10
特克斯县	Tekes County	4.09	3.09	12.69	11.99	4.79
尼勒克县	Nilka County	4.10	3.25	14.33	13.44	4.99
塔城地区	**Tacheng [Tarbagatai] Administrative Offices**	**76.67**	**47.55**	**27.81**	**49.34**	**55.14**
塔城市	Tacheng [Qoqek] City	17.05	10.69		6.36	10.69
乌苏市	Usu City	22.77	8.01		14.76	8.01
额敏县	Emin [Dorbiljin] County	9.52	9.08	12.27	8.75	13.04
沙湾县	Shawan County	18.45	12.28	3.16	8.24	13.37
托里县	Toli County	4.43	3.57	5.58	5.90	4.11
裕民县	Yumin [Qagantokay] County	2.02	1.96	3.89	2.94	2.97
和布克赛尔蒙古自治县	Hoboksar Mongol Autonomous County	2.43	1.96	2.91	2.39	2.95
阿勒泰地区	**Altay Administrative Offices**	**36.92**	**27.31**	**29.97**	**33.66**	**33.23**
阿勒泰市	Altay City	23.48	15.24		8.24	15.24
布尔津县	Burqin County	2.01	1.93	5.21	4.48	2.74
富蕴县	Fuyun [Koktokay] County	3.25	2.87	6.28	5.56	3.97
福海县	Fuhai [Burultokay] County	2.96	2.79	4.58	3.63	3.91
哈巴河县	Habahe [Kaba] County	1.93	1.79	6.82	5.67	3.08
青河县	Qinghe [Qinggil] County	1.93	1.52	4.50	4.12	2.31
吉木乃县	Jemnay County	1.36	1.17	2.58	1.96	1.98
博尔塔拉蒙古自治州	**Bortala Mongol Autonomous Prefecture**	**40.82**	**24.32**	**7.91**	**22.21**	**26.52**
博乐市	Bole [Bortala] City	26.69	16.44		10.25	16.44
精河县	Jinghe [Jing] County	9.59	4.63	4.85	8.17	6.27
温泉县	Wenquan [Araxang] County	4.54	3.25	3.06	3.79	3.81
巴音郭楞蒙古自治州	**Bayangol Mongol Autonomous Prefecture**	**108.07**	**61.84**	**28.53**	**71.44**	**65.16**
库尔勒市	Korla City	54.20	33.89		20.31	33.89
轮台县	Luntai [Bugur] County	7.04	2.38	4.57	8.78	2.83
尉犁县	Yuli [Lopnur] County	6.19	5.00	4.78	5.41	5.56
若羌县	Ruoqiang [Qarkilik] County	1.73	1.39	1.63	1.71	1.65
且末县	Qiemo [Qarqan] County	2.03	1.64	4.51	4.28	2.26
焉耆回族自治县	Yanji Hui Autonomous County	11.91	5.14	4.96	11.18	5.69
和静县	Hejing County	17.42	8.03	2.00	11.07	8.35
和硕县	Hoxud County	4.41	2.76	3.12	4.42	3.11
博湖县	Bohu [Bagrax] County	3.14	1.61	2.96	4.28	1.82

3-9 续表 2 Continued

单位：万人 (10 000 persons)

地　区	Region	城镇人口 Urban Population	#非农业人口 Non-agri-cultural Population	乡村人口 Rural Population	农业人口 Agricul-tural Population	非农业人口 Non-agri-cultural Population
阿克苏地区	**Aksu Administrative Offices**	**150.62**	**68.22**	**88.35**	**163.98**	**74.99**
阿克苏市	Aksu City	49.62	26.77		22.85	26.77
温宿县	Wensu [Onsu] County	16.41	6.05	8.16	17.44	7.13
库车县	Kuqa County	33.52	15.06	13.41	30.42	16.51
沙雅县	Xayar County	18.51	5.18	7.35	20.36	5.50
新和县	Xinhe [Toksu] County	5.30	2.68	11.66	13.52	3.44
拜城县	Baicheng [Bay] County	8.77	4.24	14.32	18.06	5.03
乌什县	Wushi [Uxturpan] County	3.80	3.03	17.95	17.99	3.76
阿瓦提县	Awat County	13.82	4.53	11.45	19.80	5.47
柯坪县	Kalpin County	0.87	0.68	4.05	3.54	1.38
克孜勒苏柯尔克孜自治州	**Kizilsu Kirgiz Autonomous Prefecture**	**32.29**	**13.73**	**23.14**	**38.95**	**16.48**
阿图什市	Artux City	25.09	8.59		16.50	8.59
阿克陶县	Akto County	4.12	2.33	16.11	16.63	3.60
阿合奇县	Akqi County	1.25	0.98	3.02	2.58	1.69
乌恰县	Wuqia [Ulugqat] County	1.83	1.83	4.01	3.24	2.60
喀什地区	**Kashgar [Kaxgar] Administrative Offices**	**145.20**	**79.23**	**265.00**	**317.32**	**92.88**
喀什市	Kashgar [Kaxgar] City	48.02	28.66		19.36	28.66
疏附县	Shufu County	3.21	2.04	30.37	30.13	3.45
疏勒县	Shule County	10.59	3.80	23.74	29.30	5.03
英吉沙县	Yengisar County	4.01	3.09	23.38	23.24	4.15
泽普县	Zepu [Poskam] County	5.81	4.83	15.08	14.81	6.08
莎车县	Shache [Yarkant] County	36.13	10.86	45.25	68.66	12.72
叶城县	Yecheng [Kagilik] County	7.53	7.17	38.18	37.06	8.65
麦盖提县	Makit County	6.91	6.57	18.70	17.79	7.82
岳普湖县	Yopurga County	4.57	2.38	11.43	12.65	3.35
伽师县	Jiashi [Payzawat] County	4.59	3.20	35.27	35.21	4.65
巴楚县	Bachu [Maralbexi] County	12.26	5.47	21.36	26.46	7.16
塔什库尔干塔吉克自治县	Taxkorgan Tajik Autonomous County	1.57	1.16	2.24	2.65	1.16
和田地区	**Hotan Administrative Offices**	**68.29**	**27.24**	**139.29**	**172.57**	**35.01**
和田市	Hotan City	32.14	13.80		18.34	13.80
和田县	Hotan County	5.81	0.37	21.34	25.83	1.32
墨玉县	Moyu [Karakax] County	7.48	2.75	45.63	48.48	4.63
皮山县	Pishan [Guma] County	7.53	4.07	19.03	20.81	5.75
洛浦县	Lop County	3.93	1.66	20.14	21.36	2.71
策勒县	Qira County	3.09	1.63	12.43	13.15	2.37
于田县	Yutian [Keriya] County	6.84	2.19	18.43	21.91	3.36
民丰县	Minfeng [Niya] County	1.47	0.77	2.29	2.69	1.07
自治区直辖县级市	**Municpality Country-LevelCity directly under the Central Govern-ment**	**106.69**	**91.56**		**15.13**	**91.56**
石河子市	Shihezi City	62.44	56.86		5.58	56.86
阿拉尔市	Aral City	19.10	11.99		7.11	11.99
图木舒克市	Tumxuk City	16.05	13.99		2.06	13.99
五家渠市	Wujiaqu City	9.10	8.72		0.38	8.72

3-10 各地、州、市采取各种避孕措施情况

Condition of Adopting Various Contraceptions by Prefecture, Autonomous Prefecture, City and County

单位：%　　(2011 年)　　(%)

地　区	Region	男性绝育 Masculine Sterilization	女性绝育 Female Sterilization	宫内节育器 IUD Intrauterine Device	皮下埋植 Subdermal Implant
总　计	**Total**	**0.07**	**5.57**	**79.07**	**0.31**
城　镇	Urban	0.10	3.12	76.52	0.21
农　村	Rural	0.06	6.96	80.51	0.37
乌鲁木齐市	Urumqi City	0.09	3.06	57.03	0.24
克拉玛依市	Karamay City	0.24	4.82	62.25	0.39
吐鲁番地区	Turpan Administrative Offices		2.09	86.83	0.37
哈密地区	Hami [Kumul] Administrative Offices	0.01	3.70	73.63	0.80
昌吉回族自治州	Changji Hui Autonomous Prefecture	0.01	6.45	78.15	0.37
伊犁州直属县(市)	Counties (Cities) Direct Under Ili Prefecture	0.18	4.38	78.65	0.18
塔城地区	Tacheng [Tarbagatai] Administrative Offices		7.67	76.91	1.08
阿勒泰地区	Altay Administrative Offices		3.28	77.25	0.47
博尔塔拉蒙古自治州	Bortala Mongol Autonomous Prefecture		8.04	73.04	0.75
巴音郭楞蒙古自治州	Bayangol Mongol Autonomous Prefecture		7.19	80.40	0.13
阿克苏地区	Aksu Administrative Offices	0.11	7.42	84.25	0.53
克孜勒苏柯尔克孜自治州	Kizilsu Kirgiz Autonomous Prefecture	0.62	2.83	88.57	0.10
喀什地区	Kashgar [Kaxgar] Administrative Offices	0.01	4.31	90.88	0.12
和田地区	Hotan Administrative Offices		10.49	83.93	0.02

地　区	Region	口服药及注射针 Medicine and Entry Needle	避孕套 Contraceptives	外用药 Drug for Exterior Use	其他 Other
总　计	**Total**	**0.55**	**13.48**	**0.74**	**0.07**
城　镇	Urban	0.59	18.96	0.36	0.10
农　村	Rural	0.53	10.39	0.96	0.06
乌鲁木齐市	Urumqi City	0.87	38.34	0.22	0.09
克拉玛依市	Karamay City	0.56	31.04	0.36	0.24
吐鲁番地区	Turpan Administrative Offices	0.72	9.69	0.24	
哈密地区	Hami [Kumul] Administrative Offices	0.45	21.12	0.20	0.01
昌吉回族自治州	Changji Hui Autonomous Prefecture	0.41	14.30	0.11	0.01
伊犁州直属县(市)	Counties (Cities) Direct Under Ili Prefecture	0.40	15.84	0.21	0.18
塔城地区	Tacheng [Tarbagatai] Administrative Offices	0.35	13.63	0.07	
阿勒泰地区	Altay Administrative Offices	0.28	18.48	0.11	
博尔塔拉蒙古自治州	Bortala Mongol Autonomous Prefecture	0.54	16.85	0.25	
巴音郭楞蒙古自治州	Bayangol Mongol Autonomous Prefecture	0.18	11.23	0.10	
阿克苏地区	Aksu Administrative Offices	1.02	5.11	1.33	0.11
克孜勒苏柯尔克孜自治州	Kizilsu Kirgiz Autonomous Prefecture	1.55	4.06	2.26	0.62
喀什地区	Kashgar [Kaxgar] Administrative Offices	0.53	2.18	1.90	0.01
和田地区	Hotan Administrative Offices	0.10	4.31	1.12	

注：表 3-10、3-11 根据自治区计生委 2011 年计划生育统计年报整理，不包括兵团。
Note: In table 3-10 and 3-11,data are compiled on statistic annals of the family planning in Xinjiang Uygur Autonomous Region in 2011.

3-11 各地、州、市计划生育及领证情况

Family Planning and Certificate Receiving by Prefecture, Autonomous Prefecture and City

(2011 年)

地　　区	Region	计划生育率 (%) Family Planning Rate (%)	领证率 (%) Coverage of One-child Certificate (%)	领取计划生育证人数 (人) Number of Persons Receiving Certificates of Honor (person)	领取独生子女证人数 (人) Number of Married Couples with One-child Certificate (person)
总　计	**Total**	**99.74**	**34.93**	**814002**	**619914**
城　镇	Urban	99.64	52.99	547572	215623
农　村	Rural	99.77	25.17	266430	404291
乌鲁木齐市	Urumqi City	99.81	48.76	192302	50783
克拉玛依市	Karamay City	99.82	65.72	45529	9733
吐鲁番地区	Turpan Administrative Offices	99.97	29.66	17353	24627
哈密地区	Hami [Kumul] Administrative Offices	99.98	61.26	48732	12645
昌吉回族自治州	Changji Hui Autonomous Prefecture	99.77	45.91	113790	23506
伊犁州直属县(市)	Counties (Cities) Direct Under Ili Prefecture	99.84	33.35	75507	102042
塔城地区	Tacheng [Tarbagatai] Administrative Offices	99.81	36.59	45700	25931
阿勒泰地区	Altay Administrative Offices	99.77	42.95	22050	29135
博尔塔拉蒙古自治州	Bortala Mongol Autonomous Prefecture	99.78	40.18	20592	11173
巴音郭楞蒙古自治州	Bayangol Mongol Autonomous Prefecture	99.12	33.95	55598	45917
阿克苏地区	Aksu Administrative Offices	99.83	25.30	48038	75081
克孜勒苏柯尔克孜自治州	Kizilsu Kirgiz Autonomous Prefecture	99.90	35.22	9554	25255
喀什地区	Kashgar [Kaxgar] Administrative Offices	99.69	23.63	70835	112707
和田地区	Hotan Administrative Offices	99.72	30.37	48422	71379

3-12 主要年份新疆生产建设兵团人口情况

Population of Xinjiang Production and Construction Group in Main Years

单位：人 (person)

年　份 Year	总人口 Total Population	男 Male	女 Female	农业人口 Agricultural Population	非农业人口 Non-Agricultural Population	出生人口 Birth Population	死亡人口 Death Population	出生率 (‰) Birth Rate (‰)	死亡率 (‰) Death Rate (‰)	自然增长率 (‰) Natural Growth Rate (‰)
1978	2119835	1090674	1029161			32749	6203	16.56	3.14	13.42
1980	2200755	1127050	1073705			26972	7162	12.27	3.26	9.01
1985	2222350	1142630	1079720	1182415	1039935	16893	7977	7.55	3.57	3.98
1990	2143528	1110475	1033053	1132435	1044093	24589	9305	11.48	4.35	7.13
1995	2287896	1194166	1093730	1230151	1057745	22519	10044	9.98	4.45	5.53
2000	2427920	1272719	1155201	1379913	1048007	22674	12525	9.40	5.20	4.20
2001	2453575	1289954	1163621	1325998	1127577	19061	9014	7.80	3.70	4.10
2002	2501189	1311750	1189439	1355526	1145663	18179	9842	7.37	3.99	3.38
2003	2542170	1330666	1211504	1377224	1164946	17218	9914	6.84	3.94	2.90
2004	2563837	1341213	1222624	1413197	1150640	15860	9864	6.21	3.86	2.35
2005	2569756	1346901	1222855	1332458	1237298	16381	11934	6.38	4.65	1.73
2006	2579435	1352541	1226894	1312908	1266527	14687	11858	5.71	4.61	1.10
2007	2584732	1353053	1231679	1316590	1268142	13289	10131	5.15	3.92	1.23
2008	2573077	1344445	1228632	1289450	1283627	14612	11183	5.67	4.34	1.33
2009	2573145	1346229	1226918	1296755	1276390	14447	11285	5.61	4.39	1.22
2010	2607184	1376580	1230604			19205	10572	6.30	4.08	2.22
2011	2613724	1372606	1241118	1244796	1368928	13838	12198	5.33	4.70	0.63

3-13 按县、市分列的团场户数、人口数

Household and Population of Regiment Farms by City and County

(2011 年)

团场	Regiment Farm	户数(户) Number of Households (household)	人口数(人) Population (person)
总计	**Total**	**625304**	**1803533**
乌鲁木齐市	**Urumqi City**	**26618**	**81793**
市辖区	Areas under Municipality	17699	55948
104 团	No.104 Regiment Farm	6641	20883
三坪农场	Sanping Farm	3319	11223
五一农场	May Ist Farm	4261	11932
头屯河农场	Tou Tunhe Farm	3478	11910
米东新区	Miquan County	6918	19909
102 团	No.102 Regiment Farm	6918	19909
乌鲁木齐县	Urumqi County	2001	5936
西山农场	Xishan Farm	2001	5936
克拉玛依市	**Karamay City**	**6827**	**19046**
136 团	No.136 Regiment Farm	3566	10175
137 团	No.137 Regiment Farm	3261	8871
石河子市	**Shihezi City**	**20173**	**56310**
152 团	No.152 Regiment Farm	2895	8672
石河子总场	General Shihezi Farm	17278	47638
吐鲁番地区	**Turpan Administrative Offices**	**1692**	**6268**
吐鲁番市	Turpan City	1692	6268
221 团	No.221 Regiment Farm	1692	6268
哈密地区	**Hami [Kumul] Administrative Offices**	**24732**	**76398**
哈密市	Hami [Kumul] City	20439	62543
红星一场	Red Star No.1 Farm	3369	8395
红星二场	Red Star No.2 Farm	2892	6514
红星四场	Red Star No.4 Farm	2520	7712
黄田农场	Huangtian Farm	3037	10569
火箭农场	Huojian Farm	5285	18656
柳树泉农场	Liu Shuquan Farm	3336	10697
巴里坤哈萨克自治县	Barkol Kazak AutonomousCounty	3585	11442
红山农场	Hongshan Farm	3585	11442
伊吾县	Yiwu [Araturuk] County	708	2413
淖毛湖农场	Zhuo Maohu Farm	708	2413
昌吉回族自治州	**Changji Hui Autonomous Prefecture**	**114796**	**301948**
昌吉市	Changji City	19200	48878
101 团	No.101 Regiment Farm	3752	10906
103 团	No.103 Regiment Farm	6811	15236
共青团农场	Communist League Farm	3102	8828
军户农场	Junhu Farm	5535	13908
呼图壁县	Hutubi County	29570	77719
105 团	No.105 Regiment Farm	4554	13628
106 团	No.106 Regiment Farm	2961	6088
芳草湖农场	Fang Caohu Farm	22055	58003
玛纳斯县	Manas County	40890	110178
147 团	No.147 Regiment Farm	5864	15346
148 团	No.148 Regiment Farm	9954	26497
149 团	No.149 Regiment Farm	6843	17784
150 团	No.150 Regiment Farm	5499	14628
新湖农场	Xinhu Farm	12730	35923
奇台县	Qitai County	11395	30864
奇台农场	Qitai Farm	10520	27352
北塔山牧场	Bei Tashan Ranch	875	3512
阜康市	Fukang City	8609	21720
222 团	No.222 Regiment Farm	4427	10882
土墩子农场	Tu Dunzi Farm	2040	5161
六运湖农场	Liu Yunhu Farm	2142	5677
吉木萨尔县	Jimsar County	5132	12589
红旗农场	Red Flag Farm	5132	12589
伊犁哈萨克自治州	**Ili Kazak Autonomous Prefecture**	**226572**	**611498**
伊犁州直属县(市)	**Counties (Cities) Direct UnderIli Prefecture**	**70306**	**197887**
奎屯市	Kuytun City	8999	20231
131 团	No.131 Regiment Farm	8999	20231
伊宁县	Yining [Gulja] County	4186	10332
70 团	No.70 Regiment Farm	4186	10332
察布查尔锡伯自治县	Qapqal Xibe Autonomous County	8900	27037
67 团	No.67 Regiment Farm	3649	12595
68 团	No.68 Regiment Farm	3215	8271
69 团	No.69 Regiment Farm	2036	6171
霍城县	Huocheng [Korgas] County	27452	80999
61 团	No.61 Regiment Farm	3955	10987
62 团	No.62 Regiment Farm	4912	15729
63 团	No.63 Regiment Farm	3243	8617
64 团	No.64 Regiment Farm	6876	21108

注：总计中包括农一师的阿拉尔农场、南口农场和幸福城农场，三个农场共计 7107 户、23246 人。
Note: Total in this table includes Alaer,Nankou and Xinfu farms of division 1,there are 7107 households and 23246 persons in this three farms.

3-13 续表 1 Continued

团 场	Regiment Farm	户数(户) Number of Households (household)	人口数(人) Population (person)	团 场	Regiment Farm	户数(户) Number of Households (household)	人口数(人) Population (person)
66 团	No.66 Regiment Farm	8466	24558	133 团	No.133 Regiment Farm	8365	22661
巩留县	Gongliu [Tokkuztara] County	2787	7145	134 团	No.134 Regiment Farm	7090	18604
73 团	No.73 Regiment Farm	2787	7145	141 团	No.141 Regiment Farm	4011	10312
新源县	Xinyuan [Kunes] County	7744	21306	142 团	No.142 Regiment Farm	10616	28717
71 团	No.71 Regiment Farm	3704	10987	143 团	No.143 Regiment Farm	13981	32546
72 团	No.72 Regiment Farm	4040	10319	144 团	No.144 Regiment Farm	5156	12626
昭苏县	Zhaosu [Mongolkure] County	7234	21238	托里县	Toli County	811	2777
74 团	No.74 Regiment Farm	1197	3190	170 团	No.170 Regiment Farm	811	2777
75 团	No.75 Regiment Farm	1096	2849	裕民县	Yumin [Qagantokay] County	2036	5608
76 团	No.76 Regiment Farm	2977	8776	161 团	No.161 Regiment Farm	2036	5608
77 团	No.77 Regiment Farm	1964	6423	和布克赛尔蒙古自治县	Hoboksar Mongol Autonomous County	2095	6380
特克斯县	Tekes County	1726	5080	184 团	No.184 Regiment Farm	2095	6380
78 团	No.78 Regiment Farm	1726	5080	**阿勒泰地区**	**Altay Administrative Offices**	**16269**	**43626**
尼勒克县	Nilka County	1278	4519	阿勒泰市	Altay City	3334	9784
79 团	No.79 Regiment Farm	1278	4519	181 团	No.181 Regiment Farm	3334	9784
塔城地区	**Tacheng [Tarbagatai] Administrative Offices**	**139997**	**369985**	福海县	Fuhai [Burultokay] County	10850	27956
塔城市	Tacheng City	4898	14616	182 团	No.182 Regiment Farm	1664	4750
163 团	No.163 Regiment Farm	3021	9047	183 团	No.183 Regiment Farm	3107	8042
164 团	No.164 Regiment Farm	1877	5569	187 团	No.187 Regiment Farm	2173	5806
额敏县	Emin [Dorbiljin] County	11198	29999	188 团	No.188 Regiment Farm	3906	9358
165 团	No.165 Regiment Farm	1677	5256	哈巴河县	Habahe [Kaba] County	1223	3533
166 团	No.166 Regiment Farm	2438	7552	185 团	No.185 Regiment Farm	1223	3533
167 团	No.167 Regiment Farm	1939	5431	吉木乃县	Jeminay County	862	2353
168 团	No.168 Regiment Farm	3947	8734	186 团	No.186 Regiment Farm	862	2353
团结农场	Tuanjie Farm	1197	3026	**博尔塔拉蒙古自治州**	**Bortala Mongol Autonomous Prefecture**	**29486**	**90016**
乌苏市	Usu City	54479	146238	博乐市	Bole [Bortala] City	17639	56353
123 团	No.123 Regiment Farm	9537	24076	81 团	No.81 Regiment Farm	3289	10556
124 团	No.124 Regiment Farm	8190	19095	84 团	No.84 Regiment Farm	2139	7357
125 团	No.125 Regiment Farm	7225	19837	86 团	No.86 Regiment Farm	4481	14793
126 团	No.126 Regiment Farm	4589	12622	89 团	No.89 Regiment Farm	4661	14696
127 团	No.127 Regiment Farm	5564	15531	90 团	No.90 Regiment Farm	3069	8951
128 团	No.128 Regiment Farm	5666	16314	精河县	Jinghe [Jing] County	8739	25148
129 团	No.129 Regiment Farm	6763	18597	83 团	No.83 Regiment Farm	7273	21435
130 团	No.130 Regiment Farm	6945	20166	91 团	No.91 Regiment Farm	1466	3713
沙湾县	Shawan County	64480	164367	温泉县	Wenquan [Araxang] County	3108	8515
121 团	No.121 Regiment Farm	15261	38901	87 团	No.87 Regiment Farm	1596	4309

3-13 续表 2 Continued

团　场	Regiment Farm	户数(户) Number of House-holds (house-hold)	人口数(人) Popula-Tion (person)
88 团	No.88 Regiment Farm	1512	4206
巴音郭楞蒙古自治州	**Bayangol Mongol Autonomous Prefecture**	**49787**	**137767**
库尔勒市	Korla City	10759	30311
29 团	No.29 Regiment Farm	7696	21253
30 团	No.30 Regiment Farm	3063	9058
尉犁县	Yuli [Lopnur] County	11798	33208
31 团	No.31 Regiment Farm	3270	8873
33 团	No.33 Regiment Farm	4872	13146
34 团	No.34 Regiment Farm	3656	11189
若羌县	Ruoqiang [Qarkilik] County	2485	7705
36 团	No.36 Regiment Farm	2485	7705
且末县	Qiemo County	662	2648
38 团	No.38 Regiment Farm	662	2648
焉耆回族自治县	Yanji Hui Autonomous County	4635	10981
27 团	No.27 Regiment Farm	4635	10981
和静县	Hejing County	13222	35694
21 团	No.21 Regiment Farm	3853	10436
22 团	No.22 Regiment Farm	6257	17579
223 团	No.223 Regiment Farm	3112	7679
和硕县	Hoxud County	3990	11687
24 团	No.24 Regiment Farm	3990	11687
博湖县	Bohu [Bagrax] County	2236	5533
25 团	No.25 Regiment Farm	2236	5533
阿克苏地区	**Aksu Administrative Offices**	**55696**	**170435**
阿克苏市	Aksu City	39812	122166
1 团	No.1 Regiment Farm	7081	20686
2 团	No.2 Regiment Farm	3473	9434
7 团	No.7 Regiment Farm	3786	11395
8 团	No.8 Regiment Farm	3350	10003
10 团	No.10 Regiment Farm	5580	16200
11 团	No.11 Regiment Farm	3202	10422
12 团	No.12 Regiment Farm	2444	8265
13 团	No.13 Regiment Farm	3865	14855
14 团	No.14 Regiment Farm	2662	7829
16 团	No.16 Regiment Farm	4369	13077
温宿县	Wensu [Onsu] County	8451	27790
5 团	No.5 Regiment Farm	5696	18364
6 团	No.6 Regiment Farm	2755	9426
乌什县	Wushi [Uxturpan] County	1977	5945
4 团	No.4 Regiment Farm	1977	5945
阿瓦提县	Awat County	5456	14534
3 团	No.3 Regiment Farm	5456	14534
克孜勒苏柯尔克孜自治州	**Kizilsu Kirgiz Autonomous Prefecture**	**1198**	**4523**
阿图什市	Artux City	924	3656
红旗农场	Red Flag Farm	924	3656
乌恰县	Wuqia [Ulugqat] County	274	867
托云牧场	Tuoyun Ranch	274	867
喀什地区	**Kashgar [Kaxgar] Administrative Offices**	**48334**	**186114**
疏勒县	Shule County	2101	6098
41 团	No.41 Regiment Farm	2101	6098
英吉莎县	Yengisar County	456	1524
东风农场	Dong Feng Farm	456	1524
叶城县	Yecheng [Kagilik] County	330	1129
叶城牧场	Yechen Ranch	330	1129
麦盖提县	Makit County	9427	30564
45 团	No.45 Regiment Farm	8187	27051
46 团	No.46 Regiment Farm	1240	3513
岳普湖县	Yopurga County	1287	3111
42 团	No.42 Regiment Farm	1287	3111
伽师县	Jiashi [Payzawat] County	3598	11466
伽师总场	General Jiashi Farm	3598	11466
巴楚县	Bachu [Maralbexi] County	31135	132222
44 团	No.44 Regiment Farm	6400	26038
48 团	No.48 Regiment Farm	2033	6557
49 团	No.49 Regiment Farm	4148	14872
50 团	No.50 Regiment Farm	4356	18555
51 团	No.51 Regiment Farm	9196	45138
53 团	No.53 Regiment Farm	5002	21062
和田地区	**Hotan Administrative Offices**	**12286**	**38171**
墨玉县	Moyu [Karakax] County	4177	13091
47 团	No.47 Regiment Farm	1475	4075
224 团	No.224 Regiment Farm	2702	9016
皮山县	Pishan [Guma] County	7267	23185
皮山农场	Pishan Farm	7267	23185
策勒县	Qira County	842	1895
一牧场	No.1Ranch	842	1895

3-14 主要年份按三次产业分的就业人员

Number of Employed Persons by Three Strata of Industry in Main Years

单位：万人 (10 000 persons)

年 份 Year	经济活动人口 Economically Active Population	就业人员合计 Total Number of Employed persons	第一产业 Primary Industry	第二产业 Secondary Industry
1978		491.25	353.99	70.42
1980		506.35	354.49	75.12
1985		565.81	363.24	89.64
1990		617.70	378.47	107.42
1995		676.00	388.16	124.21
1996		684.00	390.98	119.39
1997		715.40	421.30	105.40
1998		680.92	387.80	106.22
1999		694.34	385.57	104.51
2000		672.50	387.90	92.70
2001	697.45	685.38	388.19	92.19
2002	714.17	701.49	391.84	95.82
2003	734.02	721.27	397.20	95.69
2004	755.36	744.49	403.31	98.49
2005	802.75	791.62	408.00	122.81
2006	823.73	811.75	414.45	111.28
2007	842.12	830.42	417.73	118.34
2008	859.35	847.58	421.32	120.05
2009	878.01	866.15	427.48	127.28
2010	905.64	894.65	438.13	132.75
2011	964.46	953.34	463.91	149.04

年 份 Year		构成(合计=100) (%) Composition in Percentage (total=100)(%)		
	第三产业 Tertiary Industry	第一产业 Primary Industry	第二产业 Secondary Industry	第三产业 Tertiary Industry
1978	66.84	72.06	14.33	13.61
1980	76.71	70.01	14.84	15.15
1985	112.93	64.20	15.84	19.96
1990	131.81	61.27	17.39	21.34
1995	163.63	57.42	18.37	24.21
1996	173.63	57.16	17.45	25.39
1997	188.70	58.89	14.73	26.38
1998	186.90	56.95	15.60	27.45
1999	204.26	55.53	15.05	29.42
2000	191.90	57.68	13.78	28.54
2001	205.00	56.64	13.45	29.91
2002	213.83	55.86	13.66	30.48
2003	228.38	55.07	13.27	31.66
2004	242.69	54.17	13.23	32.60
2005	260.81	51.54	15.51	32.95
2006	286.02	51.06	13.71	35.23
2007	294.35	50.30	14.25	35.45
2008	306.21	49.71	14.16	36.13
2009	311.39	49.35	14.70	35.95
2010	323.77	48.97	14.84	36.19
2011	340.39	48.66	15.63	35.71

3-15 分地区从业人员(年末数)

Number of Employed Persons at Year-end by Region

单位：人　　(2011 年)　　(person)

项　目 Item	合　计 Total	私　营 Private	个　体 Self-employed Individuals
总　计 **Total**	**9533372**	**757767**	**957514**
乌鲁木齐市 Urumqi City	1160688	164010	229859
克拉玛依市 Karamay City	238048	24982	36694
石河子市 Shihezi City	164086	26852	25887
吐鲁番地区 Turpan Administrative Offices	392116	31645	35747
哈密地区 Hami [Kumul] Administrative Offices	239083	17804	31226
昌吉回族自治州 Changji Hui Autonomous Prefecture	790583	101279	76702
伊犁哈萨克自治州 Ili Kazak Autonomous Prefecture	2046668	129654	170091
伊犁州直属县(市) Counties (Cities) Direct Under Ili Prefecture	1136036	63519	99633
塔城地区 Tacheng [Tarbagatai] Administrative Offices	601866	37170	43639
阿勒泰地区 Altay Administrative Offices	308766	28965	26819
博尔塔拉蒙古自治州 Bortala Mongol Autonomous Prefecture	231929	19736	23548
巴音郭楞蒙古自治州 Bayangol Mongol Autonomous Prefecture	601660	76204	82857
阿克苏地区 Aksu Administrative Offices	1156289	71958	92158
克孜勒苏柯尔克孜自治州 Kizilsu Kirgiz Autonomous Prefecture	222405	9422	10866
喀什地区 Kashgar [Kaxgar] Administrative Offices	1481112	56287	82347
和田地区 Hotan Administrative Offices	808705	27934	59532

3-16 主要年份城镇登记失业人数及失业率

Number of Registered Unemployed Persons in Urban Areas and Unemployment Rate in Main Years

单位：万人 (10 000 persons)

年 份 Year	城镇登记失业人数 Number of Registered Unemployment Persons in Urban Area	城镇登记失业率(%) Registered Unemployment Rate in Urban Areas (%)	年 份 Year	城镇登记失业人数 Number of Registered Unemployment Persons in Urban Area	城镇登记失业率(%) Registered Unemployment Rate in Urban Areas (%)
1980	13.55	7.5	2000	11.00	3.8
1985	4.04	1.9	2001	12.07	3.7
1990	9.60	3.8	2002	12.68	3.6
1991	9.95	3.8	2003	12.75	3.8
1992	9.81	3.7	2004	10.87	3.8
1993	9.50	3.6	2005	11.13	3.9
1994	10.00	3.8	2006	11.98	3.9
1995	10.24	3.9	2007	11.70	3.9
1996	9.81	3.8	2008	11.77	3.7
1997	10.20	3.8	2009	11.86	3.8
1998	11.06	3.9	2010	10.99	3.2
1999	10.30	3.7	2011	11.12	3.2

3-17 各地、州、市城镇登记失业率

Registered Unemployment Rate in Urban Area by Prefecture, Autonomous Prefecture and City

单位：% (%)

地 区	Region	2010	2011
总 计	**Total**	**3.23**	**3.22**
乌鲁木齐市	Urumqi City	3.72	3.93
克拉玛依市	Karamay City	1.48	0.71
石河子市	Shihezi City	1.69	1.98
吐鲁番地区	Turpan Administrative Offices	2.86	3.28
哈密地区	Hami [Kumul] Administrative Offices	3.24	2.93
昌吉回族自治州	Changji Hui Autonomous Prefecture	3.37	3.23
伊犁州直属县(市)	Counties (Cities) Direct Under Ili Prefecture	3.97	3.82
塔城地区	Tacheng [Tarbagatai] Administrative Offices	1.96	0.71
阿勒泰地区	Altay Administrative Offices	2.95	2.80
博尔塔拉蒙古自治州	Bortala Mongol Autonomous Prefecture	3.64	3.98
巴音郭楞蒙古自治州	Bayangol Mongol Autonomous Prefecture	2.85	2.75
阿克苏地区	Aksu Administrative Offices	3.53	2.73
克孜勒苏柯尔克孜自治州	Kizilsu Kirgiz Autonomous Prefecture	4.07	2.89
喀什地区	Kashgar [Kaxgar] Administrative Offices	3.96	5.50
和田地区	Hotan Administrative Offices	3.20	2.81

3-18 各地区按行业分城镇单位就业人员(年末数)

Number of Employed Persons in Urban Units at Year-end by Sectors and Region

单位：人 (2011 年) (person)

项　目	Item	合 计 Total	国有单位 State-owned Units	城镇集体 Urban Collective-Owned Units	其他单位 Units of Other Types Of Ownership
总　计	**Total**	**2793842**	**1923188**	**33888**	**836766**
按国民经济行业分组	**Grouped by Sectors**				
农林牧渔业	Farming, Forestry, Animal Husbandry and Fishery	579367	567489	69	11809
采 矿 业	Mining	187089	28208	727	158154
制 造 业	Manufacturing	300715	35890	3998	260827
电力、燃气及水的生产和供应业	Production and Supply of Electricity, Gas and Water	75924	34325	168	41431
建 筑 业	Construction	206389	45008	5823	155558
交通运输、仓储和邮政业	Traffic Transport, Storage and Post	123005	92077	1398	29530
信息传输、计算机服务和软件业	Information Transmission, Computer Servcie and Software	24953	10811	4	14138
批发和零售业	Wholesale and Retail Trades	85038	26465	4753	53820
住宿和餐饮业	Hotels and Catering Services	28885	13535	1066	14284
金 融 业	Financial Intermediation	80947	31986	9717	39244
房地产业	Real Estate	27712	6279	637	20796
租赁和商务服务业	Leasing and Business Services	53260	27558	3758	21944
科学研究、技术服务和地质勘查业	Scientific Research, Technical Service and Geological Prospecting	49873	44487	68	5318
水利、环境和公共设施管理业	Management of Water Conservancy, Environment and PublicFacility	52984	50090	2	2892
居民服务和其他服务业	Services to households and Other Services	16149	14087	89	1973
教 育	Education	339488	337145	120	2223
卫生、社会保障和社会福利业	Health, Social Security and Social Welfare	148038	145782	1475	781
文化、体育和娱乐业	Culture, Sports and Entertainment	32161	30156	4	2001
公共管理和社会组织	Public Management and Social Organizations	381865	381810	12	43
按地区分	**By Region**				
乌鲁木齐市	Urumqi City	627007	359075	8747	259185
克拉玛依市	Karamay City	175074	53708	4497	116869
吐鲁番地区	Turpan Administrative Offices	76255	37305	584	38366
哈密地区	Hami [Kumul] Administrative Offices	88611	60355	813	27443
昌吉回族自治州	Changji Hui Autonomous Prefecture	205546	135979	2634	66933
伊犁哈萨克自治州	Ili Kazak Autonomous Prefecture	602913	501641	4820	96452
伊犁州直属县(市)	Counties (Cities) Direct Under Ili Prefecture	273352	209535	2330	61487
塔城地区	Tacheng [Tarbagatai] Administrative Offices	216508	195018	1664	19826
阿勒泰地区	Altay Administrative Offices	113053	97088	826	15139
博尔塔拉蒙古自治州	Bortala Mongol Autonomous Prefecture	95235	87241	658	7336
巴音郭楞蒙古自治州	Bayangol Mongol Autonomous Prefecture	200453	135703	2419	62331
阿克苏地区	Aksu Administrative Offices	193249	141785	2584	48880
克孜勒苏柯尔克孜自治州	Kizilsu Kirgiz Autonomous Prefecture	43829	41337	436	2056
喀什地区	Kashgar [Kaxgar] Administrative Offices	204753	162533	4765	37455
和田地区	Hotan Administrative Offices	97145	84713	690	11742
石河子市	Shihezi City	100223	52686	241	47296
阿拉尔市	Aral City	41966	38055		3911
图木舒克市	Tumxuk City	16729	14260		2469
五家渠市	Wujiaqu City	24854	16812		8042

3-19 各地区年底单位在岗职工人数
Number of Staff and Workers at Year-end by Region

单位：万人 (10 000 persons)

年 份 Year	地 区 Region	合 计 Total	国有单位 State-owned Units	城镇集体 Urban Collective-owned Units	其他单位 Units of Other Types of Ownership
	2002	242.26	189.26	9.31	43.69
	2003	237.94	184.02	7.55	46.37
	2004	235.97	182.80	6.43	46.74
	2005	237.84	181.92	5.96	49.96
	2006	238.95	182.91	5.19	50.85
	2007	239.45	181.46	4.58	53.41
	2008	239.16	180.29	3.64	55.23
	2009	239.54	175.90	3.54	60.10
	2010	245.48	178.40	3.00	64.08
	2011	270.77	187.78	3.00	79.99
乌鲁木齐市	Urumqi City	61.27	35.27	0.89	25.11
克拉玛依市	Karamay City	16.73	5.21	0.19	11.33
吐鲁番地区	Turpan Administrative Offices	7.38	3.58	0.05	3.75
哈密地区	Hami [Kumul] Administrative Offices	8.60	5.97	0.06	2.57
昌吉回族自治州	Changji Hui Autonomous Prefecture	19.78	13.34	0.25	6.19
伊犁哈萨克自治州	Ili Kazak Autonomous Prefecture	59.19	49.40	0.47	9.32
伊犁州直属县(市)	Counties (Cities) Direct Under Ili Prefecture	26.93	20.73	0.23	5.97
塔城地区	Tacheng [Tarbagatai] Administrative Offices	21.28	19.20	0.16	1.92
阿勒泰地区	Altay Administrative Offices	10.98	9.47	0.08	1.43
博尔塔拉蒙古自治州	Bortala Mongol Autonomous Prefecture	9.27	8.51	0.06	0.70
巴音郭楞蒙古自治州	Bayangol Mongol Autonomous Prefecture	18.96	12.76	0.24	5.96
阿克苏地区	Aksu Administrative Offices	19.28	14.16	0.25	4.87
克孜勒苏柯尔克孜自治州	Kizilsu Kirgiz Autonomous Prefecture	4.06	3.90	0.04	0.12
喀什地区	Kashgar [Kaxgar] Administrative Offices	18.86	15.60	0.42	2.84
和田地区	Hotan Administrative Offices	9.17	8.03	0.06	1.08
石河子市	Shihezi City	10.01	5.26	0.02	4.73
阿拉尔市	Aral City	4.20	3.81		0.39
图木舒克市	Tumxuk City	1.62	1.38		0.24
五家渠市	Wujiaqu City	2.39	1.60		0.79

3-20 分行业年底单位在岗职工(含劳务派遣工)人数

Number of Staff and Workers at Year-end by Sectors(including the dispatched workers)

单位：人 (2011 年) (person)

项 目	Item	合 计 Total	国有单位 State-owned Units	城镇集体 Urban Collective-owned Units	其他单位 Units of Other Types of Ownership
总 计	**Total**	**2707666**	**1877784**	**30003**	**799879**
农林牧渔业	**Farming, Forestry, Animal Husbandry and Fishery**	**569031**	**557530**	**63**	**11438**
农 业	Farming	451925	446876	30	5019
林 业	Forestry	8850	6449		2401
畜 牧 业	Animal Husbandry	76852	74700	9	2143
渔 业	Fishery	263	204		59
农林牧渔服务业	Services in Support of Agriculture	31141	29301	24	1816
采 矿 业	**Mining**	**184873**	**27426**	**727**	**156720**
#煤炭开采和洗选业	Mining and Washing of Coal	51439	5119	590	45730
石油和天然气开采业	Extraction of Petroleum and Natural Gas	116030	19937	6	96087
制 造 业	**Manufacturing**	**297047**	**35244**	**3933**	**257870**
#农副食品加工业	Processing of Food from Agriculture Products	20791	1653	32	19106
食品制造业	Manufacture of Food	15661	1344	142	14175
饮料制造业	Manufacture of Beverage	11116	453	75	10588
纺织业	Manufacture of Textile	22637	4107	35	18495
造纸及纸制品业	Manufacture of Paper and Paper Products	5193	37	115	5041
印刷业和记录媒介的复制	Printing and Record Medium Reproduction	3499	2270	67	1162
石油加工、炼焦及核燃料加工业	Oil processing, Refining and Nuclear-fuel processing	39270	10914	5	28351
化学原料及化学制品制造业	Raw Chemical Materials and Chemical Products	45201	1863	689	42649
塑料制品业	Plastic Products	9420	325	178	8917
非金属矿物制品业	Manufacture of Non-metal Mineral Products	42807	2264	1013	39530
黑色金属冶炼及压延加工业	Smelting and Pressing of Ferrous Metals	25880	669	763	24448
有色金属冶炼及压延加工业	Smelting and Pressing of Nonferrous Metals	10286	2186	79	8021
通用设备制造业	Manufacturing of Equipment for General Purpose	2673	220	46	2407
电力、燃气及水的生产和供应业	**Production and Distribution of Electricity, Gas and Water**	**74542**	**33962**	**168**	**40412**
电力、热力的生产和供应业	Production and Distribution of Electric Power, Thermal Power	64551	29279	97	35175
燃气生产和供应业	Production and Distribution of Gas	2793	56		2737
水的生产和供应业	Production and Distribution of Water	7198	4627	71	2500
建 筑 业	**Construction**	**189069**	**44300**	**3029**	**141740**
房屋和土木工程建筑业	Construction of Buildings and Civil Engineering	167795	36540	1934	129321
建筑安装业	Building Installation	15523	2824	1091	11608
建筑装饰业	Building Decoration	433	80	4	349

3-20 续表 1 Continued

单位：人 (person)

项　目	Item	合 计 Total	国有单位 State-owned Units	城镇集体 Urban Collective-owned Units	其他单位 Units of Other Types of Ownership
其他建筑业	Other Construction	5318	4856		462
交通运输、仓储和邮政业	**Transport Storage and Post**	**121810**	**91278**	**1394**	**29138**
铁路运输业	Railway Transport	40782	40339	401	42
道路运输业	Road Transportat	26640	19835	224	6581
城市公共交通业	Urban Public Transport	15766	798	6	14962
航空运输业	Air Transportat	10891	5557		5334
管道运输业	Via Pipe Transportat	5194	3662		1532
装卸搬运和其他运输服务业	Loading and Discharging; Other Transportation Service	7486	6503	726	257
仓储业	Storage	3771	3336	5	430
邮政业	Post	11123	11123		
信息传输、计算机服务和软件业	**Information Transmission, Computer Service and Software**	**24788**	**10655**	**4**	**14129**
电信和其他信息传输服务业	Telecommunication and Other I.T Transmission Service	23107	10194	4	12909
计算机服务业	Computer Service	480	287		193
软件业	Software	1201	174		1027
批发和零售业	**Wholesale and Retail Trades**	**83164**	**26118**	**4348**	**52698**
批发业	Wholesale Trades	51576	20717	3865	26994
零售业	Retail Trades	31588	5401	483	25704
住宿和餐饮业	**Hotels and Catering Services**	**27465**	**12449**	**1048**	**13968**
住宿业	Hotels	21389	10616	956	9817
餐饮业	Catering Services	6076	1833	92	4151
金 融 业	**Financial Intermediation**	**65048**	**29957**	**9476**	**25615**
银行业	Banking	46366	24370	9476	12520
证券业	Security Activities	716	112		604
保险业	Insurance	16324	4938		11386
其他金融活动	Other Finance Activities	1642	537		1105
房地产业	**Real Estate**	**26699**	**5855**	**430**	**20414**
#房地产开发经营	Development and Management of Real Estate	12620	1174	165	11281
物业管理	Real Estate Management	11605	3457	133	8015
房地产中介服务	Agency Service for Real Estate	674	340	6	328
租赁和商务服务业	**Leasing and Business Service**	**51826**	**26827**	**3724**	**21275**
租赁业	Leasing	484	143		341
商务服务业	Business Service	51342	26684	3724	20934

3-20 续表 2 Continued

单位：人 (person)

项　目	Item	合 计 Total	国有单位 State-owned Units	城镇集体 Urban Collective-owned Units	其他单位 Units of Other Types of Ownership
科学研究、技术服务和地质勘查业	**Scientific Research, Technology Service and Geological Prospecting**	**47906**	**43168**	**14**	**4724**
研究与试验发展	Research and Experiment Development	6224	6147		77
专业技术服务业	Professional Technique Service	23395	19132	14	4249
科技交流和推广服务业	Services of Science and Technology Exchanges and Promotion	9071	8750		321
地质勘查业	Geologica Prospecting	9216	9139		77
水利、环境和公共设施管理业	**Management of Water Conservancy, Environment and Public Facility**	**50121**	**47254**	**2**	**2865**
水利管理业	Management of Water Conservance	21089	21089		
环境管理业	Environmental Management	15994	15667		327
公共设施管理业	Management of Public Facilities	13038	10498	2	2538
居民服务和其他服务业	**Service to Households and Other Services**	**15856**	**13801**	**83**	**1972**
居民服务业	Services to Households	11562	11209	8	345
其他服务业	Other Services	4294	2592	75	1627
教　育	**Education**	**336011**	**333757**	**120**	**2134**
#初等教育	Junior Education	133879	133409		470
中等教育	Secondary Education	156815	156192	15	608
高等教育	Senior Education	28030	28030		
卫生、社会保障和社会福利业	**Health, Social Security and Social Welfare**	**144842**	**142686**	**1424**	**732**
卫　生	Health	135903	133927	1413	563
社会保障业	Social Security	5870	5821		49
社会福利业	Social Welfare	3069	2938	11	120
文化、体育和娱乐业	**Culture, Sports and Entertainment**	**31269**	**29271**	**4**	**1994**
新闻出版业	Journalism and Publishing Activities	6257	4434		1823
广播、电影、电视和音像业	Broadcasting, Movies, Televisions and Audiovisual Activities	10427	10416	4	7
文化艺术业	Culture and Art Activities	10211	10178		33
体　育	Sports	3985	3985		
娱乐业	Entertainment	389	258		131
公共管理和社会组织	**Public Management and Social Organization**	**366299**	**366246**	**12**	**41**
#中国共产党机关	Organs of Communist Party of China	21404	21404		
国家机构	Government Agencies	338418	338418		
人民政协和民主党派	People's Political Consultative Conference and Democratic Parties	2461	2461		
群众团体、社会团体和宗教组织	Non-Governmental Organizations, Social Organizations and Religion Organizations	4016	3963	12	41

3-21 各地、州、市分行业年底单位在岗职工(含劳务派遣工)人数

Number of Staff and Workers at Year-end by Sector and Prefecture, Autonomous Prefecture and City(including the dispatched workers)

单位：人　　　　(2011 年)　　　　(person)

年 份 Year	地 区 Region	合 计 Total	农林牧渔业 Farming, Forestry, Animal Husbandry and Fishery	采 矿 业 Mining	制 造 业 Manufacturing	电力、燃气及水的生产和供应业 Production and Distribution of Power, Gas and Water
总　　计	**Total**	**2707666**	**569031**	**184873**	**297047**	**74542**
乌鲁木齐市	Urumqi City	612670	11138	20509	91846	21665
克拉玛依市	Karamay City	167334	8568	73671	29976	42
吐鲁番地区	Turpan Administrative Offices	73824	3513	24852	8209	2227
哈密地区	Hami [Kumul] Administrative Offices	85966	19439	14755	6033	2807
昌吉回族自治州	Changji Hui Autonomous Prefecture	197849	58549	6475	32046	7187
伊犁哈萨克自治州	Ili Kazak Autonomous Prefecture	591852	243024	15609	41808	12411
伊犁州直属县(市)	Counties (Cities) Direct Under Ili Prefecture	269242	72197	3626	30165	6868
塔城地区	Tacheng [Tarbagatai] Administrative Offices	212826	124633	6295	9116	3066
阿勒泰地区	Altay Administrative Offices	109784	46194	5688	2527	2477
博尔塔拉蒙古自治州	Bortala Mongol Autonomous Prefecture	92734	43437	233	4183	2298
巴音郭楞蒙古自治州	Bayangol Mongol Autonomous Prefecture	189596	47214	19641	20533	3444
阿克苏地区	Aksu Administrative Offices	192824	40533	8094	17097	6514
克孜勒苏柯尔克孜自治州	Kizilsu Kirgiz Autonomous Prefecture	40601	2577	47	986	423
喀什地区	Kashgar [Kaxgar] Administrative Offices	188589	19763	214	8574	5535
和田地区	Hotan Administrative Offices	91726	13530	773	1186	2289
石河子市	Shihezi City	100052	12156		26659	5992
阿拉尔市	Aral City	41961	28552		2027	382
图木舒克市	Tumxuk City	16162	9206		650	458
五家渠市	Wujiaqu City	23926	7832		5234	868

年 份 Year	地 区 Region	建 筑 业 Construction	交通运输、仓储和邮政业 Transport Storage and Post	信息传输、计算机服务和软件业 Information Transmission, Computer Servcie and Software	批发和零售业 Wholesale and Retail Trades	住宿和餐饮业 Hotels and Catering Services
总　　计	**Total**	**189069**	**121810**	**24788**	**83164**	**27465**
乌鲁木齐市	Urumqi City	98741	82625	8361	37788	15155
克拉玛依市	Karamay City	12128	2245	1371	2690	762
吐鲁番地区	Turpan Administrative Offices	1152	1386	823	1702	443
哈密地区	Hami [Kumul] Administrative Offices	1373	1208	957	1832	915
昌吉回族自治州	Changji Hui Autonomous Prefecture	7546	3114	1521	3895	419
伊犁哈萨克自治州	Ili Kazak Autonomous Prefecture	11266	11344	4600	11799	5331
伊犁州直属县(市)	Counties (Cities) Direct Under Ili Prefecture	6711	6708	2355	8257	2816
塔城地区	Tacheng [Tarbagatai] Administrative Offices	3018	2341	1029	2292	647
阿勒泰地区	Altay Administrative Offices	1537	2295	1216	1250	1868
博尔塔拉蒙古自治州	Bortala Mongol Autonomous Prefecture	915	1582	589	1275	483
巴音郭楞蒙古自治州	Bayangol Mongol Autonomous Prefecture	8283	4703	1416	4573	1335
阿克苏地区	Aksu Administrative Offices	7031	3343	1827	7268	473
克孜勒苏柯尔克孜自治州	Kizilsu Kirgiz Autonomous Prefecture	345	1037	335	398	169
喀什地区	Kashgar [Kaxgar] Administrative Offices	7978	5380	1053	6635	1204
和田地区	Hotan Administrative Offices	4803	2561	840	1302	203
石河子市	Shihezi City	23031	1088	1050	683	558
阿拉尔市	Aral City	1825	17		1066	
图木舒克市	Tumxuk City	1758			25	15
五家渠市	Wujiaqu City	894	177	45	233	

3-21 续表 Continued

单位：人 (person)

年 份 Year	地 区 Region	金融业 Financial Intermedia-tion	房地产业 Real Estate	租赁和商务服务业 Leasing and Business Services	科学研究、技术服务和地质勘查业 Scientific Research, Technology Service and Geological Prospecting	水利、环境和公共设施管理业 Management of Water Conservancy, Environment and Public Facility
总 计	**Total**	**65048**	**26699**	**51826**	**47906**	**50121**
乌鲁木齐市	Urumqi City	19904	10753	16057	18958	5625
克拉玛依市	Karamay City	2800	3481	8129	427	976
吐鲁番地区	Turpan Administrative Offices	1901	115	285	1296	962
哈密地区	Hami [Kumul] Administrative Offices	2173	279	994	2416	3457
昌吉回族自治州	Changji Hui Autonomous Prefecture	4616	2425	5025	4158	5285
伊犁哈萨克自治州	Ili Kazak Autonomous Prefecture	10720	3832	5948	6986	10346
伊犁州直属县(市)	Counties (Cities) Direct Under Ili Prefecture	6024	3138	4898	3642	4836
塔城地区	Tacheng [Tarbagatai] Administrative Offices	2760	274	638	1334	3599
阿勒泰地区	Altay Administrative Offices	1936	420	412	2010	1911
博尔塔拉蒙古自治州	Bortala Mongol Autonomous Prefecture	1690	371	5419	1067	1717
巴音郭楞蒙古自治州	Bayangol Mongol Autonomous Prefecture	3808	1362	4016	3308	4529
阿克苏地区	Aksu Administrative Offices	5285	1506	1839	2223	5752
克孜勒苏柯尔克孜自治州	Kizilsu Kirgiz Autonomous Prefecture	846	51	505	1701	570
喀什地区	Kashgar [Kaxgar] Administrative Offices	4740	1825	786	2614	3766
和田地区	Hotan Administrative Offices	2101	174	350	1249	1516
石河子市	Shihezi City	3436	166	2067	1020	1852
阿拉尔市	Aral City	37	18	170	133	2901
图木舒克市	Tumxuk City			110	19	251
五家渠市	Wujiaqu City	991	341	126	331	616

年 份 Year	地 区 Region	居民服务和其他服务业 Service to Households and Other Services	教 育 Education	卫生、社会保障和社会福利业 Health, Social Security and Social Welfare	文化、体育和娱乐业 Culture, Sports and Entertainment	公共管理和社会组织 Public Management and Social Organizations
总 计	**Total**	**15856**	**336011**	**144842**	**31269**	**366299**
乌鲁木齐市	Urumqi City	990	47716	31182	11571	62086
克拉玛依市	Karamay City	18	7514	2947	163	9426
吐鲁番地区	Turpan Administrative Offices	4	9252	3143	492	12067
哈密地区	Hami [Kumul] Administrative Offices	200	9724	4870	990	11544
昌吉回族自治州	Changji Hui Autonomous Prefecture	4	21810	10595	996	22183
伊犁哈萨克自治州	Ili Kazak Autonomous Prefecture	455	75194	30805	4931	85443
伊犁州直属县(市)	Counties (Cities) Direct Under Ili Prefecture	331	42641	17454	2533	44042
塔城地区	Tacheng [Tarbagatai] Administrative Offices	95	20180	8346	1201	21962
阿勒泰地区	Altay Administrative Offices	29	12373	5005	1197	19439
博尔塔拉蒙古自治州	Bortala Mongol Autonomous Prefecture	15	9402	3923	622	13513
巴音郭楞蒙古自治州	Bayangol Mongol Autonomous Prefecture	121	20688	10168	1106	29348
阿克苏地区	Aksu Administrative Offices	1759	31734	11732	1516	37298
克孜勒苏柯尔克孜自治州	Kizilsu Kirgiz Autonomous Prefecture	2752	10448	6077	958	10376
喀什地区	Kashgar [Kaxgar] Administrative Offices	5476	54112	14972	5834	38128
和田地区	Hotan Administrative Offices	268	25947	7781	1434	23419
石河子市	Shihezi City	1686	7463	4894	367	5884
阿拉尔市	Aral City	2106	1419	287	178	843
图木舒克市	Tumxuk City		1358	352		1960
五家渠市	Wujiaqu City	2	2230	1114	111	2781

3-22 分行业城镇单位年底女性就业人员
Number of Female Employed in Urban Units at Year-end by Sectors

单位：人 (2011 年) (person)

项 目	Item	合 计 Total	国有单位 State-owned Units	城镇集体 Urban Collective-owned Units	其他单位 Units of Other Types of Ownership
总 计	**Total**	**1149365**	**864359**	**11685**	**273321**
农林牧渔业	Farming, Forestry, Animal Husbandry and Fishery	254912	249777	20	5115
采 矿 业	Mining	54235	4727	108	49400
制 造 业	Manufacturing	100207	13285	1378	85544
电力、燃气及水的生产和供应业	Production and Distribution of Electricity, Gas and Water	23135	10476	39	12620
建 筑 业	Construction	33726	8127	878	24721
交通运输、仓储和邮政业	Transport, Storage and Post	37172	27655	702	8815
信息传输、计算机服务和软件业	Information Transmission, Computer Servcie and Software Industries	11335	4858		6477
批发和零售业	Wholesale and Retail Trades	35451	10795	1658	22998
住宿和餐饮业	Hotels and Catering Services	15952	7576	550	7826
金 融 业	Financial Intermediation	45140	16520	4037	24583
房地产业	Real Estate	12497	3050	199	9248
租赁和商务服务业	Leasing and Business Services	19334	9682	909	8743
科学研究、技术服务和地质勘查业	Scientific Research, Technology Service and Geological Prospecting	16948	15400	18	1530
水利、环境和公共设施管理业	Management of Water Conservancy, Environment and Public Facility	23272	21727	1	1544
居民服务和其他服务业	Services to households and Other Services	10145	8716	75	1354
教 育	Education	206931	205611	68	1252
卫生、社会保障和社会福利业	Health, Social Security and Social Welfare	99487	97916	1042	529
文化、体育和娱乐业	Culture, Sports and Entertainment	14157	13153	1	1003
公共管理和社会组织	Public Management and Social Organizations	135329	135308	2	19

3-23 单位在岗职工工资总额及构成

Total Wages of Staff and Workers and Its Composition

年份 Year	地区 Region	工资总额（万元） Total wages Bill(10 000 yuan) 合计 Total	国有单位 State-owned Units	城镇集体单位 Urban Collective-owned Units	其他单位 Units of Other Types of Ownership	构成(总计=100)(%) composition (total=100)(%) 国有单位 State-owned Units	城镇集体单位 Urban Collective-owned Units	其他单位 Units of Other Types of owner-ship
	1978	159409	148278	11131		93.0	7.0	
	1980	212446	196711	15735		92.6	7.4	
	1985	339110	304999	33789	322	89.9	10.0	0.1
	1990	668808	601300	65858	1650	90.0	9.8	0.2
	1995	1677257	1521670	135990	19597	90.7	8.1	1.2
	2000	2344694	2007823	125510	211361	85.6	5.4	9.0
	2001	2677431	2092155	105861	479415	78.1	4.0	17.9
	2002	2915398	2211411	93605	610382	75.9	3.2	20.9
	2003	3315399	2497369	77460	740570	75.3	2.3	22.4
	2004	3563312	2691462	78224	793626	75.5	2.2	22.3
	2005	3874068	2871542	75971	926555	74.1	2.0	23.9
	2006	4429959	3318694	77978	1033287	74.9	1.8	23.3
	2007	5332395	3951882	82215	1298298	74.1	1.5	24.4
	2008	6198976	4428784	84187	1686005	71.4	1.4	27.2
	2009	6912058	4796811	91488	2023759	69.4	1.3	29.3
	2010	8286857	5669760	105413	2511684	68.4	1.3	30.3
	2011	11034557	7021538	140410	3872609	63.6	1.3	35.1
乌鲁木齐市	Urumqi City	3205009	1886979	37654	1280376	58.9	1.2	39.9
克拉玛依市	Karamay City	950758	288524	6198	656036	30.3	0.7	69.0
吐鲁番地区	Turpan Administrative Offices	338235	135781	1732	200722	40.1	0.5	59.4
哈密地区	Hami [Kumul] Administrative Offices	324766	203819	1745	119202	62.8	0.5	36.7
昌吉回族自治州	Changji Hui Autonomous Prefecture	780941	513524	16655	250762	65.8	2.1	32.1
伊犁哈萨克自治州	Ili Kazak Autonomous Prefecture	1783066	1402674	26468	353924	78.7	1.5	19.8
伊犁州直属县(市)	Counties (Cities) Direct Under Ili Prefecture	853259	617508	12762	222989	72.4	1.5	26.1
塔城地区	Tacheng [Tarbagatai] Administrative Offices	611539	535168	6932	69439	87.5	1.1	11.4
阿勒泰地区	Altay Administrative Offices	318268	249998	6774	61496	78.5	2.1	19.4
博尔塔拉蒙古自治州	Bortala Mongol Autonomous Prefecture	268781	237431	10276	21074	88.3	3.8	7.9
巴音郭楞蒙古自治州	Bayangol Mongol Autonomous Prefecture	805282	428890	10878	365514	53.3	1.4	45.3
阿克苏地区	Aksu Administrative Offices	705113	469795	10489	224829	66.6	1.5	31.9
克孜勒苏柯尔克孜自治州	Kizilsu Kirgiz Autonomous Prefecture	134107	130268	890	2949	97.1	0.7	2.2
喀什地区	Kashgar [Kaxgar] Administrative Offices	683397	551984	12611	118802	80.8	1.8	17.4
和田地区	Hotan Administrative Offices	347531	311836	2778	32917	89.7	0.8	9.5
石河子市	Shihezi City	448428	249770	2036	196622	55.7	0.5	43.8
阿拉尔市	Aral City	129433	115232		14201	89.0		11.0
图木舒克市	Tumxuk City	49703	41238		8465	83.0		17.0
五家渠市	Wujiaqu City	80007	53793		26214	67.2		32.8

注：含劳务派遣工.
Note: Including the dispatched workers.

3-24 主要年份在岗职工工资总额指数

Indices of Total Wages of Staff and Workers in Main Years

年 份 Year	指数(上年=100) Indices (preceding year=100)				指数(1978 年=100) Indices (1978=100)			
	合 计 Total	国有单位 State-owned Units	城镇集体单位 Urban Collective-owned Units	其他单位 Units of Other Types of Ownership	合 计 Total	国有单位 State-owned Units	城镇集体单位 Urban Collective-owned Units	其他单位 Units of Other Types of Ownership
1978	114.2	114.5	109.6		100.0	100.0	100.0	
1980	120.5	120.1	125.2		133.3	132.7	141.4	
1985	117.4	117.5	116.0	167.5	212.7	205.7	303.6	100.0
1990	116.6	116.3	126.9	132.6	419.6	405.5	591.7	513.4
1995	126.3	126.8	119.3	146.6	1052.2	1026.2	1221.7	6097.7
2000	110.7	108.1	91.4	171.0	1470.9	1354.1	1127.6	65762.7
2001	114.2	104.2	84.3	226.8	1679.6	1411.0	951.0	149164.7
2002	108.9	105.7	88.4	127.3	1828.9	1491.4	840.9	189913.4
2003	113.7	112.9	82.8	121.3	2079.8	1684.2	695.9	230420.0
2004	107.5	107.8	101.0	107.2	2235.3	1815.1	702.8	246927.8
2005	108.7	106.7	97.1	116.7	2430.3	1936.6	682.5	288287.3
2006	114.3	115.6	102.6	111.5	2779.0	2238.2	700.5	321896.3
2007	120.4	119.1	105.4	125.6	3345.1	2665.2	738.6	403198.1
2008	116.3	112.1	102.4	129.9	3888.7	2986.8	756.3	523604.0
2009	111.5	108.3	108.7	120.0	4336.1	3235.0	821.9	628496.6
2010	119.9	118.2	115.2	124.1	5198.5	3823.7	947.0	780026.1
2011	133.2	123.8	133.2	154.2	6922.2	4735.4	1261.4	1202673.7

注：2000 年起职工工资总额指数由在岗职工工资总额计算而得。
Note:. Since 2000,total wages of staff and worders were caculated by indices of total wages of stuff and workers.

3-25 主要年份在岗职工工资情况

Wages of Full-Employed Staff and Workers in Main Years

年 份 Year	在岗职工工资总额(万元) Total Wages of staff and workers (10 000 yuan)	国有单位 State-owned Units	城镇单位 Urban Collective-owned Units	其他单位 Units of Other Types of Ownership	在岗职工平均工资(元) Average Wage of Staff and Workers (yuan)	国有单位 State-owned Units	城镇单位 Urban Collective-owned Units	其他单位 Units of Other Types of Ownership
1999	2118609	1857722	137261	123626	7611	7614	6815	8681
2000	2344694	2007823	125510	211361	8717	8731	7489	9498
2001	2677431	2092155	105861	479415	10278	10145	8197	11594
2002	2915398	2211411	93605	610382	11605	11435	9353	12767
2003	3315399	2497369	77460	740570	13255	13199	9966	13937
2004	3563312	2691462	78224	793626	14484	14477	11594	14870
2005	3874068	2871542	75971	926555	15558	15364	12738	16503
2006	4429959	3318694	77978	1033287	17819	17704	14209	18566
2007	5332395	3951882	82215	1298298	21434	21369	17780	21921
2008	6198976	4428784	84187	1686005	24687	24016	22060	26815
2009	6912058	4796811	91488	2023759	27753	26872	22862	30409
2010	8286857	5669760	105413	2511684	32361	31390	31997	34807
2011	11034557	7021538	140410	3872609	38820	36752	40102	43177

3-26 主要年份在岗职工平均货币工资
Average Money Wage of Staff and Workers in Main Years

单位：元 (yuan)

年 份 Year	全 部 职 工 Full Staff and Workers	国有单位 State-owned Units	城镇集体单位 Urban Collective-owned Units	其他单位 Units of Other Types of Ownership
1978	717	726	614	
1980	882	904	676	
1985	1277	1310	1038	1707
1990	2272	2345	1765	2498
1995	5348	5431	4509	5973
2000	8717	8731	7489	9498
2001	10278	10145	8197	11594
2002	11605	11435	9353	12767
2003	13255	13199	9966	13937
2004	14484	14477	11594	14870
2005	15558	15364	12738	16503
2006	17819	17704	14209	18566
2007	21434	21369	17780	21921
2008	24687	24016	22060	26815
2009	27753	26872	22862	30409
2010	32361	31390	31997	34807
2011	38820	36752	40102	43177

3-27 主要年份在岗职工平均工资指数
Indices of Average Wage of Staff and Workers in Main Years

(上年=100) (preceding year=100)

年 份 Year	货币工资 Money Wage				实际工资 Real Wage			
	合 计 Total	国有单位 State-owned Units	城镇集体单位 Urban Collective-owned Units	其他单位 Units of Other Types of Ownership	合 计 Total	国有单位 State-owned Units	城镇集体单位 Urban Collective-owned Units	其他单位 Units of Other Types of Ownership
1978		105.2				103.9		
1980	114.5	115.3	108.3		109.3	110.0	103.4	
1985	115.7	116.0	112.5	124.6	105.9	106.0	102.7	113.7
1990	113.2	113.3	113.6	96.5	108.3	108.4	108.7	92.3
1995	125.8	125.7	125.8	120.9	105.7	105.6	105.7	101.6
2000	114.5	114.7	109.9	109.4	115.2	115.4	110.6	110.1
2001	117.9	116.2	109.5	122.1	113.4	111.7	105.3	117.4
2002	112.9	112.7	114.1	110.1	113.6	113.4	114.8	110.8
2003	114.2	115.4	106.6	109.2	113.6	114.8	106.1	108.7
2004	109.3	109.7	116.3	106.7	107.0	107.4	113.9	104.5
2005	107.4	106.1	109.9	111.0	106.7	105.4	109.1	110.2
2006	114.5	115.2	111.5	112.5	113.7	114.4	110.7	111.7
2007	120.3	120.7	125.1	118.1	114.0	114.4	118.6	111.9
2008	115.2	112.4	124.1	122.3	106.6	104.0	114.8	113.1
2009	112.4	111.9	103.6	113.4	111.6	111.1	102.9	112.6
2010	116.6	116.8	140.0	114.5	111.8	112.0	134.2	109.7
2011	120.0	117.1	125.3	124.0	113.3	110.6	118.3	117.1

3-28 各地、州、市分行业单位在岗职工(含劳务派遣工)平均货币工资

Average Money Wage of Staff and Workers by Sector and by Prefecture, Autonomous Prefecture and City(including the dispatched workers)

单位：元 (2011 年) (yuan)

年 份 Year	地 区 Region	合 计 Total	农林牧渔业 Farming, Forestry, Animal Husbandry and Fishery	采 矿 业 Mining	制 造 业 Manufacturing	电力、燃气及水的生产和供应业 Production and Distribution of Power, Gas and Water
总 计	**Total**	**38820**	**22849**	**63568**	**40123**	**51281**
乌鲁木齐市	Urumqi City	47747	25624	66985	46011	56536
克拉玛依市	Karamay City	58657	25664	73253	60063	55909
吐鲁番地区	Turpan Administrative Offices	45239	18167	60823	33332	65568
哈密地区	Hami [Kumul] Administrative Offices	38202	24022	53280	34375	62074
昌吉回族自治州	Changji Hui Autonomous Prefecture	36417	28720	45298	31232	54012
伊犁哈萨克自治州	Ili Kazak Autonomous Prefecture	29142	19263	37983	30376	49382
伊犁州直属县(市)	Counties (Cities) Direct Under Ili Prefecture	30802	20121	36821	31078	52430
塔城地区	Tacheng [Tarbagatai] Administrative Offices	27825	21219	40969	28163	43716
阿勒泰地区	Altay Administrative Offices	27662	12588	35387	29324	48007
博尔塔拉蒙古自治州	Bortala Mongol Autonomous Prefecture	28391	21579	36292	23652	39748
巴音郭楞蒙古自治州	Bayangol Mongol Autonomous Prefecture	37851	22970	66038	43603	39312
阿克苏地区	Aksu Administrative Offices	34998	23160	59787	37757	50112
克孜勒苏柯尔克孜自治州	Kizilsu Kirgiz Autonomous Prefecture	33131	28652	5191	28857	25275
喀什地区	Kashgar [Kaxgar] Administrative Offices	36088	25918	32183	23204	57165
和田地区	Hotan Administrative Offices	37664	19885	29700	25398	38637
石河子市	Shihezi City	38909	34518		37563	39549
阿拉尔市	Aral City	35193	33914		30658	40976
图木舒克市	Tumxuk City	30684	26514		29510	37220
五家渠市	Wujiaqu City	33570	23349		26889	33018

年 份 Year	地 区 Region	建 筑 业 Construction	交通运输、仓储和邮政业 Transport, Storage and Post	信息传输、计算机服务和软件业 Information Transmission, Computer Servcie and Software	批发和零售业 Wholesale and Retail Trades	住宿和餐饮业 Hotels and Catering Services
总 计	**Total**	**36197**	**53501**	**48217**	**40730**	**28106**
乌鲁木齐市	Urumqi City	36954	63815	55809	47349	31797
克拉玛依市	Karamay City	38631	42274	48856	48991	33322
吐鲁番地区	Turpan Administrative Offices	37083	24705	48086	46861	24853
哈密地区	Hami [Kumul] Administrative Offices	29155	35286	51038	53361	22842
昌吉回族自治州	Changji Hui Autonomous Prefecture	37076	28240	37185	40819	22951
伊犁哈萨克自治州	Ili Kazak Autonomous Prefecture	33508	32516	39661	28318	21485
伊犁州直属县(市)	Counties (Cities) Direct Under Ili Prefecture	34867	28793	42362	26542	19819
塔城地区	Tacheng [Tarbagatai] Administrative Offices	29443	37691	36143	28365	18727
阿勒泰地区	Altay Administrative Offices	34463	38460	37502	39589	24737
博尔塔拉蒙古自治州	Bortala Mongol Autonomous Prefecture	28547	35369	44886	43500	22854
巴音郭楞蒙古自治州	Bayangol Mongol Autonomous Prefecture	36470	31118	43613	40338	21214
阿克苏地区	Aksu Administrative Offices	37543	32889	47102	30951	25916
克孜勒苏柯尔克孜自治州	Kizilsu Kirgiz Autonomous Prefecture	34503	34235	29663	21507	23071
喀什地区	Kashgar [Kaxgar] Administrative Offices	48813	34973	60683	27562	26778
和田地区	Hotan Administrative Offices	23006	30359	35705	33790	26946
石河子市	Shihezi City	32405	47285	52634	63268	28580
阿拉尔市	Aral City	30358	19111		45387	
图木舒克市	Tumxuk City	36815			49958	20067
五家渠市	Wujiaqu City	42668	33276	36867	39031	

3-28 续表 Continued

单位：元 (yuan)

年 份 Year	地 区 Region	金融业 Financial Intermedition	房地产业 Real Estate	租赁和商务服务业 Leasing and Business Services	科学研究、技术服务和地质勘查业 Scientific Research, Technology Service and Geological Prospecting	水利、环境和公共设施管理业 Management of Water Conservancy, Environment and Public Facility
总 计	**Total**	**69405**	**32609**	**27349**	**46264**	**29490**
乌鲁木齐市	Urumqi City	94116	38993	40955	54999	45451
克拉玛依市	Karamay City	79677	23465	27242	44443	26574
吐鲁番地区	Turpan Administrative Offices	51291	20720	16625	38391	33706
哈密地区	Hami [Kumul] Administrative Offices	65863	21933	23741	38724	20469
昌吉回族自治州	Changji Hui Autonomous Prefecture	69558	29264	17052	39981	33853
伊犁哈萨克自治州	Ili Kazak Autonomous Prefecture	63932	26224	20354	41277	26483
伊犁州直属县(市)	Counties (Cities) Direct Under Ili Prefecture	62136	25711	19883	39015	24254
塔城地区	Tacheng [Tarbagatai] Administrative Offices	64500	28356	21121	45898	29979
阿勒泰地区	Altay Administrative Offices	68575	28323	24799	42287	25845
博尔塔拉蒙古自治州	Bortala Mongol Autonomous Prefecture	76059	28420	10706	46842	27575
巴音郭楞蒙古自治州	Bayangol Mongol Autonomous Prefecture	64084	18238	24008	43999	25370
阿克苏地区	Aksu Administrative Offices	46756	26319	25481	41760	22473
克孜勒苏柯尔克孜自治州	Kizilsu Kirgiz Autonomous Prefecture	34092	29353	16140	31867	34452
喀什地区	Kashgar [Kaxgar] Administrative Offices	39140	20505	26578	29392	28586
和田地区	Hotan Administrative Offices	50635	27223	36601	42324	33776
石河子市	Shihezi City	53338	370588	34164	54027	39846
阿拉尔市	Aral City	28474	21000	22818	28844	26170
图木舒克市	Tumxuk City			28829	41105	30120
五家渠市	Wujiaqu City	64674	27635	36984	54427	24693

年 份 Year	地 区 Region	居民服务和其他服务业 Services to households and Other Services	教 育 Education	卫生、社会保障和社会福利业 Health, Social Security and Social Welfare	文化、体育和娱乐业 Culture, Sports and Entertainment	公共管理和社会组织 Public Administration and Social Organizations
总 计	**Total**	**31306**	**40917**	**39031**	**38723**	**40840**
乌鲁木齐市	Urumqi City	24567	42940	47137	43028	48977
克拉玛依市	Karamay City	52611	52008	53140	50517	51393
吐鲁番地区	Turpan Administrative Offices	26000	38304	37087	32725	38118
哈密地区	Hami [Kumul] Administrative Offices	21186	41145	35966	32935	39713
昌吉回族自治州	Changji Hui Autonomous Prefecture	14250	46564	43566	41827	43356
伊犁哈萨克自治州	Ili Kazak Autonomous Prefecture	23379	37981	34864	33505	36762
伊犁州直属县(市)	Counties (Cities) Direct Under Ili Prefecture	23266	36831	32566	32453	35185
塔城地区	Tacheng [Tarbagatai] Administrative Offices	23000	39160	37551	34626	38411
阿勒泰地区	Altay Administrative Offices	26217	40031	38101	34612	38452
博尔塔拉蒙古自治州	Bortala Mongol Autonomous Prefecture	33400	40067	36729	39634	36523
巴音郭楞蒙古自治州	Bayangol Mongol Autonomous Prefecture	26302	40523	36368	36584	39770
阿克苏地区	Aksu Administrative Offices	41711	35848	32743	35362	37254
克孜勒苏柯尔克孜自治州	Kizilsu Kirgiz Autonomous Prefecture	15683	38264	28670	32486	38554
喀什地区	Kashgar [Kaxgar] Administrative Offices	36316	40487	31587	36399	36282
和田地区	Hotan Administrative Offices	34307	43857	41548	39637	44167
石河子市	Shihezi City	19576	53094	51872	44280	49243
阿拉尔市	Aral City	44334	50731	77738	48277	43298
图木舒克市	Tumxuk City		35128	29012		41454
五家渠市	Wujiaqu City	45500	42710	45054	43818	48670

3-29 各地、州、市、县(市)在岗职工(含劳务派遣工)平均货币工资
Average Wages of Fully Employed Staff and Workers by Prefecture, Autonomous Prefecture, City and County

单位：元 (2011 年) (yuan)

地　区	Region	合　计 Total	国有单位 State-owned Units	城镇集体单位 Urban Collective-owned Units	其他单位 Units of Other Types of Ownership
总　计	**Total**	**38820**	**36752**	**40102**	**43177**
乌鲁木齐市	**Urumqi City**	**47747**	**51310**	**40650**	**43517**
天山区	Tianshan District	49109	53478	45501	41303
沙依巴克区	Shayibak District	41289	44393	37523	38204
新市区	Xinshi District	46114	45842	43261	46372
水磨沟区	Shui Mogou Distric	40565	44229	10453	37572
头屯河区	Tou Tunhe District	41538	31500	48182	49157
达坂城区	Da Bancheng District	58594	41191	29729	62801
米东区	Midong District	50138	58270	43134	43280
乌鲁木齐县	Urumqi County	57652	56243		92025
克拉玛依市	**Karamay City**	**58657**	**57385**	**29784**	**59788**
独山子区	Dushanzi District	62945	50036	28268	67498
克拉玛依区	Karamay District	59123	59955	29116	59023
乌尔河区	Urhe District	46620	54831	22000	60736
白碱滩区	Bai Jiantan District	28733	25179	94595	42483
吐鲁番地区	**Turpan Administrative Offices**	**45239**	**37942**	**29806**	**52273**
吐鲁番市	Turpan City	36909	37366	18523	36672
鄯善县	Shanshan [Piqan] County	54810	37531	65287	62683
托克逊县	Toksun County	39985	40582	25139	39653
哈密地区	**Hami [Kumul] Administrative Offices**	**38202**	**34388**	**30445**	**47357**
哈密市	Hami [Kumul] City	39873	35768	26568	47531
巴里坤哈萨克自治县	Barkol Kazak Autonomous County	29309	28500	38660	38548
伊吾县	Yiwu [Araturuk] County	39218	37845	20113	60248
昌吉回族自治州	**Changji Hui Autonomous Prefecture**	**36417**	**36579**	**49584**	**35470**
昌吉市	Changji City	38685	41930	54029	34896
阜康市	Fukang City	36767	36124	64717	37127
呼图壁县	Hutubi County	30592	29802	66847	31760
玛纳斯县	Manas County	36447	35430	32729	42686
奇台县	Qitai County	33451	33914	49726	31155
吉木萨尔县	Jimsar County	40189	40627	49350	35316
木垒哈萨克自治县	Mori Kazak Autonomous County	42606	43795	52198	25836
伊犁哈萨克自治州	**Ili Kazak Autonomous Prefecture**	**29142**	**28024**	**48168**	**33446**
伊犁州直属县(市)	**Counties (Cities) Direct Under Ili Prefecture**	**30802**	**29795**	**40906**	**33463**
伊宁市	Yining [Gulja] City	33525	32711	35128	34517
奎屯市	Kuytun City	34397	34907	26162	32631
伊宁县	Yining [Gulja] County	23580	22772	9976	27641
察布查尔锡伯自治县	Qapqal Xibe Autonomous County	28759	29019	34833	25149
霍城县	Huocheng [Korgas] County	26931	26145	42861	34386
巩留县	Gongliu [Tokkuztara] County	30885	31388	41262	

3-29 续表 1 Continued

单位：元 (yuan)

地　　区	Region	合　计 Total	国　有 单　位 State-owned Units	城镇集体 单　位 Urban Collective-owned Units	其　他 单　位 Units of Other Types of Ownership
新源县	Xinyuan [Kunes] County	31756	31576	79290	31559
昭苏县	Zhaosu [Mongolkure] County	28837	28077	63438	33290
特克斯县	Tekes County	33730	33596	101289	30186
尼勒克县	Nilka County	35069	30656	48307	51597
塔城地区	**Tacheng [Tarbagatai] Administrative Offices**	**27825**	**27219**	**43513**	**32197**
塔城市	Tacheng [Qoqek] City	33388	30777	27781	48434
乌苏市	Usu City	23119	22018	33100	31170
额敏县	Emin [Dorbiljin] County	21127	20187	66699	28606
沙湾县	Shawan County	32503	33033	65407	16979
托里县	Toli County	36362	38751	23986	26406
裕民县	Yumin [Qagantokay] County	24281	24266	30239	19452
和布克赛尔蒙古自治县	Hoboksar Mongol Autonomous County	26865	24782	55927	33914
阿勒泰地区	**Altay Administrative Offices**	**27662**	**25864**	**86620**	**34911**
阿勒泰市	Altay City	28425	27536	109391	31695
布尔津县	Burqin County	28520	27243	33936	33175
富蕴县	Fuyun [Koktokay] County	22587	18344	121890	33660
福海县	Fuhai [Burultokay] County	25450	25125	84029	26143
哈巴河县	Habahe [Kaba] County	31559	27655	85778	39774
青河县	Qinghe [Qinggil] County	35083	30677	130690	65790
吉木乃县	Jeminay County	27395	26904	44057	32396
博尔塔拉蒙古自治州	**Bortala Mongol Autonomous Prefecture**	**28391**	**27942**	**35133**	**31106**
博乐市	Bole [Bortala] City	31050	30689	76706	33163
精河县	Jinghe [Jing] County	25445	24753	30994	25599
温泉县	Wenquan [Araxang] County	22661	22280	93826	21015
巴音郭楞蒙古自治州	**Bayangol Mongol Autonomous Prefecture**	**37851**	**32783**	**45080**	**45971**
库尔勒市	Korla City	40982	36137	28405	45470
轮台县	Luntai [Bugur] County	34001	32950	71461	41126
尉犁县	Yuli [Lopnur] County	32204	31837	51240	21479
若羌县	Ruoqiang [Qarkilik] County	57389	32484	116827	102183
且末县	Qiemo [Qarqan] County	34421	34661	36520	31918
焉耆回族自治县	Yanji Hui Autonomous County	31732	30642	71687	64642
和静县	Hejing County	32579	29015	26301	40241
和硕县	Hoxud County	25881	25391	71698	24224
博湖县	Bohu [Bagrax] County	28356	27690	87990	24640
阿克苏地区	**Aksu Administrative Offices**	**34998**	**33404**	**40127**	**38618**
阿克苏市	Aksu City	37593	36281	35622	41862
温宿县	Wensu [Onsu] County	25787	26614	28542	23449
库车县	Kuqa County	42056	35032	41771	49913
沙雅县	Xayar County	30607	30807	46384	29389
新和县	Xinhe [Toksu] County	34331	34696	67622	29022

3-29 续表 2 Continued

单位：元 (yuan)

地　区	Region	合计 Total	国有单位 State-owned Units	城镇集体单位 Urban Collective-owned Units	其他单位 Units of Other Types of Ownership
拜城县	Baicheng [Bay] County	36623	32098	43895	42112
乌什县	Wushi [Uxturpan] County	33045	33894	43145	22084
阿瓦提县	Awat County	31594	33399	29290	26408
柯坪县	Kalpin County	30827	30738	34500	37000
克孜勒苏柯尔克孜自治州	**Kizilsu Kirgiz Autonomous Prefecture**	**33131**	**33444**	**22413**	**26116**
阿图什市	Artux City	32046	32378	20517	28020
阿克陶县	Akto County	41170	41947	22801	10630
阿合奇县	Akqi County	25831	25856	26440	19333
乌恰县	Wuqia [Ulugqat] County	32632	32674	27053	19000
喀什地区	**Kashgar [Kaxgar] Administrative Offices**	**36088**	**35687**	**28212**	**39308**
喀什市	Kashgar [Kaxgar] City	39261	36456	19770	43797
疏附县	Shufu County	35317	35725	33155	17244
疏勒县	Shule County	32379	33488	25354	20624
英吉沙县	Yengisar County	33818	33642	39042	29239
泽普县	Zepu [Poskam] County	35908	37192	31301	19332
莎车县	Shache [Yarkant] County	34354	34901	26981	20780
叶城县	Yecheng [Kagilik] County	43370	48288	31649	26463
麦盖提县	Makit County	30270	30486	34711	26939
岳普湖县	Yopurga County	33489	33482	33883	
伽师县	Jiashi [Payzawat] County	32295	32343	29833	19500
巴楚县	Bachu [Maralbexi] County	33801	34468	18059	25704
塔什库尔干塔吉克自治县	Taxkorgan Tajik Autonomous County	41033	41033		
和田地区	**Hotan Administrative Offices**	**37664**	**38896**	**44454**	**28686**
和田市	Hotan City	40201	44566	43991	28407
和田县	Hotan County	50213	50622		41058
墨玉县	Moyu [Karakax] County	33638	33804	26234	30966
皮山县	Pishan [Guma] County	29857	29905	62352	24685
洛浦县	Lop County	40828	40978	40522	34063
策勒县	Qira County	36115	37887	57788	24358
于田县	Yutian [Keriya] County	42756	42988		38829
民丰县	Minfeng [Niya] County	40903	41208	26106	36878
自治区直辖县级市	**Municpality Country-LevelCity Directly under the Central Government**	**36841**	**36426**	**93811**	**37452**
石河子市	Shihezi City	38909	39248	93811	38257
阿拉尔市	Aral City	35193	35209		35064
图木舒克市	Tumxuk City	30684	29900		35181
五家渠市	Wujiaqu City	33570	33343		34044

主要统计指标解释

人口数 指一定时点、一定地区范围内的有生命的个人的总和。

年度统计的年末人口数指每年 12 月 31 日 24 时的人口数。

市、镇、县人口 其定义有两种口径：

第一种口径(按行政建制)

市人口：市管辖区域内的全部人口(含市辖镇，不含市辖区县)；

镇人口：县辖镇的全部人口(不含市辖镇)；

县人口：县辖乡人口。

第二种口径(按常住人口划分)

市人口：设区的市的区人口和不设区的市所辖的街道人口；

镇人口：不设区的市所辖镇的居民委员会人口和县辖镇的居民委员会人口；

县人口：除上述两种人口以外的全部人口。

出生率(又称粗出生率) 指在一定时期内(通常为一年)平均每千人所出生的人数的比率，一般用千分率表示。计算公式为：

出生率＝年出生人数 / 年平均人数×1000‰

式中：出生人数指活产婴儿，即胎儿脱离母体时(不管怀孕月数)，有过呼吸或其他生命现象。年平均人数指年初、年底人口数的平均数，也可用年中人口数代替。

死亡率(又称粗死亡率) 指在一定时期内(通常为一年)一定地区的死亡人数与同期平均人数(或期中人数)之比，一般用千分率表示。计算公式为：

死亡率＝年死亡人数 / 年平均人数×1000‰

人口自然增长率 指在一定时期内(通常为一年)人口自然增加数(出生人数减死亡人数)与该时期内平均人数(或期中人数)之比，一般用千分率表示。计算公式为：

人口自然增长率＝(本年出生人数－本年死亡人数) / 年平均人数×1000‰＝人口出生率－人口死亡率

经济活动人口 指在 16 岁以上，有劳动能力，参加或要求参加社会经济活动的人口；包括就业人员和失业人员。

就业人口 指 16 周岁及以上从事一定的社会劳动并取得劳动报酬或经营收入的人员。这一指标反应了一定时期内全部劳动力资源的实际利用情况，是研究我国基本国情国力的重要指标。

单位就业人员 指在各级国家机关、政党机关、社会团体及企业、事业单位中工作，取得工资或其他形式的劳动报酬的全部人员。包括在岗职工、再就业的离退休人员、民办教师以及在各单位中工作的外方人员和港澳台方人员、兼职人员、借用的外单位人员和第二职业者。不包括离开本单位仍保留劳动关系的职工。各单位的就业人员反映了各单位实际参加生产或工作的全部劳动力。

国有单位 指资产归国家所有的经济组织。包括按《中华人民共和国企业法人登记管理条例》规定登记注册的非公司制的经济组织，以及中央、地方各级国家机关、事业单位和社会团体。

集体单位 指生产资料归集体所有，并按《中华人民共和国企业法人登记管理条例》规定登记注册的经济组织。

其他单位 包括股份合作单位、联营单位、有限责任公司、股份有限公司、港澳台商投资单位以及外商投资单位等其他登记注册类型单位。

城镇私营和个体就业人员 城镇私营就业人员指在工商管理部门注册登记，其经营地址设在县城关镇(含城关镇)以上的私营企业从业人员；包括私营企业投资者和雇工。城镇个体就业人员指在工商管理部门注册登记，并持有城镇户口或在城镇长期居住，经批准从事个体工商经营的从业人员；包括个体经营者和在个体工商户劳动的家庭帮工和雇工。

在岗职工 指在本单位工作并由单位支付工资的人员，以及有工作岗位，但由于学习、病伤产假等原因暂未工作，仍由单位支付工资的人员。

工资总额 指各单位在一定时期内直接支付给本单位全部就业人员的劳动报酬总额。工资总额的计算原则应以直接支付给就业人员的全部劳动报酬为根据。各单位支付给就业人员的劳动报酬以及其他根据有关规定支付的工资，不论是计入成本的还是不计入成本的，不论是按国家规定列入计征奖金税项目的，还是未列入计征奖金税项目的，不论是以货币形式支付的还是以实物形式支付的，均包括在工资总额内。

平均工资 指企业、事业、机关单位的就业人员在一定时期内平均每人所得的货币工资额。它表明一定时期职工工资收入的高低程度，是反映就业人员工资水平的主要指标。计算公式为：

平均工资＝报告期实际支付的全部就业人员工资总额 / 报告期全部就业人员平均人数

平均工资指数 指报告期就业人员平均工资与基期就业人员平均工资的比率，是反映不同时期就业人员货币工资水平变动情况的相对数。计算公式为：

平均工资指数＝报告期就业人员平均工资 / 基期就业人员平均工资

平均实际工资指数 就业人员平均实际工资指扣除物价变动因素后的职工平均工资。就业人员平均实际工资指数是反映实际工资变动情况的相对数，表明就业人员实际工资水平提高或降低的程度。计算公式为：

平均实际工资指数＝报告期就业人员平均工资指数 / 报告期城镇居民消费价格指数×100%

城镇登记失业人员 指有非农业户口，在一定的劳动年龄内（16 周岁至退休年龄），有劳动能力，无业而要求就业，并在当地劳动保障部门进行失业登记的人员。

城镇登记失业率 指城镇登记失业人员与城镇单位就业人员（扣除使用的农村劳动力、聘用的离退休人员、港澳台及外方人员）、城镇单位中不在岗职工、城镇私营业主、个体户主、城镇私营企业和个体就业人员、城镇登记失业人数之和的比。计算公式为：

城镇登记失业率=城镇登记失业人数 / {(城镇单位就业人数-使用的农村劳动力-聘用的离退休人员-聘用的港澳台及外方人员)+ 不在岗职工+城镇私营业主+城镇个体户主+城镇私营企业及个体就业人员+城镇登记失业人数)}×100%

Explanatory Notes on Main Statistical Indicators

Total Population refers to the total number of people alive at a certain point of time within a given area.

The annual statistics on total population is taken at midnight, the 3lst of December.

City,Town and County Population Urban Population and Rural Population.

There are two definitions.The first definition (according to the administrative organizational system):

City Population Total population under the jurisdiction of City (including population of the town under the jurisdiction of City. excluding the population of counties under the jurisdiction of City).

Town Population Total population of town under the jurisdiction of County (excluding the population of town under the jurisdiction of City).

County Population Total population of country under the jurisdiction of County).

The second definition (classified by the permanent population):

City Population Total population of districts under the jurisdiction of City with district establishment and the population of street under the jurisdiction of City without district establishment.

Town Population Total resident-committees population of towns under the jurisdiction of City without district establishment and the resident-committees population of towns under the jurisdiction of County.

County Population Total population except City population and town population.

Birth Rate(or Crude Birth Rate) refers to the ratio of the number of births to the average population during a certain period of time(usually a year) which is often expressed in‰. The following formula is used:

Brith Rate= Number of Births/Annual Average Number of Population

Number of births refers to live births i.e. the births when babies had showed any vital phenomena regardless of the length of pregnancy.

Annual average number of population is the average of the number of population at the beginning of the year and that at the end of the year. Sometimes it is substituted for with the mid year population.

Death Rate(or Crude Death Rate) refers to the ratio of the number of deaths to the average population (or mid year population) during a certain period of time (usually a year) which is often expressed in‰. The following formula is used:

Death Rate =Number of Deaths/ Annual Average Number of Population

Natural Growth Rate of Population refers to the ratio of natural increase in population(number of births minus number of deaths)in a certain period of time(usually a year)to the average population(or mid year population)of the same period which is often expressed in‰. The following formula is applied:

Natural Growth Rate of Population= Number of Births-Number of Deaths / Average Number of Population

Natural Growth Rate of Population=Birth Rate-Death Rate

Economically Active Population refers to the population aged 16 and over who are capable to work, are participating in or willing to participate in economic activities, including employed persons and unemployed persons.

Employed Population refers to population aged 15 or over engaging in social labour which generates income.

Persons Employed in Various Units refer to all the persons working in government agencies of various levels, political and party organizations, social organizations, enterprises and institutions, and receiving wages or other forms of payment. They include fully-employed staff and workers, re-employed retirees, teachers in schools run by the local people, foreigners and Chinese compatriots from Hong Kong, Macao, and Taiwan working in various units, part-time employees, employees of other units working temporarily at current posts, and employees holding the second job, but exclude staff and workers who have left their working units while keeping their labour contract (employment relation) unchanged. This indicator reflects the total number of laborers actually engaged in production or other operations in various units.

State-owned Units refer to economic units whose assets are owned by the state.Included are non-corporation units registered according to Regulation of the People's Republic of China on the Registration of Enterprises and Corporation ,state argans,institutions and social organizations at the central and local levels.

Collective-owned Units refer to economic units registered according to Regulation of the People's Republic of China on the Registration of Enterprises and Corporations where the means of production are collectively owned.

Units of Other Types of Ownership refer to units registered with other types of ownership,including cooperative units,joint ownership units,limited companies,share holding corporation,units invested by entrepreneurs from Hong Kong,

Macao,and Taiwan,and foreign-invested units.

Persons Employed in Private Enterprises and Self-Employed Individuals in Urban Areas Persons employed in private enterprises refer to the persons employed in the private enterprises which have been registered at the departments of industrial and commercial administration and are situated at a County town (i.e. a town where the County government is located) for business operation or at urban areas with the level higher than a County town. The self-employed individuals in urban areas refer to persons who hold the certificates of residence in urban areas or have resided in the urban areas for a long time and have been registered at the departments of industrial and commercial administration and approved to be engaged in individual industrial or commercial business, including self-employed persons as well as helpers and hired labourers who work in the individual households engaged in industrial or commercial business.

Staff and Workers refer to the persons who work in(and receive payment therefrom)enterprises and institutions of state ownership, collective ownership, joint ownership, share holding, foreign ownership, and ownership by entrepreneurs from Hong Kong, Macao, and Taiwan, and other types of ownership and their affiliated units, excluding the retired persons invited to work in the units again, teachers in the schools run by the local people and foreigners and persons coming from Hong Kong, Macao and Taiwan and working in the state-owned economic units. (Number of staff and workers in this yearbook include only fully employed staff and workers, excluding those who have left their working units while keeping their labour contract/employment relation unchanged).

Total Wages refer to the total remuneration payment to staff and workers in various units during a certain period of time. The calculation of total wages is based on the total remuneration payment to the staff and workers. Therefore, all the wages and salaries and other payments to staff and workers are included in the total wages regardless of their sources, category, and forms (in kind or cash). (Total wages of staff and workers in this yearbook include only total wages of fully employed staff and workers, excluding the living allowances distributed to those who have left their working units while keeping their labour contract/employment relation unchanged).

Average Wage refers to the average wage in money terms per person during a certain period of time for staff and workers in enterprises, institutions, and government agencies, which reflects the general level of wage income during a certain period of time and is calculated as follows:

Average Wage of Staff and Workers =Total Wages of Staff and Workers in Reference Period/Average Number of Staff and Workers in Reference Period.

Index of Average Wage refers to the ratio of average wage of staff and workers at the report time to that at the reference time. It reflects the relative changing degree of average wage in money terms at the various of time, which is calculated as following:

Index of Average Wage of Staff and Worker = average wage of staff and workers at the report time/average wage of staff and workers at the reference time

Index of Average Real Wage refers to the average wage which has removed the factor of price change. Index of average real wage of staff and worker reflects the relative changing degree of average real wage, and indicates the degree of the rising or declining degree of real wage of staff and worker, which is calculated as following:

Index of Average Real Wage of Staff and Worker = Index of Average Wage of Staff and Worker at the Report Time/Urban Consumer Prices Index at the Report Time

Registered Unemployed Persons in Urban Areas refer to the persons with non-agricultural household registration at certain working ages (16 years old to retirement age), who are capable of working, unemployed and willing to work, and have been registered at the local employment service agencies to apply for a job.

Registered Unemployment Rate in Urban Areas refers to the ratio of the number of the registered unemployed persons to the sum of the number of persons employed in various units (minus the employed rural labour force, re-employed retirees, and Hong Kong, Macao, Taiwan or foreign employees), laid-off staff and workers in urban units, owners of private enterprises in urban areas, owners of self-employed individuals in urban areas, employees of private enterprises in urban areas, employyee of self-employed individuals in urban areas, and the registered unemployed persons in urban areas. The formula is as follows:

$$\text{Registered unemployment rate in urban areas} = \frac{\text{number of registered urban unemployed persons}}{\begin{array}{c}\text{number of persons employed in urban units - employed rural labour force} \\ \text{re - employed retirees - Hong Kong, Macao, Taiwan or foreign employees} \\ + \text{laid - off staff and workers} + \text{owners of urban private enterprises} + \text{owners of} \\ \text{urban self - employed individuals} + \text{employees of urban private enterprises} + \text{employees of} \\ \text{urban self - employed individuals} + \text{registered unemployed persons in urban areas}\end{array}} \times 100\%$$

2012

新疆统计年鉴

XINJIANG STATISTICAL YEARBOOK

第四篇 固定资产投资

CHAPTER 4 Investment in Fixed Assets

简要说明
Brief Introduction

本篇资料的主要内容及来源

本篇资料包括主要年份全社会固定资产投资及其主要分组；2011年及同期的全区固定资产投资及其细化分组；2011年新增主要产品生产能力(或效益)；房地产开发企业基本情况；农村非农户及农户固定资产投资情况

农村固定资产投资来自国家统计局新疆调查总队商业和投资建筑业调查处；其余资料均来自新疆维吾尔自治区统计局固定资产投资统计处。

本篇的统计调查方法除农户固定资产投资统计采用抽样调查方法外，其他均为全面统计报表。

Main Content and Source of Data

Statistics in this chapter cover the total investment in fixed assets of the whole society and its composition, total investment in fixed assets and its refining grouping by region in 2011; newly increased production capacity of major production in 2011; basic condition of enterprises for real estate development, basic condition of individual investment in fixed assets of farm households and non-farm households. The data of individual investment in fixed assets in rural areas come from the Trade and Fixed Assets and Construction Census Division of NBS Survey Office in Xinjiang; Others data come from the Division of Investment in Fixed Assets, Xinjiang Bureau of Statistics.Method of data collection: All data on the investment in fixed assets are collected by the statistical reporting system with complete enumeration, except data on the investment in fixed assets in rural areas which are collected through sample surveys,others are Comprehensive statistics.

4-1 1978-2011 年历年全社会固定资产投资

Total Investment in Fixed Assets in the Whole Country by Period(1978-2011)

单位：万元 (10 000 yuan)

年份 Year	合计 Total	城镇 Urban Area	#房地产 Real Estate Development	农村 Rural Area	非农户 Non-Farm Households	农村个人 Farm Individuals
1978	129999	129999				
1979	138253	138253				
1980	204652	203489		1163		1163
1981	183986	171706		12280	10000	2280
1982	247382	233668		13714	9693	4021
1983	277923	262027		15896	8804	7092
1984	337250	305713		31537	11089	20448
1985	444758	408435		36323	11528	24795
1986	484658	443631		41027	13934	27093
1987	512479	469898		42581	14714	27867
1988	684119	622041		62078	16848	45230
1989	750698	664243		86455	18841	67614
1990	887775	791555	9456	96220	20578	75642
1991	1249325	1130155	16886	119170	26946	92224
1992	1700326	1571456	23941	128870	33202	95668
1993	2484352	2336810	53616	147542	40738	106804
1994	2854786	2614211	86244	240575	70349	170226
1995	3333404	3035386	171238	298018	92118	205900
1996	3878472	3495942	156232	382530	111936	270594
1997	4468148	3987127	169906	481021	131063	349958
1998	5197673	4709794	148577	487879	136402	351477
1999	5346468	4847597	234481	498871	150744	348127
2000	6103843	5568492	574347	535351	171862	363489
2001	7059970	6469753	979184	590217	210040	380177
2002	8130223	7474024	877060	656199	252891	403308
2003	10021256	9213289	1024908	807967	327137	480830
2004	11615245	10608048	1125577	1007197	463358	543839
2005	13522757	12232255	1016618	1290502	573585	716917
2006	15670521	14180110	1208786	1490411	699084	791327
2007	18508415	16591894	1683160	1916521	1080611	835910
2008	22599746	20256393	2286267	2343353	1412796	930557
2009	28272359	25358648	2358805	2913711	1874325	1039386
2010	35396941	31815829	3477185	3581112	2395698	1185414
2011	47127699	42044959	5163895	5082740	3211176	1871564

4-2 全社会固定资产投资

Total Investment in Fixed Assets in the Whole Country

单位：万元　　(2011 年)　　(10 000 yuan)

项　目	Item	合 计 Total	城　镇 Urban	#房地产 Real Estate Development
投资总额	**Total Investment**	**47127699**	**42044959**	**5163895**
#住 宅	Residential Buildings	8929754	7678276	4163926
#国有经济控股	State-holding	27527833	25602506	626785
按构成分	**Grouped by Use of Funds**			
建筑工程	Construction	29541315	26408010	3972278
安装工程	Installation	3362813	3215031	336780
设备工器具购置	Purchase of Equipment and Instruments	10626129	9155476	53225
其他费用	Other Expenses	3597442	3266442	801612
按三次产业分	**Grouped by Three Strata of Industry**			
第一产业	Primary Industry	2377851	1018114	
第二产业	Secondary Industry	24653475	23161011	
第三产业	Tertiary Industry	20096373	17865834	5163895
按登记注册类型分	**Grouped by Types of Registration**			
内资企业	Domestic Fund Enterprises	44446004	41353527	5133333
国 有	State-owned	17004520	15232942	128505
集 体	Collective-owned	85477	43536	1500
股份合作	Share-holding Cooperative	46449	45379	439
联营企业	Joint Ownership Enterprises	91035	61166	
国有联营企业	State Joint Ownership Enterprises	42911	42011	
集体联营企业	Collective-owned Joint Ownership Enterprises	2041	2041	
其他联营企业	Others	46083	17114	
有限责任公司	Limited Liability Corporations	13269168	12565450	2570342
国有独资公司	State-funded Corporations	925519	921862	160644
其他有限责任公司	Other Limited Liability Corporations	12343649	11643588	2409698
股份有限公司	Share-holding Corporations Ltd	7025593	6902764	9451
私营企业	Private Enterprises	6096718	5768588	2397080
其他企业	Others	827044	733702	26016

4-2 续表 1 Continued

单位：万元 (10 000 yuan)

项　目	Item	农　村 Rural	非农户 Non-Rural Households	农村个人 Rural Individuals
投资总额	**Total Investment**	**5082740**	**3211176**	**1871564**
#住　宅	Residential Buildings	1251478	470543	780935
#国有经济控股	State-holding	1925327	1925327	
按构成分	**Grouped by Use of Funds**			
建筑工程	Construction	3133305	2234227	899078
安装工程	Installation	147782	147782	
设备工器具购置	Purchase of Equipment and Instruments	1470653	672389	798264
其他费用	Other Expenses	331000	156778	174222
按三次产业分	**Grouped by Three Strata of Industry**			
第一产业	Primary Industry	1359737	658798	700939
第二产业	Secondary Industry	1492464	1387235	105229
第三产业	Tertiary Industry	2230539	1165143	1065396
按登记注册类型分	**Grouped by Types of Registration**			
内资企业	Domestic Fund	3092477	3092477	
国　有	State-owned	1771578	1771578	
集　体	Collective-owned	41941	41941	
股份合作	Share holding Cooperative	1070	1070	
联营企业	Joint Ownership Enterprises	29869	29869	
国有联营企业	State Joint Ownership Enterprises	900	900	
集体联营企业	Collective Joint Ownership Enterprises			
其他联营企业	Others	28969	28969	
有限责任公司	Limited Liability Corporations	703718	703718	
国有独资公司	State-funded Corporations	3657	3657	
其他有限责任公司	Other Limited Liability Corporations	700061	700061	
股份有限公司	Share-holding Corporations Ltd	122829	122829	
私营企业	Private Enterprises	328130	328130	
其他企业	Others Enterprises	93342	93342	

4-2 续表 2 Continued

单位：万元 (10 000 yuan)

项　目	Item	合 计 Total	城 镇 Urban	＃房地产 Real Estate Development
港澳台商投资企业	Enterprises With Funds from Hong Kong, Macao and Taiwan	234928	203323	30562
合资经营企业(港或澳、台资)	Joint-venture Enterprises (Hongkong,Macao and Taiwan)	138021	109016	23569
港、澳、台商独资经营企业	Enterprises With Sole Investment	72028	70028	6993
港、澳、台商投资股份有限公司	Share-holding Corporation Ltd.	24879	24279	
外商投资企业	Foreign Funded Enterprises	384156	382159	
中外合资经营企业(港或澳、台资)	Joint-venture Enterprises (Hongkong,Macao and Taiwan)	41420	41420	
中外合作经营企业(港或澳、台资)	Cooperation Enterprises (Hongkon,Macao and Taiwan)	48110	46573	
外资企业	Enterprises With Sole Funds	204069	203609	
外商投资股份有限公司	Share-holding Corporations Ltd.	90557	90557	
个体经营	Individual Operate	2062611	105950	
＃个 体 户	Self-employed Personel	170671	90680	
个人合伙	Individual Partnership	20376	15270	
按隶属关系分	**By Administrative Relationship**			
中 央	Central Government	11815177	11237905	175468
地 方	Local	35312522	30807054	4988427
资金来源小计	**All Sources**	**51265602**	**45779280**	**6843313**
国家预算内资金	State Budget Funds	6266348	5264602	
国内贷款	Domestic Loans	6679368	6183760	731550
债 券	Bonds	22559	21737	
利用外资	Foreign Investment	137967	131659	1666
自筹资金	Self-raising Funds	30523848	27037657	2314233
其他资金来源	Others	7635512	7139865	3795864
本年新增固定资产	**Newly Increased Fixed Assets**	**27216158**	**23185817**	**2321411**
房屋施工面积(万平方米)	**Floor Space of Buildings (10 000 sq.m)**	**16804.88**	**13686.08**	**5481.44**
＃住 宅	Residential Buildings	11357.36	8883.89	4574.72
房屋竣工面积(万平方米)	**Floor Space of Buildings Completed (10 000 sq.m)**	**5899.06**	**3628.85**	**1270.48**
＃住 宅	Residential Buildings	4504.94	2621.59	1108.02

4-2 续表 3 Continued

单位：万元 (10 000 yuan)

项 目	Item	农 村 Rural	非农户 Non-Rural Households	农村个人 Rural Individuals
港澳台商投资企业	Enterprises With Funds from Hong Kong, Macao and Taiwan	31605	31605	
合资经营企业(港或澳、台资)	Joint-venture Enterprises (Honkong,Macao and Taiwan)	29005	29005	
港、澳、台商独资经营企业	Enterprises With Sole Investment	2000	2000	
港、澳、台商投资股份有限公司	Share-holding Corporation Ltd.	600	600	
外商投资企业	Foreign Funded			
中外合资经营企业(港或澳、台资)	Joint-venture Enterprises (Honkong,Macao and Taiwan)			
中外合作经营企业(港或澳、台资)	Cooperation Enterprises (Honkong,Macao and Taiwan)	1537	1537	
外资企业	Enterprises With Sole Funds	460	460	
外商投资股份有限公司	Share-holding Corporations Ltd.			
个体经营	Individual Operate	1956661	85097	1871564
#个 体 户	Self-employed Personel	79991	79991	
个人合伙	Individual Partnership	5106	5106	
按隶属关系分	**By Administrative Relationship**			
中 央	Central Government	577272	577272	
地 方	Local	4505468	2633904	1871564
资金来源小计	**All Sources**	**5486322**	**3614758**	**1871564**
国家预算内资金	State Budget Funds	1001746	1001746	
国内贷款	Domestic Loans	495608	177709	317899
债 券	Bonds	822	822	
利用外资	Foreign Investment	6308	6308	
自筹资金	Self-raising Funds	3486191	2045605	1440586
其他资金来源	Others	495647	382568	113079
本年新增固定资产	**Newly Increased Fixed Assets**	**4030341**	**2158777**	**1871564**
房屋施工面积(万平方米)	**Floor Space of Buildings (10 000 sq.m)**	**3118.8**	**1223.34**	**1895.46**
#住 宅	Residential Buildings	2473.47	744.25	1729.22
房屋竣工面积(万平方米)	**Floor Space of Buildings Completed (10 000 sq.m)**	**2270.21**	**547.39**	**1722.82**
#住 宅	Residential Buildings	1883.35	322.04	1561.31

4-3 按构成分全社会固定资产投资

Structure of Total Investment in Fixed Assets in the whole Country

单位：万元 (10 000 yuan)

年 份 Year	地 区 Region	合计 Total	建筑工程 Construction Works	安装工程 Installation Works	设备工具器具购置 Purchase of Equipment and Instruments	其他费用 Others
	1978	129999	86667		35686	7646
	1985	444758	323395		93254	28109
	1990	887775	571461		274647	41667
	1995	3333404	2145762		810995	376647
	1996	3878472	2245924	278445	929463	424640
	1997	4468148	2725428	310687	988070	443963
	1998	5197673	3435120	278895	920992	562666
	1999	5346468	3245779	344130	1039617	716942
	2000	6103843	3833328	416759	1254077	599679
	2001	7059970	4232768	454765	1616907	755530
	2002	8130223	4815707	593242	1787899	933375
	2003	10021256	6075091	690459	2030335	1225371
	2004	11615245	7133323	806705	2304931	1370286
	2005	13522757	8499303	993311	2637777	1392366
	2006	15670521	9776613	1014851	3166617	1712440
	2007	18508415	10667717	1517359	4312525	2010814
	2008	22599746	13071829	1773200	5488261	2266456
	2009	28272359	17511739	1938944	5855684	2965992
	2010	35396941	22224487	1943535	7960420	3268499
	2011	47127699	29541315	3362813	10626129	3597442
乌鲁木齐市	Urumqi City	6539156	3857740	559844	1565527	556045
克拉玛依市	Karamay City	2130936	1390529	358495	264708	117204
吐鲁番地区	Turpan Administrative Offices	1270996	701423	103451	374683	91439
哈密地区	Hami [Kumul] Administrative Offices	2135256	978431	234621	720331	201873
昌吉回族自治州	Changji Hui Autonomous Prefecture	5631443	3045920	320587	1880796	384140
伊犁哈萨克自治州	Ili Kazak Autonomous Prefecture	8331104	5422491	539151	1641429	728033
伊犁州直属县(市)	Counties (Cities) Direct Under Ili Prefecture	4585258	2860085	354721	970004	400448
塔城地区	Tacheng [Tarbagatai] Administrative Offices	2316119	1639711	129002	437704	109702
阿勒泰地区	Altay Administrative Offices	1429727	922695	55428	233721	217883
博尔塔拉蒙古自治州	Bortala Mongol Autonomous Prefecture	815624	509124	43061	182343	81096
巴音郭楞蒙古自治州	Bayangol Mongol Autonomous Prefecture	3883539	2700825	288402	607958	286354
阿克苏地区	Aksu Administrative Offices	2462047	1523099	228927	611211	98810
克孜勒苏柯尔克孜自治州	Kizilsu Kirgiz Autonomous Prefecture	466943	347648	12835	82244	24216
喀什地区	Kashgar [Kaxgar] Administrative Offices	3935437	3044507	254721	463117	173092
和田地区	Hotan Administrative Offices	1208289	925173	29834	104519	148763
石河子市	Shihezi City	1638136	694354	178859	613832	151091
阿拉尔市	Aral City	547654	312267	24338	186562	24487
图木舒克市	Tumxuk City	236067	144135	5782	60109	26041
五家渠市	Wujiaqu City	956599	413874	128215	341895	72615
跨地区投资	Trans-regional Investment	3066909	2630697	51690	126601	257921

注：各地区投资中不包括农村个人投资。
Note: Investment classified in different regions does not include rural individual investment.

4-4 全社会固定资产投资资金来源情况

Sources of Funds of Total Investment in Fixed Assets in the Whole Country

单位：万元 (10 000 yuan)

年份 Year	地区 Region	合计 Total	国家预算内资金 State Budget	国内贷款 Domestic Loans	债券 Bonds	利用外资 Foreign Investment	自筹及其他资金 Self-raising Fund And Others
	1978	129999	102693				27306
	1985	444758	117439	72227		7708	247384
	1990	887775	105423	294985		40927	446440
	1995	3333404	98004	818914		307619	2108867
	1996	3878472	128725	756412		324532	2668803
	1997	4468148	269106	749345		109629	3340068
	1998	5197673	384195	1116497		133936	3563045
	1999	5346468	512364	1097949	12376	93895	3629884
	2000	6103843	506867	1346175	19429	99942	4131430
	2001	7059970	545176	1321317	8340	64834	5120303
	2002	8130223	1323660	1607535	30504	62992	5105532
	2003	10021256	1626261	1896104	21586	95287	6382018
	2004	11490824	1799593	1555105	46095	87388	8002643
	2005	13543432	2093022	1677020	15428	109968	9647994
	2006	15773966	2119253	1854512	8193	88675	11703333
	2007	19070184	2258779	2480410	5526	110034	14215435
	2008	22725814	3388141	3020001	3410	90233	16224029
	2009	30345365	5813486	5246186	54636	94000	19137057
	2010	37844438	6347565	5750361	11544	120367	25614601
	2011	51265602	6266348	6679368	22559	137967	38159360
乌鲁木齐市	Urumqi City	7981776	285950	1740506	450	29277	5925593
克拉玛依市	Karamay City	2152806	194083	16000			1942723
吐鲁番地区	Turpan Administrative Offices	1352795	55564	340156	525	4489	952061
哈密地区	Hami [Kumul] Administrative Offices	2304734	201167	495774	565		1607228
昌吉回族自治州	Changji Hui Autonomous Prefecture	6639539	485720	812575		10380	5330864
伊犁哈萨克自治州	Ili Kazak Autonomous Prefecture	8977293	1452383	1030586	1766	38420	6454138
伊犁州直属县(市)	Counties (Cities) Direct Under Ili Prefecture	5048093	715997	661243	312	14259	3656282
塔城地区	Tacheng [Tarbagatai] Administrative Offices	2710804	447010	195044	1363	13068	2054319
阿勒泰地区	Altay Administrative Offices	1218396	289376	174299	91	11093	743537
博尔塔拉蒙古自治州	Bortala Mongol Autonomous Prefecture	871969	167564	46014	920	9436	648035
巴音郭楞蒙古自治州	Bayangol Mongol Autonomous Prefecture	3891078	354243	254347	3563	2491	3276434
阿克苏地区	Aksu Administrative Offices	3000480	445829	207276	12587	4200	2330588
克孜勒苏柯尔克孜自治州	Kizilsu Kirgiz Autonomous Prefecture	403686	112087	43600		141	247858
喀什地区	Kashgar [Kaxgar] Administrative Offices	4461422	1121359	123603	383	14201	3201876
和田地区	Hotan Administrative Offices	1308321	565530	4447	1800		736544
石河子市	Shihezi City	1567936	58994	134910		24932	1349100
阿拉尔市	Aral City	755576	69361	277489			408726
图木舒克市	Tumxuk City	217042	97884	40222			78936
五家渠市	Wujiaqu City	969651	30656	1344			937651
跨地区投资	Trans-regional Investment	2537934	567974	792620			1177340

注：1.自 2004 年起资金来源为本年实际到位资金。2.各地区资金来源中不包括农村个人资金。
Note: a) Sources of capital caculated on actual arrived investment from 2004. b) Sources of Capital from different regions excludes rural individdual fund.

4-5 按行业分全社会固定资产投资

Total Investment in Fixed Assets in the Whole Country by Sector

单位：万元 (10 000 yuan)

行 业	Sector	2010	2011
总 计	**Total**	**35396941**	**47127699**
农、林、牧、渔业	**Agriculture, Forestry, Animal Husbandry and Fishery**	**2114275**	**2377851**
农 业	Agriculture	450471	361651
林 业	Forestry	151687	173081
畜牧业	Animal Husbandry	189623	195970
渔 业	Fishing	1007	4401
农、林、牧、渔服务业	Services in Support of Agriculture	825600	941809
采矿业	**Mining**	**6103290**	**6518237**
#煤炭开采和洗选业	Mining and Washing of Coal	1457434	1333439
石油和天然气开采业	Extraction of Petroleum and Natural Gas	3898628	4313859
#天然原油和天然气开采	Extraction of Ores Crude Oil and Natural Gas Extraction	3814989	4105324
黑色金属矿采选业	Mining and Processing of Ferrous Metals Ores	289312	307947
#铁矿采选	Mining and Processing of Iron Ore	240194	282066
有色金属矿采选业	Mining and Processing of Non-ferrous Metals Ores	345735	439009
#常用有色金属矿采选	Mining and Processing of Common Non-ferrous Metal	269480	334930
非金属矿采选业	Mining and Processing of Nonmetal Ores	112181	113173
#土砂石开采	Mining of Earth and Gravel	53726	64469
化学矿采选	Extracting of Chemical Ore	42826	40422
制造业	**Manufacturing**	**6203672**	**11568245**
#农副食品加工业	Processing of Food from Agricultural Products	407465	422099
食品制造业	Manufacture of Food	272215	351975
#液体乳及乳制品制造	Manufacture of Liquid Milk and Dairy Products	18060	11412
饮料制造业	Manufacture of Beverage	143675	104779
烟草制品业	Manufacture of Tobacco	2885	77838
纺织业	Manufacture of Textile	248669	473103
#棉、化纤纺织及印染精加工	Cotton, Chemical Fiber, Dying, Printing and Processing	216760	454990
皮革、毛皮、羽绒及其制品业	Leather, Fur, Feather and Related Products Manufacturing	1241	
木材加工及竹、藤、棕、草制品业	Processing of Timber, Wood, Bamboo, Cane, Grass Products	35088	52916
家具制造业	Furniture Manufacturing	28944	10130
造纸及纸制品业	Paper and Paper Products Manufacturing	71405	161811
印刷业、记录媒介的复制	Printing and Copying of Medium for Record	21925	13777
石油加工及炼焦业	Oil Processing, Coking and Nuclear Fuel Processing	1113217	1250754
#精炼石油产品的制造	Manufacture of Oil Products	527028	697361
炼 焦	Coking	586189	553393
化学原料及化学制品制造业	Raw Chemical Material and Chemical Products	1258730	2387322
#基础化学原料制造	Basic Chemical Material	486289	1166221
肥料制造	Fertilizer Making	332691	523466
医药制造业	Medicine Manufacturing	31019	120057
#中药饮片加工	Processing of Chinese Herbs and Tablet	11081	8175
中成药制造	Manufacture of Chinese Herbs and Patent Medicine	16036	7397
化学纤维制造业	Chemical Fiber Manufacturing	98801	146273

注：该表门类包括农村个人投资，大类未包括。
Note: The major category contains rural individual investment while sub-category excludes it.

4-5 续表 1 Continued

单位：万元 (10 000 yuan)

行　业	Sector	2010	2011
橡胶制品业	Manufacture of Rubber	25630	51034
塑料制品业	Manufacture of Plastic	145562	181500
非金属矿物制品业	Manufacture of Non-metallic Mineral Products	1010184	2223317
#水泥、石灰和石膏的制造	Cement Manufacturing	536239	1147369
黑色金属冶炼及压延加工业	Smelting and Pressing of Non-Ferrous Metals	428391	1111071
#钢压延加工	Steel Rolling	82301	133192
有色金属冶炼及压延加工业	Smelting and Pressing of Nonferrous Metals	366537	1560191
#常用有色金属冶炼	Smeltering of Common Non-ferrous Metal	342064	1534710
金属制品业	Manufacture of Metal Products	122182	252552
通用设备制造业	Manufacture of General Purpose Machinery	86164	68925
专用设备制造业	Manufacture of Special Purpose Machinery	143701	182358
交通运输设备制造业	Manufacture of Transport Equipment	15609	79904
#汽车制造	Manufacture of Car	11835	68378
电气机械及器材制造业	Manufacture of Electricial Equipment and Machinery	50934	194847
电力、燃气及水的生产和供应业	**Production and Supply of Electricity Gas and Water**	**3950975**	**5700481**
电力、热力的生产和供应业	Production and Supply of Electric Power and Heat Power	3485983	4755198
电力生产	Production of Electric Power	2469999	3771666
电力供应	Distribution of Electric Power	817756	723663
热力生产和供应	Production and Supply of Heat Power	198228	259869
燃气生产和供应业	Production and Supply of Gas	254207	625197
水的生产和供应业	Production and Supply of Water	210785	320086
#自来水的生产和供应	Production and Distribution of Running Water	146352	243487
污水处理及其再生利用	Treatment and Recycle of Waste Water	64433	74853
建筑业	**Construction**	**412694**	**866512**
#房屋和土木工程建筑业	Construction of Buildings and Givil Engineering	291129	722749
建筑安装业	Building Installation	23675	12922
交通运输、仓储和邮政业	**Transport, Storage and Post**	**5320635**	**3940920**
铁路运输业	Railway Transport	2272319	814209
道路运输业	Road Transport	2451150	2199116
城市公共交通业	Urban Public Transport	2618	53317
航空运输业	Air Transport	100143	34130
管道运输业	Via Pipeline Transport	20438	280873
装卸搬运和其他运输服务业	Loading, Unloading and Other Transport Services	24775	25172
仓储业	Storage	234921	244189
邮政业	Post	1275	16744
信息传输、计算机服务和软件业	**Information Transmission, Computer Services and Software**	**420315**	**481474**
#电信和其他信息传输服务业	Telecommunication and Other Information Transmission Services	416935	473099
#电　信	Telecommunication	385146	457363
批发和零售业	**Wholesal and Retail Trades**	**283876**	**468815**
批发业	Wholesale Trade	190923	260950
零售业	Retail Trade	92953	207865
住宿和餐饮业	**Hotels and Catering Services**	**138710**	**212911**
住宿业	Hotels	124232	196139
#旅游饭店	Tourist Restaurant	91078	138411
餐饮业	Catering Service	13914	16772
金融业	**Financial Intermediation**	**71712**	**51154**
银行业	Banks	62576	46792

4-5 续表 2 Continued

单位：万元 (10 000 yuan)

行　业	Sector	2010	2011
保险业	Insurance	9021	1200
其他金融活动	Other Financial Activities	115	3162
房地产业	**Real Estate**	**6251295**	**9935788**
#房地产开发与经营业	Real Estate Development and Operation	3758227	5706972
物业管理	Real Estate Management	2210	12526
租赁和商务服务业	**Leasing and Business Services**	**113650**	**172723**
租赁业	Leasing	11315	10645
商务服务业	Business Service	102335	153226
科学研究、技术服务和地质勘查业	**Scientific Research, Technical Services and Geological Prospecting**	**172180**	**186848**
研究与试验发展	Research and Experimental Development	3694	585
专业技术服务业	Professional Technical Service	14292	55561
科技交流和推广服务业	Services of Science and Technology Exchanges and Promotion	31510	20230
地质勘查业	Geologic Prospecting	122684	110472
水利、环境和公共设施管理业	**Management of Water Conservancy, Environment and Public Facilities**	**1957772**	**2032966**
水利管理业	Management of Water Conservancy	673343	735946
环境管理业	Management of Environmental	109044	123440
公共设施管理业	Management of Public Facilities	1175385	1173443
市政公共设施管理	Management of Public Facilities	1047890	911840
城市绿化管理	Urban Greening Management	44854	172685
游览景区管理	Scenic-Spot Management	82641	88918
居民服务和其他服务业	**Services to Households and Other Services**	**38130**	**48747**
教　育	**Education**	**568427**	**662563**
#初等教育	Junion Education	107592	116519
中等教育	Secondary Education	260587	299962
高等教育	Senior Education	77415	67151
卫生、社会保障和社会福利业	**Health, Social Security and Social Welfare**	**314415**	**351039**
卫　生	Health Care	278867	284314
#医　院	Hospital	200665	206077
专科疾病防治活动	Control Over Special Diseases	2578	1130
疾病预防控制及防疫活动	Prevention and Control of Diseases	835	1461
社会保障业	Social Security	10034	32593
社会福利业	Social Welfare	25514	34132
文化、体育和娱乐业	**Culture, Sports and Entertainment**	**172127**	**181151**
新闻出版业	Journalism and Publishing Activities	7302	4556
广播、电视、电影和音像业	Broadcasting,Movies,Televisions and Audiovisual Activites	19689	12396
文化艺术业	Culture and Art Activities	103963	95277
体　育	Sports	32991	19246
娱乐业	Entertainment	8182	49676
公共管理和社会组织	**Public Management and Social Organization**	**788791**	**1369274**
中国共产党机关	Orgars of Communist Party of China	20470	30419
国家机构	Govemment Agencies	752701	1312136
人民政协和民主党派	People's Political Consultative Conference and Democratic Parties	819	200
群众团体、社会团体和宗教组织	Non-Govemmental Institutions,Social Organizations and Religion Organizations	6774	5973
基层群众自治组织	Grass Roots Self-governing Organizations	8027	20546

4-6 全社会房屋施工面积、竣工面积

Floor Space of Buildings under Construction and Completed in Whole Country

单位：万平方米 (10 000 sq.m)

年 份 Year	地 区 Region	施工面积 Floor Space of Buildings under Construction	#住 宅 Residential Buildings	竣工面积 Floor Space of Buildings Completed	#住 宅 Residential Buildings	房屋建筑面积竣工率(%) Rate of Floor Space of Building Completed (%)	#住 宅 Residential Buildings
	1985	1670.30	945.76	1327.69	816.26	79.5	86.3
	1990	1740.94	1074.98	1337.06	912.57	76.8	84.9
	1995	2420.38	1368.84	1634.33	1064.14	67.5	77.7
	1996	2952.02	1901.01	2095.58	1441.22	71.0	75.8
	1997	2574.79	1732.19	1903.96	1393.11	73.9	80.4
	1998	2946.76	2057.08	2148.75	1604.68	72.9	78.0
	1999	3439.11	2470.41	2618.98	2020.89	76.2	81.8
	2000	4485.77	2509.17	2633.23	1881.88	58.7	75.0
	2001	4940.70	3282.51	3386.60	2411.78	68.5	73.5
	2002	3986.81	2358.04	2706.44	1790.82	67.9	75.9
	2003	5004.13	2863.92	3599.74	2347.04	71.9	82.0
	2004	5290.77	2999.85	4273.02	2298.56	80.8	76.6
	2005	6677.06	4522.20	4705.07	3618.78	70.5	80.0
	2006	7854.43	5694.75	4773.93	3785.46	60.8	66.5
	2007	8028.32	5915.83	5441.23	4458.77	67.8	75.4
	2008	8317.15	5938.78	5184.01	4125.67	62.3	69.5
	2009	9511.02	6344.39	4598.79	3412.43	48.4	53.8
	2010	11361.96	7640.58	4649.89	3291.89	40.9	43.1
	2011	16804.88	11357.36	5899.06	4504.94	35.1	39.7
乌鲁木齐市	Urumqi City	2544.85	1860.02	442.67	333.48	17.4	17.9
克拉玛依市	Karamay City	209.79	138.84	71.96	67.18	34.3	48.4
吐鲁番地区	Turpan Administrative Offices	179.14	138.23	51.45	30.93	28.7	22.4
哈密地区	Hami [Kumul] Administrative Offices	560.50	460.59	173.16	145.83	30.9	31.7
昌吉回族自治州	Changji Hui Autonomous Prefecture	1239.86	780.43	276.98	185.42	22.3	23.8
伊犁哈萨克自治州	Ili Kazak Autonomous Prefecture	3109.18	2091.53	993.72	736.46	32.0	35.2
伊犁州直属县(市)	Counties (Cities) Direct Under Ili Prefecture	1785.79	1146.68	559.77	432.20	31.3	37.7
塔城地区	Tacheng [Tarbagatai] Administrative Offices	881.20	609.60	261.22	182.30	29.6	29.9
阿勒泰地区	Altay Administrative Offices	442.19	335.25	172.73	121.96	39.1	36.4
博尔塔拉蒙古自治州	Bortala Mongol Autonomous Prefecture	388.84	297.06	93.98	71.37	24.2	24.0
巴音郭楞蒙古自治州	Bayangol Mongol Autonomous Prefecture	1131.38	785.95	350.51	237.82	31.0	30.3
阿克苏地区	Aksu Administrative Offices	1054.94	664.24	358.44	227.03	34.0	34.2
克孜勒苏柯尔克孜自治州	Kizilsu Kirgiz Autonomous Prefecture	237.70	157.05	114.11	75.31	48.0	48.0
喀什地区	Kashgar [Kaxgar] Administrative Offices	2270.16	930.06	367.35	184.53	16.2	19.8
和田地区	Hotan Administrative Offices	902.94	734.64	507.58	446.55	56.2	60.8
石河子市	Shihezi City	506.91	246.56	167.93	86.98	33.1	35.3
阿拉尔市	Aral City	176.31	90.82	122.03	69.82	69.2	76.9
图木舒克市	Tumxuk City	100.15	63.62	30.64	19.60	30.6	30.8
五家渠市	Wujiaqu City	231.57	127.85	34.91	8.14	15.1	6.4
跨地区投资	Trans-regional Investment	65.20	60.65	18.82	17.18	28.8	28.3

注：分地区房屋施工面积、竣工面积未包括农村个人。
Note: Floor space under construction and completed floor space by sectors exclude those in rural areas.

4-7 按构成及建设性质分城镇固定资产投资

Investment in Fixed Assets in Urban Area by Composition of Funds and Type of Construction

单位：万元 (10 000 yuan)

年份 Year	地区 Region	合计 Total	按构成分 By Composition of Funds 建筑安装工程 Construction and Installation	设备工具器具购置 Purchase of Equipment and Instruments	#用于更新的设备 Update Equipment	其他费用 Others
	1978	129999	86667	35686		7646
	1985	408435	314651	67295	5499	26489
	1990	782099	516443	224673	25153	40983
	1995	2864148	1817364	754369	64612	292415
	1996	3339710	2167304	825067	66119	347339
	1997	3817221	2600884	858958	61094	357379
	1998	4561217	3333948	792449	71986	434820
	1999	4613116	3294346	831951	82363	486819
	2000	4994145	3531280	1103399	104850	359466
	2001	5490569	3638754	1392920	186605	458895
	2002	6596964	4379556	1558818	181920	658590
	2003	8188381	5599787	1718853	105728	869741
	2004	9482471	6451184	2047000	232343	984287
	2005	11215637	7926905	2230165	145514	1058567
	2006	12971324	8943879	2686125	188170	1341320
	2007	14908734	9646247	3746476	177062	1516011
	2008	17970126	11542024	4772937	311014	1655165
	2009	22999843	15632380	5026513	552733	2340950
	2010	28338644	18973774	6938417	346525	2426453
	2011	36881064	25313983	9102251	726850	2464830
乌鲁木齐市	Urumqi City	4343646	2550317	1491402	233761	301927
克拉玛依市	Karamay City	1993665	1644121	264457	66822	85087
吐鲁番地区	Turpan Administrative Offices	1242315	779169	374276	4171	88870
哈密地区	Hami [Kumul] Administrative Offices	1874333	1013925	719664	8395	140744
昌吉回族自治州	Changji Hui Autonomous Prefecture	4356079	2496823	1565219	180857	294037
伊犁哈萨克自治州	Ili Kazak Autonomous Prefecture	6159228	4153919	1496463	74153	508846
伊犁州直属县(市)	Counties (Cities) Direct Under Ili Prefecture	3204801	2063904	879309	63577	261588
塔城地区	Tacheng [Tarbagatai] Administrative Offices	1701872	1265408	388862	10086	47602
阿勒泰地区	Altay Administrative Offices	1252555	824607	228292	490	199656
博尔塔拉蒙古自治州	Bortala Mongol Autonomous Prefecture	643430	441131	154882	2866	47417
巴音郭楞蒙古自治州	Bayangol Mongol Autonomous Prefecture	3349974	2534504	592225	40954	223245
阿克苏地区	Aksu Administrative Offices	1986846	1358297	562564	17707	65985
克孜勒苏柯尔克孜自治州	Kizilsu Kirgiz Autonomous Prefecture	417606	316778	80844	40034	19984
喀什地区	Kashgar [Kaxgar] Administrative Offices	3303322	2818076	399011	33681	86235
和田地区	Hotan Administrative Offices	1144577	911957	98068	1519	134552
石河子市	Shihezi City	1507501	774879	613487	5183	119135
阿拉尔市	Aral City	443750	248915	180985	100	13850
图木舒克市	Tumxuk City	172841	116679	41520		14642
五家渠市	Wujiaqu City	875042	472106	340583		62353
跨地区投资	Trans-regional Investment	3066909	2682387	126601	16647	257921

注：城镇投资额未含房地产投资，以下同。
Note: Urban Investment exclude real estate, the following the same as follows.

4-7 续表 Continued

单位：万元 (10 000 yuan)

年 份 Year	地 区 Region	按建设性质分 By Type of Construction			
		新 建 New Construction	扩 建 Expansion	改 建 Reconstruction	其 他 Others
	1978	93462	34399		2138
	1985	110236	160639	116006	21554
	1990	299356	148222	277007	57514
	1995	1067281	886882	646081	263904
	1996	1240585	820966	967022	311137
	1997	1405259	911902	1155121	344939
	1998	1648622	1017786	1338994	555815
	1999	1381764	1226797	1326775	677780
	2000	1410065	1424339	1558514	601227
	2001	891146	2373927	1614961	610535
	2002	1429874	2687996	1984657	494437
	2003	2207269	3128374	2237752	614986
	2004	2358662	3595847	2781101	746861
	2005	3397472	3657464	3063457	1097244
	2006	3633284	5436397	2430373	1471270
	2007	3759028	7439715	2386806	1323185
	2008	5350574	8078708	2759536	1781308
	2009	9465044	7634515	4113649	1786635
	2010	13612835	8408038	4177527	2140244
	2011	19799225	9910989	4216233	2954617
乌鲁木齐市	Urumqi City	1368893	1988417	404653	581683
克拉玛依市	Karamay City	1664231	44405	258831	26198
吐鲁番地区	Turpan Administrative Offices	647532	453035	60846	80902
哈密地区	Hami [Kumul] Administrative Offices	724656	926547	156056	67074
昌吉回族自治州	Changji Hui Autonomous Prefecture	3065102	314542	752831	223604
伊犁哈萨克自治州	Ili Kazak Autonomous Prefecture	3259338	1568967	609090	721833
伊犁州直属县(市)	Counties (Cities) Direct Under Ili Prefecture	1996867	635824	268486	303624
塔城地区	Tacheng [Tarbagatai] Administrative Offices	859567	335283	255246	251776
阿勒泰地区	Altay Administrative Offices	402904	597860	85358	166433
博尔塔拉蒙古自治州	Bortala Mongol Autonomous Prefecture	228242	197735	93028	124425
巴音郭楞蒙古自治州	Bayangol Mongol Autonomous Prefecture	2339194	623514	168598	218668
阿克苏地区	Aksu Administrative Offices	1313607	423897	82238	167104
克孜勒苏柯尔克孜自治州	Kizilsu Kirgiz Autonomous Prefecture	362961	22689	11298	20658
喀什地区	Kashgar [Kaxgar] Administrative Offices	2513253	467218	74212	248639
和田地区	Hotan Administrative Offices	54429	825770	44025	220353
石河子市	Shihezi City	1057999	296542	68330	84630
阿拉尔市	Aral City	314017	18547	23511	87675
图木舒克市	Tumxuk City	20903	91711	13153	47074
五家渠市	Wujiaqu City	316649	484891	39405	34097
跨地区投资	Trans-regional Investment	548219	1162562	1356128	

4-8 分行业城镇固定资产投资主要指标

Main Indicators of Investment in Fixed Assets in Urban Area by Sector

(2011 年)

行业	Sector	投资额(万元) Total Investment (10 000 yuan)	#地方 Local	施工项目个数(个) Number of Projects under Construction (unit)	竣工项目个数(个) Number of Projects Completed (unit)	本年新增固定资产(万元) Newly Increased Fixed Assets (10 000 yuan)
总计	**Total**	**36881064**	**25818627**	**10382**	**6528**	**20864406**
农、林、牧、渔业	**Agriculture, Forestry, Animal Husbandry and Fishery**	**1018114**	**841627**	**1039**	**838**	**877202**
农业	Agriculture	195931	165332	149	113	141001
林业	Forestry	118933	113063	189	165	125697
畜牧业	Animal Husbandry	103157	85207	125	102	105822
渔业	Fishing	1663	350	4	3	1313
农、林、牧、渔服务业	Service in Support of Agriculture	598430	477675	572	455	503369
采矿业	**Mining**	**6310817**	**1888989**	**403**	**216**	**4560215**
#煤炭开采和洗选业	Mining and Washing of Coal	1205245	1123365	124	42	288161
石油和天然气开采业	Extraction of Petroleum and Natural Gas	4313859	49961	27	19	3334253
#天然原油和天然气开采	Extraction of Ores Crude Oil and Natural Gas Extraction	4105324	3711	14	10	3130823
黑色金属矿采选业	Mining and Processing of Ferrous Metals Ores	305468	283797	86	54	214806
#铁矿采选	Mining and Processing of Iron Ore	280187	258516	78	49	183357
有色金属矿采选业	Mining and Processing of Non-ferrous Metals Ores	394067	365219	109	66	210360
#常用有色金属矿采选	Mining and Processing of Common Non-ferrous Metal	318183	289335	70	43	166980
非金属矿采选业	Mining and Processing of Nonmetal Ores	81368	55837	55	33	497235
#土砂石开采	Mining of Earth and Gravel	48749	43417	44	26	25975
化学矿采选	Extracting of Chemical Ore	25422	6090	4	4	467293
制造业	**Manufacturing**	**10813017**	**9736180**	**1608**	**833**	**5019085**
#农副食品加工业	Processing of Food from Agricultural Products	374671	315322	212	119	260868
食品制造业	Manufacture of Foods	318939	308108	80	52	155005
#液体乳及乳制品制造	Manufacture of Liquid Milk and Dairy Products	10612	10612	7	4	10580
饮料制造业	Manufacture of Beverages	93381	83676	48	23	66907
烟草制品业	Manufacture of Tobacco	77838	77838	2		
纺织业	Manufacture of Textile	457784	387530	60	26	98816
#棉、化纤纺织及印染精加工	Cotton, Chemical Fiber Dyeing, Printing and Processing	440871	371114	46	15	88013
纺织服装、鞋、帽制造业	Manufacture of Textile Wearing Apparel, Footware and Caps	11825	11025	4	3	12758
木材加工及竹、藤、棕、草制品业	Processing of Timber, Wood, Bamboo, Cane, Grass Products	52792	52792	14	9	6368
家具制造业	Manufacture of Furniture	10070	10070	6	2	1900
造纸及纸制品业	Manufacture of Paper and Paper Products	153280	152300	32	18	56436
印刷业、记录媒介的复制	Printing,Reproduction,of Recording Media	13147	13147	10	5	6116
石油加工及炼焦业	Processing of Petroleum,Coking	1233720	1032691	67	17	301145
#精炼石油产品的制造	Manufacture of Oil Products	697361	520847	33	9	171181
炼焦	Coking	536359	511844	34	8	129964

4-8 续表 1 Continued

行业	Sector	投资额（万元） Total Investment (10 000 yuan)	#地方 Local	施工项目个数（个） Number of Projects under Construction (unit)	竣工项目个数（个） Number of Projects Completed (unit)	本年新增固定资产（万元） Newly Increased Fixed Assets (10 000 yuan)
化学原料及化学制品制造业	Manufacture of Raw Chemical Material and Chemical Products	2307349	2089715	140	62	1588286
#基础化学原料制造	Manufacture of Basic Chemical Material	1139771	1083726	42	18	775396
肥料制造	Fertilizer Making	492312	386829	44	21	224241
医药制造业	Manufacture of Medicine	120057	119163	21	7	10375
#中药饮片加工	Manufacture and Processing of Chinese Herbs and Tablet	8175	7885	7	3	6156
中成药制造	Manufacture of Chinese Medicine	7397	6793	5	2	3269
化学纤维制造业	Manufacture of Chemical Fibers	142073	142073	11	5	37460
橡胶制品业	Manufacture of Rubber Products	45222	45222	6	3	5100
塑料制品业	Manufacture of Plastic Products	170340	156298	86	51	79276
非金属矿物制品业	Manufacture of Non-metallic Mineral Products	1977003	1810586	479	292	1160095
#水泥、石灰和石膏的制造	Cement Manufacturing	1060047	930261	108	60	467395
黑色金属冶炼及压延加工业	Smelting and Pressing of Ferrous Metals	1110871	868871	80	35	455290
#钢压延加工	Steel Rolling	133092	133092	22	9	31163
有色金属冶炼及压延加工业	Smelting and Pressing of Nonferrous Metals	1360763	1350487	30	9	324997
#常用有色金属冶炼	Smeltering of Common Non-ferrous Metal	1335282	1335282	21	7	323227
金属制品业	Manufacture of Metal Products	212398	204783	76	39	133972
通用设备制造业	Manufacture of General Purpose Machinery	64845	64495	31	14	19761
专用设备制造业	Manufacture of Special Purpose Machinery	172392	166437	43	12	119301
交通运输设备制造业	Manufacture of Transport Equipment	79904	71535	14	6	11132
#汽车制造	Manufacture of Car	68378	60009	10	4	4832
电气机械及器材制造业	Manufacture of Electric Equipment and Machinery	180153	132283	33	11	78079
电力、燃气及水的生产和供应业	**Production and Supply of Electricity,Gas and Water**	**5420642**	**3525619**	**800**	**467**	**2497006**
电力、热力的生产和供应业	Production and Supply of Electricity Power and Heat Power	4498917	2694836	518	299	2173760
电力生产	Production of Electric Power	3574502	2250894	178	60	1458801
电力供应	Supply of Electric Power	675349	313393	222	164	585228
热力生产和供应	Production and Supply of Heat Power	249066	130549	118	75	129731
燃气生产和供应业	Production and Supply of Gas	616887	567784	89	50	113451
水的生产和供应业	Production and Supply of Water	304838	262999	193	118	209795
#自来水的生产和供应	Production and Distribution of Running Water	228989	204442	144	88	137519
污水处理及其再生利用	Treatment and Recycle of Waste Water	74103	56811	46	29	71415
建筑业	**Construction**	**616535**	**557793**	**307**	**184**	**339883**
#房屋和土木工程建筑业	Buildings and Givil Engineering Construction	579875	522010	272	164	320313
建筑安装业	Building Installation	12922	12045	6	2	4395

4-8 续表 2 Continued

行业	Sector	投资额(万元) Total Investment (10 000 yuan)	#地方 Local	施工项目个数(个) Number of Projects under Construction (unit)	竣工项目个数(个) Number of Projects Completed (unit)	本年新增固定资产(万元) Newly Increased Fixed Assets (10 000 yuan)
交通运输、仓储和邮政业	**Transport Storage and Post**	**3458999**	**2101098**	**684**	**415**	**1494590**
铁路运输业	Railway Transport	814209	27781	33	7	219911
道路运输业	Road Transport	2013731	1744713	517	326	636487
城市公共交通业	Urban Public Transport	52607	52607	9	5	44871
航空运输业	Air Transportation	34130	23293	11	7	281579
管道运输业	Via Pipelines Transport	280873	7534	4	2	146780
装卸搬运和其他运输服务业	Loading,Unloading and Other Transport Services	25172	23761	14	12	22991
仓储业	Storage	221533	206565	88	52	133994
邮政业	Post	16744	14844	8	4	7977
信息传输、计算机服务和软件业	**Information Transmission, Computer Services and Software**	**481274**	**167973**	**105**	**71**	**227826**
#电信和其他信息传输服务业	Telecommunication and Other Information Transmission Services	472899	165598	103	71	227826
#电　信	Telecommunication	457363	151711	84	60	221667
批发和零售业	**Wholesale&Retail Trades**	**455673**	**408152**	**205**	**126**	**178564**
批发业	Wholesale Trades	252946	214600	93	51	78541
零售业	Retail Trades	202727	193552	112	75	100023
住宿和餐饮业	**Hotels and Catering Services**	**203120**	**166338**	**109**	**54**	**96473**
#住宿业	Hotels	187281	150844	91	41	80250
#旅游饭店	Tourist Restaurant	131683	96746	49	21	58929
金融业	**Financial Intermediation**	**49034**	**18570**	**43**	**34**	**58106**
银行业	Bank	44872	15470	39	30	47644
保险业	Insurance	1200	200	3	3	7500
其他金融活动	Other Financial Activities	2962	2900	1	1	2962
房地产业	**Real Estate**	**3621776**	**2518044**	**1287**	**698**	**2043256**
#房地产开发与经营业	Real Estate Development and Operation	526626	502996	192	89	218229
物业管理	Management of Real Estate	12526	3557	7	6	11926
租赁和商务服务业	**Leasing and Business Services**	**156301**	**155931**	**62**	**38**	**174548**
租赁业	Leasing	8445	8445	8	3	3445
商务服务业	Business Service	147856	147486	54	35	171103
科学研究、技术服务和地质勘查业	**Scientific Research, Technical Service and Geological Prospecting**	**178246**	**163252**	**125**	**95**	**172505**
研究与试验发展	Research and Experiment Development	585	585	5	3	260
专业技术服务业	Professional Technical Service	55289	53039	35	28	41908
科技交流和推广服务业	Services of Science and Technology Exchanges and Difussion	14453	11631	23	16	19320

4-8 续表 3 Continued

行　业	Sector	投资额（万元）Total Investment (10 000 yuan)	#地方 Local	施工项目个数（个）Number of Projects under Construction (unit)	竣工项目个数（个）Number of Projects Completed (unit)	本年新增固定资产（万元）Newly Increased Fixed Assets (10 000 yuan)
地质勘查业	Geologic Prospection	107919	97997	62	48	111017
水利、环境和公共设施管理业	**Management of Water Conservancy, Environment and Public Facilities**	**1823859**	**1508393**	**1200**	**822**	**1242985**
水利管理业	Management of Water Conservancy	572325	490155	405	261	328069
环境管理业	Environmental Management	107873	103539	101	63	139904
公共设施管理业	Management of Public Facilities	1143661	914699	694	498	775012
市政公共设施管理	Management of Public Facilities	885046	661569	557	394	596621
城市绿化管理	Management of Urban Greening	172617	167531	66	56	102551
游览景区管理	Scenic-Spot Management	85998	85599	71	48	75840
居民服务和其他服务业	**Resident Service and Other Services**	**46853**	**41166**	**56**	**37**	**33941**
教　育	**Education**	**626062**	**548312**	**872**	**619**	**510188**
#初等教育	Elementary Education	107416	86070	218	164	85234
中等教育	Secondary Education	294397	252805	348	210	247765
高等教育	Higher Education	67151	64954	23	14	31512
卫生、社会保障和社会福利业	**Health, Social Security and Social Welfare**	**339890**	**307812**	**346**	**211**	**262478**
卫　生	Health Care	274578	249603	272	165	220888
#医　院	Hospital	205667	184532	155	89	170560
专科疾病防治活动	Prerention and Control of Special Diseases	1130	240	2	1	890
疾病预防控制及防疫活动	Prevention and Control of Diseases	1461	1211	9	7	1134
社会保障业	Social Security	31599	31599	12	8	26244
社会福利业	Social Welfare	33713	26610	62	38	15346
文化、体育和娱乐业	**Culture, Sports and Entertainment**	**174394**	**149897**	**184**	**120**	**121502**
新闻出版业	Journalism and Publishing Activities	4556	4556	5	3	4392
广播、电视、电影和音像业	Broadcasting,Movies,Televisions and Audiovisual Activites	12110	11897	14	10	13641
文化艺术业	Cultural and Art Activities	91906	71483	121	78	58269
体　育	Sports	18946	16505	19	11	15286
娱乐业	Entertainment	46876	45456	25	18	29914
公共管理和社会组织	**Public Management and Social Organization**	**1086458**	**1013481**	**947**	**650**	**954053**
中国共产党机关	Organ of Communist Party of China	28366	28366	31	24	26171
国家机构	Government Agencies	1036801	963824	867	593	912675
人民政协和民主党派	People's Political Consultative Conference and Democratic Parties	200	200	1		
群众团体、社会团体和宗教组织	Non-Governmental Institutions,Social Organizations and Religion Organizations	5473	5473	12	11	4386
基层群众自治组织	Grass Roots Self-governing Organizations	15618	15618	36	22	10821

4-9 分行业城镇固定资产投资资金来源情况

单位：万元 (2011 年)

行　业	Sector	本年资金来源小计 Sub-total Funds This Year
总　计	**Total**	**38935967**
农、林、牧、渔业	**Agriculture, Forestry, Animal Husbandry and Fishery**	**1037667**
农　业	Agriculture	198969
林　业	Forestry	112001
畜牧业	Animal Husbandry	109234
渔　业	Fishing	2313
农、林、牧、渔服务业	Activities for Agriculture, Forestry, Animal Husbandry and Fishing	615150
采矿业	**Mining and Quarrying**	**6535581**
#煤炭开采和洗选业	Mining and Washing of Coal	1382195
石油和天然气开采业	Extraction of Petroleum and Natural Gas	4177782
#天然原油和天然气开采	Extraction of Ores Crude Oil and Natural Gas Extraction	3970604
黑色金属矿采选业	Mining and Processing of Ferrous Metals Ores	457920
#铁矿采选	Mining and Processing of Iron Ore	431529
有色金属矿采选业	Mining and Processing of Non-ferrous Metals Ores	420066
#常用有色金属矿采选	Mining and Processing of Common Non-ferrous Metal	336971
非金属矿采选业	Processing of Nonmetal Ores	86808
#土砂石开采	Mining of Earth and Gravel	51641
化学矿采选	Extracting of Chemical Ore	25600
制造业	**Manufacturing**	**12096040**
#农副食品加工业	Processing of Food from Agricultural Products	435374
食品制造业	Manufacture of Foods	332146
#液体乳及乳制品制造	Manufacture of Liquid Milk and Dairy Products	10550
饮料制造业	Manufacture of Beverages	106363
烟草制品业	Manufacture of Tabauo	182900
纺织业	Manufacture of Textile	457346
#棉、化纤纺织及印染精加工	Cotton, Chemical Fiber Dyeing, Printing and Processing	441062
麻纺织	Manufacture of Flax Textile	
纺织服装、鞋、帽制造业	Manufacture of Textile Wearing Apparel ,Footware and Caps	10588
木材加工及竹、藤、棕、草制品业	Processing of Timber, Manufacture of Cane, Grass Products	53350
家具制造业	Manufacture of Furniture	9670
造纸及纸制品业	Manufacture of Paper and Paper Products	168573
印刷业、记录媒介的复制	Printing, Reproduction of Recording Media	13148
石油加工及炼焦业	Processing of Petroleum, Coking	1315213
#精炼石油产品的制造	Manufacture of Oil Products	728172
炼　焦	Coking	587041

Sources of Funds of Investment in Fixed Assets in Urban Area by Sector

(10 000 yuan)

国家预算内资金 State Budget	国内贷款 Domestic Loans	债券 Bonds	利用外资 Foreign Investment	自筹资金 Self-raising Funds	其他资金来源 Others
5264602	**5452210**	**21737**	**129993**	**24723424**	**3344001**
393404	**48241**	**6404**	**4475**	**452619**	**132524**
36014	4424			117661	40870
43946			4475	45755	17825
34641	6171			39870	28552
20				2293	
278783	37646	6404		247040	45277
13560	**828664**		**6480**	**5103629**	**583248**
2609	161293		6380	1164754	47159
5766	558409			3200817	412790
1266	531659			3024889	412790
4850	56015			360192	36863
4850	56015			349443	21221
	52807			297410	69849
	52807			217315	66849
335	140		100	80456	5777
335	140			47316	3850
				25600	
71434	**1389194**		**45833**	**10313260**	**276319**
7529	13940			398117	15788
176	3350		11860	313600	3160
	250			10300	
2600	4720			94548	4495
				182900	
3260	63525			384307	6254
3260	63525			368977	5300
				10588	
				49718	3632
	1500			6170	2000
70	42578		4000	121371	554
88	410			11650	1000
50000	25000		2202	1231010	7001
50000			2202	668969	7001
	25000			562041	

4-9 续表 1

单位：万元

行　业	Sector	本年资金来源小计 Sub-total Funds This Year
化学原料及化学制品制造业	Manufacture of Raw Chemical Material and Chemical Products	2792729
#基础化学原料制造	Manufacture of Basic Chemical Material	1376856
肥料制造	Making of Fertilizer	536430
医药制造业	Manufacture of Medicine	162483
#中药饮片加工	Manufacture of Chinese Herbs and Tablet	8622
中成药制造	Manufacture of Chinese Medicines	9393
化学纤维制造业	Manufacture of Chemical Fibers	124374
橡胶制品业	Manufacture of Rubber Products	7848
塑料制品业	Manufacture of Plastic Products	185773
非金属矿物制品业	Manufacture of Non-metallic Mineral Products	2419658
#水泥、石灰和石膏的制造	Manufacture of Cement	1393664
黑色金属冶炼及压延加工业	Smelting and Pressing of Ferrous Metals	1211965
#钢压延加工	Steel Rolling	198158
有色金属冶炼及压延加工业	Smelting and Pressing of Non-ferrous Metals	1348340
#常用有色金属冶炼	Smeltering of Common Non-ferrous Metal	1327947
金属制品业	Manufacture of Metal Products	213102
通用设备制造业	Manufacture of General Purpose Machinery	59056
专用设备制造业	Manufacture of Special Purpose Machinery	123788
交通运输设备制造业	Manufacture of Transport Equipment	91051
#汽车制造	Manufacture of Car	77525
电气机械及器材制造业	Manufacture of Electrical Equipment and Machinery	199441
电力、燃气及水的生产和供应业	**Production and Supply of Electricity, Gas and Water**	**5732413**
电力、热力的生产和供应业	Production and Supply of Electric Power and Heat Power	4769255
电力生产	Production of Electric Power	3826703
电力供应	Supply of Electric Power	651559
热力生产和供应	Production and Supply of Heat Power	290993
燃气生产和供应业	Production and Supply of Gas	659156
水的生产和供应业	Production and Supply of Water	304002
#自来水的生产和供应	Production and Distribution of Running Water	224256
污水处理及其再生利用	Treatment and Recycle of Waste Water	78000
建筑业	**Construction**	**688337**
#房屋和土木工程建筑业	Buildings and Givil Engineering Construction	653485
建筑安装业	Building Installation	12923

Continued

(10 000 yuan)

国家预算内资金 State Budget	国内贷款 Domestic Loans	债券 Bonds	利用外资 Foreign Investment	自筹资金 Self-raising Funds	其他资金来源 Others
830	866083		21600	1903836	380
	574973			801853	30
830	160600			375000	
	4100			158183	200
				8422	200
				9393	
	19000			97973	7401
				7848	
180	7300		3800	169495	4998
1060	150234		2371	2080127	185866
1000	127000			1128812	136852
	89606			1107126	15233
	500			195425	2233
	66080			1282260	
	63580			1264367	
	5598			197362	10142
	5500			52356	1200
304	16050			105189	2245
	200			90271	580
	200			77125	200
4000	1000			192241	2200
445256	**1922453**	**4736**	**35464**	**3130116**	**194388**
274615	1600163	3795	29277	2735606	125799
145297	1220009		29277	2361475	70645
75437	288679	3795		248010	35638
53881	91475			126121	19516
11571	311605			326995	8985
159070	10685	941	6187	67515	59604
121475	10685	941	1073	48980	41102
36464			5114	18535	17887
179085	**76959**	**51**	**15201**	**360877**	**56164**
170560	74188	51	15201	338621	54864
468				12455	

4-9 续表 2

单位：万元

行　业	Sector	本年资金来源小计 Sub-total Funds This Year
交通运输、仓储和邮政业	**Transport,Storage and Post**	**3185973**
铁路运输业	Railway Transport	865225
道路运输业	Road Transport	1599536
城市公共交通业	City Public Transport	60103
航空运输业	Air Transportation	42708
管道运输业	Via Pipeline Transport	343591
装卸搬运和其他运输服务业	Loading,Unloading and Other Transport Services	31168
仓储业	Storage	225535
邮政业	Post	18107
信息传输、计算机服务和软件业	**Information Transmission, Computer Services and Software**	**519244**
#电信和其他信息传输服务业	Telecommunications and Other Information Transmission Services	510395
#电　信	Telecommunication	492005
批发和零售业	**Wholesale&Retail Trades**	**496242**
批发业	Wholesale Trades	282506
零售业	Retail Trades	213736
住宿和餐饮业	**Hotels and Catering Services**	**204707**
#住宿业	Hotels	187761
#旅游饭店	Tourist Restaurant	126904
金融业	**Financial Intermediation**	**52956**
银行业	Banks	48994
保险业	Insurance	1000
其他金融活动	Others Financial Activities	2962
房地产业	**Real Estate**	**3682582**
#房地产开发与经营业	Real Estate Development and Operation	557435
物业管理	Real Estate Management	12527
租赁和商务服务业	**Leasing and Business Services**	**120559**
租赁业	Leasing	8495
商务服务业	Business Service	112064
科学研究、技术服务和地质勘查业	**Scientific Research, Technical Service and Geological Prospecting**	**166675**
研究与试验发展	Research and Experiment Development	1398
专业技术服务业	Professional Technical Service	54853
科技交流和推广服务业	Services of Science and Technology Exchanges and Difussion	11547

Continued

(10 000 yuan)

国家预算内资金 State Budget	国内贷款 Domestic Loans	债券 Bonds	利用外资 Foreign Investment	自筹资金 Self-raising Funds	其他资金来源 Others
1093208	**786206**		**7729**	**944815**	**354015**
469647	118431			185184	91963
557859	334631		6629	449275	251142
44765	3800			6396	5142
4400				38308	
	312149			31442	
65				31103	
13575	17195		1100	189087	4578
2897				14020	1190
11701	**44111**			**446645**	**16787**
11161	44111			439005	16118
7205	44111			425833	14856
12250	**18300**			**438898**	**26794**
6414	18200			244848	13044
5836	100			194050	13750
15791	**2822**		**1666**	**156901**	**27527**
14788	2822		1666	142048	26437
13370	1500		1666	101668	8700
3813			**800**	**47826**	**517**
913				47564	517
			800	200	
2900				62	
1014698	**92839**	**3595**		**1356285**	**1215165**
103615	10663	554		378351	64252
238				12197	92
16118	**16693**		**400**	**82820**	**4528**
	300			8195	
16118	16393		400	74625	4528
17835				**119201**	**29639**
530				500	368
11500				17674	25679
5705				3731	2111

4-9 续表 3

单位：万元

行业	Sector	本年资金来源小计 Sub-total Funds This Year
地质勘查业	Geologic Prospecting	98877
水利、环境和公共设施管理业	**Management of Water Conservancy, Environment and Public Facilities**	**1977418**
水利管理业	Management of Water Conservancy	764643
环境管理业	Environmental Management	183023
公共设施管理业	Management of Public Facilities	1029752
市政公共设施管理	Management of Public Facilities	848863
城市绿化管理	Management of Urban Greening	94441
游览景区管理	Scenic-Spot Management	86448
居民服务和其他服务业	**Services to Households and Other Services**	**113174**
教　育	**Education**	**664653**
#初等教育	Elementary Education	112969
中等教育	Secondary Education	329592
高等教育	Higher Education	59895
卫生、社会保障和社会福利业	**Health, Social Security and Social Welfare**	**358575**
卫　生	Health Care	289707
#医　院	Hospital	214664
专科疾病防治活动	Prerention and Control of Special Diseases	1190
疾病预防控制及防疫活动	Prevention and Control of Diseases	1318
社会保障业	Social Security	31537
社会福利业	Social Welfare	37331
文化、体育和娱乐业	**Culture, Sport and Entertainment**	**192939**
新闻出版业	Journalism and Publishing Activities	5559
广播、电视、电影和音像业	Broadcasting,Movies,Televisions and Audiovisual Activites	11970
文化艺术业	Culture and Art Activities	108680
体　育	Sports Activities	23255
娱乐业	Entertainment	43475
公共管理和社会组织	**Public Management and Social Organization**	**1110232**
中国共产党机关	Organ of Communist Party of China	24239
国家机构	Government Agencies	1064095
人民政协和民主党派	People's Political Consultative Conference and Democratic Parties	200
群众团体、社会团体和宗教组织	Non-Governmental Organizations,Social Organizations and Religion Organizations	5319
基层群众自治组织	Grass Root Self-governing Organizations	16379

Continued

(10 000 yuan)

国家预算内资金 State Budget	国内贷款 Domestic Loans	债券 Bonds	利用外资 Foreign Investment	自筹资金 Self-raising Funds	其他资金来源 Others
100				97296	1481
798138	**149481**	**606**	**10784**	**925106**	**93303**
284371	39936		2000	382133	56203
91121	54285		1177	32349	4091
422646	55260	606	7607	510624	33009
353516	41588	606	7317	424095	21741
50523	8522			31261	4135
18607	5150		290	55268	7133
6704	**4000**			**99523**	**2947**
430631	**33887**	**3856**	**1161**	**105998**	**89120**
84792		2523	391	18809	6454
221871	16285	1193		30947	59296
11922	17602			26571	3800
176167	**11162**	**1008**		**112809**	**57429**
138708	7894	1008		90210	51887
105144	4300	315		71494	33411
				1190	
1111				192	15
11747	3268			15722	800
25712				6877	4742
53990	**17600**	**525**		**93364**	**27460**
350				3709	1500
7968				3002	1000
27241	17600	525		41604	21710
13030				10225	
5401				34824	3250
510819	**9598**	**956**		**432732**	**156127**
8952		10		9597	5680
487798	9598	833		418075	147791
					200
1823				2284	1212
12246		113		2776	1244

4-10 各地、州、市、县(市)城镇固定资产投资和新增固定资产

Total Investment and Newly Increased Fixed Assets in Urban Area by Prefecture, Autonomous Prefecture, City and County

单位：万元　　(2011 年)　　(10 000 yuan)

地　区 Region	投资总额 Total Investment	第一产业 Primary Industry	第二产业 Secondary Industry	第三产业 Tertiary Industry	新增固定资产 Newly Increased Fixed Assets	房屋建筑面积(万平方米) Floor Space of Buildings (10 000 sq.m) 施工面积 Floor Space Under Construction	竣工面积 Floor Space Completed
总　计 Total	**36881064**	**1018114**	**23161011**	**12701939**	**20864406**	**8204.64**	**2358.37**
按隶属关系分 By Administrative Relationship							
中　央 Central Government	11062437	176487	7452430	3433520	7311350	1617.02	595.08
地　方 Local	25818627	841627	15708581	9268419	13553056	6587.62	1763.29
按区域分 Grouped by Region							
乌鲁木齐市 Urumqi City	**4343646**	**19626**	**2321789**	**2002231**	**2434909**	**559.32**	**92.54**
天山区 Tianshan District	566721		355692	211029	444406	70.91	18.98
沙依巴克区 Shayibak District	435004	2550	76796	355658	106143	42.43	9.45
新市区 Xinshi District	1482563	1900	753372	727291	824944	151.34	2.27
水磨沟区 Shui Mogou District	222610		15524	207086	364945	95.25	24.45
头屯河区 Tou Tunhe District	630755	2167	330890	297698	387545	132.48	12.38
达坂城区 Da Bancheng District	214361		213081	1280	11346	3.22	
米东区 Midong District	696903	7169	547168	142566	237627	55.20	18.61
乌鲁木齐县 Urumqi County	94729	5840	29266	59623	57953	8.48	6.41
克拉玛依市 Karamay City	**1993665**	**1710**	**1828820**	**163135**	**1855097**	**77.63**	**9.40**
独山子区 Dushanzi District	151607		113502	38105	110191		
克拉玛依区 Karamay District	1817633	1354	1705442	110837	1719507	71.26	5.88
乌尔河区 Urhe District	12863	356	4365	8142	14006	3.51	3.51
白碱滩区 Bai Jiantan District	11562		5511	6051	11393	2.85	
吐鲁番地区 Turpan Administrative Offices	**1242315**	**33077**	**1021420**	**187818**	**670036**	**122.15**	**19.99**
吐鲁番市 Turpan City	242461	15185	124713	102563	102949	85.78	17.24
鄯善县 Shanshan [Piqan] County	682845	13310	592975	76560	398636	30.91	2.43
托克逊县 Toksun County	317009	4582	303732	8695	168451	5.45	0.33
哈密地区 Hami [Kumul] Administrative Offices	**1874333**	**37876**	**1435878**	**400579**	**757390**	**280.59**	**104.22**
哈密市 Hami [Kumul] City	1165188	26744	875643	262801	626300	237.58	102.55
巴里坤哈萨克自治县 Barkol Kazak Autonomous County	253535	7347	176727	69461	110314	40.66	1.02
伊吾县 Yiwu [Araturuk] County	455610	3785	383508	68317	20776	2.35	0.65
昌吉回族自治州 Changji Hui Autonomous Prefecture	**4356079**	**85669**	**3343753**	**926657**	**1934270**	**683.97**	**148.04**
昌吉市 Changji City	714113	26801	383856	303456	168401	145.05	12.01
阜康市 Fukang City	776458	4985	729930	41543	789777	18.15	14.64

4-10 续表 1 Continued

单位：万元 (10 000 yuan)

地　区 Region	投资总额 Total Investment	第一产业 Primary Industry	第二产业 Secondary Industry	第三产业 Tertiary Industry	新增固定资产 Newly Increased Fixed Assets	房屋建筑面积(万平方米) Floor Space of Buildings (10 000 sq.m) 施工面积 Floor Space Under Construction	 竣工面积 Floor Space Completed
呼图壁县 Hutubi County	463330	10884	286501	165945	200031	99.92	48.05
玛纳斯县 Manas County	588118	22300	385184	180634	430643	158.57	37.77
奇台县 Qitai County	615346	20699	407970	186677	262612	109.04	35.56
吉木萨尔县 Jimsar County	1172950		1146132	26818	64924	123.09	
木垒哈萨克自治县 Mori Kazak Autonomous County	25764		4180	21584	17882	30.15	
伊犁哈萨克自治州 Ili Kazak Autonomous Prefecture	**6159228**	**334670**	**3748465**	**2076093**	**2904741**	**1583.25**	**433.66**
伊犁州直属县(市) Counties (Cities) Direct Under Ili Prefecture	**3204801**	**79642**	**2180484**	**944675**	**1247020**	**809.63**	**168.23**
伊宁市 Yining [Gulja] City	764991	2230	484600	278161	237546	240.86	13.40
奎屯市 Kuytun City	582150	4882	359502	217766	126253	161.38	16.30
伊宁县 Yining [Gulja] County	484304	26966	415566	41772	60675	49.53	17.58
察布查尔锡伯自治县 Qapqal Xibe Autonomous County	306246	2278	251869	52099	200271	52.21	11.87
霍城县 Huocheng [Korgas] County	299470	5165	133754	160551	161258	136.34	36.44
巩留县 Gongliu [Tokkuztara] County	128061	20279	76350	31432	96567	30.83	16.34
新源县 Xinyuan [Kunes] County	197526	8201	122288	67037	176254	38.09	23.66
昭苏县 Zhaosu [Mongolkure] County	62654	1007	26703	34944	26603	30.47	7.33
特克斯县 Tekes County	115864	7209	58525	50130	112334	42.50	23.12
尼勒克县 Nilka County	263535	1425	251327	10783	49259	27.41	2.19
塔城地区 Tacheng [Tarbagatai] Administrative Offices	**1701872**	**133585**	**942367**	**625920**	**945513**	**528.64**	**149.99**
塔城市 Tacheng [Qoqek] City	177342	31974	38998	106370	77074	105.02	7.24
乌苏市 Usu City	351416	14940	288886	47590	204585	69.10	37.08
额敏县 Emin Ciunty	269045	39592	111980	117473	203530	64.75	26.94
沙湾县 Shawan County	412690	27339	172072	213279	247426	206.35	51.30
托里县 Toli County	148832	5483	95484	47865	68522	25.37	22.86
裕民县 Yumin [Qagantokay] County	32720	1363	9701	21656	24969	12.71	2.83
和布克赛尔蒙古自治县 Hoboksar Mongol Autonomous County	309827	12894	225246	71687	119407	45.35	1.74
阿勒泰地区 Altay Administrative Offices	**1252555**	**121443**	**625614**	**505498**	**712208**	**244.98**	**115.44**
阿勒泰市 Altay City	255755	29805	79585	146365	107864	64.49	31.53
布尔津县 Burqin County	129561	25469	36681	67411	89271	25.90	9.46
富蕴县 Fuyun [Koktokay] County	290267	3513	227872	58882	84436	18.60	7.89
福海县 Fuhai [Burultokay] County	131255	23556	36346	71353	70442	33.41	10.77

4-10 续表 2 Continued

单位：万元 (10 000 yuan)

地区 Region	投资总额 Total Investment	第一产业 Primary Industry	第二产业 Secondary Industry	第三产业 Tertiary Industry	新增固定资产 Newly Increased Fixed Assets	房屋建筑面积(万平方米) Floor Space of Buildings (10 000 sq.m) 施工面积 Floor Space Under Construction	竣工面积 Floor Space Completed
哈巴河县 Habahe [Kaba] County	202727	24134	100281	78312	129406	53.33	19.91
青河县 Qinghe [Qinggil] County	148691	10293	91468	46930	140571	26.70	19.77
吉木乃县 Jeminay County	94299	4673	53381	36245	90218	22.55	16.12
博尔塔拉蒙古自治州 Bortala Mongol Autonomous Prefecture	**643430**	**57030**	**242965**	**343435**	**521459**	**309.08**	**78.28**
博乐市 Bole [Bortala] City	428995	32735	189061	207199	420168	214.49	65.15
精河县 Jinghe [Jing] County	149414	14027	48658	86729	53740	65.86	
温泉县 Wenquan [Araxang] County	65021	10268	5246	49507	47551	28.73	13.12
巴音郭楞蒙古自治州 Bayangol Mongol Autonomous Prefecture	**3349974**	**76909**	**2571303**	**701762**	**2217841**	**505.19**	**179.84**
库尔勒市 Korla City	1982258	8193	1746168	227897	1128824	130.50	69.57
轮台县 Luntai [Bugur] County	206539	5371	152334	48834	109084	36.91	7.63
尉犁县 Yuli [Lopnur] County	55809	10682	17279	27848	51220	26.96	2.29
若羌县 Ruoqiang [Qarkilik] County	301528	10305	195574	95649	632295	87.89	7.85
且末县 Qiemo [Qarqan] County	101450	6722	13698	81030	59913	49.91	6.95
焉耆回族自治县 Yanqi Hui Autonomous County	128096	13076	52038	62982	64947	45.24	26.91
和静县 Hejing County	446781	6568	362774	77439	94862	55.78	37.52
和硕县 Hoxud County	75032	11467	19424	44141	52377	40.71	20.21
博湖县 Bohu [Bagrax] County	52481	4525	12014	35942	24319	31.30	0.90
阿克苏地区 Aksu Administrative Offices	**1986846**	**54692**	**1250900**	**681254**	**876195**	**671.32**	**178.43**
阿克苏市 Aksu City	500163	16569	317759	165835	285113	265.67	59.13
温宿县 Wensu [Onsu] County	202693	7741	110194	84758	44431	38.67	8.91
库车县 Kuqa County	604756	5750	386955	212051	214211	140.78	42.12
沙雅县 Xayar County	141801		115550	26251	155025	21.65	3.00
新和县 Xinhe [Toksu] County	100750	10476	43506	46768	63293	47.48	34.30
拜城县 Baicheng [Bay] County	276379		212613	63766	34090	59.13	6.31
乌什县 Wushi [Uxturpan] County	47250	8475	3335	35440	22897	27.31	12.43
阿瓦提县 Awat County	85248	2484	42574	40190	40681	59.69	8.07
柯坪县 Kalpin County	27806	3197	18414	6195	16454	10.94	4.17
克孜勒苏柯尔克孜自治州 Kizilsu Kirgiz Autonomous Prefecture	**417606**	**8411**	**242618**	**166577**	**238738**	**191.96**	**100.53**
阿图什市 Artux City	108698		76101	32597	83348	55.63	23.86
阿克陶县 Akto County	143664	6046	58983	78635	77094	80.15	57.13

4-10 续表 3 Continued

单位：万元 (10 000 yuan)

地　区 Region	投资总额 Total Investment	第一产业 Primary Industry	第二产业 Secondary Industry	第三产业 Tertiary Industry	新增固定资产 Newly Increased Fixed Assets	房屋建筑面积(万平方米) Floor Space of Buildings (10 000 sq.m)	
						施工面积 Floor Space Under Construction	竣工面积 Floor Space Completed
阿合奇县 Akqi County	78427	236	73663	4528	7389	13.78	
乌恰县 Wuqia [Ulugqat] County	86817	2129	33871	50817	70907	42.40	19.55
喀什地区 Kashgar [Kaxgar] Administrative Offices	**3303322**	**167981**	**1415016**	**1720325**	**2374691**	**1729.66**	**234.01**
喀什市 Kashgar [Kaxgar] City	516141	3108	133483	379550	324563	70.90	0.29
疏附县 Shufu County	228595	9103	177359	42133	119081	156.82	51.93
疏勒县 Shule County	623236	46643	294844	281749	336077	358.49	2.73
英吉沙县 Yengisar County	250394	9535	211437	29422	90869	119.01	0.25
泽普县 Zepu [Poskam] County	190472	14065	120997	55410	179062	264.23	
莎车县 Shache [Yarkant] County	250976	18884	73634	158458	140143	208.91	1.25
叶城县 Yecheng [Kagilik] County	297401	12113	78360	206928	337825	214.04	0.44
麦盖提县 Makit County	179054	21719	48928	108407	171991	21.35	14.41
岳普湖县 Yopurga County	124769	12050	79333	33386	118499	17.35	3.34
伽师县 Jiashi [Payzawat] County	272583	17657	69005	185921	174744	76.43	2.22
巴楚县 Bachu [Maralbexi] County	221568		82402	139166	233704	199.90	148.15
塔什库尔干塔吉克自治县 Taxkorgan Tajik Autonomous County	148133	3104	45234	99795	148133	22.23	9.01
和田地区 Hotan Administrative Offices	**1144577**	**88332**	**273992**	**782253**	**953392**	**748.60**	**478.46**
和田市 Hotan City	307160	13734	75749	217677	210147	204.80	90.15
和田县 Hotan County	190190	23230	65953	101007	126843	153.43	124.26
墨玉县 Moyu [Karakax] County	214561	18436	31572	164553	206009	160.94	130.45
皮山县 Pishan [Guma] County	89043	1096	1403	86544	88967	41.70	26.08
洛浦县 Lop County	81314	4582	15733	60999	93008	42.93	17.08
策勒县 Qira County	79954	14407	10176	55371	68167	69.26	42.65
于田县 Yutian [Keriya] County	142048	11001	66356	64691	132413	41.58	39.36
民丰县 Minfeng [Niya] County	40307	1846	7050	31411	27838	33.96	8.43
自治区直辖县级市 Municpality Country-LevelCity directly under the Central Government	**2999134**	**52131**	**2422235**	**524768**	**1948801**	**676.72**	**282.15**
石河子市 Shihezi City	1507501	32711	1252995	221795	944896	328.26	129.92
阿拉尔市 Aral City	443750	12745	318909	112096	311117	127.15	92.36
图木舒克市 Tumxuk City	172841	4877	52997	114967	109109	81.16	26.17
五家渠市 Wujiaqu City	875042	1798	797334	75910	583679	140.15	33.70
跨地区投资 Trans-regional Investment	**3066909**		**1041857**	**2025052**	**1176846**	**65.20**	**18.82**

4-11 各地、州、市分行业城镇固定资产投资

单位：万元 (2011 年)

行业 Sector	合计 Total	乌鲁木齐市 Urumqi City	克拉玛依市 Karamay City	吐鲁番地区 Turpan Administrative Offices	哈密地区 Hami [Kumul] Administrative Offices	昌吉回族自治州 Changji Hui Autonomous Prefecture	伊犁哈萨克自治州 Ili Kazak Autonomous Prefecture	伊犁州直属县(市) Counties (Cities) Direct Under Ili Prefecture
总计 Total	**36881064**	**4343646**	**1993665**	**1242315**	**1874333**	**4356079**	**6159228**	**3204801**
农、林、牧、渔业 Farming, Forestry, Animal Husbandry and Fishery	1018114	19626	1710	33077	37876	85669	334670	79642
采矿业 Mining	6310817	121517	1511039	438205	720111	298529	410755	175302
制造业 Manufacturing	10813017	1380081	257468	396542	186253	2317711	1846924	1337288
电力、燃气及水的生产和供应业 Production and Supply of Electricity, Gas and Water	5420642	753062	23391	186673	529514	727045	1453132	637519
建筑业 Construction	616535	67129	36922			468	37654	30375
交通运输、仓储及邮政业 Transport, Storage, Postal and Telecommunications Services	3458999	470369	3643	31065	68957	179146	289892	149913
信息传输、计算机服务和软件业 Information Transmission, Computer Services and Software	481274	341950	764		18280	11237	35532	20156
批发和零售业 Wholesale&Retail Trades	455673	141796	17029	12891	12678	35653	73704	57184
住宿和餐饮业 Hotels and Catering Services	203120	12528	302	10780	2803	34340	33831	10825
金融业 Financial Intermediation	49034	31642	107	736	1478	1515	1691	511
房地产业 Real Estate	3621776	259388	21516	30397	191281	384116	786197	370008
租赁和商务服务业 Leasing and Business Services	156301	61841	269			20400	16524	15239
科学研究、技术服务和地质勘查业 Scientific Research, Technical Service and Geological Prospection	178246	22362	24720	21072	145	256	77990	7723
水利、环境和公共设施管理业 Management of Water Conservancy, Environment and Public Facilities	1823859	433063	24356	18910	64651	136400	383802	115158
居民服务和其他服务业 Service to Households and Others Services	46853	12018	1297	549	555	3408	4550	1089
教育 Education	626062	68581	24365	11364	17980	35967	119663	59649
卫生、社会保障和社会福利业 Health, Social Securities and Social Welfare	339890	37953	8159	3457	8805	21873	72888	43632
文化、体育和娱乐业 Culture, Sports and Entertainment	174394	12246	9066	555	4320	41848	23803	3672
公共管理和社会组织 Public Management and Social Organization	1086458	96494	27542	46042	8646	20498	156026	89916

Investment in Fixed Assets in Urban Area by Sectors in Prefecture, Autonomous Prefecture and City

(10 000 yuan)

塔城地区 Tacheng [Tarbagatai] Administra-tive Offices	阿勒泰地区 Altay Administra-tive Offices	博尔塔拉蒙古自治州 Bortala Mongol Autono-mous Prefecture	巴音郭楞蒙古自治州 Bayangol Mongol Autono-mous Prefecture	阿克苏地区 Aksu Administra-tive Offices	克孜勒苏柯尔克孜自治州 Kizilsu Kirgiz Autono-mous Prefecture	喀什地区 Kashgar [Kaxgar] Administra-tive Offices	和田地区 Hotan Administra-tive Offices	石河子市 Shihezi City	阿拉尔市 Aral City	图木舒克市 Tumxuk City	五家渠市 Wujiaqu City	跨地区投资 Trans-regional Investment
1701872	**1252555**	**643430**	**3349974**	**1986846**	**417606**	**3303322**	**1144577**	**1507501**	**443750**	**172841**	**875042**	**3066909**
133585	121443	57030	76909	54692	8411	167981	88332	32711	12745	4877	1798	
95566	139887	7359	1514570	68405	18332	145557	29531			100		1026807
421300	88336	146498	880237	895887	86432	772236	100704	776726	233063	44872	491383	
418801	396812	56346	175566	237617	118877	135276	136304	472967	85846	8025	305951	15050
6700	579	32762	930	48991	18977	361947	7453	3302				
66451	73528	38794	89916	59046	6194	121327	60495	24419	5355	400	13029	1996952
9223	6153	12178	1072	674	1380	36234	15137	6541		295		
3248	13272	19063	23732	28417	650	63838	19345	1000	1175	3702	1000	
10817	12189	5146	16663	6330		44481	14820	13176	750	6870	300	
250	930	1740	1510	689	465	4826	2635					
297489	118700	113369	242062	207707	75844	713534	352039	76901	87137	46514	33774	
1285		1200	12707	25576		14104	3680					
3096	67171	1958	2527	5179	3861	11160	4394		792	1830		
112313	156331	66458	164447	66147	12152	184968	94830	87472	5493	32435	20175	28100
2909	552	2533	6420	331	553	10700	560		1510	634	1235	
36692	23322	15416	34456	68581	13271	142126	53825	1893	5997	10577	2000	
20531	8725	6069	20247	30561	4614	84574	28831	4893	2370	4596		
13843	6288	4433	1378	1439	4439	46268	13498	5500	300	1144	4157	
47773	18337	55078	84625	180577	43154	242185	118164		1217	5970	240	

4-12 城镇固定资产投资效果指标
Investment Result of Urban Investment

指 标	Item	2010	2011
建设周期(年)	Construction Cycle (year)	3	4
计划总投资(万元)	Total Planned Investment (10 000 yuan)	80276938	131077233
本年完成投资(万元)	Completed Invetsment for the Current Year (10 000 yuan)	28338644	36881064
本年新增固定资产(万元)	Newly Increased Fixed Assets for the Current Year (10 000 yuan)	15042603	20864406
固定资产交付使用率(%)	Rate of Projects of Fixed Assets Completed and Put into Operation (%)	53.1	56.6
施工项目个数(个)	Number of Projects under Construction (unit)	8179	10382
竣工项目个数(个)	Number of Projects Completed (unit)	5369	6528
建设项目投产率(%)	Rate of Projects Completed&Put into Use (%)	65.6	62.9
施工面积(万平方米)	Construction Area (10 000 sq.m)	5400.16	8204.64
#住 宅	Residential Buildings	2717.34	4309.17
竣工面积(万平方米)	Completed Area (10 000 sq.m)	2147.84	2358.37
#住 宅	Residential Buildings	1168.34	1513.57
房屋面积竣工率(%)	Rate of Floor Space of Buildings Completed (%)	39.8	28.7
#住 宅	Residential Buildings	43.0	35.1

4-13 主要年份房地产开发企业基本情况

Basic Condition of Enterprises for Real Estate Development in Main Years

指　标	Item	2005	2010	2011
企业单位数(个)	**Number of Enterprises (unit)**	**756**	**1233**	**1421**
#亏损企业	Loss- Suffering Enterprises	410	606	695
主要财务指标（万元）	**Main Financial Indices (10 000 yuan)**			
年末资产负债情况	Situation of Year-end Liabilities			
资产总计	Total Assets	4861415	12591584	18885515
固定资产累计折旧	Accumulated Depreciation of Fixed Assets	81096	156739	229200
#本年折旧	Depreciation for the Current Year	17981	34814	42418
负债总计	Total Liabilities	2932694	9422446	14297295
所有者权益合计	Total of Owner's Right and Interest	1928721	3169138	4588220
实收资本	Total of Actual Capital	970103	2109245	2645950
#国家资本	State-owned Capital	59976	162505	
损益情况	Situation of Profit and Loss			
经营收入总计	Total Income of Business	1084796	4119413	5148232
#土地转让收入	Income of Land Transfer	11295	19029	14287
商品房销售收入	Sales Income of Commercial Flat	1047965	4022490	5024930
房屋出租收入	Income of Renting House	15773	39343	62576
其他收入	Others	9763	38550	46439
经营成本	Operating Cost	871320	3040741	3666103
经营税金及附加	Operating Tax and Extra Charges	63562	295011	370039
销售费用	Expenses of sales	27319	100896	129878
其他业务利润	Other Business Profits	9161	28592	26302
管理费用及财务费用	Expenses of Both Management and Finance	80949	257405	414662
投资收益及营业外收入	Income of Investment earnings and Extra-business	7829	14881	61315
营业外支出	Expenditure of Extra-business	3456	14909	27276
利润总额	Total Profits	34320	454814	663318

注：2004 年以后，企业个数包括了没有开发量的企业数，而往年未包括。
Note: Urban Investment exclude real estate, the following the same as follows.

4-14 主要年份房地产投资主要指标
Main Indicators of Real Estate Investment in Main Years

指　标	Item	2005	2010	2011
本年购置土地面积(万平方米)	**Land Area Purchased for the Current Year (10 000 sq. m)**	**447.30**	**557.69**	**980.87**
房地产开发投资额(万元)	**Total Investment of Real-Estate Development (10 000 yuan)**	**1016618**	**3477185**	**5163895**
按中央和地方分	Grouped by Central and Local			
中央企业	Central Enterprises	54128	175564	175468
地方企业	Local Enterprises	962490	3301621	4988427
按投资构成分	Classified by Use of Funds			
建筑工程	Construction Works	810003	2742491	3972278
安装工程	Works of Installation	49559	161703	336780
设备工器具购置	Purchase of Equipment and Instruments	14135	51777	53225
其他费用	Other Expenses	142921	521214	801612
#土地购置费	Expenses of Land Purchase	94230	313568	425236
按工程用途分	Grouped by Purpose of Projects			
住　宅	Residential buildings	679521	2815620	4163926
办公楼	Office Building	40977	102895	155400
商业营业用房	Houses for Commercial and Business Purpose	247033	380275	572602
其　他	Others	49087	178395	271967
本年资金来源小计（万元）	**Sub-total of Capital Sources for the Current Year (10 000 yuan)**	**1137693**	**5380739**	**6843313**
国内贷款	Domestic Loans	113887	684191	731550
利用外资	Foreign Investment	160		1666
自筹资金	Self-raising Funds	479948	1397982	2314233
其它资金	Others	543698	3298566	3795864

4-15 按用途分房地产开发企业（单位）投资完成额

Investment Actually Completed by Enterprises for Real Estate Development by Use

单位：万元　　　　(10 000 yuan)

年份 Year	地区 Region	企业个数(个) Number of Enterprises (unit)	本年完成投资 Investment Completed This Year	住宅 Residential Buildings	#别墅、高档公寓 Villas, High-grade Apartments	#经济适用房 Economically Affordable Housing
1996		139	156232	80728		4489
1997			169906	81886	1668	21474
1998			148577	95225	1000	27388
1999		165	234481	174446	2994	55345
2000		209	574347	500381	2390	236923
2001		293	979184	757490	3126	350362
2002		335	877060	570643	11001	236731
2003		492	1024908	547770	20212	243651
2004		709	1125577	599276	29585	207447
2005		756	1016618	679521	26634	245022
2006		824	1208786	899482	48542	304890
2007		909	1683160	1390360	57776	164429
2008		1130	2286267	1937460	94256	164559
2009		1159	2358805	1882530	148916	160840
2010		1233	3477185	2815620	194136	99339
2011		1421	5163895	4163926	258846	
乌鲁木齐市	Urumqi City	364	1980381	1612908	84747	
克拉玛依市	Karamay City	42	133246	96139	2188	
吐鲁番地区	Turpan Administrative Offices	17	24103	17132		
哈密地区	Hami [Kumul] Administrative Offices	91	227494	200370	2149	
昌吉回族自治州	Changji Hui Autonomous Prefecture	129	497167	448014	10805	
伊犁哈萨克自治州	Ili Kazak Autonomous Prefecture	270	969191	773686	3975	
伊犁州直属县(市)	Counties (Cities) Direct Under Ili Prefecture	144	580807	448758	2235	
塔城地区	Tacheng [Tarbagatai] Administrative Offices	61	267227	236724	1740	
阿勒泰地区	Altay Administrative Offices	65	121157	88204		
博尔塔拉蒙古自治州	Bortala Mongol Autonomous Prefecture	45	68339	46101	2155	
巴音郭楞蒙古自治州	Bayangol Mongol Autonomous Prefecture	141	458166	365690	150946	
阿克苏地区	Aksu Administrative Offices	124	203683	168792	985	
克孜勒苏柯尔克孜自治州	Kizilsu Kirgiz Autonomous Prefecture	12	9406	6349	100	
喀什地区	Kashgar [Kaxgar] Administrative Offices	84	328274	206076		
和田地区	Hotan Administrative Offices	3	3254	2097		
石河子市	Shihezi City	57	127819	113915	80	
阿拉尔市	Aral City	14	41004	32133		
图木舒克市	Tumxuk City	6	16700	12975		
五家渠市	Wujiaqu City	22	75668	61549	716	

4-15 续表 Continued

单位：万元 (10 000 yuan)

年 份 Year	地 区 Region	办公楼 Office buildings	商业营业用房 Houses for Business Use	其 他 Other
	1996	18108	42562	14834
	1997	25347	41935	20738
	1998	17394	22027	13931
	1999	9133	27068	23834
	2000	13171	42601	18194
	2001	41911	111028	68755
	2002	81119	153498	71800
	2003	81497	286896	108745
	2004	77843	390566	57892
	2005	40977	247033	49087
	2006	28233	236945	44126
	2007	27629	205590	59581
	2008	56358	221418	71031
	2009	81926	281946	112403
	2010	102895	380275	178395
	2011	155400	572602	271967
乌鲁木齐市	Urumqi City	72426	138448	156599
克拉玛依市	Karamay City	23357	2930	10820
吐鲁番地区	Turpan Administrative Offices	2335	3966	670
哈密地区	Hami [Kumul] Administrative Offices	6128	16825	4171
昌吉回族自治州	Changji Hui Autonomous Prefecture	8276	23556	17321
伊犁哈萨克自治州	Ili Kazak Autonomous Prefecture	16482	145062	33961
伊犁州直属县(市)	Counties (Cities) Direct Under Ili Prefecture	13049	105614	13386
塔城地区	Tacheng [Tarbagatai] Administrative Offices	1344	12133	17026
阿勒泰地区	Altay Administrative Offices	2089	27315	3549
博尔塔拉蒙古自治州	Bortala Mongol Autonomous Prefecture	248	20994	996
巴音郭楞蒙古自治州	Bayangol Mongol Autonomous Prefecture	5793	63313	23370
阿克苏地区	Aksu Administrative Offices	2772	27704	4415
克孜勒苏柯尔克孜自治州	Kizilsu Kirgiz Autonomous Prefecture		1157	1900
喀什地区	Kashgar [Kaxgar] Administrative Offices	15426	92506	14266
和田地区	Hotan Administrative Offices	442	445	270
石河子市	Shihezi City	1159	11080	1665
阿拉尔市	Aral City		8871	
图木舒克市	Tumxuk City	36	3609	80
五家渠市	Wujiaqu City	520	12136	1463

4-16 房地产开发企业（单位）资金来源
Sources of Funds of Enterprises for Real Estate Development

单位：万元 (10 000 yuan)

年 份 Year	地 区 Region	合 计 Total	国内贷款 Domestic Loans	利用外资 Foreign Investment	自筹资金 Self-raising Funds	其他资金来源 Others
	1996	154995	51048	742	45104	58101
	1997	161399	51443	500	60573	48883
	1998	151094	22419	500	49427	78748
	1999	244252	29665	5770	73899	134918
	2000	701332	113823	600	232768	354141
	2001	890102	106794	1278	303975	478055
	2002	1064031	158511		455707	449813
	2003	1117659	208348		448441	460870
	2004	1215850	125553		546282	544015
	2005	1137693	113887	160	479948	543698
	2006	1446593	145340		478871	822382
	2007	2243755	217380		766344	1260031
	2008	2427323	253427		961343	1212553
	2009	3683795	453692	50	915219	2314834
	2010	5380739	684191		1397982	3298566
	2011	6843313	731550	1666	2314233	3795864
乌鲁木齐市	Urumqi City	3117756	475294		756325	1886137
克拉玛依市	Karamay City	133650	1300		94065	38285
吐鲁番地区	Turpan Administrative Offices	25661			19150	6511
哈密地区	Hami [Kumul] Administrative Offices	265358	17452		66450	181456
昌吉回族自治州	Changji Hui Autonomous Prefecture	624172	84721		178944	360507
伊犁哈萨克自治州	Ili Kazak Autonomous Prefecture	1133745	52472		538843	542430
伊犁州直属县(市)	Counties (Cities) Direct Under Ili Prefecture	730380	43082		208957	478341
塔城地区	Tacheng [Tarbagatai] Administrative Offices	289449	4450		244846	40153
阿勒泰地区	Altay Administrative Offices	113916	4940		85040	23936
博尔塔拉蒙古自治州	Bortala Mongol Autonomous Prefecture	83821	1569		56556	25696
巴音郭楞蒙古自治州	Bayangol Mongol Autonomous Prefecture	453383	28943		166148	258292
阿克苏地区	Aksu Administrative Offices	254306	18730		101035	134541
克孜勒苏柯尔克孜自治州	Kizilsu Kirgiz Autonomous Prefecture	9854			7906	1948
喀什地区	Kashgar [Kaxgar] Administrative Offices	449888	39596		228593	181699
和田地区	Hotan Administrative Offices	6106			6106	
石河子市	Shihezi City	155329	11130	1666	34919	107614
阿拉尔市	Aral City	41144			40937	207
图木舒克市	Tumxuk City	13010			6290	6720
五家渠市	Wujiaqu City	76130	343		11966	63821

4-17 房地产开发企业（单位）施工、销售和待售情况

单位：万平方米

年 份 Year	地 区 Region	本年施工房屋面积 Floor Space of Building under Construction This Year	#住宅 Residential Buildings	#商业营业用房 Houses for Business Use	本年新开工房屋面积 Floor Space Started This Year	#住宅 Residential Buildings	#商业营业用房 Houses for Business Use
	1996	224.90	150.80	41.67	103.87	69.84	19.52
	1997	222.20	144.50	47.68	90.24	70.08	12.81
	1998	252.61	188.38	40.72	133.26	120.95	6.35
	1999	343.38	295.62	34.33	212.73	194.77	12.48
	2000	771.86	665.30	74.20	453.63	397.77	43.00
	2001	1433.54	1207.89	150.63	912.06	778.55	97.24
	2002	1246.89	946.11	204.52	577.04	433.57	98.13
	2003	1382.14	962.89	298.51	782.78	557.28	175.73
	2004	1333.03	863.19	357.53	771.47	550.66	178.43
	2005	1371.15	941.58	340.63	793.55	639.98	130.90
	2006	1567.70	1188.61	307.19	1035.59	875.99	131.90
	2007	2053.76	1715.00	271.52	1347.11	1216.39	101.82
	2008	2639.06	2247.80	259.78	1703.86	1500.75	129.11
	2009	3064.41	2560.67	305.81	1718.17	1482.86	158.07
	2010	3980.80	3317.68	410.96	2177.24	1852.88	214.50
	2011	5481.44	4574.72	543.12	2974.51	2510.68	304.46
乌鲁木齐市	Urumqi City	1913.41	1563.18	123.22	599.70	491.92	33.88
克拉玛依市	Karamay City	131.63	122.41	2.93	85.35	79.49	2.52
吐鲁番地区	Turpan Administrative Offices	56.99	45.29	5.65	18.01	14.52	1.32
哈密地区	Hami [Kumul] Administrative Offices	276.44	235.45	27.90	163.48	145.60	13.36
昌吉回族自治州	Changji Hui Autonomous Prefecture	454.61	420.80	19.83	339.13	315.98	13.47
伊犁哈萨克自治州	Ili Kazak Autonomous Prefecture	987.35	831.87	128.78	655.62	555.61	81.40
伊犁州直属县(市)	Counties (Cities) Direct Under Ili Prefecture	569.44	473.50	78.06	361.96	296.08	52.38
塔城地区	Tacheng [Tarbagatai] Administrative Offices	249.11	228.98	15.28	201.45	186.48	12.69
阿勒泰地区	Altay Administrative Offices	168.79	129.39	35.44	92.21	73.05	16.33
博尔塔拉蒙古自治州	Bortala Mongol Autonomous Prefecture	73.84	52.42	20.71	48.69	34.30	14.25
巴音郭楞蒙古自治州	Bayangol Mongol Autonomous Prefecture	605.94	516.99	62.69	395.24	335.94	40.77
阿克苏地区	Aksu Administrative Offices	249.32	204.44	37.52	161.85	132.74	24.92
克孜勒苏柯尔克孜自治州	Kizilsu Kirgiz Autonomous Prefecture	11.44	6.67	3.20	4.82	3.25	
喀什地区	Kashgar [Kaxgar] Administrative Offices	389.20	301.12	67.75	247.62	182.05	51.41
和田地区	Hotan Administrative Offices	6.68	5.08	0.92	1.15	0.40	0.14
石河子市	Shihezi City	178.65	150.14	18.13	121.24	109.05	7.02
阿拉尔市	Aral City	38.76	26.91	11.85	34.26	26.31	7.95
图木舒克市	Tumxuk City	15.74	12.15	3.56	15.12	11.53	3.56
五家渠市	Wujiaqu City	91.44	79.80	8.48	83.23	71.99	8.49

Condition of Under Construction, Sale and Idle of Enterprises for Real Estate Development

(10 000 sq.m)

本年竣工房屋面积 Floor Space of Buindings Completed This Year	#住宅 Residential Buildings	#商业营业用房 Houses for Business Use	本年房屋销售面积 Floor Space of Building Sold This Year	#住宅 Residential Buildings	#商业营业用房 Houses for Business Use	房屋销售额（万元） Sales Value of Buildings (10 000 yuan)	#住宅 Residential Buildings	#商业营业用房 Houses for Business Use
81.19	64.51	8.14	45.60	41.29	2.91	67514	57024	5883
93.56	73.32	6.93	55.43	52.48	0.98	75110	67585	1569
94.28	79.92	6.23	83.29	75.97	3.46	118386	98803	8544
159.99	143.93	13.52	127.48	120.44	4.67	177683	158304	12599
330.11	298.79	23.07	262.52	250.95	9.82	373801	333166	35153
633.25	559.91	57.01	419.87	381.67	31.77	643814	537818	90441
727.21	616.12	85.03	506.66	455.68	46.34	879287	658157	208821
791.14	626.50	126.42	587.02	516.48	53.44	1066640	768012	224579
704.25	511.61	156.54	635.53	538.33	81.27	1106143	784408	281856
717.43	553.48	121.37	687.20	606.48	68.16	1235410	915191	288747
679.06	551.63	104.13	892.41	806.46	73.96	1658176	1358136	265450
890.55	798.12	72.07	1144.34	1078.28	51.57	2381520	2113425	211508
1049.29	943.40	67.30	954.35	886.35	51.22	2137859	1861169	212861
1032.72	900.87	76.28	1406.55	1326.67	65.81	3662638	3271682	317310
1012.90	859.92	98.40	1564.90	1450.02	94.42	4830392	4164140	523153
1270.48	1108.02	109.66	1728.23	1570.56	123.12	6133128	5162366	779898
340.99	291.43	18.89	481.84	436.15	20.15	2494793	2136451	207611
62.03	59.21	1.95	50.37	47.65	1.42	134165	124958	4918
31.45	28.18	2.92	27.99	25.37	2.62	56027	45425	10602
68.10	58.11	4.52	77.06	72.87	3.37	236780	205327	28547
101.24	94.32	6.64	207.57	200.44	6.56	649648	610458	36713
277.27	252.47	21.60	319.08	295.24	22.07	901280	778244	117006
172.26	159.67	10.38	211.85	197.27	13.68	630711	544836	81600
51.73	48.57	2.55	52.00	49.26	2.43	135229	128356	6381
53.28	44.23	8.67	55.23	48.71	5.96	135340	105052	29025
13.83	9.07	4.34	36.96	30.95	6.01	98721	68187	30534
168.70	144.08	17.26	196.88	182.70	14.08	543674	465641	77743
79.16	69.28	9.19	149.92	130.33	16.81	405264	312557	75123
6.62	3.42	3.20	8.56	5.60	2.94	41728	12630	28933
59.50	52.51	4.94	51.52	38.68	12.20	191927	108133	80035
1.63	0.40	0.70	7.82	6.55	0.99	20209	17398	2180
38.01	31.16	5.96	52.14	44.97	6.44	201357	159114	40241
19.28	11.95	7.33	19.16	13.29	5.87	56528	24765	31763
1.45	1.45		7.94	7.20	0.75	14699	10915	3784
1.22	0.98	0.22	33.42	32.57	0.84	86328	82163	4165

4-17 续表 Continued

单位：万平方米 (10 000 sq.m)

年份 Year	地区 Region	房屋待售面积 Floor Space At Idle	#住宅 Residential Buildings	#商业营业用房 Houses for Business Use
	1996	33.20	27.41	4.44
	1997	36.33	25.58	3.76
	1998	27.20	20.33	2.78
	1999	63.01	49.00	8.91
	2000	69.75	58.92	6.35
	2001	200.46	169.78	20.26
	2002	353.23	285.87	51.33
	2003	422.11	313.93	84.81
	2004	400.40	248.38	125.31
	2005	460.99	269.07	151.02
	2006	406.25	208.02	157.83
	2007	289.22	115.39	150.68
	2008	389.70	245.81	119.10
	2009	419.83	254.36	121.41
	2010	348.98	195.47	106.55
	2011	367.02	220.45	92.77
乌鲁木齐市	Urumqi City	127.94	54.14	34.00
克拉玛依市	Karamay City	4.86		2.85
吐鲁番地区	Turpan Administrative Offices	3.01	1.41	1.60
哈密地区	Hami [Kumul] Administrative Offices	4.59	2.11	0.61
昌吉回族自治州	Changji Hui Autonomous Prefecture	30.53	24.14	5.95
伊犁哈萨克自治州	Ili Kazak Autonomous Prefecture	88.33	67.65	18.39
伊犁州直属县(市)	Counties (Cities) Direct Under Ili Prefecture	31.67	19.86	9.82
塔城地区	Tacheng [Tarbagatai] Administrative Offices	52.71	45.58	7.01
阿勒泰地区	Altay Administrative Offices	3.95	2.21	1.56
博尔塔拉蒙古自治州	Bortala Mongol Autonomous Prefecture	5.35	3.25	2.09
巴音郭楞蒙古自治州	Bayangol Mongol Autonomous Prefecture	39.15	25.88	11.52
阿克苏地区	Aksu Administrative Offices	26.81	19.98	4.75
克孜勒苏柯尔克孜自治州	Kizilsu Kirgiz Autonomous Prefecture	3.13	1.08	0.50
喀什地区	Kashgar [Kaxgar] Administrative Offices	19.97	15.44	2.76
和田地区	Hotan Administrative Offices	2.94	2.40	0.29
石河子市	Shihezi City	4.45	2.06	2.39
阿拉尔市	Aral City	4.56	0.45	4.11
图木舒克市	Tumxuk City	0.19	0.15	0.03
五家渠市	Wujiaqu City	1.21	0.31	0.93

4-18 新增主要产品生产能力
Newly Increased Production Capacity of Major Products

项　目	Item	2010	2011
原煤开采(万吨/年)	Coal Mining (10 000 tons/year)	4874.90	2706.00
焦炭(万吨/年)	Coke (10 000 tons/year)	564.00	190.00
天然原油开采(万吨/年)	Petroleum Extractin (10 000 tons/year)	330.55	1092.80
天然气开采(亿立方米/年)	Natural Gas Extraction (100 million cu.m/year)	20.00	23.00
石油加工	Petroleum Processing		
裂化设备能力(处理万吨/年)	Cracking Equipment Capabillity(handle 10 000 tons/year)		8.00
催化重整设备能力(万吨/年)	Catalytic Reforming Equipment Capability (10 000 tons/year)		0.63
铁矿石开采(原矿) (万吨/年)	Iron-Ore Mining (10 000 tons/year)	486.70	907.60
铁矿选矿处理原矿量(万吨/年)	Iron-ore Dressing (10 000 tons/year)	62.00	62.50
铁矿石成品矿(万吨/年)	Eed Products of Iron Ore Mine(10 000 tons/year)	58.00	86.00
生铁(万吨/年)	Pig Iron(10 000 tons/year)	88.50	520.60
粗钢(万吨/年)	Crude Steel(10 000 tons/year)	160.00	270.00
转炉钢	Converter Steel		150.00
热轧钢材(万吨/年)	Hot-rolled Steel(10 000 tons/year)	60.00	122.30
铜采矿(原矿)(万吨/年)	Copper Ore Mining (10 000 tons/year)	627.00	92.15
铜选矿	Copper Ore Dressing		
处理原矿(万吨/年)	Raw Ore Treatment (10 000 tons/year)	686.25	152.52
铅锌采矿(原矿) (万吨/年)	Plumbum/Zinc Ore Mining (10 000 tons/year)	3.03	5.00
铝加工(吨/年)	Aluminium Processing (ton/year)	29500	74000
黄金(公斤/年)	Gold (kg/year)	475	394
发电机组容量(万千瓦)	Capacity of Generating Setes (10 000 kw/year)		
水力发电	Hydropower	39.42	37.05
火力发电	Thermal Power	97.10	237.32
其他发电	Others	29.75	68.15
输电线路长度(11 万伏及以上)(公里)	Transmission Line (110 000V)(km)	6967.70	2881.84
水泥(万吨/年)	Cement (10 000 tons/year)	863.00	2071.80

4-18 续表 Continued

项　　目	Item	2010	2011
石墨及炭素制品(吨/年)	Graphite and Carbon Products(ton/year)	450050	332895
电石(吨/年)	Calcium Carbide (ton/year)	780000	1810000
农用氮、磷、钾化学肥料(吨/年)	Farm-use Nitrogen, Phosphorus and Potassium Fertilizer (ton/year)		
氮肥	Nitrogen Fertilizer	316500	962907
磷肥	Phoshate Fertilizer	4150	14500
钾肥	Potash Fertilizer	850453	1209000
塑料树脂及共聚物(吨/年)	Plastic Colophony and Polymer (ton/year)	368000	437010
化学纤维(吨/年)	Chemical Fiber (ton/year)	10199	113000
粘胶纤维(吨/年)	Viscose Fiber(ton/year)	100	100000
棉纺锭(锭)	Cotton Spindle (spindle)	430560	160000
酒(万吨/年)	Liquors (10 000 tons/year)	14.74	1.98
其他酒	Others	5.62	1.98
程控交换机安装能力(万线/年)	Program-Controlled Telephone Exchange (10 000 lines/year)	3.00	40.00
新建公路(公里)	Length of New Highways (km)	2915.00	2140.11
二级公路	Second Class highway	252.00	202.73
改建公路(公里)	Length of Reconstructed Highways(km)	10490.00	7691.18
二级公路	Second Class highway	1412.00	1524.96
新建独立公路桥梁(延长米)	New-Built Separate Highway and Bridge (Extended Length m)	5159.00	2084.54
(座)	(unit)	12	5
新(扩)建客、货运站(个)	Number of newly-Built or Expanded Passenger and Freight Stations (unit)	11	14
(平方米)	(sq.m)	11171	22802
民航机场跑道(条)	Length of runway(unit)	1	
(米)	(m)	2600	
城市自来水供水能力(万吨/日)	Capacity of City Tap Water Supply (10 000 tons/day)	4.21	17.25
城市公共交通车辆购置(辆)	Purchase of City Communiting Vehicles (unit)	107	230
城市污水处理能力(万吨/日)	Disposal Capacity of Sewer (10 000 tons/day)	26.70	11.36

4-19 农村非农户固定资产投资情况
Investment in Fixed Assets of Non-Rural Households in Rural Areas

单位：万元 (10 000 yuan)

指　　标	Item	2010	2011
新增固定资产	**Newly Increased Investment in Fixed Assets**	**2040850**	**2158777**
固定资产投资完成额	**Completed Investment in Fixed Assets**	**2395698**	**3211176**
按投资构成分	By Use of Funds		
建筑工程	Construction Works	1680923	2234227
安装工程	Installation Works	84491	147782
设备工器具购置	Purchase of Equipment and Instruments	441866	672389
#用于更新的设备	Renew of Equipment and Instruments	24961	48911
其　他	Others	188418	156778
按投资方向分	By Sector of Investment		
农、林、牧、渔业	Agriculture, Forestry, Animal Husbandry and Fishing	625516	658798
采矿业	Mining	148357	207420
制造业	Manufacturing	377963	749671
电力、燃气及水的生产及供应业	Production and Supply of Electricity Gas and Water	166265	279839
建筑业	Construction	55750	150305
交通运输、仓储和邮政业	Transport, Storage and Post	254073	208751
信息传输、计算机服务和软件业	Information Transmission, Computer Servcies and Software	6775	200
批发和零售业	Wholesale and Retail Trades	23603	13142
住宿和餐饮业	Hotel and Catering Service	5025	9791
金融业	Financial Intermediation	929	2120
房地产业	Real Estate	327223	367474
租赁和商务服务业	Leasing and Business Service Industries	11362	7570
科学研究、技术服务和地质勘查业	Scientific Research, Technology Service and Geological Prospecting	7765	8602
水利、环境和公共设施管理业	Water Conservancy, Environment and Public Facility Management	195734	208970
居民服务和其他服务业	Community Service and Other Services	2538	1300
教　育	Education	31606	36501
卫生、社会保障和社会福利业	Health, Social Security and Social Welfare	26533	11149
文化、体育和娱乐业	Culture, Sports and Entertainment	11228	6757
公共管理和社会组织	Public Management and Social Organizations	117453	282816
资金来源	**Sub-total Funds**	**2437138**	**3614758**
国家预算内资金	State Budgetary Funds	779907	1001746
国内贷款	Domestic Loans	140959	177709
债　券	Bonds		822
利用外资	Foreign Investment	1294	6308
自筹资金	Self-raising Funds	1246453	2045605
其他资金	Others	268525	382568
本年施工房屋面积(万平方米)	**Floor Space of Buildings Under Construction (10 000 sq.m)**	**856.62**	**1223.34**
#住　宅	Residential Building	526.44	744.25
本年竣工房屋面积(万平方米)	**Floor Space of Completed Building (10 000 sq.m)**	**450.52**	**547.39**
#住　宅	Residential Building	269.21	322.04

4-20 农户固定资产投资情况
Investment in Fixed Assets of Rural Households in Rural Areas

单位:万元 (抽样调查 Sampled Survey) (10 000 yuan)

指 标	Item	2010	2011
新增固定资产原值	**Newly Increased Investment in Fixed Assets**	**1185414**	**1871564**
固定资产投资完成额	**Complete Investment in Fixed Assets**	**1185414**	**1871564**
按投资来源分	By Source of Fund		
国内贷款	Domestic Loans	202133	317899
自筹资金	Self-raising Funds	947111	1440585
其他资金	Others	36170	113080
按投资构成分	By Use of Funds		
建筑工程	Construction	524640	899078
#水 利	Water Conservancy	34805	34617
房 屋	Building	485835	859660
#住 宅	Residential Building	466781	780935
设备工、器具购置	Purchase of Equipment And Instruments	528360	798264
#生产设备	Production of Equipment	424014	618222
其 它	Others	132414	174222
按投资方向分	By Sector of Funds		
第一产业	Primary	495887	700939
第二产业	Secondary	87764	105229
第三产业	Tertiary	601763	1065396
按具体投资项目分	By Project of Investment		
房 屋	Building	485835	859660
#住 宅	Residential Building	466781	780935
道 路	Road		137
设 备	Equipment	528360	798264
水 利	Water Conservancy	34805	34617
其 他	Others	136414	178886
本年施工房屋面积(万平方米)	**Floor Space of Buildings Under Construction (10 000 sq.m)**	**1124.38**	**1895.46**
#住 宅	Residential Building	1079.12	1729.22
本年竣工房屋面积(万平方米)	**Floor Space of Completed Building (10 000 sq.m)**	**1038.63**	**1722.82**
#住 宅	Residential Building	994.42	1561.31
调查户总人口(人)	**Total Number of Households (person)**	**7169**	**6655**

主要统计指标解释

全社会固定资产投资　以货币形式表现的在一定时期内全社会建造和购置固定资产的工作量以及与此有关的费用的总称。该指标是反映固定资产投资规模、结构和发展速度的综合性指标,又是观察工程进度和考核投资效果的重要依据。全社会固定资产投资按登记注册类型可分为国有、集体、个体、联营、股份制、外商、港澳台商、其他等。

城镇固定资产投资　指城镇各种登记注册类型的企业、事业、行政单位及个体户进行的计划总投资500万元以上的建设项目投资和房地产开发投资。县城及以上区域内发生的投资，县及县以上各级政府及主管部门直接领导、管理的建设项目和企业事业单位的投资均为城镇固定资产投资。

房地产开发投资　指各种登记注册类型的房地产开发公司、商品房建设公司及其他房地产开发法人单位和附属于其他法人单位实际从事房地产开发或经营活动的单位统一开发的包括统代建、拆迁还建的住宅、厂房、仓库、饭店、宾馆、度假村、写字楼、办公楼等房屋建筑物和配套的服务设施，土地开发工程(如道路、给水、排水、供电、供热、通讯、平整场地等基础设施工程)的投资;不包括单纯的土地交易活动。

农村投资　包括在农村区域范围内进行固定资产投资活动的企业、事业、行政单位及农户投资。

建设总规模　是指在报告期内所有施工项目的计划总投资。这个指标和施工项目相对应。

在建总规模　是指在报告期末所有在建项目的计划总投资。

在建净规模　是指报告期末所有在建项目建成投产尚需的投资总量。

在建净规模＝在建总规模－未投产项目（期末在建）累计完成投资。

固定资产投资的资金来源　根据固定资产投资的资金来源不同，分为国家预算内资金、国内贷款、利用外资、自筹资金和其他资金来源。

(1)国家预算内资金:分为财政拨款和财政安排的贷款两部分。包括中央财政的基本建设基金(分经营性基金和非经营性基金两部分)、专项支出、收回再贷、贴息资金，财政安排的挖潜改造和新产品试制支出、城建支出、商业部门简易建筑支出、不发达地区发展基金等资金中用于固定资产投资的资金;地方财政中由国家统筹安排的资金等。

(2)国内贷款:指报告期固定资产投资单位向银行及非银行金融机构借入的用于固定资产投资的各种国内借款，包括银行利用自有资金及吸收的存款发放的贷款、上级主管部门拨入的国内贷款、国家专项贷款、地方财政专项资金安排的贷款、国内储备贷款、周转贷款等。

(3)利用外资:指报告期收到的用于固定资产建造和购置的国外资金(包括设备、材料、技术在内)。包括对外借款(外国政府、国际金融组织贷款、出口信贷、外国银行商业贷款、对外发行债券和股票)、外商直接投资及外商其他投资。不包括我国自有外汇资金(国家外汇、地方外汇、留成外汇、调剂外汇和中国银行自有资金发行的外汇贷款等)。计算利用外资时，需要折算成人民币，折算中所使用的外汇汇率按现汇计算，即按使用外汇时的汇率计算。

(4)自筹资金:指固定资产投资单位报告期收到的，由各地区、各部门及企、事业单位筹集用于固定资产投资的预算外资金，包括中央各部门、各级地方和企、事业单位的自筹资金。

(5)其他资金:指在报告期收到的除以上各种资金之外其他用于固定资产投资的资金，包括企业或金融机构通过发行各种债券筹集到的资金、社会集资、个人资金、无偿捐赠的资金及其他单位拨入的资金等。

固定资产投资按国民经济行业分　根据现有企业、事业、行政单位和建设项目建成投产后的主要产品种类或主要用途及社会经济活动性质来确定国民经济行业。一般情况下，一个建设项目或一个企业、事业单位只能属于一种国民经济行业。

固定资产投资按建设性质分　根据建设项目情况来确定。 建设项目的性质一般分为新建、扩建、改建和技术改造、单纯建造生活设施、迁建、恢复、单纯购置。房地产开发单位、农户投资不划分建设性质。

(1)新建:一般指从无到有开始建设的企业、事业和行政单位或建设项目。有的单位原有基础很小，经过建设后新增的固定资产价值超过该企、事业、行政单位原有固定资产价值(原值)三倍以上的也应作为新建。

(2)扩建:指在厂内或其他地点，为扩大原有产品的生产能力(或效益)或增加新的产品生产能力，而增建主要的生产车间(或主要工程)、分厂、独立的生产线。行政、事业单位在原单位增建业务用房(如学校增建教学用房、医院增建门诊部、病房等)也作为扩建。

现有企、事业单位为扩大原有主要产品生产能力或增加新的产品生产能力，增建一个或几个主要生产车间(或主要工程)、分厂，同时进行一些更新改造工程的，也应作为扩建。

(3)改建和技术改造:指现有企业、事业单位，对原有设施进行技术改造或更新(包括相应配套的辅助性生产、生活福利设施)的建设项目。现有企业、事业单位为适应市场变化的需要，而改变企业的主要产品种类(如军工企业转产民品等) 的建设项目，应作为改建。原有产品生产作业线由于各工序(车间)之间能力不平衡，为填平补齐充分发挥原有生产能力而增建不增加本企业主要产品设计能力的车间，也应作为改建。技术改造是指企业、事业单位在现有基础上，用先进的技术代替落后的技术，用先进的工艺和装备代替落后的工艺和装备，以改变企业落后的技术经济面貌，实现以内涵为主的扩大再生产，达到提高产品质量、促进产品更新换代、节约能源、降低消耗、扩大生产规模、全面提高社会经济效益的目的。技术改造具体包括以下内容：机器设备和工具的更新改造；生产工艺改革、节约能源和原材料的改造；厂房建筑和公共设施的改造；劳动条件和生产环境的改造等。

固定资产投资按构成分　固定资产投资活动按其工作内容和实现方式分为建筑安装工程，设备工具器具购置和其他费用三个部分。

(1)建筑安装工程(建筑安装工作量):指各种房屋、建筑物的建造工程和各种设备、装置的安装工程。包括各种房屋建造工程；各种用途设备基础和各种工业窑炉的砌筑工程及金属结构工程;为施工而进行的各种准备工作和临时工程以及完工后的清理工作等;铁路、道路的铺设，矿井的开凿及石油管道的架设等;水利工程;防空地下建筑等特殊工程;列入房屋工程预算内的暖气、卫生、通风、照明、煤气等设备的价值及装设油饰工程;列入建筑工程预算内的各种管道(蒸汽、压缩空气、石油、给排水等管道)、电力、电讯电缆导线等的敷设工程;以及各种机械设备的安装工程;为测定安装工程质量，对设备进行的试运工作;房地产开发单位进行的商品房屋开发建设工程、土地开发工程。

在建筑安装工程中，不包括被安装设备本身的价值。

(2)设备工具器具购置:指建设单位或企、事业单位购置或自制的，达到固定资产标准的设备、工具、器具的价值。新建单位及扩建单位的新建车间，按照设计或计划要求购置或自制的全部设备、工具、器具，不论是否达到固定资产标准均计入“设备工具器具购置”中。

(3)其他费用:指在固定资产建造和购置过程中发生的，除上述几项内容以外的各种应分摊计入固定资产的费用。

施工项目　指报告期内所有施工的建设项目个数，包括本年新开工的项目和以前年度开工在本年继续施工的建设项目。凡是报告期内施过工的建设项目，不论施工时间长短，均作为施工项目统计。施工项目个数可以反映一定时期固定资产投资的实际规模，与同期全部建成投产的建设项目个数相比，可以从建设速度的角度反映固定资产投资的效果。

全部建成投产项目　指报告期内按设计文件规定的全部生产能力（或效益）建成投产、经验收合格交付使用的建设项目。

新增生产能力(或工程效益)　指通过固定资产投资活动而增加的设计能力(或工程效益)，主要指标包括建设规模、本年施工规模、自开始建设累计新增生产能力（或工程效益）、本年新增生产能力（或工程效益）等。

房屋建筑面积　指房屋建筑物勒脚以上外墙外围的水平截面面积，包括房屋建筑物的有效面积和结构面积。该指标是从实物形态上反映建设规模和建设成果的重要指标之一，也是检查工程形象进度、计算工程造价、分析投资效果、研究施工任务和建筑材料之间平衡情况的重要依据。

施工房屋面积　指报告期内施工的全部房屋（包括地下室、半地下室以及被配套房屋）建筑面积。包括本期新开工的面积和上期开工跨入本期继续施工的房屋面积，以及上期已停建在本期恢复施工的房屋面积。本期竣工和本期施工后又停缓建的房屋，其建筑面积仍计入本期房屋施工面积中。

竣工房屋面积　指在报告期内房屋建筑按照设计要求已经全部完工，达到住人和使用条件，经验收鉴定合格(或达到竣工验收标准)，可正式移交使用单位的各栋房屋建筑面积的总和。

房屋建筑面积竣工率　指一定时期内房屋竣工面积占同期房屋施工面积的比率。该指标从房屋建筑施工速度的角度反映投资效果的指标。

新增固定资产　指报告期内已经完成建造和购置过程，并已交付生产或使用单位的固定资产价值。该指标是表示固定资产投资成果的价值指标，也是反映建设进度，计算固定资产投资效果的重要指标。

建设项目投产率　指一定时期内全部建成投产项目个数与同期施工项目个数的比率。该指标是从建设单位建设速度的角度反映投资效果的指标。

固定资产交付使用率　指一定时期新增固定资产与同期完成投资额的比率。该指标是反映固定资产动用速度，衡量建设过程中宏观投资效果的综合指标。由于新增固定资产是较长时期内形成的结果，而投资额则是当年完成的，因此，该指标一般适宜于反映较长时期内固定资产的动用情况。

商品房销售面积　指报告期内出售商品房屋的合同总面积（即双方签署的正式买卖合同中所确定的建筑面积）。由现房销售建筑面积和期房销售建筑面积两部分组成。

商品房销售额　指报告期内出售商品房屋的合同总价款（即双方签署的正式买卖合同中所确定的合同总价）。该指标与商品房销售面积同口径，由现房销售建筑面积和期房销售建筑面积两部分组成。

经济适用房　指根据国家经济适用房计划安排建设的政策性住宅。经济是指房屋建筑造价和销售价格低于一般商品住宅;适用是指适合中低收入家庭购买使用。经济适用房主要是由国家统一下达投资计划，房地产公司开发，对外销售;用地一般采用行政划拨或招标投标方式，免收土地出让金;对各种经批准的收费减半征收，开发利润不超过3%;销售价格实行政府指导价。该指标可以分析房地产投资结构，反映中低收入家庭商品住宅的供求平衡情况。

Explanatory Notes on Main Statistical Indicators

Total Investment in Fixed Assets in the Whole Country refers to the volume of activities in construction and purchases of fixed assets and related fees, expressed in monetary terms. It is a comprehensive indicatorwhich shows the size, structure and growth of the investment in fixed assets, providing basis for observing the progress of construction projects and evaluating results of investment. Total investment in fixed assets in the whole country includes, by type of ownership, the investment by the state-owned units, collective units, individuals, joint ownership units, share-holding units, as well as investment by businessmen from foreign countries and from Hong Kong, Macau and Taiwan, and by other units.

Urban Investment in Fixed Assets refer to construction projects involving a total planned (or required) investment of 5 million yuan and over by urban enterprises and institutions of various types of ownership, by administrative units and by individuals, investment in real estate development, and housing investment by individuals in urban areas and in industrial and mining areas. In other words, all investments that take place in county towns and urban areas, investment in construction projects under the direct leadership and management of government agencies at and above county levels and investments by enterprises and institutions at and above county levels are covered in urban investment in fixed assets.

Investment in Real Estate Development refers to the investment by the real estate development companies, commercial buildings construction companies and other real estate development units of various types of ownership in the construction of house buildings, such as residential buildings, factory buildings, warehouses, hotels, guesthouses, holiday villages, office buildings, and the complementary service facilities and land development projects, such as roads, water supply, water drainage, power supply, heating, telecommunications, land leveling and other projects of infrastructure. It excludes the activities in pure land transactions.

Investment in Rural Areas refers to investment in fixed assets by enterprises, institutions and individuals in rural areas.

Total Size of Construction refers to the planned total investment for all construction projects during the reference period.

Total Size of Investment in Projects under Construction refers to the planned total investment of all projects under construction at the end of the reference period.

Net Size of Investment in Projects under Construction refers to the required investment of all projects under construction at the end of the reference period.

Net Size of Investment = Total Size of Investment – accumulated completed investment of projects under construction

Sources of Funds for Investment in Fixed Assets include fund from state budget, domestic loans, foreign investment, self-raised funds, and others depending on the source of investment. (1) Fund from state budget consists of budgetary appropriation and loans from state budget. More specifically, it includes, from the budget of the central government, capital construction fund (operation fund and non-operational fund), special expenses (e.g. expenses on substituting petroleum with coal), loans from repayment, discount fund, expenses on innovation and trial production of new products, expenses on urban construction, expenses on temporary construction by Trades departments, development fund for less developed areas, as well as local budgetary fund transferred from the central budget. (2) Domestic loans refer to loans of various forms borrowed by investing units from banks and non-bank financial institutions during the reference period for the purpose of investment in fixed assets, including loans issued by banks from their self-owned funds and deposit, loans appropriated by higher responsible authorities, special loans by government (including loan for substituting petroleum with coal, special loan for reform-through-labour coal mines), loans arranged by local government from special funds, domestic reserve loan, and working loan, etc. (3) Foreign Investment refers to foreign funds received during the reference period for the construction and purchase of investment in fixed assets (covering equipment, materials and technology), including foreign borrowings (loans from foreign governments and international financial institutions, export credit, commercial loans from foreign banks, issue of bonds and stocks overseas), foreign direct investment and other foreign investment. Excluded in this category are capitals in foreign exchanges owned by China (foreign exchanges owned by the central and local governments, foreign exchanges retained by enterprises, foreign exchanges by enterprises through regulating mechanism, loans in foreign exchanges issued by the Bank of China with its own fund, etc.). In calculating the utilization of foreign capitals, foreign currencies are converted into Chinese Renminbi applying the current exchange rate when the foreign capitals are actually used. (4) Self-raised funds refer to extra-budgetary funds for investment in fixed assets received by investing units from central government ministries, local governments, enterprises and institutions, including their self-raised funds. (5) Others refer to funds for investment in fixed assets received from the sources other than those listed above, including capitals raised through issuing bonds by enterprises or financial institutions, funds raised from individuals and through donations, and funds transferred from other units.

Investment in Fixed Assets by Sector The classification of construction projects by sector is determined by the major products or the purpose of the projects when they are put into production or use, and by the nature of their social economic activities. In general, one project or one enterprise or institution can only be classified into one sector.

Investment in Fixed Assets by Type of Construction The construction projects in general can be classified, by the type of construction, into new construction, expansion, reconstruction and technical transformation, moving and restoration. However, investment by type of construction is not applied to investment by real-estate development units, investment in rural areas and investment in housing by urban individuals.

(1) New construction in general refers to newly constructed enterprises, institutions, administrative agencies or independent projects from scratch. Construction in the existing enterprises, institutions or agencies is not considered as new construction. In case the assets of the existing unit is quite small, and the value of newly added fixed assets exceeds the original value of assets by three times, the expansion will be considered as new construction

(2) Expansion refers to construction of new major production workshop, branch factory or independent production line within a factory or in other locations, for the purpose of increasing the production capacity (or improving efficiency) of the original products. Newly constructed houses for the operation of institutions and administrative organizations (such as the newly constructed buildings for teaching in schools, buildings for clinics or wards in hospitals, etc.) are also classified as expansion.Also included in the expansion are investments by existing enterprises or institutions in building major production line(s) or branch factory(ies) along with some work on innovation, for the purpose of expending the production capacity of original products or producing new products.

(3) Reconstruction refers to construction projects by existing enterprises or institutions in innovation or technical transformation of the old facilities (including auxiliary production equipment and welfare facilities). Also considered as reconstruction is the construction of new workshops by the existing enterprises or institutions to change the variety of products to meet the market demand (such as the production of civil products by defence industries), or to bring the designed production capacity into full play through a more balanced production process on production lines. Technical transformation refers to replacement of old technology or equipment by new technology or equipment, in order to expand the reproduction through improvement of technology contents in production, to improve product quality, to promote new products, to save energy and reduce consumption and to improve overall social-economic efficiency. Contents of technical transformation include: updating of machinery, equipment and tools; reforming production process by using energy or materials saving technology; construction of factory workshops and transformation of public facilities; improvement of working conditions and environment, etc.

Investment in Fixed Assets by Structure By their contents, investment activities are classified into 3 categories, i.e. construction and installation, purchase of equipment and instrument, and other expenses.(1) Construction and installation (work volume of construction and installation) refers to the construction of various houses and buildings and installation of various kinds of equipment and instruments. They include construction of various houses; equipment foundations, industrial kilns and stoves, and metal structure work; preparation works for project construction, and clearing up works post project construction; pavement of railways and roads, drilling of mines and putting up of oil pipes; construction of projects of water conservancy; construction of underground air-raid shelters and construction of other special projects; value of equipment for heating, sanitation, ventilation, lighting, gas, painting, etc. that are covered by the budget of housing projects; laying out of various pipelines (for steam, compressed air, petroleum, tap water and sewage) and lines for electric power and for communications; installation of various machinery equipment, testing operation for pre-testing the quality of installation projects, and land and other development work conducted by real estate developers for commercial housing. The value of equipment installed is not included in the value of installation projects.(2) Purchase of equipment and instruments refers to the total value of equipment, tools, and instruments purchased or self-produced which come up to standards for fixed assets by the construction units or investing enterprises or institutions. Equipment, tools and instruments purchased or self-produced for new workshops by newly established or expanded units are categorized as "purchase of equipment and instruments" no matter whether they come up to the standards for fixed assets.(3) Other expenses refer to expenses occurring during the construction or purchase of fixed assets other than those mentioned above.

Projects under Construction refer to number of all projects construction activities newly started in current year or left-over from the previous year in the reference period. All projects that have construction activities undertaken during the reference period are reported as projects under construction irrespective of the length of construction work. The number of projects under construction can reflect the actual size of investment in fixed assets during a given period, and when compared with the number of projects completed and put into use during the same period, it demonstrates the results of investment in fixed assets. Depending on the nature of const ruction activities, projects under construction can also be classified into projects under construct ion in current y ear, winding-up projects in current year and stopped or suspended projects in previous years (with preservation work in current year).

Projects Completed and Put into Use refer to projects have been completed in accordance with the design documents, rusulting in forming production capacity (efficiency) and have been checked and accepted after relevant tests,and have been formaally delivered for use.

Newly Increased Production Capacity (or Project Efficiency) refers to the increase in design capacity (or project efficiency) through investment in fixed assets, The main indicator include:construction scal,scale of projects under production capacity since the start of projects and the newly increased production capacity(project efficiency) of current year.

The newly increased product ion capaCity (project efficiency) are usually expressed in one of the following forms: (1) output of products, i.e. the output that the project can produce during a given period (usually a year). For instance, the capaCity in coal mining is expressed in 10, 000 tons/year , the capaCity in producing chemical pesticides expressed in ton/year, the capaCity in producing tractors in tractor/year, etc. For some chemical products where the effective contents differ significantly, the production capaCity is expressed as the designed effective content equivalent, such as in the case of sulphuric acid, soda ash, caustic soda, etc; (2) raw materials processing capaCity, i.e. the volume of raw materials that could be processed by the project per day (or per hour), such as tons of materials processed per day by a sugar refining project or edible vegetable oil project, or tons of urban sewage processed per day; (3) number or capaCity of major equipment increased, such as number of cotton or silk looms increased, wool spindles in-creased, or capaCity (in kilowatt s) of power generators increased; (4) saved raw materials, fuels or power, which are mainly used for the efficiency of innovation and transformation projects; and (5) physical measures (volume, capaCity, area, and length) of construction, which is typical for non industrial projects, for instance, the length of new railways or highways, the capaCity of reservoirs, the floor space of housing projects, capaCity f or new students in schools or beds in hospitals, areas under new irrigation project, etc. Features of projects sometimes call for combined use of two or more measurement to reflect the increased production capaCity (or project efficiency), for instance, the new capaCity for the production of internal combustion engines are expressed in set s per year and kilowatts per year simultaneously. To standardize the nomenclature and unit of measurement for new production capaCity (or project efficiency), the National Bureau of Statistics has developed Nomenclature for New Production CapaCity (Project Efficiency) and Nomenclature for Saving Raw Materials, Fuels and Power. All reporting units with investment activities are required to follow these two nomenclatures in reporting statistics on new production capaCity (project efficiency).

Floor Space of Buildings under Construction refers to total floor space of the horizontal section of outer walls above the plinth of the building, including the effective area and the area occupied by the structure. This indicator is one of the important indicators in physical terms to reflect the scale and accomplishment of the construction industry, and important basis for monitoring the pr ogress, calculating the cost, analyzing the efficiency and studying the sup ply of building materials in relation with the construction projects.

Floor Space of Residential Buildings refers to the floor space of the residential buildings among the total space of buildings under construction or completed.

Floor Space under Construction refers to total floor space of all buildings under construct ion during the reference period, including floor space of newly start ed buildings during the reference period, floor space of construction extended from the previous period to the current period, and floor space of construction suspended during the previous period and resumed in the current period. Floor space of const ruction completed in the current period, and floor space of const ruction started and then suspended in the current period are also included in the floor space under const ruction of the current year.

Floor Space of Buildings Completed refers to the floor space of all buildings completed in the reference period, which have been appraised and accepted (or come up to the designed standards) and have been transferred to the owners for use.

Completion Rate of Floor Space of Buildings refers to the ratio of the floor space of buildings completed in certain period of time to the floor space of buildings under const ruction in the same period. This indicator reflects the investment result from the perspective of t he speed of construction.

Newly Increased Fixed Assets refer to the newly

in-creased value of fixed assets, constructed or purchased, that have been transfer red to the investors. This is an indicator that demonstrates the results of investment in fixed assets in monetary terms, and an important indicator to reflect the speed of construct ion and to calculate the efficiency of investment.

Rate of Construction Projects Completed and Put into Use refers to the ratio of the number of construction projects completed and put into use in certain period of time to the number of projects under construction in the same period. This reflects the investment efficiency from the perspective of the speed of projects construction.

Rate of Projects of Fixed Assets Completed and Put into Operation refers to the ratio of the newly increased fixed assets to the total investment made in the same period. This is a comprehensive indicator reflecting the speed of the employment of fixed assets and the investment efficiency at the macro-level. As the newly increase fixed assets is the result of a long period while the investment is completed in the current year, this indicator is expected to be used to reflect the employment of fixed assets over a long period of time.

Area of Commercialized Housing Sold refers to total contracted area of commercialized housing (i.e. area of floor space as designated in the formal contracts signed by both sides) during the reference time. It constitutes floor space of completed housing and floor space of future housing.

Value of Commercialized Housing Sold refers to the total contracted value (i.e. value of sales/purchase for selling/purchase of commercialized housing as designated in the contract signed by both sides) during the reference time. This indicator has the same coverage as the area of commercialized housing sold, which constitutes floor space of completed housing and floor space of housing yet to be completed.

Economically Affordable Housing refers to housing constructed according to the state plan for economically affordable housing. Houses of this category featured in low cost in construct ion and low prices, and therefore are affordable to mid-income or low-income households. Economically affordable housing projects are developed by real estate companies under the state investment plan, with the land provided through government allocation or tendering procedures. Developers are exempted from land utilization fees and enjoy another 50% exemption of all other legitimate fees, while their profits are limited to less than 3%, and the completed houses are sold under the government guided prices. This indicator helps to analyze the investment structure of the real estate industry and the demand and supply of housing for mid or low income households.

2012

新疆统计年鉴

XINJIANG STATISTICAL YEARBOOK

第五篇
对外经济贸易和旅游

CHAPTER 5
Foreign Trade & Economic Cooperation and Tourism

简要说明
Brief Introduction

本篇资料的主要内容及来源

本篇内容包括海关进出口额、主要进出口商品数量及金额、对外承包工程和劳务合作、利用外资、外国和港澳台地区在新疆直接投资情况、新疆在国外和港澳台地区直接投资、经济技术开发（合作）主要情况、旅游情况等。

海关进出口额、利用外资、旅游资料由新疆维吾尔自治区统计局贸易外经统计处分别根据乌鲁木齐海关、新疆维吾尔自治区对外经济贸易厅、新疆维吾尔自治区工商管理局和新疆维吾尔自治区旅游局的有关资料加工整理。

Main Content and Source of Data

Data in this chapter cover mainly total imports and exports at customs, main imports and exports in volume and value, contracted projects and labor services cooperation, utilization of foreign capital, basic condition of direct investment in Xinjiang by foreign countries and compatriots from Hong Kong, Macao and Taiwan, main condition of economic and technological development and cooperation zones, condition of tourism. Data on imports and exports, utilization of foreign capitals, tourism are collected and processed by the Department of Trade Statistics, the Xinjiang Bureau of Statistics in accordance with the data from custom of Urumqi, Foreign Economic and Trade Commission of Xinjiang,Xinjiang Administration for Industry and Commerce, Tourist Bureau of Xingjiang.

5-1 进出口贸易总额
Total Value of Imports and Exports

单位：万美元 (USD 10 000)

年 份 Year	地 区 Region	进出口总额 Total Imports and Exports	出口额 Exports	#一般贸易 Ordinary Trade	#边境贸易 Border Trade	进口额 Imports	#一般贸易 Ordinary Trade	#边境贸易 Border Trade
	1978	2346	937			1409		
	1985	29197	18020			11177		
	1990	41025	33530		3506	7495		3416
	1995	142798	76880	44550	27562	65918	17640	41888
	1996	140367	54975	30281	18647	85392	25982	54484
	1997	144667	66547	36061	22962	78120	24061	52031
	1998	153214	80789	32268	37599	72425	20972	49354
	1999	176534	102743	37120	57329	73791	25723	44976
	2000	226399	120408	55060	58020	105991	28020	73950
	2001	177148	66849	29523	18418	110299	24895	79661
	2002	269186	130849	54404	47218	138337	26028	107152
	2003	477198	254221	71115	160411	222977	72510	143504
	2004	563563	304658	50194	223782	258905	101540	147058
	2005	794189	504024	88036	386237	290165	108894	167648
	2006	910327	713923	158842	522038	196404	61915	126429
	2007	1371623	1150311	294000	806885	221312	75418	134778
	2008	2221680	1929925	290237	1576911	291755	92279	187279
	2009	1382771	1082325	168078	754206	300446	128702	157390
	2010	1712834	1296981	208909	767478	415853	154567	236745
	2011	2282225	1682886	476788	881882	599339	170863	401754
乌鲁木齐市	Urumqi City	902984	669589			233395		
克拉玛依市	Karamay City	46888	42810			4078		
石河子市	Shihezi City	90975	87854			3121		
吐鲁番地区	Turpan Administrative Offices	3054	2410			644		
哈密地区	Hami [Kumul] Administrative Offices	2615	1974			641		
昌吉回族自治州	Changji Hui Autonomous Prefecture	211336	194570			16766		
伊犁哈萨克自治州	Ili Kazak Autonomous Prefecture	697825	423254			274571		
伊犁州直属县(市)	Counties (Cities) Direct Under Ili Prefecture	557956	306435			251521		
塔城地区	Tacheng [Tarbagatai] Administrative Offices	53944	31224			22720		
阿勒泰地区	Altay Administrative Offices	85925	85595			330		
博尔塔拉蒙古自治州	Bortala Mongol Autonomous Prefecture	161098	102555			58543		
巴音郭楞蒙古自治州	Bayangol Mongol Autonomous Prefecture	16492	14775			1717		
阿克苏地区	Aksu Administrative Offices	32209	30966			1243		
克孜勒苏柯尔克孜自治州	Kizilsu Kirgiz Autonomous Prefecture	15548	11435			4113		
喀什地区	Kashgar [Kaxgar] Administrative Offices	100761	100269			492		
和田地区	Hotan Administrative Offices	440	425			15		

注：1998 年以前的资料由外经贸厅提供，1998 年以后资料由乌鲁木齐海关提供(5-2、5-3、5-4 表相同)。
Note: The data prior to 1998 is offered by the Bureau of Foreign Economic and Trades , data after 1998 is offered by Urumqi Customs (The same in the 5-2, 5-3, 5-4 tables).

5-2 主要进出口商品数量和金额
Main Imports and Exports in Volume and Value

项目	Item	2010		2011	
		数量 Volume	金额(万美元) Value (USD 10 000)	数量 Volume	金额(万美元) Value (USD 10 000)
主要出口商品	**Main Export Commodities**				
棉纱(吨)	Cotton Yarn (ton)	2925	1306	2849	1478
棉机织物(万米)	Cotton Woven Fabrics(10 000 m)	9734	9169	18749	24153
肠衣(吨)	Casings (ton)	617	2073	491	2809
番茄酱(万吨)	Tomato Jam (10 000 tons)	60	41574	68	50926
电视机(万台)	TV Sets (10 000 sets)	2	224	2	262
地毯(吨)	Carpets (ton)	1904	722	2619	1442
药材(吨)	Medical Materials (ton)	250	126	91	56
鞋 类	Shoes		155524		190232
主要进口商品	**Main Import Commodities**				
羊毛及条(吨)	Wool and Wool Tops (ton)	5425	719	9476	800
钢材(万吨)	Rolled Steel (10 000 tons)	20	17550	16	16677
纸及纸板(未切成型的)(吨)	Paper and Paperboard in Rolls (ton)	35	7	57	12
原木(万立方米)	Logs (10 000 cu.m)	1	161	1	170
医疗仪器及器械	Medical Equipment and Apparatus		3592		4441
肥料(万吨)	Fertilizers (10 000 tons)	10	3159	3	1328
原油(万吨)	Crude Oil (10 000 tons)	296	166080	370	283746
成品油(万吨)	Oil Product (10 000 tons)	24	9552	71	44792
牛皮革及马皮革(吨)	Cattle and Horse Leather (ton)	13840	1806	15203	1774

5-3 新疆同各国(地区)海关进出口总额

Value of Xinjiang's Imports and Exports by Countries(Region) of Destination

单位：万美元 (USD 10 000)

国别(地区)	Country (Territory)	2010 进出口总额 Total Value Imports and Exports	2010 出口额 Exports	2010 进口额 Imports	2011 进出口总额 Total Value Imports and Exports	2011 出口额 Exports	2011 进口额 Imports
总 计	**Total**	**1712834**	**1296981**	**415853**	**2282225**	**1682886**	**599339**
亚 洲	**Asia**	**1482222**	**1162187**	**320035**	**1885418**	**1402547**	**482871**
阿富汗	Afghanistan	441	438	3	365	355	10
巴 林	Bahrain	112	112		166	166	
孟加拉国	Bangladesh	275	274	1	910	910	
不 丹	Bhutan				314	314	
文 莱	Brunei	67	67		124	124	
缅 甸	Myanmar	194	194		150	150	
柬埔寨	Cambodia	114	64	50	863	863	
塞浦路斯	Cyprus	32	32		13	13	
朝 鲜	Korea DPR	7	7		95	95	
香 港	Hong Kong, China	2511	1704	807	4483	4176	307
印 度	India	3488	1668	1820	7524	5729	1795
印度尼西亚	Indonesia	4538	4354	184	4306	3897	409
伊 朗	Iran	2497	2006	491	5167	4488	679
伊拉克	Iraq	574	517	57	258	62	196
以色列	Israel	604	402	202	2455	2164	291
日 本	Japan	16951	6087	10864	22299	8649	13650
约 旦	Jordan	151	151		396	396	
科威特	Kuwait	171	165	6	70	70	
老 挝	Laos	14	14		7	7	
黎巴嫩	Lebanon	123	123		355	355	
马来西亚	Malaysia	6894	6767	127	12087	11645	442
蒙 古	Mongolia	27181	24908	2273	42105	34755	7350
尼泊尔	Nepal	34	34		66	66	
阿 曼	Aman	171	171		431	431	
巴基斯坦	Pakistan	12728	12534	194	38202	37983	219
巴勒斯坦	Palestine	1	1		52	52	
菲律宾	Philppines	1650	1293	357	2279	1908	371
卡塔尔	Qatar	59	59		125	125	
沙特阿拉伯	Saudi Arbia	2306	2203	103	4602	4478	124
新加坡	Singapore	1339	308	1031	4188	3209	979
韩 国	Korea Rep.	8277	1738	6539	8513	4255	4258
斯里兰卡	Sri Lanka	123	117	6	446	427	19
叙利亚	Syria	356	125	231	154	146	8
泰 国	Thailand	2614	2372	242	4646	4549	97
土耳其	Turkey	2007	1129	878	2830	1420	1410
阿拉伯联合酋长国	Unitd Arab Emirates	3159	3146	13	6230	6116	114
也门共和国	Republic of Yemen	701	701		962	962	
越 南	Viet Nam	2961	2838	123	5576	5495	81
中华人民共和国	P.R.China	315		315	423		423
台湾省	Taiwan, China	2237	1690	547	2766	2238	528
东帝汶	Timor Leste	5	5				
哈萨克斯坦	Kazakhstan	925918	682821	243097	1059664	666499	393165
吉尔吉斯斯坦	Kirghizia	265725	258836	6889	380556	372071	8485
塔吉克斯坦	Tadzhikistan	107574	106057	1517	172229	168395	3834

5-3 续表 1 Continued

单位：万美元 (USD 10 000)

国 别 (地 区)	Country (Territory)	2010			2011		
		进出口总额 Total Value Imports and Exports	出口额 Exports	进口额 Imports	进出口总额 Total Value Imports and Exports	出口额 Exports	进口额 Imports
土库曼斯坦	Turkmenistan	12883	10989	1894	11824	10640	1184
乌兹别克斯坦	Uzbekistan	62140	22966	39174	74142	31699	42443
非 洲	**Africa**	**19581**	**17052**	**2529**	**23160**	**22282**	**878**
阿尔及利亚	Algeria	2334	2334		2108	2108	
安哥拉	Angola	47	47		447	447	
贝 宁	Benin	34	34		265	265	
布隆迪	Burundi				30	30	
喀麦隆	Cameroon	195	193	2	423	423	
佛得角	Cape Verde	2	2				
刚 果	Congo	11	11		18	18	
吉布提	Djibouti	31	31	1	67	67	
埃 及	Egypt	317	286	31	2749	2436	313
赤道几内亚	Equatorial Guinea				43	43	
埃塞俄比亚	Ethiopia	139	139		513	513	
加 纳	Ghana	831	825	6	1583	1583	
冈比亚	Gambia	17	17		21	21	
加 蓬	Gabon	8	8		143	33	110
几内亚	Guinea	14	14		77	77	
科特迪瓦共和国	Cote d'lvoire	45	45		297	297	
肯尼亚	Kenya	69	69		287	287	
利比里亚	Liberia				4	4	
利比亚	Libya	1213	1213		28	28	
马达加斯加	Madagascar	21	21		47	47	
马拉维	Malawi				12	12	
马 里	Mali				338	338	
毛里塔尼亚	Mauritania	18	18		21	21	
毛里求斯	Mauritius	298	298		589	589	
摩洛哥	Morocco	221	221		392	392	
莫桑比克	Mozambique	22	22		73	69	4
纳米比亚	Mozanmbique	171	171		30	30	
尼日利亚	Nigeria	1043	1041	2	4082	4082	
留尼汪	Reunion	1	1				
圣多美和普林西比	Monetary	2	2		2	2	
塞内加尔	Senegal	193	193		507	507	
塞拉利昂	SierraLeone	207	207		97	97	
索马里	Somalia				2	2	
南 非	South Africa	845	698	147	3578	3133	445
苏 丹	Sudan	8310	8310		3079	3079	
坦桑尼亚	Tanzania	109	109		479	475	4
多 哥	Togo	66	66		374	374	
突尼斯	Tunisia	226	226		64	64	
刚果（金）	Congo DR	42	42		154	154	
赞比亚	Zambia	2462	121	2341	128	128	
莱索托	Lesotho	14	14				
津巴布韦	Zimbabwe				7	5	2
马约特岛	Mayotte	3	3		2	2	

5-3 续表 2 Continued

单位：万美元 (USD 10 000)

国 别 (地 区)	Country (Territory)	2010			2011		
		进出口总额 Total Value Imports and Exports	出口额 Exports	进口额 Imports	进出口总额 Total Value Imports and Exports	出口额 Exports	进口额 Imports
欧 洲	**Europe**	**175167**	**103156**	**72011**	**260755**	**171352**	**89403**
比利时	Belgium	1986	695	1291	4718	4243	475
丹 麦	Denmark	565	82	483	730	470	260
英 国	United Kingdom	3331	2118	1213	10802	9889	913
德 国	Germany	24092	4846	19246	39035	16705	22330
法 国	France	3176	721	2455	6626	4300	2326
爱尔兰	Ireland	306	172	134	468	253	215
意大利	Italy	11534	7301	4233	18718	13267	5451
荷 兰	Netherlands	1261	1023	238	9940	9511	429
希 腊	Greece	93	84	9	443	385	58
葡萄牙	Portugal	91	89	2	359	356	3
西班牙	Spain	707	479	228	4087	3907	180
阿尔巴尼亚	Albania	12	12		23	23	
安道尔	Andorra				1	1	
奥地利	Austria	1127	215	912	971	469	502
保加利亚	Bulgaria	242	242		145	145	
芬 兰	Finland	15849	229	15620	10233	279	9954
匈牙利	Hungary	69	43	26	96	96	
冰 岛	Iceland	5	5		3	3	
马耳他	Malta	67	67		632	632	
挪 威	Norway	541	474	67	543	471	72
波 兰	Poland	1745	1744	1	2447	2442	5
罗马尼亚	Romania	1628	1069	559	597	585	12
瑞 典	Sweden	951	130	821	1545	365	1180
瑞 士	Switzerland	3617	965	2652	3872	943	2929
爱沙尼亚	Estonia	21	21		71	70	1
拉脱维亚	Latvia	293	293		188	188	
立陶宛	Lithuania	272	272		395	394	1
格鲁吉亚	Georgia	372	360	12	285	264	21
亚美尼亚	Argentina	1314	1314		587	587	
阿塞拜疆	Azerbajan	35494	35473	21	43960	43439	521
白俄罗斯	Belorussia	274	88	186	641	59	582
摩尔多瓦	Moldova	5	5		9	9	
俄罗斯	Russia	56889	35348	21541	92778	51892	40886
乌克兰	Ukraine	6796	6778	18	3897	3808	89
斯洛文尼亚	Slovenia	60	60		191	191	
克罗地亚	Croatia	96	96		131	131	
捷 克	Czecho	249	206	43	545	539	6
前南马其顿	Macedonia				5	5	
波 黑	Bosnia	10	10				
塞尔维亚	Serbia	21	21		37	35	2
黑 山	Montenegro	6	6		1	1	

5-3 续表 3 Continued

单位：万美元 (USD 10 000)

国 别 (地 区)	Country (Territory)	2010 进出口总额 Total Value Imports and Exports	2010 出口额 Exports	2010 进口额 Imports	2011 进出口总额 Total Value Imports and Exports	2011 出口额 Exports	2011 进口额 Imports
拉丁美洲	**Latin America**	**5789**	**3791**	**1998**	**12746**	**12580**	**166**
阿根廷	Argentina	723	418	305	2407	2388	19
巴哈马	Bahamas	3	3		3	3	
巴巴多斯	Barbados	3	3		11	11	
伯利兹	Belize	1	1		5	5	
巴 西	Brazil	2757	1450	1307	2206	2158	48
智 利	Chile	682	314	368	1293	1293	
哥伦比亚	Colombia	180	180		514	514	
多米尼加	Dominica	12	12				
哥斯达黎加	Costarica	71	71		71	71	
古 巴	Cuba	14	14		4		4
多米尼加共和国	Dominica Rep.	30	29	1	29	23	6
厄瓜多尔	Ecuador	116	116		208	208	
格林纳达	Granada				12	12	
危地马拉	Guatemala	128	128		77	77	
圭亚那	Guyana	2	2				
海 地	Hayti	175	175		91	91	
洪都拉斯	Honduras	39	39		35	35	
牙买加	Jamaica	82	82		316	316	
墨西哥	Mexico	160	143	17	1310	1224	86
尼加拉瓜	Nicaragua	1	1		6	6	
巴拿马	Panama	56	56		2498	2498	
巴拉圭	Paraguay	116	116		146	146	
秘 鲁	Peru	300	300		809	806	3
波多黎各	Puerto Rico	25	25		42	42	
圣卢西亚	Saint Lucia	1	1				
圣文森特和格林纳丁斯	Saint Vincent and the Grenadines	1	1				
萨尔瓦多	El. Salvador	21	21		15	15	
苏里南	Surinam				33	33	
特立尼达和多巴哥	Trinidada and Tobago	27	27		9	9	
乌拉圭	Uruguay	39	39		314	314	
委内瑞拉	Venezuela	24	24		282	282	
北美洲	**North America**	**26107**	**9209**	**16898**	**89951**	**68498**	**21453**
加拿大	Canada	1680	1356	324	5814	5022	792
美 国	United States	24427	7853	16574	84137	63476	20661
大洋洲	**Oceania**	**3968**	**1586**	**2382**	**10195**	**5627**	**4568**
澳大利亚	Australia	2799	1168	1631	8826	4781	4045
斐 济	Fiji	35	35		28	28	
新喀里多尼亚	New Caledonia	11	11		12	12	
瓦努阿图	Vanuatu	5	5				
新西兰	New Zealand	688	331	357	1161	781	380
巴布亚新几内亚	Papua New Guinea	430	36	394	159	16	143
所罗门群岛	Solomon Is.				5	5	
萨摩亚	Samoa				4	4	

5-4 按贸易方式和登记注册类型分的海关进出口额
Total Volue of Imports and Exports by Customs Regime and Registration (Customs Statiatics)

单位：万美元 (USD 10 000)

项目	Item	2010			2011		
		进出口总额 Total Imports and Exports	出口额 Exports	进口额 Imports	进出口总额 Total Imports and Exports	出口额 Exports	进口额 Imports
总计	**Total**	**1712834**	**1296981**	**415853**	**2282225**	**1682886**	**599339**
按贸易方式分	**By Customs Regime**						
一般贸易	Ordinary Trades	363476	208909	154567	647651	476788	170863
加工贸易	Processing Trades	32690	30404	2286	26470	23493	2977
边境小额贸易	Petty-volume Border Trades	1004223	767478	236745	1283636	881882	401754
其它贸易	Other Trades	312445	290190	22255	324468	300723	23745
按登记注册类型分	**By Registration Status**						
国有经济	State-owned Units	470176	170865	299311	687378	198333	489045
集体经济	Collective-owned Units	27094	22977	4117	21965	15929	6036
私营经济	Private-owned Units	1179989	1085210	94779	1539587	1449389	90198
三资企业	Three Kinds of Ventures	35518	17872	17646	33290	19230	14060
其它经济	Other Types of Ownership	57	57		5	5	

5-5 主要年份人民币对主要外币年平均汇价(中间价)
Average Exchange Rate of RMB Yuan Against Main Convertible Currences in Main Years (Medium Rate)

单位：人民币元 (RMB yuan)

年份 Year	100 美元 100 US Dollars	100 日元 100 JapaneseYen	100 港元 100 Hong Kong Dollars	100 欧元 100 Euros
1985	293.66	1.25	37.57	
1990	478.32	3.32	61.39	
1995	835.10	8.92	107.96	
1996	831.42	7.64	107.51	
1997	828.98	6.86	107.09	
1998	827.91	6.35	106.88	
1999	827.83	7.29	106.66	
2000	827.84	7.69	106.18	
2001	827.70	6.81	106.08	
2002	827.70	6.62	106.07	800.58
2003	827.70	7.15	106.24	936.13
2004	827.68	7.66	106.23	1029.00
2005	819.17	7.45	105.30	1019.53
2006	797.18	6.86	102.62	1001.90
2007	760.40	6.46	97.46	1041.75
2008	694.51	6.74	89.19	1022.27
2009	683.10	7.29	88.12	952.70
2010	676.95	7.73	87.13	897.25
2011	645.88	8.11	82.97	900.11

5-6 对外承包工程和劳务合作
Contracted Projects in Foreign Countries or Territories

单位：个、万美元 (unit,USD 10 000)

项　　目	Item	2010	2011
承包工程	**Contracted Projects**		
新签合同数	Number of Newly Signed Contracts	54	51
新签合同金额	Newly Signed Contracted Value	55366	46987
实际营业额	Actual Business Volume	93714	97167

5-7 外商直接投资
Direct Foreign Investments

单位：个、万美元 (unit, USD 10 000)

指　　标	Item	2010			2011		
		项　目 Number of Projects	合同金额 Contract Value	实际使用金额 Used Value	项　目 Number of Projects	合同金额 Contract Value	实际使用金额 Used Value
总　　计	**Total**	**59**	**30091**	**23742**	**69**	**55834**	**33485**
独资经营企业	Foreign Investment Enterprises	28	9070	14571	45	35214	11394
合资经营企业	Joint Ventures Enterprises	28	8988	7991	23	8701	9206
合作经营企业	Cooperative Operation Enterprises	3	2880	752	1	1238	3587
股份制企业	Share-holding Corporations Ltd.		9153	428		10681	9298

5-8 外国和港澳台地区在华直接投资情况

Basic Conditions of Direct Investment in China by Foreign Countries and Compatriots from Hongkong, Macao and Taiwan

单位：个、万美元 (2011 年) (unit, USD 10 000)

项　目	Item	签订协议情况 Signed Agreements		客商实际投资额	年末实有企业个数
		合同数 Number of Contracts	客商投资额 Actually Used Amount of Region Investment	Used Amount of Foreign Investment	Number of Enterprises at Year-end
总　计	**Total**	**69**	**55834**	**33485**	**491**
按投资方式分	**Grouped by Investment Mode**				
独资经营企业	Foreign Investment Enterprises	45	35214	11394	214
合资经营企业	Joint Ventures Enterprises	23	8701	9206	239
合作经营企业	Cooperative Operation Enterprises	1	1238	3587	29
外商投资股份制企业	Foreign Investment Share Enterprises		10681	9298	9
按国民经济行业分	**Grouped by Economic Sector**				
农、林、牧、渔业	Farming, Forestry, Animal Husbandry and Fishery	5	4278	2669	26
采矿业	Mining and Quarrying	4	13071	8142	29
制造业	Manufacturing	23	26841	9831	183
电力、煤气及水的生产和供应业	Production and Distribution of Electricity, Gas and Water		322	181	8
建筑业	Construction	1	273		5
交通运输、仓储及邮电通讯业	Transport, Storage, Post and Telecommunications		10545	10323	12
信息传输、计算机服务和软件业	Information Transmission, Computer Service and Software	1	30		4
批发和零售业	Wholesale and Retail Trades	23	-945	360	131
住宿和餐饮业	Accommodation and Catering Service	3	138	15	26
金融业	Financial Intermediation	1	250		1
房地产业	Real Estate	1	10	898	13
租赁和商务服务业	Leasing and Business Services	3	959	479	25
科学研究、技术服务和地质勘察业	Scientific Research, Technical Service and Geological Prospecting	2	45	587	15
水利、环境和公共设施管理业	Water Conservancy, Environment and Public Facility Management				6
居民服务和其他服务业	Services to Households and Other Services	2	17		2
教育	Education				2
文化、体育和娱乐业	Culture,Sports and Entertainment				3
按国别、地区分	**By Country or Territory**				
中国香港	Hong Kong，China	33	33280	11048	192
中国台湾	Taiwan，China	3	2026	53	20
日　本	Japan		-568		10
美　国	United States	4	815	11	27
加拿大	Canada	2	23		10
丹　麦	Denmark			408	3
意大利	Italy	1	136		2
德　国	Federal Republic of Germany			22	4
土耳其	Turkey	3	33	110	12
英　国	United Kingdom			67	3
泰　国	Thailand				2
新加坡	Singapore		900	603	13
澳大利亚	Australia	3	57	450	11
独联体	Commonwealth of Independent States	7	-71	1575	75
马来西亚	Malaysia			5	2
韩　国	Republic of Korea	3	23	22	18

5-9 各地、州、市利用外商直接投资情况
Conditions of Foreign Direct Investment Used by Prefecture, Autonomous Prefecture and City

单位：个、万美元 (unit, USD 10 000)

地 区	Region	2010			2011		
		签订合同数 Number of Contracts	合同金额 Contract Value	实际使用投资 Amount of Foreingn Capital Actually Used	签订合同数 Number of Contracts	合同金额 Contract Value	实际使用投资 Amount of Foreign Capital Actually Used
总 计	**Total**	**59**	**30091**	**23742**	**69**	**55834**	**33485**
乌鲁木齐市	Urumqi City	28	15125	5038	38	10331	11702
克拉玛依市	Karamay City				1	3320	1500
石河子市	Shihezi City	9	2683	1171	11	15702	8384
吐鲁番地区	Turpan Administrative Offices	1	18				
哈密地区	Hami [Kumul] Administrative Offices	2	-453	2282	2	4876	2012
昌吉回族自治州	Changji Hui Autonomous Prefecture	6	4418	2471	4	7033	3629
伊犁哈萨克自治州	Ili Kazak Autonomous Prefecture	5	2781	9955	4	1653	2496
伊犁州直属县(市)	Counties (Cities) Direct Under Ili Prefecture	5	2781	5908	3	773	1609
塔城地区	Tacheng [Tarbagatai] Administrative Offices				1	880	
阿勒泰地区	Altay Administrative Offices			4047			887
博尔塔拉蒙古自治州	Bortala Mongol Autonomous Prefecture						
巴音郭楞蒙古自治州	BayangolMongol Autonomous Prefecture	2	733	1764	2	5300	2470
阿克苏地区	Aksu Administrative Offices	3	3848		3	6089	586
克孜勒苏柯尔克孜自治州	Kizilsu Kirgiz Autonomous Prefecture		661	876			661
喀什地区	Kashgar [Kaxgar] Administrative Offices	1	13	185	4	1530	
和田地区	Hotan Administrative Offices	2	264				45

5-10 新疆在外国和港澳台地区直接投资
Direct Investment in Foreign Countries and Hong Kong， Macao and Taiwan Made by Xinjiang Partner

单位：个、万美元 (unit, USD 10 000)

项 目	Item	2010		2011	
		合同数 Number of Contracts	我方投资额 National Investment	合同数 Number of Contracts	我方投资额 National Investment
总 计	**Total**	**39**	**47809**	**37**	**41803**
独资经营企业	Foreign Investment Enterprises	24	46569	29	41446
合资经营企业	Joint Ventures Enterprises	15	1240	8	357

5-11 主要年份旅游事业发展情况
Development of Tourism in Main Years

项　　目	Item	1995	2000	2011
旅行社总数（个）	**Total Number of Travel Agencies (unit)**	**79**	**130**	**391**
入境旅游人数（人）	**Total Number of Overseas Vistor Arrivals (person)**	**203579**	**256082**	**1324989**
外国人	Foreigners	185514	208374	1248983
#日　本	Japan	43983	51974	28085
新加坡	Singapore	2048	5137	6992
美　国	United States	5595	10231	25965
英　国	United Kingdom	2422	3702	8788
法　国	France	3062	5218	10197
德　国	Federal Republic of Germany	4892	6310	7412
独联体	Commonwealth of Independent States	93578	76966	987627
香港同胞	Compatriots from Hong Kong		12710	21295
澳门同胞	Compatriots from Macao		1387	5122
台湾同胞	Compatriots from Taiwan	8816	33611	49589
按地区分	**By Regions**			
乌鲁木齐市	Urumqi City	63275	144830	291497
克拉玛依市	Karamay City		505	1188
石河子市	Shihezi City		532	687
吐鲁番地区	Turpan Administrative Offices	27230	43641	64680
哈密地区	Hami [Kumul] Administrative Offices	1220	624	21736
昌吉回族自治洲	Changji Hui Autonomous Prefecture	224	213	4989
伊犁哈萨克自治州	Ili Kazak Autonomous Prefecture	68948	18204	788021
伊犁州直属县(市)	Counties (Cities) Direct Under Ili Prefecture	67651	15356	696705
塔城地区	Tacheng [Tarbagatai] Administrative Offices	1297	298	30062
阿勒泰地区	Altay Administrative Offices		2550	61254
博尔塔拉蒙古自治州	Bortala Mongol Autonomous Prefecture	354	672	44866
巴音郭楞蒙古自治州	BayangolMongol Autonomous Prefecture	1738	7313	8002
阿克苏地区	Aksu Administrative Offices	5737	6028	6047
克孜勒苏柯尔克孜自治州	Kizilsu Kirgiz Autonomous Prefecture	2485	2100	12530
喀什地区	Kashgar [Kaxgar] Administrative Offices	31102	27510	58981
和田地区	Hotan Administrative Offices	1266	3910	21765
国内旅游人数（万人）	**Number of Domestic Visitors (10 000 persons)**	**514**	**758**	**3829**
疆内居民出境游（人）	**Number of Domestic Resident Outbound Visitors (person)**	**591**	**4535**	**13255**
旅游收入	**Income of Tourism**			
入境旅游收入(万美元)	Foreign Exchange Earnings from International Tourism (USD 10 000)	5268	9494	46519
国内旅游收入(亿元)	Earnings from Domestic Tourism (100 million yuan)	7.10	62.67	411.00

注：1.1998 年以后的旅游外汇收入根据抽样调查取得。
　　2.2010 年国际旅游人数统计口径有所变化增加了口岸旅游购物人数。.

Note: a) The Foreign Exchange Earnings from Tourism after 1998 are obtained from Sampled Survey.
　　b) International tourist arrivals statistics have changed,increased the number of tourist in the custom offices to the shopping.

5-12 各地、州、市旅行社及旅游宾馆(酒店)基本情况

Accommodation of Travel Agencies and Tourist Hotels by Prefecture, Autonomous Prefecture and City

(2011 年)

地区	Region	旅行社(个) Number of Travel Agencies (unit)	星级宾馆(个) Number of Tourist Hotels (unit)	客房(间) Number of Rooms (unit)	床位(张) Number of Beds (unit)
总计	**Total**	**391**	**462**	**48382**	**89304**
乌鲁木齐市	Urumqi City	221	98	14279	25408
克拉玛依市	Karamay City	14	17	1514	2542
石河子市	Shihezi City	5	16	1878	4512
吐鲁番地区	Turpan Administrative Offices	4	20	1829	3516
哈密地区	Hami [Kumul] Administrative Offices	10	17	1965	3710
昌吉回族自治洲	Changji Hui Autonomous Prefecture	6	32	1783	3517
伊犁哈萨克自治州	Ili Kazak Autonomous Prefecture	70	123	11120	21681
伊犁州直属县(市)	Counties (Cities) Direct Under Ili Prefecture	25	65	5894	11478
塔城地区	Tacheng [Tarbagatai] Administrative Offices	4	13	877	1707
阿勒泰地区	Altay Administrative Offices	41	45	4349	8496
博尔塔拉蒙古自治州	Bortala Mongol Autonomous Prefecture	6	10	842	1577
巴音郭楞蒙古自治州	Bayangol Mongol Autonomous Prefecture	16	45	4745	8543
阿克苏地区	Aksu Administrative Offices	8	34	3503	6208
克孜勒苏柯尔克孜自治州	Kizilsu Kirgiz Autonomous Prefecture	1	3	225	438
喀什地区	Kashgar [Kaxgar] Administrative Offices	28	30	3303	5453
和田地区	Hotan Administrative Offices	2	17	1396	2199

5-13 各地、州、市旅游收入情况

Income of Tourism by Prefecture, Autonomous Prefecture and City

(2011 年)

地区	Region	入境旅游收入 (万美元) Foreign Exchange Earnings from International Tourism (USD 10 000)	国内旅游收入 (万元) Earnings from Domestic Tourism (10 000 yuan)
总计	**Total**	**46519**	**4110021**
乌鲁木齐市	Urumqi City	15459	1886527
克拉玛依市	Karamay City	45	102656
石河子市	Shihezi City	31	121221
吐鲁番地区	Turpan Administrative Offices	3960	305106
哈密地区	Hami [Kumul] Administrative Offices	986	164534
昌吉回族自治州	Changji Hui Autonomous Prefecture	150	134142
伊犁哈萨克自治州	Ili Kazak Autonomous Prefecture	18886	710232
伊犁州直属县(市)	Counties (Cities) Direct Under Ili Prefecture	17015	251385
塔城地区	Tacheng [Tarbagatai] Administrative Offices	614	95459
阿勒泰地区	Altay Administrative Offices	1257	363388
博尔塔拉蒙古自治州	Bortala Mongol Autonomous Prefecture	801	38776
巴音郭楞蒙古自治州	BayangolMongol Autonomous Prefecture	593	150009
阿克苏地区	Aksu Administrative Offices	327	110964
克孜勒苏柯尔克孜自治州	Kizilsu Kirgiz Autonomous Prefecture	726	22948
喀什地区	Kashgar [Kaxgar] Administrative Offices	3543	282751
和田地区	Hotan Administrative Offices	1012	80155

5-14 入境旅游收入及构成

Foreign Exchange Earnings from International Tourism and Composition

单位：万美元、% (USD 10 000,%)

指　　标	Item	2010 金　额 Value	2010 比 重 Percentage	2011 金　额 Value	2011 比 重 Percentage
总　计	**Total**	**36844**	**100**	**46519**	**100**
长途交通费	Long Distance Transportation	9543	25.9	11304	24.3
民　航	Air	6374	17.3	3442	7.4
铁　路	Railway	1326	3.6	3954	8.5
汽　车	Highway	1843	5.0	3908	8.4
游　览	Visiting	1769	4.8	1489	3.2
住　宿	Accommodation	2984	8.1	3582	7.7
餐　饮	Catering	2026	5.5	2000	4.3
商品销售	Commodity Sales	13374	36.3	17677	38.0
娱　乐	Entertainment	516	1.4		
邮电通信	Post and Communication Services	1216	3.3	1303	2.8
市内交通	Local Transportation	921	2.5	1861	4.0
其他服务	Other Services	4495	12.2	7303	15.7

5-15 接待外国旅游人数(按国别分)

Number of Foreign Tourists Received by Country

单位：人 (person)

国　别	Country	2010	2011	国　别	Country	2010	2011
总　计	**Total**	**1010294**	**1248983**	法　国	France	9818	10197
亚　洲	**Asia**	**723612**	**957530**	意大利	Italy	3599	2619
印　度	India	2319	1310	西班牙	Spain	2709	1420
印度尼西亚	Indonesia	1694	949	瑞　典	Sweden	3573	1529
日　本	Japan	28629	28085	瑞　士	Switzerland	4505	2189
马来西亚	Malaysia	4950	5257	独联体(欧洲部分)	Commonwealth of Independent States (Europe)	180076	197531
蒙　古	Mongolia	39052	41246	其　他	Others	6745	6505
菲律宾	The Philppines	1246	321	**北美洲**	**North America**	**35543**	**39097**
新加坡	Singapore	6269	6992	加拿大	Canada	6394	6880
韩　国	Republic of Korea	13613	17841	美　国	United States	22603	25965
泰　国	Thailand	4413	3108	其　他	Others	6546	6252
巴基斯坦	Pakistan	35340	41325	**大洋洲**	**Oceania**	**10127**	**8636**
其　他	Others	586087	811096	澳大利亚	Australia	5875	6135
非　洲	**Africa**	**841**	**765**	新西兰	New Zealand	1929	1438
欧　洲	**Europe**	**233854**	**238190**	其　他	Others	2323	1063
英　国	United Kingdom	14289	8788	**其他小计**	**Other sub-total**	**6317**	**4765**
德　国	Federal Republic of Germany	8540	7412				

注：表中独联体仅指独联体在欧洲部分的国家。
Note: Commonwealth of Independent State in the table only refer to the part of the countries in Europe.

主要统计指标解释

进出口总额 指实际进出我国国境的货物总金额。包括对外贸易实际进出口货物，来料加工装配进出口货物，国家间、联合国及国际组织无偿援助物资和赠送品，华侨、港澳台同胞和外籍华人捐赠品，租赁期满归承租人所有的租赁货物，进料加工进出口货物，边境地方贸易及边境地区小额贸易进出口货物(边民互市贸易除外)，中外合资企业、中外合作经营企业、外商独资经营企业进出口货物和公用物品，到、离岸价格在规定限额以上的进出口货样和广告品(无商业价值、无使用价值和免费提供出口的除外)，从保税仓库提取在中国境内销售的进口货物，以及其他进出口货物。该指标可以观察一个国家在对外贸易方面的总规模。我国规定出口货物按离岸价格统计，进口货物按到岸价格统计。

利用外资 指我国各级政府、部门、企业和其他经济组织通过对外借款、吸收外商直接投资以及用其他方式筹措的境外现汇、设备、技术等。

外商直接投资 指外国企业和经济组织或个人(包括华侨、港澳台胞以及我国在境外注册的企业)按我国有关政策、法规，用现汇、实物、技术等在我国境内开办外商独资企业、与我国境内的企业或经济组织共同举办中外合资经营企业、合作经营企业或合作开发资源的投资(包括外商投资收益的再投资)，以及经政府有关部门批准的项目投资总额内企业从境外借入的资金。

对外承包工程 指我国境内企业法人或者其他经济组织按照国际通行做法，在国外及港澳台地区承揽、实施工程建设项目的勘察、设计、施工、监理、设备材料采购、安装调试、工程咨询、工程管理等经营活动。

对外劳务合作 指我国境内企业法人与国（境）外允许招收或雇用外籍劳务人员的公司、中介机构或私人雇主签订合同，并按合同约定的条件有组织地招聘、选拔、派遣我国公民到国（境）外为外方雇主提供劳务服务并进行管理的经济活动。

旅游人数 包括入境旅游人数、出境人数和国内旅游人数。

(1)入境旅游人数：指报告期内来我国观光、度假、探亲访友、就医疗养、购物、参加会议或从事经济、文化、体育、宗教活动的外国人、港澳台同胞等入境游客。统计时，外国人、港澳台同胞每入境一次统计1人次。

(2)出境人数：指中国（大陆）居民因公或因私出境前往其他国家、中国香港特别行政区、澳门特别行政区和台湾省观光、度假、探亲访友、就医疗养、购物、参加会议或从事经济、文化、体育、宗教活动的人数，即出境游客。统计时，按每出境一次统计1人次。

(3)国内旅游人数：指在报告期内在中国（大陆）观光游览、度假、探亲访友、就医疗养、购物、参加会议或从事经济、文化、体育、宗教活动的中国（大陆）居民人数，其出游的目的不是通过所从事的活动谋取报酬。统计时，国内游客按每出游一次统计1人次。

国际旅游(外汇)收入 指入境游客在中国（大陆）境内旅行、游览过程中用于交通、参观游览、住宿、餐饮、购物、娱乐等全部花费。

国内旅游收入 又称旅游总花费指国内游客在国内旅行、游览过程中用于交通、参观游览、住宿、餐饮、购物、娱乐等全部花费。

国际旅行社 指经营业务范围包括入境旅游业务、出境旅游业务和国内旅游业务的旅行社。

国内旅行社 指经营范围仅限于国内旅游业务的旅行社。

星级饭店 指设备、设施、服务符合《旅游饭店星级的划分与评定》（GB/T14308-2003），通过相关旅游管理部门评定，并取得星级饭店称号的饭店（含预备星级饭店）。

Explanatory Notes on Main Statistical Indicators

Total Imports and Exports at Customs refer to the real value of commodities imported and exported across the border of China. They include the actual imports and exports through foreign trade, imported and exported goods under the processing and assembling trades and materials, supplies and gifts as aid given gratis between governments and by the United Nations and other international organizations, and contributions donated by overseas Chinese, compatriots in Hong Kong and Macao and Chinese with foreign citizenship, leasing commodities owned by tenant at the expiration of leasing period, the imported and exported commodities processed with imported materials, commodities trading in border areas (excluding mutual exchange goods), the imported and exported commodities and articles for public use of the Sino-foreign joint ventures, cooperative enterprises and ventures with sole foreign investment. Also included is import or export of samples and advertising goods for which CIF or FOB value are beyond the permitted ceiling (excluding goods of no trading or use value and free commodities for export), imported goods sold in China from bonded warehouses and other imported or exported goods. The indicator of the total imports and exports at customs can be used to observe the total size of external trade in a country. In accordance with the stipulation of the Chinese government, imports are calculated at CIF, while exports are calculated at FOB.

Utilization of Foreign Capitals refers to remittance, equipment and technology financed from abroad, by loans, foreign direct investment and other forms undertaken by the Chinese governments at all levels, by various departments, enterprises and other economic units.

Foreign Direct Investment refers to the investments inside China by foreign enterprises and economic organizations or individuals (including overseas Chinese, compatriots from Hong Kong, Macao and Taiwan, and Chinese enterprises registered abroad), following the relevant policies and laws of China, for the establishment of ventures exclusively with foreign own investment, Sino-foreign joint ventures and cooperative enterprises or for co-operative exploration of resources with enterprises or economic organizations in China. It includes the re- investment of the foreign entrepreneurs with the profits gained from the investment and the funds that enterprises borrow from abroad in the total investment of projects which are approved by the relevant department of the government.

Overseas Contracted Project refers to in accordance with the international common practice, domestic corporates or other economic organizations contract and implement construction projects in foreign countries, Hong Kong SAR, Macao SAR and Taiwan province including reconnaissance, design, construction, supervision, purchasing of equipment and materials, installation and testing, engineering consulting and project management.

Overseas Labour Services refer to domestic corporates which signed contracts with overseas corporations, intermediary agencies and private employers which are allowed to recruit or hire foreign labour forces, they will send Chinese citizens to go abroad to provide labour services to foreign employers through organized recruitment and selection according to the signed contracts and relevant management activities.

Number of Tourists include international tourists entering into China, Chinese residents going abroad and domestic tourists.

(1) International tourists refer to foreigners, overseas Chinese, Chinese compatriots from Hong Kong, Macao and Taiwan coming to China for sightseeing, visits, tours, family reunions, vacations, study tours, conferences and other activities of a business, scientific and technological, cultural, educational and religious nature. It does not include representatives and employees of resident institutions of foreign countries in China such as embassies, consulates, news agencies and offices of foreign companies and organizations, nor does it include long-term foreign experts or students residing in China, or persons in transition without spending a night in China.

(2) Chinese residents going abroad refer to Chinese residents going abroad for short terms for either public business or private purposes. Chinese employees working on international transport carriers are included in those going abroad for public business purpose, not in those for private purpose.

(3) Domestic tourists refer to residents of the mainland of China who stay for one night at least but no more than 6 months at tourist facilities in other places than their permanent residence within the territory of the mainland China, including foreigners, overseas Chinese and Chinese compatriots from Hong Kong, Macao and Taiwan who have resided in China for over one year.

Foreign Exchange Earnings from International Tourism refer to the total expenditures of foreigners, overseas Chinese, Chinese compatriots from Hong Kong, Macao and Taiwan during their stay in the mainland of China, which are earnings of foreign exchange from international tourism from the point of view from China.

Earning from domestic travel refer to the domestic tourists during their stay in the mainland of China ,which are earnings of transportaion,inviting,hoteling,catering,shopping and entertainment

International Travel Agencies refer to travel agencies engaged in the promotion, solicitation, organization and reception of tours to the mainland of China by foreigners, overseas Chinese, Chinese compatriots from Hong Kong, Macao and Taiwan.

Domestic Travel Agencies refer to travel agencies engaged in the promotion, solicitation, organization and reception of domestic tourists, and in the reception of foreigners, overseas Chinese, Chinese compatriots from Hong Kong, Macao and Taiwan organized by international travel agencies or other departments concerned, without their own promotion and solicitation programmes.

Start-Hotels refer to hotels that are able, with the approval of departments concerned, to accommodate foreigners, overseas Chinese, Chinese compatriots from Hong Kong, Macao and Taiwan Province.

2012

新疆统计年鉴

XINJIANG STATISTICAL YEARBOOK

第六篇
能源生产和消费

CHAPTER 6
Production and Consumption of Energy

简要说明
Brief Introduction

本篇资料的主要内容及来源

本篇包括的主要内容有能源生产、消费总量及品种构成，综合能源平衡表和主要能源品种单项平衡表，分行业、分主要能源品种的消费量，能源生产和消费弹性系数，能源加工转换效率及生活用能源消费量等。

从2006年度开始，能源生产、消费等指标需经国家审定后方可公布，因国家审定、公布各省的这部分指标数据为每年的八月份，时间在年鉴出版时间之后，为此，这部分数据采取错年上，即2011年上2010年数据。

本篇资料由新疆维吾尔自治区统计局能源与资源统计处依据能源年报整理提供。

Main Content and Source of Data

Data in this chapter cover mainly the energy production and consumption and their composition, the overall balance of energy and the balance by different types of energy, the consumption of energy by sector and by types of energy the elasticity ratio of energy production and consumption, efficiency of energy conversion and the consumption of energy for non-production uses.

Since 2006, data on production and consumption of energy are announced after NBS authorized. Time of publication is August every year. So the data on energy in 2011 Statistical Yearbook is data in 2010. Data in this chapter are provided and processed in accordance with the statistical reporting scheme on energy by the Department of Industry and Transport of the Xinjiang Bureau of Statistics.

6-1 主要年份能源生产总量及构成
Total Production of Energy and Its Composition in Main Years

年 份 Year	能源生产总量 (万吨标准煤) Total Energy Production (10 000 tons of SCE)	占能源生产总量的比重(%) Percentage of Total Energy Production (%)			
		原 煤 Coal	原 油 Crude Oil	天然气 Natural Gas	水风电 Hydro- Power and Wind Power
1978	1410.75	60.0	35.8	2.4	1.8
1980	1527.72	58.4	36.5	3.1	2.0
1985	2092.47	60.0	34.1	3.5	2.4
1990	2801.57	58.8	35.8	2.4	3.0
1995	4266.06	50.1	43.5	3.6	2.8
2000	5419.77	40.6	48.7	7.9	2.8
2001	5720.04	38.7	48.6	9.7	3.0
2002	6156.05	39.5	47.3	10.5	2.7
2003	6657.43	41.1	46.0	10.2	2.7
2004	7112.95	41.4	45.3	10.7	2.6
2005	8175.74	37.9	42.1	17.3	2.7
2006	9528.72	37.3	37.1	22.9	2.7
2007	10735.84	36.7	34.7	26.0	2.6
2008	12669.13	41.9	30.6	24.8	2.7
2009	13542.33	46.5	26.5	24.1	2.9
2010	15000.47	50.3	24.4	22.2	3.1

注：电力折算标准煤的系数根据当年平均发电煤耗计算，并将历史资料做了调整，下表同。

Note: The coefficient for conversion of electric power into SCE (standard coal equivalent) is calculated on the basic of the data on the average coal consumption in generating electric power in the same year. The same is as in the following tables.

6-2 主要年份能源消费总量及构成
Total Consumption of Energy and Its Composition in Main Years

年 份 Year	能源消费总量 (万吨标准煤) Total Energy Consumption (10 000 tons of SCE)	占能源消费总量的比重(%) As percentage of Total Energy Consumption (%)			
		煤 炭 Coal	石 油 Crude Oil	天然气 Natural Gas	水风电 Hydro- Power and Wind Power
1978	979.27	72.5	21.5	3.4	2.6
1980	1026.45	71.3	21.1	4.6	3.0
1985	1410.84	72.0	19.3	5.1	3.6
1990	1924.38	69.6	22.5	3.5	4.4
1995	2733.04	66.2	23.8	5.6	4.4
2000	3316.03	63.6	23.3	8.6	4.5
2001	3496.44	60.4	21.6	13.2	4.8
2002	3622.40	62.2	20.5	12.7	4.6
2003	4064.43	60.3	21.7	13.1	4.9
2004	4784.83	61.0	20.1	15.0	3.9
2005	5506.49	56.1	26.2	13.7	4.0
2006	6047.27	56.7	24.7	14.3	4.3
2007	6575.92	57.8	23.9	14.1	4.2
2008	7069.39	61.7	20.3	13.1	4.9
2009	7525.56	65.9	16.9	12.0	5.2
2010	8290.20	65.8	15.8	12.4	5.6

6-3 主要年份综合能源平衡表
Overall Energy Balance Sheet in Main Years

单位:万吨标准煤 (10 000 tons of SCE)

项　　目	Item	1990	1995	2000	2005	2010
可供消费的能源总量	**Total Energy Available for Consumption**	**2045.32**	**2883.61**	**3430.05**	**5349.17**	**8285.44**
一次能源生产量	Primary Energy Output	2801.57	4266.06	5419.77	8175.74	15000.47
进口量	Imports			107.39	130.80	1417.54
外省调入量	Inflow from other Provinces (Autonomons Regions and Municipalities)	2.26	8.29	25.59	58.17	175.17
出口量(-)	Exports (-)	4.84	1.04	31.90	60.80	18.49
本区调出量(-)	Outflow (-)	694.89	1414.05	2144.79	3172.41	8119.06
年初年末库存差额	Stock Changes in the Year	-58.78	24.35	53.99	95.71	-171.00
能源消费总量	**Total Energy Consumption**	**1924.45**	**2733.01**	**3316.03**	**5506.49**	**8290.20**
在总量中：	Consumption by Sector					
农、林、牧、渔、水利业	Farming, Forestry, Animal Husbandry, Fishery and Water Conservancy	134.91	189.13	274.97	314.25	416.74
工　业	Industry	1095.22	1571.88	1860.26	3440.83	5903.00
建筑业	Construction	41.16	63.01	81.73	43.22	75.86
交通运输和邮电通讯业	Transportation, Post and Telecommunications Services	99.72	152.77	189.76	413.77	635.41
商业、饮食、物资供销和仓储业	Commerce, Catering Services, Materials Supply, Marketing and Storage	26.28	51.37	93.83	138.39	182.27
其　他	Others	99.12	205.04	164.57	177.51	218.02
生活消费	Residential Consumption	428.04	499.84	650.91	978.54	858.90
在总量中：	Consumption by Usage					
终端消费	End-use Consumption	1825.44	2587.35	3148.77	5086.96	7300.36
#工　业	Industry	996.27	1426.22	1692.96	3021.27	5027.82
加工转换损失量	Losses During the Process of Energy Conversion	27.90	62.06	91.25	228.26	634.69
#炼　焦	Coking	13.00	27.56	72.05	77.60	289.29
炼　油	Petroleum Refining	13.16	33.49	75.99	62.18	70.58
损失量	Energy Losses	71.05	83.60	76.05	191.27	310.06
平衡差额	**Balance**	**120.87**	**150.60**	**114.02**	**-157.32**	**27.18**

注：1.村办工业包括在工业中(下同)。
2.电力、热力按等价热值折算，因此加工转换损失量中不包括发电、供热损失量。
3.进口量包括新疆飞机在国外加油量，出口量包括外国飞机在新疆的加油量。

Note: a) Data on industry includes the data of village-run industry. (The same is as in the following tables).
b) Electric power and heat are converted on the basic of equal caloric value. Therefore, losses in processing and transformation exclude losses in power generation and heating.
c) Data on imports include the petroleum consumed by the Xinjiang airplanes in refueling abroad. Data on exports include the petroleum consumed by the foreign airplanes in refueling in Xinjiang.

6-4 主要年份石油平衡表
Petroleum Balance Sheet in Main Years

单位:万吨 (10 000 tons)

项　　目	Item	1990	1995	2000	2005	2010
可供量	**Total Energy Available for Consumption**	**333.19**	**496.35**	**616.14**	**1021.31**	**869.02**
生产量	Output	701.26	1299.83	1848.43	2408.32	2558.16
进口量	Imports			75.16	91.54	993.43
外省调入量	Inflow from other Provinces (Autonomons Regions and Municipalities)	1.44	3.31	10.85	14.85	
出口量(-)	Exports (-)	3.29	0.63	11.17	5.18	1.08
本区调出量(-)	Outflow (-)	353.59	849.63	1285.38	1525.72	2682.12
年初年末库存差额	Stock Changes in the Year	-12.63	43.47	-21.75	37.50	0.63
消费量	**Total Energy Consumption**	**300.16**	**451.26**	**527.71**	**1014.84**	**869.02**
在消费量中：	Consumption by Sector					
农、林、牧、渔、水利业	Farming, Forestry, Animal Husbandry, Fishery and Water Conservancy	42.46	44.56	63.65	70.68	71.27
工　业	Industry	171.96	269.79	273.95	611.18	298.42
建筑业	Construction	16.87	16.67	32.10	15.36	23.81
交通运输和邮电通讯业	Transportation, Post and Telecommunications Services	48.30	76.55	86.89	210.00	360.79
商业、饮食、物资供销和仓储业	Commerce, Catering Services, Materials Supply, Marketing and Storage	3.66	8.80	18.78	31.91	40.15
其　他	Others	8.48	20.25	32.70	46.20	44.91
生活消费	Residential Consumption	8.43	14.64	19.64	29.51	29.67
在消费量中：	Consumption by Sector					
终端消费	Final Consumption	257.06	411.94	457.99	936.88	687.45
#工　业	Industry	128.86	230.47	204.23	533.22	197.11
中间消费(用于加工转换)	Intermediate Consumption	15.69	10.01	17.34	47.37	101.31
#发　电	Power Generation	15.69	10.01	2.10	8.65	13.31
供　热	Heating			1.24	1.04	27.43
此外：当年炼油投入量	Petroleum Refining Input	464.29	692.40	1001.32	1531.68	2182.96
平衡差额	**Balance**	**33.03**	**45.09**	**88.43**	**6.47**	

注：1.生产量为原油产量。
2.进口量包括新疆飞机在国外加油量，出口量包括外国飞机在新疆的加油量。

Note: a) Data on output refer to the output of crude oil.
b) Data on imports include the petroleum consumed by the Xinjiang Airplanes in refueling abroad. Data on exports include the petroleum consumed by the foreign airplanes in refueling in Xinjiang.

6-5 主要年份煤炭平衡表
Coal Balance Sheet in Main Years

单位:万吨 (10 000 tons)

项　　目	Item	1990	1995	2000	2005	2010
可供量	**Total Energy Available for Consumption**	**1816.32**	**2444.21**	**2702.81**	**3702.32**	**8106.35**
生产量	Output	2100.20	2720.74	2798.90	3942.29	9926.73
外省调入量	Inflow from other Provinces (Autonomons Regions and Municipalities)		1.40	10.70	30.40	213.43
进口量	Imports				0.03	0.52
出口量(-)	Exports (-)	0.01	0.14	0.22	0.01	
本区调出量(-)	Outflow (-)	232.76	221.00	203.12	323.47	1916.20
年初年末库存差额	Stock Changes in the Year	-51.11	-56.79	96.55	53.08	-118.13
消费量	**Total Energy Consumption**	**1716.11**	**2327.52**	**2702.40**	**3859.91**	**8106.35**
在消费量中：	Consumption by Sector					
农、林、牧、渔、水利业	Farming, Forestry, Animal Husbandry, Fishery and Water Conservancy	23.96	80.44	100.00	103.30	101.00
工　业	Industry	1080.07	1452.19	1801.40	3110.44	7593.35
建筑业	Construction	11.67	26.02	26.00	17.00	19.00
交通运输和邮电通讯业	Transportation, Post and Telecommunications Services	25.42	32.56	55.00	56.60	50.00
商业、饮食、物资供销和仓储业	Commerce, Catering Services, Materials Supply, Marketing and Storage	20.50	33.00	40.00	31.78	47.00
其　他	Others	79.48	176.31	90.00	40.00	44.00
生活消费	Residential Consumption	479.37	527.00	590.00	500.79	252.00
在消费量中：	Consumption by Sector					
终端消费	Final Consumption	1163.46	1427.87	1502.63	1503.83	2350.51
#工　业	Industry	523.06	552.54	601.63	754.36	1837.51
中间消费(用于加工转换)	Intermediate Consumption	525.51	842.96	1199.77	2356.08	5755.84
#发　电	Power Generation	372.01	575.88	849.20	1363.96	2501.72
供　热	Heating	32.32	102.93	204.46	585.51	1096.50
炼　焦	Coking	111.39	158.93	137.77	380.90	1988.54
平衡差额	**Balance**	**100.21**	**116.69**	**0.41**	**-157.59**	

注：生产量为原煤产量。
Note: Data on output refer to the output of crude coal.

6-6 主要年份电力平衡表
Electricity Balance Sheet in Main Years

单位:亿千瓦小时 (100 million kwh)

项目	Item	1990	1995	2000	2005	2010
可供量	**Total Energy Available for Consumption**	**69.79**	**120.43**	**182.98**	**310.14**	**661.96**
生产量	Output	69.79	120.43	182.98	310.14	665.06
水 电	Hydropower	14.25	22.82	30.54	46.49	97.07
风 电	Wind Power	0.08	0.34	1.73	2.32	30.02
火 电	Thermal Power	55.46	97.27	150.71	261.33	538.63
消费量	**Total Energy Consumption**	**69.79**	**120.37**	**182.98**	**310.14**	**661.96**
在消费量中:	Consumption by Sector					
农、林、牧、渔、水利业	Farming, Forestry, Animal Husbandry, Fishery and Water Conservancy	9.16	11.50	22.30	28.72	61.12
工 业	Industry	48.86	83.53	118.85	221.67	494.94
建筑业	Construction	1.18	3.20	3.50	1.44	6.86
交通运输和邮电通讯业	Transportation, Post and Telecommunications Services	1.48	2.73	4.00	4.74	6.68
商业、饮食、物资供销和仓储业	Commerce, Catering Services, Materials Supply, Marketing and Storage	0.81	2.30	6.90	11.09	16.74
其 他	Others	4.08	7.00	9.83	15.38	28.52
生活消费	Residential Consumption	4.22	10.11	17.60	27.10	47.10
在消费量中:	Consumption by Sector					
终端消费	Final Consumption	65.74	112.87	170.86	282.42	608.71
#工 业	Industry	44.81	76.03	106.73	193.95	441.69
输配电损失量	Losses in Transmission	4.05	7.50	12.12	27.72	53.25

6-7 分行业能源消费总量和主要能源消费量

(2010 年)

行业	Sector	能源消费总量(万吨标准煤) Total Energy Consumption (10 000 tons of SCE)	煤炭消费量(万吨) Coal Consumption (10 000 tons)	焦炭消费量(万吨) Coke Consumption (10 000 tons)
消费总量	**Total Consumption**	**8290.20**	**8106.35**	**648.21**
农、林、牧、渔业	**Farming, Forestry, Animal Husbandry, and Fishery**	**416.74**	**101.00**	
工　业	**Industry**	**5903.00**	**7593.35**	**648.21**
采 矿 业	**Mining and Quarrying**	**1022.02**	**415.74**	**2.59**
煤炭开采和洗选业	Mining and Washing of Coal	180.92	312.49	0.10
石油和天然气开采业	Extraction of Petroleum and Natural Gas	752.09	55.88	
黑色金属矿采选业	Mining and Processing of Ferrous Metals Ores	51.39	25.50	1.07
有色金属矿采选业	Mining and Processing of Nonferrous Metals Ores	25.65	9.41	1.42
非金属矿采选业	Mining and Processing of Non-metal Ores	11.54	12.30	
其他采矿业	Mining of Other Ores	0.43	0.17	
制 造 业	**Manufacturing**	**4191.48**	**4383.58**	**645.62**
农副食品加工业	Processing of Food from Agricultural Products	91.50	110.71	2.68
食品制造业	Manufacture of Food	61.88	59.39	
饮料制造业	Manufacture of Beverage	19.95	14.27	
烟草制品业	Manufacture of Tobacco	1.10	0.99	
纺织业	Manufacture of Textile	71.90	24.71	
纺织服装、鞋、帽制造业	Manufacture of Textile Wearing Apparel,Footware and Caps	0.31	0.07	
皮革、毛皮、羽绒及其制品业	Manufacture of Leather, Fur, Feather and Related Products	0.37	0.38	
木材加工及木、竹、藤、棕、草制品业	Timber Production, Wood, Bamboo, Cane and Grass	6.36	6.42	
家具制造业	Manufacture of Furniture	1.39	0.79	
造纸及纸制品业	Manufacture of Paper and Paper Products	29.58	30.40	
印刷业和记录媒介的复制	Printing and Copying of Medium for Record	1.05	0.22	
石油加工、炼焦及核燃料加工业	Processing of Oil Processing, Coking and Nuclear Fuel	1415.62		

Consumption of Total Energy and Its Main Varieties by Sector

原油消费量 (万吨) Crude Oil Consumption (10 000 tons)	汽油消费量 (万吨) Gasoline Consumption (10 000 tons)	煤油消费量 (万吨) Kerosene Consumption (10 000 tons)	柴油消费量 (万吨) Diesel Oil Consumption (10 000 tons)	燃料油消费量 (万吨) Fuel Oil Consumption (10 000 tons)	天然气消费量 (亿立方米) Natural Gas Consumption (100 million cu.m)	电力消费量 (亿千瓦小时) Electricity Consumption (100 million kwh)
2308.44	**131.17**	**33.33**	**363.72**	**14.95**	**80.15**	**661.96**
	9.86	**0.41**	**60.00**		**0.01**	**61.12**
2228.18	**7.45**	**0.07**	**64.01**	**14.95**	**70.70**	**494.94**
83.07	**3.13**		**51.15**	**0.56**	**49.67**	**57.67**
	0.66		26.59			12.86
83.07	2.22		18.99	0.56	49.56	32.59
	0.12		4.39		0.12	6.87
	0.09		0.62			4.57
	0.03		0.56			0.70
			0.02			0.08
2145.09	**3.09**	**0.07**	**11.71**	**14.37**	**20.60**	**322.42**
	0.29		0.29		0.02	5.90
	0.18		0.28		0.04	4.47
	0.10		0.03		0.03	1.38
	0.01					0.11
	0.10		0.05			13.47
	0.01		0.01			0.02
	0.01					0.03
	0.01		0.05			0.81
	0.02		0.02			0.17
	0.03		0.06	0.13		2.33
	0.06		0.01			0.13
2145.09	0.34	0.04	0.65	14.22	8.12	36.23

6-7 续表

行业	Sector	能源消费总量(万吨标准煤) Total Energy Consumption (10 000 tons of SCE)	煤炭消费量(万吨) Coal Consumption (10 000 tons)	焦炭消费量(万吨) Coke Consumption (10 000 tons)
化学原料及化学制品制造业	Manufacture of Raw Chemical Material and Chemical Products	825.70	2371.47	117.75
医药制造业	Manufacture of Medicine	4.80	524.91	
化学纤维制造业	Manufacture of Chemical Fiber	71.85	5.40	
橡胶制品业	Manufacture of Rubber Products	3.42	75.91	
塑料制品业	Manufacture of Plastic Products	12.25	3.52	
非金属矿物制品业	Manufacture of Non-metallic Mineral Products	491.73	2.11	5.77
黑色金属冶炼及压延加工业	Smelting and Pressing of Ferrous Metals	866.09	477.37	511.15
有色金属冶炼及压延加工业	Smelting and Pressing of Non-ferrous Metals	94.59	604.09	4.29
金属制品业	Metal Products Manufacturing	70.00	23.23	3.82
通用设备制造业	Manufacture of General Purpose Machinery	2.75	1.13	0.12
专用设备制造业	Manufacture of Special Purpose Machinery	3.17	0.91	0.01
交通运输设备制造业	Manufacture of Transport Equipment	1.62	3.06	0.03
电气机械及器材制造业	Manufacture of Electric Equipment and Machinery	5.81	0.37	
通信设备、计算机及其他电子设备制造业	Communication Equipment, Computer and Other Electronic Equipment	36.01	2.65	
仪器仪表及文化办公用机械制造业	Manufacture of Equipment, Meter, Culture and Office Machinery	0.06	39.08	
工艺品及其他制造业	Manufacture of Artwork and Other Manufacturing Sector	0.62	0.01	
电力、燃气及水的生产和供应业	**Electric Power, Gas and Water Production and Supply**	**689.49**	**2794.03**	
电力、热力的生产和供应业	Production and Distribution of Power, Steam and Hot Water	679.70	2787.01	
燃气生产和供应业	Production and Supply of Gas	3.05	3.05	
水的生产和供应业	Production and Supply of Water	6.74	3.97	
建筑业	**Construction**	**75.86**	**19.00**	
交通运输、仓储及邮电通信业	**Transportation, Storage, Post & Telecommunications Services**	**635.41**	**50.00**	
批发和零售贸易业、餐饮业	**Wholesale, Retail Trades and Catering Services**	**182.27**	**47.00**	
其他行业	**Others**	**218.02**	**44.00**	
生活消费	**Household Consumption**	**858.90**	**252.00**	

Continued

原油消费量 (万吨) Crude Oil Consumption (10 000 tons)	汽油消费量 (万吨) Gasoline Consumption (10 000 tons)	煤油消费量 (万吨) Kerosene Consumption (10 000 tons)	柴油消费量 (万吨) Diesel Oil Consumption (10 000 tons)	燃料油消费量 (万吨) Fuel Oil Consumption (10 000 tons)	天然气消费量 (亿立方米) Natural Gas Consumption (100 million cu.m)	电力消费量 (亿千瓦小时) Electricity Consumption (100 million kwh)
	0.41	0.03	2.62		11.98	99.32
	0.04		0.02	0.01	0.01	0.19
	0.03		0.05			5.68
	0.01		0.01			0.27
	0.11		0.05		0.02	2.60
	0.55		5.43		0.26	47.60
	0.22		1.53		0.04	51.95
	0.07		0.30		0.02	21.06
	0.12		0.10		0.04	17.58
	0.12		0.03		0.01	0.36
	0.10		0.02			0.32
	0.04		0.02		0.02	0.10
	0.07		0.03			0.98
	0.02		0.04			9.22
	0.01					
						0.13
0.01	**1.23**		**1.15**	**0.02**	**0.42**	**114.85**
0.01	1.13		1.04	0.02	0.26	113.02
	0.03		0.05		0.14	0.43
	0.07		0.06		0.02	1.40
	3.10	**0.16**	**12.50**		**0.02**	**6.86**
80.26	**69.71**	**32.00**	**172.00**		**3.12**	**6.68**
	10.60	**0.05**	**25.50**		**1.22**	**16.74**
	20.00	**0.30**	**23.20**		**0.48**	**28.52**
	10.45	**0.34**	**6.51**		**4.60**	**47.10**

6-8 主要年份能源生产弹性系数

Elasticity Ration of Energy Production in Main Years

年 份 Year	能源生产比上年增长(%) Growth Rate of Energy Production Over Preceding Year(%)	电力生产比上年增长(%) Growth Rate of Electricity Production over Preceding Year(%)	新疆生产总值比上年增长(%) Growth Rate of Gross Domestic Product (GDP) Over Preceding Year(%)	能源生产弹性系数 Elasticity Cofficient of Energy Production	电力生产弹性系数 Elasticity Ratio of Electricity Production
1980	7.8	3.6	7.2	1.08	0.50
1985	11.6	11.5	16.9	0.69	0.68
1990	5.8	10.8	11.7	0.50	0.92
1995	7.8	13.4	9.0	0.87	1.49
2000	3.3	8.1	8.2	0.40	0.99
2001	5.5	8.0	8.1	0.68	0.99
2002	7.6	7.4	8.1	0.94	0.91
2003	8.1	10.5	10.8	0.75	0.97
2004	6.8	13.3	11.1	0.61	1.20
2005	14.9	16.6	10.9	1.37	1.52
2006	16.6	15.2	11.0	1.51	1.38
2007	12.7	16.7	12.2	1.04	1.37
2008	18.0	16.0	11.0	1.64	1.45
2009	6.9	14.3	8.1	0.85	1.77
2010	10.8	21.4	10.6	1.02	2.02

注：新疆生产总值增速按可比价格计算，下表同。
Note: The growth rate of GDP in Xinjiang is calculated at comparable prices and the same as in the following tables.

6-9 主要年份能源消费弹性系数

Elasticity Ration of Energy Consumption in Main Years

年 份 Year	能源消费比上年增长(%) Growth Rate of Energy Consumption Over Preceding Year(%)	电力消费比上年增长(%) Growth Rate of Electricity Consumption over Preceding Year(%)	新疆生产总值比上年增长(%) Growth Rate of Gross Domestic Product (GDP) Over Preceding Year(%)	能源消费弹性系数 Elasticity Ration of Energy Consumption	电力消费弹性系数 Elasticity Ration of Electricity Consumption
1980	4.5	3.6	7.2	0.63	0.50
1985	13.6	11.5	16.9	0.80	0.68
1990	9.3	10.8	11.7	0.79	0.92
1995	4.9	13.4	9.0	0.54	1.49
2000	3.1	8.1	8.2	0.38	0.99
2001	5.4	8.0	8.1	0.67	0.99
2002	3.6	7.4	8.1	0.44	0.91
2003	12.2	10.5	10.8	1.13	0.97
2004	17.7	13.3	11.1	1.59	1.20
2005	15.1	16.6	10.9	1.39	1.52
2006	9.8	14.8	11.0	0.89	1.35
2007	8.7	16.0	12.2	0.71	1.31
2008	7.5	16.0	11.0	0.68	1.45
2009	6.5	14.3	8.1	0.80	1.77
2010	10.2	20.8	10.6	0.96	1.96

6-10 主要年份能源加工转换效率
Efficiency of Energy Procession and Conversion in Main Years

单位：% (%)

年份 Year	总效率 Total Efficiency	发电 Electricity Generation	供热 Heating	炼焦 Coking	炼油 Petroleum Refining
1980	73.9	21.2		72.0	96.9
1985	74.9	21.1		75.5	98.1
1990	73.9	20.9	69.4	85.5	98.0
1995	72.7	23.6	71.2	78.6	96.6
2000	73.6	26.6	75.0	89.4	94.7
2001	73.7	26.1	74.6	78.2	97.4
2002	73.6	26.8	73.5	83.4	96.8
2003	73.8	26.0	78.0	92.0	97.9
2004	70.2	25.9	70.3	78.8	96.2
2005	72.3	27.0	77.7	75.7	97.1
2006	74.8	27.8	76.7	85.0	97.6
2007	73.3	28.6	73.5	86.3	96.4
2008	73.8	30.0	76.6	84.8	96.6
2009	73.5	30.4	77.4	82.2	96.3
2010	75.6	33.5	76.8	81.5	96.1

6-11 主要年份平均每天各种能源消费量
Average Daily Energy Consumption by Type of Energy in Main Years

能源品种	Variey of Energy	1990	1995	2000	2005	2010
总计(万吨标准煤)	**Total (10 000 tons of SCE)**	**5.41**	**7.60**	**9.09**	**15.09**	**22.71**
煤炭(万吨)	Coal (10 000 tons)	5.04	6.67	7.48	10.58	22.21
焦炭(万吨)	Coke (10 000 tons)	0.16	0.20	0.20	0.50	1.78
原油(万吨)	Crude Oil (10 000 tons)	1.33	1.99	2.94	4.46	6.32
燃料油(万吨)	Fuel Oil (10 000 tons)	0.25	0.32	0.16	0.50	0.04
汽油(万吨)	Gasoline (10 000 tons)	0.20	0.28	0.28	0.29	0.36
煤油(万吨)	Kerosene (10 000 tons)	0.01	0.04	0.06	0.07	0.09
柴油(万吨)	Diesel Oil (10 000 tons)	0.24	0.33	0.43	0.83	1.00
天然气(万立方米)	Natural Gas (10 000 cu.m)	137.53	314.52	642.19	1546.85	2195.89
电力(亿千瓦时)	Electricity (100 million kwh)	0.19	0.33	0.50	0.85	1.81

6-12 主要年份分品种生活能源年消费总量

Average Annual Energy Consumption for Household by Variety in Main Years

年 份 Year	合 计(万吨标准煤) Total (10 000 tons of SCE)	煤 炭(万吨) Coal (10 000 tons)	煤 油(万吨) Kerosene (10 000 tons)	液化石油气(万吨) Liquefied Petroleum Gas (10 000 tons)	天然气(亿立方米) Natural Gas (100 million cu.m)	热 力(万百万千焦) Heat (10 billion kilo-joule)	电 力(亿千瓦小时) Electricity (100 million kwh)
1980	330.44	404.10					1.70
1985	355.65	421.72	0.71	3.00			2.38
1990	428.04	479.37	0.58	5.35		160.02	4.22
1995	499.84	527.00	0.50	8.94		177.29	10.11
2000	650.91	590.00	0.75	10.89	0.13	1611.81	17.60
2001	703.97	600.00	0.67	12.31	0.46	2209.66	19.50
2002	752.10	610.00	0.10	14.22	0.32	3112.58	19.20
2003	782.21	625.04		16.62	0.60	3191.14	20.37
2004	901.88	605.00		17.00	1.00	3363.45	24.26
2005	978.54	500.79	0.55	12.96	1.92	6219.00	27.10
2006	612.66	211.00	0.55	14.10	2.60	5008.00	31.90
2007	652.36	213.00	0.42	14.53	2.70	5097.43	33.52
2008	752.73	232.20	0.35	11.60	2.89	7371.00	38.55
2009	855.56	255.00	0.35	13.50	3.90	9073.84	42.62
2010	858.90	252.00	0.34	12.30	4.60	10511.04	47.10

注：表 6-12 和 6-13 中，2006 年以前数据未按新口径进行调整。
Note: Figures in table6-12 and6-13 did not adjusted at new coverage, except for figures in 2006.

6-13 主要年份每人年平均生活用能源

Annual Per-Capital Energy Consumption of Households in Main Years

年 份 Year	平均每人生活消费能源(公斤标准煤/人) Annual Per Capita Consumption for Household (kg of SCE/person)	煤 炭(公斤) Coal (kg)	电 力(千瓦小时) Electricity (kwh)	煤 油(公斤) Kerosene (kg)	液化石油气(公斤) Liquefied Petroleum Gas (kg)	天然气(立方米) Natural Gas (cu.m)
1980	258	315	13.25			
1985	261	310	17.49	0.52	2.20	
1990	268	313	27.60	0.38	3.50	
1995	301	317	65.60	0.30	5.33	
2000	353	320	95.33	0.41	5.90	0.70
2001	375	320	103.93	0.36	6.56	2.45
2002	395	320	100.78	0.05	7.46	1.68
2003	404	323	105.33		8.59	3.10
2004	459	308	123.58		8.66	5.09
2005	487	249	134.80	0.27	6.45	9.55
2006	302	104	157.13	0.27	6.95	12.81
2007	311	102	159.99	0.20	6.93	12.89
2008	352	109	180.92	0.16	5.44	13.56
2009	396	118	197.44	0.16	6.25	18.07
2010	394	116	215.92	0.16	5.64	21.09

6-14 各地、州、市规模以上工业企业能源消费量

Energy Consumption of Industry above Designated Size by Prefecture, Autonomous Prefecture and City

(2010 年)

能源品种	Item	合计 Total	乌鲁木齐市 Urumqi City	克拉玛依市 Karamay City	吐鲁番地区 Turpan Administrative Offices
原煤(吨)	Coal (ton)	67116290	16005532	3341491	3426884
洗精煤(吨)	Washed Coal(ton)	5958871	4074813		
其他洗煤(吨)	Other Washed Coal (ton)	140662	68186		
焦炭(吨)	Coke (ton)	6482054	3085717		675657
焦炉煤气(万立方米)	Coke Oven Gas (10 000 cu.m)	129615	99281		9816
高炉煤气(万立方米)	High Oven Gas (10 000 cu.m)	944977	944977		
天然气(万立方米)	Natural Gas (10 000 cu.m)	707001	89172	265662	60627
原油(吨)	Coal (ton)	22281803	5352902	13526811	72740
汽油(吨)	Gasoline (ton)	45761	13755	9690	1005
煤油(吨)	Kerosene (ton)	731	384	342	
柴油(吨)	Diesel Oil (ton)	630085	55000	167470	34914
燃料油(吨)	Fuel Oil (ton)	143273	140540	831	172
液化石油气(吨)	Liquefied Petroleum Gas (ton)	96425	94	65028	17028
炼厂干气(吨)	Refinary Dry Gas (ton)	771149	169309	471005	
其他石油制品(吨)	Other Oil Product (ton)	592913	378344		41978
热力(百万千焦)	Heat (million KJ)	79124771	20833601	30422442	1589124
电力(万千瓦时)	Electricity (10 000 kwh)	4727076	1345792	469095	220619
其他燃料(吨标准煤)	Other (ton of SCE)	149883	21543		7115
能源合计(吨标准煤)	Energy Total (ton of SCE)	116706217	33016297	27970046	5059423

能源品种	Item	哈密地区 Hami [kumul] Administrative Offices	昌吉回族自治州 Changji Hui Autonomous Prefecture	博尔塔拉蒙古自治州 Bortala Mongol Autonomous Prefecture	伊犁州直属县(市) Counties (Cities) Direct Under Ili Prefecture
原煤(吨)	Coal (ton)	3764706	16696249	568271	4285821
洗精煤(吨)	Washed Coal (ton)				680385
其他洗煤(吨)	Other Washed Coal (ton)	5816	600		
焦炭(吨)	Coke (ton)	110390	113115	156146	720242
焦炉煤气(万立方米)	Coke Oven Gas (10 000 cu.m)		522		18965
高炉煤气(万立方米)	High Oven Gas (10 000 cu.m)				
天然气(万立方米)	Natural Gas (10 000 cu.m)		5664		95
原油(吨)	Coal (ton)		33558		
汽油(吨)	Gasoline (ton)	2351	3006	341	2656
煤油(吨)	Kerosene (ton)				5
柴油(吨)	Diesel Oil (ton)	20864	244878	1815	13117
燃料油(吨)	Fuel Oil (ton)				
液化石油气(吨)	Liquefied Petroleum Gas (ton)				2
炼厂干气(吨)	Refinary Dry Gas (ton)				
其他石油制品(吨)	Other Oil Product (ton)		10048	1108	38718
热力(百万千焦)	Heat (million KJ)	2345	1761921	156847	767709
电力(万千瓦时)	Electricity (10 000 kwh)	117284	395628	27885	390262
其他燃料(吨标准煤)	Other (ton of SCE)				
能源合计(吨标准煤)	Energy Total (ton of SCE)	3031485	13276830	601889	4988277

注：各地区数含兵团工业在内。
Note:Figures in different prefectures include data of XPCG enterprises.

6-14 续表 Continued

名称	Variey of Energy	塔城地区 Tacheng [Tarbagatai] Administrative Office	阿勒泰地区 Altay Administrative Offices	巴音郭楞蒙古自治州 Bayangol Mongol Autonomous Prefecture	阿克苏地区 Aksu Administrative Offices
原煤(吨)	Coal (ton)	2348705	690944	2929880	4710045
洗精煤(吨)	Washed Coal (ton)			79467	571788
其他洗煤(吨)	Other Washed Coal (ton)			21079	44960
焦炭(吨)	Coke (ton)	30014	87659	568557	43000
焦炉煤气(万立方米)	Coke Oven Gas (10 000 cu.m)				238
高炉煤气(万立方米)	High Oven Gas (10 000 cu.m)				
天然气(万立方米)	Natural Gas (10 000 cu.m)			202662	73816
原油(吨)	Coal (ton)			778383	2517401
汽油(吨)	Gasoline (ton)	1387	1268	6182	1801
煤油(吨)	Kerosene (ton)		1		
柴油(吨)	Diesel Oil (ton)	5404	29835	30085	14667
燃料油(吨)	Fuel Oil (ton)			1551	16
液化石油气(吨)	Liquefied Petroleum Gas (ton)			14263	11
炼厂干气(吨)	Refinary Dry Gas (ton)			31045	99790
其他石油制品(吨)	Other Oil Product (ton)			465	122075
热力(百万千焦)	Heat (million KJ)	1181314	751	10625649	1848490
电力(万千瓦时)	Electricity (10 000 kwh)	152894	81966	302786	175889
其他燃料(吨标准煤)	Other (ton of SCE)	250		36746	44229
能源合计(吨标准煤)	Energy Total (ton of SCE)	1989050	728472	7305579	9318398

名称	Variey of Energy	克孜勒苏柯尔克孜自治州 Kizilsu Kirgiz Autonomous Prefecture	喀什地区 Kashgar [kaxgar] Administrative Offices	和田地区 Hotan Administrative Offices	石河子市 Shihezi City
原煤(吨)	Coal (ton)	117860	974687	269099	6986117
洗精煤(吨)	Washed Coal (ton)				552418
其他洗煤(吨)	Other Washed Coal (ton)				20
焦炭(吨)	Coke (ton)		128178		763379
焦炉煤气(万立方米)	Coke Oven Gas (10 000 cu.m)				793
高炉煤气(万立方米)	High Oven Gas (10 000 cu.m)				
天然气(万立方米)	Natural Gas (10 000 cu.m)	3464	3197	21	2620
原油(吨)	Coal (ton)				8
汽油(吨)	Gasoline (ton)	323	680	529	788
煤油(吨)	Kerosene (ton)				
柴油(吨)	Diesel Oil (ton)	1937	3069	1448	5582
燃料油(吨)	Fuel Oil (ton)			2	161
液化石油气(吨)	Liquefied Petroleum Gas (ton)				
炼厂干气(吨)	Refinary Dry Gas (ton)				
其他石油制品(吨)	Other Oil Product (ton)	125			52
热力(百万千焦)	Heat (million KJ)				9934577
电力(万千瓦时)	Electricity (10 000 kwh)	12825	47096	27117	959938
其他燃料(吨标准煤)	Other (ton of SCE)		40000		
能源合计(吨标准煤)	Energy Total (ton of SCE)	149458	972850	235726	8062437

主要统计指标解释

能源生产总量 指一定时期内，一个地区一次能源生产量的总和。该指标是观察一个地区能源生产水平、规模、构成和发展速度的总量指标。一次能源生产量包括原煤、原油、天然气、水电、核能及其他动力能(如风能、地热能等)发电量，不包括低热值燃料生产量、生物质能、太阳能等的利用和由一次能源加工转换而成的二次能源产量。

能源消费总量 指一定时期内，一个地区和居民生活消费的各种能源的总和，该指标是观察能源消费水平、构成和增长速度的总量指标。能源消费总量包括原煤和原油及其制品、天然气、电力，不包括低热值燃料、生物质能和太阳能等的利用。能源消费总量分为终端能源消费量、能源加工转换损失量和损失量三部分。

(1)终端能源消费量：指一定时期内，一个地区生产和生活消费的各种能源在扣除了用于加工转换二次能源消费量和损失量以后的数量。

(2)能源加工转换损失量：指一定时期内，一个地区投入加工转换的各种能源数量之和与产出各种能源产品之和的差额，该指标是观察能源在加工转换过程中损失量变化的指标。

(3)能源损失量：指一定时期内，能源在输送、分配、储存过程中发生的损失和由客观原因造成的各种损失量，不包括各种气体能源放空、放散量。

能源生产弹性系数 是研究能源生产增长速度与国民经济增长速度之间关系的指标。计算公式为：

能源生产弹性系数＝能源生产总量年平均增长速度／国民经济年平均增长速度

国民经济年平均增长速度，可根据不同的目的或需要，用国民生产总值、国内生产总值等指标来计算，本年鉴是采用国内生产总值指标计算的。

电力生产弹性系数 是研究电力生产增长速度与国民经济增长速度之间关系的指标。一般来说，电力的发展应当快于国民经济的发展，也就是说电力应超前发展。计算公式为：

电力生产弹性系数＝电力生产量年平均增长速度／国民经济年平均增长速度

能源消费弹性系数 是反映能源消费增长速度与国民经济增长速度之间比例关系的指标。计算公式为：

能源消费弹性系数＝能源消费量年平均增长速度／国民经济年平均增长速度

电力消费弹性系数 反映电力消费增长速度与国民经济增长速度之间比例关系的指标。计算公式为：

电力消费弹性系数＝电力消费量年平均增长速度／国民经济年平均增长速度

能源加工转换效率 指一定时期内，能源经过加工、转换后，产出的各种能源产品的数量与同期内投入加工转换的各种能源数量的比率。该指标是观察能源加工转换装置和生产工艺先进与落后、管理水平高低等的重要指标。计算公式为：

能源加工转换效率＝能源加工、转换产出量／能源加工、转换投入量×100%

单位国内生产总值能耗 指一定时期内，一个国家或地区每生产一个单位的国内生产总值所消耗的能源。计算公式为：

单位国内生产总值能耗=能源消费总量/国内生产总值

单位国内生产总值电耗 指一定时期内，一个国家或地区每生产一个单位的国内生产总值所消耗的电力。计算公式为：

单位国内生产总值电耗=全社会用电量/国内生产总值

单位工业增加值能耗 指一定时期内，一个国家或地区每生产一个单位的工业增加值所消耗的能源。计算公式为：

单位工业增加值能耗=工业能源消费量/工业增加值

Explanatory Notes on Main Statistical Indicators

Total Energy Production refers to the total production of primary energy by all energy producing enterprises in the country in a given period of time. It is a comprehensive indicator to show the level, scale, composition and pace of development of energy production of the country. The production of primary energy includes that of coal, crude oil, natural gas, hydro-power and electricity generated by nuclear energy and other means such as wind power and geothermal power. However, it does not include the production of fuels of low calorific value, bio-energy, solar energy and secondary energy converted from primary energy.

Total Energy Consumption refers to the total consumption of energy of various kinds by the production sectors and the households in the country in a given period of time. It is a comprehensive indicator to show the scale, composition and pace of increase of energy consumption. Total energy consumption includes that of coal, crude oil and their products, natural gas and electricity. However, it does not include the consumption of fuel of low calorific value, bio-energy and solar energy. Total energy consumption can be divided into three parts: end-use energy consumption; loss during the process of energy conversion; and energy loss.

(1)End-use Energy Consumption: It refers to the total energy consumption by the production sectors and the households in the country (region) in a given period of time. It does not include the consumption during the conversion of primary energy into secondary energy and the loss in the process of energy conversion.

(2)Loss During the Process of Energy Conversion: It refers to the total input of various kinds of energy for conversion, minus the total output of various kinds of energy in the country in a given period of time. It is an indicator to show the loss that occurs during the process of energy conversion.

(3)Energy Loss: It refers to the total of the loss of energy during the course of energy transport, distribution and storage and the loss caused by any objective reason in a given period of time. The loss of various kinds of gas due to gas discharges and stocktaking is not included.

Elasticity Ratio of Energy Production is an indicator to show the relationship between the growth rate of energy production and the growth rate of the national economy. The formula is:

$$\text{Elasticity Ratio of Energy Production} = \frac{\text{Average Annual Growth Rate of Energy Production}}{\text{Average Annual Growth Rate of National Economy}}$$

The average annual growth rate of the national economy can be measured by indicators such as the Gross National Product and the Gross Domestic Product, depending on the purposes or needs. The Gross Domestic Product has been used in the calculation of the ratio in this Yearbook.

Elasticity Ratio of Electricity Production is an indicator to show the relationship between the growth rate of electricity production and the growth rate of the national economy. Generally speaking, the growth rate of electricity production should be higher than that of the national economy.

Its formula is:

$$\text{Elasticity Ratio of Electricity Production} = \frac{\text{Average Annual Growth Rate of Electricity Production}}{\text{Average Annual Growth Rate of National Economy}}$$

Elasticity Ratio of Energy Consumption is an indicator to show the relationship between the growth rate of energy consumption and the growth rate of the national economy. The formula is:

$$\text{Elasticity Ratio of Energy Consumption} = \frac{\text{Average Annual Growth Rate of Energy Consumption}}{\text{Average Annual Growth Rate of National Economy}}$$

Elasticity Ratio of Electricity Consumption is an indicator to show the relationship between the growth rate of electricity consumption and the growth rate of the national economy. The formula is:

$$\text{Elasticity Ratio of Electricity Consumption} = \frac{\text{Average Annual Growth Rate of Electricity Consumption}}{\text{Average Annual Growth Rate of National Economy}}$$

Efficiency of Energy Processing and Conversion refers to the ratio of the total output of energy products of various kinds after processing and conversion to the total input of energy of various kinds for processing and conversion in the same reference period. It is an important indicator to show the current conditions of energy processing and conversion equipment, production technique and management. The formula is:

$$\text{Efficiency of Energy Processing \& Conversion} = \frac{\text{Output of Energy After Processing \& Conversion}}{\text{Input of Energy for Processing \& Conversion}} \times 100\%$$

Energy Consumption per Unit of GDP refers to the energy consumption per unit of Gross Domestic Product in a country or the Gross Regional Product in a region in the same reference period. The formula is:

$$\text{Energy Consumption per Unit of GDP} = \frac{\text{Total Energy Consumption}}{\text{Gross Domestic Product}}$$

Electricity Consumption per Unit of GDP refers to the electricity consumption per unit of Gross Domestic Product in a country or the Gross Regional Product in a region in the same reference period. The formula is:

$$\text{Electricity Consumption per Unit of GDP} = \frac{\text{Total Electricity Consumption}}{\text{Gross Domestic Product}}$$

Energy Consumption per Unit of Industrial Value-added refers to the energy consumption per unit of industrial value-added in a country or region in the same reference period. The formula is:

$$\text{Energy Consumptionper Unit Of Industrial Value-added} = \frac{\text{energy consumption of industry}}{\text{Industrial Value-added}}$$

2012

新疆统计年鉴

XINJIANG STATISTICAL YEARBOOK

第七篇
财政、金融和保险

CHAPTER 7
Government Finance, Financial Intermediation and Insurance

简要说明
Brief Introduction

本篇资料的主要内容及来源

本篇反映自治区财政、金融、证券和保险业发展情况，有以下四个部分：一是地方财政预算收支情况；二是金融机构存贷等活动情况；三是保险业务情况；四是证券上市情况。

地方财政预算收支情况取自新疆维吾尔自治区财政厅年度总决算；金融资料来自中国人民银行乌鲁木齐中心支行金融机构信贷统计月报及年报；保险业务情况资料取自中国保险监督管理委员会新疆监管局编制的保险统计资料；证券及上市公司情况来自新疆证监会。

本篇章数据由新疆维吾尔自治区统计局国民经济综合统计处根据上述部门所提供的资料整理。

Main Content and Source of Data

The data in this chapter show the development of Xinjiang Uygur Autonomous region government finance, banking, securities and insurance, in the following 4 aspects(1)The government revenue and expenditure;(2)The financial activities of banking institutions;(3)The business of insurance;(4)The condition of listed securities.Data on the government revenue and expenditure come from the final state financial accounts, Data on financial intermediation come from the credit funds sheet of financial institutions of Urumqi municipal sub-branches, People's Bank of China; Data on insurance come from Xinjiang Insurance Regulatory Bureau of CIRC. Data on listed securities are from Xinjiang Security Regulatory Bureau of CSRC.Data in this chapter are compiled and collected by the Division of comprehensive of the Xinjing Bureau of Statistics on the basis of data from the relative departments.

7-1 主要年份地方财政一般预算收支及增长速度
The General Budgetary Revenue & Expenses and Growth Rate of Local Finance in Main Years

单位：万元 (10 000 yuan)

年 份 Year	地方财政一般预算收入 General Budgetary Revenue in Local Finance	地方财政一般预算支出 General Budgetary Expenditure in Local Finance	收支差额 Balance	指数(上年=100) Indices (precding year=100)	
				地方财政一般预算收入 General Budgetary Revenue in Local Finance	地方财政一般预算支出 General Budgetary Expenditure in Local Finance
1978	71416	170169	-98753	196.5	153.3
1980	40309	162159	-121850	73.4	95.4
1985	84663	286031	-201368	117.2	122.6
1990	217784	476210	-258426	118.9	114.2
1995	382818	964021	-581203	133.4	135.6
2000	790724	1909529	-1118805	110.9	114.8
2001	950933	2633232	-1682299	120.3	137.9
2002	1164724	3611729	-2447005	122.5	137.2
2003	1282218	3684676	-2402458	110.1	102.0
2004	1557040	4210446	-2653406	121.4	114.3
2005	1803184	5190179	-3386995	115.8	123.3
2006	2194628	6784723	-4590095	121.7	130.7
2007	2858600	7951540	-5092940	130.3	117.2
2008	3610616	10593638	-6983022	126.3	133.2
2009	3887848	13469125	-9581277	107.7	127.1
2010	5005759	16989126	-11983367	128.8	126.1
2011	7204324	22844864	-15640540	143.9	134.5

7-2 主要年份地方财政一般预算收入占新疆生产总值的比重
Ration of the General Budgetary Revenue in Local Finance to GDP of Xinjiang in Main Years

单位：亿元 (100 million yuan)

年 份 Year	地方财政一般预算收入 General Budgetary Revenue in Local Finance	新疆生产总值 Gross Domestic Product in Xinjiang	地方财政一般预算收入相当于新疆生产总值的比例(%) Proportion of Local Financial Revenue to GDP of Xinjiang (%)
1978	7.14	39.07	18.27
1980	4.03	53.24	7.57
1985	8.47	112.24	7.56
1990	21.78	261.44	8.34
1995	38.28	814.85	4.70
2000	79.07	1363.56	5.80
2001	95.09	1491.60	6.37
2002	116.47	1612.65	7.22
2003	128.22	1886.35	6.79
2004	155.70	2209.09	7.05
2005	180.32	2604.14	6.92
2006	219.46	3045.26	7.21
2007	285.86	3523.16	8.11
2008	361.06	4183.21	8.63
2009	388.78	4277.05	9.09
2010	500.58	5437.47	9.21
2011	720.43	6610.05	10.90

7-3 地方财政收支情况

Statistics on Total Government Revenue and Expenditures in Local Finance

单位：万元 (10 000 yuan)

项　　目	Item	2010	2011
收入合计	**Total Revenue**	**6932683**	**10404200**
地方财政一般预算收入	General Budgetary Revenue in Local Finance	5005759	7204324
税收收入	Taxes Revenue	4162343	5934094
增值税	Value-added Tax	753113	966950
营业税	Business Tax	1512668	2098421
企业所得税（含退税）	Corporate Income Tax	400152	634266
个人所得税	Individual Income Tax	273834	383380
资源税	Resources Tax	324678	650089
城市维护建设税	City Maintenance and Construction Tax	318406	412565
房产税	House Property Tax	123506	146694
契　税	Contract Tax	152583	218633
其他税收收入	Other Revenues	303403	423096
非税收入	Non-tax Revenues	843416	1270230
专项收入	Special Program Receipts	324350	463920
行政性收费收入	Charge of Administrative and Institutional Units	196106	365662
罚没收入	Penalty Receipts	123790	139960
其他收入	Other Revenues	199170	300688
基金预算收入	Fund Budgetary Revenues	1926924	3199876
支出合计	**Total Expenditures**	**18855622**	**25996664**
地方财政一般预算支出	General Budgetary Expenditure in Local Finance	16989126	22844864
一般公共服务	Expenditure for General Public Services	1955676	2453616
教　育	Expenditure for Education	3138356	3998031
科学技术	Expenditure for Science and Technology	201869	264349
文化体育与传媒	Expenditure for Culture Sports and Media	339222	477003
社会保障和就业	Expenditure for Social Safety Net and Employment Effort	1664041	2016411
医疗卫生	Expenditure for Medical and Health Care	1035599	1324305
节能环保	Expenditure for Environmental Protection	510155	536738
城乡社区事务	Expenditure for Urban and Rural Community Affairs	952755	1401039
农林水事务	Expenditure for Agriculture, Forestry and Water Conservancy	2204962	2975868
交通运输	Expenditure for Transportation	915385	2068252
资源勘探电力信息等事务	Expenditure for Miming and Quarrying,Electriaty and Information Technology	385301	475963
其他各项支出	Other Expenditures	3685805	4853289
基金预算支出	Fund Budgetary Expenditure	1866496	3151800

7-4 各地、州、市、县(市)地方财政一般预算收支

Government Revenue and Expenditures by Prefecture, Autonomous Prefecture, City and County

单位：万元　　(2011 年)　　(10 000 yuan)

地　区	Region	收　入 Revenue	支　出 Expenditures
总　计	**Total**	**7204324**	**22844864**
自治区本级	Autonomous regional Level	908934	6275338
乌鲁木齐市	**Urumqi City and Changji Prefecture**	**2062035**	**2384851**
乌鲁木齐市本级	Urumqi and Changji Level	1221069	1368457
乌鲁木齐县	Urumqi County	24169	64589
天山区	Tianshan District	163476	181020
沙依巴克区	Shayibak District	127578	158261
新市区	Xinshi District	123041	131320
水磨沟区	Shui Mogou District	134094	149743
头屯河区	Tou Tunhe District	61997	66892
米东区	Midong District	162786	195432
达坂城区	Da Bancheng District	43825	69137
昌吉回族自治州	Changji Hui Autonomous Prefecture	**482221**	**1213830**
昌吉州本级	Changji Prefecture Level	42428	193707
昌吉市	Changji City	161803	247955
阜康市	Fukang City	85967	158386
呼图壁县	Hutubi County	39489	116392
玛纳斯县	Manas County	43289	109329
奇台县	Qitai County	47006	166403
吉木萨尔县	Jimsar County	47505	122921
木垒哈萨克自治县	Mori Kazak Autonomous County	14734	98737
克拉玛依市	**Karamay City**	**509650**	**633033**
市本级	City Level	322200	368390
克拉玛依区	Karamay District	110010	130430
独山子区	Dushanzi District	50493	82539
白碱滩区	Bai Jiantan District	21249	40816
乌尔河区	Urhe District	5698	10858
吐鲁番地区	**Turpan Administrative Offices**	**203580**	**452426**
地区本级	Prefecture Level	40223	63794
吐鲁番市	Turpan City	48796	136192
鄯善县	Shanshan [Piqan] County	76775	148736
托克逊县	Toksun County	37786	103704
哈密地区	**Hami [Kumul] Administrative Offices**	**235153**	**562908**
地区本级	Prefecture Level	11835	128459
哈密市	Hami [Kumul] City	187218	260267
巴里坤哈萨克自治县	Barkol Kazak Autonomous County	20716	110935
伊吾县	Yiwu [Araturuk] County	15384	63247
伊犁哈萨克自治州	**Ili Kazak Autonomous Prefecture**	**904482**	**3477638**
伊犁州直属县(市)	**Counties (Cities) Direct Under Ili Prefecture**	**446529**	**1697966**
州本级	Autonomous Prefecture Level	28225	196512
伊宁市	Yining [Gulja] City	140904	281702
奎屯市	Kuytun City	109119	156992
伊宁县	Yining [Gulja] County	28865	182311
察布查尔锡伯自治县	Qapqal Xibe Autonomous County	20003	126242
霍城县	Huocheng [Korgas] County	23673	146876

7-4 续表 1 Continued

单位：万元 (10 000 yuan)

地　区	Region	收 入 Revenue	支 出 Expenditures
巩留县	Gongliu [Tokkuztara] County	11500	118755
新源县	Xinyuan [Kunes] County	39403	147855
昭苏县	Zhaosu [Mongolkure] County	8207	120414
特克斯县	Tekes County	9559	107463
尼勒克县	Nilka County	27071	112844
塔城地区	**Tacheng [Tarbagatai] Administrative Office**	**257936**	**899382**
地区本级	Prefecture Level	5813	62304
塔城市	Tacheng [Qoqek] City	27186	116460
乌苏市	Usu City	63387	178351
额敏县	Emin [Dorbiljin] County	17335	117388
沙湾县	Shawan County	40585	138446
托里县	Toli County	20153	94002
裕民县	Yumin [Qagantokay] County	3516	64159
和布克赛尔蒙古自治县	Hoboksar Mongol Autonomous County	79961	128272
阿勒泰地区	**Altay Administrative Offices**	**200017**	**880290**
地区本级	Prefecture Level	23084	117920
阿勒泰市	Altay City	24027	151201
布尔津县	Burqin County	12836	82642
富蕴县	Fuyun [Koktokay] County	67381	148875
福海县	Fuhai [Burultokay] County	16366	85942
哈巴河县	Habahe [Kaba] County	35648	108426
青河县	Qinghe [Qinggil] County	17745	113896
吉木乃县	Jeminay County	2930	71388
博尔塔拉蒙古自治州	**Bortala Mongol Autonomous Prefecture**	**82127**	**410284**
州本级	Autonomous Prefecture Level	23749	129798
博乐市	Bole [Bortala] City	40080	119795
精河县	Jinghe [Jing] County	13901	92132
温泉县	Wenquan [Araxang] County	4397	68559
巴音郭楞蒙古自治州	**Bayangol Mongol Autonomous Prefecture**	**491289**	**1281237**
州本级	Autonomous Prefecture Level	48968	196751
库尔勒市	Korla City	210035	325879
轮台县	Luntai [Bugur] County	62092	100094
尉犁县	Yuli [Lopnur] County	13508	77942
若羌县	Ruoqiang [Qarkilik] County	43864	96812
且末县	Qiemo [Qarqan] County	30218	112473
焉耆回族自治县	Yanqi Hui Autonomous County	17645	89283
和静县	Hejing County	46970	155198
和硕县	Hoxud County	9946	67414
博湖县	Bohu [Bagrax] County	8043	59391
阿克苏地区	**Aksu Administrative Offices**	**621052**	**1576440**
地区本级	Prefecture Level	21005	167970
阿克苏市	Aksu City	109909	213794
温宿县	Wensu [Onsu] County	22901	139187

7-4 续表 2 Continued

单位：万元 (10 000 yuan)

地　　区	Region	收入 Revenue	支出 Expenditure
库车县	Kuqa County	260766	344461
沙雅县	Xayar County	70820	140393
新和县	Xinhe [Toksu] County	41899	120969
拜城县	Baicheng [Bay] County	75445	150003
乌什县	Wushi [Uxturpan] County	6745	121363
阿瓦提县	Awat County	9151	120800
柯坪县	Kalpin County	2411	57500
克孜勒苏柯尔克孜自治州	**Kizilsu Kirgiz Autonomous Prefecture**	**55227**	**552425**
州本级	Autonomous Prefecture Level	8269	107184
阿图什市	Artux City	14789	136088
阿克陶县	Akto County	14214	148535
阿合奇县	Akqi County	4452	68833
乌恰县	Wuqia [Ulugqat] County	13503	91785
喀什地区	**Kashgar [Kaxgar] Administrative Offices**	**287506**	**2409603**
地区本级	Prefecture Level	10960	171605
喀什市	Kashgar [Kaxgar] City	104278	416923
疏附县	Shufu County	11333	154117
疏勒县	Shule County	20167	142388
英吉沙县	Yengisar County	9349	131719
泽普县	Zepu [Poskam] County	16267	122794
莎车县	Shache [Yarkant] County	24006	359489
叶城县	Yecheng [Kagilik] County	23710	246736
麦盖提县	Makit County	15030	123942
岳普湖县	Yopurga County	6293	98341
伽师县	Jiashi [Payzawat] County	21387	190173
巴楚县	Bachu [Maralbexi] County	17331	174381
塔什库尔干塔吉克自治县	Taxkorgan Tajik Autonomous County	7395	76995
和田地区	**Hotan Administrative Offices**	**93231**	**1256735**
地区本级	Prefecture Level	9593	119509
和田市	Hotan City	32272	176836
和田县	Hotan County	9619	138841
墨玉县	Moyu [Karakax] County	12170	220989
皮山县	Pishan [Guma] County	7960	146568
洛浦县	Lop County	5938	125000
策勒县	Qira County	4930	116305
于田县	Yutian [Keriya] County	6625	146616
民丰县	Minfeng [Niya] County	4124	66071
自治区直辖县级市	**Municpality Country-LevelCity directly under the Central Govern-ment**	**267837**	**358116**
石河子市	Shihezi City	192822	252565
阿拉尔市	Aral City	26682	34539
图木舒克市	Tumxuk City	10670	21356
五家渠市	Wujiaqu City	37663	49656

7-5 1978-2011 年历年金融机构各项存款和各项贷款余额

Banlance of Deposits and Loans of National Banking System (1978-2011)

单位：亿元 (100 million yuan)

年 份 Year	各项存款合计 Total Deposits	#单位存款 Deposits by Units	#储蓄存款 Savings Deposit	各项贷款合计 Total Loans
1978	32.07	6.86	6.42	18.26
1979	33.44	7.03	7.21	21.19
1980	38.56	9.60	9.52	24.74
1981	45.59	12.21	12.29	28.84
1982	53.47	15.23	15.30	32.86
1983	61.94	17.95	19.01	38.85
1984	73.63	23.35	24.31	52.02
1985	82.96	29.87	29.55	72.68
1986	102.75	38.15	40.37	93.18
1987	124.93	44.13	53.25	111.14
1988	141.10	47.41	66.25	139.43
1989	167.03	52.76	83.33	173.02
1990	221.80	71.23	114.13	233.72
1991	282.21	92.78	145.01	299.59
1992	336.58	119.51	175.62	380.26
1993	397.39	129.98	220.45	467.81
1994	634.44	214.13	347.71	632.32
1995	838.42	274.24	477.18	843.38
1996	1012.47	364.51	575.79	1016.20
1997	1180.78	442.76	676.13	1215.39
1998	1336.58	461.02	759.14	1318.41
1999	1548.72	544.22	824.68	1386.78
2000	1863.48	702.21	908.55	1403.13
2001	1972.55	691.74	994.00	1584.73
2002	2225.31	705.82	1137.87	1801.15
2003	2661.65	763.49	1371.59	2099.09
2004	2959.78	832.50	1534.67	2214.66
2005	3427.48	909.45	1816.38	2272.08
2006	4040.78	1106.42	2035.63	2412.69
2007	4614.62	1452.25	2054.91	2685.00
2008	5399.34	1473.24	2550.95	2826.53
2009	6845.07	2043.54	3049.91	3782.92
2010	8870.72	2791.72	3713.47	4973.16
2011	10387.00	5573.38	4421.93	6270.21

注：单位存款 2010 年及以前年份为企业存款。
Note: Before 2010 the deposits of units refer to the deposits of enterprises.

7-6 金融机构和人员数
Number of Financial Institutions and Staff

单位：个、人 (2011 年) (unit, person)

项 目	Item	合 计 Total		自治区级 Level of Autonomous Region		地区级 Prefectural Level	
		机 构 Institutions	人 员 Employees	机 构 Institutions	人 员 Employees	机 构 Institutions	人 员 Employees
总 计	**Total**	**3381**	**60331**	**19**	**4681**	**144**	**15365**
人民银行	**The People's Bank of China**	**68**	**3533**	**1**	**440**	**14**	**1819**
银监会新疆监管局	**China Banking Regulatory Commission Xingjiang Bureau**	**55**	**910**	**1**	**145**	**14**	**622**
中资全国性大型银行	**Large National Bank of Chinese Investment**	**1878**	**36151**	**9**	**3384**	**77**	**10017**
工商银行	Industrial and Commercial Bank	291	8589	1	711	15	3015
农业银行	Agricultural Bank	364	8388	1	346	15	2417
农业银行兵团分行	Agricultural Bank, XPCG Branch	252	3888	1	252	3	502
中国银行	Bank of China	164	3861	1	736	13	1050
建设银行	Bank of Construction	190	5684	1	732	14	2164
国家开发银行	State Development Bank	1	143	1	143		
中国进出口银行	Export and Import Bank of China	1	29	1	29		
交通银行	Bank of Communication	28	829	1	338	1	42
邮政储蓄银行	Postal Savings Bank	587	4740	1	97	16	827
中资全国性中小银行	**Small and Medium-sized National Bank of Chinese Investment**	**156**	**4694**	**4**	**448**	**25**	**1623**
农业发展银行	Agricultural Development Bank	90	2383	1	158	17	726
中信银行`	China Citic Bank	3	160			1	119
光大银行	Guang Da Bank	1	72			1	72
华夏银行	Hua Xia Bank	6	225			1	138
招商银行	Merchants Bank	11	431			1	230
浦发银行	Shanghai PuDong Development Bank	10	284	1	153	1	19
兴业银行	Xing Ye Bank	9	341	1	116		
昆仑银行	KunLun Bank	26	798	1	21	3	319
中资区域性中小银行	**Small and Medium-sized Regional Bank of Chinese Investment**	**164**	**2920**			**10**	**990**
城市商业银行	City Commercial Bank	129	2335			9	961
农村商业银行	Rural Commercila Bank	4	64			1	29
村镇银行	County Bank	14	270				
农村合作银行	Rural Cooperation Bank	17	251				
外资银行	**Foreign Bank**	**2**	**93**			**1**	**83**
农村信用社	**Rural Credit Cooperative**	**1052**	**11702**	**1**	**147**		
财务公司	**Finance Company**	**1**	**13**			**1**	**13**
信托投资公司	**Trust and Investment Company**	**1**	**123**			**1**	**123**
金融租赁公司	**Financial Leasing Company**	**1**	**75**			**1**	**75**
资产管理公司	**Assets Management Company**	**3**	**117**	**3**	**117**		
信达公司	Xinda Firm	1	32	1	32		
华融公司	Huarong Firm	1	42	1	42		
长城公司	Great Wall Firm	1	43	1	43		

7-6 续表 Continued

单位：个、人 (unit, person)

项　目	Item	县　级 County Level		营业网点 Business Outlets	
		机 构 Institutions	人 员 Employees	机 构 Institutions	人 员 Employees
总　计	**Total**	**950**	**21735**	**2268**	**18550**
人民银行	**The People's Bank of China**	**53**	**1274**		
银监会新疆监管局	**China Banking Regulatory Commission Xingjiang Bureau**	**40**	**143**		
中资全国性大型银行	**Large National Bank of Chinese Investment**	**657**	**13668**	**1135**	**9082**
工商银行	Industrial and Commercial Bank	216	4167	59	696
农业银行	Agricultural Bank	146	3589	202	2036
农业银行兵团分行	Agricultural Bank, XPCG Branch	40	1128	208	2006
中国银行	Bank of China	33	843	117	1232
建设银行	Bank of Construction	62	1441	113	1347
国家开发银行	State Development Bank				
中国进出口银行	Export and Import Bank of China				
交通银行	Bank of Communication	26	449		
邮政储蓄银行	Postal Savings Bank	134	2051	436	1765
中资全国性中小银行	**Small and Medium-sized National Bank of Chinese Investment**	**104**	**2128**	**23**	**495**
农业发展银行	Agricultural Development Bank	72	1499		
中信银行`	China Citic Bank	2	41		
光大银行	Guang Da Bank				
华夏银行	Hua Xia Bank			5	87
招商银行	Merchants Bank			10	201
浦发银行	Shanghai PuDong Development Bank	8	112		
兴业银行	Xing Ye Bank	1	33	7	192
昆仑银行	KunLun Bank	21	443	1	15
中资区域性中小银行	**Small and Medium-sized Regional Bank of Chinese Investment**	**13**	**478**	**141**	**1452**
城市商业银行	City Commercial Bank	2	134	118	1240
农村商业银行	Rural Commercila Bank	3	35		
村镇银行	County Bank	7	207	7	63
农村合作银行	Rural Cooperation Bank	1	102	16	149
外资银行	**Foreign Bank**			**1**	**10**
农村信用社	**Rural Credit Cooperative**	**83**	**4044**	**968**	**7511**
财务公司	**Finance Company**				
信托投资公司	**Trust and Investment Company**				
金融租赁公司	**Financial Leasing Company**				
资产管理公司	**Assets Management Company**				
信达公司	Xinda Firm				
华融公司	Huarong Firm				
长城公司	Great Wall Firm				

7-7 金融机构人民币信贷资金平衡表
Balance Sheet of Credit Funds of Financial Institutions

单位：亿元 (100 million yuan)

项　　目	Item	2011
资金来源合计	**All Sources**	**9863.79**
各项存款	Total Deposits	10387.00
单位存款	Deposits by Enterprises	5573.38
活期存款	Current Deposits	4046.86
定期存款	Time Deposits	859.92
个人存款	Personal Desposits	4431.19
#储蓄存款	Savings Desposits	4421.93
其他存款	Other Desposits	382.43
中长期借款	Medium and Long-term Loans	33.05
应付及暂收款	Payable and Temporary Collection	159.60
同业往来(来源方)	Inter-bank Transactions	57.28
外汇买卖(来源方)	Foreign Exchange Trading	425.27
各项准备金	Various Preparations	143.28
所有者权益	Owner's Right and Interest	431.69
其　他	Others	-1773.38
资金运用合计	**All Uses**	**9863.79**
各项贷款	Total Loans	6270.21
#境内贷款	Domestic Loans	6269.94
短期贷款	Short-term Loans	2250.61
个人贷款及透支	Personal loans and overdrafts	420.42
#个人消费贷款	Personal Consumption Loans	22.00
单位贷款及透支	Unit loans and overdrafts	1635.67
#经营贷款	Loans to Business	1627.43
固定资产贷款	Loans to fixed Assets	8.07
银团贷款	Syndicated Loans	104.28
贸易融资	Trade finance	90.18
境外筹资转贷款	Overseas Financing Loans	0.07
中长期贷款	Medium & Long-term Loans	3757.93
个人贷款	Personal loans	860.32
#个人消费贷款	Personal Consumption Loans	581.81
单位普通贷款	Common Unit Loans	2397.50
#经营贷款	Loans to Business	621.39
固定资产贷款	Loans to fixed Assets	1776.11
普通并购贷款	Ordinary　Loans	11.00
银团贷款	Syndicated Loans	488.15
境外筹资转贷款	Overseas Financing Loans	0.96
融资租赁	Finance leasing	92.44
票据融资	Bills financing	168.04
各项垫付	The various funds	0.92
境外贷款	Foreign Loans	0.27
有价证券及投资	Portfolio Investment	421.70
系统内资金往来(运用方)	Capital Transaction inside the System	2331.16
外汇买卖（运用方）	Foreign Exchang Trading	425.53
固定资产	Fixed assets	125.31
其　他	Others	289.88

7-8 各地区金融机构存贷款年底余额
Deposits and Loans of Financial Institution by Region

单位：亿元 (2011 年) (100 million yuan)

项 目	Item	各项存款余额 Balance of Deposits	#单位存款 #Deposits by Units	各项贷款余额 Banlance of Loans	#中长期贷款 #Medium and Long-term
总 计	**Total**	**10386.99**	**5573.35**	**6270.21**	**3757.93**
乌鲁木齐市	Urumqi City	4080.50	2308.78	2553.98	1588.56
克拉玛依市	Karamay City	860.80	860.80	132.67	83.23
吐鲁番地区	Turpan Administrative Offices	148.94	59.02	82.84	47.15
哈密地区	Hami [Kumul] Administrative Offices	315.25	145.95	153.28	104.48
昌吉回族自治州	Changji Hui Autonomous Prefecture	655.02	312.42	435.34	209.10
博尔塔拉蒙古自治州	Bortala Mongol Autonomous Prefecture	195.26	98.08	92.26	24.38
巴音郭楞蒙古自治州	Bayangol Mongol Autonomous Prefecture	664.86	294.89	361.56	150.25
阿克苏地区	Aksu Administrative Offices	699.13	318.32	358.82	145.09
克孜勒苏柯尔克孜自治州	Kizilsu Kirgiz Autonomous Prefecture	92.33	55.89	29.71	15.90
喀什地区	Kashgar [Kaxgar] Administrative Offices	698.78	373.30	217.10	117.83
和田地区	Hotan Administrative Offices	274.72	161.73	55.17	29.23
伊犁哈萨克自治州直属	Ili Kazak Autonomous Prefecture	708.29	328.25	349.49	170.33
塔城地区	Tacheng [Tarbagatai] Administrative Offices	303.52	117.54	158.68	50.83
阿勒泰地区	Altay Administrative Offices	239.94	139.08	95.38	51.86
石河子市	Shihezi City	356.19	127.57	248.05	74.36

7-9 个人消费贷款情况
Basic Conditons of Personal Consumption Loans

单位：亿元 (100 million yuan)

项 目	Item	2010	2011
个人消费贷款	**Personal Consumption Loans**	**457.76**	**603.81**
短期个人消费贷款	Short-term Loans for Personal Consumption	17.36	22.00
住房贷款	Housing Loans	0.56	0.83
汽车贷款	Auto Loans	0.20	0.13
其他贷款	Other Loans	11.64	13.10
个人卡透支	Personalized Card is Overdrawn	4.96	7.94
长期个人消费贷款	Long-term Loans for Personal Consumption	440.40	581.81
住房贷款	Housing Loans	376.58	496.23
汽车贷款	Auto Loans	14.08	16.32
助学贷款	Student Loans	0.88	0.73
其他贷款	Other Loans	48.86	65.36

7-10 主要年份国内保险业务情况

Conditions of Domestic Insurance Service in Main Years

单位：亿元 (100 million yuan)

年 份 Year	承保额 Amount Insured		保 费 Premium		赔款及给付 Claim and Payment	
	财产险 Property Insurance	人身险 Life Insurance	财产险 Property Insurance	人身险 Life Insurance	财产险 Property Insurance	人身险 Life Insurance
1980	4		0.01			
1985	70	2	0.40	0.01	0.15	…
1990	241	41	1.04	0.53	0.47	0.08
1995	613	168	4.59	2.06	2.38	0.41
2000	1612	1711	12.49	15.72	5.99	3.72
2001	2112	1371	14.17	19.98	7.43	4.37
2002	2283	3524	16.48	35.25	7.84	5.02
2003	5588	1362	19.12	43.06	10.36	7.10
2004	6401	1735	20.04	48.09	10.65	7.70
2005	8949	9418	20.93	51.57	12.60	7.65
2006	8333	27028	24.61	60.79	12.92	10.34
2007	12188	13081	34.67	70.95	18.78	18.64
2008	13641	17555	44.25	108.26	23.61	20.79
2009	16296	19819	51.82	104.87	26.60	21.51
2010	17431	18129	63.00	127.92	29.21	20.12
2011	23575	13649	78.51	125.11	34.24	23.24

7-11 保险业务经济技术指标

Economic and Technical Indicators of Insurance Company

单位：万元 (10 000 yuan)

项 目	Item	保 费 Premium		赔款及给付 Claim and Payment	
		2010	2011	2010	2011
财产保险业务	**Property Insurance Companies**	**630010**	**785100**	**292149**	**342350**
企业财产险	Insurance of Enterprise Property	43282	54112	14045	17104
家庭财产险	Insurance of Family Property	5018	6534	1278	735
机动车辆险	Insurance of Mobile Vehicles	390415	492578	178104	225335
工程保险	Engineering Insurance	9861	25790	3291	5771
责任保险	Insurance of Liability	22343	30346	7223	8030
信用保险	Insurance of Credit	-3		13	
保证保险	Insurance of Guaranty	11715	13128	1061	1427
船舶险	Insurance of Snip	3	5		
货物运输险	Insurance of Cargo Transportation	7747	10153	1408	1635
特殊风险保险	Special insurance against risk	980	62	467	748
农业保险	Insurance of Agriculture	138642	152358	85257	81570
其他险	Other Insurance	6	33		-4
人身保险业务	**Life Insurance Companies**	**1279229**	**1251055**	**201203**	**232443**
寿 险	Life Insurance	1086009	1028580	131278	155002
健康险	Health Insurance	143927	153246	58355	62381
人身意外伤害险	Unforeseen Human Injury Insurance	49292	69229	11569	15059

7-12 新疆辖区保险机构

Number of Insurance Institutions in Xinjiang

单位：个 (2011 年) (unit)

项目	Item	机构数 Number of Institution	自治区分公司 Xinjiang Branch Company
总计	**Total**	**1514**	**27**
中国人民财产保险股份有限公司	The People's Insurance Corporation Ltd.of china	450	1
中国人寿保险股份有限公司	The Life Insurance Corporation Ltd.of China	377	1
中国大地财产保险股份有限公司	Da Di Property Insurance Corporation Ltd of China	13	1
中华联合财产保险股份有限公司	The Pacific Insurance Corporation Ltd.Property Insruance Company of China	234	1
中国太平洋财产保险股份有限公司	The Pacific Insurance Corporation Ltd., Property Insurance Company of China	18	1
中国太平洋人寿保险股份有限公司	The Pacific Insurance Corporation Ltd.,Life Insurance Company of China	30	1
中国平安财产保险股份有限公司	The Ping An Insurance Corporation Ltd., Property Insurance Company of China	43	1
中国平安人寿保险股份有限公司	The Ping An Insurance Corporation Ltd.,Life Insurance Company of China	65	1
新华人寿保险股份有限公司	Xin Hua Life Insurance Corporation Ltd.	44	1
泰康人寿保险股份有限公司	Tai Kang Life Insurance Corporation Ltd.	63	1
天安保险股份有限公司	Tian An Property Insurance Corporation Ltd.	14	1
永安财产保险股份有限公司	Yong An Property Insurance Corporation Ltd.	53	1
太平人寿保险有限公司	Taiping Life Insurance Corporation Ltd.	6	1
中银保险有限公司	Zhongyin Insurance Corporation Ltd.	1	1
生命人寿保险股份有限公司	The Life Insurance Corporation Ltd.	1	1
永诚财产保险股份有限公司	Yong chen Insurance Corporation Ltd.	2	1
平安养老保险股份有限公司	The Pingan Old-age Pension Insurance Company	1	1
合众人寿保险股份有限公司	Union Life Insurance Corporation Ltd.	12	1
中国人民健康保险股份有限公司	PICC Health Insurance Corporation Ltd.	6	1
阳光财产保险股份有限公司	Sunshine Property Insurance Corporation Ltd.	23	1
都邦财产保险股份有限公司	Du-bang Property Insurance Corporation Ltd.	1	1
渤海财产保险股份有限公司	Bohai Property Insurance Corporation Ltd.	4	1
中国人民人寿保险股份有限公司	PICC Life Insurance Corporation Ltd.of China	19	1
中国人寿财产保险股份有限公司	The Life Insurance Corporation Ltd.,Property Insurance Company	1	1
阳光人寿保险股份有限公司	The Sun of Life Insurance Corporation Ltd.	3	1
信达财产保险股份有限公司	Xinda Property Insurance Corporation Ltd.	2	1
安邦财产保险股份有限公司	An Bang Property Insurance Corporation Ltd.	28	1

7-12 续表 Continued

单位：个　　(2011 年)　　(unit)

项　　目	Item	地区级中心支公司 Branch Company at Prefecture Level	县　级支公司 Branch Company at County Level	营　销服务部 Marke-Ting Depart-ment
总　计	**Total**	**174**	**416**	**897**
中国人民财产保险股份有限公司	The People's Insurance Corporation Ltd.of china	15	94	340
中国人寿保险股份有限公司	The Life Insurance Corporation Ltd.of China	15	68	293
中国大地财产保险股份有限公司	Da Di Property Insurance Corporation Ltd of China	1	1	10
中华联合财产保险股份有限公司	The Pacific Insurance Corporation Ltd.Property Insruance Company of China	16	145	72
中国太平洋财产保险股份有限公司	The Pacific Insurance Corporation Ltd., Property Insurance Company of China	8	9	
中国太平洋人寿保险股份有限公司	The Pacific Insurance Corporation Ltd.,Life Insurance Company of China	8	19	2
中国平安财产保险股份有限公司	The Ping An Insurance Corporation Ltd., Property Insurance Company of China	14	11	17
中国平安人寿保险股份有限公司	The Ping An Insurance Corporation Ltd.,Life Insurance Company of China	12	12	40
新华人寿保险股份有限公司	Xin Hua Life Insurance Corporation Ltd.	10	10	23
泰康人寿保险股份有限公司	Tai Kang Life Insurance Corporation Ltd.	11	16	35
天安保险股份有限公司	Tian An Property Insurance Corporation Ltd.	6		7
永安财产保险股份有限公司	Yong An Property Insurance Corporation Ltd.	14	2	36
太平人寿保险有限公司	Taiping Life Insurance Corporation Ltd.	4	1	
中银保险有限公司	Zhongyin Insurance Corporation Ltd.			
生命人寿保险股份有限公司	The Life Insurance Corporation Ltd.			
永诚财产保险股份有限公司	Yong chen Insurance Corporation Ltd.	1		
平安养老保险股份有限公司	The Pingan Old-age Pension Insurance Company			
合众人寿保险股份有限公司	Union Life Insurance Corporation Ltd.	7	4	
中国人民健康保险股份有限公司	PICC Health Insurance Corporation Ltd.	1		4
阳光财产保险股份有限公司	Sunshine Property Insurance Corporation Ltd.	6	10	6
都邦财产保险股份有限公司	Du-bang Property Insurance Corporation Ltd.			
渤海财产保险股份有限公司	Bohai Property Insurance Corporation Ltd.	3		
中国人民人寿保险股份有限公司	PICC Life Insurance Corporation Ltd.of China	10	8	
中国人寿财产保险股份有限公司	The Life Insurance Corporation Ltd.,Property Insurance Company			
阳光人寿保险股份有限公司	The Sun of Life Insurance Corporation Ltd.	2		
信达财产保险股份有限公司	Xinda Property Insurance Corporation Ltd.	1		
安邦财产保险股份有限公司	An Bang Property Insurance Corporation Ltd.	9	6	12

7-13 新疆辖区保险事业发展情况

Statistics on Development of Insurance in Xinjiang

单位：万元　　(2011 年)　　(10 000 yuan)

项　目	Item	承保额(亿元) Amount Insured (100 million yuan)	保 费 Premium	赔款及给付 Claim and Payment
总　计	**Total**	**37224.54**	**2036154.79**	**574792.91**
产险公司小计	**Sub-total**	**25336.35**	**849358.88**	**368650.07**
中国人民财产保险股份有限公司	The People's Insurance Corporation Ltd.of China	11035.57	445769.65	181862.00
中华联合财产保险股份有限公司	The Property Insurance Corporation Ltd.XPCG	5811.50	183850.68	95352.37
中国平安财产保险股份有限公司	The Ping An Insurance Corporation Ltd., Property Insurance Company of China	3852.73	82782.41	32546.23
中国太平洋财产保险股份有限公司	The Pacific Insurance Corporation Ltd., Property Insurance Company of China	2181.17	55963.23	26366.91
永安财产保险股份有限公司	Yong An Property Insurance Corporation Ltd.	496.59	21531.92	8812.61
天安保险股份有限公司	Tian An Property Insurance Corporation Ltd.	180.48	7437.83	4071.60
安邦财产保险股份有限公司	An Bang Property Insurance Corporation Ltd.	65.51	5989.33	2517.18
中国大地财产保险股份有限公司	Da Di Property Insurance Corporation Ltd.	386.49	10024.25	4836.95
阳光财产保险股份有限公司	Sunshine Property Insurance Corporation Ltd.	735.01	21985.30	9072.34
都邦财产保险股份有限公司	Du-bang Property Insurance Corporation Ltd.	60.88	1030.23	911.65
渤海财产保险股份有限公司	Bohai Property Insurance Corporation Ltd.	39.23	2999.12	767.68
永诚财产保险股份有限公司	Yongcheng Property Insurance Corporation Ltd.	354.56	5812.99	1133.02
中银财产保险股份有限公司	Zhongyin Property Insurance Corporation Ltd.	40.51	383.72	12.87
信达财产保险股份有限公司	Xinda Property Insurance Corporation Ltd.	59.25	2642.53	285.93
中国人寿财产保险股份有限公司	The Life Insurance Corporation Ltd.,Property Insurance Company	36.87	1155.69	100.73
寿险公司小计	**Sub-total**	**11888.19**	**1186795.91**	**206142.84**
中国人寿保险股份有限公司	The Life Insurance Corporation Ltd.of China	7420.40	494019.36	136495.01
中国平安人寿保险股份有限公司	The Ping An Insurance Corporation Ltd.,Life Insurance Company of China	661.48	156372.03	31130.29
中国太平洋人寿保险股份有限公司	The Pacific Insurance Corporation Ltd.,Life Insurance Company of China	560.04	187742.89	14539.54
新华人寿保险股份有限公司	Xin Hua Life Insurance Corporation Ltd.	290.61	140375.07	6877.92
泰康人寿保险股份有限公司	Tai Kang Life Insurance Corporation Ltd.	1033.10	99090.29	4700.01
中国人民人寿保险股份有限公司	PICC Life Insurance Corporation Ltd.of China	268.59	31614.24	1232.60
太平人寿保险有限公司	Taiping Life Insurance Corporation Ltd.	26.89	27549.87	1407.26
中国人民健康保险股份有限公司	PICC Health Insurance Corporation Ltd.	690.59	9936.49	5922.43
合众人寿保险股份有限公司	Union Life Insurance Corporation Ltd.	51.41	26317.13	629.33
平安养老保险股份有限公司	The Pingan Old-age Pension Insurance Company	736.79	4506.37	2830.48
阳光人寿保险股份有限公司	The Sun of Life Insurance Corporation Ltd.	138.17	5250.34	13.49
生命人寿保险股份有限公司	The Life Insurance Corporation Ltd.	10.12	4021.83	364.48

7-14 各地区保险业务情况
Conditions of Insurance Service by Region

单位：万元 (2011 年) (10 000 yuan)

地　区	Region	全部业务 All Insurance Business		财产保险公司业务 Property Insurance Business	
		保费收入 Premium Income	比上年增长(%) Increase Rate Over preceding year(%)	保费收入 Premium Income	比上年增长(%) Increase Rate Over preceding year(%)
总　计	**Total**	**2036154.79**	**13.93**	**849358.88**	**24.84**
乌鲁木齐市	Urumqi City	670061.69	18.64	228496.98	38.32
昌吉回族自治州	Changji Hui Autonomous Prefecture	192441.56	12.61	85865.33	24.80
伊犁州直属县(市)	Counties (Cities) Direct Under Ili Prefecture	125857.43	8.19	61150.87	18.64
克拉玛依市	Karamay City	119056.47	1.82	41147.83	10.34
博尔塔拉蒙古自治州	Bortala Mongol Autonomous Prefecture	50131.47	9.67	23233.94	6.35
石河子市	Shihezi City	102622.06	13.82	42709.65	37.38
奎屯市	Kuytun City	50964.26	15.28	22464.54	23.74
阿勒泰地区	Altay Administrative Offices	46573.42	8.31	20733.99	12.53
塔城地区	Tacheng [Tarbagatai] Administrative Offices	73249.83	11.19	27193.36	17.12
克孜勒苏柯尔克孜自治州	Kizilsu Kirgiz Autonomous Prefecture	10028.90	27.27	7266.66	40.62
和田地区	Hotan Administrative Offices	31655.59	23.43	21200.56	35.83
喀什地区	Kashgar [Kaxgar] Administrative Offices	121826.93	13.10	74296.15	22.68
巴音郭楞蒙古自治州	Bayangol Mongol Autonomous Prefecture	166640.73	12.61	71549.63	14.75
阿克苏地区	Aksu Administrative Offices	148462.03	16.29	75089.73	23.44
吐鲁番地区	Turpan Administrative Offices	44882.46	10.40	20673.79	17.34
哈密地区	Hami [Kumul] Administrative Offices	81699.97	13.97	26285.86	16.03

地　区	Region	人寿保险公司业务 Life Insurance Business		保险密度(元) Insurance Density (yuan)	保险深度(%) Insurance Depth(%)
		保费收入 Premium Income	比上年增长(%) Increase Rate Over preceding year(%)		
总　计	**Total**	**1186795.91**	**7.23**	**922**	**3.08**
乌鲁木齐市	Urumqi City	441564.71	10.50	2687	3.97
昌吉回族自治州	Changji Hui Autonomous Prefecture	106576.23	4.39	1380	2.74
伊犁州直属县(市)	Counties (Cities) Direct Under Ili Prefecture	64706.56	-0.13	488	2.54
克拉玛依市	Karamay City	77908.64	-2.17	4217	1.49
博尔塔拉蒙古自治州	Bortala Mongol Autonomous Prefecture	26897.53	12.70	1029	3.31
石河子市	Shihezi City	59912.41	1.42	1644	6.01
奎屯市	Kuytun City	28499.72	9.39	1657	5.67
阿勒泰地区	Altay Administrative Offices	25839.43	5.15	696	2.85
塔城地区	Tacheng [Tarbagatai] Administrative Offices	46056.47	7.96	701	1.74
克孜勒苏柯尔克孜自治州	Kizilsu Kirgiz Autonomous Prefecture	2762.24	1.83	181	2.08
和田地区	Hotan Administrative Offices	10455.02	4.15	152	2.50
喀什地区	Kashgar [Kaxgar] Administrative Offices	47530.78	0.80	297	2.90
巴音郭楞蒙古自治州	Bayangol Mongol Autonomous Prefecture	95091.10	11.05	1220	2.08
阿克苏地区	Aksu Administrative Offices	73372.30	9.78	621	2.93
吐鲁番地区	Turpan Administrative Offices	24208.66	5.10	710	2.03
哈密地区	Hami [Kumul] Administrative Offices	55414.11	13.02	1399	3.70

7-15 新疆辖区证券、期货经营机构和人员数
Operators and Staff of Securities and Futures in Xinjiang

单位：个、人 (2011 年) (unit, person)

公司名称	Name of Enterprise	机构数 Number of Institution	人员 Staff	营业部数量 Number of Business Department	人员 Staff
总 计	**Total**	**3**	**4856**	**70**	**1732**
新疆辖区证券机构	**Stock Instituions in the Territory of Xinjiang**	**1**	**4614**	**60**	**1609**
宏源证券股份有限公司	Hongyuan Securities Stock Limited Company	1	4614	38	784
异地证券公司营业部	Business Department, Non-local Stock Company			22	825
长江证券股份有限公司	Dapeng Securities Liability Corporation Ltd.			2	91
光大证券股份有限公司	Everbright Securities Liability Corporation Ltd.			1	27
广发证券股份有限公司	Guangfa Securities Liability Corporation Ltd.			1	91
国泰君安证券股份有限公司	Jun'an Securities Stock Corporation Ltd.			1	50
海通证券股份有限公司	Haitong Securities Company			1	71
平安证券有限责任公司	Pin'An Securities Liability Corporation Ltd.			1	69
申银万国股份有限公司	Shenyin Universal Stock Corporation Ltd.			1	42
湘财证券有限责任公司	Xiangcai Securities Liability Corporation Ltd.			2	53
中国银河证券股份有限公司	China Yinhe Securities Liability Corporation Ltd.			1	64
中国民族证券有限责任公司	Nationality Securities Company			1	41
金元证券股份有限公司	Jinyuan Securities Company			1	47
华融证券股份有限公司	Huarong Securities Company			4	68
华龙证券股份有限公司	Hualong Securities Compang			1	51
齐鲁证券有限责任公司	QiLU Securities Liability Corporation Ltd.			1	18
中信建投证券有限责任公司	China Securities Corporation Ltd.			1	13
国信证券股份有限公司	Guoxin Securities Liability Corporation Ltd.			1	22
华泰证券股份有限公司	Huatai Securities Liability Corporation Ltd.			1	7
新疆辖区期货经纪公司	**Xinjiang Futures Broker's Company**	**2**	**242**	**10**	**123**
新疆天利期货经纪有限公司	Xinjiang Tianli Futures Broker's Company	1	59	3	18
新疆金石期货经纪有限公司	Xinjiang Jingshi Futures Broker's Company	1	183	5	57
万达期货经纪有限公司	Henan Wanda Futures Broker's Company			1	24
宏源期货有限公司	Hongyuan Futures Broker's Company			1	24

7-16 上市公司基本情况表

Basic Condition of Listed Companies

公司简称 Names of Businesses		上市时间 Listed Time	上市交易所 Listing Stock Exchange	发行时股本(万股) Total Capital Stock (10 000 share)		发行募集资金(万元) Floated Raised Funds (10 000 yuan)	2011 年末股本(万股) Stock Capital by 2011 (10 000 share)		2011 年累计募集资金(万元) Capital Raised by 2011 (10 000 yuan)
				总股本 Total Stock Capital	流通股本 Circulating Capital Stock		总股本 Total Stock Capital	流通股本 Circulating Stock Capital	
总　计	**Total**			**557884**	**155975**	**1250008**	**2317692**	**1930686**	**6180850**
宏源证券	Hongyuan Trust	1994	深交所	17500	4500	10550	146120	146117	339250
新疆众和	Xijiang Zhonghe	1996	上交所	7953	2025	9690	41104	35206	370702
百花村	Bai Huacun	1996	上交所	6128	2700	11800	26885	11996	113071
渤海租赁	Bohai Leasing	1996	深交所	5000	1250	7062	97635	30029	626265
友好集团	Youhao Group	1996	上交所	10700	2700	10607	31149	30884	54991
中粮屯河	Zhongliang Tunhe	1997	上交所	7000	1750	9400	100560	80560	168978
啤酒花	Hop	1997	上交所	8000	3000	11523	36792	36792	25981
新疆天业	Xinjiang Tianye	1997	上交所	6300	2430	16896	43859	43859	45333
特变电工	Toban Electric Engineering	1997	上交所	8168	3000	14820	263556	263556	615823
中葡股份	Suntime International	1997	上交所	8600	2700	24071	80992	46446	233625
天山纺织	Tianshan Textile	1998	深交所	18782	4230	20783	36346	36346	41783
天山股份	Tianshan Stock	1999	上交所	12946	4500	26394	38895	33566	199936
新农开发	Xinnong Development	1999	上交所	29400	9000	32905	32100	32100	65790
伊力特	Yilite	1999	上交所	22050	7500	45375	44100	44100	46950
新中基	Xin Zhongji	2000	上交所	12459	4500	21011	48205	43285	121952
广汇股份	Guanghui Stock	2000	上交所	35378	5000	31652	194687	107876	547000
国际实业	Industry International	2000	深交所	17179	7000	39837	48114	48114	84741
美克股份	Markor Stock	2000	上交所	9208	4000	50923	63268	58637	298195
天利高科	Tianli High-Tech	2000	上交所	17000	6000	42653	57815	57815	93114
天宏纸业	Xinjinag Tianhong	2001	上交所	8016	3000	16633	8016	8016	16922
香梨股份	Fragrant Pear Stock	2001	上交所	16050	5000	23141	14771	14771	24700
天富热电	Tianfu Thermoelectricity	2002	上交所	16909	6000	42000	65570	65570	153331
八一钢铁	August 1st Steel	2002	上交所	40943	13000	92254	76645	76645	215940
冠农股份	Guannong Stock	2003	上交所	12000	4000	21610	36210	36210	65920
青松建化	Qubgsibg Cement	2003	上交所	18493	6000	24265	47870	47870	167017
新疆城建	Xinjiang Urban Construction	2003	上交所	16054	6000	33546	67579	67579	108737
新赛股份	Xinsai Stock	2003	上交所	15000	5000	31441	30271	30271	64216
中泰化学	Zhongtai Chemical	2006	深交所	23600	8000	66000	115434	96090	676208
天康生物	TianKang Animal	2006	深交所	6400	1280	15868	29458	26594	58319
金风科技	Goldwind	2007	深交所	50000	5000	180000	269459	212141	180000
国统股份	Guotong Stock	2008	深交所	8000	2000	15380	11615	9839	58994
准油股份	Zhunyou Stock	2008	深交所	9946	2500	19625	9946	8469	19625
北新路桥	Beixin Road&Bridge	2009	深交所	18945	3800	37635	42871	20601	80755
西部建设	West Construction	2009	深交所	14000	2800	48473	21000	9745	52500
西部牧业	Xinjiang Western Animal Husbandry	2010	深交所	11700	3000	35700	11700	6142	35700
光正钢构	Guangzheng Steel Structure	2010	深交所	9038	1810	34307	18076	4520	34307
新研股份	Research Shares Corporation	2010	深交所	3040		74179	9020	2332	74179

主要统计指标解释

财政收入 指国家财政参与社会产品分配所取得的收入，是实现国家职能的财力保证。主要包括：

(1)**各项税收**：包括国内增值税、国内消费税、进口货物增值税和消费税、出口货物退增值税和消费税、营业税、企业所得税、个人所得税、资源税、城市维护建设税、房产税、印花税、城镇土地使用税、土地增值税、车船税、船舶吨税、车辆购置税、关税、耕地占用税、契税、烟叶税等。

(2)**非税收入**：包括专项收入、行政事业性收费、罚没收入和其他收入。

地方财政收入 包括营业税（不含铁道部门、各银行总行、各保险公司总公司集中交纳的营业税），地方企业上交利润，城市维护建设税（不含铁道部门、各银行总行、各保险公司总公司集中交纳的部分），房产税，城镇土地使用税，土地增值税，车船税，耕地占用税，契税，烟叶税，印花税，增值税25%部分，纳入共享范围的企业所得税40%部分，个人所得税40%部分，证券交易印花税3%部分，海洋石油资源税以外的其他资源税，地方非税收入等。

地方财政支出 包括一般公共服务，公共安全支出，地方统筹的各项社会事业支出等。

信贷资金 指金融机构以信用方式积聚和分配的货币资金。金融机构信贷资金的来源有各项存款、金融债券、对国际金融机构负债、流通中现金、其他项目等；信贷资金的运用有各项贷款、有价证券及投资、金银占款、外汇占款、财政借款及在国际金融机构中的资产等。

存款 指企业、机关、团体或居民根据资金必须收回的原则，把货币资金存入银行或其他信贷机构保管并取得一定利息的一种信用活动形式。根据存款对象或性质的不同可划分为企业存款、财政存款、机关团体存款、城乡储蓄存款、农业存款、信托及委托类存款、其他存款等科目。它是银行信贷资金的主要来源。

贷款 指银行或其他信用机构根据资金必须归还的原则，按一定利率，为企业、个人等提供资金的一种信用活动形式。我国银行贷款分为短期贷款、委托及信托类贷款、其他类贷款等

保险金额 指保险人承担赔偿或者给付保险金责任的最高限额。

保费 指投保人为取得保险人在约定范围内所承担赔偿责任而支付给保险人的费用。

赔款 指保险人根据保险合同的规定，向被保险人支付的赔偿保险责任损失的金额。

给付 包括死伤医疗给付和满期给付。死伤医疗给付是指保险人根据人寿保险及长期健康保险合同的规定，因被保险人在保险期内发生保险责任范围内的保险事故支付给被保险人(或受益人)的金额。满期给付是指被保险人生存期满，保险人按人寿保险合同规定支付给被保险人的满期保险金额。

Explanatory Notes on Main Statistical Indicators

Government Revenue refer to the revenue of the government finance by means of participating in the distribution of the social products,which is the financial resources for ensuring the government to function,The contents of government revenue have been changed several times.Now it includes the following main items:

(1)Various tax revenue including value added tax,business tax,consumption tax,land value added tax,tax on city maintenance and construction,resources tax,tax on use of urban land,enterprise income tax,personal income tax,tariff,stamp tax on security transactions,tax on purchase of motor vehicles,tax on agriculture and animal husbandary and tax on occupancy of cultivated land,etc.

(2)Non-tax revenue including Special income, Administrative fees, Incomes from imposition and oter incomes.

Revenue of the Local Governments includes business tax (excluding the part of the Ministry of Railways, head offices of banks, head offices of insurance company, which are handed over to the government in a centralized way), profit handed in by the local enterprises, city maintenance and construct tax (excluding the part of the Ministry of Railways, head offices of banks, head offices of insurance company, which are handed over to the government in a centralized way), house property tax, urban land use tax, land appreciation tax, tax on vehicles and boat operation, farm land occupation tax, deed tax, and tobacco leaf tax, stamp tax, 25% of the value added tax, 40% the share part of the corporate income tax, 40% of individual income tax, 3% of stamp tax on securities transactions, resource tax other than the tax on offshore petroleum resources, local non-tax revenue, etc.

Expenditure of the Local Governments includes mainly the expenditure for general public services, expenditure for public security, and expenditures for social development which are planed by local governments, etc.

Credit Funds refer to the funds issued as loans by banking institutions. The sources of credit funds of the banking institutions included deposits, liabilities to international financial institutions, currency in circulation, self-owned funds and current retained profits, etc. The credit funds can be used in forms of loans, gold, foreign exchange, government debt and assets in the international financial institutions.

Deposit is a form of credit by which enterprises, institutions, organizations or households can put money into banks and other credit institutions for safekeeping and interest earning under the principle of free withdrawal. According to different depositors, deposits are divided into enterprise deposits,treasury deposits, deposits of government agencies and organizations,capital construction deposits, urban savings deposits, rural deposits and other deposits. Deposits are major sources of the credit funds of banks.

Loan is a form of credit by which banks and other credit institutions provide funds at certain interest rate to enterprises and individuals in the light of the principle of unconditional repayment. Loans from Chinese banks include circulating capital loans, fixed assets loans, loans to urban and rural individuals engaged in industrial and commercial business and agricultural loans.

Amount Insured refers to the maximum that the insurant will get for the claim of the case insured.

Premium is the fee paid by the insurant to the insurer to obtain the obligation of compensation from the insurance within the agreed terms.

Settled Claim is the compensation paid by the insurer to the insurant in accordance with the insurance contract.

Payment includes payment for death, injury or medical treatment and mature payment. Payment for death, injury or medical treatment refers to the money paid to the insurant (or the beneficiary) in accordance with the life or health insurance contract when the insurant encounters accidents within the insured period covered in the contract. Mature payment refers to the mature payment to the insurant in accordance with the life insurance contract at the end of the insured period.

2012

新疆统计年鉴

XINJIANG STATISTICAL YEARBOOK

第八篇
价格指数

CHAPTER 8
Price Indices

简要说明
Brief Introduction

本篇资料的主要内容及来源

本篇价格指数资料，反映生产、流通、消费与投资环节的价格变动趋势和变动幅度，主要包括居民消费价格指数、商品零售价格指数、农业生产资料价格指数、工业品出厂价格指数、工业品购进价格指数、固定资产投资价格指数。居民消费价格指数、商品零售价格指数和农业生产资料价格指数出自国家统计局新疆调查总队消费价格调查处；工业品出厂价格指数、工业品购进价格指数、固定资产投资价格指数出自国家统计局新疆调查总队生产投资价格调查处。

Main Content and Source of Data

Data on the price indices in this chapter show the changing trend and the change rates in production, circulation, consumption and investment, including mainly consumer price indices of residents, retail price indices, price indices of agricultural means of production, purchasing price indices of farm products, producers' price indices of industrial products, purchasing price indices of raw materials, fuels and power, price indices of investment in fixed assets, and real estate price indices.Data on the consumer price index, retail price index and price indices of agriculture production come from Division of Consumer Price of NBS Survey Office in Xinjiang; Data on the price indices of industrial products, indices of purchasing price of raw materials, fuels and power, price indices of investment in fixed assets, price indices for real estate come from Division of Consumer Price of NBS Survey Office in Xinjiang.

8-1 主要年份各种物价指数
Price Indices in Main Years

年　份 Year	居民消费价格指数 Consumer Price Index	城市居民消费价格指数 Urban Household	农村居民消费价格指数 Rural Household	商品零售价格指数 Retail Price Index
上年=100 Preceding year=100				
1978	101.2	101.4	100.3	101.4
1980	102.8	104.1	102.0	104.2
1985	107.8	109.5	106.4	108.1
1990	105.0	104.5	105.9	104.1
1995	119.7	118.4	122.5	116.7
1996	110.5	110.4	110.6	108.8
1997	103.7	103.5	103.9	101.8
1998	100.2	99.9	100.8	99.7
1999	97.4	97.7	96.8	96.2
2000	99.4	100.1	97.6	98.3
2001	104.0	104.0	103.8	102.5
2002	99.4	98.9	100.9	97.9
2003	100.4	100.5	100.2	99.2
2004	102.7	102.1	104.5	100.7
2005	100.7	100.6	101.2	99.4
2006	101.3	101.0	102.0	101.8
2007	105.5	104.6	107.2	105.1
2008	108.1	107.3	109.5	108.5
2009	100.7	100.2	102.0	100.4
2010	104.3	103.6	105.8	104.6
2011	105.9	105.5	106.8	105.1
1978 年=100 Year 1978 =100				
1978	100.0	100.0	100.0	100.0
1980	105.1	106.6	103.8	107.8
1985	120.9	125.6	117.9	124.2
1990	194.3	206.0	184.0	197.6
1995	392.7	422.7	364.2	381.0
1996	433.9	466.7	402.9	414.6
1997	450.0	483.0	418.6	422.0
1998	450.9	482.5	421.9	420.8
1999	439.2	471.4	408.4	404.8
2000	436.5	471.9	398.6	397.9
2001	454.0	490.8	413.8	407.8
2002	451.3	485.4	417.5	399.3
2003	453.1	487.8	418.3	396.1
2004	465.3	498.1	437.1	398.9
2005	468.6	501.1	442.3	396.5
2006	474.7	506.1	451.1	403.6
2007	500.8	529.4	483.6	424.2
2008	541.4	568.0	529.5	460.3
2009	545.2	569.1	540.1	462.1
2010	568.6	589.6	571.4	483.4
2011	602.1	622.0	610.3	508.1

8-2 居民消费价格分类指数
Consumer Price Indices by Category

(上年=100) (2011 年) (preceding year=100)

项　　目	Item	全　区 Autonomous Region	城　市 Urban Indices	农　村 Rural Indices
居民消费价格总指数	**Consumer Price Index**	**105.9**	**105.5**	**106.8**
食　品	**Food**	**112.6**	**112.4**	**112.7**
粮　食	Grain	108.7	108.6	108.8
大　米	Rice	110.7	110.8	110.6
面　粉	Flour	107.8	106.8	108.7
粮食制品	Grain Products	107.8	108.8	102.7
其　它	Others	107.9	103.0	111.8
淀　粉	Starches and Tubers	107.7	109.3	105.7
干豆类及豆制品	Beans and Its Products	107.4	108.0	106.4
油　脂	Oil or Fat	112.6	110.4	115.5
肉禽及其制品	Meat, Poultry and Processed Products	120.1	121.4	117.9
蛋	Eggs	112.2	113.8	110.0
水产品	Aquatic Products	110.7	110.2	111.3
菜	Vegetables	104.6	101.4	110.2
鲜　菜	Fresh Vegetables	104.4	101.1	110.1
干菜及菜制品	Dried Vegetables and Vegetable Products	107.6	109.2	104.5
薯　类	Tubers	108.2	102.4	124.8
调味品	Flavoring	104.5	106.2	102.0
糖	Carbohydrate	115.0	111.7	118.6
食　糖	Sugar	129.5	125.0	133.5
糖　果	Candy	109.9	108.2	111.8
巧克力制品	Chocolate Goods	103.7	99.3	108.9
糖类小食品	Carbohydrate Products	110.7	111.0	110.2
茶及饮料	Tea and Beverages	102.6	103.9	100.8
干鲜瓜果	Dried and Fresh Melons and Fruits	120.1	120.0	120.2
鲜瓜果	Fresh Fruits	120.4	120.2	120.6
干(坚)果	Drie (nut) Fruits	119.5	119.7	119.0
糕点饼干	Cake and Biscuit	105.9	105.8	106.2
液体乳及乳制品	Milk and Its Products	107.0	106.7	107.6
在外用膳食品	Dining Out	110.9	111.3	109.4
主　食	Staple Food	115.4	116.2	111.9
炒　菜	Fried Dishes	106.7	107.8	103.1
地方小吃	Local Snack	111.8	111.2	114.4
其他	Others	109.3	107.2	112.5
其他食品	Other Foods	105.6	104.8	107.6
烟酒及用品	**Tobacco, Liquor and Articles**	**103.3**	**103.6**	**102.9**
烟　草	Tobacco	100.1	100.3	99.7
酒	Liquor	106.9	107.5	106.0
衣　着	**Clothing**	**101.1**	**100.8**	**101.8**
服　装	Garments	101.1	101.2	100.7
衣着材料	Clothing Material	106.7	108.1	105.4
棉　布	Cotton Cloth	116.5	119.8	113.8

8-2 续表 Continued

(上年=100) (preceding year=100)

项　目	Item	全　区 Autonomous Region	城　市 Urban Areas	农　村 Rural Areas
化纤布	Chemical Fiber Cloth	103.8	104.8	102.9
毛　线	Wool	102.7	103.2	102.1
其　他	Others	102.1	103.6	100.9
鞋袜帽	Footwear and Hats	100.0	98.8	102.9
鞋	Shoes	99.6	98.1	103.4
袜　子	Socks and Stockings	101.9	102.0	101.7
帽　子	Hats	101.9	102.9	99.3
衣着加工服务费	Clothing Processing	107.8	107.9	107.8
家庭设备用品及维修服务	**Household Facilities,Articles and Services**	**102.4**	**102.1**	**102.9**
耐用消费品	Durable Consumer Goods	99.8	98.9	101.4
家　具	Furniture	100.3	99.6	101.3
家庭设备	Household Facilities	99.6	98.5	101.4
室内装饰品	Interior Decorations	102.2	102.3	101.9
床上用品	Bed Articles	103.7	105.1	101.2
家庭日用杂品	Daily Use Household Articles	102.4	102.6	101.9
家庭服务及加工维修服务	Household Service and Mainteance and Renovation	114.8	113.2	118.1
医疗保健和个人用品	**Health Care and Personal Articles**	**104.3**	**103.6**	**105.7**
医疗保健	Health Cares	102.7	102.5	103.4
医疗器具及用品	Medical Instruments and Articles	99.5	100.6	97.9
中药材及中成药	Traditional Chinese Medicine	111.4	110.5	113.9
西　药	Western Medicine	101.0	101.1	100.5
保健器具及用品	Constitutional Appliances and Articles	100.5	100.8	99.6
医疗保健服务	Medical and Health Service	100.3	100.1	100.9
个人用品及服务	Personal Articles and Services	106.3	105.6	106.9
交通和通信	**Transportation and Communication**	**100.5**	**99.9**	**101.5**
交　通	Transportation	103.0	102.3	104.3
通　信	Communication	98.1	97.8	98.5
娱乐教育文化用品及服务	**Recreation, Education, Culture Articles**	**101.1**	**100.1**	**103.1**
文娱用耐用消费品及服务	Durable Consumer Goods for Cultural and Recreationl Use and Services	95.2	93.4	98.8
教　育	Education	102.8	101.9	104.5
文化娱乐	Culture and Recreation Articles	100.6	99.7	102.8
文化娱乐用品	Cultural and Recreational Articles	100.1	99.1	102.5
书报杂志	Newspapers and Magazines	102.2	101.1	104.5
文娱费	Expenditure on Culture and Recreation	100.1	99.4	101.8
旅　游	Touring and Outing	105.6	105.7	105.4
居　住	**Housing**	**105.4**	**104.9**	**106.2**
建房及装修材料	Building and Building Decoration Materials	104.8	104.1	106.6
住房租金	Renting	102.9	102.7	104.1
自有住房	Private Housing	106.6	106.3	107.1
水、电、燃料	Water, Electricity and Fuels	103.7	103.9	103.4
服务项目价格指数	**Services**	**104.0**	**103.1**	**105.8**

8-3 各市县居民消费价格分类指数

(上年=100) (2011 年)

项 目	Item	乌鲁木齐市 Urumqi City	喀什市 Kashgar [Kaxgar] City	伊宁市 Yining [Gulja] City	和田市 Hotan City	克拉玛依市 Karamay City	哈密市 Hami [Kumul] City
居民消费价格总指数	**Consumer Price Index**	**104.5**	**106.0**	**106.7**	**106.9**	**105.8**	**105.3**
食 品	**Food**	**112.2**	**114.6**	**112.4**	**113.6**	**110.2**	**110.9**
粮 食	Grain	108.5	109.7	107.0	109.8	110.0	107.6
大 米	Rice	107.6	113.8	107.6	105.9	114.8	113.9
面 粉	Flour	109.2	108.9	108.6	109.6	100.3	102.1
粮食制品	Grain Products	110.5	108.6	103.2	116.1	117.5	108.9
其 它	Others	96.6	93.4	111.1	121.5	99.4	103.8
淀 粉	Starches and Tubers	116.2	106.7	99.0	120.6	90.8	100.0
干豆类及豆制品	Beans and Its Products	109.3	108.3	127.5	106.3	106.3	110.6
油 脂	Oil or Fat	113.7	113.7	113.8	105.2	105.6	112.3
肉禽及其制品	Meat, Poultry and Their Products	121.4	120.3	119.5	118.8	122.7	119.2
蛋	Eggs	114.4	108.4	113.3	103.5	115.2	116.0
水产品	Aquatic Products	109.2	110.6	119.2	112.6	110.7	108.3
菜	Vegetables	98.9	109.3	103.3	115.3	98.4	100.1
鲜 菜	Fresh Vegetables	98.6	109.0	101.7	116.1	97.5	98.5
干菜及菜制品	Dried Vegetables and Vegetable Products	105.8	109.6	119.6	102.2	111.2	123.8
薯 类	Tubers	100.7	122.5	105.1	139.6	96.6	93.7
调味品	Flavoring	103.0	110.8	106.8	106.8	104.9	110.0
糖	Carbohydrate Products	107.2	110.5	119.6	109.5	116.3	108.6
食 糖	Sugar	123.3	113.1	136.2	126.8	120.6	126.1
糖 果	Candy	105.9	113.0	116.4	103.6	113.9	100.5
巧克力制品	Chocolate Goods	91.5	94.8	108.3	100.3	102.3	102.5
糖类小食品	Carbohydrate	110.9	115.6	107.0	101.0	134.9	102.7
茶及饮料	Tea and Beverages	103.8	102.6	101.4	106.1	101.5	113.9
干鲜瓜果	Dried and Fresh Melons and Fruits	118.9	126.3	116.8	128.0	113.6	117.9
鲜瓜果	Fresh Fruits	120.3	127.9	117.2	131.1	112.8	122.8
干(坚)果	Dried(nut)Fruits	115.6	123.4	115.8	120.7	116.9	110.5
糕点饼干面包	Cake, Cookie	106.8	108.8	104.3	105.1	99.9	121.8
液体乳及乳制品	Milk and Its Products	106.7	116.8	109.0	101.3	106.1	106.3
在外用膳食品	Dining Out	114.2	111.4	112.2	112.8	107.0	108.3
主 食	Staple Food	127.4	108.1	117.5	112.7	108.8	102.0
炒 菜	Fried Dishes	105.3	112.2	106.6	116.9	107.0	116.5
地方小吃	Local Snack	115.6	117.4	116.0	102.7	107.2	104.4
其 他	Others	110.8	113.9	100.3	114.4	100.2	101.1
其他食品	Other Foods	107.1	107.3	101.4	100.2	106.2	101.5
烟酒及用品	**Tobacco, Liquor and Articles**	**103.7**	**102.5**	**103.6**	**107.8**	**102.1**	**103.6**
烟 草	Tobacco	100.0	100.0	100.0	100.0	100.0	100.0
酒	Liquor	108.3	105.3	106.7	115.8	103.8	107.1
衣 着	**Clothing**	**97.2**	**103.9**	**110.4**	**102.5**	**102.8**	**93.7**
服 装	Garments	98.1	104.4	109.8	101.3	102.8	85.7
衣着材料	Clothing Material	106.0	110.7	110.1	111.6	108.8	111.9
棉 布	Cotton Cloth	115.8	124.5	115.3	120.7	117.8	136.2

Consumer Price Indices by Category in Cities and Counties

(preceding year=100)

昌吉市 Changji City	库尔勒市 Korla City	阿克苏市 Aksu City	焉耆回族自治县 Yanqi Hui Autonomous County	塔城市 Tacheng [Qoqek] City	阿勒泰市 Altay City	乌苏市 Usu City	博乐市 Bole [Bortala] City	吐鲁番市 Turpan City	库车县 Kuqa County	阿图什市 Artux City	莎车县 Shache [Yarkant] County	奎屯市 Kuytun City	石河子市 Shihezi City
105.3	**105.6**	**106.8**	**108.0**	**105.7**	**105.5**	**105.3**	**106.0**	**105.7**	**106.1**	**105.9**	**107.3**	**105.2**	**105.4**
110.5	**111.1**	**113.0**	**113.3**	**111.4**	**112.2**	**109.7**	**113.2**	**112.3**	**111.7**	**113.9**	**111.0**	**110.6**	**110.5**
108.1	108.9	104.5	107.4	109.3	106.6	109.9	110.2	108.1	109.1	111.1	107.2	107.8	109.3
110.8	115.9	114.0	109.9	115.6	107.5	111.8	110.6	107.5	113.5	113.1	109.9	121.3	112.8
108.7	106.9	97.5	106.7	114.2	107.1	107.9	113.1	111.1	106.3	110.9	106.7	100.0	104.7
100.3	102.6	102.9	105.4	103.6	102.8	111.3	102.4	104.5	104.4	106.4	95.7	102.2	113.8
105.7	114.2	100.8	104.2	107.1	107.1	100.0	110.2	105.4	119.0	105.9	127.1	117.4	103.4
113.8	102.5	104.8	102.5	117.4	100.0	98.2	121.4	100.0	102.3	100.0	102.7	109.3	109.1
102.1	99.6	103.6	104.7	106.5	102.5	103.0	110.1	92.6	105.9	114.3	117.5	99.1	109.7
108.0	105.4	113.4	116.2	116.9	120.9	113.3	114.7	122.0	106.9	109.7	120.5	104.5	115.1
118.2	117.7	121.4	117.2	124.8	122.9	117.3	119.3	117.0	115.8	111.1	110.7	126.5	116.6
118.7	113.5	113.0	114.2	113.1	111.4	123.3	108.1	116.6	103.9	107.2	104.7	116.6	110.9
106.3	109.5	108.5	109.2	113.5	109.2	105.4	109.6	111.2	111.8	115.5	108.4	106.9	108.5
102.4	105.2	107.2	103.3	100.9	102.6	100.8	111.2	101.1	105.6	115.6	118.7	95.3	102.8
102.4	105.3	105.8	103.0	96.4	101.4	96.5	113.4	98.0	104.0	115.8	119.9	95.1	100.1
102.6	102.6	120.5	105.2	110.9	100.9	115.1	88.4	107.6	116.6	113.8	90.2	100.3	112.8
115.8	109.8	110.0	104.2	134.5	112.4	124.5	161.8	115.9	118.7	111.3	131.1	101.2	121.0
112.6	101.9	109.8	110.0	107.2	105.0	100.6	101.3	102.5	103.6	111.2	92.4	100.0	103.1
110.8	111.0	115.0	113.4	114.7	115.9	126.9	112.3	110.9	113.6	108.1	128.6	114.0	110.2
131.0	125.7	130.8	139.3	131.2	154.3	173.9	120.8	121.3	128.8	119.1	137.3	138.5	113.0
104.3	110.2	112.4	100.4	106.9	100.0	115.1	111.0	107.6	106.5	102.8	129.3	100.7	102.6
104.3	104.4	115.8	94.7	100.0	103.5	100.0	112.8	100.0	105.8	100.7	130.1	105.2	100.4
104.7	100.0	100.1	100.3	122.5	100.0	117.5	100.0	100.0	100.0	101.8	115.8	100.0	123.8
106.6	101.3	105.7	101.2	102.1	102.3	100.7	101.4	94.5	103.2	99.4	99.2	100.0	102.6
112.8	129.1	125.2	115.7	109.8	125.8	109.7	119.4	122.7	136.5	148.3	109.6	117.2	107.8
105.6	131.0	126.4	116.7	110.7	125.0	110.7	121.2	130.5	142.6	158.0	102.1	113.9	108.0
129.0	123.2	122.0	113.8	107.1	128.5	106.9	115.1	108.3	121.6	126.1	127.0	124.2	107.4
101.5	105.6	102.9	117.8	107.9	101.7	104.4	108.3	111.3	100.4	100.1	105.8	107.2	102.4
110.7	103.5	103.9	112.1	107.7	108.1	114.5	111.4	97.3	102.4	108.6	120.2	101.0	109.3
109.2	102.6	112.7	120.1	107.2	105.5	105.2	109.0	119.6	109.2	105.9	106.7	106.2	115.1
102.4	101.5	107.8	130.8	107.8	104.1	105.2	101.0	128.5	111.0	102.5	115.1	111.7	120.1
119.0	101.4	120.7	114.5	100.0	100.8	103.5	118.1	111.5	101.5	108.8	89.6	105.5	103.2
105.7	110.4	112.2	114.1	136.7	120.4	107.3	104.5	124.8	120.4	110.2	110.1	108.5	148.9
122.6	100.0	100.0	126.7	100.0	105.6	106.4	100.0	100.0	106.8	100.0	124.3	100.0	107.5
104.2	100.0	103.8	104.2	105.9	100.0	100.0	108.3	100.0	100.2	102.3	122.8	100.0	103.0
104.2	**100.6**	**102.2**	**102.7**	**103.7**	**104.9**	**102.3**	**102.3**	**106.9**	**102.7**	**104.5**	**106.6**	**102.5**	**101.0**
101.5	100.0	100.0	100.0	100.0	99.8	100.0	100.1	101.7	98.0	100.3	109.7	100.0	100.1
107.5	101.2	105.0	105.8	106.6	110.9	104.6	104.8	112.3	108.2	108.9	103.2	105.0	102.0
102.5	**103.0**	**107.3**	**106.5**	**98.3**	**102.6**	**105.9**	**102.1**	**100.3**	**103.1**	**101.3**	**100.4**	**102.4**	**104.8**
101.9	103.9	104.5	106.5	96.5	104.0	102.1	102.1	100.5	100.9	100.4	98.7	102.3	103.3
101.3	101.2	112.0	116.2	149.4	103.1	102.4	110.7	106.3	103.4	107.7	97.6	101.8	99.4
107.2	106.0	130.5	137.9	190.2	103.9	103.3	128.6	128.6	108.2	109.1	97.6	105.0	100.0

8-3 续表

(上年=100)

项　　目	Item	乌鲁木齐市 Urumqi City	喀什市 Kashgar [Kaxgar] City	伊宁市 Yining [Gulja] City	和田市 Hotan City	克拉玛依市 Karamay City	哈密市 Hami [Kumul] City
化纤布	Chemical Fiber Cloth	105.4	107.0	106.7	107.2	98.8	106.3
毛　线	Wool	105.2	107.1	105.4	106.8	106.4	104.5
其　他	Others	100.0	100.0	118.0	109.5	100.6	100.0
鞋袜帽	Footgear and Hats	92.8	100.0	112.8	102.0	101.2	100.0
鞋	Shoes	92.0	100.0	114.6	102.4	101.1	100.0
袜　子	Socks and Stockings	100.0	99.8	101.7	100.0	100.1	100.0
帽　子	Hats	102.6	100.3	103.7	103.8	103.3	100.0
衣着加工服务费	Clothing Manufacturing Services	109.8	112.1	103.0	112.2	110.2	123.1
家庭设备用品及维修服务	**Household Facilities and Articles and Services**	**102.1**	**102.3**	**102.4**	**100.3**	**101.7**	**105.2**
耐用消费品	Durable Consumer Goods	96.7	97.7	99.8	100.2	100.5	100.4
家　具	Furniture	97.4	99.0	99.9	101.9	100.9	101.0
家庭设备	Household Facilities	96.4	96.8	99.7	99.0	100.2	100.1
室内装饰品	Interior Decorations	105.0	100.0	106.4	101.1	99.5	100.0
床上用品	Bed Articles	111.5	100.0	102.3	100.2	100.0	99.8
家庭日用杂品	Daily Use Household Articles	104.3	109.2	100.6	100.5	101.7	114.7
家庭服务及加工维修服务	Household Services and Maintenance and Renovation	121.2	109.8	118.3	100.0	111.3	116.7
医疗保健和个人用品	**Health Care and Personal Articles**	**103.3**	**105.8**	**104.3**	**104.3**	**103.5**	**107.9**
医疗保健	Health Cares	102.2	103.3	105.0	104.0	101.8	107.9
医疗器具及用品	Medical Appliances and Articles	93.9	99.9	102.6	100.0	104.2	106.4
中药材及中成药	Traditional Chinese Medicine	105.5	111.9	118.9	106.8	104.8	114.8
西　药	Western Medicine	101.6	99.5	101.5	105.6	101.8	107.7
保健器具及用品	Constitutional Appliances and Articles	100.8	98.2	100.0	99.9	99.8	102.0
医疗保健服务	Medical and Health Service	100.0	102.3	100.0	100.0	99.1	100.0
个人用品及服务	Personal Articles and Services	105.7	109.7	103.2	105.2	105.4	107.9
交通和通信	**Transportation and Communication**	**99.8**	**99.6**	**99.6**	**100.6**	**100.4**	**99.3**
交　通	Transportation	102.1	102.4	100.7	105.9	101.9	102.4
通　信	Communication	97.3	96.1	98.6	96.5	98.7	95.6
娱乐教育文化用品及服务	**Recreation, Education and Culture Articles and Services**	**99.2**	**101.1**	**103.6**	**100.2**	**103.0**	**101.9**
文娱用耐用消费品及服务	Durable Consumer Goods for Cultural and Recreationl Use and Services	87.0	92.6	96.7	98.7	97.1	96.3
教　育	Education	100.7	104.0	101.5	100.0	108.1	105.0
文化娱乐	Culture and Recreation Articles	99.7	99.9	101.4	101.8	100.3	101.8
文化娱乐用品	Cultural and Recreational Articles	97.5	98.3	100.0	100.6	100.3	101.6
书报杂志	Newspapers and Magazines	100.6	101.6	104.9	100.0	100.7	102.9
文娱费	Expenditure on Culture and Recreation	101.5	100.4	99.7	104.5	100.0	100.9
旅　游	Touring and Outing	104.3	105.8	116.5	105.6	109.0	104.0
居　住	**Residence**	**102.9**	**98.0**	**102.0**	**108.7**	**109.8**	**107.1**
建房及装修材料	Building and Building Decoration Materials	101.7	109.8	101.6	107.1	108.4	101.6
住房租金	Renting	105.1	90.8	100.0	100.0	104.7	104.3
自有住房	Private Housing	107.0	96.7	101.4	112.7	115.3	110.4
水、电、燃料	Water, Electricity and Fuels	102.6	103.8	111.3	110.0	99.8	102.7
服务项目价格指数	**Services**	**102.4**	**100.8**	**102.1**	**104.2**	**107.3**	**106.8**

Continued

(preceding year=100)

昌吉市 Changji City	库尔勒市 Korla City	阿克苏市 Aksu City	焉耆回族自治县 Yanqi Hui Autonomous County	塔城市 Tacheng [Qoqek] City	阿勒泰市 Altay City	乌苏市 Usu City	博乐市 Bole [Bortala] City	吐鲁番市 Turpan City	库车县 Kuqa County	阿图什市 Artux City	莎车县 Shache [Yarkant] County	奎屯市 Kuytun City	石河子市 Shihezi City
99.0	100.0	108.6	109.1	104.6	101.2	105.4	106.4	105.1	100.0	100.9	96.4	100.0	100.2
100.0	100.0	100.6	111.8	118.9	100.0	100.0	101.9	97.0	113.1	100.0	96.3	101.9	102.5
100.0	100.0	107.5	100.0	100.0	105.6	100.0	100.0	93.1	91.7	117.5	100.0	100.0	96.9
102.6	101.9	108.6	102.0	100.5	100.0	115.7	99.7	97.5	106.7	101.5	103.5	103.1	105.2
102.7	101.9	104.1	102.5	100.0	100.0	127.1	98.9	94.9	106.5	101.3	104.8	104.3	106.7
102.1	101.9	125.7	99.6	105.4	100.0	100.0	100.0	110.3	108.7	102.7	99.3	100.0	99.2
99.3	104.3	109.1	100.0	100.0	100.0	100.0	110.1	101.6	104.4	100.0	89.0	101.1	113.2
114.0	100.0	117.2	111.7	137.5	101.0	100.0	103.5	108.8	112.0	102.0	112.9	100.0	127.3
103.2	**101.0**	**106.1**	**102.9**	**102.1**	**100.0**	**101.9**	**100.7**	**107.1**	**100.7**	**101.1**	**106.7**	**103.9**	**102.7**
100.7	100.2	99.8	102.4	98.4	100.2	100.0	100.0	104.2	97.3	101.0	104.4	98.8	99.4
102.0	100.7	101.5	106.9	100.0	100.3	100.1	100.2	100.0	98.3	100.8	103.9	99.2	101.2
100.5	99.9	98.6	99.9	97.6	100.1	100.0	99.9	105.9	96.3	101.2	104.7	98.7	98.6
100.5	100.3	104.3	105.8	100.0	100.0	100.0	102.8	101.1	109.5	100.0	100.6	104.0	107.9
101.7	106.4	111.2	105.0	100.0	100.2	100.0	100.0	106.5	100.1	105.3	99.7	118.7	103.7
106.5	101.1	109.4	103.1	101.4	99.7	103.2	101.6	100.6	98.7	100.0	105.1	103.2	104.4
111.5	101.6	124.8	100.2	143.3	100.0	109.9	100.0	139.9	117.2	100.0	135.3	115.1	106.7
103.0	**102.6**	**101.4**	**105.8**	**108.3**	**104.5**	**99.8**	**104.1**	**101.0**	**102.4**	**101.6**	**107.4**	**103.6**	**104.1**
101.8	101.0	101.0	107.4	106.7	105.4	98.6	102.5	97.1	96.9	100.7	108.7	100.9	104.1
100.0	102.6	100.0	104.2	114.3	100.0	100.0	97.6	87.1	98.1	98.7	96.0	99.2	95.4
111.0	104.4	102.1	121.3	122.4	118.1	97.5	107.4	106.1	100.5	104.7	126.7	103.5	116.9
98.0	99.1	100.4	104.7	111.5	101.6	98.3	102.8	90.7	92.7	99.3	101.2	100.0	103.3
103.4	100.4	100.0	100.0	102.8	100.0	99.9	100.0	96.4	97.4	100.0	103.3	99.7	97.0
100.1	100.0	101.1	97.7	100.0	100.0	100.0	100.1	100.3	99.0	100.0	104.8	100.0	100.0
105.6	105.2	102.2	103.3	112.7	103.0	101.4	106.5	107.7	111.3	102.8	105.4	107.8	104.1
100.5	**103.5**	**102.4**	**103.1**	**102.2**	**99.4**	**98.8**	**101.1**	**101.5**	**102.9**	**99.2**	**102.0**	**99.4**	**100.3**
102.0	106.4	105.1	107.0	103.7	104.0	103.3	102.7	103.7	104.5	102.5	104.3	100.5	101.3
99.0	99.5	98.2	100.2	100.3	94.4	94.8	99.6	99.4	100.3	95.9	99.4	98.4	99.1
100.9	**103.3**	**99.0**	**103.6**	**102.9**	**99.5**	**100.5**	**103.6**	**101.7**	**106.2**	**99.4**	**101.6**	**101.3**	**100.8**
96.6	99.5	96.0	99.5	93.8	96.4	99.9	99.0	99.2	100.3	96.5	99.8	99.4	95.9
100.8	107.3	100.1	106.5	108.7	100.0	101.0	107.9	103.9	104.9	100.3	100.4	100.4	100.5
100.7	101.3	100.6	101.8	100.0	102.7	100.7	101.2	101.0	104.2	100.8	108.1	100.6	99.9
101.8	100.6	99.8	99.9	98.5	99.8	100.0	102.0	101.7	101.1	102.0	111.3	100.3	99.7
100.1	102.5	101.8	105.3	103.5	102.4	102.7	100.0	102.3	104.1	100.0	111.8	100.0	100.0
100.4	101.0	100.3	101.1	100.4	109.3	100.0	100.9	98.8	108.3	100.0	100.0	101.4	100.0
104.6	100.5	99.9	101.5	110.5	99.4	100.0	105.8	99.4	121.1	99.2	104.1	107.7	108.9
105.5	**103.5**	**106.0**	**108.8**	**102.9**	**104.1**	**108.6**	**102.1**	**103.0**	**103.5**	**105.7**	**111.5**	**104.3**	**104.4**
110.0	105.0	106.7	107.7	112.0	103.5	103.2	103.7	112.1	102.4	105.6	109.4	103.8	108.9
107.3	100.0	113.2	105.7	100.0	102.3	111.8	103.8	100.0	102.7	103.8	106.1	104.2	104.4
104.1	104.4	104.1	111.6	101.2	104.3	110.3	101.2	101.9	104.7	106.3	115.7	104.8	103.4
100.4	102.6	99.9	103.2	105.8	104.2	104.0	104.0	100.4	100.3	104.1	102.8	102.1	102.3
103.5	**103.5**	**104.6**	**105.8**	**104.1**	**102.3**	**105.9**	**102.7**	**103.6**	**106.3**	**102.5**	**107.8**	**104.0**	**103.2**

8-4 商品零售价格分类指数
Retail Price Indices by Category

(上年=100) (2011 年) (preceding year=100)

项目	Item	全区 Autonomous Region	城市 Urban Indices	农村 Rural Indices
商品零售价格总指数	**Retail Price Index**	**105.1**	**104.5**	**106.6**
食品	**Food**	**112.5**	**112.4**	**112.7**
粮食	Grain	108.3	108.4	108.0
油脂	Oil or Fat	113.8	112.2	116.1
肉禽及其制品	Meat, Poultry and Processed Products	120.2	120.7	119.0
猪肉	Pork	149.3	150.2	147.1
牛肉	Beef	111.8	113.2	109.4
羊肉	Mutton	114.5	115.8	111.5
鸡	Chicken	115.6	114.9	117.1
鲜蛋	Fresh Eggs	113.0	114.1	110.8
水产品	Aquatic Products	109.4	109.2	109.8
鲜瓜果	Fresh Melons and Fruits	119.5	119.9	118.8
糕点、饼干、面包	Cake、Biscuit and Bread	106.7	106.6	106.8
饮料、烟酒	**Beverages, Tobacco and Liquor**	**103.5**	**103.6**	**103.5**
茶及饮料	Tea and Beverages	102.4	103.6	100.2
#饮料	Beverages	102.1	103.3	99.8
烟草	Tobacco	100.7	100.1	102.5
酒	Liquor	107.3	107.6	106.6
服装鞋帽	**Garments, Shoes and Hats**	**99.5**	**98.7**	**101.4**
服装	Garments	99.7	99.4	100.4
鞋袜帽	Footgear and Hats	99.1	97.2	103.7
#鞋	Shoes	98.3	96.0	104.1
纺织品	**Textiles**	**101.8**	**100.6**	**104.7**
棉布	Cotton Cloth	118.7	118.3	119.1
化纤布	Chemical Fiber Cloth	104.1	104.5	103.1
毛线	Wool	101.7	102.6	99.7
其他	Others			
家用电器及音响器材	**Household Appliances,Music and Video Equipment**	**96.4**	**94.8**	**99.7**
家庭设备	Household Facilities	98.6	97.3	101.5
文娱用耐用消费品	Durable Consuming Goods for Entertainment	93.6	91.4	97.8
专业音像器材	Sound Apparatus	98.5	97.7	99.9

8-4 续表 Continued

(上年=100) (preceding year=100)

项目	Item	全区 Autonomous Region	城市 Urban Indices	农村 Rural Indices
文化办公用品	**Cultural and Office Goods**	**98.7**	**96.2**	**104.1**
日用品	**Articles for Daily Use**	**103.6**	**104.3**	**102.1**
日用百货	General Merchandise for Daily Use	102.1	101.5	103.0
日用杂品	Miscellaneous for Daily Use	100.0	99.3	101.5
洗涤用品	Washing and Cleaning Goods	108.5	109.9	103.2
其他日用品	Other Daily-use Goods	101.7	102.5	100.3
体育娱乐用品	**Sports and Entertainment Goods**	**101.6**	**101.9**	**100.9**
体育用品	Sports Articles	101.9	101.9	102.0
娱乐用品	Recreational Articles	101.4	101.9	100.0
交通、通信用品	**Traffic and Telecommunication Goods**	**92.3**	**90.2**	**97.6**
交通运输机械	Traffic and Transport Machinery	93.1	90.6	99.8
通信器材	Telecommunication Apparatus	91.4	89.7	95.2
家　具	**Furniture**	**100.2**	**99.8**	**101.2**
化妆品	**Cosmetics**	**101.3**	**101.2**	**101.4**
金银珠宝	**Gold and Silver Jewelry**	**118.5**	**116.8**	**123.9**
中西药品及医疗保健用品	**Chinese and Western Medicine, Medical-care and Healthy Goods**	**103.5**	**102.6**	**105.5**
医疗器具及用品	Medical-care Apparatus and Goods	96.6	96.3	97.2
中药材及中成药	Chinese Herbs and Patent Medicine	111.4	108.1	117.3
西　药	Western Medicine	100.8	101.2	99.6
保健器具及用品	Healthy Devices and Goods	100.5	100.8	99.5
书报杂志及电子出版物	**Books, Magazines and Electronic Publications**	**100.7**	**100.1**	**102.3**
教材及参考书	Texts and Reference Books	101.8	101.4	102.7
书报杂志	Newspapers and Magazines	101.5	100.9	103.6
电子音像制品	Electronic Audio and Video Products	97.6	96.6	99.8
燃　料	**Fuels**	**109.6**	**109.4**	**110.1**
煤炭及制品	Coal and Its Products	105.2	103.1	107.5
石油及制品	Oil and Its Products	111.4	111.1	112.3
建筑材料及五金电料	**Building Apparatus, Hardwares and Electrical Apparatus**	**104.8**	**104.1**	**105.9**
建筑装璜材料	Building Decoration Materials	105.3	103.8	108.2
五金电料	Hardwares and Electrical Apparatus	103.2	105.0	100.3

8-5 各市县商品零售价格分类指数

(上年=100) (2011 年)

项 目	Item	乌鲁木齐市 Urumqi City	喀什市 Kashgar [Kaxgar] City	伊宁市 Yining [Gulja] City	和田市 Hotan City	克拉玛依市 Karamay City	哈密市 Hami [Kumul] City
商品零售价格总指数	**General Retail Price Index**	**104.1**	**106.0**	**107.5**	**106.9**	**104.8**	**104.7**
食 品	**Food**	**112.7**	**114.9**	**112.8**	**114.0**	**110.5**	**110.3**
粮 食	Grain	108.6	109.8	107.0	108.4	110.1	107.2
油 脂	Oil or Fat	113.2	114.5	114.0	105.3	105.6	112.4
肉禽及其制品	Meat, Poultry and Their Products	121.2	120.9	119.8	118.1	123.5	119.7
猪 肉	Pork	150.8	158.6	151.4	142.0	139.9	144.9
牛 肉	Beef	114.5	104.9	114.1	108.2	112.3	117.4
羊 肉	Mutton	116.6	116.2	112.7	117.5	109.6	115.3
鸡	Chicken	113.8	121.5	110.6	119.9	129.9	111.9
鲜 蛋	Fresh Egg	114.6	107.9	113.4	103.2	118.6	114.5
水产品	Aquatic Products	109.2	109.2	119.2	112.8	110.7	107.4
鲜瓜果	Fresh Fruits	120.3	127.9	117.2	131.1	112.8	122.8
糕点、饼干、面包	Cake、Biscuit and Bread	106.8	109.0	104.3	105.1	99.9	122.2
饮料、烟酒	**Beverages, Tobacco and Liquor**	**103.7**	**101.7**	**102.9**	**109.0**	**102.0**	**105.5**
茶及饮料	Tea and Beverages	103.8	102.9	101.3	110.4	101.4	114.2
#饮 料	Beverages	103.8	101.4	101.3	102.1	99.1	113.6
烟 草	Tobacco	100.0	100.0	100.0	100.0	100.0	100.0
酒	Liquor	108.4	104.6	105.9	115.8	103.8	106.9
服装鞋帽	**Garments, Shoes and Hats**	**96.5**	**102.9**	**110.8**	**101.6**	**102.2**	**92.1**
服 装	Garments	98.2	104.2	109.8	101.3	102.8	86.2
鞋袜帽	Footgear and Hats	92.7	100.0	112.8	102.2	101.1	100.0
#鞋	Shoes	91.9	100.0	114.6	102.7	101.1	100.0
纺织品	**Textiles**	**98.5**	**105.9**	**106.8**	**106.3**	**102.5**	**106.1**
棉 布	Cotton Cloth	115.8	124.5	115.3	120.7	117.8	136.2
化纤布	Chemical Fiber Cloth	105.4	107.0	106.7	107.2	98.8	106.3
毛 线	Wool	105.2	107.1	105.4	106.8	106.4	104.5
其 他	Others	100.0	100.0	118.0	109.5	100.6	100.0
家用电器及音响器材	**Household Appliances, Music and Sound Apparatus**	**93.4**	**95.2**	**98.1**	**98.7**	**98.6**	**97.9**
家庭设备	Household Facilities	96.3	97.3	99.7	98.9	99.7	100.1
文娱用耐用消费品	Durable Consuming Goods for Entertainment	89.3	92.6	95.7	98.4	96.9	95.3
专业音像器材	Sound Apparatus	94.2	97.4	99.4	100.0	100.0	99.5

Retail Price Indices by Category in Cities and Counties

(receding year=100)

昌吉市 Changji City	库尔勒市 Korla City	阿克苏市 Aksu City	焉耆回族自治县 Yanqi Hui Autonomous County	塔城市 Tacheng [Qoqek] City	阿勒泰市 Altay City	乌苏市 Usu City	博乐市 Bole [Bortala] City	吐鲁番市 Turpan City	库车县 Kuqa County	阿图什市 Artux City	莎车县 Shache [Yarkant] County	奎屯市 Kuytun City	石河子市 Shihezi City
105.8	**105.3**	**107.0**	**107.7**	**106.5**	**106.1**	**105.0**	**106.4**	**105.5**	**104.4**	**105.8**	**107.7**	**104.8**	**105.6**
111.2	**111.0**	**113.2**	**113.5**	**111.5**	**112.1**	**110.7**	**113.5**	**113.0**	**109.2**	**114.1**	**112.2**	**108.9**	**110.9**
108.8	109.2	104.2	107.0	109.3	106.6	109.9	109.6	108.1	109.2	111.4	106.5	108.0	108.9
115.7	105.5	113.2	116.5	116.9	120.1	113.3	113.1	121.6	104.0	109.8	122.5	104.7	113.8
119.6	117.5	121.4	116.9	124.8	121.9	118.0	119.1	117.0	114.0	111.0	113.1	121.5	116.0
147.6	153.2	150.9	156.2	161.3	147.6	134.7	146.9	140.5	148.1	122.3	147.3	159.4	146.4
114.1	105.4	107.9	105.9	112.9	119.0	113.3	109.2	113.6	103.7	105.8	104.9	113.3	104.2
117.3	111.9	109.1	107.1	117.2	111.9	113.6	116.1	117.0	113.4	112.0	103.5	111.1	114.3
109.5	117.0	109.9	114.5	115.6	129.6	120.1	122.7	107.8	119.3	112.8	117.0	112.1	106.0
117.1	113.6	112.8	114.3	112.1	109.6	125.6	109.9	117.1	108.3	108.2	103.3	117.0	114.0
106.4	108.7	108.5	108.8	113.5	110.5	104.9	110.5	111.2	109.1	115.8	110.9	106.3	108.7
105.6	131.0	126.4	116.7	110.7	125.0	110.7	121.2	130.5	142.6	158.0	102.1	113.9	108.0
101.5	106.2	102.9	117.8	107.9	101.8	103.4	111.1	111.3	100.7	100.1	106.7	107.5	102.3
104.0	**100.8**	**102.6**	**102.4**	**102.5**	**104.7**	**101.9**	**101.3**	**102.4**	**103.3**	**101.8**	**106.1**	**101.2**	**102.3**
106.7	101.2	105.1	100.9	102.1	103.0	100.6	101.5	94.5	103.4	99.4	102.2	100.0	104.8
107.2	102.1	105.2	101.5	101.4	103.0	100.8	100.9	93.0	106.7	99.5	102.8	100.0	106.8
101.5	100.0	100.0	100.0	100.0	99.7	100.0	99.8	105.9	97.1	100.3	110.6	100.0	100.6
106.9	101.4	105.0	106.2	106.6	110.7	104.3	103.3	112.3	108.0	107.0	103.6	103.5	102.2
102.6	**103.3**	**106.7**	**104.2**	**97.6**	**102.0**	**108.6**	**101.3**	**99.6**	**103.0**	**100.7**	**100.0**	**102.4**	**104.5**
102.7	104.0	104.7	106.0	96.5	103.5	102.1	101.2	100.6	100.7	100.1	98.8	101.9	103.9
102.6	102.2	109.9	101.4	100.5	100.0	116.1	101.6	97.5	106.7	101.6	103.5	103.3	106.0
102.7	101.9	104.1	102.3	100.0	100.0	124.8	99.3	94.9	106.5	101.5	106.4	104.4	106.8
102.3	**103.5**	**114.1**	**111.0**	**114.0**	**101.4**	**101.3**	**106.0**	**107.8**	**102.5**	**105.6**	**98.5**	**104.6**	**102.6**
107.2	106.0	130.5	137.9	190.2	103.9	103.3	128.6	128.6	108.2	109.1	97.6	105.0	100.0
99.0	100.0	108.6	109.1	104.6	101.2	105.4	106.4	105.1	100.0	100.9	96.4	100.0	100.2
100.0	100.0	100.6	111.8	118.9	100.0	100.0	101.9	97.0	113.1	100.0	96.3	101.9	102.5
100.0	100.0	107.5	100.0	100.0	105.6	100.0	100.0	93.1	91.7	117.5	100.0	100.0	96.9
99.8	**99.9**	**97.4**	**99.8**	**95.5**	**97.6**	**99.5**	**99.5**	**103.0**	**97.6**	**99.5**	**102.2**	**99.1**	**97.1**
100.9	100.0	98.6	99.9	97.6	100.1	100.0	100.0	105.8	95.6	102.0	104.1	99.8	99.1
98.5	99.5	96.0	99.5	92.9	94.3	98.9	98.8	99.1	100.3	96.0	99.8	98.2	94.4
96.2	101.1	100.0	101.1	100.0	100.0	100.0	99.8	100.0	99.8	100.0	100.0	99.5	100.0

8-5 续表

(上年=100)

项　目	Item	乌鲁木齐市 Urumqi City	喀什市 Kashgar [Kaxgar] City	伊宁市 Yining [Gulja] City	和田市 Hotan City	克拉玛依市 Karamay City	哈密市 Hami [Kumul] City
文化办公用品	**Cultural and Office Appliances**	**94.4**	**96.6**	**99.1**	**100.3**	**98.5**	**101.1**
日用品	**Articles for Daily Use**	**106.7**	**101.0**	**101.5**	**102.1**	**102.7**	**106.9**
日用百货	General Merchandise for Daily Use	101.7	99.2	99.6	101.7	100.7	101.3
日用杂品	Miscellaneous for Daily Use	97.9	99.7	100.2	100.0	100.7	106.2
洗涤用品	Washing and Cleaning Goods	112.3	103.7	100.3	104.0	106.3	114.6
其他日用品	Other Daily-use Goods	103.2	99.0	104.5	103.2	102.2	100.2
体育娱乐用品	**Sports and Entertainment Goods**	**102.7**	**100.1**	**101.9**	**101.5**	**101.1**	**99.7**
体育用品	Sports Articles	102.7	100.2	99.0	102.1	99.4	102.7
娱乐用品	Recreational Articles	102.6	100.1	104.0	100.8	102.8	96.1
交通、通信用品	**Traffic and Telecommunication Goods**	**86.0**	**95.8**	**96.7**	**97.3**	**97.4**	**94.6**
交通运输机械	Traffic and Transport Machinery	84.4	102.5	99.3	99.6	99.6	98.1
通信器材	Telecommunication Apparatus	87.9	86.4	94.6	94.1	95.0	90.0
家　具	**Furniture**	**99.0**	**99.2**	**99.9**	**102.2**	**100.9**	**101.0**
化妆品	**Cosmetics**	**101.3**	**100.4**	**101.4**	**103.7**	**100.7**	**102.9**
金银珠宝	**Gold and Silver Jewelry**	**115.7**	**107.7**	**114.9**	**116.4**	**115.2**	**111.2**
中西药品及医疗保健用品	**Chinese and Western Medicine, Medical-care and Healthy Goods**	**102.6**	**104.1**	**107.2**	**105.4**	**102.4**	**109.5**
医疗器具及用品	Medical-care Apparatus and Goods	93.9	99.9	102.6	100.0	104.2	106.4
中药材及中成药	Chinese Herbs and Patent Medicine	107.6	112.5	119.4	106.8	104.8	114.8
西　药	Western Medicine	101.7	101.2	101.5	106.1	101.5	108.1
保健器具及用品	Healthy Devices and Goods	100.8	98.6	100.0	99.9	99.8	102.1
书报杂志及电子出版物	**Books, Magazines and Electronic Publications**	**99.7**	**101.3**	**101.7**	**100.0**	**102.3**	**100.9**
教材及参考书	Texts and Reference Books	100.5	101.7	100.0	100.1	106.5	100.6
书报杂志	Newspapers and Magazines	100.6	101.5	105.0	100.0	100.7	103.1
电子音像制品	Electronic Audio and Video Products	96.9	100.0	99.5	100.0	95.7	97.3
燃　料	**Fuels**	**110.6**	**108.0**	**117.8**	**109.4**	**107.2**	**107.2**
煤炭及制品	Coal and Its Products	100.0	103.2	102.2	104.1	105.1	103.6
石油及制品	Oil and Its Products	111.2	110.0	120.1	110.7	108.3	109.1
建筑材料及五金电料	**Building Apparatus, Hardwares and Electrical Apparatus**	**103.4**	**109.4**	**102.1**	**105.1**	**106.7**	**102.9**
建筑装璜材料	Building Decoration Materials	102.4	110.0	103.1	106.3	108.9	102.6
五金电料	Hardwares and Electrical Apparatus	106.6	106.8	98.6	102.4	102.8	103.4

Continued

(preceding year=100)

昌吉市 Changji City	库尔勒市 Korla City	阿克苏市 Aksu City	焉耆回族自治县 Yanqi Hui Autonomous County	塔城市 Tacheng [Qoqek] City	阿勒泰市 Altay City	乌苏市 Usu City	博乐市 Bole [Bortala] City	吐鲁番市 Turpan City	库车县 Kuqa County	阿图什市 Artux City	莎车县 Shache [Yarkant] County	奎屯市 Kuytun City	石河子市 Shihezi City
96.6	**100.2**	**96.6**	**99.5**	**95.4**	**99.7**	**100.0**	**101.3**	**99.2**	**104.5**	**100.7**	**113.4**	**126.3**	**98.5**
102.2	**101.5**	**103.4**	**104.1**	**100.7**	**100.2**	**102.6**	**103.0**	**100.9**	**104.1**	**100.3**	**103.0**	**102.2**	**104.3**
101.1	101.0	102.3	100.7	100.0	99.8	101.4	99.4	101.7	107.2	100.0	106.2	101.0	101.7
99.7	100.6	105.0	100.9	101.0	99.8	100.0	102.7	100.0	103.1	100.0	102.3	106.3	105.0
104.1	103.2	108.0	110.1	104.3	101.1	106.2	107.6	100.9	101.0	100.2	101.9	100.0	107.0
100.3	100.1	100.1	101.2	99.5	100.0	99.4	99.9	100.0	103.8	102.4	97.2	101.3	101.8
100.1	**100.7**	**101.2**	**100.7**	**100.0**	**100.0**	**100.0**	**100.1**	**107.0**	**100.1**	**100.5**	**99.4**	**100.7**	**100.2**
99.9	102.0	100.0	101.0	100.0	100.0	100.0	100.0	111.7	100.0	101.0	98.7	102.0	103.5
100.2	99.2	101.8	100.4	100.0	100.0	100.0	100.2	100.0	100.2	100.0	100.0	99.9	96.7
98.0	**99.6**	**97.9**	**92.4**	**100.7**	**94.5**	**95.1**	**99.3**	**98.0**	**96.6**	**94.6**	**98.4**	**97.7**	**96.1**
97.6	100.0	99.1	100.0	100.1	100.9	100.0	100.1	96.5	98.5	100.0	100.5	100.0	96.8
98.6	98.7	96.1	89.2	102.0	89.1	91.4	98.3	98.8	94.7	90.2	96.9	96.1	95.2
101.9	**100.8**	**101.7**	**106.9**	**100.0**	**100.4**	**100.1**	**100.5**	**100.0**	**98.7**	**100.7**	**103.7**	**98.3**	**100.0**
101.6	**102.7**	**97.1**	**100.9**	**100.0**	**100.6**	**100.2**	**103.0**	**100.2**	**104.3**	**100.8**	**101.7**	**102.4**	**100.4**
134.8	**111.5**	**127.7**	**120.7**	**116.2**	**142.2**	**118.9**	**112.5**	**117.0**	**135.3**	**113.4**	**130.7**	**102.2**	**118.7**
102.9	**101.5**	**100.9**	**109.5**	**115.6**	**106.2**	**98.1**	**103.0**	**94.9**	**96.7**	**101.0**	**108.5**	**100.5**	**106.2**
100.0	102.6	100.0	104.2	114.3	100.0	100.0	97.6	87.1	98.1	98.7	96.0	99.2	95.4
112.1	105.1	102.1	119.2	122.4	116.7	97.4	106.7	104.9	100.6	105.2	129.5	103.3	116.9
98.5	99.2	100.4	105.1	111.5	101.0	98.2	102.8	90.3	93.5	99.1	100.9	100.0	103.5
103.7	100.5	100.0	100.0	102.8	100.0	99.8	100.0	96.5	96.0	100.0	102.6	97.0	96.9
100.1	**103.9**	**100.7**	**113.2**	**100.9**	**100.8**	**101.0**	**100.0**	**100.9**	**102.4**	**100.0**	**108.9**	**100.2**	**99.8**
101.0	112.1	100.4	117.8	100.0	100.0	100.0	100.0	99.9	103.1	100.0	103.8	100.6	100.0
100.1	101.6	101.8	107.9	103.5	102.2	102.4	100.0	102.3	104.1	100.0	115.2	100.0	100.0
99.4	100.0	100.0	100.0	98.5	100.0	100.0	100.0	100.0	100.0	100.0	100.0	100.0	99.2
106.6	**108.7**	**114.1**	**114.6**	**113.6**	**109.7**	**107.0**	**112.7**	**105.8**	**104.0**	**111.7**	**111.8**	**107.3**	**109.5**
103.4	101.2	118.6	115.6	113.1	101.0	99.0	108.4	104.2	101.2	125.7	115.8	101.6	108.7
106.7	111.1	112.6	114.0	113.8	114.7	113.3	114.5	107.0	106.8	107.9	110.0	110.3	109.7
107.4	**105.2**	**106.4**	**106.5**	**110.7**	**102.3**	**103.7**	**102.9**	**108.2**	**102.2**	**103.6**	**107.9**	**104.7**	**105.0**
109.4	107.1	107.7	107.7	111.7	103.0	106.7	104.2	112.3	104.6	105.8	110.0	104.7	107.1
100.6	101.1	101.1	103.2	95.9	100.8	100.0	100.3	100.0	99.8	100.1	101.2	104.4	101.2

8-6 主要年份农业生产资料价格分类指数

Price Indices for Means of Agricultural Production by Category in Main Years

(上年=100) (preceding year=100)

项 目	Item	2005	2010	2011
农业生产资料价格指数	**Price Indices for Means of Agricultural Production**	**105.3**	**103.1**	**106.6**
农用手工工具	Farm Handtools	104.9	101.0	100.8
饲料类	Forage	101.3	114.0	106.7
产品畜	Commodity Animals	89.4	127.1	120.7
半机械化农具	Semi-mechanized Farm Tools	100.9	101.7	102.5
机械化农具	Mechanized Farm Machinery	102.5	100.1	104.2
化学肥料	Chemical Fertilizer	110.2	95.3	102.1
农药及农药械	Pesticide and Its Appliances	102.8	101.7	100.1
农用机油	Oil for Farm Machinery	111.0	110.1	111.7
其他农业生产资料	Other Means of Agricultural Production	105.5	100.7	118.3
农业生产服务	Service for Agriculture Production		102.0	105.8

8-7 各市县农业生产资料价格指数

Price Indices for Means of Agricultural Production in Cities and Counties

(上年=100) (2011 年) (preceding year=100)

项 目	Item	塔城市 Kashgar [Kaxgar] City	阿勒泰市 Altay City	乌苏市 Usu City	博乐市 Bole [Bortala] City	吐鲁番市 Turpan City	库车县 Kuqa County	阿图什市 Artux City	莎车县 Shache [Yarkant] County	焉耆回族自治县 Yanqi Hui Autonomous County
农业生产资料价格指数	**Price Indices for Means of Agricultural Production**	**109.1**	**105.6**	**107.3**	**103.0**	**109.9**	**102.6**	**108.0**	**104.1**	**109.5**
农用手工工具	Farm Handtools	100.0	100.0	100.0	103.4	97.9	100.0	100.0	101.6	100.0
饲料类	Forage	102.6	111.5	117.6	113.4	110.9	108.4	118.4	91.9	102.9
产品畜	Commodity Animals	168.3	117.8	108.5	115.9	130.1	133.4	105.0	115.4	129.0
半机械化农具	Semi-mechanized Farm Tools	125.2	109.9	100.0	100.0	100.0	100.0	100.0	100.4	100.2
机械化农具	Mechanized Farm Machinery	101.5	107.0	100.0	100.5	100.0	100.0	100.7	106.5	111.5
化学肥料	Chemical Fertilizer	108.0	103.2	109.6	99.0	109.7	99.5	106.9	94.2	112.0
农药及农药械	Pesticide and Its Appliances	101.0	101.4	100.0	101.4	101.2	99.8	103.2	97.0	105.0
农用机油	Oil for Farm Machinery	111.6	109.4	113.8	105.8	111.2	110.4	109.3	112.8	117.8
其他农业生产资料	Other Means of Agricultural Production	106.7	103.5	98.8	100.0	105.0	96.2	114.5	141.7	107.9
农业生产服务	Service for Agriculture Production	104.9	100.5	102.6	100.4	119.9	97.3	103.4	104.6	101.3

8-8 主要年份工业生产者出厂价格分类指数
Producer Price Indices for Manufactured Goods by Category in Main Years

(上年=100) (preceding year=100)

项 目	Item	2005	2010	2011
全部工业品	**Total Industrial Products**	**116.6**	**125.3**	**114.8**
按轻、重工业分	**By Light and Heavy Industry**			
轻工业	Light Industry	99.6	108.9	110.1
以农产品为原料	Using Farm Produces as Raw Materials	98.4	111.2	110.8
以非农产品为原料	Using Non-farm Produces as Raw Materials	101.9	104.6	106.5
重工业	Heavy Industry	122.5	128.7	115.6
采 掘	Mining and Quarrying	136.2	153.1	127.9
原 料	Raw Materials	114.2	114.0	111.9
加 工	Processing	104.1	105.6	106.1
按部类分	**By Sector**			
生产资料	Means of Production	118.4	127.1	115.6
采 掘	Mining and Quarrying	136.0	151.9	127.9
原 料	Raw Materials	114.3	115.1	111.5
加 工	Processing	100.4	107.3	109.0
生活资料	Consumer Goods	101.3	104.1	106.4
食 品	Food	101.7	104.4	107.2
衣 着	Clothing	96.4	101.5	100.4
一般日用品	Articles for Daily Use	101.1	101.4	104.1
耐用消费品	Durable Consumer Goods	99.2	102.3	96.9
按工业部门分	**Division of Industrial Setors**			
冶金工业	Metallurgical Industry	101.9	114.4	112.7
电力工业	Power Industry	100.9	100.7	100.9
煤炭及炼焦工业	Coal and Coking Industry	109.4	104.0	103.1
石油工业	Petroleum Industry	130.5	141.6	123.6
化学工业	Chemical Industry	106.1	112.1	111.7
机械工业	Machine Manufacturing Industry	112.4	97.4	91.7
建筑材料工业	Building Materials Industry	99.4	101.1	108.2
森林工业	Timber Industry	99.9	101.7	96.5
食品工业	Food Industry	101.1	104.9	106.8
纺织工业	Textile Industry	92.1	122.8	131.2
缝纫工业	Tailoring Industry	96.3	101.5	100.1
皮革工业	Leather Industry	100.0	101.1	121.4
造纸工业	Paper Industry	102.6	127.8	105.8
文教艺术用品工业	Cultural, Educational and Handicrafts Articles	99.7	101.1	100.8
其他工业	Other Industry	104.0	107.7	106.5

8-9 主要年份工业生产者购进价格分类指数
Purchasing Prices Indices for Raw Material, Fuels and Power by Category in Main Years

(上年=100) (preceding year=100)

项　　目	Iterm	2005	2010	2011
全部原材料价格指数	**Total of Raw Material**	**110.7**	**123.9**	**117.8**
燃料、动力类	Fuel and Power	132.0	137.6	132.9
黑色金属材料类	Ferrous Metals	113.8	105.0	109.4
#钢　材	Rolled Steel	112.9	102.5	106.9
其　他	Others	114.9	112.3	114.0
有色金属材料和电线类	Nonferrous Metals and Wire Type	108.5	139.6	111.9
化工原料类	Raw Chemistry Material	113.0	106.8	106.7
木材及纸浆类	Timber and Paper Pulp	102.0	104.0	103.7
建筑材料及非金属矿类	Building Material and Non-metal Ore	103.9	103.0	104.0
其他工业原材料及半成品类	Other Industrial Raw Material and Semi-finished Category	105.5	101.1	102.9
农副产品类	Agricultural Products	91.9	118.7	109.6
纺织原料类	Textile Raw Materials	93.0	144.2	118.3

8-10 主要年份固定资产投资价格指数
Price Indices for Investment in Fixed Assets in Main Years

(上年=100) (preceding year=100)

项　　目	Item	2005	2010	2011
固定资产投资价格指数	**Investment in Fixed Assets**	**102.8**	**104.6**	**107.1**
建筑安装工程	**Construction and Installtion**	**102.7**	**105.9**	**110.3**
人工费	Manpower Expenses	103.8	110.6	116.1
材料费	Material Expenses	102.3	104.8	108.9
#钢　材	Rolled Steel	101.7	104.4	109.1
木　材	Timber	102.5	104.8	107.3
水　泥	Cement	100.1	104.7	112.2
地方材料	Local Material	102.0	104.6	110.8
化工材料	Chemical Material	109.1	104.9	108.4
电　料	Electrical Wire	104.0	105.1	106.4
其他材料	Other Material	99.9	101.7	103.7
机械使用费	Expenses of Machine Use	102.3	103.3	109.0
设备工器具	**Purchase of Equipment,Tools and Instruments**	**104.8**	**100.4**	**98.4**
其他费用	**Others**	**100.0**	**105.2**	**103.7**

主要统计指标解释

居民消费价格指数 简称CPI，是反映一定时期内城乡居民所购买的生活消费品价格和服务项目价格变动趋势和程度的相对数，是对城市居民消费价格指数和农村居民消费价格指数进行综合汇总计算的结果。该指数可以观察和分析消费品的零售价格和服务价格变动对城乡居民实际生活费支出的影响程度。

商品零售价格指数 是反映一定时期内城乡商品零售价格变动趋势和程度的相对数。商品零售物价的变动直接影响到城乡居民的生活支出和国家的财政收入，影响居民购买力和市场供需的平衡，影响到消费与积累的比例关系。因此，该指数可以从一个侧面对上述经济活动进行观察和分析。

农业生产资料价格指数 指反映一定时期内农业生产资料价格变动趋势和程度的相对数。其编制目的是了解农业生产中物质资料投入价格的变动状况，服务于国民经济核算。1994年以前，农业生产资料价格指数仅仅是商品零售价格指数的一个类别，此后，从商品零售价格指数中分离出来，单独编制。

工业生产者出厂价格指数 简称PPI，是反映一定时期内全部工业产品出厂价格（工业企业产品第一次出售时的价格）总水平的变动趋势和程度的相对数，包括工业企业售给本企业以外所有单位的各种产品和直接售给居民用于生活消费的产品。该指数可以观察出厂价格变动对工业总产值及增加值的影响。

工业生产者购进价格指数 是反映工业企业作为生产投入而从物资交易市场和能源、原材料生产企业购买原材料、燃料和动力产品时，所支付的价格水平变动趋势和程度的相对数。是扣除工业企业物质消耗成本承担价格变动影响的重要依据。

固定资产投资价格指数 是反映一定时期内固定资产投资品及费用项目的价格变动趋势和程度的相对数。固定资产投资额是由建筑安装工程投资完成额、设备工器具购置投资完成额和其他费用投资完成额三部分组成的。编制固定资产投资价格指数应首先分别编制上述三部分投资的价格指数，然后采用加权算术平均法求出固定资产投资价格总指数。

该指数可以准确地反映固定资产投资中涉及的各类投资品和取费项目价格变动趋势和变动幅度，消除按现价计算的固定资产投资指标中的价格变动因素，真实地反映固定资产投资的规模、速度、结构和效益，为国家科学地制定、检查固定资产投资计划并提高宏观调控水平，为完善国民经济核算体系提供科学的、可靠的依据。

Explanatory Notes on Main Statistical Indicators

Consumer Price Indices reflect the trend and degree of changes in prices of consumer goods and services purchased by urban households during a given period,and is a composite index derived from the urban consumer price index and the rural consumer price index. Consumer price index can be used to analyze the impact of consumer price change on actual expenditure for living cost of urban and rural residents.

Retail Price Indices reflect the trend and degree of change in retail prices of commodities during a given period. The change in retail prices of commodities directly affect the living expenses of urban and rural residents, government revenue, purchasing power of residents and the equilibrium of market supply and demand, and the ratio of consumption to accumulation. Therefore, the retail price indices are useful from an oblique perspective for observing and analyzing the changes of the above economic activities.

Price Indices for Means of Agricultural Production reflect the trend and degree of changes in the prices of the means of agricultural production during a given period. Compilation of these indices helps to understand the changes in prices of input into agricultural production and facilitate the compilation of national accounts statistics. Before 1994, price indices for means of agricultural production were a sub-category in the retail price indices for commodities, and it has been compiled separately since 1994.

Producer Price Indices for Manufactured Goods reflect the trend and degree of changes in general ex-factory prices of all manufactured goods during a given period, including sales of manufactured goods by an industrial enterprise to all units outside the enterprise, as well as sales of consumer goods to residents. It can be used to analyze the impact of ex-factory prices on gross output value and value-added of the industrial sector.

Indices of Purchasing Prices of Raw Materials,Fuels and Power reflect changes in the levels and degree of prices paid by industrial enterprises when they purchase production input such as raw materials ,fuels and power from the market or from other energy or raw materials producing enterprises,These indices provide important basis for measuring the material consumption of industrial enterprises afer removing influence of price changes.

Price Indices for Investment in Fixed Assets reflect the trend and degree of changes in prices of investment goods and projects in fixed assets during a given period. The investment in fixed assets consists of three components, namely the investment in construction and installation, the investment in purchases of equipment and instrument, and the investment in other items. Price indices for investment in fixed assets are calculated as the weighted arithmetic mean of the price indices for the three components of investment in fixed assets.

Removing the factor of price change in the aggregates of investment at current prices, this indicator shows the changes in the prices of commodities and fees involved in the investment of fixed assets, and can be used to observe the actual size, growth, structure, and efficiency of investment in fixed assets and provides reliable and scientific data for government planning, management, decisionmaking, and further improving the current national accounting system.

Price Indices for Real Estate reflect the trend and degree of changes in prices of real estate during a given period, including sale price indices for houses, price indices for renting houses, price indices for land transactions and price indices for management of properties. The methods for the compilation of these four sets of indices are similar in that they all use the bottom-up approach under which data are reported from lower level to higher level

2012

新疆统计年鉴

XINJIANG STATISTICAL YEARBOOK

第九篇
人民生活和社会保障

CHAPTER 9
People′s Living Conditions and Social Security

简要说明
Brief Introduction

本篇资料的主要内容及来源

本篇资料反映新疆城乡人民生活现状及变化以及城镇居民社会保障情况，分为城镇居民生活和农村居民生活两部分，主要包括居民家庭基本情况、家庭收入、支出情况、主要商品购买数量及支出金额、居住状况和耐用消费品的拥有量等。

城镇居民生活状况的数据来源于国家统计局新疆调查总队城镇住户调查处。

农村居民生活状况的数据来源于国家统计局新疆调查总队农村住户调查处。

城镇居民社会保障情况数据来源于新疆维吾尔自治区人力资源和社会保障厅。

Main Content and Source of Data

Data in this chapter show the condition of people's livelihood in Xinjiang and social security in urban and rural, consisting of two parts on the life of urban and rural households respectively, including mainly basic condition of people's household, income of households, income and expenditure of the household, the quantity and the expenditure on major commodities purchased, the housing condition and the possession of the durable consumer goods, etc.

Data on the livelihood of the urban residents are from the Department of Urban households Survey , NBS Survey office in Xinjiang.

Data on the livelihood of the rural residents are from the Department of Rural households Surveys, NBS Survey Office in Xinjiang

Data on social security in urban and rural are from Bureau of Human Resources and Social Security of Xinjiang Uygur Autonomous Region.

9-1 主要年份人民物质文化生活情况

People's Material and Cultural Living Conditions in Main Years

项目	Item	2000	2005	2010	2011
就 业	**Employment**				
城镇居民家庭每户就业人口(人)	Average Number of Employed Persons Per Urban Household (person)	1.55	1.48	1.54	1.49
农村居民家庭每户整半劳动力(人)	Average Number of Full/Semi Laborer Per (person)	3.06	2.92	3.14	2.85
每一农村劳动力负担人数(人)	Number of Dependents Per Laborer of Rural Household (person)	1.74	1.62	1.47	1.51
每一城镇就业者负担人数(人)	Number of Dependents Per Employee of Urban Household (person)	2.03	2.04	1.94	1.95
城镇登记失业率(%)	Registered Urban Unemployment Rate (%)	3.8	3.9	3.2	3.2
收入与支出	**Income and Expenditure**				
城镇居民家庭人均可支配收入(元)	Annual Per capita Disposable Income of Urban Household Residents (yuan)	5645	7990	13644	15514
农村居民家庭人均纯收入(元)	Annual per Capita Net Income of Rural Household (yuan)	1618	2482	4643	5442
城镇居民人均消费性支出(元)	Annual Per capita Net Income of Rural Household (yuan)	4423	6208	10197	11839
农村居民人均生活消费支出(元)	Annual per Capita Living Expencliture of Urban (yuan)	1236	1924	3458	4398
人均储蓄存款余额(元)	Per Capita Balance of Saving Deposit (yuan)	4913	9035	17113	20145
生活质量(元)	**Annual Per capita Consumption (yuan)**				
居民家庭恩格尔系数 (%)	Household's Engel;s Coefficient (%)				
城 镇	Urban	36.4	36.4	36.2	38.3
农 村	Rural	50.0	41.8	40.3	36.1
居住条件	Residence Condition				
城镇人均住房建筑面积(平方米)	Per Capita Building Space in Urban Area (sq.m)	26.75	26.02	27.25	28.92
农村人均住房面积(平方米)	Per Capita Living Space in Rural Area (sq.m)	17.25	21.23	24.00	26.14
交 通	Traffic				
城镇每百户拥有汽车(辆)	Number of Automobile per 100 Households in Urban Areas (unit)	0.82	2.81	8.63	12.32
农村每百户拥有摩托车(辆)	Number of Motor Cycles Per 100 Rural Household (unit)	18.33	45.42	62.84	77.23
通信条件	Communication Condition				
电话普及率(固定电话)(部/百人)	Telephone Popularization Rate (Fixed Telephone)(set/100 persons)	15.0	30.8	25.4	25.0
移动电话普及率(部/百人)	Popularization Rate of Mobile Telephone (set/100 persons)	4.3	26.7	63.0	77.4
城镇公用事业	Public Utilities in Urban Areas				
自来水普及率 (%)	Coverage Rate of Population with Access to Tap Water (%)	98.8	97.9	99.2	99.2

9-1 续表 Continued

项　　目	Item	2000	2005	2010	2011
燃气普及率（%）	Coverage Rate of Population with Access to Gas(%)	92.8	89.3	95.8	96.2
文化、教育和卫生	**Culture,Education and Health Care**				
文 化	Culture				
广播综合人口覆盖率（%）	Radio Coverage Rate of Population (%)	89.77	93.14	94.90	94.90
电视综合人口覆盖率（%）	TV Coverage Rate of Population (%)	92.15	92.78	95.28	95.29
每百户彩色电视机拥有量（部/百户）	Number of Color TV Per 100 Household (set/100 Households)				
城 镇	Urban	102.57	105.70	105.61	106.42
农 村	Rural	31.87	61.81	89.87	99.03
居民家庭文教娱乐支出比重（%）	Percentage of Household Expenditure on Education, Culture and Entertainment				
城 镇	Urban	13.58	11.94	9.93	9.48
农 村	Rural	3.76	3.70	4.92	5.22
教 育	Education				
各级普通学校毕业生升学率（%）	Rate of Entering Higher School				
高中升学率	Promotion Rate from Senion Secondary Schools to Higher Education	80.46	64.84	84.59	85.02
初中升学率	Promotion Rate from Junior Secondary Schools to Senior Secondary Schools	30.30	39.13	45.40	47.64
小学升学率	Promotion Rate from Primary Schools to Junior Secondary Schools	92.01	99.33	100.53	99.47
卫 生	Public Health				
每万人有医院、卫生院床位(张)	Number of Hospital Beds per 10 000 Population (unit)	35.6	37.8	50.4	53.9
每万人有医生数(人)	Number of Doctors per 10 000 Population (person)	24.6	20.6	22.3	22.5
居民家庭医疗保健支出比重（%）	Percentage of Resident Expenditure on Health Care				
城 镇	Urban	7.48	8.04	6.94	7.71
农 村	Rural	2.61	3.93	9.10	8.57
社会保障	Social Security				
参加城镇职工基本养老保险人数（万人）	Number of Employees Joining Urban Basic Pension Insurance (10 000persons)	140.34	181.87	259.67	291.99
参加城镇职工基本医疗保险人数（万人）	Number of Persons Joining Urban Basic Medical Care System (10 000persons)	88.20	211.85	296.72	322.73
参加失业保险人数（万人）	Number of Employees Joining Unemploy ment Insurance (10 000persons)	122.10	140.82	180.29	196.72
参加工伤保险人数（万人）	Number of Employees Joining Injury Insurance (10 000persons)		79.51	184.13	208.18
参加生育保险人数（万人）	Number of persons Joining Maternity Insurance (10 000persons)		103.48	188.23	206.14

9-2 主要年份城乡居民储蓄存款年底余额和年增加额
Savings Deposit of Urban and Rural Households at Year-end in Main Years

单位: 亿元 (100 million yuan)

年 份 Year l	年末余额 Total	年增加额 Year-on-year Increase	年 份 Year l	年末余额 Total	年增加额 Year-on-year Increase
1978	6.42		2004	1534.67	162.85
1980	9.52	2.31	2005	1816.38	281.71
1985	29.55	5.24	2006	2035.63	219.25
1990	114.13	35.68	2007	2054.91	19.29
1995	477.18	129.47	2008	2550.95	499.45
2000	908.55	83.86	2009	3049.91	498.79
2001	994.00	85.46	2010	3713.47	662.61
2002	1137.87	143.85	2011	4421.93	709.38
2003	1371.59	233.81			

9-3 主要年份城乡居民家庭人均收入及指数
Per Capita Annual Income of Urban and Rural Households and the Related Index in Main Years

年 份 Year	农村居民家庭人均纯收入 Per capita Annual Net Income of Rural Households		城镇居民家庭人均年可支配收入 Per capita Annual Disposable Income of Urban Households		农村居民家庭恩格尔系数 (%) Engel's Coefficient of Rural Households (%)	城镇居民家庭恩格尔系数 (%) Engel's Coefficient of Urban Households (%)
	绝对数（元） Value (yuan)	指数(1978=100) Index	绝对数（元） Value (yuan)	指数(1978=100) Index		
1978	119	100.0	319	100.0		
1980	201	168.9	427	133.9	60.8	57.3
1985	394	331.1	735	230.4	57.9	46.8
1990	684	574.8	1314	411.8	53.7	47.8
1995	1137	955.5	4163	1172.3	50.1	44.8
2000	1618	1359.3	5645	1589.4	50.0	36.4
2001	1710	1437.0	6215	1749.9	50.4	34.8
2002	1863	1564.9	6554	1979.1	49.0	33.9
2003	2106	1768.3	7006	2115.7	45.5	35.9
2004	2245	1885.0	7503	2265.9	45.2	36.1
2005	2482	2084.0	7990	2412.9	41.8	36.4
2006	2737	2300.0	8871	2679.0	39.9	35.5
2007	3183	2674.8	10313	3114.5	39.9	35.1
2008	3503	2943.7	11432	3452.4	42.5	37.3
2009	3883	3263.0	12258	3701.8	41.6	36.3
2010	4643	3901.7	13644	4120.0	40.3	36.2
2011	5442	4573.1	15514	4684.4	36.1	38.3

注: 1992 年以前城镇居民人均年可支配收入为人均年生活费收入。
Note: Per capita disposal income of urban households before the year 1992 is Per capita annual income as life expense.

9-4 主要年份城镇居民家庭生活基本情况

Basic Living Conditions of Urban Households in Main Years

(抽样调查 Sampled Survey)

项　　目	Item	2000	2005	2010	2011
调查户数（户）	**Number of Households Surveyed (household)**	**790**	**1380**	**1560**	**1460**
平均每户家庭人口(人)	**Average Household Size (person)**	**3.15**	**3.02**	**2.98**	**2.91**
平均每户就业人口(人)	**Average Number of Employed Persons Per Household (person)**	**1.55**	**1.48**	**1.54**	**1.49**
平均每户就业面 (%)	**Proportion of Employment per Household (%)**	**49.21**	**49.01**	**51.68**	**51.20**
平均每一就业者负担人数(包括就业者本人)(人)	**Number of Dependents Per Employee (including the employee himself or herself) (person)**	**2.03**	**2.04**	**1.94**	**1.95**
平均每人全部年收入(元)	**Per Capita Annual Income (yuan)**	**5686.52**	**8693.67**	**15421.59**	**17631.15**
#可支配收入	Disposable Income	5644.86	7990.15	13643.77	15513.62
工资性收入	Income from Wages and Salaries	4128.29	6553.47	11327.91	12653.43
工资及补贴收入	Salary & Subsidy	4027.36	6331.74	11208.19	12551.87
其他劳动收入	Part-time Income	100.93	221.73	119.72	101.56
经营净收入	Net Business Income	230.29	522.14	1131.78	1412.32
财产性收入	Income from Porperties	38.03	54.51	151.94	149.06
转移性收入	Income from Transfer	1243.55	1563.54	2809.96	3416.35
平均每人消费性支出(元)	**Per Capita Annual Consumption Expenditures (yuan)**	**4422.92**	**6207.52**	**10197.09**	**11839.40**
平均每人消费性支出构成(%)(人均消费支出=100)	**Composition of Per Capita Annual Consumption (%)**	**100**	**100**	**100**	**100**
食　品	Food	36.38	36.37	36.23	38.33
衣　着	Clothing	13.05	13.31	14.84	14.49
家庭设备用品及服务	Household Facilities,Articles and Service	9.29	4.99	6.57	6.68
医疗保健	Health Care and Medical Service	7.48	8.04	6.94	7.71
交通通讯	Transport and Communication	7.48	12.20	12.32	11.64
教育文化娱乐服务	Education , Cultural and Recreation Services	13.58	11.94	9.93	9.48
居　住	Residence	7.76	9.21	8.81	7.50
其他商品和服务	Miscellaneous Goods and Services	4.98	3.94	4.36	4.17

9-5 城镇居民家庭基本情况
Basic Conditions of Urban Households

(2011 年) (抽样调查 Sampled Survey)

项目	Item	全区 Whole Region	最低收入户 Lowest Income Households	#困难户 Poor Households	低收入户 Low Income Households
调查户数(户)	Number of Households Surveyed (household)	1460	145	74	145
比重(%)	Proportion (%)	100	10	5	10
平均每户家庭人口(人)	Average Household Size (person)	2.91	3.92	4.15	3.33
平均每户就业人口(人)	Average Number of Employees per Household (person)	1.49	1.17	1.12	1.47
平均每户就业面(%)	Proportion of Employment per Household (%)	51.20	29.85	26.99	44.14
平均每一就业者负担人数(包括就业者本人)(人)	Number of Dependents per Employee (Including the employee himself or herself) (person)	1.95	3.35	3.71	2.27
平均每人全部年收入(元)	Per Capita Annual Income (yuan)	17631.15	5428.85	4548.87	9528.22
平均每人可支配收入(元)	Per Capita Disposable Income (yuan)	15513.62	4707.66	3907.22	8222.87
平均每人消费性支出(元)	Per Capita Annual Consumption Expenditure (yuan)	11839.40	5262.41	4638.05	7395.11

项目	Item	中等偏下户 Lower Middle Income Households	中等收入户 Middle Income Households	中等偏上户 Upper Middle Income Households	高收入户 High Income Households	最高收入户 Highest Income Households
调查户数(户)	Number of Households Surveyed (household)	295	296	294	146	139
比重(%)	Proportion (%)	20	20	20	10	10
平均每户家庭人口(人)	Average Household Size (person)	3.18	2.83	2.53	2.51	2.11
平均每户就业人口(人)	Average Number of Employees per Household (person)	1.67	1.65	1.42	1.51	1.26
平均每户就业面(%)	Proportion of Employed Persons per Household (%)	52.52	58.30	56.13	60.16	59.72
平均每一就业者负担人数(包括就业者本人)(人)	Number of Dependents per Employee (Including the employee himself or herself) (person)	1.90	1.72	1.78	1.66	1.67
平均每人全部年收入(元)	Per Capita Annual Income (yuan)	13393.86	17882.95	23408.55	30283.30	42047.87
平均每人可支配收入(元)	Per Capita Disposable Income (yuan)	11528.83	15711.64	20843.16	26612.31	37845.82
平均每人消费性支出(元)	Per Capita Annual Consumption Expenditure (yuan)	9859.01	11624.58	15986.47	18134.39	23022.88

9-6 城镇居民家庭平均每人全年消费性支出
Per Capita Annual Living Expenditure of Urban Households

单位：元 (2011 年) (抽样调查 Sampled Survey) (yuan)

项目	Item	总平均 Total Average	最低收入户 Lowest Income Households	#困难户 Poor Households	低收入户 Low Income Households
消费性支出	**Consumption Expenditures**	**11839.40**	**5262.41**	**4638.05**	**7395.11**
食品	Food	4537.46	2584.64	2364.22	3438.73
#粮食	Grain	441.69	470.67	474.08	467.75
肉禽及其制品	Meat, Poultry and Processed Products	1048.21	780.78	727.45	924.35
蛋类	Eggs	85.84	65.62	58.48	72.59
水产品	Aquatic Products	100.17	39.62	21.67	69.75
奶及奶制品	Milk and Processed Products	197.70	101.41	93.85	112.97
衣着	Clothing	1715.94	666.20	561.58	988.42
#服装	Garments	1209.04	441.07	370.91	667.12
家庭设备用品及服务	Household Appliances and Services	791.43	245.99	200.19	426.57
#耐用消费品	Durable Consumer Goods	279.89	57.50	43.80	119.86
医疗保健	Health Care and Medical Services	912.99	530.28	493.08	421.61
交通通讯	Transport and Communication Services	1377.67	422.28	360.63	689.30
教育文化娱乐服务	Education , Cultural and Recreation Services	1122.18	257.39	158.33	670.15
#文化娱乐用品	Recreation Articles	326.80	63.63	44.40	208.67
居住	Residence	888.16	479.00	442.66	582.99
#住房	Housing	200.17	90.71	102.16	100.51
其他商品和服务	Miscellaneous Goods and Services	493.56	76.63	57.35	177.35

项目	Item	中等偏下户 Lower Middle Income Households	中等收入户 Middle Income Households	中等偏上户 Upper Middle Income Households	高收入户 High Income Households	最高收入户 Highest Income Households
消费性支出	**Consumption Expenditures**	**9859.01**	**11624.58**	**15986.47**	**18134.39**	**23022.88**
食品	Food	3893.75	4467.30	5603.19	6465.87	7988.09
#粮食	Grain	380.75	409.70	486.93	462.78	484.85
肉禽及其制品	Meat, Poultry and Processed Products	852.76	1014.16	1321.89	1370.91	1489.36
蛋类	Eggs	71.66	91.12	107.62	106.67	103.30
水产品	Aquatic Products	88.63	120.00	117.91	136.98	177.03
奶及奶制品	Milk and Processed Products	172.52	255.70	208.59	315.38	305.19
衣着	Clothing	1383.40	1837.73	2348.61	2677.65	3265.89
#服装	Garments	967.96	1272.64	1685.36	1903.68	2407.91
家庭设备用品及服务	Household Appliances and Services	636.05	844.33	1146.58	1207.54	1582.68
#耐用消费品	Durable Consumer Goods	210.18	301.15	473.61	428.51	544.41
医疗保健	Health Care and Medical Services	857.43	780.11	1395.57	1146.54	1722.88
交通通讯	Transport and Communication Services	960.07	1220.47	2193.99	2277.37	3370.20
教育文化娱乐服务	Education , Cultural and Recreation Services	1008.53	1113.57	1487.86	2121.94	1984.18
#文化娱乐用品	Recreation Articles	277.40	323.47	500.47	474.65	650.97
居住	Residence	756.56	919.47	1142.69	1346.97	1454.12
#住房	Housing	136.73	170.69	328.88	352.87	396.15
其他商品和服务	Miscellaneous Goods and Services	363.22	441.61	667.98	890.50	1654.84

9-7 城镇居民家庭平均每人全年消费性支出构成
Composition of Per Capita Living Expenditure of Urban Households

单位：% (2011 年) (抽样调查 Sampled Survey) (%)

项目	Item	总平均 Total Average	最低收入户 Lowest Income Households	#困难户 Poor Households	低收入户 Low Income Households
消费性支出	**Consumption Expenditures**	**100**	**100**	**100**	**100**
食 品	Food	38.33	49.12	50.97	46.50
衣 着	Clothing	14.49	12.66	12.11	13.37
家庭设备用品及服务	Household Facilities, Articles and Services	6.68	4.67	4.32	5.77
医疗保健	Health Care and Medical Services	7.71	10.08	10.63	5.70
交通通讯	Transport and Communication Services	11.64	8.02	7.78	9.32
教育文化娱乐服务	Education , Cultural and Recreation Services	9.48	4.89	3.41	9.06
居 住	Residence	7.50	9.10	9.54	7.88
其他商品和服务	Miscellaneous Goods and Services	4.17	1.46	1.24	2.40

项目	Item	中等偏下户 Lower Middle Income Households	中等收入户 Middle Income Households	中等偏上户 Upper Middle Income Households	高收入户 High Income Households	最高收入户 Highest Income Households
消费性支出	**Consumption Expenditures**	**100**	**100**	**100**	**100**	**100**
食 品	Food	39.49	38.43	35.05	35.66	34.70
衣 着	Clothing	14.03	15.81	14.69	14.77	14.19
家庭设备用品及服务	Household Facilities, Articles and Services	6.45	7.26	7.17	6.66	6.87
医疗保健	Health Care and Medical Services	8.70	6.71	8.73	6.32	7.48
交通通讯	Transport and Communication Services	9.74	10.50	13.72	12.56	14.64
教育文化娱乐服务	Education , Cultural and Recreation Services	10.23	9.58	9.31	11.70	8.62
居 住	Residence	7.67	7.91	7.15	7.43	6.32
其他商品和服务	Miscellaneous Goods and Services	3.68	3.80	4.18	4.91	7.19

9-8 主要年份城镇居民家庭年人均购买的主要商品数量

Per Capita Annual Purchases of Major Commodities of Urban Households in Main Years

(抽样调查 Sampled Survey)

项 目	Item	2000	2005	2010	2011
粮食(千克)	Grain (kg)	81.91	88.38	89.76	100.75
鲜菜(千克)	Fresh Vegetables (kg)	90.56	109.45	96.15	104.01
食用植物油(千克)	Edible Vegetable Oil (kg)	9.69	11.01	10.94	11.44
猪肉(千克)	Pork (kg)	5.17	6.37	7.33	7.10
牛肉(千克)	Beef (kg)	3.62	3.51	3.86	4.83
羊肉(千克)	Mutton(kg)	13.06	11.99	9.87	10.06
禽类(千克)	Poultry (kg)	6.11	6.71	8.14	8.52
鲜蛋(千克)	Fresh Eggs (kg)	7.39	7.44	7.91	8.66
水产品(千克)	Aquatic Products (kg)	4.35	4.98	5.27	4.43
鲜乳品(千克)	Fresh Dairy Products (kg)	18.44	26.26	21.80	21.46
鲜瓜果(千克)	Fresh Fruits & Melons(kg)	64.31	66.99	57.36	62.99
服装(件)	Clothes(piece)	6.36	7.51	8.60	8.57
管道天然气(立方米)	Natural Gas (cu.m)	1.93	22.12	39.68	52.42
煤炭(千克)	Coal (kg)	123.78	133.57	84.07	58.87

9-9 主要年份城镇居民家庭平均每百户年底耐用消费品拥有量

Number of Major Durable Consumer Goods Owned Per-100 Urban Households at Year-end in Main Years

项 目	Item	2000	2005	2010	2011
摩托车(辆)	Motorcycle (unit)	8.53	16.04	18.53	13.79
助力车(辆)	Aided Power Bicycle (unit)		2.29	8.60	13.77
家用汽车(辆)	Automobil (unit)	0.82	2.81	8.63	12.32
洗衣机(台)	Washing Machine (unit)	95.48	88.53	93.43	96.10
电冰箱(台)	Refrigerator (unit)	81.76	79.72	90.20	94.34
彩色电视机(台)	Color TV Set (set)	102.57	105.70	105.61	106.42
家用电脑(台)	Household Computer (set)	5.68	23.86	47.68	61.20
组合音响(套)	Hi-Fi Stereo Component System (set)	17.53	16.10	15.06	15.10
摄相机(架)	Pickug Camera (set)	1.02	3.12	4.57	7.98
照相机(架)	Camera (set)	33.71	37.42	26.83	29.24
钢琴(架)	Piano (set)	1.38	2.23	2.04	1.36
其他中高档乐器(件)	Other Medium and High Grade Musical Instrument (piece)	9.09	5.97	6.54	5.05
微波炉(台)	Oven (unit)	5.39	19.68	34.84	37.75
空调器(台)	Air Conditioner (unit)	2.78	7.02	12.42	11.87
淋浴热水器(台)	Shower (unit)	47.91	59.58	74.27	76.53
消毒碗柜(台)	Disinfectant Machine (unit)		4.56	3.80	4.76
健身器材(台)	Healthy Equipment (unit)	2.35	3.89	2.65	1.08
固定电话(部)	Telephone (unit)	71.69	87.23	82.42	77.15
移动电话(部)	Mobile Phone (unit)	4.81	108.61	159.79	181.54
接入有线电视电视机(台)	Cable Tv (unit)		97.86	88.34	83.85
接入互连网计算机(台)	Internet Computer (unit)		12.43	32.20	48.17
接入互连网移动电话(台)	Internet Mobile Phone (unit)		0.52	7.89	23.05

9-10 按收入等级分城镇居民家庭平均每人全年购买商品数量

Per Capita Annual Purchases of Major Commodities of Urban Households by Level of Income

(2011 年) (抽样调查 Sampled Survey)

项　目	Item	总平均 Total Average	最低收入户 Lowest Income Households	#困难户 Poor Households	低收入户 Low Income Households
粮　食(千克)	Grain (kg)	100.75	117.79	119.16	108.31
油脂类(千克)	Oil and Fats (kg)	11.48	11.26	11.80	12.47
食用植物油(千克)	Edible Vegetable Oil (kg)	11.44	11.22	11.78	12.43
肉　类(千克)	Meat (kg)	24.77	17.36	15.80	21.39
猪　肉(千克)	Pork (kg)	7.10	2.36	0.97	5.15
牛　肉(千克)	Beef (kg)	4.83	2.62	1.99	4.30
羊　肉(千克)	Mutton (kg)	10.06	11.39	12.15	10.24
禽　类(千克)	Poultry (kg)	8.52	4.67	3.07	6.66
蛋　类(千克)	Fresh Eggs (kg)	9.16	7.40	6.70	7.94
鱼　(千克)	Fish (kg)	4.43	2.23	1.21	3.39
虾　(千克)	Shrimp (kg)	0.40	0.10	0.04	0.24
鲜　菜(千克)	Fresh Vegetables (kg)	104.01	77.18	70.57	93.40
酒　类(千克)	Liquor (kg)	3.41	1.14	0.89	2.07
白　酒(千克)	Liquor (kg)	1.15	0.33	0.37	0.64
果　酒(千克)	Fruit Wine (kg)	0.19	0.01	0.01	0.13
啤　酒(千克)	Beer (kg)	2.06	0.79	0.51	1.31
鲜　果(千克)	Fresh Fruits (kg)	32.47	19.73	17.62	22.66
鲜　瓜(千克)	Fresh Melon (kg)	30.52	23.31	22.86	23.01
糕　点(千克)	Cake (kg)	4.20	1.66	1.39	3.00
鲜乳品(千克)	Fresh Dairy Products (kg)	21.64	15.56	14.75	14.25
奶　粉(千克)	Milk Powder (kg)	0.26	0.07	0.05	0.09
酸　奶(千克)	Yogurt (kg)	4.14	1.87	1.39	2.55
服　装(件)	Clothing (piece)	8.57	4.47	3.88	6.03
鞋　类(双)	Shoes (pair)	2.81	1.96	1.73	2.31
水(吨)	Water (ton)	26.43	20.38	22.14	24.46
电(度)	Electricity (kw)	323.85	178.37	164.41	271.62
煤　炭(千克)	Coal (kg)	58.87	172.19	188.42	57.24
罐装液化石油气(千克)	Liquefied Gas (kg)	6.54	5.81	6.33	4.80
管道天然气(立方米)	Gas Pipeline (cu.m)	52.42	26.28	21.39	49.75

9-10 续表 Continued

项目	Item	中等偏下户 Lower Middle Income Households	中等收入户 Middle Income Households	中等偏上户 Upper Middle Income Households	高收入户 High Income Households	最高收入户 Highest Income Households
粮　食(千克)	Grain (kg)	85.18	96.15	108.7	99.63	97.06
油脂类(千克)	Oil and Fats (kg)	10.19	11.67	12.33	11.62	11.34
食用植物油(千克)	Edible Vegetable Oil (kg)	10.18	11.60	12.30	11.61	11.27
肉　类(千克)	Meat (kg)	20.60	24.54	31.16	32.07	35.88
猪　肉(千克)	Pork (kg)	6.43	7.61	10.34	8.83	11.09
牛　肉(千克)	Beef (kg)	4.34	6.07	4.84	6.73	6.04
羊　肉(千克)	Mutton (kg)	7.62	8.31	12.77	12.02	10.62
禽　类(千克)	Poultry (kg)	7.74	9.11	10.31	11.12	13.17
蛋　类(千克)	Fresh Eggs (kg)	7.68	9.77	11.60	10.44	10.50
鱼　(千克)	Fish (kg)	3.85	5.52	5.23	5.71	6.19
虾　(千克)	Shrimp (kg)	0.37	0.43	0.52	0.47	0.89
鲜　菜(千克)	Fresh Vegetables (kg)	91.60	106.33	128.30	115.42	139.62
酒　类(千克)	Liquor (kg)	3.50	3.94	4.50	4.00	5.54
白　酒(千克)	Liquor (kg)	1.22	1.34	1.24	1.84	2.04
果　酒(千克)	Fruit Wine (kg)	0.17	0.21	0.19	0.31	0.49
啤　酒(千克)	Beer (kg)	2.06	2.38	3.07	1.85	3.02
鲜　果(千克)	Fresh Fruits (kg)	27.68	35.03	40.44	44.94	50.85
鲜　瓜(千克)	Fresh Melon (kg)	28.98	33.03	33.75	34.79	44.99
糕　点(千克)	Cake (kg)	3.72	4.65	5.43	5.63	7.28
鲜乳品(千克)	Fresh Dairy Products (kg)	18.98	26.11	22.62	32.64	28.33
奶　粉(千克)	Milk Powder (kg)	0.19	0.55	0.19	0.34	0.46
酸　奶(千克)	Yogurt (kg)	3.38	5.02	5.52	5.19	7.29
服　装(件)	Clothing (piece)	7.83	9.10	10.94	12.17	12.29
鞋　类(双)	Shoes (pair)	2.46	3.13	3.26	3.69	3.53
水(吨)	Water (ton)	21.19	27.79	32.14	36.36	28.79
电(度)	Electricity (kw)	283.43	344.17	397.92	436.65	472.49
煤　炭(千克)	Coal (kg)	62.01	25.04	31.71	35.32	13.62
罐装液化石油气(千克)	Liquefied Gas (kg)	7.59	7.29	6.30	6.90	5.93
管道天然气(立方米)	Gas Pipeline (cu.m)	28.83	37.21	106.41	70.81	71.25

9-11 按收入等级分城镇居民家庭平均每百户年底耐用消费品拥有量

Ownership of Durable Consumer Goods Per100 Urban Households at Year-end by Level of Income

(2011 年) (抽样调查 Sampled Survey)

项目	Item	总平均 Total Average	最低收入户 Lowest Income Households	#困难户 Poor Households	低收入户 Low Income Households
摩托车(辆)	Motorcycle(unit)	13.79	19.12	15.76	12.50
助力车(辆)	Aided Power Bicycle (unit)	13.77	15.43	14.40	12.11
家用汽车(辆)	Automobile(unit)	12.32	4.28	2.16	6.11
洗衣机(台)	Washing Machine (unit)	96.10	92.85	93.92	91.50
电冰箱(台)	Refrigerator (unit)	94.34	80.11	72.68	89.94
彩色电视机(台)	Color TV (set)	106.42	100.00	100.00	105.08
家用电脑(台)	Household Computer (set)	61.20	24.91	17.25	51.54
组合音响(套)	Hi-Fi Stereo Sound System (set)	15.10	3.70		12.78
摄像机(架)	Pickup Camera (set)	7.98	1.87	0.35	3.57
照相机(架)	Camera (set)	29.24	5.28	2.68	23.17
钢　琴(架)	Piano (set)	1.36			0.75
其他中高档乐器(件)	Other Medium and High Grade Musical Instrument (piece)	5.05			9.31
微波炉(台)	Microwave Oven (unit)	37.75	6.49	2.16	26.11
空调器(台)	Air Conditioner (unit)	11.87	1.94	1.05	6.09
淋浴热水器(台)	Water Heater for Shower (unit)	76.53	44.32	29.58	60.00
消毒碗柜(台)	Disinfectant Machine (unit)	4.76	0.60	0.70	1.85
健身器材(件)	Health Equipment (unit)	1.08			0.18
固定电话(部)	Fixed Telephone (unit)	77.15	66.33	70.49	69.25
移动电话(部)	Mobile Telephone (unit)	181.54	129.91	107.30	162.31
接入有线电视电视机(台)	Cable Tv (unit)	83.85	57.42	45.37	79.37
接入互连网计算机(台)	Internet Computer (unit)	48.17	15.03	10.85	38.98
接入互连网移动电话(台)	Internet Mobile Phone (unit)	23.05	6.04	7.16	9.61

项目	Item	中等偏下户 Lower Middle Income Households	中等收入户 Middle Income Households	中等偏上户 Upper Middle Income Households	高收入户 High Income Households	最高收入户 Highest Income Households
摩托车(辆)	Motorcycle(unit)	17.17	13.74	8.57	12.35	14.76
助力车(辆)	Aided Power Bicycle (unit)	17.98	11.35	13.40	13.84	10.48
家用汽车(辆)	Automobile(unit)	9.91	12.30	13.27	24.94	18.32
洗衣机(台)	Washing Machine (unit)	96.08	97.48	95.61	101.94	97.18
电冰箱(台)	Refrigerator (unit)	90.63	98.96	97.89	99.39	101.10
彩色电视机(台)	Color TV (set)	107.34	101.72	110.40	111.49	108.97
家用电脑(台)	Household Computer (set)	65.80	59.95	70.33	74.89	71.71
组合音响(套)	Hi-Fi Stereo Sound System (set)	18.34	16.41	15.38	18.52	16.53
摄像机(架)	Pickup Camera (set)	9.67	8.09	7.30	9.55	15.98
照相机(架)	Camera (set)	28.72	31.74	29.80	39.15	47.27
钢　琴(架)	Piano (set)	0.66	1.13	1.48	3.82	2.66
其他中高档乐器(件)	Other Medium and High Grade Musical Instrument (piece)	6.06	6.69	4.42	2.86	3.53
微波炉(台)	Microwave Oven (unit)	35.50	39.13	44.59	52.28	58.51
空调器(台)	Air Conditioner (unit)	9.84	8.65	17.79	15.70	24.49
淋浴热水器(台)	Water Heater for Shower (unit)	80.76	77.47	85.81	86.49	91.04
消毒碗柜(台)	Disinfectant Machine (unit)	4.23	3.61	5.38	6.68	13.16
健身器材(件)	Health Equipment (unit)		0.32	0.71	2.69	6.34
固定电话(部)	Fixed Telephone (unit)	79.33	79.27	76.34	86.88	80.80
移动电话(部)	Mobile Telephone (unit)	202.65	186.33	187.79	195.84	177.82
接入有线电视电视机(台)	Cable Tv (unit)	86.00	85.05	90.05	90.05	91.68
接入互连网计算机(台)	Internet Computer (unit)	50.47	50.32	52.90	61.69	62.06
接入互连网移动电话(台)	Internet Mobile Phone (unit)	29.63	35.24	22.40	22.45	21.17

9-12 按收入等级分城镇居民家庭年末住房情况

Living Conditions of Urban Households by level of Income at Year-end

(2011 年) (抽样调查 Sampled Survey)

项 目	Item	总平均 Total Average	最低收入户 Lowest Income Households	#困难户 Poor Households	低收入户 Low Income Households
家庭居住人口数(人/户)	Number of Permanent Residents (person/household)	2.89	3.91	4.13	3.28
现住房总建筑面积(平方米/人)	Floor Space of Buildings (Sq.m/person)	28.92	22.31	20.86	23.75
现住房屋总使用面积(平方米/人)	Floor Space of Using(Sq.m/person)	21.70	16.74	15.65	17.82
房屋产权 (%)	House Ownership (%)				
租赁公房	Renting of Publicly-Funded House	2.00	7.46	9.44	1.28
租赁私房	Renting of Private House	4.14	8.56	9.65	8.07
原有私房	Original Private House	9.43	40.24	50.63	14.41
房改私房	Private House Obtained from House Reform	47.56	24.12	15.99	43.90
商品房	Commercial House	32.41	17.73	13.15	26.57
其他	Others	4.45	1.89	1.12	5.77
住宅建筑式样 (%)	Architectural Style of Dwelling (%)				
单栋住宅	Building	0.29			
四居室	Four-Room House	1.42			0.85
三居室	Three-Room House	34.01	16.33	13.42	30.91
二居室	Two-Room House	42.74	24.91	14.90	40.14
一居室	One-Room House	3.73	6.00	5.78	5.93
普通楼房	Ordinary Multi-Storey Building	5.90	4.08	5.03	2.38
平房及其他	A Single-Storey House and Others	11.90	48.68	60.87	19.79
装修状况 (%)	Decoration Situation (%)				
有装修	Decoration	64.64	38.80	32.16	57.51
未装修	Without Decoration	35.36	61.20	67.84	42.49
饮水情况 (%)	Condition of Drinking Water (%)				
# 自来水	Tap Water	97.64	95.04	94.82	94.39
纯净水	Purified Water	0.61			0.92
井、河水	Well Water、River Water	1.75	4.96	5.18	4.69
用水情况 (%)	By Tap Water Facilities (%)				
独用自来水	Tap Water Owner Per Household	98.15	95.04	94.82	95.05
公用自来水	Public Tap Water	0.07			
井、河水	Well Water、River Water	1.73	4.96	5.18	4.51
卫生设备 (%)	By Health Facilities (%)				
无卫生设备	Without Toilet Room	4.75	12.42	17.77	8.71
有厕所浴室	Bathroom and Toilet Room Owned by Household	76.13	41.42	29.58	60.75
有厕所无浴室	Toilet Room Owned by Household and Without bathroom	17.05	35.77	44.68	26.56
公用	Public Toilet Room	2.07	10.39	7.97	3.98
取暖设备 (%)	By Heating Facilities (%)				
无取暖设备	Without Heating Facilities				
暖气	Warm Gas	89.42	54.90	42.91	83.99
其他	Other	10.54	45.10	57.09	16.01
炊用燃料使用情况 (%)	By Fuel Types (%)				
管道天然气	Pipeline gas	62.45	33.53	24.35	60.51
罐装液化石油气	LPG	25.60	18.44	14.52	22.38
煤炭	Coal	11.70	47.62	60.42	17.12
其他	Others	0.17	0.40	0.70	
通信设备使用情况	By General Equipment Usage				
固定电话(部/百户)	Fixed Telephone (unit /100 Households)	77.15	66.33	70.49	69.25
移动电话(部/百户)	Mobile Telephone (unit /100 Households)	181.54	129.91	107.30	162.31
使用互联网(条/百户)	The use of Internet (unit /100 Households)	48.17	15.03	10.85	38.98

9-12 续表 Continued

项　　目	Item	中等偏下户 Lower Middle Income Households	中等收入户 Middle Income Households	中等偏上户 Upper Middle Income Households	高收入户 High Income Households	最高收入户 Highest Income Households
家庭居住人口数(人/户)	Number of Permanent Residents	3.18	2.83	2.50	2.47	2.07
现住房总建筑面积(平方米/人)	Floor Space of Buildings (Sq.m/person)	25.67	29.55	32.86	35.50	43.45
现住房屋总使用面积(平方米/人)	Floor Space of Using(Sq.m/person)	19.26	22.17	24.65	26.63	32.60
房屋产权 (%)	House Ownership (%)					
租赁公房	Renting of Publicly-Funded House	2.17	0.51	1.37		3.14
租赁私房	Renting of Private House	3.72	2.05	3.35	3.14	2.31
原有私房	Original Private House	7.61	5.91	1.62	5.93	0.66
房改私房	Private House Obtained from House Reform	49.06	47.16	57.46	45.20	57.37
商品房	Commercial House	35.26	40.07	31.86	35.89	31.27
其他	Others	2.18	4.29	4.35	9.84	5.25
住宅建筑式样 (%)	Architectural Style of Dwelling (%)					
单栋住宅	Building	1.17	0.06	0.21		
四居室	Four-Room House	0.56	3.13	1.06	1.04	3.20
三居室	Three-Room House	28.47	33.03	38.89	48.49	45.38
二居室	Two-Room House	49.21	46.82	46.64	36.89	41.45
一居室	One-Room House	5.50	1.92	2.99	1.56	2.34
普通楼房	Ordinary Multi-Storey Building	6.45	7.53	6.74	5.67	6.26
平房及其他	A Single-Storey House and Others	8.64	7.51	3.46	6.34	1.38
装修状况 (%)	Decoration Situation (%)					
有装修	Decoration	65.77	69.02	69.28	67.40	77.87
未装修	Without Decoration	34.23	30.98	30.72	32.60	22.13
饮水情况 (%)	Condition of Drinking Water (%)					
# 自来水	Tap Water	97.38	98.38	99.46	99.24	98.08
纯净水	Purified Water	0.63	0.56	0.54	0.76	0.93
井、河水	Well Water、River Water	2.00	1.07			0.99
用水情况 (%)	By Tap Water Facilities (%)					
独用自来水	Tap Water Owner Per Household	97.9	98.87	99.94	100.00	98.75
公用自来水	Public Tap Water	0.10	0.06	0.06		0.26
井、河水	Well Water、River Water	2.00	1.07			0.99
卫生设备 (%)	By Health Facilities (%)					
无卫生设备	Without Toilet Room	5.49	4.76	1.48	1.45	0.26
有厕所浴室	Bathroom and Toilet Room Owned by Household	79.86	77.47	85.81	85.59	92.03
有厕所无浴室	Toilet Room Owned by Household and Without bathroom	14.04	17.01	12.24	12.06	6.71
公用	Public Toilet Room	0.61	0.76	0.47	0.90	0.99
取暖设备 (%)	By Heating Facilities (%)					
无取暖设备	Without Heating Facilities					
暖气	Warm Gas	92.14	92.55	97.23	95.78	98.62
其他	Other	7.86	7.26	2.77	4.22	1.38
炊用燃料使用情况 (%)	By Fuel Types (%)					
管道天然气	Pipeline gas	63.39	61.70	69.44	67.39	76.25
罐装液化石油气	LPG	28.19	29.67	24.48	30.46	20.51
煤炭	Coal	8.42	8.52	6.08	1.10	2.31
其他	Others		0.11		1.05	
通信设备使用情况	By General Equipment Usage					
固定电话(部/百户)	Fixed Telephone (unit /100 Households)	79.33	79.27	76.34	86.88	80.80
移动电话(部/百户)	Mobile Telephone (unit /100 Households)	202.65	186.33	187.79	195.84	177.82
使用互联网(条/百户)	The use of Internet (unit /100 Households)	50.47	50.32	52.90	61.69	62.06

9-13 城镇居民家庭就业情况
Employment Conditions of Urban Households

(抽样调查 Sampled Survey)

项 目	Item	2010	2011
调查户数(户)	**Number of Households Surveyed (household)**	**1560**	**1460**
平均每户家庭人口数(人)	**Average Household Size (person)**	**2.98**	**2.91**
有收入者人数	Number of person having income	1.91	1.89
就业人数	Number of person Employed	1.54	1.49
国有经济单位职工人数	Employed Person in State-owned Units	0.93	0.85
城镇集体经济单位职工人数	Employed Person in Collective-owned Units	0.03	0.04
其他各种经济类型单位职工	Employed Person in Other Varions Economic Units	0.09	0.09
城镇个体经营者人员数	Number of Employed Person by himself in Town	0.17	0.17
城镇个体被雇人员数	Number of Employed Person in Town	0.26	0.28
离退休再就业人员	Retired and resigned person reemployed	0.01	0.01
其他就业人员	Person employed in other way	0.05	0.05
离退休人员	Number of Retired and Resinged Person	0.32	0.36
其他有收入者人数	Number of other person having income	0.04	0.04
无收入者人数	Number of person having no income	1.07	1.03

9-14 主要年份农村居民家庭基本情况
Basic Conditions of Rural Households in Main Years

(抽样调查 Sampled Survey)

项 目	Item	2000	2005	2010	2011
调查户数(户)	**Number of Households Surveyed(household)**	**1500**	**1550**	**1550**	**1550**
调查户人口(人)	**Number of Residents Surveyed (person)**	**7999**	**7315**	**7169**	**6644**
平均每户常住人口	Average Number of Permanent Residents per Household	5.33	4.72	4.63	4.29
平均每户整半劳动力	Average Number of Full/semi Labour Force per Household	3.06	2.92	3.14	2.85
平均每个劳动力负担人口(含本人)	Average Number of Dependents per Labour Force (Including the laborer himself and herself)	1.74	1.62	1.47	1.51
平均每人经营耕地面积(亩)	Average Number of Management of Cultivated Land Area(Mu)	4.20	4.20	4.76	5.73
年内每户新建(购)房屋面积(平方米)	Space of Rooms per Household Newly Built Within the Year (sq.m)	2.03	6.45	3.68	4.52
年底人均居住面积(平方米)	Per Capita Net Living Rooms Space in Rural Area (sq.m)	17.25	21.13	24.00	26.14
平均每人年收入(元)	**Per Capita Annual Income(yuan)**				
总收入	Total Income	3129.35	4604.90	8806.87	11590.94
工资性收入	Income from Wages and Salaries	104.58	195.51	556.26	804.73
家庭经营收入	Income from Household Operations	2926.75	4252.96	7795.26	9988.44
财产性收入	Income from Properties	40.42	33.87	126.53	147.14
转移性收入	Income from Transfers	57.60	122.56	328.82	650.63
现金收入	Cash Income	2444.30	3921.17	7517.22	10258.65
工资性收入	Income from Wages and Salaries	104.46	195.51	556.26	804.57
家庭经营收入	Income from Household Operations	2245.31	3580.44	6525.27	8682.46
财产性收入	Income from Properties	37.87	22.84	106.87	121.94
转移性收入	Income from Transfers	56.66	122.38	328.82	649.68
平均每人年支出(元)	**Per Capita Annual Expenditures(yuan)**				
总支出	Total Expenditure	2819.77	4302.26	8241.28	11250.23
家庭经营费用支出	Expenditure for Household Operations	1198.23	1928.63	3800.24	5620.97
购置生产性固定资产	Purchase of Productive Fixed Assets	115.19	258.79	568.14	775.98
税费支出	Taxes and Fees	177.24	14.36	7.83	7.84
生活消费支出	Expenditure on Household Consumption	1236.45	1924.41	3458.14	4397.82
转移性和财产性支出	Expenditure for Transfer and Property	92.66	176.07	406.93	447.62
现金支出	Cash Expenditure	2353.45	3855.34	7464.48	10585.98
家庭经营费用支出	Expenditure for Household Operations	1100.43	1823.95	3643.29	5465.40
购置生产性固定资产	Purchase of Productive Fixed Assets	115.19	258.79	568.14	775.98
税费支出	Taxes and Fees	177.22	14.36	7.83	7.78
生活消费支出	Expenditure on Household Consumption	871.37	1582.17	2838.29	3889.69
转移性和财产性支出	Expenditure for Transfer and Property	89.24	176.07	406.93	447.13
平均每人年纯收入(元)	**Per Capita Annual Net Income (yuan)**	**1618.08**	**2482.15**	**4642.67**	**5442.15**
工资性收入	Income from Wages and Salaries	104.58	195.51	556.26	804.73
家庭经营纯收入	Income from Household Business	1451.33	2140.76	3649.98	3887.15
财产性收入	Income from Properties	40.43	33.87	126.52	147.14
转移性收入	Income from Transfers	21.74	112.01	309.91	603.13

9-15 农村居民家庭人均年总收入、纯收入和构成
Per Capita Annual Gross and Net Income and Its Composition of Rural Households

单位：元 (抽样调查 Sampled Survey) (yuan)

项　　目	Item	2010	2011	构成(%) Composition 2010	2011
全年总收入	**Annual Gross Income**	**8806.87**	**11590.94**	**100**	**100**
工资性收入	Income from Wages and Salaries	556.26	804.73	6.32	6.94
家庭经营收入	Income from Household Operations	7795.26	9988.44	88.51	86.18
财产性收入	Income from Transfers	126.53	147.14	1.44	1.27
转移性收入	Income from Properties	328.82	650.63	3.73	5.61
全年总支出	**Annual Gross Expenditure**	**8241.28**	**11250.23**	**100**	**100**
#家庭经营费用支出	Expenditure for Household Business	3800.24	5620.97	46.11	49.96
生活消费支出	Expenditure for Consumption	3458.14	4397.82	41.96	39.09
全年纯收入	**Annual Net Income**	**4642.67**	**5442.15**	**100**	**100**
基本纯收入	Basic Net Income	4206.24	4691.88	90.60	86.22
转移性纯收入	Income from Transfers	309.91	603.13	6.67	11.08
财产性纯收入	Income from Properties	126.52	147.14	2.73	2.70

9-16 主要年份农村居民家庭平均每人总收入和纯收入
Per Capita Annual Gross and Net Income of Rural Households in Main Years

单位：元 (抽样调查 Sampled Survey) (yuan)

项　　目	Item	2000	2005	2010	2011
总 收 入	**Gross Income**	**3129.35**	**4604.9**	**8806.87**	**11590.94**
基本收入	Basic Income	3031.33	4448.47	8351.52	10793.17
工资性收入	Income from Wages and Salaries	104.58	195.51	556.26	804.73
家庭经营收入	Income from Household Operations	2926.75	4252.96	7795.26	9988.44
转移性和财产性收入	Income from Transfers and Properties	98.02	156.43	455.35	797.77
纯收入	**Net Income**	**1618.08**	**2482.15**	**4642.67**	**5442.15**
基本收入	Basic Income	1555.91	2336.27	4206.24	4691.88
工资性收入	Income from Wages and Salaries	104.58	195.51	556.26	804.73
家庭经营纯收入	Income from Household Operations	1451.33	2140.76	3649.98	3887.15
农业收入	Farming	1109.39	1618.33	2670.60	2662.94
林业收入	Forestry	22.51	61.65	172.01	186.72
牧业收入	Animal Husbandry	171.18	245.10	469.08	646.78
渔业收入	Fishery				1.56
工业收入	Industry	6.35	18.84	34.65	46.53
建筑业收入	Construction	4.31	15.22	22.71	30.42
交通、运输和邮电业收入	Transportation, Post and Telecommunications Services	26.48	30.06	94.88	72.01
批发和零售贸易业、饮食业收入	Wholesale, Retail Trades and Catering Services	23.8	86.86	128.47	186.35
社会服务业收入	Services Trades	15.01	9.43	22.70	23.22
文教卫生业收入	Cultural, Education, Medicines and Medical Services			10.53	12.59
其他行业收入	Others	72.30	55.27	24.36	18.03
转移性和财产性收入	Income from Transfers and Properties	62.17	145.88	436.43	750.27

9-17 主要年份农村居民家庭人均主要消费品消费量
Per Capita Consumption of Major Consumer Goods of Rural Households in Main Years

单位:千克　　(抽样调查 Sampled Survey)　　(kg)

项　目	Item	2000	2005	2010	2011
粮食(原粮)	Grain(Unprocessed)	244.83	235.66	236.10	236.81
#小 麦	Wheat	199.83	188.38	191.28	195.95
稻 谷	Rice	15.19	19.93	23.20	27.04
豆类及豆制品	Soybeans and Processed Products	0.5	0.83	0.56	0.65
蔬 菜	Fresh Vegetable	89.24	67.89	77.72	77.93
食 油	Edible Oil	9.64	10.90	10.74	12.77
#植物油	Vegetable Oil	9.56	10.79	10.69	12.74
肉禽及制品	Meats,Poultry and Processed Products	12.41	14.31	15.38	17.87
#猪 肉	Pork	1.95	0.67	1.04	1.31
牛 肉	Beef	1.95	2.56	2.32	3.60
羊 肉	Mutton	7.03	8.99	9.18	9.66
家 禽	Poultry	1.36	1.70	2.27	2.85
蛋及制品	Eggs and Processed Products	1.2	1.00	1.92	2.96
食 糖	Sugar	0.42	0.45	0.49	0.40
酒	Liquor	1.12	1.27	1.06	1.59
水果及制品	Fruits and Processed Products	46.89	34.81	25.30	22.64
茶 叶	Tea	0.37	0.45	0.43	0.30

9-18 主要年份农村居民家庭平均每百户耐用消费品拥有量
Number of Durable Consumer Goods Owned by Per100 Rural Households in Main Years

(抽样调查 Sampled Survey)

项　目	Item	2000	2005	2010	2011
洗衣机(台)	Washing Machine (unit)	20.87	28.26	47.94	72.77
电冰箱(台)	Refrigerator (unit)	9.93	20.13	43.48	63.94
空调机(台)	Air Conditioner (unit)		0.39	0.65	1.03
抽油烟机(台)	Exhaust Fan(unit)	1.13	1.23	2.77	4.58
自行车(辆)	Bicycle (unit)	136.60	80.97	78.52	62.58
摩托车(辆)	Motorcycle (unit)	18.33	45.42	62.84	77.23
电话机(部)	Telephone(unit)	15.07	36.26	38.97	34.00
移动电话(部)	Mobile phone (unit)	0.33	21.29	84.32	141.87
黑白电视机(台)	Black and White TV (set)	59.33	35.16	11.61	4.58
彩色电视机(台)	Color TV (set)	31.87	61.81	89.87	99.03
照像机(架)	Camera (set)	2.20	3.23	3.29	2.90
影碟机(台)	Video Disc Player (set)	3.60		31.94	31.48
微波炉(台)	Microwave Oven (unit)			1.81	3.87

9-19 农村居民人均生活消费支出及构成
Composition of Per Capita Living Expendture of Rural Households

单位：元 (抽样调查 Sampled Survey) (yuan)

项目	Item	2010	2011	构成(%) Composition(%)	
				2010	2011
生活消费支出	**Expenditure for Consumption**	**3458.14**	**4397.82**	**100**	**100**
食　品	Food	1394.65	1589.46	40.33	36.14
#主 食	Staple Food	432.02	422.70	12.49	9.61
副食及其他食品	Non-staple Food and others	830.25	992.34	24.01	22.56
衣　着	Clothing	303.66	372.10	8.78	8.46
居　住	Residence	695.17	1025.28	20.11	23.32
家庭设备、用品及服务	Household Facilities,Articles and Services	137.69	198.57	3.98	4.52
医疗保健	Health Care and Medical Services	314.73	376.87	9.10	8.57
交通和通讯	Transport and Communications	382.14	530.59	11.05	12.06
文教娱乐用品及服务	Cultural, Education ,Recreation and Services	170.15	229.66	4.92	5.22
其他商品和服务	Other Commodities and Services	59.94	75.28	1.73	1.71

9-20 农村居民家庭平均每百户耐用消费品拥有量
Number of Durable Consumer Goods Owned by Per100 Rural Households

(抽样调查 Sampled Survey)

项目	Item	2010	2011
自行车(辆)	Bicycle (unit)	78.52	62.58
黑白电视机(台)	Black and White TV (set)	11.61	4.58
彩色电视机(台)	Color TV (set)	89.87	99.03
抽油烟机(台)	Exhaust Fan(unit)	2.77	4.58
照像机(架)	Camera (set)	3.29	2.90
移动电话(部)	Mobile phone (unit)	84.32	141.87
洗衣机(台)	Washing Machine (unit)	47.94	72.77
电冰箱(台)	Refrigerator (unit)	43.48	63.94
摩托车(辆)	Motorcycle (unit)	62.84	77.23
影碟机(台)	Video Disc Player (set)	31.94	31.48
微波炉(台)	Microwave Oven (unit)	1.81	3.87

9-21 农村居民家庭人均商品性和自给性生活消费品支出

Per Capita Self-Sufficiency and Consumption on Commodity Goods of Living Expenditure in Rural Households

(抽样调查 Sampled Survey)

项　　目	Item	2010			2011		
		合 计 Total	货币性 In Money	实物性 In Kind	合 计 Total	货币性 In Money	实物性 In Kind
生活消费支出合计(元/人)	**Expenditure for Consumption (yuan/person)**	**3458.14**	**2838.29**	**619.85**	**4397.82**	**3889.69**	**508.13**
食　品	Food	1394.65	850.35	544.30	1589.46	1138.12	451.34
衣　着	Clothing	303.66	301.17	2.49	372.10	368.37	3.73
居　住	Residence	695.17	625.91	69.26	1025.28	976.36	48.92
家庭设备、用品及服务	Household Appliances and Services	137.69	133.90	3.79	198.57	194.43	4.14
医疗保健	Health Care and Medical Services	314.73	314.73		376.87	376.87	
交通和通讯	Transportation and Communications	382.14	382.14		530.59	530.59	
文教娱乐用品及服务	Cultural, Education and Recreational Articles and Services	170.15	170.15		229.66	229.66	
其他商品和服务	Other Commodities and Services	59.94	59.94		75.28	75.28	
生活消费支出构成(%)	**Composition of Living Expenditures (%)**	**100**	**100**	**100**	**100**	**100**	**100**
食　品	Food	40.33	29.96	87.81	36.14	29.26	88.82
衣　着	Clothing	8.78	10.61	0.40	8.46	9.47	0.73
居　住	Residence	20.11	22.06	11.18	23.32	25.10	9.64
家庭设备、用品及服务	Household Facilities,Articles and Services	3.98	4.72	0.61	4.52	5.00	0.81
医疗保健	Health Care and Medical Services	9.10	11.09		8.57	9.69	
交通和通讯	Transportation and Communications	11.05	13.46		12.06	13.64	
文教娱乐用品及服务	Cultural, Education and Recreational Articles and Services	4.92	5.99		5.22	5.90	
其他商品和服务	Other Commodities and Services	1.73	2.11		1.71	1.94	
生活消费支出中货币性和实物性比重(%)	**Percentage of Expenditure for Consumption in Money and Kind (%)**	**100**	**82.08**	**17.92**	**100**	**88.45**	**11.55**
食　品	Food	100	60.97	39.03	100	71.60	28.40
衣　着	Clothing	100	99.18	0.82	100	99.00	1.00
居　住	Residence	100	90.04	9.96	100	95.23	4.77
家庭设备、用品及服务	Household Facilities,Articles and Services	100	97.25	2.75	100	97.92	2.08
医疗保健	Health Care and Medical Services	100	100		100		
交通和通讯	Transportation and Communications	100	100		100		
文教娱乐用品及服务	Cultural, Education and Recreational Articles and Services	100	100		100		
其他商品和服务	Other Commodities and Services	100	100		100		

9-22 分地区农村居民家庭人均总收入和纯收入

单位：元 (2011 年)

项 目 Item	自治区 Autonomous Region	乌鲁木齐市 Urumqi City	吐鲁番地区 Turpan Administrative Offices	哈密地区 Hami [Kumul] Administrative Offices
调查县、市(个) Number of Counties and Cities Surveyed (unit)	**33**	**3**	**2**	**2**
调查户数(户) Number of Households Surveyed (household)	**1550**	**300**	**180**	**180**
常住人口(人) Number of Permanent Residents In the Households Surveyed (person)	**6644**	**1088**	**818**	**628**
总收入 Annual Gross Income	**11590.94**	**15267.29**	**10971.02**	**11283.08**
工资性收入 Income from Wages and Salaries	804.73	2369.86	606.71	2086.53
在非企业组织中劳动得到的 From Non-enterprise Organization	148.28	274.79	179.96	510.72
在本地企业中劳动得到的 From Local Enterprise	339.90	2005.62	340.20	1009.41
常住人口外出从业得到的 Out of Migrant Workers	316.54	89.46	86.55	566.40
家庭经营收入 Income From Household Business	9988.44	12410.13	9805.27	8227.08
农业收入 Farming	7324.47	6612.64	7178.36	5761.24
林业收入 Forestry	249.72	50.55	19.37	28.58
牧业收入 Animal Husbandry	1680.31	3557.81	1106.57	1954.15
渔业收入 Fishery	1.60			
工业收入 Industry	86.11			3.71
建筑业收入 Construction	57.26	30.33	0.73	
交通、运输和邮电业收入 Transportation, Post and Telecommunications Services	182.09	1460.10	101.42	238.13
批发和零售贸易、餐饮业收入 Wholesale, Retail Trades and Catering Services	299.23	566.28	1272.96	203.70
社会服务业收入 Social Services	32.04	132.43	63.48	25.92
文教卫生业收入 Cultural, Education, Medicines and Medical Services	34.80		61.30	
其他家庭经营收入 Others	40.83		1.08	11.65
财产性收入 Income from Properties	147.14	73.77	268.81	214.84
#利 息 Interest	1.68	2.00	0.24	0.45
租 金 Rent	17.00	39.31	17.24	56.08
转移性收入 Income from Transfer	650.63	413.53	290.23	754.63
全年家庭人均纯收入 Annual Net Income	**5442.15**	**8485.24**	**6060.36**	**7143.09**

Per Capita Annual Gross and Net Income of Rural Households by Region

(抽样调查 Sampled Survey) (yuan)

昌吉回族自治州 Changji Hui Autonomous Prefecture	伊犁州直属县(市) Counties (Cities) Direct Under Ili Prefecture	塔城地区 Tacheng [Tarbagatai] Administrative Offices	阿勒泰地区 Altay Administrative Offices	博尔塔拉蒙古自治州 Bortala Mongol Autonomous Prefecture	巴音郭楞蒙古自治州 Bayangol Mongol Autonomous Prefecture	阿克苏地区 Aksu Administrative Offices	克孜勒苏克尔克孜自治州 Kizilsu Kirgiz Autonomous Prefecture	喀什地区 Kashgar [Kaxgar] Adminis-trative Offices	和田地区 Hotan Adminis-trative Offices
4	**5**	**5**	**6**	**2**	**4**	**6**	**3**	**7**	**4**
400	**400**	**400**	**300**	**200**	**400**	**400**	**240**	**560**	**400**
1334	**1554**	**1393**	**1158**	**713**	**1573**	**1732**	**1189**	**2597**	**1706**
33649.80	**14138.46**	**23428.22**	**10629.99**	**34887.83**	**14547.18**	**11404.32**	**4012.53**	**7810.94**	**6216.05**
1604.35	1505.93	589.59	906.19	858.45	1010.87	335.26	491.72	786.55	984.51
151.10	374.96	172.67	210.50	244.37	317.24	107.00	88.24	93.25	96.56
1237.33	887.22	359.29	622.39	341.30	603.35	200.08	112.41	275.24	386.75
215.92	243.75	57.64	73.30	272.78	90.28	28.18	291.06	418.06	501.19
30453.10	11086.48	22150.25	8747.56	33322.10	12560.40	10531.47	3108.07	6465.72	4575.90
26811.16	6695.04	19754.66	5298.20	30903.25	10135.27	7964.61	1677.17	4600.64	2023.49
8.07	71.80	32.95	75.72	0.72	76.43	871.50	48.81	224.26	482.90
2792.06	2802.70	1953.63	3086.54	1642.76	1997.96	1567.52	931.93	1189.85	1135.18
			14.28	0.29			0.67		
80.41	221.33	0.07	83.67	13.34	30.26	3.46	6.30	24.84	377.98
3.63	64.67	161.16	0.34	1.26	0.10	6.96	20.08	45.27	38.54
551.44	522.39	49.74	98.32	220.77	115.01	8.24	247.17	138.78	175.81
178.97	404.05	170.61	34.99	520.40	182.90	80.49	119.94	113.70	208.36
19.13	133.08	3.71	35.89	0.18	22.47	21.32	49.01	27.26	54.92
2.74	122.42	21.53	1.73			1.27		1.50	
5.48	49.00	2.19	17.90	19.12		6.10	6.98	99.62	78.72
542.06	506.45	220.44	192.85	143.49	531.15	232.84	2.61	91.97	24.63
33.28	1.61	4.04	0.22	10.85	0.03	0.08			
175.28	12.58	23.32	5.77	3.29	67.37	16.86		1.33	
1050.28	1039.59	467.94	783.39	563.80	444.77	304.74	410.14	466.70	631.01
10198.64	**6389.41**	**9207.76**	**5159.21**	**8267.66**	**8689.98**	**5894.83**	**2698.45**	**4026.03**	**3554.92**

9-23 分地区农村居民家庭平均每人总支出

单位：元 (2011 年)

项目 Item	自治区 Autonomous Region	乌鲁木齐市 Urumqi City	吐鲁番地区 Turpan Administrative Offices	哈密地区 Hami [Kumul] Administrative Offices	昌吉回族自治州 Changji Hui Autonomous Prefecture
全年总支出 Annual Total Expenditure	**11250.23**	**15784.54**	**11862.14**	**11260.25**	**35503.32**
家庭经营费用支出 Expenditure for Household Business	**5620.97**	**6129.77**	**4115.54**	**3566.97**	**21689.55**
农业生产 Farming	4407.09	3280.22	2530.40	2421.87	19320.01
林业生产 Forestry	62.74	69.64	8.68	1.89	76.51
牧业生产 Animal Husbandry	871.55	2257.67	969.77	1020.25	1862.92
渔业生产 Fishery	0.04				4.29
工业生产 Industry	37.19		0.49	0.73	41.20
建筑业生产 Construction	19.85	4.60	0.98	0.02	11.99
交通、运输和邮电业支出 Transportation, Post and Telecommunications Services	70.51	330.19	21.47	102.80	260.06
批发和零售贸易、餐饮业支出 Wholesale, Retail Trades and Catering Services	105.26	177.17	509.70	13.48	102.98
社会服务业支出 Social Services	6.01	10.28	47.92	1.84	4.39
文教卫生业支出 Cultural, Education, Medicines and Medical Services	19.56		24.39		0.64
其他经营支出 Others	21.17		1.75	4.09	4.55
购置生产用固定资产支出 Expenditure for Productive Fixed Assets	**775.98**	**1275.22**	**467.50**	**602.45**	**1782.45**
税费支出 Taxes and Fee	**7.84**		**2.14**	**1.11**	**0.12**
生活消费支出 Expenditure for Consumption	**4397.82**	**7657.08**	**6696.03**	**6433.41**	**10629.28**
食品 Food	1589.46	2652.80	2319.22	1850.86	3262.71
#主食 Staple Food	422.70	475.97	511.58	389.89	455.75
副食及其他食品 Non-staple Food and Others	992.34	1784.16	1538.83	1331.68	2179.95
衣着 Clothing	372.10	680.97	526.28	582.71	729.13
居住 Residence	1025.28	1820.43	1012.43	1698.77	2950.15
家庭设备、用品及服务 Household Facilities, Articles and Services	198.57	344.33	262.20	242.05	435.17
医疗保健 Health Care and Medical Services	376.87	680.92	988.72	682.56	1028.49
交通和通讯 Transportation and Communications	530.59	896.72	1158.44	959.82	1328.64
文化教育娱乐用品及服务 Cultural, Education and Recreational Articles and Services	229.66	480.90	302.10	331.72	624.00
其他商品和服务 Other Commodities and Services	75.28	100.01	126.64	84.92	270.99
附：生产用固定资产折旧 Depreciation Charge for Productive Fixed Assets	472.49	588.61	712.76	471.91	1678.98

Per Capita Total Expenditure of Rural Household by Region

(抽样调查 Sampled Survey) (yuan)

伊犁州直属县(市) Counties (Cities) Direct Under Ili Prefecture	塔城地区 Tacheng [Tarbagatai] Administrative Offices	阿勒泰地区 Altay Administrative Offices	博尔塔拉蒙古自治州 Bortala Mongol Autonomous Prefecture	巴音郭楞蒙古自治州 Bayangol Mongol Autonomous Prefecture	阿克苏地区 Aksu Administrative Offices	克孜勒苏克尔克孜自治州 Kizilsu Kirgiz Autonomous Prefecture	喀什地区 Kashgar [Kaxgar] Administrative Offices	和田地区 Hotan Administrative Offices
15755.90	**22922.25**	**10803.07**	**39139.47**	**12824.44**	**12167.52**	**3375.36**	**8002.66**	**6752.29**
7144.99	**13302.56**	**4485.04**	**25800.09**	**5384.01**	**4883.36**	**1072.37**	**3655.19**	**2520.35**
3953.09	12269.18	2840.08	23499.89	4095.60	3783.29	621.27	2785.25	936.85
76.16	45.93	220.09	31.87	28.49	141.01	4.93	38.43	151.69
2272.75	834.93	1327.32	1600.80	1171.80	886.60	362.94	687.89	954.45
3.04	0.08	0.31	0.04		0.53			
244.92	0.37	17.70	0.12	8.03	0.35	0.02	12.17	97.36
30.92	78.97	15.96	5.43		5.67	4.35	7.00	78.04
227.52	3.88	44.45	79.08	35.53	7.28	67.12	33.11	82.69
223.22	23.73	7.35	566.17	44.10	27.69	10.91	34.04	205.79
15.46		4.06		0.45	19.38	0.01	4.98	0.61
86.45	23.83	1.76					1.16	4.45
11.47	21.66	5.95	16.68		11.57	0.82	51.16	8.43
1038.73	**1329.62**	**468.62**	**1010.20**	**673.38**	**1428.60**	**178.01**	**483.63**	**220.58**
0.95	**14.09**	**0.11**	**9.15**	**3.34**	**52.08**		**2.68**	**19.23**
6748.48	**7401.42**	**5343.31**	**10902.41**	**6423.43**	**5544.94**	**1984.90**	**3703.88**	**3825.76**
1915.68	2575.00	1864.14	2823.77	2121.53	1888.42	985.94	1600.67	1292.58
398.18	456.20	422.28	372.06	519.55	531.14	371.56	587.49	364.89
1255.78	1755.73	1274.14	1945.70	1437.76	1113.57	566.72	893.41	822.40
514.66	595.92	539.40	609.30	482.73	598.70	190.87	458.50	416.73
1921.85	1551.06	960.19	3456.57	1211.13	1095.84	310.49	770.96	1028.60
368.83	381.64	260.40	430.36	264.46	252.13	83.77	140.08	169.15
715.52	660.10	701.49	856.51	561.35	545.51	191.55	311.91	275.02
784.58	1077.91	769.47	1751.65	1512.40	897.43	194.42	328.68	537.00
423.98	368.71	199.64	722.39	246.89	153.47	18.68	59.68	47.54
103.38	191.06	48.59	251.86	22.94	113.44	9.17	33.41	59.14
466.00	885.96	935.35	725.43	455.13	565.61	221.58	119.71	107.01

9-24 分地区农村居民家庭人均现金收支

单位：元 (2011 年)(抽样调查 Sampled Survey) (yuan)

项目	Item	自治区 Autonomous Region	乌鲁木齐市 Urumqi City	吐鲁番地区 Turpan Administrative Offices	哈密地区 Hami [Kumul] Administrative Offices
期内现金收入	**Annual Total Income In Cash**	**10258.65**	**15009.36**	**10783.05**	**10513.50**
工资性收入	Income from Wages and Salaries	804.57	2367.91	606.71	2083.08
在非企业组织中劳动得到的	From Non-enterprise Organization	148.19	272.84	179.96	509.45
在本地企业中劳动得到的	From Local Enterprises	339.83	2005.62	340.20	1007.23
常住人口外出从业得到的	Out of Migrant Workers	316.54	89.46	86.55	566.40
家庭经营收入	Income of Household Operation	8682.46	12166.80	9783.67	7481.68
农业现金收入	Cash Income from Farming	6155.46	6513.71	7331.40	5142.72
#出售农产品收入	Sale of Agricultural Products	5879.18	6466.50	6883.67	5004.95
林业现金收入	Cash Income from Forestry	213.96	50.55	19.37	28.58
#出售林业产品收入	Sale of Forestry Products	212.49	50.55	14.84	14.39
牧业现金收入	Cash Income from Animal Husbandry	1579.19	3413.41	931.92	1827.27
#出售牧业产品收入	Sale of Animal Husbandry Products	1566.38	3406.33	891.09	1787.61
渔业现金收入	Cash Income from Fishery	1.51			
#出售渔业产品收入	Sale of Fishery Products	1.51			
工业收入	Income from Industry	86.11			3.71
#出售工业产品收入	Sale of Industrial Products	48.53			
工业服务性收入	Income from Industrial services	37.57			3.71
建筑业收入	Income from Construction	57.26	30.33	0.73	
#出售建筑业产品收入	Sale of Constructive Products	0.75			
建筑业服务性收入	Income from Constructive services	56.51	30.33	0.73	
交通、运输、邮电业收入	Income from Transport,Post and Telecommunication Servies	182.09	1460.10	101.42	238.13
批零贸易业、饮食业收入	Income from Wholesale and Retail Trades and Catering Servies	299.23	566.28	1272.96	203.70
社会服务业收入	Income from Social Services	32.04	132.43	63.48	25.92
文教卫生业收入	Income from Culture,Edcuation and Health Care	34.80		61.30	
其他行业收入	Others	34.98		61.36	2.14
财产性收入	Property Income	121.94	73.77	102.60	194.46
#利 息	Interest	1.68	2.00	0.24	0.45
租 金	Rent	17.00	39.31	17.24	56.08
转移性收入	Transfer Income	649.68	400.88	290.08	754.29
非收入所得	**Non-income Gain**	**3427.34**	**1301.70**	**2834.90**	**3912.58**
#从银行信用社得到的贷款	Credit	1909.14	329.04	1443.52	1229.45
借入款	Borrowed Money	389.21	189.98	378.58	997.53
收回借出款	Recall Loaned Money	168.55	30.61	30.75	90.79
从银行信用社取回存款	Take Deposit back	466.98	112.59	460.02	735.06
出售财产所得款	Sold Property	130.84	79.26	106.26	13.55
期内现金支出	**Annual Expenditure in Cash**	**10585.98**	**15501.29**	**11489.53**	**10737.88**
生产费用支出	Producing Expenditure	6241.38	7398.31	4579.43	4003.37
家庭经营费用支出	Expenditure for Household Business	5465.40	6123.10	4111.93	3400.92
农业生产支出	Farming	4367.47	3279.13	2530.40	2369.68
林业生产支出	Forestry	62.74	69.64	8.68	1.89
牧业生产支出	Animal Husbandry	755.61	2252.09	966.16	906.39

Per Capita Income and Expenditure in Cash of Rural Household by Region

单位：元 (yuan)

昌吉回族自治州 Changji Hui Autonomous Prefecture	伊犁州直属县(市) Counties (Cities) Direct Under Ili Prefecture	塔城地区 Tacheng [Tarbagatai] Administrative Offices	阿勒泰地区 Altay Administrative Offices	博尔塔拉蒙古自治州 Bortala Mongol Autonomous Prefecture	巴音郭楞蒙古自治州 Bayangol Mongol Autonomous Prefecture	阿克苏地区 Aksu Administrative Offices	克孜勒苏克尔克孜自治州 Kizilsu Kirgiz Autonomous Prefecture	喀什地区 Kashgar [Kaxgar] Administrative Offices	和田地区 Hotan Administrative Offices
30780.06	**13991.47**	**22301.98**	**9213.30**	**30840.26**	**14147.53**	**9874.36**	**3240.91**	**6679.50**	**5072.30**
1589.34	1505.29	575.08	906.19	858.45	1010.87	334.91	491.72	786.55	983.51
141.06	374.96	166.05	210.50	244.37	317.24	107.00	88.24	93.25	96.56
1232.35	886.59	351.39	622.39	341.30	603.35	199.74	112.41	275.24	385.76
215.92	243.75	57.64	73.30	272.78	90.28	28.18	291.06	418.06	501.19
27718.74	11228.27	21044.78	7591.53	29193.20	12274.20	9028.79	2341.08	5341.27	3442.30
24338.67	6748.57	18791.56	4508.74	26727.07	9976.42	6981.69	1045.86	3554.17	903.58
23362.62	6146.37	18302.07	4370.72	26331.98	9688.68	6486.13	857.88	3323.25	860.45
5.47	72.06	32.95	76.40	4.51	76.24	499.61	48.46	215.66	467.82
4.65	68.36	32.95	47.65	3.95	72.93	492.71	45.56	215.08	467.33
2533.41	2890.69	1812.12	2719.58	1686.25	1870.81	1419.66	796.60	1120.48	1069.88
2530.89	2828.98	1809.25	2637.43	1683.95	1867.25	1412.69	704.97	1119.89	1069.15
			13.98	0.29			0.67		
			13.98	0.29			0.67		
80.41	221.33	0.07	83.67	13.34	30.26	3.46	6.30	24.84	444.68
75.98	57.73	0.07	9.85	12.21	3.69			0.19	359.97
4.43	163.60		73.82	1.13	26.57	3.46	6.30	24.65	84.71
3.63	64.67	161.16	0.34	1.26	0.10	6.96	20.08	45.27	38.54
2.73		0.22	0.34		0.10	0.23		2.05	
0.90	64.67	160.94		1.26		6.74	20.08	43.21	38.54
551.44	522.39	49.74	98.32	220.77	115.01	8.24	247.17	138.78	175.81
178.97	404.05	170.61	34.99	520.40	182.90	80.49	119.94	113.70	208.36
19.13	133.08	3.71	35.89	0.18	22.47	21.32	49.01	27.26	54.92
2.74	122.42	21.53	1.73			1.27		1.50	
7.60	123.86	21.75	5.23	10.51		1.27		1.50	0.72
486.75	219.51	214.18	165.48	224.82	417.77	205.95	0.16	84.98	15.48
33.28	1.61	4.04	0.22	10.85	0.03	0.08			
175.28	12.58	23.32	5.77	3.29	67.37	16.86		1.33	
985.23	1038.40	467.94	550.10	563.80	444.69	304.71	407.95	466.70	631.01
14185.01	**3803.94**	**7453.52**	**4304.34**	**7354.57**	**2317.64**	**3310.92**	**638.23**	**1653.75**	**766.79**
7382.36	2104.64	6017.76	2697.85	3884.54	1493.75	1743.18	320.67	989.79	474.86
2017.37	598.84	165.75	423.96	1402.96	102.38	459.81	203.23	93.14	95.25
1034.46	122.62	176.89	275.59	376.94	65.61	36.22	2.03	10.73	36.53
2582.27	308.95	932.64	624.56	825.07	164.93	571.24		239.52	16.75
278.01	172.16	36.16	1.04	246.22	360.51	234.24	44.00	143.98	30.55
34463.01	**15369.78**	**22623.29**	**10135.62**	**38849.09**	**12460.12**	**11436.06**	**2909.22**	**7075.82**	**6027.62**
23186.01	8100.51	14590.92	4793.72	26747.11	5960.03	6255.24	1104.38	3908.75	2614.20
21403.57	7061.79	13261.30	4325.10	25736.91	5286.65	4826.63	926.37	3425.12	2393.62
19286.62	3944.48	12246.24	2835.96	23471.95	4095.60	3764.39	584.34	2723.56	884.64
76.51	76.16	45.93	220.09	31.87	28.49	141.01	4.93	38.43	151.69
1610.33	2192.32	817.43	1171.49	1565.56	1074.44	848.77	247.21	519.30	843.19

9-24 续表

单位：元 (yuan)

项目	Item	自治区 Autonomous Region	乌鲁木齐市 Urumqi City	吐鲁番地区 Turpan Administrative Offices	哈密地区 Hami [Kumul] Administrative Offices
渔业生产支出	Fishery	0.04			
工业生产支出	Industry	37.19		0.49	0.73
建筑业生产支出	Construction	19.85	4.60	0.98	0.02
交通运输支出	Transportation	70.51	330.19	21.47	102.80
批发和零售贸易、餐饮业	Wholesale Retail Trades and Catering services	105.26	177.17	509.70	13.48
社会服务业支出	Social Services	6.01	10.28	47.92	1.84
文教卫生业	Cultural, Education, Medicines and Medical Services	19.56		24.39	
其他经营支出	Others	21.17		1.75	4.09
购置生产性固定资产支出	Expenditure for Productive Fixed Assets	775.98	1275.22	467.50	602.45
税费支出	Taxes and Fee	7.78		2.14	1.11
生活消费支出	Expenditure for Consumption	3889.69	7380.67	6327.03	6077.21
财产性支出	Expenditure for Properties	22.31		2.43	0.16
转移性支出	Expenditure for Transfers	424.81	722.31	578.51	656.02
非消费性现金付出	**Expenditure for Non-consumption**	**3098.09**	**1206.85**	**1659.83**	**3760.91**
#归还银行信用社贷款	Loan Returned to Bank	1374.34	205.92	533.02	974.90
借出款	Lending Money	102.25	45.50	125.47	116.98
归还借款	Return Borrowed Money	476.22	229.63	183.12	424.36
存入银行信用社	Deposit	652.65	3.95	70.90	1129.33
期末金融资产余额	**Balance of Financial Assets in Year-end**	**3002.04**	**5488.40**	**3223.07**	**4269.40**
#银行存款	Deposit	2088.54	4388.33	2215.75	3087.62
手存现金	Cash	904.03	1095.48	970.65	974.85
期末债务余额	**Balance of Debt in Year-end**	**1638.78**	**4482.90**	**1916.63**	**3237.56**
#银行、信用社贷款	Loan from Bank and Credit Cooperatives	1136.83	3587.22	1443.77	2299.72
个人借(欠)款	Borrowed Money from Individual	477.02	661.31	351.47	926.70
生活消费支出的现金	**Expenditure for Consumption**	**3889.69**	**7380.67**	**6327.03**	**6077.21**
食品	Food	1138.12	2376.39	1954.62	1494.74
#主食	Staple Food	196.61	460.33	511.58	265.37
副食	Non-staple Food	767.09	1523.40	1174.22	1100.09
衣着	Clothing	368.37	680.97	525.77	582.71
居住	Residence	976.36	1820.43	1012.43	1698.77
家庭设备、用品及服务	Household Facilities，Articles and Services	194.43	344.33	258.31	241.97
医疗保健	Health Care and Medical Services	376.87	680.92	988.72	682.56
交通和通讯	Transportation and Communications	530.59	896.72	1158.44	959.82
文化教育、娱乐用品及服务	Cultural，Education and Recreational Articles and Services	229.66	480.90	302.10	331.72
#文化教育、娱乐用品	Cultural，Education and Recreational Articles	51.95	140.67	37.06	92.68
文化教育、娱乐服务	Cultural，Education and Recreational Services	177.71	340.23	265.04	239.04
其他商品和服务	Other Commodities and Services	75.28	100.01	126.64	84.92
在生活消费支出的现金中	Expenditure for Consumption				
商品性支出	Commodities	2787.37	5291.44	4096.26	4261.45
服务支出	Services	1102.32	2089.23	2230.77	1815.77

Continued

单位：元 (yuan)

昌吉回族自治州 Changji Hui Autonomous Prefecture	伊犁州直属县(市) Counties (Cities) Direct Under Ili Prefecture	塔城地区 Tacheng [Tarbagatai] Administrative Offices	阿勒泰地区 Altay Administrative Offices	博尔塔拉蒙古自治州 Bortala Mongol Autonomous Prefecture	巴音郭楞蒙古自治州 Bayangol Mongol Autonomous Prefecture	阿克苏地区 Aksu Administrative Offices	克孜勒苏克尔克孜自治州 Kizilsu Kirgiz Autonomous Prefecture	喀什地区 Kashgar [Kaxgar] Administrative Offices	和田地区 Hotan Administrative Offices
4.29	3.04	0.08	0.31	0.04		0.53			
41.20	244.92	0.37	17.70	0.12	8.03	0.35	0.02	12.17	145.95
11.99	30.92	78.97	15.96	5.43		5.67	4.35	7.21	75.69
260.06	227.52	3.88	44.45	79.08	35.53	7.28	75.46	33.11	86.74
102.98	229.03	22.91	7.35	566.17	44.10	27.69	9.23	34.04	197.06
4.39	15.46		4.06		0.45	19.38	0.01	4.98	0.61
0.64	86.45	23.83	1.76					1.16	4.45
4.55	11.47	21.66	5.95	16.68		11.57	0.82	51.16	3.61
1782.45	1038.73	1329.62	468.62	1010.20	673.38	1428.60	178.01	483.63	220.58
0.12	0.95	12.90	0.11	9.15	3.34	51.87		2.68	19.23
9901.46	6446.76	7144.92	4840.63	10675.42	6156.76	4873.28	1664.77	3007.10	3227.82
0.49	47.25		0.72	5.95	0.04	12.50	18.62	31.29	0.02
1374.93	774.30	874.56	500.44	1411.47	339.94	243.18	121.44	126.01	166.35
14087.93	**3786.92**	**5880.86**	**1826.83**	**6366.09**	**2505.86**	**2837.44**	**218.28**	**1757.43**	**581.45**
5527.62	1675.63	4310.85	822.55	3068.06	1541.94	1685.40	37.96	772.75	301.58
372.21	141.68	66.57	13.35	797.72	10.67	58.61	1.22	7.64	11.07
2320.55	713.93	829.89	223.69	1048.94	148.98	201.32	71.59	126.17	139.08
4890.59	385.07	177.28	235.01	423.15	214.85	429.85	6.73	667.13	29.36
10131.76	**3892.92**	**7494.22**	**3072.90**	**9547.48**	**5312.13**	**1821.14**	**371.72**	**888.11**	**674.14**
9204.72	3085.47	6864.02	1864.71	8187.90	3496.74	1274.84	19.35	462.21	8.50
927.05	807.45	630.20	1208.19	1345.56	1815.39	533.02	352.37	405.53	665.64
2607.92	**3462.66**	**2519.65**	**4591.14**	**2511.74**	**1918.14**	**792.59**	**528.89**	**286.89**	**187.92**
1866.42	2243.73	2158.84	4010.43	1840.87	1324.69	534.97	350.28	229.00	130.10
741.50	1070.77	360.81	514.40	646.34	532.41	248.46	178.48	57.89	28.52
9901.46	**6446.76**	**7144.92**	**4840.63**	**10675.42**	**6156.76**	**4873.28**	**1664.77**	**3007.10**	**3227.82**
2542.56	1653.89	2318.57	1361.74	2628.02	1856.42	1330.12	714.37	979.69	766.09
293.54	259.78	439.02	391.58	353.94	411.69	239.67	166.50	182.67	95.18
1622.01	1132.39	1516.48	802.45	1768.07	1280.51	846.74	500.21	677.26	565.63
729.13	514.66	595.85	539.40	609.30	481.17	587.26	190.87	450.69	412.25
2944.02	1881.92	1551.06	960.19	3425.33	1211.13	995.12	266.07	711.18	980.37
433.62	368.83	381.64	260.11	430.36	264.46	250.93	79.63	131.87	150.41
1028.49	715.52	660.10	701.49	856.51	561.35	545.51	191.55	311.91	275.02
1328.64	784.58	1077.91	769.47	1751.65	1512.40	897.43	194.42	328.68	537.00
624.00	423.98	368.71	199.64	722.39	246.89	153.47	18.68	59.68	47.54
204.00	127.18	117.63	64.61	214.75	73.73	40.04	8.21	16.27	15.30
420.00	296.81	251.08	135.04	507.64	173.16	113.43	10.48	43.41	32.23
270.99	103.38	191.06	48.59	251.86	22.94	113.44	9.17	33.41	59.14
7137.93	4442.33	5266.72	3376.19	8053.91	4698.25	3568.48	1233.59	2205.12	2571.22
2763.53	2004.43	1878.20	1464.44	2621.52	1458.51	1304.80	431.18	801.99	656.60

9-25 农村居民家庭人均纯收入分组

Rural Households Grouped by Per Capita Annual Net Income

(2011 年) (抽样调查 Sampled Survey)

项 目	Item	合 计 Total	0-400 元 0-400 yuan	400-600 元 400-600 yuan	600-800 元 600-800 yuan	800-1000 元 800-1000 yuan	1000-1200 元 1000-1200 yuan
调查户数(户)	**Number of Households Surveyed (household)**	**1550**	**46**	**16**	**16**	**24**	**23**
构成(%)	Percentage (%)	100	2.97	1.03	1.03	1.55	1.48
常住人口(人)	**Number of Permanent Residents in the Households Surveyed (person)**	**6644**	**183**	**91**	**81**	**133**	**117**
构成(%)	Percentage (%)	100	2.76	1.37	1.22	2.01	1.75
人均纯收入(元)	**Per Capita Net Income (yuan)**	**5442.15**	**-588.27**	**500.15**	**691.13**	**925.78**	**1113.90**

项 目	Item	1200-1500 元 1200-1500 yuan	1500-1700 元 1500-1700 yuan	1700-2000 元 1700-2000 yuan	2000-2500 元 2000-2500 yuan	2500-3000 元 2500-3000 yuan
调查户数(户)	**Number of Households Surveyed (household)**	**35**	**49**	**79**	**135**	**104**
构成(%)	Percentage (%)	2.26	3.16	5.10	8.71	6.71
常住人口(人)	**Number of Permanent Residents in the Households Surveyed (person)**	**169**	**235**	**379**	**633**	**479**
构成(%)	Percentage (%)	2.54	3.54	5.70	9.52	7.21
人均纯收入(元)	**Per Capita Net Income (yuan)**	**1388.05**	**1599.42**	**1856.22**	**2237.14**	**2761.88**

项 目	Item	3000-3500 元 3000-3500 yuan	3500-4000 元 3500-4000 yuan	4000-4500 元 4000-4500 yuan	4500-5000 元 4500-5000 yuan	5000 元以上 over 5000 yuan
调查户数(户)	**Number of Households Surveyed (household)**	**91**	**107**	**86**	**77**	**662**
构成(%)	Percentage (%)	5.87	6.90	5.55	4.97	42.71
常住人口(人)	**Number of Permanent Residents in the Households Surveyed (person)**	**416**	**502**	**394**	**336**	**2497**
构成(%)	Percentage (%)	6.26	7.55	5.93	5.05	37.59
人均纯收入(元)	**Per Capita Net Income (yuan)**	**3233.77**	**3730.65**	**4246.49**	**4770.99**	**10157.68**

9-26 主要年份农村居民家庭房屋使用情况
Housing Conditions of Rural Households in Main Years

(抽样调查 Sampled Survey)

项 目	Item	2000	2005	2010	2011
本年新建(购)房屋	**Houses Newly built This Year**				
面积(平方米/人)	Per Capita Floor Space of Houses (sq.m/person)	0.38	1.37	0.73	1.06
价值(元/平方米)	Value of Houses (yuan/sq.m)	169.37	225.20	442.00	843.42
住房结构(平方米/人)	Structure of Houses (sq.m/person)				
#钢筋混凝土结构	Reinforced Concrete Structure	0.03	0.08	0.22	0.32
砖木结构	Brick and Wood Structure	0.16	1.04	0.50	0.71
生活用房面积(平方米/人)	Per Capita Living Rooms Space (sq.m/person)	0.38	0.72	0.80	1.06
年末住房情况	**Houses at Year-end**				
住房面积(平方米/人)	Per Capita Floor Space of Houses (sq.m/person)	17.25	21.23	24.00	26.14
住房价值(元/平方米)	Value of Houses (yuan/sq.m)	120.86	160.99	252.79	452.36
住房结构(平方米/人)	Structure of House (sq.m/person)				
#钢筋混凝土结构	Reinforced Concrete Structure	0.53	0.98	1.83	2.30
砖木结构	Brick and Wood Structure	2.75	6.48	10.95	13.47

9-27 主要年份城乡新建住宅面积和居民住房情况
Floor Space of Newly Built Residential Buildings and Housing Conditions of Urban and Rural Residents in Main Years

年份 Year	城镇新建住宅面积(万平方米) Floor Space of Newly Built Residential Buildings In Urban Areas (10 000 sq.m)	农村新建住宅面积(万平方米) Floor Space of Newly Built Residential Buildings in Rural Areas (10 000 sq.m)	城镇人均使用面积(平方米) Per Capita Gross Living Space in Urban Areas (sq.m)	城镇人均建筑面积(平方米) Per Capita Floor Space of Residential Building in Urban Areas (sq.m)	农村人均居住面积(平方米) Per Capita Floor Space of Residential Building in Rural Areas (sq.m)
1985	353.26	463.00	10.70	14.27	12.75
1990	381.61	393.96	13.55	18.07	14.04
1995	567.54	496.6	16.57	22.09	16.12
1996	683.51	757.71	17.61	23.48	16.12
1997	673.58	719.53	13.62	18.16	16.13
1998	874.97	729.71	18.95	25.27	16.20
1999	1315.89	705.00	19.76	26.35	16.90
2000	1327.29	554.59	20.06	26.75	17.25
2001	1517.22	894.56	20.60	27.47	18.04
2002	1256.72	534.10	18.17	23.78	18.56
2003	1546.23	800.81	17.91	23.36	18.62
2004	1565.72	732.84	18.82	24.44	19.10
2005	2226.97	1391.81	20.15	26.02	21.23
2006	2212.08	1573.38	20.33	26.31	21.96
2007	2491.60	1967.17	20.38	27.17	22.45
2008	2584.23	1541.44	20.47	27.29	22.79
2009	1994.28	1418.15	20.42	27.16	23.45
2010	2028.26	1263.63	20.49	27.25	24.00
2011	2621.59	1883.35	21.70	28.92	26.14

9-28 分地区农村居民家庭平均每人粮食收支平衡表
Per Capita Grain Banlance of Debit and Credit by Region

单位：公斤 (2011 年)(抽样调查 Sampled Survey) (kg)

项 目	Item	自治区 Autonomous Region	乌鲁木齐市 Urumqi City	吐鲁番地区 Turpan Administrative Offices	哈密地区 Hami [Kumul] Administrative Offices
年初粮食结存	**Inventory of Grain at Beginning of Year**	**297.56**	**306.48**	**15.75**	**137.84**
粮食收入合计	**Total of Debit**	**1509.31**	**990.91**	**257.50**	**689.45**
家庭经营生产的	From Household Business	1314.36	703.37	21.49	414.51
购 入	Purchases	194.41	287.54	236.02	274.75
其他粮食收入	Others	0.55			0.19
粮食支出合计	**Total of Expenditure**	**1264.17**	**969.85**	**237.76**	**634.67**
主食用粮	Staple Food	236.81	167.56	219.25	174.04
出 售	Sales	812.64	673.25	0.40	199.89
种 籽	Seeds	39.03	29.78	5.94	32.95
饲 料	Fodder	172.04	99.27	12.17	227.71
其他粮食支出	Others	3.65			0.07
年末粮食结存(实际数)	**Inventory of Grain at Year-end**	**434.77**	**309.09**	**42.47**	**277.48**

项 目	Item	昌吉回族自治州 Changji Hui Autonomous Prefecture	伊犁州直属县(市) Counties (Cities) Direct Under Ili Prefecture	塔城地区 Tacheng [Tarbagatai] Administrative Offices	阿勒泰地区 Altay Administrative Offices	博尔塔拉蒙古自治州 Bortala Mongol Autonomous Prefecture
年初粮食结存	**Inventory of Grain at Beginning of Year**	**108.12**	**930.70**	**339.94**	**83.20**	**538.98**
粮食收入合计	**Total of Debit**	**4600.80**	**2392.67**	**2891.08**	**1420.54**	**5940.32**
家庭经营生产的	From Household Business	4130.46	2073.49	2555.09	1103.99	5542.36
购 入	Purchases	470.08	319.11	335.99	316.44	397.96
其他粮食收入	Others	0.26	0.06		0.10	
粮食支出合计	**Total of Expenditure**	**4133.28**	**2226.08**	**2691.82**	**1197.00**	**4259.47**
主食用粮	Staple Food	216.60	190.16	204.38	173.05	153.59
出 售	Sales	3457.43	1771.77	2322.93	844.12	3808.11
种 籽	Seeds	110.73	49.72	87.02	49.75	108.53
饲 料	Fodder	348.15	214.34	77.49	130.08	189.24
其他粮食支出	Others	0.38	0.08			
年末粮食结存(实际数)	**Inventory of Grain at Year-end**	**712.46**	**921.68**	**333.67**	**182.00**	**672.82**

项 目	Item	巴音郭楞蒙古自治州 Bayangol Mongol Autonomous Prefecture	阿克苏地区 Aksu Administrative Offices	克孜勒苏克尔克孜自治州 Kizilsu Kirgiz Autonomous Prefecture	喀什地区 Kashgar [Kaxgar] Administrative Offices	和田地区 Hotan Administrative Offices
年初粮食结存	**Inventory of Grain at Beginning of Year**	**170.72**	**253.86**	**31.73**	**117.49**	**139.28**
粮食收入合计	**Total of Debit**	**674.59**	**860.08**	**589.24**	**881.06**	**705.78**
家庭经营生产的	From Household Business	414.31	677.23	504.70	779.04	655.76
购 入	Purchases	260.25	182.82	84.54	98.41	50.02
其他粮食收入	Others	0.03	0.03		3.61	
粮食支出合计	**Total of Expenditure**	**557.67**	**739.91**	**470.19**	**714.86**	**451.51**
主食用粮	Staple Food	216.41	247.50	182.93	296.21	193.09
出 售	Sales	167.93	357.04	188.42	204.31	128.67
种 籽	Seeds	21.57	24.72	28.64	28.67	19.24
饲 料	Fodder	151.76	110.53	70.20	173.59	108.26
其他粮食支出	Others		0.12		12.07	2.25
年末粮食结存(实际数)	**Inventory of Grain at Year-end**	**259.61**	**331.95**	**94.69**	**203.02**	**325.98**

9-29 主要年份农村居民家庭平均每户饲养畜禽、其他小动物生产情况

Output of Livestock, Poultry and Other Small Animals Per Rural Households in Main Years

单位：公斤　　(抽样调查)(Sampled Surrey)　　(kg)

年 份 Year	出售自宰猪肉产量 Output of Pork Sold and Self-slaugutered	出售自宰羊肉产量 Output of Mutton Sold and Self-slaughtered	羊毛产量 Output of Wool	牛羊奶产量 Output of Cow and Sheep Milk	出售自宰家禽产量 Output of Poultry Sold and Self-slaughtered	禽蛋产量 Output of Poultry and Eggs	蚕茧产量 Output of Silkworm
1985	16.76	47.54	10.51	51.53		13.95	0.26
1990	24.97	45.72	15.86	67.16		17.68	1.26
1995	23.42	61.41	14.86	66.16	28.86	23.14	1.69
1996	23.10	62.09	7.61	34.93	7.61	8.20	0.89
1997	12.46	73.78	7.37	33.57	9.87	7.97	1.08
1998	10.18	84.42	5.40	42.53	7.39	8.78	1.58
1999	12.91	100.45	4.06	34.92	7.65	13.90	1.38
2000	16.48	94.55	5.49	34.27	13.03	25.26	1.01
2001	13.24	91.54			16.92	35.71	
2002	11.01	110.97			16.09	41.07	
2003	13.16	86.23	4.51	91.91	12.48	37.10	0.66
2004	10.30	105.20	4.09	89.54	12.75	6.03	0.23
2005	8.29	107.11	6.28	134.36	14.95	49.14	0.23
2006	4.28	114.78	6.91	112.72	12.33	71.07	0.14
2007	2.70	112.08	7.05	144.28	12.25	40.59	0.02
2008	9.39	105.70	5.06	169.98	18.43	62.33	0.03
2009	9.64	102.68	5.19	136.18	25.58	67.18	
2010	11.64	108.72	4.05	145.32	19.16	36.26	
2011	22.81	105.84	5.79	83.25	23.02	58.02	

注：因调查户调整，部分指标数据与往年相比变动较大。
Note:Beceucse of Households Surveyed adjustment, Parts of Index sign data quite changed compared to last yesr.

9-30 主要年份农村居民家庭平均每户饲养畜禽、其他小动物出售量

Quantities of Livestock, Poultry and Other Small Animals Sold Per Rural Households in Main Years

(抽样调查) (Sampled Surrey)

年 份 Year	猪(头) Pork (head)	牛(头) Cattle (head)	羊(只) Sheep (head)	家禽(只) Poultry (head)	蛋类(公斤) Eggs (kg)	羊毛(公斤) Wool (kg)	牛羊奶(公斤) Milk (kg)
1985	0.10		1.94	3.30	7.68	6.87	5.68
1990	0.22	0.11	1.50	4.15	8.25	9.63	17.47
1995	0.17	0.22	2.21	11.69	17.28	5.80	26.76
1996	0.24	0.14	2.14	1.98	3.08	3.13	12.43
1997	0.11	0.16	2.74	3.00	3.51	4.16	11.56
1998	0.07	0.15	3.47	2.14	4.30	2.23	18.04
1999	0.08	0.25	3.89	2.70	9.23	1.67	12.75
2000	0.14	0.39	3.81	4.89	21.27	1.82	21.30
2001	0.12	0.37	3.85	7.55	31.60	1.43	39.77
2002	0.11	0.35	4.61	6.64	34.55	1.95	55.33
2003	0.18	0.35	4.14	3.60	33.55	1.81	73.94
2004	0.12	0.32	4.55	4.28	3.01	1.86	77.30
2005	0.09	0.39	6.03	4.42	46.51	4.54	117.65
2006	0.06	0.59	7.21	4.12	68.19	5.19	91.42
2007	0.03	0.65	6.03	3.54	38.11	5.43	123.35
2008	0.11	0.56	4.92	6.35	59.54	3.28	148.16
2009	0.12	0.43	4.62	9.63	63.91	3.06	119.28
2010	0.12	0.39	4.32	6.12	33.01	2.88	129.76
2011	0.43	0.41	4.47	7.17	54.03	4.71	71.60

9-31 社会保险基本情况
Basic Conditions on Social Insurance

单位：万元 (10 000 yuan)

指　　标	Item	2010	2011
基本养老保险	**Basic Endowment Insurance**		
职工基本养老保险	Employee Basic Pension Insurance		
年末参保人数(万人)	Contributors at Year-end (10 000 persons)	259.67	291.99
#参保职工	Staff and Workers	193.07	214.66
离退休人员	Number of Retirees	66.60	77.33
新型农村社会养老保险	New Rural Old-age Insurance		
年末参保人数(万人)	Contributors at Year-end (10 000 persons)		490.58
享受待遇人数（万人）	Beneficiaries at Year-end (10000 persons)		84.68
城镇居民社会养老保险	Urban Employee Basic Pension Insurance		
年末参保人数(万人)	Contributors at Year-end (10 000 persons)		27.49
享受待遇人数（万人）	Beneficiaries at Year-end (10000 persons)		4.48
基本医疗保险	Basic Medical Care Insurance		
职工基本医疗保险	Employee Basic Medical Care Insurance		
年末参保人数(万人)	Contributors at Year-end (10 000 persons)	296.72	322.73
城镇居民基本医疗保险	Urban Employee Basic Medical Care Insurance		
年末参保人数(万人)	Contributors at Year-end (10 000 persons)	274.60	282.68
工伤保险	**Work Injury Insurance**		
年末参保人数(万人)	Contributors at Year-end (10 000 persons)	184.13	208.18
年末享受待遇人次数（万人次）	Beneficiaries at Year-end (10 000 persons)	1.48	1.42
失业保险	**Unemployment Insurance**		
年末参保人数(万人)	Year-end Contributors (10 000 persons)	180.29	196.72
年末享受待遇人数（万人）	Beneficiaries at Year-end (10 000 persons)	5.88	5.55
生育保险	**Maternity Insurance**		
年末参保人数(万人)	Contributors at Year-end (10 000 persons)	188.23	206.14
年末享受待遇人次数（万人次）	Beneficiaries at Year-end (10000 persons)	4.67	5.26

注：基本医疗保险数据不含新型农村合作医疗。
Note: Statistics on basic endowment insuranse didn't coner data on new rural old-age insurance.

9-32 各地、州、市社会保险年末参保人数

Number of Social Insured Persons at the Year-end by Prefecture, Autonomous Prefecture and City

单位：万人 (10 000 persons)

年 份 Year	地 区 Region	基本养老保险 Basic Endowment Insurance			职工基本医疗保险 Employee Basic Medical Care Insurance
		职工基本养老保险 Employee Basic Pension Insurance	新型农村社会养老保险 New Rural Old-age Insurance	城镇居民社会养老保险 Urban Non-employment Social Pension Insurance	
	2001	148.08			116.17
	2002	152.06			148.12
	2003	160.04			176.37
	2004	173.76			195.97
	2005	181.88			211.85
	2006	191.97			227.15
	2007	205.00			244.78
	2008	222.17			263.54
	2009	232.08			279.09
	2010	259.67			296.72
	2011	291.99	490.58	27.49	322.73
乌鲁木齐市	Urumqi City	94.74	10.30	0.80	99.13
克拉玛依市	Karamay City	4.25	0.09	0.05	3.95
吐鲁番地区	Turpan Administrative Offices	4.95	19.07	0.55	7.47
哈密地区	Hami [Kumul] Administrative Offices	9.27	8.53	0.24	10.06
昌吉回族自治州	Changji Hui Autonomous Prefecture	19.94	30.59	0.64	22.52
伊犁州直属县(市)	Counties (Cities) Direct Under Ili Prefecture	23.65	51.49	5.35	25.34
塔城地区	Tacheng [Tarbagatai] Administrative Offices	11.77	19.43	1.56	12.21
阿勒泰地区	Altay Administrative Offices	7.81	12.92	0.79	11.23
博尔塔拉蒙古自治州	Bortala Mongol Autonomous Prefecture	5.10	7.16	0.23	5.73
巴音郭楞蒙古自治州	Bayangol Mongol Autonomous Prefecture	20.49	20.38	1.50	24.01
阿克苏地区	Aksu Administrative Offices	11.64	64.51	2.43	17.12
克孜勒苏柯尔克孜自治州	Kizilsu Kirgiz Autonomous Prefecture	3.17	17.36	1.17	6.65
喀什地区	Kashgar [Kaxgar] Administrative Offices	13.95	137.92	9.51	23.71
和田地区	Hotan Administrative Offices	4.82	90.84	2.67	10.26

注：基本医疗保险数据不含新型农村合作医疗。

9-32 续表 Continued

单位：万人 (10 000 persons)

年份 Year	地区 Region	基本养老保险 Basic Endowment Insurance / 城镇居民基本医疗保险 Urban Non-employment Basic Medical Insurance	工伤保险 Work Injury Insurance	失业保险 Unemployment Insurance	生育保险 Maternity Insurance
	2001		30.53	126.47	30.52
	2002		29.45	131.29	29.72
	2003		41.08	135.12	32.16
	2004		60.93	138.58	59.23
	2005		79.51	140.82	103.48
	2006		102.40	145.04	135.90
	2007		132.55	151.55	151.60
	2008	175.07	151.08	162.76	165.02
	2009	256.90	167.70	169.60	176.07
	2010	274.60	184.13	180.29	188.23
	2011	282.68	208.18	196.72	206.14
乌鲁木齐市	Urumqi City	56.27	66.14	67.99	57.59
克拉玛依市	Karamay City	7.58	5.02	3.99	4.40
吐鲁番地区	Turpan Administrative Offices	9.28	4.70	3.98	3.97
哈密地区	Hami [Kumul] Administrative Offices	9.89	8.80	5.90	5.97
昌吉回族自治州	Changji Hui Autonomous Prefecture	21.03	21.82	12.61	16.42
伊犁州直属县(市)	Counties (Cities) Direct Under Ili Prefecture	33.56	14.46	13.78	16.33
塔城地区	Tacheng [Tarbagatai] Administrative Offices	11.51	6.28	6.03	7.28
阿勒泰地区	Altay Administrative Offices	12.39	7.29	5.21	6.36
博尔塔拉蒙古自治州	Bortala Mongol Autonomous Prefecture	7.80	3.98	3.40	3.97
巴音郭楞蒙古自治州	Bayangol Mongol Autonomous Prefecture	19.09	14.86	14.82	15.14
阿克苏地区	Aksu Administrative Offices	26.87	8.52	9.20	10.40
克孜勒苏柯尔克孜自治州	Kizilsu Kirgiz Autonomous Prefecture	6.53	3.74	3.43	4.12
喀什地区	Kashgar [Kaxgar] Administrative Offices	42.92	13.87	14.06	15.51
和田地区	Hotan Administrative Offices	17.95	6.08	5.98	7.09

Note: Data of basic medical care insurance did not include new cooperative health care in agricultural and pastoral areas.

主要统计指标解释

一、城镇住户

城镇家庭人口 指居住在一起,经济上合在一起共同生活的家庭成员。凡计算为家庭人口的成员其全部收入包括在家庭中。

城镇就业者负担人数 指家庭人口与就业人口之比。

城镇家庭总收入 指家庭成员得到的工薪收入、经营净收入、财产性收入、转移性收入之和，不包括出售财物收入和借贷收入。

城镇家庭可支配收入 指家庭成员得到可用于最终消费支出和其它非义务性支出以及储蓄的总和，即居民家庭可以用来自由支配的收入。它是家庭总收入扣除交纳的所得税、个人交纳的社会保障支出以及记账补贴后的收入。计算公式为：

可支配收入=家庭总收入-交纳个人所得税-个人交纳的社会保障支出-记帐补贴

城镇家庭消费性支出 指家庭用于日常生活的支出,包括食品、衣着、家庭设备用品及服务、医疗保健、交通和通信、娱乐教育文化服务、居住、其他商品和服务等八大类支出。

城镇家庭服务性消费支出 指家庭用于支付社会提供的各种非商品性服务费用。

城镇家庭收入分组方法 是将所有调查户依户人均可支配收入由低到高排队，按10%，10%，20%，20%，20%，10%，10%的比例依次分成：最低收入户、低收入户、中等偏下收入户、中等收入户、中等偏上收入户、高收入户、最高收入户等七组。总体中最低5%的户为困难户。

恩格尔系数 指食物支出金额在消费性总支出金额中所占的比例。计算公式为：

恩格尔系数=食品支出金额/生活消费总支出金额×100%

二、农村住户

总收入 指调查期内农村住户和住户成员从各种来源渠道得到的收入总和。按收入的性质划分为工资性收入、家庭经营收入、财产性收入和转移性收入。

工资性收入 指农村住户成员受雇于单位或个人，靠出卖劳动所而获得的收入。

家庭经营收入 指农村住户以家庭为生产经营单位进行生产筹划和管理而获得的收入。农村住户家庭经营活动按行业划分为农业、林业、牧业、渔业、工业、建筑业、交通运输业邮电业、批发和零售贸易餐饮业、社会服务业、文教卫生业和其他家庭经营。

财产性收入 指金融资产或有形非生产性资产的所有者向其他机构单位提供资金或将有形非生产性资产供其支配，作为回报而从中获得的收入。

转移性收入 指农村住户和住户成员无须付出任何对应物而获得的货物、服务、资金或资产所有权等，不包括无偿提供的用于固定资本形成的资金。一般情况下，是指农村住户在二次分配中的所有收入。

现金收入 指农村住户和住户成员在调查期内得到以现金形态表现的收入。按来源分成工资性收入、家庭经营现金收入、财产性收入、转移性收入。

纯收入 指农村住户当年从各个来源得到的总收入相应地扣除所发生的费用后的收入总和。计算方法：

纯收入=总收入-家庭经营费用支出-税费支出-生产性固定资产折旧-赠送农村外部亲友支出

纯收入主要用于再生产投入和当年生活消费支出，也可用于储蓄和各种非义务性支出。“农民人均纯收入”按人口平均的纯收入水平，反映的是一个地区农村居民的平均收入水平。

总支出 指农村住户用于生产、生活和再分配的全部支出。包括家庭经营费用支出、购置生产性固定资产支出、税费支出、生活消费支出、财产性支出和转移性支出。

三、社会保险

城镇职工基本养老保险

1.参加保险职工人数：指报告期末按照国家法律、法规和有关政策规定参加基本养老保险并在社保经办机构已建立缴费记录档案的职工人数。包括中断缴费但未终止养老关系的职工人数，不包括只登记未建立缴费记录档案的人数。

2.参加保险离退休人员人数：指报告期末参加基本养老保险的离休、退休和退职人员的人数。

3.基本养老保险基金收入：指根据国家有关规定，由纳入基本养老保险范围的缴费单位和个人按照国家规定的缴费基数和缴费比例缴纳的养老保险基金，以及通过其他方式取得的形成基金来源的收入。包括单位和职工个人缴纳的基本养老保险费、基本养老基金利息收入、上级补助收入、下级上解收入、转移收入、财政补贴和其他收入。

4.基本养老保险基金支出：指按照国家政策规定的开支范围和开支标准从基本养老保险基金中支付给参加基本养老保险的个人的养老金、丧葬抚恤补助，以及由于保险关系转移、上下级之间调剂资金等原因而发生的支出。包括:离休金、退休金、退职金、各种补贴、医疗费、死亡丧葬补助费、抚恤救济费、社会保险经办机构管理费、补助下级支出、上解上级支出、转移支出、其他支出等。

5.基本养老保险基金累计结余：指截止报告期末基本养老基金收支相抵后的累计余额。

基本医疗保险

1.参保人数：指报告期末按国家有关规定参加基本医疗保险的人数。

2.基金收入：指由用人单位和个人按照国家规定的缴费基数、缴费比例或缴费标准缴纳的基本医疗保险基金，财政补助资金以及通过其他方式取得的形成基金来源的款项，包括：单位缴纳收入、个人缴纳收入、财政补助收入（含医疗救助补助个人收入）、财政补贴收入、利息收入和其他收入。

3.基金支出：指按照国家政策规定的开支范围和开支标准从社会统筹基金中支付给参加基本医疗保险的职工和退休人员的医疗保险待遇支出，和从个人帐户基金中支付给参加基本医疗保险的职工和退休人员的医疗费用支出，以及其他支出。包括：住院医疗费用支出、门急诊医疗费用支出、个人账户基金支出、其他支出。

4.基金累计结余：指截止报告期末基本医疗保险基金累计结余金额。

失业保险

1.参加保险人数：指报告期末按照国家法律、法规和有关政策规定参加了失业保险的城镇企业、事业单位的职工及地方政府规定参加失业保险的其他人员的人数。

2.失业保险基金收入：指报告期内筹集的失业保险基金的总额，包括失业保险费收入、利息收入、财政补贴收入、其他收入、转移收入、上级补助收入、下级上解收入。

3.失业保险基金支出：指报告期内为保障失业人员基本生活、促进其再就业等支出的基金总额，包括失业保险金支出、医疗补助金支出、丧葬补助金和抚恤金支出、职业培训和职业介绍补贴支出、农民合同制工人一次性生活补助支出、其他支出、转移支出、上级补助支出、下级上解支出。

4.基金累计结余：指截止报告期末失业保险基金收支相抵后的累计余额。

工伤保险

1.参加保险人数：指报告期末依据国家有关规定参加工伤保险的职工人数和有雇工的个体工商户的雇工数。

2.享受保险待遇人数：指年初至报告期末因工伤或职业病而享受工伤保险待遇的人数。为享受工伤医疗待遇中未评定等级的人数、享受伤残待遇人数以及享受因工死亡待遇人数之和。

3.基金收入：指根据国家有关规定，由参加工伤保险的单位按国家规定的缴费基数和缴费比例缴纳的工伤保险基金，以及通过其他形式取得的形成基金来源的款项。包括：单位缴纳的社会统筹基金收入、财政补贴收入、利息收入、其他收入。

4.基金支出：指按照国家政策规定的开支范围和开支标准从工伤保险基金中支付给参加工伤保险的人员及供养直系亲属工伤保险待遇支出及其他支出。包括工伤医疗费、伤残补助金、工亡补助金、护理费、丧葬补助费、工伤预防费用、职业康复费用和其他支出。

5.基金累计结余：指截止报告期末工伤保险基金累计结余金额。

生育保险

1.参保人数：指报告期末依据有关规定参加生育保险的人数。

2.基金收入：指根据国家有关规定，由参加生育保险的单位按照国家规定的缴费基数和缴费比例缴纳的生育保险基金，以及通过其他方式取得的形成基金来源的款项，包括：单位缴纳的基金收入、利息收入和其他收入。

3.基金支出：指按照国家政策规定的开支范围和开支标准，从生育保险基金中支付给参加生育保险的职工，因妊娠、分娩和计划生育手术而享受的待遇及其他支出。包括：生育津贴、医疗费用支出及其他支出。

4.基金累计结余：指截止报告期末生育保险基金累计结余金额。

Explanatory Notes on Main Statistical Indicators

I. Urban Households

Population of Urban Households refer to members of households living and sharing economically together in the urban areas. All the income and expenditure of all the members of such households are included in the income and expenditure of the household.

Number of Dependents per Urban Employee refers to the ratio between number of persons in an urban household and the number of employed persons.

Total Income of Urban Households refers to the sum of wage and salary; net business income; income from properties; and income from transfers of members of the households. Income from selling of properties and income from borrowing are not included.

Disposable Income of Urban Households refers to the actual income at the disposal of members of the households which can be used for final consumption, other non-compulsory expenditure and savings. This equals to total income minus income tax, personal contribution to social security and subsidy for keeping diaries in being a sample household. The following formula is used:

Disposable income = total household income - income tax - personal contribution to social security - subsidy for keeping diaries for a sampled household.

Consumption Expenditure of Urban Households refers to total expenditure of households for consumption in daily life, including expenditure on the eight categories of food; clothing; housing; household appliances and services; health care and medical services; transport and communications; recreation, education and cultural services; and miscellaneous goods and services.

Expenditure of Urban Households on Consumption of Services refers to expenditure of households on various kinds of non-commercial services provided by society.

Urban Households by Income Group All households in the sample are grouped, by per capita disposable income of the household, into groups of lowest income, low income, lower middle income, middle income, upper middle income, high income and highest income, each group consisting of 10%, 10%, 20%, 20%, 20%, 10% and 10% of all households respectively. The lowest 5% of households are also referred to as poor households.

Engel's Coefficient refers to the percentage of expenditure on food in the total consumption expenditure, using the following formula:

$$\text{Engel's Coefficient} = \frac{\text{expenditure on food}}{\text{total consumption expenditure}} \times 100\%$$

II. Rural Household

Total Income refers to the sum of income earned from various sources by the rural households and their members during the reference period, and is classified as income from wages and salaries, income from household operations, income from properties and income from transfers.

Income from Wages and Salaries refers to income from labour earned by the members of rural households employed by other units or individuals.

Income from Household Operations refers to income by the rural households as units of production and operation. Operations by rural households are classified according to their economic activities namely agriculture, forestry, animal husbandry, fishery, manufacturing, construction, transportation, post and telecommunications, wholesale, retail and catering, social service, culture, education, health, and other household operations.

Income from Properties refers to the income received as returns by owners of financial assets or tangible non-productive assets by providing capitals or tangible non-productive assets to other institutional units.

Income from Transfers refers to the receipt by rural households and their members of goods, services, capital or rights of assets without giving or repaying accordingly, excluding capital provided to them for the formation of fixed assets. In general, it refers to all income received by rural households through redistribution.

Cash Income refers to income received by rural households and their members in the form of cash during the reference period. It is classified, by source of income, into income from wages and salaries, cash income from household operations, income from properties and income from transfers.

Net Income refers to the total income of rural households from all sources minus all corresponding expenses. The formula for calculation is as follows:

Net income = total income - taxes and fees paid - household operation expenses - taxes and fees depreciation of fixed assets for production - gifts to non-rural relatives

Net income is mainly used as input for reinvestment in production and as consumption expenditure of the year, and also used for savings and non-compulsory expenses of various forms. "Per capita net income of farmers" is the level of net income averaged by population, reflecting the average income level of rural households in a given area.

Total Expenditure refers to total expenses of rural households on production, consumption and redistribution, including expenditure on household operations; purchase of productive fixed assets; depreciation of productive fixed assets; taxes and fees; expenses on household consumption; expenses on properties; and expenses on transfers.

Ⅲ.Social Insurance

Basic Pension Insurance

1. Number of staff and workers covered refer to staff and workers participating in the basic pension insurance programme according to national laws, regulations and related policies at the end of the reference period, who have already had payment records in social security management agencies, including those who have interrupt payment without terminating the insurance programme. Those who have registered in the programme but with no payment records are not included.

2. Number of retirees participating in basisc pension insurance programme refer to number retirees participating in basic pension insurance programme by the end of reference period.

3. Revenue of the basic pension insurance programme refers to payments made by employers and individuals participating in the pension insurance programme in accordance with the basis and proportion stipulated in State regulations, and income from other sources that become source of pension insurance fund, including the premium paid by employers and staff and workers, interest income, subsidies from higher level agencies, income as transfer from subordinate agencies, transferred income, government financial subsidies and other income.

4. Expenditure of basic pension insurance programme refers to payment made on pensions and funeral subsidies to those retired and resigned people covered in pension insurance programmes according to related national policies on scopeand standard of expenditure. Also included are expenditure which arises due to shift of the insurance relationship or adjustment of funds among agencies. More specifically, included are pensions for resigned people, pensions for retired people, pension for people quitting jobs, various subsidies, medical fees, funeral subsidies, compensation payments, management fees for social security agencies, expenses on subsidies to lower subordinates, expenses as transfer to agencies at higher level, transferred expenditure and other expenditures on properties; and expenses on transfers.

5. Balance of basic pension insurance programme refers to the balance of basic pension insurance funds at the end of the reference period after deducting expenses from revenue.

Basic Medical Care Insurance

1. Number of people participating in the insurance programme refers to people participating in the basic medical care insurance programme according to related regulations as at the end of reference period, including number of staff and workers and retirees participating in this insurance programme.

2. Revenue of the insurance programme refers to payments made by employers and individuals participating in the medical care insurance programme in accordance with the basis and proportion stipulated in State regulations, and income from other sources that become source of medical insurance fund, including income paid by units, individual paid income, financial assistance's income (including individual income from medicaid), financial subsidies' income, interest income and other income.

3. Expenditure of the insurance programme refers to payment made from social comprehensive funds to those retired and resigned people covered in basic medical care insurance within the scope and standards of expenditure according to related national policies, and medical care payment made from individual accounts to staff and workers and retirees, and other expenses, including medical expenses of hospital inpatients, medical expenses for outpatients and emergency patients, payment from individual accounts and other expenditure.

4. Balance of the basic medical care insurance programme refers to the balance of medical care insurance funds at the end of the reference period.

Unemployment Insurance

1. Number of people covered refers to staff and workers in urban enterprises or institutions who have participated in the unemployment insurance programme according to relevant policies and regulations, and other people who have participated according to local government regulations, as at the end of reference period.

2. Revenue of the unemployment insurance programme refers to the total unemployment insurance funds raised in the reference period, including unemployment insurance premium, interest income, financial subsidies, other income, transferred income, subsidies from higher level agencies and income as transfer from subordinate agencies .

3. Expenditure of the unemployment insurance programme refers to total expenses during the reference period to guarantee the basic livelihood of unemployed people, and to encourage their re-employment. Included are unemployment relief, medical fees, funeral subsidies, compensation payments, training expenses, management fees for unemployment insurance agencies, subsidies to lower level agencies, expenses as transfer to higher level agencies, transferred expenditure and other expenditure.

4. Balance of the unemployment insurance programme refers to the balance of revenue of the programme after deducting expenses at the end of the reference period.

Work Injury Insurance

1. Number of people covered refers to staff and workers who have participated in the work injury insurance programme and number of employees in private business according to relevant national regulations at the end of the reference period.

2. Number of beneficiaries refers to number of people benefited from work injury insurance, as a result of work injury or occupational disease. It is the sum of beneficiaries from the work injury medical treatment withut rating, disabilities and deaths at work places.

3. Revenue of the work injury insurance programme refers to payments made by employers participating in the work injury insurance programme in accordance with the basis and proportion stipulated in State regulations, and income from other sources that become source of work injury insurance fund, including income of social comprehensive funds paid by employers, government financial subsidies, interest income and other income.

4. Expenditure of the work injury insurance programme refers to payments made from work injury insurance funds to those who participated in the work injury insurance programme and their direct dependents within the scope and standards of expenditure according to related national policies, and other expenditure, including medical fees for work injury, injury and disability subsidies, death subsidies, nursing fees, funeral subsidies, injury prevention fees, occupational rehabilitation fees and other expenditure.

5. Balance of the work injury insurance programme refers to the balance of the work injury funds at the end of the reference period, including bank savings, special fiscal account, investment in bonds and others.

Maternity Insurance

1. Number of people covered refers to staff and workers who have participated in the maternity insurance programme according to relevant regulation at the end of the reporting period.

2. Revenue of maternity insurance refers to payments made by employers participating in the maternity insurance programme in accordance with the basis and proportion stipulated in State regulations, and income from other sources that become source of maternity insurance fund, including income of funds paid by employers, interest income and other income.

3. Expenditure of the maternity insurance programme refers to payments made from maternity insurance funds to staff and workers who participate in the maternity insurance programme within the scope and standards of expenditure in accordance with related national policies, expenses paid for pregnancy, child delivery or surgeries related to family planning, and other expenditure, including allowance for child bearing, medical fees and other expenditure.

4. Balance of the maternity programme refers to the balance of the maternity insurance funds at the end of reference period, including bank savings, special fiscal account, investment in funds and others.

2012

新疆统计年鉴

XINJIANG STATISTICAL YEARBOOK

第十篇
城市概况

CHAPTER 10
General Survey of Cities

简要说明
Brief Introduction

本篇资料的主要内容及来源

本篇资料反映新疆城市社会、经济发展和城市建设的基本情况。

城市概况资料主要包括城市公用事业基本情况、主要经济指标、市政设施、园林绿化、环境卫生、供水供气等。

本篇资料由新疆维吾尔自治区统计局国民经济综合统计处根据新疆维吾尔自治区建设厅和新疆维吾尔自治区统计局相关处室提供的年度数据整理。

Main Content and Source of Data

Data in this chapter show the social and economic development and the urban construction of Xinjiang.

Data on the general survey cities include the basic condition of urban public facilities, main economic indicators, civil facilities, urban greenery, environment and sanitation, supply of gas and heating, public transportation, etc.

Data on this chapter are compiled by the Department of National Accounts of the Xinjiang Bureau of Statistics according to the data of yearly statistics, which are provided by the Construction Bureau of Xinjiang Uygur Autonomous Region and related departments of Statistics Bureau of Xinjiang Uygur Autonomous Region.

10-1 城市公用事业基本情况
Basic Statistics on City Public Utilities

项　　目	Item	2010	2011
城市及建筑物面积	**City Areas and Floor Space of Buildings**		
建成区面积(平方公里)	Area of Built Districts(sq.km)	838	922
征用土地面积(平方公里)	Land Put in Requisition for State Construction Projects (sq. km)	17.7	15.7
城市人口密度(人/平方公里)	Population Density of City Districts(persons/sq.km)	4977	4563
供水、供气及供热	**Water Supply, Gas Supply and Heating**		
自来水年供水量(万立方米)	Annual Volume of Tap Water Supply (10 000 cu.m)	77263	80894
#生活用水量	Water Consumption for Residential use	26078	28091
平均每人日生活用水量(升)	Per -Capita Water Consumption for Residential Use (litre)	150.8	160.0
用水普及率(%)	Coverage Rate of Population with Access to Tap Water (%)	99.2	99.2
人工煤气供气量(万立方米)	Gaswork Gas Supply (10 000 cu.m)	1752	1999
#家庭用量	Consumption of Gaswork Gas for Residential Use	1752	1999
天然气供气量(万立方米)	Natural Gas Supply (10 000 cu.m)	134711	184413
#家庭用量	Consumption of Coal Gas for Residential Use	40067	45859
液化石油气供气量(吨)	Liquefied Petroleum Gas (ton)	79617	82993
#家庭用量	Consumption of Liquefied Gas for Residential Use	61050	67827
天然气、煤气管道长度(公里)	Length of Gas Pipelines (km)	7298	8765
燃气普及率(%)	Goverage Rate of Urban Population with Access to Gas (%)	95.8	96.2
集中供热面积(万平方米)	Area of Centralized Heating (10 000 sq.m)	19162	21064
#住 宅	Residential Buildings	13298	14716
市政工程	**Municipal Engineering**		
铺装道路长度(公里)	Length of Paved Roads (km)	5178	5476
平均每万人拥有 (公里)	Length of Paved Roads per 10 000 Population (km)	6.1	6.2
铺装道路面积(万平方米)	Area of Paved Roads (10 000 sq.m)	8323	8964
平均每人拥有(平方米)	Area of Paved Roads per Population (sq.m)	9.7	10.1
下水道长度(公里)	Length of Sewer Pipelines (km)	4372	4592
平均每万人拥有 (公里)	Length of Sewer Pipelines per 10 000 Population (km)	5.1	5.2
城市绿化	**City Greening**		
建成区绿化覆盖面积(公顷)	Green Areas of Completed Area (hectare)	30530	33772
每万人建成区绿地面积(公顷)	Green Areas of Completed Area per 10 000 Population (hectare)	35.7	38.1
公园数(个)	Number of Parks and Zoos(unit)	131	137
公园面积(公顷)	Area of Parks (hectare)	3156	3274
环境卫生	**Environmental Sanitation**		
清运生活垃圾(万吨)	Volume of Garbage Disposal (10 000 tons)	317	344
清运粪便(万吨)	Volume of Disposal of Excrement and Urine (10 000 tons)	4.1	3.4
每万人拥有公共厕所(座)	Number of Public Lavatories per 10 000 Population (unit)	2.5	2.4

10-2 各城市主要经济指标

Major Economic Indicators by Cities

单位：万元 (2011 年) (10 000 yuan)

城市名称	City	地区生产总值（当年价格） Gross Region Production (current-year price)	第一产业 Primary Industry	第二产业 Secondary Industry	#工业 Industry
乌鲁木齐市	Urumqi City	16900347	220550	7590607	6590607
克拉玛依市	Karamay City	8016856	41509	7162011	6988211
吐鲁番市	Turpan City	586534	104968	229202	190803
哈 密 市	Hami [Kumul] City	1766951	180746	873590	592020
昌 吉 市	Changji City	2213651	297309	1036261	861414
阜 康 市	Fukang City	1031019	180386	650619	585724
伊 宁 市	Yining [Gulja] City	1139000	56838	316484	177047
奎 屯 市	Kuytun City	900159	47806	494798	409330
塔 城 市	Tacheng [Qoqek] City	501824	119919	135273	78518
乌 苏 市	Usu City	1207499	395426	582910	449050
阿勒泰市	Altay City	403595	65967	84311	51611
博 乐 市	Bole [Bortala] City	999142	264366	232897	162105
库尔勒市	Korla City	5582944	318190	4497423	4021762
阿克苏市	Aksu City	1429142	263367	485573	372478
阿图什市	Artux City	232925	39711	52396	33940
喀 什 市	Kashgar [Kaxgar] City	1075965	46000	369500	264500
和 田 市	Hotan City	351173	33574	122552	45688
石河子市	Shi Hezi City	1705948	110015	943672	772178
阿拉尔市	Aral City				
图木舒克市	Tumxuk City				
五家渠市	Wujiaqu City				

城市名称	City	第三产业 Tertiary Industry	#交通运输、仓储和邮政业 Transport, Storage and Post	人均地区生产总值（元） Per Capita GDP (yuan)
乌鲁木齐市	Urumqi City	9089190	1759876	52649
克拉玛依市	Karamay City	813336	130882	129105
吐鲁番市	Turpan City	252364	72200	21267
哈 密 市	Hami [Kumul] City	712615	197229	39060
昌 吉 市	Changji City	880081	158608	46118
阜 康 市	Fukang City	200014	27874	62373
伊 宁 市	Yining [Gulja] City	765678	62888	23615
奎 屯 市	Kuytun City	357555	59114	59066
塔 城 市	Tacheng [Qoqek] City	246632	31946	29442
乌 苏 市	Usu City	229163	28780	35778
阿勒泰市	Altay City	253317	24841	21456
博 乐 市	Bole [Bortala] City	501879	88473	37661
库尔勒市	Korla City	767332	94816	99094
阿克苏市	Aksu City	680201	79685	29714
阿图什市	Artux City	140818	16255	9284
喀 什 市	Kashgar [Kaxgar] City	660465	73054	19962
和 田 市	Hotan City	195047	14109	5954
石河子市	Shi Hezi City	652261	61303	54037
阿拉尔市	Aral City			
图木舒克市	Tumxuk City			
五家渠市	Wujiaqu City			

10-2 续表 Continued

单位: 万元 (10 000 yuan)

城市名称	City	城镇固定资产投资总额 Investment in Fixed Assets in Urban Area	规模以上工业总产值（当年价格） Gross Industrial Output Value above Designated Size (At Current Prices)	地方财政一般预算收入 General Budgetary Revenue in Local Finance	地方财政一般预算支出 General Budgetary Expenditure in Local Finance
乌鲁木齐市	Urumqi City	4343646	19925799	2062035	2384851
克拉玛依市	Karamay City	1993665	16390366	509650	633033
吐鲁番市	Turpan City	242461	438564	48796	136192
哈 密 市	Hami [Kumul] City	1165188	1146666	187218	260267
昌 吉 市	Changji City	714113	1941621	161803	247955
阜 康 市	Fukang City	776458	977402	85967	158386
伊 宁 市	Yining [Gulja] City	764991	356020	140904	281702
奎 屯 市	Kuytun City	582150	927688	109119	156992
塔 城 市	Tacheng [Qoqek] City	177342	97806	27186	116460
乌 苏 市	Usu City	351416	625339	63387	178351
阿勒泰市	Altay City	255755	122340	24027	151201
博 乐 市	Bole [Bortala] City	428995	298875	40080	119795
库尔勒市	Korla City	1982258	5773626	210035	325879
阿克苏市	Aksu City	500163	821826	109909	213794
阿图什市	Artux City	108698	100750	14789	136088
喀 什 市	Kashgar [Kaxgar] City	516141	403555	104278	416923
和 田 市	Hotan City	307160	81209	32272	176836
石河子市	Shi Hezi City	1507501	2893433	192822	252565
阿拉尔市	Aral City	443750	278036	26682	34539
图木舒克市	Tumxuk City	172841	79822	10670	21356
五家渠市	Wujiaqu City	875042	904473	37663	49656

城市名称	City	居民消费价格指数(上年=100) Consumer Price Index (preceding year=100)	社会消费品零售总额 Total Retail Sales of Consumer Goods	在岗职工人数(万人) Number of Fully-employed Staff and Workers (10 000 persons)	在岗职工平均货币工资(元) Average Money Wage of Staff and Workers (yuan)
乌鲁木齐市	Urumqi City	104.5	6497286	61.27	47747
克拉玛依市	Karamay City	105.8	435790	16.73	58657
吐鲁番市	Turpan City	105.7	133093	2.93	36909
哈 密 市	Hami [Kumul] City	105.3	415857	6.90	39873
昌 吉 市	Changji City	105.3	552568	6.57	38685
阜 康 市	Fukang City		183647	2.73	36767
伊 宁 市	Yining [Gulja] City	106.7	430038	7.21	33525
奎 屯 市	Kuytun City	105.2	156436	3.01	34397
塔 城 市	Tacheng [Qoqek] City	105.7	105081	2.89	33388
乌 苏 市	Usu City	105.3	99297	5.50	23119
阿勒泰市	Altay City	105.5	156414	4.03	28425
博 乐 市	Bole [Bortala] City	106.0	156741	5.61	31050
库尔勒市	Korla City	105.6	517285	9.77	40982
阿克苏市	Aksu City	106.8	405197	6.72	37593
阿图什市	Artux City	105.9	65343	1.93	32046
喀 什 市	Kashgar [Kaxgar] City	106.0	420174	5.54	39261
和 田 市	Hotan City	106.9	111711	2.85	40201
石河子市	Shi Hezi City	105.4	523755	10.01	38909
阿拉尔市	Aral City			4.20	35193
图木舒克市	Tumxuk City			1.62	30684
五家渠市	Wujiaqu City			2.39	33570

10-3 各城市市区设施水平

Level of Urban Public Facilities in Cities

(2011 年)

城市名称	City	城市用水普及率(%) Coverage Rate of Urban Population with Access to Tap Water (%)	城市燃气普及率(%) Coverage Rate of Population with Access to Gas (%)	人均铺装道路面积(平方米) Per Capital Area of Paved Roads (sq.m)	人均公园绿地面积(平方米) Per Capital Area of Parks and Green Land (sq.m)	排水管道密度(公里/平方公里) Density of Sewage Pipelines (km/sq.km)
总　计	**Total**	99.17	96.19	13.74	9.48	4.98
乌鲁木齐市	Urumqi City	99.94	99.51	7.42	9.07	3.18
克拉玛依市	Karamay City	100.00	100.00	24.31	9.22	6.86
吐鲁番市	Turpan City	100.00	92.59	16.85	11.11	3.97
哈 密 市	Hami [Kumul] City	100.00	99.91	17.40	9.61	10.28
昌 吉 市	Changji City	100.00	100.00	9.68	8.72	3.22
阜 康 市	Fukang City	90.04	83.93	15.12	6.26	8.22
伊 宁 市	Yining [Gulja] City	99.97	92.32	17.80	9.01	11.86
奎 屯 市	Kuytun City	100.00	90.91	13.74	8.64	8.99
塔 城 市	Tacheng [Qoqek] City	93.25	79.38	15.71	12.63	7.97
乌 苏 市	Usu City	89.44	70.00	17.65	6.89	7.24
阿勒泰市	Altay City	95.01	79.06	9.15	31.07	7.34
博 乐 市	Bole [Bortala] City	99.21	56.20	9.69	10.99	3.76
库尔勒市	Korla City	100.00	100.00	27.54	10.75	4.74
阿克苏市	Aksu City	100.00	99.81	12.97	6.99	6.76
阿图什市	Artux City	99.43	95.17	15.97	1.85	3.54
喀 什 市	Kashgar [Kaxgar] City	100.00	95.83	17.53	10.69	3.15
和 田 市	Hotan City	96.97	97.71	16.75	8.88	4.09
石河子市	Shihezi City	100.00	98.98	24.62	10.12	10.62
阿拉尔市	Aral City	95.45	90.91	24.51	11.52	3.44
图木舒克市	Tumxuk City	64.84	64.52	46.82	26.13	6.93
五家渠市	Wujiaqu City	93.31	98.76	55.74	8.86	6.60
北 屯 市	Beitun City	93.33	93.33	25.34	10.13	2.54

10-4 主要年份城市自来水情况

Basic Statistics on Tap Water Supply in Cities in Main Years

指　标	Item	2000	2010	2011
年末水厂生产能力(万吨/日)	Production Capacity of TapWater Supply (10 000 tons/day)	292	373	385
年末供水管道总长度(公里)	Length of Water Supply Piplines (km)	4448	6507	6888
全年供水总量(亿立方米)	Total Annual Volume of Water supply (100 millon cu.m)	5.0	7.7	8.1
#生活用水	For Residential Use	2.5	2.6	2.8
生产用水	For Productive Use	2.0	2.1	2.3
平均每人日生活用水量(升)	Per-Capitall Daily Consumption of Tap Water for Residential Use (litre)	165.1	150.8	160.0
用水人口(万人)	Number of Residents with Access to Tap Water (10 000 persons)	418	626	647

10-5 主要年份城市市政建设情况

Statistics on City Construction in Cities in Main Years

指　　标	Item	2000	2010	2011
实有道路长度(公里)	Length of Paved Roads (km)	2809	5178	5476
实有道路面积(万平方米)	Area of Paved Roads (10 000 sq.m)	3654	8323	8964
城市桥梁(座)	Number of City Bridges (unit)	253	384	409
防洪堤长度(公里)	Length of Dyke for Control of Flood (km)	130	262	255
城市下水道总长度(公里)	Length of Sewer Pipelines (km)	2008	4372	4592
城市污水日处理能力(万立方米)	Daily Disposal Capacity of Sewage (10 000 cu.m)	46	157	191
城市路灯盏数(千盏)	Number of Street Light (1 000 units)	72.9	400.1	423.6

注：城市污水日处理能力指污水处理厂处理能力，不包括其他污水处理设施处理量。
Note: The daily treatment capacity in urban area refers to the treatment capacity of a waste- water treatment plant, excluding the volume handled by other polluted-water treatment facility.

10-6 主要年份城市园林绿化情况

Basic Statistics on Parks and Green Areas in Cities in Main Years

指　　标	Item	2000	2010	2011
城市园林绿地面积(公顷)	Area of Park and Green Land (hectare)	19124	37686	44097
#建成区绿地面积	Green Land of Completed Area		27773	30672
每万人建成区绿地面积(公顷)	Green Areas of Completed Area Per 10 000 Population (hectare)	53.4	35.7	38.1
建成区绿化覆盖率(%)	Green Covrage Rate of Completed Area (%)	29.1	36.4	36.6
平均每人公园绿地面积(平方米)	Per Capita Parks Green Areas (sq.m)	6.4	8.6	9.5
公园数(个)	Number of Parks and Zoos (unit)	84	131	137
公园面积(公顷)	Area of Parks (hectare)	1568	3156	3274

10-7 主要年份城市环境卫生情况

Basic Statistics on Urban Environment in Cities in Main Years

指　　标	Item	2000	2010	2011
环卫专用车辆设备数量(辆)	Number of Special Vehicles for Environmental Sanitation (unit)	767	1690	2335
公共厕所(座)	Number of Public Lavatories (unit)	1684	2119	2128
每万人拥有公共厕所(座)	Number of Public Lavatories Per 10 000 Population (unit)	4.7	2.5	2.4
道路清扫面积(万平方米)	Area under Cleaning Program (10 000 sq.m)	3224	8080	9951
#机械化	Mechanization		3163	4041
清运生活垃圾(万吨)	Volum of Garbage Disposal (10 000 tons)	259	317	344
清运粪便 (万吨)	Volum of Excrement and Urine Disposal (10 000 tons)	16	4	3

10-8 主要年份城市煤气、液化石油气、天然气情况
Basic Statistics on Supply of Gas, Liquefied Petroleum Gas and Natural Gas in Cities in Main Years

指　　标	Item	2000	2010	2011
人工煤气生产能力(万立方米/日)	Production Capacity of Gaswork Gas (10 000 cu.m/day)		49	46
管道长度(公里)	Length of Gas Pipelines (km)	385	7298	8765
人工煤气	Coal Gas		71	71
液化石油气	Liquefied Petroleum Gas		82	81
天然气	Natural Gas	385	7145	8613
全年供气总量(万立方米)	Volume of Gas Supply (10 000 cu.m)			
人工煤气	Coal Gas		1752	1999
液化石油气(吨)	Liquefied Petroleum Gas (ton)	244018	79617	82993
天然气	Natural Gas	5385	134711	184413
用气人口(万人)	Population with Access to Gas (10 000 persons)		604.37	627.50
人工煤气	Coal Gas		8.75	6.20
液化石油气	Liquefied Petroleum Gas	305.70	150.64	130.96
天然气	Natural Gas	27.00	444.98	490.34

10-9 主要年份城市集中供热情况
Basic Statistics on Heating in Cities in Main Years

指　　标	Item	2000	2010	2011
供应能力	**Heating Capacity**			
蒸汽(吨/小时)	Steam (ton/hour)	1638	1376	1460
热水(兆瓦)	Hot Water (1 billion kw)	6145	18897	20465
供热总量(万吉焦)	**Quantity of Heating Supplied (10 000 gigajoules)**			
蒸 汽	Steam		1242	974
热 水	Hot Water		16866	15524
管道长度(公里)	**Length of Heating Pipelines (km)**			
蒸 汽	Steam	250	207	340
热 水	Hot Water	2064	5912	6434
供热面积(万平方米)	**Area of Centralized Heating (10 000 sq.m)**	**5170**	**19162**	**21064**
#住 宅	Residential Buildings		13298	14716

主要统计指标解释

供水综合生产能力　指按供水设施取水、净化、送水、出厂输水干管等环节设计能力计算的综合生产能力。包括在原设计能力的基础上，经挖、革、改增加的生产能力。计算时，以四个环节中最薄弱的环节为主确定能力。

年末供水管道长度　指从送水泵到用户水表之间所有管道的长度。不包括新安装尚未使用、水厂内以及用户建筑物内的管道。

全年供水总量　指报告期供水企业(单位)供出的全部水量。包括有效供水量和漏损水量。

生活用水量　包括公共服务用水和居民家庭用水。公共服务用水指为城市社会公共生活服务的用水。包括行政事业单位、部队营区和公共设施服务、社会服务业、批发零售业、住宿餐饮业以及其他公共服务业等单位的用水。居民家庭用水指城市范围内所有居民家庭的日常生活用水。包括城市居民、农民家庭、公共供水站用水。

用水普及率　指城市用水人口数与城市人口总数的比率。计算公式为：

用水普及率＝城市用水人口数／城市人口总数×100%

人工煤气生产能力　指报告期末人工煤气生产厂制气、净化、输送等环节的综合生产能力，不包括备用设备能力。一般按设计能力计算，如果实际生产能力大于设计能力时，应按实际测定的生产能力计算。测定时应以制气、净化、输送三个环节中最薄弱的环节为主。

供气管道长度　指报告期末从气源厂压缩机的出口或门站出口至各类用户引入管之间的全部已经通气投入使用的管道长度。不包括煤气生产厂、输配站、液化气储存站、灌瓶站、储配站、气化站、混气站、供应站等厂(站)内的管道。

全年供气总量　指全年燃气企业(单位)向用户供应的燃气数量。包括销售量和损失量。

燃气普及率　指报告期末使用煤气的城市人口数)与城市人口总数的比率。计算公式为：

燃气普及率＝城市用气人口数／城市人口总数×100%

城市供热能力　指供热企业（单位）向城市热用户输送热源的设计能力。

城市供热总量　指在报告期供热企业（单位）向城市热用户输送全部蒸汽和热水的总热量。

城市供热管道长度　指从各种热源到热用户建筑物接入口之间的全部蒸汽和热水的管道长度。不包括各类热源厂内部的管道长度。

年末道路长度　指年末道路长度和与道路相通的桥梁、隧道的长度，按车行道中心线计算。在统计时只统计路面宽度在3.5米（含3.5米）以上的各种铺装道路，包括开放型工业区和住宅区道路在内。

城市桥梁　指为跨越天然或人工障碍物而修建的构筑物。包括跨河桥、立交桥、人行天桥以及人行地下通道等。按使用年限分为永久性桥和半永久性桥。

城市排水道总长度　指所有排水总管、干管、支管、检查井及连接井进出口等长度之和。

城市污水日处理能力　指污水处理厂（污水处理处理装置）每昼夜处理污水量的设计能力。

城市绿地面积　指报告期末用作园林和绿化的各种绿地面积。包括园林绿地、公共绿地、防护绿地、附属绿地和其他绿地面积。

公园绿地　城市中向公众开放的以游憩为主要功能，有一定的游憩设施和服务设施，同时兼有健全生态、美化景观，防灾减灾等综合作用的绿化用地。包括综合公园、社区公园、专类公园、带状公园和街旁绿地。其中综合公园、专类公园和带状公园面积之和为公园面积。

清扫保洁面积　指报告期末对城市道路和公共场所（主要包括城市行车道、人行道、车行隧道、人行过街地下通道、道路附属绿地、地铁站、高架路、人行过街天桥、立交桥、广场、停车场及其他设施等）进行清扫保洁的面积。一天清扫多次的，按清扫保洁面积最大的一次计算。

市容环卫专用车辆　指用于环境卫生作业、监察的专用车辆和设备，包括用于道路清扫、冲洗、洒水、除雪、垃圾粪便清运、市容监察以及与其配套使用的车辆和设备。

Explanatory Notes on Main Statistical Indicators

Production Capacity of Water Supply refers to the designed overall production capacity of water facilities, covering the four segments of water collection, purification, conveyance, and outflow through trunk pipelines. Increased capacity through transformation and innovation projects is included as well. The capacity is determined mainly on the weakest of the above-mentioned four segments.

Length of Water Supply Pipelines at Year-end refers to the total length of all the pipelines between the water pumps and the user water meters, excluding pipelines newly installed but not used yet, pipeline in the water factory,and pipeline in the user's buildings.

Annual Volume of Water Supply refers to the total volume of water supplied by water-works (units) during the reference period, including both the effective water supply and loss during the water supply.

Consumption of Water for Residential Use refers to water consumption of households for daily life and water consumption of public service facilities. The latter refers to water consumption for urban public services, including the consumption of government agencies and public institutions, military barracks, public facilities, wholesale and retail outlets, restaurants, hotels, and other units providing public services. Household water consumption refers to consumption of water for daily life of all households within the boundary of cities, including households of urban residents and farmers, and public water supply stations.

Coverage Rate of Urban Population with Access to Tap Water refers to the ratio of the urban population with access to tap water to the total urban population. The formula is:

$$\text{Coverage of urban population with access to tap water} = \frac{\text{Urban population with access to tap water}}{\text{Urban population}} \times 100\%$$

Production Capacity of Gaswork Gas refers to the overall production capacity of the urban gasworks in gas generation, purification and delivery at the end of the reference period, excluding capacity of the reserved facilities. In general, it is determined by the designed capacity, and when actual production capacity is larger than the designed capacity, the capacity is determined by the actual measurement on the weakest segment in the production, purification and delivery.

Length of Gas Pipelines refers to the total length of pipelines in use between the outlet of the compressor of gas-work or outlet of gas stations and the leading pipe of users, excluding pipelines within gasworks, delivery stations, LPG storage stations, refilling stations, gas-mixing stations and supply stations.

Volume of Gas Supply refers to the total volume of gas provided to users by gas-producing enterprises (units) in a year, including the volume sold and the volume lost.

Coverage Rate of Urban Population with Access to Gas refers to the ratio of the urban population with access to gas to the total urban population at the end of the reference period. The formula is:

$$\text{Coverage rate of urban population with access to gas} = \frac{\text{Urban population with access to gas}}{\text{Urban population}} \times 100\%$$

Heating Capacity in Urban Areas refers to the designed capacity of heating enterprises (units) in supplying heating energy to urban users during the reference period.

Quantity of Heat Supplied in Urban Areas refers to the total quantity of heat from steam and hot water supplied to urban users by heating enterprises (units) during the reference period.

Length of Urban Heating Pipelines refers to the total length of steam or hot water pipelines for sources of heat to the leading pipelines of the buildings of the users, excluding internal pipelines in heat generating enterprises.

Length of Paved Roads at Year-end refers to the length of roads with paved surface including bridges and tunnels connected with roads by the end of the year. Length of the roads is measured by the central lines for vehicles for paved roads with a width of 3.5 meters and over, including roads in open-ended factory compounds and residential quarters.

Urban Bridges refer to bridges built to cross over natural or man-made barriers, including bridges over rivers, overpasses for traffic and for pedestrians, underpasses for pedestrians, etc. Both permanent and semi-permanent bridges are included.

Length of Urban Sewage Pipes refers to the total length of general drainage, trunks, branch and inspection wells, connection wells, inlets and outlets, etc.

Daily Disposal Capacity of Urban Sewage refers to the designed 24-hour capacity of sewage disposal by the sewage treatment works or facilities.

Area of Urban Green Areas refers to the total area occupied for green projects at the end of the reference period, including park green land, production green land, protection green land, green land attached to institutions, and other green areas.

Park Green Area refers to green areas open to the public for amusement and rest with the facilities of amusement, rest and services. Its function includes perfecting ecology, beautifying landscape, and preventing and reducing disaster. Park green areas include comprehensive park, community park, topic park, belt-shaped park and green area nearby street. Total areas of comprehensive park, topic park and belt-shaped is the area of park.

Area Cleaned refers to the area which are regularly cleaned, as at the end of the reference period, at urban roads and public places (mainly including urban roadways, pedestrian walkways, vehicular tunnels, pedestrian underpasses, underground railway stations, lifted roads, pedestrians walk bridges, overpasses, plazas, carparks and other facilities). If there are several times of cleaning in a day at a location, the area of that time of cleaning with the largest area cleaned will be taken.

Vehicles Dedicated to Urban Cleanliness and Environmental Sanitation refer to vehicles and facilities dedicated for use in the operation, management and monitoring of environmental hygiene work. They include vehicles for road cleaning, washing, showering, ice removal, disposal of garbage and human wastes, cleanliness monitoring and related activities.

第十一篇 自然资源与环境保护

CHAPTER 11 Natural Resources and Environment Protection

简要说明
Brief Introduction

本篇资料的主要内容及来源

本篇主要反映新疆维吾尔自治区自然资源、自然状况及环境保护事业发展情况等资料。主要内容包括自然资源储量和自然状况及水环境、大气环境、固体废物、声环境、生态环境、环境污染治理投资等内容。

水资源、城市生活垃圾清运及处理、地质灾害与防治、矿产资源资料、土地资源和土地利用情况、林木资源等资料分别由新疆维吾尔自治区水利厅、建设厅、地震局、国土资源厅、林业厅提供；气象资料由新疆维吾尔自治区气象局提供。环境污染与治理、声环境、工业污染治理投资等情况由新疆维吾尔自治区环境保护厅依据年报资料整理提供。

2009年国家进行了第二次全国土地调查，我区调查数据目前国土资源部尚未反馈，为此，2011年年鉴中涉及土地资源、矿产资源及相关内容表式仍然沿用2008年度数据。

Main Content and Source of Data

This chapter contain information that reflect the natural conditions and natural resources and data on development of environment protection in Xinjiang Uygur Autonomous Region, including natural resources and natural condition, total water resources, atmosphere environment, solid wastes, environmental noise, eco-environment protection and investments in the treatment of environmental pollution etc.

Data on water resource, collection and disposal of urban consumption wastes, geological disasters, land use, forest resource, etc. are provided respectively by Bureau of Water Conservancy, Bureau of Construction, Seismological Bureau, Bureau of Land and Resources, Forestry Bureau in Xinjiang Uygur Autonomous Region; Meteorological data are provided by the Xinjiang Uygur Autonomous Region Meteorological Bureau. Data on environment pollution and treatment, noise monitoring and on investment in the treatment of industrial pollution are provided by the Xinjiang Environmental Protection Bureau.

Data of the Second National Land Survey did not feedback.So data in 2012 Statistical Yearbook of land and mineral resource followed data in 2008.

11-1 自 然 资 源
Natural Resources

指　标	Item	2011
自然状况	**State of the Nature**	
经纬度	Longitude and Latitude	
东　经	East Longitude	73°40′～96°23′
北　纬	North Latitude	34°25′～49°10′
气　候	Climate	
年平均气温(摄氏度)	Annual Average Temperature (℃)	10.0
北　疆	North Xinjiang	7.6
南　疆	South Xinjiang	12.9
东　疆	East Xinjiang	13.2
年平均降水量(毫米)	Annual Average Precipitation (mm)	167.1
北　疆	North Xinjiang	256.6
南　疆	South Xinjiang	66.4
东　疆	East Xinjiang	16.1
平均日照时数(小时)	Average Sunny Hours (hour)	2797.0
北　疆	North Xinjiang	2759.5
南　疆	South Xinjiang	2859.8
东　疆	East Xinjiang	3137.4
自然资源	**Natural Resources**	
土地资源(万公顷)	Land Resources (10 000 hectares)	
土地总面积	Total Land Area	16648.97
农用地	Land for farm use	6308.48
耕地面积	Area of Cultivated Land	412.46
园地面积	Garden Area	36.42
林地面积	Woodland Area	676.48
牧草地面积	Pastureland Area	5111.38
其他农用地	Other Land for Agriculture	71.75
建设用地	Land for Construction	123.98
未利用地	Land yet to be Used	10216.51
土地利用率(%)	Land utilization rate (%)	38.64
林木资源	Forest resources	
活立木总蓄积量(万立方米)	Total Standing Stock Volume (10 000 cu.m)	33914.50
林地蓄积量(万立方米)	Woodland Stock Volume (10 000 cu.m)	30100.54

11-1 续表 Continued

指　　标	Item	2011
有林地面积(万公顷)	Woodland Area (10 000 hectares)	201.62
灌木林地面积(万公顷)	Bush Woodland Area (10 000 hectares)	462.78
四旁树(万株)	Surrounding Woods (10 000 trees)	23696.00
森林覆盖率(%)	Forest coverage Rate (%)	4.02
水资源(亿立方米)	Water Resources (100 million cu.m)	
水资源总量	Total Water Resources Volume	1124.00
地表水水资源量	Surface Water Volume	1063.00
地下水水资源量	Underground Water Volume	624.30
重复计算量	Volume of Repeated Computation	563.20
主要矿产资源保有储量	**Reserve of Main Mineral Resources**	
铁矿(万吨)	Iron Ore (10 000 tons)	101875.89
铬矿(万吨)	Chromium Ore (10 000 tons)	170.88
铜矿(金属)(万吨)	Copper Ore (10 000 tons)	246.99
铅矿(金属)(万吨)	Lead Ore (10 000 tons)	98.91
锌矿(金属)(万吨)	Zinc Ore (10 000 tons)	205.69
铝土矿(万吨)	Bauxite(10 000 tons)	55.32
镍矿(金属)(万吨)	Nickel Ore (10 000 tons)	96.59
煤(亿吨)	Coal (100 million tons)	1977.25
耐火粘土(万吨)	Fire-proof Clay (10 000 tons)	709.50
钠硝石(万吨)	Nitratite (10 000 tons)	6164.70
芒硝(Na_2SO_4) (万吨)	Mirabilite(Na_2SO_4) (10 000 tons)	3777799.50
盐矿(NaCl) (万吨)	Solidum Salt(NaCI) (10 000 tons)	743420.20
钾盐(KCl) (万吨)	Potassium(KCI) (10 000 tons)	9186.90
石棉(万吨)	Asbest (10 000 tons)	830.60
云母(吨)	Mica (ton)	54416.87
蛭石(万吨)	Roseite (10 000 tons)	1335.60
水泥用灰岩(万吨)	Limestone Used for Cement (10 000 tons)	157905.48
膨润土(万吨)	Bentonite (10 000 tons)	36049.40
饰面用花岗岩(万立方米)	Granite as Veneer (10 000 cu.m)	12268.40

注：1.水资源为 2010 年数据。2.林木资源为 2006 年自治区森林资源第五次复查数据（2009 年公布）。3.因 2009 年第二次全国土地调查数据国家尚未反馈，土地资源及主要矿产资源保有储量仍沿用 2008 年度数据。

Note: a) Water-resources is based on the data in 2010.b) Figures of 2006 forest resources were form the fifth Autonomous Region Forest Survey(2009 announced).c) Because data of the Second National Land Survey in 2009 don't feedback, so data of land resources and ensured reserves of major mineral followed in 2008.

11-2 主要城市平均气温
Monthly Average Temperature of Major Cities

单位：摄氏度 (2011 年) (℃)

城 市	City	一月 Jan.	二月 Feb.	三月 Mar.	四月 Apr.	五月 May	六月 June	七月 July
乌鲁木齐市	Urumqi City	-18.8	-8.7	-5.2	13.2	17.1	23.1	24.6
克拉玛依市	Karamay City	-23.1	-9.4	-4.5	15.9	19.4	26.0	27.9
石河子市	Shihezi City	-22.8	-8.6	-4.4	15.4	19.6	25.7	25.7
阜康市	Fukang City	-23.0	-10.0	-6.3	14.6	18.8	25.3	25.8
米泉市	Miquan City	-19.9	-8.0	-4.1	15.3	19.4	25.7	26.8
伊宁市	Yining [Gulja] City	-12.6	-2.7	2.7	15.4	18.4	22.5	23.8
塔城市	Tacheng [Qoqek] City	-15.6	-6.1	-2.8	13.3	16.3	22.7	24.3
阿勒泰市	Altay City	-23.2	-11.8	-8.3	11.0	15.1	21.4	21.6
博乐市	Bole [Bor tala] City	-21.9	-8.9	-3.9	14.0	17.9	23.9	24.3
库尔勒市	Korla City	-10.7	1.5	4.8	18.6	21.4	26.3	28.3
阿克苏市	Aksu City	-10.9	0.9	4.8	17.3	20.8	24.2	25.2
阿图什市	Artux City	-8.5	1.5	5.3	18.1	22.6	26.8	27.3
喀什市	Kashgar [Kaxgar] City	-7.5	1.5	5.8	17.6	21.9	26.2	26.3
和田市	Hotan City	-6.8	2.6	7.1	18.6	23.3	26.3	27.1
吐鲁番市	Turpan City	-11.2	2.9	8.2	22.8	26.9	32.2	34.2
哈密市	Hami [Kumul] City	-16.4	-2.1	2.6	17.2	20.7	26.5	28.1

城 市	City	八月 Aug.	九月 Sept.	十月 Oct.	十一月 Nov.	十二月 Dec.	全年平均 Annual Average
乌鲁木齐市	Urumqi City	23.2	18.0	9.9	0.2	-9.1	7.3
克拉玛依市	Karamay City	25.7	20.4	11.3	2.1	-11.6	8.3
石河子市	Shi Hezi City	24.1	18.1	10.4	1.6	-9.9	7.9
阜康市	Fukang City	24.0	17.7	9.8	0.3	-10.8	7.2
米泉市	Miquan City	25.2	19.5	11.1	0.8	-9.1	8.6
伊宁市	Yining [Gulja] City	22.5	17.6	10.5	2.3	-6.5	9.5
塔城市	Tacheng [Qoqek] City	23.1	17.7	9.9	0.6	-7.5	8.0
阿勒泰市	Altay City	20.8	15.1	8.0	-1.6	-13.5	4.6
博乐市	Bole [Bor tala] City	23.3	17.5	9.5	1.0	-9.7	7.3
库尔勒市	Korla City	27.1	21.6	13.0	4.7	-4.5	12.7
阿克苏市	Aksu City	24.4	20.3	13.0	4.3	-4.8	11.6
阿图什市	Artux City	26.8	21.6	15.2	6.1	-4.7	13.2
喀什市	Kashgar [Kaxgar] City	25.9	21.0	14.6	6.2	-4.7	12.9
和田市	Hotan City	27.1	22.1	15.6	6.7	-3.3	13.9
吐鲁番市	Turpan City	32.0	25.1	15.0	6.1	-4.2	15.8
哈密市	Hami [Kumul] City	26.3	18.3	10.0	2.4	-7.7	10.5

11-3 主要城市降水量
Monthly Precipitation of Major Cities

单位：毫米　　　　(2011 年)　　　　(millimeter)

城　市	City	一月 Jan.	二月 Feb.	三月 Mar.	四月 Apr.	五月 May	六月 June	七月 July
乌鲁木齐市	Urumqi City	11.0	17.2	20.1	46.6	43.5	22.4	64.9
克拉玛依市	Karamay City	4.4	3.7	2.8	7.6	34.8	37.8	8.4
石河子市	Shi Hezi City	6.3	14.9	12.0	47.8	46.8	11.7	23.5
阜康市	Fukang City	7.0	9.9	11.5	25.3	32.0	18.6	69.0
米泉市	Miquan City	10.0	17.9	14.7	29.6	39.4	13.6	55.5
伊宁市	Yining [Gulja] City	2.4	19.4	24.2	3.4	55.5	20.3	42.1
塔城市	Tacheng [Qoqek] City	3.6	14.0	15.1	4.4	39.3	17.8	10.0
阿勒泰市	Altay City	31.9	17.4	3.7	11.5	44.1	15.3	3.6
博乐市	Bole [Bortala] City	5.9	8.9	16.5	13.2	26.7	15.5	43.2
库尔勒市	Korla City	0.1		0.9	1.1	1.1	2.7	2.1
阿克苏市	Aksu City		3.1	1.4	0.3	8.9	9.4	7.2
阿图什市	Artux City		42.6	5.4	0.1	19.1	2.7	6.4
喀什市	Kashgar [Kaxgar] City		20.9	6.7	0.4	7.9	2.4	13.1
和田市	Hotan City		0.6			4.4	0.3	0.2
吐鲁番市	Turpan City		0.4				2.0	0.3
哈密市	Hami [Kumul] City	1.3	0.2	4.9		1.0	4.3	2.4

城　市	City	八月 Aug.	九月 Sept.	十月 Oct.	十一月 Nov.	十二月 Dec.	全年合计 Annual Total
乌鲁木齐市	Urumqi City	55.4	1.7	36.9	12.7	12.1	344.5
克拉玛依市	Karamay City	45.5	0.8	17.5	8.0	7.1	178.4
石河子市	Shihezi City	39.2		32.9	10.7	7.5	253.3
阜康市	Fukang City	33.5	1.4	30.3	10.2	6.5	255.2
米泉市	Miquan City	42.5		37.0	10.0	7.0	277.2
伊宁市	Yining [Gulja] City	25.7	20.0	13.3	49.7	22.4	298.4
塔城市	Tacheng [Qoqek] City	12.3	13.1	21.8	35.0	15.3	201.7
阿勒泰市	Altay City	14.0	15.1	4.4	39.3	17.8	208.0
博乐市	Bole [Bortala] City	73.9	2.9	60.0	19.2	6.9	292.8
库尔勒市	Korla City	0.9		3.1	1.7	0.3	14.0
阿克苏市	Aksu City	35.1	1.8	0.2	0.3	3.6	71.3
阿图什市	Artux City	15.2	16.1	1.9		27.8	137.3
喀什市	Kashgar [Kaxgar] City	9.1	12.1			25.2	97.8
和田市	Hotan City	1.0	1.4			3.5	11.4
吐鲁番市	Turpan City	0.1	0.1	6.2	0.2		9.3
哈密市	Hami [Kumul] City	1.6		0.4	6.7		22.8

11-4 主要城市日照时数
Monthly Sunshine Hours of Major Cities

单位：小时 (2011 年) (hour)

城　　市	City	一月 Jan.	二月 Feb.	三月 Mar.	四月 Apr.	五月 May	六月 June	七月 July
乌鲁木齐市	Urumqi City	109.5	89.2	238.4	307.4	319.6	310.4	361.6
克拉玛依市	Karamay City	123.8	97.3	247.0	257.6	322.5	302.3	351.2
石河子市	Shi Hezi City	110.4	86.4	235.0	309.8	325.2	324.4	369.0
阜康市	Fukang City	95.1	91.7	217.9	278.5	301.8	325.3	362.6
米泉市	Miquan City	38.7	59.0	209.3	286.9	305.6	295.6	341.4
伊宁市	Yining [Gulja] City	197.6	128.3	245.8	280.9	323.4	322.5	374.3
塔城市	Tacheng [Qoqek] City	190.3	160.8	272.8	285.4	301.0	318.6	372.0
阿勒泰市	Altay City	348.8	337.5	321.1	239.4	103.7	159.5	190.3
博乐市	Bole [Bortala] City	158.6	110.4	232.3	241.5	273.9	277.8	332.0
库尔勒市	Korla City	204.8	176.3	210.8	262.3	288.1	263.2	335.9
阿克苏市	Aksu City	224.5	156.1	205.9	272.1	296.9	305.6	298.2
阿图什市	Artux City	178.5	133.1	137.7	261.4	295.1	339.9	339.4
喀什市	Kashgar [Kaxgar] City	211.5	152.1	168.3	300.1	325.2	352.7	356.8
和田市	Hotan City	186.7	159.3	147.2	249.7	307.7	289.6	238.2
吐鲁番市	Turpan City	63.7	161.2	239.4	271.7	309.0	291.9	336.5
哈密市	Hami [Kumul] City	229.8	247.6	312.1	341.5	398.5	341.6	389.0

城　　市	City	八月 Aug.	九月 Sept.	十月 Oct.	十一月 Nov.	十二月 Dec.	全年合计 Annual Total
乌鲁木齐市	Urumqi City	297.9	315.2	243.9	114.0	60.4	2767.5
克拉玛依市	Karamay City	293.9	302.1	225.7	89.4	111.6	2724.4
石河子市	Shi Hezi City	299.5	323.1	256.6	102.4	57.7	2799.5
阜康市	Fukang City	293.5	296.5	230.4	90.3	21.2	2604.8
米泉市	Miquan City	296.3	290.0	214.9	66.9	8.5	2413.1
伊宁市	Yining [Gulja] City	296.0	308.6	235.8	110.1	95.5	2918.8
塔城市	Tacheng [Qoqek] City	317.9	289.7	218.8	106.4	140.2	2973.9
阿勒泰市	Altay City	160.8	272.8	285.4	301.0	318.6	3140.0
博乐市	Bole [Bortala] City	275.1	289.4	160.8	54.9	86.4	2493.1
库尔勒市	Korla City	284.4	284.9	272.5	210.9	158.0	2952.1
阿克苏市	Aksu City	292.7	258.5	242.1	177.6	149.8	2880.0
阿图什市	Artux City	306.4	240.6	226.7	171.3	127.2	2757.3
喀什市	Kashgar [Kaxgar] City	327.9	256.5	239.6	183.2	141.3	3015.2
和田市	Hotan City	237.3	225.2	276.1	214.7	162.5	2694.2
吐鲁番市	Turpan City	291.7	274.9	202.9	110.9	50.2	2604.0
哈密市	Hami [Kumul] City	364.4	327.3	274.1	215.8	229.0	3670.7

11-5 环境保护基本情况
Basic Statistics on Environmental Protection

项目	Item	2010	2011
水环境	**Water**		
废水排放总量(亿吨)	Volume of Waste Water Discharged (100 million tons)	8.37	9.09
#工业废水排放量	Volume of Industrial Waste Water Discharged	2.54	2.88
城镇生活废水排放量	Volume of Non-industrial Waste Water Discharged	5.83	6.21
集中式治理设施废水排放量	Volume of Centralized Treatment for Waste Water Facilities		0.0038
化学需氧量排放量(万吨)	Amount of COD Discharged (10 000 tons)	29.60	67.29
#工业化学需氧量排放量	Amount of COD Discharged by industry	16.29	18.76
城镇生活化学需氧量排放量	Amount of COD Discharged by Non-industry	13.32	12.97
农业化学需氧量排放量	Amount of COD Discharged by Agricutral		35.10
集中式治理设施化学需氧量排放量	Amount of Centralized Treatment for COD Facilities		0.45
氨氮排放量(万吨)	Ammonia Nitrogen Discharged (10 000 tons)	2.66	4.68
#工业氨氮排放量	Industrial Ammonia Nitrogen Discharged	0.63	1.21
城镇生活氨氮排放量	Non-industrial Ammonia Nitrogen Discharged	2.04	2.21
农业氨氮排放量	Agricultural Ammonia Nitrogen Discharged		1.23
集中式治理设施氨氮排放量	Amount of Centralized Treatment for Ammonia Nitrogen Facilities		0.03
大气环境	**Atmosphere Environment**		
工业废气排放量(亿标立方米)	Industrial Waste Air Emission (100 million cu.m)	9309.61	11867.99
二氧化硫排放量(万吨)	Volume of Sulphur Dioxide Emission (10 000 tons)	58.85	76.31
#工业二氧化硫排放量	Volume of Sulphur Dioxide Emission by Industry	51.84	66.91
城镇生活二氧化硫排放量	Volume of Sulphur Dioxide Emission by Consumption	7.00	9.40
集中式治理设施二氧化硫排放量	Amount of Centralized Treatment for Sulphur Dioxide Facilities		0.0002
氮氧化物排放量(万吨)	Ammonia Nitrogen Discharged (10 000 tons)		75.51

注：2011 年自然保护区只包含自治区及国家级自然保护区。
Note: The nature reserves contain the municipality and state leuel nature protection area.

11-5 续表 1 Continued

项　　　目	Item	2010	2011
#工业氮氧化物排放量	Industrial Ammonia Nitrogen Discharged		45.23
城镇生活氮氧化物排放量	Non-industrial Ammonia Nitrogen Discharged		1.64
机动车氮氧化物排放量	Agricultural Ammonia Nitrogen Discharged		28.64
集中式治理设施氮氧化物排放量	Amount of Centralized Treatment for Ammonia Nitrogen Facilities		0.0006
烟(粉)尘排放量(万吨)	Volume of Soot Emission (10 000 tons)	34.40	53.27
#工业烟(粉)尘排放量	Volume of Industrial Soot Emission		44.13
城镇生活烟(粉)尘排放量	Volume of Soot Emission by Consumption	24.84	6.97
机动车烟(粉)尘排放量(总颗粒物排放量)	Volume of Soot Emission by Consumption	9.56	2.16
集中式治理设施氮氧化物排放量	Amount of Centralized Treatment for Ammonia Nitrogen Facilities	18.46	0.01
固体废物	**Solid Wastes**		
一般工业固体废物产生量(万吨)	Industrial Solid Wastes Produced (10 000 tons)	3914.12	5219.09
一般工业固体废物综合利用量(万吨)	Industrial Solid Wastes Utilized (10 000 tons)	1876.86	2838.11
一般工业固体废物处置量(万吨)	Ratio of Industrial Solid Wastes Utilized (%)		620.92
一般工业固体废物储存量(万吨)	Industrial Solid Wastes Discharged (10 000 tons)		1702.43
一般工业固体废物倾倒丢弃量(万吨)	General volume of industrial solid wastes dumping of discarded (10 000 tons)	62.79	88.731
危险废物产生量（万吨）	Amount of hazardous waste generated (10 000 tons)		470.14
生态环境	**Eco-Environment Protection**		
当年造林面积(万公顷)	Area of Reforestation of the Year (10 000 hectares)	21.94	20.58
自然保护区数(个)	Number of Nature Reserves (unit)	34	28
#国家级	National Level	9	9
自然保护区面积(万公顷)	Area of Nature Reserves (10 000 hectares)	2257.60	2096.00
#国家级	National Level	1275.86	1365.53

11-5 续表 2 Continued

项　　目	Item	2010	2011
自然保护区面积占辖区面积比重(%)	Area of Nature Reserves in Regions (%)	13.56	12.63
农村生态示范建设个数(个)	Number of Demonstration Zones of Ecology (unit)		84
国家级生态乡镇数(个)	Number of National Eco-towns (unit)		15
国家级生态村数(个)	Number of National Eco-village (unit)		7
自然灾害	**Natural Disaster**		
发生地质灾害起数(次)	Geological Disaster(case)	69	24
发生地震灾害次数(次)	Seismic Disaster(case)	2	8
#5.0 级以上	Magnitude above 5 Richter Scale	2	8
森林火灾次数(次)	Forest Fire (case)	34	59
森林火灾受灾面积（公顷)	Fire-Affected Forest Area (hectare)	43.82	150.16
森林病虫害发生面积(万公顷)	Forest Area Affected by Disease and Pests (10 000 hectares)	105.11	122.36
森林病虫害防治面积(万公顷)	Forest Area Provented and Cured from Disease and Pests (10 000 hectares)	57.10	54.72
森林病虫害防治率(%)	Rate of Prevention and Cure (%)	54.3	45.0
环境污染治理投资	**Investment in the Treaiment of Environmental Pollution**		
环境污染治理投资总额(亿元)	Total Investment in Pollution Treatment (10 000 yuan)	65.02	194.04
城镇环境基础设施建设投资额	Investment in Urban Environment Infrastructure	32.87	122.61
工业污染治理项目年完成投资总额	Investment Completed in Treatment Projects Industrial Pollution	6.68	23.17
当年完成环保验收项目环保投资总额	Investment Completed in Treatment Projects Industrial Pollution	25.47	48.26
环境污染治理投资总额相当于新疆生产总值比例(%)	Investment in Pollution Treatment Out of XJ GDP (%)	1.20	2.95
当年施工工业污染治理项目数(个)	Number of Projects in Industrial Pollution Treatment under Construction of The Year (unit)	56	154
当年竣工工业污染治理项目数(个)	Number of Projects Completed in Industrial Pollution Treatment of the Year Projects (unit)	48	92

11-6 水资源情况
Water Resource

年 份 Year	地 区 Region	水资源总量(亿立方米) Total Amount Of Water Resources (100 million cu.m)	地表水资源量 Surface Water Resources	地下水资源量 Ground Water Resources	地下水与地下水资源重复量 Duplicated Measurement Between surface Water and Groundwater	人均水资源量(立方米/人) Per Capita Water Resources (cu.m/person)
	2000	952.40	897.10	636.29	580.99	5255
	2001	1024.40	966.90	692.31	634.81	5500
	2002	1068.60	1006.00	724.85	662.25	5652
	2003	920.10	863.20	604.30	547.40	4793
	2004	855.40	809.20	502.60	456.40	4390
	2005	962.82	910.66	562.57	510.41	4789
	2006	953.12	903.84	554.13	504.85	4695
	2007	863.80	816.60	514.10	466.90	4168
	2008	802.60	759.50	518.50	475.36	3798
	2009	754.29	713.64	470.47	429.82	3517
	2010	1124.00	1063.00	624.30	563.20	5120
乌鲁木齐市	Urumqi City	9.55	9.25	4.03	3.74	388
克拉玛依市	Karamay City	0.92	0.09	1.96	1.13	328
石河子市	Shihezi City	0.18	0.09	1.18	1.08	57
吐鲁番地区	Turpan Administrative Offices	8.37	6.32	7.38	5.32	1334
哈密地区	Hami [Kumul] Administrative Offices	16.69	13.84	11.15	8.30	2888
昌吉回族自治州	Changji Hui Autonomous Prefecture	37.69	33.29	23.15	18.75	2685
伊犁州直属县(市)	Counties (Cities) Direct Under Ili Prefecture	229.10	224.80	100.10	95.76	8039
塔城地区	Tacheng [Tarbagatai] Administrative Offices	87.86	81.78	52.13	46.04	8466
阿勒泰地区	Altay Administrative Offices	161.60	154.80	71.89	65.07	24281
博尔塔拉蒙古自治州	Bortala Mongol Autonomous Prefecture	31.05	28.60	18.30	15.86	6403
巴音郭楞蒙古自治州	Bayangol Mongol Autonomous Prefecture	129.50	122.40	75.13	68.08	9632
阿克苏地区	Aksu Administrative Offices	83.24	75.60	63.52	55.88	3512
克孜勒苏柯尔克孜自治州	Kizilsu Kirgiz Autonomous Prefecture	82.35	80.89	52.58	51.12	15053
喀什地区	Kashgar [Kaxgar] Administrative Offices	92.87	86.47	69.76	63.35	2287
和田地区	Hotan Administrative Offices	152.70	144.40	72.03	63.76	7421

11-7 供水和用水情况

Water Supply and Water Used

单位：亿立方米　　(2010 年)　　(100 million cu.m)

年 份 Year	地 区 Region	供水总量 Water Supply	地表水 Surface Water	地下水 Ground Water	中水利用量 Use of Intermediate Water	用水总量 Water Used	生 产 Production
总 计	**Total**	**535.08**	**439.19**	**95.15**	**0.74**	**535.08**	**510.69**
乌鲁木齐市	Urumqi City	11.12	5.69	4.97	0.46	11.12	9.13
克拉玛依市	Karamay City	6.01	5.35	0.51	0.14	6.01	2.92
石河子市	Shihezi City	15.01	11.80	3.21		15.01	14.56
吐鲁番地区	Turpan Administrative Offices	13.35	5.69	7.65	0.01	13.35	12.63
哈密地区	Hami [Kumul] Administrative Offices	10.37	4.40	5.96	0.01	10.37	9.63
昌吉回族自治州	Changji Hui Autonomous Prefecture	35.01	20.96	14.05		35.01	34.36
伊犁州直属县(市)	Counties (Cities) Direct Under Ili Prefecture	52.89	48.69	4.15	0.05	52.89	51.28
塔城地区	Tacheng [Tarbagatai] Administrative Offices	17.65	9.38	8.27		17.65	16.71
阿勒泰地区	Altay Administrative Offices	42.46	41.96	0.50		42.46	34.65
博尔塔拉蒙古自治州	Bortala Mongol Autonomous Prefecture	14.84	10.70	4.14		14.84	14.64
巴音郭楞蒙古自治州	Bayangol Mongol Autonomous Prefecture	44.10	35.04	9.01	0.05	44.10	42.33
阿克苏地区	Aksu Administrative Offices	100.24	93.19	7.05		100.24	98.49
克孜勒苏柯尔克孜自治州	Kizilsu Kirgiz Autonomous Prefecture	8.83	7.83	1.00		8.83	8.63
喀什地区	Kashgar [Kaxgar] Administrative Offices	116.81	95.85	20.95	0.01	116.81	115.69
和田地区	Hotan Administrative Offices	46.40	42.66	3.74		46.4	45.02

年 份 Year	地 区 Region	第一产业 Primary Industry	第二产业 Secondary Industry	第三产业 Tertiary Industry	居民生活 Consumption	生态环境 Ecological Protection	人均用水量(立方米/人) Per Capita Water Used (cu.m/person)
总 计	**Total**	**495.95**	**13.60**	**1.14**	**7.00**	**17.39**	**2453**
乌鲁木齐市	Urumqi City	6.65	2.27	0.21	1.57	0.43	357
克拉玛依市	Karamay City	1.76	1.13	0.03	0.15	2.47	2007
石河子市	Shihezi City	13.29	1.23	0.04	0.25	0.20	2363
吐鲁番地区	Turpan Administrative Offices	12.10	0.47	0.06	0.16	0.55	2143
哈密地区	Hami [Kumul] Administrative Offices	9.22	0.39	0.02	0.24	0.50	1812
昌吉回族自治州	Changji Hui Autonomous Prefecture	32.46	1.81	0.09	0.51	0.60	2483
伊犁州直属县(市)	Counties (Cities) Direct Under Ili Prefecture	48.87	2.30	0.11	0.94	0.69	2131
塔城地区	Tacheng [Tarbagatai] Administrative Offices	16.18	0.43	0.10	0.44	0.50	1448
阿勒泰地区	Altay Administrative Offices	34.31	0.33	0.01	0.15	7.66	7038
博尔塔拉蒙古自治州	Bortala Mongol Autonomous Prefecture	14.47	0.17		0.20		3345
巴音郭楞蒙古自治州	Bayangol Mongol Autonomous Prefecture	40.90	1.32	0.11	0.51	1.26	3289
阿克苏地区	Aksu Administrative Offices	97.50	0.86	0.13	0.60	1.16	4228
克孜勒苏柯尔克孜自治州	Kizilsu Kirgiz Autonomous Prefecture	8.54	0.07	0.02	0.13	0.07	1680
喀什地区	Kashgar [Kaxgar] Administrative Offices	114.96	0.64	0.09	0.78	0.34	2935
和田地区	Hotan Administrative Offices	44.73	0.16	0.13	0.40	0.98	2303

11-8 主要年份环保系统机构、人员数

Number of Environmental Protection Agencies and Persons Engaged in Main Years

年 份 Year	机构数（个） Number of Agencies (unit)	人员数（人） Total Number of Staff & Workers (person)	#科技人员 Scientific and Technical Personnel	#监测人员 Monitoring Personnel	#监察人员 Supervising and Administrative Personnel
2000	208	1965	110	654	416
2001	208	2096	109	636	420
2002	238	2386	99	692	523
2003	275	2588	107	766	671
2004	288	2694	107	763	701
2005	304	2796	120	758	790
2006	326	2968	125	777	923
2007	326	2962	77	786	955
2008	296	2962	100	812	993
2009	319	3197	103	857	998
2010	324	3237	109	936	1126
2011	335	3372	121	967	1194

注：本表数据从 2009 年开始不包含兵团数据。(11-12、11-13、11-14 同)
Note: The date of this table don't cover the date of XJPCC from 2009.(the same as the table of 11-12,11-13,11-14)

11-9 工业按行业重点调查工业企业废气及污染物排放情况

Emission and Treatment of Waste Water and Pollutant in Industrial Enterprises by Sector

单位：吨　　(2011 年)　　(ton)

行业	Sector	工业废气排放量（亿立方米） Total Volume of Industrial Waste Gas Emission (100 million cu.m)	工业二氧化硫排放量 Volume of Sulphur Dioxide Emission by Industry	工业氮氧化物排放量 Volume of Nitrogen Dioxide Emission by Industry	工业烟(粉)尘排放量 Volume of Industrial Soot Emission
合　计	**Total**	**11867.98**	**640083.08**	**438996.49**	**406844.21**
黑色金属矿采选业	Processing of Ferrous Metals Ores	68.21	1247.73	317.30	2515.75
有色金属矿采选业	Processing of Nonferrous Metals Ores	11.99	482.38	187.26	1499.19
农副产品加工业	Processing of Food from Agricultural Products	89.05	9531.53	9031.61	3692.43
造纸及纸制品业	Paper and Paper Products Manufacturing	31.73	4749.77	1191.84	1970.60
石油加工炼焦及核燃料加工业	Oil Processing, Coking and Nuclear Fuel Processing	1143.27	102743.08	45007.47	44226.40
化学原料及化学制品制造业	Raw Chemical Material and Chemical Products	945.18	38408.76	20690.49	13040.43
非金属矿物制品业	Nonmetal Mineral Products Manufacturing	2120.76	16840.73	46995.67	129654.03
水泥行业	Cement Industry	1329.79	5608.80	40807.82	42369.03
黑色金属冶炼及压延加工业	Smelting and Pressing of Ferrous Metals	2163.08	56992.90	25577.20	32092.93
钢铁冶炼行业	Iron and Steel Industry	705.09	46975.37	8607.83	16994.58
有色金属冶炼及压延加工业	Smelting and Pressing of Nonferrous Metals	391.93	106581.03	7153.77	10622.73
电力、热力的生产和供应业	Electricity and Thermal Production and Supply	4210.51	278571.51	267879.99	92469.19
其他行业	Ohters	692.27	23933.68	14963.88	75060.52

11-10 工业按行业重点调查工业企业废水及污染物排放情况

Emission and Treatment of Waste Water and Pollutant in Industrial Enterprises by Sector

(2011 年)

行业	Sector	工业废水排放量（万吨） Volume Of Waste Water Discharged (10 000 tons)	工业废水中化学需氧量排放量（吨） COD Discharge From Industrial WasteWater (ton)	工业废水中氨氮排放量（吨） Ammonia Nitrogen Discharge form Industrial Waste Water (ton)
合　计	**Total**	**26709.69**	**178436.27**	**11870.98**
农副食品加工业	Processing of Food from Agricultural Products	1586.69	25055.54	540.22
食品制造业	Food Manufacturing	2464.15	11782.82	560.96
酒、饮料和精制茶制造业		875.74	18709.70	249.47
纺织业	Textile Industry	479.37	442.63	39.81
造纸及纸制品业	Paper and Paper Products Manufacturing	2192.12	12114.76	170.12
石油加工、炼焦及核燃料加工业	Oil Processing, Coking and Nuclear Fuel Processing	1684.10	1984.00	605.44
化学原料及化学制品制造业	Raw Chemical Material and Chemical Products	3724.87	3780.39	7006.41
化学纤维制造业	Chemical Fiber Manufacturing	5794.01	97126.75	1747.03
黑色金属冶炼及压延加工业	Smelting and Pressing of Ferrous Metals	1794.95	1682.26	674.21
电力、热力的生产和供应业	Electricity and Thermal Production and Supply	2953.25	992.35	34.32
其他行业	Ohters	3160.45	4765.08	243.01

11-11 工业按行业重点调查一般工业企业固体废物产生量及处理利用情况

Productian and Treatment of Waste Solid in Industrial Enterprises by Region

单位：万吨　　(2011 年)　　(10 000 ton)

行业 Sector	工业固体废物产生量 Volume of Industrial Solid Wastes Produced	工业固体废物综合利用量 Volume of Industrial Solid Wastes Utilized	工业固体废物贮存量 Volume of Industrial Solid Wastes in Stocks	工业固体废物处置量 Volume of Industrial Solid Wastes Treated	工业固体废物倾倒丢弃量 General Volume of Industrial Solid Wastes Dumping of Discarded (10 000 tons)
合　计 **Total**	**5018.01**	**2686.69**	**600.18**	**1680.33**	**77.40**
煤炭开采和洗选业 Mining and Washing of Coal	406.50	372.89	20.42	11.97	1.32
黑色金属矿采选业 Processing of Ferrous Metals Ores	1055.57	196.64	8.74	830.32	19.87
有色金属矿采选业 Processing of Nonferrous Metals Ores	738.73	132.41	157.00	415.38	33.95
农副产品加工业 Processing of Food from Agricultural Products	47.13	37.54	8.68	0.87	0.04
食品制造业 Food Manufacturing	30.90	30.46	0.44		0.05
纺织业 Textile Manufacturing	1.17	1.16			
化学原料及化学制品制造业 Raw Chemical Material and Chemical Products	393.91	235.68	145.58	12.65	
非金属矿物制品业 Nonmetal Mineral Products Manufacturing	159.10	157.02	1.91	0.12	0.05
黑色金属冶炼及压延加工业 Smelting and Pressing of Ferrous Metals	1061.14	580.45	205.24	262.14	13.32
电力、热力的生产和供应业 Electricity and Thermal Production and Supply	730.09	647.39	24.66	57.98	0.09
其他行业 Ohters	393.77	295.06	27.49	88.90	8.71

11-12 环境污染治理投资
Investment in the Treatment of Environment Pollution

项　　目	Item	2010	2011
环境污染治理投资总额(万元)	**Total Investment in the Treatment of Environment Pollution (10 000 yuan)**	**650247**	**1940404**
城镇环境基础设施建设投资	Investment in Urban Environmental Infrastructure	328690	1226067
#污水处理	Volume of Waste Water	14999	31296
垃圾处理	Volume of Garbage Disposal	2229	53631
燃　气	Gas Supply	57891	220336
集中供热	Centralized Heating	144444	524178
园林绿化	Gardening and Greening	109127	396626
工业污染源治理投资	Investment in the Treatment of Industrial Pollution	66813	231696
#工业废水治理项目	Number of Project in Industrial Waste water Treatment	19687	36028
工业废气脱硫治理项目	Number of Project in Industrial Waste Gas Treatment	46276	42004
工业废气脱硝治理项目	Number of Project in Industrial Waste Gas Treatment	800	135457
污染物自动在线监测仪器安装项目	Number of Project Installation Pollution	50	146
当年完成环保验收项目环保投资	Investment in the Treatment of Industrial Pollution	254744	482641
#废水治理环保投资	Investment of Pollution in Waste Water Treatment		153260
废气治理环保投资	Investment of Pollution in Waste Gas Treatment		153914
固体废物治理环保投资	Investment of Pollution in Solid Wastes Treatment		31988
噪声治理环保投资	Investment of Pollution in Noise Treatment		23338
绿化及生态环保投资	Investment of Pollution in Landscape and Greening		120140
环境污染治理投资总额相当于新疆生产总值比例(%)	**Investment in the Treatment of Environmental Pollution as Percent of GDP (%)**	**1.20**	**2.95**

11-13 主要年份工业污染治理投资完成情况
Investment Completed in the Treatment of Industrial Pollution in Main Years

年 份 Year	汇总工业企业数(个) Number of Industrial Enterprises (unit)	污染治理项目本年完成投资(万元) Investment In the Treatment of Industrial Pollution (10 000 yuan)	治理废水 Treatment of Waste Water	治理废气 Treatment of Waste Gas	治理固体废物 Treatment of Solid Waste	治理噪声 Treatment of Noise Pollution	治理其他 Treatment of Other Pollution	本年施工项目数(个) Projects Under Construction (unit)	本年竣工项目数(个) Projects Completed (unit)
2000	154	22311	8528	9116	349	4109	209	203	198
2001	113	32009	25917	4886	723	66	416	113	106
2002	89	16952	5015	8241	2206	261	1229	129	85
2003	83	26509	9298	9514	4865	21	2811	104	94
2004	94	29622	12334	13114	2756	92	1327	146	110
2005	97	44008	23549	9656	371	321	10111	162	153
2006	92	45229	26876	12036	2582	32	3703	143	132
2007	90	60138	29958	23891	1676	219	4394	117	103
2008	72	68004	33123	31999	1964	270	648	120	120
2009	99	125435	22242	99849	600	170	2574	109	100
2010	66	66813	19687	46276	800		50	56	48
2011	81	231693	36028	195202			317	154	92

11-14 工业污染治理投资来源

Source of Investment in the Treatment of Industrial Pollution

单位：万元 (10 000 yuan)

项　　目	Item	2010	2011
施工项目本年投资来源	Source of Current Investment	66813	231693
排污费补助	Pollution Charges Subsidies	270	402
政府其他补助	Other Government Subsidies	1169	3876
企业自筹	Self-raising Funds	65374	227415
#银行贷款	Bank Loans	10	

11-15 主要城市空气质量指标

Ambient Air Quality in Main Cities

单位:毫克/立方米 (2011 年) (milligram/cu.m)

城　市	City	可吸入颗粒物 (PM10) Paticulate Matters	二氧化硫 (SO_2)	二氧化氮 (NO_2)	空气质量达到及好于二级的天数(天) Days of Air Quality Equal to or Above Grade II (day)
乌鲁木齐市	Urumqi City	0.131	0.079	0.068	276
克拉玛依市	Karamay City	0.066	0.016	0.024	354
石河子市	Shihezi City	0.068	0.042	0.029	329
吐鲁番市	Turpan City	0.155	0.017	0.018	249
哈 密 市	Hami [Kumul] City	0.087	0.027	0.019	353
昌 吉 市	Changji City	0.080	0.031	0.049	327
阜 康 市	Fukang City	0.095	0.038	0.027	317
奎 屯 市	Kuytun City	0.082	0.023	0.025	343
伊 宁 市	Yining [Gulja] City	0.073	0.033	0.034	357
塔 城 市	Tacheng [Qoqek] City	0.046	0.018	0.015	365
乌 苏 市	Usu City	0.072	0.022	0.023	344
阿勒泰市	Altay City	0.039	0.018	0.012	364
博 乐 市	Bole [Bortala] City	0.049	0.014	0.018	365
库尔勒市	Korla City	0.111	0.015	0.031	312
阿克苏市	Aksu City	0.154	0.016	0.016	254
阿图什市	Artux City	0.151	0.014	0.015	247
喀 什 市	Kashgar [Kaxgar] City	0.281	0.036	0.019	128
和 田 市	Hotan City	0.288	0.020	0.030	110
五家渠市	Wujiaqu City	0.095	0.018	0.020	321

11-16 主要城市道路交通噪声监测情况
Monitoring of Urban Road Traffic Noise in Major Cities

(2011 年)

城 市	City	等效声级 dB(A) Average Noise ValuedB(A)
乌鲁木齐市	Urumqi City	67.0
克拉玛依市	Karamay City	65.8
石河子市	Shihezi City	67.0
吐鲁番市	Turpan City	67.5
哈 密 市	Hami [Kumul] City	67.6
昌 吉 市	Changji City	68.4
阜 康 市	Fukang City	64.5
奎 屯 市	Kuytun City	65.7
伊 宁 市	Yining [Gulja] City	66.4
塔 城 市	Tacheng [Qoqek] City	60.9
阿勒泰市	Altay City	66.4
博 乐 市	Bole [Bortala] City	63.8
库尔勒市	Korla City	64.9
阿克苏市	Aksu City	67.4
阿图什市	Artux City	65.2
喀 什 市	Kashgar [Kaxgar] City	68.2
和 田 市	Hotan City	64.7

11-17 主要城市区域环境噪声监测情况
Monitoring of Urban Environment Noise in Major Cities under National Control Programme

(2011 年)

城 市	City	等效声级 dB(A) Average Noise ValuedB(A)
乌鲁木齐市	Urumqi City	52.6
克拉玛依市	Karamay City	53.2
石河子市	Shihezi City	51.0
吐鲁番市	Turpan City	49.8
哈 密 市	Hami [Kumul] City	52.3
昌 吉 市	Changji City	52.7
阜 康 市	Fukang City	55.0
奎 屯 市	Kuytun City	52.6
伊 宁 市	Yining [Gulja] City	51.0
塔 城 市	Tacheng [Qoqek] City	53.9
阿勒泰市	Altay City	57.2
博 乐 市	Bole [Bortala] City	48.0
库尔勒市	Korla City	51.5
阿克苏市	Aksu City	49.5
阿图什市	Artux City	52.8
喀 什 市	Kashgar [Kaxgar] City	60.8
和 田 市	Hotan City	58.9

11-18 主要年份自然保护区基本情况
Basic Situation of Natural Protection in Main Years

年 份 Year	自然保护区个数 (个) Number of Nature Reserves (unit)	#国家级 Nation level	自然保护区面积 (万公顷) Area of Nature Reserves (10 000 hectares)	#国家级 Nation Level	自然保护区占辖区面积比重 (%) Percentage of Nature Reserves in the Region (%)
2000	23	5	1594.05	869.08	9.6
2001	26	7	2042.40	1105.50	12.3
2005	28	8	2183.49	1275.86	13.1
2006	28	8	2162.49	1275.86	13.0
2007	34	8	2257.60	1275.86	13.6
2008	34	8	2257.60	1275.86	13.6
2009	34	8	2257.60	1275.86	13.6
2010	34	8	2257.60	1275.86	13.6
2011	28	9	2096.00	1365.53	12.6

11-19 各地区城市生活垃圾清运和处理情况
Collection, Transport and Disposal of Consumption Wastes in Cities by Region

(2011 年)

城 市	City	生活垃圾清运量 (万吨) Consumption Wastes Collected and Transported (10 000 tons)	生活垃圾处理量 (万吨) Disposal of Consumption Wastes Treatment (10 000 tons)	无害化处理厂数 (座) Number of Factories for Wastes Treatment (unit)	无害化处理能力 (吨/日) Treatment Capacity (m ton/day)	无害化处理量 (万吨) Volume of Wastes Disposed (10 000 tons)	生活垃圾处理率 (%) Treatment Rate of Consumption Wastes (%)
总 计	**Total**	**344.48**	**317.61**	**19**	**7004**	**273.78**	**92.20**
乌鲁木齐市	Urumqi City	129.34	118.81	2	2600	106.26	91.86
克拉玛依市	Karamay City	16.11	16.11	3	450	15.64	100.00
吐鲁番市	Turpan City	9.56	8.50	1	300	8.50	88.91
哈 密 市	Hami [Kumul] City	18.07	17.80	1	350	17.80	98.51
昌 吉 市	Changji City	14.88	14.40	1	450	14.40	96.77
阜 康 市	Fukang City	2.57	2.49	1	150	2.49	96.89
伊 宁 市	Yining [Gulja] City	20.10	18.10	1	600	18.10	90.05
奎 屯 市	Kuytun City	5.20	4.60	1	200	4.60	88.46
塔 城 市	Tacheng [Qoqek] City	6.50	6.30	1	190	6.30	96.92
乌 苏 市	Usu City	12.00	11.04	1	165	11.04	92.00
阿勒泰市	Altay City	4.00	3.90	1	140	3.90	97.50
博 乐 市	Bole [Bortala] City	8.41	7.79	1	149	7.79	92.63
库尔勒市	Korla City	25.68	24.56	1	500	24.56	95.64
阿克苏市	Aksu City	12.70	12.70				100.00
阿图什市	Artux City	3.00	2.90	1	80	2.90	96.67
喀 什 市	Kashgar [Kaxgar] City	19.00	17.00	1	500	17.00	89.47
和 田 市	Hotan City	14.27	12.50	1	180	12.50	87.60
石河子市	Shihezi City	14.30	14.30				100.00
阿拉尔市	Aral City	2.40	2.30				95.83
图木舒克市	Tumxuk City	1.00					
五家渠市	Wujiaqu City	3.65					
北 屯 市	Beitur City	1.74	1.51				86.78

注：表中无害化处理数据均为二级以上无害化处理厂数据。
Note: Data on wastes disposed are provided by secondary and above factories for wastes treatment.

11-20 各地区土地利用情况
Land Use by Region

单位:万公顷 (10 000 hectares)

年份 Year 地区 Region	土地调查面积 Area under Land Survey	农用地 Land for Agriculture Use	#园地 Garden Land	#牧草地 Grazing and Pasture Land	建设用地 Land for Construction	居民点及工矿用地 Land for Living Quarters, Mining and Manufacturing Sites	交通用地 Land for Transport Facilities	水利设施用地 Land for Water Conservancy Facilities
2000	16648.97	6346.21	19.22	5136.05	154.38	88.69	22.3	43.39
2001	16648.97	6295.64	19.68	5135.35	112.11	88.88	5.25	17.98
2002	16648.97	6297.36	22.21	5135.75	118.2	94.63	5.49	18.08
2003	16648.97	6301.54	29.58	5131.49	119.96	96.12	5.76	18.08
2004	16648.97	6304.57	33.59	5121.58	121.05	97.02	5.89	18.14
2005	16648.97	6306.07	35.43	5116.07	122.07	97.62	6.12	18.33
2006	16648.97	6307.61	36.37	5112.47	122.66	98.15	6.16	18.35
2007	16648.97	6308.05	36.45	5111.92	123.43	98.86	6.21	18.36
2008	16648.97	6308.48	36.42	5111.38	123.98	99.33	6.27	18.38
乌鲁木齐市 Urumqi City	113.84	90.75	0.34	78.05	4.41	3.88	0.35	0.18
克拉玛依市 Karamay City	86.54	35.99	0.03	23.13	6.5	5.91	0.37	0.22
石河子市 Shihezi City	4.60	3.44	0.07	0.61	0.62	0.57	0.05	...
吐鲁番地区 Turpan Administrative Offices	675.63	84.37	2.19	72.97	2.95	2.49	0.35	0.11
哈密地区 Hami [Kumul] Administrative Offices	1420.95	443.06	1.34	374.21	18.57	17.94	0.51	0.12
昌吉回族自治州 Changji Hui Autonomous Prefecture	776.39	602.96	0.87	497.76	11.69	9.89	0.71	1.1
伊犁州直属县(市) Counties (Cities) Direct Under Ili Prefecture	563.81	476.23	2.14	360.56	9.15	8.31	0.51	0.33
塔城地区 Tacheng [Tarbagatai] Administrative Offices	946.98	765.34	0.57	643.19	9.86	8.13	0.52	1.22
阿勒泰地区 Altay Administrative Offices	1176.99	1069.72	0.03	962.91	4.43	3.08	0.31	1.03
博尔塔拉蒙古自治州 Bortala Mongol Autonomous Prefecture	249.34	192.61	0.36	159.74	2.22	1.92	0.17	0.13
巴音郭楞蒙古自治州 Bayangol Mongol Autonomous Prefecture	4709.54	970.86	7.43	824.19	11.37	8.89	0.84	1.64
阿克苏地区 Aksu Administrative Offices	1313.41	542.5	6.32	403.7	12.67	8.00	0.41	4.26
克孜勒苏柯尔克孜自治州 Kizilsu Kirgiz Autonomous Prefecture	724.68	324.82	0.63	298.14	1.55	1.20	0.16	0.19
喀什地区 Kashgar [Kaxgar] Administrative Offices	1394.8	302.46	10.55	160.61	18.61	13.08	0.53	5.00
和田地区 Hotan Administrative Offices	2491.47	403.37	3.55	251.61	9.38	6.04	0.48	2.85

11-21 造林面积

Area of Afforestation

单位:公顷 (hectare)

年份 地区 Year Region	造林总面积 Total Area of Afforestation	按造林方式分 By Approach			按林种用途分 By Function of Forest				
		人工造林 Manual Planting	飞机播种 Airplane Planting	无林地和疏林地新封 Area without Forest or of Sparse Forest	用材林 Timber Forests	经济林 By-product Forests	防护林 Protection Forests	薪炭林 Fuel Forests	特种用途林 Forests for Special Purpose
2000	64173	63793	200		1605	44564	16512	1012	480
2001	106771	106771			2149	78203	24536	1424	459
2002	216924	216924			3034	78302	134723	706	159
2003	263781	253781	10000		10152	59777	191380	2390	82
2004	176540	176540			3897	73103	96897	2638	5
2005	136990	130323	6667		3226	40523	92449	738	54
2006	97424	97424			1780	38495	56548	588	13
2007	146632	124642		21990	2991	71667	71325	589	60
2008	239951	217429		22522	8744	136046	94820	341	
2009	301438	266301		35137	9387	155503	135584	954	10
2010	199629	156964		42665	1996	104527	90546	2298	262
2011	186197	140262		45935	823	92656	89942	2356	420
乌鲁木齐市 Urumqi City	2975	2975					2975		
克拉玛依市 Karamay City	1739	406		1333			1739		
石河子市 Shihezi City	84	84					84		
吐鲁番地区 Turpan Administrative Offices	4436	3303		1133	128	976	2765	167	400
哈密地区 Hami [Kumul] Administrative Offices	5214	2214		3000		1097	3917	200	
昌吉回族自治州 Changji Hui Autonomous Prefecture	26296	12960		13336	27	3535	22734		
伊犁州直属县(市) Counties (Cities) Direct Under Ili Prefecture	29071	28871		200	570	25594	2361	546	
塔城地区 Tacheng [Tarbagatai] Administrative Offices	15313	6979		8334	98	806	13450	939	20
阿勒泰地区 Altay Administrative Offices	19802	10069		9733		1679	18123		
博尔塔拉蒙古自治州 Bortala Mongol Autonomous Prefecture	4068	2068		2000		104	3964		
巴音郭楞蒙古自治州 Bayangol Mongol Autonomous Prefecture	13843	10777		3066		8967	4577	299	
阿克苏地区 Aksu Administrative Offices	22500	22500				17864	4636		
克孜勒苏柯尔克孜自治州 Kizilsu Kirgiz Autonomous Prefecture	2839	2372		467		1212	1627		
喀什地区 Kashgar [Kaxgar] Administrative Offices	21750	20083		1667		18607	3074	69	
和田地区 Hotan Administrative Offices	16267	14601		1666		12215	3916	136	

11-22 林业重点工程造林面积
Area of Key Afforestation Projects

单位:公顷 (hectare)

年 份 Year	地区 Region	造林总面积 Total Area of Afforestation	#退耕还林工程 Grain for Green Projects	#三北及长江流域等防护林工程 Project on Protection Forests in North China and Yangtze River Basin
	2001	102317	13173	
	2002	199324	113010	
	2003	235924	175314	
	2004	152967	82838	70129
	2005	133778	62457	71321
	2006	88744	38160	50584
	2007	138700	32926	105774
	2008	187318	50977	136341
	2009	270997	48120	222877
	2010	177674	38034	139640
	2011	186197	31066	107390
乌鲁木齐市	Urumqi City	2975	670	2295
克拉玛依市	Karamay City	1739	300	1200
石河子市	Shihezi City	84		
吐鲁番地区	Turpan Administrative Offices	4436	1732	2704
哈密地区	Hami [Kumul] Administrative Offices	5214	258	4956
昌吉回族自治州	Changji Hui Autonomous Prefecture	26296	6561	19735
伊犁州直属县(市)	Counties (Cities) Direct Under Ili Prefecture	29071	3956	17929
塔城地区	Tacheng [Tarbagatai] Administrative Offices	15313	3678	11635
阿勒泰地区	Altay Administrative Offices	19802	3058	16744
博尔塔拉蒙古自治州	Bortala Mongol Autonomous Prefecture	4068	521	3258
巴音郭楞蒙古自治州	Bayangol Mongol Autonomous Prefecture	13843	3340	7619
阿克苏地区	Aksu Administrative Offices	22500	3301	3771
克孜勒苏柯尔克孜自治州	Kizilsu Kirgiz Autonomous Prefecture	2839	604	2235
喀什地区	Kashgar [Kaxgar] Administrative Offices	21750	1470	5903
和田地区	Hotan Administrative Offices	16267	1617	7406

11-23 各地区天然湿地面积
Area of Wetlands by Region

单位:百公顷 (2008 年) (100 hectares)

地 区 Region	天然湿地面积 Area of Natural Wetlands	河 流 Rivers	湖 泊 Lakes	沼 泽 Marshland	天然湿地面积占土地总面积比重(%) Proportion of Natural Wetlands in Total Area of Territory(%)
总 计 Total	**12673.56**	**4732.99**	**4763.91**	**3176.66**	**0.76**
乌鲁木齐市 Urumqi City	74.72	20.98	39.37	14.37	0.66
克拉玛依市 Karamay City	214.69	23.59	154.58	36.52	2.48
石河子市 Shihezi City	4.92	4.77		0.15	1.07
吐鲁番地区 Turpan Administrative Offices	127.84	5.99	0.18	121.67	0.19
哈密地区 Hami [Kumul] Administrative Offices	179.00	35.73	122.34	20.93	0.13
昌吉回族自治州 Changji Hui Autonomous Prefecture	264.46	50.27	2.58	211.61	0.34
伊犁州直属县(市) Counties (Cities) Direct Under Ili Prefecture	543.92	246.61	6.59	290.72	0.96
塔城地区 Tacheng [Tarbagatai] Administrative Offices	352.75	113.36	5.98	233.41	0.37
阿勒泰地区 Altay Administrative Offices	1353.84	353.78	845.49	154.57	1.15
博尔塔拉蒙古自治州 Bortala Mongol Autonomous Prefecture	1331.27	28.88	1176.41	125.98	5.34
巴音郭楞蒙古自治州 Bayangol Mongol Autonomous Prefecture	4034.70	979.74	2098.16	956.80	0.86
阿克苏地区 Aksu Administrative Offices	1018.86	709.19	68.68	240.99	0.78
克孜勒苏柯尔克孜自治州 Kizilsu Kirgiz Autonomous Prefecture	326.89	94.18	46.61	186.10	0.45
喀什地区 Kashgar [Kaxgar] Administrative Offices	1056.83	556.60	88.55	411.68	0.76
和田地区 Hotan Administrative Offices	1788.87	1509.32	108.39	171.16	0.72

11-24 森林火灾情况

Forest Fires

年 份 Year	地 区 Region	森林火灾次数(次) Forest Fires (case)	一般火灾 Ordinary Fires	较大火灾 Large Fires	火场总面积(公顷) Total Area of Fires (hectare)
	2005	28	1		42.33
	2006	35	5		258.27
	2007	47	13		137.09
	2008	67	19		191.38
	2009	51	35	16	83.58
	2010	34	27	7	65.95
	2011	59	46	13	713.72
乌鲁木齐市	Urumqi City				
克拉玛依市	Karamay City				
石河子市	Shihezi City				
吐鲁番地区	Turpan Administrative Offices				
哈密地区	Hami [Kumul] Administrative Offices	3	3		0.001
昌吉回族自治州	Changji Hui Autonomous Prefecture	16	16		1.566
伊犁州直属县(市)	Counties (Cities) Direct Under Ili Prefecture	12	8	4	99.690
塔城地区	Tacheng [Tarbagatai] Administrative Offices	2	2		0.516
阿勒泰地区	Altay Administrative Offices	18	13	5	379.312
博尔塔拉蒙古自治州	Bortala Mongol Autonomous Prefecture	1		1	109.000
巴音郭楞蒙古自治州	Bayangol Mongol Autonomous Prefecture	3	2	1	14.070
阿克苏地区	Aksu Administrative Offices	3	2	1	21.510
克孜勒苏柯尔克孜自治州	Kizilsu Kirgiz Autonomous Prefecture				
喀什地区	Kashgar [Kaxgar] Administrative Offices				
和田地区	Hotan Administrative Offices				
五家渠市	Wujiaqu City	1		1	88.050

年 份 Year	地 区 Region	受灾森林总面积(公顷) Destructed Forest Area (hectare)	#天然林 Natural Forest	#人工林 Man-made Forest	经济损失(万元) Economic Loss (10 000 yuan)
	2005	11.62	10.63	0.99	12.52
	2006	94.10	78.28	1.39	9.26
	2007	75.34	31.44	39.37	19.47
	2008	122.74	58.39	65.64	145.53
	2009	72.66	8.24	49.86	52.29
	2010	43.82	17.56	15.70	5.48
	2011	150.16	114.36	35.80	1426.91
乌鲁木齐市	Urumqi City				
克拉玛依市	Karamay City				
石河子市	Shihezi City				
吐鲁番地区	Turpan Administrative Offices				
哈密地区	Hami [Kumul] Administrative Offices	0.001		0.001	0.30
昌吉回族自治州	Changji Hui Autonomous Prefecture	1.566		1.566	21.30
伊犁州直属县(市)	Counties (Cities) Direct Under Ili Prefecture	31.978	0.018	31.960	
塔城地区	Tacheng [Tarbagatai] Administrative Offices	0.516	0.250	0.266	
阿勒泰地区	Altay Administrative Offices	40.172	38.162	2.010	485.18
博尔塔拉蒙古自治州	Bortala Mongol Autonomous Prefecture	6.900	6.900		
巴音郭楞蒙古自治州	Bayangol Mongol Autonomous Prefecture	12.300	12.300		
阿克苏地区	Aksu Administrative Offices	21.510	21.510		
克孜勒苏柯尔克孜自治州	Kizilsu Kirgiz Autonomous Prefecture				
喀什地区	Kashgar [Kaxgar] Administrative Offices				
和田地区	Hotan Administrative Offices				
五家渠市	Wujiaqu City	35.220	35.220		920.13

11-25 森林病虫害防治情况
Prevention of Forest Diseases and Pests

单位：公顷 (hectare)

年份 Year	地区 Region	合计 Total			森林病害 Forest Diseases		
		发生面积 Area of Occurrence	防治面积 Area of Prevention	防治率(%) Prevention Rate (%)	发生面积 Area of Occurrence	防治面积 Area of Prevention	防治率(%) Prevention Rate (%)
	2005	241713	221720	91.7	4467	3440	77.0
	2006	400127	344146	86.0	21993	19273	87.6
	2007	787087	441533	56.1	30194	23393	77.5
	2008	1066659	609457	57.1	147035	92811	63.1
	2009	990580	572735	57.8	82273	68525	83.3
	2010	1051060	570973	54.3	80820	73573	91.0
	2011	1223633	547200	45.0	73747	61240	83.0
乌鲁木齐市	Urumqi City	8274	8155	98.6	6	6	100.0
吐鲁番地区	Turpan Administrative Offices	3050	2246	73.6			
哈密地区	Hami [Kumul] Administrative Offices	15947	10196	63.9	1200	1100	91.7
昌吉回族自治州	Changji Hui Autonomous Prefecture	415844	10053	2.4	1554	1547	99.6
伊犁州直属县(市)	Counties (Cities) Direct Under Ili Prefecture	21727	13724	63.2	2801	2207	78.8
塔城地区	Tacheng [Tarbagatai] Administrative Offices	8769	3336	38.0	188	155	82.6
阿勒泰地区	Altay Administrative Offices	25911			222		
博尔塔拉蒙古自治州	Bortala Mongol Autonomous Prefecture	31280	1071	3.4			
巴音郭楞蒙古自治州	Bayangol Mongol Autonomous Prefecture	80843	19266	23.8	221	209	94.6
阿克苏地区	Aksu Administrative Offices	184416	180239	97.7	8671	8401	96.9
克孜勒苏柯尔克孜自治州	Kizilsu Kirgiz Autonomous Prefecture	63893	3528	5.5	5871	1947	33.2
喀什地区	Kashgar [Kaxgar] Administrative Offices	224677	192359	85.6	20339	17244	84.8
和田地区	Hotan Administrative Offices	106423	97349	91.5	29619	27959	94.4
自治区林业厅	Xinjiang Forestry Bureau	32579	5678	1.2	3055	465	15.2

年份 Year	地区 Region	森林虫害 Forest Diseases			森林鼠害 Forest Rat Plague		
		发生面积 Area of Occurrence	防治面积 Area of Prevention	防治率(%) Prevention Rate (%)	发生面积 Area of Occurrence	防治面积 Area of Prevention	防治率(%) Prevention Rate (%)
	2005	221500	199700	89.9	21747	18580	85.4
	2006	340320	290693	85.4	37813	34180	90.4
	2007	350592	331735	94.6	406301	86405	21.3
	2008	527465	446766	84.7	392159	69880	17.8
	2009	474213	431197	90.9	434093	73013	16.8
	2010	470961	432316	91.8	499279	65084	13.0
	2011	582653	457627	79.0	567233	28333	5.0
乌鲁木齐市	Urumqi City	6068	6016	99.1	2200	2133	97.0
吐鲁番地区	Turpan Administrative Offices	3050	2246	73.6			
哈密地区	Hami [Kumul] Administrative Offices	8760	7922	90.4	5987	1174	19.6
昌吉回族自治州	Changji Hui Autonomous Prefecture	5899	4225	71.6	408391	4281	1.1
伊犁州直属县(市)	Counties (Cities) Direct Under Ili Prefecture	15969	10376	65.0	2957	1141	38.6
塔城地区	Tacheng [Tarbagatai] Administrative Offices	2601	2057	79.0	5980	1124	18.8
阿勒泰地区	Altay Administrative Offices	9972			15717		
博尔塔拉蒙古自治州	Bortala Mongol Autonomous Prefecture	4835	1058	21.9	26445	13	0.1
巴音郭楞蒙古自治州	Bayangol Mongol Autonomous Prefecture	18616	17484	93.9	62006	1573	2.5
阿克苏地区	Aksu Administrative Offices	175745	171838	97.8			
克孜勒苏柯尔克孜自治州	Kizilsu Kirgiz Autonomous Prefecture	53429	981	1.8	4593	600	13.1
喀什地区	Kashgar [Kaxgar] Administrative Offices	185878	159516	85.8	18460	15599	84.5
和田地区	Hotan Administrative Offices	76210	68842	90.3	594	548	92.2
自治区林业厅	Xinjiang Forestry Bureau	15621	5066	32.4	13903	147	1.1

注：自治区林业厅数据中包括石河子市和克拉玛依市的数据。
Note: The data on Bureau of Forestry include the data of Shihezi City and Karamay City.

11-26 地震灾害情况
Earthquake Disasters

年份 Year	地区 Region	地震次数(次) Number of Earthquakes (case)	5.0-5.9 级 5.0-5.9 Richterscale	6.0-6.9 级 6.0-6.9 Richterscale	7.0 级以上 Over 7.0 Richterscale
2005		**4**	**3**	**1**	
2006		**2**	**2**		
2007		**1**	**1**		
特克斯县	Tekes County	1	1		
2008		**4**	**2**	**1**	**1**
于田县、策勒县	Yutian [Keriya] County, Qira County	1			1
裕民县	Yumin [Qagantokay] County	1	1		
和静县	Hejing County	1	1		
乌恰县	Wuqia [Ulugqat] County	1		1	
2009		**6**	**6**		
察布查尔县、昭苏县	Qapqai Xibe Autonomous County, Zhaosu[Mongolrure] County	1	1		
柯坪县、阿合齐县	Kalpin County, Akqi County	1	1		
阿合齐县、乌什县	Akqi County, Wushi[Uxtnrpan] County	1	1		
阿图什市	Artux City	1	1		
叶城县、皮山县	Yecheng[Kagilik] County, Pishan[Guma] County	1	1		
哈密市	Hami[Kumul] City	1	1		
2010		**2**	**2**		
乌恰县	Wuqia [Ulugqat] County	2	2		
2011		**8**	**7**	**1**	
乌恰县	Wuqia [Ulugqat] County	1	1		
托克逊县	Toksun County	1	1		
青河县	Qinghe[Qinggil]County	1	1		
阿图什-伽师交界	Artux City border on Jiashi[payzawat] County	1	1		
于田县	Yutian[Keriya] County	1	1		
精河县	Jinghe[Jing] County	1	1		
尼勒克、巩留交界	Nilka County border on Gongliu[Tokkuztara] County	1		1	
莎车县	Shache[Yarkant]County	1	1		

注：本表数据由自治区地震局提供。
Note: The data in this table is Provided by theBureau of Earthquake.

11-26 续表 Continued

年份 Year	地区 Region	人员伤亡(人) Casualties (person)	#死亡人数 Deaths	经济损失(万元) Economic Losses (10 000 yuan)	失去住所(户) Homeless (household)
2005				**16316**	**5823**
2006				**126**	
2007				**11060**	**5074**
特克斯县	Tekes County			11060	5074
2008				**38437**	**5702**
于田县、策勒县	Yutian [Keriya] County, Qira County			19480	3004
裕民县	Yumin [Qagantokay] County			8585	2302
和静县	Hejing County			3644	220
乌恰县	Wuqia [Ulugqat] County			6728	176
2009				**20498**	**4393**
察布查尔县、昭苏县	Qapqai Xibe Autonomous County, Zhaosu[Mongolrure] County			4612	1396
柯坪县、阿合齐县	Kalpin County, Akqi County			9068	1706
阿合齐县、乌什县	Akqi County, Wushi[Uxtnrpan] County			4636	708
阿图什市	Artux City			2182	583
叶城县、皮山县	Yecheng[Kagilik] County, Pishan[Guma] County				
哈密市	Hami[Kumul] City				
2010				**2408**	**675**
乌恰县	Wuqia [Ulugqat] County			2408	675
2011				**105059**	**15964**
乌恰县	Wuqia [Ulugqat] County				
托克逊县	Toksun County			9225	4757
青河县	Qinghe[Qinggil]County			3330	915
阿图什-伽师交界	Artux City border on Jiashi[payzawat] County			18322	1994
于田县	Yutian[Keriya] County			292	
精河县	Jinghe[Jing] County			1185	324
尼勒克、巩留交界	Nilka County border on Gongliu[Tokkuztara] County			67846	7598
莎车县	Shache[Yarkant]County			4859	376

11-27 林业系统营林固定资产投资完成情况
Completed Investment in Fixed Assets for Afforestation in Forest System

单位：万元　　(10 000 yuan)

年 份 Year	地 区 Region	本年完成投资 Investment Completed During the Year	#国家投资 State Investment	本年新增固定资产 Newly Increased Fixed Assets
	2000	23582	11686	4542
	2001	45890	23725	12492
	2002	68861	35835	
	2003	71277	40821	27223
	2004	60631	43475	23047
	2005	80150	57680	24988
	2006	96062	82235	31047
	2007	115523	94094	33091
	2008	158416	129294	55295
	2009	193818	153538	52765
	2010	168930	142678	28725
	2011	85365	39304	41378
克拉玛依市	Karamay City	15030		15030
石河子市	Shihezi City	2108		
吐鲁番地区	Turpan Administrative Offices	819	819	760
哈密地区	Hami [Kumul] Administrative Offices	3186	170	3186
昌吉回族自治州	Changji Hui Autonomous Prefecture	1820	1820	3036
伊犁州直属县(市)	Counties (Cities) Direct Under Ili Prefecture	2200	1230	1230
塔城地区	Tacheng [Tarbagatai] Administrative Offices	2943	915	134
阿勒泰地区	Altay Administrative Offices	8682	7152	2082
博尔塔拉蒙古自治州	Bortala Mongol Autonomous Prefecture	4422	4306	4422
巴音郭楞蒙古自治州	Bayangol Mongol Autonomous Prefecture	1736	1736	
阿克苏地区	Aksu Administrative Offices	14539	8026	10487
克孜勒苏柯尔克孜自治州	Kizilsu Kirgiz Autonomous Prefecture	12111	12111	
自治区林业厅	Xinjiang Forestry Bureau	15769	1019	1011

注：2011 年固定资产投资统计范围为单项投资 500 万元以上项目，2010 年及以前年份统计范围是只要形成固定资产的投资均需统计。
Note: In 2011,Statistical range of investment in fixed assets is above of 5million yuan single investment project.Before 2010,Statistical range is the formation of the investment fixed assets required statistics.

主要统计指标解释

国土 指一个主权国家管辖下的领土、领海和领空。

气候 指地球与大气之间长期能量交换与质量交换所形成的一种自然环境状态，它是多种因素综合作用的结果。气候既是人类生活和生产的环境要素之一，又是供给人类生活和生产的重要资源。气温、降水、湿度等气象要素的多年平均值是用来描述一个地区气候状况的主要参数，而各种气象要素某年、某月的平均值(或总量)则可以反映出该时期天气气候状况的重要特征。

自然资源 指人类可以直接从自然界获得，并用于生产和生活的物质资源。自然资源一般可以分成可再生资源和非再生资源两大类。可再生资源指在较短时间内可以再生、可以循环利用的资源，包括土地资源、水资源、气候资源、生物资源和海洋资源等。非再生资源指在使用后不能再生的资源，包括矿产资源和地热能源。

土地资源 土地指陆地的表层部分，它主要由岩石、岩石的风化物和土壤构成。土地资源按利用类型可以分为农用地、建筑用地和未利用地。农用地包括耕地、园地、林地、牧草地和水面。建筑用地包括居民点及工矿用地、交通用地和水利设施用地。未利用地指农用地和建筑用地以外的土地，包括滩涂、荒漠、戈壁、冰川和石山等。

耕地面积 指经过开垦用以种植农作物并经常进行耕耘的土地面积。包括种有作物的土地面积、休闲地、新开荒地和抛荒未满三年的土地面积。

林业用地面积 指生长乔木、竹类、灌木、沿海红树林等林木的土地面积，包括有林地、灌木林、疏林地、未成林造林地、迹地、苗圃等。

草地面积 指牧区和农区用于放牧牲畜或割草，植被盖度在5%以上的草原、草坡、草山等面积。包括天然的和人工种植或改良的草地面积。

森林面积 包括郁闭度0.2以上的乔木林地面积和竹林面积，国家特别规定的灌木林地面积，农田林网以及村旁、路旁、水旁、宅旁林木的覆盖面积。

森林蓄积量 指一定森林面积上存在着的林木树干部分的总材积。它是反映一个国家或地区森林资源总规模和水平的基本指标之一，也是反映森林资源的丰富程度、衡量森林生态环境优劣的重要依据。

森林覆盖率 以行政区域为单位，森林面积占区域土地总面积的百分比。计算公式为：

森林覆盖率(%)=森林面积／土地总面积×100%

活立木总蓄积量 指一定范围内土地上全部树木蓄积的总量，包括森林蓄积、疏林蓄积、散生木蓄积和四旁树蓄积。

内陆水域总面积 指江、河、湖泊、池塘、塘堰、水库等各种流水或蓄水的水面占地面积。

径流 指陆地上接受降水后扣除损耗外，从地表和地下向流域出口断面汇集的水流。径流可分为地表径流、地下径流和壤中流。地表径流指沿地表向河流、湖泊、沼泽、海洋等汇集的水流；地下径流指沿潜水层或隔水层间的含水层，向河流、湖泊、沼泽、海洋等汇集的地下水水流。

径流量 指在一定时段内通过河流某一过水断面的水量，用以反映一个国家或地区水资源的丰歉程度。计算公式为：

径流量=降水量-蒸发量

流域 每条河流都有自己的干流和支流，干支流共同组成这条河流的水系。每条河流都有自己的集水区域，这个集水区域就称为该河流的流域。

外流河 指直接或间接流入海洋的河流。供给外流河河水的区域称为外流区域。

内陆河 指在陆地内部干燥地区，河水沿途消失于沙漠或注入内陆湖泊的河流。供给内陆河河水的区域称为内陆区域。

矿产资源 矿产指由地质作用形成，富集于地壳中或出露于地表达到工农业利用要求的有用矿物。矿产是一种重要的自然资源，是社会发展的重要物质基础。从某种意义上讲，一个国家对矿产资源开发利用的广度和深度，可以作为这个国家经济发展水平的标志。

矿产保有储量 指探明的矿产储量(包括工业储量和远景储量)，扣除已开采部分和地下损失量后的年末实有储量，是反映国家矿产资源现状的重要指标。

气温 指空气的温度，我国一般以摄氏度(℃)为单位表示。气象观测的温度表是放在离地面约1.5米处通风良好的百叶箱里测量的，因此，通常说的气温指的是离地面1.5米处百叶箱中的温度。其统计计算方法为：

月平均气温是将全月各日的平均气温相加，除以该月的天数而得。

年平均气温是将12个月的月平均气温累加后除以12而得。

降水量 指从天空降落到地面的液态或固态(经融化后)水，未经蒸发、渗透、流失而在地面上积聚的深度。其统计计算方法为：

月降水量是将全月各日的降水量累加而得。

年降水量是将12个月的月降水量累加而得。

日照时数 指太阳实际照射地面的时间。其统计方法与降水量相同。

水资源总量 指评价区内降水形成的地表和地下产水总量，即地表产流量与降水入渗补给地下水量之和，不包括过境水量。

地表水资源量 指评价区内河流、湖泊、冰川等地表水体中可以逐年更新的动态水量，即当地天然河川径流量。

地下水资源量 指评价区内降水和地表水对饱水岩土层的补给量，包括降水入渗补给量和河道、湖库、渠系、渠灌田间等地表水体的入渗补给量。

地表水与地下水资源重复计算量 指地表水和地下水相互转化的部分，即天然河川径流量中的地下水排泄量和地下水补给量中来源于地表水的入渗量。

供水总量 指各种水源工程为用户提供的包括输水损失在内的毛供水量之和。

地表水源供水量 指地表水体工程的取水量，按蓄、引、提、调四种形式统计。从水库、塘坝中引水或提水，均属蓄水工程供水量；从河道或湖泊中自流引水的，无论有闸或无闸，均属引水工程供水量；利用扬水站从河道或湖泊中直接取水的，属提水工程供水量；跨流域调水指水资源一级区或独立流域之间的跨流域调配水量，不包括在蓄、引、提水量中。

地下水源供水量 指水井工程的开采量，按浅层谈水、深层承压水和微咸水分别统计。城市地下水源供水量包括自来水厂的开采量和工矿企业自备井的开采量。

其他水源供水量 包括污水处理再利用、集雨工程、海水淡化等水源工程的供水量。

用水总量 指分配给各类用户的包括输水损失在内的毛用水量之和。

农业用水 指农田灌溉用水、林果地灌溉用水、草地灌溉用水和鱼塘补水。

工业用水 指工矿企业在生产过程中用于制造、加工、冷却、空调、净化、洗涤等方面的用水，按新水取用量计，不包括企业内部的重复利用水量。

生活用水 包括城镇生活用水和农村生活用水。城镇生活用水由居民用水和公共用水(含第三产业及建筑业等用水)组成；农村生活用水除居民生活用水外，还包括畜用水在内。

生态环境补水 仅包括人为措施供给的城镇环境用水和部分河湖、湿地补水，而不包括降水、径流自然满足的水量。

工业废水排放量 指经过企业厂区所有排放口排到企业外部的工业废水量。包括生产废水、外排的直接冷却水、超标排放的矿井地下水和与工业废水混排的厂区生活污水，不包括外排的间接冷却水(清污不分流的间接冷却水应计算在内)。

工业废水排放达标量 指报告期内废水中各项污染物指标都达到国家或地方排放标准的外排工业废水量，包括未经处理外排达标的，经废水处理设施处理后达标排放的，以及经污水处理厂处理后达标排放的。

工业废水排放达标率 指工业废水排放达标量占工业废水排放量的百分率，计算公式为：

工业废水排放达标率=工业废水排放达标量/工业废水排放量×100%

化学需氧量(COD) 只指用化学氧化剂氧化水中有机污染物时所需要的氧量。COD 值越高，表示水中有机污染物污染越重。

工业废气排放量 指报告期内企业厂区内燃料燃烧和生产工艺过程中产生的各种排入大气的含有污染物的气体的总量，以标准状态(273K，101325Pa)计算。测算公式为：

工业废气排放量=燃料燃烧过程中废气排放量+生产工艺过程中废气排放量

工业烟尘排放量 指企业厂区内燃料燃烧过程中产生的烟气中夹带的颗粒物排放量。

工业粉尘排放量 指企业在生产工艺过程中排放的能在空气中悬浮一定时间的固体颗粒物排放量。如钢铁企业的耐火材料粉尘、焦化企业的筛焦系统粉尘、烧结机的粉尘、石灰窑的粉尘、建材企业的水泥粉尘等。不包括电厂排入大气的烟尘。

工业固体废物产生量 指报告期内企业在生产过程中产生的固体状、半固体状和高浓度液体状废弃物的总量，包括危险废物、冶炼废渣、粉煤灰、炉渣、煤矸石、尾矿、放射性废物和其他废物等；不包括矿山开采的剥离废石和掘进废石(煤矸石和呈酸性或碱性的废石除外)。酸性或碱性废石指采掘的废石其流经水、雨淋水的 pH 值小于 4 或 pH 值大于 10.5 者。

工业固体废物综合利用量 指报告期内企业通过回收、加工、循环、交换等方式，从固体废物中提取或者使其转化为可以利用的资源、能源和其他原材料的固体废物量(包括当年利用往年的工业固体废物贮存量)，如用作农业肥料、生产建筑材料、筑路等。综合利用量由原产生固体废物的单位统计。

工业固体废物综合利用率 指工业固体废物综合利用量占工业固体废物产生量(包括综合利用往年贮存量)的百分率。计算公式为：

工业固体废物综合利用率=工业固体废物综合利用量/(工业固体废物产生量+综合利用往年贮存量)×100%

工业固体废物贮存量 指报告期内企业以综合利用或处置为目的，将固体废物暂时贮存或堆存在专设的贮存设施或专设的集中堆存场所内的数量。专设的固体废物贮存场所或贮存设施必须有防扩散、防流失、防渗漏、防止污染大气、水体的措施。

工业固体废物处置量 指报告期内企业将固体废物焚烧或者最终置于符合环境保护规定要求的场所，并不再回取的工业固体废物量(包括当年处置往年的工业固体废物贮存量)。处置方式有填埋(其中危险废物应安全填埋)、焚烧、专业贮存场(库)封场处理、深层灌注、回填矿井及海洋处置(经海洋管理部门同意投海处置)等。

工业固体废物排放量 指报告期内企业将所产生的固体废物排到固体废物污染防治设施、场所以外的数量，不包括矿山开采的剥离废石和掘进废石(煤矸石和呈酸性或碱性的废石除外)。

生活垃圾清运量 指报告期内收集和运送到垃圾处理厂(场)的生活垃圾数量。生活垃圾指城市日常生活或为城市日常生活提供服务的活动中产生的固体废物以及法律行政规定的视为城市生活垃圾的固体废物。包括：居民生活垃圾、商业垃圾、集市贸易市场垃圾、街道清扫垃圾、公共场所垃圾和机关、学校、厂矿等单位的生活垃圾。

生活垃圾无害化处理率 指报告期生活垃圾无害化处理量与生活垃圾产生量比率。在统计上，由于生活垃圾产生量不易取得，可用清运量代替。计算公式为：

生活垃圾无害化处理率=生活垃圾无害化处理量/生活垃圾产生量×100%

农用地 指直接用于农业生产的土地，包括耕地、园地、林地、牧草地及其他农用地。

人工林面积 指由人工播种、植苗或扦插造林形成的生长稳定，(一般造林 3-5 年后或飞机播种 5-7 年后)每公顷保存株数大于或等于造林设计植树株数 80%或郁闭度 0.20 以上(含 02.0)的林分面积。

造林总面积 指在宜林荒山荒地、宜林沙荒地、无立木林地、疏林地和退耕地等其它宜林地上通过人工措施形成或恢复森林、林木、灌木林的过程。用材林 指以生产木材为主要目的的森林和林木，包括以生产竹材为主要目的的竹林。

经济林 指以生产果品，食用油料、饮料、调料，工业原料和药材为主要目的的林木。经济林是人们为了取得林木的果实、叶片、皮层、胶液等产品作为工业原料或者供食用所营造的林木，如油茶、油桐、核桃、樟树、花椒、茶、桑、果等。

防护林 指以防护为主要目的的森林、林木和灌木丛。包括水源涵养林，水土保持林，防风固沙林，农田、牧场防护林，护岸林，护路林等。

薪炭林 指以生产燃料为主要目的的林木。

天然林保护工程 是我国林业的"天"字号工程、一号工程，也是投资最大的生态工程。具体包括三个层次:全面停止长江上游、黄河上中游地区天然林采伐；大幅度调减东北、内蒙古等重点国有林区的木材产量；同时保护好其他地区的天然林资源。主要解决这些区域天然林资源的休养生息和恢复发展问题。

退耕还林还草工程 是我国林业建设上涉及面最广、政策性最强、工序最复杂、群众参与度最高的生态建设工程。主要解决重点地区的水土流失问题。

三北和长江流域等重点防护林体系建设工程 三北和长江中下游地区等重点防护林体系建设工程，是我国涵盖面最大、内容最丰富的防护林体系建设工程。具体包括三北防护林四期工程、长江中下游及淮河太湖流域防护林二期工程、沿海防护林二期工程、珠江防护林二期工程、太行山绿化二期工程和平原绿化二期工程。主要解决三北地区的防沙治沙问题和其他区域各不相同的生态问题。

野生动植物保护及自然保护区建设工程 野生动植物保护及自然保护区建设工程，是一个面向未来，着眼长远，具有多项战略意义的生态保护工程，也是呼应国际大气候、树立中国良好国际形象的"外交工程"。主要解决基因保存、生物多样性保护、自然保护、湿地保护等问题。

湿地 指天然或人工、长久或暂时性的沼泽地、泥炭地或水域地带，包括静止或流动、淡水、半咸水、咸水体，低潮时水深不超过6米的水域以及海岸地带地区的珊瑚滩和海草床、滩涂、红树林、河口、河流、淡水沼泽、沼泽森林、湖泊、盐沼及盐湖。

自然保护区 指为了保护自然环境和自然资源，促进国民经济的持续发展，将一定面积的陆地和水体划分出来，并经各级人民政府批准而进行特殊保护和管理的区域个数。根据保护对象，自然保护区分为自然生态系统类、野生生物类、自然遗迹类。风景名胜区、文物保护区不计在内。

滑坡 指斜坡上不稳定的岩土体在重力作用下沿一定软面(或滑动带)整体向下滑动的物理地质现象。地表水和地下水的作用以及人为的不合理工程活动对斜坡岩、土体稳定性的破坏，经常是促使滑坡发生的主要因素。在露天采矿、水利、铁路、公路等工程中，滑坡往往造成严重危害。

崩塌 指陡坡上大块的岩土体在重力作用下突然脱离母体崩落的物理地质现象。它可因多裂隙的岩体经强烈的物理风化、雨水渗入或地震而造成，往往毁坏建筑物，堵塞河道或交通路线。

泥石流 指山地突然爆发的包含大量泥沙、石块的特殊洪流，多见于半干旱山地高原地区。其形成条件是地形陡峻，松散堆积物丰富，有特大暴雨或大量冰融水的流出。

地面塌陷 指地表岩、土体在自然或人为因素作用下向下陷落，并在地面形成塌陷坑(洞)的一种动力地质现象。由于其发育的地质条件和作用因素的不同，地面塌陷可分为：岩溶塌陷、非岩溶塌陷。

突发环境事件 指突然发生，造成或可能造成重大人员伤亡、重大财产损失和对全国或者某一地区的经济社会稳定、政治安定构成重大威胁和损害，有重大社会影响的涉及公共安全的环境事件。

环境污染治理投资 指在污染源治理和城市环境基础设施建设的资金投入中，用于形成固定资产的资金，其中污染源治理投资包括工业污染源治理投资和"三同时"项目环保投资两部分。环境污染治理投资为城市环境基础设施投资、工业污染源治理投资与"三同时"项目环保投资之和。

林业建设到位资金 报告期内林业建设项目实施单位专项账户上实际收到的用于林业建设的资金合计。

林业建设本年完成投资 指从本年 1 月 1 日起至本年最后一天止完成的全部投资额。本年完成投资是反映本年的实际投资规模，计算有关投资效果，进行年度国民经济平衡分析的重要指标。

Explanatory Notes on Main Statistical Indicators

Territory refers to territorial land, sea and air space under the administration of the People's Republic of China.

Climate refers to the natural environmental status formed by the long-term exchange of energy and mass between the earth and the atmosphere, and is the result of interaction of many factors. Climate is both one of the environment factors and also the important resources for living and production activities of the human being. The average values across several years of meteorological factors such as temperature, rainfall and humidity are used as important parameters to describe the climate of a region, while the average values (or total values) of a given year or month of meteorological factors reflect the key characteristics of climate for that period of time.

Natural Resources refer to material resources that could be obtained from the nature by human being and used for production and living. Natural resources in general can be classified as renewable resources and non-renewable resources. Renewable resources refer to resources that could be renewed and recycled during a relatively short period of time, including land resource, water resource, climate resource, biology resource and marine resource. Non-renewable resources include resources that could not be renewed, such as minerals and geothermal resource.

Land Resource Land refers to the surface of the earth, consisting of mainly rocks and its weathering and earth. Land resource can be classified, by its utilization, as land for agriculture, land for construction and unused land. Land for agriculture includes cultivated land, plantation land, forestland, grassland and waters. Land for construction includes land for residential purpose, for manufacturing and mining, for transportation and for water-conservancy projects. Unused land refers to land other than land for agriculture and construction, including beaches, deserts, Gobi, glaciers and rock mountains.

Area of Cultivated Land refers to area of land reclaimed for the regular cultivation of various farm crops, including crop-cover land, fallow, newly reclaimed land and land laid idle for less than 3 years.

Area of Afforested Land refers to area for land for trees bamboo, bushes and mangrove, including forest-covered land, bush-covered land, sparse forest land, land planned for afforestation and nurseries of young trees.

Area of Grassland refers to area of grassland, grass-slopes and grass-covered hills with a vegetation-covering rate of over 5% that are used for animal husbandry or harvesting of grass. It includes natural, cultivated and improved grassland areas.

Forest Area refers to the area of trees and bamboo grow with canopy density above 0.2, the area of shrubby tree according to regulations of the government, the area of forest land inside farm land and the area of trees planted by the side of villages, farm houses and along roads and rivers.

Stock Volume of Forest refers to total stock volume of wood growing in forest area, which shows the total size and level of forest resources of a country or a region. It is also an important indicator illustrating the richness of forest resource and the status of forest ecological environment.

Forest Coverage Rate Taking the administrative jurisdiction as the unit, the percentage of area of afforested land to the area of total land. The formula for calculating forest coverage rate is as follows:

$$\text{Forestry coverage rate (\%)} = \frac{\text{Area of Afforested Land}}{\text{Area of Total Land}} \times 100\ \%$$

Total Standing Stock Volume refers to the total stock volume of trees growing in land, including trees in forest, trees in sparse forest, scattered trees and trees planted by the side of villages, farm houses and along roads and rivers.

Water Resource Water exists in the nature in solid, liquid and gaseous states, is distributed in the ocean, land (including earth) and air, and constitutes the water resource through the circulation of water. Water resource includes the surface water and underground water that is controlled by the human being for irrigation, power-generation, water supply, navigation and cultivation. It also includes rivers, lakes, wells, springs, tides, gulf and water area for cultivation. Water resource as an important natural resource is indispensable for the development of the national economy.

Runoff refers to the water gathered at the way out of the cross section of drainage area either from the surface or underground after deducting the wastage of the precipitation on the land. Runoff can be divided into surface runoff, underground runoff and within soil runoff. Surface runoff refers to water flowing to the rivers, lakes, swamps, and seas on the surface of the earth. Underground runoff refers to water flow to rivers, lakes, swamps, and seas through the water-bearing stratum of confined layer or unconfined layer.

Volume of Runoff refers to the total volume of water running through a certain cross section of a river during a certain period of time, reflecting the water resource condition in a country or a region. The formula for calculating volume of runoff is as follows:

Runoff =Precipitation-Evaporation

Drainage Area Each river has its own main stream and branches to form the water system of the river. Each river has its own catchment's area, which is also called as the drainage area of the river.

Out-flowing Rivers refer to rivers directly or indirectly flowing into the sea. The area providing water to the out-flowing rivers is called as out-flowing area.

Inland Rivers refer to rivers in inland dry areas that die away in desert on the way or infuse into inland lakes. The area providing water to the inland rivers is called as inland area.

Mineral Resources refer to useful minerals that can be used for industrial or agricultural purposes enriched in lithosphere or on earth due to the geological process.

Ensured Mineral Reserves refer to the actual mineral reserves, which equal to the proven mineral reserves (including industrial reserves and prospective reserves) minus extracted parts and underground losses. This indicator shows the current condition of the mineral resources of a Country.

Temperature refers to the air temperature. China uses

centigrade as the unit. The thermometry used for weather observation is put in a breezy shutter, which is 1.5 meters high from the ground. Therefore, the commonly used temperature refers to the temperature in the breezy shutter 1.5 meters away from the ground. The calculation method is as follows:

Monthly average temperature is the summation of average daily temperature of one month divided by the actual days of that particular month.

Annual average temperature is the summation of monthly average of a year divided by 12 months.

Volume of Precipitation refers to the deepness of liquid state or solid state (thawed) water falling from the sky to the ground that has not been evaporated, infiltrated or run off. The calculation method is as follows:

Monthly precipitation is the summation of daily precipitation of a month.

Annual precipitation is the summation of 12 months precipitation of a year.

Sunshine Hours refer to the actual hours of sun irradiating the earth. The calculation method is the same as that of the precipitation.

Total Water Resources refers to total volume of water resources measured as run-off for surface water from rainfall and recharge for groundwater in a given area, excluding transit water.

Surface Water Resources refers to total renewable resources which exist in rivers, lakes, glaciers and other collectors from rainfall and are measured as run-off of rivers.

Groundwater Resources refers to replenishment of aquifers with rainfall and surface water.

Duplicated Measurement between Surface Water and Groundwater refers to mutual exchange between surface water and groundwater, i.e. run-off of rivers includes some depletion into groundwater while groundwater includes some replenishment from surface water.

Water Supply refers to gross water supply by supply systems from sources to consumers, including losses during distribution.

Surface Water Supply refers to withdrawals by surface water supply system, broken down with storage, flow, pumping and transfer. Supply from storage projects includes withdrawals from reservoirs; supply from flow includes withdrawals from rivers and lakes with natural flows no matter if there are locks or not; supply from pumping projects includes withdrawals from rivers or lakes with pumping stations; and supply from transfer refers to water supplies transferred from first-level regions of water resources or independent river drainage areas to others, and should not be covered under supplies of storage, flow and pumping.

Groundwater Supply refers to withdrawals from supplying wells, broken down with shallow layer freshwater, deep layer freshwater and slightly brackish water. Groundwater supply for urban areas includes water mining by both waterworks and own wells of enterprises.

Other Water Supply Sources include supplies by waste-water treatment, rain collection, seawater desalinization and other water projects.

Water Use refers to gross water use distributed to users, including loss during transportation, broken down into use by agriculture, industry, living consumption and ecological protection.

Water Use by Agriculture includes uses of water by irrigation of farming fields and by forestry, animal husbandry and fishing. Water use by forestry, animal husbandry and fishery includes irrigation of forestry and orchards, irrigation of grassland and replenishment of fishing farms.

Water Use by Industry refers to new withdrawals of water, excluding reuse of water within enterprises.

Water Use by Living Consumption includes use of water for living consumption in both urban and rural areas. Urban water use by living consumption is composed of household use and public use (including services, commerce, restaurants, cargo transportation, posts, telecommunications and construction). Rural water use by living consumption includes both households and animals.

Water Use by Ecological Protection includes replenishment of rivers and lakes and use for urban environment.

Waste Water Discharged by Industry refers to the volume of waste water discharged by industrial enterprises through all their outlets, including waste water from production process, directly cooled water, groundwater from mining wells which does not meet discharge standards and sewage from households mixed with waste water produced by industrial activities, but excluding indirectly cooled water discharged (It should be included if the discharge is not separated from waste water).

Industrial Waste Water Meeting Discharge Standards refers to volume of industrial waste water discharge which, with or without treatment, reaches national or local standards with regard to all pollutants.

Ratio of Industrial Waste Water Meeting Discharge Standards refers to percentage of industrial waste water meeting discharge standards over total industrial waste water discharge. It is calculated as:

$$\text{Ratio of industrial waste water meeting discharge standards} = \frac{\text{industrial waste water meeting discharge standards}}{\text{total industrial waste water discharge}}$$

Chemical Oxygen Demand (COD) refers to the amount of oxygen required when chemical oxidants are used to oxidize organic pollutants in water. A higher value of COD corresponds to more serious pollution by organic pollutants.

Industrial Waste Air Emission refers to discharge into atmosphere of waste air containing pollutants generated from fuel burning and production process in enterprises within a given period of time. It is converted into standard (273K, 101325Pa) with the following formula:

Emission=emission from fuel burning+ emission through production process

Industrial Soot Emission refers to the volume of soot in smoke emitted in the process of fuel burning in the premises of enterprises.

Industrial Dust Emission refers to volume of dust emitted by production process of enterprises and suspended in the air for a given period of time, including dust from refractory material of iron and steel works, dust from coke-screening systems and sintering machines of coke plants, dust from lime kilns and dust from cement production in building material enterprises, but excluding soot and dust emitted from power plants.

Industrial Solid Wastes Produced refers to total volume of solid, semi-solid and high concentration liquid residues produced by industrial enterprises from production process in a given period of time, including hazardous wastes, slag, coal ash, gangue, tailings, radioactive residues and other wastes, but excluding stones stripped or dug out in mining - gangue and acid or alkaline stones not included (a stone is acid or alkaline according to the pH value of the water being below 4 or above 10.5 when the stone is in, or soaked by water).

Industrial Solid Wastes Utilized refers to volume of solid wastes from which useful materials can be extracted or which can be converted into usable resources, energy or other materials by means of reclamation, processing, recycling and exchange (including utilizing in the year the stocks of industrial solid wastes of the previous year). Examples of such utilizations include fertilizers, building materials and road materials. The information shall be collected by the producing units of the wastes.

Rate of Utilization of Industrial Solid Wastes refers to the percentage of industrial solid wastes utilized over industrial solid wastes produced (including stocks of the previous years). It is calculated as:

$$\text{Rate of utilization of industrial solid wastes} = \frac{\text{volume of industrial solid wastes utilized}}{\text{industrial solid wastes produced} + \text{stock of previous years}} \times 100\%$$

Stock of Industrial Solid Wastes refers to the volume of solid wastes placed in special facilities or special sites for purposes of utilization or disposal. The sites or facilities should take measures against dispersion, loss, seepage, and air and water contamination.

Industrial Solid Wastes Disposed refers to the quantity of industrial solid wastes which are burnt or placed ultimately in the sites meeting the requirements for environmental protection and not salvaged or recycled (including disposition in the year of those wastes of previous years). The disposition includes landfill (Safe landfills should be conducted for hazardous wastes), incineration, containment spaces, deep underground disposal, backfill in mining pits and disposal at sea.

Industrial Solid Wastes Discharged refers to the volume of industrial solid wastes discharged by producing enterprises to disposal facilities or to other sites. The wastes exclude stones stripped or dug from mining (gangue and acid or alkaline waste stones not included).

Consumption Wastes Transported refers to volume of consumption wastes collected and transported to disposal factories or sites. Consumption wastes are solid wastes produced from urban households or from service activities for urban households, and solid wastes regarded by laws and regulations as urban consumption wastes, including those from households, commercial activities, markets, cleaning of streets, public sites, offices, schools, factories, mining units and other sources.

Ratio of Consumption Wastes Treated refers to consum- ption wastes treated over that produced. In practical statistics, as it is difficult to estimate, the volume of consumption wastes produced is replaced with that transported. It is calculated as:

$$\text{Ratio of consumption treated} = \frac{\text{consumption wastes treated}}{\text{consumption wastes produced}} \times 100\%$$

Land for Agriculture Use refers to land directly used for agriculture production, including land for cultivation, gardening, forests, herbage and other agriculture activities.

Area of Man-made Forests refer to the area of stable growing forests, planted manually or by airplanes, with a survival rate of 80% or higher of the designed number of trees per hectare, or with a canopy density of or above 0.20 after 3-5 years of manual planting or 5-7 years of airplane planting.

Total Area of Afforestation refers to the total area of land suitable for afforestation, including barren hills, idle land, sand dunes, "grain for green" land, on which acres of arbores or bushes are planted through manual planting, airplane planting, plant seedlings, etc. in accordance with the required density standards of the Technical Procedures of Afforestation, and with a survival rate of over 85% in line with the Implementing Rules of the Forest Law of the People's Republic of China (or a survival rate of 75% in areas with less that 400 mm of annual rainfall and without irrigation facilities). Included in the this category are trees planted alone the roadsides, riversides, or next to houses that occupy an area over 0.066 hectares, or where more than 4 lines of trees are planted. Total area of afforestation is further classified by ownership (state-owned, state-collective, collective or private), by approach of planting (manual, airplane), and by type of forests (timber, by-products, protection, fuel, special use, etc.).

By-product Forests refer to forests that mainly produce fruits, nuts, edible oil, beverages, indigents, raw materials and medicine materials. By-product forests are planted to harvest the fruits, leaves, bark or liquid of trees, and consume them as food or raw materials for the manufacturing industry, such as tea-oil trees, tung oil trees, walnut trees, camphor trees, tea bushes, mulberry trees, fruit trees, etc.

Protection Forests refer to forests, trees and bushes planted mainly for protection or preservation purpose, including water resource conservation forests, water and soil conservation forests, windbreak and dune-fixing forests, farmland and pasture protection forests, riverside protection forests, roadside protection forests, etc.

Fuel Forests refer to forests planted mainly for fuels.

Project on Preservation of Natural Forests is the Number One ecological project in China's forest industry that involves the largest investment. It consists of 3 components: 1) Complete halt of all cutting and logging activities in the natural forests at the upper stream of Yangtze River and the upper and middle streams of the Yellow River. 2) Significant reduction of timber production of key state forest zones in northeast provinces and in Inner Mongolia. 3) Better protection of natural forests in other regions through rehabilitation programmes.

Projects on Converting Cultivated Land to Forests and Grassland (Grain for Green Projects) aiming at preventing soil erosion in key regions, these projects are ecological construction projects in the development of forest industry that have the widest coverage and most sophisticated procedures, with strong policy implications and most active participation of the people.

Projects on Protection Forests in North China and Yangtze River Basin covering the widest areas in China with a rich variety of contents, these projects aim at solving the problem of sand and dust in northeastern China, northern China and northwestern China and the ecological issues in other areas. More specifically, they include phase IV of Project on North China protection forests, phase II of Project on protection forests at the middle and lower streams of Yangtze River and at the Huihe River and Taihu Lake valley, phase II of Project on coastal protection forests, phase II of Project on Pearl River protection forests, phase II Project on greenery of Taihang Mountain and phase II Projects on greenery of plains.

Projects on Preserving Wild Animals and Plants and on Construction of Natural Reserves aiming at gene preservation and protection of bio-diversity, nature and wetlands, these projects are forward-looking with strategic perspectives in line with international trends and practices.

Wetlands refer to marshland and peat bog, whether natural or man-made, permanent or temporary; water covered areas, whether stagnant or flowing, with fresh or semi-fresh or salty water that is less than 6 meters deep at low tide; as well as coral beach, weed beach, mud beach, mangrove, river outlet, rivers, fresh-water marshland, marshland forests, lakes, salty bog and salt lakes along the coastal areas.

Natural Reserves refer to certain areas of land, waters or sea demarked and approved by relevant governments at all levels to put under special protection and management in order to protect the natural environment and natural resources and to promote the sustainable development of the national economy. According to the objects be protected, the natural reserves are classified into classes of natural ecosystem, wild life and natural heritage. Scenic spots and cultural preservation zones are not included.

Landslides refer to the geological phenomenon of unstable rocks and earth on slopes sliding down along certain soft surface as a result of gravitational force. Role of surface water and underground water, and destruction of the stability of slopes by irrational construction work are usually main factors triggering the landslides. Several damages are often caused by landslides in open mining, in water conservancy projects, and in the construction of railways and highways.

Collapse refers to the geological phenomenon of large mass of rocks or earth suddenly collapsing from the mountain or cliff as a result of gravitational force. Usually caused by weathering of rocks, permeance of rain or earthquakes, collapse often destructs buildings and blocks river course or transport routes.

Mud-rock Flow refers to the sudden rush of flood torrents containing large amount of mud and rocks in mountainnous areas. It is found mostly in semi-arid hills or plateaus. High and precipitous topographic features, loose soil mass, heavy rains or melting water contribute to the mud-rock flow.

Land Subside refers to the geological phenomenon of surface rocks or earth subsiding into holes or pits as a result of natural or human factors. Land subside can be classified as karst subside and non-karst subside.

Environmental Emergencies refer to environmental emergencies that caused or likely to cause significant causalities, serious property damages and pose a major threat and damage to the economic, social or political stability of the country or a region, or have significant social impact that related to the public safety.

Environment Pollution and Destruction Accidents refer to sudden accidents, due to economic or social activities that are contrary to environment protection laws or due to unforeseen factors or natural disasters, that lead to environment pollution, destruction of protected wild animals, plants or nature reserves, damage to human health, economic and property losses, and other negative impacts on the society.

Funds Allocated to Afforestation refers to the total funds which have been transfered into the specific accounts of the agencies responsible for afforestation projects at reporting period.

Completed Investment for Afforestation during the Year reflecting the actual size of investment completed during January 1 and December 31 of the reference year, this indicator is important in estimating investment efficiency and in making annual analysis of the performance of the national economy.

2012

新疆统计年鉴

XINJIANG STATISTICAL YEARBOOK

第十二篇 农业

CHAPTER 12 Agriculture

简要说明
Brief Introduction

本篇资料的主要内容及来源

本篇资料反映新疆维吾尔自治区农业生产和农村经济基本情况，主要内容包括农村基层组织情况、乡村从业人员、国有农、林、牧、渔场情况、主要农业生产条件、耕地、农林牧渔业产值、主要农产品生产情况、特色农作物生产情况、乡镇企业情况等。

本篇资料除表12－4来自新疆维吾尔自治区国土资源厅，表12－10、12－11、12－12来自新疆维吾尔自治区水利厅，乡镇企业主要指标来自新疆维吾尔自治区乡镇企业局外，其余资料均由新疆维吾尔自治区统计局农村统计处提供。

Main Content and Source of Data

The data in this chapter show the basic conditions of agricultural production and rural economy in Xinjiang Uygur Autonomous Region, including mainly rural grassroots units rural population, rural employed labor force, basic conditions of township enterprises, statistic on forest products, cultivated land, gross output value farming, forest, animal husbandry and fishery, output of major farm products and condition on the township enterprises, ect.

Statistics on agriculture cover all agriculture production activities expect horse raising for military purpose and activities undertaken by agriculture research institutions. Included in agriculture statistics are production activities in crop cultivation, forestry, animal husbandry and fishery undertaken by rural economic units of various types and by rural households, production activities of farms specializing in crop cultivation, forestry, animal husbandry and fishery undertaken by rural economic units of various types and by rural households, production activities of farms specializing in crop cultivation, forestry, animal husbandry and fishery; production activities undertaken by government agencies, institutions, schools and military units, production activities in agriculture undertaken by collective farms run by townships and villages, and production activities in crop cultivation, forest, animal husbandry and fishery undertaken by manufacturing and mining enterprises.

Data on this chapter are provided by the Xinjiang Bureau of Water Resources except 12-10,12-11,12-12. the data on the township enterprises are from the Xinjiang Bureau of Township Enterprises. Others are provided by the Department of Rural statistics, Xinjiang Bureau of Statistics.

12-1 主要年份农村基层组织情况
Basic Conditions of Rural Grass-roots Unit in Main Years

指　　标	Item	2000	2010	2011
乡镇政府(个)	**Number of Township and Town Governments (unit)**	**794**	**801**	**806**
#镇政府	Number of Township Governments	124	183	188
村民委员会(个)	Number of Villager's Committees (unit)	9378	8796	8770
乡村户数(户)	Number of Rural Households (household)	2008794	2551479	2627329
乡村人口(人)	Rural Population (person)	9131922	10737179	10963329
乡村从业人员(人)	**Number of Rural Laborers (person)**	**3540789**	**4650560**	**5024249**
按性别分	Grouped by Gender			
男	Male	1950559	2558491	2755912
女	Female	1590230	2092069	2268337
按行业分	Grouped by Sector			
农林牧渔业	Agriculture, Forestry, Animal Husbandry & Fishery	3144461	3758972	4023995
工　业	Industry	84766	161325	193152
建筑业	Construction	49126	162427	184503
交通运输、仓储和邮政业	Transportation,Storage, Postal and Telecommunication Services		145132	155326
信息传输、计算机服务和软件业	Information Transmission, Computer Service and Software Sector		13915	18200
批发与零售业	Wholesale and Retail Trades	76727	157457	175192
住宿和餐饮业	Hotels and Catering Serives	109217	106191	116347
其　他	Others	76492	145141	157534

12-2 国有农林牧渔场基本情况
Basic Conditions of State Agriculture, Forestry, Animal Husbandry and Fishery

指　　标	Item	2010	2011
场数合计(个)	**Total (unit)**	**472**	**484**
农　场	Number of Farms	285	287
林　场	Number of Forest Farms	44	52
牧　场	Number of Ranch	130	133
渔　场	Number of Fishing Ground	13	12
场内户数(户)	**Number of Households on a Farm (household)**	**803022**	**831339**
#牧业户数	Number of Stock-breeding Household	68284	72561
场内人口(人)	**Farm Population (person)**	**2538956**	**2532728**
#牧业人口	Stock-breeding Population	252044	257247
场内实有从业人员(人)	**Persons Actually Engaged on a Farm (person)**	**1035763**	**1087919**
男	Male	578631	602929
女	Female	457132	484990
农　业	Employed Persons in Agriculture	768773	783833
工　业	Employed Persons in Industry	56237	66877
建筑业	Employed Persons in Construction	25444	29834
交通运输、仓储和邮政业	Transportation,Storage, Post and Telecommunications Services	30382	34944
信息传输、计算机服务和软件业	Information Transmission, Computer Service and Software Sector	910	1160
批发与零售业	Wholesale and Retail Trades	48775	53556
住宿和餐饮业	Hotels and Catering Serives	20767	25268
其　他	Others	84475	92447

12-3 各地、州、市、县(市)农村基层组织情况

(2011 年)

地　　区	Region	乡镇数(个) Number of Township and Town Govern-ments (unit)	#镇 town	村民委员会(个) Number of Villager's Committees (unit)	乡村户数(户) Number of Rural House-Holds (household)	#牧业户数 Stock-breeding households
总　计	**Total**	**806**	**188**	**8770**	**2627329**	**343251**
乌鲁木齐市	**Urumqi City**	**22**	**8**	**176**	**64710**	**7822**
#乌鲁木齐县	Urumqi County	6	1	41	10902	3567
克拉玛依市	**Karamay City**	**2**		**6**	**601**	**73**
吐鲁番地区	**Turpan Administrative Offices**	**24**	**7**	**170**	**104942**	**3265**
吐鲁番市	Turpan City	9	1	60	41979	2105
鄯善县	Shanshan [piqan]County	9	4	65	38834	352
托克逊县	Toksun County	6	2	45	24129	808
哈密地区	**Hami [Kumul]Administrative Offices**	**31**	**7**	**170**	**52493**	**14372**
哈密市	Hami [Kumul]City	15	4	91	31542	7448
巴里坤哈萨克自治县	Barkol KazakAutonomous County	10	2	47	18136	5889
伊吾县	Yiwu [Araturuk]County	6	1	32	2815	1035
昌吉回族自治州	**Changji Hui Autonomous Prefecture**	**67**	**34**	**545**	**181111**	**29799**
昌吉市	Changji City	10	7	87	33209	6038
阜康市	Fukang City	6	3	106	18573	2940
呼图壁县	Hutubi County	6	5	48	20613	3994
玛纳斯县	Manas County	11	6	87	26298	3436
奇台县	Qitai County	15	6	102	34469	4417
吉木萨尔县	Jimsar County	9	5	55	26538	2657
木垒哈萨克自治县	Mori Kazak Autonomous County	10	2	60	21411	6317
伊犁哈萨克自治州	**Ili Kazak Autonomous Prefecture**	**212**	**54**	**1936**	**558916**	**88636**
伊犁州直属县(市)	**Counties (Cities) Direct Under Ili Prefecture**	**99**	**22**	**656**	**329435**	**42685**
伊宁市	Yining [Gulja]City	9	1	46	32396	601
奎屯市	Kuytun City	1		4	409	374
伊宁县	Yining [Gulja]County	18	2	130	71887	4604
察布查尔锡伯自治县	Qapqal Xibe Autonomous County	13	2	64	32936	2127
霍城县	Huocheng [korgas]County	10	5	75	51850	2324
巩留县	Gongliu [Tokkuzlara]County	8	2	53	25567	4102
新源县	Xinyuan [kunes]County	11	6	77	38912	7145
昭苏县	Zhaosu [mongolkure]County	10	1	73	24875	6369
特克斯县	Tekes County	8	2	59	21461	6918
尼勒克县	Nilka County	11	1	75	29142	8121
塔城地区	**Tacheng [Tarbagatai] Administrative Offices**	**62**	**21**	**781**	**146245**	**17791**
塔城市	Tacheng [Qoqek] City	6	1	115	19262	2051
乌苏市	Usu City	14	7	134	31201	520
额敏县	Emin [Dorbiljin] County	12		139	19569	1277
沙湾县	Shawan County	12	9	227	45952	1686
托里县	Toli County	7	3	66	16057	8210
裕民县	Yumin [Qagantokay] County	5		45	7212	2007
和布克赛尔蒙古自治县	Hoboksar Mongol Autonomous County	6	1	55	6992	2040
阿勒泰地区	**Altay Administrative Offices**	**51**	**11**	**499**	**83236**	**28160**
阿勒泰市	Altay City	10	2	97	15901	3466
布尔津县	Burqin County	7	2	63	14510	5527
富蕴县	Fuyun [Koktokay] County	9	3	71	11250	4027
福海县	Fuhai [Burultokay] County	5		62	9167	3267
哈巴河县	Habahe [Kaba] County	7	1	113	16782	5422
青河县	Qinghe [Qinggil] County	7	2	52	8798	4975
吉木乃县	Jeminay County	6	1	41	6828	1476

Basic Conditions of Rural Grass-roots Units by Prefecture, Autonomous Prefecture, City and County

乡村人口数(人) Rural Population (person)	#牧业人口数 Population Engaged in Livestocks	乡村从业人员(人) Number of Rural Laborers (person)	#男 Male	农林牧渔业 Agriculture, Forestry, Animal Husbandry & Fishery	工业 Industry	建筑业 Construction	交通仓储和邮政业 Transport, Storage, Post and Telecommunication Services	信息传输、计算机服务和软件业 Information Transmission, Computer Servcie and Software Industries	批发与零售业 Retail and Wholesale Trades	住宿和餐饮业 Hotels and Catering Serives	其他 Others
10963329	**1392969**	**5024249**	**2755912**	**4023995**	**193152**	**184503**	**155326**	**18200**	**175192**	**116347**	**157534**
224518	**27538**	**139812**	**75272**	**85205**	**10978**	**2143**	**12052**	**322**	**9101**	**10461**	**9550**
40356	14132	24100	12571	18379	183	90	1181	79	763	951	2474
2056	**266**	**1298**	**670**	**1153**			**20**		**28**	**97**	
427632	**16666**	**248469**	**135101**	**201487**	**4992**	**6413**	**10437**	**1175**	**11249**	**8322**	**4394**
178105	11660	101485	56390	78601	2143	2524	5240	223	5806	5254	1694
160708	1308	96574	52167	82576	1596	2261	3377	821	3730	2063	150
88819	3698	50410	26544	40310	1253	1628	1820	131	1713	1005	2550
179320	**54644**	**101442**	**54314**	**75222**	**3758**	**3854**	**7946**	**443**	**3847**	**2742**	**3630**
111660	26381	64583	34430	50929	1768	1465	4251	235	2574	1435	1926
59560	24157	31984	17206	19968	1972	2357	3645	203	1161	1248	1430
8100	4106	4875	2678	4325	18	32	50	5	112	59	274
670771	**110853**	**382202**	**207522**	**308586**	**14969**	**7048**	**13577**	**629**	**11966**	**9497**	**15930**
119129	19144	64311	34821	49550	3268	1361	2441	112	2018	1582	3979
66920	12255	42044	23048	31103	2412	1404	1254	34	1448	1756	2633
81700	16299	44806	24323	38433	1156	150	1848	106	1333	803	977
91736	11287	51095	27311	39422	4290	483	2480	87	1610	1095	1628
147958	19566	81712	45143	65412	1543	1941	3219	197	3016	2652	3732
92558	9512	56051	30798	46720	1172	927	1762	47	1745	1259	2419
70770	22790	42183	22078	37946	1128	782	573	46	796	350	562
2311493	**394554**	**1144010**	**642253**	**891028**	**58203**	**50835**	**38027**	**5350**	**40927**	**27184**	**32456**
1475469	**213670**	**699532**	**399927**	**527358**	**36471**	**38087**	**28054**	**4284**	**27927**	**17740**	**19611**
144338	3205	71473	39332	38329	6344	7270	6860	205	6172	3050	3243
1449	1351	923	496	853	18	27	8		15	2	
328838	24258	167470	99269	126105	11445	9741	5110	1763	5497	3676	4133
123865	9245	63988	37935	53650	2520	1930	1146	158	1774	1110	1700
209508	11682	122110	65220	97069	3246	4233	5833	873	3653	3946	3257
119560	21337	42405	25018	36868	1326	851	1381	26	1755	163	35
202395	37480	82145	48131	60298	5710	4059	3314	500	3552	2090	2622
110931	32603	41820	26949	32003	1907	2524	1534	212	1668	687	1285
108881	36771	54442	28325	42070	2166	4892	608	387	1548	1713	1058
125704	35738	52756	29252	40113	1789	2560	2260	160	2293	1303	2278
531407	**68047**	**304549**	**164100**	**258996**	**13337**	**5961**	**6006**	**606**	**7904**	**5416**	**6323**
64820	6320	38517	19712	31477	1913	553	857	139	1249	548	1781
113428	1782	63506	34280	53323	3600	1021	1130	115	1744	1715	858
83761	5071	48280	28968	42887	1043	635	1022	91	1523	523	556
154933	6756	92563	48518	77713	4917	1803	1787	168	2314	1934	1927
58931	33253	35359	19094	30349	1357	1638	751	44	509	354	357
33915	8364	17859	9287	16002	274	210	348	5	391	307	322
21619	6501	8465	4241	7245	233	101	111	44	174	35	522
304617	**112837**	**139929**	**78226**	**104674**	**8395**	**6787**	**3967**	**460**	**5096**	**4028**	**6522**
63195	15120	30845	18495	23878	2317	919	794	111	926	498	1402
48697	18578	22712	12461	16610	489	930	447	107	1093	1149	1887
43324	16182	17834	9458	11309	1955	1178	752	86	577	389	1588
35976	16429	19138	10731	14710	693	1960	715	51	419	406	184
56267	19737	21996	11430	16968	1059	1023	467	37	1116	921	405
39253	22378	18351	9767	13164	1864	777	773	68	830	541	334
17905	4413	9053	5884	8035	18		19		135	124	722

12-3 续表

地 区	Region	乡镇数(个) Number of Township and Town Governments (unit)	#镇 town	村民委员会(个) Number of Villagers' Committees (unit)	乡村户数(户) Number of Rural Households (unit)	#牧业户数 Stock-Breeding households
博尔塔拉蒙古自治州	**Bortala Mongol Autonomous Prefecture**	**13**	**5**	**249**	**53296**	**5880**
博乐市	Bole [Bortala] City	5	3	129	19615	2137
精河县	Jinghe [Jing] County	4	1	55	20945	1812
温泉县	Wenquan [Araxang] County	4	1	65	12736	1931
巴音郭楞蒙古自治州	**Bayangol Mongol Autonomous Prefecture**	**73**	**12**	**409**	**122860**	**11749**
库尔勒市	Korla City	10	1	59	19251	423
轮台县	Luntai [Bugur] County	10	3	65	18487	929
尉犁县	Yuli [Lopnur] County	7		50	13228	1975
若羌县	Ruoqiang [Qarkilik] County	5		26	6132	202
且末县	Qiemo [Qarqan] County	11		53	8554	1239
焉耆回族自治县	Yanqi Hui Autonomous County	7	3	49	18741	577
和静县	Hejing County	11	4	55	20083	3929
和硕县	Hoxud County	6		26	10168	1969
博湖县	Bohu [Bagrax] County	6	1	26	8216	506
阿克苏地区	**Aksu Administrative Offices**	**76**	**22**	**1105**	**340901**	**28963**
阿克苏市	Aksu City	6	2	122	35883	6671
温宿县	Wensu [Onsu] County	9	4	104	36279	3711
库车县	Kuqa County	14	8	210	68713	4117
沙雅县	Xayar County	9	3	150	45407	4087
新和县	Xinhe [Toksu] County	7	1	110	33650	3923
拜城县	Baicheng [Bay] County	12	2	150	34983	3140
乌什县	Wushi [Uxturpan] County	8		107	41672	1525
阿瓦提县	Awat County	7	2	119	36318	1050
柯坪县	Kalpin County	4		33	7996	739
克孜勒苏柯尔克孜自治州	**Kizilsu Kirgiz Autonomous Prefecture**	**35**	**3**	**238**	**94304**	**28404**
阿图什市	Artux City	7		77	37795	8115
阿克陶县	Akto County	13	2	109	40011	8647
阿合奇县	Akqi County	6	1	18	7696	4618
乌恰县	Wuqia [Ulugqat] County	9		34	8802	7024
喀什地区	**Kashgar [Kaxgar] Administrative Offices**	**160**	**24**	**2350**	**633516**	**92048**
喀什市	Kashgar [Kaxgar] City	8	2	106	38575	2200
疏附县	Shufu County	12	1	165	62523	9450
疏勒县	Shule County	14	2	223	55800	2505
英吉沙县	Yengisar County	14	1	163	53309	5483
泽普县	Zepu [Poskam] County	11	1	138	26947	1602
莎车县	Shache [Yarkant] County	28	6	502	132923	28343
叶城县	Yecheng [Kagilik] County	19	2	309	70961	12193
麦盖提县	Makit County	10	1	129	31371	1288
岳普湖县	Yopurga County	9	2	87	27284	4130
伽师县	Jiashi [Payzawat] County	13	2	297	75744	7913
巴楚县	Bachu [Maralbexi] County	11	3	186	52228	11090
塔什库尔干塔吉克自治县	Taxkorgan Tajik Autonomous County	11	1	45	5851	5851
和田地区	**Hotan Administrative Offices**	**89**	**12**	**1387**	**412455**	**31878**
和田市	Hotan City	8	2	113	39740	3263
和田县	Hotan County	11	1	211	61371	2874
墨玉县	Moyu [Karakax] County	16	1	364	105907	8646
皮山县	Pishan [Guma] County	16	3	169	46957	2312
洛浦县	Lop County	9	1	207	54622	4800
策勒县	Qira County	8	1	123	39297	5375
于田县	Yutian [Keriya] County	15	2	170	58153	3102
民丰县	Minfeng [Niya] County	6	1	30	6408	1506
生产建设兵团	**Xinjiang Production and Construction Group**	**2**		**29**	**7224**	**362**

Continued

乡 村人口数(人) Rural Population (person)	#牧 业人口数 Population Engaged in Livestocks	乡村从业人员(人) Number of Rural Laborers (person)	#男 Male	农林牧渔业 Agriculture, Forestry, Animal Husbandry & Fishery	工 业 Industry	建筑业 Construction	交通仓储和邮政业 Transport, Storage, Post and Telecommunication Services	信息传输、计算机服务和软件业 Information Transmission, Computer Servcie and Software Industries	批发与零售业 Retail and Wholesale Trades	住宿和餐饮业 Hotels and Catering Serives	其他 Others
196927	**22634**	**93410**	**51087**	**65912**	**4113**	**3684**	**3476**	**225**	**3989**	**3251**	**8760**
87945	9967	42178	23780	26928	2416	1841	2063	130	2085	1727	4988
68783	6179	28494	15375	21624	787	813	610	17	1155	1089	2399
40199	6488	22738	11932	17360	910	1030	803	78	749	435	1373
488786	**44215**	**242146**	**139849**	**190707**	**19284**	**6150**	**6903**	**658**	**8674**	**4808**	**4962**
73935	1197	38855	22926	32332	80	449	1138	169	3154	1181	352
74305	3055	33552	18454	30213	339	407	300	72	764	516	941
48840	7884	21064	11498	19374	56	216	353	107	431	204	323
24439	715	18483	13350	8508	6665	1307	1343	6	473	174	7
39514	4983	13529	7844	11000	221	1062	621	55	320	169	81
73702	2857	36108	21111	26341	3236	1291	1634	28	1103	1124	1351
82996	14439	46230	25022	32950	8119	1023	660	80	1319	892	1187
37750	7143	16991	9777	14647	171	131	375	115	615	364	573
33305	1942	17334	9867	15342	397	264	479	26	495	184	147
1486958	**100161**	**756958**	**408221**	**662589**	**11388**	**20833**	**14789**	**2125**	**18495**	**11525**	**15214**
158719	21238	66999	37345	45080	1647	6095	3724	505	3417	3030	3501
148958	12905	84676	44969	78799	485	578	613	95	1441	673	1992
314208	13621	159203	83512	130841	3246	7147	5471	687	4521	2932	4358
194170	16272	99995	59556	92829	920	2465	508	110	1546	995	622
132840	8865	67250	34821	63648	325	595	642	185	1286	465	104
156358	12559	71737	40271	66413	827	506	1121	86	1471	629	684
171547	6702	107210	54677	95489	2042	1865	1217	253	2582	1215	2547
173827	5007	82437	43211	73942	1533	1056	1193	186	1858	1325	1344
36331	2992	17451	9859	15548	363	526	300	18	373	261	62
412311	**123054**	**158288**	**88417**	**124281**	**6911**	**6328**	**5487**	**128**	**6437**	**3706**	**5010**
179252	34003	69277	39558	46707	4833	3192	3746	108	4403	3071	3217
166164	37708	67449	37263	59011	1424	2393	1292		1056	610	1663
30570	22927	7686	4381	6866	75	170	100	20	300	25	130
36325	28416	13876	7215	11697	579	573	349		678		
2863363	**382089**	**1120996**	**618094**	**931061**	**22929**	**45109**	**26361**	**4955**	**39040**	**23844**	**27697**
179000	8200	67814	44079	30350	1709	7500	4100		5480	6915	11760
275000	38730	95000	55600	71194	2920	5306	2790	150	5540	2600	4500
283000	6730	61195	38345	55700	1780	1490	1300	120	333	252	220
233869	27415	111008	57706	103312	809	1666	1333	83	1888	1444	473
113021	5928	35190	17122	30057	426	1420	1154	50	957	76	1050
625292	123321	231356	120855	193876	4951	11725	5265	1146	8148	1591	4654
328662	51180	190083	106047	155714	5777	7681	4429	2686	7726	6070	
126613	4960	56055	29056	49015	1335	2080	375	84	829	295	2042
121594	22211	51472	25817	43892	633	1822	1283	295	1257	1569	721
349467	34817	131500	68380	119498	1495	2345	2918	191	2455	2495	103
201843	32595	80135	49695	69795	850	1402	1260	150	4215	483	1980
26002	26002	10188	5392	8658	244	672	154		212	54	194
1674473	**114352**	**624094**	**329636**	**477302**	**35187**	**32046**	**16066**	**2190**	**21063**	**10840**	**29400**
173154	13125	58126	33132	35683	5516	2789	2741	564	3653	2192	4988
257638	9810	94736	51593	71297	12526	3117	2187	99	2663	1540	1307
475276	29830	148298	78613	106235	8507	11993	4261	438	7170	3580	6114
189686	7114	73802	37042	58513	1116	1999	1666		1040	462	9006
213238	15103	98854	51828	82343	4164	5383	1766	612	2371	863	1352
131285	21040	53463	27559	46833	988	2189	729	135	1360	753	476
211608	12642	89628	45699	71246	2225	4228	2200	322	2537	1075	5795
22588	5688	7187	4170	5152	145	348	516	20	269	375	362
24721	**1943**	**11124**	**5476**	**9462**	**440**	**60**	**185**		**376**	**70**	**531**

12-4 各地、州、市、县(市)耕地面积

Area of Cultivated land by Prefecture, Autonomous Prefecture, City and County

单位：公顷 (2008 年) (hectare)

地 区	Region	年末耕地面积 Cultivated Land at Year-end	#水浇地 # Irrigable Land	#旱地 Arid Land
总 计	**Total**	**4124563.70**	**3812247.55**	**204501.81**
乌鲁木齐市	**Urumqi City**	**96950.66**	**78328.45**	**4035.06**
#乌鲁木齐县	Urumqi County	55412.44	48787.55	2206.13
克拉玛依市	**Karamay City**	**41926.31**	**41150.26**	**34.34**
石河子市	**Shihezi City**	**21886.21**	**21444.27**	
吐鲁番地区	**TurpanAdministrative Offices**	**48182.08**	**47560.93**	
吐鲁番市	Turpan City	17365.34	16883.43	
鄯善县	Shanshan [piqan]County	13707.94	13577.23	
托克逊县	Toksun County	17108.80	17100.27	
哈密地区	**Hami [Kumul]Administrative Offices**	**87087.69**	**83783.52**	**2617.09**
哈密市	Hami [Kumul]City	48101.16	47484.37	0.91
巴里坤哈萨克自治县	Barkol KazakAutonomous County	33793.67	31248.76	2494.56
伊吾县	Yiwu [Araturuk]County	5192.86	5050.39	121.62
昌吉回族自治州	**Changji Hui Autonomous Prefecture**	**629255.41**	**575551.19**	**48255.72**
昌吉市	Changji City	81216.70	79559.30	
阜康市	Fukang City	45008.84	43705.99	438.04
呼图壁县	Hutubi County	108240.93	107083.42	
玛纳斯县	Manas County	142651.23	140149.81	1646.14
奇台县	Qitai County	141463.80	125593.52	15405.67
吉木萨尔县	Jimsar County	59196.71	54743.95	4118.61
木垒哈萨克自治县	Mori Kazak Autonomous County	51477.20	24715.20	26647.26
伊犁哈萨克自治州	**Ili Kazak Autonomous Prefecture**	**1370619.63**	**1206934.23**	**147541.35**
伊犁州直属县(市)	**Counties (Cities) Direct Under Ili Prefecture**	**565724.94**	**462766.85**	**93380.19**
伊宁市	Yining [Gulja]City	13143.75	12397.65	157.73
奎屯市	Kuytun City	13830.81	13416.21	
伊宁县	Yining [Gulja]County	91060.36	87325.21	3074.98
察布查尔锡伯自治县	Qapqal Xibe Autonomous County	78010.92	67482.83	8691.95
霍城县	Huocheng [korgas]County	90103.57	86672.14	2627.72
巩留县	Gongliu [Tokkuzlara]County	42300.77	34067.58	5769.73
新源县	Xinyuan [kunes]County	69968.00	64130.84	3631.87
昭苏县	Zhaosu [mongolkure]County	89646.90	46655.06	42897.45
特克斯县	Tekes County	29857.44	23166.80	6399.81
尼勒克县	Nilka County	47802.42	27452.53	20128.95
塔城地区	**Tacheng [Tarbagatai] Administrative Offices**	**623638.56**	**574819.09**	**44346.27**
塔城市	Tacheng [Qoqek] City	116362.76	111668.61	4375.15
乌苏市	Usu City	90090.34	88675.34	
额敏县	Emin [Dorbiljin] County	147338.60	125362.73	21758.60
沙湾县	Shawan County	189499.02	186954.94	254.66
托里县	Toli County	24924.02	24791.30	70.37
裕民县	Yumin [Qagantokay] County	44247.45	26309.92	17887.49
和布克赛尔蒙古自治县	Hoboksar Mongol Autonomous County	11176.37	11056.25	
阿勒泰地区	**Altay Administrative Offices**	**181256.13**	**169348.29**	**9814.89**
阿勒泰市	Altay City	40931.04	40585.26	24.04
布尔津县	Burqin County	20584.37	16887.53	3469.38
富蕴县	Fuyun [Koktokay] County	14892.11	11654.88	2860.36
福海县	Fuhai [Burultokay] County	48402.20	47386.39	105.63
哈巴河县	Habahe [Kaba] County	31714.03	29103.31	2462.77
青河县	Qinghe [Qinggil] County	9825.27	8902.88	892.71
吉木乃县	Jeminay County	14907.11	14828.04	

12-4 续表 Continued

单位：公顷 (hectare)

地　区	Region	年末耕地面积 Cultivated Land at Year-end	#水浇地 # Irrigable Land	#旱地 Arid Land
博尔塔拉蒙古自治州	**Bortala Mongol Autonomous Prefecture**	**135223.32**	**133774.95**	**23.79**
博乐市	Bole [Bortala] City	65574.44	64586.74	
精河县	Jinghe [Jing] County	36147.89	35728.97	23.79
温泉县	Wenquan [Araxang] County	33500.99	33459.24	
巴音郭楞蒙古自治州	**Bayangol Mongol Autonomous Prefecture**	**322556.95**	**312340.71**	
库尔勒市	Korla City	63399.62	55645.29	
轮台县	Luntai [Bugur] County	32947.41	32914.37	
尉犁县	Yuli [Lopnur] County	68263.86	67857.08	
若羌县	Ruoqiang [Qarkilik] County	7132.15	7070.05	
且末县	Qiemo [Qarqan] County	15088.73	15059.49	
焉耆回族自治县	Yanqi Hui Autonomous County	36128.76	35999.77	
和静县	Hejing County	45540.81	45088.93	
和硕县	Hoxud County	36168.43	35167.26	
博湖县	Bohu [Bagrax] County	17887.18	17538.47	
阿克苏地区	**Aksu Administrative Offices**	**614943.17**	**585562.62**	**1674.65**
阿克苏市	Aksu City	168847.83	161536.10	394.20
温宿县	Wensu [Onsu] County	78711.69	67549.42	831.61
库车县	Kuqa County	65204.00	63182.13	6.41
沙雅县	Xayar County	56653.34	56359.21	
新和县	Xinhe [Toksu] County	37933.16	34910.01	
拜城县	Baicheng [Bay] County	72601.88	71028.51	
乌什县	Wushi [Uxturpan] County	46465.29	43538.75	
阿瓦提县	Awat County	79372.13	78323.46	442.43
柯坪县	Kalpin County	9153.85	9135.03	
克孜勒苏柯尔克孜自治州	**Kizilsu Kirgiz Autonomous Prefecture**	**52859.60**	**50149.91**	**252.68**
阿图什市	Artux City	15715.38	15293.50	223.54
阿克陶县	Akto County	29250.53	27006.77	11.71
阿合奇县	Akqi County	6164.41	6140.43	
乌恰县	Wuqia [Ulugqat] County	1729.28	1709.21	17.43
喀什地区	**Kashgar [Kaxgar] Administrative Offices**	**530457.07**	**516515.12**	**66.56**
喀什市	Kashgar [Kaxgar] City	7165.97	6271.21	
疏附县	Shufu County	51747.77	48541.95	
疏勒县	Shule County	49364.21	47766.47	
英吉沙县	Yengisar County	5718.17	5537.15	60.69
泽普县	Zepu [Poskam] County	37625.15	36203.14	
莎车县	Shache [Yarkant] County	98935.41	95867.11	
叶城县	Yecheng [Kagilik] County	53928.82	52503.91	4.67
麦盖提县	Makit County	50533.09	50138.07	
岳普湖县	Yopurga County	22224.51	22149.50	
伽师县	Jiashi [Payzawat] County	52288.15	51455.31	0.54
巴楚县	Bachu [Maralbexi] County	96950.39	96108.71	0.66
塔什库尔干塔吉克自治县	Taxkorgan Tajik Autonomous County	3975.44	3972.59	
和田地区	**Hotan Administrative Offices**	**172615.60**	**159151.39**	**0.57**
和田市	Hotan City	5996.45	5300.40	
和田县	Hotan County	30130.79	27035.19	
墨玉县	Moyu [Karakax] County	34013.32	28767.52	
皮山县	Pishan [Guma] County	27499.96	27193.71	
洛浦县	Lop County	26977.43	26784.99	
策勒县	Qira County	16489.41	16046.82	0.57
于田县	Yutian [Keriya] County	27445.86	24235.45	
民丰县	Minfeng [Niya] County	4062.38	3787.31	

12-5 农、林、牧、渔业总产值

Gross Output Value of Agriculture, Forestry, Animal Husbandry and Fishery

单位：万元 (10 000 yuan)

年份 Year	地区 Region	农林牧渔业总产值 Total	农业产值 Farming	林业产值 Forestry	牧业产值 Animal Husbandry	渔业产值 Fishery	农林牧渔服务业产值 Output Value of Services for Farming, Forestry, Animal Husbandary and Fishery
1978		191184	142460	3397	44990	337	
1980		220135	164187	5394	50148	406	
1985		565699	429519	25906	108598	1676	
1990		1446535	1104742	38152	294963	8678	
1995		4057332	3150055	56381	823351	27545	
1996		4309617	3340735	61940	875560	31382	
1997		4764743	3738602	64913	925923	35305	
1998		4992355	3873616	74394	1008783	35562	
1999		4611503	3409380	75565	1092279	34279	
2000		4872005	3605405	83451	1145142	38007	
2001		4968125	3488409	100847	1340236	38633	
2002		5250446	3627669	110897	1480382	31498	
2003		6883187	4827597	136936	1619823	32065	266766
2004		7506792	5150018	138204	1874660	42985	300925
2005		8310614	5958464	152851	1835206	43405	320688
2006		8835409	6385954	171994	1890700	46945	339816
2007		10634648	7669468	208623	2315097	70149	371311
2008		11766907	7841922	231830	3182256	99097	411802
2009		12976109	8986167	266451	3183730	111403	428358
2010		18461828	13768852	352701	3757905	126663	455707
2011		19553884	14378900	380808	4150000	141653	502523
乌鲁木齐市	Urumqi City	302681	136767	5300	152197	7064	1353
克拉玛依市	Karamay City	95011	33712	14885	31650	668	14096
吐鲁番地区	Turpan Administrative Offices	448620	355353	4038	81437	448	7344
哈密地区	Hami [Kumul] Administrative Offices	363691	188891	11570	156795	2029	4406
昌吉回族自治州	Changji Hui Autonomous Prefecture	2409379	1079122	22107	1266695	16813	24642
伊犁哈萨克自治州	Ili Kazak Autonomous Prefecture	3706518	2160534	76998	1396879	18649	53458
伊犁州直属县(市)	Counties (Cities) Direct Under Ili Prefecture	1577240	796691	52413	690441	10385	27310
塔城地区	Tacheng [Tarbagatai] Administrative Offices	1619187	1115512	12122	472682	2606	16265
阿勒泰地区	Altay Administrative Offices	510091	248331	12463	233756	5658	9883
博尔塔拉蒙古自治州	Bortala Mongol Autonomous Prefecture	591080	457991	6163	98633	2705	25588
巴音郭楞蒙古自治州	Bayangol Mongol Autonomous Prefecture	1891953	1442903	68307	315674	11264	53805
阿克苏地区	Aksu Administrative Offices	1851959	1460786	31230	282147	9733	68063
克孜勒苏柯尔克孜自治州	Kizilsu Kirgiz Autonomous Prefecture	180891	102015	3689	63367	211	11609
喀什地区	Kashgar [Kaxgar] Administrative Offices	3077305	2075708	76456	846015	11241	67885
和田地区	Hotan Administrative Offices	839222	570630	30714	221713	2672	13493
生产建设兵团	Xinjiang Production and Construction Group	6758492	5136154	63397	1077165	39130	442646

注：本表按当年价格计算。

Note：The number in this form is caculated by current price.

12-6 主要年份农、林、牧、渔业总产值指数

Indices of Gross Output Value of Agriculture, Forestry, Animal Husbandry and Fishery in Main Years

年 份 Year	农林牧渔业总产值 Total	#农业产值 Farming	#林业产值 Forestry	#牧业产值 Animal Husbandry	#渔业产值 Fishery
(上年=100) (preceding year=100)					
1978	113.0	118.6	108.8	105.4	106.7
1980	108.9	108.4	151.2	104.4	112.7
1985	110.9	111.5	131.3	104.6	135.1
1990	115.1	119.2	95.2	102.0	111.3
1995	107.1	107.0	88.5	109.0	127.0
1996	104.2	103.3	101.0	107.7	112.3
1997	109.5	109.6	100.5	110.2	108.6
1998	110.8	111.5	105.5	109.0	102.0
1999	104.8	103.9	100.9	108.1	106.3
2000	105.3	104.2	110.3	108.0	116.4
2001	104.5	103.9	116.1	105.8	104.2
2002	105.2	103.9	111.5	108.9	102.1
2003	106.3	105.2	120.7	108.7	101.7
2004	106.4	104.5	100.7	112.0	108.2
2005	107.4	107.0	105.8	109.0	105.3
2006	107.5	107.7	106.5	107.8	105.3
2007	108.2	108.9	108.6	106.0	115.2
2008	106.7	106.1	107.5	109.4	107.5
2009	105.1	107.8	106.5	98.5	106.9
2010	104.9	104.7	106.4	105.1	105.5
2011	106.9	108.3	105.9	102.0	107.1
(1978 年=100) (1978=100)					
1978	100.0	100.0	100.0	100.0	100.0
1980	115.9	115.5	158.8	111.1	120.5
1985	188.4	194.3	245.4	160.0	140.9
1990	303.7	322.6	244.4	243.7	442.4
1995	420.7	453.3	247.4	325.5	863.7
1996	438.4	468.1	249.8	350.6	970.0
1997	480.2	512.8	251.1	386.4	1053.2
1998	531.8	571.7	265.1	421.1	1073.9
1999	557.1	593.8	267.5	455.3	1141.6
2000	586.3	618.8	295.0	491.9	1328.4
2001	612.9	642.8	342.5	520.6	1384.1
2002	644.8	668.1	381.9	566.9	1413.2
2003	685.4	702.6	460.9	616.0	1437.2
2004	729.3	734.2	464.1	689.9	1555.1
2005	783.3	785.6	491.0	752.0	1637.5
2006	842.0	846.1	522.9	810.7	1724.3
2007	911.0	921.4	567.9	859.3	1986.4
2008	972.0	977.6	610.5	940.1	2135.4
2009	1021.6	1053.9	650.2	926.0	2282.7
2010	1071.7	1103.4	691.8	973.2	2408.2
2011	1145.6	1195.0	732.6	992.7	2579.2

12-7 各地、州、市、县(市)农林牧渔业总产值
Gross Output Value of Agriculture, Forestry, Animal Husbandry and Fishery by Prefecture, Autonomous Prefecture, City and County

单位：万元 (2011 年) (10 000 yuan)

地 区	Region	农林牧渔业总产值 Total	农业产值 Farming	林业产值 Forestry	牧业产值 Animal Husbandry	渔业产值 Fishery	农林牧渔服务业产值 Output Value of Services for Farming, Forestry, Animal Husbandary and Fishery
总 计	**Total**	**19553884**	**14378900**	**380808**	**4150000**	**141653**	**502523**
乌鲁木齐市	**Urumqi City**	**302681**	**136767**	**5300**	**152197**	**7064**	**1353**
＃乌鲁木齐县	Urumqi County	76474	30117	1361	43313	383	1300
克拉玛依市	**Karamay City**	**95011**	**33712**	**14885**	**31650**	**668**	**14096**
吐鲁番地区	**TurpanAdministrative Offices**	**448620**	**355353**	**4038**	**81437**	**448**	**7344**
吐鲁番市	Turpan City	174127	139000	1785	29050	321	3971
鄯善县	Shanshan [piqan]County	169041	138341	1388	27797	92	1423
托克逊县	Toksun County	105452	78012	865	24590	35	1950
哈密地区	**Hami [Kumul]Administrative Offices**	**363691**	**188891**	**11570**	**156795**	**2029**	**4406**
哈密市	Hami [Kumul]City	183822	124515	6283	49020	1788	2216
巴里坤哈萨克自治县	Barkol KazakAutonomous County	126415	43667	458	81077	223	990
伊吾县	Yiwu [Araturuk]County	53454	20709	4829	26698	18	1200
昌吉回族自治州	**Changji Hui Autonomous Prefecture**	**2409379**	**1079122**	**22107**	**1266695**	**16813**	**24642**
昌吉市	Changji City	365170	164780	3120	184152	9778	3340
阜康市	Fukang City	275157	123117	1873	148585	353	1229
呼图壁县	Hutubi County	426123	167863	3329	241178	3196	10557
玛纳斯县	Manas County	460834	255505	1885	193367	2258	7819
奇台县	Qitai County	508214	216992	5221	285737		264
吉木萨尔县	Jimsar County	201251	88667	5318	105027	1228	1011
木垒哈萨克自治县	Mori Kazak Autonomous County	172630	62198	1361	108649		422
伊犁哈萨克自治州	**Ili Kazak Autonomous Prefecture**	**3706518**	**2160534**	**76998**	**1396879**	**18649**	**53458**
伊犁州直属县(市)	**Counties (Cities) Direct Under Ili Prefecture**	**1577240**	**796691**	**52413**	**690441**	**10385**	**27310**
伊宁市	Yining [Gulja]City	99645	62159	1290	31723	1961	2512
奎屯市	Kuytun City	12974	6506	174	5248		1046
伊宁县	Yining [Gulja]County	320807	174907	5604	128870	6226	5200
察布查尔锡伯自治县	Qapqal Xibe Autonomous County	164709	111491	3551	46169	490	3008
霍城县	Huocheng [korgas]County	195792	101955	5026	84348	210	4253
巩留县	Gongliu [Tokkuzlara]County	150495	76164	2599	70687	743	302
新源县	Xinyuan [kunes]County	261715	119188	29022	109349	618	3538
昭苏县	Zhaosu [mongolkure]County	116261	50848	436	63428		1549
特克斯县	Tekes County	119096	49274	2032	66765	75	950
尼勒克县	Nilka County	135746	44199	2679	83854	62	4952

注：本表按当年价格计算。
Note: The number in this form is caculated by current price.

12-7 续表 1 Continued

单位：万元 (10 000 yuan)

地　区	Region	农林牧渔业总产值 Total	农业产值 Farming	林业产值 Forestry	牧业产值 Animal Husbandry	渔业产值 Fishery	农林牧渔服务业产值 Output Value of Services for Farming, Forestry, Animal Husbandary and Fishery
塔城地区	**Tacheng [Tarbagatai] Administrative Offices**	**1619187**	**1115512**	**12122**	**472682**	**2606**	**16265**
塔城市	Tacheng [Qoqek] City	221153	160199	844	58099	545	1466
乌苏市	Usu City	406939	303636	5797	92548	501	4457
额敏县	Emin [Dorbiljin] County	236362	155007	459	79798	168	930
沙湾县	Shawan County	543798	405331	2252	129196	1307	5712
托里县	Toli County	71637	26056	1088	42751		1742
裕民县	Yumin [Qagantokay] County	75107	43678	1202	29444	52	731
和布克赛尔蒙古自治县	Hoboksar Mongol Autonomous County	64191	21605	480	40846	33	1227
阿勒泰地区	**Altay Administrative Offices**	**510091**	**248331**	**12463**	**233756**	**5658**	**9883**
阿勒泰市	Altay City	89942	45560	870	41500	542	1470
布尔津县	Burqin County	49623	21424	1792	24698	240	1469
富蕴县	Fuyun [Koktokay] County	95310	34326	1710	57827	142	1305
福海县	Fuhai [Burultokay] County	110023	65655	1992	35199	4251	2926
哈巴河县	Habahe [Kaba] County	90923	49195	3731	36694	365	938
青河县	Qinghe [Qinggil] County	46603	19805	2021	23867	78	832
吉木乃县	Jeminay County	27667	12366	347	13971	40	943
博尔塔拉蒙古自治州	**Bortala Mongol Autonomous Prefecture**	**591080**	**457991**	**6163**	**98633**	**2705**	**25588**
博乐市	Bole [Bortala] City	239332	182638	2028	45060	242	9364
精河县	Jinghe [Jing] County	264746	223789	3258	25190	1201	11308
温泉县	Wenquan [Araxang] County	87002	51564	877	28383	1262	4916
巴音郭楞蒙古自治州	**Bayangol Mongol Autonomous Prefecture**	**1891953**	**1442903**	**68307**	**315674**	**11264**	**53805**
库尔勒市	Korla City	426110	350329	15829	49937	1061	8954
轮台县	Luntai [Bugur] County	236735	200089	1073	32489	266	2818
尉犁县	Yuli [Lopnur] County	202743	168831	3366	15627	9	14910
若羌县	Ruoqiang [Qarkilik] County	173536	160450	1324	9982		1780
且末县	Qiemo [Qarqan] County	121011	87352	3456	23273	393	6537
焉耆回族自治县	Yanqi Hui Autonomous County	188214	111359	19533	49812	614	6896
和静县	Hejing County	222743	116779	4954	95762	304	4944
和硕县	Hoxud County	211326	171134	13205	21787	72	5128
博湖县	Bohu [Bagrax] County	109535	76580	5567	17005	8545	1838
阿克苏地区	**Aksu Administrative Offices**	**1851959**	**1460786**	**31230**	**282147**	**9733**	**68063**
阿克苏市	Aksu City	284306	222774	2253	44828	2745	11706
温宿县	Wensu [Onsu] County	297157	219483	8107	48426	2130	19011
库车县	Kuqa County	319208	238119	7901	69367	476	3345

12-7 续表 2 Continued

单位：万元 (10 000 yuan)

地 区	Region	农林牧渔业总产值 Total	农业产值 Farming	林业产值 Forestry	牧业产值 Animal Husbandry	渔业产值 Fishery	农林牧渔服务业产值 Output Value of Services for Farming, Forestry, Animal Husbandary and Fishery
沙雅县	Xayar County	224255	194458	4764	20282	385	4366
新和县	Xinhe [Toksu] County	193416	160126	2421	18201	122	12546
拜城县	Baicheng [Bay] County	144550	100385	2834	35417	3688	2226
乌什县	Wushi [Uxturpan] County	110251	84724	1240	20653	94	3540
阿瓦提县	Awat County	244611	216199	1220	17294	93	9805
柯坪县	Kalpin County	34205	24518	490	7679		1518
克孜勒苏柯尔克孜自治州	**Kizilsu Kirgiz Autonomous Prefecture**	**180891**	**102015**	**3689**	**63367**	**211**	**11609**
阿图什市	Artux City	76242	43279	1170	26750	183	4860
阿克陶县	Akto County	78109	51584	1738	19999	28	4760
阿合奇县	Akqi County	13178	3389	590	8277		922
乌恰县	Wuqia [Ulugqat] County	13362	3763	191	8341		1067
喀什地区	**Kashgar [Kaxgar] Administrative Offices**	**3077305**	**2075708**	**76456**	**846015**	**11241**	**67885**
喀什市	Kashgar [Kaxgar] City	129819	64638	4929	55298	854	4100
疏附县	Shufu County	309415	202115	7688	92652	960	6000
疏勒县	Shule County	281142	182258	9684	88268	540	392
英吉沙县	Yengisar County	158542	102518	4609	46555	60	4800
泽普县	Zepu [Poskam] County	204247	138420	1509	57754	3480	3084
莎车县	Shache [Yarkant] County	575921	411446	27276	115930	3185	18084
叶城县	Yecheng [Kagilik] County	451850	317893	7132	121626	942	4257
麦盖提县	Makit County	201845	145649	2437	46575	220	6964
岳普湖县	Yopurga County	116044	71061	4237	38435	144	2167
伽师县	Jiashi [Payzawat] County	326451	217864	6865	92666	456	8600
巴楚县	Bachu [Maralbexi] County	306328	219741	90	77597	400	8500
塔什库尔干塔吉克自治县	Taxkorgan Tajik Autonomous County	15701	2105		12659		937
和田地区	**Hotan Administrative Offices**	**839222**	**570630**	**30714**	**221713**	**2672**	**13493**
和田市	Hotan City	76432	45724	2787	25616	697	1608
和田县	Hotan County	143273	109804	3287	27755	1046	1381
墨玉县	Moyu [Karakax] County	188855	127739	4806	53367	410	2533
皮山县	Pishan [Guma] County	109384	78677	4396	23268	27	3016
洛浦县	Lop County	94632	65914	3690	23246	252	1530
策勒县	Qira County	83367	59781	2937	19677	34	938
于田县	Yutian [Keriya] County	119617	75339	4480	37573	153	2072
民丰县	Minfeng [Niya] County	23662	7652	4331	11211	53	415
生产建设兵团	**Xinjiang Production and ConstructionGroup**	**6758492**	**5136154**	**63397**	**1077165**	**39130**	**442646**

12-8 各地、州、市、县(市)农业机械拥有量
Agricultural Machinery by Prefecture, Autonomous Prefecture, City and County

(2011 年)

地 区	Region	农业机械总动力(千瓦) Total Power of Agricultural Machinery (kw)	农用大中型拖拉机 Large and Medium Agricultural Tractors		小型拖拉机 Small Tractors	
			数量(台) Number (unit)	动力(千瓦) Capacity (kw)	数量(台) Number (unit)	动力(千瓦) Capacity (kw)
总 计	**Total**	**17959388**	**295245**	**8737483**	**349061**	**4346267**
乌鲁木齐市	**Urumqi City**	**285453**	**2851**	**84115**	**5546**	**66690**
#乌鲁木齐县	Urumqi County	138673	2069	48696	3614	45295
克拉玛依市	**Karamay City**	**28708**	**444**	**14041**	**96**	**1212**
吐鲁番地区	**TurpanAdministrative Offices**	**511705**	**2198**	**74542**	**10085**	**117047**
吐鲁番市	Turpan City	210974	791	28574	4188	51240
鄯善县	Shanshan [piqan]County	201373	605	18333	3621	40577
托克逊县	Toksun County	99358	802	27635	2276	25230
哈密地区	**Hami [Kumul]Administrative Offices**	**323122**	**2868**	**91036**	**10981**	**128829**
哈密市	Hami [Kumul]City	168317	1625	48470	4891	58905
巴里坤哈萨克自治县	Barkol KazakAutonomous County	125984	962	31472	5177	58843
伊吾县	Yiwu [Araturuk]County	28821	281	11094	913	11081
昌吉回族自治州	**Changji Hui Autonomous Prefecture**	**1853424**	**17800**	**677186**	**51236**	**631697**
昌吉市	Changji City	310711	2197	123788	9455	122893
阜康市	Fukang City	310899	4196	144354	6515	89367
呼图壁县	Hutubi County	309575	3911	122572	8891	117630
玛纳斯县	Manas County	437513	2981	120194	11279	124069
奇台县	Qitai County	189979	1279	50900	6082	72895
吉木萨尔县	Jimsar County	143424	1617	54804	5287	63603
木垒哈萨克自治县	Mori Kazak Autonomous County	151323	1619	60574	3727	41240
伊犁哈萨克自治州	**Ili Kazak Autonomous Prefecture**	**3806847**	**65055**	**1964068**	**75608**	**969323**
伊犁州直属县(市)	**Counties (Cities) Direct Under Ili Prefecture**	**1417753**	**23797**	**767678**	**26781**	**329718**
伊宁市	Yining [Gulja]City	70520	1010	35363	1196	15309
奎屯市	Kuytun City	10284	282	9940	47	344
伊宁县	Yining [Gulja]County	256473	3997	150544	5246	65019
察布查尔锡伯自治县	Qapqal Xibe Autonomous County	170296	2897	87379	2343	28753
霍城县	Huocheng [korgas]County	196293	4485	108308	4662	49464
巩留县	Gongliu [Tokkuzlara]County	166960	2127	73014	4858	61352
新源县	Xinyuan [kunes]County	219266	4378	138709	1755	21928
昭苏县	Zhaosu [mongolkure]County	124809	1444	62765	2891	38518
特克斯县	Tekes County	88498	1676	46393	1391	17935
尼勒克县	Nilka County	114354	1501	55263	2392	31096
塔城地区	**Tacheng [Tarbagatai] Administrative Offices**	**1782119**	**30655**	**895079**	**33016**	**429544**
塔城市	Tacheng [Qoqek] City	253860	4071	131926	4616	58623
乌苏市	Usu City	244509	2721	77391	4014	64676
额敏县	Emin [Dorbiljin] County	516227	9605	275329	10747	135345
沙湾县	Shawan County	528510	10952	308789	9961	123093
托里县	Toli County	79636	1060	29610	988	12481
裕民县	Yumin [Qagantokay] County	122239	1595	52761	2055	27365
和布克赛尔蒙古自治县	Hoboksar Mongol Autonomous County	37138	651	19272	635	7961
阿勒泰地区	**Altay Administrative Offices**	**606975**	**10603**	**301311**	**15811**	**210061**
阿勒泰市	Altay City	148007	2190	82229	4050	51840
布尔津县	Burqin County	74938	1221	29207	2685	34850
富蕴县	Fuyun [Koktokay] County	88611	1657	38033	2274	33642
福海县	Fuhai [Burultokay] County	108891	2881	73481	1684	21041
哈巴河县	Habahe [Kaba] County	115284	1288	39897	3486	45858
青河县	Qinghe [Qinggil] County	49051	900	25141	1170	17199
吉木乃县	Jeminay County	22193	466	13323	462	5631

12-8 续表 1 Continued

地　　区	Region	农业机械总动力(千瓦) Total Power of Agricultural Machinery (kw)	农用大中型拖拉机 Large and Medium Agricultural Tractors		小型拖拉机 Small Tractors	
			数量(台) Number (unit)	动力(千瓦) Capacity (kw)	数量(台) Number (unit)	动力(千瓦) Capacity (kw)
博尔塔拉蒙古自治州	**Bortala Mongol Autonomous Prefecture**	**521726**	**8306**	**234203**	**14169**	**174677**
博乐市	Bole [Bortala] City	229170	3694	104700	5225	64431
精河县	Jinghe [Jing] County	181009	3169	86044	6560	81401
温泉县	Wenquan [Araxang] County	111547	1443	43459	2384	28845
巴音郭楞蒙古自治州	**Bayangol Mongol Autonomous Prefecture**	**1442595**	**26499**	**766250**	**28639**	**366993**
库尔勒市	Korla City	376879	6157	185894	10334	136822
轮台县	Luntai [Bugur] County	123548	2087	55457	3864	47301
尉犁县	Yuli [Lopnur] County	212346	5779	169599	1335	18354
若羌县	Ruoqiang [Qarkilik] County	46085	1145	25675	282	3599
且末县	Qiemo [Qarqan] County	80872	1862	46218	2154	29762
焉耆回族自治县	Yanqi Hui Autonomous County	192013	2517	82705	3686	45798
和静县	Hejing County	167068	3474	89450	2165	28664
和硕县	Hoxud County	115066	1517	53866	1317	16455
博湖县	Bohu [Bagrax] County	128718	1961	57386	3502	40238
阿克苏地区	**Aksu Administrative Offices**	**2056377**	**37370**	**1011777**	**64592**	**779301**
阿克苏市	Aksu City	210085	3825	98269	7360	91158
温宿县	Wensu [Onsu] County	352010	7326	214373	7347	84564
库车县	Kuqa County	263661	4364	115740	8559	111267
沙雅县	Xayar County	236260	5105	148866	6735	75722
新和县	Xinhe [Toksu] County	152563	2461	48829	5076	60912
拜城县	Baicheng [Bay] County	274442	3982	96331	10472	131206
乌什县	Wushi [Uxturpan] County	182985	4261	93144	5780	84966
阿瓦提县	Awat County	345428	5313	174741	12654	131465
柯坪县	Kalpin County	38943	733	21484	609	8041
克孜勒苏柯尔克孜自治州	**Kizilsu Kirgiz Autonomous Prefecture**	**293122**	**7550**	**176152**	**6156**	**78354**
阿图什市	Artux City	97419	1885	50558	1708	21517
阿克陶县	Akto County	158311	4160	94065	3986	50628
阿合奇县	Akqi County	17304	698	15789	145	1986
乌恰县	Wuqia [Ulugqat] County	20088	807	15740	317	4223
喀什地区	**Kashgar [Kaxgar] Administrative Offices**	**2282442**	**70213**	**1447824**	**37061**	**454917**
喀什市	Kashgar [Kaxgar] City	64745	2080	36422	1198	14054
疏附县	Shufu County	279194	6821	138879	5929	72273
疏勒县	Shule County	251665	8071	170869	4902	59341
英吉沙县	Yengisar County	129354	3138	68068	3262	40032
泽普县	Zepu [Poskam] County	154184	5522	110350	2421	29459
莎车县	Shache [Yarkant] County	428918	11707	273314	8526	104562
叶城县	Yecheng [Kagilik] County	180761	7442	135177	1146	16846
麦盖提县	Makit County	188441	5707	130195	2170	26713
岳普湖县	Yopurga County	102721	3699	78517	1507	17868
伽师县	Jiashi [Payzawat] County	200857	6354	67804	3685	45220
巴楚县	Bachu [Maralbexi] County	281139	8882	224654	2146	26476
塔什库尔干塔吉克自治县	Taxkorgan Tajik Autonomous County	20463	790	13575	169	2073
和田地区	**Hotan Administrative Offices**	**591309**	**14074**	**401217**	**9360**	**121436**
和田市	Hotan City	61734	1622	47742	582	8695
和田县	Hotan County	75778	1494	30700	1416	18691
墨玉县	Moyu [Karakax] County	136576	3101	72701	1815	21820
皮山县	Pishan [Guma] County	61063	1629	35936	736	9745
洛浦县	Lop County	84535	2259	54258	1106	14245
策勒县	Qira County	61121	1036	31284	1705	22423
于田县	Yutian [Keriya] County	86863	2374	53094	1547	19400
民丰县	Minfeng [Niya] County	23639	559	75502	453	6417
生产建设兵团	**Xinjiang Production and Construction Group**	**3962558**	**40017**	**1795072**	**35532**	**455791**

12-8 续表 2 Continued

地　　区	Region	大中型拖拉机配套农具(部) Number of Large and Medium Tractor Towing Farm Machinery (unit)	小型拖拉机配套农具(部) Number of Small Tractor Towing Farm Machinery (unit)	农用排灌柴油机 Diesel Engines 数　量(台) Number (unit)	动　力(千瓦) Capacity (kw)
总　计	**Total**	**519425**	**634110**	**14037**	**208061**
乌鲁木齐市	**Urumqi City**	**3559**	**4618**	**5**	**33**
＃乌鲁木齐县	Urumqi County	2080	3273	5	33
克拉玛依市	**Karamay City**	**852**	**156**	**1**	**15**
吐鲁番地区	**TurpanAdministrative Offices**	**4440**	**17675**	**13**	**158**
吐鲁番市	Turpan City	1749	5874		
鄯善县	Shanshan [piqan]County	842	4408		
托克逊县	Toksun County	1849	7393	13	158
哈密地区	**Hami [Kumul]Administrative Offices**	**7824**	**19724**		
哈密市	Hami [Kumul]City	4808	6789		
巴里坤哈萨克自治县	Barkol KazakAutonomous County	2477	11101		
伊吾县	Yiwu [Araturuk]County	539	1834		
昌吉回族自治州	**Changji Hui Autonomous Prefecture**	**36045**	**63943**	**138**	**2607**
昌吉市	Changji City	5786	11905		
阜康市	Fukang City	9865	15096		
呼图壁县	Hutubi County	5917	16742	15	183
玛纳斯县	Manas County	6916	7782		
奇台县	Qitai County	2441	4898		
吉木萨尔县	Jimsar County	1646	3488	123	2424
木垒哈萨克自治县	Mori Kazak Autonomous County	3474	4032		
伊犁哈萨克自治州	**Ili Kazak Autonomous Prefecture**	**137815**	**128940**	**5337**	**70169**
伊犁州直属县(市)	**Counties (Cities) Direct Under Ili Prefecture**	**44347**	**23579**	**786**	**8071**
伊宁市	Yining [Gulja]City	2607	841	25	420
奎屯市	Kuytun City	648	62		
伊宁县	Yining [Gulja]County	5566	5022	223	2156
察布查尔锡伯自治县	Qapqal Xibe Autonomous County	6317	3542	45	793
霍城县	Huocheng [korgas]County	6728	5594	219	1642
巩留县	Gongliu [Tokkuzlara]County	3049	2478	34	746
新源县	Xinyuan [kunes]County	8199	2802	70	951
昭苏县	Zhaosu [mongolkure]County	2654	249	72	
特克斯县	Tekes County	4602	1624	8	382
尼勒克县	Nilka County	3977	1365	90	981
塔城地区	**Tacheng [Tarbagatai] Administrative Offices**	**80023**	**94324**	**2633**	**38354**
塔城市	Tacheng [Qoqek] City	9766	6835	35	741
乌苏市	Usu City	10536	15329	1374	22589
额敏县	Emin [Dorbiljin] County	27640	36490	1050	12084
沙湾县	Shawan County	26304	30711	81	937
托里县	Toli County	1455	989	75	1835
裕民县	Yumin [Qagantokay] County	3911	3821		
和布克赛尔蒙古自治县	Hoboksar Mongol Autonomous County	411	149	18	168
阿勒泰地区	**Altay Administrative Offices**	**13445**	**11037**	**1918**	**23744**
阿勒泰市	Altay City	3510	1850	51	601
布尔津县	Burqin County	921	1900	173	2249
富蕴县	Fuyun [Koktokay] County	3614	1037	634	8437
福海县	Fuhai [Burultokay] County	3341	2612	333	3986
哈巴河县	Habahe [Kaba] County	698	1802	492	4741
青河县	Qinghe [Qinggil] County	836	1032	217	3417
吉木乃县	Jeminay County	525	804	18	313

12-8 续表 3 Continued

地　区	Region	大中型拖拉机配套农具(部) Number of Large and Medium Tractor Towing Farm Machinery (unit)	小型拖拉机配套农具(部) Number of Small Tractor Towing Farm Machinery (unit)	农用排灌柴油机 Diesel Engines 数量(台) Number (unit)	农用排灌柴油机 Diesel Engines 动力(千瓦) Capacity (kw)
博尔塔拉蒙古自治州	**Bortala Mongol Autonomous Prefecture**	**12036**	**11389**	**8**	**187**
博乐市	Bole [Bortala] City	5784	3452	3	33
精河县	Jinghe [Jing] County	4238	6941		
温泉县	Wenquan [Araxang] County	2014	996	5	154
巴音郭楞蒙古自治州	**Bayangol Mongol Autonomous Prefecture**	**45266**	**69614**	**2291**	**28628**
库尔勒市	Korla City	12131	28056	1268	13314
轮台县	Luntai [Bugur] County	3985	8268		
尉犁县	Yuli [Lopnur] County	4771	7123	722	9025
若羌县	Ruoqiang [Qarkilik] County	1924	1839	191	5137
且末县	Qiemo [Qarqan] County	2185	3675		
焉耆回族自治县	Yanqi Hui Autonomous County	7147	8477	4	92
和静县	Hejing County	7605	4775	46	700
和硕县	Hoxud County	3034	2897	60	360
博湖县	Bohu [Bagrax] County	2484	4504		
阿克苏地区	**Aksu Administrative Offices**	**78912**	**147888**	**857**	**9933**
阿克苏市	Aksu City	15790	18110	38	558
温宿县	Wensu [Onsu] County	7246	11430	51	630
库车县	Kuqa County	10910	19554	50	670
沙雅县	Xayar County	12606	15555	550	5686
新和县	Xinhe [Toksu] County	3671	11240	62	683
拜城县	Baicheng [Bay] County	9484	26968	2	26
乌什县	Wushi [Uxturpan] County	6337	12917	19	240
阿瓦提县	Awat County	11874	30346	46	721
柯坪县	Kalpin County	994	1768	39	719
克孜勒苏柯尔克孜自治州	**Kizilsu Kirgiz Autonomous Prefecture**	**9240**	**9611**	**1**	**4**
阿图什市	Artux City	3861	3485		
阿克陶县	Akto County	4038	5139		
阿合奇县	Akqi County	1233	781		
乌恰县	Wuqia [Ulugqat] County	108	206	1	4
喀什地区	**Kashgar [Kaxgar] Administrative Offices**	**95790**	**109897**	**1901**	**27122**
喀什市	Kashgar [Kaxgar] City	948	2915		
疏附县	Shufu County	4139	24128		
疏勒县	Shule County	19522	29497		
英吉沙县	Yengisar County	3500	8714		
泽普县	Zepu [Poskam] County	6197	6832		
莎车县	Shache [Yarkant] County	16688	10301	469	8292
叶城县	Yecheng [Kagilik] County	15127	10619		
麦盖提县	Makit County	5569	5325	306	4498
岳普湖县	Yopurga County	5454	4139	30	264
伽师县	Jiashi [Payzawat] County	9550	6030	225	394
巴楚县	Bachu [Maralbexi] County	8116	846	871	13674
塔什库尔干塔吉克自治县	Taxkorgan Tajik Autonomous County	980	551		
和田地区	**Hotan Administrative Offices**	**12698**	**16590**	**40**	**921**
和田市	Hotan City	1510	465		
和田县	Hotan County	1738	1687	12	132
墨玉县	Moyu [Karakax] County	2977	1691	11	153
皮山县	Pishan [Guma] County	1535	3624	5	65
洛浦县	Lop County	1370	2680		
策勒县	Qira County	910	3061	8	424
于田县	Yutian [Keriya] County	2250	2900		
民丰县	Minfeng [Niya] County	408	482	4	147
生产建设兵团	**Xinjiang Production and Construction Group**	**74948**	**34065**	**3445**	**68284**

12-9 各地、州、市、县(市)农村电气化和农田水利情况
Statistics on Water Conservancy and Electrification in Rural Areas by Prefecture, Autonomous Prefecture, City and County

(2011 年)

地　　区	Region	有效灌溉面积(千公顷) Irrigated Area (1000 hectares)	化肥施用量(吨)(折纯) Consumption of Chemical Fertilizer (ton) (100% Purity)	#氮肥 Nitrogenous Fertilizer	#磷肥 Phosphate Fertilizer	#钾肥 Potash Fertilizer
总　计	**Total**	**4209.61**	**1837858**	**855622**	**462770**	**117293**
乌鲁木齐市	**Urumqi City**	**46.26**	**9266**	**5849**	**1759**	**699**
#乌鲁木齐县	Urumqi County	12.85	1832	876	510	282
克拉玛依市	**Karamay City**	**10.47**	**4239**	**1543**	**1108**	**349**
吐鲁番地区	**TurpanAdministrative Offices**	**35.19**	**19570**	**8212**	**3367**	**2176**
吐鲁番市	Turpan City	14.36	10948	4665	563	1312
鄯善县	Shanshan [piqan]County	10.07	4583	2581	629	354
托克逊县	Toksun County	10.76	4039	966	2175	510
哈密地区	**Hami [Kumul]Administrative Offices**	**43.74**	**17720**	**8611**	**2860**	**1130**
哈密市	Hami [Kumul]City	21.13	9748	5119	2050	859
巴里坤哈萨克自治县	Barkol KazakAutonomous County	17.33	6004	2664	160	21
伊吾县	Yiwu [Araturuk]County	5.28	1968	828	650	250
昌吉回族自治州	**Changji Hui Autonomous Prefecture**	**436.12**	**134603**	**69667**	**32329**	**7321**
昌吉市	Changji City	88.36	26454	12336	6376	2643
阜康市	Fukang City	40.89	8478	4869	1709	6
呼图壁县	Hutubi County	72.25	30367	16728	8881	1343
玛纳斯县	Manas County	68.74	30464	15301	8520	775
奇台县	Qitai County	104.52	21741	11504	4002	581
吉木萨尔县	Jimsar County	39.62	12561	7474	1424	1384
木垒哈萨克自治县	Mori Kazak Autonomous County	21.74	4538	1455	1417	589
伊犁哈萨克自治州	**Ili Kazak Autonomous Prefecture**	**879.19**	**266249**	**108290**	**58803**	**17361**
伊犁州直属县(市)	**Counties (Cities) Direct Under Ili Prefecture**	**313.77**	**103266**	**32165**	**16741**	**5932**
伊宁市	Yining [Gulja]City	16.07	3754	1814	120	42
奎屯市	Kuytun City	4.10	2799	1114	1120	80
伊宁县	Yining [Gulja]County	69.38	29029	9092	4048	1524
察布查尔锡伯自治县	Qapqal Xibe Autonomous County	50.03	12975	4143	3780	1316
霍城县	Huocheng [korgas]County	40.10	12392	3140	2974	1260
巩留县	Gongliu [Tokkuzlara]County	34.80	9193	4002		
新源县	Xinyuan [kunes]County	37.98	11157	3116	1399	531
昭苏县	Zhaosu [mongolkure]County	18.79	6544	2170	1084	956
特克斯县	Tekes County	19.96	3814	868	852	
尼勒克县	Nilka County	22.56	11609	2706	1364	223
塔城地区	**Tacheng [Tarbagatai] Administrative Offices**	**404.23**	**137418**	**61362**	**34229**	**9224**
塔城市	Tacheng [Qoqek] City	85.37	23606	10149	8909	1523
乌苏市	Usu City	82.71	26461	15573	3091	1462
额敏县	Emin [Dorbiljin] County	74.21	23461	7886	7007	441
沙湾县	Shawan County	102.97	50598	22106	12831	5711
托里县	Toli County	24.56	4900	2300	1400	
裕民县	Yumin [Qagantokay] County	24.93	4676	1923	725	7
和布克赛尔蒙古自治县	Hoboksar Mongol Autonomous County	9.48	3716	1425	266	80
阿勒泰地区	**Altay Administrative Offices**	**161.19**	**25565**	**14763**	**7833**	**2205**
阿勒泰市	Altay City	25.02	5074	3223	1716	73
布尔津县	Burqin County	17.13	1626	849	777	
富蕴县	Fuyun [Koktokay] County	17.66	1518	1023	406	24
福海县	Fuhai [Burultokay] County	50.89	11042	5704	3087	1714
哈巴河县	Habahe [Kaba] County	28.40	2824	1674	690	374
青河县	Qinghe [Qinggil] County	12.60	2841	1890	945	1
吉木乃县	Jeminay County	9.49	640	400	212	19

12-9 续表 1 Continued

地　　区	Region	有效灌溉面积(千公顷) Irrigated Area(1000 hectares)	化肥施用量(吨)(折纯) Consumption of Chemical Fertilizer (ton) (100% Purity)	#氮肥 Nitrogenous Fertilizer	#磷肥 Phosphate Fertilizer	#钾肥 Potash Fertilizer
博尔塔拉蒙古自治州	**Bortala Mongol Autonomous Prefecture**	**128.89**	**44637**	**21220**	**13330**	**2268**
博乐市	Bole [Bortala] City	47.01	16197	6755	4725	994
精河县	Jinghe [Jing] County	48.50	17161	8680	4468	589
温泉县	Wenquan [Araxang] County	33.38	11279	5785	4137	685
巴音郭楞蒙古自治州	**Bayangol Mongol Autonomous Prefecture**	**245.01**	**130240**	**68628**	**35737**	**8919**
库尔勒市	Korla City	55.00	26319	14729	7977	1818
轮台县	Luntai [Bugur] County	30.54	20513	11170	4033	445
尉犁县	Yuli [Lopnur] County	36.67	23131	10922	7645	2675
若羌县	Ruoqiang [Qarkilik] County	7.27	6095	3344	857	300
且末县	Qiemo [Qarqan] County	16.16	7468	5036	745	40
焉耆回族自治县	Yanqi Hui Autonomous County	25.25	14601	7579	2663	1520
和静县	Hejing County	26.33	9805	4245	3815	1109
和硕县	Hoxud County	32.41	12665	6759	5077	210
博湖县	Bohu [Bagrax] County	15.38	9643	4844	2925	802
阿克苏地区	**Aksu Administrative Offices**	**509.95**	**248542**	**112016**	**90856**	**10412**
阿克苏市	Aksu City	62.49	57793	23636	25190	2092
温宿县	Wensu [Onsu] County	67.86	23410	10911	7395	2256
库车县	Kuqa County	72.25	42812	18754	12181	1246
沙雅县	Xayar County	77.33	38553	17736	16190	1542
新和县	Xinhe [Toksu] County	50.00	19153	6028	10784	936
拜城县	Baicheng [Bay] County	56.06	20755	7664	9282	1331
乌什县	Wushi [Uxturpan] County	31.21	12395	8825	821	
阿瓦提县	Awat County	82.00	30682	16910	7576	1009
柯坪县	Kalpin County	10.75	2989	1552	1437	
克孜勒苏柯尔克孜自治州	**Kizilsu Kirgiz Autonomous Prefecture**	**37.40**	**18051**	**9015**	**6687**	**1007**
阿图什市	Artux City	12.27	9045	4404	4641	
阿克陶县	Akto County	18.33	8883	4522	2012	1007
阿合奇县	Akqi County	4.42	47	30	17	
乌恰县	Wuqia [Ulugqat] County	2.38	76	59	17	
喀什地区	**Kashgar [Kaxgar] Administrative Offices**	**580.05**	**301300**	**139846**	**97373**	**15164**
喀什市	Kashgar [Kaxgar] City	11.65	4800	1800	1800	
疏附县	Shufu County	40.00	26125	13200	12100	825
疏勒县	Shule County	50.92	22300	11350	8000	1750
英吉沙县	Yengisar County	37.33	15597	7154		
泽普县	Zepu [Poskam] County	25.83	19723	8394	8243	1410
莎车县	Shache [Yarkant] County	109.27	69588	26908	18182	1697
叶城县	Yecheng [Kagilik] County	75.68	30385	17103	6624	3893
麦盖提县	Makit County	61.33	16520	11162	4738	59
岳普湖县	Yopurga County	32.03	29044	13479	7944	2660
伽师县	Jiashi [Payzawat] County	63.29	30224	16950	9630	854
巴楚县	Bachu [Maralbexi] County	67.97	35899	12096	20093	2016
塔什库尔干塔吉克自治县	Taxkorgan Tajik Autonomous County	4.73	1095	250	19	
和田地区	**Hotan Administrative Offices**	**165.85**	**65334**	**35973**	**19229**	**3961**
和田市	Hotan City	10.01	5221	3284	1651	250
和田县	Hotan County	22.50	9982	5515	3067	940
墨玉县	Moyu [Karakax] County	35.25	13123	5625	2499	1246
皮山县	Pishan [Guma] County	29.51	10730	7086	2341	542
洛浦县	Lop County	21.23	8447	4902	3545	
策勒县	Qira County	16.30	5475	3740	1632	73
于田县	Yutian [Keriya] County	28.33	10198	4610	3647	864
民丰县	Minfeng [Niya] County	2.73	2158	1211	847	46
生产建设兵团	**Xinjiang Production and Construction Group**	**1091.49**	**578107**	**266752**	**99332**	**46526**

12-9 续表 2 Continued

地 区	Region	乡村及村以下办水电站 Hydropower Station in Village or Below		农村用电量(万千瓦小时) Electricity Consumed in Rural Areas (10 000 kwh)
		装机容量(万千瓦) Installed Capacity (10 000 kw)	发电量(万千瓦) Generating Capacity (10 000 kw)	
总　计	**Total**	**19.30**	**28638**	**716538**
乌鲁木齐市	**Urumqi City**			**17481**
＃乌鲁木齐县	Urumqi County			682
克拉玛依市	**Karamay City**			**486**
吐鲁番地区	**TurpanAdministrative Offices**			**42396**
吐鲁番市	Turpan City			16861
鄯善县	Shanshan [piqan]County			20217
托克逊县	Toksun County			5318
哈密地区	**Hami [Kumul]Administrative Offices**			**22497**
哈密市	Hami [Kumul]City			18786
巴里坤哈萨克自治县	Barkol KazakAutonomous County			3171
伊吾县	Yiwu [Araturuk]County			540
昌吉回族自治州	**Changji Hui Autonomous Prefecture**	**0.35**	**900**	**79500**
昌吉市	Changji City			19689
阜康市	Fukang City			5682
呼图壁县	Hutubi County			16695
玛纳斯县	Manas County			8715
奇台县	Qitai County			22899
吉木萨尔县	Jimsar County	0.35	900	2733
木垒哈萨克自治县	Mori Kazak Autonomous County			3087
伊犁哈萨克自治州	**Ili Kazak Autonomous Prefecture**	**2.26**	**3413**	**69383**
伊犁州直属县(市)	**Counties (Cities) Direct Under Ili Prefecture**	**0.92**	**2059**	**24197**
伊宁市	Yining [Gulja]City			1686
奎屯市	Kuytun City			1700
伊宁县	Yining [Gulja]County	0.08	84	3692
察布查尔锡伯自治县	Qapqal Xibe Autonomous County			1519
霍城县	Huocheng [korgas]County			7103
巩留县	Gongliu [Tokkuzlara]County	0.09	350	965
新源县	Xinyuan [kunes]County	0.24	1440	3645
昭苏县	Zhaosu [mongolkure]County	0.51	20	937
特克斯县	Tekes County		165	917
尼勒克县	Nilka County			2033
塔城地区	**Tacheng [Tarbagatai] Administrative Offices**			**30607**
塔城市	Tacheng [Qoqek] City			6014
乌苏市	Usu City			3975
额敏县	Emin [Dorbiljin] County			2456
沙湾县	Shawan County			9577
托里县	Toli County			3500
裕民县	Yumin [Qagantokay] County			3625
和布克赛尔蒙古自治县	Hoboksar Mongol Autonomous County			1460
阿勒泰地区	**Altay Administrative Offices**	**1.34**	**1354**	**14579**
阿勒泰市	Altay City	1.00	198	814
布尔津县	Burqin County	0.10		1624
富蕴县	Fuyun [Koktokay] County	0.04	69	3764
福海县	Fuhai [Burultokay] County			1270
哈巴河县	Habahe [Kaba] County			860
青河县	Qinghe [Qinggil] County	0.20	1087	5737
吉木乃县	Jeminay County			510

12-9 续表 3 Continued

地　区	Region	乡村及村以下办水电站 HydroPower Station inVillage or Below		农村用电量（万千瓦小时）
		装机容量(万千瓦) Installed Capacity (10 000 kw)	发电量(万千瓦) Generating Capacity (10 000 kw)	Electricity Consumed in Rural Areas (10 000 kwh)
博尔塔拉蒙古自治州	**Bortala Mongol Autonomous Prefecture**	**0.52**	**1714**	**21727**
博乐市	Bole [Bortala] City	0.15	722	8212
精河县	Jinghe [Jing] County	0.37	992	12097
温泉县	Wenquan [Araxang] County			1418
巴音郭楞蒙古自治州	**Bayangol Mongol Autonomous Prefecture**			**50728**
库尔勒市	Korla City			14907
轮台县	Luntai [Bugur] County			7250
尉犁县	Yuli [Lopnur] County			5229
若羌县	Ruoqiang [Qarkilik] County			1422
且末县	Qiemo [Qarqan] County			365
焉耆回族自治县	Yanqi Hui Autonomous County			3056
和静县	Hejing County			1521
和硕县	Hoxud County			14079
博湖县	Bohu [Bagrax] County			2899
阿克苏地区	**Aksu Administrative Offices**	**6.00**	**96**	**41396**
阿克苏市	Aksu City			3867
温宿县	Wensu [Onsu] County	6.00	96	2056
库车县	Kuqa County			8643
沙雅县	Xayar County			8158
新和县	Xinhe [Toksu] County			9407
拜城县	Baicheng [Bay] County			1595
乌什县	Wushi [Uxturpan] County			1890
阿瓦提县	Awat County			4152
柯坪县	Kalpin County			1628
克孜勒苏柯尔克孜自治州	**Kizilsu Kirgiz Autonomous Prefecture**	**0.12**	**253**	**3485**
阿图什市	Artux City	0.12	253	1388
阿克陶县	Akto County			1538
阿合奇县	Akqi County			307
乌恰县	Wuqia [Ulugqat] County			252
喀什地区	**Kashgar [Kaxgar] Administrative Offices**	**3.00**	**25**	**36043**
喀什市	Kashgar [Kaxgar] City			675
疏附县	Shufu County	3.00	25	1705
疏勒县	Shule County			1125
英吉沙县	Yengisar County			3655
泽普县	Zepu [Poskam] County			2245
莎车县	Shache [Yarkant] County			3851
叶城县	Yecheng [Kagilik] County			1147
麦盖提县	Makit County			6161
岳普湖县	Yopurga County			2245
伽师县	Jiashi [Payzawat] County			5165
巴楚县	Bachu [Maralbexi] County			8025
塔什库尔干塔吉克自治县	Taxkorgan Tajik Autonomous County			44
和田地区	**Hotan Administrative Offices**	**1.47**	**3158**	**26649**
和田市	Hotan City	0.08		3581
和田县	Hotan County			4298
墨玉县	Moyu [Karakax] County	1.00	1995	5822
皮山县	Pishan [Guma] County			1387
洛浦县	Lop County	0.36	1163	5243
策勒县	Qira County	0.02		2367
于田县	Yutian [Keriya] County			2842
民丰县	Minfeng [Niya] County	0.01		1109
生产建设兵团	**Xinjiang Production and Construction Group**	**5.58**	**19079**	**304767**

12-10 灌溉、水库和除涝、治水情况

Irrigation, Reservoirs, Flood Prevention, Water and Soil Conservation

项　　目	Item	2009	2010
灌溉面积(千公顷)	Irrigated Areas (1000 hectares)	3933.54	4031.26
有效灌溉面积	Effective Irrigated Areas	2666.46	2739.25
林地灌溉面积	Irrigated Wooded-land Areas	458.57	483.90
果园灌溉面积	Irrigated Orchard Areas	407.37	425.42
牧草灌溉面积	Irrigated Pasture-land Areas	340.46	326.98
其他灌溉面积	Other Irrigated Areas	60.68	55.71
水库(座)	Number of Reservoirs (unit)	452	450
大型水库	Large Reservoir	13	13
中型水库	Medium-sized Reservoir	86	86
小型水库	Small Reservoir	353	351
水库库容量 (亿立方米)	Capacity of Reservoirs (100 million cu.m)	102.83	102.95
大型水库	Large Reservoir	70.17	70.17
中型水库	Medium-sized Reservoir	25.17	25.32
小型水库	Small Reservoir	7.49	7.46
节水灌溉面积 (千公顷)	Water-saving Irrigated Areas (1000 hectares)	1995.11	2140.68
除涝面积 (千公顷)	Areas wish Flood Prevention Measures (1000 hectares)	39.52	42.92
水土流失治理面积(千公顷)	Area of Soil Erosion under Control (1000 hectares)	336.91	358.85
堤防长度 (公里)	Total Length of Dikes (km)	6717.55	6899.75
堤防保护耕地面积 (千公顷)	Area of Land Protected by Dikes (1000 hectares)	1531.97	1547.45

注: 1.大型水库库容: 1 亿立方米以上; 中型水库库容: 1 千万至 1 亿立方米;小型水库库容: 10 万至 1 千万立方米。2.本表和 12-11，12-12 表资料由水利厅提供。

Note: a) The capacity of the large reservoirs is over 100 million cubic meters, while that of the medium ones is from 10 million to 100 million cubic meters, and that of the small ones is from 100 000 to 10 million cubic meters. b) The data in the table is offered by the Bureau of Water Conservancy, together with table 12-11,12-12.

12-11 各地、州、市水利设施和除涝面积

Water Conservancy Facilities and Area with Flood Prevention Measures by Prefecture, Autonomous Prefecture and City

(2010 年)

地 区	Region	水库数 (座) Number of Reservoirs (unit)	水库总库容量 (万立方米) Capacity of Reservoirs (10 000 cu.m)	除涝面积 (千公顷) Area with Flood Prevention Measures (1 000 hectares)	水土流失治理面积 (千公顷) Area of Soil Erosion under Control (1 000 hectares)
总 计	**Total**	**450**	**1029547**	**42.92**	**358.85**
乌鲁木齐市	Urumqi City	32	16536	3.00	18.18
克拉玛依市	Karamay City	7	28680		7.58
吐鲁番地区	Turpan Administrative Offices	15	10448		8.84
哈密地区	Hami [Kumul]Administrative Offices	37	10557		22.89
昌吉回族自治州	Changji HuiAutonomous Prefecture	78	34419		28.92
伊犁州直属县(市)	Counties (Cities) Direct Under Ili Prefecture	14	255535	20.35	57.07
塔城地区	Tacheng [Tarbagatai] Administrative Offices	58	25162		9.86
阿勒泰地区	Altay Administrative Offices	65	101495		11.30
博尔塔拉蒙古自治州	Bortala Mongol Autonomous Prefecture	4	6838		12.34
巴音郭楞蒙古自治州	Bayangol Mongol Autonomous Prefecture	16	20690		79.42
阿克苏地区	Aksu Administrative Offices	6	22829	19.04	33.77
克孜勒苏柯尔克孜自治州	Kizilsu Kirgiz Autonomous Prefecture	12	10525		1.63
喀什地区	Kashgar [Kaxgar] Administrative Offices	50	79598		13.27
和田地区	Hotan Administrative Offices	43	31011		40.20
其 他	Others	13	375224	0.53	13.58

12-12 各地、州、市农村饮水安全情况

Basic Statistics on Security of Drinking Water in Rural Area by Prefecture, Autonomous Prefecture and City

单位:万人 (2010 年) (10 000 persons)

地 区	Region	农村饮水安全达标人口 Reach the Standards in Security of Drinking Water of Rural Population	本年新增饮水安全达标人口 Increased in Security of Drinking Water of Rural Population This Year	农村饮水安全未达标人口 Not Reach the Standards in Security of Drinking Water of Rural Populaition
总 计	**Total**	**771.91**	**120.00**	**343.24**
乌鲁木齐市	Urumqi City	19.47	3.89	8.50
克拉玛依市	Karamay City	2.38		0.35
吐鲁番地区	Turpan Administrative Offices	19.89	6.11	17.13
哈密地区	Hami [Kumul]Administrative Offices	15.48	3.33	6.59
昌吉回族自治州	Changji HuiAutonomous Prefecture	51.72	16.44	26.94
伊犁州直属县(市)	Counties (Cities) Direct Under Ili Prefecture	101.52	18.80	43.70
塔城地区	Tacheng [Tarbagatai] Administrative Offices	33.28	8.58	26.55
阿勒泰地区	Altay Administrative Offices	25.10	6.01	15.20
博尔塔拉蒙古自治州	Bortala Mongol Autonomous Prefecture	17.81	4.00	10.30
巴音郭楞蒙古自治州	Bayangol Mongol Autonomous Prefecture	29.59	7.30	27.04
阿克苏地区	Aksu Administrative Offices	93.81	14.26	43.82
克孜勒苏柯尔克孜自治州	Kizilsu Kirgiz Autonomous Prefecture	27.77	3.95	12.07
喀什地区	Kashgar [Kaxgar] Administrative Offices	210.74	16.53	56.45
和田地区	Hotan Administrative Offices	109.51	10.16	35.37
其 他	Others	13.84	0.64	13.23

12-13 主要年份农作物播种面积

Total Sown Areas of Farm Crops in Main Years

单位：千公顷 (1 000 hectares)

年 份 Year	农作物播种面积 Total Sown Area	粮食作物播种面积 Sown Area of Grain Crops	谷 物 Cereal	#水 稻 Rice	#小 麦 Wheat	#玉 米 Corn	#大 麦 Barley	豆 类 Soybeans	薯 类 Tubers	棉 花 Cotton
1978	3021.67	2310.71	2297.44	105.59	1348.82	621.39	50.01	13.27	23.09	150.42
1980	2993.71	2162.37	2147.60	98.39	1354.83	555.79	23.24	14.77	17.55	181.22
1985	2846.63	1853.04	1844.47	74.50	1278.43	418.43	13.63	8.57	10.56	253.52
1990	2979.51	1826.61	1813.16	84.13	1180.11	442.40	42.92	13.45	10.67	435.22
1995	3051.44	1593.29	1528.62	73.38	952.58	439.16	41.58	64.67	10.34	742.90
2000	3388.76	1445.77	1353.99	78.15	838.99	382.45	33.50	91.78	22.59	1012.39
2001	3404.12	1394.96	1281.38	73.28	744.27	410.29	34.11	113.58	20.77	1129.72
2002	3478.37	1493.96	1386.81	74.96	749.74	501.93	36.45	107.15	20.65	943.97
2003	3470.28	1307.02	1202.61	67.16	626.09	454.14	38.25	104.41	23.89	1037.05
2004	3571.89	1378.61	1273.03	66.77	658.08	505.69	24.53	105.58	24.23	1127.55
2005	3728.11	1471.76	1371.89	69.07	761.84	497.64	27.42	99.87	20.51	1157.99
2006	4206.28	1465.82	1369.68	68.00	740.11	496.43	50.96	96.14	22.79	1664.43
2007	4394.25	1379.00	1300.58	70.95	634.02	528.91	55.86	78.42	33.15	1782.60
2008	4536.87	1649.97	1554.43	70.12	877.97	545.39	54.68	95.54	36.02	1668.01
2009	4710.26	1993.50	1867.77	73.49	1153.32	598.38	31.73	125.73	37.68	1409.31
2010	4758.64	1991.61	1879.36	66.93	1120.01	653.82	28.94	112.25	36.99	1460.60
2011	4983.48	2000.36	1916.10	70.59	1077.98	728.00	24.81	84.26	47.12	1638.06

年 份 Year	#长绒棉 Long-Staple Cotton	油 料 Oil Bearing Crops	#油 菜 Rapeseeds	#胡 麻 Flax	#葵 花 Helianthus	甜 菜 Beetroots	蔬 菜 Vegetables	果用瓜 Melon	#甜 瓜 Musk-melon	苜 蓿 Lucerne
1978	29.05	202.13	90.90	65.49	23.68	17.67	55.12	41.95		174.90
1980	38.50	269.39	107.47	81.85	50.08	24.27	46.99	39.54		191.65
1985	26.28	294.78	89.82	81.12	111.39	15.51	54.91	53.69	27.95	132.07
1990	62.69	269.27	117.35	46.04	96.11	66.87	58.07	28.84	15.09	159.34
1995	8.35	306.70	130.11	26.75	140.10	71.10	71.54	25.15	9.72	120.25
2000	49.29	310.07	96.23	24.57	157.05	55.75	127.75	55.99	26.01	120.49
2001	67.69	217.64	72.85	17.10	99.76	85.54	125.96	58.19	26.55	165.06
2002	46.30	215.05	70.00	23.84	96.60	85.32	164.21	82.47	48.47	235.11
2003	70.13	226.38	74.48	22.30	100.07	67.31	163.84	62.45	32.82	294.13
2004	70.63	215.47	67.52	13.74	85.55	59.88	185.60	61.29	36.07	301.10
2005	73.38	185.49	59.92	17.37	84.62	69.90	176.66	70.57	36.02	275.91
2006	106.94	151.73	49.25	14.28	64.29	94.42	186.82	74.02	41.27	242.38
2007	142.53	176.47	59.48	12.32	96.41	94.02	234.88	103.40	62.81	231.36
2008	132.18	286.68	83.67	9.51	172.44	71.14	258.04	110.60	68.22	171.42
2009	82.60	270.05	76.95	12.43	155.74	63.74	262.17	143.47	86.70	165.34
2010	96.79	273.37	70.15	8.75	164.87	75.27	303.59	122.78	69.44	150.14
2011	83.87	264.28	64.47	7.83	163.65	75.43	322.61	118.85	57.78	145.29

注：粮食、棉花及蔬菜播种面积为国家审定数。
Note: Total sown areas of grain,cotton and vegetable refer to the statistical data of state approved.

12-14 各地、州、市、县(市)农作物播种面积

单位：千公顷 (2011 年)

地　区	Region	农作物播种面积 Total Sown Area	粮食 Grain Crops	谷物 Cereal	#水稻 Rice	#小麦 Wheat	#玉米 Corn	豆类 Soy-beans
总　计	**Total**	**4983.48**	**2000.36**	**1916.10**	**70.59**	**1077.98**	**728.00**	**84.26**
乌鲁木齐市	**Urumqi City**	**55.16**	**25.49**	**24.34**	**6.79**	**10.13**	**4.27**	**1.15**
#乌鲁木齐县	Urumqi County	15.13	4.92	4.70		1.51	0.18	0.21
克拉玛依市	**Karamay City**	**10.44**	**0.44**	**0.44**		**0.05**	**0.39**	
吐鲁番地区	**TurpanAdministrative Offices**	**47.35**	**4.74**	**4.72**		**0.04**	**1.77**	**0.01**
吐鲁番市	Turpan City	14.10	0.97	0.97				
鄯善县	Shanshan [piqan]County	11.90	1.31	1.31		0.01	1.01	
托克逊县	Toksun County	21.35	2.45	2.44		0.03	0.76	…
哈密地区	**Hami [Kumul]Administrative Offices**	**60.71**	**26.07**	**25.92**		**18.54**	**2.94**	**0.15**
哈密市	Hami [Kumul]City	30.97	6.44	6.38		2.10	2.55	0.05
巴里坤哈萨克自治县	Barkol KazakAutonomous County	24.11	18.18	18.18		16.02		
伊吾县	Yiwu [Araturuk]County	5.63	1.45	1.36		0.42	0.39	0.10
昌吉回族自治州	**Changji Hui Autonomous Prefecture**	**541.79**	**286.98**	**257.38**	**0.99**	**178.66**	**73.37**	**29.61**
昌吉市	Changji City	92.12	37.64	35.87	0.59	25.55	9.59	1.77
阜康市	Fukang City	47.12	27.33	24.43	0.09	16.44	7.81	2.91
呼图壁县	Hutubi County	90.25	33.93	32.31	0.20	22.12	9.99	1.62
玛纳斯县	Manas County	71.02	17.61	17.46	0.10	3.82	13.42	0.15
奇台县	Qitai County	143.21	105.97	93.12		68.00	22.75	12.85
吉木萨尔县	Jimsar County	48.90	25.30	24.74		19.90	4.48	0.56
木垒哈萨克自治县	Mori Kazak Autonomous County	49.15	39.21	29.46		22.82	5.33	9.74
伊犁哈萨克自治州	**Ili Kazak Autonomous Prefecture**	**1097.65**	**591.97**	**541.58**	**14.30**	**322.39**	**195.11**	**50.39**
伊犁州直属县(市)	**Counties (Cities) Direct Under Ili Prefecture**	**471.31**	**329.31**	**290.54**	**13.50**	**178.09**	**95.19**	**38.77**
伊宁市	Yining [Gulja]City	21.39	14.80	12.97	0.55	5.20	7.21	1.84
奎屯市	Kuytun City	4.13	1.47	1.47		1.35	0.12	
伊宁县	Yining [Gulja]County	91.52	75.81	63.03		22.88	40.15	12.78
察布查尔锡伯自治县	Qapqal Xibe Autonomous County	69.03	47.54	43.68	10.87	24.17	8.62	3.87
霍城县	Huocheng [korgas]County	46.00	25.99	24.98		11.40	13.58	1.01
巩留县	Gongliu [Tokkuzlara]County	54.72	43.50	31.42	0.31	22.37	8.74	12.09
新源县	Xinyuan [kunes]County	60.14	46.27	39.90	1.77	28.60	9.25	6.38
昭苏县	Zhaosu [mongolkure]County	52.80	25.34	25.34		24.36		
特克斯县	Tekes County	33.84	19.81	19.36		15.30	2.70	0.44
尼勒克县	Nilka County	37.74	28.77	28.40		22.45	4.82	0.38
塔城地区	**Tacheng [Tarbagatai] Administrative Offices**	**445.03**	**204.53**	**203.56**	**0.80**	**116.58**	**81.74**	**0.97**
塔城市	Tacheng [Qoqek] City	89.05	66.70	66.70		36.55	28.75	
乌苏市	Usu City	85.07	19.40	19.39	0.80	10.14	8.41	0.01
额敏县	Emin [Dorbiljin] County	90.35	55.53	55.53		38.08	15.74	
沙湾县	Shawan County	106.41	23.02	22.15		13.72	8.24	0.87
托里县	Toli County	24.37	17.16	17.09		7.93	8.06	0.07
裕民县	Yumin [Qagantokay] County	38.33	21.29	21.29		9.11	12.18	
和布克赛尔蒙古自治县	Hoboksar Mongol Autonomous County	11.46	1.42	1.40		1.04	0.36	0.02
阿勒泰地区	**Altay Administrative Offices**	**181.31**	**58.13**	**47.48**		**27.72**	**18.18**	**10.65**
阿勒泰市	Altay City	25.02	8.53	6.23		2.36	3.86	2.30
布尔津县	Burqin County	22.71	6.44	3.33		1.94	1.26	3.12
富蕴县	Fuyun [Koktokay] County	24.55	10.92	9.35		6.12	2.27	1.57
福海县	Fuhai [Burultokay] County	48.87	4.74	4.74		2.34	2.41	
哈巴河县	Habahe [Kaba] County	36.67	14.81	11.37		3.88	7.03	3.45
青河县	Qinghe [Qinggil] County	14.00	7.93	7.72		7.35	0.36	0.21
吉木乃县	Jeminay County	9.49	4.74	4.74		3.73	1.01	

注:全区农作物播种面积及棉花面积合计不等于地方和生产建设兵团汇总数。

Sown Areas of Farm Crops by Prefecture, Autonomous Prefecture, City and County

(1 000 hectares)

薯类 Tubers	棉花 Cotton	#长绒棉 Longstaple Cotton	油料 Oil Bearing Crops	#油菜 Rapeseeds	#胡麻 Flax	#葵花 Helianthus	甜菜 Beetroots	蔬菜 Vegetables	果用瓜 Melon	#甜瓜 Muskmelon	苜蓿 Lucerne
47.12	**1638.06**	**83.87**	**264.28**	**64.47**	**7.83**	**163.65**	**75.43**	**322.61**	**118.85**	**57.78**	**145.29**
4.68	**1.39**	**0.14**	**4.43**	**0.27**	**0.01**	**3.31**	**0.06**	**12.71**	**0.17**	**0.01**	**2.47**
3.30			1.10	0.17		0.93		2.77			2.00
0.01	**7.80**		**0.07**			**0.07**		**0.44**	**0.16**	**0.00**	**0.30**
	21.58		**0.11**					**6.27**	**6.97**	**4.06**	**0.48**
	5.08							2.89	3.81	1.48	0.24
	5.61							1.88	2.55	2.07	0.07
	10.89		0.11					1.51	0.61	0.51	0.17
1.45	**15.82**		**2.45**	**2.29**	**0.01**	**0.15**		**3.30**	**5.15**	**4.49**	**3.28**
0.04	15.60		1.43	1.29	0.01	0.14		2.36	2.57	1.91	0.65
1.34	0.19		0.26	0.25		0.01		0.91	0.17	0.17	1.74
0.07	0.03		0.76	0.75				0.03	2.41	2.41	0.89
12.33	**105.50**		**27.16**	**0.14**	**0.53**	**21.60**	**8.93**	**50.65**	**6.17**	**0.70**	**5.12**
0.06	33.08		4.19	0.04		3.52	0.86	10.48	3.46	0.11	0.07
1.24	0.36		4.57			4.29	0.59	7.17	0.30	0.07	0.56
0.50	33.30		2.10			1.81	0.85	9.03	0.78	0.11	2.04
0.52	38.77		3.07			2.08	0.21	6.41	0.41		0.51
4.08			7.51			5.59	5.84	6.48	0.37	0.09	0.07
4.57			3.16	0.03		2.36	0.37	10.35	0.71	0.27	0.78
1.34			2.57	0.08	0.53	1.96	0.22	0.73	0.14	0.03	1.11
11.54	**138.66**		**137.57**	**29.76**	**4.05**	**88.80**	**27.34**	**43.14**	**3.44**	**1.21**	**31.95**
6.56	**15.71**		**56.24**	**24.95**	**4.05**	**25.84**	**22.10**	**18.95**	**1.38**	**0.06**	**2.67**
0.06			0.94	0.04		0.90	0.47	3.71	0.23		0.02
0.01	1.82		0.58			0.58		0.15			
0.78	0.17		4.88	1.55	0.02	3.30	3.14	4.89	0.63		0.71
0.03	11.88		3.79		0.98	2.63	0.63	1.34	0.19	0.04	0.70
0.22	1.84		4.42		0.06	3.29	7.68	3.17	0.09		
0.03			3.49	0.12		3.37	2.53	1.51	0.04		0.30
2.26			4.47	0.71	0.01	3.61	3.46	1.10	0.09		0.57
2.25			23.19	21.31	0.83	1.05	1.16	0.16			
0.16			7.75	0.82	0.30	6.63	1.37	1.65	0.08	0.02	
0.75			2.74	0.40	1.85	0.48	1.65	1.28	0.03		0.36
1.48	**122.95**		**30.54**	**4.81**		**12.17**	**4.71**	**22.29**	**0.72**	**0.15**	**8.08**
0.19			1.76	1.21		0.41	0.63	2.47	0.03		2.47
0.23	52.77		2.27			2.27	0.60	7.78	0.31	0.09	0.13
0.13			8.27	2.17		5.60	2.69	0.95			2.23
0.50	63.67		3.02			2.93	0.79	11.02	0.38	0.06	0.28
0.06	0.23		3.63	1.41		0.63		0.03			2.27
0.28			11.26	0.03				0.04			0.34
0.09	6.28		0.34			0.34		0.02			0.36
3.50			**50.79**			**50.79**	**0.53**	**1.90**	**1.34**	**1.00**	**21.20**
0.26			6.64			6.64	0.19	0.26	0.68	0.65	2.96
0.10			9.24			9.24		0.39	0.08	0.08	1.42
0.34			7.24			7.24		0.31	0.09	0.03	2.85
0.03			18.65			18.65	0.34	0.10	0.14	0.12	5.57
1.60			6.41			6.41		0.65	0.35	0.12	3.78
0.36			0.76			0.76		0.11			3.93
0.81			1.86			1.86		0.07			0.68

Note:Total of sown areas of farm crops and cotton areas by region do not mean that summary number of local and Production&Construction Corps.

12-14 续表

单位：千公顷

地　区	Region	农作物播种面积 Total Sown Area	粮食 Grain Crops	谷物 Cereal	#水稻 Rice	#小麦 Wheat	#玉米 Corn	豆类 Soy-beans
博尔塔拉蒙古自治州	**Bortala Mongol Autonomous Prefecture**	**130.10**	**44.98**	**44.85**	**0.12**	**14.95**	**29.77**	**0.13**
博乐市	Bole [Bortala] City	48.01	17.67	17.59	0.12	2.08	15.40	0.07
精河县	Jinghe [Jing] County	48.71	3.08	3.08		1.71	1.37	
温泉县	Wenquan [Araxang] County	33.38	24.23	24.17		11.16	13.01	0.06
巴音郭楞蒙古自治州	**Bayangol Mongol Autonomous Prefecture**	**298.66**	**55.71**	**55.22**	**0.18**	**38.38**	**15.54**	**0.49**
库尔勒市	Korla City	57.32	2.53	2.53		2.03	0.50	
轮台县	Luntai [Bugur] County	51.44	14.16	14.16		7.98	6.18	
尉犁县	Yuli [Lopnur] County	37.46	0.27	0.27		0.20	0.07	
若羌县	Ruoqiang [Qarkilik] County	12.21	2.77	2.53		1.85	0.68	0.24
且末县	Qiemo [Qarqan] County	21.27	6.23	6.17		3.61	2.47	0.06
焉耆回族自治县	Yanqi Hui Autonomous County	32.77	12.02	11.83		9.67	2.16	0.19
和静县	Hejing County	30.29	8.99	8.99		6.28	1.68	
和硕县	Hoxud County	33.12	4.20	4.20	0.02	3.48	0.71	
博湖县	Bohu [Bagrax] County	22.78	4.53	4.53	0.17	3.28	1.09	
阿克苏地区	**Aksu Administrative Offices**	**582.17**	**198.69**	**197.75**	**14.58**	**110.26**	**72.26**	**0.94**
阿克苏市	Aksu City	74.57	15.57	15.57	2.42	8.04	5.12	
温宿县	Wensu [Onsu] County	71.19	29.96	29.93	8.86	14.35	6.68	0.03
库车县	Kuqa County	93.00	35.22	35.07		22.13	12.94	0.15
沙雅县	Xayar County	91.18	26.02	26.02		15.03	10.99	
新和县	Xinhe [Toksu] County	55.12	17.35	17.35		10.10	7.25	
拜城县	Baicheng [Bay] County	52.65	27.44	26.93	1.14	13.24	12.01	0.51
乌什县	Wushi [Uxturpan] County	34.53	23.20	22.94	2.17	13.50	7.23	0.25
阿瓦提县	Awat County	99.16	19.54	19.54		10.87	8.67	
柯坪县	Kalpin County	10.77	4.39	4.39		3.00	1.39	
克孜勒苏柯尔克孜自治州	**Kizilsu Kirgiz Autonomous Prefecture**	**56.90**	**44.31**	**44.16**	**0.52**	**24.65**	**18.06**	**0.15**
阿图什市	Artux City	18.86	13.38	13.38	0.05	8.79	4.51	
阿克陶县	Akto County	30.57	25.33	25.33	0.47	12.83	11.93	
阿合奇县	Akqi County	4.42	3.56	3.48		1.80	0.97	0.08
乌恰县	Wuqia [Ulugqat] County	3.04	2.03	1.96		1.22	0.66	0.07
喀什地区	**Kashgar [Kaxgar] Administrative Offices**	**853.67**	**415.71**	**389.53**	**7.40**	**214.13**	**166.56**	**26.18**
喀什市	Kashgar [Kaxgar] City	19.06	11.84	11.84	1.52	6.91	3.41	
疏附县	Shufu County	69.32	44.20	44.20	0.20	26.67	17.33	
疏勒县	Shule County	72.68	36.49	36.49	0.15	20.67	15.67	
英吉沙县	Yengisar County	47.93	29.84	29.31		15.84	13.47	0.53
泽普县	Zepu [Poskam] County	44.53	29.07	17.41	0.27	11.81	5.33	11.67
莎车县	Shache [Yarkant] County	182.23	95.78	87.18	4.67	43.33	39.17	8.60
叶城县	Yecheng [Kagilik] County	89.21	53.79	49.24	0.60	26.19	22.13	4.55
麦盖提县	Makit County	79.59	22.32	22.27		12.07	10.20	0.05
岳普湖县	Yopurga County	39.73	14.90	14.90		8.42	6.48	
伽师县	Jiashi [Payzawat] County	84.75	42.43	42.10		23.45	18.65	0.33
巴楚县	Bachu [Maralbexi] County	120.31	31.33	31.33		16.67	14.67	
塔什库尔干塔吉克自治县	Taxkorgan Tajik Autonomous County	4.32	3.71	3.27		2.09	0.04	0.44
和田地区	**Hotan Administrative Offices**	**231.78**	**158.01**	**157.13**	**7.80**	**79.50**	**69.62**	**0.88**
和田市	Hotan City	18.02	13.60	13.57	0.45	7.42	5.71	0.03
和田县	Hotan County	33.58	25.37	25.29	2.41	12.83	10.05	0.09
墨玉县	Moyu [Karakax] County	54.41	40.93	40.90	2.13	21.40	17.37	0.03
皮山县	Pishan [Guma] County	31.15	18.05	17.66		8.82	8.83	0.38
洛浦县	Lop County	31.35	21.53	21.53	0.01	10.80	10.72	
策勒县	Qira County	25.37	13.92	13.62		6.77	6.71	0.31
于田县	Yutian [Keriya] County	33.99	22.09	22.04	2.80	10.16	9.03	0.04
民丰县	Minfeng [Niya] County	3.91	2.51	2.51		1.31	1.20	
生产建设兵团	**Xinjiang Production and Construction Group**	**1114.08**	**244.45**	**235.21**	**20.68**	**128.07**	**79.18**	**9.24**

Continued

(1 000 hectares)

薯类 Tubers	棉花 Cotton	#长绒棉 Longstaple Cotton	油料 Oil Bearing Crops	#油菜 Rapeseeds	#胡麻 Flax	#葵花 Helianthus	甜菜 Beetroots	蔬菜 Vegetables	果用瓜 Melon	#甜瓜 Muskmelon	苜蓿 Lucerne
0.06	**63.50**		**7.32**			**7.30**	**2.35**	**1.53**	**0.21**		**1.40**
	26.86		0.60			0.60	1.29	1.09	0.08		0.12
	36.64		0.05			0.03	0.10	0.25	0.08		0.21
0.06			6.66			6.66	0.95	0.18	0.06		1.08
0.45	**171.60**		**4.10**	**1.68**		**2.43**	**3.92**	**41.23**	**6.53**	**5.69**	**0.73**
	53.43							1.19	0.14	0.05	
	36.35		0.01	0.01				0.25	0.67	0.63	
	36.70							0.08	0.42	0.13	
	3.99							0.18	4.77	4.72	
	13.27		0.02	0.02				0.32	0.08	0.05	0.64
	2.41		1.46	0.30		1.16	2.38	6.41	0.02	0.01	
0.37	4.47		1.51	1.25		0.26	1.20	11.48	0.11	0.02	
0.08	15.71		0.33	0.09		0.24	0.14	11.62	0.11	0.02	0.07
	5.27		0.77	…		0.77	0.20	9.71	0.21	0.06	0.01
4.99	**315.24**	**70.50**	**4.66**	**3.27**	**0.81**	**0.52**	**5.56**	**25.31**	**13.69**	**5.04**	**8.78**
	44.83	9.59					0.07	4.86	3.45	2.61	5.68
0.32	34.67		1.11	1.05			0.53	1.36	1.31	0.17	0.94
0.74	50.43		0.62	0.62			0.08	2.71	2.61	0.96	0.58
0.02	61.50	0.10	0.26	0.23		0.02	1.11	0.93	1.22	0.57	0.12
	35.33		0.03	0.03				1.04	0.86	0.29	0.32
3.80	0.21		1.93	0.98	0.48	0.47	2.73	9.82	2.29	0.10	0.80
0.10	6.33		0.68	0.35	0.32		0.49	3.14	0.35	0.07	
	76.67	60.81						1.07	1.44	0.12	0.33
	5.25		0.03			0.03	0.55	0.38	0.17	0.14	
0.07	**5.88**		**0.71**	**0.36**	**0.29**	**0.04**		**1.36**	**0.71**	**0.34**	**1.66**
0.02	2.15		0.09	0.02	0.01	0.03		0.44	0.27	0.26	0.63
	3.72		0.01			0.01		0.68	0.42	0.08	0.09
0.03			0.50	0.22	0.27			0.06			0.28
0.02	0.01		0.12	0.12				0.18	0.02		0.66
8.09	**210.67**		**8.93**	**3.95**	**0.95**	**2.23**		**54.19**	**61.27**	**28.62**	**28.44**
	0.13							6.15	0.67	0.13	0.26
0.53	4.67		0.13		0.13			10.43	9.33	3.01	
	15.29							6.26	10.45	4.63	4.20
0.03	8.00		1.95	1.95				3.57	2.21	0.67	2.33
2.67	7.33		0.07		0.07			1.53	1.87	0.52	
2.47	43.33		5.00	2.01	0.54	1.21		11.18	11.29	5.85	1.33
2.25	6.67		1.44		0.21	0.82		7.71	1.35	0.45	5.75
	38.39		0.15					1.49	2.66	0.85	3.23
	13.33		0.20			0.20		0.39	3.18	1.42	4.07
	20.00							4.15	12.40	9.10	5.19
	53.33							1.11	5.87	2.01	2.00
0.13	0.20							0.21			0.07
1.39	**24.78**	**0.02**	**3.45**	**1.30**	**1.09**	**0.43**		**13.06**	**4.93**	**2.04**	**21.44**
	1.40	0.02	0.07	0.07				1.48	0.57	0.24	0.52
0.64	3.00		0.47	0.33	0.10			1.60	0.50	0.16	1.31
0.06	4.00		0.24	0.17	0.02			2.07	1.45	0.57	5.03
0.25	4.14		0.55	0.43		0.11		2.35	0.10	0.03	5.31
0.07	3.37		0.77	0.01	0.71	0.01		1.61	0.58	0.21	2.97
0.10	3.90		0.89	0.07	0.26	0.32		1.45	0.70	0.20	3.21
0.26	4.97		0.42	0.21				2.32	0.50	0.14	2.49
0.01			0.04	0.03	0.01			0.18	0.53	0.50	0.60
7.89	**534.62**	**13.20**	**63.33**	**21.44**	**0.11**	**36.77**	**27.27**	**84.43**	**9.44**	**5.58**	**39.22**

12-15 主要年份农作物种植结构
Planting Structure of Major Farm Crops in Main Years

单位：% (%)

项 目	Item	1995	2000	2010	2011
农作物总播种面积	**Total Sown Areas of Farm Crops**	**100**	**100**	**100**	**100**
粮食作物	Grain Crops	52.21	42.66	41.85	40.14
谷 物	Cereal	50.10	39.95	39.49	38.45
稻 谷	Rice	2.40	2.31	1.41	1.42
小 麦	Wheat	31.22	24.75	23.54	21.63
玉 米	Corn	14.39	11.29	13.74	14.61
谷 子	Millet	0.02	0.04	0.02	0.01
高 粱	Jowar	0.47	0.39	0.12	0.20
其它谷物	Other Cereal	1.59	1.18	0.67	0.09
豆 类	Soybeans	2.12	2.71	2.36	1.69
#大 豆	Soja	0.94	1.85	1.56	1.56
杂 豆	Miscellaneous Beans	1.18	0.20	0.80	0.13
薯 类	Tubers	0.34	0.66	0.78	0.95
油 料	Oil-bearing Crops	10.05	9.15	5.74	5.30
#花 生	Peanuts		0.14	0.08	0.07
油菜籽	Rapeseeds	4.26	2.84	1.47	1.29
芝 麻	Sesame		0.02	0.03	0.01
胡麻籽	Benne	0.88	0.72	0.18	0.16
向日葵	Helianthus	4.59	4.63	3.46	3.28
棉 花	Cotton	24.35	29.87	30.69	32.87
麻 类	Fiber Crops	0.14	0.21	0.05	0.08
甜 菜	Beetroots	2.33	1.65	1.58	1.51
烟 叶	Tobacco	0.03	0.08	0.02	
药 材	Medicinal Materials	0.22	0.38	0.42	0.46
蔬菜、瓜类	Vegetables and Melon	3.17	5.42	8.96	8.86
#蔬 菜	Vegetables	2.34	3.77	6.38	6.47
其他农作物	Other Farm Crops	7.16	9.92	9.91	9.83
#青饲料	Succulence	3.94	3.56	1.26	1.13

12-16 主要年份农作物产品产量

Output of Major Farm Crops in Main Years

单位：万吨 (10 000 tons)

年 份 Year	粮 食 Grain Crops	谷 物 Cereal	#水 稻 Rice	#小 麦 Wheat	#玉 米 Corn	#大 麦 Barley	豆 类 Soybeans	薯 类 Tubers	棉 花 Cotton	#长绒棉 Long-staple Cotton
1978	370.01	367.71	27.39	180.02	134.45	5.01	2.30	22.91	5.50	1.19
1980	386.13	384.16	25.62	213.19	126.43	3.50	1.97	16.03	7.92	1.74
1985	496.65	495.16	30.63	314.52	139.38	1.93	1.49	15.14	18.78	1.40
1990	676.89	673.18	47.27	390.80	209.42	10.51	3.71	22.57	46.88	3.48
1995	730.16	716.83	48.25	381.21	266.74	12.82	13.33	26.43	93.50	1.13
1996	818.20	808.67	51.49	420.32	312.54	17.39	9.53	32.50	94.04	1.72
1997	825.34	813.07	55.27	437.60	294.31	17.92	12.27	26.73	115.00	3.10
1998	830.00	814.54	49.56	444.00	302.25	11.00	15.46	33.12	140.00	1.39
1999	838.78	821.70	54.14	423.29	323.06	8.00	17.08	46.06	140.75	1.67
2000	808.60	782.93	60.35	405.80	298.22	11.75	25.67	64.01	150.00	6.16
2001	796.00	767.53	56.79	374.14	318.41	11.86	28.47	60.02	157.00	9.71
2002	875.87	849.48	60.62	386.44	379.05	13.78	26.39	62.41	150.00	6.67
2003	801.64	774.62	50.73	335.67	366.25	14.33	27.02	71.80	160.00	10.10
2004	828.53	800.04	51.31	345.94	388.12	8.06	28.49	70.79	175.25	11.22
2005	877.21	852.00	54.18	400.71	380.36	10.23	25.22	65.86	195.70	11.87
2006	895.22	870.21	59.27	400.31	386.80	17.85	25.01	76.50	267.53	18.59
2007	867.04	846.35	62.52	359.22	396.00	24.26	20.69	101.36	290.00	25.02
2008	909.00	885.99	56.50	395.69	416.41	14.75	23.01	107.62	301.55	19.73
2009	1152.00	1119.77	58.30	630.70	439.38	14.30	32.23	126.06	252.40	11.04
2010	1150.20	1121.88	58.98	623.49	421.61	12.54	28.32	102.50	247.90	13.03
2011	1200.75	1171.64	60.64	576.64	517.67	11.06	29.11	119.75	289.77	12.16

年 份 Year	油 料 Oil bearing Crops	#油 菜 Rapeseeds	#胡 麻 Flax	#葵 花 Helianthus	甜 菜 Beetroots	蔬 菜 Vegetables	果用瓜 Melons	#甜 瓜 Muskmelon	苜 蓿 Lucerne
1978	10.33	3.30	3.14	2.29	16.37	91.26	44.05		
1980	17.59	5.59	5.17	4.59	38.52	73.44	55.68		
1985	34.25	7.29	8.10	16.90	40.69	111.08	103.18	47.02	49.69
1990	38.96	12.17	6.32	18.17	224.37	187.42	93.38	37.75	89.29
1995	49.41	15.12	3.79	29.06	288.14	269.56	68.75	18.31	82.62
1996	30.95	10.15	3.12	16.91	354.52	301.94	67.16	17.33	75.42
1997	29.95	8.92	2.53	17.69	388.71	295.59	86.78	25.90	70.05
1998	37.52	12.32	2.53	20.82	513.12	321.79	88.32	29.45	67.56
1999	60.46	16.37	2.75	35.69	354.24	406.18	143.49	46.38	69.98
2000	60.14	14.75	3.60	35.47	292.65	527.84	151.03	51.22	76.32
2001	42.64	12.19	2.47	23.31	455.12	486.74	156.87	56.86	103.12
2002	44.37	12.90	3.69	23.26	466.81	674.96	233.40	107.49	149.93
2003	50.13	15.43	3.49	25.80	381.65	761.00	189.32	77.61	249.60
2004	44.54	12.16	2.10	21.90	344.21	919.13	186.06	92.54	273.04
2005	38.94	9.22	2.39	21.69	419.12	862.23	220.65	95.58	295.74
2006	32.82	9.73	2.52	16.17	555.53	958.04	237.28	109.98	240.15
2007	40.30	9.60	1.58	25.39	586.93	1173.99	338.67	192.63	205.47
2008	56.85	10.67	1.23	42.87	438.88	970.67	404.17	248.81	150.83
2009	63.91	15.72	1.89	41.40	418.41	1383.21	491.20	286.30	154.90
2010	66.62	15.14	1.32	44.11	486.97	1734.40	435.00	222.58	132.93
2011	66.76	15.18	1.23	45.36	518.95	1866.15	434.31	193.06	139.94

注：粮食、棉花及蔬菜总产量为国家审定数。
Note:Total grain output refers to the number of state approved.

12-17 各地、州、市、县(市)主要农产品产量

单位：吨 (2011 年)

地 区	Region	粮食作物 Grain Crops	谷物 Cereal	#水稻 Rice	#小麦 Wheat	#玉米 Corn	豆类 Soy-beans
总 计	**Total**	**12007445**	**11716393**	**606400**	**5766404**	**5176689**	**291052**
乌鲁木齐市	**Urumqi City**	**168687**	**164320**	**61802**	**52405**	**37953**	**4367**
#乌鲁木齐县	Urumqi County	19675	18981		6616	909	694
克拉玛依市	**Karamay City**	**3500**	**3500**		**158**	**3342**	
吐鲁番地区	**TurpanAdministrative Offices**	**24066**	**24050**		**173**	**10433**	**16**
吐鲁番市	Turpan City	4440	4440				
鄯善县	Shanshan [piqan]County	6443	6443		30	5300	
托克逊县	Toksun County	13183	13167		143	5133	16
哈密地区	**Hami [Kumul]Administrative Offices**	**132817**	**132379**		**90397**	**25698**	**438**
哈密市	Hami [Kumul]City	38723	38500		10067	23637	223
巴里坤哈萨克自治县	Barkol KazakAutonomous County	88306	88306		78338	35	
伊吾县	Yiwu [Araturuk]County	5788	5573		1992	2026	215
昌吉回族自治州	**Changji Hui Autonomous Prefecture**	**1802649**	**1750179**	**8535**	**1020347**	**705173**	**52470**
昌吉市	Changji City	270423	267260	4879	157332	104849	3163
阜康市	Fukang City	186067	178975	873	104712	72995	7092
呼图壁县	Hutubi County	208281	206645	1839	135045	69761	1636
玛纳斯县	Manas County	149718	149081	944	25206	122693	637
奇台县	Qitai County	666869	645049		403060	232859	21820
吉木萨尔县	Jimsar County	159690	158475		111369	46036	1215
木垒哈萨克自治县	Mori Kazak Autonomous County	161601	144694		83623	55980	16907
伊犁哈萨克自治州	**Ili Kazak Autonomous Prefecture**	**4348951**	**4211142**	**134213**	**1765809**	**2276137**	**137809**
伊犁州直属县(市)	**Counties (Cities) Direct Under Ili Prefecture**	**2367949**	**2264527**	**125813**	**1003641**	**1121208**	**103422**
伊宁市	Yining [Gulja]City	119763	114419	5907	28183	80317	5344
奎屯市	Kuytun City	6714	6714		5570	1144	
伊宁县	Yining [Gulja]County	651056	617502		126696	490806	33554
察布查尔锡伯自治县	Qapqal Xibe Autonomous County	331710	319418	104676	124963	89733	12292
霍城县	Huocheng [korgas]County	230110	226625		70765	155860	3485
巩留县	Gongliu [Tokkuzlara]County	262900	236200	2708	135134	98358	26700
新源县	Xinyuan [kunes]County	330758	311885	12522	183209	115633	18873
昭苏县	Zhaosu [mongolkure]County	127701	127701		123212		
特克斯县	Tekes County	118020	116158		75724	34677	1862
尼勒克县	Nilka County	189217	187905		130185	54680	1312
塔城地区	**Tacheng [Tarbagatai] Administrative Offices**	**1647212**	**1643934**	**8400**	**626486**	**991677**	**3278**
塔城市	Tacheng [Qoqek] City	536045	536045		184807	345017	
乌苏市	Usu City	193058	193028	8400	68505	115923	30
额敏县	Emin [Dorbiljin] County	410738	410738		203325	199537	
沙湾县	Shawan County	198308	195303		86701	107714	3005
托里县	Toli County	119711	119492		37109	80197	219
裕民县	Yumin [Qagantokay] County	182306	182306		42935	139371	
和布克赛尔蒙古自治县	Hoboksar Mongol Autonomous County	7046	7022		3104	3918	24
阿勒泰地区	**Altay Administrative Offices**	**333790**	**302681**		**135682**	**163252**	**31109**
阿勒泰市	Altay City	48169	40643		11704	28929	7526
布尔津县	Burqin County	30007	20416		8747	11509	9591
富蕴县	Fuyun [Koktokay] County	58164	54795		28085	23885	3369
福海县	Fuhai [Burultokay] County	33928	33928		8464	25464	
哈巴河县	Habahe [Kaba] County	93569	83483		18160	64632	10086
青河县	Qinghe [Qinggil] County	43737	43200		40576	2563	537
吉木乃县	Jeminay County	26216	26216		19946	6270	

注: 1.地方与生产建设兵团粮食产量合计不等于全区总计数。2.全区总计数为国家统计局审定数。

Output of Major Farm Crops by Prefecture, Autonomous Prefecture, City and County

(ton)

薯 类 Tubers	棉 花 Cotton	#长绒棉 Longstaple Cotton	油 料 Oil Bearing Crops	#油 菜 Rapeseeds	#胡 麻 Flax	#葵 花 Helianthus	甜 菜 Beetroots	蔬 菜 Vegetables	果用瓜 Melon	#甜 瓜 Muskmelon	苜 蓿 Lucerne
1197478	**2897747**	**121584**	**667647**	**151789**	**12334**	**453586**	**5189502**	**18661502**	**4343080**	**1930583**	**1399399**
109276	**1669**	**110**	**8934**	**571**		**7816**	**4960**	**576596**	**3923**	**770**	**14548**
71312			2068	389		1679		80735	27		9846
250	**12674**		**264**			**264**		**18169**	**6628**	**71**	**3328**
	29125		**479**					**241301**	**188660**	**101776**	**11042**
	5705							131085	100205	36700	3367
	7578							59850	71520	51216	1330
	15842		479					50366	16935	13860	6345
61252	**27800**		**1714**	**1272**	**22**	**420**		**148708**	**177482**	**138996**	**25092**
1153	27430		661	232	19	410		105943	95614	57128	8960
57975	336		427	418		9		41198	2405	2405	12146
2124	34		626	622	3	1		1567	79463	79463	3986
457754	**199219**		**82309**	**228**	**738**	**69983**	**563686**	**3023852**	**348461**	**25907**	**56716**
1949	54153		14090	95		10006	57632	773570	227933	3599	474
53835	475		15041			14544	35200	276532	11672	1263	6530
16115	63948		3657			3223	60610	550204	36220	4230	20779
12861	80643		10950			7315	17600	489600	27209		6872
177722			22828			21146	357236	303946	10830	3463	400
153041			9439	30		8286	25540	605143	29068	12167	13668
42231			6304	103	738	5463	9868	24857	5529	1185	7993
369063	**246176**		**331710**	**71348**	**6200**	**233285**	**1723232**	**2533448**	**143167**	**30890**	**252413**
213840	**18006**		**139066**	**62177**	**6200**	**65250**	**1384670**	**880921**	**65487**	**2575**	**25016**
2375			2298	75	5	2157	31265	255508	8502		354
500	1911		1726			1726		11968			
27965	199		13165	4377	64	8656	197807	156900	35720		8493
1190	13790		8718		1295	6382	43174	53607	8280	1725	6189
5980	2106		10921		175	7660	509375	138500	3153		
810			9152	345		8807	165080	73150	740		1389
90075			12106	1516	20	9387	197818	72230	4721	100	6523
53790			57478	52828	1490	3160	69560	5933			
3525			17927	1835	373	15719	79064	59400	2871	750	
27630			5575	1201	2778	1596	91527	53725	1500		2068
51911	**228170**		**61392**	**9171**		**36783**	**314780**	**1591931**	**36237**	**4388**	**61506**
8271			3448	2344		904	40238	98547	655	80	11466
10874	98317		7673			7673	50338	787412	15030	2072	943
3430			19213	3805		14690	177128	78481			18704
17979	120045		11295			10727	47076	624738	20552	2236	1970
879	395		6687	2989		1544		1668			14007
10365			11831	33				880			6221
113	9413		1245			1245		205			8195
103312			**131252**			**131252**	**23782**	**60596**	**41443**	**23927**	**165891**
5935			20426			20426	9793	13100	13100	12870	31100
5103			25244			25244		7934	2526	2526	9598
8143			16494			16494		11559	3772	1072	19897
1163			43938			43938	13989	4328	3725	3245	43420
55680			18461			18461		19663	18320	4214	34776
8886			1625			1625		3268			23598
18402			5064			5064		744			3502

Note:a) The region total output of grain is not equal to the sum of local and Production and Construction Groups.b) The region total data of grain refer to approvable data by NBS.

12-17 续表

单位：吨

地区	Region	粮食作物 Grain Crops	谷物 Cereal	#水稻 Rice	#小麦 Wheat	#玉米 Corn	豆类 Soy-beans
博尔塔拉蒙古自治州	**Bortala Mongol Autonomous Prefecture**	**511178**	**510749**	**1243**	**88916**	**420581**	**429**
博乐市	Bole [Bortala] City	233092	232842	1243	13147	218452	250
精河县	Jinghe [Jing] County	27365	27365		10461	16904	
温泉县	Wenquan [Araxang] County	250721	250542		65308	185225	179
巴音郭楞蒙古自治州	**Bayangol Mongol Autonomous Prefecture**	**353022**	**352143**	**1072**	**232190**	**116494**	**879**
库尔勒市	Korla City	11367	11363		8901	2462	4
轮台县	Luntai [Bugur] County	77360	77360		43530	33830	
尉犁县	Yuli [Lopnur] County	1270	1270		716	554	
若羌县	Ruoqiang [Qarkilik] County	12489	12193		9395	2798	296
且末县	Qiemo [Qarqan] County	35991	35848		22429	13134	143
焉耆回族自治县	Yanqi Hui Autonomous County	89549	89113		63045	26068	436
和静县	Hejing County	62460	62460		40630	19728	
和硕县	Hoxud County	28453	28453	91	20500	7862	
博湖县	Bohu [Bagrax] County	34083	34083	981	23044	10058	
阿克苏地区	**Aksu Administrative Offices**	**1462257**	**1459553**	**150536**	**720798**	**586328**	**2704**
阿克苏市	Aksu City	118256	118256	25514	53689	39053	
温宿县	Wensu [Onsu] County	235462	235436	93293	94301	47665	26
库车县	Kuqa County	234265	234122		148849	85256	143
沙雅县	Xayar County	184536	184536		101582	82946	
新和县	Xinhe [Toksu] County	114127	114127		66872	47255	
拜城县	Baicheng [Bay] County	242080	240684	9821	83110	146231	1396
乌什县	Wushi [Uxturpan] County	175199	174060	21908	81708	70277	1139
阿瓦提县	Awat County	131103	131103		72603	58500	
柯坪县	Kalpin County	27229	27229		18084	9145	
克孜勒苏柯尔克孜自治州	**Kizilsu Kirgiz Autonomous Prefecture**	**263244**	**262763**	**4446**	**139613**	**116499**	**481**
阿图什市	Artux City	72617	72617	292	46023	26252	
阿克陶县	Akto County	168877	168877	4154	80713	83810	
阿合奇县	Akqi County	13068	12771		7078	3915	297
乌恰县	Wuqia [Ulugqat] County	8682	8498		5799	2522	184
喀什地区	**Kashgar [Kaxgar] Administrative Offices**	**2575333**	**2513330**	**66469**	**1231764**	**1211254**	**62003**
喀什市	Kashgar [Kaxgar] City	72695	72695	11967	37228	23500	
疏附县	Shufu County	290490	290490	1530	156100	132860	
疏勒县	Shule County	233943	233943	1282	121044	111617	
英吉沙县	Yengisar County	182793	181593		90768	90825	1200
泽普县	Zepu [Poskam] County	144335	111966	1560	69917	40489	32369
莎车县	Shache [Yarkant] County	583808	572068	44100	254488	273474	11740
叶城县	Yecheng [Kagilik] County	370984	355835	6030	153812	194893	15149
麦盖提县	Makit County	136837	136738		63763	72975	99
岳普湖县	Yopurga County	95615	95615		48034	47581	
伽师县	Jiashi [Payzawat] County	249656	249031		134412	114619	625
巴楚县	Bachu [Maralbexi] County	202830	202830		95868	106962	
塔什库尔干塔吉克自治县	Taxkorgan Tajik Autonomous County	11347	10526		6330	1459	821
和田地区	**Hotan Administrative Offices**	**1061599**	**1059047**	**55866**	**481849**	**520718**	**2552**
和田市	Hotan City	95568	95521	3571	44875	47075	47
和田县	Hotan County	163539	163007	15944	77979	69084	532
墨玉县	Moyu [Karakax] County	268977	268943	16352	130443	122148	34
皮山县	Pishan [Guma] County	128223	127192		51431	75727	1031
洛浦县	Lop County	141353	141353	30	66307	75016	
策勒县	Qira County	97235	96425		40692	55362	810
于田县	Yutian [Keriya] County	150206	150108	19969	62532	67398	98
民丰县	Minfeng [Niya] County	16498	16498		7590	8908	
生产建设兵团	**Xinjiang Production and Construction Group**	**1618642**	**1592438**	**180218**	**742785**	**635879**	**26204**

Continued

(ton)

薯 类 Tubers	棉 花 Cotton	#长绒棉 Longstaple Cotton	油 料 Oil Bearing Crops	#油 菜 Rapeseeds	#胡 麻 Flax	#葵 花 Helianthus	甜 菜 Beetroots	蔬 菜 Vegetables	果用瓜 Melon	#甜 瓜 Muskmelon	苜 蓿 Lucerne
1537	**135884**		**21037**			**21006**	**146607**	**94339**	**8280**	**94**	**7835**
	56972		1820			1820	86099	67916	2657		808
	78912		112			81	4400	10899	2580	94	1446
1537			19105			19105	56108	15524	3043		5581
14277	**352013**		**7372**	**2079**		**5267**	**347186**	**2942897**	**117918**	**70266**	**7858**
	108196						70	84765	4986	883	
	74211		50	50				13052	11941	11248	
	83729							2239	17790	4100	
	7142							4864	55385	49370	
	26634		29	29				7591	1347	910	6950
	3053		3007	389		2618	213978	570190	843	318	
11795	7105		2087	1502		585	107795	598216	7646	875	
2482	30885		622	104		492	8985	942227	6422	1152	788
	11058		1577	5		1572	16358	719753	11558	1410	120
159969	**534839**	**94516**	**9827**	**5587**	**1522**	**1356**	**344614**	**934977**	**400328**	**151042**	**152249**
	95044	15071					3806	304476	133265	102486	110652
4825	56602		1747	1656			24027	25557	37400	3400	10100
24575	83882		801	800	1		3125	69025	59803	20153	12398
1378	107230	156	438	398		40	18440	13022	18851	8201	2542
	62593		43	43				45104	21252	5552	6576
125441	279		5378	1946	888	1273	254706	329806	81617	3030	4981
3750	9095		1377	744	633		33057	108360	11545	3345	
	112125	79289						33900	34595	2875	5000
	7989		43			43	7453	5727	2000	2000	
552	**8956**		**978**	**560**	**293**	**55**		**33200**	**20064**	**9020**	**16898**
407	3259		159	31	22	36		14262	6153	5886	7485
	5689		19			19		15200	13743	3134	1601
75			574	303	271			1184			2310
70	8		226	226				2554	168		5502
297263	**346846**		**15091**	**6206**	**1506**	**4573**		**2419229**	**2394415**	**1190447**	**254350**
	200							267919	25480	5096	
20800	7196		240		240			443564	394320	128600	
	23657							290939	468382	235816	50400
1530	11441		3796	3796				145608	92778	29093	22050
80000	7700		170		170			63072	78313	21753	
60200	66475		5675	2410	651	1456		495533	351669	240169	10000
133333	11353		4750		445	2877		418149	64133	22780	64655
	70455		220					75108	118265	36740	38800
200	20978		240			240		16776	97875	45085	30502
	28088							148423	441300	341015	22201
	99088							51152	261900	84300	15000
1200	215							2986			742
41245	**45413**	**37**	**9231**	**2455**	**1754**	**2611**		**438087**	**152418**	**49417**	**296795**
	2183	37	225	225				60128	25790	9460	6248
19275	5756		917	616	221			61772	12257	3419	9685
1875	7626		540	335	10	5		54050	32183	13072	63311
5080	7883		2474	744	2	1645		65260	4415	806	65226
2165	5920		1108	15	1036	13		67358	24278	7739	91355
4215	7376		2089	91	467	946		53838	35974	8480	24824
8615	8669		1846	422				70793	14331	3968	30654
20			32	7	18	2		4888	3190	2473	5492
271440	**1293053**	**26921**	**178701**	**61483**	**299**	**106950**	**2059217**	**6256699**	**381336**	**161887**	**300275**

12-18 各地、州、市、县(市)农作物单位面积产量

Output of Major Farm Products Per Hectare by Prefecture, Autonomous Prefecture, City and County

单位：公斤/公顷　　　　(2011 年)　　　　(kg / hectare)

地　区	Region	粮　食 Grain	#谷　物 Cereal	#小　麦 Wheat	#玉　米 Corn	棉 花 Cotton	油 料 Oil-Bearing Crops	甜 菜 Beetroots
总　计	**Total**	**6003**	**6115**	**5349**	**7111**	**1769**	**2526**	**68800**
乌鲁木齐市	**Urumqi City**	**6619**	**6752**	**5174**	**8892**	**1197**	**2019**	**83596**
#乌鲁木齐县	Urumqi County	4002	4035	4385	5179		1880	
克拉玛依市	**Karamay City**	**7999**	**7999**	**3131**	**8634**	**1624**	**3960**	
吐鲁番地区	**TurpanAdministrative Offices**	**5080**	**5091**	**4325**	**5894**	**1350**	**4491**	
吐鲁番市	Turpan City	4562	4562			1123		
鄯善县	Shanshan [piqan]County	4906	4906	4500	5249	1350		
托克逊县	Toksun County	5379	5401	4290	6750	1455	4491	
哈密地区	**Hami [Kumul]Administrative Offices**	**5095**	**5107**	**4877**	**8748**	**1757**	**700**	
哈密市	Hami [Kumul]City	6018	6032	4790	9277	1758	460	
巴里坤哈萨克自治县	Barkol KazakAutonomous County	4857	4857	4890	9052	1801	1649	
伊吾县	Yiwu [Araturuk]County	3984	4105	4799	5251	1114	829	
昌吉回族自治州	**Changji Hui Autonomous Prefecture**	**6281**	**6800**	**5711**	**9611**	**1888**	**3031**	**63113**
昌吉市	Changji City	7184	7452	6158	10937	1637	3362	66900
阜康市	Fukang City	6807	7327	6368	9347	1324	3295	60000
呼图壁县	Hutubi County	6138	6396	6106	6982	1921	1739	71587
玛纳斯县	Manas County	8502	8539	6596	9143	2080	3565	82500
奇台县	Qitai County	6293	6927	5927	10234		3041	61176
吉木萨尔县	Jimsar County	6313	6406	5596	10268		2992	69440
木垒哈萨克自治县	Mori Kazak Autonomous County	4122	4911	3665	10509		2457	45685
伊犁哈萨克自治州	**Ili Kazak Autonomous Prefecture**	**7347**	**7776**	**5477**	**11666**	**1779**	**2411**	**63026**
伊犁州直属县(市)	**Counties (Cities) Direct Under Ili Prefecture**	**7191**	**7794**	**5636**	**11779**	**1146**	**2473**	**62659**
伊宁市	Yining [Gulja]City	8092	8825	5417	11147		2449	66249
奎屯市	Kuytun City	4561	4561	4112	9750	1050	3001	
伊宁县	Yining [Gulja]County	8588	9797	5537	12225	1199	2700	63000
察布查尔锡伯自治县	Qapqal Xibe Autonomous County	6977	7313	5171	10405	1160	2301	68012
霍城县	Huocheng [korgas]County	8854	9072	6209	11475	1143	2468	66300
巩留县	Gongliu [Tokkuzlara]County	6043	7518	6042	11250		2619	65280
新源县	Xinyuan [kunes]County	7148	7817	6405	12502		2710	57139
昭苏县	Zhaosu [mongolkure]County	5040	5040	5057			2478	59966
特克斯县	Tekes County	5958	5999	4950	12840		2314	57750
尼勒克县	Nilka County	6576	6617	5798	11351		2038	55500
塔城地区	**Tacheng [Tarbagatai] Administrative Offices**	**8053**	**8076**	**5374**	**12132**	**1860**	**2010**	**66755**
塔城市	Tacheng [Qoqek] City	8036	8036	5056	12000		1964	63480
乌苏市	Usu City	9949	9953	6759	13785	1863	3375	83249
额敏县	Emin [Dorbiljin] County	7396	7396	5339	12675		2324	65850
沙湾县	Shawan County	8614	8816	6319	13080	1886	3740	59812
托里县	Toli County	6976	6993	4678	9945	1693	1844	
裕民县	Yumin [Qagantokay] County	8563	8563	4711	11445		1050	
和布克赛尔蒙古自治县	Hoboksar Mongol Autonomous County	4964	5018	2981	10934	1500	3683	
阿勒泰地区	**Altay Administrative Offices**	**5742**	**6375**	**4894**	**8978**		**2584**	**45053**
阿勒泰市	Altay City	5646	6526	4950	7500		3075	52500
布尔津县	Burqin County	4656	6136	4515	9150		2732	
富蕴县	Fuyun [Koktokay] County	5325	5858	4592	10518		2279	
福海县	Fuhai [Burultokay] County	7151	7151	3618	10587		2356	40983
哈巴河县	Habahe [Kaba] County	6317	7345	4680	9195		2881	
青河县	Qinghe [Qinggil] County	5516	5596	5520	7199		2130	
吉木乃县	Jeminay County	5527	5527	5341	6219		2726	

注：个别县(市)油料等作物种植在边角地头，未计面积，故单产偏高。

Note: The oil-bearing crop planted at the edge or margin of fields in small number of counties (cities), whose area is not calculated, thus per-unit output is relatively higher.

12-18 续表 Continued

单位：公斤/公顷 (kg/ hectare)

地 区	Region	粮 食 Grain	#谷 物 Cereal	#小 麦 Wheat	#玉 米 Corn	棉 花 Cotton	油 料 Oil-Bearing Crops	甜 菜 Beet-roots
博尔塔拉蒙古自治州	**Bortala Mongol Autonomous Prefecture**	**11365**	**11388**	**5946**	**14125**	**2140**	**2875**	**62466**
博乐市	Bole [Bortala] City	13194	13234	6314	14190	2121	3010	66771
精河县	Jinghe [Jing] County	8873	8873	6106	12332	2154	2327	42581
温泉县	Wenquan [Araxang] County	10349	10366	5853	14238		2867	58801
巴音郭楞蒙古自治州	**Bayangol Mongol Autonomous Prefecture**	**6336**	**6377**	**6050**	**7499**	**2051**	**1796**	**88487**
库尔勒市	Korla City	4486	4488	4385	4905	2025		52500
轮台县	Luntai [Bugur] County	5465	5465	5457	5475	2042	3750	
尉犁县	Yuli [Lopnur] County	4704	4704	3562	8029	2281		
若羌县	Ruoqiang [Qarkilik] County	4505	4814	5070	4117	1791		
且末县	Qiemo [Qarqan] County	5778	5807	6220	5310	2007	1719	
焉耆回族自治县	Yanqi Hui Autonomous County	7447	7532	6521	12050	1267	2064	90000
和静县	Hejing County	6947	6947	6465	11775	1590	1380	89999
和硕县	Hoxud County	6773	6773	5896	11117	1966	1868	62715
博湖县	Bohu [Bagrax] County	7516	7516	7020	9264	2098	2045	80291
阿克苏地区	**Aksu Administrative Offices**	**7360**	**7381**	**6537**	**8114**	**1697**	**2110**	**61975**
阿克苏市	Aksu City	7595	7595	6679	7635	2120		55427
温宿县	Wensu [Onsu] County	7858	7866	6573	7135	1633	1573	45000
库车县	Kuqa County	6652	6675	6725	6591	1663	1291	37500
沙雅县	Xayar County	7092	7092	6760	7546	1743	1711	16680
新和县	Xinhe [Toksu] County	6579	6579	6621	6521	1772	1290	
拜城县	Baicheng [Bay] County	8822	8937	6275	12180	1325	2787	93185
乌什县	Wushi [Uxturpan] County	7553	7586	6052	9720	1436	2028	67500
阿瓦提县	Awat County	6709	6709	6677	6750	1463		
柯坪县	Kalpin County	6205	6205	6028	6587	1521	1518	13650
克孜勒苏柯尔克孜自治州	**Kizilsu Kirgiz Autonomous Prefecture**	**5942**	**5951**	**5664**	**6449**	**1523**	**1373**	
阿图什市	Artux City	5426	5426	5236	5824	1513	1784	
阿克陶县	Akto County	6667	6667	6290	7023	1528	2938	
阿合奇县	Akqi County	3671	3665	3932	4050		1150	
乌恰县	Wuqia [Ulugqat] County	4272	4337	4735	3838	1600	1922	
喀什地区	**Kashgar [Kaxgar] Administrative Offices**	**6195**	**6452**	**5753**	**7272**	**1646**	**1689**	
喀什市	Kashgar [Kaxgar] City	6138	6138	5385	6885	1500		
疏附县	Shufu County	6572	6572	5854	7665	1542	1800	
疏勒县	Shule County	6412	6412	5835	7124	1548		
英吉沙县	Yengisar County	6126	6196	5730	6744	1430	1950	
泽普县	Zepu [Poskam] County	4965	6432	5922	7592	1050	2550	
莎车县	Shache [Yarkant] County	6095	6562	5873	6981	1534	1135	
叶城县	Yecheng [Kagilik] County	6896	7227	5872	8805	1703	3299	
麦盖提县	Makit County	6131	6141	5284	7154	1835	1500	
岳普湖县	Yopurga County	6416	6416	5705	7340	1573	1200	
伽师县	Jiashi [Payzawat] County	5883	5915	5731	6147	1404		
巴楚县	Bachu [Maralbexi] County	6473	6473	5752	7293	1858		
塔什库尔干塔吉克自治县	Taxkorgan Tajik Autonomous County	3061	3222	3024	36475	1075		
和田地区	**Hotan Administrative Offices**	**6719**	**6740**	**6061**	**7480**	**1832**	**2674**	
和田市	Hotan City	7027	7038	6052	8249	1555	3375	
和田县	Hotan County	6445	6446	6079	6873	1919	1955	
墨玉县	Moyu [Karakax] County	6571	6576	6095	7033	1907	2223	
皮山县	Pishan [Guma] County	7104	7200	5832	8580	1903	4481	
洛浦县	Lop County	6565	6565	6140	6996	1756	1440	
策勒县	Qira County	6985	7082	6013	8251	1891	2340	
于田县	Yutian [Keriya] County	6801	6810	6155	7461	1746	4381	
民丰县	Minfeng [Niya] County	6564	6564	5779	7423		845	
生产建设兵团	**Xinjiang Production and Construction Group**	**6622**	**6770**	**5800**	**8030**	**2419**	**2822**	**75525**

12-19 各地、州、市、县(市)特色农作物播种面积

Soun Areas of Characteristic Farm Crops by Prefecture,Autonomous Prefecture ,City and County

单位：千公顷 (2011 年) (1000 hectares)

地 区	Region	番 茄 Tomato	工业用番 茄 Tonato in Industry	辣 椒 Peppers	工业用辣 椒 Capsicum	打瓜籽 Melon Seeds	啤酒花 Hop
总 计	**Total**	**110.88**	**91.89**	**67.80**	**46.10**	**138.37**	**3.24**
乌鲁木齐市	**Urumqi City**	**0.83**	**0.31**	**0.92**		**0.07**	**0.01**
＃市辖区	Municipal Districts	0.82	0.31	0.60		0.07	0.01
乌鲁木齐县	Urumqi County	0.01		0.32			
克拉玛依市	**Karamay City**	**0.08**	**0.05**	**0.06**		**0.72**	
吐鲁番地区	**TurpanAdministrative Offices**	**0.87**		**0.47**			
吐鲁番市	Turpan City	0.33		0.07			
鄯善县	Shanshan [piqan]County	0.32		0.19			
托克逊县	Toksun County	0.22		0.21			
哈密地区	**Hami [Kumul]Administrative Offices**	**0.26**		**0.31**			
哈密市	Hami [Kumul]City	0.22		0.26			
巴里坤哈萨克自治县	Barkol KazakAutonomous County	0.04		0.05			
伊吾县	Yiwu [Araturuk]County						
昌吉回族自治州	**Changji Hui Autonomous Prefecture**	**22.24**	**20.13**	**5.51**	**1.50**	**15.43**	**0.27**
昌吉市	Changji City	6.33	6.03	0.42	0.12	0.59	0.03
阜康市	Fukang City	1.48	0.76	1.11	0.25	4.80	
呼图壁县	Hutubi County	5.69	5.65	1.22	1.08	0.79	0.23
玛纳斯县	Manas County	2.96	2.83	0.38	0.03	0.59	
奇台县	Qitai County	1.89	1.33	0.85		4.66	
吉木萨尔县	Jimsar County	3.86	3.53	1.27	0.02	1.34	0.01
木垒哈萨克自治县	Mori Kazak Autonomous County	0.04		0.26		2.68	
伊犁哈萨克自治州	**Ili Kazak Autonomous Prefecture**	**11.07**	**8.82**	**6.68**	**0.44**	**77.36**	**0.34**
伊犁州直属县(市)	**Counties(Cities) Direct Under Ili Prefecture**	**2.81**	**0.97**	**2.32**	**0.44**	**2.46**	
伊宁市	Yining [Gulja]City	0.52		0.56			
奎屯市	Kuytun City	0.15	0.15			0.09	
伊宁县	Yining [Gulja]County	0.74		0.61		0.09	
察布查尔锡伯自治县	Qapqal Xibe Autonomous County	0.17	0.01	0.45	0.24		
霍城县	Huocheng [korgas]County	0.84	0.81	0.23	0.20	1.41	
巩留县	Gongliu [Tokkuzlara]County	0.03		0.25			
新源县	Xinyuan [kunes]County	0.06		0.07		0.17	
昭苏县	Zhaosu [mongolkure]County			0.01			
特克斯县	Tekes County	0.26		0.08			
尼勒克县	Nilka County	0.04		0.06		0.70	

12-19 续表 1 Continued

单位：千公顷 (1000 hectares)

地 区	Region	番 茄 Tomato	工业用番 茄 Tonato in Industry	辣 椒 Peppers	工业用辣 椒 Capsicum	打瓜籽 Melon Seeds	啤酒花 Hop
塔城地区	**Tacheng[Tarbagatai] Administrative Officess**	**8.12**	**7.84**	**4.17**		**43.17**	**0.26**
塔城市	Tacheng [Qoqek] City	0.26	0.05	0.15		14.61	0.13
乌苏市	Usu City	3.91	3.91	0.10		0.59	
额敏县	Emin [Dorbiljin] County	0.81	0.79			20.55	
沙湾县	Shawan County	3.13	3.09	3.92		1.18	0.13
托里县	Toli County					0.99	
裕民县	Yumin [Qagantokay] County					4.89	
和布克赛尔蒙古自治县	Hoboksar Mongol Autonomous County	0.01				0.36	
阿勒泰地区	**Altay Administrative Offices**	**0.15**		**0.19**		**31.73**	**0.08**
阿勒泰市	Altay City	0.02		0.02		3.19	
布尔津县	Burqin County	0.01		0.01		4.09	
富蕴县	Fuyun [Koktokay] County	0.02		0.01		1.87	
福海县	Fuhai [Burultokay] County	0.01				15.91	0.08
哈巴河县	Habahe [Kaba] County	0.08		0.12		6.12	
青河县	Qinghe [Qinggil] County	0.01		0.01		0.49	
吉木乃县	Jeminay County	0.01		0.01		0.06	
博尔塔拉蒙古自治州	**Bortala Mongol Autonomous Prefecture**	**0.70**	**0.54**	**0.14**	**0.01**	**0.44**	
博乐市	Bole [Bortala] City	0.47	0.34	0.10	0.01	0.26	
精河县	Jinghe [Jing] County	0.06	0.03	0.04		0.09	
温泉县	Wenquan [Araxang] County	0.17	0.17			0.09	
巴音郭楞蒙古自治州	**Bayangol Mongol Autonomous Prefecture**	**14.82**	**13.89**	**18.79**	**18.06**	**3.16**	**0.05**
库尔勒市	Korla City	0.13		0.20			
轮台县	Luntai [Bugur] County	0.02					
尉犁县	Yuli [Lopnur] County	0.01		0.01			
若羌县	Ruoqiang [Qarkilik] County	0.01		0.01			
且末县	Qiemo [Qarqan] County	0.03		0.06	0.03		
焉耆回族自治县	Yanqi Hui Autonomous County	3.55	3.44	2.20	2.15	1.26	
和静县	Hejing County	2.87	2.61	8.03	7.69	0.69	
和硕县	Hoxud County	3.96	3.62	5.21	5.15	0.51	
博湖县	Bohu [Bagrax] County	4.23	4.22	3.06	3.04	0.69	0.05
阿克苏地区	**Aksu Administrative Offices**	**5.97**	**4.40**	**5.48**	**4.36**	**0.44**	**0.08**
阿克苏市	Aksu City	0.42		0.18			
温宿县	Wensu [Onsu] County	0.11		0.14			
库车县	Kuqa County	0.28	0.02	0.17			

12-19 续表 2 Continued

单位：千公顷 (1000 hectares)

地区	Region	番茄 Tomato	工业用番茄 Tonato in Industry	辣椒 Peppers	工业用辣椒 Capsicum	打瓜籽 Melon Seeds	啤酒花 Hop
沙雅县	Xayar County	0.08		0.07			
新和县	Xinhe [Toksu] County	0.29		0.08			
拜城县	Baicheng [Bay] County	2.29	2.01	4.67	4.36	0.40	0.08
乌什县	Wushi [Uxturpan] County	2.37	2.37	0.08			
阿瓦提县	Awat County	0.13		0.08		0.04	
柯坪县	Kalpin County	0.01		0.01			
克孜勒苏柯尔克孜自治州	**Kizilsu Kirgiz Autonomous Prefecture**	**0.24**		**0.10**			
阿图什市	Artux City	0.02		0.01			
阿克陶县	Akto County	0.13		0.08			
阿合奇县	Akqi County	0.01					
乌恰县	Wuqia [Ulugqat] County	0.08		0.01			
喀什地区	**Kashgar [Kaxgar] Administrative Offices**	**7.39**	**0.49**	**13.93**	**8.07**	**0.13**	
喀什市	Kashgar [Kaxgar] City	0.80		0.11			
疏附县	Shufu County	1.49		1.25			
疏勒县	Shule County	0.43		0.23			
英吉沙县	Yengisar County	0.47		0.51			
泽普县	Zepu [Poskam] County	0.11		0.69	0.67		
莎车县	Shache [Yarkant] County	0.56	0.49	8.27	5.86	0.13	
叶城县	Yecheng [Kagilik] County	1.04		2.39	1.49		
麦盖提县	Makit County	0.15		0.09	0.05		
岳普湖县	Yopurga County	0.07		0.03			
伽师县	Jiashi [Payzawat] County	2.17		0.24			
巴楚县	Bachu [Maralbexi] County	0.10		0.13			
塔什库尔干塔吉克自治县	Taxkorgan Tajik Autonomous County						
和田地区	**Hotan Administrative Offices**	**1.69**	**0.36**	**1.19**	**0.40**		
和田市	Hotan City	0.27		0.12			
和田县	Hotan County	0.12		0.29			
墨玉县	Moyu [Karakax] County	0.09		0.24	0.24		
皮山县	Pishan [Guma] County	0.45	0.36	0.23			
洛浦县	Lop County	0.11		0.05			
策勒县	Qira County	0.02		0.01			
于田县	Yutian [Keriya] County	0.59		0.23	0.16		
民丰县	Minfeng [Niya] County	0.04		0.01			
生产建设兵团	**Xinjiang Production and Construction Group**	**49.89**	**47.19**	**19.53**	**16.65**	**40.64**	**2.50**

12-20 各地、州、市、县(市)特色农作物产量

Output of Characteristic Farm Crops by Prefecture,Autonomous Prefectura,City and County

单位：吧 (2011 年) (ton)

地 区	Region	番 茄 Tomato	工业用番 茄 Tonato in Industry	辣 椒 Peppers	工业用辣 椒 Capsicum	枸 杞 Medlar	打瓜籽 Melon Seeds	啤酒花 Hop
总 计	**Total**	**9888480**	**8870756**	**2395133**	**1446866**	**19551**	**237053**	**12964**
乌鲁木齐市	**Urumqi City**	**52421**	**18132**	**43115**		**156**	**84**	**40**
#市辖区	Municipal Districts	51791	18132	32181		156	84	40
乌鲁木齐县	Urumqi County	630		10934				
克拉玛依市	**Karamay City**	**6685**	**4440**	**1962**			**1267**	
吐鲁番地区	**TurpanAdministrative Offices**	**39852**		**8520**				
吐鲁番市	Turpan City	13708		1018				
鄯善县	Shanshan [piqan]County	10460		2870				
托克逊县	Toksun County	15684		4632				
哈密地区	**Hami [Kumul]Administrative Offices**	**14421**		**12758**				
哈密市	Hami [Kumul]City	13041		11273				
巴里坤哈萨克自治县	Barkol KazakAutonomous County	1380		1352				
伊吾县	Yiwu [Araturuk]County			133				
昌吉回族自治州	**Changji Hui Autonomous Prefecture**	**1855602**	**1741651**	**187436**	**49851**	**114**	**32302**	**1800**
昌吉市	Changji City	565340	537822	15898	2600		4834	413
阜康市	Fukang City	96966	74400	34505	11890	27	10696	
呼图壁县	Hutubi County	402551	400031	37924	31701		1754	1367
玛纳斯县	Manas County	302839	284897	16226	2940	87	1205	
奇台县	Qitai County	117370	98316	27757			6879	5
吉木萨尔县	Jimsar County	368296	346185	45634	720		3008	15
木垒哈萨克自治县	Mori Kazak Autonomous County	2240		9492			3926	
伊犁哈萨克自治州	**Ili Kazak Autonomous Prefecture**	**1157803**	**1044713**	**230188**	**6804**	**890**	**111158**	**3408**
伊犁州直属县(市)	**Counties (Cities) Direct Under Ili Prefecture**	**158050**	**60164**	**102903**	**6804**		**3866**	
伊宁市	Yining [Gulja]City	41321	88	46316			6	
奎屯市	Kuytun City	11968	11968				195	
伊宁县	Yining [Gulja]County	29268		20425			211	
察布查尔锡伯自治县	Qapqal Xibe Autonomous County	9949	1081	14804	3454			
霍城县	Huocheng [korgas]County	48123	47027	3750	3350		2065	
巩留县	Gongliu [Tokkuzlara]County	1750		9300				
新源县	Xinyuan [kunes]County	5181		3256			289	
昭苏县	Zhaosu [mongolkure]County			540				
特克斯县	Tekes County	8550		2622				
尼勒克县	Nilka County	1940		1890			1100	

注：特色农作物产量为国家审定数，分地州合计数不等于全区总计数。
Note: The oil-bearing crop planted at the edge or margin of fields in small number of counties (cities), whose area is not calculated, thus per-unit output is relatively higher.

12-20 续表 1 Continued

单位：吨 (ton)

地 区	Region	番 茄 Tomato	工业用番 茄 Tonato in Industr	辣 椒 Peppers	工业用辣 椒 Capsicum	枸 杞 Medlar	打瓜籽 Melon Seeds	啤酒花 Hop
塔城地区	**Tacheng[Tarbagatai] Administrative Officess**	**994621**	**984549**	**121950**		**527**	**56467**	**2928**
塔城市	Tacheng [Qoqek] City	11667	3100	4950			18985	2000
乌苏市	Usu City	625172	625172	709		305	1679	
额敏县	Emin [Dorbiljin] County	73088	72650				26187	
沙湾县	Shawan County	284627	283627	116281		222	2630	926
托里县	Toli County	14		10			1335	
裕民县	Yumin [Qagantokay] County						5299	
和布克赛尔蒙古自治县	Hoboksar Mongol Autonomous County	53					352	2
阿勒泰地区	**Altay Administrative Offices**	**5132**		**5335**		**363**	**50825**	**480**
阿勒泰市	Altay City	1184		1016			5984	
布尔津县	Burqin County	48		480			5515	
富蕴县	Fuyun [Koktokay] County	883		431			3379	
福海县	Fuhai [Burultokay] County	238		94		363	24182	480
哈巴河县	Habahe [Kaba] County	2264		2990			11023	
青河县	Qinghe [Qinggil] County	275		204			663	
吉木乃县	Jeminay County	240		120			79	
博尔塔拉蒙古自治州	**Bortala Mongol Autonomous Prefecture**	**60849**	**54395**	**3690**	**200**	**14606**	**736**	
博乐市	Bole [Bortala] City	41624	35934	2667	200	8	414	
精河县	Jinghe [Jing] County	4174	3410	1023		14598	219	
温泉县	Wenquan [Araxang] County	15051	15051				103	
巴音郭楞蒙古自治州	**Bayangol Mongol Autonomous Prefecture**	**1604754**	**1512445**	**757761**	**724424**		**6042**	**700**
库尔勒市	Korla City	10486		15243				
轮台县	Luntai [Bugur] County	1050		216				
尉犁县	Yuli [Lopnur] County	440		174				
若羌县	Ruoqiang [Qarkilik] County	685		361				
且末县	Qiemo [Qarqan] County	620		1605	900			
焉耆回族自治县	Yanqi Hui Autonomous County	393692	381337	98406	96798		2834	
和静县	Hejing County	311860	282111	253787	242239		1249	
和硕县	Hoxud County	439509	404048	259596	256923		865	
博湖县	Bohu [Bagrax] County	446412	444949	128373	127564		1094	700
阿克苏地区	**Aksu Administrative Offices**	**347506**	**266625**	**40365**	**21991**		**886**	**230**
阿克苏市	Aksu City	29616		4821				
温宿县	Wensu [Onsu] County	1570		1560				
库车县	Kuqa County	7531	744	3064				

12-20 续表 2 Continued

单位：吨 (ton)

地　区	Region	番　茄 Tomato	工业用番　茄 Tonato in Industr	辣　椒 Peppers	工业用辣　椒 Capsicum	枸　杞 Medlar	打瓜籽 Melon Seeds	啤酒花 Hop
沙雅县	Xayar County	825		831				
新和县	Xinhe [Toksu] County	13035		1784				
拜城县	Baicheng [Bay] County	205986	184493	24532	21991		886	230
乌什县	Wushi [Uxturpan] County	81388	81388	305				
阿瓦提县	Awat County	7450		3390				
柯坪县	Kalpin County	105		78				
克孜勒苏柯尔克孜自治州	**Kizilsu Kirgiz Autonomous Prefecture**	**5101**		**4276**				
阿图什市	Artux City	1086		733				
阿克陶县	Akto County	2140		3440				
阿合奇县	Akqi County	330		30				
乌恰县	Wuqia [Ulugqat] County	1545		73				
喀什地区	**Kashgar [Kaxgar] Administrative Offices**	**339007**	**22200**	**626510**	**219609**		**226**	
喀什市	Kashgar [Kaxgar] City	43560		4015				
疏附县	Shufu County	78050		18750				
疏勒县	Shule County	14439		5000				
英吉沙县	Yengisar County	12410		9371				
泽普县	Zepu [Poskam] County	6400		28766	28000			
莎车县	Shache [Yarkant] County	22215	22200	409200	100703		226	
叶城县	Yecheng [Kagilik] County	59660		133152	88106			
麦盖提县	Makit County	9200		4216	2800			
岳普湖县	Yopurga County	4720		760				
伽师县	Jiashi [Payzawat] County	83653		7200				
巴楚县	Bachu [Maralbexi] County	4700		6080				
塔什库尔干塔吉克自治县	Taxkorgan Tajik Autonomous County							
和田地区	**Hotan Administrative Offices**	**79912**	**16489**	**27928**	**4348**			
和田市	Hotan City	14560		6184				
和田县	Hotan County	6055		9053				
墨玉县	Moyu [Karakax] County	3486		2790	2790			
皮山县	Pishan [Guma] County	20900	16489	5521				
洛浦县	Lop County	3756		1013				
策勒县	Qira County	744		416				
于田县	Yutian [Keriya] County	29205		2770	1558			
民丰县	Minfeng [Niya] County	1206		181				
生产建设兵团	**Xinjiang Production and Construction Group**	**4854454**	**4665017**	**695077**	**568231**	**3785**	**84352**	**6786**

12-21 各地、州、市林业生产情况
Condition on Forest Products by Prefecture, Autonomous Prefecture, City

单位:公顷 (2011 年) (hectare)

地区	Region	当年造林面积 Planting Area in the Current Year	用材林 Timber Forest	经济林 Economic Forest	防护林 Windbreak	薪炭林 Firewood Forest	特种用途林 Forest for Special Purpose
总计	**Total**	**205796**	**843**	**93779**	**108345**	**2356**	**473**
乌鲁木齐市	Urumqi City	2975			2975		
克拉玛依市	Karamay City	1739			1739		
吐鲁番地区	Turpan Administrative Offices	4436	128	976	2765	167	400
哈密地区	Hami [Kumul]Administrative Offices	5214		1097	3917	200	
昌吉回族自治州	Changji Hui Autonomous Prefecture	26296	27	3535	22734		
伊犁哈萨克自治州	Ili Kazak Administrative Prefecture	64186	668	28079	33934	1485	20
伊犁州直属县(市)	Counties (Cities) Direct Under Ili Prefecture	29071	570	25594	2361	546	
塔城地区	Tacheng [Tarbagatai] Administrative Offices	15313	98	806	13450	939	20
阿勒泰地区	Altay Administrative Offices	19802		1679	18123		
博尔塔拉蒙古自治州	Bortala Mongol Autonomous Prefecture	4068		104	3964		
巴音郭楞蒙古自治州	Bayangol Mongol Autonomous Prefecture	13843		8967	4577	299	
阿克苏地区	Aksu Administrative Offices	22500		17864	4636		
克孜勒苏柯尔克孜自治州	Kizilsu Kirgiz Autonomous Prefecture	2839		1212	1627		
喀什地区	Kashgar [Kaxgar] Administrative Offices	21750		18607	3074	69	
和田地区	Hotan Administrative Offices	16267		12215	3916	136	
生产建设兵团	Xinjiang Production and Construction Group	19599	20	1123	18403		53

地区	Region	迹地更新面积 Renewing Area in Slash	当年零星植树(万株) Fragmentary Planting (10 000 trees)	年末实有育苗面积 Actual Sapling Breeding Area	幼林抚育作业面积 Tending Area of Young Growth	成林抚育面积 Tending Area of Full Growth	核桃产量(吨) Walnut Output (ton)	村及村以下木材采伐量(立方米) Timber Felling Output in Village or Below (cu.m)
总计	**Total**	**1566**	**2096.72**	**14325**	**2836121**	**2017942**	**235860**	**315631**
乌鲁木齐市	Urumqi City		6.00	220		85		496
克拉玛依市	Karamay City		129.00	460	2800	9295		
吐鲁番地区	Turpan Administrative Offices	17		103	5000	6367	170	1350
哈密地区	Hami[Kumul] Administrative Offices			112	103323	23133		845
昌吉回族自治州	Changji Hui Autonomous Prefecture		71.21	5547	42205	37929		54646
伊犁哈萨克自治州	Ili Kazak Administrative Prefecture	348	522.96	1362	339468	355828	646	92153
伊犁州直属县(市)	Counties (Cities) Direct Under Ili Prefecture	253	368.90	971	211004	70694	646	58783
塔城地区	Tacheng [Tarbagatai] Administrative Offices	95	31.06	267	39231	124678		30618
阿勒泰地区	Altay Administrative Offices		123.00	124	89233	160456		2752
博尔塔拉蒙古自治州	Bortala Mongol Autonomous Prefecture	77	33.50	100	17157	14323	2	10864
巴音郭楞蒙古自治州	Bayangol Mongol Autonomous Prefecture	39	70.07	650	173684	49294	207	29576
阿克苏地区	Aksu Administrative Offices	337	44.73	298	1185869	710584	74314	45219
克孜勒苏柯尔克孜自治州	Kizilsu Kirgiz Autonomous Prefecture		10.00	195	13750	23165	560	5255
喀什地区	Kashgar [Kaxgar] Administrative Offices	318	601.10	1130	456903	250164	96139	54324
和田地区	Hotan Administrative Offices	311	449.83	1615	230401	170399	62672	20903
生产建设兵团	Xinjiang Production and Construction Group	119	153.51	2235	263931	349097	1150	

12-22 各地、州、市水果种植面积
Planted Area of Fruits by Prefecture, Autonomous Prefecture, City

单位:公顷 (2011 年) (hectare)

地区	Region	合计 Total	苹果 Apples	梨 Pears	葡萄 Grapes	#无核葡萄 Seedless Grapes
总计	**Total**	**990313**	**83326**	**69923**	**135509**	**43019**
乌鲁木齐市	Urumqi City	807	72	2	429	
克拉玛依市	Karamay City					
吐鲁番地区	TurpanAdministrative Offices	40604		20	30334	27717
哈密地区	Hami [Kumul] Administrative Offices	28846	34	39	3739	3017
昌吉回族自治州	Changji Hui Autonomous Prefecture	14952	3159	23	7082	
伊犁哈萨克自治州	Ili Kazak Autonomous Prefecture	71207	44838	183	6204	
伊犁州直属县(市)	Counties (Cities) Direct Under Ili Prefecture	69027	43761	146	5404	
塔城地区	Tacheng [Tarbagatai] Administrative Offices	1727	1060	37	374	
阿勒泰地区	Altay Administrative Offices	453	17		426	
博尔塔拉蒙古自治州	Bortala MongolAutonomous Prefecture	345	86	6	233	
巴音郭楞蒙古自治州	Bayangol Mongol Autonomous Prefecture	95534	339	36213	13466	
阿克苏地区	Aksu Administrative Offices	201148	14268	13363	7417	
克孜勒苏柯尔克孜自治州	Kizilsu Kirgiz Autonomous Prefecture	27319	128	17	6671	
喀什地区	Kashgar [Kaxgar] Administrative Offices	255707	3881	1427	5034	
和田地区	Hotan Administrative Offices	68074	1156	494	11631	2412
生产建设兵团	Xinjiang Production and Construction Group	185770	15365	18136	43268	9872

地区	Region	桃 Peaches	杏 Apricots	红枣 Jujubes	石榴 Pomegraniate	其它 Others
总计	**Total**	**12893**	**193591**	**456074**	**14237**	**24761**
乌鲁木齐市	Urumqi City	131	70	31		73
克拉玛依市	Karamay City					
吐鲁番地区	TurpanAdministrative Offices	6	1993	7811	440	
哈密地区	Hami [Kumul] Administrative Offices	31	2326	21906		770
昌吉回族自治州	Changji Hui Autonomous Prefecture	706	2120	94		1768
伊犁哈萨克自治州	Ili Kazak Autonomous Prefecture	1935	12284	490		5274
伊犁州直属县(市)	Counties (Cities) Direct Under Ili Prefecture	1805	12273	468		5170
塔城地区	Tacheng [Tarbagatai] Administrative Offices	123	10	22		101
阿勒泰地区	Altay Administrative Offices	7				3
博尔塔拉蒙古自治州	Bortala Mongol Autonomous Prefecture	10	7	2		2
巴音郭楞蒙古自治州	Bayangol Mongol Autonomous Prefecture	277	16801	26518	4	1915
阿克苏地区	Aksu Administrative Offices	418	31791	130431	103	3357
克孜勒苏柯尔克孜自治州	Kizilsu Kirgiz Autonomous Prefecture	860	16579	1824	215	1023
喀什地区	Kashgar [Kaxgar] Administrative Offices	5311	87104	136114	9191	7645
和田地区	Hotan Administrative Offices	1163	17778	29009	4255	2588
生产建设兵团	Xinjiang Production and Construction Group	2044	4739	101843	30	346

12-23 各地、州、市水果产量

Output of Fruits by Prefecture, Autonomous Prefecture, City

单位：吨 (2011 年) (ton)

地区	Region	合计 Total	苹果 Apples	梨 Pears	葡萄 Grapes	#无核葡萄 Seedless Grapes
总计	**Total**	**6016470**	**715136**	**605731**	**1754725**	**801231**
乌鲁木齐市	Urumqi City	10651	1158		6803	
克拉玛依市	Karamay City					
吐鲁番地区	TurpanAdministrative Offices	642226		197	617068	562032
哈密地区	Hami [Kumul] Administrative Offices	93182	159	393	81522	58786
昌吉回族自治州	Changji Hui Autonomous Prefecture	157860	16850	99	123243	7
伊犁哈萨克自治州	Ili Kazak Autonomous Prefecture	287730	145173	1448	75318	8
伊犁州直属县(市)	Counties (Cities) Direct Under Ili Prefecture	268014	138689	763	66099	
塔城地区	Tacheng [Tarbagatai] Administrative Offices	18758	6000	685	8914	8
阿勒泰地区	Altay Administrative Offices	958	484		305	
博尔塔拉蒙古自治州	Bortala MongolAutonomous Prefecture	2439	1032	19	1243	
巴音郭楞蒙古自治州	Bayangol Mongol Autonomous Prefecture	311336	2526	133399	22598	
阿克苏地区	Aksu Administrative Offices	1334567	243308	255914	113093	
克孜勒苏柯尔克孜自治州	Kizilsu Kirgiz Autonomous Prefecture	186867	307	43	65213	
喀什地区	Kashgar [Kaxgar] Administrative Offices	1336923	89079	14224	84118	
和田地区	Hotan Administrative Offices	376448	10999	3930	184093	56066
生产建设兵团	Xinjiang Production and Construction Group	1276241	204545	196065	380413	124332

地区	Region	桃 Peachs	杏 Apricots	红枣 Jujubes	石榴 Pomegranate	其它 Others
总计	**Total**	**109212**	**1607632**	**1057983**	**56506**	**109545**
乌鲁木齐市	Urumqi City	1193	634	8		855
克拉玛依市	Karamay City					
吐鲁番地区	TurpanAdministrative Offices	47	9035	14858	1021	
哈密地区	Hami [Kumul] Administrative Offices	93	1651	9364		
昌吉回族自治州	Changji Hui Autonomous Prefecture	8548	4215	304		4601
伊犁哈萨克自治州	Ili Kazak Autonomous Prefecture	19218	38982	1121		6470
伊犁州直属县(市)	Counties (Cities) Direct Under Ili Prefecture	17491	38864	985		5123
塔城地区	Tacheng [Tarbagatai] Administrative Offices	1588	118	136		1317
阿勒泰地区	Altay Administrative Offices	139				30
博尔塔拉蒙古自治州	Bortala MongolAutonomous Prefecture	139	6			
巴音郭楞蒙古自治州	Bayangol Mongol Autonomous Prefecture	1206	81699	65502	1	4405
阿克苏地区	Aksu Administrative Offices	143	376661	316714	45	28689
克孜勒苏柯尔克孜自治州	Kizilsu Kirgiz Autonomous Prefecture	505	115764	710	811	3514
喀什地区	Kashgar [Kaxgar] Administrative Offices	39259	842851	180863	36652	49877
和田地区	Hotan Administrative Offices	6997	111963	34028	17926	6512
生产建设兵团	Xinjiang Production and Construction Group	31864	24171	434511	50	4622

12-24 主要年份牲畜饲养情况
Number of Livestock in Main Years

单位：万头(只) (10 000 heads)

年 份 Year	大牲畜年底头数 Large Animals (year-end)	牛 Cattle and Buffaloes	马 Horses	驴 Donkeys	骡 Mules	骆驼 Camels	在大牲畜中役畜 Draught Animals
1978	446.19	222.39	112.39	96.61	1.61	13.19	148.34
1980	482.55	250.65	106.89	108.88	1.72	14.41	154.86
1985	517.55	293.26	99.54	106.57	2.17	16.05	197.29
1990	575.88	338.22	104.58	112.96	2.69	17.43	209.95
1995	580.04	343.54	100.47	117.04	2.77	16.22	213.61
1996	589.41	349.78	101.16	119.36	2.76	16.34	215.05
1997	600.12	359.81	100.32	120.74	2.87	16.38	207.15
1998	606.79	364.29	100.26	123.45	2.80	15.99	205.31
1999	615.91	370.52	101.47	124.99	2.78	16.15	189.86
2000	632.93	384.98	102.57	125.94	2.74	16.70	173.37
2001	630.67	386.40	99.38	126.06	2.84	15.99	172.08
2002	654.46	414.13	99.71	122.22	2.59	15.81	169.51
2003	694.53	453.06	99.39	124.02	2.48	15.58	163.72
2004	716.56	482.30	95.78	120.82	2.36	15.30	151.49
2005	739.72	504.16	94.19	123.90	2.38	15.09	134.81
2006	736.33	502.86	92.09	124.94	2.14	14.30	145.97
2007	702.03	486.98	86.09	113.92	1.83	13.20	120.79
2008	543.41	336.00	83.85	109.25	1.45	12.86	96.56
2009	536.83	330.76	84.60	107.17	1.35	12.95	99.48
2010	536.82	330.47	85.29	106.96	1.19	12.91	108.93
2011	523.00	318.20	85.66	104.73	1.08	13.33	158.20

年 份 Year	猪年底头数 Hogs (year-end)	羊年底只数 Sheep and Goats (year-end)	山羊 Goats	绵羊 Sheep	牲畜出栏头数 Slanghtered Fattened Animals withina Year	#猪 Pork Pig	#牛 Beef Cattle	#羊 Mutton Sheep
1978	103.25	1927.34	349.63	1577.91	460.41	50.75	18.75	382.76
1980	84.62	2105.43	388.89	1716.54	584.09	67.32	24.22	477.81
1985	66.58	2431.91	394.79	2037.12	836.39	49.07	42.33	723.51
1990	89.71	2830.81	449.43	2381.38	1242.89	78.93	70.10	1070.43
1995	135.26	3009.02	471.38	2537.64	1709.93	122.32	101.20	1448.72
1996	138.18	3136.21	498.10	2638.11	1859.28	153.75	116.25	1550.65
1997	145.73	3261.81	514.60	2747.21	2096.67	173.06	125.72	1753.88
1998	169.82	3447.38	528.05	2919.33	2222.27	197.39	140.82	1837.57
1999	188.34	3592.29	555.21	3037.08	2223.89	203.87	145.95	1820.71
2000	201.53	3690.21	586.70	3103.51	2455.99	224.46	154.53	2017.36
2001	208.23	3764.88	601.14	3163.74	2633.83	246.00	179.32	2147.31
2002	219.08	3908.23	626.42	3281.81	2878.39	259.05	188.65	2363.02
2003	227.71	4104.30	657.15	3447.15	3201.99	307.74	202.23	2626.94
2004	223.08	4266.73	669.47	3597.26	3437.59	352.83	220.80	2790.53
2005	238.38	4355.50	659.75	3695.75	3756.92	358.71	249.41	3081.88
2006	243.88	4359.50	654.26	3705.24	4063.52	390.82	278.69	3317.99
2007	237.90	4083.44	608.10	3475.34	4108.28	393.70	271.76	3361.99
2008	177.00	3025.70	453.85	2571.85	3388.09	265.50	207.30	2842.30
2009	180.42	3127.50	469.13	2658.37	3135.72	254.23	210.89	2604.48
2010	171.96	3013.37	528.73	2484.64	3498.52	262.72	216.69	2947.22
2011	158.20	3016.40	489.70	2526.70	3450.77	256.10	203.90	2913.80

注：牲畜出栏数 1999 年以后计算口径与 1998 年以前不同。
Note: The calculating norm of cattles out of stock after 1999 was different from that prior to that in 1998.

12-25 各地、州、市、县(市)牲畜年底头数

Number of Livestock at the Year-end by Prefecture, Autonomous Prefecture, City and County

单位：万头(只)　　　　(2011 年)　　　　(10 000 heads)

地　区	Region	合 计 Total	#牛 Cattle and Buffaloes	#马 Horses	#驴 Donkeys	#猪 Hogs	#山羊 Goats	#绵羊 Sheep
总　计	**Total**	**3697.60**	**318.20**	**85.66**	**104.73**	**158.20**	**489.70**	**2526.70**
乌鲁木齐市	**Urumqi City**	**70.18**	**7.84**	**1.67**	**0.23**	**7.13**	**18.35**	**34.62**
#乌鲁木齐县	Urumqi County	25.56	2.68	1.28	0.12	0.04	3.68	17.69
克拉玛依市	**Karamay City**	**13.46**	**0.72**	**0.06**	**0.01**	**6.89**	**1.89**	**3.86**
吐鲁番地区	**TurpanAdministrative Offices**	**105.33**	**4.82**	**0.34**	**2.21**	**2.28**	**17.96**	**77.30**
吐鲁番市	Turpan City	34.82	1.54	0.03	0.64	1.33	7.53	23.72
鄯善县	Shanshan [piqan]County	33.71	0.80	0.07	0.53	0.90	4.02	27.24
托克逊县	Toksun County	36.80	2.48	0.24	1.04	0.05	6.41	26.34
哈密地区	**Hami [Kumul]Administrative Offices**	**113.76**	**6.91**	**1.21**	**0.86**	**11.65**	**19.91**	**72.18**
哈密市	Hami [Kumul]City	41.70	2.38	0.28	0.33	2.65	8.02	27.7
巴里坤哈萨克自治县	Barkol KazakAutonomous County	54.54	3.33	0.69	0.43	4.74	8.24	36.61
伊吾县	Yiwu [Araturuk]County	17.52	1.20	0.24	0.10	4.26	3.65	7.87
昌吉回族自治州	**Changji Hui Autonomous Prefecture**	**403.38**	**45.21**	**5.22**	**1.33**	**53.57**	**44.25**	**251.94**
昌吉市	Changji City	73.16	8.44	0.95	0.08	17.51	10.84	35.08
阜康市	Fukang City	26.22	4.05	0.35	0.05	3.00	5.92	12.73
呼图壁县	Hutubi County	58.19	9.30	1.23	0.04	6.84	5.72	34.80
玛纳斯县	Manas County	54.08	4.98	0.74	0.12	7.91	1.68	38.45
奇台县	Qitai County	86.05	9.58	0.69	0.41	9.18	7.96	57.87
吉木萨尔县	Jimsar County	52.13	6.05	0.59	0.26	6.20	4.84	34.10
木垒哈萨克自治县	Mori Kazak Autonomous County	53.55	2.81	0.67	0.37	2.93	7.29	38.91
伊犁哈萨克自治州	**Ili Kazak Autonomous Prefecture**	**1341.62**	**226.62**	**58.48**	**3.15**	**51.38**	**127.77**	**867.64**
伊犁州直属县(市)	**Counties (Cities) Direct Under Ili Prefecture**	**624.59**	**128.09**	**38.75**	**2.86**	**31.97**	**24.47**	**397.82**
伊宁市	Yining [Gulja]City	22.64	4.73	0.39	0.22	1.85	1.16	14.26
奎屯市	Kuytun City	3.17	0.12	0.01		2.42	0.14	0.48
伊宁县	Yining [Gulja]County	86.66	17.16	2.55	0.55	10.25	6.50	49.50
察布查尔锡伯自治县	Qapqal Xibe Autonomous County	40.85	6.84	1.33	0.92	2.69	3.19	25.88
霍城县	Huocheng [korgas]County	70.72	12.21	1.74	0.65	4.42	1.69	49.90
巩留县	Gongliu [Tokkuzlara]County	56.00	12.35	3.73	0.37	2.95	2.61	33.95
新源县	Xinyuan [kunes]County	100.88	22.64	7.98	0.05	2.17	2.08	65.95
昭苏县	Zhaosu [mongolkure]County	84.85	16.10	8.21	0.02	2.87	1.44	56.16
特克斯县	Tekes County	69.45	16.71	4.54	0.03	0.95	2.46	44.73
尼勒克县	Nilka County	89.37	19.23	8.27	0.05	1.40	3.20	57.01
塔城地区	**Tacheng [Tarbagatai] Administrative Offices**	**443.66**	**44.13**	**9.49**	**0.27**	**17.69**	**66.53**	**303.46**
塔城市	Tacheng [Qoqek] City	62.94	6.55	1.40	0.09	2.01	5.51	47.18
乌苏市	Usu City	72.36	4.60	0.82	0.09	4.15	12.44	49.92
额敏县	Emin [Dorbiljin] County	71.72	6.24	1.35		1.69	10.13	52.13
沙湾县	Shawan County	61.37	8.23	0.70	0.02	9.07	6.78	36.40
托里县	Toli County	65.97	8.41	1.87	0.05	0.22	10.93	43.98
裕民县	Yumin [Qagantokay] County	60.68	5.78	1.92		0.35	8.92	43.30
和布克赛尔蒙古自治县	Hoboksar Mongol Autonomous County	48.62	4.32	1.43	0.02	0.20	11.82	30.55
阿勒泰地区	**Altay Administrative Offices**	**273.37**	**54.40**	**10.24**	**0.02**	**1.72**	**36.77**	**166.36**
阿勒泰市	Altay City	49.62	12.02	1.95	0.01	0.42	2.88	31.70
布尔津县	Burqin County	31.09	11.06	1.79		0.22	3.49	14.07
富蕴县	Fuyun [Koktokay] County	60.99	7.11	2.70	0.01	0.08	8.54	41.28
福海县	Fuhai [Burultokay] County	41.32	7.19	0.70		0.81	5.54	26.44
哈巴河县	Habahe [Kaba] County	40.29	11.39	1.52		0.09	5.83	21.10
青河县	Qinghe [Qinggil] County	28.65	3.02	0.84		0.05	7.40	17.10
吉木乃县	Jeminay County	21.41	2.61	0.74		0.05	3.09	14.67

注：1.全区总计不等于地方与生产建设兵团汇总数。2.全区总计数为国家统计局审定数。

Note:a)The region total data is not equal to the sum of local and Production and Construction Groups.b)The region total data refer to approvable data of NBS.

12-25 续表 Continued

单位：万头(只) (10 000 heads)

地　　区	Region	合 计 Total	#牛 Cattle and Buffaloes	#马 Horses	#驴 Donkeys	#猪 Hogs	#山羊 Goats	#绵羊 Sheep
博尔塔拉蒙古自治州	**Bortala Mongol Autonomous Prefecture**	**108.90**	**7.11**	**1.36**	**0.18**	**5.25**	**12.45**	**82.32**
博乐市	Bole [Bortala] City	38.45	2.86	0.33	0.10	2.79	2.99	29.26
精河县	Jinghe [Jing] County	36.85	1.63	0.38	0.02	1.23	6.56	26.99
温泉县	Wenquan [Araxang] County	33.60	2.62	0.65	0.06	1.23	2.90	26.07
巴音郭楞蒙古自治州	**Bayangol Mongol Autonomous Prefecture**	**303.22**	**14.84**	**3.68**	**2.93**	**28.20**	**56.49**	**196.38**
库尔勒市	Korla City	29.39	1.08	0.07	0.15	8.40	3.27	16.42
轮台县	Luntai [Bugur] County	36.30	1.30	0.02	0.75	1.45	8.62	24.14
尉犁县	Yuli [Lopnur] County	34.12	0.66	0.05	0.17	0.41	19.01	13.81
若羌县	Ruoqiang [Qarkilik] County	9.88	0.35	0.05	0.24	0.74	1.30	7.16
且末县	Qiemo [Qarqan] County	36.12	1.89	0.10	1.13	0.82	8.80	23.15
焉耆回族自治县	Yanqi Hui Autonomous County	24.99	1.78	0.08	0.06	1.80	0.76	20.51
和静县	Hejing County	92.33	6.37	2.51	0.38	3.83	8.60	70.52
和硕县	Hoxud County	22.15	0.81	0.55	0.03	3.25	5.03	12.21
博湖县	Bohu [Bagrax] County	17.94	0.60	0.25	0.02	7.50	1.10	8.46
阿克苏地区	**Aksu Administrative Offices**	**441.03**	**33.38**	**5.27**	**10.57**	**16.61**	**110.09**	**264.15**
阿克苏市	Aksu City	50.23	3.12	0.33	0.56	8.43	5.19	32.60
温宿县	Wensu [Onsu] County	57.97	3.58	0.87	0.95	1.77	9.70	41.05
库车县	Kuqa County	69.97	4.99	0.57	1.32	2.08	19.64	41.22
沙雅县	Xayar County	43.65	2.64	0.48	1.38	1.78	18.72	18.52
新和县	Xinhe [Toksu] County	23.09	3.11	0.60	1.25	0.29	1.61	16.18
拜城县	Baicheng [Bay] County	87.71	7.76	0.79	2.65	1.71	23.12	51.64
乌什县	Wushi [Uxturpan] County	52.51	5.27	1.34	1.71	0.13	18.10	25.78
阿瓦提县	Awat County	37.40	2.63	0.25	0.30	0.42	4.91	28.88
柯坪县	Kalpin County	18.50	0.28	0.04	0.45		9.10	8.28
克孜勒苏柯尔克孜自治州	**Kizilsu Kirgiz Autonomous Prefecture**	**162.64**	**16.28**	**2.55**	**3.32**	**0.47**	**37.45**	**101.77**
阿图什市	Artux City	47.00	4.60	0.35	1.00	0.28	11.50	29.02
阿克陶县	Akto County	52.00	9.38	0.21	1.78	0.13	8.17	32.19
阿合奇县	Akqi County	34.05	1.05	1.58	0.11	0.06	10.24	20.95
乌恰县	Wuqia [Ulugqat] County	29.59	1.25	0.41	0.43		7.54	19.61
喀什地区	**Kashgar [Kaxgar] Administrative Offices**	**821.04**	**91.99**	**1.79**	**45.51**	**12.96**	**40.66**	**627.74**
喀什市	Kashgar [Kaxgar] City	27.04	1.57	0.01	0.96	1.99	0.35	22.16
疏附县	Shufu County	105.50	10.60	0.11	3.97	1.63	3.54	85.60
疏勒县	Shule County	79.50	10.00	0.04	4.25	5.30	0.64	59.22
英吉沙县	Yengisar County	38.20	5.80	0.04	2.60	0.35	0.40	28.99
泽普县	Zepu [Poskam] County	40.00	5.73	0.18	2.30	1.12	1.43	29.24
莎车县	Shache [Yarkant] County	121.30	15.50	0.30	6.00	0.40	2.98	96.12
叶城县	Yecheng [Kagilik] County	120.49	16.23	0.30	6.88	0.51	6.60	89.85
麦盖提县	Makit County	57.24	6.92	0.21	2.09	0.47	4.18	43.36
岳普湖县	Yopurga County	38.31	5.00	0.12	7.73	0.14	3.10	22.20
伽师县	Jiashi [Payzawat] County	102.00	6.05	0.28	6.68	0.20	6.25	82.53
巴楚县	Bachu [Maralbexi] County	71.91	5.17	0.12	1.47	0.85	5.53	58.77
塔什库尔干塔吉克自治县	Taxkorgan Tajik Autonomous County	19.55	3.42	0.08	0.58		5.66	9.70
和田地区	**Hotan Administrative Offices**	**500.95**	**29.88**	**1.40**	**33.13**	**1.93**	**29.39**	**404.57**
和田市	Hotan City	33.06	2.42	0.05	1.34	1.23	0.65	27.36
和田县	Hotan County	77.74	5.98	0.18	5.23	0.08	2.32	63.87
墨玉县	Moyu [Karakax] County	116.72	9.10	0.25	8.29	0.07	2.21	96.79
皮山县	Pishan [Guma] County	50.80	1.22	0.14	3.69	0.12	2.81	42.73
洛浦县	Lop County	51.11	4.60	0.06	3.55	0.14	1.07	41.67
策勒县	Qira County	50.68	1.22	0.24	2.66	0.08	2.75	43.65
于田县	Yutian [Keriya] County	89.70	4.91	0.42	7.33	0.17	8.68	67.98
民丰县	Minfeng [Niya] County	31.14	0.43	0.06	1.04	0.04	8.90	20.52
生产建设兵团	**Xinjiang Production and Construction Group**	**668.79**	**40.56**	**2.63**	**1.30**	**183.62**	**42.88**	**397.39**

12-26 主要年份畜产品产量

Output of Livestock Products in Main Years

年份 Year	肉类产量(万吨) Output of meat (10 000 tons)	#牛 Beef	#马 Horse Meat	#骆驼 Camels	#猪 Pork	#羊 Mutton	#禽兔肉 Poultry and Rabbit Meat
1978	9.65	1.85			2.48	5.32	
1980	12.70	2.20	0.60	0.05	3.29	6.48	
1985	18.37	4.23	0.86	0.15	3.09	9.97	
1990	30.46	7.08	1.18	0.18	4.93	15.75	1.22
1995	52.38	13.14	2.05	0.40	8.37	24.48	3.61
1996	60.31	15.18	2.24	0.38	10.43	26.93	4.82
1997	64.40	16.40	2.55	0.38	11.52	27.72	5.38
1998	75.19	19.19	2.82	0.47	13.60	32.49	6.16
1999	81.36	20.61	2.93	0.62	16.02	33.57	6.94
2000	90.00	22.24	3.57	0.63	17.18	37.50	7.76
2001	97.00	23.99	3.55	0.72	18.36	40.48	8.66
2002	105.44	25.90	3.65	0.68	19.70	43.06	10.38
2003	115.00	28.77	3.88	0.69	22.41	45.54	11.46
2004	128.13	30.42	4.34	0.70	24.58	52.65	13.27
2005	141.46	34.22	4.67	0.77	26.18	59.89	13.46
2006	158.21	39.25	4.80	0.90	28.78	66.99	14.92
2007	160.58	42.25	5.09	0.94	31.73	65.02	13.74
2008	114.74	32.40	4.29	0.95	22.30	45.40	7.89
2009	115.31	33.88	4.33	0.73	22.03	43.77	8.52
2010	121.74	35.47	4.67	0.78	23.05	46.95	8.71
2011	120.04	33.80	4.86	0.73	22.50	46.40	9.50

年份 Year	羊毛(万吨) Wool (10 000 tons)	#绵羊毛 Sheep Wool	山羊绒(吨) Cashmere (ton)	驼毛(吨) Camel Hair (ton)	牛奶(万吨) Cow Milk (10 000 tons)	羊奶(万吨) Sheep Milk (10 000 tons)	牛皮(万张) Oxhide (10 000 sheets)	羊皮(万张) Sheep Skin (10 000 sheets)	禽蛋(万吨) Poultry Eggs (10 000 tons)
1978	3.08	3.00	324	371	4.50	0.75	17.36	300.05	
1980	3.31	3.21	263	353	5.84	1.44	18.22	338.32	
1985	7.07	3.91	325	530	16.43	3.27	35.72	587.69	4.29
1990	5.09	4.93	607	656	30.81	4.83	56.76	839.69	6.30
1995	5.66	5.45	716	716	45.21	4.60	91.54	1125.72	9.51
1996	5.99	5.77	780	787	48.76	5.46	92.31	1178.39	10.33
1997	6.25	6.01	813	742	54.18	4.60	96.88	1326.69	12.16
1998	6.48	6.22	811	768	59.96	5.06	110.12	1391.77	13.34
1999	6.76	6.50	849	727	64.81	5.62	118.35	1569.50	16.68
2000	6.98	6.67	893	757	72.54	5.69	125.62	1686.03	18.53
2001	7.30	6.99	973	736	81.09	6.76	143.13	1689.24	20.37
2002	7.78	7.44	1034	824	94.87	5.84	139.87	1801.67	22.64
2003	8.21	7.84	1143	793	113.00	6.21	141.57	1692.35	23.62
2004	8.91	8.49	1228	770	133.32	6.41	150.15	1981.82	24.99
2005	9.38	8.98	1258	730	152.22	5.62	169.53	2022.61	24.99
2006	9.62	8.96	1263	746	179.81	5.60	196.97	2300.73	25.80
2007	9.34	8.92	1265	946	196.23	5.54	191.90	2409.84	28.37
2008	9.03	8.40	1157	1040	137.40	4.96	208.07	2441.52	28.92
2009	7.60	7.16	1261	578	120.88	4.27	193.52	2358.98	23.20
2010	8.69	8.40	1324	602	128.60	4.22	204.14	2403.25	24.35
2011	9.01	8.69	1261	610	130.50	3.41	221.35	2535.63	25.60

12-27 各地、州、市、县(市)总产肉量

Total Output of Meat by Prefecture, Autonomous Prefecture, City and County

单位：吨　　(2011 年)　　(ton)

地　区	Region	合 计 Total	#牛 Beef	#马 Horse	#骆 驼 Camels	#猪 Pork	#山 羊 Goats	#绵 羊 Sheep	#禽 肉 Poultry Meat	#兔肉 Rabbit Meat
总　计	**Total**	**1200439**	**338000**	**48614**	**7308**	**225000**	**72000**	**392000**	**88000**	**7000**
乌鲁木齐市	**Urumqi City**	**57429**	**16164**	**1936**	**199**	**17252**	**5117**	**10022**	**6527**	**21**
#乌鲁木齐县	Urumqi County	10193	2969	1307	108	67	1840	3050	770	9
克拉玛依市	**Karamay City**	**10436**	**516**	**42**		**8595**	**142**	**493**	**648**	
吐鲁番地区	**TurpanAdministrative Offices**	**41134**	**10454**	**265**	**146**	**1674**	**3799**	**23879**	**882**	**35**
吐鲁番市	Turpan City	22480	4494	133	12	724	2171	14853	93	
鄯善县	Shanshan [piqan]County	9679	1860	72	72	670	860	5730	415	
托克逊县	Toksun County	8975	4100	60	62	280	768	3296	374	35
哈密地区	**Hami [Kumul]Administrative Offices**	**49535**	**6974**	**566**	**715**	**18164**	**2954**	**17357**	**2458**	**1**
哈密市	Hami [Kumul]City	21948	4004	131	102	3986	1685	10258	1628	1
巴里坤哈萨克自治县	Barkol KazakAutonomous County	19431	2400	222	480	9308	642	5557	679	
伊吾县	Yiwu [Araturuk]County	8156	570	213	133	4870	627	1542	151	
昌吉回族自治州	**Changji Hui Autonomous Prefecture**	**500322**	**73518**	**3968**	**1344**	**173186**	**9650**	**88241**	**149700**	**237**
昌吉市	Changji City	87676	13311	1134	325	33441	1939	13792	23490	176
阜康市	Fukang City	68122	9449	507	112	14028	2351	11282	30386	
呼图壁县	Hutubi County	81605	13135	744	126	19302	545	12366	35345	24
玛纳斯县	Manas County	65736	5953	566	126	21971	720	11746	24632	22
奇台县	Qitai County	113796	14497	163	105	66070	1621	18635	12570	12
吉木萨尔县	Jimsar County	50103	10422	300	33	9774	977	11367	17157	3
木垒哈萨克自治县	Mori Kazak Autonomous County	33284	6751	554	517	8600	1497	9053	6120	
伊犁哈萨克自治州	**Ili Kazak Autonomous Prefecture**	**470239**	**161421**	**31728**	**2878**	**80580**	**20582**	**131898**	**39294**	**559**
伊犁州直属县(市)	**Counties (Cities) Direct Under Ili Prefecture**	**234278**	**87241**	**21531**	**207**	**40003**	**3390**	**56621**	**24044**	**117**
伊宁市	Yining [Gulja]City	12051	4409	510	18	3260	175	2322	1268	2
奎屯市	Kuytun City	3567	75			3080	6	86	320	
伊宁县	Yining [Gulja]County	38742	18879	1455	32	5472	1141	6868	4425	
察布查尔锡伯自治县	Qapqal Xibe Autonomous County	17435	5641	735		5670	329	3279	1440	41
霍城县	Huocheng [korgas]County	31598	6612	1830		7746	275	7335	7680	22
巩留县	Gongliu [Tokkuzlara]County	26999	10745	2880	30	3976	321	4719	4160	40
新源县	Xinyuan [kunes]County	35004	12340	4680		5383	279	10712	1594	9
昭苏县	Zhaosu [mongolkure]County	24251	10200	3570	15	2130	121	7541	657	2
特克斯县	Tekes County	16805	7658	1260	16	1120	399	5743	600	1
尼勒克县	Nilka County	27826	10682	4611	96	2166	344	8016	1900	

注：同 12-25 表。
Note:The same applies to 12-25 table following.

12-27 续表 1 Continued

单位：吨 (ton)

地　区	Region	合计 Total	#牛 Beef	#马 Horse	#骆驼 Camels	#猪 Pork	#山羊 Goats	#绵羊 Sheep	#禽肉 Poultry Meat	#兔肉 Rabbit Meat
塔城地区	**Tacheng [Tarbagatai] Administrative Officess**	**162328**	**41408**	**7215**	**1316**	**36292**	**12236**	**51935**	**11728**	**44**
塔城市	Tacheng [Qoqek] City	15303	4396	887	110	1357	430	6764	1325	1
乌苏市	Usu City	33334	5763	2074	414	12405	3839	7664	1050	10
额敏县	Emin [Dorbiljin] County	24347	5700	816	162	6060	1803	8851	955	
沙湾县	Shawan County	47787	12128	421	89	15120	1592	10399	8001	31
托里县	Toli County	17948	6016	972	117	520	1553	8770		
裕民县	Yumin [Qagantokay] County	11094	3949	695	244	478	859	4515	352	2
和布克赛尔蒙古自治县	Hoboksar Mongol Autonomous County	12515	3456	1350	180	352	2160	4972	45	
阿勒泰地区	**Altay Administrative Offices**	**73633**	**32772**	**2982**	**1355**	**4285**	**4956**	**23342**	**3522**	**398**
阿勒泰市	Altay City	15080	7900	689	360	464	680	4812	154	8
布尔津县	Burqin County	10521	6386	276	40	1012	444	1928	435	
富蕴县	Fuyun [Koktokay] County	15209	4526	533	260	233	1049	6658	1579	371
福海县	Fuhai [Burultokay] County	11729	3982	308	259	2312	546	3952	365	5
哈巴河县	Habahe [Kaba] County	10753	6599	308	130	104	650	2630	330	2
青河县	Qinghe [Qinggil] County	6266	2175	612	198	75	1341	1315	546	4
吉木乃县	Jeminay County	4075	1204	256	108	85	246	2047	113	8
博尔塔拉蒙古自治州	**Bortala Mongol Autonomous Prefecture**	**20710**	**3249**	**614**	**62**	**5409**	**1027**	**8738**	**1574**	**13**
博乐市	Bole [Bortala] City	8620	1279	118	27	2853	223	3114	993	
精河县	Jinghe [Jing] County	5731	759	96	5	1165	564	2742	391	8
温泉县	Wenquan [Araxang] County	6359	1211	400	30	1391	240	2882	190	5
巴音郭楞蒙古自治州	**Bayangol Mongol Autonomous Prefecture**	**84631**	**15319**	**1695**	**293**	**25777**	**6264**	**24782**	**9278**	**170**
库尔勒市	Korla City	18654	2018	3		5625	526	4233	6128	39
轮台县	Luntai [Bugur] County	8090	793	25		2237	1056	3360	448	2
尉犁县	Yuli [Lopnur] County	5098	879	14		619	1613	1542	360	12
若羌县	Ruoqiang [Qarkilik] County	2052	229	33	8	842	128	516	98	5
且末县	Qiemo [Qarqan] County	7607	1814	106	82	800	1015	3269	106	30
焉耆回族自治县	Yanqi Hui Autonomous County	10203	3567	50		2064	744	2862	808	72
和静县	Hejing County	22051	5090	1354	63	7484	396	7184	383	7
和硕县	Hoxud County	5412	508	68	132	2152	586	1276	675	
博湖县	Bohu [Bagrax] County	5464	421	42	8	3954	200	540	272	3
阿克苏地区	**Aksu Administrative Offices**	**171487**	**40428**	**3642**	**628**	**29725**	**13133**	**48480**	**27059**	
阿克苏市	Aksu City	43344	5143	264		15931	897	10245	10514	
温宿县	Wensu [Onsu] County	17848	4202	540	58	2081	1506	5145	4059	
库车县	Kuqa County	45200	13764	1060		3456	4188	15234	5342	

12-27 续表 2 Continued

单位：吨 (ton)

地　区	Region	合计 Total	#牛 Beef	#马 Horse	#骆驼 Camels	#猪 Pork	#山羊 Goats	#绵羊 Sheep	#禽肉 Poultry Meat	#兔肉 Rabbit Meat
沙雅县	Xayar County	10012	2235	60		1927	1574	2362	1758	
新和县	Xinhe [Toksu] County	6401	2114	113		269	189	1733	1859	
拜城县	Baicheng [Bay] County	18945	5520	280	60	4778	1538	4819	1208	
乌什县	Wushi [Uxturpan] County	15523	5302	1244	310	460	1932	3910	1780	
阿瓦提县	Awat County	11802	1860	36		783	805	4132	230	
柯坪县	Kalpin County	2412	288	45	200	40	504	900	309	
克孜勒苏柯尔克孜自治州	**Kizilsu Kirgiz Autonomous Prefecture**	**35510**	**13523**	**1300**	**453**	**691**	**3581**	**12641**	**3321**	
阿图什市	Artux City	13832	5709	88	41	531	1670	4593	1200	
阿克陶县	Akto County	12084	5712	67	51	44	803	4067	1340	
阿合奇县	Akqi County	4514	1104	780	56	98	569	1811	96	
乌恰县	Wuqia [Ulugqat] County	5080	998	365	305	18	539	2170	685	
喀什地区	**Kashgar [Kaxgar] Administrative Offices**	**375256**	**88664**	**780**	**134**	**21262**	**27221**	**135701**	**89523**	**2995**
喀什市	Kashgar [Kaxgar] City	24701	5788			3114	214	13655	1880	
疏附县	Shufu County	41633	13780	20	15	2576	592	19440	4775	
疏勒县	Shule County	39964	10580		30	5937	108	13959	8175	
英吉沙县	Yengisar County	20716	8310	30	15	238	63	7610	3585	
泽普县	Zepu [Poskam] County	26202	3528	24		3856	156	7223	11189	
莎车县	Shache [Yarkant] County	50562	8800	230		1832	1346	23214	11900	2950
叶城县	Yecheng [Kagilik] County	54403	13060	144	48	485	21379	891	16701	45
麦盖提县	Makit County	20728	4250	48		1123	463	10267	4272	
岳普湖县	Yopurga County	15098	3540	24		144	410	5904	4301	
伽师县	Jiashi [Payzawat] County	43133	6400	150		240	1032	19511	13000	
巴楚县	Bachu [Maralbexi] County	32713	7660	80		1717	776	12425	9745	
塔什库尔干塔吉克自治县	Taxkorgan Tajik Autonomous County	5403	2968	30	26		682	1602		
和田地区	**Hotan Administrative Offices**	**82192**	**17808**	**370**	**195**	**1981**	**2221**	**49470**	**10095**	**52**
和田市	Hotan City	11356	2928	10		1603	31	5358	1426	
和田县	Hotan County	10251	2760	20	15	28	106	6284	1037	1
墨玉县	Moyu [Karakax] County	19663	5436	40	30	42	111	12098	1899	7
皮山县	Pishan [Guma] County	8856	624	30	30	91	265	5396	2408	12
洛浦县	Lop County	8395	2340	20	15	56	84	5088	783	9
策勒县	Qira County	6613	444	40	45	42	174	4909	958	1
于田县	Yutian [Keriya] County	13056	3060	190	30	77	633	8201	843	22
民丰县	Minfeng [Niya] County	4002	216	20	30	42	817	2136	741	
生产建设兵团	**Xinjiang Production and Construction Group**	**382317**	**44218**	**1708**	**261**	**213477**	**11828**	**75477**	**31317**	**2800**

12-28 水产品产量和养殖面积
Output of Aquatic Products and Cultured Area

年 份 Year	地 区 Region	水产品产量(吨) Aquatic Products (ton)	#养殖产量 Cultured Output	养殖面积(公顷) Culture Area (hectare)
1985		8958	3403	32775
1990		23217	15401	68838
1995		44432	35341	72538
1996		47890	38876	79006
1997		52366	42656	75895
1998		53391	44557	67473
1999		55840	48068	70524
2000		60065	50974	69806
2001		60876	50902	63340
2002		63906	55159	62629
2003		67278	57244	67374
2004		73296	60405	74996
2005		79320	65571	76037
2006		84539	71440	76606
2007		88879	78639	77590
2008		92587	82040	73909
2009		97037	87863	73433
2010		101063	90913	73289
2011		116916	103315	74000
乌鲁木齐市	Urumqi City	7801	7801	3624
克拉玛依市	Karamay City	528	418	68
吐鲁番地区	Turpan Administrative Offices	380	380	42
哈密地区	Hami [Kumul] Administrative Offices	1056	1014	675
昌吉回族自治州	Changji Hui Autonomous Prefecture	17000	17000	2787
伊犁哈萨克自治州	Ili Kazak Autonomous Prefecture	22119	18617	18203
伊犁州直属县(市)	Counties (Cities) Direct Under Ili Prefecture	12776	12584	880
塔城地区	Tacheng [Tarbagatai] Administrative Offices	2557	1833	1656
阿勒泰地区	Altay Administrative Offices	6786	4200	15667
博尔塔拉蒙古自治州	Bortala Mongol Autonomous Prefecture	3160	900	527
巴音郭楞蒙古自治州	Bayangol Mongol Autonomous Prefecture	11220	5168	3027
阿克苏地区	Aksu Administrative Offices	11121	10627	1157
克孜勒苏柯尔克孜自治州	Kizilsu Kirgiz Autonomous Prefecture	250		
喀什地区	Kashgar [Kaxgar] Administrative Offices	9405	9162	8424
和田地区	Hotan Administrative Offices	1979	1816	379
生产建设兵团	Xinjiang Production and Construction Group	30897	30412	35087

12-29 乡镇企业主要指标
Main Indicators of Township Enterprises

单位：万元 (10 000 yuan)

年 份 Year	地 区 Region	企业个数 (个) Number of Enterprises (unit)	从业人数 (人) Employees of Enterprises (person)	总产值 Total Output Value
	1985	98826	367753	75179
	1990	144281	464027	222218
	1991	145762	472332	314765
	1992	155711	498132	402139
	1993	202274	600687	553616
	1994	250037	686425	924082
	1995	281130	745291	1319217
	1996	282733	781784	1622442
	1997	43548	355585	1219032
	1998	269048	712490	2457410
	1999	297147	749205	2736766
	2000	316524	806368	3022076
	2001	334694	824499	3316049
	2002	307963	866661	3629499
	2003	354640	880874	4119555
	2004	368553	933473	4562898
	2005	366883	954411	4994156
	2006	368724	990365	5574730
	2007	377385	1037023	4265895
	2008	378343	1063023	8629234
	2009	378983	1115703	8486719
	2010	383653	1167548	9574341
	2011	391680	1219552	12067084
乌鲁木齐市	Urumqi City	19852	67545	1039185
克拉玛依市	Karamay City	179	1513	14024
石河子市	Shihezi City	2964	19520	134728
吐鲁番地区	Turpan Administrative Offices	21062	48048	370861
哈密地区	Hami [Kumul] Administrative Offices	9963	29765	218475
昌吉回族自治州	Changji Hui Autonomous Prefecture	39097	141754	2793398
伊犁州直属县(市)	Counties (Cities) Direct Under Ili Prefecture	52042	165503	1689640
塔城地区	Tacheng [Tarbagatai] Administrative Offices	26288	105753	1542690
阿勒泰地区	Altay Administrative Offices	24684	58136	399933
博尔塔拉蒙古自治州	Bortala Mongol Autonomous Prefecture	8685	34476	337226
巴音郭楞蒙古自治州	Bayangol Mongol Autonomous Prefecture	25799	79371	1999973
阿克苏地区	Aksu Administrative Offices	43373	136023	594653
克孜勒苏柯尔克孜自治州	Kizilsu Kirgiz Autonomous Prefecture	9223	20787	38007
喀什地区	Kashgar [Kaxgar] Administrative Offices	63700	171380	585845
和田地区	Hotan Administrative Offices	44769	139978	308446

12-29 续表 Continued

单位：万元 (10 000 yuan)

年 份 Year	地 区 Region	营业收入 Business Income	利润总额 Total Profits	上缴税金
	1985	105072	9357	3136
	1990	249906	8614	5206
	1991	299890	25974	13747
	1992	374810	34644	16976
	1993	584089	51880	27354
	1994	957701	75439	69494
	1995	1493924	110656	76479
	1996	1927425	136410	76479
	1997	1128271	43337	48945
	1998	2455629	156578	82365
	1999	2742029	164949	93490
	2000	3071497	191764	100444
	2001	3377589	211439	108864
	2002	3739524	225723	126732
	2003	4276322	264661	137880
	2004	4757808	304998	152243
	2005	5164593	294021	164604
	2006	5806803	332070	190833
	2007	6776709	318943	228386
	2008	7548573	563293	249122
	2009	8547580	671806	271759
	2010	9596967	756277	306105
	2011	12287481	937847	374096
乌鲁木齐市	Urumqi City	1050605	52289	26436
克拉玛依市	Karamay City	13706	1228	774
石河子市	Shihezi City	181648	5604	2530
吐鲁番地区	Turpan Administrative Offices	306399	32516	14493
哈密地区	Hami [Kumul] Administrative Offices	197019	14429	12255
昌吉回族自治州	Changji Hui Autonomous Prefecture	2919293	223039	85605
伊犁州直属县(市)	Counties (Cities) Direct Under Ili Prefecture	1817910	95196	34176
塔城地区	Tacheng [Tarbagatai] Administrative Offices	1470504	155489	38703
阿勒泰地区	Altay Administrative Offices	450811	38871	16614
博尔塔拉蒙古自治州	Bortala Mongol Autonomous Prefecture	328810	11856	7888
巴音郭楞蒙古自治州	Bayangol Mongol Autonomous Prefecture	2052982	174639	86657
阿克苏地区	Aksu Administrative Offices	577578	43077	19366
克孜勒苏柯尔克孜自治州	Kizilsu Kirgiz Autonomous Prefecture	41670	4108	2068
喀什地区	Kashgar [Kaxgar] Administrative Offices	578850	59710	15110
和田地区	Hotan Administrative Offices	299696	25796	11421

主要统计指标解释

农林牧渔业总产值 指以货币表现的农、林、牧、渔业全部产品和对农林牧渔业生产活动进行的各种支持性服务活动的价值总量，它反映一定时期内农林牧渔业生产总规模和总成果。1957年以前的农林牧渔业总产值中包括了厩肥和农民自给性手工业(如农民自制衣服、鞋、袜，自己从事粮食初步加工等)。1958年及以后，林业中增加了村及村以下竹木采伐产值；牧业中取消了厩肥产值；副业中取消了农民自给性手工业产值，增加了村及村以下办的工业产值； 渔业中增加了海洋捕捞水产品产值。1980年及以后，在副业中增加了农民家庭兼营工业商品部分的产值。从1984年起村及村以下工业产值划归工业。从1993年起取消副业，将野生动物的捕猎划入牧业，野生植物采集和农民家庭兼营商品性工业划归农业。从2003年起，执行新的国民经济行业分类标准，农林牧渔业总产值中包括了农林牧渔服务业产值。林业中增加了森林采运业产值。农业中取消了家庭兼营商品性工业产值，将野生林产品的采集划归林业。第一次农业普查以后，由于畜牧业产品年报数据与普查数据之间存在一定的差距，国家统计局农调总队对畜牧业年报数据与普查数据进行衔接，对畜牧业产值进行相应调整。

农林牧渔业总产值的计算方法通常是按农、林、牧、渔业产品及其副产品的产量分别乘以各自单位产品价格求得；少数生产周期较长，当年没有产品或产品产量不易统计的，则采用间接方法匡算其产值；然后将四业产品产值及农林牧渔服务业产值相加即为农林牧渔业总产值。

粮食产量 指全社会的产量。包括国有经济经营的、集体统一经营的和农民家庭经营的粮食产量，还包括工矿企业办的农场和其他生产单位的产量。粮食除包括稻谷、小麦、玉米、高粱、谷子及其他杂粮外，还包括薯类和豆类。其产量计算方法，豆类按去豆荚后的干豆计算；薯类(包括甘薯和马铃薯，不包括芋头和木薯)1963年以前按每4公斤鲜薯折1公斤粮食计算，从1964年开始改为按5公斤鲜薯折1公斤粮食计算。城市郊区作为蔬菜的薯类(如马铃薯等)按鲜品计算，并且不作粮食统计。其他粮食一律按脱粒后的原粮计算。1989年以前全国粮食产量数据主要靠全面报表取得，1989年开始使用抽样调查数据。

棉花产量 指全社会的产量。包括春播棉和夏播棉。产量按皮棉计算。不包括木棉。

油料产量 指全部油料作物的生产量。包括花生、油菜籽、芝麻、向日葵籽、胡麻籽(亚麻籽)和其他油料。不包括大豆、木本油料和野生油料。花生以带壳干花生计算。

水产品产量 指人工养殖的水产品和天然生长的水产品的捕捞量。包括海水的鱼类、虾蟹类、贝类和藻类以及内陆水域的鱼类、虾蟹类和贝类，不包括淡水生植物。水产品产量是通过各级水产和统计部门逐级上报取得数据。1995年及以前，贝类中牡蛎按鲜肉计算; 蚶、蛤、蛏按 5 斤鲜品折1斤计算。1996 年以后则统一按鲜品计算。

猪、牛、羊肉产量 指当年出栏并已屠宰、除去头蹄下水后带骨肉(即胴体重)的重量。包括全社会范围内的产量。1996年前为各级逐级上报数据。1996年第一次农业普查以后，由于畜牧业产品年报数据与普查数据之间存在一定的差距，国家统计局农调总队对畜牧业年报数据与普查数据进行衔接。1999年以后，国家统计局在部分地区开展了猪、牛、羊、禽等主要畜禽品种的抽样调查，并用抽样数据作为国家定案数据使用。未开展抽样调查的地区和品种，仍使用各级统计部门逐级上报数据。

期初(末)畜禽存栏头(只)数 指报告期初(末)农村各种合作经济组织和国营农场、农民个人、机关、团体、学校、工矿企业、部队等单位以及城镇居民饲养的大牲畜、猪、羊、家禽等畜禽的存栏数。数据上报方式及数据调整情况同猪、牛、羊肉产量。

农作物播种面积 指实际播种或移植有农作物的面积。凡是实际种植农作物的面积，不论种植在耕地上还是种植在非耕地上，均包括在农作物播种面积中。在播种季节基本结束后，因遭灾而重新改种和补种的农作物面积，也包括在内。该指标可以反映我国耕地面积的利用情况。目前，农作物播种面积主要包括粮食、棉花、油料、糖料、麻类、烟叶、蔬菜和瓜类、药材和其它农作物等十大类。

有效灌溉面积 指具有一定的水源，地块比较平整，灌溉工程或设备已经配套，在一般年景下，当年能够进行正常灌溉的耕地面积。在一般情况下，有效灌溉面积应等于灌溉工程或设备已经配备，能够进行正常灌溉的水田和水浇地面积之和。它是反映我国耕地抗旱能力的一个重要指标。

农用化肥施用量 指本年内实际用于农业生产的化肥数量，包括氮肥、磷肥、钾肥和复合肥。化肥施用量要求按折纯量计算数量。折纯量是指把氮肥、磷肥、钾肥分别按含氮、含五氧化二磷、含氧化钾的百分之百成份进行折算后的数量。复合肥按其所含主要成分折算。公式为:

折纯量= 实物量×某种化肥有效成份含量的百分比

农业机械总动力　指主要用于农、林、牧、渔业的各种动力机械的动力总和。包括耕作机械、排灌机械、收获机械、农用运输机械、植物保护机械、牧业机械、林业机械、渔业机械和其他农业机械〔内燃机按引擎马力折成瓦(特)计算、电动机按功率折成瓦(特)计算〕。不包括专门用于乡、镇、村、组办工业、基本建设、非农业运输、科学试验和教学等非农业生产方面用的动力机械与作业机械。这个指标的统计数据主要来源于农机部门。

Explanatory Notes on Main Statistical Indicators

Gross Output Value of Agriculture, Forestry, Animal Husbandry and Fishery refers to the total value of products of agriculture, forestry, animal husbandry and fishery, and total value of services in support of agriculture, forestry, animal husbandry and fishery activities. It reflects the total scale and results of agricultural production during a given period. Prior to 1957, China's gross agricultural output value included barnyard manure and handicraft products for self-consumption (clothes, shoes, stockings, and initial grain processing undertaken by peasants). Since 1958, cutting and felling of bamboo and trees by villages and other cooperative organizations under villages have been included in forestry; value of barnyard manure has been excluded from animal husbandry; self consumed handicrafts have not been included from sideline occupations, while the output value of industries run by villages and cooperative organizations under village has been included in sideline occupations; and the output value of fish catches by motor fishing boats has been added to fishery. Since 1980, the value of handicraft products made for sale by individuals in households has been added to sideline occupations. Since 1984, industries run by villages and under villages have been included in the sector of industry. Since 1993, the subdivision of sideline occupations has been cancelled, and the hunting of wild animals has been classified into animal husbandry, and the gathering of wild plants and commodity industry run by rural household have been included in farming. A new industrial classification of economic activities was introduced in 2003. Under the new classification, value of services to agriculture, forestry, animal husbandry and fishery is included in the gross output value of agriculture, value of wood felling and transport is included in forestry, value of industrial output by rural households is not included in agriculture, and the collection of wild forest products is taken from agriculture and included in forestry. The First Agriculture Census of China revealed some discrepancy between the production of animal products from the annual reports and that from the census. Efforts were made by the Rural Survey of NBS to adjust the output value of animal husbandry to make the figures from the annual reports consistent with the census data.

Gross output value of agriculture is obtained by multiplying the output of each product or by-product by its price, resulting in the output value of each single item. For a small number of products, annual output of which is not available or difficult to get due to the long production (growing) process involved, the output value is estimated through an indirect approach. The sum of output values of all products of agriculture, forestry, animal husbandry and fishery and services in support to those industries is then equal to the gross output value of agriculture.

Grain Output refers to the total output in the whole country including grains produced by State farms, collective units, rural households, as well as by farms affiliated to industrial and mining enterprises and other production units. Grain includes rice, wheat, corn, sorghum, millet and other miscellaneous grains as well as tubers and beans. Output of beans refers to dry beans without pods. The output of tubers (sweet potatoes and potatoes, not including taros and cassava) are converted into that of grain at the ratio 4:1, i.e. 4 kilograms of fresh tubers were equivalent to 1 kilogram of grain up to 1963. Since 1964 the ratio for conversion has been 5:1. Tubers supplied as vegetables (such as potatoes) in cities and suburbs are calculated as fresh vegetables and their output is not included in the output of grain. Output of all other grains refers to husked grain. Data on grain production before 1989 were obtained through the Comprehensive Statistical Reporting System. Since 1989, data from sample surveys are used.

Cotton Output refers to cotton production in the whole country including cotton planted in spring and in autumn. Output is measured as the weight of ginned cotton. Ceiba is not included.

Output of Oil-bearing Crops refers to the total Production of oil-bearing crops of various kinds, including peanuts (dry, in shell), rapeseeds, sesame, sunflower seeds, flax seeds, and other oil-bearing crops. Soybeans, oil-bearing woody plants, and wild oil-bearing crops are not included.

Output of Aquatic Products refers to catches of both artificially cultured and naturally grown aquatic products, including fish, shrimps, crabs and shellfish in sea and inland water as well as seaweed. Freshwater plants are not included. Data on output of aquatic products are reported by aquatic product and statistical agencies level by level. Before 1995, among the shellfish, oyster was counted as fresh meat; 5 kilograms of ark shell, clams and frogs are equivalent to 1 kilogram of fresh aquatic products; they have all been counted as fresh aquatic products since 1996.

Output of Pork, Beef, and Mutton refers to the meat of slaughtered hogs, cattle, sheep and goats with head, feet, and offal taken away. Data refers to the production of the whole country. The First Agricultural Census of China in 1996 revealed some discrepancy between the production of animal products from the annual reports and that from the census. Efforts were made by the Rural Survey Organization of the NBS to adjust the output value of animal husbandry to make the figures from the annual reports consistent with the census data. Since 1999, the NBS conducted sample surveys for the major animal husbandry products, such as hogs, cattle, sheep and goats and fowls, and the data from sample surveys are used as national finalized data. Those products, which are not covered by the sample survey, are still reported by statistical agencies level by level.

Number of Livestock or Poultry in Stock at Beginning (or End) of Period refers to the total number of large animals, pigs, sheep, fowls, etc. raised by rural cooperative organizations, State farms, rural individuals, government agencies, schools, industrial and mining enterprises, army, and urban residents at the beginning (or end) of the reference period. Data reporting system and data adjustment are the same as that in the output of pork, beef and mutton.

Sown Area of Crops refer to area of land sown or transplanted with crops regardless of being in cultivated area of noncultivated area, Area of land re-sown due to natural disaster is also included.This is an important indicator that can reflect the utilization comdition of the cultivated land in China,At present,the sown area of crops mainly include the following categories of crops:grain,cotton,oil-bearing crops ,sugar crops,fiber crops,Tobacco,Vegetables and melons,medical materials and other farm crops.

Irrigated Area refers to area of land that are effectively irrigated, i.e. relatively level land, where there are water sources or complete sets of irrigation facilities to lift and move adequate water for irrigation purpose under normal conditions. Under normal situations, irrigated area is the sum of watered fields and irrigated fields where irrigation systems or equipment have been installed for regular irrigation purpose. This important indicator reflects drought resistance capacity of the cultivated land in China.

Consumption of Chemical Fertilizers in Agriculture refers to the quantity of chemical fertilizers applied in agriculture in the year, including nitrogenous fertilizer, phosphate fertilizer, potash fertilizer, and compound fertilizer. The consumption of chemical fertilizers is calculated in terms of volume of effective components by means of converting the gross weight of the respective fertilizers into weight containing effective component (e.g. nitrogen content in nitrogenous fertilizer, phosphorous pentoxide contents in phosphate fertilizer, and potassium oxide contents in potash fertilizer). Compound fertilizer is converted in regard to its major components. The formula is:

Volume of effective component= physical quantity× effective component of certain chemical fertilizer (%)

Total Power of Agricultural Machinery refers to total mechanical power of machinery used in agriculture, forestry, animal husbandry and fishery, including machinery for ploughing, irrigation and drainage, harvesting, transport, plant protection, animal husbandry, forestry and fishery and other agricultural machineries. (For the power of internal combustion engines, it is converted from its horsepower into watts while for electric motors the output power is converted into watts.) Machinery employed for non-agricultural purposes, such as the machines used in township-run and village-run industry, construction, non-agricultural transport, scientific experiments and teaching, are not included. Data are mainly from agricultural machinery agencies.

2012

新疆统计年鉴

XINJIANG STATISTICAL YEARBOOK

第十三篇 工 业

CHAPTER 13 Industry

简要说明
Brief Introduction

本篇资料的主要内容及来源

本篇资料反映新疆维吾尔自治区工业经济方面的基本情况，包括所辖地（州、市）、县（市、区）的主要工业经济统计数据：

1、主要年份工业总产值及工业总产值指数。

2、全区规模以上工业企业主要经济指标，以及按企业登记注册类型、轻重工业、企业规模、工业行业大类和按地（州、市）、县（市、区）分组的主要经济指标和经济效益指标。

3、国有控股工业企业按工业行业大类和按地（州、市）、县（市、区）分组的主要经济指标和经济效益指标。

4、大中型工业企业按工业行业大类分组的主要经济指标和经济效益指标。

5、主要工业产品产量和生产能力。

6、国有控股和重点行业主要指标占全区规模以上工业比重。

主要年份工业总产值、工业总产值指数及主要工业产品产量的统计范围为全部工业企业；其他资料的统计范围均为年主营业务收入在2000万元以上工业企业（即规模以上工业企业）。

本篇资料由新疆维吾尔自治区统计局工业交通统计处根据工业统计年度报表中有关资料整理汇总。

Main Content and Source of Data

Data in this chapter reflect the basic condition of industrial sector including the gross industrial output and indices of industrial enterprises; Main indicator on economic and economic benefit of industrial enterprises above designated size by status of registration, light & heavy industries, size of enterprises, industrial sector. Main indicators including number of enterprises, gross industrial output value, value added of industry, total assets, total liabilities, revenue from principal business, cost of principle business, taxes and other charges on principal business, total profits, value added tax payable, ratio of total assets to industrial output value, assets liability ration, ratio of profits to cost, output of major industrial products, main economic indicator of state-owned and non-state-owned industrial enterprises.

This chapter covers main indicators on economic and economic benefit of all state-owned and non-state-owned industrial enterprises, cooperative enterprises, industrial enterprises with funds from Hong Kong, Macao and Taiwan, foreign funded industrial enterprises, and large & medium-sized enterprises.

Statistical scope of data on output of major industrial products is all industrial enterprises.

Data in this chapter are collected and compiled by the Department of Industry and transport, XBS in accordance with the annual report of industrial statistics.The scopes of gross industrial output value,indicies of gross industrial output value and output industrial products are all industrial enterprises;The scope of others are industrial enterprises with revenur from principal business over 20 million yuan.(industrial enterprises above designated size).

13-1 主要年份工业总产值
Gross Industrial Output Value in Main Years

单位:亿元 (100 million yuan)

年 份 Year	工业总产值 Gross Industrial Output Value	国有工业 State-owned Enterprises	集体工业 Collective-owned Enterprises	其它经济类型工业 Enterprises of Other Types of Ownership
1978	33.91	30.22	3.69	
1980	40.71	36.20	4.50	0.01
1985	86.78	73.18	11.93	1.67
1990	219.92	176.52	36.72	6.68
1995	593.43	461.31	89.24	42.88
2000	1061.29	258.93	72.78	729.58
2001	1084.22	155.26	53.31	875.65
2002	1133.38	159.73	46.39	927.26
2003	1330.15	161.94	35.69	1132.52
2004	1756.18	224.63	19.14	1512.41
2005	2358.83	236.18	17.29	2105.36
2006	2894.88	272.06	16.14	2606.68
2007	3471.51	358.28	17.29	3095.94
2008	4639.02	387.53	15.70	4235.79
2009	4184.50	404.01	15.61	3764.88
2010	5766.51	382.00	25.54	5358.97
2011	7105.31	654.79	29.44	6421.08

13-2 主要年份工业总产值指数
Indices of Gross Industrial Output Value in Main Years

(1978 年=100)

年 份 Year	工业总产值 Gross Industrial Output Value	国有工业 State-owned Enterprises	集体工业 Collective-owned Enterprises	其它经济类型工业 Enterprises of Other Types of Ownership
1978	100.0	100.0	100.0	
1980	117.7	118.0	113.2	(1981 年=100)
1985	220.6	199.5	428.2	851.7
1990	380.3	326.0	915.9	2096.1
1995	670.8	506.1	2104.5	7441.5
2000	1000.4	227.3	1763.6	66265.2
2001	1077.8	151.0	1311.5	87376.0
2002	1180.9	149.3	1123.1	99435.1
2003	1306.7	152.9	837.3	113823.3
2004	1567.8	210.4	442.4	135173.5
2005	1821.8	218.2	388.9	160072.4
2006	2057.1	246.3	344.8	180922.4
2007	2322.8	319.9	339.3	201240.8
2008	2707.5	336.5	272.4	237624.5
2009	2942.2	353.4	289.2	259031.4
2010	3331.8	325.7	431.9	298801.3
2011	3721.3	527.1	451.7	323156.5

13-3 规模以上工业企业分行业、地区增加值(GB/T4754-2011)

Value-added of Industrial Enterprises above Designated Size by Sector and Region (GB/T4754-2011)

单位: 万元

行　业	Sector	2010	2011
总　计	**Total**	**20857522.3**	**25635749.7**
按行业分	Grouped by Industrial Sector		
煤炭开采和洗选业	Mining and Washing of Coal	823701.9	1125752.9
石油和天然气开采业	Extraction of Petroleum and Natural Gas	9186066.2	13118622.6
黑色金属矿采选业	Mining and Processing of Ferrous Metals Ores	393639.6	493050.7
有色金属矿采选业	Mining and Processing of Nonferrous Metals Ores	333452.4	417964.0
非金属矿采选业	Mining and Processing of Nonmetal Ores	50340.0	69693.0
开采辅助活动	Mining Activities	370559.4	543976.1
农副食品加工业	Processing of Food from Agricultural Products	356912.2	407736.7
食品制造业	Manufacture of Food	205265.0	228323.5
酒、饮料和精制茶制造业	Manufacture of Beverage	226447.1	278720.3
烟草制品业	Manufacture of Tobacco	188122.6	236486.5
纺织业	Manufacture of Textile	290203.2	259999.1
纺织服装、服饰业	Manufacture of Textile Wearing Apparel, Footware and Caps	4122.0	8119.5
皮革、毛皮、羽毛(绒)及其制品业	Leather, Fur, Feather and Related Products Manufacturing	8110.9	18521.1
木材加工及木、竹、藤、棕、草制品业	Processing of Timber, Wood, Bamboo, Cane, Grass Products	16305.3	12561.8
家具制造业	Manufacture of Furniture	26534.5	26916.6
造纸及纸制品业	Manufacture of Paper and Paper Products	44806.7	47117.2
印刷业和记录媒介的复制	Printing and Copying of Medium for Record	14678.4	14617.8
文教、工美、体育和娱乐用品制造业	Manufacture of Articles for Culture,Education,Sports and Entertainment	1204.2	1372.8
石油加工、炼焦及核燃料加工业	Oil Processing, Coking and Nuclear Fuel Processing	3265478.6	2022820.5
化学原料及化学制品制造业	Raw Chemical Material and Chemical Products	925374.0	1382059.8
医药制造业	Manufacture of Medicine	32029.1	40289.0
化学纤维制造业	Manufacture of Chemical Fiber	194286.0	151251.4
橡胶和塑料制品业	Manufacture of Rubber Products	100770.9	130528.3
非金属矿物制品业	Manufacture of Nonmetal Mineral Products	588674.8	811437.1
黑色金属冶炼及压延加工业	Smelting and Pressing of Ferrous Metals	733353.6	868133.9
有色金属冶炼及压延加工业	Smelting and Pressing of Nonferrous Metals	171191.2	312094.1
金属制品业	Manufacture of Metal Products	87636.2	103312.9

13-3 续表 Continued

单位：万元

行　　业	Sector	2010	2011
通用设备制造业	Manufacture of General Purpose Machinery	13814.6	17264.7
专用设备制造业	Manufacture of Special Purpose Machinery	41267.7	62778.8
汽车制造业	Manufacture of Automobile	6343.0	1070.4
铁路、船舶、航空航天和其他运输设备制造业	Manufouture of Railroads,Ships,Aerospace and Other Transportation Equipment	1005.4	1085.3
电气机械及器材制造业	Manufacture of Electric Equipment and Machinery	667856.6	460713.4
计算机、通信和其他电子设备制造业	Manufalture of Communication Equipment Computers and Other Electronic Equipment	53547.8	60933.0
仪器仪表制造业	Manufacture of Measuring Instruments	3102.8	1547.9
其他制造业	Others		10027.4
废弃资源综合利用业	Recycling and Disposal of Waste	4963.1	21707.3
金属制品、机械和设备修理业	Manufacture and Repair of Metal Products and Machinery	5952.2	2856.4
电力、热力生产和供应业	Production and Supply of Electricity and Therma	1347266.7	1769022.4
燃气生产和供应业	Production and Supply of Gas	54341.1	72113.9
水的生产和供应业	Production and Supply of Water	18795.5	23149.8
按地区分	**Grouped by Region**		
乌鲁木齐市	Urumqi City	4930416.5	5560049.9
克拉玛依市	Karamay City	6410107.0	6959226.5
吐鲁番地区	Turpan Administrative Offices	897848.0	1135817.7
哈密地区	Hami [Kumul] Administrative Offices	361880.0	496934,5
昌吉回族自治州	Changji Hui Autonomous Prefecture	948444.0	1154269.3
伊犁州直属县(市)	Counties (Cities) Direct Under Ili Prefecture	705349.2	878370.6
塔城地区	Tacheng [Tarbagatai] Administrative Offices	456921.0	605612.4
阿勒泰地区	Altay Administrative Offices	423203.3	566053.2
博尔塔拉蒙古自治州	Bortala Mongol Autonomous Prefecture	71785.9	85768.3
巴音郭楞蒙古自治州	Bayangol Mongol Autonomous Prefecture	3472695.9	5045854.7
阿克苏地区	Aksu Administrative Offices	616355.6	880862.9
克孜勒苏柯尔克孜自治州	Kizilsu Kirgiz Autonomous Prefecture	36781.9	55105.5
喀什地区	Kashgar [Kaxgar] Administrative Offices	123712.3	245208.7
和田地区	Hotan Administrative Offices	39632.1	47266.6
生产建设兵团	Xinjiang Production and Construction Group	1362389.6	1919349.0

13-4 规模以上工业企业分行业、地区增加值(GB/T4754-2002)

Value-added of Industrial Enterprises above Designated Size by Sector and Region (GB/T4754-2002)

单位: 万元

行　　业	Sector	2010	2011
总　　计	**Total**	**20857522.3**	**25635749.7**
按行业分	Grouped by Industrial Sector		
煤炭开采和洗选业	Mining and Washing of Coal	823701.9	1125752.9
石油和天然气开采业	Extraction of Petroleum and Natural Gas	9538659.7	13641591.5
黑色金属矿采选业	Mining and Processing of Ferrous Metals Ores	393639.6	493050.7
有色金属矿采选业	Mining and Processing of Nonferrous Metals Ores	333452.4	417964.0
非金属矿采选业	Mining and Processing of Nonmetal Ores	50340.0	69531.8
农副食品加工业	Processing of Food from Agricultural Products	368205.9	413636.6
食品制造业	Manufacture of Food	197435.4	222423.6
饮料制造业	Manufacture of Beverage	226037.7	278720.3
烟草制品业	Manufacture of Tobacco	188122.6	236486.5
纺织业	Manufacture of Textile	290021.4	257303.6
纺织服装、鞋、帽制造业	Manufacture of Textile Wearing Apparel, Footware and Caps	3974.1	10427.8
皮革、毛皮、羽毛(绒)及其制品业	Leather, Fur, Feather and Related Products Manufacturing	8110.9	18521.1
木材加工及木、竹、藤、棕、草制品业	Processing of Timber, Wood, Bamboo, Cane, Grass Products	16305.3	12561.8
家具制造业	Manufacture of Furniture	26534.5	26916.6
造纸及纸制品业	Manufacture of Paper and Paper Products	43056.1	47117.2
印刷业和记录媒介的复制	Printing and Copying of Medium for Record	14678.4	14617.8
石油加工、炼焦及核燃料加工业	Oil Processing, Coking and Nuclear Fuel Processing	3265478.6	2022820.5
化学原料及化学制品制造业	Raw Chemical Material and Chemical Products	940633.3	1398941.4
医药制造业	Manufacture of Medicine	32029.1	40289.0
化学纤维制造业	Manufacture of Chemical Fiber	194286.0	151251.4
橡胶和塑料制品业	Manufacture of Rubber Products	10994.5	16912.2
塑料制品业	Manufacture of Plastics	91856.6	114003.4
非金属矿物制品业	Manufacture of Nonmetal Mineral Products	588227.6	810661.1
黑色金属冶炼及压延加工业	Smelting and Pressing of Ferrous Metals	757864.1	880799.6
有色金属冶炼及压延加工业	Smelting and Pressing of Nonferrous Metals	162024.1	317181.0
金属制品业	Manufacture of Metal Products	65637.6	79736.3

13-4 续表 Continued

单位: 万元

行业	Sector	2010	2011
通用设备制造业	Manufacture of General Purpose Machinery	25312.1	29368.1
专用设备制造业	Manufacture of Special Purpose Machinery	42048.3	62778.8
交通运输设备制造业	Manufacture of Transport Equipment	7348.4	2155.7
电气机械及器材制造业	Manufacture of Electrical Machinery and Equipment	666448.5	460713.4
通信设备、计算机及其他电子设备制造业	Manufacture of Communication Equipment,Computers and Other Electronic Equipment	53547.8	60933.0
仪器仪表及文化、办公用机械制造业	Manufacture of Measuring Instruments and Machinery for Cultural Activity and Office Work	3102.8	1547.9
工艺品及其他制造业	Manufacture of Artwork and Other Manufacturing	3040.7	13040.0
废弃资源和废旧材料回收加工业	Recycling and Disposal of Waste	4963.1	21707.3
电力、热力生产和供应业	Production and Supply of Electric Power and Heat Power	1347266.7	1769022.4
燃气生产和供应业	Production and Supply of Gas	54341.1	72113.9
水的生产和供应业	Production and Supply of Water	18795.5	23149.8
按地区分	**Grouped by Region**		
乌鲁木齐市	Urumqi City	4930416.5	5560049.9
克拉玛依市	Karamay City	6410107.0	6959226.5
吐鲁番地区	Turpan Administrative Offices	897848.0	1135817.7
哈密地区	Hami [Kumul] Administrative Offices	361880.0	496934.5
昌吉回族自治州	Changji Hui Autonomous Prefecture	948444.0	1154269.3
伊犁州直属县(市)	Counties (Cities) Direct Under Ili Prefecture	705349.2	878370.6
塔城地区	Tacheng [Tarbagatai] Administrative Offices	456921.0	605612.4
阿勒泰地区	Altay Administrative Offices	423203.3	566053.2
博尔塔拉蒙古自治州	Bortala Mongol Autonomous Prefecture	71785.9	85768.3
巴音郭楞蒙古自治州	Bayangol Mongol Autonomous Prefecture	3472695.9	5045854.7
阿克苏地区	Aksu Administrative Offices	616355.6	880862.9
克孜勒苏柯尔克孜自治州	Kizilsu Kirgiz Autonomous Prefecture	36781.9	55105.5
喀什地区	Kashgar [Kaxgar] Administrative Offices	123712.3	245208.7
和田地区	Hotan Administrative Offices	39632.1	47266.6
生产建设兵团	Xinjiang Production and Construction Group	1362389.6	1919349.0

13-5 规模以上工业企业主要经济指标

单位: 万元 (2011 年)

项　　目	Item	企业单位数(个) Number of Enterprises (unit)	#亏损企业 Loss- Suffering Enterprises	工业总产值(当年价格) Gross Industrial Output Value (At Current Prices)
总　　计	**Total**	**1738**	**357**	**67208461.8**
按登记注册类型分	**By Status of Registration**			
内资企业	Domestic Funded Enterprises	1663	341	65799794.1
国有企业	State-owned Enterprises	110	25	5809723.1
#中央企业	Central Enterprises	53	10	4629669.1
地方企业	Local Enterprises	57	15	1180054.0
#自治区属企业	Autonomous	23	7	675940.2
地区(州、市)属企业	Prefecture or City	9	3	212647.0
县(市)属企业	County or City	18	3	120662.6
集体企业	Collective-owned Enterprises	13	1	251908.8
#自治区属企业	Autonomous	5		105790.9
地区(州、市)属企业	Prefecture or City	1		7540.5
县(市)属企业	County or City	5	1	32385.5
镇属企业	Town	1		10311.7
股份合作企业	Cooperative Enterprises	11	3	311914.2
联营企业	Joint Ownership Enterprises	7	2	32976.7
#国有联营企业	State Joint Ownership Enterprises	4	1	16181.3
国有与集体联营企业	Joint State-collective Enterprises	1		4050.0
其他联营企业	Other Joint Ownership Enterprises	2	1	12745.4
有限责任公司	Limited Liability Corporations	768	169	19854341.5
#国有独资公司	State Sole funded Corporations	52	5	3564752.4
其他有限责任公司	Other Limited Liability Corporations	716	164	16289589.1
股份有限公司	Share-holding Corporations Ltd.	80	16	31750976.9
私营企业	Private Enterprises	674	125	7787952.9
#私营独资企业	Private-funded Enterprises	51	4	322463.3
私营合伙企业	Private Partnership Enterprises	8	3	50666.1
私营有限责任公司	Private Limited Liability Corporations	594	111	5718570.3
私营股份有限公司	Private Share-holding Corporations Ltd.	21	7	1696253.2
港、澳、台商投资企业	Enterprises with Funds from Hong Kong, Macao and Taiwan	28	9	477108.8
外商投资企业	Foreign Funded Enterprises	47	7	931558.9
在总计中: 国有控股企业	Of the Total : State-owned and State-holding Enterprises	459	89	48665888.6
在总计中: 农村工业	Of the Total : Rural Industry	7	1	13883.3
按轻、重工业分(GB/T4754-2011)	**Grouped by Light & Heavy Industry (GB/T4754-2011)**			
轻工业	Light Industry	632	158	7994906.1
以农产品为原料	Using Farm Produces as Raw Materials	587	151	7666923.1
以非农产品为原料	Using Non-Farm Produces as Raw Materials	45	7	327983.0
重工业	Heavy Industry	1106	199	59213555.7
采掘工业	Mining and Quarrying	262	41	19142060.1
原料工业	Raw Material Industry	443	98	33469328.7
加工工业	Manufacturing Industry	401	60	6602166.9
按轻、重工业分(GB/T4754-2002)	**Grouped by Light & Heavy Industry (GB/T4754-2002)**			
轻工业	Light Industry	631	157	7992452.9
以农产品为原料	Using Farm Produces as Raw Materials	585	150	7658459.9
以非农产品为原料	Using Non-Farm Produces as Raw Materials	46	7	333993.0
重工业	Heavy Industry	1107	200	59216008.9
采掘工业	Mining and Quarrying	261	42	19099529.5
原料工业	Raw Material Industry	439	97	33492125.9
加工工业	Manufacturing Industry	407	61	6624353.5
按企业规模分(新标准)	**Grouped by Size of Enterprises (New Standard)**			
大型企业	Large Enterprises	73	15	41836437.0
中型企业	Medium-sized Enterprises	290	65	13049571.9
小型企业	Small Enterprises	1239	245	11511915.5
微型企业	Min Enterprises	136	32	810537.4
按企业规模分(旧标准)	**Grouped by Size of Enterprises (Old Standard)**			
大型企业	Large Enterprises	35	6	38369617.5
中型企业	Medium-sized Enterprises	320	76	16401985.0
小型企业	Small Enterprises	1383	275	12436859.3

Main Economic Indicators of Industrial Enterprises above Designated Size

(10 000 yuan)

工业增加值 Value-added	工业销售产值(当年价) Sales Value of Industry Products (At Current Prices)	出口交货值 Delivery Value of Industry Export	实收资本 Total Capital Hold	资产合计 Total Assets	流动资产合计 Total Working Capitals	#产成品 Finished Product	固定资产原价 Net Value of Fixed Assets
25635749.7	**65996909.7**	**704655.1**	**31198256.3**	**93049478.0**	**30149057.3**	**3312397.7**	**69398719.4**
25276412.4	64670919.8	637356.7	30685363.9	91390639.8	29355445.6	3137496.9	68485761.9
2389302.7	5741809.2	37364.7	2957352.5	10876176.0	2522165.6	187198.6	10321775.8
2002162.2	4594968.1	6227.8	2279727.3	7866663.0	1802701.5	112964.0	7828903.0
387140.5	1146841.1	31136.9	677625.2	3009513.0	719464.1	74234.6	2492872.8
249775.1	666770.7	15527.0	513281.7	1712569.0	274148.7	23087.3	1589173.9
43763.5	193119.9		94684.5	663991.5	293788.9	36737.0	435670.8
58727.5	116201.3		32452.0	369698.4	83279.8	3060.6	310976.2
51578.5	257132.6		15686.9	169961.8	88802.0	12529.3	89192.9
15596.9	106125.7		3089.2	48447.0	38138.9	4258.7	14211.5
662.5	7538.8		272.1	1661.9	1498.8	318.3	396.6
11258.8	32423.4		7569.4	29694.1	20301.6	2446.2	15279.9
10040.4	10311.7		195.0	7159.7	4790.5		2559.6
59876.1	292378.2	15149.0	77788.8	453632.7	268658.7	41778.4	169377.6
10802.7	32883.0		13222.0	54440.1	23446.9	1669.4	33333.3
6112.9	16197.0		10867.4	42176.6	17220.5	234.9	25545.4
1629.1	4050.0		1154.6	2895.4	990.3		2815.6
3060.7	12636.0		1200.0	9368.1	5236.1	1434.5	4972.3
5886193.4	19286951.5	247650.7	7560961.8	31119208.2	10582746.3	1374963.8	18178591.3
1126485.2	3545835.1	743.1	1225871.9	4662576.0	1392110.9	67006.8	3301186.0
4759708.2	15741116.4	246907.6	6335089.9	26456632.2	9190635.4	1307957.0	14877405.3
15076253.2	31647794.8	192913.7	18235558.7	38446135.7	10410367.3	862014.1	36641717.6
1802405.7	7411970.5	144278.6	1824793.2	10271085.3	5459258.8	657343.3	3051773.4
114409.5	303585.4	2637.9	119895.5	388845.4	143608.7	27566.0	177497.2
18657.1	48741.7		5773.2	19694.2	9653.4	2417.6	13053.7
1285411.0	5476913.2	66218.7	1309949.5	6787953.3	3238860.2	468107.9	2714690.3
383928.1	1582730.2	75422.0	389175.0	3074592.4	2067136.5	159251.8	146532.2
129271.9	430795.1	49026.6	190774.3	584838.7	328349.6	82207.7	330000.3
230065.4	895194.8	18271.8	322118.1	1073999.5	465262.1	92693.1	582957.2
20918681.6	48307739.5	384013.6	25679116.9	64283377.6	16723746.3	1668703.4	58772698.1
3402.7	13272.7		7034.2	27109.2	6206.3	872.5	17419.1
1798430.1	7619493.1	347746.3	2448287.9	10801271.6	5460568.4	1255689.9	5194915.1
1699997.7	7295290.1	347335.7	2146218.6	9816326.0	5130468.0	1230059.4	4575881.5
98432.4	324203.0	410.6	302069.3	984945.6	330100.4	25630.5	619033.6
23837319.5	58377416.6	356908.8	28749968.4	82248206.4	24688488.9	2056707.8	64203804.3
15769059.3	18985485.0	5925.8	16074968.2	31397561.4	7040829.2	450892.8	32730911.6
6422166.2	33098765.5	191300.1	10808211.9	39318153.9	11283600.3	1078487.4	28500644.5
1646094.0	6293166.1	159682.9	1866788.3	11532491.1	6364059.4	527327.6	2972248.2
1799230.8	7619439.6	347746.3	2447012.4	10808487.6	5471401.5	1258258.7	5194238.0
1697806.9	7288844.1	347335.7	2139467.6	9803163.8	5126178.2	1229985.3	4573294.9
101423.8	330595.5	410.6	307544.8	1005323.8	345223.3	28273.4	620943.1
23548931.9	58377470.1	356908.8	28751243.9	82240990.4	24677655.8	2054139.0	64204481.4
15460303.9	18941586.2	5925.8	16064068.2	31356013.6	7013082.0	450811.9	32722913.0
6453188.0	33119064.3	191300.1	10829241.7	39350917.0	11308370.0	1079005.2	28517580.8
1635440.0	6316819.6	159682.9	1857934.0	11534059.8	6356203.8	524321.9	2963987.6
18461010.5	41502794.6	293484.0	22843045.4	56731818.5	15015317.1	1144122.7	50801916.9
4106073.9	12699786.4	169387.8	4284381.4	19998291.0	8120029.1	922691.5	9818387.1
2975470.9	11007214.1	233396.7	3867236.5	15535051.7	6630540.7	1182427.9	8410797.5
93194.3	787114.6	8386.6	203593.0	784316.8	383170.4	63155.6	367617.9
17430191.1	38185173.7	123439.9	21242781.7	48585169.6	12225117.7	872335.3	47189319.6
4777439.9	15896462.3	364543.9	5445547.5	26840494.2	10684635.5	1203331.3	12605408.3
3140531.6	11915273.7	216671.3	4509927.1	17623814.2	7239304.1	1238012.6	9603991.5

13-5 续表

单位: 万元

项 目	Item	流动负债合计 Total Working Liabilities	长期负债合计 Long-term Liabilities	所有者权益合计 Total Owners' Equities
总 计	**Total**	**31943282.3**	**17138745.2**	**42857163.3**
按登记注册类型分	**By Status of Registration**			
内资企业	Domestic Funded Enterprises	31141725.2	16992232.7	42152362.6
国有企业	State-owned Enterprises	3450397.1	2804577.2	4167973.4
#中央企业	Central Enterprises	2620854.9	1931023.2	3303987.6
地方企业	Local Enterprises	829542.2	873554.0	863985.8
#自治区属企业	Autonomous	296514.7	386882.8	624546.4
地区(州、市)属企业	Prefecture or City	256918.3	333229.3	73708.4
县(市)属企业	County or City	196029.9	61106.5	74891.6
集体企业	Collective-owned Enterprises	80740.3	39058.4	47203.1
#自治区属企业	Autonomous	23599.2	101.8	21786.2
地区(州、市)属企业	Prefecture or City	1083.3		578.6
县(市)属企业	County or City	14312.7	486.3	14894.9
镇属企业	Town	3998.9		3160.8
股份合作企业	Cooperative Enterprises	169872.4	60286.2	196016.6
联营企业	Joint Ownership Enterprises	39670.1	3974.6	10780.7
#国有联营企业	State Joint Ownership Enterprises	28981.3	3974.6	9220.7
国有与集体联营企业	Joint State-collective Enterprises	1450.4		1445.0
其他联营企业	Other Joint Ownership Enterprises	9238.4		115.0
有限责任公司	Limited Liability Corporations	13124198.5	6102504.1	11433382.3
#国有独资公司	State Sole funded Corporations	1618644.5	967960.8	1973040.0
其他有限责任公司	Other Limited Liability Corporations	11505554.0	5134543.3	9460342.3
股份有限公司	Share-holding Corporations Ltd.	9439091.6	7006143.0	21987574.4
私营企业	Private Enterprises	4837755.2	975689.2	4309432.1
#私营独资企业	Private-funded Enterprises	154537.3	14739.8	163714.4
私营合伙企业	Private Partnership Enterprises	9122.3	440.9	10131.0
私营有限责任公司	Private Limited Liability Corporations	3207080.0	858697.3	2636493.3
私营股份有限公司	Private Share-holding Corporations Ltd.	1467015.6	101811.2	1499093.4
港、澳、台商投资企业	Enterprises with Funds from Hong Kong, Macao and Taiwan	268577.0	16759.6	297416.9
外商投资企业	Foreign Funded Enterprises	532980.1	129752.9	407383.8
在总计中: 国有控股企业	Of the Total : State-owned and State-holding Enterprises	18668510.6	13548143.7	31388707.3
在总计中: 农村工业	Of the Total : Rural Industry	15792.7	168.8	9159.4
按轻、重工业分(GB/T4754-2011)	**Grouped by Light & Heavy Industry(GB/T4754-2011)**			
轻工业	Light Industry	5667395.6	1169712.3	3848402.8
以农产品为原料	Using Farm Produces as Raw Materials	5236556.4	1009202.2	3466792.2
以非农产品为原料	Using Non-Farm Produces as Raw Materials	430839.2	160510.1	381610.6
重工业	Heavy Industry	26275886.7	15969032.9	39008760.5
采掘工业	Mining and Quarrying	7975928.9	6511242.2	16803017.6
原料工业	Raw Material Industry	13722854.2	7807205.8	16969208.2
加工工业	Manufacturing Industry	4577103.6	1650584.9	5236534.7
按轻、重工业分(GB/T4754-2002)	**Grouped by Light & Heavy Industry(GB/T4754-2002)**			
轻工业	Light Industry	5670638.0	1169033.2	3848862.3
以农产品为原料	Using Farm Produces as Raw Materials	5232917.6	1008712.0	3457759.1
以非农产品为原料	Using Non-Farm Produces as Raw Materials	437720.4	160321.2	391103.2
重工业	Heavy Industry	26272644.3	15969712.0	39008301.0
采掘工业	Mining and Quarrying	7979712.0	6511232.2	16757696.8
原料工业	Raw Material Industry	13729689.5	7803737.7	16998797.8
加工工业	Manufacturing Industry	4563242.8	1654742.1	5251806.4
按企业规模分(新标准)	**Grouped by Size of Enterprises (New Standard)**			
大型企业	Large Enterprises	16389752.4	11776237.6	28473395.5
中型企业	Medium-sized Enterprises	8372465.2	3079737.3	7841869.5
小型企业	Small Enterprises	6780271.6	2190037.8	6288729.8
微型企业	Mini Enterprises	400793.1	92732.5	253168.5
按企业规模分(旧标准)	**Grouped by Size of Enterprises (Old Standard)**			
大型企业	Large Enterprises	13583918.1	9867525.4	25132495.3
中型企业	Medium-sized Enterprises	10900857.7	4698610.7	10835711.0
小型企业	Small Enterprises	7458506.5	2572609.1	6888957.0

Continued

(10 000 yuan)

主营业务收入 Revenue from Principal Business	#主营业务成本 Cost of Principal Business	主营业务税金及附加 Taxes and Other Charges on Principal Business	营业利润 Business Profit	利润总额 Total Profit	亏损企业亏损总额 Losses Value of Loss-Suffering Enterprises	利税总额 Total Profits and Taxes	本年应交增值税 Value-added Taxes Payable	全部从业人员年平均人数(人) Annual Average Employed Persons (person)
67822512.9	**49660271.4**	**3344787.0**	**9308890.8**	**9637368.2**	**1498145.3**	**16102161.6**	**3120006.4**	**589851**
66381248.1	48522693.2	3330188.7	9183079.8	9504955.5	1486373.9	15907611.7	3072467.5	571845
5671370.5	4610753.8	206887.2	436566.3	469408.0	146943.1	910654.5	234359.3	73300
4570602.6	3660355.7	200483.3	409354.3	435124.6	85036.0	823077.4	187469.5	54756
1100767.9	950398.1	6403.9	27212.0	34283.4	61907.1	87577.1	46889.8	18544
621390.4	550900.0	2884.9	7504.6	3287.8	47764.7	36497.1	30324.4	11463
189551.8	169217.1	317.4	-3752.8	110.7	6881.7	2992.1	2564.0	2526
113892.3	76829.7	2660.5	8801.0	14453.0	7148.5	23872.0	6758.5	2997
276143.6	246624.6	1933.5	15004.9	16404.7	179.7	26369.6	8031.4	3143
117093.0	109642.6	424.8	2813.2	3528.2		6718.9	2765.9	1099
7538.8	7288.9	23.4	57.0	48.5		84.8	12.9	113
33941.3	25804.6	888.8	7733.0	8360.3	179.7	11090.8	1841.7	522
10685.7	4707.8	192.3	4199.1	4199.1		6208.0	1816.6	230
262316.0	236265.1	1099.8	13551.8	13501.9	1461.5	20946.8	6345.1	4963
31596.3	26344.7	429.3	2175.6	2520.9	547.3	4921.2	1971.0	973
16375.6	12850.4	271.8	1470.4	1635.2	2.3	3154.3	1247.3	364
4050.0	2582.1	28.2	1265.9	1378.1		1407.4	1.1	39
11170.7	10912.2	129.3	-560.7	-492.4	545.0	359.5	722.6	570
18989429.0	15376712.2	395344.9	1508640.2	1651427.8	341566.9	2883590.9	836818.2	237595
3642050.6	2916324.9	261576.9	218965.3	240987.8	68029.7	673512.0	170947.3	39252
15347378.4	12460387.3	133768.0	1289674.9	1410440.0	273537.2	2210078.9	665870.9	198343
33205705.7	21631027.5	2685130.0	6416239.3	6513280.3	940829.0	10964292.0	1765881.7	156235
7944687.0	6394965.3	39364.0	790901.7	838411.9	54846.4	1096836.7	219060.8	95636
307367.2	234546.3	1783.9	44414.0	43467.1	1170.2	62459.5	17208.5	7000
47647.6	35091.5	280.9	7105.1	5586.1	155.2	9977.7	4110.7	591
5753731.0	4744650.4	34449.2	457132.5	490077.7	47623.1	702143.2	177616.3	81136
1835941.2	1380677.1	2850.0	282250.1	299281.0	5897.9	322256.3	20125.3	6909
440186.0	328930.8	2282.3	47147.9	49308.9	2926.7	67031.6	15440.4	7786
1001078.8	808647.4	12316.0	78663.1	83103.8	8844.7	127518.3	32098.5	10220
49136691.5	34406033.0	3225271.7	7654407.9	7876122.1	1311681.1	13579598.2	2478204.4	349653
11452.9	9693.0	29.6	674.3	692.2	14.2	944.9	223.1	408
8033994.5	6622951.0	198161.3	366248.7	420112.8	211075.0	846825.6	228551.5	131188
7705865.3	6371428.3	196579.3	350133.7	399460.0	200660.3	810899.7	214860.4	122793
328129.2	251522.7	1582.0	16115.0	20652.8	10414.7	35925.9	13691.1	8395
59788518.4	43037320.4	3146625.7	8942642.1	9217255.4	1287070.3	15255336.0	2891454.9	458663
19698421.4	8380730.6	1407080.3	7605978.2	7726311.7	129503.7	10982206.2	1848814.2	182420
33324050.6	29315679.8	1701411.9	592600.0	652890.8	1123798.4	3214938.2	860635.5	205133
6766046.4	5340910.0	38133.5	744063.9	838052.9	33768.2	1058191.6	182005.2	71110
8039806.9	6626382.0	198099.8	367670.4	421919.5	211074.9	848362.3	228343.0	131255
7699208.0	6366166.7	196512.6	349465.1	399175.1	200660.2	810140.9	214453.2	122564
340598.9	260215.3	1587.2	18205.3	22744.4	10414.7	38221.4	13889.8	8691
59782706.0	43033889.4	3146687.2	8941220.4	9215448.7	1287070.4	15253799.3	2891663.4	458596
19659246.3	8352926.7	1405743.0	7595936.7	7715297.8	132743.4	10968538.3	1847497.5	181446
33337586.1	29324036.5	1702343.8	595217.6	655922.3	1123664.8	3219273.5	861007.4	205911
6785873.6	5356926.2	38600.4	750066.1	844228.6	30662.2	1065987.5	183158.5	71239
42271992.6	29301675.2	2803356.4	7039048.8	7214735.7	1119867.2	12173170.7	2155078.6	271995
13265855.1	10418670.6	453199.4	1256860.3	1335692.5	219020.6	2327291.2	538399.3	169042
11497251.1	9310566.2	85436.0	992102.6	1062058.2	145977.4	1562751.3	415257.1	145372
787414.1	629359.4	2795.2	20879.1	24881.8	13280.1	38948.4	11271.4	3442
38811110.3	26469030.7	2776188.3	6773305.2	6921817.1	1026924.8	11700762.5	2002757.1	226538
16656040.1	13213863.1	480290.4	1507796.9	1613439.0	314550.4	2771791.8	678062.4	218576
12355362.5	9977377.6	88308.3	1027788.7	1102112.1	156670.1	1629607.3	439186.9	144737

13-6 按行业分规模以上工业企业主要经济指标(GB/T4754-2011)

单位: 万元 (2011 年)

行业	Sector	企业单位数(个) Number of Enterprises (unit)	#亏损企业 Loss- Suffering Enterprises	工业总产值(当年价格) Gross Industrial Output Value (At Current Prices)
总计	**Total**	**1738**	**357**	**67208461.8**
煤炭开采和洗选业	Mining and Washing of Coal	111	24	1891207.7
石油和天然气开采业	Extraction of Petroleum and Natural Gas	6		14130667.7
黑色金属矿采选业	Mining and Processing of Ferrous Metals Ores	73	10	1043029.9
有色金属矿采选业	Mining and Processing of Nonferrous Metals Ores	30	4	567792.1
非金属矿采选业	Mining and Processing of Nonmetal Ores	22	2	180196.2
#采盐	Extraction of Salt	4		40529.3
农副食品加工业	Processing of Food from Agricultural Products	256	68	2689141.9
#谷物磨制	Grain Grinding	47	6	362996.5
饲料加工	Fodder Processing	29	4	410548.8
制糖	Sugar Making	14		296444.0
食品制造业	Manufacture of Food	118	36	1145998.6
#罐头制造	Manufacture of can	57	25	478361.2
酒、饮料和精制茶制造业	Manufacture of Wine,Beverages and Refined Tea	57	5	753181.2
#酒的制造	Manufacture of Wine	39	3	470404.7
烟草制品业	Manufacture of Tobacco	1		302740.4
纺织业	Manufacture of Textile	83	25	1217671.9
#棉、化纤纺织及印染精加工	Cotton, Chemical Fiber, Dyeing, Printing and Processing	68	22	1124650.6
毛纺织和染整精加工	Wool Textile, Dyeing and Printing	6	2	23638.3
纺织服装、鞋、帽制造业	Manufacture of Textile Wearing Apparel, Footware and Caps	4	2	31802.5
皮革、毛皮、羽毛(绒)及其制品业	Leather, Fur, Feather and Related Products Manufacturing	4		71943.0
#皮革鞣制加工	Leather Tanning and Processing	4		71943.0
木材加工及木、竹、藤、棕、草制品业	Processing of Timber, Wood, Bamboo, Cane, Grass Products	10	3	65059.9
家具制造业	Manufacture of Furniture	6	2	71795.7
造纸及纸制品业	Manufacture of Paper and Paper Products	24	4	182908.4
印刷业和记录媒介的复制	Printing and Copying of Medium for Record	10	1	45481.4
石油加工、炼焦及核燃料加工业	Oil Processing, Coking and Nuclear Fuel Processing	87	25	15720006.4
#炼焦	Coking	52	16	968351.9
化学原料及化学制品制造业	Raw Chemical Material and Chemical Products	109	14	4548905.2
#基础化学原料制造	Basic Chemical Material	26	8	858875.3
肥料制造	Fertilizer Making	22	1	739433.6
合成材料制造	Manufacture of Synthetic Materials	13	2	2480208.4
医药制造业	Manufacture of Medicine	19	1	133602.6
化学纤维制造业	Manufacture of Chemical Fiber	14	9	1073793.0
橡胶和塑料制品业	Manufacture of Rubber Products	81	12	694903.0
非金属矿物制品业	Manufacture of Nonmetal Mineral Products	213	35	2715796.3
#水泥制造	Manufacture of Cement	65	8	1337206.4
黑色金属冶炼及压延加工业	Smelting and Pressing of Ferrous Metals	62	18	6795822.6
有色金属冶炼及压延加工业	Smelting and Pressing of Nonferrous Metals	28	5	1299808.2
金属制品业	Manufacture of Metal Products	58	11	825426.4
通用设备制造业	Manufacture of General Purpose Machinery	17		59801.8
专用设备制造业	Manufacture of Special Purpose Machinery	22	2	283766.0
汽车制造业	Manufacture of Automobile	7	6	72839.3
电气机械及器材制造业	Manufacture of Electric Equipment and Machinery	31	1	2141944.3
计算机、通信和其他电子设备制造业	Telecom Equipment, Computer and Other Electronic Equipment	2		191767.0
仪器仪表制造业	Measuring Instruments and Machinery for Cultural Activify and Office Work	2		10306.1
金属制品、机械和设备修理业	Manufacture and Repairing of Metal Prodults,Mouhinery and Equipment	1		15350.7
电力、热力的生产和供应业	Electricity and Thermal Production and Supply	118	26	4593579.5
#电力生产和电力供应	Electricity Production and Supply	81	16	4364559.7
燃气生产和供应业	Gas Production and Supply	19	1	182362.4
水的生产和供应业	Water Production and Supply	8	3	49284.4

Main Economic Indicators of Industrial Enterprises above Designated Size by Sectors (GB/T4754-2011)

(10 000 yuan)

工业增加值 Value-added	工业销售产值(当年价) Sales Value of Industry Products (At Current Prices)	出口交货值 Delivery Value of Industry Export	实收资本 Total Capital Hold	资产合计 Total Assets	流动资产合计 Total Working Capitals	#产成品 Finished Product	固定资产原价 Original Value of Fixed Assets
25635749.7	**65996909.7**	**704655.1**	**31198256.3**	**93049478.0**	**30149057.3**	**3312397.0**	**69398719.4**
1125752.9	1888320.7		1486339.0	5338382.2	1369770.7	97325.1	1991613.6
13118622.6	14096222.2		13057131.0	21241104.8	3493935.9	148074.4	28431645.6
493050.7	979981.0		333332.5	1815909.7	975084.4	130904.3	642485.8
417964.0	528371.4		198752.0	1231729.5	356400.5	60973.3	543843.4
69693.0	163843.7	3539.1	42868.6	156401.1	88465.2	11253.0	56911.3
23150.0	34410.8		16307.1	47779.7	28336.5	4232.9	15197.7
407736.7	2578321.6	20756.1	509680.9	2494105.0	1550060.6	469986.1	900986.2
36574.0	355982.4		50236.8	239100.3	129784.9	8232.0	87572.8
58735.5	395250.2	5.3	57315.1	347506.6	192986.3	24526.8	94058.1
117426.7	327667.3		87288.8	369034.8	202858.7	94761.8	272090.5
228323.5	1071819.3	208711.1	466930.3	1959007.1	1016916.6	352555.7	1044935.5
60927.6	419731.1	183784.6	269017.6	1257454.0	739045.8	313827.0	623427.7
278720.3	729783.0		246688.8	977614.8	525316.2	57293.2	437934.0
208820.5	460164.2		186015.0	765291.3	450968.9	40862.3	307338.5
236486.5	302055.5		18741.7	371707.0	261354.0		129728.0
259999.1	1157568.3	68220.4	509779.6	2093332.0	999165.3	206516.4	1100643.8
236462.3	1071486.7	56072.9	415685.6	1894465.2	917956.4	193519.3	995176.0
5173.2	27876.9	314.3	16847.4	27490.8	15713.4	3410.2	19632.2
8119.5	29387.7	538.8	5127.9	21892.6	14390.9	1486.5	9145.7
18521.1	71361.1		6556.4	23742.0	16694.8	1708.5	9936.3
18521.1	71361.1		6556.4	23742.0	16694.8	1708.5	9936.3
12561.8	63860.4		17419.1	63815.5	29227.3	8575.1	34309.2
26916.6	76709.0	47442.9	70894.0	312879.8	48282.1	7823.1	47905.0
47117.2	174819.9		44906.1	284311.1	130927.6	24102.8	184436.8
14617.8	44980.3		17900.2	70629.6	30674.7	3071.7	58885.2
2022820.5	15598128.7	14644.8	4756845.4	8825292.7	3175486.5	330677.7	7757845.3
267939.3	924896.1	14644.8	315834.9	1244679.7	482543.2	68542.8	596443.5
1382059.8	4342820.3	156035.6	1747539.3	7577741.8	2226112.3	310240.9	4159540.4
264090.1	844226.6	51222.5	492610.9	2800384.8	706858.7	43943.9	843720.0
392389.8	615907.7	849.8	181333.6	1210964.3	475528.9	61093.3	802266.3
596202.5	2423659.9	103721.1	959061.6	3048985.0	766962.0	184335.3	2333614.8
40289.0	128488.5	1870.7	63017.2	238499.3	139329.2	24400.8	92194.0
151251.4	985381.0		216148.0	1091771.1	461909.6	90045.4	608288.8
130528.3	646083.3	7614.4	226214.9	821384.6	442501.9	105604.7	370021.4
811437.1	2615885.6	15609.9	1241780.2	4994823.9	1919216.4	123055.5	2326902.7
506835.5	1289591.6		903340.7	3339057.1	1101203.6	54744.6	1614110.9
868133.9	6709361.5	19073.8	1101969.9	5851771.6	2337582.6	384650.5	3103840.7
312094.1	1278649.1	2637.9	426592.1	2517652.4	829664.9	54626.4	1148389.1
103312.9	886065.9	6769.1	167298.4	638703.4	400623.3	38766.6	165440.5
17264.7	60584.9	1645.8	22288.2	79099.8	59903.0	9092.4	26760.3
62778.8	226783.5	29208.0	59779.6	350692.1	262222.3	48424.9	85149.2
1070.4	74697.5	50.8	36508.2	149839.6	78342.5	13049.2	52783.6
460713.4	2070321.7	45846.0	639005.0	5319272.1	3233208.1	176970.1	263162.0
60933.0	195554.4	52053.2	41404.2	708640.6	368332.9	11415.9	169170.5
1547.9	9752.9		4500.0	19255.2	12498.8	2406.4	504.8
2856.4	14438.3		900.6	17172.4	13355.3	941.4	4208.9
1769022.4	4579646.6		2083848.7	12516049.3	2129741.9	133.8	11533032.5
1678880.8	4351084.6		1921072.2	11586678.9	1803080.0	133.8	10712486.2
72113.9	160751.3		109356.8	482804.3	186426.7	585.2	290883.2
23149.8	49284.4		223601.5	516391.7	110898.8		397177.0

13-6 续表

单位：万元

行业	Sector	流动负债合计 Total Working Liabilities	长期负债合计 Long-term Liabilities	所有者权益合计 Total Owners' Equities
总计	**Total**	**31943282.3**	**17138745.2**	**42857163.3**
煤炭开采和洗选业	Mining and Washing of Coal	1814635.1	1268972.2	2161965.7
石油和天然气开采业	Extraction of Petroleum and Natural Gas	3909036.8	4718550.2	12612287.9
黑色金属矿采选业	Mining and Processing of Ferrous Metals Ores	993721.8	158499.6	656509.6
有色金属矿采选业	Mining and Processing of Nonferrous Metals Ores	387567.5	162380.7	679916.8
非金属矿采选业	Mining and Processing of Nonmetal Ores	78758.2	5388.8	70096.1
#采盐	Extraction of Salt	14379.2	3373.0	30027.5
农副食品加工业	Processing of Food from Agricultural Products	1480907.6	104543.7	860243.8
#谷物磨制	Grain Grinding	121610.3	11822.2	104760.6
饲料加工	Fodder Processing	128186.4	40156.3	177652.1
制糖	Sugar Making	174812.0	4785.4	188637.2
食品制造业	Manufacture of Food	1230848.4	103523.7	601404.0
#罐头制造	Manufacture of can	909426.4	75187.7	254025.1
酒、饮料和精制茶制造业	Manufacture of Wine,Beverages and Refined Tea	462248.4	206228.4	308966.4
#酒的制造	Manufacture of Wine	339385.5	199611.4	226122.9
烟草制品业	Manufacture of Tobacco	98051.0		273656.0
纺织业	Manufacture of Textile	995806.3	360083.5	725804.2
#棉、化纤纺织及印染精加工	Cotton, Chemical Fiber, Dyeing, Printing and Processing	912439.0	344630.0	626037.4
毛纺织和染整精加工	Wool Textile, Dyeing and Printing	17778.0	42.7	9670.1
纺织服装、鞋、帽制造业	Manufacture of Textile Wearing Apparel, Footware and Caps	11436.9	14936.7	-4480.9
皮革、毛皮、羽毛(绒)及其制品业	Leather, Fur, Feather and Related Products Manufacturing	12829.3	1818.1	8244.0
#皮革鞣制加工	Leather Tanning and Processing	12829.3	1818.1	8244.0
木材加工及木、竹、藤、棕、草制品业	Processing of Timber, Wood, Bamboo, Cane, Grass Products	29337.9	5003.2	29472.5
家具制造业	Manufacture of Furniture	35345.0	18436.6	255798.1
造纸及纸制品业	Manufacture of Paper and Paper Products	145818.8	20126.2	107531.3
印刷业和记录媒介的复制	Printing and Copying of Medium for Record	27951.3	7376.2	35301.8
石油加工、炼焦及核燃料加工业	Oil Processing, Coking and Nuclear Fuel Processing	2665228.2	812667.3	5336398.7
#炼焦	Coking	545275.8	203326.3	485280.7
化学原料及化学制品制造业	Raw Chemical Material and Chemical Products	1891927.5	2003503.5	3666991.7
#基础化学原料制造	Basic Chemical Material	753376.0	692399.0	1345222.3
肥料制造	Fertilizer Making	381717.4	302841.3	526145.1
合成材料制造	Manufacture of Synthetic Material	547105.7	972354.7	1526032.9
医药制造业	Manufacture of Medicine	99143.1	10562.5	127958.4
化学纤维制造业	Manufacture of Chemical Fiber	685374.7	168794.9	232318.7
橡胶和塑料制品业	Manufacture of Rubber Products	364194.0	108613.8	334511.9
非金属矿物制品业	Manufacture of Nonmetal Mineral Products	1701327.6	822351.6	2308604.4
#水泥制造	Manufacture of Cement	976624.2	630719.4	1590932.5
黑色金属冶炼及压延加工业	Smelting and Pressing of Ferrous Metals	3307363.8	678733.9	1843806.0
有色金属冶炼及压延加工业	Smelting and Pressing of Nonferrous Metals	1774704.2	125972.3	568447.2
金属制品业	Manufacture of Metal Products	336978.3	39084.7	250235.3
通用设备制造业	Manufacture of General Purpose Machinery	39096.1	1518.6	36533.6
专用设备制造业	Manufacture of Special Purpose Machinery	137194.9	15928.0	191160.3
汽车制造业	Manufacture of Automobile	119438.8	10424.4	19616.3
电气机械及器材制造业	Manufacture of Electric Equipment and Machinery	2216852.2	554548.9	2542160.7
计算机、通信和其他电子设备制造业	Telecom Equipment, Computer and Other Electronic Equipment	85004.3	269028.4	354607.9
仪器仪表制造业	Measuring Instruments and Machinery for Cultunal Activify and Office Work	6327.1	1219.1	11709.0
金属制品、机械和设备修理业	Manufacture and Repairing of Metal Products, Machinery and Equipment	14651.4		2520.9
电力、热力的生产和供应业	Electricity and Thermal Production and Supply	3496044.8	3862968.9	4575383.2
#电力生产和电力供应	Electricity Production and Supply	3171785.6	3511100.0	4351984.6
燃气生产和供应业	Gas Production and Supply	185518.4	127907.4	162216.8
水的生产和供应业	Water Production and Supply	113296.6	157679.0	236027.5

Continued

(10 000 yuan)

主营业务收入 Revenue from Principal Business	#主营业务成本 Cost of Principal Business	主营业务税金及附加 Taxes and Other Charges on Principal Business	营业利润 Business Profit	利润总额 Total Profit	亏损企业亏损总额 Losses Value of Loss-Suffering Enterprises	利税总额 Total Profits and Taxes	本年应交增值税 Value-added Taxes Payable	全部从业人员年平均人数(人) Annual Average Employed Persons (person)
67822512.9	**49660271.4**	**3344787.0**	**9308890.8**	**9637368.2**	**1498145.3**	**16102161.6**	**3120006.4**	**589851**
1919296.7	1278292.6	49092.0	281050.2	275618.4	50099.6	519028.5	194318.1	59749
14797418.6	4962169.1	1310434.3	6853199.3	6952227.6		9687694.3	1425032.4	72579
1043936.4	614709.3	23144.1	270693.9	270884.5	6542.6	388181.0	94152.4	9565
529431.6	205211.2	8257.7	245948.7	246046.1	4947.0	310168.9	55865.1	9136
154462.9	90673.3	3814.4	16132.5	17020.4	290.7	39663.6	18828.8	3509
34452.9	10919.2	2818.2	5732.7	5793.7		12840.7	4228.8	1283
2725218.0	2354786.8	4145.1	132558.4	139441.1	45227.9	193806.6	50220.4	27233
358765.8	329329.5	257.3	12928.4	13753.7	1507.6	16642.5	2631.5	2531
402380.8	340213.0	336.9	24772.1	27658.2	782.9	34442.8	6447.7	3131
314887.4	230673.1	2409.7	45348.6	46248.8		74892.2	26233.7	6667
1115733.0	883332.4	3815.5	32670.5	39699.9	56755.6	68223.7	24708.3	20710
423893.8	344621.9	1225.0	-32539.5	-31881.6	53320.6	-29480.2	1176.4	8799
743040.8	498292.3	47011.9	101803.8	112644.0	5596.1	195477.3	35821.4	11063
461613.2	280698.9	45413.9	66911.7	76507.8	4837.4	151530.7	29609.0	8174
302058.0	106288.0	134892.0	40736.0	40648.0		210392.0	34852.0	885
1254465.3	1126922.2	3437.1	32402.3	47047.6	35408.2	91146.2	40661.5	39803
1161100.6	1046982.1	3120.7	30410.4	42469.6	33320.5	84239.7	38649.4	35016
26556.8	24689.0	74.3	-1570.4	-1454.5	2087.6	-573.5	806.7	1593
47156.8	43824.9	30.3	-829.8	-286.9	1028.1	-132.2	124.4	1225
71277.8	65076.0	87.3	5231.6	5531.2		6558.4	939.9	559
71277.8	65076.0	87.3	5231.6	5531.2		6558.4	939.9	559
57322.8	48638.9	186.3	4024.6	5230.7	116.3	7361.8	1944.8	981
77236.2	64599.1	412.2	2506.3	2893.1	380.0	3719.9	414.6	3229
173052.4	146226.1	871.1	12517.3	16322.7	2601.9	23207.1	6013.3	5201
46788.5	39525.8	164.2	729.1	2559.3	71.6	4068.9	1345.4	1614
16016213.8	14404372.1	1636022.5	-724313.4	-753763.7	996105.4	1140743.3	258484.5	43088
905338.9	713660.9	8515.3	111161.8	110339.5	7280.0	156929.5	38074.7	11907
3996385.9	2962863.3	40860.1	621565.6	677372.8	13616.6	907984.8	189751.9	45646
1092525.0	881674.4	4192.0	88281.2	88190.4	11975.1	136202.3	43819.9	16011
612089.0	294772.9	18859.9	200314.3	240131.2	20.9	292682.7	33691.6	6336
1792800.8	1394742.2	14365.5	268507.1	282068.4	1319.9	386325.5	89891.6	16664
115854.8	68448.4	848.3	14249.9	14222.4	397.3	21329.0	6258.3	3398
1082061.4	998265.2	1361.9	-20918.5	-16719.8	53819.6	1328.4	16686.3	9896
687500.7	592470.3	2939.1	34950.3	38486.0	7220.9	57563.9	16138.8	11816
2636837.4	2074918.5	13387.1	308964.0	340092.6	18558.7	474106.4	120626.7	47443
1276797.0	908268.7	8006.4	234571.4	260450.3	6427.4	340150.5	71693.8	25684
6969285.6	6395559.8	17721.1	210071.7	213451.9	10669.1	355171.3	123998.3	35950
1211833.3	1093756.7	1387.5	71486.0	75968.8	13743.3	123738.8	46382.5	12037
839695.8	777953.5	2162.8	26455.1	27997.9	1675.3	38874.2	8713.5	7906
62680.1	48263.1	635.1	4824.9	7236.7		9353.9	1482.1	1594
278534.2	218415.0	737.9	27714.0	30511.3	924.7	34352.3	3103.1	4357
151842.1	151198.6	105.2	-11321.8	-10408.8	10533.8	-9680.2	623.4	1824
2368344.4	1842996.6	3971.7	302611.4	337750.0	77.1	397259.1	55537.4	9289
185797.5	139881.3	484.8	27732.9	29428.1		29916.8	3.9	4058
9752.9	7504.4	37.7	731.8	784.2		1064.1	242.2	70
13587.7	12527.7	58.6	197.0	184.9		709.2	465.7	257
4557462.0	3896459.0	17118.5	414479.4	453165.3	83163.9	682093.1	211809.3	50879
4323068.5	3687814.8	16395.7	419257.8	442606.2	76330.0	663916.5	204914.6	44665
192091.6	119201.6	2167.9	25283.1	25893.0	203.3	33951.9	5891.0	2597
56533.5	43594.4	334.5	-11634.7	-7695.4	9761.8	-5162.4	2198.5	1983

13-7 按行业分规模以上工业企业主要经济指标(GB/T4754-2002)

单位：万元 (2011 年)

行业	Sector	企业单位数(个) Number of Enterprises (unit)	#亏损企业 Loss- Suffering Enterprises	工业总产值(当年价格) Gross Industrial Output Value (At Current Prices)
煤炭开采和洗选业	Mining and Washing of Coal	111	24	1891207.7
石油和天然气开采业	Extraction of Petroleum and Natural Gas	24	1	15412392.0
#天然原油和天然气开采	Extraction of Ores Crude Oil and Natural Gas Extraction	6		14130667.7
黑色金属矿采选业	Mining and Processing of Ferrous Metals Ores	73	10	1043029.9
有色金属矿采选业	Mining and Processing of Nonferrous Metals Ores	30	4	567792.1
非金属矿采选业	Mining and Processing of Nonmetal Ores	23	3	185107.8
#采　盐	Extraction of Salt	4		40529.3
农副食品加工业	Processing of Food from Agricultural Products	257	69	2740306.4
#谷物磨制	Grain Grinding	47	6	362996.5
饲料加工	Fodder Processing	29	4	410548.8
制　糖	Sugar Making	14		296444.0
食品制造业	Manufacture of Food	117	35	1094834.1
#罐头制造	Manufacture of can	56	24	427196.7
饮料制造业	Manufacture of Beverage	57	5	753181.2
#酒的制造	Manufacture of Wine	41	3	463976.0
烟草制品业	Manufacture of Tobacco	1		302740.4
纺织业	Manufacture of Textile	83	26	1211101.0
#棉、化纤纺织及印染精加工	Cotton, Chemical Fiber, Dyeing, Printing and Processing	67	22	1113697.9
毛纺织和染整精加工	Wool Textile, Dyeing and Printing	6	2	23638.3
纺织服装、鞋、帽制造业	Manufacture of Textile Wearing Apparel, Footware and Caps	3		36535.6
皮革、毛皮、羽毛(绒)及其制品业	Leather, Fur, Feather and Related Products Manufacturing	4		71943.0
#皮革鞣制加工	Leather Tanning and Processing	3		52212.6
木材加工及木、竹、藤、棕、草制品业	Processing of Timber, Wood, Bamboo, Cane, Grass Products	10	3	65059.9
家具制造业	Manufacture of Furniture	6	2	71795.7
造纸及纸制品业	Manufacture of Paper and Paper Products	24	4	182908.4
印刷业和记录媒介的复制	Printing and Copying of Medium for Record	10	1	45481.4
石油加工、炼焦及核燃料加工业	Oil Processing, Coking and Nuclear Fuel Processing	87	25	15720006.4
#炼　焦	Coking	52	16	968351.9
化学原料及化学制品制造业	Raw Chemical Material and Chemical Products	109	13	4577273.6
#基础化学原料制造	Basic Chemical Material	25	7	854478.8
肥料制造	Fertilizer Making	22	1	739433.6
医药制造业	Manufacture of Medicine	19	1	133602.6
化学纤维制造业	Manufacture of Chemical Fiber	14	9	1073793.0
橡胶制品业	Manufacture of Rubber Products	2	1	112370.3
塑料制品业	Manufacture of Plastic Products	80	12	584370.5
非金属矿物制品业	Manufacture of Nonmetal Mineral Products	213	35	2714085.5
#水泥制造	Manufacture of Cement	62	8	1320174.6
黑色金属冶炼及压延加工业	Smelting and Pressing of Ferrous Metals	59	19	6797932.0
有色金属冶炼及压延加工业	Smelting and Pressing of Nonferrous Metals	28	4	1304065.1
金属制品业	Manufacture of Metal Products	59	11	786067.4
通用设备制造业	Manufacture of General Purpose Machinery	20		119525.7
专用设备制造业	Manufacture of Special Purpose Machinery	22	2	283766.0
交通运输设备制造业	Manufacture of Transport Equipment	8	7	76078.5
电气机械及器材制造业	Manufacture of Electric Equipment and Machinery	31	1	2141944.3
通信设备、计算机及其他电子设备制造业	Telecom Equipment, Computer and Other Electronic Equipment	2		191767.0
仪器仪表及文化、办公用机械制造业	Measuring Instruments and Machinery for Cultunal Activify and Office Work	2		10306.1
工艺品及其他制造业	Art work and Other Manufacturing Sector	3		38015.5
电力、热力的生产和供应业	Electricity and Thermal Production and Supply	118	26	4593579.5
#电力生产和电力供应	Electricity Production and Supply	81	16	4364559.7
燃气生产和供应业	Gas Production and Supply	19	1	182362.4
水的生产和供应业	Water Production and Supply	8	3	49284.4

Main Economic Indicators of Industrial Enterprises above Designated Size by Sectors (GB/T4754-2002)

(10 000 yuan)

工业增加值 Value-added	工业销售产值(当年价) Sales Value of Industry Products (At Current Prices)	出口交货值 Delivery Value of Industry Export	实收资本 Total Capital Hold	资产合计 Total Assets	流动资产合计 Total Working Capitals	#产成品 Finished Product	固定资产原价 Original Value of Fixed Assets
1125752.9	1888320.7		1486339.0	5338382.2	1369770.7	97325.1	1991613.6
13641591.5	15377576.0	2386.7	13995676.1	22793438.2	4215712.3	148963.3	29473664.0
13118622.6	14096222.2		13057131.0	21241104.8	3493935.9	148074.4	28431645.6
493050.7	979981.0		333332.5	1815909.7	975084.4	130904.3	642485.8
417964.0	528371.4		198752.0	1231729.5	356400.5	60973.3	543843.4
69531.8	167337.1	3539.1	49968.6	176554.0	96114.1	12645.9	71306.2
23150.0	34410.8		16307.1	47779.7	28336.5	4232.9	15197.7
413636.6	2608465.4	20756.1	607132.1	2666844.2	1652965.4	500205.0	985239.3
36574.0	355982.4		50236.8	239100.3	129784.9	8232.0	87572.8
58735.5	395250.2	5.3	57315.1	347506.6	192986.3	24526.8	94058.1
117426.7	327667.3		87288.8	369034.8	202858.7	94761.8	272090.5
222423.6	1041675.5	208711.1	369479.1	1786267.9	914011.8	322336.8	960682.4
55027.7	389587.3	183784.6	171566.4	1084714.8	636141.0	283608.1	539174.6
278720.3	729783.0		246688.8	977614.8	525316.2	57293.2	437934.0
210535.1	453800.5		189932.0	752671.1	441609.7	40597.8	304123.8
236486.5	302055.5		18741.7	371707.0	261354.0		129728.0
257303.6	1151813.8	63605.3	510311.5	2077527.8	987286.0	204420.3	1100003.1
233307.1	1060495.4	51457.8	414435.6	1878157.5	905363.9	190639.2	993122.7
5173.2	27876.9	314.3	16847.4	27490.8	15713.4	3410.2	19632.2
10427.8	33304.4	5153.9	3595.0	34111.5	24188.6	3455.8	8088.5
18521.1	71361.1		6556.4	23742.0	16694.8	1708.5	9936.3
16542.7	51921.8		6256.4	20849.4	14470.7	954.1	9267.8
12561.8	63860.4		17419.1	63815.5	29227.3	8575.1	34309.2
26916.6	76709.0	47442.9	70894.0	312879.8	48282.1	7823.1	47905.0
47117.2	174819.9		44906.1	284311.1	130927.6	24102.8	184436.8
14617.8	44980.3		17900.2	70629.6	30674.7	3071.7	58885.2
2022820.5	15598128.7	14644.8	4756845.4	8825292.7	3175486.5	330677.7	7757845.3
267939.3	924896.1	14644.8	315834.9	1244679.7	482543.2	68542.8	596443.5
1398941.4	4371138.7	156035.6	1756034.3	7610561.9	2249799.4	310169.4	4176981.8
264113.9	839830.1	51222.5	492105.9	2799307.9	706217.9	43741.1	843140.9
392389.8	615907.7	849.8	181333.6	1210964.3	475528.9	61093.3	802266.3
40289.0	128488.5	1870.7	63017.2	238499.3	139329.2	24400.8	92194.0
151251.4	985381.0		216148.0	1091771.1	461909.6	90045.4	608288.8
16912.2	107100.6	6472.4	38620.0	128146.1	47475.5	11790.2	56015.6
114003.4	540820.5	1142.0	188595.9	696823.8	397108.0	93941.3	315703.7
810661.1	2615684.4	15609.9	1235885.2	4976993.1	1913532.7	121534.0	2313100.2
502383.8	1272559.8		901040.7	3322157.7	1093887.7	54413.2	1603069.0
880799.6	6717698.3	19073.8	1102499.7	5860563.0	2332382.1	386111.4	3118735.1
317181.0	1273868.3	2637.9	440597.1	2524166.9	842152.1	53951.5	1143606.8
79736.3	851073.8	6769.1	151833.6	604751.0	375933.5	37356.0	154073.1
29368.1	117748.4	1645.8	32318.8	139637.1	99497.3	12000.9	35329.2
62778.8	226783.5	29208.0	59779.6	350692.1	262222.3	48424.9	85149.2
2155.7	77936.7	50.8	45686.8	160452.3	86754.6	13049.2	55556.6
460713.4	2070321.7	45846.0	639005.0	5319272.1	3233208.1	176970.1	263162.0
60933.0	195554.4	52053.2	41404.2	708640.6	368332.9	11415.9	169170.5
1547.9	9752.9		4500.0	19255.2	12498.8	2406.4	504.8
13040.0	37470.0		18988.0	200695.3	61684.6	1188.8	126342.2
1769022.4	4579646.6		2083848.7	12516049.3	2129741.9	133.8	11533032.5
1678880.8	4351084.6		1921072.2	11586678.9	1803080.0	133.8	10712486.2
72113.9	160751.3		109356.8	482804.3	186426.7	585.2	290883.2
23149.8	49284.4		223601.5	516391.7	110898.8		397177.0

13-7 续表

单位：万元

行　　业	Sector	流动负债合计 Total Working Liabilities	长期负债合计 Long-term Liabilities	所有者权益合计 Total Owners' Equities
煤炭开采和洗选业	Mining and Washing of Coal	1814635.1	1268972.2	2161965.7
石油和天然气开采业	Extraction of Petroleum and Natural Gas	4682448.9	4915990.9	13191636.2
#天然原油和天然气开采	Extraction of Ores Crude Oil and Natural Gas Extraction	3909036.8	4718550.2	12612287.9
黑色金属矿采选业	Mining and Processing of Ferrous Metals Ores	993721.8	158499.6	656509.6
有色金属矿采选业	Mining and Processing of Nonferrous Metals Ores	387567.5	162380.7	679916.8
非金属矿采选业	Mining and Processing of Nonmetal Ores	101338.7	5388.8	67668.5
#采　盐	Extraction of Salt	14379.2	3373.0	30027.5
农副食品加工业	Processing of Food from Agricultural Products	1552495.2	134624.1	931315.0
#谷物磨制	Grain Grinding	121610.3	11822.2	104760.6
饲料加工	Fodder Processing	128186.4	40156.3	177652.1
制　糖	Sugar Making	174812.0	4785.4	188637.2
食品制造业	Manufacture of Food	1159260.8	73443.3	530332.8
#罐头制造	Manufacture of can	837838.8	45107.3	182953.9
饮料制造业	Manufacture of Beverage	462248.4	206228.4	308966.4
#酒的制造	Manufacture of Wine	329345.0	195699.7	227454.9
烟草制品业	Manufacture of Tobacco	98051.0		273656.0
纺织业	Manufacture of Textile	986961.7	367937.3	710994.9
#棉、化纤纺织及印染精加工	Cotton, Chemical Fiber, Dyeing, Printing and Processing	902536.6	341118.6	623147.5
毛纺织和染整精加工	Wool Textile, Dyeing and Printing	17778.0	42.7	9670.1
纺织服装、鞋、帽制造业	Manufacture of Textile Wearing Apparel,Footware and Caps	19040.0	6592.7	8474.8
皮革、毛皮、羽毛(绒)及其制品业	Leather, Fur, Feather and Related Products Manufacturing	12829.3	1818.1	8244.0
#皮革鞣制加工	Leather Tanning and Processing	11166.3	1749.6	7944.0
木材加工及木、竹、藤、棕、草制品业	Processing of Timber, Wood, Bamboo, Cane, Grass Products	29337.9	5003.2	29472.5
家具制造业	Manufacture of Furniture	35345.0	18436.6	255798.1
造纸及纸制品业	Manufacture of Paper and Paper Products	145818.8	20126.2	107531.3
印刷业和记录媒介的复制	Printing and Copying of Medium for Record	27951.3	7376.2	35301.8
石油加工、炼焦及核燃料加工业	Oil Processing, Coking and Nuclear Fuel Processing	2665228.2	812667.3	5336398.7
#炼　焦	Coking	545275.8	203326.3	485280.7
化学原料及化学制品制造业	Raw Chemical Material and Chemical Products	1906550.8	2003503.5	3685163.1
#基础化学原料制造	Basic Chemical Material	751042.0	692399.0	1346454.0
肥料制造	Fertilizer Making	381717.4	302841.3	526145.1
医药制造业	Manufacture of Medicine	99143.1	10562.5	127958.4
化学纤维制造业	Manufacture of Chemical Fiber	685374.7	168794.9	232318.7
橡胶制品业	Manufacture of Rubber Products	50274.0	33368.1	44504.0
塑料制品业	Manufacture of Plastic Products	315161.5	75735.9	291861.5
非金属矿物制品业	Manufacture of Nonmetal Mineral Products	1682217.6	822570.5	2309909.1
#水泥制造	Manufacture of Cement	969835.3	627251.3	1584509.2
黑色金属冶炼及压延加工业	Smelting and Pressing of Ferrous Metals	3323119.6	678733.9	1836845.0
有色金属冶炼及压延加工业	Smelting and Pressing of Nonferrous Metals	1756750.3	125972.3	592915.5
金属制品业	Manufacture of Metal Products	321651.6	39084.7	230165.3
通用设备制造业	Manufacture of General Purpose Machinery	72194.8	1528.6	65403.0
专用设备制造业	Manufacture of Special Purpose Machinery	137194.9	15928.0	191160.3
交通运输设备制造业	Manufacture of Transport Equipment	124340.1	10424.4	25327.6
电气机械及器材制造业	Manufacture of Electric Equipment and Machinery	2216852.2	554548.9	2542160.7
通信设备、计算机及其他电子设备制造业	Telecom Equipment, Computer and Other Electronic Equipment	85004.3	269028.4	354607.9
仪器仪表及文化、办公用机械制造业	Measuring Instruments and Machinery for Cultural Activify and Office Work	6327.1	1219.1	11709.0
工艺品及其他制造业	Art work and Other Manufacturing Sector	175761.4	500.6	24214.2
电力、热力的生产和供应业	Electricity and Thermal Production and Supply	3496044.8	3862968.9	4575383.2
#电力生产和电力供应	Electricity Production and Supply	3171785.6	3511100.0	4351984.6
燃气生产和供应业	Gas Production and Supply	185518.4	127907.4	162216.8
水的生产和供应业	Water Production and Supply	113296.6	157679.0	236027.5

Continued

(10 000 yuan)

主营业务收入 Revenue from Principal Business	#主营业务成本 Cost of Principal Business	主营业务税金及附加 Taxes and Other Charges on Principal Business	营业利润 Business Profit	利润总额 Total Profit	亏损企业亏损总额 Losses Value of Loss-Suffering Enterprises	利税总额 Total Profits and Taxes	本年应交增值税 Value-added Taxes Payable	全部从业人员年平均人数(人) Annual Average Employed Persons (person)
1919296.7	1278292.6	49092.0	281050.2	275618.4	50099.6	519028.5	194318.1	59749
16007529.7	6160644.3	1321401.2	6784887.4	6908968.1	67623.8	9714651.4	1484282.1	99357
14797418.6	4962169.1	1310434.3	6853199.3	6952227.6		9687694.3	1425032.4	22098
1043936.4	614709.3	23144.1	270693.9	270884.5	6542.6	388181.0	94152.4	9565
529431.6	205211.2	8257.7	245948.7	246046.1	4947.0	310168.9	55865.1	9136
159051.9	94069.3	3848.0	13356.5	13780.7	3530.4	36508.5	18879.8	3639
34452.9	10919.2	2818.2	5732.7	5793.7		12840.7	4228.8	1283
2755361.8	2378941.6	4145.1	130982.4	138915.6	45753.4	193281.1	50220.4	27931
358765.8	329329.5	257.3	12928.4	13753.7	1507.6	16642.5	2631.5	2531
402380.8	340213.0	336.9	24772.1	27658.2	782.9	34442.8	6447.7	3131
314887.4	230673.1	2409.7	45348.6	46248.8		74892.2	26233.7	6667
1085589.2	859177.6	3815.5	34246.5	40225.4	56230.1	68749.2	24708.3	20012
393750.0	320467.1	1225.0	-30963.5	-31356.1	52795.1	-28954.7	1176.4	8101
743040.8	498292.3	47011.9	101803.8	112644.0	5596.1	195477.3	35821.4	11063
457585.2	273627.5	45202.5	67638.8	76893.7	4837.4	152518.4	30422.2	8483
302058.0	106288.0	134892.0	40736.0	40648.0		210392.0	34852.0	885
1248916.3	1122423.1	3437.7	30948.7	45590.4	36436.2	89494.0	40465.9	39198
1150108.3	1036850.2	3113.5	30432.0	42040.4	33320.5	83664.4	38510.5	34230
26556.8	24689.0	74.3	-1570.4	-1454.5	2087.6	-573.5	806.7	1593
50868.0	46813.4	20.4	625.8	1170.4		1434.6	243.8	1745
71277.8	65076.0	87.3	5231.6	5531.2		6558.4	939.9	559
51838.5	45783.7	61.9	5212.5	5512.1		6196.2	622.2	503
57322.8	48638.9	186.3	4024.6	5230.7	116.3	7361.8	1944.8	981
77236.2	64599.1	412.2	2506.3	2893.1	380.0	3719.9	414.6	3229
173052.4	146226.1	871.1	12517.3	16322.7	2601.9	23207.1	6013.3	5201
46788.5	39525.8	164.2	729.1	2559.3	71.6	4068.9	1345.4	1614
16016213.8	14404372.1	1636022.5	-724313.4	-753763.7	996105.4	1140743.3	258484.5	43088
905338.9	713660.9	8515.3	111161.8	110339.5	7280.0	156929.5	38074.7	11907
4021076.2	2978837.9	41918.7	626209.0	682493.4	13483.0	915157.2	190745.1	46622
1088128.5	877203.6	4185.3	88414.8	88324.0	11841.5	136289.0	43779.7	15981
612089.0	294772.9	18859.9	200314.3	240131.2	20.9	292682.7	33691.6	6336
115854.8	68448.4	848.3	14249.9	14222.4	397.3	21329.0	6258.3	3398
1082061.4	998265.2	1361.9	-20918.5	-16719.8	53819.6	1328.4	16686.3	9896
93293.4	80818.6	1397.0	128.7	419.8	1084.7	5495.2	3678.4	1652
596045.1	513162.3	1551.4	34819.6	38066.1	6136.3	52154.1	12536.6	10249
2635257.5	2075514.0	13388.4	310961.9	342554.6	15452.6	476372.6	120429.6	47231
1259194.8	893905.5	7909.8	232712.1	258627.4	6427.4	337598.5	71061.3	25411
6975049.8	6404592.0	17901.1	206011.7	209531.1	12253.8	353369.6	125937.4	36302
1207060.3	1086325.7	1162.9	75352.2	79596.1	12158.6	125141.2	44382.2	11621
807728.6	748706.4	2154.7	24271.3	25921.8	1675.3	36689.8	8613.3	7692
118993.0	96462.7	1017.0	9956.2	12379.4		15810.5	2414.1	2167
278534.2	218415.0	737.9	27714.0	30511.3	924.7	34352.3	3103.1	4357
157815.2	156053.2	163.8	-12198.0	-11393.9	11518.9	-10259.1	971.0	1969
2368344.4	1842996.6	3971.7	302611.4	337750.0	77.1	397259.1	55537.4	9289
185797.5	139881.3	484.8	27732.9	29428.1		29916.8	3.9	4058
9752.9	7504.4	37.7	731.8	784.2		1064.1	242.2	70
34662.6	29806.9	22.3	3026.7	3029.2		6403.3	3351.8	793
4557462.0	3896459.0	17118.5	414479.4	453165.3	83163.9	682093.1	211809.3	50879
4323068.5	3687814.8	16395.7	419257.8	442606.2	76330.0	663916.5	204914.6	44665
192091.6	119201.6	2167.9	25283.1	25893.0	203.3	33951.9	5891.0	2597
56533.5	43594.4	334.5	-11634.7	-7695.4	9761.8	-5162.4	2198.5	1983

13-8 各地、州、市、县(市)规模以上工业企业主要经济指标

单位: 万元 (2011 年)

地　区	Region	企业单位数(个) Number of Enterprises (unit)	#亏损企业 Loss- Suffering Enterprises	工业总产值(当年价格) Gross Industrial Output Value (At Current Prices)
总　计	**Total**	**1738**	**357**	**67208461.8**
乌鲁木齐市	**Urumqi City**	**343**	**66**	**19925798.7**
天山区	Tianshan District	16	3	2017409.4
沙依巴克区	Shayibak District	24	3	487819.1
新市区	Xinshi District	142	29	6361728.2
水磨沟区	Shui Mogou District	21	4	344538.3
头屯河区	Tou Tunhe District	47	10	5389102.6
达坂城区	Da Bancheng District	7		183338.5
米东区	Midong District	84	17	5111709.0
乌鲁木齐县	Urumqi County	2		30153.6
克拉玛依市	**Karamay City**	**62**	**9**	**16390365.6**
独山子区	Dushanzi District	10	4	5772355.7
克拉玛依区	Karamay District	43	4	10492862.9
白碱滩区	Bai Jiantan District	7		102243.9
乌尔河区	Urhe District	2	1	22903.1
吐鲁番地区	**Turpan Administrative Offices**	**66**	**11**	**2220534.8**
吐鲁番市	Turpan City	19	4	438563.5
鄯善县	Shanshan [Piqan] County	28	1	1440749.2
托克逊县	Toksun County	19	6	341222.1
哈密地区	**Hami [Kumul] Administrative Offices**	**84**	**12**	**1319855.1**
哈密市	Hami [Kumul] City	71	10	1146665.8
巴里坤哈萨克自治县	Barkol Kazak Autonomous County	11	1	129724.6
伊吾县	Yiwu [Araturuk] County	2	1	43464.7
昌吉回族自治州	**Changji Hui Autonomous Prefecture**	**290**	**60**	**4753317.6**
昌吉市	Changji City	109	10	1941621.1
阜康市	Fukang City	46	9	977401.5
呼图壁县	Hutubi County	50	18	429171.3
玛纳斯县	Manas County	34	14	784199.8
奇台县	Qitai County	29	1	380808.0
吉木萨尔县	Jimsar County	19	6	207805.0
木垒哈萨克自治县	Mori Kazak Autonomous County	3	2	32310.9
伊犁哈萨克自治州	**Ili Kazak Autonomous Prefecture**	**357**	**88**	**5679016.2**
伊犁州直属县(市)	**Counties (Cities) Direct Under Ili Prefecture**	**189**	**49**	**2948603.2**
伊宁市	Yining [Gulja] City	27	3	356020.3
奎屯市	Kuytun City	40	12	927687.5
伊宁县	Yining [Gulja] County	35	12	400341.3
察布查尔锡伯自治县	Qapqal Xibe Autonomous County	13	2	108664.0
霍城县	Huocheng [Korgas] County	25	6	172794.0
巩留县	Gongliu [Tokkuztara] County	8	4	58628.6
新源县	Xinyuan [Kunes] County	16	4	586765.0
昭苏县	Zhaosu [Mongolkure] County	13	3	111079.3
特克斯县	Tekes County	4	2	46103.8
尼勒克县	Nilka County	8	1	180519.4
塔城地区	**Tacheng [Tarbagatai] Administrative Offices**	**96**	**32**	**1742036.1**
塔城市	Tacheng [Qoqek] City	5	2	97806.2
乌苏市	Usu City	18	5	625339.2
额敏县	Emin [Dorbiljin] County	12	5	124330.7

Main Economic Indicators of Industrial Enterprises above Designated Size by Prefecture, Autonomous Prefecture, City and County

(10 000 yuan)

工业增加值 Value-added	工业销售产值(当年价) Sales Value of Industry Products (At Current Prices)	出口交货值 Delivery Value of Industry Export	实收资本 Total Capital Hold	资产合计 Total Assets	流动资产合计 Total Working Capitals	#产成品 Finished Product	固定资产原价 Original Value of Fixed Assets
25635749.7	**65996909.7**	**704655.1**	**31198256.3**	**93049478.0**	**30149057.3**	**3312397.7**	**69398719.4**
5647380.8	**19715616.2**	**282208.5**	**7597126.4**	**28079712.0**	**9618023.2**	**805036.1**	**18151109.9**
569094.5	2004347.4	21371.5	395215.1	4085608.3	765700.7	46717.0	3770759.9
131093.7	499370.9	35301.7	428027.0	2636754.3	657751.4	16919.2	728784.3
3508569.8	6179250.9	194849.8	3342065.6	10908680.9	4475620.1	355604.0	6939203.7
104640.7	345112.1		91300.1	596236.1	209983.6	14891.0	546397.8
509655.0	5436910.0	19022.0	885970.0	4390779.3	1458629.9	203136.1	2427827.6
115598.1	177397.9		124563.9	419516.6	78010.7	8816.9	230843.6
683246.9	5043399.8	11663.5	2267218.5	4806535.3	1936704.4	158951.9	3304785.9
25482.3	29827.2		62766.2	235601.2	35622.4		202507.1
6962583.6	**16398601.3**	**17996.6**	**10737038.3**	**17001472.3**	**4502946.3**	**196357.8**	**18269647.8**
551231.8	5776663.6	15609.9	3161884.1	4827565.9	1395421.0	119378.1	4537033.3
6377488.0	10499732.8		7556524.3	12028759.2	3007559.8	74478.6	13683451.8
27277.9	100746.8	2386.7	17369.9	126413.0	87792.4	1996.2	40391.4
6586.0	21458.1		1260.0	18734.2	12173.1	504.9	8771.3
1136819.4	**2186197.4**	**10377.0**	**1326525.1**	**4030316.2**	**1425650.7**	**153216.7**	**3899929.9**
131449.0	434387.6	4438.5	117492.2	663328.7	322682.4	26774.5	308334.2
856328.0	1409555.3	5938.5	973531.6	2245175.1	638055.7	108467.1	3068090.2
149042.4	342254.5		235501.3	1121812.4	464912.6	17975.1	523505.5
560224.8	**1286097.5**	**1166.2**	**953573.2**	**3103073.0**	**986350.2**	**107521.4**	**1246307.5**
458241.2	1116421.9	1166.2	610972.7	2028663.1	856843.9	95389.8	1081844.2
72514.7	127798.8		39100.5	241282.3	77879.8	11391.5	126961.3
29468.9	41876.8		303500.0	833127.6	51626.5	740.1	37502.0
1240406.5	**4538147.0**	**70703.0**	**1316887.7**	**6877724.4**	**2969885.9**	**402582.0**	**2596756.7**
493118.8	1940491.1	44175.0	534715.0	3423116.8	1654688.2	162010.5	832977.7
282887.7	946103.0		389484.5	1429530.2	428700.8	56779.8	652668.1
59906.4	392581.8	1.7	51725.6	254080.7	100305.7	26954.5	139096.8
229012.7	711084.2	17728.2	171326.3	1000003.9	481704.1	57409.0	600757.2
104460.6	346108.7		64709.5	363672.5	187491.8	72496.7	142373.1
60495.0	172397.2	8798.1	100726.8	368461.6	97253.0	23570.1	209290.0
10525.3	29381.0		4200.0	38858.7	19742.3	3361.4	19593.8
2424299.5	**5427522.3**	**94190.4**	**1741626.2**	**8903900.3**	**3184097.0**	**482684.9**	**5318072.3**
1131675.1	**2902103.5**	**48329.5**	**1170483.4**	**5278305.1**	**1931504.6**	**233949.2**	**3074370.2**
116842.9	352405.7	2851.6	63174.9	415097.0	127467.5	8106.2	397460.5
366377.1	932519.4	37392.3	203139.0	1369303.4	655040.9	71650.3	729170.6
115701.5	410566.4		133085.3	546925.8	209498.1	30422.6	286302.1
25411.4	105681.1		36913.7	224819.3	77859.3	14210.4	69055.1
51441.6	165367.3	6751.6	75155.0	254185.3	110536.7	36717.7	151151.2
27466.6	59367.3		299679.8	746179.9	100703.8	5398.5	453764.7
286694.5	561288.7	1334.0	209947.4	949443.0	464691.3	56613.3	461392.3
26281.7	101072.8		15810.0	71626.9	50153.0	6842.5	26245.0
11692.4	42616.5		30510.0	73731.5	33552.2	2445.9	44669.0
103765.5	171218.3		103068.3	626993.0	102001.8	1541.8	455159.7
708263.6	**1567928.4**	**45860.9**	**361701.7**	**1979195.8**	**744074.6**	**168877.1**	**1265481.2**
33746.9	98713.8		11594.0	113834.8	18481.3	1132.7	127896.6
388227.0	592085.9	40859.8	79874.2	725627.9	201448.3	61835.7	477580.6
43377.4	117342.3		64090.7	177287.4	80080.5	30917.6	148155.7

13-8 续表 1

单位：万元

地　　区	Region	企业单位数（个）Number of Enterprises (unit)	#亏损企业 Loss- Suffering Enterprises	工业总产值（当年价格）Gross Industrial Output Value (At Current Prices)
沙湾县	Shawan County	39	15	522667.3
托里县	Toli County	10	3	207288.8
裕民县	Yumin [Qagantokay] County			
和布克赛尔蒙古自治县	Hoboksar Mongol Autonomous County	12	2	164603.9
阿勒泰地区	**Altay Administrative Offices**	**72**	**7**	**988376.9**
阿勒泰市	Altay City	14	4	122340.1
布尔津县	Burqin County	7	1	58219.2
富蕴县	Fuyun [Koktokay] County	17	2	428256.7
福海县	Fuhai [Burultokay] County	9		46588.3
哈巴河县	Habahe [Kaba] County	6		302083.7
青河县	Qinghe [Qinggil] County	18		26434.6
吉木乃县	Jeminay County	1		4454.3
博尔塔拉蒙古自治州	**Bortala Mongol Autonomous Prefecture**	**38**	**9**	**366244.0**
博乐市	Bole [Bortala] City	28	8	298875.2
精河县	Jinghe [Jing] County	9	1	64657.2
温泉县	Wenquan [Araxang] County	1		2711.6
巴音郭楞蒙古自治州	**Bayangol Mongol Autonomous Prefecture**	**119**	**22**	**7316459.2**
库尔勒市	Korla City	57	11	5773625.8
轮台县	Luntai [Bugur] County	12	1	227684.9
尉犁县	Yuli [Lopnur] County	1	1	976.9
若羌县	Ruoqiang [Qarkilik] County	5	2	430623.9
且末县	Qiemo [Qarqan] County			
焉耆回族自治县	Yanqi Hui Autonomous County	10	3	78603.1
和静县	Hejing County	25	3	755750.1
和硕县	Hoxud County	6		27333.4
博湖县	Bohu [Bagrax] County	3	1	21861.1
阿克苏地区	**Aksu Administrative Offices**	**144**	**25**	**3970304.1**
阿克苏市	Aksu City	43	7	821825.5
温宿县	Wensu [Onsu] County	19	3	101245.0
库车县	Kuqa County	32	6	2422454.2
沙雅县	Xayar County	10	2	144039.0
新和县	Xinhe [Toksu] County	8		60578.6
拜城县	Baicheng [Bay] County	21	4	361489.6
乌什县	Wushi [Uxturpan] County	2		9253.3

Continued

(10 000 yuan)

工业增加值 Value-added	工业销售产值(当年价) Sales Value of Industry Products (At Current Prices)	出口交货值 Delivery Value of Industry Export	实收资本 Total Capital Hold	资产合计 Total Assets	流动资产合计 Total Working Capitals		固定资产原价 Original Value of Fixed Assets
						#产成品 Finished Product	
54687.8	456723.1	5001.1	88627.3	430357.0	248348.1	53873.9	224951.9
105563.7	185513.1		64526.2	306678.2	127227.2	14180.1	140542.9
82660.9	117550.2		52989.3	225410.5	68489.2	6937.1	146353.5
584360.8	**957490.4**		**209441.1**	**1646399.4**	**508517.8**	**79858.6**	**978220.9**
38696.9	120450.5		33223.1	233286.2	59153.0	3074.6	197057.3
27596.9	59338.1		24580.7	247260.7	34990.8	840.3	224327.7
269003.6	401182.5		65179.3	725998.0	254985.7	61598.5	320296.5
17039.5	45532.5		23175.6	69460.4	37972.9	7100.7	53193.9
222506.0	301817.9		50660.0	313504.8	104335.7	6256.3	142542.7
6184.2	24714.6		3044.4	17750.8	12810.2	988.2	5881.7
3333.7	4454.3		9578.0	39138.5	4269.5		34921.1
114694.8	**359400.4**	**4028.6**	**128236.9**	**697548.2**	**281700.5**	**62721.4**	**461561.6**
96775.2	291071.0	4028.6	109439.6	609272.9	236090.0	51861.2	433371.5
17303.7	65955.6		18689.3	86339.6	44600.2	10481.7	27184.6
615.9	2373.8		108.0	1935.7	1010.3	378.5	1005.5
5146033.8	**7116393.9**	**64920.5**	**4257004.4**	**10460016.2**	**2485754.1**	**357244.3**	**10784009.5**
4563725.8	5732494.2	23393.6	3939986.7	8260391.9	1621842.0	124541.2	9468999.7
48999.0	220734.7		53639.0	354256.8	177205.6	46262.5	166481.0
-120.3	890.6		1740.0	2924.9	450.8	167.2	2365.0
285961.2	356080.0		60499.9	751123.1	293631.0	35074.8	466671.2
25167.3	85520.1	12762.3	38591.4	116525.8	56950.0	19276.6	80659.1
213359.8	669337.5	1977.8	145135.1	893905.2	286711.1	105711.1	541748.3
6259.9	30539.7	12808.4	7310.9	44330.0	27627.9	9678.7	23114.4
2681.1	20797.1	13978.4	10101.4	36558.5	21335.7	16532.2	33970.8
1021426.6	**3872335.3**	**6390.0**	**1228134.4**	**4418033.6**	**1496297.9**	**197553.8**	**2340765.0**
249564.0	744400.3	1666.4	414009.1	1543356.2	490153.0	86307.3	758033.0
42885.7	96073.0		60951.5	288554.5	71581.5	10148.5	135361.1
498084.5	2439844.0	35.9	537928.2	1580571.7	469865.6	31397.9	953056.4
37288.3	131802.4		60606.8	226640.3	110734.6	14348.1	118549.4
19494.1	46598.6		23022.9	113443.9	69460.5	3703.2	30751.0
158393.6	360489.8		116705.9	586867.1	243021.5	38512.1	303510.9
3197.2	6921.8	4687.7	4000.0	17239.9	9491.6	5434.2	9372.0

13-8 续表 2

单位：万元

地　　区	Region	企业单位数（个） Number of Enterprises (unit)	#亏损企业 Loss- Suffering Enterprises	工业总产值（当年价格） Gross Industrial Output Value (At Current Prices)
阿瓦提县	Awat County	8	2	46874.9
柯坪县	Kalpin County	1	1	2544.0
克孜勒苏柯尔克孜自治州	**Kizilsu Kirgiz Autonomous Prefecture**	**18**	**8**	**167746.2**
阿图什市	Artux City	8	2	100749.5
阿克陶县	Akto County	6	3	35802.3
阿合奇县	Akqi County			
乌恰县	Wuqia [Ulugqat] County	4	3	31194.4
喀什地区	**Kashgar [Kaxgar] Administrative Offices**	**58**	**13**	**796319.8**
喀什市	Kashgar [Kaxgar] City	19	3	403555.2
疏附县	Shufu County	1	1	4100.2
疏勒县	Shule County	7	1	34926.4
英吉沙县	Yengisar County	2		6689.4
泽普县	Zepu [Poskam] County	4		25889.7
莎车县	Shache [Yarkant] County	6	2	75171.1
叶城县	Yecheng [Kagilik] County	4	2	47499.5
麦盖提县	Makit County	7		46693.7
岳普湖县	Yopurga County	1		6643.0
伽师县	Jiashi [Payzawat] County	2		105841.7
巴楚县	Bachu [Maralbexi] County	4	4	31068.1
塔什库尔干塔吉克自治县	Taxkorgan Tajik Autonomous County	1		8241.8
和田地区	**Hotan Administrative Offices**	**16**	**5**	**146736.4**
和田市	Hotan City	8	3	81209.4
和田县	Hotan County	3	1	26035.6
墨玉县	Moyu [Karakax] County	1		18373.7
皮山县	Pishan [Guma] County	2	1	9356.5
洛浦县	Lop County	2		11761.2
策勒县	Qira County			
于田县	Yutian [Keriya] County			
民丰县	Minfeng [Niya] County			
自治区直辖县级市	**Municpality Country-LevelCity directly under the Central Government**	**143**	**29**	**4155764.1**
石河子市	Shihezi City	83	22	2893433.3
阿拉尔市	Aral City	22	3	278035.9
图木舒克市	Tumxuk City	8		79822.1
五家渠市	Wujiaqu City	30	4	904472.8

Continued

(10 000 yuan)

工业增加值 Value-added	工业销售产值（当年价） Sales Value of Industry Products (At Current Prices)	出口交货值 Delivery Value of Industry Export	实收资本 Total Capital Hold	资产合计 Total Assets	流动资产合计 Total Working Capitals	#产成品 Finished Product	固定资产原价 Original Value of Fixed Assets
12281.5	44362.0		9990.0	57588.0	29194.0	7702.5	30983.9
237.7	1843.4		920.0	3772.0	2795.6		1147.3
55105.5	**168556.8**		**112454.7**	**319754.0**	**149060.2**	**28944.1**	**143803.6**
29124.1	94757.3		64313.7	183144.3	87589.7	8501.5	98551.6
16841.3	44586.6		45947.0	112643.5	43651.4	12666.1	37533.9
9140.0	29212.9		2194.0	23966.2	17819.1	7776.5	7718.1
246480.4	**787274.7**	**1437.2**	**139904.5**	**1012514.2**	**370385.7**	**68295.1**	**827222.3**
124195.7	404429.8	1437.2	53070.8	563642.2	158089.3	22016.7	622930.5
519.3	4089.2		1000.0	1361.0	644.4	278.7	1312.8
8091.7	31699.8		10820.0	43648.1	31208.1	6764.9	14101.6
2069.3	6689.4		600.0	4162.9	2555.1		2068.1
6676.1	25023.2		4320.0	22233.2	8599.8	2587.3	15705.6
19116.5	63428.7		10070.0	66697.0	47681.2	12218.6	17689.3
9137.5	48500.5		31199.0	95857.1	26933.7	7169.8	68609.5
11373.7	46320.5		11754.7	54895.4	41254.8	7392.3	12945.2
1691.3	6568.0		1000.0	8881.2	4680.6	75.9	4509.7
51319.6	115518.7		3900.0	92306.1	31909.1	2251.3	39374.0
10019.1	28139.3		12050.0	35263.9	14310.8	7388.2	24197.8
2270.6	6867.6		120.0	23566.1	2518.8	151.4	3778.2
59609.7	**141757.5**	**406.1**	**184650.9**	**365497.5**	**73608.3**	**5449.4**	**377981.2**
25879.0	80161.8		16176.1	121383.3	24261.3	961.6	154453.1
18534.4	22908.3		148537.2	161497.9	15572.1	1731.5	163043.1
7815.1	18470.0		15237.0	40384.9	11076.6	42.9	36251.8
2780.4	8489.8	406.1	1773.6	24601.1	10468.4	1103.3	16637.3
4600.9	11727.6		2927.0	17630.3	12229.9	1610.1	7595.9
1020684.4	**3999009.4**	**150831.0**	**1475093.6**	**7779916.1**	**2605297.3**	**444790.7**	**4981552.1**
704017.8	2798657.1	136186.2	1047357.5	4595769.8	1604002.1	311810.9	3091546.0
46078.4	261085.3		102992.8	480944.0	173729.4	44279.9	340059.6
20046.0	75125.6		34575.2	197088.0	93812.7	26624.9	105678.5
250542.1	864141.4	14644.8	290168.1	2506114.3	733753.1	62075.0	1444268.0

13-8 续表 3

单位: 万元

地　　区	Region	流动负债合计 Total Working Liabilities	长期负债合计 Long-term Liabilities	所有者权益合计 Total Owners' Equities
总　计	**Total**	**31943282.3**	**17138745.2**	**42857163.3**
乌鲁木齐市	**Urumqi City**	**10211667.0**	**4513852.8**	**13307528.3**
天山区	Tianshan District	1347625.7	1049373.5	1686841.1
沙依巴克区	Shayibak District	578263.0	720919.8	1334271.1
新市区	Xinshi District	4162291.0	1140934.5	5574498.1
水磨沟区	Shui Mogou District	176400.2	37650.5	380447.8
头屯河区	Tou Tunhe District	2334321.1	650285.1	1402068.0
达坂城区	Da Bancheng District	138267.2	27410.5	253838.6
米东区	Midong District	1385034.3	806758.7	2609947.2
乌鲁木齐县	Urumqi County	89464.5	80520.2	65616.4
克拉玛依市	**Karamay City**	**3656183.3**	**2862102.2**	**10481795.0**
独山子区	Dushanzi District	1145498.3	447035.2	3235032.1
克拉玛依区	Karamay District	2416295.9	2413265.5	7198892.8
白碱滩区	Bai Jiantan District	84627.3	1523.2	39176.2
乌尔河区	Urhe District	9761.8	278.3	8693.9
吐鲁番地区	**Turpan Administrative Offices**	**1217305.3**	**894835.2**	**1864922.1**
吐鲁番市	Turpan City	318897.1	52586.1	288882.9
鄯善县	Shanshan [Piqan] County	562075.8	557242.9	1106624.4
托克逊县	Toksun County	336332.4	285006.2	469414.8
哈密地区	**Hami [Kumul] Administrative Offices**	**986481.6**	**838189.7**	**1265618.7**
哈密市	Hami [Kumul] City	778374.2	426720.7	813362.8
巴里坤哈萨克自治县	Barkol Kazak Autonomous County	85153.5	48116.9	105434.3
伊吾县	Yiwu [Araturuk] County	122953.9	363352.1	346821.6
昌吉回族自治州	**Changji Hui Autonomous Prefecture**	**2972533.8**	**1193237.1**	**2632773.9**
昌吉市	Changji City	1376227.7	477221.7	1554726.5
阜康市	Fukang City	565011.0	289447.6	571068.3
呼图壁县	Hutubi County	135132.3	9652.0	68296.4
玛纳斯县	Manas County	425188.0	346620.4	220526.8
奇台县	Qitai County	213888.2	33065.3	112192.9
吉木萨尔县	Jimsar County	227978.4	39303.7	96212.5
木垒哈萨克自治县	Mori Kazak Autonomous County	29108.2	-2073.6	9750.5
伊犁哈萨克自治州	**Ili Kazak Autonomous Prefecture**	**3598949.6**	**1253213.0**	**3521739.2**
伊犁州直属县(市)	**Counties (Cities) Direct Under Ili Prefecture**	**1884177.6**	**848536.2**	**2079780.5**
伊宁市	Yining [Gulja] City	134584.8	86111.5	175491.9
奎屯市	Kuytun City	504207.2	285705.4	578940.3
伊宁县	Yining [Gulja] County	214680.0	90988.4	227760.5
察布查尔锡伯自治县	Qapqal Xibe Autonomous County	97870.1	23310.0	64307.8
霍城县	Huocheng [Korgas] County	100647.4	34752.1	115790.7
巩留县	Gongliu [Tokkuztara] County	83383.0	3442.1	268730.2
新源县	Xinyuan [Kunes] County	496711.2	35815.3	416916.4
昭苏县	Zhaosu [Mongolkure] County	45102.1	2142.0	24382.0
特克斯县	Tekes County	34897.8	6583.3	32247.8
尼勒克县	Nilka County	172094.0	279686.1	175212.9
塔城地区	**Tacheng [Tarbagatai] Administrative Offices**	**1089175.1**	**150318.2**	**721399.9**
塔城市	Tacheng [Qoqek] City	59058.1	16290.7	36543.0
乌苏市	Usu City	439550.5	50496.7	235594.8
额敏县	Emin [Dorbiljin] County	73265.3	3059.9	99529.7

Continued

(10 000 yuan)

主营业务收入 Revenue from Principal Business	#主营业务成本 Cost of Principal Business	主营业务税金及附加 Taxes and Other Charges on Principal Business	营业利润 Business Profit	利润总额 Total Profit	亏损企业亏损总额 Losses Value of Loss-Suffering Enterprises	利税总额 Total Profits and Taxes	本年应交增值税 Value-added Taxes Payable	全部从业人员年平均人数(人) Annual Average Employed Persons (person)
67822512.9	**49660271.4**	**3344787.0**	**9308890.8**	**9637368.2**	**1498145.3**	**16102161.6**	**3120006.4**	**589851**
20388825.5	**16131238.9**	**1097550.1**	**1651275.6**	**1749132.2**	**502038.1**	**3505189.3**	**658507.0**	**131617**
1975875.7	1782403.4	3153.4	136885.4	147403.9	41403.7	204542.9	53985.6	14540
526545.3	411154.2	5040.6	55274.0	62297.9	9921.4	89078.5	21740.0	9440
6473834.7	3528917.6	623624.4	1561876.4	1627043.5	32726.7	2621981.4	371313.5	45580
351570.4	292677.1	1858.9	23567.1	28211.7	5810.7	47850.9	17780.3	4869
5588177.5	5184170.0	14727.5	108087.4	109231.7	5399.3	217450.5	93491.3	18941
179022.8	113931.6	2143.9	37497.6	40771.6		56239.4	13323.9	6694
5265017.6	4805988.0	447001.4	-283296.5	-279263.0	406776.3	251333.7	83595.3	31486
28781.5	11997.0		11384.2	13434.9		16712.0	3277.1	67
17331756.2	**12659628.4**	**1308766.0**	**2321527.1**	**2434693.5**	**595034.3**	**4642877.7**	**899418.2**	**105334**
5848812.2	5480694.2	544238.9	-499495.5	-501895.1	526155.3	127645.0	85301.2	19359
11344183.1	7062671.3	762929.4	2810067.6	2925025.6	68617.5	4495831.9	807876.9	82971
117846.7	97716.0	902.3	7561.7	8293.8		14171.6	4975.5	2715
20914.2	18546.9	695.4	3393.3	3269.2	261.5	5229.2	1264.6	289
2318182.3	**1458113.9**	**66479.0**	**525823.5**	**532218.1**	**4058.5**	**724179.7**	**125482.6**	**23856**
463923.4	367472.3	1921.4	59706.3	62343.0	1198.6	84042.0	19777.6	6654
1514602.8	850094.3	58748.6	427015.2	430122.0	88.3	572378.7	83508.1	9596
339656.1	240547.3	5809.0	39102.0	39753.1	2771.6	67759.0	22196.9	7606
1296092.0	**954351.8**	**20079.1**	**172725.1**	**174748.5**	**5517.0**	**272813.4**	**77985.8**	**29497**
1132499.1	856707.0	14787.9	133394.6	132435.0	2367.3	212005.8	64782.9	24370
121716.1	63691.3	3905.7	37505.2	39985.2	327.0	55176.8	11285.9	2654
41876.8	33953.5	1385.5	1825.3	2328.3	2822.7	5630.8	1917.0	2473
4543743.1	**3772992.2**	**27213.2**	**347786.7**	**362421.9**	**81193.1**	**552810.6**	**163175.5**	**53640**
2000891.0	1616261.8	5250.6	213173.6	217042.6	8022.7	295441.9	73148.7	20638
962227.3	807300.9	3318.1	91874.4	93996.6	12011.6	133463.7	36149.0	13606
327057.6	281184.7	1651.4	20662.5	22222.0	5967.7	31835.3	7961.9	4077
721783.0	654806.6	7260.9	-11111.2	-4225.4	39960.0	28039.1	25003.6	7880
338506.0	256172.3	4633.6	37053.8	37625.3	648.8	53893.5	11634.6	3570
166444.0	136034.3	4268.3	-5068.1	-5290.8	13388.4	5087.4	6109.9	3617
26834.2	21231.6	830.3	1201.7	1051.6	1193.9	5049.7	3167.8	252
5442206.0	**3920650.0**	**192147.0**	**709450.7**	**720899.7**	**74983.7**	**1181731.3**	**268684.6**	**78825**
2871295.4	**2134151.9**	**165859.5**	**300655.2**	**302362.6**	**35945.2**	**609096.1**	**140874.0**	**43381**
351087.6	282712.2	2951.9	36199.8	38511.2	399.8	56181.1	14718.0	6204
980659.5	703939.2	137267.5	56347.2	51800.8	25766.5	243687.0	54618.7	9370
392444.2	307838.9	1695.9	40142.7	42831.0	4966.8	60440.8	15913.9	7848
104495.7	80431.8	553.0	13873.2	12308.6	270.1	15714.1	2852.5	1505
175944.6	143692.7	379.6	20041.3	20482.6	754.9	26624.4	5762.2	3248
60580.0	38836.1	252.3	-983.9	-836.3	1640.0	3722.2	4306.2	1110
495190.7	358291.3	19920.1	78339.4	80982.9	1030.1	123736.5	22833.5	10064
100256.0	85840.1	212.5	9136.2	10498.0	651.2	12082.2	1371.7	1232
39392.2	28428.6	338.2	1426.0	1396.5	83.8	3246.7	1512.0	723
171244.9	104141.0	2288.5	46133.3	44387.3	382.0	63661.1	16985.3	2077
1580782.8	**1265766.7**	**10646.6**	**75346.1**	**81225.3**	**33790.5**	**132961.8**	**41089.9**	**24169**
95943.5	92488.8	1027.5	-1279.8	-1322.5	4980.8	1661.4	1956.4	1442
623841.0	466616.1	3744.7	27316.5	24567.6	7068.0	38276.1	9963.8	6394
118402.1	93264.5	512.6	13194.1	14055.9	1160.6	20253.2	5684.7	2276

13-8 续表 4

单位: 万元

地　区	Region	流动负债合计 Total Working Liabilities	长期负债合计 Long-term Liabilities	所有者权益合计 Total Owners' Equities
沙湾县	Shawan County	268281.5	24054.9	125647.7
托里县	Toli County	138368.5	36930.1	130870.7
裕民县	Yumin [Qagantokay] County			
和布克赛尔蒙古自治县	Hoboksar Mongol Autonomous County	110651.2	19485.9	93214.0
阿勒泰地区	**Altay Administrative Offices**	**625596.9**	**254358.6**	**720558.8**
阿勒泰市	Altay City	71179.7	98502.6	62308.1
布尔津县	Burqin County	137338.1	55155.1	32767.4
富蕴县	Fuyun [Koktokay] County	316591.5	59429.4	349977.0
福海县	Fuhai [Burultokay] County	30469.3	1285.2	23705.3
哈巴河县	Habahe [Kaba] County	55603.9	20984.6	236916.3
青河县	Qinghe [Qinggil] County	7341.7	-1498.3	3318.9
吉木乃县	Jeminay County	7072.7	20500.0	11565.8
博尔塔拉蒙古自治州	**Bortala Mongol Autonomous Prefecture**	**321952.2**	**192612.0**	**180763.5**
博乐市	Bole [Bortala] City	265302.3	189523.8	152226.3
精河县	Jinghe [Jing] County	55603.1	3088.2	27648.3
温泉县	Wenquan [Araxang] County	1046.8		888.9
巴音郭楞蒙古自治州	**Bayangol Mongol Autonomous Prefecture**	**2789453.8**	**2567246.0**	**5084457.1**
库尔勒市	Korla City	1807603.9	2143143.1	4294442.9
轮台县	Luntai [Bugur] County	159641.0	24778.0	167697.8
尉犁县	Yuli [Lopnur] County	1530.0		1394.9
若羌县	Ruoqiang [Qarkilik] County	258136.8	229339.1	263587.2
且末县	Qiemo [Qarqan] County			
焉耆回族自治县	Yanqi Hui Autonomous County	68795.7	4655.6	42997.7
和静县	Hejing County	443284.3	164894.7	284345.7
和硕县	Hoxud County	26221.1	189.0	17919.9
博湖县	Bohu [Bagrax] County	24241.0	246.5	12071.0
阿克苏地区	**Aksu Administrative Offices**	**1733842.0**	**703039.4**	**1745878.4**
阿克苏市	Aksu City	607896.9	273323.1	580892.7
温宿县	Wensu [Onsu] County	120798.1	94724.8	72747.6
库车县	Kuqa County	588110.0	129691.1	741524.7
沙雅县	Xayar County	98643.0	55041.3	70172.6
新和县	Xinhe [Toksu] County	68289.4	6590.0	31274.4
拜城县	Baicheng [Bay] County	209887.6	137850.0	229828.1
乌什县	Wushi [Uxturpan] County	8125.4	400.0	8714.5

Continued

(10 000 yuan)

主营业务收入 Revenue from Principal Business	#主营业务成本 Cost of Principal Business	主营业务税金及附加 Taxes and Other Charges on Principal Business	营业利润 Business Profit	利润总额 Total Profit	亏损企业亏损总额 Losses Value of Loss-Suffering Enterprises	利税总额 Total Profits and Taxes	本年应交增值税 Value-added Taxes Payable	全部从业人员年平均人数(人) Annual Average Employed Persons (person)
472963.2	424732.7	789.7	12620.6	17391.2	9752.9	26699.1	8518.2	5962
163448.7	122594.3	1103.5	9446.7	11171.0	10447.4	17654.9	5380.4	4102
106184.3	66070.3	3468.6	14048.0	15362.1	380.8	28417.1	9586.4	3993
990127.8	**520731.4**	**15640.9**	**333449.4**	**337311.8**	**5248.0**	**439673.4**	**86720.7**	**11275**
122082.4	110277.8	601.0	3545.7	3811.8	1184.8	7785.2	3372.4	2426
59398.4	34307.9	347.2	9658.7	11189.6	1007.4	15467.1	3930.3	674
426778.6	203077.9	9784.6	147897.9	149192.4	3055.8	204375.9	45398.9	5055
45783.9	33180.5	417.0	8833.6	8862.4		10939.4	1660.0	871
301840.1	111761.0	4418.3	161258.6	161995.1		197629.2	31215.8	2077
29790.1	26450.7	71.9	272.6	272.7		1487.9	1143.3	156
4454.3	1675.6	0.9	1982.3	1987.8		1988.7		16
397530.4	**334129.2**	**1837.2**	**24029.5**	**29091.2**	**5742.5**	**45279.1**	**14350.7**	**7527**
319809.3	267158.7	1717.8	17844.4	21325.5	5087.5	35229.0	12185.7	6278
75347.3	65088.1	119.4	5794.6	7212.2	655.0	9384.8	2053.2	1219
2373.8	1882.4		390.5	553.5		665.3	111.8	30
7295185.3	**3182653.4**	**342045.5**	**2920602.9**	**2956117.1**	**19209.2**	**3848257.7**	**550095.1**	**45432**
5772552.6	2133943.7	311493.9	2637147.6	2638137.3	9617.0	3433320.3	483689.1	30345
217851.0	180683.8	5821.3	17922.6	18834.5	1581.9	28092.9	3437.1	1882
1050.8	997.1		-308.9	-308.9	308.9	-308.9		56
349293.0	112924.7	19303.4	151100.8	184443.3	1226.9	237141.8	33395.1	3297
83466.7	58549.9	1343.5	7574.8	7112.9	4244.2	13845.0	5388.6	1199
819669.8	652826.6	3854.9	106568.7	106718.4	904.3	133652.1	23078.8	7607
30577.4	25945.4	133.7	1401.8	2040.0		3155.4	981.7	690
20724.0	16782.2	94.8	-804.5	-860.4	1326.0	-640.9	124.7	356
4032431.3	**3251837.2**	**256380.5**	**274369.4**	**275342.3**	**89184.9**	**675496.4**	**143773.6**	**33494**
865173.6	688941.3	3951.6	104147.4	111458.6	8116.9	145115.9	29705.7	12548
99446.2	68740.3	1461.0	13624.0	12720.8	796.5	18999.5	4817.7	2878
2472690.4	2078443.3	244793.1	45325.4	46304.5	75650.2	366475.2	75377.6	7922
120186.0	91145.0	115.2	18583.1	9629.6	214.4	11408.4	1663.6	1737
54781.7	36906.9	49.9	13756.3	13496.4		14361.9	815.6	953
368537.1	243782.0	5275.6	76108.7	78594.6	3499.8	114430.2	30560.0	6195
6921.0	4112.9	646.6	920.9	918.4		1788.7	223.7	196

13-8 续表 5

单位: 万元

地　　区	Region	流动负债合计 Total Working Liabilities	长期负债合计 Long-term Liabilities	所有者权益合计 Total Owners' Equities
阿瓦提县	Awat County	28655.0	5419.1	10388.5
柯坪县	Kalpin County	3436.6		335.3
克孜勒苏柯尔克孜自治州	**Kizilsu Kirgiz Autonomous Prefecture**	**196192.7**	**3515.6**	**121736.0**
阿图什市	Artux City	116835.0	2953.1	65053.6
阿克陶县	Akto County	56598.3	562.5	55482.7
阿合奇县	Akqi County			
乌恰县	Wuqia [Ulugqat] County	22759.4		1199.7
喀什地区	**Kashgar [Kaxgar] Administrative Offices**	**417524.6**	**335270.7**	**242083.9**
喀什市	Kashgar [Kaxgar] City	189165.4	271959.5	95494.5
疏附县	Shufu County	1592.4		-231.4
疏勒县	Shule County	27300.0	917.5	15057.2
英吉沙县	Yengisar County	3567.7		287.7
泽普县	Zepu [Poskam] County	9474.1		8079.8
莎车县	Shache [Yarkant] County	51274.4	7255.4	7970.0
叶城县	Yecheng [Kagilik] County	25489.5	39214.9	31072.0
麦盖提县	Makit County	33494.4	30.0	17140.1
岳普湖县	Yopurga County	6531.5		2349.6
伽师县	Jiashi [Payzawat] County	27606.7	6550.0	58149.3
巴楚县	Bachu [Maralbexi] County	18332.2	8958.4	7230.3
塔什库尔干塔吉克自治县	Taxkorgan Tajik Autonomous County	23696.3	385.0	-515.2
和田地区	**Hotan Administrative Offices**	**68718.8**	**75969.8**	**209031.6**
和田市	Hotan City	49861.9	67142.0	4279.3
和田县	Hotan County	-3694.6	5250.4	149279.0
墨玉县	Moyu [Karakax] County	3600.6	283.6	36500.7
皮山县	Pishan [Guma] County	10743.4	3293.8	9549.9
洛浦县	Lop County	8207.5		9422.7
策勒县	Qira County			
于田县	Yutian [Keriya] County			
民丰县	Minfeng [Niya] County			
自治区直辖县级市	**Municpality Country-LevelCity directly under the Central Government**	**3772477.6**	**1705661.7**	**2198835.6**
石河子市	Shihezi City	1405534.6	1362855.4	1746244.8
阿拉尔市	Aral City	285348.9	119163.1	75565.7
图木舒克市	Tumxuk City	70727.4	86733.7	39626.9
五家渠市	Wujiaqu City	2010866.7	136909.5	337398.2

Continued

(10 000 yuan)

主营业务收入 Revenue from Principal Business	#主营业务成本 Cost of Principal Business	主营业务税金及附加 Taxes and Other Charges on Principal Business	营业利润 Business Profit	利润总额 Total Profit	亏损企业亏损总额 Losses Value of Loss-Suffering Enterprises	利税总额 Total Profits and Taxes	本年应交增值税 Value-added Taxes Payable	全部从业人员年平均人数(人) Annual Average Employed Persons (person)
41278.5	36505.9	87.5	1882.0	2801.6	324.9	3498.8	609.7	1014
3416.8	3259.6		21.6	-582.2	582.2	-582.2		51
171969.2	**151832.7**	**2288.3**	**4669.9**	**4973.1**	**7242.5**	**15982.5**	**8721.1**	**2917**
96359.9	88803.0	194.7	955.1	1468.0	4790.8	4045.2	2382.5	1536
44586.6	34234.0	1725.9	4035.5	3861.3	1866.7	9773.4	4186.2	898
31022.7	28795.7	367.7	-320.7	-356.2	585.0	2163.9	2152.4	483
811226.9	**720033.5**	**4392.5**	**43847.9**	**43943.0**	**35579.6**	**90697.6**	**42362.1**	**14219**
416406.3	394464.7	3065.1	-1891.9	-1816.4	29464.0	20001.2	18752.5	7730
3389.8	3423.1	13.9	-144.4	-144.8	144.8	8.8	139.7	164
39407.4	35086.1	92.1	2033.4	1995.4	42.9	3757.2	1669.7	475
5700.0	4350.7	55.8	444.8	447.3		952.1	449.0	248
22615.1	20163.0	67.4	1609.3	1635.2		2411.6	709.0	944
63776.6	60471.3	73.5	10137.7	10101.4	224.6	10944.0	769.1	774
47782.6	38964.6	296.1	-66.2	-92.5	782.3	3778.3	3574.7	1540
53227.7	43708.9	42.4	7346.8	7658.5		7717.2	16.3	741
6643.4	5778.3	12.1	865.1	1027.0		1135.4	96.3	78
104796.0	68925.0	639.5	28200.1	27171.8		43758.7	15947.4	1020
40582.0	42246.6	20.3	-5571.0	-4921.0	4921.0	-4900.7		387
6900.0	2451.2	14.3	884.2	881.1		1133.8	238.4	118
147073.1	**132579.8**	**535.9**	**-4959.1**	**-1598.9**	**18943.9**	**9527.8**	**10590.8**	**3467**
80811.3	80836.1	329.2	-10340.5	-10307.0	15234.8	-5708.6	4269.2	1630
28029.6	21807.3	24.0	1932.7	2990.2	3499.0	6595.4	3581.2	539
17999.2	13956.6	39.0	2481.3	3943.7		5437.1	1454.4	212
8150.1	7620.2	77.5	-267.2	233.0	210.1	930.5	620.0	441
12082.9	8359.6	66.2	1234.6	1541.2		2273.4	666.0	645
3646291.6	**2990230.4**	**25072.7**	**317741.6**	**355386.5**	**59418.0**	**537318.5**	**156859.3**	**60026**
2469937.3	1968618.0	18090.6	272632.0	308205.5	29108.1	422759.1	96463.0	45082
264670.5	224228.4	1032.6	1337.6	1381.2	21040.1	12351.8	9938.0	3724
70904.9	59076.3	58.4	5145.2	5120.8		6623.2	1444.0	1431
840778.9	738307.7	5891.1	38626.8	40679.0	9269.8	95584.4	49014.3	9789

13-9 规模以上工业企业主要经济效益指标

单位: %　　(2011 年)

项　　目	Item	产值利税率 Ratio of Profits and Taxes to Industrial Output Value
总　　计	**Total**	**24.0**
按登记注册类型分	**Grouped by Registry Type**	
内资企业	Domestic Funded Enterprises	24.2
国有企业	State-owned Enterprises	15.7
#中央企业	Central Enterprises	17.8
地方企业	Local Enterprises	7.4
#自治区属企业	Autonomous	5.4
地区(州、市)属企业	Prefecture or City	1.4
县(市)属企业	County or City	19.8
集体企业	Collective-owned Enterprises	10.5
#自治区属企业	Autonomous	6.4
地区(州、市)属企业	Prefecture or City	1.1
县(市)属企业	County or City	34.2
镇属企业	Town	60.2
股份合作企业	Share-holding Cooperative Enterprises	6.7
联营企业	Joint Ownership Enterprises	14.9
#国有联营企业	State Joint Ownership Enterprises	19.5
国有与集体联营企业	Joint State-collective Enterprises	34.8
其他联营企业	Other Joint Ownership Enterprises	2.8
有限责任公司	Limited Liability Corporations	14.5
#国有独资公司	State Sole funded Corporations	18.9
其他有限责任公司	Other Limited Liability Corporations	13.6
股份有限公司	Share-holding Corporations Ltd.	34.5
私营企业	Private Enterprises	14.1
#私营独资企业	Private-funded Enterprises	19.4
私营合伙企业	Private Partnership Enterprises	19.7
私营有限责任公司	Private Limited Liability Corporations	12.3
私营股份有限公司	Private Share-holding Corporations Ltd.	19.0
港、澳、台商投资企业	Enterprises with Funds from Hong Kong, Macao and Taiwan	14.0
外商投资企业	Foreign Funded Enterprises	13.7
在总计中: 国有控股企业	Of the Total: State-owned and State-holding Enterprises	27.9
在总计中: 农村工业	Of the Total: Rural Industry	6.8
按轻、重工业分(GB/T4754-2011)	**Grouped by Light & Heavy Industry (GB/T4754-2011)**	
轻工业	Light Industry	10.6
以农产品为原料	Using Farm Produces as Raw Materials	10.6
以非农产品为原料	Using Non-Farm Produces as Raw Materials	11.0
重工业	Heavy Industry	25.8
采掘工业	Mining and Quarrying	57.4
原料工业	Raw Materials Industry	9.6
加工工业	Manufacturing Industry	16.0
按轻、重工业分(GB/T4754-2002)	**Grouped by Light & Heavy Industry (GB/T4754-2002)**	
轻工业	Light Industry	10.6
以农产品为原料	Using Farm Produces as Raw Materials	10.6
以非农产品为原料	Using Non-Farm Produces as Raw Materials	11.4
重工业	Heavy Industry	25.8
采掘工业	Mining and Quarrying	57.4
原料工业	Raw Materials Industry	9.6
加工工业	Manufacturing Industry	16.1
按企业规模分(新标准)	**Grouped by Size of Enterprises (New Standard)**	
大型企业	Large Enterprises	29.1
中型企业	Medium-sized Enterprises	17.8
小型企业	Small Enterprises	13.6
微型企业	Mini Enterprises	4.8
按企业规模分(旧标准)	**Grouped by Size of Enterprises (Old Standard)**	
大型企业	Large Enterprises	30.5
中型企业	Medium-sized Enterprises	16.9
小型企业	Small Enterprises	13.1

Main Indicators on Economic Efficiency of Industrial Enterprises above Designated Size

(%)

总资产贡献率 Ratio of Total Assets to Industrial Output Value	资本保值增值率 Ratio of Capital-hold and Rise	资产负债率 Assets Liability Ratio	流动资产周转次数(次/年) Number of Times of Annual TurnoverWorking Capitals (times/year)	成本费用利润率 Ratio of Profits to Industrial Cost	全员劳动生产率 Overall Labour Productivity
18.4	**113.6**	**53.8**	**2.2**	**17.5**	**43.5**
18.5	113.6	53.7	2.3	17.7	44.2
9.7	153.7	61.6	2.2	9.3	32.6
11.7	186.8	57.9	2.5	11.0	36.6
4.5	91.6	71.3	1.5	3.2	20.9
3.4	89.1	63.5	2.3	0.5	21.8
2.0	151.9	88.9	0.6	0.1	17.3
8.7	105.8	79.7	1.4	14.1	19.6
15.6	102.3	72.2	3.1	6.3	16.4
14.1	114.5	55.0	3.1	3.1	14.2
5.1	106.6	65.2	5.0	0.6	5.9
37.4	84.8	49.8	1.7	29.6	21.6
86.7	378.6	55.9	2.2	66.7	43.7
5.4	500.9	55.1	1.0	5.2	12.1
9.8	91.8	80.2	1.3	8.3	11.1
8.4	92.3	78.1	1.0	10.6	16.8
49.3	342.1	50.1	4.1	50.0	41.8
3.8	8.7	98.7	2.1	-4.1	5.4
10.8	133.0	62.9	1.8	9.6	24.8
16.0	104.1	57.7	2.6	7.6	28.7
9.9	141.2	63.9	1.7	10.1	24.0
29.2	101.3	42.8	3.2	27.4	96.5
12.1	107.8	57.8	1.5	11.7	18.8
16.9	169.3	56.6	2.1	16.5	16.3
52.9	54.7	48.6	4.9	13.9	31.6
12.0	142.4	60.9	1.8	9.3	15.8
11.4	73.8	51.3	0.9	19.1	55.6
12.3	140.5	49.1	1.3	12.7	16.6
13.9	100.1	62.1	2.2	8.9	22.5
22.2	109.0	51.1	2.9	20.8	59.8
4.8	24.1	66.2	1.8	6.4	8.3
9.5	109.9	64.2	1.5	5.6	13.7
10.0	109.0	64.5	1.5	5.6	13.8
4.4	118.8	61.3	1.0	6.7	11.7
19.6	113.9	52.4	2.4	19.4	52.0
35.6	104.3	46.4	2.8	76.8	86.4
9.6	125.3	56.6	3.0	2.1	31.3
10.2	114.6	54.5	1.1	13.9	23.1
9.5	109.9	64.2	1.5	5.6	13.7
10.0	109.0	64.6	1.5	5.6	13.9
4.6	119.3	60.7	1.0	7.1	11.7
19.6	113.9	52.4	2.4	19.4	51.4
35.6	104.2	46.5	2.8	76.9	85.2
9.6	125.2	56.6	2.9	2.1	31.3
10.3	115.1	54.4	1.1	13.9	23.0
22.4	105.6	49.7	2.8	22.4	67.9
13.0	147.9	60.6	1.6	11.4	24.3
11.7	116.6	59.3	1.7	10.1	20.5
6.5	305.2	67.6	2.1	3.7	27.1
24.9	107.8	48.3	3.2	24.0	76.9
11.7	121.3	59.3	1.6	10.9	21.9
10.8	125.3	60.7	1.7	9.8	21.7

13-10 分行业规模以上工业企业主要经济效益指标(GB/T4754-2011)

单位: % (2011 年)

行 业	Sector	产值利税率 Ratio of Profits and Taxes to Industrial Output Value
总 计	**Total**	**24.0**
煤炭开采和洗选业	Mining and Washing of Coal	27.4
石油和天然气开采业	Extraction of Petroleum and Natural Gas	68.6
黑色金属矿采选业	Mining and Processing of Ferrous Metals Ores	37.2
有色金属矿采选业	Mining and Processing of Nonferrous Metals Ores	54.6
非金属矿采选业	Mining and Processing of Nonmetal Ores	22.0
#采 盐	Extraction of Salt	31.7
农副食品加工业	Processing of Food from Agricultural Products	7.2
#谷物磨制	Grain Grinding	4.6
饲料加工	Fodder Processing	8.4
制 糖	Sugar Making	25.3
食品制造业	Manufacture of Food	6.0
#罐头制造	Manufacture of can	-6.2
酒、饮料和精制茶制造业	Manufacture of Wine,Beverages and Refined Tea	26.0
#酒的制造	Manufacture of Wine	32.2
烟草制品业	Manufacture of Tobacco	69.5
纺织业	Manufacture of Textile	7.5
#棉、化纤纺织及印染精加工	Cotton, Chemical Fiber, Dyeing, Printing and Processing	7.5
毛纺织和染整精加工	Wool Textile, Dyeing and Printing	-2.4
纺织服装、鞋、帽制造业	Manufacture of Textile Wearing Apparel,Footware and Caps	-0.4
皮革、毛皮、羽毛(绒)及其制品业	Leather, Fur, Feather and Related Products Manufacturing	9.1
#皮革鞣制加工	Leather Tanning and Processing	9.1
木材加工及木、竹、藤、棕、草制品业	Processing of Timber, Wood, Bamboo, Cane, Grass Products	11.3
家具制造业	Manufacture of Furniture	5.2
造纸及纸制品业	Manufacture of Paper and Paper Products	12.7
印刷业和记录媒介的复制	Printing and Copying of Medium for Record	9.0
石油加工、炼焦及核燃料加工业	Oil Processing, Coking and Nuclear Fuel Processing	7.3
#炼 焦	Coking	16.2
化学原料及化学制品制造业	Raw Chemical Material and Chemical Products	20.0
#基础化学原料制造	Basic Chemical Material	15.9
肥料制造	Fertilizer Making	39.6
合成材料制造	Manufacture of Synthetic Materials	15.6
医药制造业	Manufacture of Medicine	16.0
化学纤维制造业	Manufacture of Chemical Fiber	0.1
橡胶制品业	Manufacture of Rubber Products	8.3
非金属矿物制品业	Manufacture of Nonmetal Mineral Products	17.5
#水泥制造	Manufacture of Cement	25.4
黑色金属冶炼及压延加工业	Smelting and Pressing of Ferrous Metals	5.2
有色金属冶炼及压延加工业	Smelting and Pressing of Nonferrous Metals	9.5
金属制品业	Manufacture of Metal Products	4.7
通用设备制造业	Manufacture of General Purpose Machinery	15.6
专用设备制造业	Manufacture of Special Purpose Machinery	12.1
汽车制造业	Manufacture of Automobile	-13.3
电气机械及器材制造业	Manufacture of Electric Equipment and Machinery	18.6
计算机、通信和其他电子设备制造业	Telecom Equipment, Computer and Other Electronic Equipment	15.6
仪器仪表制造业	Measuring Instruments and Machinery for Cultunal Activify and OfficeWork	10.3
金属制品、机械和设备修理业	Manufacture of Repairing of Metal Products,Machinery and Equipment	4.6
电力、热力的生产和供应业	Electricity and Thermal Production and Supply	14.9
#电力生产和电力供应	Electricity Production and Supply	15.2
燃气生产和供应业	Gas Production and Supply	18.6
水的生产和供应业	Water Production and Supply	-10.5

Main Indicators on Economic Efficiency of Industrial Enterprises above Designated Size by Sectors(GB/T4754-2011)

(%)

总资产贡献率 Ratio of Total Assets to Industrial Output Value	资本保值增值率 Ratio of Capital-hold and Rise	资产负债率 Assets Liability Ratio	流动资产周转次数(次/年) Number of Times of Annual Turnover Working Capitals (times/year)	成本费用利润率 Ratio of Profits to Industrial Cost	全员劳动生产率 Overall Labour Productivity
18.4	**113.6**	**53.8**	**2.3**	**17.5**	**43.5**
10.5	171.1	59.2	1.4	17.4	18.8
46.1	96.0	40.6	4.2	116.0	180.7
22.6	113.0	63.9	1.1	35.9	51.5
25.9	122.2	44.8	1.5	88.3	45.7
25.9	143.3	53.8	1.8	12.6	19.9
27.3	172.7	37.2	1.2	22.5	18.0
10.1	114.7	65.4	1.8	5.4	15.0
8.5	94.2	56.0	2.8	4.0	14.5
11.9	122.0	48.9	2.1	7.3	18.8
21.0	144.7	48.9	1.6	17.0	17.6
5.3	97.4	69.2	1.1	3.7	11.0
	74.1	79.7	0.6	-7.2	6.9
20.8	116.1	68.4	1.4	18.6	25.2
20.6	111.6	70.4	1.0	21.5	25.5
56.6	229.6	26.4	1.2	32.1	267.2
5.7	110.0	65.0	1.3	3.8	6.5
5.9	108.6	66.6	1.3	3.7	6.8
-1.7	67.5	64.8	1.7	-5.2	3.2
0.3	-93.7	120.5	3.3	-0.6	6.6
28.8	217.8	64.1	4.3	8.3	33.1
28.8	217.8	64.1	4.3	8.3	33.1
13.2	79.0	53.8	2.0	9.8	12.8
1.8	94.8	18.2	1.6	3.8	8.3
9.4	111.1	62.2	1.3	10.0	9.1
6.5	114.6	50.0	1.5	5.5	9.1
13.4	119.6	39.4	5.0	-5.0	46.9
14.4	126.9	60.4	1.9	14.0	22.5
13.7	119.5	51.6	1.8	20.0	30.3
6.3	105.1	52.0	1.6	8.5	16.5
25.8	155.5	56.6	1.3	60.9	61.9
14.7	123.6	49.9	2.3	18.6	35.8
9.7	141.7	46.3	0.8	14.1	11.9
2.9	69.8	78.2	2.3	-1.5	15.3
7.9	148.0	58.8	1.6	5.9	11.0
10.9	113.2	52.4	1.4	14.3	17.1
11.5	126.4	50.4	1.2	24.0	19.7
8.0	125.5	68.3	3.0	3.1	24.1
5.5	220.8	77.4	1.5	6.5	25.9
7.0	105.2	60.8	2.1	3.4	13.1
12.4	88.2	53.8	1.1	12.4	10.8
10.5	413.4	45.5	1.1	12.3	14.4
-5.2	76.9	86.9	1.9	-6.4	0.6
8.3	104.5	52.2	0.7	16.2	49.6
4.9	162.4	50.0	0.5	18.7	15.0
6.3	62.3	39.2	0.8	8.8	22.1
4.9	45.9	85.3	1.0	1.3	11.1
7.4	133.9	63.4	2.1	10.6	34.8
7.7	134.6	62.4	2.4	11.0	37.6
8.5	116.3	65.9	1.0	15.6	27.8
-0.1	110.1	54.3	0.5	-11.4	11.7

13-11 分行业规模以上工业企业主要经济效益指标(GB/T4754-2002)

单位: % (2011 年)

行 业	Sector	产值利税率 Ratio of Profits and Taxes to Industrial Output Value
煤炭开采和洗选业	Mining and Washing of Coal	27.4
石油和天然气开采业	Extraction of Petroleum and Natural Gas	63.0
#天然原油和天然气开采	Extraction of Ores Crude Oil and Natural Gas Extraction	68.6
黑色金属矿采选业	Mining and Processing of Ferrous Metals Ores	37.2
有色金属矿采选业	Mining and Processing of Nonferrous Metals Ores	54.6
非金属矿采选业	Mining and Processing of Nonmetal Ores	19.7
#采 盐	Extraction of Salt	31.7
农副食品加工业	Processing of Food from Agricultural Products	7.1
#谷物磨制	Grain Grinding	4.6
饲料加工	Fodder Processing	8.4
制 糖	Sugar Making	25.3
食品制造业	Manufacture of Food	6.3
#罐头制造	Manufacture of can	-6.8
饮料制造业	Manufacture of Beverage	26.0
#酒的制造	Manufacture of Wine	32.9
烟草制品业	Manufacture of Tobacco	69.5
纺织业	Manufacture of Textile	7.4
#棉、化纤纺织及印染精加工	Cotton, Chemical Fiber, Dyeing, Printing and Processing	7.5
毛纺织和染整精加工	Wool Textile, Dyeing and Printing	-2.4
纺织服装、鞋、帽制造业	Manufacture of Textile Wearing Apparel,Footware and Caps	3.9
皮革、毛皮、羽毛(绒)及其制品业	Leather, Fur, Feather and Related Products Manufacturing	9.1
#皮革鞣制加工	Leather Tanning and Processing	11.9
木材加工及木、竹、藤、棕、草制品业	Processing of Timber, Wood, Bamboo, Cane, Grass Products	11.3
家具制造业	Manufacture of Furniture	5.2
造纸及纸制品业	Manufacture of Paper and Paper Products	12.7
印刷业和记录媒介的复制	Printing and Copying of Medium for Record	9.0
石油加工、炼焦及核燃料加工业	Oil Processing, Coking and Nuclear Fuel Processing	7.3
#炼 焦	Coking	16.2
化学原料及化学制品制造业	Raw Chemical Material and Chemical Products	20.0
#基础化学原料制造	Basic Chemical Material	16.0
肥料制造	Fertilizer Making	39.6
医药制造业	Manufacture of Medicine	16.0
化学纤维制造业	Manufacture of Chemical Fiber	0.1
橡胶制品业	Manufacture of Rubber Products	4.9
塑料制品业	Manufacture of Plastic Products	8.9
非金属矿物制品业	Manufacture of Nonmetal Mineral Products	17.6
#水泥制造	Manufacture of Cement	25.6
黑色金属冶炼及压延加工业	Smelting and Pressing of Ferrous Metals	5.2
有色金属冶炼及压延加工业	Smelting and Pressing of Nonferrous Metals	9.6
金属制品业	Manufacture of Metal Products	4.7
通用设备制造业	Manufacture of General Purpose Machinery	13.2
专用设备制造业	Manufacture of Special Purpose Machinery	12.1
交通运输设备制造业	Manufacture of Transport Equipment	-13.5
电气机械及器材制造业	Manufacture of Electric Equipment and Machinery	18.6
通信设备、计算机及其他电子设备制造业	Telecom Equipment, Computer and Other Electronic Equipment	15.6
仪器仪表及文化、办公用机械制造业	Measuring Instruments and Machinery for Cultunal Activify and OfficeWork	10.3
工艺品及其他制造业	Art work and Other Manufacturing Sector	16.8
电力、热力的生产和供应业	Electricity and Thermal Production and Supply	14.9
#电力生产和电力供应	Electricity Production and Supply	15.2
燃气生产和供应业	Gas Production and Supply	18.6
水的生产和供应业	Water Production and Supply	-10.5

Main Indicators on Economic Efficiency of Industrial Enterprises above Designated Size by Sectors(GB/T4754-2002)

(%)

总资产贡献率 Ratio of Total Assets to Industrial Output Value	资本保值增值率 Ratio of Capital-hold and Rise	资产负债率 Assets Liability Ratio	流动资产周转次数(次/年) Number of Times of Annual Turnover Working Capitals (times/year)	成本费用利润率 Ratio of Profits to Industrial Cost	全员劳动生产率 Overall Labour Productivity
10.5	171.1	59.2	1.4	17.4	18.8
43.2	96.7	42.1	3.8	95.1	137.3
46.1	96.0	40.6	4.2	116.0	593.7
22.6	113.0	63.9	1.1	35.9	51.5
25.9	122.2	44.8	1.5	88.3	45.7
21.5	138.3	60.5	1.7	9.7	19.1
27.3	172.7	37.2	1.2	22.5	18.0
9.6	108.4	65.0	1.7	5.3	14.8
8.5	94.2	56.0	2.8	4.0	14.5
11.9	122.0	48.9	2.1	7.3	18.8
21.0	144.7	48.9	1.6	17.0	17.6
5.6	103.8	70.2	1.2	3.9	11.1
-0.4	78.6	83.0	0.6	-7.6	6.8
20.8	116.1	68.4	1.4	18.6	25.2
21.1	110.4	69.8	1.0	21.9	24.8
56.6	229.6	26.4	1.2	32.1	267.2
5.7	108.0	65.5	1.3	3.7	6.6
5.9	108.6	66.5	1.3	3.7	6.8
-1.7	67.0	64.8	1.7	-5.2	3.2
5.5	181.2	75.1	2.1	2.3	6.0
28.8	217.8	64.1	4.3	8.3	33.1
30.8	228.0	62.0	3.6	11.7	32.9
13.2	79.0	53.8	2.0	9.8	12.8
1.8	94.8	18.2	1.6	3.8	8.3
9.4	119.7	62.2	1.3	10.0	9.1
6.5	114.6	50.0	1.5	5.5	9.1
13.4	119.6	39.4	5.0	-5.0	46.9
14.4	126.9	60.4	1.9	14.0	22.5
13.7	119.5	51.6	1.8	20.0	30.0
6.3	104.7	51.9	1.5	8.5	16.5
25.8	155.5	56.6	1.3	60.9	61.9
9.7	141.7	46.3	0.8	14.1	11.9
2.9	69.8	78.2	2.3	-1.5	15.3
4.7	484.7	65.3	2.0	0.5	10.2
8.5	129.6	57.5	1.5	6.8	11.1
10.9	113.0	52.2	1.4	14.4	17.2
11.5	126.3	50.3	1.2	24.1	19.8
7.9	125.1	68.5	3.0	3.1	24.3
5.6	213.0	76.5	1.4	6.9	27.3
7.0	108.6	61.9	2.2	3.3	10.4
11.9	106.1	53.2	1.2	11.0	13.6
10.5	409.2	45.5	1.1	12.3	14.4
-5.2	80.2	84.2	1.8	-6.7	1.1
8.3	104.6	52.2	0.7	16.2	49.6
4.9	162.4	50.0	0.5	18.7	15.0
6.3	62.3	39.2	0.8	8.8	22.1
3.5	518.7	87.9	0.6	9.8	16.4
7.4	133.9	63.4	2.1	10.6	34.8
7.7	134.6	62.4	2.4	11.0	37.6
8.5	116.3	65.9	1.0	15.6	27.8
-0.1	110.1	54.3	0.5	-11.4	11.7

13-12 各地、州、市、县(市)规模以上工业企业主要经济效益指标

单位: % (2011 年)

地 区	Region	产值利税率 Ratio of Profits and Taxes to Industrial Output Value
总 计	**Total**	**24.0**
乌鲁木齐市	**Urumqi City**	**17.6**
天山区	Tianshan District	10.1
沙依巴克区	Shayibak District	18.3
新市区	Xinshi District	41.2
水磨沟区	Shui Mogou District	13.9
头屯河区	Tou Tunhe District	4.0
达坂城区	Da Bancheng District	30.7
米东区	Midong District	4.9
乌鲁木齐县	Urumqi County	55.4
克拉玛依市	**Karamay City**	**28.3**
独山子区	Dushanzi District	2.2
克拉玛依区	Karamay District	42.9
白碱滩区	Bai Jiantan District	13.9
乌尔河区	Urhe District	22.8
吐鲁番地区	**Turpan Administrative Offices**	**32.6**
吐鲁番市	Turpan City	19.2
鄯善县	Shanshan [Piqan] County	39.7
托克逊县	Toksun County	19.9
哈密地区	**Hami [Kumul] Administrative Offices**	**20.7**
哈密市	Hami [Kumul] City	18.5
巴里坤哈萨克自治县	Barkol Kazak Autonomous County	42.5
伊吾县	Yiwu [Araturuk] County	13.0
昌吉回族自治州	**Changji Hui Autonomous Prefecture**	**11.6**
昌吉市	Changji City	15.2
阜康市	Fukang City	13.7
呼图壁县	Hutubi County	7.4
玛纳斯县	Manas County	3.6
奇台县	Qitai County	14.2
吉木萨尔县	Jimsar County	2.5
木垒哈萨克自治县	Mori Kazak Autonomous County	15.6
伊犁哈萨克自治州	**Ili Kazak Autonomous Prefecture**	**20.8**
伊犁州直属县(市)	**Counties (Cities) Direct Under Ili Prefecture**	**20.7**
伊宁市	Yining [Gulja] City	15.8
奎屯市	Kuytun City	26.3
伊宁县	Yining [Gulja] County	15.1
察布查尔锡伯自治县	Qapqal Xibe Autonomous County	14.5
霍城县	Huocheng [Korgas] County	15.4
巩留县	Gongliu [Tokkuztara] County	6.4
新源县	Xinyuan [Kunes] County	21.1
昭苏县	Zhaosu [Mongolkure] County	10.9
特克斯县	Tekes County	7.0
尼勒克县	Nilka County	35.3
塔城地区	**Tacheng [Tarbagatai] Administrative Offices**	**7.6**
塔城市	Tacheng [Qoqek] City	1.7
乌苏市	Usu City	6.1
额敏县	Emin [Dorbiljin] County	16.3

Main Indicators on Economic Benefit of Industrial Enterprises above Designated Size by Prefecture, Autonomous Prefecture, City and County

(%)

总资产贡献率 Ratio of Total Assets to Industrial Output Value	资本保值增值率 Ratio of Capital-hold and Rise	资产负债率 Assets Liability Ratio	流动资产周转次数(次/年) Number of Times of Annual TurnoverWorking Capitals (times/year)	成本费用利润率 Ratio of Profits to Industrial Cost	全员劳动生产率 Overall Labour Productivity
18.4	**113.6**	**53.8**	**2.3**	**17.5**	**43.5**
13.7	**109.1**	**52.6**	**2.1**	**9.9**	**42.9**
6.8	153.6	58.7	2.6	7.8	39.1
4.5	91.1	49.4	0.8	12.0	13.9
25.1	93.0	48.9	1.5	37.7	77.0
11.0	107.7	36.0	1.7	8.7	21.5
7.0	121.4	68.1	3.8	2.0	26.9
13.7	107.9	39.5	2.3	30.2	17.3
5.6	141.7	45.7	2.7	-5.5	21.7
10.0	112.5	72.2	0.8	69.4	380.3
27.8	**110.8**	**38.4**	**3.9**	**17.9**	**66.1**
3.1	122.7	33.0	4.2	-8.6	28.5
37.9	106.1	40.2	3.8	38.5	76.9
12.1	131.6	69.0	1.3	7.7	10.0
28.5	103.1	53.6	1.7	16.5	22.8
19.0	**104.9**	**53.5**	**1.6**	**31.7**	**47.7**
14.6	117.8	56.5	1.4	15.0	19.8
26.1	89.4	50.4	2.4	44.6	89.2
7.3	159.6	58.2	0.7	13.5	19.6
9.7	**156.0**	**59.2**	**1.3**	**15.7**	**19.0**
11.7	111.4	59.9	1.3	13.4	18.8
24.3	171.1	56.3	1.6	49.8	27.3
0.7	1754.7	58.4	0.8	6.0	11.9
9.4	**111.6**	**61.6**	**1.5**	**8.6**	**23.1**
9.6	116.2	54.5	1.2	11.9	23.9
10.8	117.7	59.9	2.2	10.7	20.8
14.9	47.1	73.1	3.3	7.3	14.7
4.8	97.5	77.8	1.5	-0.6	29.1
16.6	131.6	68.7	1.8	12.4	29.3
2.7	133.8	73.9	1.7	-3.3	16.7
12.9	109.2	74.9	1.4	4.2	41.8
14.7	**131.4**	**60.4**	**1.7**	**16.1**	**30.8**
12.8	**130.6**	**60.6**	**1.5**	**12.4**	**26.1**
15.3	142.9	57.7	2.8	12.4	18.8
19.0	159.9	57.7	1.5	6.6	39.1
12.5	134.6	58.4	1.9	12.0	14.7
8.6	227.8	71.4	1.3	13.7	16.9
11.7	134.8	54.4	1.6	12.8	15.8
1.6	91.0	64.0	0.6	-1.4	24.7
14.1	113.8	56.1	1.1	19.6	28.5
18.6	112.0	66.0	2.0	11.5	21.3
7.3	355.3	56.3	1.2	3.7	16.2
11.3	133.5	72.1	1.7	36.2	50.0
8.4	**136.5**	**63.2**	**2.1**	**5.8**	**29.3**
2.7	117.2	67.7	5.2	-1.4	23.4
7.3	166.7	67.6	3.1	4.9	60.7
12.8	193.3	43.9	1.5	13.2	19.1

13-12 续表 1

单位: %

地区	Region	产值利税率 Ratio of Profits and Taxes to Industrial Output Value
沙湾县	Shawan County	5.1
托里县	Toli County	8.5
裕民县	Yumin [Qagantokay] County	
和布克赛尔蒙古自治县	Hoboksar Mongol Autonomous County	17.3
阿勒泰地区	**Altay Administrative Offices**	**44.5**
阿勒泰市	Altay City	6.4
布尔津县	Burqin County	26.6
富蕴县	Fuyun [Koktokay] County	47.7
福海县	Fuhai [Burultokay] County	23.5
哈巴河县	Habahe [Kaba] County	65.4
青河县	Qinghe [Qinggil] County	5.6
吉木乃县	Jeminay County	44.7
博尔塔拉蒙古自治州	**Bortala Mongol Autonomous Prefecture**	**12.4**
博乐市	Bole [Bortala] City	11.8
精河县	Jinghe [Jing] County	14.5
温泉县	Wenquan [Araxang] County	24.5
巴音郭楞蒙古自治州	**Bayangol Mongol Autonomous Prefecture**	**52.6**
库尔勒市	Korla City	59.5
轮台县	Luntai [Bugur] County	12.3
尉犁县	Yuli [Lopnur] County	-31.6
若羌县	Ruoqiang [Qarkilik] County	55.1
且末县	Qiemo [Qarqan] County	
焉耆回族自治县	Yanqi Hui Autonomous County	17.6
和静县	Hejing County	17.7
和硕县	Hoxud County	11.5
博湖县	Bohu [Bagrax] County	-2.9
阿克苏地区	**Aksu Administrative Offices**	**17.0**
阿克苏市	Aksu City	17.7
温宿县	Wensu [Onsu] County	18.8
库车县	Kuqa County	15.1
沙雅县	Xayar County	7.9
新和县	Xinhe [Toksu] County	23.7
拜城县	Baicheng [Bay] County	31.7
乌什县	Wushi [Uxturpan] County	19.3

Continued

(%)

总资产贡献率 Ratio of Total Assets to Industrial Output Value	资本保值增值率 Ratio of Capital-hold and Rise	资产负债率 Assets Liability Ratio	流动资产周转次数(次/年) Number of Times of Annual TurnoverWorking Capitals (times/year)	成本费用利润率 Ratio of Profits to Industrial Cost	全员劳动生产率 Overall Labour Productivity
8.0	103.1	69.3	1.9	3.8	9.2
7.4	118.3	57.2	1.3	7.3	25.7
13.5	129.5	58.6	1.6	17.1	20.7
28.3	**128.6**	**56.2**	**2.0**	**52.1**	**51.8**
5.3	129.7	73.3	2.1	3.2	16.0
10.1	155.5	86.8	1.7	22.5	40.9
29.1	129.8	51.8	1.7	54.8	53.2
16.3	102.0	65.9	1.2	24.2	19.6
63.8	124.3	24.4	2.9	118.8	107.1
11.6	43.6	81.3	2.3	0.9	39.6
7.4	0.0	70.5	1.0	69.1	208.4
8.5	**129.1**	**74.1**	**1.4**	**7.7**	**15.2**
7.8	126.4	75.0	1.4	7.0	15.4
13.0	175.5	68.0	1.7	10.3	14.2
36.9	23.7	54.1	2.4	27.9	20.5
37.7	**113.4**	**51.4**	**2.9**	**78.3**	**113.3**
42.3	109.5	48.0	3.6	103.4	150.4
9.0	117.5	52.1	1.2	9.5	26.0
-10.3	54.3	52.3	2.3	-22.7	-2.1
33.6	213.2	64.9	1.2	102.2	86.7
13.7	107.9	63.1	1.5	9.5	21.0
17.2	128.3	68.0	2.9	14.8	28.0
8.5	108.8	59.6	1.1	7.0	9.1
-0.6	101.0	67.0	1.0	-4.1	7.5
16.9	**116.5**	**58.6**	**2.7**	**7.8**	**30.5**
11.0	116.9	58.8	1.8	14.5	19.9
8.3	320.1	74.8	1.4	14.7	14.9
24.6	98.9	52.0	5.3	2.1	62.9
7.4	201.6	67.8	1.1	9.4	21.5
14.2	246.8	72.4	0.8	32.7	20.5
21.2	138.9	59.4	1.5	27.4	25.6
11.7	109.1	49.5	0.7	16.3	16.3

13-12 续表 2

单位: %

地 区	Region	产值利税率 Ratio of Profits and Taxes to Industrial Output Value
阿瓦提县	Awat County	7.5
柯坪县	Kalpin County	-22.9
克孜勒苏柯尔克孜自治州	**Kizilsu Kirgiz Autonomous Prefecture**	**9.5**
阿图什市	Artux City	4.0
阿克陶县	Akto County	27.3
阿合奇县	Akqi County	
乌恰县	Wuqia [Ulugqat] County	6.9
喀什地区	**Kashgar [Kaxgar] Administrative Offices**	**11.4**
喀什市	Kashgar [Kaxgar] City	5.0
疏附县	Shufu County	0.2
疏勒县	Shule County	10.8
英吉沙县	Yengisar County	14.2
泽普县	Zepu [Poskam] County	9.3
莎车县	Shache [Yarkant] County	14.6
叶城县	Yecheng [Kagilik] County	8.0
麦盖提县	Makit County	16.5
岳普湖县	Yopurga County	17.1
伽师县	Jiashi [Payzawat] County	41.3
巴楚县	Bachu [Maralbexi] County	-15.8
塔什库尔干塔吉克自治县	Taxkorgan Tajik Autonomous County	13.8
和田地区	**Hotan Administrative Offices**	**6.5**
和田市	Hotan City	-7.0
和田县	Hotan County	25.3
墨玉县	Moyu [Karakax] County	29.6
皮山县	Pishan [Guma] County	9.9
洛浦县	Lop County	19.3
策勒县	Qira County	
于田县	Yutian [Keriya] County	
民丰县	Minfeng [Niya] County	
自治区直辖县级市	**Municpality Country-LevelCity directly under the Central Government**	**12.9**
石河子市	Shihezi City	14.6
阿拉尔市	Aral City	4.4
图木舒克市	Tumxuk City	8.3
五家渠市	Wujiaqu City	10.6

Continued

(%)

总资产贡献率 Ratio of Total Assets to Industrial Output Value	资本保值增值率 Ratio of Capital-hold and Rise	资产负债率 Assets Liability Ratio	流动资产周转次数(次/年) Number of Times of Annual TurnoverWorking Capitals (times/year)	成本费用利润率 Ratio of Profits to Industrial Cost	全员劳动生产率 Overall Labour Productivity
8.3	132.3	82.0	1.4	7.1	12.1
-14.6	56.1	91.1	1.2	-17.2	4.7
5.4	**140.2**	**62.5**	**1.2**	**3.0**	**18.9**
2.5	108.3	65.4	1.1	1.6	19.0
9.3	190.4	50.7	1.0	9.9	18.8
9.1	-50.0	95.0	1.7	-1.1	18.9
11.2	**157.8**	**75.6**	**2.2**	**5.5**	**17.3**
6.4	129.6	83.0	2.6	-0.4	16.1
0.7	288.9	117.0	5.3	-4.0	3.2
9.9	147.7	65.5	1.3	5.3	17.0
25.9	-219.3	93.1	2.2	8.6	8.3
12.1	207.3	58.7	2.6	7.5	7.1
18.9	239.3	88.1	1.3	15.7	24.7
5.5	2091.7	67.6	1.8	-0.2	5.9
15.3	146.4	61.5	1.3	16.1	15.3
12.9	148.0	73.5	1.4	16.5	21.7
47.9	158.5	37.0	3.3	34.7	50.3
-9.6	60.2	79.5	2.8	-10.4	25.9
4.8	54.5	102.2	2.7	14.1	19.2
3.8	**101.5**	**39.9**	**2.0**	**-1.1**	**17.2**
-1.7	33.5	96.4	3.3	-12.0	15.9
4.1	102.6	1.0	1.8	11.6	34.4
13.5	106.9	9.6	1.6	26.3	36.9
4.5	197.5	61.2	0.8	2.6	6.3
15.4	109.1	46.6	1.0	14.3	7.1
8.5	**117.3**	**71.6**	**1.4**	**10.6**	**17.0**
11.1	119.3	61.9	1.5	13.9	15.6
5.3	61.0	84.2	1.5	0.5	12.4
5.8	140.5	79.9	0.8	7.5	14.0
4.7	130.8	86.2	1.2	5.1	25.6

13-13 国有控股工业企业主要经济指标

单位: 万元 (2011 年)

项　　目	Item	企业单位数（个） Number of Enterprises (unit)	#亏损企业 Loss- Suffering Enterprises	工业总产值（当年价格） Gross Industrial Output Value (At Current Prices)
总　　计	**Total**	**459**	**89**	**48665888.6**
按登记注册类型分	**Grouped by Registry Type**			
内资企业	DomesticFunded Enterprises	454	89	48601979.6
国有企业	State-owned Enterprises	110	25	5809723.1
#中央企业	Central Enterprises	53	10	4629669.1
地方企业	Local Enterprises	57	15	1180054.0
#自治区属企业	Autonomous	23	7	675940.2
地区(州、市)属企业	Prefecture or City	9	3	212647.0
县(市)属企业	County or City	18	3	120662.6
股份合作企业	Share-holding Cooperative Enterprises	3	1	22366.5
联营企业	Joint Ownership Enterprises	5	1	20231.3
#国有联营企业	State Joint Enterprises Ownership	4	1	16181.3
国有与集体联营企业	Joint State-collective OwnershipEnterprises	1		4050.0
有限责任公司	Limited Liability Corporations	285	49	12609110.6
#国有独资公司	Sole State-funded Corporations	52	5	3564752.4
其他有限责任公司	Other Limited Liability Corporations	233	44	9044358.2
股份有限公司	Share-holding Corporations Ltd.	51	13	30140548.1
港、澳、台商投资企业	Enterprises with Funds from Hongkong,Macao and Taiwan	1		6404.7
外商投资企业	Foreign Funded Enterprises	4		57504.3
在总计中: 国有控股企业	Of the Total : State-owned and State-holding Enterprises	459	89	48665888.6
按轻、重工业分(GB/T4754-2011)	**Grouped by Light & Heavy Industry(GB/T4754-2011)**			
轻工业	Light Industry	141	40	2452599.2
以农产品为原料	Using Farm Produces as Raw Materials	123	36	2352203.1
以非农产品为原料	Using Non-Farm Produces as Raw Materials	18	4	100396.1
重工业	Heavy Industry	318	49	46213289.4
采掘工业	Mining and Quarrying	73	8	17078018.9
原料工业	Raw Material Industry	163	32	26940509.5
加工工业	Manufacturing Industry	82	9	2194761.0
按轻、重工业分(GB/T4754-2002)	**Grouped by Light & Heavy Industry(GB/T4754-2002)**			
轻工业	Light Industry	141	40	2452599.2
以农产品为原料	Using Farm Produces as Raw Materials	124	36	2354703.1
以非农产品为原料	Using Non-Farm Produces as Raw Materials	17	4	97896.1
重工业	Heavy Industry	318	49	46213289.4
采掘工业	Mining and Quarrying	73	8	17078018.9
原料工业	Raw Material Industry	163	32	26979729.0
加工工业	Manufacturing Industry	82	9	2155541.5
按企业规模分(新标准)	**Grouped by Size of Enterprises (New Standard)**			
大型企业	Large Enterprises	52	11	38511258.9
中型企业	Medium-sized Enterprises	132	29	6940442.5
小型企业	Small Enterprises	252	44	2767392.5
微型企业	Mini Enterprises	23	5	446794.7
按企业规模分(旧标准)	**Grouped by Size of Enterprises (Old Standard)**			
大型企业	Large Enterprises	27	5	36416828.2
中型企业	Medium-sized Enterprises	151	36	8873323.9
小型企业	Small Enterprises	281	48	3375736.5

Main Economic Indicators Efficiency of State-holding Industrial Enterprises

(10 000 yuan)

工业增加值 Value-added	工业销售产值(当年价) Sales Value of Industry Products (At Current Prices)	出口交货值 Delivery Value of Industry Export	实收资本 Total Capital Hold	资产合计 Total Assets	流动资产合计 Total Working Capitals	#产成品 Finished Product	固定资产原价 Original Value of Fixed Assets
20918681.7	**48307739.5**	**384013.6**	**25679116.9**	**64283377.6**	**16723746.3**	**1668703.4**	**58772698.1**
20881489.4	48243585.7	384013.6	25573494.9	63998681.9	16661120.4	1667431.0	58584620.7
2389302.8	5741809.2	37364.7	2957352.5	10876176.0	2522165.6	187198.6	10321775.8
2002162.2	4594968.1	6227.8	2279727.3	7866663.0	1802701.5	112964.0	7828903.0
387140.5	1146841.1	31136.9	677625.2	3009513.0	719464.1	74234.6	2492872.8
249775.1	666770.7	15527.0	513281.7	1712569.0	274148.7	23087.3	1589173.9
43763.5	193119.9		94684.5	663991.5	293788.9	36737.0	435670.8
58727.5	116201.3		32452.0	369698.4	83279.8	3060.6	310976.2
7005.7	19221.6		10408.0	38207.3	22361.1	3245.0	26830.2
7742.0	20247.0		12022.0	45072.0	18210.8	234.9	28361.0
6112.9	16197.0		10867.4	42176.6	17220.5	234.9	25545.4
1629.1	4050.0		1154.6	2895.4	990.3		2815.6
3896713.9	12394674.1	208175.6	4903204.0	18817068.8	5662280.0	786378.7	12633609.2
1126485.2	3545835.1	743.1	1225871.9	4662576.0	1392110.9	67006.8	3301186.0
2770228.7	8848839.0	207432.5	3677332.1	14154492.8	4270169.1	719371.9	9332423.2
14580725.1	30067633.8	138473.3	17690508.4	34222157.8	8436102.9	690373.8	35574044.5
3646.8	6404.7		13000.0	36047.5	6105.3		34348.2
33545.4	57749.1		92622.0	248648.2	56520.6	1272.4	153729.2
20918681.7	48307739.5	384013.6	25679116.9	64283377.6	16723746.3	1668703.4	58772698.1
752805.8	2386629.5	173301.6	1106166.7	4166852.2	2128678.2	511825.2	2342451.5
712934.6	2285444.8	173097.3	873780.0	3594345.2	1964278.0	503280.5	1948710.4
39871.2	101184.7	204.3	232386.7	572507.0	164400.2	8544.7	393741.1
20165875.9	45921110.0	210712.0	24572950.2	60116525.4	14595068.1	1156878.2	56430246.6
14745658.7	17008890.1		14996112.0	27228587.8	5519963.9	304426.5	31199549.9
4764544.5	26818452.9	172574.9	8968017.1	29924334.9	7651596.4	658664.8	23804849.6
655672.7	2093767.0	38137.1	608821.1	2963602.7	1423507.8	193786.9	1425847.1
752805.8	2386629.5	173301.6	1106166.7	4166852.2	2128678.2	511825.2	2342451.5
713770.0	2287944.8	173097.3	874530.0	3596028.2	1964841.6	503694.3	1949897.1
39035.8	98684.7	204.3	231636.7	570824.0	163836.6	8130.9	392554.4
20165875.9	45921110.0	210712.0	24572950.2	60116525.4	14595068.1	1156878.2	56430246.6
14745658.7	17008890.1		14996112.0	27228587.8	5519963.9	304426.5	31199549.9
4787008.2	26853225.6	172574.9	8983017.1	29956410.9	7676014.8	660537.9	23813410.0
633208.9	2058994.3	38137.1	593821.1	2931526.7	1399089.4	191913.8	1417286.7
17567435.9	38308767.5	197996.0	21808930.7	48408871.8	11561844.7	868793.0	47956734.2
2379916.6	6833033.7	74727.6	2161810.6	9443749.8	3148488.6	419448.2	6253728.8
927380.8	2739643.7	111290.0	1582652.5	5995225.5	1853633.9	347363.9	4307869.8
43948.4	426294.6		125723.1	435530.5	159779.1	33098.3	254365.3
16869728.5	36265937.8	31016.4	20610590.9	42434108.9	9726445.8	681218.4	45331095.3
2986631.9	8721604.2	256997.4	2930964.0	14143080.0	4803693.5	610059.9	8032717.2
1062321.2	3320197.5	95999.8	2137562.0	7706188.7	2193607.0	377425.1	5408885.6

13-13 续表

单位：万元

项　　目	Item	流动负债合计 Total Working Liabilities	长期负债合计 Long-term Liabilities	所有者权益合计 Total Owners' Equities
总　　计	**Total**	**18668510.6**	**13548143.7**	**31388707.3**
按登记注册类型分	**Grouped by Registry Type**			
内资企业	DomesticFunded Enterprises	18585281.6	13487156.4	31248227.9
国有企业	State-owned Enterprises	3450397.1	2804577.2	4167973.4
#中央企业	Central Enterprises	2620854.9	1931023.2	3303987.6
地方企业	Local Enterprises	829542.2	873554.0	863985.8
#自治区属企业	Autonomous	296514.7	386882.8	624546.4
地区(州、市)属企业	Prefecture or City	256918.3	333229.3	73708.4
县(市)属企业	County or City	196029.9	61106.5	74891.6
股份合作企业	Share-holding Cooperative Enterprises	27028.4		5989.2
联营企业	Joint Ownership Enterprises	30431.7	3974.6	10665.7
#国有联营企业	State Joint Enterprises Ownership	28981.3	3974.6	9220.7
国有与集体联营企业	Joint State-collective OwnershipEnterprises	1450.4		1445.0
有限责任公司	Limited Liability Corporations	6994074.8	4438610.1	7176680.1
#国有独资公司	Sole State-funded Corporations	1618644.5	967960.8	1973040.0
其他有限责任公司	Other Limited Liability Corporations	5375430.3	3470649.3	5203640.1
股份有限公司	Share-holding Corporations Ltd.	8083349.6	6239994.5	19886919.5
港、澳、台商投资企业	Enterprises with Funds from Hongkong,Macao and Taiwan	2823.1		33224.4
外商投资企业	Foreign Funded Enterprises	80405.9	60987.3	107255.0
在总计中：国有控股企业	Of the Total : State-owned and State-holding Enterprises	18668510.6	13548143.7	31388707.3
按轻、重工业分(GB/T4754-2011)	**Grouped by Light & Heavy Industry(GB/T4754-2011)**			
轻工业	Light Industry	2091594.9	400842.5	1639563.3
以农产品为原料	Using Farm Produces as Raw Materials	1942374.3	260960.5	1365826.9
以非农产品为原料	Using Non-Farm Produces as Raw Materials	149220.6	139882.0	273736.4
重工业	Heavy Industry	16576915.7	13147301.2	29749144.0
采掘工业	Mining and Quarrying	6311809.8	5884738.8	15002069.0
原料工业	Raw Material Industry	9126614.3	6736748.2	13450573.0
加工工业	Manufacturing Industry	1138491.6	525814.2	1296502.0
按轻、重工业分(GB/T4754-2002)	**Grouped by Light & Heavy Industry(GB/T4754-2002)**			
轻工业	Light Industry	2091594.9	400842.5	1639563.3
以农产品为原料	Using Farm Produces as Raw Materials	1943435.0	260960.5	1366449.2
以非农产品为原料	Using Non-Farm Produces as Raw Materials	148159.9	139882.0	273114.1
重工业	Heavy Industry	16576915.7	13147301.2	29749144.0
采掘工业	Mining and Quarrying	6311809.8	5884738.8	15002069.0
原料工业	Raw Material Industry	9142569.9	6736748.2	13466693.4
加工工业	Manufacturing Industry	1122536.0	525814.2	1280381.6
按企业规模分(新标准)	**Grouped by Size of Enterprises (New Standard)**			
大型企业	Large Enterprises	12585939.7	10574905.2	25246766.6
中型企业	Medium-sized Enterprises	3823406.0	1432902.6	3622978.5
小型企业	Small Enterprises	2080149.4	1458685.2	2373324.9
微型企业	Mini Enterprises	179015.5	81650.7	145637.3
按企业规模分(旧标准)	**Grouped by Size of Enterprises (Old Standard)**			
大型企业	Large Enterprises	10671875.9	8975274.6	22785727.9
中型企业	Medium-sized Enterprises	5547248.9	2778847.0	5643531.2
小型企业	Small Enterprises	2449385.8	1794022.1	2959448.2

Continued

(10 000 yuan)

主营业务收入 Revenue from Principal Business	#主营业务成本 Cost of Principal Business	主营业务税金及附加 Taxes and Other Charges on Principal Business	营业利润 Business Profit	利润总额 Total Profit	亏损企业亏损总额 Losses Value of Loss-Suffering Enterprises	利税总额 Total Profits and Taxes	本年应交增值税 Value-added Taxes Payable	全部从业人员年平均人数(人) Annual Average Employed Persons (person)
49136691.5	**34406033.0**	**3225271.7**	**7654407.9**	**7876122.1**	**1311681.1**	**13579598.2**	**2478204.4**	**349653**
49073150.3	34363356.4	3224616.5	7642859.1	7862727.5	1311681.1	13559842.6	2472498.6	348781
5671370.5	4610753.8	206887.2	436566.3	469408.0	146943.1	910654.5	234359.3	73300
4570602.6	3660355.7	200483.3	409354.3	435124.6	85036.0	823077.4	187469.5	54756
1100767.9	950398.1	6403.9	27212.0	34283.4	61907.1	87577.1	46889.8	18544
621390.4	550900.0	2884.9	7504.6	3287.8	47764.7	36497.1	30324.4	11463
189551.8	169217.1	317.4	-3752.8	110.7	6881.7	2992.1	2564.0	2526
113892.3	76829.7	2660.5	8801.0	14453.0	7148.5	23872.0	6758.5	2997
19322.9	15498.3	294.1	1063.4	755.3	737.6	1242.6	193.2	690
20425.6	15432.5	300.0	2736.3	3013.3	2.3	4561.7	1248.4	403
16375.6	12850.4	271.8	1470.4	1635.2	2.3	3154.3	1247.3	364
4050.0	2582.1	28.2	1265.9	1378.1		1407.4	1.1	39
11987272.5	9553069.9	348482.2	998503.1	1101442.0	223794.0	1978017.4	528093.2	138876
3642050.6	2916324.9	261576.9	218965.3	240987.8	68029.7	673512.0	170947.3	39252
8345221.9	6636745.0	86905.3	779537.8	860454.2	155764.3	1304505.4	357145.9	99624
31374758.8	20168601.9	2668653.0	6203990.0	6288108.9	940204.1	10665366.4	1708604.5	135512
5406.3	2046.0		1782.2	2828.6		2828.6		28
58134.9	40630.6	655.2	9766.6	10566.0		16927.0	5705.8	844
49136691.5	34406033.0	3225271.7	7654407.9	7876122.1	1311681.1	13579598.2	2478204.4	349653
2455328.8	1850957.8	166128.0	89816.4	106131.5	108119.6	392430.8	120171.3	46464
2351275.2	1773221.6	165390.9	95750.6	108064.3	98355.5	388901.0	115445.8	42231
104053.6	77736.2	737.1	-5934.2	-1932.8	9764.1	3529.8	4725.5	4233
46681362.7	32555075.2	3059143.7	7564591.5	7769990.6	1203561.5	13187167.4	2358033.1	303189
17700027.9	7059092.5	1367041.5	7252338.6	7376512.1	99702.1	10408042.6	1664489.0	142750
26796888.3	23817982.7	1666851.5	33740.0	68969.1	1091142.2	2354235.6	618415.0	135424
2184446.5	1678000.0	25250.7	278512.9	324509.4	12717.2	424889.2	75129.1	25015
2455328.8	1850957.8	166128.0	89816.4	106131.5	108119.6	392430.8	120171.3	46464
2353859.2	1775208.2	165392.5	96282.7	108596.4	98355.5	389451.7	115462.8	42267
101469.6	75749.6	735.5	-6466.3	-2464.9	9764.1	2979.1	4708.5	4197
46681362.7	32555075.2	3059143.7	7564591.5	7769990.6	1203561.5	13187167.4	2358033.1	303189
17700027.9	7059092.5	1367041.5	7252338.6	7376512.1	99702.1	10408042.6	1664489.0	142750
26832024.0	23850784.4	1666814.6	34994.1	70128.2	1091142.2	2355481.2	618538.4	135599
2149310.8	1645198.3	25287.6	277258.8	323350.3	12717.2	423643.6	75005.7	24840
38815629.2	26387614.2	2790769.9	6796145.2	6950141.8	1088393.6	11763771.9	2022860.2	226708
7092746.6	5552650.8	414749.5	545176.4	568897.6	162304.1	1309306.4	325659.3	86403
2802474.7	2163486.2	18920.4	304171.6	343993.9	53042.1	488557.0	125642.7	36282
425841.0	302281.8	831.9	8914.7	13088.8	7941.3	17962.9	4042.2	260
36745963.7	24711171.9	2770465.5	6609019.7	6742396.5	1020177.5	11453130.2	1940268.2	197629
9000384.4	7134322.0	434558.1	699995.5	742560.4	232185.6	1569878.5	392760.0	115678
3390343.4	2560539.1	20248.1	345392.7	391165.2	59318.0	556589.5	145176.2	36346

13-14 分行业国有控股工业企业主要经济指标(GB/T4754-2011)

单位: 万元 (2011 年)

行业	Sector	企业单位数(个) Number of Enterprises (unit)	#亏损企业 Loss- Suffering Enterprises	工业总产值(当年价格) Gross Industrial Output Value (At Current Prices)
总计	**Total**	**459**	**89**	**48665888.6**
煤炭开采和洗选业	Mining and Washing of Coal	33	6	909323.4
石油和天然气开采业	Extraction of Petroleum and Natural Gas	5		14058213.6
黑色金属矿采选业	Mining and Processing of Ferrous Metals Ores	10		614797.0
有色金属矿采选业	Mining and Processing of Nonferrous Metals Ores	15	1	419639.1
非金属矿采选业	Mining and Processing of Nonmetal Ores	8		74190.1
#采盐	Extraction of Salt	4		40529.3
农副食品加工业	Processing of Food from Agricultural Products	46	10	741528.3
#谷物磨制	Grain Grinding	12	2	70299.3
饲料加工	Fodder Processing	5		148530.0
制糖	Sugar Making	11		260976.2
食品制造业	Manufacture of Food	34	14	477433.6
#罐头制造	Manufacture of can	21	13	259221.8
酒、饮料和精制茶制造业	Manufacture of Wine,Beverages and Refined Tea	13	2	208878.3
#酒的制造	Manufacture of Wine	12	2	206082.1
烟草制品业	Manufacture of Tobacco	1		302740.4
纺织业	Manufacture of Textile	13	6	298171.7
#棉、化纤纺织及印染精加工	Cotton, Chemical Fiber, Dyeing, Printing and Processing	10	6	267493.9
毛纺织和染整精加工	Wool Textile, Dyeing and Printing	2		5355.1
纺织服装、鞋、帽制造业	Manufacture of Textile Wearing Apparel,Footware and Caps	2	1	26209.7
造纸及纸制品业	Manufacture of Paper and Paper Products	4		71629.0
印刷业和记录媒介的复制	Printing and Copying of Medium for Record	5	1	24180.7
石油加工、炼焦及核燃料加工业	Oil Processing, Coking and Nuclear Fuel Processing	10	5	14062859.0
#炼焦	Coking	2	1	96232.6
化学原料及化学制品制造业	Raw Chemical Material and Chemical Products	30	5	3393833.0
#基础化学原料制造	Basic Chemical Material	9	4	509667.5
肥料制造	Fertilizer Making	6		574827.9
合成材料制造	Manufacture of Synthetic Material	7	1	2224126.5
医药制造业	Manufacture of Medicine	7		67920.8
化学纤维制造业	Manufacture of Chemical Fiber	3	2	168411.1
橡胶制品业	Manufacture of Rubber Products	20	5	330128.3
非金属矿物制品业	Manufacture of Nonmetal Mineral Products	61	4	1266872.9
#水泥制造	Manufacture of Cement	32	3	758686.5
黑色金属冶炼及压延加工业	Smelting and Pressing of Ferrous Metals	5	1	4821364.8
有色金属冶炼及压延加工业	Smelting and Pressing of Nonferrous Metals	8	1	385176.1
金属制品业	Manufacture of Metal Products	7	1	446979.6
通用设备制造业	Manufacture of General Purpose Machinery	1		3252.7
专用设备制造业	Manufacture of Special Purpose Machinery	8		88115.5
汽车制造业	Manufacture of Automobile	3	3	50537.6
电气机械及器材制造业	Manufacture of Electric Equipment and Machinery	4		28129.0
仪器仪表制造业	Manufacture of Measuring Instruments and Machinery	1		6016.1
电力、热力的生产和供应业	Electric Power and Thermal Production and Supply	90	17	4169741.7
#电力生产和电力供应	Electric Power Production and Supply	68	13	4009177.6
燃气生产和供应业	Gas Production and Supply	2		88113.0
水的生产和供应业	Water Production and Supply	7	3	38326.8

Main Economic Indicators of State-holding Industrial Enterprises by Sectors (GB/T4754-2011)

(10 000 yuan)

工业增加值 Value-added	工业销售产值(当年价) Sales Value of Industry Products (At Current Prices)	出口交货值 Delivery Value of Industry Export	实收资本 Total Capital Hold	资产合计 Total Assets	流动资产合计 Total Working Capitals	#产成品 Finished Product	固定资产原价 Net Value of Fixed Assets
20918681.7	**48307739.5**	**384013.6**	**25679116.9**	**64283377.6**	**16723746.3**	**1668703.4**	**58772698.1**
614037.4	954183.0		831173.6	2856458.8	704335.8	37211.2	1204801.4
13080155.5	14024241.8		12950531.0	21158637.5	3455624.2	147035.3	28376963.5
265463.8	574519.0		173276.0	1035143.3	566730.5	76366.0	346046.7
328802.6	390955.2		126208.4	898920.9	226762.9	37755.8	389373.5
36409.1	63493.2		24581.5	78013.1	42827.8	6058.2	28551.9
23150.0	34410.8		16307.1	47779.7	28336.5	4232.9	15197.7
166279.9	741971.0		186264.5	866845.3	500226.0	190459.1	393897.6
11407.3	72056.6		11940.4	53100.2	23780.9	1482.2	23162.5
30269.0	140478.4		31248.8	229765.7	117515.1	16267.8	44511.1
105308.7	298540.0		81028.8	308421.8	166551.6	78365.1	234118.8
84237.0	443065.8	121168.1	250832.1	1087129.0	580113.5	206461.1	606221.1
15683.5	233171.1	111092.3	203727.0	862438.4	505663.2	194535.2	443810.0
110799.1	207006.8		108370.8	319494.1	157305.4	9137.8	139356.8
110067.5	204592.6		108169.8	318255.4	156654.1	8963.7	138669.3
236486.5	302055.5		18741.7	371707.0	261354.0		129728.0
56328.6	280167.7	49724.0	193450.6	470123.0	264221.2	48444.3	342383.0
48306.1	254557.8	37890.8	150406.5	394342.3	219529.2	46706.9	296502.2
2080.7	5795.2		6698.5	9002.0	5672.9	621.7	9902.5
7417.4	23745.6	538.8	4707.9	19957.2	12813.7	1382.8	8660.5
19662.2	67355.9		22911.5	143510.5	61797.0	6434.6	106810.8
9528.2	24741.3		11354.2	51348.0	21868.5	1850.3	46054.0
1687545.1	14008279.3	14644.8	4332695.2	7333440.6	2531527.1	222012.4	7120129.5
33060.6	91804.3	14644.8	32313.0	272498.3	86872.9	6221.3	178617.0
1080883.0	3256121.6	147482.0	1442545.5	6053823.2	1569168.7	239006.5	3420822.3
130486.3	505898.3	51222.5	343298.7	2058128.6	438536.9	21241.1	462222.5
339794.4	494846.8		120384.7	946305.5	361848.8	48040.9	670885.4
572299.6	2170607.1	96259.5	941424.8	2932285.7	716788.3	166888.9	2261049.9
17550.7	69438.7	1870.7	32889.5	130647.8	82077.9	16903.1	47677.4
15185.2	162459.3		63800.0	215631.9	68151.7	29316.6	160839.5
55369.8	291148.6	6472.4	132523.8	406876.1	237108.1	72316.0	169546.4
403904.6	1272871.5	15609.9	729171.8	2906835.6	1088187.4	42484.8	1247407.7
283739.8	756977.4		607638.4	2175852.7	734057.1	24297.9	964901.4
496507.6	4832685.8	10448.1	841114.8	4080030.6	1297902.9	202381.8	2374962.4
81548.9	378839.4		57024.5	330708.8	138205.9	21362.4	158118.8
51545.3	492713.5		81305.4	201818.8	110714.6	9959.7	56446.4
685.1	3443.0		500.0	2851.0	2176.0	615.7	1410.3
17671.9	80362.7	16004.0	18347.5	132367.8	92966.7	24594.1	40186.2
-929.2	46862.4	50.8	16578.2	93047.7	44338.1	9889.3	32846.6
4741.0	24492.4		11357.9	71398.3	55464.3	7184.3	17826.0
616.6	6016.1		1500.0	7078.0	6961.4	1786.4	220.1
1510960.7	4156606.4		1841320.7	11006900.9	1791331.3	0.3	10458326.9
1452803.3	3996600.1		1720285.2	10298848.1	1559390.5	0.3	9839964.7
22215.7	66752.3		67664.0	250033.2	113697.3	293.5	118063.7
19453.9	38326.8		208234.5	468617.9	104171.6		350807.6

13-14 续表

单位: 万元

行业	Sector	流动负债合计 Total Working Liabilities	长期负债合计 Long-term Liabilities	所有者权益合计 Total Owners' Equities
总计	**Total**	**18668510.6**	**13548143.7**	**31388707.3**
煤炭开采和洗选业	Mining and Washing of Coal	954545.4	766134.9	1108695.6
石油和天然气开采业	Extraction of Petroleum and Natural Gas	3882919.4	4706015.1	12568473.1
黑色金属矿采选业	Mining and Processing of Ferrous Metals Ores	573593.6	129939.6	331570.6
有色金属矿采选业	Mining and Processing of Nonferrous Metals Ores	268033.8	118941.1	510483.3
非金属矿采选业	Mining and Processing of Nonmetal Ores	33849.1	3630.0	40378.8
#采盐	Extraction of Salt	14379.2	3373.0	30027.5
农副食品加工业	Processing of Food from Agricultural Products	446979.5	52144.0	356916.9
#谷物磨制	Grain Grinding	20936.7	8340.6	23523.7
饲料加工	Fodder Processing	76635.3	34105.0	118011.8
制糖	Sugar Making	138540.2	4325.5	165556.1
食品制造业	Manufacture of Food	743132.1	81925.8	257778.3
#罐头制造	Manufacture of can	640654.3	72095.7	145440.7
酒、饮料和精制茶制造业	Manufacture of Wine,Beverages and Refined Tea	158728.8	3264.2	157501.0
#酒的制造	Manufacture of Wine	158063.7	3264.2	156927.4
烟草制品业	Manufacture of Tobacco	98051.0		273656.0
纺织业	Manufacture of Textile	239812.3	37866.5	188969.5
#棉、化纤纺织及印染精加工	Cotton, Chemical Fiber, Dyeing, Printing and Processing	207279.2	37560.6	146027.9
毛纺织和染整精加工	Wool Textile, Dyeing and Printing	9153.9	42.7	-194.6
纺织服装、鞋、帽制造业	Manufacture of Textile Wearing Apparel,Footware and Caps	9826.7	14936.7	-4806.2
造纸及纸制品业	Manufacture of Paper and Paper Products	64613.8	6251.3	65989.8
印刷业和记录媒介的复制	Printing and Copying of Medium for Record	19569.1	5520.4	26258.3
石油加工、炼焦及核燃料加工业	Oil Processing, Coking and Nuclear Fuel Processing	2069804.3	646602.8	4617033.2
#炼焦	Coking	144613.6	83107.8	44776.9
化学原料及化学制品制造业	Raw Chemical Material and Chemical Products	1275333.4	1757548.6	3020715.4
#基础化学原料制造	Basic Chemical Material	488681.9	542355.1	1026866.1
肥料制造	Fertilizer Making	265729.7	249916.9	430658.8
合成材料制造	Manufacture of Synthetic Material	498400.1	950667.1	1483218.3
医药制造业	Manufacture of Medicine	54681.5	5212.2	70519.6
化学纤维制造业	Manufacture of Chemical Fiber	132764.6	59434.8	23432.5
橡胶制品业	Manufacture of Rubber Products	186994.6	39515.0	178373.1
非金属矿物制品业	Manufacture of Nonmetal Mineral Products	935444.8	541587.4	1387600.9
#水泥制造	Manufacture of Cement	658642.8	437375.8	1038432.5
黑色金属冶炼及压延加工业	Smelting and Pressing of Ferrous Metals	2220840.2	620523.7	1238666.7
有色金属冶炼及压延加工业	Smelting and Pressing of Nonferrous Metals	175321.3	8407.9	146979.6
金属制品业	Manufacture of Metal Products	100557.4	6384.6	94876.7
通用设备制造业	Manufacture of General Purpose Machinery	2173.0		678.0
专用设备制造业	Manufacture of Special Purpose Machinery	70657.1	7448.0	54262.4
汽车制造业	Manufacture of Automobile	87422.7	533.2	5091.7
电气机械及器材制造业	Manufacture of Electric Equipment and Machinery	34784.8	24227.0	12386.4
仪器仪表制造业	Manufacture of Measuring Instruments and Machinery for Cultural Activity and Office Work	5008.3		2069.7
电力、热力的生产和供应业	Electric Power and Thermal Production and Supply	3011069.1	3530315.8	3896744.2
#电力生产和电力供应	Electric Power Production and Supply	2796165.3	3205253.9	3756760.4
燃气生产和供应业	Gas Production and Supply	105732.7	67276.0	77024.5
水的生产和供应业	Water Production and Supply	105747.4	133279.0	220202.9

Continued

(10 000 yuan)

主营业务收入 Revenue from Principal Business	#主营业务成本 Cost of Principal Business	主营业务税金及附加 Taxes and Other Charges on Principal Business	营业利润 Business Profit	利润总额 Total Profit	亏损企业亏损总额 Losses Value of Loss-Suffering Enterprises	利税总额 Total Profits and Taxes	本年应交增值税 Value-added Taxes Payable	全部从业人员年平均人数(人) Ann Employed Persons (person)
49136691.5	**34406033.0**	**3225271.7**	**7654407.9**	**7876122.1**	**1311681.1**	**13579598.2**	**2478204.4**	**349653**
993683.0	647209.6	29993.0	134815.6	132684.2	29084.0	267147.7	104470.5	37451
14724881.3	4921246.4	1309986.0	6824921.4	6923929.7		9654477.0	1420561.3	72419
603518.9	354151.6	11774.6	174049.5	174859.3		233162.8	46528.9	4457
393735.6	138742.7	5719.9	202201.9	204148.5	2994.3	250608.0	40739.6	5569
52760.3	21484.8	3151.4	7512.2	8164.2		16727.7	5412.1	2340
34452.9	10919.2	2818.2	5732.7	5793.7		12840.7	4228.8	1283
751798.5	609339.0	2637.6	58493.8	60221.4	13353.2	91004.5	28145.5	10296
72535.9	64842.6	124.3	3981.9	4556.5	573.6	5783.9	1103.1	832
150781.9	114773.6	316.6	16019.7	16808.8		19526.5	2401.1	1071
281242.8	206137.9	2039.5	41462.9	41964.0		67329.0	23325.5	5548
450390.2	368754.6	2163.1	-13186.1	-9864.4	47916.3	2018.3	9719.6	8472
236291.9	204708.2	911.7	-45957.0	-44171.7	47584.8	-42623.2	636.8	4934
200365.7	109428.3	23744.5	30632.0	33722.2	3135.0	74364.7	16898.0	4338
197883.6	107769.5	23727.6	30558.9	33621.2	3135.0	74103.2	16754.4	4232
302058.0	106288.0	134892.0	40736.0	40648.0		210392.0	34852.0	885
321051.1	299173.6	771.6	-14704.4	-16008.4	18526.6	-2579.3	12657.5	11173
294223.1	276031.3	618.3	-13046.1	-16200.2	18526.6	-3630.1	11951.8	9694
5445.9	4512.3		176.8	179.8		458.8	279.0	230
39696.3	36356.3	15.1	-578.7	-50.8	731.2	-16.2	19.5	1091
66215.9	55554.1	364.7	4994.1	7805.5		11120.2	2950.0	2570
25778.0	21523.0	85.0	-227.9	1462.8	71.6	2157.6	609.8	1115
14358714.3	13002503.5	1617635.6	-866406.3	-892873.7	987433.0	938184.7	213422.8	30368
103570.0	77304.8	5770.9	4915.8	4880.5	65.5	15664.6	5013.2	2537
2859542.0	2086579.2	36413.6	501360.1	548297.5	11344.6	729508.7	144797.6	33464
738983.8	650840.2	2958.8	35368.8	33644.3	10049.5	55821.4	19218.3	11068
495452.0	212746.9	18680.7	182109.2	218907.0		269310.5	31722.8	4637
1539159.2	1165113.9	13949.6	258706.0	270197.5	1295.1	370870.8	86723.7	15813
56874.8	38398.4	355.3	4943.1	5575.8		7902.1	1971.0	1896
166778.0	146549.1	672.2	-13225.7	-12803.7	14621.6	-3336.5	8795.0	1756
301482.3	265640.3	1801.0	6652.0	8038.0	3338.5	19580.8	9741.8	5728
1316072.0	1023382.7	6908.8	189143.8	212886.1	5009.9	283898.9	64104.0	20932
751301.3	541058.5	5208.2	144515.6	164191.8	4825.2	213638.0	44238.0	14418
4911729.8	4566140.5	13149.5	83602.5	82202.0	1622.6	176853.3	81501.8	14821
353202.8	303526.6	334.5	29402.7	31321.2	5277.3	33642.3	1986.6	4223
467396.3	448240.6	561.9	12025.7	11995.1	32.3	15634.4	3077.4	1880
3527.0	2919.0	71.0	95.0	84.0		195.0	40.0	84
92862.9	76233.1	141.1	5602.6	6637.0		7358.1	580.0	2374
67322.9	67457.7	89.4	-9825.9	-9164.0	9164.0	-8620.3	454.3	1203
24358.7	20069.4	62.6	-1016.7	573.8		1100.6	464.2	756
6016.1	5000.7	18.0	66.4	78.2		196.4	100.2	50
4134604.3	3581480.4	13588.5	348315.6	379885.0	80639.5	564603.6	171130.1	44551
3973004.0	3434248.3	13257.7	354646.4	376995.5	75066.3	558192.0	167938.8	40734
91929.8	63307.5	1216.3	3603.5	4042.6		7067.4	1808.5	993
45575.9	36236.0	334.5	-11250.9	-7930.7	9761.8	-5397.7	2198.5	1866

13-15 分行业国有控股工业企业主要经济指标(GB/T4754-2002)

单位: 万元 (2011 年)

行业	Sector	企业单位数(个) Number of Enterprises (unit)	#亏损企业 Loss- Suffering Enterprises	工业总产值(当年价格) Gross Industrial Output Value (At Current Prices)
煤炭开采和洗选业	Mining and Washing of Coal	33	6	909323.4
石油和天然气开采业	Extraction of Petroleum and Natural Gas	7	1	15060069.3
#天然原油和天然气开采	Extraction of Ores Crude Oil and Natural Gas Extraction	5		14058213.6
黑色金属矿采选业	Mining and Processing of Ferrous Metals Ores	10		614797.0
有色金属矿采选业	Mining and Processing of Nonferrous Metals Ores	15	1	419639.1
非金属矿采选业	Mining and Processing of Nonmetal Ores	8		74190.1
#采　盐	Extraction of Salt	4		40529.3
农副食品加工业	Processing of Food from Agricultural Products	47	11	792692.8
#谷物磨制	Grain Grinding	12	2	70299.3
饲料加工	Fodder Processing	5		148530.0
制　糖	Sugar Making	11		260976.2
食品制造业	Manufacture of Food	33	13	426269.1
#罐头制造	Manufacture of can	20	12	208057.3
饮料制造业	Manufacture of Beverage	13	2	208878.3
#酒的制造	Manufacture of Wine	12	2	206082.1
烟草制品业	Manufacture of Tobacco	1		302740.4
纺织业	Manufacture of Textile	13	7	288750.1
#棉、化纤纺织及印染精加工	Cotton, Chemical Fiber, Dyeing, Printing and Processing	9	6	256541.2
毛纺织和染整精加工	Wool Textile, Dyeing and Printing	2		5355.1
纺织服装、鞋、帽制造业	Manufacture of Textile Wearing Apparel,Footware and Caps	2		35631.3
造纸及纸制品业	Manufacture of Paper and Paper Products	4		71629.0
印刷业和记录媒介的复制	Printing and Copying of Medium for Record	5	1	24180.7
石油加工、炼焦及核燃料加工业	Oil Processing, Coking and Nuclear Fuel Processing	10	5	14062859.0
#炼　焦	Coking	2	1	96232.6
化学原料及化学制品制造业	Raw Chemical Material and Chemical Products	30	5	3393833.0
#基础化学原料制造	Basic Chemical Material	9	4	509667.5
肥料制造	Fertilizer Making	6		574827.9
医药制造业	Manufacture of Medicine	7		67920.8
化学纤维制造业	Manufacture of Chemical Fiber	3	2	168411.1
橡胶制品业	Manufacture of Rubber Products	2	1	112370.3
塑料制品业	Manufacture of Plastic Products	18	4	217758.0
非金属矿物制品业	Manufacture of Nonmetal Mineral Products	61	4	1266872.9
#水泥制造	Manufacture of Cement	31	3	752411.3
黑色金属冶炼及压延加工业	Smelting and Pressing of Ferrous Metals	5	1	4821364.8
有色金属冶炼及压延加工业	Smelting and Pressing of Nonferrous Metals	9	1	430670.8
金属制品业	Manufacture of Metal Products	6	1	401484.9
通用设备制造业	Manufacture of General Purpose Machinery	1		3252.7
专用设备制造业	Manufacture of Special Purpose Machinery	8		88115.5
交通运输设备制造业	Manufacture of Transport Equipment	3	3	50537.6
电气机械及器材制造业	Manufacture of Electric Equipment and Machinery	4		28129.0
仪器仪表及文化、办公用机械制造业	Manufacture of Measuring Instruments and Machinery for Cultural Activity and Office Work	1		6016.1
电力、热力的生产和供应业	Electric Power and Thermal Production and Supply	90	17	4169741.7
#电力生产和电力供应	Electric Power Production and Supply	68	13	4009177.6
燃气生产和供应业	Gas Production and Supply	2		88113.0
水的生产和供应业	Water Production and Supply	7	3	38326.8

Main Economic Indicators of State-holding Industrial Enterprises by Sectors (GB/T4754-2002)

(10 000 yuan)

工业增加值 Value-added	工业销售产值(当年价) Sales Value of Industry Products (At Current Prices)	出口交货值 Delivery Value of Industry Export	实收资本 Total Capital Hold	资产合计 Total Assets	流动资产合计 Total Working Capitals	#产成品 Finished Product	固定资产原价 Net Value of Fixed Assets
614037.4	954183.0		831173.6	2856458.8	704335.8	37211.2	1204801.4
13500945.9	15025739.7		13840872.5	22360051.7	3979306.9	147035.3	29230776.4
13080155.5	14024241.8		12950531.0	21158637.5	3455624.2	147035.3	28376963.5
265463.8	574519.0		173276.0	1035143.3	566730.5	76366.0	346046.7
328802.6	390955.2		126208.4	898920.9	226762.9	37755.8	389373.5
36409.1	63493.2		24581.5	78013.1	42827.8	6058.2	28551.9
23150.0	34410.8		16307.1	47779.7	28336.5	4232.9	15197.7
172179.9	772114.8		283715.7	1039584.5	603130.8	220678.0	478150.7
11407.3	72056.6		11940.4	53100.2	23780.9	1482.2	23162.5
30269.0	140478.4		31248.8	229765.7	117515.1	16267.8	44511.1
105308.7	298540.0		81028.8	308421.8	166551.6	78365.1	234118.8
78337.0	412922.0	121168.1	153380.9	914389.8	477208.7	176242.2	521968.0
9783.5	203027.3	111092.3	106275.8	689699.2	402758.4	164316.3	359556.9
110799.1	207006.8		108370.8	319494.1	157305.4	9137.8	139356.8
110067.5	204592.6		108169.8	318255.4	156654.1	8963.7	138669.3
236486.5	302055.5		18741.7	371707.0	261354.0		129728.0
53739.7	271562.5	45108.9	194883.5	457312.7	253877.8	46473.7	343361.3
45150.8	243566.5	33275.7	149156.5	378034.6	206936.7	43826.8	294448.9
2080.7	5795.2		6698.5	9002.0	5672.9	621.7	9902.5
10006.3	32350.8	5153.9	3275.0	32767.5	23157.1	3353.4	7682.2
19662.2	67355.9		22911.5	143510.5	61797.0	6434.6	106810.8
9528.2	24741.3		11354.2	51348.0	21868.5	1850.3	46054.0
1687545.1	14008279.3	14644.8	4332695.2	7333440.6	2531527.1	222012.4	7120129.5
33060.6	91804.3	14644.8	32313.0	272498.3	86872.9	6221.3	178617.0
1080883.0	3256121.6	147482.0	1442545.5	6053823.2	1569168.7	239006.5	3420822.3
130486.3	505898.3	51222.5	343298.7	2058128.6	438536.9	21241.1	462222.5
339794.4	494846.8		120384.7	946305.5	361848.8	48040.9	670885.4
17550.7	69438.7	1870.7	32889.5	130647.8	82077.9	16903.1	47677.1
15185.2	162459.3		63800.0	215631.9	68151.7	29316.6	160839.5
16912.2	107100.6	6472.4	38620.0	128146.1	47475.5	11790.2	56015.6
38457.6	184048.0		93903.8	278730.0	189632.6	60525.8	113530.8
403904.6	1272871.5	15609.9	729171.8	2906835.6	1088187.4	42484.8	1247407.7
282433.8	750702.2		606638.4	2168685.7	728968.7	24297.9	961934.1
496507.6	4832685.8	10448.1	841114.8	4080030.6	1297902.9	202381.8	2374962.4
105318.6	419887.3		73024.5	369951.8	167712.7	23235.5	169646.5
27775.5	451665.6		65305.4	162575.8	81207.8	8086.6	44918.7
685.1	3443.0		500.0	2851.0	2176.0	615.7	1410.3
17671.9	80362.7	16004.0	18347.5	132367.8	92966.7	24594.1	40186.2
-929.2	46862.4	50.8	16578.2	93047.7	44338.1	9889.3	32846.6
4741.0	24492.4		11357.9	71398.3	55464.3	7184.3	17826.0
616.6	6016.1		1500.0	7078.0	6961.4	1786.4	220.1
1510960.7	4156606.4		1841320.7	11006900.9	1791331.3	0.3	10458326.9
1452803.3	3996600.1		1720285.2	10298848.1	1559390.5	0.3	9839964.7
22215.7	66752.3		67664.0	250033.2	113697.3	293.5	118063.7
19453.9	38326.8		208234.5	468617.9	104171.6		350807.6

13-15 续表

单位: 万元

行　业	Sector	流动负债合　计 Total Working Liabilities	长期负债合　计 Long-term Liabilities	所有者权益合计 Total Owners' Equities
煤炭开采和洗选业	Mining and Washing of Coal	954545.4	766134.9	1108695.6
石油和天然气开采业	Extraction of Petroleum and Natural Gas	4481787.9	4866093.2	13010940.7
#天然原油和天然气开采	Extraction of Ores Crude Oil and Natural Gas Extraction	3882919.4	4706015.1	12568473.1
黑色金属矿采选业	Mining and Processing of Ferrous Metals Ores	573593.6	129939.6	331570.6
有色金属矿采选业	Mining and Processing of Nonferrous Metals Ores	268033.8	118941.1	510483.3
非金属矿采选业	Mining and Processing of Nonmetal Ores	33849.1	3630.0	40378.8
#采　盐	Extraction of Salt	14379.2	3373.0	30027.5
农副食品加工业	Processing of Food from Agricultural Products	518567.1	82224.4	427988.1
#谷物磨制	Grain Grinding	20936.7	8340.6	23523.7
饲料加工	Fodder Processing	76635.3	34105.0	118011.8
制　糖	Sugar Making	138540.2	4325.5	165556.1
食品制造业	Manufacture of Food	671544.5	51845.4	186707.1
#罐头制造	Manufacture of can	569066.7	42015.3	74369.5
饮料制造业	Manufacture of Beverage	158728.8	3264.2	157501.0
#酒的制造	Manufacture of Wine	158063.7	3264.2	156927.4
烟草制品业	Manufacture of Tobacco	98051.0		273656.0
纺织业	Manufacture of Textile	231418.1	46210.5	176213.4
#棉、化纤纺织及印染精加工	Cotton, Chemical Fiber, Dyeing, Printing and Processing	197376.8	34049.2	143138.0
毛纺织和染整精加工	Wool Textile, Dyeing and Printing	9153.9	42.7	-194.6
纺织服装、鞋、帽制造业	Manufacture of Textile Wearing Apparel,Footware and Caps	18220.9	6592.7	7949.9
造纸及纸制品业	Manufacture of Paper and Paper Products	64613.8	6251.3	65989.8
印刷业和记录媒介的复制	Printing and Copying of Medium for Record	19569.1	5520.4	26258.3
石油加工、炼焦及核燃料加工业	Oil Processing, Coking and Nuclear Fuel Processing	2069804.3	646602.8	4617033.2
#炼　焦	Coking	144613.6	83107.8	44776.9
化学原料及化学制品制造业	Raw Chemical Material and Chemical Products	1275333.4	1757548.6	3020715.4
#基础化学原料制造	Basic Chemical Material	488681.9	542355.1	1026866.1
肥料制造	Fertilizer Making	265729.7	249916.9	430658.8
医药制造业	Manufacture of Medicine	54681.5	5212.2	70519.6
化学纤维制造业	Manufacture of Chemical Fiber	132764.6	59434.8	23432.5
橡胶制品业	Manufacture of Rubber Products	50274.0	33368.1	44504.0
塑料制品业	Manufacture of Plastic Products	136720.6	6146.9	133869.1
非金属矿物制品业	Manufacture of Nonmetal Mineral Products	935444.8	541587.4	1387600.9
#水泥制造	Manufacture of Cement	654362.1	437375.8	1035546.2
黑色金属冶炼及压延加工业	Smelting and Pressing of Ferrous Metals	2220840.2	620523.7	1238666.7
有色金属冶炼及压延加工业	Smelting and Pressing of Nonferrous Metals	195557.6	8407.9	165986.3
金属制品业	Manufacture of Metal Products	80321.1	6384.6	75870.0
通用设备制造业	Manufacture of General Purpose Machinery	2173.0		678.0
专用设备制造业	Manufacture of Special Purpose Machinery	70657.1	7448.0	54262.4
交通运输设备制造业	Manufacture of Transport Equipment	87422.7	533.2	5091.7
电气机械及器材制造业	Manufacture of Electric Equipment and Machinery	34784.8	24227.0	12386.4
仪器仪表及文化、办公用机械制造业	Manufacture of Measuring Instruments and Machinery for Cultural Activity and Office Work	5008.3		2069.7
电力、热力的生产和供应业	Electric Power and Thermal Production and Supply	3011069.1	3530315.8	3896744.2
#电力生产和电力供应	Electric Power Production and Supply	2796165.3	3205253.9	3756760.4
燃气生产和供应业	Gas Production and Supply	105732.7	67276.0	77024.5
水的生产和供应业	Water Production and Supply	105747.4	133279.0	220202.9

Continued

(10 000 yuan)

主营业务收入 Revenue from Principal Business	#主营业务成本 Cost of Principal Business	主营业务税金及附加 Taxes and Other Charges on Principal Business	营业利润 Business Profit	利润总额 Total Profit	亏损企业亏损总额 Losses Value of Loss-Suffering Enterprises	利税总额 Total Profits and Taxes	本年应交增值税 Value-added Taxes Payable	全部从业人员年平均人数（人） Ann Employed Persons (person)
993683.0	647209.6	29993.0	134815.6	132684.2	29084.0	267147.7	104470.5	37451
15656330.1	5897503.8	1316402.6	6733759.4	6856655.9	67623.8	9640396.4	1467337.9	92933
14724881.3	4921246.4	1309986.0	6824921.4	6923929.7		9654477.0	1420561.3	21938
603518.9	354151.6	11774.6	174049.5	174859.3		233162.8	46528.9	4457
393735.6	138742.7	5719.9	202201.9	204148.5	2994.3	250608.0	40739.6	5569
52760.3	21484.8	3151.4	7512.2	8164.2		16727.7	5412.1	2340
34452.9	10919.2	2818.2	5732.7	5793.7		12840.7	4228.8	1283
781942.3	633493.8	2637.6	56917.8	59695.9	13878.7	90479.0	28145.5	10994
72535.9	64842.6	124.3	3981.9	4556.5	573.6	5783.9	1103.1	832
150781.9	114773.6	316.6	16019.7	16808.8		19526.5	2401.1	1071
281242.8	206137.9	2039.5	41462.9	41964.0		67329.0	23325.5	5548
420246.4	344599.8	2163.1	-11610.1	-9338.9	47390.8	2543.8	9719.6	7774
206148.1	180553.4	911.7	-44381.0	-43646.2	47059.3	-42097.7	636.8	4236
200365.7	109428.3	23744.5	30632.0	33722.2	3135.0	74364.7	16898.0	4338
197883.6	107769.5	23727.6	30558.9	33621.2	3135.0	74103.2	16754.4	4232
302058.0	106288.0	134892.0	40736.0	40648.0		210392.0	34852.0	885
312481.1	291047.4	779.5	-15863.1	-17168.8	19257.8	-3851.2	12538.1	10593
283230.8	265899.4	611.1	-13024.5	-16629.4	18526.6	-4205.4	11812.9	8908
5445.9	4512.3		176.8	179.8		458.8	279.0	230
48266.3	44482.5	7.2	580.0	1109.6		1255.7	138.9	1671
66215.9	55554.1	364.7	4994.1	7805.5		11120.2	2950.0	2570
25778.0	21523.0	85.0	-227.9	1462.8	71.6	2157.6	609.8	1115
14358714.3	13002503.5	1617635.6	-866406.3	-892873.7	987433.0	938184.7	213422.8	30368
103570.0	77304.8	5770.9	4915.8	4880.5	65.5	15664.6	5013.2	2537
2859542.0	2086579.2	36413.6	501360.1	548297.5	11344.6	729508.7	144797.6	33464
738983.8	650840.2	2958.8	35368.8	33644.3	10049.5	55821.4	19218.3	11068
495452.0	212746.9	18680.7	182109.2	218907.0		269310.5	31722.8	4637
56874.8	38398.4	355.3	4943.1	5575.8		7902.1	1971.0	1896
166778.0	146549.1	672.2	-13225.7	-12803.7	14621.6	-3336.5	8795.0	1756
93293.4	80818.6	1397.0	128.7	419.8	1084.7	5495.2	3678.4	1652
208188.9	184821.7	404.0	6523.3	7618.2	2253.8	14085.6	6063.4	4076
1316072.0	1023382.7	6908.8	189143.8	212886.1	5009.9	283898.9	64104.0	20932
745381.3	536571.2	5164.3	143625.9	163308.3	4825.2	212710.6	44238.0	14359
4911729.8	4566140.5	13149.5	83602.5	82202.0	1622.6	176853.3	81501.8	14821
394258.5	340815.6	341.5	31546.5	33363.8	5277.3	35815.3	2110.0	4457
426340.6	410951.6	554.9	9881.9	9952.5	32.3	13461.4	2954.0	1646
3527.0	2919.0	71.0	95.0	84.0		195.0	40.0	84
92862.9	76233.1	141.1	5602.6	6637.0		7358.1	580.0	2374
67322.9	67457.7	89.4	-9825.9	-9164.0	9164.0	-8620.3	454.3	1203
24358.7	20069.4	62.6	-1016.7	573.8		1100.6	464.2	756
6016.1	5000.7	18.0	66.4	78.2		196.4	100.2	50
4134604.3	3581480.4	13588.5	348315.6	379885.0	80639.5	564603.6	171130.1	44551
3973004.0	3434248.3	13257.7	354646.4	376995.5	75066.3	558192.0	167938.8	40734
91929.8	63307.5	1216.3	3603.5	4042.6		7067.4	1808.5	993
45575.9	36236.0	334.5	-11250.9	-7930.7	9761.8	-5397.7	2198.5	1866

13-16 各地、州、市、县(市)国有控股工业企业主要经济指标

单位: 万元 (2011 年)

地 区	Region	企业单位数(个) Number of Enterprises (unit)	#亏损企业 Loss- Suffering Enterprises	工业总产值(当年价格) Gross Industrial Output Value (At Current Prices)
总 计	**Total**	**459**	**89**	**48665888.6**
乌鲁木齐市	**Urumqi City**	**110**	**17**	**15749851.5**
天山区	Tianshan District	13	2	2001777.4
沙依巴克区	Shayibak District	16	2	444033.3
新市区	Xinshi District	42	6	3473487.9
水磨沟区	Shui Mogou District	6	1	285861.4
头屯河区	Tou Tunhe District	13	3	5063928.2
达坂城区	Da Bancheng District	4		171667.6
米东区	Midong District	14	3	4278942.1
乌鲁木齐县	Urumqi County	2		30153.6
克拉玛依市	**Karamay City**	**13**	**5**	**15580611.5**
独山子区	Dushanzi District	6	3	5728849.6
克拉玛依区	Karamay District	7	2	9851761.9
白碱滩区	Bai Jiantan District			
乌尔河区	Urhe District			
吐鲁番地区	**Turpan Administrative Offices**	**15**	**1**	**1149995.7**
吐鲁番市	Turpan City	4	1	50734.5
鄯善县	Shanshan [Piqan] County	4		972472.9
托克逊县	Toksun County	7		126788.3
哈密地区	**Hami [Kumul] Administrative Offices**	**34**	**1**	**950204.2**
哈密市	Hami [Kumul] City	28	1	848820.2
巴里坤哈萨克自治县	Barkol Kazak Autonomous County	5		87394.1
伊吾县	Yiwu [Araturuk] County	1		13989.9
昌吉回族自治州	**Changji Hui Autonomous Prefecture**	**19**	**6**	**493115.4**
昌吉市	Changji City	5		67604.6
阜康市	Fukang City	4	2	312301.1
呼图壁县	Hutubi County	2		39261.4
玛纳斯县	Manas County	4	2	28082.5
奇台县	Qitai County	1		23005.9
吉木萨尔县	Jimsar County	3	2	22859.9
木垒哈萨克自治县	Mori Kazak Autonomous County			
伊犁哈萨克自治州	**Ili Kazak Autonomous Prefecture**	**111**	**22**	**3283154.8**
伊犁州直属县(市)	**Counties (Cities) Direct Under Ili Prefecture**	**53**	**12**	**1676935.6**
伊宁市	Yining [Gulja] City	6	2	223377.3
奎屯市	Kuytun City	16	6	626270.6
伊宁县	Yining [Gulja] County	8	1	207860.4
察布查尔锡伯自治县	Qapqal Xibe Autonomous County	4		24175.3
霍城县	Huocheng [Korgas] County	6	1	97310.0
巩留县	Gongliu [Tokkuztara] County	1	1	27668.3
新源县	Xinyuan [Kunes] County	7	1	367475.7
昭苏县	Zhaosu [Mongolkure] County	2		11778.0
特克斯县	Tekes County			
尼勒克县	Nilka County	3		91020.0
塔城地区	**Tacheng [Tarbagatai] Administrative Offices**	**31**	**7**	**932043.0**
塔城市	Tacheng [Qoqek] City	3	2	69618.1
乌苏市	Usu City	7	1	469970.2
额敏县	Emin [Dorbiljin] County	5	1	66937.8

Main Economic Indicators of State-holding Industrial Enterprises by Prefecture, Autonomous Prefecture, City and County

(10 000 yuan)

工业增加值 Value-added	工业销售产值(当年价) Sales Value of Industry Products (At Current Prices)	出口交货值 Delivery Value of Industry Export	实收资本 Total Capital Hold	资产合计 Total Assets	流动资产合计 Total Working Capitals	#产成品 Finished Product	固定资产原价 Net Value of Fixed Assets
20918681.7	**48307739.5**	**384013.6**	**25679116.9**	**64283377.6**	**16723746.3**	**1668703.4**	**58772698.1**
4849574.2	**15696008.5**	**95181.2**	**6305777.4**	**20871212.4**	**5572774.0**	**490138.5**	**16637880.3**
566393.3	1988725.4	21371.5	391715.1	4070228.4	757646.8	46436.9	3758719.4
123555.5	455828.4	28231.4	416527.0	2589366.9	628202.4	14531.9	694560.5
2873135.0	3436948.4	27888.0	2340485.1	4874662.9	1106953.8	134974.4	5911791.0
93447.7	288199.2		64301.9	512347.5	166045.0	7047.2	489849.0
469310.0	5114166.2	15267.5	824245.4	4099025.4	1292675.7	185223.1	2341313.6
111380.3	166221.0		122163.9	406443.3	68914.5	5579.5	222199.4
586870.3	4216092.7	2422.8	2083572.8	4083536.8	1516713.4	96345.5	3016940.3
25482.3	29827.2		62766.2	235601.2	35622.4		202507.1
6757466.5	**15596119.1**	**15609.9**	**10556175.5**	**16235536.3**	**4088244.5**	**166160.5**	**17908286.5**
540101.2	5737813.8	15609.9	3132115.0	4715926.2	1363646.2	114138.7	4453037.8
6217365.3	9858305.3		7424060.5	11519610.1	2724598.3	52021.8	13455248.7
802961.9	**1128506.8**		**936663.3**	**2303656.6**	**368968.7**	**69616.4**	**3366734.4**
23880.3	47282.3		35296.8	154247.3	18938.8	597.5	134665.0
726975.3	959718.3		809152.8	1683210.7	262384.6	68244.2	2913886.9
52106.3	121506.2		92213.7	466198.6	87645.3	774.7	318182.5
429256.8	**919476.8**		**525176.0**	**1801817.2**	**719929.5**	**73427.8**	**978534.3**
367871.4	820167.1		502875.5	1603799.7	638491.0	65450.5	885088.6
51861.5	86907.7		22200.5	172566.3	59432.8	7237.2	88514.0
9524.0	12402.0		100.0	25451.2	22005.7	740.1	4931.7
121283.8	**487100.3**	**29002.9**	**135458.5**	**723981.9**	**259112.0**	**54839.6**	**397446.0**
21618.3	60347.6	4914.6	10662.2	57254.0	29534.0	7141.0	26187.3
68363.4	305071.6		112261.5	453447.0	168314.0	14442.3	207040.0
5945.1	39214.4		1030.0	16830.7	7381.2	1233.7	13097.8
9172.3	34602.3	15290.2	2754.8	84361.3	27652.7	14906.7	51783.3
9099.2	31064.5		1000.0	28625.0	8250.4	4969.5	25638.0
7085.6	16799.9	8798.1	7750.0	83463.9	17979.7	12146.4	73699.6
1735121.2	**3243151.2**	**53383.0**	**1196577.9**	**6100581.3**	**1798766.3**	**242300.6**	**3925371.9**
792322.8	**1680814.2**	**35435.3**	**871831.2**	**3708335.0**	**1165305.0**	**127069.1**	**2263876.0**
87484.4	221972.3		33448.1	306033.1	71561.2	2106.4	341917.9
304951.5	630035.8	35435.3	148723.1	1062660.7	476892.1	52482.9	600410.7
85521.5	218595.3		86787.6	374107.5	122706.6	8205.9	191873.6
6002.4	19798.2		27330.0	113800.0	30975.5	4383.5	8158.9
32372.6	105230.4		35527.8	139189.7	61118.4	24108.2	89532.9
21145.1	27668.3		291061.8	713417.4	84932.1		436915.8
190850.1	361925.0		152371.0	505903.3	264470.9	32854.0	226179.2
4134.6	13870.0		1100.0	7460.1	4764.7	1422.6	3675.7
59860.6	81718.9		95481.8	485763.2	47883.5	1505.6	365211.3
518900.0	**900001.9**	**17947.7**	**179412.0**	**1136048.5**	**314981.6**	**64247.8**	**856026.9**
22360.8	70443.4		9811.0	96309.0	9878.3	110.4	118764.4
342095.7	468974.1	12946.6	32476.0	516454.5	78183.3	16112.0	386833.4
24193.3	63375.9		56208.4	121953.4	48859.6	15854.0	105047.6

13-16 续表 1

单位: 万元

地　区	Region	企业单位数(个) Number of Enterprises (unit)	#亏损企业 Loss- Suffering Enterprises	工业总产值(当年价格) Gross Industrial Output Value (At Current Prices)
沙湾县	Shawan County	6	2	128907.7
托里县	Toli County	4	1	119898.6
裕民县	Yumin [Qagantokay] County			
和布克赛尔蒙古自治县	Hoboksar Mongol Autonomous County	6		76710.6
阿勒泰地区	**Altay Administrative Offices**	**27**	**3**	**674176.2**
阿勒泰市	Altay City	7	2	100390.2
布尔津县	Burqin County	6		55851.0
富蕴县	Fuyun [Koktokay] County	5	1	221241.6
福海县	Fuhai [Burultokay] County	4		16533.4
哈巴河县	Habahe [Kaba] County	4		275705.7
青河县	Qinghe [Qinggil] County			
吉木乃县	Jeminay County	1		4454.3
博尔塔拉蒙古自治州	**Bortala Mongol Autonomous Prefecture**	**13**	**5**	**154153.6**
博乐市	Bole [Bortala] City	12	5	149900.6
精河县	Jinghe [Jing] County	1		4253.0
温泉县	Wenquan [Araxang] County			
巴音郭楞蒙古自治州	**Bayangol Mongol Autonomous Prefecture**	**34**	**2**	**5672790.3**
库尔勒市	Korla City	20	1	5062540.9
轮台县	Luntai [Bugur] County			
尉犁县	Yuli [Lopnur] County			
若羌县	Ruoqiang [Qarkilik] County	3		413949.9
且末县	Qiemo [Qarqan] County			
焉耆回族自治县	Yanqi Hui Autonomous County	3		28988.5
和静县	Hejing County	5		142756.6
和硕县	Hoxud County	1		4981.3
博湖县	Bohu [Bagrax] County	2	1	19573.1
阿克苏地区	**Aksu Administrative Offices**	**37**	**5**	**2679356.1**
阿克苏市	Aksu City	10	1	369633.8
温宿县	Wensu [Onsu] County	9	1	45369.9
库车县	Kuqa County	9	1	2178236.9
沙雅县	Xayar County			
新和县	Xinhe [Toksu] County			
拜城县	Baicheng [Bay] County	6	2	71658.3
乌什县	Wushi [Uxturpan] County	2		9253.3

Continued

(10 000 yuan)

工业增加值 Value-added	工业销售产值(当年价) Sales Value of Industry Products (At Current Prices)	出口交货值 Delivery Value of Industry Export	实收资本 Total Capital Hold	资产合计 Total Assets	流动资产合计 Total Working Capitals	#产成品 Finished Product	固定资产原价 Net Value of Fixed Assets
21372.1	115375.4	5001.1	18289.0	109674.8	56356.9	18378.4	91638.4
65829.7	110732.7		32000.0	190886.6	84034.7	9516.2	85528.2
43048.4	71100.4		30627.6	100770.2	37668.8	4276.8	68214.9
423898.4	**662335.1**		**145334.7**	**1256197.8**	**318479.7**	**50983.7**	**805469.0**
34402.0	99918.9		20622.0	187532.4	38024.3	1197.5	184554.3
27441.0	55868.0		19580.7	233942.9	32050.5	381.5	215294.2
139870.7	206297.1		38152.0	493869.2	144668.3	46232.2	212243.3
7915.3	16505.2		17922.0	39413.0	19201.4	1025.9	37058.5
210935.7	279291.6		39480.0	262301.8	80265.7	2146.6	121397.6
3333.7	4454.3		9578.0	39138.5	4269.5		34921.1
58473.1	**152726.2**		**73909.8**	**445025.0**	**133404.4**	**37172.6**	**374704.7**
56193.4	148125.2		72983.8	437069.3	131494.4	36865.0	371836.4
2279.6	4601.0		926.0	7955.7	1910.0	307.6	2868.3
4781645.4	**5593093.3**	**39146.5**	**3869921.3**	**8242206.6**	**1526935.2**	**145869.6**	**9679528.2**
4415798.7	5067788.6	19854.5	3714429.5	7046783.5	1142884.5	67078.6	8875481.6
282130.3	339579.4		57899.9	701300.7	258765.0	33894.8	462650.4
14030.4	35774.0		14186.4	22726.4	8179.9	3719.3	23654.7
66779.9	124104.6		72869.1	429917.4	90885.5	21954.3	281612.3
1083.9	7337.6	5313.6	1450.0	7674.3	5323.4	3014.0	5282.6
1822.2	18509.1	13978.4	9086.4	33804.3	20896.9	16208.6	30846.6
625177.6	**2654293.0**	**6354.1**	**759118.3**	**2418214.1**	**567398.4**	**54056.4**	**1511944.9**
125317.6	334230.4	1666.4	264809.9	815622.0	153922.8	25434.2	486721.2
26455.3	42664.8		44121.5	234589.4	39879.0	828.8	115086.1
420413.2	2196820.7		433194.2	1198429.5	308426.0	15616.0	798350.4
48946.1	70435.9		11992.7	135221.9	45021.9	6743.2	95626.5
3197.2	6921.8	4687.7	4000.0	17239.9	9491.6	5434.2	9372.0

13-16 续表 2

单位：万元

地　　区	Region	企业单位数（个） Number of Enterprises (unit)	#亏损企业 Loss- Suffering Enterprises	工业总产值（当年价格） Gross Industrial Output Value (At Current Prices)
阿瓦提县	Awat County	1		5203.9
柯坪县	Kalpin County			
克孜勒苏柯尔克孜自治州	**Kizilsu Kirgiz Autonomous Prefecture**	**2**		**26236.4**
阿图什市	Artux City	2		26236.4
阿克陶县	Akto County			
阿合奇县	Akqi County			
乌恰县	Wuqia [Ulugqat] County			
喀什地区	**Kashgar [Kaxgar] Administrative Offices**	**8**	**3**	**248428.0**
喀什市	Kashgar [Kaxgar] City	7	2	244327.8
疏附县	Shufu County	1	1	4100.2
疏勒县	Shule County			
英吉沙县	Yengisar County			
泽普县	Zepu [Poskam] County			
莎车县	Shache [Yarkant] County			
叶城县	Yecheng [Kagilik] County			
麦盖提县	Makit County			
岳普湖县	Yopurga County			
伽师县	Jiashi [Payzawat] County			
巴楚县	Bachu [Maralbexi] County			
塔什库尔干塔吉克自治县	Taxkorgan Tajik Autonomous County			
和田地区	**Hotan Administrative Offices**	**7**	**3**	**89297.5**
和田市	Hotan City	3	1	56745.2
和田县	Hotan County	2	1	12871.3
墨玉县	Moyu [Karakax] County	1		18373.7
皮山县	Pishan [Guma] County	1	1	1307.3
洛浦县	Lop County			
策勒县	Qira County			
于田县	Yutian [Keriya] County			
民丰县	Minfeng [Niya] County			
自治区直辖县级市	**Municpality Country-LevelCity directly under the Central Government**	**56**	**19**	**2588693.6**
石河子市	Shihezi City	37	13	2170942.2
阿拉尔市	Aral City	6	3	171781.3
图木舒克市	Tumxuk City	6		66153.4
五家渠市	Wujiaqu City	7	3	179816.7

Continued

(10 000 yuan)

工业增加值 Value-added	工业销售产值(当年价) Sales Value of Industry Products (At Current Prices)	出口交货值 Delivery Value of Industry Export	实收资本 Total Capital Hold	资产合计 Total Assets	流动资产合计 Total Working Capitals	#产成品 Finished Product	固定资产原价 Net Value of Fixed Assets
848.3	3219.4		1000.0	17111.4	10657.1		6788.7
8933.5	**26062.9**		**37733.9**	**65591.9**	**29576.5**	**673.8**	**35646.4**
8933.5	26062.9		37733.9	65591.9	29576.5	673.8	35646.4
82799.2	**245966.2**		**28056.7**	**376142.7**	**55390.3**	**12047.7**	**529665.8**
82279.9	241877.0		27056.7	374781.7	54745.9	11769.0	528353.0
519.3	4089.2		1000.0	1361.0	644.4	278.7	1312.8
38066.7	**88033.6**	**406.1**	**154636.8**	**291112.3**	**35625.5**	**1371.1**	**331490.7**
18772.2	56745.2		10362.6	101429.0	11780.3		144127.3
11344.1	12412.3		128537.2	143938.7	10899.8	400.9	147657.1
7815.1	18470.0		15237.0	40384.9	11076.6	42.9	36251.8
135.5	406.1	406.1	500.0	5359.7	1868.8	927.3	3454.5
627921.7	**2477201.6**	**144929.9**	**1099911.5**	**4408299.3**	**1567621.0**	**321028.8**	**3095464.0**
561897.1	2098058.2	130285.1	827922.5	3436399.4	1192994.0	229816.1	2456046.4
13029.9	164997.3		84008.6	316067.1	78353.6	25842.2	258814.9
16411.7	63008.1		32879.2	182816.4	85791.7	25103.3	98372.5
36583.0	151138.0	14644.8	155101.2	473016.4	210481.7	40267.2	282230.2

13-16 续表 3

单位：万元

地　　区	Region	流动负债合计 Total Working Liabilities	长期负债合计 Long-term Liabilities	所有者权益合计 Total Owners' Equities
总　计	**Total**	**16723746.3**	**1668703.4**	**31388707.3**
乌鲁木齐市	**Urumqi City**	**5572774.0**	**490138.5**	**9780192.3**
天山区	Tianshan District	757646.8	46436.9	1682923.7
沙依巴克区	Shayibak District	628202.4	14531.9	1318961.8
新市区	Xinshi District	1106953.8	134974.4	2468889.9
水磨沟区	Shui Mogou District	166045.0	7047.2	348736.4
头屯河区	Tou Tunhe District	1292675.7	185223.1	1273618.2
达坂城区	Da Bancheng District	68914.5	5579.5	245931.5
米东区	Midong District	1516713.4	96345.5	2375514.4
乌鲁木齐县	Urumqi County	35622.4		65616.4
克拉玛依市	**Karamay City**	**4088244.5**	**166160.5**	**10109531.5**
独山子区	Dushanzi District	1363646.2	114138.7	3200614.7
克拉玛依区	Karamay District	2724598.3	52021.8	6908916.8
白碱滩区	Bai Jiantan District			
乌尔河区	Urhe District			
吐鲁番地区	**Turpan Administrative Offices**	**368968.7**	**69616.4**	**1014537.1**
吐鲁番市	Turpan City	18938.8	597.5	50406.4
鄯善县	Shanshan [Piqan] County	262384.6	68244.2	835558.3
托克逊县	Toksun County	87645.3	774.7	128572.4
哈密地区	**Hami [Kumul] Administrative Offices**	**719929.5**	**73427.8**	**687770.6**
哈密市	Hami [Kumul] City	638491.0	65450.5	625403.1
巴里坤哈萨克自治县	Barkol Kazak Autonomous County	59432.8	7237.2	59041.7
伊吾县	Yiwu [Araturuk] County	22005.7	740.1	3325.8
昌吉回族自治州	**Changji Hui Autonomous Prefecture**	**259112.0**	**54839.6**	**143603.4**
昌吉市	Changji City	29534.0	7141.0	30788.5
阜康市	Fukang City	168314.0	14442.3	81224.4
呼图壁县	Hutubi County	7381.2	1233.7	9014.0
玛纳斯县	Manas County	27652.7	14906.7	18567.2
奇台县	Qitai County	8250.4	4969.5	5085.8
吉木萨尔县	Jimsar County	17979.7	12146.4	-1076.5
木垒哈萨克自治县	Mori Kazak Autonomous County			
伊犁哈萨克自治州	**Ili Kazak Autonomous Prefecture**	**1798766.3**	**242300.6**	**2458242.2**
伊犁州直属县(市)	**Counties (Cities) Direct Under Ili Prefecture**	**1165305.0**	**127069.1**	**1447229.2**
伊宁市	Yining [Gulja] City	71561.2	2106.4	124158.9
奎屯市	Kuytun City	476892.1	52482.9	448699.4
伊宁县	Yining [Gulja] County	122706.6	8205.9	166132.2
察布查尔锡伯自治县	Qapqal Xibe Autonomous County	30975.5	4383.5	27629.6
霍城县	Huocheng [Korgas] County	61118.4	24108.2	67496.4
巩留县	Gongliu [Tokkuztara] County	84932.1		253398.2
新源县	Xinyuan [Kunes] County	264470.9	32854.0	241486.1
昭苏县	Zhaosu [Mongolkure] County	4764.7	1422.6	1932.8
特克斯县	Tekes County			
尼勒克县	Nilka County	47883.5	1505.6	116295.6
塔城地区	**Tacheng [Tarbagatai] Administrative Offices**	**314981.6**	**64247.8**	**461107.8**
塔城市	Tacheng [Qoqek] City	9878.3	110.4	29807.2
乌苏市	Usu City	78183.3	16112.0	162954.3
额敏县	Emin [Dorbiljin] County	48859.6	15854.0	75681.5

Continued

(10 000 yuan)

主营业务收入 Revenue from Principal Business	#主营业务成本 Cost of Principal Business	主营业务税金及附加 Taxes and Other Charges on Principal Business	营业利润 Business Profit	利润总额 Total Profit	亏损企业亏损总额 Losses Value of Loss-Suffering Enterprises	利税总额 Total Profits and Taxes	本年应交增值税 Value-added Taxes Payable	全部从业人员年平均人数(人) Annual Average Employed Persons (person)
58772698.1	**18668510.6**	**13548143.7**	**31388707.3**	**49136691.5**	**34406033.0**	**3225271.7**	**7654407.9**	**349653**
16637880.3	**7443271.5**	**3623028.6**	**9780192.3**	**15985301.0**	**12519006.6**	**1082576.9**	**1296037.5**	**88286**
3758719.4	1336743.2	1048873.5	1682923.7	1960433.1	1769132.9	3049.9	137186.6	14199
694560.5	552468.0	717936.8	1318961.8	481557.3	369867.0	4800.8	56208.5	8583
5911791.0	2015699.9	367280.6	2468889.9	3465480.7	1200764.2	612749.8	1224103.9	19247
489849.0	129340.1	34270.8	348736.4	292313.7	239696.1	1529.5	23593.4	3500
2341313.6	2201705.0	623463.7	1273618.2	5220847.5	4851454.1	13829.1	101748.6	15499
222199.4	133721.1	26790.5	245931.5	167221.1	106378.0	2120.3	35521.6	6440
3016940.3	984129.7	723892.5	2375514.4	4368666.1	3969717.3	444497.5	-293709.3	20751
202507.1	89464.5	80520.2	65616.4	28781.5	11997.0		11384.2	67
17908286.5	**3318196.1**	**2807508.5**	**10109531.5**	**16453201.6**	**11907795.8**	**1291548.5**	**2266414.6**	**92634**
4453037.8	1108545.8	406765.5	3200614.7	5804773.8	5441861.9	544124.8	-501289.6	17690
13455248.7	2209650.3	2400743.0	6908916.8	10648427.8	6465933.9	747423.7	2767704.2	74944
3366734.4	**479289.4**	**780603.0**	**1014537.1**	**1199522.0**	**568226.1**	**57824.2**	**392399.3**	**9274**
134665.0	60276.9	43563.9	50406.4	50141.3	35535.6	426.6	7910.8	1175
2913886.9	323559.1	524093.3	835558.3	1022871.8	440453.0	55748.1	368777.1	5746
318182.5	95453.4	212945.8	128572.4	126508.9	92237.5	1649.5	15711.4	2353
978534.3	**661421.8**	**447535.3**	**687770.6**	**928489.9**	**670104.7**	**15716.8**	**137565.3**	**20511**
885088.6	575426.7	400458.0	625403.1	835993.9	628964.2	11922.2	103093.7	18948
88514.0	63869.7	47077.3	59041.7	80094.0	36998.2	3452.9	29324.1	1364
4931.7	22125.4		3325.8	12402.0	4142.3	341.7	5147.5	199
397446.0	**436946.1**	**143432.4**	**143603.4**	**495872.4**	**438270.4**	**1796.3**	**12112.0**	**8403**
26187.3	21387.4	5078.1	30788.5	77576.3	64521.4	113.0	6483.7	1875
207040.0	260550.0	111672.5	81224.4	305071.6	279501.7	824.2	6363.9	4067
13097.8	7639.9	176.8	9014.0	39250.8	33524.4	22.7	2893.4	246
51783.3	39310.5	26483.7	18567.2	27268.9	20751.5	376.2	-226.3	813
25638.0	23539.2		5085.8	26126.1	19306.7	225.1	3747.8	383
73699.6	84519.1	21.3	-1076.5	20578.7	20664.7	235.1	-7150.5	1019
3925371.9	**2077839.1**	**1078309.7**	**2458242.2**	**3183985.7**	**2130025.5**	**173288.8**	**474307.9**	**43148**
2263876.0	**1071074.0**	**742101.8**	**1447229.2**	**1635503.6**	**1113431.9**	**159562.6**	**182955.2**	**22994**
341917.9	86366.0	81580.8	124158.9	220385.7	173400.7	1246.5	26374.6	3753
600410.7	358937.7	255027.4	448699.4	630870.8	403239.9	136393.3	34046.0	5429
191873.6	127095.1	76829.9	166132.2	216721.7	148458.8	1251.1	38817.6	4067
8158.9	46839.0		27629.6	20499.3	16294.0	273.2	3132.8	547
89532.9	38598.3	33094.9	67496.4	108050.0	86956.6	318.7	11944.9	1925
436915.8	69394.6		253398.2	28156.0	10786.8	167.4	-1134.9	285
226179.2	243974.5	20442.7	241486.1	315940.2	223141.5	18353.9	40628.1	6108
3675.7	5527.3		1932.8	13870.0	9994.8	30.4	3301.6	170
365211.3	94341.5	275126.1	116295.6	81009.9	41158.8	1528.1	25844.5	710
856026.9	**555752.2**	**116928.8**	**461107.8**	**885402.6**	**679111.4**	**4907.6**	**46894.0**	**12585**
118764.4	49169.8	15589.0	29807.2	67178.5	70421.1	135.4	-4527.6	1152
386833.4	311249.8	42250.2	162954.3	488709.1	365700.6	1131.6	10969.8	3680
105047.6	43698.3	2573.5	75681.5	61854.9	48368.1	192.1	10358.4	1175

13-16 续表 4

单位: 万元

地　　区	Region	流动负债合计 Total Working Liabilities	长期负债合计 Long-term Liabilities	所有者权益合计 Total Owners' Equities
沙湾县	Shawan County	51779.3	16944.1	40951.3
托里县	Toli County	67642.1	21896.3	100842.1
裕民县	Yumin [Qagantokay] County			
和布克赛尔蒙古自治县	Hoboksar Mongol Autonomous County	32212.9	17675.7	50871.4
阿勒泰地区	**Altay Administrative Offices**	**451012.9**	**219279.1**	**549905.2**
阿勒泰市	Altay City	58295.0	86408.1	42829.2
布尔津县	Burqin County	126805.4	55155.1	29982.3
富蕴县	Fuyun [Koktokay] County	209285.7	54131.3	230452.2
福海县	Fuhai [Burultokay] County	8585.0		16827.6
哈巴河县	Habahe [Kaba] County	40969.1	3084.6	218248.1
青河县	Qinghe [Qinggil] County			
吉木乃县	Jeminay County	7072.7	20500.0	11565.8
博尔塔拉蒙古自治州	**Bortala Mongol Autonomous Prefecture**	**162521.6**	**177615.1**	**102875.3**
博乐市	Bole [Bortala] City	161100.8	175471.9	98483.6
精河县	Jinghe [Jing] County	1420.8	2143.2	4391.7
温泉县	Wenquan [Araxang] County			
巴音郭楞蒙古自治州	**Bayangol Mongol Autonomous Prefecture**	**1630922.3**	**2299992.8**	**4296676.5**
库尔勒市	Korla City	1234555.9	1919973.6	3877698.9
轮台县	Luntai [Bugur] County			
尉犁县	Yuli [Lopnur] County			
若羌县	Ruoqiang [Qarkilik] County	205440.4	229339.1	266461.2
且末县	Qiemo [Qarqan] County			
焉耆回族自治县	Yanqi Hui Autonomous County	8090.0	200.8	14435.7
和静县	Hejing County	155344.8	150232.8	124339.8
和硕县	Hoxud County	4318.7		3355.6
博湖县	Bohu [Bagrax] County	23172.5	246.5	10385.3
阿克苏地区	**Aksu Administrative Offices**	**824767.9**	**482681.4**	**1009764.4**
阿克苏市	Aksu City	225720.0	246453.0	342866.8
温宿县	Wensu [Onsu] County	93956.2	93881.7	46751.4
库车县	Kuqa County	443224.0	87964.1	573093.2
沙雅县	Xayar County			
新和县	Xinhe [Toksu] County			
拜城县	Baicheng [Bay] County	41915.1	53982.6	38248.0
乌什县	Wushi [Uxturpan] County	8125.4	400.0	8714.5

Continued

(10 000 yuan)

主营业务收入 Revenue from Principal Business	#主营业务成本 Cost of Principal Business	主营业务税金及附加 Taxes and Other Charges on Principal Business	营业利润 Business Profit	利润总额 Total Profit	亏损企业亏损总额 Losses Value of Loss-Suffering Enterprises	利税总额 Total Profits and Taxes	本年应交增值税 Value-added Taxes Payable	全部从业人员年平均人数(人) Annual Average Employed Persons (person)
116871.2	100884.2	349.9	7049.3	8721.5	2179.3	12153.6	3082.2	1563
86378.3	60057.9	449.3	10358.2	10962.2	8496.1	12378.1	966.6	2824
64410.6	33679.5	2649.3	12685.9	13912.2		23349.7	6788.2	2191
663079.5	**337482.2**	**8818.6**	**244458.7**	**247966.8**	**3441.8**	**314048.1**	**57262.7**	**7569**
99480.9	90901.5	557.3	2777.7	2850.3	447.5	6304.9	2897.3	1896
55928.3	31811.3	279.0	10644.7	12197.0		16050.1	3574.1	548
207285.8	103010.6	3711.5	69141.0	70559.5	2994.3	94724.5	20453.5	3149
16638.6	11663.1	268.0	3779.7	3787.9		5143.6	1087.7	313
279291.6	98420.1	4001.9	156133.3	156584.3		189836.3	29250.1	1647
4454.3	1675.6	0.9	1982.3	1987.8		1988.7		16
179769.8	**153931.9**	**753.6**	**4671.0**	**5912.1**	**4696.7**	**14823.1**	**8157.4**	**4098**
175725.2	151311.4	656.1	4064.7	5297.6	4696.7	13778.8	7825.1	3878
4044.6	2620.5	97.5	606.3	614.5		1044.3	332.3	220
5558794.2	**1755291.0**	**329577.6**	**2779836.4**	**2811107.9**	**1593.8**	**3641896.1**	**501210.6**	**26567**
5039819.5	1534618.4	308698.5	2588313.2	2585429.2	267.8	3353479.4	459351.7	20885
332792.4	98269.5	18695.6	152190.0	185670.2		235620.5	31254.7	3018
35128.2	25399.4	308.4	6650.2	6665.0		10930.2	3956.8	581
125207.4	76491.8	1755.5	33448.0	34164.6		42281.5	6361.4	1754
7337.6	5601.0	28.1	304.2	304.0		522.6	190.5	73
18509.1	14910.9	91.5	-1069.2	-1125.1	1326.0	-938.1	95.5	256
2674158.8	**2234334.9**	**248378.8**	**88426.2**	**92757.3**	**74289.2**	**430874.5**	**89738.4**	**15182**
334799.5	279286.1	2155.6	37027.3	39966.9	5315.4	59352.6	17230.1	6506
42427.4	25699.8	504.8	7795.0	7714.6	152.9	11050.7	2831.3	1437
2211693.7	1884683.8	243311.1	20416.8	21939.6	66382.2	326706.6	61455.9	4753
75097.8	37602.5	1738.7	22175.7	22127.3	2438.7	31859.8	7993.8	2162
6921.0	4112.9	646.6	920.9	918.4		1788.7	223.7	196

13-16 续表 5

单位: 万元

地　　区	Region	流动负债合　计 Total Working Liabilities	长期负债合　计 Long-term Liabilities	所有者权益合计 Total Owners' Equities
阿瓦提县	Awat County	11827.2		90.5
柯坪县	Kalpin County			
克孜勒苏柯尔克孜自治州	**Kizilsu Kirgiz Autonomous Prefecture**	**22887.2**	**1103.5**	**41556.1**
阿图什市	Artux City	22887.2	1103.5	41556.1
阿克陶县	Akto County			
阿合奇县	Akqi County			
乌恰县	Wuqia [Ulugqat] County			
喀什地区	**Kashgar [Kaxgar] Administrative Offices**	**105022.7**	**247239.4**	**23860.4**
喀什市	Kashgar [Kaxgar] City	103430.3	247239.4	24091.8
疏附县	Shufu County	1592.4		-231.4
疏勒县	Shule County			
英吉沙县	Yengisar County			
泽普县	Zepu [Poskam] County			
莎车县	Shache [Yarkant] County			
叶城县	Yecheng [Kagilik] County			
麦盖提县	Makit County			
岳普湖县	Yopurga County			
伽师县	Jiashi [Payzawat] County			
巴楚县	Bachu [Maralbexi] County			
塔什库尔干塔吉克自治县	Taxkorgan Tajik Autonomous County			
和田地区	**Hotan Administrative Offices**	**54564.8**	**72564.1**	**163983.3**
和田市	Hotan City	38882.2	67030.1	-4483.3
和田县	Hotan County	6968.5	5250.4	131719.8
墨玉县	Moyu [Karakax] County	3600.6	283.6	36500.7
皮山县	Pishan [Guma] County	5113.5		246.1
洛浦县	Lop County			
策勒县	Qira County			
于田县	Yutian [Keriya] County			
民丰县	Minfeng [Niya] County			
自治区直辖县级市	**Municpality Country-LevelCity directly under the Central Government**	**1450860.1**	**1386529.9**	**1556114.2**
石河子市	Shihezi City	1001580.4	1072887.8	1353449.1
阿拉尔市	Aral City	175342.5	108903.8	31469.7
图木舒克市	Tumxuk City	60194.7	86733.7	35888.0
五家渠市	Wujiaqu City	213742.5	118004.6	135307.4

Continued

(10 000 yuan)

主营业务收　入 Revenue from Principal Business	#主营业务成　本 Cost of Principal Business	主营业务税金及附加 Taxes and Other Charges on Principal Business	营业利润 Business Profit	利润总额 Total Profit	亏损企业亏损总额 Losses Value of Loss-Suffering Enterprises	利税总额 Total Profits and Taxes	本年应交增值税 Value-added Taxes Payable	全部从业人员年平均人数(人) Annual Average Employed Persons (person)
3219.4	2949.8	22.0	90.5	90.5		116.1	3.6	128
25375.7	**19601.8**	**60.0**	**3575.1**	**3557.7**		**3806.2**	**188.5**	**365**
25375.7	19601.8	60.0	3575.1	3557.7		3806.2	188.5	365
239268.6	**247696.2**	**1276.8**	**-20113.3**	**-23157.6**	**29598.0**	**-10003.6**	**11877.2**	**5323**
235878.8	244273.1	1262.9	-19968.9	-23012.8	29453.2	-10012.4	11737.5	5159
3389.8	3423.1	13.9	-144.4	-144.8	144.8	8.8	139.7	164
88327.6	**86930.1**	**250.6**	**-13014.1**	**-12268.6**	**18156.3**	**-5067.3**	**6950.7**	**1827**
56710.7	61104.8	187.6	-13608.3	-13558.4	14447.2	-10296.6	3074.2	1213
13227.9	11696.2	24.0	-1680.8	-2443.8	3499.0	2.3	2422.1	363
17999.2	13956.6	39.0	2481.3	3943.7		5437.1	1454.4	212
389.8	172.5		-206.3	-210.1	210.1	-210.1		39
2124624.2	**1674818.0**	**22222.8**	**232190.0**	**255363.0**	**42749.3**	**369457.9**	**91872.1**	**34035**
1735895.1	1339724.5	16034.0	247122.3	269051.6	19186.7	362854.0	77768.4	27754
167681.2	154747.3	589.2	-20494.0	-20450.4	21040.1	-11782.4	8078.8	2070
58787.4	49473.4	45.2	3726.1	3701.7		4978.4	1231.5	941
162260.5	130872.8	5554.4	1835.6	3060.1	2522.5	13407.9	4793.4	3270

13-17 国有控股工业企业主要经济效益指标

单位: % (2011 年)

项 目	Item	产 值 利税率 Ratio of Profits and Taxes to Industrial Output Value
总 计	**Total**	**27.9**
按登记注册类型分	**By Status of Registration**	
内资企业	Domestic Funded Enterprises	27.9
国有企业	State-owned Enterprises	15.7
#中央企业	Central Enterprises	17.8
地方企业	Local Enterprises	7.4
#自治区属企业	Autonomous	5.4
地区(州、市)属企业	Prefecture or City	1.4
县(市)属企业	County or City	19.8
股份合作企业	Share-holding Cooperative Enterprises	5.6
联营企业	Joint Ownership Enterprises	22.5
#国有联营企业	State Joint Enterprises Ownership	19.5
集体联营企业	Collective Joint Ownership Enterprises	
国有与集体联营企业	Joint State-collectiue Enterprises	34.8
其他联营企业	Other Joint Ownership Enterprises	
有限责任公司	Limited Liability Corporations	15.7
#国有独资公司	Sole State-funded Corporations	18.9
其他有限责任公司	Other Limited Liability Corporations	14.4
股份有限公司	Share-holding Corporations Ltd.	35.4
港、澳、台商投资企业	Enterprises with Funds from Hongkong,Macao and Taiwan	44.2
外商投资企业	Foreign Funded Enterprises	29.4
国有控股企业	Of the Total : State-owned and State-holding Enterprises	27.9
农村工业	Village Industry	
按轻、重工业分(GB/T4754-2011)	**Grouped by Light & Heavy Industry(GB/T4754-2011)**	
轻工业	Light Industry	16.0
以农产品为原料	Using Farm Produces as Raw Materials	16.5
以非农产品为原料	Using Non-Farm Produces as Raw Materials	3.5
重工业	Heavy Industry	28.5
采掘工业	Mining and Quarrying	60.9
原料工业	Raw Materials Industry	8.7
加工工业	Manufacturing Industry	19.4
按轻、重工业分(GB/T4754-2002)	**Grouped by Light & Heavy Industry(GB/T4754-2002)**	
轻工业	Light Industry	16.0
以农产品为原料	Using Farm Produces as Raw Materials	16.5
以非农产品为原料	Using Non-Farm Produces as Raw Materials	3.0
重工业	Heavy Industry	28.5
采掘工业	Mining and Quarrying	60.9
原料工业	Raw Materials Industry	8.7
加工工业	Manufacturing Industry	19.7
按企业规模分(新标准)	**Grouped by Size of Enterprises (New Standard) (Old Standard)**	
大型企业	Large Enterprises	30.5
中型企业	Medium-sized Enterprises	18.9
小型企业	Small Enterprises	17.7
微型企业	Mini Enterprises	4.0
按企业规模分(旧标准)	**Grouped by Size of Enterprises (Old Standard)**	
大型企业	Large Enterprises	31.5
中型企业	Medium-sized Enterprises	17.7
小型企业	Small Enterprises	16.5

Main Indicators on Economic Efficiency of State-holding Industrial Enterprises

(%)

总资产贡献率 Ratio of Total Assets to Industrial Output Value	资本保值增值率 Ratio of Capital-hold and Rise	资产负债率 Assets Liability Ratio	流动资产周转次数(次/年) Number of Times of Annual TurnoverWorking Capitals (times/year)	成本费用利润率 Ratio of Profits to Industrial Cost	全员劳动生产率 Overall Labour Productivity
22.2	**109.0**	**51.1**	**2.9**	**20.8**	**59.8**
22.3	108.9	51.2	2.9	20.8	59.9
9.7	153.7	61.6	2.2	9.3	32.6
11.7	186.8	57.9	2.5	11.0	36.6
4.5	91.6	71.3	1.5	3.2	20.9
3.4	89.1	63.5	2.3	0.5	21.8
2.0	151.9	88.9	0.6	0.1	17.3
8.7	105.8	79.7	1.4	14.1	19.6
4.4	42.3	84.3	0.9	4.2	10.2
11.0	102.4	76.3	1.1	16.6	19.2
8.4	92.3	78.1	1.0	10.6	16.8
49.3	342.1	50.1	4.1	50.0	41.8
12.3	125.6	61.8	2.1	10.4	28.1
16.0	104.1	57.7	2.6	7.6	28.7
11.0	136.3	63.2	2.0	11.6	27.8
31.8	98.3	41.9	3.7	28.4	107.6
11.3		7.8	0.9	78.1	130.2
8.2	97.7	56.9	1.0	21.8	39.7
22.2	109.0	51.1	2.9	20.8	59.8
10.9	107.0	60.6	1.2	4.9	16.2
12.5	105.9	61.9	1.2	5.2	16.9
1.2	113.0	52.2	0.6	-1.8	9.4
23.0	109.1	50.5	3.2	21.8	66.5
38.8	99.5	44.9	3.2	87.4	103.3
9.3	119.9	55.0	3.5	0.3	35.2
15.7	133.5	56.2	1.5	17.1	26.2
10.9	107.0	60.6	1.2	4.9	16.2
12.5	105.6	61.9	1.2	5.2	16.9
1.1	114.7	52.1	0.6	-2.3	9.3
23.0	109.1	50.5	3.2	21.8	66.5
38.8	99.5	44.9	3.2	87.4	103.3
9.3	119.7	55.0	3.5	0.3	35.3
15.8	135.9	56.3	1.5	17.3	25.5
25.2	108.7	47.8	3.4	24.1	77.5
15.3	108.9	61.6	2.3	9.2	27.5
10.0	107.7	60.3	1.5	13.7	25.6
6.1	345.5	66.6	2.7	4.1	169.0
27.8	106.5	46.3	3.8	25.0	85.4
12.6	109.3	60.1	1.9	9.3	25.8
8.9	131.8	61.5	1.5	13.2	29.2

13-18 分行业国有控股工业企业主要经济效益指标(GB/T4754-2011)

单位: % (2011 年)

行 业	Sector	产值利税率 Ratio of Profits and Taxes to Industrial Output Value
总 计	**Total**	**27.9**
煤炭开采和洗选业	Mining and Washing of Coal	29.4
石油和天然气开采业	Extraction of Petroleum and Natural Gas	68.7
黑色金属矿采选业	Mining and Processing of Ferrous Metals Ores	37.9
有色金属矿采选业	Mining and Processing of Nonferrous Metals Ores	59.7
非金属矿采选业	Mining and Processing of Nonmetal Ores	22.6
#采 盐	Extraction of Salt	31.7
农副食品加工业	Processing of Food from Agricultural Products	12.3
#谷物磨制	Grain Grinding	8.2
饲料加工	Fodder Processing	13.2
制 糖	Sugar Making	25.8
食品制造业	Manufacture of Food	0.4
#罐头制造	Manufacture of can	-16.4
酒、饮料和精制茶制造业	Manufacture of Wine,Beverages and Refined Tea	35.6
#酒的制造	Manufacture of Wine	36.0
烟草制品业	Manufacture of Tobacco	69.5
纺织业	Manufacture of Textile	-0.9
#棉、化纤纺织及印染精加工	Cotton, Chemical Fiber, Dyeing, Printing and Processing	-1.4
毛纺织和染整精加工	Wool Textile, Dyeing and Printing	8.6
纺织服装、鞋、帽制造业	Manufacture of Textile Wearing Apparel, Footware and Caps	-0.1
造纸及纸制品业	Manufacture of Paper and Paper Products	15.5
印刷业和记录媒介的复制	Printing and Copying of Medium for Record	8.9
石油加工、炼焦及核燃料加工业	Oil Processing, Coking and Nuclear Fuel Processing	6.7
#炼 焦	Coking	16.3
化学原料及化学制品制造业	Raw Chemical Material and Chemical Products	21.5
#基础化学原料制造	Basic Chemical Material	11.0
肥料制造	Fertilizer Making	46.9
合成材料制造	Manufacture of Synthetic Material	16.7
医药制造业	Manufacture of Medicine	11.6
化学纤维制造业	Manufacture of Chemical Fiber	-2.0
橡胶制品业	Manufacture of Rubber Products	5.9
非金属矿物制品业	Manufacture of Nonmetal Mineral Products	22.4
#水泥制造	Manufacture of Cement	28.2
黑色金属冶炼及压延加工业	Smelting and Pressing of Ferrous Metals	3.7
有色金属冶炼及压延加工业	Smelting and Pressing of Nonferrous Metals	8.7
金属制品业	Manufacture of Metal Products	3.5
通用设备制造业	Manufacture of General Purpose Machinery	6.0
专用设备制造业	Manufacture of Special Purpose Machinery	8.4
汽车制造业	Manufacture of Automobile	-17.1
电气机械和器材制造业	Manufacture of Electric Equipment and Machinery	3.9
仪器仪表制造业	Manufacture of Measuring Instruments and Machinery	3.3
电力、热力的生产和供应业	Electricity and Thermal Production and Supply	13.5
#电力生产和电力供应	Electricity Production and Supply	13.9
燃气生产和供应业	Gas Production and Supply	8.0
水的生产和供应业	Water Production and Supply	-14.1

Main Indicators on Economic Efficiency of State-holding Industrial Enterprises by Sectors(GB/T4754-2011)

(%)

总资产贡献率 Ratio of Total Assets to Industrial Output Value	资本保值增值率 Ratio of Capital-hold and Rise	资产负债率 Assets Liability Ratio	流动资产周转次数(次/年) Number of Times of Annual TurnoverWorking Capitals (times/year)	成本费用利润率 Ratio of Profits to Industrial Cost	全员劳动生产率 Overall Labour Productivity
22.2	**109.0**	**51.2**	**2.9**	**20.8**	**59.8**
10.3	141.3	61.2	1.4	16.2	16.4
46.1	95.8	40.6	4.3	116.4	180.6
23.6	102.9	68.0	1.1	41.8	59.6
28.4	119.2	43.2	1.7	108.0	59.0
22.1	145.8	48.0	1.2	19.4	15.6
27.3	172.7	37.2	1.2	22.5	18.0
12.3	126.6	58.8	1.5	8.7	16.1
11.9	102.9	55.1	3.1	6.6	13.7
10.8	114.9	48.6	1.3	12.4	28.3
22.5	148.6	46.3	1.7	17.4	19.0
2.5	71.8	76.3	0.8	-2.2	9.9
-2.4	55.1	83.1	0.5	-16.3	3.2
24.1	101.6	50.7	1.3	23.0	25.5
24.1	101.6	50.7	1.3	23.3	26.0
56.6	229.6	26.4	1.2	32.1	267.2
0.8	98.1	59.1	1.2	-4.9	5.0
0.4	104.8	62.1	1.3	-5.4	5.0
5.1	-2.1	102.2	1.0	3.4	9.0
0.8	-102.7	124.1	3.1	-0.1	6.8
9.1	101.4	54.0	1.1	12.2	7.7
4.8	115.8	48.9	1.2	5.5	8.5
13.1	118.9	37.0	5.7	-6.6	55.6
7.9	110.6	83.6	1.2	5.3	13.0
13.7	117.4	50.1	1.8	23.1	32.3
3.8	102.8	50.1	1.7	4.5	11.8
30.1	137.0	54.5	1.4	73.9	73.3
14.6	122.8	49.4	2.2	21.3	36.2
6.5	133.2	46.0	0.7	10.8	9.3
2.4	31.0	89.1	2.5	-7.6	8.6
5.6	137.8	56.1	1.3	2.7	9.7
11.1	117.2	52.2	1.2	18.3	19.3
11.1	116.0	52.2	1.0	25.5	19.7
6.4	113.7	69.6	3.8	1.7	33.5
10.4	238.4	55.6	2.6	9.5	19.3
8.5	109.4	53.0	4.2	2.6	27.4
8.2	109.9	76.2	1.6	2.5	8.2
6.8	-1075.1	59.0	1.0	7.7	7.4
-7.9	33.6	94.5	1.5	-12.0	-0.8
1.9	106.5	82.7	0.4	2.3	6.3
2.8	94.2	70.8	0.9	1.3	12.3
7.1	126.6	64.5	2.3	9.7	33.9
7.4	127.3	63.5	2.6	10.1	35.7
4.1	104.5	69.2	0.8	4.7	22.4
-0.5	110.9	53.0	0.4	-14.2	10.4

13-19 分行业国有控股工业企业主要经济效益指标(GB/T4754-2002)

单位: %　　(2011 年)

行　　业	Sector	产　值 利税率 Ratio of Profits and Taxes to Industrial Output Value
煤炭开采和洗选业	Mining and Washing of Coal	29.4
石油和天然气开采业	Extraction of Petroleum and Natural Gas	64.0
#天然原油和天然气开采	Extraction of Ores Crude Oil and Natural Gas Extraction	68.7
黑色金属矿采选业	Mining and Processing of Ferrous Metals Ores	37.9
有色金属矿采选业	Mining and Processing of Nonferrous Metals Ores	59.7
非金属矿采选业	Mining and Processing of Nonmetal Ores	22.6
#采　盐	Extraction of Salt	31.7
农副食品加工业	Processing of Food from Agricultural Products	11.4
#谷物磨制	Grain Grinding	8.2
饲料加工	Fodder Processing	13.2
制　糖	Sugar Making	25.8
食品制造业	Manufacture of Food	0.6
#罐头制造	Manufacture of can	-20.2
饮料制造业	Manufacture of Beverage	35.6
#酒的制造	Manufacture of Wine	36.0
烟草制品业	Manufacture of Tobacco	69.5
纺织业	Manufacture of Textile	-1.3
#棉、化纤纺织及印染精加工	Cotton, Chemical Fiber, Dyeing, Printing and Processing	-1.6
毛纺织和染整精加工	Wool Textile, Dyeing and Printing	8.6
纺织服装、鞋、帽制造业	Manufacture of Textile Wearing Apparel, Footware and Caps	3.5
造纸及纸制品业	Manufacture of Paper and Paper Products	15.5
印刷业和记录媒介的复制	Printing and Copying of Medium for Record	8.9
石油加工、炼焦及核燃料加工业	Oil Processing, Coking and Nuclear Fuel Processing	6.7
#炼　焦	Coking	16.3
化学原料及化学制品制造业	Raw Chemical Material and Chemical Products	21.5
#基础化学原料制造	Basic Chemical Material	11.0
肥料制造	Fertilizer Making	46.9
医药制造业	Manufacture of Medicine	11.6
化学纤维制造业	Manufacture of Chemical Fiber	-2.0
橡胶制品业	Manufacture of Rubber Products	4.9
塑料制品业	Manufacture of Plastic Products	6.5
非金属矿物制品业	Manufacture of Nonmetal Mineral Products	22.4
#水泥制造	Manufacture of Cement	28.3
黑色金属冶炼及压延加工业	Smelting and Pressing of Ferrous Metals	3.7
有色金属冶炼及压延加工业	Smelting and Pressing of Nonferrous Metals	8.3
金属制品业	Manufacture of Metal Products	3.4
通用设备制造业	Manufacture of General Purpose Machinery	6.0
专用设备制造业	Manufacture of Special Purpose Machinery	8.4
交通运输设备制造业	Manufacture of Transport Equipment	-17.1
电气机械及器材制造业	Manufacture of Electric Equipment and Machinery	3.9
仪器仪表及文化、办公用机械制造业	Manufacture of Measuring Instruments and Machinery for Cultural Activity and Office Work	3.3
电力、热力的生产和供应业	Electricity and Thermal Production and Supply	13.5
#电力生产和电力供应	Electricity Production and Supply	13.9
燃气生产和供应业	Gas Production and Supply	8.0
水的生产和供应业	Water Production and Supply	-14.1

Main Indicators on Economic Efficiency of State-holding Industrial Enterprises by Sectors(GB/T4754-2002)

(%)

总资产贡献率 Ratio of Total Assets to Industrial Output Value	资本保值增值率 Ratio of Capital-hold and Rise	资产负债率 Assets Liability Ratio	流动资产周转次数(次/年) Number of Times of Annual TurnoverWorking Capitals (times/year)	成本费用利润率 Ratio of Profits to Industrial Cost	全员劳动生产率 Overall Labour Productivity
10.3	141.3	61.2	1.4	16.2	16.4
43.6	96.3	41.8	3.9	98.3	145.3
46.1	95.8	40.6	4.3	116.4	596.2
23.6	102.9	68.0	1.1	41.8	59.6
28.4	119.2	43.2	1.7	108.0	59.0
22.1	145.8	48.0	1.2	19.4	15.6
27.3	172.7	37.2	1.2	22.5	18.0
10.7	109.3	58.8	1.3	8.2	15.7
11.9	102.9	55.1	3.1	6.6	13.7
10.8	114.9	48.6	1.3	12.4	28.3
22.5	148.6	46.3	1.7	17.4	19.0
2.5	74.1	79.6	0.9	-2.2	10.1
-3.6	48.2	89.2	0.5	-18.2	2.3
24.1	101.6	50.7	1.3	23.0	25.5
24.1	101.6	50.7	1.3	23.3	26.0
56.6	229.6	26.4	1.2	32.1	267.2
0.5	91.5	60.7	1.2	-5.3	5.1
0.2	105.0	61.2	1.4	-5.7	5.1
5.1	-2.1	102.2	1.0	3.4	9.0
5.1	170.0	75.7	2.1	2.3	6.0
9.1	101.4	54.0	1.1	12.2	7.7
4.8	115.8	48.9	1.2	5.5	8.5
13.1	118.9	37.0	5.7	-6.6	55.6
7.9	110.6	83.6	1.2	5.3	13.0
13.7	117.5	50.1	1.8	23.1	32.3
3.8	102.8	50.1	1.7	4.5	11.8
30.1	137.0	54.5	1.4	73.9	73.3
6.5	133.2	46.0	0.7	10.8	9.3
2.4	31.0	89.1	2.5	-7.6	8.6
4.7	563.8	65.3	2.0	0.5	10.2
6.0	110.1	51.9	1.1	3.7	9.4
11.1	117.2	52.2	1.2	18.3	19.3
11.1	115.9	52.2	1.0	25.6	19.7
6.4	112.3	69.6	3.8	1.7	33.5
10.0	209.7	55.1	2.4	9.1	23.6
9.1	136.8	53.3	5.3	2.4	16.9
8.2	109.9	76.2	1.6	2.5	8.2
6.8	-1075.1	59.0	1.0	7.7	7.4
-7.9	33.6	94.5	1.5	-12.0	-0.8
1.9	106.5	82.7	0.4	2.3	6.3
2.8	94.2	70.8	0.9	1.3	12.3
7.1	126.6	64.5	2.3	9.7	33.9
7.4	127.3	63.5	2.6	10.1	35.7
4.1	104.5	69.2	0.8	4.7	22.4
-0.5	110.9	53.0	0.4	-14.2	10.4

13-20 各地、州、市、县(市)国有控股工业企业主要经济效益指标

单位: % (2011 年)

地区	Region	产值利税率 Ratio of Profits and Taxes to Industrial Output Value
总　计	**Total**	**27.7**
乌鲁木齐市	**Urumqi City**	**18.3**
天山区	Tianshan District	5.0
沙依巴克区	Shayibak District	19.6
新市区	Xinshi District	62.1
水磨沟区	Shui Mogou District	15.9
头屯河区	Tou Tunhe District	4.0
达坂城区	Da Bancheng District	31.0
米东区	Midong District	5.1
乌鲁木齐县	Urumqi County	55.4
克拉玛依市	**Karamay City**	**29.1**
独山子区	Dushanzi District	2.2
克拉玛依区	Karamay District	44.8
白碱滩区	Bai Jiantan District	
乌尔河区	Urhe District	
吐鲁番地区	**Turpan Administrative Offices**	**44.3**
吐鲁番市	Turpan City	27.1
鄯善县	Shanshan [Piqan] County	48.3
托克逊县	Toksun County	18.9
哈密地区	**Hami [Kumul] Administrative Offices**	**22.6**
哈密市	Hami [Kumul] City	19.4
巴里坤哈萨克自治县	Barkol Kazak Autonomous County	49.5
伊吾县	Yiwu [Araturuk] County	53.0
昌吉回族自治州	**Changji Hui Autonomous Prefecture**	**5.7**
昌吉市	Changji City	11.9
阜康市	Fukang City	4.6
呼图壁县	Hutubi County	10.0
玛纳斯县	Manas County	5.5
奇台县	Qitai County	27.3
吉木萨尔县	Jimsar County	-27.6
木垒哈萨克自治县	Mori Kazak Autonomous County	
伊犁哈萨克自治州	**Ili Kazak Autonomous Prefecture**	**25.6**
伊犁州直属县(市)	**Counties (Cities) Direct Under Ili Prefecture**	**26.8**
伊宁市	Yining [Gulja] City	17.9
奎屯市	Kuytun City	34.0
伊宁县	Yining [Gulja] County	25.3
察布查尔锡伯自治县	Qapqal Xibe Autonomous County	17.3
霍城县	Huocheng [Korgas] County	17.8
巩留县	Gongliu [Tokkuztara] County	8.8
新源县	Xinyuan [Kunes] County	21.6
昭苏县	Zhaosu [Mongolkure] County	28.6
特克斯县	Tekes County	
尼勒克县	Nilka County	41.0
塔城地区	**Tacheng [Tarbagatai] Administrative Offices**	**8.2**
塔城市	Tacheng [Qoqek] City	-4.5
乌苏市	Usu City	3.7
额敏县	Emin [Dorbiljin] County	20.8

Main Indicators on Economic Efficiency of State-holding Industrial Enterprises by Prefecture, Autonomous Prefecture, City and County

(%)

总资产贡献率 Ratio of Total Assets to Industrial Output Value	资本保值增值率 Ratio of Capital-hold and Rise	资产负债率 Assets Liability Ratio	流动资产周转次数(次/年) Number of Times of Annual TurnoverWorking Capitals (times/year)	成本费用利润率 Ratio of Profits to Industrial Cost	全员劳动生产率 Overall Labour Productivity
22.1	**109.0**	**51.2**	**2.9**	**20.5**	**59.8**
15.1	**106.3**	**53.1**	**2.9**	**9.0**	**54.9**
4.3	153.6	58.6	2.6	2.3	39.9
4.4	91.5	49.1	0.8	13.1	14.4
45.4	74.0	49.4	3.1	75.7	149.3
12.3	108.0	31.9	1.8	10.4	26.7
7.0	116.9	68.9	4.0	2.0	30.3
13.4	107.8	39.5	2.4	30.9	17.3
5.7	145.5	41.8	2.9	-7.0	28.3
10.0	112.5	72.2	0.8	68.2	380.3
28.4	**110.3**	**37.7**	**4.0**	**18.6**	**72.9**
3.1	121.9	32.1	4.3	-8.7	30.5
38.8	105.6	40.0	3.9	41.3	83.0
23.9	**79.0**	**56.0**	**3.3**	**59.2**	**86.6**
11.2	174.1	67.3	2.7	22.0	20.3
29.6	72.7	50.4	3.9	71.7	126.5
7.3	120.9	72.4	1.4	14.8	22.1
13.1	**112.7**	**61.8**	**1.3**	**17.5**	20.9
11.4	113.5	61.0	1.3	13.7	19.4
27.0	148.9	65.8	1.4	67.3	38.0
28.9	16.8	86.9	0.6	74.5	47.9
5.1	92.6	81.1	1.9	2.6	14.4
15.6	186.8	46.2	2.6	8.9	11.5
4.2	87.1	82.1	1.8	2.2	16.8
26.0	113.4	86.8	5.2	8.5	24.2
4.1	67.7	78.0	1.0	-0.9	11.3
21.5	370.8	82.2	3.2	16.9	23.8
-6.9	-15.0	101.3	1.1	-28.0	7.0
15.0	**132.0**	**59.7**	**1.8**	**19.6**	**40.2**
13.2	**127.0**	**61.0**	**1.4**	**14.2**	**34.5**
14.9	150.8	59.4	3.1	14.0	23.3
21.2	161.9	57.8	1.3	7.3	56.2
15.2	145.8	55.6	1.8	21.4	21.0
3.7	1952.6	75.7	0.7	19.1	11.0
13.4	119.3	51.5	1.8	12.8	16.8
1.4	88.9	64.5	0.3	-3.8	74.2
16.4	104.8	52.3	1.2	16.0	31.2
45.8	64.7	74.1	2.9	31.3	24.3
8.9	129.8	76.1	1.7	48.1	84.3
8.3	**150.0**	**59.4**	**2.8**	**6.6**	**41.2**
-1.9	107.2	69.1	6.8	-6.3	19.4
5.6	224.7	68.5	6.3	2.6	93.0
13.0	254.9	37.9	1.3	19.6	20.6

13-20 续表 1

单位: %

地　区	Region	产值利税率 Ratio of Profits and Taxes to Industrial Output Value
沙湾县	Shawan County	9.4
托里县	Toli County	10.3
裕民县	Yumin [Qagantokay] County	
和布克赛尔蒙古自治县	Hoboksar Mongol Autonomous County	30.4
阿勒泰地区	**Altay Administrative Offices**	**46.6**
阿勒泰市	Altay City	6.3
布尔津县	Burqin County	28.7
富蕴县	Fuyun [Koktokay] County	42.8
福海县	Fuhai [Burultokay] County	31.1
哈巴河县	Habahe [Kaba] County	68.9
青河县	Qinghe [Qinggil] County	
吉木乃县	Jeminay County	44.7
博尔塔拉蒙古自治州	**Bortala Mongol Autonomous Prefecture**	**9.6**
博乐市	Bole [Bortala] City	9.2
精河县	Jinghe [Jing] County	24.6
温泉县	Wenquan [Araxang] County	
巴音郭楞蒙古自治州	**Bayangol Mongol Autonomous Prefecture**	**64.2**
库尔勒市	Korla City	66.2
轮台县	Luntai [Bugur] County	
尉犁县	Yuli [Lopnur] County	
若羌县	Ruoqiang [Qarkilik] County	56.9
且末县	Qiemo [Qarqan] County	
焉耆回族自治县	Yanqi Hui Autonomous County	37.7
和静县	Hejing County	29.6
和硕县	Hoxud County	10.5
博湖县	Bohu [Bagrax] County	-4.8
阿克苏地区	**Aksu Administrative Offices**	**16.1**
阿克苏市	Aksu City	16.1
温宿县	Wensu [Onsu] County	24.4
库车县	Kuqa County	15.0
沙雅县	Xayar County	
新和县	Xinhe [Toksu] County	
拜城县	Baicheng [Bay] County	44.5
乌什县	Wushi [Uxturpan] County	19.3

Continued

(%)

总资产贡献率 Ratio of Total Assets to Industrial Output Value	资本保值增值率 Ratio of Capital-hold and Rise	资产负债率 Assets Liability Ratio	流动资产周转次数(次/年) Number of Times of Annual TurnoverWorking Capitals (times/year)	成本费用利润率 Ratio of Profits to Industrial Cost	全员劳动生产率 Overall Labour Productivity
11.8	129.4	62.7	2.1	8.0	13.7
7.5	113.9	46.9	1.0	14.1	23.3
23.8	89.0	49.5	1.7	28.0	19.6
26.4	**132.2**	**56.2**	**2.1**	**59.7**	**56.0**
5.5	150.9	77.2	2.6	2.9	18.1
10.9	300.2	87.2	1.8	26.6	50.1
19.7	121.9	53.3	1.4	51.3	44.4
13.2	126.9	57.3	0.9	30.0	25.3
72.7	124.5	16.8	3.5	131.2	128.1
7.4		70.5	1.0	69.1	208.4
5.6	**121.9**	**76.9**	**1.4**	**3.3**	**14.3**
5.4	132.1	77.5	1.3	3.0	14.5
14.9	72.5	44.8	2.1	17.7	10.4
44.9	**112.4**	**47.9**	**3.6**	**129.4**	**180.0**
48.0	108.6	45.0	4.4	139.3	211.4
35.6	212.9	62.0	1.3	114.5	93.5
49.1	84.2	36.5	4.3	23.4	24.1
12.2	131.9	71.1	1.4	34.7	38.1
8.0	110.5	56.3	1.4	4.4	14.8
-1.5	90.9	69.3	0.9	-5.9	7.1
19.3	**103.2**	**58.2**	**4.7**	**3.9**	**41.2**
8.7	109.2	57.9	2.2	13.1	19.3
6.5	473.8	80.1	1.1	21.4	18.4
28.7	92.6	52.2	7.2	1.1	88.5
26.3	141.3	71.7	1.7	43.0	22.6
11.7	109.1	49.5	0.7	16.3	16.3

13-20 续表 2

单位: %

地　区	Region	产值利税率 Ratio of Profits and Taxes to Industrial Output Value
阿瓦提县	Awat County	2.2
柯坪县	Kalpin County	
克孜勒苏柯尔克孜自治州	**Kizilsu Kirgiz Autonomous Prefecture**	**14.5**
阿图什市	Artux City	14.5
阿克陶县	Akto County	
阿合奇县	Akqi County	
乌恰县	Wuqia [Ulugqat] County	
喀什地区	**Kashgar [Kaxgar] Administrative Offices**	**-4.0**
喀什市	Kashgar [Kaxgar] City	-4.1
疏附县	Shufu County	0.2
疏勒县	Shule County	
英吉沙县	Yengisar County	
泽普县	Zepu [Poskam] County	
莎车县	Shache [Yarkant] County	
叶城县	Yecheng [Kagilik] County	
麦盖提县	Makit County	
岳普湖县	Yopurga County	
伽师县	Jiashi [Payzawat] County	
巴楚县	Bachu [Maralbexi] County	
塔什库尔干塔吉克自治县	Taxkorgan Tajik Autonomous County	
和田地区	**Hotan Administrative Offices**	**-5.7**
和田市	Hotan City	-18.2
和田县	Hotan County	
墨玉县	Moyu [Karakax] County	29.6
皮山县	Pishan [Guma] County	-16.1
洛浦县	Lop County	
策勒县	Qira County	
于田县	Yutian [Keriya] County	
民丰县	Minfeng [Niya] County	
自治区直辖县级市	**Municpality Country-LevelCity directly under the Central Government**	**14.5**
石河子市	Shihezi City	17.1
阿拉尔市	Aral City	-6.9
图木舒克市	Tumxuk City	7.5
五家渠市	Wujiaqu City	7.5

Continued

(%)

总资产贡献率 Ratio of Total Assets to Industrial Output Value	资本保值增值率 Ratio of Capital-hold and Rise	资产负债率 Assets Liability Ratio	流动资产周转次数(次/年) Number of Times of Annual TurnoverWorking Capitals (times/year)	成本费用利润率 Ratio of Profits to Industrial Cost	全员劳动生产率 Overall Labour Productivity
1.4	11.9	99.5	0.3	2.9	6.6
5.9	**133.7**	**36.6**	**0.9**	**16.8**	**24.5**
5.9	133.7	36.6	0.9	16.8	24.5
0.7	**87.4**	**93.7**	**4.3**	**-8.8**	**15.6**
0.7	88.0	93.6	4.3	-8.9	15.9
0.7	288.9	117.0	5.3	-4.0	3.2
-0.5	**91.8**	**43.7**	**2.5**	**-12.8**	**20.8**
-6.6	-40.7	104.4	4.8	-20.7	15.5
	99.0	8.5	1.2	-16.6	31.3
13.5	106.9	9.6	1.6	26.3	36.9
-1.8	53.9	95.4	0.2	-48.9	3.5
10.6	**111.6**	**64.5**	**1.4**	**13.4**	**18.4**
12.6	118.7	60.5	1.5	17.8	20.2
-0.4	37.3	90.0	2.1	-11.5	6.3
5.3	144.5	80.4	0.7	6.4	17.4
5.4	93.7	70.1	0.8	2.0	11.2

13-21 分行业大中型工业企业主要经济指标(GB/T4754-2011)

单位：万元 (2011 年)

行　业	Sector	企业单位数（个） Number of Enterprises (unit)	#亏损企业 Loss- Suffering Enterprises	工业总产值（当年价格） Gross Industrial Output Value (At Current Prices)
总　计	**Total**	**363**	**80**	**54886008.9**
煤炭开采和洗选业	Mining and Washing of Coal	38	11	1292172.3
石油和天然气开采业	Extraction of Petroleum and Natural Gas	4		13748213.6
黑色金属矿采选业	Mining and Processing of Ferrous Metals Ores	7	1	560840.0
有色金属矿采选业	Mining and Processing of Nonferrous Metals Ores	7	1	360525.8
非金属矿采选业	Mining and Processing of Nonmetal Ores	3		43897.9
#采　盐	Extraction of Salt	2		28919.9
农副食品加工业	Processing of Food from Agricultural Products	21	2	538329.8
#饲料加工	Fodder Processing	1		113564.2
制　糖	Sugar Making	14		296444.0
食品制造业	Manufacture of Food	13	1	426280.3
#罐头制造	Manufacture of can	2	1	87956.9
酒、饮料和精制茶制造业	Manufacture of Wine,Beverages and Refined Tea	9	2	339820.8
#酒的制造	Manufacture of Wine	6	1	266233.2
烟草制品业	Manufacture of Tobacco	1		302740.4
纺织业	Manufacture of Textile	41	15	1004962.7
#棉、化纤纺织及印染精加工	Cotton, Chemical Fiber, Dyeing, Printing and Processing	36	14	939883.0
毛纺织和染整精加工	Wool Textile, Dyeing and Printing	2	1	15201.2
纺织服装、鞋、帽制造业	Manufacture of Textile Wearing Apparel, Footware and Caps	1		24678.6
家具制造业	Manufacture of Furniture	1		45707.2
造纸及纸制品业	Manufacture of Paper and Paper Products	4	1	79456.9
印刷业和记录媒介的复制	Printing and Copying of Medium for Record	1		6499.0
石油加工、炼焦及核燃料加工业	Oil Processing, Coking and Nuclear Fuel Processing	19	6	14803983.0
#炼　焦	Coking	12	3	605632.5
化学原料及化学制品制造业	Raw Chemical Material and Chemical Products	31	6	3774521.7
#基础化学原料制造	Basic Chemical Material	14	5	714138.0
肥料制造	Fertilizer Making	4		598451.5
合成材料制造	Manufacture of Synthetic Material	8	1	2365592.1
医药制造业	Manufacture of Medicine	2		27343.1
化学纤维制造业	Manufacture of Chemical Fiber	11	7	969935.1
橡胶制品业	Manufacture of Rubber Products	6	2	266407.1
非金属矿物制品业	Manufacture of Nonmetal Mineral Products	38	6	1339601.0
#水泥制造	Manufacture of Cement	28	5	937805.7
黑色金属冶炼及压延加工业	Smelting and Pressing of Ferrous Metals	20	4	6134780.3
有色金属冶炼及压延加工业	Smelting and Pressing of Nonferrous Metals	12	4	1047451.1
金属制品业	Manufacture of Metal Products	5		309659.6
专用设备制造业	Manufacture of Special Purpose Machinery	3		55100.8
汽车制造业	Manufacture of Automobile	2	2	42494.9
电气机械和器材制造业	Manufacture of Electric Equipment and Machinery	8		2014635.2
计算机、通信和其他电子设备制造业	Telecom Equipment, Computer and Other Electronic Equipment	1		187597.2
电力、热力的生产和供应业	Electricity and Thermal Production and Supply	40	7	3753066.2
#电力生产和电力供应	Electricity Production and Supply	32	6	3631350.1
燃气生产和供应业	Gas Production and Supply	1		83757.9
水的生产和供应业	Water Production and Supply	1	1	16072.5

Main Indicators of Large-scale and Medium-scale Industrial Enterprises by Sectors(GB/T4754-2011)

(10 000 yuan)

工业增加值 Value-added	工业销售产值(当年价) Sales Value of Industry Products (At Current Prices)	出口交货值 Delivery Value of Industry Export	实收资本 Total Capital Hold	资产合计 Total Assets	流动资产合计 Total Working Capitals	#产成品 Finished Product	固定资产原价 Original Value of Fixed Assets
22567084.4	**54202581.0**	**462871.8**	**27127426.8**	**76730109.5**	**23135346.2**	**2066814.20**	**60620304.0**
814762.5	1315217.5		1314533.5	4515247.6	1135463.3	73747.8	1564499.7
13080155.5	13714241.8		12950531.0	21110930.8	3455624.2	147035.3	28376963.5
249906.3	516373.8		167477.2	919645.7	546239.8	71326.7	301598.7
290815.6	337775.0		103393.4	737098.2	187217.0	32106.5	318040.2
23529.1	35988.5		17499.9	46085.4	27993.8	4048.1	17407.4
18748.5	23706.5		14500.0	36685.2	24611.5	3475.5	11791.3
168799.4	555436.0	3067.8	159737.3	771743.6	431186.0	142796.0	348502.6
27474.2	105695.2		29475.8	217042.1	107773.1	15773.9	39609.8
117426.7	327667.3		87288.8	369034.8	202858.7	94761.8	272090.5
91602.7	393057.4	46804.7	123170.6	674660.7	317322.9	64323.4	371243.7
-5194.6	58924.6	38040.2	53441.0	352436.5	211135.8	47376.5	146306.4
156926.9	330115.0		120853.4	577750.6	347298.7	15646.1	227059.8
138972.9	259740.9		103473.5	516079.7	316972.8	5518.8	179784.7
236486.5	302055.5		18741.7	371707.0	261354.0		129728.0
217747.2	952107.6	68220.4	436721.5	1777381.0	807330.7	171670.8	958641.0
203197.1	894367.0	56072.9	360268.9	1620662.1	747770.7	164624.1	881608.4
2712.4	18999.7	314.3	8607.0	16341.1	9443.7	2788.0	7574.0
6851.1	21359.5	538.8	2025.0	16459.8	10564.6	473.3	5628.9
23957.8	50897.1	37983.1	63268.0	285766.3	34155.6	7091.5	41660.6
22324.5	76623.0		25388.0	162596.2	82527.5	9847.9	100203.2
3741.3	6568.4		5727.4	24893.0	8004.1	1479.3	26280.9
1863957.0	14743886.6	14644.8	4538277.7	8092129.5	2799578.5	260424.0	7452880.9
183735.9	590570.6	14644.8	218248.6	903793.8	325105.7	42651.0	441765.8
1207648.6	3630739.4	154979.5	1555387.0	6795977.2	1823554.7	255033.3	3817339.1
223374.8	706240.9	51222.5	426232.9	2607974.7	628086.3	34139.8	729140.7
353169.9	518464.3		148649.7	1041914.1	379685.0	38323.0	748622.7
584377.7	2308802.6	103721.1	943424.8	2987549.5	741872.3	180235.8	2294324.8
6899.2	28950.6	204.3	10960.6	61935.5	37268.5	5240.5	21355.1
138016.4	907198.7		204148.0	1033453.6	433855.9	86211.1	580134.6
42221.4	241132.7	6472.4	118538.1	354273.7	167742.2	58549.6	182580.0
429850.2	1303472.8	15609.9	743313.8	3278154.9	1129291.1	62172.0	1404374.3
347789.9	914840.7		663825.3	2771139.4	897637.0	42195.1	1205661.7
784766.8	6074395.3	16386.6	1007023.8	5412496.5	2043303.0	337522.5	2965400.7
255334.1	1016150.6	2637.9	388121.5	2384721.0	768561.4	46785.4	1086560.6
25566.3	319039.5		36783.5	234348.8	153169.2	13400.4	52472.8
16854.7	47842.2	477.0	22373.2	141498.9	115966.1	13061.4	21243.9
-1898.0	38096.2	50.8	10015.8	81764.0	35827.5	8868.5	29196.5
442221.6	1944038.0	45846.0	583334.8	5130707.6	3100558.7	165386.5	226157.3
60501.8	189440.9	46561.1	41104.2	706678.3	366480.9	11259.5	168859.8
1351083.2	3746806.2		1185599.3	8751003.9	1552578.7	0.3	8341922.9
1302402.8	3625090.1		1097353.7	8197585.9	1335933.9	0.3	7884633.9
21868.1	62433.6		67634.0	249777.8	113602.8	385.5	117802.5
7271.6	16072.5		151700.0	314053.2	68496.3		224394.6

13-21 续表

单位：万元

行　　业	Sector	流动负债合计 Total Working Liabilities	长期负债合计 Long-term Liabilities
总　　计	**Total**	**24762217.6**	**14855974.9**
煤炭开采和洗选业	Mining and Washing of Coal	1387770.2	1217100.0
石油和天然气开采业	Extraction of Petroleum and Natural Gas	3882919.4	4706015.1
黑色金属矿采选业	Mining and Processing of Ferrous Metals Ores	576172.0	49359.3
有色金属矿采选业	Mining and Processing of Nonferrous Metals Ores	216065.0	98556.9
非金属矿采选业	Mining and Processing of Nonmetal Ores	21232.4	1229.8
#采　盐	Extraction of Salt	12109.4	1229.8
农副食品加工业	Processing of Food from Agricultural Products	338209.7	47520.4
#饲料加工	Fodder Processing	71219.7	34105.0
制　糖	Sugar Making	174812.0	4785.4
食品制造业	Manufacture of Food	455034.1	37630.1
#罐头制造	Manufacture of can	300572.3	28485.0
酒、饮料和精制茶制造业	Manufacture of Wine,Beverages and Refined Tea	226895.3	188931.3
#酒的制造	Manufacture of Wine	191251.8	188656.8
烟草制品业	Manufacture of Tobacco	98051.0	
纺织业	Manufacture of Textile	788866.4	340678.9
#棉、化纤纺织及印染精加工	Cotton, Chemical Fiber, Dyeing, Printing and Processing	732460.3	325789.3
毛纺织和染整精加工	Wool Textile, Dyeing and Printing	7920.1	
纺织服装、鞋、帽制造业	Manufacture of Textile Wearing Apparel, Footware and Caps	8318.5	3081.3
家具制造业	Manufacture of Furniture	19909.2	18336.6
造纸及纸制品业	Manufacture of Paper and Paper Products	86869.4	7196.3
印刷业和记录媒介的复制	Printing and Copying of Medium for Record	10122.3	2907.1
石油加工、炼焦及核燃料加工业	Oil Processing, Coking and Nuclear Fuel Processing	2351356.9	779030.1
#炼　焦	Coking	393268.6	177792.3
化学原料及化学制品制造业	Raw Chemical Material and Chemical Products	1545634.7	1934643.7
#基础化学原料制造	Basic Chemical Material	698274.2	648884.5
肥料制造	Fertilizer Making	279820.9	300395.9
合成材料制造	Manufacture of Synthetic Materials	529584.4	961857.2
医药制造业	Manufacture of Medicine	17707.5	901.0
化学纤维制造业	Manufacture of Chemical Fiber	640943.7	168794.9
橡胶制品业	Manufacture of Rubber Products	132154.5	73642.8
非金属矿物制品业	Manufacture of Nonmetal Mineral Products	1016101.7	652905.6
#水泥制造	Manufacture of Cement	830406.7	564793.5
黑色金属冶炼及压延加工业	Smelting and Pressing of Ferrous Metals	3000861.5	666353.7
有色金属冶炼及压延加工业	Smelting and Pressing of Nonferrous Metals	1719770.6	112913.5
金属制品业	Manufacture of Metal Products	124504.8	15239.9
专用设备制造业	Manufacture of Special Purpose Machinery	41395.2	6075.1
汽车制造业	Manufacture of Automobile	82750.0	533.2
电气机械和器材制造业	Manufacture of Electric Equipment and Machinery	2132519.6	527350.3
计算机、通信和其他电子设备制造业	Telecom Equipment, Computer and Other Electronic Equipment	83703.3	269028.4
电力、热力的生产和供应业	Electricity and Thermal Production and Supply	2656480.4	2571853.1
#电力生产和电力供应	Electricity Production and Supply	2495037.8	2323827.9
燃气生产和供应业	Gas Production and Supply	105619.8	67276.0
水的生产和供应业	Water Production and Supply	68496.3	94729.0

Continued

(10 000 yuan)

所有者权益合计 Total Owners' Equities	主营业务收入 Revenue from Principal Business	#主营业务成本 Cost of Principal Business	主营业务税金及附加 Taxes and Other Charges on Principal Business	营业利润 Business Profit	利润总额 Total Profit	亏损企业亏损总额 Losses Value of Loss-Suffering Enterprises	利税总额 Total Profits and Taxes	本年应交增值税 Value-added Taxes Payable	全部从业人员年平均人数（人） Ann Employed Persons (person)
36315265.0	**55537847.7**	**39720345.8**	**3256555.8**	**8295909.1**	**8550428.2**	**1338887.8**	**14500461.9**	**2693477.9**	**441037**
1828540.1	1346415.5	896775.4	37355.7	173813.4	171371.6	34262.7	343770.0	135042.7	49081
12520766.4	14414881.3	4704246.4	1309986.0	6824921.4	6922127.1		9652674.4	1420561.3	72419
295846.5	557754.0	330277.2	11358.0	163366.9	163913.8	2552.2	218959.7	43687.9	4277
422476.3	332513.9	107959.5	4923.3	183232.7	184470.6	2994.3	226615.3	37221.4	5198
23623.2	30288.2	11880.4	2323.3	4962.1	4997.7		10614.3	3293.3	1541
23346.0	24710.4	7619.3	2286.2	4936.3	4989.1		10537.4	3262.1	923
385113.2	566386.6	421723.1	2869.1	71265.3	74636.8	2287.4	107503.8	29997.9	9864
111717.4	113200.2	79583.7	316.6	15213.1	16003.7		18721.4	2401.1	846
188637.2	314887.4	230673.1	2409.7	45348.6	46248.8		74892.2	26233.7	6667
181967.2	415805.3	315674.1	1755.7	9578.1	10686.5	36267.0	27256.4	14814.2	8083
23349.9	66652.2	62843.0	132.0	-32220.4	-33612.1	36267.0	-33480.1		2531
161923.9	336910.6	204065.3	31947.1	47242.3	55154.5	2001.1	112370.7	25269.1	6123
136171.0	257755.3	142506.2	31484.6	43281.1	49734.8	1702.4	103231.2	22011.8	4887
273656.0	302058.0	106288.0	134892.0	40736.0	40648.0		210392.0	34852.0	885
636474.3	1050693.7	942064.9	2974.0	24350.3	37929.3	32877.8	76258.3	35355.0	34357
551054.2	984867.3	883676.6	2684.8	25831.8	36876.5	30805.7	73455.9	33894.6	30674
8421.0	19068.7	18403.1	74.3	-1818.8	-1705.9	2072.1	-1112.1	519.5	1313
5060.0	37274.0	34350.6		601.6	680.4		680.4		885
247520.4	50860.6	41445.5	329.7	2639.5	2622.4		2952.1		2613
61874.9	76832.3	64398.4	441.1	5272.4	8701.0	2061.8	12548.4	3406.3	3281
11863.5	6631.6	5300.7	37.0	-911.7	148.3		466.0	280.7	519
4954384.6	15071039.1	13599722.3	1620425.6	-784158.4	-809352.4	987700.7	1051170.4	240097.2	36910
325375.3	586542.6	457171.5	8058.1	78552.1	81205.4	2921.1	117924.1	28660.6	7850
3315472.8	3245572.5	2351025.2	37452.0	552636.3	600274.5	11671.6	801930.2	164203.7	37999
1260590.4	947402.5	768842.3	3467.9	73269.3	72008.1	10376.5	111436.6	35960.6	14314
461697.2	515955.4	220551.0	18679.7	188973.1	225865.3		276255.3	31710.3	4789
1496107.6	1677298.3	1288951.8	14164.8	264562.2	276204.3	1295.1	378522.1	88153.0	16141
43092.7	23064.9	14752.0	194.2	1668.5	1755.3		2698.8	749.3	963
218432.3	1013864.0	928115.6	1151.9	-17309.9	-13520.2	50042.9	2108.7	14477.0	9345
148476.3	226538.2	201086.0	1564.7	3758.0	4755.1	1247.3	11243.6	4923.8	5169
1483860.6	1292283.6	981167.4	7132.0	192640.0	212387.0	8198.8	277589.9	58070.9	26118
1251205.1	901212.1	639686.6	6023.8	167728.0	186961.2	5760.7	241762.5	48777.5	19786
1726819.8	6271448.1	5745307.0	16823.0	190371.0	191985.8	5690.3	323537.9	114729.1	29695
504072.8	962062.6	881207.1	894.4	42973.9	44029.0	13739.7	78978.2	34054.8	9554
94603.8	305959.5	288012.4	661.3	10170.8	11076.4		13335.2	1597.5	2457
94028.6	56596.6	40493.4	114.1	7179.4	8856.9		9130.8	159.8	2039
-1519.2	58728.4	59662.4	24.5	-9496.0	-8834.1	8834.1	-8436.9	372.7	809
2470782.1	2243877.0	1734302.8	3811.0	299409.3	332654.9		388686.2	52220.3	6992
353946.6	179462.0	134024.9	484.8	27583.0	29232.3		29721.0	3.9	3967
3033302.3	3743648.9	3300786.7	13014.9	300709.3	311854.6	59537.3	484956.7	160087.2	41116
2903279.5	3619332.7	3194648.2	12804.9	300348.7	305698.2	54418.8	475840.9	157337.8	38524
76882.0	87574.7	59298.0	1208.2	3526.1	3965.2		6911.8	1738.4	976
150827.8	23609.2	20805.3	132.3	-12322.6	-9297.0	9297.0	-8045.4	1119.3	832

13-22 分行业大中型工业企业主要经济指标(GB/T4754-2002)

单位: 万元 (2011 年)

行业	Sector	企业单位数(个) Number of Enterp-rises (unit)	#亏损企业 Loss- Suffering Enterprises	工业总产值(当年价格) Gross Industrial Output Value (At Current Prices)
煤炭开采和洗选业	Mining and Washing of Coal	36	11	1240559.6
石油和天然气开采业	Extraction of Petroleum and Natural Gas	14	1	14972035.7
#天然原油和天然气开采	Extraction of Ores Crude Oil and Natural Gas Extraction	4		13748213.6
黑色金属矿采选业	Mining and Processing of Ferrous Metals Ores	8	1	575783.1
有色金属矿采选业	Mining and Processing of Nonferrous Metals Ores	9	2	408908.6
非金属矿采选业	Mining and Processing of Nonmetal Ores	3		43897.9
#采 盐	Extraction of Salt	2		28919.9
农副食品加工业	Processing of Food from Agricultural Products	22	3	559687.2
#饲料加工	Fodder Processing	1		113564.2
制 糖	Sugar Making	13		291860.3
食品制造业	Manufacture of Food	16	4	467978.0
#罐头制造	Manufacture of can	6	4	164560.9
饮料制造业	Manufacture of Beverage	8	2	331540.8
#酒的制造	Manufacture of Wine	6	1	264307.9
烟草制品业	Manufacture of Tobacco	1		302740.4
纺织业	Manufacture of Textile	36	13	968825.2
#棉、化纤纺织及印染精加工	Cotton, Chemical Fiber, Dyeing, Printing and Processing	31	12	903745.5
毛纺织和染整精加工	Wool Textile, Dyeing and Printing	2	1	15201.2
纺织服装、鞋、帽制造业	Manufacture of Textile Wearing Apparel,Footware and Caps	2		35631.3
家具制造业	Manufacture of Furniture	1		45707.2
造纸及纸制品业	Manufacture of Paper and Paper Products	4	1	79456.9
印刷业和记录媒介的复制	Printing and Copying of Medium for Record	1		6499.0
石油加工、炼焦及核燃料加工业	Oil Processing, Coking and Nuclear Fuel Processing	20	6	14816933.7
#炼 焦	Coking	13	3	618583.2
化学原料及化学制品制造业	Raw Chemical Material and Chemical Products	32	6	3807286.6
#基础化学原料制造	Basic Chemical Material	14	5	714138.0
肥料制造	Fertilizer Making	4		598451.5
医药制造业	Manufacture of Medicine	2		27343.1
化学纤维制造业	Manufacture of Chemical Fiber	10	7	947534.8
橡胶制品业	Manufacture of Rubber Products	2	1	112370.3
塑料制品业	Manufacture of Plastic Products	4	1	154036.8
非金属矿物制品业	Manufacture of Nonmetal Mineral Products	36	6	1316789.9
#水泥制造	Manufacture of Cement	25	5	858488.3
黑色金属冶炼及压延加工业	Smelting and Pressing of Ferrous Metals	23	5	6240848.5
有色金属冶炼及压延加工业	Smelting and Pressing of Nonferrous Metals	10	3	949222.3
金属制品业	Manufacture of Metal Products	4		249657.7
专用设备制造业	Manufacture of Special Purpose Machinery	4		94974.8
交通运输设备制造业	Manufacture of Transport Equipment	2	2	42494.9
电气机械及器材制造业	Manufacture of Electric Equipment and Machinery	6		1996879.0
通信设备、计算机及其他电子设备制造业	Telecom Equipment, Computer and Other Electronic Equipment	1		187597.2
工艺品及其他制造业	Manufacture of Handicrafts and Others	1		28889.9
电力、热力的生产和供应业	Electricity and Thermal Production and Supply	35	6	3659661.7
#电力生产和电力供应	Electricity Production and Supply	30	5	3555723.2
燃气生产和供应业	Gas Production and Supply	1		83757.9
水的生产和供应业	Water Production and Supply	1	1	16072.5

Main Indicators of Large-scale and Medium-scale Industrial Enterprises by Sectors(GB/T4754-2002)

(10 000 yuan)

工业增加值 Value-added	工业销售产值（当年价） Sales Value of Industry Products (At Current Prices)	出口交货值 Delivery Value of Industry Export	实收资本 Total Capital Hold	资产合计 Total Assets	流动资产合计 Total Working Capitals	#产成品 Finished Product	固定资产原价 Original Value of Fixed Assets
785419.3	1280176.6		1298506.6	4419783.7	1076850.2	52502.9	1555548.4
13580585.6	14937706.1	2386.7	13880574.6	22602961.0	4149998.7	147825.0	29378881.4
13080155.5	13714241.8		12950531.0	21110930.8	3455624.2	147035.3	28376963.5
261586.7	531455.5		182477.2	976482.8	566953.6	71326.7	335204.5
331117.3	386871.5		105893.4	822133.8	216214.6	33741.0	358472.1
23529.1	35988.5		17499.9	46085.4	27993.8	4048.1	17407.4
18748.5	23706.5		14500.0	36685.2	24611.5	3475.5	11791.3
172373.0	574318.9	3067.8	165537.3	789396.6	435996.5	147920.8	360211.6
27474.2	105695.2		29475.8	217042.1	107773.1	15773.9	39609.8
116387.4	323644.1		83588.8	359010.8	195891.6	91487.7	266278.1
102822.1	422537.4	71916.7	133763.4	782121.1	391176.3	112608.3	427618.3
11622.3	123300.3	63152.2	65033.8	476472.2	292275.9	96987.1	215517.6
153940.2	321835.0		120753.4	572909.5	343921.7	15410.1	224805.0
138603.2	257318.6		107373.5	519213.6	318377.3	6998.3	180862.7
236486.5	302055.5		18741.7	371707.0	261354.0		129728.0
208160.0	918435.8	63605.3	431507.4	1709024.2	747452.8	164941.5	945446.0
193609.9	860695.2	51457.8	355054.8	1552305.3	687892.8	157894.8	868413.4
2712.4	18999.7	314.3	8607.0	16341.1	9443.7	2788.0	7574.0
10006.3	32350.8	5153.9	3275.0	32767.5	23157.1	3353.4	7682.2
23957.8	50897.1	37983.1	63268.0	285766.3	34155.6	7091.5	41660.6
22324.5	76623.0		25388.0	162596.2	82527.5	9847.9	100203.2
3741.3	6568.4		5727.4	24893.0	8004.1	1479.3	26280.9
1867469.0	14757358.1	14644.8	4540758.3	8103071.3	2807672.8	260762.5	7458833.8
187247.9	604042.1	14644.8	220729.2	914735.6	333200.0	42989.5	447718.7
1224506.5	3663454.3	154979.5	1564387.0	6829874.2	1847882.6	255164.6	3835359.6
223374.8	706240.9	51222.5	426232.9	2607974.7	628086.3	34139.8	729140.7
353169.9	518464.3		148649.7	1041914.1	379685.0	38323.0	748622.7
6899.2	28950.6	201.3	10960.6	61935.5	37268.5	5240.5	21355.1
133007.4	885288.3		199148.0	1018973.9	426448.3	81196.5	570564.5
16912.2	107100.6	6472.4	38620.0	128146.1	47475.5	11790.2	56015.6
25309.2	134032.1		79918.1	226127.6	120266.7	46759.4	126564.4
408224.2	1282073.5	15609.9	698020.3	3134993.4	1081309.2	61727.5	1291624.4
308358.7	835478.9		617671.8	2598382.6	830515.6	41327.8	1083739.6
810842.6	6182992.4	16386.6	1017233.2	5477702.8	2081399.8	343708.6	2994681.2
220599.5	923101.9	2637.9	381126.5	2310040.0	714994.8	34437.4	1066023.9
21454.5	259037.6		31783.5	189907.9	118350.5	9323.1	46717.7
25234.2	65096.2	477.0	27373.2	154404.0	126156.1	13061.4	23419.0
-1898.0	38096.2	50.8	10015.8	81764.0	35827.5	8868.5	29196.5
437864.1	1926995.5	45846.0	574834.8	5103527.8	3075614.2	159884.6	222905.8
60501.8	189440.9	46561.1	41104.2	706678.3	366480.9	11259.5	168859.8
10027.4	28889.9		15000.0	189242.0	54526.1		120231.8
1283074.9	3653401.7		785798.4	7546815.9	1420224.1	0.3	7511028.1
1245235.3	3549463.2		720810.1	7046490.2	1215508.9	0.3	7112019.9
21868.1	62433.6		67634.0	249777.8	113602.8	385.5	117802.5
7271.6	16072.5		151700.0	314053.2	68496.3		224394.6

13-22 续表

单位: 万元

行　　业	Sector	流动负债合计 Total Working Liabilities	长期负债合计 Total Owners' Equities
煤炭开采和洗选业	Mining and Washing of Coal	1336717.1	1205098.7
石油和天然气开采业	Extraction of Petroleum and Natural Gas	4618378.9	4902176.6
＃天然原油和天然气开采	Extraction of Ores Crude Oil and Natural Gas Extraction	3882919.4	4706015.1
黑色金属矿采选业	Mining and Processing of Ferrous Metals Ores	588792.9	54352.3
有色金属矿采选业	Mining and Processing of Nonferrous Metals Ores	241525.4	98606.9
非金属矿采选业	Mining and Processing of Nonmetal Ores	21232.4	1229.8
＃采　盐	Extraction of Salt	12109.4	1229.8
农副食品加工业	Processing of Food from Agricultural Products	345525.9	49010.4
＃饲料加工	Fodder Processing	71219.7	34105.0
制　糖	Sugar Making	167089.9	4785.4
食品制造业	Manufacture of Food	540358.3	37576.7
＃罐头制造	Manufacture of can	393423.5	28608.4
饮料制造业	Manufacture of Beverage	225961.9	188931.3
＃酒的制造	Manufacture of Wine	194332.4	188656.8
烟草制品业	Manufacture of Tobacco	98051.0	
纺织业	Manufacture of Textile	731012.1	335937.5
＃棉、化纤纺织及印染精加工	Cotton, Chemical Fiber, Dyeing, Printing and Processing	674606.0	321047.9
毛纺织和染整精加工	Wool Textile, Dyeing and Printing	7920.1	
纺织服装、鞋、帽制造业	Manufacture of Textile Wearing Apparel,Footware and Caps	18220.9	6592.7
家具制造业	Manufacture of Furniture	19909.2	18336.6
造纸及纸制品业	Manufacture of Paper and Paper Products	86869.4	7196.3
印刷业和记录媒介的复制	Printing and Copying of Medium for Record	10122.3	2907.1
石油加工、炼焦及核燃料加工业	Oil Processing, Coking and Nuclear Fuel Processing	2352166.9	779030.1
＃炼 焦	Coking	394078.6	177792.3
化学原料及化学制品制造业	Raw Chemical Material and Chemical Products	1562592.0	1934643.7
＃基础化学原料制造	Basic Chemical Material	698274.2	648884.5
肥料制造	Fertilizer Making	279820.9	300395.9
医药制造业	Manufacture of Medicine	17707.5	901.0
化学纤维制造业	Manufacture of Chemical Fiber	636368.9	168794.9
橡胶制品业	Manufacture of Rubber Products	50274.0	33368.1
塑料制品业	Manufacture of Plastic Products	81880.5	40274.7
非金属矿物制品业	Manufacture of Nonmetal Mineral Products	952161.9	632508.1
＃水泥制造	Manufacture of Cement	760815.5	544396.0
黑色金属冶炼及压延加工业	Smelting and Pressing of Ferrous Metals	3055211.7	666487.3
有色金属冶炼及压延加工业	Smelting and Pressing of Nonferrous Metals	1643667.6	112716.5
金属制品业	Manufacture of Metal Products	90486.2	10577.3
专用设备制造业	Manufacture of Special Purpose Machinery	44895.0	6075.1
交通运输设备制造业	Manufacture of Transport Equipment	82750.0	533.2
电气机械及器材制造业	Manufacture of Electric Equipment and Machinery	2115787.2	527046.7
通信设备、计算机及其他电子设备制造业	Telecom Equipment, Computer and Other Electronic Equipment	83703.3	269028.4
工艺品及其他制造业	Manufacture of Handicrafts and Others	173365.4	
电力、热力的生产和供应业	Electricity and Thermal Production and Supply	2484963.9	2314193.1
＃电力生产和电力供应	Electricity Production and Supply	2339780.5	2070887.9
燃气生产和供应业	Gas Production and Supply	105619.8	67276.0
水的生产和供应业	Water Production and Supply	68496.3	94729.0

Continued

(10 000 yuan)

主营业务收入 Revenue from Principal Business	#主营业务成本 Cost of Principal Business	主营业务税金及附加 Taxes and Other Charges on Principal Business	营业利润 Business Profit	利润总额 Total Profit	亏损企业亏损总额 Losses Value of Loss-Suffering Enterprises	利税总额 Total Profits and Taxes	本年应交增值税 Value-added Taxes Payable	全部从业人员年平均人数(人) Ann Employed Persons (person)
1311375.5	881339.6	35969.5	163661.9	161511.5	34262.7	328521.8	131040.8	48508
15566830.2	5854583.4	1319195.6	6754387.3	6876129.0	67623.8	9672896.5	1477571.9	117797
14414881.3	4704246.4	1309986.0	6824921.4	6922127.1		9652674.4	1420561.3	93136
572835.7	335789.3	11855.9	168972.2	169448.7	2552.2	226664.8	45360.2	4720
381610.4	124260.1	5975.8	208717.9	208856.0	3784.9	258490.2	43658.4	5885
30288.2	11880.4	2323.3	4962.1	4997.7		10614.3	3293.3	1391
24710.4	7619.3	2286.2	4936.3	4989.1		10537.4	3262.1	932
583703.6	437756.4	2860.3	71142.4	74619.2	2804.3	107367.5	29888	10313
113200.2	79583.7	316.6	15213.1	16003.7		18721.4	2401.1	878
310864.2	227181.9	2392.7	45247.9	46130.1		74646.6	26123.8	6397
437207.4	331672.9	2122.9	7203.1	7806.4	40359.7	24022.5	14093.2	9633
122950.0	108356.7	513.8	-31779.4	-33478.8	40359.7	-32965		3917
328630.6	198714.5	31937.3	44431.8	52341.7	2001.1	109548.1	25269.1	6581
255319.1	140916.6	31789.4	41002.2	47453.6	1702.4	101558.3	22315.3	5566
302058.0	106288.0	134892.0	40736.0	40648.0		210392	34852	885
1017593.5	910807.3	2837.3	24408.9	37305.9	31163.9	74403.1	34259.9	32108
951767.1	852419.0	2548.1	25890.4	36253.1	29091.8	71600.7	32799.5	28425
19068.7	18403.1	74.3	-1818.8	-1705.9	2072.1	-1112.1	519.5	1313
48266.3	44482.5	7.2	580.0	1109.6		1255.7	138.9	1662
50860.6	41445.5	329.7	2639.5	2622.4		2952.1		2751
76832.3	64398.4	441.1	5272.4	8701.0	2061.8	12548.4	3406.3	3404
6631.6	5300.7	37.0	-911.7	148.3		466	280.7	519
15084510.6	13611400.7	1620455.7	-783092.4	-808296.9	987700.7	1052758	240599.2	38017
600014.1	468849.9	8088.2	79618.1	82260.9	2921.1	119511.7	29162.6	7661
3274659.3	2371470.6	38517.3	557146.1	605261.5	11671.6	809015.9	165237.1	39373
947402.5	768842.3	3467.9	73269.3	72008.1	10376.5	111436.6	35960.6	13952
515955.4	220551.0	18679.7	188973.1	225865.3		276255.3	31710.3	4889
23064.9	14752.0	194.2	1668.5	1755.3		2698.8	749.3	964
991953.5	909892.1	967.1	-18705.8	-15338.1	50042.9	-1445.9	12925.1	8433
93293.4	80818.6	1397.0	128.7	419.8	1084.7	5495.2	3678.4	1532
133244.8	120267.4	167.7	3629.3	4335.3	162.6	5748.4	1245.4	3081
1276065.7	985060.6	7461.2	180179.4	202672.8	8198.8	265357.1	55223.1	24506
822089.7	593444.4	5692.0	146990.1	168700.5	5760.7	216541.3	42148.8	17912
6386873.1	5852939.9	17161.5	190173.4	192571.3	7275.0	327269.1	117536.3	32563
869030.9	791597.3	662.8	34854.3	35781.8	12155.0	68375.7	31931.1	8862
274231.0	259722.2	613.3	9149.4	9766.3		11624.9	1245.3	2483
97607.3	72920.9	161.7	12046.6	13725.9		14068.3	180.7	2714
58728.4	59662.4	24.5	-9496.0	-8834.1	8834.1	-8436.9	372.7	1192
2224144.6	1718381.7	3714.0	298150.3	331263.8		386545.5	51567.7	6481
179462.0	134024.9	484.8	27583.0	29232.3		29721	3.9	3952
26177.1	23345.4		1524.4	1528.0		4575.2	3047.2	500
3648196.0	3247814.8	12370.5	288755.6	298497.5	58438.4	460174.6	149306.6	43185
3543655.7	3158390.3	12269.7	288246.9	293585.8	53319.9	454379.2	148523.7	40669
87574.7	59298.0	1208.2	3526.1	3965.2		6911.8	1738.4	1073
23609.2	20805.3	132.3	-12322.6	-9297.0	9297.0	-8045.4	1119.3	965

13-23 分行业大中型工业企业主要经济效益指标(GB/T4754-2011)

单位: % (2011 年)

行　　业	Sector	产值利税率 Ratio of Profits and Taxes to Industrial Output Value
总　　计	**Total**	**26.4**
煤炭开采和洗选业	Mining and Washing of Coal	26.6
石油和天然气开采业	Extraction of Petroleum and Natural Gas	70.2
黑色金属矿采选业	Mining and Processing of Ferrous Metals Ores	39.0
有色金属矿采选业	Mining and Processing of Nonferrous Metals Ores	62.9
非金属矿采选业	Mining and Processing of Nonmetal Ores	24.2
#采　盐	Extraction of Salt	36.4
农副食品加工业	Processing of Food from Agricultural Products	20.0
#饲料加工	Fodder Processing	16.5
制　糖	Sugar Making	25.3
食品制造业	Manufacture of Food	6.4
#罐头制造	Manufacture of can	-38.1
酒、饮料和精制茶制造业	Manufacture of Wine,Beverages and Refined Tea	33.1
#酒的制造	Manufacture of Wine	38.8
烟草制品业	Manufacture of Tobacco	69.5
纺织业	Manufacture of Textile	7.6
#棉、化纤纺织及印染精加工	Cotton, Chemical Fiber, Dyeing, Printing and Processing	7.8
毛纺织和染整精加工	Wool Textile, Dyeing and Printing	-7.3
纺织服装、鞋、帽制造业	Manufacture of Textile Wearing Apparel, Footware and Caps	2.8
家具制造业	Manufacture of Furniture	6.5
造纸及纸制品业	Manufacture of Paper and Paper Products	15.8
印刷业和记录媒介的复制	Printing and Copying of Medium for Record	7.2
石油加工、炼焦及核燃料加工业	Oil Processing, Coking and Nuclear Fuel Processing	7.1
#炼　焦	Coking	19.5
化学原料及化学制品制造业	Raw Chemical Material and Chemical Products	21.3
#基础化学原料制造	Basic Chemical Material	15.6
肥料制造	Fertilizer Making	46.2
合成材料制造	Manufacture of Synthetic Material	16.0
医药制造业	Manufacture of Medicine	9.9
化学纤维制造业	Manufacture of Chemical Fiber	0.2
橡胶制品业	Manufacture of Rubber Products	4.2
非金属矿物制品业	Manufacture of Nonmetal Mineral Products	20.7
#水泥制造	Manufacture of Cement	25.8
黑色金属冶炼及压延加工业	Smelting and Pressing of Ferrous Metals	5.3
有色金属冶炼及压延加工业	Smelting and Pressing of Nonferrous Metals	7.5
金属制品业	Manufacture of Metal Products	4.3
专用设备制造业	Manufacture of Special Purpose Machinery	16.6
汽车制造业	Manufacture of Automobile	-19.9
电气机械和器材制造业	Manufacture of Electric Equipment and Machinery	19.3
计算机、通信和其他电子设备制造业	Telecom Equipment, Computer and Other Electronic Equipment	15.8
电力、热力的生产和供应业	Electricity and Thermal Production and Supply	12.9
#电力生产和电力供应	Electricity Production and Supply	13.1
燃气生产和供应业	Gas Production and Supply	8.3
水的生产和供应业	Water Production and Supply	-50.1

Main Indicators on Economic Efficiency of Large-scale and Medium-scale Industrial Enterprises by Sectors(GB/T4754-2011)

(%)

总资产贡献率 Ratio of Total Assets to ndustrial Output Value	资本保值增值率 Ratio of Capital-hold and Rise	资产负债率 Assets Liability Ratio	流动资产周转次数(次/年) Number of Times of Annual TurnoverWorking Capitals (times/year)	成本费用利润率 Ratio of Profits to Industrial Cost	全员劳动生产率 Overall Labour Productivity
19.9	**112.6**	**52.5**	**2.4**	**19.5**	**51.2**
8.4	191.0	59.1	1.2	15.1	16.6
46.2	95.5	40.7	4.2	120.7	180.6
24.7	109.0	68.0	1.0	42.8	58.4
31.2	112.3	42.7	1.8	125.0	55.9
23.4	197.7	48.7	1.1	21.9	15.3
28.9	208.8	36.4	1.0	28.9	20.3
15.6	126.0	50.1	1.3	15.0	17.1
11.0	117.2	48.5	1.1	16.2	32.5
21.0	147.1	48.9	1.6	17.0	17.6
6.2	58.9	73.0	1.3	2.7	11.3
-6.2	12.0	93.4	0.3	-37.5	-2.1
20.2	103.1	72.0	1.0	20.5	25.6
20.7	104.8	73.6	0.8	25.9	28.4
56.6	229.6	26.4	1.2	32.1	267.2
5.7	112.5	63.8	1.3	3.7	6.3
6.0	109.4	65.6	1.3	3.8	6.6
-6.4	302.2	48.5	2.0	-8.3	2.1
5.2	108.2	69.3	3.5	1.9	7.7
1.6	99.6	13.4	1.5	5.4	9.2
9.2	119.9	62.0	0.9	11.7	6.8
3.0	105.9	52.3	0.8	1.8	7.2
13.4	119.6	38.7	5.4	-5.7	50.5
15.1	126.2	63.4	1.8	16.0	23.4
13.5	118.6	51.2	1.8	22.1	31.8
5.6	104.3	51.7	1.5	7.9	15.6
28.3	149.0	55.7	1.4	73.1	73.7
14.7	123.9	49.9	2.3	19.7	36.2
4.5	135.6	30.4	0.6	8.4	7.2
3.1	69.9	78.4	2.3	-1.3	14.8
3.8	154.1	58.1	1.4	2.1	8.2
9.9	121.3	53.0	1.1	18.5	16.5
10.1	128.2	52.8	1.0	24.1	17.6
8.0	125.3	68.0	3.1	3.1	26.4
3.9	228.7	78.8	1.3	4.7	26.7
6.5	222.7	59.6	2.0	3.7	10.4
6.6	-853.0	33.6	0.5	17.8	8.3
-8.7	-61.8	101.9	1.6	-13.1	-2.3
8.4	104.1	51.8	0.7	16.9	63.2
4.9	166.5	49.9	0.5	19.3	15.3
7.3	137.0	65.3	2.4	8.8	32.9
7.6	135.1	64.6	2.7	8.9	33.8
4.0	105.1	69.2	0.8	4.8	22.4
-2.1	10.8	52.0	0.3	-26.6	8.7

13-24 分行业大中型工业企业主要经济效益指标(GB/T4754-2002)

单位: % (2011 年)

行业	Sector	产值利税率 Ratio of Profits and Taxes to Industrial Output Value
煤炭开采和洗选业	Mining and Washing of Coal	26.5
石油和天然气开采业	Extraction of Petroleum and Natural Gas	64.6
#天然原油和天然气开采	Extraction of Ores Crude Oil and Natural Gas Extraction	70.2
黑色金属矿采选业	Mining and Processing of Ferrous Metals Ores	39.4
有色金属矿采选业	Mining and Processing of Nonferrous Metals Ores	63.2
非金属矿采选业	Mining and Processing of Nonmetal Ores	24.2
#采　盐	Extraction of Salt	36.4
农副食品加工业	Processing of Food from Agricultural Products	19.2
#饲料加工	Fodder Processing	16.5
制　糖	Sugar Making	25.6
食品制造业	Manufacture of Food	5.1
#罐头制造	Manufacture of can	-20.0
饮料制造业	Manufacture of Beverage	33.0
#酒的制造	Manufacture of Wine	38.4
烟草制品业	Manufacture of Tobacco	69.5
纺织业	Manufacture of Textile	7.7
#棉、化纤纺织及印染精加工	Cotton, Chemical Fiber, Dyeing, Printing and Processing	7.9
毛纺织和染整精加工	Wool Textile, Dyeing and Printing	-7.3
纺织服装、鞋、帽制造业	Manufacture of Textile Wearing Apparel,Footware and Caps	3.5
家具制造业	Manufacture of Furniture	6.5
造纸及纸制品业	Manufacture of Paper and Paper Products	15.8
印刷业和记录媒介的复制	Printing and Copying of Medium for Record	7.2
石油加工、炼焦及核燃料加工业	Oil Processing, Coking and Nuclear Fuel Processing	7.1
#炼　焦	Coking	19.3
化学原料及化学制品制造业	Raw Chemical Material and Chemical Products	21.3
#基础化学原料制造	Basic Chemical Material	15.6
肥料制造	Fertilizer Making	46.2
医药制造业	Manufacture of Medicine	9.9
化学纤维制造业	Manufacture of Chemical Fiber	-0.2
橡胶制品业	Manufacture of Rubber Products	4.9
塑料制品业	Manufacture of Plastic Products	3.7
非金属矿物制品业	Manufacture of Nonmetal Mineral Products	20.2
#水泥制造	Manufacture of Cement	25.2
黑色金属冶炼及压延加工业	Smelting and Pressing of Ferrous Metals	5.2
有色金属冶炼及压延加工业	Smelting and Pressing of Nonferrous Metals	7.2
金属制品业	Manufacture of Metal Products	4.7
专用设备制造业	Manufacture of Special Purpose Machinery	14.8
交通运输设备制造业	Manufacture of Transport Equipment	-19.9
电气机械及器材制造业	Manufacture of Electric Equipment and Machinery	19.4
通信设备、计算机及其他电子设备制造业	Telecom Equipment, Computer and Other Electronic Equipment	15.8
工艺品及其他制造业	Manufacture of Handicrafts and Others	15.8
电力、热力的生产和供应业	Electricity and Thermal Production and Supply	12.6
#电力生产和电力供应	Electricity Production and Supply	12.8
燃气生产和供应业	Gas Production and Supply	8.3
水的生产和供应业	Water Production and Supply	-50.1

Main Indicators on Economic Efficiency of Large-scale and Medium-scale Industrial Enterprises by Sectors(GB/T4754-2002)

(%)

总资产贡献率 Ratio of Total Assets to ndustrial Output Value	资本保值增值率 Ratio of Capital-hold and Rise	资产负债率 Assets Liability Ratio	流动资产周转次数(次/年) Number of Times of Annual TurnoverWorking Capitals (times/year)	成本费用利润率 Ratio of Profits to Industrial Cost	全员劳动生产率 Overall Labour Productivity
8.2	188.1	59.0	1.2	14.6	16.2
43.3	96.2	42.1	3.8	98.9	115.3
46.2	95.5	40.7	4.2	120.7	140.4
24.2	123.5	65.9	1.0	43.3	55.4
31.9	128.1	41.4	1.8	122.8	56.3
23.4	197.7	48.7	1.1	21.9	16.9
28.9	208.8	36.4	1.0	28.9	20.1
15.3	98.1	50.2	1.3	14.5	16.7
11.0	117.2	48.5	1.1	16.2	31.3
21.5	145.3	48.1	1.6	17.2	18.2
5.1	99.9	73.9	1.1	1.9	10.7
-4.1	60.2	88.6	0.4	-23.2	3.0
19.8	100.6	72.4	1.0	19.8	23.4
20.3	101.8	73.8	0.8	24.9	24.9
56.6	229.6	26.4	1.2	32.1	267.2
5.8	112.6	62.7	1.4	3.8	6.5
6.1	109.7	64.5	1.4	3.9	6.8
-6.4	302.2	48.5	2.0	-8.3	2.1
5.1	170.0	75.7	2.1	2.3	6.0
1.6	99.6	13.4	1.5	5.4	8.7
9.2	119.9	62.0	0.9	11.7	6.6
3.0	105.9	52.3	0.8	1.8	7.2
13.4	119.8	38.7	5.4	-5.7	49.1
15.1	130.1	62.7	1.8	15.9	24.4
13.5	118.2	51.2	1.8	22.1	31.1
5.6	103.9	51.7	1.5	7.9	16.0
28.3	149.0	55.7	1.4	73.1	72.2
4.5	135.6	30.4	0.6	8.4	7.2
2.7	66.7	79.0	2.3	-1.5	15.8
4.7	563.8	65.3	2.0	0.5	11.0
3.2	117.5	54.0	1.1	3.3	8.2
9.8	116.7	52.8	1.2	17.7	16.7
9.6	119.7	52.9	1.0	23.5	17.2
8.0	126.0	68.1	3.1	3.1	24.9
3.5	226.0	78.1	1.2	4.2	24.9
6.8	264.9	53.2	2.3	3.7	8.6
9.3	-938.3	33.0	0.8	16.6	9.3
-8.7	-61.8	101.9	1.6	-13.1	-1.6
8.4	103.6	51.8	0.7	17.0	67.6
4.9	166.5	49.9	0.5	19.3	15.3
2.7		91.6	0.5	6.4	20.1
8.0	119.6	64.9	2.6	8.6	29.7
8.4	118.7	63.8	2.9	8.7	30.6
4.0	105.1	69.2	0.8	4.8	20.4
-2.1	10.8	52.0	0.3	-26.6	7.5

13-25 主要工业产品产量
Output of Major Industrial Products

产品名称	Item	2010	2011
原煤(吨)	Raw Coal (ton)	99267283	119917064
天然原油(吨)	Crude Oil (ton)	25581585	26156316
天然气(万立方米)	Natural Gas (10 000 cu.m)	2499096	2353798
铁矿石原矿量(吨)	Crudeiron Ore (ton)	26914436	37140482
铜选矿含铜量(吨)	Cuproaurite (ton)	123250	100967
硫铁矿(折含 S 35%)(吨)	Pyritel with Content of (S35%)(ton)	166310	151684
原盐(吨)	Salt (ton)	1746712	2580489
发电量(万千瓦小时)	Electricity (10 000 kwh)	6793226	8751884
＃火 电	Thermalpower	5509050	7310090
水 电	Hydropower	970725	1145669
供热量(万吉焦)	Heat Supply (10 000 gigajoules)	25078	22990
大米(吨)	Rice (ton)	188694	193579
小麦粉(万吨)	Wheate Flour (10 000 tons)	274	278
精制食用植物油(吨)	Refined Edible Oil (ton)	1151673	1144978
成品糖(吨)	Sugar (ton)	450976	461056
饲料(吨)	Forage (ton)	1802771	2035077
糖果(吨)	Candy (ton)	3336	4510
乳制品(吨)	Dairy Products (ton)	321158	351904
罐头(吨)	Canned Food (ton)	1106348	1154128
＃番茄酱	Tomato Jam	1049068	1125359
味精(吨)	Mono Sodium Glutamate (ton)	21552	21607
酱油(吨)	Soy (ton)	24222	28955
方便面(吨)	Instant Noodles(ton)	37228	47721
发酵酒精(千升)	Zymolytic Alcohol (kilo-liter)	52110	64459
饮料酒(千升)	Alcohol Beverage(kilo-liter)	565041	645919
＃白 酒	Liquor	72553	73926
啤 酒	Beer	440895	510960
葡萄酒	Grape Wine	48472	58579
软饮料(吨)	Soft Drink (ton)	1137518	1485290
＃碳酸饮料	Carbonic Drink	65868	137139
果汁和蔬菜汁饮料	Fruit Juice and Vegetable Juice Drink	320695	483316
包装饮用水	Bottled Water	524400	672029
冷冻饮品(吨)	Ice Beverage (ton)	46653	47042
卷烟(万支)	Cigarettes (10 000 pieces)	1500000	1600081
纱(吨)	Yarn (ton)	415783	399094
布(万米)	Cloth (10 000 m)	15069	7303
＃棉 布	Pure Cotton Cloth	14919	7143
绒线(毛线)(吨)	Knitting Wool (ton)	741	444

注：钢材里包括钢材生产中消耗的外购国内钢。
Note: Rolled steel contain that manufacture of steel consumed outsourcing of internal steel.

13-25 续表 1 Continued

产品名称	Item	2010	2011
呢绒(万米)	Woolen Cloth Goods (10 000 m)	326	383
服装(万件)	Garments (10 000 units)	1451	1821
轻革(平方米)	Light Leather (sq.m)	3302302	4791153
皮鞋(万双)	Leather Shoes (10 000 pairs)	148	
人造板(立方米)	Artificial Board (cu.m)	1301944	1299462
#胶合板	Plywood	341805	364283
纤维板	Fiberboard	653259	529521
刨花板	Chip Board	254031	348831
家具(件)	Furniture (unit)	3115339	2659957
#木制家具	WoodenFurniture	2675416	2289328
金属家具	Steal Furniture	294196	227743
纸浆(吨)	Paper Pulp (ton)	312302	234700
纸制品(吨)	Paper produces (ton)	310529	332095
#瓦楞纸箱(纸箱)	Corrugaled Case	259086	276678
机制纸及纸板(吨)	Machine-made Paper and Paperboard (ton)	371032	422924
本册(万本)	Copy (10 000 copies)	1365	
原油加工量(吨)	Processed Crude Oil (ton)	21903701	23884140
汽油(吨)	Gasoline (ton)	2681492	2334956
溶剂油(吨)	Megilp (ton)	155930	176213
煤油(吨)	Kerosene (ton)	456263	461274
柴油(吨)	Diesel Oil (ton)	9761180	10973746
润滑油(吨)	Lubricating Oil (ton)	762322	825281
燃料油(吨)	Fuel Oil (ton)	195176	118462
石油沥青(吨)	Petroleum Bitumen (ton)	1507775	1734067
液化石油气(吨)	Liquefied Petroleum Gas (ton)	514246	528859
焦炭(吨)	Coke (ton)	11878348	13765167
#机械化焦炉生产的焦炭	Coke Turned out by Mechanized Coke Oven	8296973	9927078
煤气(万立方米)	Coal Gas (10 000 cu.m)	1240215	1269083
硫酸(折 100%)(吨)	Sulfuric Acid (ton)	326112	361779
盐酸(含量 31%以上)(吨)	Hydrochloric Acid (With Content of 31%) (ton)	281656	274338
氢氧化钠(烧碱)(折 100%)(吨)	Caustic Soda (ton)	916205	1315745
碳酸钠(纯碱)(吨)	Soda Ash (ton)	130803	151592
碳化钙(电石)(折 300 升/千克)(吨)	Calcium Carbide (ton)	1845104	2784380
合成氨(吨)	Synthetic Ammonia (ton)	1484103	1775660
农用氮、磷、钾化学肥料(折纯)(吨)	Chemical Fertilizers (ton)	1591043	2335610
#氮肥(折含 N 100%)	Nitrogen Fertilizers	1146900	1557445
#尿 素	Carbamide	1120660	1451997
磷肥(折合 P_2O_5 100%)	Phosphate Fertilizers	7911	18182

13-25 续表 2 Continued

产品名称	Item	2010	2011
乙烯(吨)	Ethylene(ton)	1193261	1039855
涂料(吨)	Paint (ton)	107849	72167
合成洗涤剂(吨)	Synthetic Detergents (ton)	46155	34461
化学原料药(吨)	Chemical Medicine (ton)	47	28
中成药(吨)	Traditional Chinese Medicine (ton)	6957	5993
轮胎外胎(条)	Outer Tyres (unit)	921296	1038487
塑料制品(吨)	Plastic Produces (ton)	830651	1041107
＃塑料薄膜	Plastic Film	157471	187406
＃农用薄膜	Farm Plastic Sheet	143888	176028
塑料型材(含板片材)	Plastic Moulding Material	33660	30685
塑料制管子及其附件(吨)	Plastic Pipe and Accessory (ton)	330431	431629
塑料编织袋(吨)	Woven Plastic Bag (ton)	93428	112257
泡沫塑料(吨)	Foamed Plastics (ton)	16986	35399
塑料包装箱及容器(吨)	Plastic Packing Case and Container (ton)	46881	46921
日用塑料制品(吨)	Household Plastic Products (ton)	27588	25775
水泥熟料(万吨)	Cement Chamotte (10 000 ton)	1879	2528
窑外分解窑熟料(预分解窑熟料)(万吨)	Clinker Cement (10 000 tons)	1314	1536
水泥(万吨)	Cement (10 000 tons)	2401	3172
水泥电杆(根)	Cement Electric Pole Piece (unit)	278519	276753
建筑涂料(吨)	Architectural Coating (ton)	3329	
商品混凝土(立方米)	Commercial Concrete (cu.m)	15872581	23814641
预应力混凝土桩 (米)	Prestressed Concrete Piles (m)	2592414	4980957
砖(折标准砖)(万块)	Brick (Standard Brick) (10 000 pieces)	1252827	1573813
瓦(万片)	Tile (10 000 pieces)	7071	9118
大理石板材(平方米)	Marble Slab (sq.m)	328249	1240465
花岗石板材(平方米)	Granite Sheet (sq.m)	9729097	12609309
石膏板(万平方米)	Plasterboard (sq.m)	672	845
平板玻璃(重量箱)	Plate Glass (weight case)	3420192	2454818
沥青和改性沥青防水卷材(平方米)	Bitumen and Rolled Waterproof Material (sq.m)	3264350	2039281
中空玻璃(平方米)	Insulating Glass (sq.m)	91863	131772
钢化玻璃(平方米)	Toughened Glass (sq.m)	118035	106297
夹层玻璃(平方米)	Laminated Glass (sq.m)	31847	21829
日用玻璃制品(吨)	Household Glass Products (ton)	112092	55926
玻璃保温容器(万个)	Glass Attemperator (10 000 units)	919	1031

13-25 续表 3 Continued

产品名称	Item	2010	2011
陶质砖(平方米)	Carbonic Bricks (sq.m)	32415720	21282306
耐火材料制品(吨)	Fire Proof Material (ton)	136074	200069
石墨及碳素制品(吨)	Graphite and Carbon Products (ton)	146398	173344
玻璃纤维增强塑料制品(吨)	Glass Fibre Reinforced Plastices Products (ton)	37368	28527
生铁(吨)	Pig Iron (ton)	9411248	10884521
粗钢(吨)	Crude Steel (ton)	8255449	8929755
钢材(吨)	Rolled Steel (ton)	8916980	9851406
中小型型钢	Medium and Small Fasioned Steel	266809	378595
钢　筋	Concrete Iron	2403164	2844017
盘　条(线材)	Wire Rod	1964219	2049975
铁合金(吨)	Ferroalloy (ton)	149759	160568
铜(吨)	Copper (ton)	6461	16721
镍(吨)	Nickel (ton)	5936	8128
铝(吨)	Aluminium (ton)	65954	294144
铝材(吨)	Aluminium Material (ton)	45174	54773
工业锅炉(蒸发量吨)	Industrial Boiler (evaporating quantity ton)	729	947
泵(台)	Pump (unit)	9033	10953
风机(台)	Fan (unit)	5605	7559
铸钢件(吨)	Steel Casting (ton)	17094	17081
铸铁件(吨)	Iron Casting (ton)	43436	31442
小型拖拉机(台)	Small-Size Tractor (unit)	1517	1448
农作物收获机械(台)	Grop Harvesting Machinery (unit)	3371	9708
汽车(辆)	Motor Vehicles(unit)	1763	1148
#载货汽车	Trucks	1763	1148
改装汽车(辆)	Modified Truck (unit)	2236	1576
发电设备(千瓦)	Power Generating Equipment (kw)	5023500	3540500
变压器(千伏安)	Transformer (kva)	35829383	48550052
电力电缆(公里)	Electric Cable (km)	35800	65961

13-26 各地、州、市主要工业产品产量

年份 Year	地区 Region	纱(吨) Yarn (ton)	布(万米) Cloth (10 000 m)	绒线(吨) Knitting Wool (ton)	呢绒(万米) Woolen Piece Goods (10 000 m)
1978		28008	15616	1239	189.37
1980		31272	16931	1614	240.08
1985		39130	21150	2396	680
1990		101941	30017	2179	1230
1995		244689	30460	2286	1262
1996		208526	27186	2202	1361
1997		247143	29862	2393	1227
1998		220332	26719	1361	979
1999		294378	27450	1349	798
2000		334307	28060	1184	754
2001		302654	25380	843	399
2002		316095	20679	811	264.58
2003		292713	15239	744	205.58
2004		291386	13989	980	205.92
2005		340864	14047	1118	283.68
2006		357324	15415	799	326.67
2007		408870	16000	637	367.51
2008		397417	15302	578	412
2009		386085	15148	533	375.76
2010		415783	15069	741	326
2011		399094	7303	444	383
乌鲁木齐市	Urumqi City	25345	444	260	
克拉玛依市	Karamay City				
吐鲁番地区	Turpan Administrative Offices	3870			
哈密地区	Hami [Kumul] Administrative Offices	11979			
昌吉回族自治州	Changji Hui Autonomous Prefecture	76461	563		156
伊犁哈萨克自治州	Ili Kazak Autonomous Prefecture	36053	939	183	
伊犁州直属县(市)	Counties (Cities) Direct Under Ili Prefecture	18002	159	3	
塔城地区	Tacheng [Tarbagatai] Administrative Offices	18051	780	180	
阿勒泰地区	Altay Administrative Offices				
博尔塔拉蒙古自治州	Bortala Mongol Autonomous Prefecture	16004	115		
巴音郭楞蒙古自治州	Bayangol Mongol Autonomous Prefecture	30159	707		
阿克苏地区	Aksu Administrative Offices	41329	216		
克孜勒苏柯尔克孜自治州	Kizilsu Kirgiz Autonomous Prefecture				
喀什地区	Kashgar [Kaxgar] Administrative Offices	27422	89		
和田地区	Hotan Administrative Offices	877			
自治区直辖县级市	Municpality Country-LevelCity directly under the Central Government				
石河子市	Shihezi City	107565	3778	1	227
阿拉尔市	Aral City	9592	137		
图木舒克市	Tumxuk City	4501	315		
五家渠市	Wujiaqu City	7939			

Output of Major Industrial Products by Prefecture, Autonomous Prefecture and City

机制纸及纸板(吨) Machine-made Paper and Paperboard (ton)	原盐(万吨) Salt (10 000 tons)	成品糖(万吨) Sugar (10 000 tons)	饮料酒(千升) Alcohol Beverage (kilo-liter)	卷烟(亿支) Cigarettes (100 million pieces)	原煤(万吨) Coal (10 000 tons)	原油(万吨) Crude Oil (10 000 tons)	天然气(万立方米) Natural gas (10 000 cu.m)	发电量(亿千瓦时) Electricity (100 million kwh)	#水电 Hydropower
19851	51.71	2.08	9336	15.05	1079.01	353.05	25100	21.17	4.64
23838	38.18	4.43	17082	15.55	1136.84	390.58	35298	23.58	5.25
41521	35.09	7.18	74809	40.20	1600.22	499.00	54556	38.11	8.64
90857	159.00	16.84	118585	61.70	2100.00	695.00	50161	69.79	14.25
180440	25.98	30.18	249481	68.05	2720.74	1267.83	114821	120.43	22.82
169789	36.54	36.34	219961	67.80	2986.00	1457.10	140609	136.03	24.49
161659	39.85	42.28	259015	66.05	3021.37	1629.25	213006	150.58	26.97
168799	27.53	47.59	271056	60.20	2926.91	1628.38	237826	157.76	28.23
180138	36.14	46.36	269453	55.00	2778.16	1739.65	310600	169.30	30.06
176477	31.78	30.76	269761	52.50	2798.90	1848.43	353930	182.98	30.53
193389	46.02	41.98	296187	55.20	2819.61	1946.95	417429	197.62	34.10
226950	50.75	51.84	307167	60.00	3098.67	2036.19	485237	212.24	34.67
233365	52.71	45.43	317260	62.50	3482.86	2141.39	502942	234.62	36.20
263066	87.32	37.26	345770	70.00	3749.40	2253.02	574805	266.30	37.08
289318	85.35	42.92	355275	70.00	3898.81	2408.32	1066437	306.92	43.27
295338	153.21	53.79	401771	85.00	4518.52	2474.74	1642099	357.15	53.43
252329	111.53	64.94	438502	100.00	5018.64	2604.31	2103348	416.87	58.78
301606	153.06	53.78	486007	120.00	6763.41	2715.13	2358941	489.17	73.84
355762	129.36	40.77	484936	135.00	8812.55	2512.86	2453887	571.31	79.84
371032	174.67	45.10	565041	150.00	9926.72	2558.16	2499096	679.33	97.07
422924	258.05	46.11	645919	160.00	11991.71	2615.63	2353798	875.19	114.57
86283	10.31		140667		1930.28	725.00	159429	241.35	
	0.09		3599		90.00	1090.01	371039	43.36	0.06
	48.60		6725		1302.05	155.00	105006	27.05	0.01
1912	19.41		28102		1804.94			29.55	0.04
119126		5.00	63548		3886.23			133.51	0.38
11525	151.86	27.79	167738	160.00	1230.88	68.00		127.34	60.84
5783		18.16	85324	160.00	554.20			72.95	44.96
5126	151.84	8.90	81014		665.76	68.00		36.65	2.35
616	0.02	0.73	1399		10.92			17.73	13.53
	5.94	2.55	1073					6.95	2.71
104066	18.94	8.05	42456		320.11	577.62	1705000	49.49	17.16
	2.91	2.28	32093		1308.62			44.94	10.92
			2		12.82			0.51	0.16
15472		0.44	28292		14.10			22.62	7.62
			185		54.87			10.28	9.94
31461			131333		27.79			126.49	4.54
								6.62	
			100					5.12	
53079			6		9.00				

13-26 续表

年 份 Year	地 区 Region	生铁(万吨) Pig Iron (10 000 tons)	粗钢(万吨) Crude Steel (10 000 tons)	大理石板材(平方米) Marble Plate (sq.m.)	钢材(万吨) Steel Rolled (10 000 tons)
	1978	17.52	8.46		6.83
	1980	15.81	10.74		8.59
	1985	22.87	19.79		16.73
	1990	40.57	36.49	9589	28.48
	1995	69.53	70.59	34169	66.55
	1996	85.64	87.47	6420	86.70
	1997	93.82	97.21	53588	99.89
	1998	100.40	107.67	9197	116.19
	1999	101.30	105.60	7807	117.30
	2000	106.42	109.70	6294	131.26
	2001	111.73	131.83	22786	134.42
	2002	122.78	175.45	34185	173.07
	2003	144.86	204.12	117306	203.10
	2004	193.89	249.13	109663	238.52
	2005	258.66	306.54	78577	326.96
	2006	324.08	394.19	176025	411.45
	2007	394.97	447.24	119926	470.94
	2008	505.70	536.60	160011	576.62
	2009	764.62	653.32	190480	690.81
	2010	941.12	825.54	328249	891.70
	2011	1088.45	892.98	1240465	985.14
乌鲁木齐市	Urumqi City	597.73	694.90	11349	791.99
克拉玛依市	Karamay City				0.03
吐鲁番地区	Turpan Administrative Offices	105.84		19001	
哈密地区	Hami [Kumul] Administrative Offices	15.20			
昌吉回族自治州	Changji Hui Autonomous Prefecture	75.15		17562	0.66
伊犁哈萨克自治州	Ili Kazak Autonomous Prefecture	125.45	76.92	110657	65.32
伊犁州直属县(市)	Counties (Cities) Direct Under Ili Prefecture	108.44	57.46	49487	56.55
塔城地区	Tacheng [Tarbagatai] Administrative Offices		19.47		8.68
阿勒泰地区	Altay Administrative Offices	17.02		61170	0.09
博尔塔拉蒙古自治州	Bortala Mongol Autonomous Prefecture	14.38		1058945	
巴音郭楞蒙古自治州	Bayangol Mongol Autonomous Prefecture	121.09	121.16	5450	121.21
阿克苏地区	Aksu Administrative Offices	5.74		15000	1.36
克孜勒苏柯尔克孜自治州	Kizilsu Kirgiz Autonomous Prefecture	15.06		2500	
喀什地区	Kashgar [Kaxgar] Administrative Offices	12.81			1.71
和田地区	Hotan Administrative Offices				
自治区直辖县级市	Municpality Country-LevelCity directly under the Central Government				
石河子市	Shihezi City				2.86
阿拉尔市	Aral City				
图木舒克市	Tumxuk City				
五家渠市	Wujiaqu City				

Continued

水 泥 (万吨) Cement (10 000 tons)	硫 酸 (吨) Sulfuric Acid (ton)	烧 碱 (吨) Caustic Soda (ton)	合成氨 (吨)(折纯) Synthetic Ammonia (ton)	农用氮、磷、钾化肥(吨) Farm Nitrogen Phophate and Potassium (ton)	碳化钙 (电石)(吨) Calcium Crbide (ton)	塑料制品 (吨) Plastic Products (ton)	小型拖拉机 (台) Small Tractor (unit)
78.15	20262	4164	33155	20276	4895	3194	843
90.89	19153	3542	13762	9207	4486	2051	137
201.05	23921	5045	85728	58080	5989	17974	11117
285.00	47732	15063	397062	287640	15976	40958	17081
489.88	88491	24732	492754	383279	12344	100739	30352
562.87	76413	28008	488337	372056	15901	129059	26671
628.00	77187	35544	581449	428711	28350	143916	14780
728.94	64836	39614	688069	520681	28999	168372	19017
805.83	68169	42161	896632	685587	40216	139497	17048
895.67	71458	51831	947511	754668	51749	197756	13472
981.29	72511	68589	884340	729034	65763	262873	12672
1029.71	70407	93362	956732	766291	73680	230729	4019
1128.98	85322	114110	1082601	854530	82057	314891	
1212.99	114046	174445	1015630	869795	115991	388270	1407
1241.74	126901	295917	1192001	1285346	290591	349151	5171
1334.50	160073	423901	1303586	1290802	501283	412032	
1536.77	183484	485880	1325017	1385279	711277	517069	5408
1672.76	201993	630314	1471312	1609409	910659	653230	4429
2049.60	300423	814393	1407674	1591027	1560762	697269	2923
2400.96	326112	916205	1484103	1591043	1845104	830651	1517
3171.71	361779	1315745	1775660	2335610	2784380	1041107	1448
552.25	9250	614437	699310	554202	163659	263630	1448
				34129		23750	
132.26	125541				512256		
172.39				8684		12890	
254.71	20605	6942		1660	380233	241733	
669.90	116767		3483	32827	149945	144962	
301.30				320	116574	39651	
252.82	26057		3483	32507	33371	95433	
115.78	90710					9878	
65.28				150		41210	
195.76		4052	742288	1252132		34284	
477.41	37556		330579	379178		48298	
70.30						223	
154.18	16015					30113	
144.09				656		1656	
267.04	36046	690314			1578287	139084	
						25498	
16.14						14015	
				71992		19762	

13-27 国有控股企业主要指标占全区规模以上工业比重

Percentage of Main Indicators in State-holding Enterprises to Enterprises above Designated Size

单位：万元　　(2011 年)　　(10 000 yuan)

指　标	Item	全区规模以上工业企业 Enterprises Above Designated Size	国　有控股企业 State-Holding Enterprises	比 重(%) Percentage (%)
企业单位数(个)	Number of Enterprises(unit)	1738	459	26.4
从业人员(人)	Employed Person (person)	589851	349653	59.3
工业总产值	Gross Industrial Output Value	67208461.8	48665888.6	72.4
工业销售产值	Sales Value of Industry Products	65996909.7	48307739.5	73.2
出口交货值	Delivery Value of Industry Export	704655.1	384013.6	54.5
资产总计	Total Assets	93049478.0	64283377.6	69.1
负债合计	Total Liabilities	50049876.1	32880103.5	65.7
所有者权益	Owner's Right and Interest	42830300.1	31382030.0	73.3
实收资本	Substantial Capital	31198256.3	25679116.9	82.3
主营业务收入	Revenue from Principal Business	67822512.9	49136691.5	72.5
主营业务税金及附加	Taes and Other Charges on Principal Business	3344488.5	3225268.0	96.4
利润总额	Total Profits	9530340.3	7772742.5	81.6
利税总额	Total Profits and Tax	15995281.7	13476205.9	84.3
亏损单位数(个)	Number of Loss-suffering Enterprises (unit)	357	89	24.9
亏损企业亏损额	Losses Value of Loss-suffering	1498984.4	1311681.1	87.5

13-28 重点行业主要指标占全区规模以上工业比重(GB/T4754-2011)

Percentage of Main Indicators in Key Industrial Sectors to Xinjiang's Industry above Designated Size(GB/T4754-2011)

(2011 年)

指　标	Item	合　计 Total	占全区比重 (%) Percentage (%)
从业人员(人)	**Employed Person (person)**	**589851**	
石油和天然气开采业	Extraction of Petroleum and Natural Gas	72579	12.3
石油加工、炼焦及核燃料加工业	Petroleum Processing,Coking and Nuclear Fuel Processing	43088	7.3
黑色金属冶炼及压延加工业	Smelting and Pressing of Ferrous Metal	35950	6.1
电力、热力的生产和供应业	Electric Power, Thermal Power Production and Supply	50879	8.6
化学原料及化学制品制造业	Raw Chemical Material and Chemical Products	49279	8.4
纺织业	Textile Industry	39803	6.7
农副食品加工业	Processing of Food from Agricultural Products	27233	4.6
工业总产值(万元)	**Gross Industrial Output Value (10 000 yuan)**	**67208461.8**	
石油和天然气开采业	Extraction of Petroleum and Natural Gas	14130667.7	21.0
石油加工、炼焦及核燃料加工业	Petroleum Processing,Coking and Nuclear Fuel Processing	15720006.4	23.4
黑色金属冶炼及压延加工业	Smelting and Pressing of Ferrous Metal	6795822.6	10.1
电力、热力的生产和供应业	Electric Power, Thermal Power Production and Supply	4593579.5	6.8
化学原料及化学制品制造业	Raw Chemical Material and Chemical Products	4548905.2	6.8
纺织业	Textile Industry	1217671.9	1.8
农副食品加工业	Processing of Food from Agricultural Products	2689141.9	4.0
工业销售产值(万元)	**Sales Value of Industry Products (10 000 yuan)**	**65996909.7**	
石油和天然气开采业	Extraction of Petroleum and Natural Gas	14096222.2	21.4
石油加工、炼焦及核燃料加工业	Petroleum Processing,Coking and Nuclear Fuel Processing	15598128.7	23.6
黑色金属冶炼及压延加工业	Smelting and Pressing of Ferrous Metal	6709361.5	10.2
电力、热力的生产和供应业	Electric Power, Thermal Power Production and Supply	4579646.6	6.9
化学原料及化学制品制造业	Raw Chemical Material and Chemical Products	4342820.3	6.6
纺织业	Textile Industry	1157568.3	1.8
农副食品加工业	Processing of Food from Agricultural Products	2578321.6	3.9

注：所列行业为工业总产值百亿元以上行业。
Note: Listed sector of gross industrial output value were above ten billion sector.

13-28 续表 Continued

指　标	Item	合　计 Total	占全区比重(%) Percentage(%)
资产总计(万元)	**Total of Assets (10 000 yuan)**	**93049478.0**	
石油和天然气开采业	Extraction of Petroleum and Natural Gas	21241104.8	22.8
石油加工、炼焦及核燃料加工业	Petroleum Processing,Coking and Nuclear Fuel Processing	8825292.7	9.5
黑色金属冶炼及压延加工业	Smelting and Pressing of Ferrous Metal	5851771.6	6.3
电力、热力的生产和供应业	Electric Power, Thermal Power Production and Supply	12516049.3	13.5
化学原料及化学制品制造业	Raw Chemical Material and Chemical Products	7577741.8	8.1
纺织业	Textile Industry	2093332.0	2.2
农副食品加工业	Processing of Food from Agricultural Products	2494105.0	2.7
利润总额(万元)	**Total Profits (10 000 yuan)**	**9637368.2**	
石油和天然气开采业	Extraction of Petroleum and Natural Gas	6952227.6	72.1
石油加工、炼焦及核燃料加工业	Petroleum Processing,Coking and Nuclear Fuel Processing	-753763.7	-7.8
黑色金属冶炼及压延加工业	Smelting and Pressing of Ferrous Metal	213451.9	2.2
电力、热力的生产和供应业	Electric Power, Thermal Power Production and Supply	453165.3	4.7
化学原料及化学制品制造业	Raw Chemical Material and Chemical Products	677372.8	7.0
纺织业	Textile Industry	47047.6	0.5
农副食品加工业	Processing of Food from Agricultural Products	139441.1	1.4
利税总额(万元)	**Total Profitsand Tax (10 000 yuan)**	**16102161.6**	
石油和天然气开采业	Extraction of Petroleum and Natural Gas	9687694.3	60.2
石油加工、炼焦及核燃料加工业	Petroleum Processing,Coking and Nuclear Fuel Processing	1140743.3	7.1
黑色金属冶炼及压延加工业	Smelting and Pressing of Ferrous Metal	355171.3	2.2
电力、热力的生产和供应业	Electric Power, Thermal Power Production and Supply	682093.1	4.2
化学原料及化学制品制造业	Raw Chemical Material and Chemical Products	907984.8	5.6
纺织业	Textile Industry	91146.2	0.6
农副食品加工业	Processing of Food from Agricultural Products	193806.6	1.2
主营业务收入(万元)	**Revenue from Principal Business (10 000 yuan)**	**67822512.9**	
石油和天然气开采业	Extraction of Petroleum and Natural Gas	14797418.6	21.8
石油加工、炼焦及核燃料加工业	Petroleum Processing,Coking and Nuclear Fuel Processing	16016213.8	23.6
黑色金属冶炼及压延加工业	Smelting and Pressing of Ferrous Metal	6969285.6	10.3
化学原料及化学制品制造业	Raw Chemical Material and Chemical Products	3996385.9	5.9
电力、热力的生产和供应业	Electric Power, Thermal Power Production and Supply	4557462.0	6.7
纺织业	Textile Industry	1254465.3	1.8
农副食品加工业	Processing of Food from Agricultural Products	2725218.0	4.0

13-29 重点行业主要指标占全区规模以上工业比重(GB/T4754-2002)

Percentage of Main Indicators in Key Industrial Sectors to Xinjiang's Industry above Designated Size(GB/T4754-2002)

(2011 年)

指　标	Item	合　计 Total	占全区比重(%) Percentage(%)
从业人员(人)	**Employed Person (person)**	**589851**	
石油和天然气开采业	Extraction of Petroleum and Natural Gas	99357	16.8
石油加工、炼焦及核燃料加工业	Petroleum Processing,Coking and Nuclear Fuel Processing	43088	7.3
黑色金属冶炼及压延加工业	Smelting and Pressing of Ferrous Metal	36302	6.2
电力、热力的生产和供应业	Electric Power, Thermal Power Production and Supply	50879	8.6
化学原料及化学制品制造业	Raw Chemical Material and Chemical Products	49279	8.4
纺织业	Textile Industry	39198	6.6
农副食品加工业	Processing of Food from Agricultural Products	27931	4.7
工业总产值(万元)	**Gross Industrial Output Value (10 000 yuan)**	**67208461.8**	
石油和天然气开采业	Extraction of Petroleum and Natural Gas	15412392.0	22.9
石油加工、炼焦及核燃料加工业	Petroleum Processing,Coking and Nuclear Fuel Processing	15720006.4	23.4
黑色金属冶炼及压延加工业	Smelting and Pressing of Ferrous Metal	6797932.0	10.1
电力、热力的生产和供应业	Electric Power, Thermal Power Production and Supply	4593579.5	6.8
化学原料及化学制品制造业	Raw Chemical Material and Chemical Products	4577273.6	6.8
纺织业	Textile Industry	1211101.0	1.8
农副食品加工业	Processing of Food from Agricultural Products	2740306.4	4.1
工业销售产值(万元)	**Sales Value of Industry Products (10 000 yuan)**	**65996909.7**	
石油和天然气开采业	Extraction of Petroleum and Natural Gas	15377576.0	23.3
石油加工、炼焦及核燃料加工业	Petroleum Processing,Coking and Nuclear Fuel Processing	15598128.7	23.6
黑色金属冶炼及压延加工业	Smelting and Pressing of Ferrous Metal	6717698.3	10.2
电力、热力的生产和供应业	Electric Power, Thermal Power Production and Supply	4579646.6	6.9
化学原料及化学制品制造业	Raw Chemical Material and Chemical Products	4371138.7	6.6
纺织业	Textile Industry	1151813.8	1.7
农副食品加工业	Processing of Food from Agricultural Products	2608465.4	4.0

注：所列行业为工业总产值百亿元以上行业。
Note: Listed sector of gross industrial output value were above ten billion sector.

13-29 续表 Continued

指　标	Item	合　计 Total	占全区比重(%) Percentage(%)
资产总计(万元)	**Total of Assets (10 000 yuan)**	**93049478.0**	
石油和天然气开采业	Extraction of Petroleum and Natural Gas	22793438.2	24.5
石油加工、炼焦及核燃料加工业	Petroleum Processing,Coking and Nuclear Fuel Processing	8825292.7	9.5
黑色金属冶炼及压延加工业	Smelting and Pressing of Ferrous Metal	5860563.0	6.3
电力、热力的生产和供应业	Electric Power, Thermal Power Production and Supply	12516049.3	13.5
化学原料及化学制品制造业	Raw Chemical Material and Chemical Products	7610561.9	8.2
纺织业	Textile Industry	2077527.8	2.2
农副食品加工业	Processing of Food from Agricultural Products	2666844.2	2.9
利润总额(万元)	**Total Profits (10 000 yuan)**	**9637368.2**	
石油和天然气开采业	Extraction of Petroleum and Natural Gas	6908968.1	71.7
石油加工、炼焦及核燃料加工业	Petroleum Processing,Coking and Nuclear Fuel Processing	-753763.7	-7.8
黑色金属冶炼及压延加工业	Smelting and Pressing of Ferrous Metal	209531.1	2.2
电力、热力的生产和供应业	Electric Power, Thermal Power Production and Supply	453165.3	4.7
化学原料及化学制品制造业	Raw Chemical Material and Chemical Products	682493.4	7.1
纺织业	Textile Industry	45590.4	0.5
农副食品加工业	Processing of Food from Agricultural Products	138915.6	1.4
利税总额(万元)	**Total Profitsand Tax (10 000 yuan)**	**16102161.6**	
石油和天然气开采业	Extraction of Petroleum and Natural Gas	9714651.4	60.3
石油加工、炼焦及核燃料加工业	Petroleum Processing,Coking and Nuclear Fuel Processing	1140743.3	7.1
黑色金属冶炼及压延加工业	Smelting and Pressing of Ferrous Metal	353369.6	2.2
电力、热力的生产和供应业	Electric Power, Thermal Power Production and Supply	682093.1	4.2
化学原料及化学制品制造业	Raw Chemical Material and Chemical Products	915157.2	5.7
纺织业	Textile Industry	89494.0	0.6
农副食品加工业	Processing of Food from Agricultural Products	193281.1	1.2
主营业务收入(万元)	**Revenue from Principal Business (10 000 yuan)**	**67822512.9**	
石油和天然气开采业	Extraction of Petroleum and Natural Gas	16007529.7	23.6
石油加工、炼焦及核燃料加工业	Petroleum Processing,Coking and Nuclear Fuel Processing	16016213.8	23.6
黑色金属冶炼及压延加工业	Smelting and Pressing of Ferrous Metal	6975049.8	10.3
化学原料及化学制品制造业	Raw Chemical Material and Chemical Products	4021076.2	5.9
电力、热力的生产和供应业	Electric Power, Thermal Power Production and Supply	4557462.0	6.7
纺织业	Textile Industry	1248916.3	1.8
农副食品加工业	Processing of Food from Agricultural Products	2755361.8	4.1

13-30 规模以上工业主要产品生产能力
Production Capacity of Major Industrial Products above Designated Size

产品名称	Item	2010	2011
原煤(吨)	Raw Coal (ton)	94730000	107859000
天然原油(吨)	Crude Oil (ton)	27314200	26325400
发电设备容量(万千瓦)	Generating Capacity (10 000 kw)	1339	1698
卷烟(万支)	Cigarettes (10 000 pieces)	1500000	2303316
化学纤维(吨)	Chemical Fiber (ton)	370000	500000
棉纺锭(环锭纺)(锭)	Cotton Hasp (unit)	3774936	4024464
气流纺锭(转杯纺)(头)	Airflow Hasp (unit)	71654	71416
棉布织机(台)	Calico Spinning Machine (set)	5129	4319
焦炭(吨)	Coke (ton)	21708000	23653088
炭化钙(电石)(折 300 升/千克)(吨)	Calcium Carbide (ton)	2240000	3708000
农用氮、磷、钾化学肥料(折纯)(吨)	Chemical Fertilizers (ton)	2268509	2755337
水泥熟料(吨)	Cement Chamotte (ton)	25690000	36593000
#窑外分解窑熟料	Decompose Cellar Chamotte	20095000	29860000
水泥(吨)	Cement (ton)	33605000	49005000
平板玻璃(重量箱)	Plate Glass (weight case)	3600000	2000000
平拉玻璃(重量箱)	Plate Drawing Glass (weight case)	2000000	2000000
生铁(吨)	Pig Iron (ton)	12052000	14347402
粗钢(吨)	Crude Steel (ton)	10350000	11440000
钢材(吨)	Rolled Steel (ton)	12131500	13186500
铁合金(吨)	Ferroalloy (ton)	218000	225000
原铝(电解铝)(吨)	Aluminium (ton)	261200	594700
汽车(辆)	Motor Vehicles(unit)	5000	5000

主要统计指标解释

工业 指从事自然资源的开采，对采掘品和农产品进行加工和再加工的物质生产部门。具体包括：(1)对自然资源的开采，如采矿、晒盐等(但不包括禽兽捕猎和水产捕捞)；(2)对农副产品的加工、再加工，如粮油加工、食品加工、缫丝、纺织、制革等；(3)对采掘品的加工、再加工，如炼铁、炼钢、化工生产、石油加工、机器制造、木材加工等，以及电力、自来水、煤气的生产和供应等；(4)对工业品的修理、翻新，如机器设备的修理、交通运输工具(包括小卧车)的修理等。

工业统计调查单位为独立核算法人工业企业。

独立核算法人工业企业指从事工业生产经营活动的单位。独立核算法人工业企业应同时具备以下条件：①依法成立，有自己的名称、组织机构和场所，能够承担民事责任；②独立拥有和使用资产，承担负债，有权与其他单位签订合同；③独立核算盈亏，并能够编制资产负债表。

本年鉴中涉及的企业登记注册类型：

国有及国有控股企业 指国有企业加上国有控股企业。国有企业(即原全民所有制工业或国营工业)指企业全部资产归国家所有，并按《中华人民共和国企业法人登记管理条例》规定登记注册的非公司制的经济组织。包括国有企业、国有独资公司和国有联营企业。1957年以前的公私合营和私营工业，后均改造为国营工业，1992年改为国有工业，这部分工业的资料不单独分列时，均包括在国有企业内。国有控股企业是对混合所有制经济的企业进行的"国有控股"分类。它是指这些企业的全部资产中国有资产(股份)相对其他所有者中的任何一个所有者占资(股)最多的企业。该分组反映了国有经济控股情况。

本篇涉及的其他企业登记注册类型的解释详见综合篇。

轻工业 指主要提供生活消费品和制作手工工具的工业。按其所使用的原料不同，可分为两大类：(1)以农产品为原料的轻工业，是指直接或间接以农产品为基本原料的轻工业。主要包括食品制造、饮料制造、烟草加工、纺织、缝纫、皮革和毛皮制作、造纸以及印刷等工业；(2)以非农产品为原料的轻工业，是指以工业品为原料的轻工业。主要包括文教体育用品、化学药品制造、合成纤维制造、日用化学制品、日用玻璃制品、日用金属制品、手工工具制造、医疗器械制造、文化和办公用机械制造等工业。

重工业 指为国民经济各部门提供物质技术基础的主要生产资料的工业。按其生产性质和产品用途，可以分为下列三类：(1)采掘(伐)工业，是指对自然资源的开采，包括石油开采、煤炭开采、金属矿开采、非金属矿开采等工业；(2)原材料工业，指向国民经济各部门提供基本材料、动力和燃料的工业。包括金属冶炼及加工、炼焦及焦炭、化学、化工原料、水泥、人造板以及电力、石油和煤炭加工等工业；(3)加工工业，是指对工业原材料进行再加工制造的工业。包括装备国民经济各部门的机械设备制造工业、金属结构、水泥制品等工业，以及为农业提供的生产资料如化肥、农药等工业。

根据上述划分原则，修理业中以重工业产品为修理作业对象的划为重工业，反之划为轻工业。

工业总产值

(1)定义：工业总产值是以货币形式表现的，工业企业在一定时期内生产的工业最终产品或提供工业性劳务活动的总价值量。它反映一定时间内工业生产的总规模和总水平。

(2)计算原则：

工业生产的原则，即凡是企业在报告期生产的经检验合格的产品，不管是否在报告期销售，均包括在内。

最终产品的原则，即凡是计入工业总产值的产品，必须是本企业生产的经检验合格的，不需要再进行任何加工的最终产品。如果企业有中间产品(半成品)对外销售，则对外销售的中间产品应视为企业的最终产品。

工厂法原则，即工业总产值是以工业企业作为基本计算(核算)单位，即按企业的最终产品计算工业总产值。按这种方法计算的工业总产值，不允许同一产品价值在企业内部重复计算，不能把企业内部各个车间(分厂)生产的成果相加，但允许企业间的重复计算。

(3)内容及计算方法：

1995年全国工业普查对工业总产值(原规定)的内容及计算原则和方法做了某些修订，修订后的工业总产值(新规定)包括三项内容：即本期生产成品价值、对外加工费收入、在制品半成品期末期初差额价值三部分。

本期生产成品价值：指企业本期生产，并在报告期内不再进行加工，经检验、包装入库的全部工业成品(半产品)价值合计，包括企业生产的自制设备及提供给本企业在建工程、其他非工业部门和福利部门等单位使用的成品价值。本期生产成品价值为按自备原材料生产的产品的数量乘以本期不含增值税(销项税额)的产品实际销售平均单价计算；会计核算中按成本价格转帐的自制设备和自产自用的成品，按成本价格计算生产成品价值。生产成品价值中不包括用定货者来料加工的成品(半产品)价值。

对外加工费收入：指企业在报告期内完成的对外承接的工业品加工(包括用定货者来料加工产品)的加工费收入和对外工业修理作业所取得的加工费收入。对外加工费收入按不含增值税(销项税额)的价格计算，可根据会计"产品销售收入"科目的有关资料取得。

对于本企业对内非工业部门提供的加工修理、设备安装的劳务收入，如果企业会计核算基础较好，能取得这部分资料，而且这部分价值所占比重较大，应包括在对外加工费收入中。

自制半成品在制品期末期初差额价值：指企业报告期在制品期末减期初的差额价值，本指标一般可以从会计核算资料中取得。如果会计产品成本核算中不计算半成品、在制品的成本，则总产值中也不包括这部分价值，反之则包括。

(4)工业总产值统计范围变化和计算方法修订情况：

1984年以前工业总产值不包括村办工业，村办工业总产值划归农业。1984年以后工业总产值包括村办工业。

1995年工业普查对工业总产值计算方法做了修订，即从1995年始按新修订(新规定)方法计算工业总产值。新规定与原规定的区别如下：

全价与加工费的计算原则不同：新规定为凡自备原材料，不论其生产繁简程度如何，一律按全价计算工业总产值；凡来料加工，允许按加工费计算工业总产值。原规定则视生产加工的繁简程度不同，规定哪些行业按全价，哪些行业按加工费计算工业总产值。

自制半成品、在产品期末期初差额价值的计算原则不同：新规定要求，凡会计产品成本核算时计算了成本的差额价值，总产值中就应包括，否则可不包括；原规定则按生产周期六个月的界限区分，凡生产周期六个月以上的企业，总产值计算中应包括这部分差额价值，否则可不包括。

计算价格不同：新规定按不含增值税(销项税额)的价格计算；原规定则按含增值税(销项税额)的价格计算。

工业增加值 指工业企业在报告期内以货币表现的工业生产活动的最终成果。

工业增加值有两种计算方法：一是生产法，即工业总产出减去工业中间投入加上应交增值税；二是收入法，即从收入的角度出发，根据生产要素在生产过程中应得到的收入份额计算，具体构成项目有固定资产折旧、劳动者报酬、生产税净额、营业盈余，这种方法也称要素分配法。本年鉴中的工业增加值是以生产法计算的。

生产法工业增加值的计算方法为：

工业增加值=工业总产出-工业中间投入+应交增值税

(1)工业总产出：指工业企业在一定时期内工业生产活动的总成果。工业总产出包括：成品生产价值，对外加工费收入，自制半成品、在产品期末期初差额价值。1995年后用新规定计算的工业总产值代替。

(2)工业中间投入：指工业企业在工业生产活动中消耗的外购物质产品和对外支付的服务费用。服务费用包括支付给物质生产部门(工业、农业、批发零售贸易业、建筑业、运输邮电业)的服务费用和支付给非物质生产部门(如保险、金融、文化教育、科学研究、医疗卫生、行政管理等)的服务费用。工业中间投入的确定须遵循以下原则：必须从外部购入的，并已计入工业总产出的产品和服务价值；必须是本期投入生产，并一次性消耗掉(包括本期摊销的低值易耗品等)的产品和服务价值。

工业中间投入包括直接材料费用、制造费用中的工业中间投入、管理费用中的工业中间投入、销售费用中的工业中间投入和利息支出五部分。

资产总计 指企业拥有或控制的能以货币计量的经济资源，包括各种财产、债权和其他权利。资产按流动性分为流动资产、长期投资、固定资产、无形资产、递延资产和其他资产。该指标根据企业会计“资产负债表”中“资产总计”项目的期末数增列。

流动资产平均余额 指企业在报告期内全部流动资产的平均余额。

固定资产净值年平均余额 指固定资产净值在报告期内余额的平均数。计算公式为：

固定资产净值年平均余额=1至12月各月月初、月末固定资产净值之和/24

该指标根据“资产负债表”中“固定资产原价”、“累计折旧”指标的期初、期末数计算填列。

固定资产净值指固定资产原价减去历年已提折旧额后的净额。计算公式为：

固定资产净值=固定资产原价-累计折旧

负债合计 指企业所承担的能以货币计量，将以资产或劳务偿付的债务，偿还形式包括货币、资产或提供劳务。负债一般按偿还期长短分为流动负债和长期负债。根据会计“资产负债表”中“负债合计”的年末数填列。

所有者权益合计 指企业投资人对企业净资产的所有权。企业净资产为企业全部资产与企业全部负债的差额，包括实收资本、资本公积、盈余公积、未分配利润等。根据会计“资产负债表”中“所有者权益”项的期末数填列。

主营业务收入 指会计“利润表”中对应指标的本年累计数。未执行2001年《企业会计制度》的企业，用“产品销售收入”的本期累计数代替。

主营业务成本 指会计“利润表”中对应指标的本年累计数。未执行2001年《企业会计制度》的企业，用“产品销售成本”的本期累计数代替。

主营业务税金及附加 指会计“利润表”中对应指标的本年累计数。未执行2001年《企业会计制度》的企业，用“产品销售税金及附加”的本期累计数代替。

利润总额 指企业在生产经营过程中各种收入扣除各种耗费后的盈余，反映企业在报告期内实现的盈亏总额，包括营业利润、补贴收入、投资净收益和营业外收支净额。根据会计“利润表”中的对应指标的本期累计数填列。

本年应交增值税 指企业按税法规定，从事货物销售或提供加工、修理修配劳务等增加货物价值的活动本期应交纳的税金。指企业在报告期应交增值税额。计算公式为：

本年应交增值税=销项税额-（进项税额-进项税额转出）-出口抵减内销产品应纳税额-减免税款+出口退税

本年进项税额指工业企业在报告期内购入货物或接受

应税劳务而支付的、准予从销项税额中抵扣的增值税额。

本年销项税额指工业企业在报告期内销售货物或提供应税劳务应收取的增值税额。

从业人员平均人数 是指报告期内每天拥有的从业人员人数。其计算公式为：

月平均人数=报告月内每天实有人数之和/报告月日历日数

季平均人数=季内各月平均人数之和/3

年平均人数=年内各月平均人数之和/12

工业经济效益综合指数 是指现行综合评价工业经济效益总体水平及工业经济运行质量的指数。它是以若干项代表性经济效益指标，分别除以各项指标的标准值，再乘以各自的权数，加总后除以总权数求得。其计算公式为：

工业经济效益综合指数=(某项经济效益指标报告期数值/该项指标标准值×权数)÷总权数

上式总权数为100。

总资产贡献率 反映企业全部资产的获利能力，是企业经营业绩和管理水平的集中体现，是评价和考核企业盈利能力的核心指标。计算公式为：

总资产贡献率（%）=(利润总额+税金总额+利息支出)/平均资金总额×100%

公式中：税金总额为产品销售税金及附加与应交增值税之和；平均资产总额为期初期末资产之和的算术平均值。

资产负债率 该指标既反映企业经营风险的大小，也反映企业利用债权人提供的资金从事经营活动的能力。计算公式为：

资产负债率（%）=负债总额/资产总额×100%

资产与负债均为报告期期末数。

流动资产周转次数 指一定时期内流动资产完成的周转次数，反映投入工业企业流动资金的周转速度。计算公式为：

流动资产周转次数=产品销售收入/全部流动资产平均余额

公式中：全部流动资产平均余额为期初和期末的流动资产之和的算术平均值。

成本费用利润率 反映企业投入的生产成本及费用的经济效益，同时也反映企业降低成本所取得的经济效益。计算公式为：

成本费用利润率（%）=利润总额/成本费用总额×100%

公式中：成本费用总额为产品销售成本、销售费用、管理费用、财务费用之和。

产品销售率 该指标反映工业产品已实现销售的程度，是分析工业产销衔接情况，研究工业产品满足社会需求的指标。计算公式为：

$$\text{产品销售率（\%）} = \frac{\text{工业销售产值}}{\text{工业总产值（现价）}} \times 100\%$$

Explanatory Notes on Main Statistical Indicators

Industry refers to the material production sector which is engaged in the extraction of natural resources and processing and reprocessing of minerals and agricultural products, including (1) extraction of natural resources, such as mining, salt production (but not including hunting and fishing); (2) processing and reprocessing of farm and sideline produces, such as rice husking, flour milling, wine making, oil pressing, silk reeling, spinning and weaving, and leather making; (3) manufacture of industrial products, such as steel making, iron smelting, chemicals manufacturing, petroleum processing, machine building, timber processing; water and gas production and electricity generation and supply; (4)repairing of industrial products such as the repairing of machinery and means of transport (including cars).

In industrial statistics surveys, the units of enquiry are corporate industrial enterprises with independent accounting systems.

Corporate industrial enterprises with independent accounting systems refer to enterprises engaging in industrial production activities, which meet the following requirements: (1) They are established legally, having their own names, organizations, location and able to take civil liability; (2) They possess and use their assets independently, assume liabilities and are entitled to sign contracts with other units; (3) They are financially independent and compile their own balance sheets.

Enterprises covered in the industrial statistics in the Yearbook include the following categories by their registration:

State-owned and State-holding Enterprises refer to state-owned enterprises plus State-holding enterprises. State-owned enterprises (originally known as State-run enterprises with ownership by the whole society) are non-corporate economic entities registered in accordance with the Regulation of the People's Republic of China on the Management of Registration of Legal Enterprises, where all assets are owned by the State. Included in this category are State-owned enterprises, State-funded corporations and State-owned joint-operation enterprises. Joint State-private industries and private industries, which existed before 1957, were transformed into state-run industries since 1957, and into State-owned industries after 1992. Statistics on those enterprises are included in the State-owned industries instead of being grouped them separately. State-holding enterprises are a sub-classification of enterprises with mixed ownership, referring to enterprises where the percentage of State assets (or shares by the State) is larger than any other single share holder of the same enterprise. This sub-classification illustrates the control of the State over a particular industry.

Light Industry refers to the industry that produces consumer goods and hand tools. It consists of two categories, depending on the materials used:

(1) Industries using farm products as raw materials. These are the branches of light industry which directly or indirectly use farm products as basic raw materials, including the manufacture of food and beverages, tobacco processing, textile, clothing, fur and leather manufacturing, paper making, printing, etc.

(2) Industries using non-farm products as raw materials. These are the branches of light industry which use manufactured goods as raw materials, including the manufacture of cultural, educational articles and sports goods, chemicals, synthetic fibre, chemical products for daily use, glass products for daily use, metal products for daily use, hand tools, medical apparatus and instruments, and the manufacture of cultural and office machinery.

Heavy Industry refers to the industry which produces capital goods, and provides various sectors of the national economy with necessary material and technical basis for production. It consists of the following three branches according to the purpose of production or the use of products:

(1) Mining, quarrying and logging industry, which refers to the industry that extracts natural resources, including extraction of petroleum, coal, metal and non-metal ores.

(2) Raw materials industry refers to the industry that provides various sectors of the national economy with raw materials, fuels and power. It includes smelting and processing of metals, coking and coke chemistry, chemical materials and building materials such as cement, plywood, and power, petroleum refining and coal dressing.

(3) Manufacturing industry which refers to the industry that processes raw materials. It includes machine-building industries which equip sectors of the national economy; industries producing metal structure and cement products; and industries producing means of agricultural production, such as chemical fertilizers and pesticides.

In accordance with the above principles of classification, the repairing trades, which are engaged primarily in repairing products of heavy industry, are classified as heavy industry while those which are engaged in repairing products of light industry are classified as light industry.

Gross Industrial Output Value

(1) Definition: Gross industrial output value is the total volume of final industrial products produced and industrial services provided during a given period. It reflects the total achievements and overall scale of industrial production during a given period.

(2) Principles for calculation:

Statistics on industrial production follow the principle that all products produced by the enterprises and accepted through quality check during the reference period are to be included no matter whether they are sold or not during the reference period.

Determination of final products follows the principle that all products that are included in the calculation of gross industrial output value are the final products of the enterprise which have been accepted through quality check and require no further processing. If an enterprise has intermediate (semi-finished) products to sell, these intermediate products are considered as the final products of the enterprise.

Gross industrial output value is calculated following the principle of factory approach, i.e. industrial enterprise is used as the basic accounting unit in calculating the gross industrial output value. By this approach, value of the same product is not to be double-counted, and the output value of different workshops (branch factories) within the enterprise should not be added. However, this approach allows the possibility of double counting between enterprises.

(3) Content and method of calculation: The old definition of gross industrial output value was modified during the 1995 National Industrial Census. The revised (new) definition of gross industrial output value consists of 3 components: value of the finished products during the reference period, income from processing for external parties, and value of change in semi-finished products between the end and the beginning of the reference period.

Value of finished products during the reference period: refers to the value of all finished (semi-finished) industrial products that are produced during the reference period without the need for further processing, checked for acceptance, packed and put into the warehouse of the enterprise, including the value of own-produced equipment and the value of products provided to the projects under construction of the enterprise, and to other non-industrial or welfare units. Value of finished products during the reference period is calculated by the quantity of products produced using own materials multiplied by the average unit prices at which products are sold (excluding value-added tax). Own-produced equipment and products produced for own use are valued at cost prices as in the case of enterprise accounting. Value of finished products does not include the value of finished products (semi-finished products) that are produced using the materials from the clients who place the orders.

Income from external processing: refers to income from contracted external processing of industrial products (including processing of industrial products using materials from the clients), and the income from industrial repairing work provided to other parties. Income from external processing is calculated using information from the item "products sales income" in the enterprise accounting at the prices with value-added tax excluded.

For income from services such as processing, repairing and installation of equipment provided to non-industrial units within the enterprise, if the accounting work of the enterprise is good enough to separate it from other records, and the share of such services is significant, it should also be included in the income from external processing.

Value of change in semi-finished products between the end and the beginning of the reference period: refers to the value of change in semi-finished products between the end and the beginning of the reference period, which generally can be obtained from accounting records of enterprises. If the enterprise accounting excludes the cost of semi-finished products, then it should not be included in the gross industrial output value, and the reverse if otherwise.

(4) Changes in the scope and method of calculation of the gross industrial output value

Prior to 1984, the value of rural industry run by villages was classified into agriculture instead of industry. Since 1984, it has been included in the gross industrial output value. Method of calculation for the gross industrial output value was modified in the industrial census in 1995. The difference in the new method as compared with the old one is outlined below:

Principle in using full value vs. processing fee: The new method stipulates that all products produced using own materials are to be calculated with full value in reporting the gross industrial output value irrespective of the complexity of production, and for external processing, it allows calculation using processing fee. In the old method, however, the use of full value or processing fee was determined by the degree of complexity of production in different branches of industries.

Principle in determining the value of change in semi-finished products: The new method requires that value of change in semi-finished products should be included in the gross industrial output value if it is included in the accounting record of the enterprise, otherwise it should not be included. In the old method, it is determined by the type of enterprises in terms of production cycle. If the production cycle is over 6 months, the value of change in semi-finished products is included in the gross industrial output value, otherwise it is not.

Difference in prices: The new method uses prices excluding value-added tax in the calculation of gross industrial output value, while the old method used prices including value-added tax.

Value-added of Industry refers to the final results of industrial production of industrial enterprises in money terms during the reference period.

Industrial value-added can be calculated by two approaches: the production approach, i.e. gross industrial output value minus intermediate input plus value-added tax, and the income approach, i.e. income for various factors used in the course of production, including depreciation of fixed assets, remuneration of labourers, net of production tax, and operating surplus. Value-added of industry in the Yearbook is calculated by the production approach as follows:

Value-added of industry = gross industrial output - industrial intermediate input + value-added tax

(1) Gross industrial output: refers to the total achievements of industrial production activities during a given period. Gross industrial output includes value of finished products, income from external processing, and value of change in semi-finished products between the end and the beginning of the reference period. Since 1995, the gross industrial output value obtained by the new method is used in the calculation.

(2) Industrial intermediate input: refers to purchased goods and paid services consumed during the industrial production of enterprises. Fees paid for services include fees paid for the services provided by material production sectors (industry, agriculture, wholesale and retail trade, construction, transport, post and telecommunications) and by non-material production sectors (insurance, banking, culture, education, scientific research, health and medical care, public administration, etc.). The determination of industrial intermediate input follows the principle that the goods and services must be purchased from outside and included in the gross industrial output, and that the goods and services are inputted into production and consumed (include low-value consumables) during the reference period.

Industrial intermediate input includes 5 components, namely direct consumption of materials, industrial intermediate input in manufacturing cost, industrial intermediate input in management cost, industrial intermediate input in marketing cost and expenditure on interest.

Total Assets refer to all economic resources, in monetary term, these are owned or controlled by enterprises, including properties, creditor's equity and other economic rights of all forms. Classified by the degree of liquidity, total assets include working capitals, long-term investment, fixed assets, intangible assets, deferred assets and other assets. Data on this indicator can be obtained by the year-end figures of total assets in the Assets and Liability Table of accounting records of enterprises.

Annual Average Value of Working Capital refers to the average value of all working capital of the enterprise during the reference period.

Annual Average of Net Value of Fixed Assets refers to the average of the net value of fixed assets during the reference period, calculated with the following formula:

$$\text{Annual Average of Net Value of Fixed Assets} = \frac{\text{sum of net value of fixed assets at the beginning and at the end of each month from January to December}}{24}$$

Information on this indicator can be obtained from the beginning and ending figures of the original value of fixed assets and cumulative depreciation from the Assets and Liability Table of enterprises.

Net value of fixed assets refers to the original value of fixed assets minus depreciation over the years, i.e.:

Net value of fixed assets = original value of fixed assets - cumulative depreciation

Total Liabilities refer to payable liabilities of enterprises that have to be repaid in terms of money, assets or labour services. In terms of payment, it can be divided into liquid liabilities and long-term liabilities. Data on this item is obtained from the ending figures on total liabilities from the Assets and Liability Table from the enterprises.

Owner's Equity refers to the ownership of net assets of enterprise by its investors. Net assets equal total assets minus total liabilities of the enterprise, including the paid-in capital, accumulation of capital and operating surplus and non-distributed profits. Data are obtained from the ending figures on "total equity" from the "balance sheets".

Revenue from Principal Business refers to the annual accumulation of the corresponding item in the "profit table" of the accountant. For enterprises that do not follow the 2001 Enterprise Accounting Standards, the year-end accumulation of revenue from the sales of products is used as a substitute.

Cost of Principal Business refers to the annual accumulation of the corresponding item in the "profit table" of the accountant. For enterprises that do not follow the 2001 Enterprise Accounting Standards, the year-end accumulation of cost for the sales of products is used as a substitute.

Tax and Extra Charges from Principal Business refer to the annual accumulation of the corresponding item in the "profit table" of the accountant. For enterprises that do not follow the 2001 Enterprise Accounting Standards, the year-end accumulation of tax and extra charges from the sales of products is used as a substitute.

Total Profits refers to the balance of various incomes minus various spendings in the course of operation, reflecting the total profits and losses of enterprises in reporting period. It includes: operating profits, income from subsidies, net investment income and net income from activities other than operation. Data are obtained from the annual accumulation of the corresponding item in the "profit table" of the accountant

Value-added Tax Payable in the Current Year refers to the payable tax of enterprises which engaged in selling of goods or providing services that bring added value to the goods, such as processing, repairing, fitting and other activities should be paid according to Tax Law. It refers to the amount of the value-added tax which should be paid by the enterprises during the reference period. The formula is as follows:

Value-added Tax Payable in the Current Year = tax on sales-(tax on purchase-transferred tax on purchase)-exports deduct tax payable on domestic sales-tax relief+the export tax rebate.

Average Annual Number of Employed Persons Employed persons refer to all those who are employed in enterprises and receive remunerations there from, including currently working employees, retirees who are re-employed, teachers of local-run schools, as well as foreigners, staff from Hong Kong, Macao and Taiwan, part-time employees and persons with second job who are employed by the enterprise, and employees of other units temporarily working in the enterprises, but excluding former employees who left the enterprise with their employment records still being kept by the enterprises.

Average number of employed persons refers to the number of employee everyday during the reference period, calculated with the following formula:

$$\text{Monthly average number} = \frac{\text{sum of actual employees everyday in reference month}}{\text{number of calendar dates in reference month}}$$

$$\text{Annual average number} = \frac{\text{sum of monthly average number in reference year}}{12}$$

$$\text{Quarterly average number} = \frac{\text{sum of monthly average number in reference quarter}}{3}$$

Ratio of Profits, Taxes and Interests to Average Assets reflects the profit-making capability of all assets of the enterprise and is a key indicator manifesting the performance and management and evaluating the profit-making potential of the enterprise. It is calculated as follows:

$$\text{Ratio of Profits, Taxes and Interests to Average Assets (\%)} = \frac{\text{total profits} + \text{total taxes} + \text{interest payment}}{\text{average assets}} \times 100\%$$

In the above formula, total taxes is the sum of tax and extra charges on the sales of products and value-added tax payable; and average assets is the arithmetic mean of the sum of beginning assets and ending assets.

Ratio of Debts to Assets reflects both the operation risk and the capability of the enterprise in making use of the capital from the creditors. It is calculated as follows:

$$\text{Ratio of Debts to Assets (\%)} = \frac{\text{total debts}}{\text{total assets}} \times 100\,\%$$

Both assets and debts are figures at the end of the reference period.

Turnover of Working Capital refers to the number of times of turnover of working capital in a given period of time, which reflects the speed of the turnover of working capital of industrial enterprises, and is calculated as follows:

$$\text{Turnover of Working Capital} = \frac{\text{sales revenue of products}}{\text{average balance of total working capital}}$$

In the above formula, average balance of total working capital refers to the arithmetic mean of the sum of working capital at the beginning and at the end of the reference period.

Ratio of Profits to Total Industrial Costs refers to the ratio of profits realized in a given period to the total costs in the same period, which reflects the economic efficiency of input cost and is calculated as follows:

$$\text{Ratio of Profits to Total Industrial Cost (\%)} = \frac{\text{total profits}}{\text{total costs}} \times 100\,\%$$

Total costs in the above formula are the sum of cost of products sold, marketing cost, management cost and financial cost.

Sales Ratio of Products is an indicator reflecting the actual sale of industrial products, analyzing the production-selling and supply-demand relations. It is calculated as:

$$\text{Sales Ratio of Products (\%)} = \frac{\text{value of industrial sales}}{\text{gross industrial output value (current prices)}} \times 100\,\%$$

2012

新疆统计年鉴

XINJIANG STATISTICAL YEARBOOK

第十四篇 建筑业

CHAPTER 14 Construction

简要说明
Brief Introduction

本篇资料的主要内容及来源

本篇资料反映在新疆维吾尔自治区注册的建筑法人企业概况及发展情况，包括建筑业企业基本情况和生产经营情况。主要指标有企业个数、从业人员和建筑企业签定合同情况、承包工程完成情况及总产值、增加值、企业技术装备情况、房屋建筑面积、利润、税金、劳动生产率等。

根据建筑业发展的实际情况，建筑业统计范围从2002年起，由原具有建筑业资质等级四级及四级以上的独立核算的建筑业企业调整为具有施工总承包、专业承包和劳务分包的法人建筑业企业。

本篇建筑业企业统计数据是根据国家统计局制定的《建筑业统计报表制度》整理汇总的。建筑业统计数据采取全面调查的方法。资料由新疆维吾尔自治区统计局固定资产投资统计处提供。

Main Content and Source of Data

Data in this chapter show the general situation and the development of the construction in Xinjiang Uygur Autonomous Region. They cover the situation of production and management of the enterprises on construction, including the number of enterprises, number of employed persons, complemet and gross output value of construction industry, value added floor space of the buildings, profits and taxes of enterprises and labor productivity, etc.

According to the development of construction industry, starting from 2002,the coverage of construction statistics has been adjusted to include all the construction enterprises of various types of ownership with qualification certificates and with independent accounting system ,instead of the original criteria that required construction enterprises of various types of ownership to have qualification certificates at or above Class 4 with independent accounting system.

Data on construction enterprises are collected in accordance with the Reporting System of Construction Statistics stipulated by the National Bureau of Statistics. Data on the construction industry are collected through comprehensive reporting system and provided by the Department of Investment in Fixed Assets Statistics, Xinjiang Bureau of Statistics.

14-1 建筑企业概况
Main Indicators on Construction Enterprises

年 份 Year	地 区 Region	企业个数(个) Number of Enterprises (unit)				从业人员(万人) Number of Persons Employed (10 000 persons)			
		合 计 Total	国 有 State-owned	集 体 Collec-tive-owned	其 他 Others	合 计 Total	国 有 State-owned	集 体 Collec-tive-owned	其 他 Others
	1985	275	117	158		25.85	19.21	6.64	
	1990	353	183	170		22.86	18.36	4.50	
	1995	928	481	432	15	35.33	26.33	8.72	0.28
	1996	886	478	386	22	24.97	18.53	6.09	0.35
	1997	650	313	312	25	30.75	20.39	8.56	1.80
	1998	682	269	348	65	22.14	14.83	6.42	0.89
	1999	711	272	344	95	19.35	13.00	4.94	1.41
	2000	690	226	293	171	26.16	17.69	4.25	4.22
	2001	594	175	152	267	25.27	14.77	2.68	7.82
	2002	730	146	109	475	23.57	8.64	1.89	13.04
	2003	776	112	77	587	20.81	6.16	1.12	13.53
	2004	932	105	51	776	33.22	7.21	0.84	25.17
	2005	881	107	43	731	34.37	8.70	0.90	24.77
	2006	914	102	39	773	33.84	8.81	0.84	24.19
	2007	967	103	35	829	37.02	9.63	0.92	26.47
	2008	998	99	32	867	42.37	11.28	0.48	30.61
	2009	993	90	28	875	48.18	12.01	0.52	35.65
	2010	1004	81	28	895	56.48	12.66	0.52	43.30
	2011	1025	89	22	914	52.73	9.89	0.40	42.44
乌鲁木齐市	Urumqi City	477	48	11	418	19.75	5.01	0.19	14.55
克拉玛依市	Karamay City	60	2	2	56	2.29	0.14	0.06	2.09
吐鲁番地区	Turpan Administrative Offices	14	1		13	0.50	0.01		0.49
哈密地区	Hami [Kumul] Administrative Offices	38	3		35	0.45	0.04		0.41
昌吉回族自治州	Changji Hui Autonomous Prefecture	75	2	1	72	3.36	0.15	0.01	3.20
伊犁哈萨克自治州	Ili Kazak Autonomous Prefecture	105	14	6	85	5.78	1.55	0.08	4.15
伊犁州直属县(市)	Counties (Cities) Direct Under Ili Prefecture	58	6	3	49	3.17	1.41	0.06	1.70
塔城地区	Tacheng [Tarbagatai] Administrative Offices	22	4	3	15	1.77	0.09	0.02	1.66
阿勒泰地区	Altay Administrative Offices	25	4		21	0.84	0.05		0.79
博尔塔拉蒙古自治州	Bortala Mongol Autonomous Prefecture	22	3	1	18	0.93	0.07	0.06	0.81
巴音郭楞蒙古自治州	Bayangol Mongol Autonomous Prefecture	51	4	1	46	5.27	0.50		4.77
阿克苏地区	Aksu Administrative Offices	61	2		59	3.23	0.04		3.19
克孜勒苏柯尔克孜自治州	Kizilsu Kirgiz Autonomous Prefecture	15	1		14	0.35			0.35
喀什地区	Kashgar [Kaxgar] Administrative Offices	46	2		44	3.29	0.04		3.24
和田地区	Hotan Administrative Offices	20			20	0.96			0.96
石河子市	Shihezi City	27	5		22	5.39	2.18		3.21
阿拉尔市	Aral City	5	1		4	0.27	0.15		0.12
图木舒克市	Tumxuk City	3			3	0.37			0.37
五家渠市	Wujiaqu City	6	1		5	0.56	0.02		0.54

注：1.2000 年至 2002 年建筑业所有指标数据均包括克拉玛依石油管理局工业部分，2003 年起将此部分扣除(以下同)。
2.2004 年建筑业所有数据为经济普查数，企业个数及其他指标包括没有工作量或者停业企业，往年未包括(以下同)。
3.根据我区建筑特点，建筑业从业人员为年平均人数。

Note: a) All the quota indices in building sector from 2000 to 2002 include the industrial part of Karamay Oil Administration. From 2003, this part was omitted. (the same as in the following) . b) All the data in architectural sector are the statistics of economic census, enterprise numbers and other quota exclude work volume or closed enterprises except for previous years. (the same as in the following) . c)In view of the features of the construction, the number of employed persons refers to the annual average.

14-2 按登记注册类型分建筑企业总产值

Total Output Value of Construction Enterprises by Registration Status

单位：万元 (10 000 yuan)

年 份 Year	地 区 Region	合 计 Total	国有经济 State-owned Units	集体经济 Collective -owned Units	其他经济 Others Units
	1985	175165	138138	37027	
	1990	273893	220574	53319	
	1995	1070085	816396	238387	15302
	1996	1284669	977358	283776	23535
	1997	1141318	828482	288081	24755
	1998	1434787	1002235	378956	53596
	1999	1569486	1085080	365588	118818
	2000	2349506	1436653	362649	550204
	2001	2742800	1394099	252076	1096625
	2002	3136257	1270601	170319	1695337
	2003	3221502	739953	147256	2334293
	2004	3439968	910264	89189	2440515
	2005	3615674	1138005	102580	2375089
	2006	3856223	1269722	88474	2498027
	2007	4541026	1548285	97418	2895323
	2008	6292562	1879497	86431	4326634
	2009	7913768	2245048	119717	5549003
	2010	9694741	2486878	119917	7087946
	2011	13278310	3302487	104738	9871085
乌鲁木齐市	Urumqi City	5342021	2181572	41926	3118523
克拉玛依市	Karamay City	884428	21624	18328	844476
吐鲁番地区	Turpan Administrative Offices	187505	7573		179932
哈密地区	Hami [Kumul] Administrative Offices	288620	85190		203430
昌吉回族自治州	Changji Hui Autonomous Prefecture	848365	27963	13300	807102
伊犁哈萨克自治州	Ili Kazak Autonomous Prefecture	1505334	419095	17183	1069056
伊犁州直属县(市)	Counties (Cities) Direct Under Ili Prefecture	812393	321982	11753	478658
塔城地区	Tacheng [Tarbagatai] Administrative Offices	419616	52501	5430	361685
阿勒泰地区	Altay Administrative Offices	273325	44612		228713
博尔塔拉蒙古自治州	Bortala Mongol Autonomous Prefecture	189358	54238	13700	121420
巴音郭楞蒙古自治州	Bayangol Mongol Autonomous Prefecture	1175377	104722	301	1070354
阿克苏地区	Aksu Administrative Offices	813526	24175		789351
克孜勒苏柯尔克孜自治州	Kizilsu Kirgiz Autonomous Prefecture	126694	6873		119821
喀什地区	Kashgar [Kaxgar] Administrative Offices	639584	12510		627074
和田地区	Hotan Administrative Offices	218870			218870
石河子市	Shihezi City	717663	293073		424590
阿拉尔市	Aral City	161005	61079		99926
图木舒克市	Tumxuk City	72894			72894
五家渠市	Wujiaqu City	107066	2800		104266

14-3 按构成分建筑企业总产值

Total Output Value of Construction Enterprises by Composition

单位：万元 (10 000 yuan)

年份 Year	地区 Region	总产值 Total Output Value	建筑工程 Output Value of Construction Projects	安装工程 Output Value of Installation Projects	其他 Others
1985		175165	154496	18042	2627
1990		273893	241574	28211	4108
1995		1070085	942158	106744	21183
1996		1284669	1124271	132079	28319
1997		1141318	1009082	105891	26345
1998		1434787	1270483	139104	25200
1999		1569486	1398179	146154	25153
2000		2349506	2073166	214425	61915
2001		2742800	2403688	279909	59203
2002		3136257	2637362	405115	93780
2003		3221502	2708269	336535	176698
2004		3439968	2836668	396509	206791
2005		3615674	2981373	487239	147062
2006		3856223	3209192	510770	136261
2007		4541026	3822922	564228	153876
2008		6292562	5359129	804719	128714
2009		7913768	6924156	867812	121800
2010		9694741	8450628	1107006	137107
2011		13278310	11850908	1223095	204307
乌鲁木齐市	Urumqi City	5342021	4847162	430670	64189
克拉玛依市	Karamay City	884428	450319	380746	53363
吐鲁番地区	Turpan Administrative Offices	187505	96257	78724	12524
哈密地区	Hami [Kumul] Administrative Offices	288620	287340	1280	
昌吉回族自治州	Changji Hui Autonomous Prefecture	848365	749683	84142	14540
伊犁哈萨克自治州	Ili Kazak Autonomous Prefecture	1505335	1456975	44456	3904
伊犁州直属县(市)	Counties (Cities) Direct Under Ili Prefecture	812393	787018	22976	2399
塔城地区	Tacheng [Tarbagatai] Administrative Offices	419616	406380	13236	
阿勒泰地区	Altay Administrative Offices	273326	263577	8244	1505
博尔塔拉蒙古自治州	Bortala Mongol Autonomous Prefecture	189358	188603	157	598
巴音郭楞蒙古自治州	Bayangol Mongol Autonomous Prefecture	1175377	1113557	29288	32532
阿克苏地区	Aksu Administrative Offices	813526	762424	45241	5861
克孜勒苏柯尔克孜自治州	Kizilsu Kirgiz Autonomous Prefecture	126694	114592	6232	5870
喀什地区	Kashgar [Kaxgar] Administrative Offices	639584	576425	55324	7835
和田地区	Hotan Administrative Offices	218870	207839	7940	3091
石河子市	Shihezi City	717663	658887	58776	
阿拉尔市	Aral City	161005	160885	120	
图木舒克市	Tumxuk City	72894	72894		
五家渠市	Wujiaqu City	107066	107066		

14-4 按行业和登记注册类型分建筑企业总产值

Total Output Value of Construction Enterprises by Registration Status and Sectors

单位：万元 (10 000 yuan)

项目	Item	2010	2011
总计	**Total**	**9694741**	**13278310**
#一、二级企业	First Grade and Second Grade Enterprises	8103645	11245324
#国有及国有控股	State-owned and State-holding	4665988	6693556
按登记注册类型分组	**Grouped by Registration Status**		
内资企业	Domestic Funded	9694418	13278168
国有企业	State-owned Enterprises	1647361	2568692
集体企业	Collective-owned Enterprises	119917	104737
股份合作企业	Share-holding Cooperative	52066	
联营企业	Joint Ownership Enterprises		320
有限责任公司	Limited Liability Corporations	5334128	7230099
国有独资公司	Sole State -funded Company	839517	733795
其他有限责任公司	Other Limited Liability Companies	4494611	6496304
股份有限公司	Share-holding Corporations Ltd	659566	698045
私营企业	Private Enterprises	1881380	2594276
#私营有限责任公司	Private Limited Liability Companies	1811565	2531826
私营股份有限公司	Private Stock Limited Companies	67808	60482
其他企业	Others		81998
港、澳、台及外商企业	Enterprises With Funds from Hong Kong, Macao , Taiwan and Foreign	323	143
#合资经营企业(港或澳、台资)	Joint-Venture	220	70
按国民经济行业分组	**Grouped by National Economic Sectors**		
房屋和土木工程建筑业	Buildings and Civil Engineering Construction	8710794	12281746
房屋工程建筑	Building Construction	5886052	8742547
土木工程建筑	Civil Engineering Construction	2824742	3539199
铁路、道路、隧道和桥梁	Railways, Roads, Tunnels and Bridges	2044836	2357550
水利和港口建筑	Water Conservancy and Seaport Construction	466486	563363
工矿工程建筑	Mine Project	43662	60574
架线和管道工程建筑	Cabling and Piping Project	221548	484035
其他土木工程建筑	Other Civil Engineering	48210	73677
建筑安装业	Construction and Installation	869919	842619
建筑装饰业	Building Decoration	60979	67103
其他建筑业	Others	53050	86842
按隶属关系分组	**Grouped by Subordination**		
中央	Central Government	2994670	4041765
地方	Local	6700071	9236545
按企业资质等级分组	**Grouped by Enterprise's Qualification**		
施工总承包	Undertaking Porjects	8924733	12380778
特级	Special Grade	148694	200534
一级	First Grade	4185541	5349783
二级	Second Grade	3287718	5115477
三级及以下	Third Grade and Below	1302780	1714984
专业承包	Specialized Undertaking	712456	824097
一级	First Grade	195129	262226
二级	Second Grade	249612	268414
三级及以下	Third Grade and Below	267715	293457
劳务分包	Work Subcontractors	57552	73435
三级及以下	Third Grade and Below	57552	73435

14-5 建筑企业增加值
Value-added of Construction Enterprises

单位：万元 (10 000 yuan)

年份 Year	地区 Region	合计 Total	按注册类型分 Grouped by Ownership 国有企业 State-owned Enterprise	集体企业 Collective-owned Enterprises	其他企业 Others	按隶属关系分 By Administrative Relationship 中央企业 Central Enterprises	地方企业 Local Enterprises
	1985	60152	52022	8130			
	1990	109923	91983	17940			
	1995	283882	207212	72598	4072	92259	191623
	1996	303370	218532	78973	5865	96996	206374
	1997	380806	284938	87437	8431	133287	247519
	1998	296444	182903	89375	24166	84239	212205
	1999	323714	198463	87477	37774	92459	213255
	2000	587341	386475	84268	116598	274836	312505
	2001	637472	340470	49298	247704	260784	376688
	2002	621430	223509	37383	360538	211988	409442
	2003	672531	143473	29333	499725	161523	511008
	2004	693070	158801	18938	515331	157382	535688
	2005	716063	199645	18265	498153	176697	539366
	2006	790466	230867	20948	538651	215766	574700
	2007	947319	304278	19234	623807	278640	668679
	2008	1349429	375318	18888	955223	427287	922142
	2009	1627342	417474	19541	1190327	492321	1135021
	2010	2053556	451108	21823	1580625	658449	1395107
	2011	2745615	564723	18348	2162544	864566	1881049
乌鲁木齐市	Urumqi City	1092963	326771	8375	757817	435308	657655
克拉玛依市	Karamay City	161080	5844	1441	153795	25754	135326
吐鲁番地区	Turpan Administrative Offices	37395	1400		35995	10666	26729
哈密地区	Hami [Kumul] Administrative Offices	32133	7663		24470	4403	27730
昌吉回族自治州	Changji Hui Autonomous Prefecture	183487	5854	1296	176337	7679	175808
伊犁哈萨克自治州	Ili Kazak Autonomous Prefecture	269750	79839	3500	186411	102775	166975
伊犁州直属县(市)	Counties (Cities) Direct Under Ili Prefecture	150752	64711	2435	83606	70475	80277
塔城地区	Tacheng [Tarbagatai] Administrative Offices	73103	7830	1065	64208	30197	42906
阿勒泰地区	Altay Administrative Offices	45895	7298		38597	2103	43792
博尔塔拉蒙古自治州	Bortala Mongol Autonomous Prefecture	33128	4843	3663	24622	4733	28395
巴音郭楞蒙古自治州	Bayangol Mongol Autonomous Prefecture	271612	30196	73	241343	21942	249670
阿克苏地区	Aksu Administrative Offices	181477	3230		178247	17563	163914
克孜勒苏柯尔克孜自治州	Kizilsu Kirgiz Autonomous Prefecture	13948	409		13539		13948
喀什地区	Kashgar [Kaxgar] Administrative Offices	146656	1252		145404	14473	132183
和田地区	Hotan Administrative Offices	39824			39824	3372	36452
石河子市	Shihezi City	212581	84314		128267	192595	19986
阿拉尔市	Aral City	23117	12154		10963	13965	9152
图木舒克市	Tumxuk City	17869			17869	8384	9485
五家渠市	Wujiaqu City	28595	954		27641	954	27641

14-6 建筑企业利税总额

Total Pre-tax Profits of Construction Enterprises

单位：万元 (10 000 yuan)

年 份 Year	地 区 Region	利税总额合计 Total Pre-tax Profits	利润总额 Total Profits	工程结算税金及附加 Taxes and Extra Charges on Project Settlement Accounts	管理费用中的税金 Taxes in Management Expenses	产值利税率(%) Ratio of Pre-tax Profits to Output Value (%)	资金利税率(%) Ratio of Pre-tax Profits to Assets (%)
	1994	28199	5535	20195	2469	3.81	4.11
	1995	30156	2974	24916	2266	3.44	3.46
	1996	20752	-8625	26816	2561	1.97	-0.93
	1997	31970	-4347	33360	2957	2.80	2.51
	1998	37596	-5875	41162	2309	2.62	2.41
	1999	64777	13359	48995	2423	4.13	3.72
	2000	19274	-48005	64614	2665	0.82	0.63
	2001	28688	-47485	74206	1967	1.05	0.84
	2002	84833	-11089	92484	3438	2.70	2.18
	2003	169594	67146	96888	5560	5.26	5.51
	2004	174255	65037	102990	6228	5.07	5.65
	2005	165236	46909	112565	5762	4.57	4.91
	2006	177102	54570	116426	6106	4.59	4.83
	2007	221117	67796	145119	8202	4.87	5.40
	2008	328484	120146	198718	9620	5.22	6.67
	2009	422062	156541	252547	12974	5.33	7.08
	2010	536197	208372	317056	10769	5.53	7.54
	2011	725740	274797	438927	12016	5.47	7.68
乌鲁木齐市	Urumqi City	283853	107175	172184	4494	5.31	6.24
克拉玛依市	Karamay City	47496	16591	29623	1282	5.37	3.95
吐鲁番地区	Turpan Administrative Offices	11355	4551	6652	152	6.06	8.16
哈密地区	Hami [Kumul] Administrative Offices	14629	6292	8164	173	5.07	6.83
昌吉回族自治州	Changji Hui Autonomous Prefecture	46511	18745	27062	704	5.48	10.59
伊犁哈萨克自治州	Ili Kazak Autonomous Prefecture	72632	20317	51371	944	4.82	11.84
伊犁州直属县(市)	Counties (Cities) Direct Under Ili Prefecture	33079	6570	26029	480	4.07	8.98
塔城地区	Tacheng [Tarbagatai] Administrative Offices	24583	8801	15662	120	5.86	20.97
阿勒泰地区	Altay Administrative Offices	14970	4946	9680	344	5.48	11.70
博尔塔拉蒙古自治州	Bortala Mongol Autonomous Prefecture	8198	630	7479	89	4.33	9.80
巴音郭楞蒙古自治州	Bayangol Mongol Autonomous Prefecture	89625	50046	38025	1554	7.63	19.06
阿克苏地区	Aksu Administrative Offices	47532	21180	25317	1035	5.84	10.36
克孜勒苏柯尔克孜自治州	Kizilsu Kirgiz Autonomous Prefecture	4983	1266	3502	215	3.93	4.87
喀什地区	Kashgar [Kaxgar] Administrative Offices	36541	10315	25595	631	5.71	9.56
和田地区	Hotan Administrative Offices	11530	715	10497	318	5.27	13.06
石河子市	Shihezi City	32644	9188	23165	291	4.55	6.85
阿拉尔市	Aral City	10038	4370	5661	7	6.24	8.61
图木舒克市	Tumxuk City	3172	1580	1502	90	4.35	5.65
五家渠市	Wujiaqu City	5001	1835	3129	37	4.67	7.94

14-7 建筑企业劳动生产率

Labor Productivity of Construction Enterprises

单位：元/人 (yuan/person)

年 份 Year	地 区 Region	按总产值计算的劳动生产率 Overall Labor Productivity in Terms of Total Output Value	#国有经济 State-owned Enterprises	#集体经济 Collective-owned Enterprises	按增加值计算的劳动生产率 Overall Labor Productivity in Terms of Added-Value	#国有经济 State-owned Enterprises	#集体经济 Collective-owned Enterprises
	1994	29871	32616	23023	9499	10546	7186
	1995	34668	38483	26617	11238	12505	8673
	1996	32606	36557	25291	10648	12286	7719
	1997	38808	40629	33658	12948	13973	10215
	1998	47698	51465	40819	9855	10044	9627
	1999	55593	61196	44235	11466	11766	10584
	2000	74994	87999	48767	25208	32781	14138
	2001	84666	94344	62458	19678	23041	12215
	2002	86302	108857	66231	17100	19149	14537
	2003	94165	98095	86190	19659	19020	17169
	2004	107150	112145	107185	21588	22365	22759
	2005	112214	137966	127587	22223	23971	22718
	2006	121506	149550	118932	24907	27794	28159
	2007	126303	134275	139988	26349	26389	27640
	2008	152795	182536	168023	32767	36451	36718
	2009	173714	204170	233869	35721	37966	38174
	2010	176404	200435	231859	37366	36358	42194
	2011	226848	284263	176207	46906	48609	30867
乌鲁木齐市	Urumqi City	240416	365606	127940	49188	54763	25558
克拉玛依市	Karamay City	357071	157611	303440	65033	42596	23857
吐鲁番地区	Turpan Administrative Offices	357903	620738		71378	114770	
哈密地区	Hami [Kumul] Administrative Offices	271412	277493		30217	24959	
昌吉回族自治州	Changji Hui Autonomous Prefecture	230353	191002	221662	49821	39986	21886
伊犁哈萨克自治州	Ili Kazak Autonomous Prefecture	217471	235341	189236	38970	44834	
伊犁州直属县(市)	Counties (Cities) Direct Under Ili Prefecture	250229	223397	201590	46434	44898	41759
塔城地区	Tacheng [Tarbagatai] Administrative Offices	149970	229764	167074	26127	34264	32772
阿勒泰地区	Altay Administrative Offices	311517	401914		52308	65751	
博尔塔拉蒙古自治州	Bortala Mongol Autonomous Prefecture	207835	238724	249091	36360	21314	66595
巴音郭楞蒙古自治州	Bayangol Mongol Autonomous Prefecture	220195	206429	231692	50884	59524	56360
阿克苏地区	Aksu Administrative Offices	242373	753106		54067	100612	
克孜勒苏柯尔克孜自治州	Kizilsu Kirgiz Autonomous Prefecture	159224	118917		17529	7071	
喀什地区	Kashgar [Kaxgar] Administrative Offices	175286	82251		40193	8234	
和田地区	Hotan Administrative Offices	239857			43642		
石河子市	Shihezi City	135823	141369		40233	40671	
阿拉尔市	Aral City	382981	334311		54989	66524	
图木舒克市	Tumxuk City	206733			50678		
五家渠市	Wujiaqu City	171114	80445		45701	27425	

14-8 建筑企业技术装备情况

Number and Power of Machinery and Equipment Owned by Construction Enterprises

年份 Year	地区 Region	自有机械设备总台数(台) Number of Machinery and Equipment Owned (set)	自有机械设备总功率(万千瓦) Total Power of Equipment and Machinery Owned (10 000 kw)	自有机械设备净值(万元) Net Value of Machinery and Equipment Owned (10 000 yuan)	技术装备率(元/人) Value of Machines Per Laborer (yuan/ person)	动力装备率(千瓦/人) Power of Machines Per Laborer (kw/person)
	1985	30307	105	29308	1332	6
	1990	34806	91	46098	2511	5
	1995	55455	138	106383	4211	5
	1996	60567	129	127572	4478	5
	1997	64252	149	139617	4747	5
	1998	72606	148	164157	7415	7
	1999	73735	155	184559	9543	8
	2000	77975	182	224485	8582	7
	2001	85981	177	238142	9425	7
	2002	96116	207	442787	18996	9
	2003	100913	207	395865	11866	6
	2004	98541	239	358397	11389	8
	2005	99324	190	326360	10372	6
	2006	96674	197	348344	11187	6
	2007	103431	203	374396	10650	6
	2008	102266	230	392371	9692	6
	2009	103285	235	407809	9136	5
	2010	97562	238	383196	7145	4
	2011	98768	246	398762	6812	4
乌鲁木齐市	Urumqi City	25259	94	161682	7276	4
克拉玛依市	Karamay City	6424	25	43798	17683	10
吐鲁番地区	Turpan Administrative Offices	1637	6	11088	21164	12
哈密地区	Hami [Kumul] Administrative Offices	4817	10	5776	5431	10
昌吉回族自治州	Changji Hui Autonomous Prefecture	9337	11	19533	5304	3
伊犁哈萨克自治州	Ili Kazak Autonomous Prefecture	15794	26	34699	5013	4
伊犁州直属县(市)	Counties (Cities) Direct Under Ili Prefecture	9025	10	16242	5003	3
塔城地区	Tacheng [Tarbagatai] Administrative Offices	4245	11	7602	2717	4
阿勒泰地区	Altay Administrative Offices	2524	5	10855	12372	6
博尔塔拉蒙古自治州	Bortala Mongol Autonomous Prefecture	3685	6	12246	13441	6
巴音郭楞蒙古自治州	Bayangol Mongol Autonomous Prefecture	10351	23	38025	7124	4
阿克苏地区	Aksu Administrative Offices	5845	16	21299	6346	5
克孜勒苏柯尔克孜自治州	Kizilsu Kirgiz Autonomous Prefecture	623	1	1681	2112	2
喀什地区	Kashgar [Kaxgar] Administrative Offices	5817	12	12231	3352	3
和田地区	Hotan Administrative Offices	4513	3	5540	6071	4
石河子市	Shihezi City	3022	8	19207	3635	2
阿拉尔市	Aral City	771	3	8410	20005	6
图木舒克市	Tumxuk City	525	2	2964	8405	6
五家渠市	Wujiaqu City	348	0	583	931	1

14-9 按登记注册类型分建筑企业技术装备情况

Number and Power of Machinery and Equipment Owned by Registration Status

(2011 年)

项　目	Item	自有机械设备年末总台数（台）Number of Machinery and Equipment Owned Year-end (set)	自有机械设备年末总功率（千瓦）Total Power of Machinery and Equipment Owned Year-end (kw)	自有机械设备年末净值（万元）Net Value of Machinery and Equipment Owned Year-end (10 000 yuan)
总　计	**Total**	**98768**	**2461704**	**398762**
#一、二级企业	First, Second Enterprises	78627	2141051	343949
#国有及国有控股	State-owned and State-holding	35759	1299213	212394
按登记注册类型分组	**Grouped by Registration Status**			
内资企业	Domestic Funede	98768	2461704	398762
国有企业	State-owned Enterprises	14521	414178	77148
集体企业	Collective-owned Enterprises	1002	27463	4491
有限责任公司	Limited Liability Corporations	53686	1392865	188816
国有独资公司	Sole State -funded Company	3027	122772	18196
其他有限责任公司	Other Limited Liability Companies	50659	1270093	170619
股份有限公司	Share-holding Corporations Ltd.	2368	165743	46040
私营企业	Private Enterprises	27132	459909	82083
#私营有限责任公司	Private Limited Liability Companies	26491	455123	81266
私营股份有限公司	Private Stock Limited Companies	627	4651	796
按国民经济行业分组	**Grouped by National Economic Sectors**			
房屋和土木工程建筑业	Buildings and Givil Engineering	88551	2234946	345773
房屋工程建筑	Building	71044	1404366	179491
土木工程建筑	Civil Engineering	17507	830580	166282
铁路、道路、隧道和桥梁	Railways, Roads, Tunnels and Bridges	7241	518777	108697
水利和港口建筑	Water Conservancy and Seaport	6617	173022	34032
工矿工程建筑	Mining Project	1077	32860	3231
架线和管道工程建筑	Cabling and Piping Project	2198	100052	18940
其他土木工程建筑	Other Civil Engineering	374	5869	1383
建筑安装业	Construction and Installation	9058	201571	43978
建筑装饰业	Building Decoration	792	9347	3045
其他建筑业	Others	367	15840	5965
按隶属关系分组	**Grouped by Subordination**			
中 央	Central Government	20933	824144	134244
地 方	Local	77835	1637560	264518
按企业资质等级分组	**Grouped by Enterprise's Qualification**			
施工总承包	Undertaking Porjects	93302	2371895	377842
特　级	Special Grade	875	28008	100
一　级	First Grade	28148	1090351	177690
二　级	Second Grade	47475	981356	155087
三　级	Third Grade	16804	272180	44965
专业承包	Specialized Undertaking	5466	89809	20920
一　级	First Grade	951	30024	6046
二　级	Second Grade	1178	11312	5027
三　级	Third Grade	3337	48473	9848

14-10 建筑企业签订合同情况
Contracts Signed by Construction Enterprises

单位：万元 (10 000 yuan)

年份 Year	地区 Region	合同总额 Total Value Of Contracts	上年结转合同 Value from Contracts Signed In Last Year	本年新签合同 Value from New Contracts Signed In This Year
	2002	3962086	988485	2973601
	2003	4312515	1236887	3075628
	2004	4725501	1351086	3374415
	2005	4857604	1557300	3300304
	2006	5692120	1483664	4208455
	2007	7220300	1986086	5234214
	2008	9907859	2906991	7000868
	2009	12473691	3859836	8613855
	2010	15883584	5459941	10423643
	2011	21956637	6083819	15872818
乌鲁木齐市	Urumqi City	9661297	3258033	6403264
克拉玛依市	Karamay City	1861916	319485	1542431
吐鲁番地区	Turpan Administrative Offices	221832	60898	160934
哈密地区	Hami [Kumul] Administrative Offices	471323	142550	328773
昌吉回族自治州	Changji Hui Autonomous Prefecture	1174955	275230	899725
伊犁哈萨克自治州	Ili Kazak Autonomous Prefecture	2152148	569280	1582868
伊犁州直属县(市)	Counties (Cities) Direct Under Ili Prefecture	1136699	336711	799988
塔城地区	Tacheng [Tarbagatai] Administrative Offices	682251	186860	495391
阿勒泰地区	Altay Administrative Offices	333198	45709	287489
博尔塔拉蒙古自治州	Bortala Mongol Autonomous Prefecture	267904	49737	218167
巴音郭楞蒙古自治州	Bayangol Mongol Autonomous Prefecture	1689922	340278	1349644
阿克苏地区	Aksu Administrative Offices	1223461	289057	934404
克孜勒苏柯尔克孜自治州	Kizilsu Kirgiz Autonomous Prefecture	156791	19513	137278
喀什地区	Kashgar [Kaxgar] Administrative Offices	926616	255395	671221
和田地区	Hotan Administrative Offices	326166	50243	275923
石河子市	Shihezi City	1375178	345361	1029817
阿拉尔市	Aral City	236056	38060	197996
图木舒克市	Tumxuk City	95174	16104	79070
五家渠市	Wujiaqu City	115901	54596	61305

注：14-10、14-11 表口径为总承包和专业承包企业。
Note:The data of the table 14-10&14-11 refer to all general construction contractors and professional contractors.

14-11 建筑企业承包工程完成情况

Completion of Contracted Projects by Construction Enterprises

单位：万元 (10 000 yuan)

年 份 Year	地 区 Region	直接从建设单位承揽工程完成产值 Completed Output Value of Projects Contracted Directly from Investors	自行完成施工产值 Own-Completed Output Value	分包出去工程产值 Output Value Of Out-Sourced Projects	从建设单位以外承揽工程产值 Completed Output Value of Projects Contracted From Non-investors
	2002	3141928	3048086	93842	88171
	2003	3238170	3135725	102445	85777
	2004	3443802	3377532	66270	62436
	2005	3634746	3563947	70799	51727
	2006	3856300	3775975	80325	80248
	2007	4534324	4420958	113366	120068
	2008	6309803	6128312	181492	164251
	2009	7993048	7805261	187787	108507
	2010	9723428	9503630	219798	191111
	2011	13382657	13026735	355922	251577
乌鲁木齐市	Urumqi City	5368547	5225299	143248	116722
克拉玛依市	Karamay City	988542	868744	119798	15684
吐鲁番地区	Turpan Administrative Offices	187505	187505		
哈密地区	Hami [Kumul] Administrative Offices	288440	288440		180
昌吉回族自治州	Changji Hui Autonomous Prefecture	845766	841348	4418	7018
伊犁哈萨克自治州	Ili Kazak Autonomous Prefecture	1497446	1444784	52662	60551
伊犁州直属县(市)	Counties (Cities) Direct Under Ili Prefecture	815556	812394	3162	
塔城地区	Tacheng [Tarbagatai] Administrative Offices	420526	371026	49500	48590
阿勒泰地区	Altay Administrative Offices	261364	261364		11961
博尔塔拉蒙古自治州	Bortala Mongol Autonomous Prefecture	189359	189359		
巴音郭楞蒙古自治州	Bayangol Mongol Autonomous Prefecture	1173746	1173746		1631
阿克苏地区	Aksu Administrative Offices	812338	812026	312	1499
克孜勒苏柯尔克孜自治州	Kizilsu Kirgiz Autonomous Prefecture	126694	126694		
喀什地区	Kashgar [Kaxgar] Administrative Offices	634705	600730	33975	38854
和田地区	Hotan Administrative Offices	218870	217361	1509	1509
石河子市	Shihezi City	709734	709734		7929
阿拉尔市	Aral City	161005	161005		
图木舒克市	Tumxuk City	72894	72894		
五家渠市	Wujiaqu City	107066	107066		

14-12 建筑企业资产及资本金

Assets and Capital Principal of Construction Enterprises

单位：万元 (10 000 yuan)

年份 Year	地区 Region	资产合计 Total Assets	流动资产合计 Total of Circulating Funds	固定资产合计 Total of Fixed Assets	固定资产净值 Net Value of Fixed Assets	本年折旧 Depreciation in the Year	资本金合计 Total of Principal Value	#国家资本金 National Principal
1995		939205	647608	240076	225084	18463	221212	110987
2000		3256421	1855185	1215525	1106384	65383	892851	208214
2001		3740312	2187385	1243161	1048023	82884	1055531	227457
2002		4244587	2527414	1364782	1179599	95565	1327186	227601
2003		3375330	2292828	787690	675947	61335	835618	219826
2004		3810825	2632242	825567	722019	62725	929293	225884
2005		3818087	2665404	826376	700835	72103	936389	184447
2006		4115800	2952267	796558	712740	69191	985436	202670
2007		4611598	3387459	804007	706591	76979	1095997	222967
2008		5527993	4040796	958379	862286	91915	1408249	429579
2009		6565349	4966204	1080129	960338	103188	1528701	396188
2010		7906943	6141713	1078910	939519	99050	1585475	412634
2011		10577644	8275111	1395723	1176365	119913	1960348	1948237
	乌鲁木齐市 Urumqi City	5157626	4078049	563155	468352	55323	858818	848676
	克拉玛依市 Karamay City	1310271	992739	232474	208168	12272	169158	168973
	吐鲁番地区 Turpan Administrative Offices	147125	119783	19928	19434	4265	38251	38251
	哈密地区 Hami [Kumul] Administrative Offices	227130	191986	25291	22230	2068	34891	34446
	昌吉回族自治州 Changji Hui Autonomous Prefecture	503763	397650	45221	41366	4722	107943	107217
	伊犁哈萨克自治州 Ili Kazak Autonomous Prefecture	668611	529786	91114	83841	10248	191714	191101
	伊犁州直属县(市) Counties (Cities) Direct Under Ili Prefecture	403039	324177	47887	44314	6010	114822	114305
	塔城地区 Tacheng [Tarbagatai] Administrative Offices	130506	103319	15255	13925	1770	32031	31935
	阿勒泰地区 Altay Administrative Offices	135066	102290	27972	25602	2468	44861	44861
	博尔塔拉蒙古自治州 Bortala Mongol Autonomous Prefecture	88905	62273	23038	21371	807	31924	31924
	巴音郭楞蒙古自治州 Bayangol Mongol Autonomous Prefecture	531731	392706	103600	77571	11799	143736	143736
	阿克苏地区 Aksu Administrative Offices	513258	392896	88721	65754	4795	111495	111495
	克孜勒苏柯尔克孜自治州 Kizilsu Kirgiz Autonomous Prefecture	112203	87557	18882	14835	682	20751	20751
	喀什地区 Kashgar [Kaxgar] Administrative Offices	447826	349627	41069	32783	2790	81383	81383
	和田地区 Hotan Administrative Offices	96597	68496	22160	19799	1625	39930	39930
	石河子市 Shihezi City	500613	406182	84276	70569	3762	102640	102640
	阿拉尔市 Aral City	124716	90718	26177	25828	3864	11289	11289
	图木舒克市 Tumxuk City	64394	52554	8653	3590	769	5874	5874
	五家渠市 Wujiaqu City	82876	62110	1965	874	122	10553	10553

14-13 建筑企业负债及所有者权益
Liabilities and Owner's Equity of Construction Enterprises

单位：万元 (10 000 yuan)

年 份 Year	地 区 Region	负债合计 Total Liabilities	流动负债 Liquid Liabilities	长期负债 Long-term Liabilities	所有者权益 Owners' Equity
	1994	540403	467895	72508	192618
	1995	699997	614110	84378	239208
	1996	815330	714429	98342	324051
	1997	1018007	901138	115032	350659
	1998	1175839	1044115	131724	385913
	1999	1325825	1205880	119945	415026
	2000	2068439	1941268	127171	1187982
	2001	2300621	2168441	132180	1439690
	2002	2717728	2585374	132354	1526859
	2003	2327382	2206412	120970	1047948
	2004	2631252	2517755	105621	1174864
	2005	2651255	2555028	96227	1159206
	2006	2886203	2797525	88678	1220298
	2007	3240248	3139697	100551	1359137
	2008	3806899	3669521	137378	1707855
	2009	4553885	4380062	173823	1996439
	2010	5798936	5466110	332826	2089888
	2011	7857731	7365272	450784	2707722
乌鲁木齐市	Urumqi City	4019261	3665958	353121	1129099
克拉玛依市	Karamay City	986241	980943	5285	323817
吐鲁番地区	Turpan Administrative Offices	108509	103203	2082	38616
哈密地区	Hami [Kumul] Administrative Offices	180096	173078	3167	46431
昌吉回族自治州	Changji Hui Autonomous Prefecture	337394	321961	15433	165268
伊犁哈萨克自治州	Ili Kazak Autonomous Prefecture	434788	405206	20200	232817
伊犁州直属县(市)	Counties (Cities) Direct Under Ili Prefecture	267654	240542	17757	134512
塔城地区	Tacheng [Tarbagatai] Administrative Offices	83051	82056	995	47321
阿勒泰地区	Altay Administrative Offices	84083	82608	1448	50984
博尔塔拉蒙古自治州	Bortala Mongol Autonomous Prefecture	56093	55170	923	32812
巴音郭楞蒙古自治州	Bayangol Mongol Autonomous Prefecture	299715	283224	10359	232016
阿克苏地区	Aksu Administrative Offices	345279	333857	7705	167979
克孜勒苏柯尔克孜自治州	Kizilsu Kirgiz Autonomous Prefecture	86302	85124	1178	25901
喀什地区	Kashgar [Kaxgar] Administrative Offices	333930	317154	1602	113896
和田地区	Hotan Administrative Offices	55158	53858	1300	41439
石河子市	Shihezi City	389301	385743	3558	111311
阿拉尔市	Aral City	100112	88501	11611	24603
图木舒克市	Tumxuk City	56490	52167	4323	7904
五家渠市	Wujiaqu City	69064	60125	8939	13812

14-14 建筑企业总收入
Total Income of Construction Enterprises

单位：万元 (10 000 yuan)

年份 Year	地区 Region	企业总收入 Total Income of Enterprises	工程结算收入 Revenue of Project Settlement Accounts	#工程结算成本 Costs of Project Settlement Accounts	#工程结算利润 Profits of Project Settlement Accounts	其他业务收入 Revenue from Other Business	#其他业务利润 Profits from Other Business
	1994	813369	714469	627830	66444	98900	9332
	1995	898810	821713	713940	82858	77097	9445
	1996	983170	904800	799183	78801	78370	8765
	1997	1210813	1081666	950091	98216	129147	17368
	1998	1454758	1346748	1193276	112310	108010	19146
	1999	1595986	1500818	1320898	130925	95167	14882
	2000	2659696	2514011	2252154	197243	145686	30012
	2001	2961754	2807549	2521902	211441	154205	34532
	2002	3360613	3199880	2854350	254428	160733	30853
	2003	3221521	3090768	2716009	254015	130753	21692
	2004	3395793	3276421	2900842	253783	119372	21601
	2005	3685197	3566042	3202712	238351	119155	23629
	2006	3766819	3643783	3255171	252876	123036	20730
	2007	4584374	4431221	3983622	285041	153154	22186
	2008	6382510	6225083	5635311	368605	157427	33187
	2009	7958865	7788105	7074708	440109	170760	39289
	2010	9849630	9610000	8752747	510265	239630	46564
	2011	13467486	13201119	12045042		266367	39679
乌鲁木齐市	Urumqi City	5451116	5282368	4805532		168748	22023
克拉玛依市	Karamay City	1161406	1118201	987067		43205	3690
吐鲁番地区	Turpan Administrative Offices	199649	199242	183905		407	1533
哈密地区	Hami [Kumul] Administrative Offices	258689	257311	234962		1378	720
昌吉回族自治州	Changji Hui Autonomous Prefecture	834100	832928	764209		1172	1767
伊犁哈萨克自治州	Ili Kazak Autonomous Prefecture	1465575	1459423	1352593		6152	2264
伊犁州直属县(市)	Counties (Cities) Direct Under Ili Prefecture	831400	827752	773147		3648	2001
塔城地区	Tacheng [Tarbagatai] Administrative Offices	384501	383199	351372		1302	185
阿勒泰地区	Altay Administrative Offices	249674	248472	228075		1202	78
博尔塔拉蒙古自治州	Bortala Mongol Autonomous Prefecture	207753	192956	181108		14797	322
巴音郭楞蒙古自治州	Bayangol Mongol Autonomous Prefecture	1037383	1028841	920390		8542	-758
阿克苏地区	Aksu Administrative Offices	785512	782465	712897		3047	1384
克孜勒苏柯尔克孜自治州	Kizilsu Kirgiz Autonomous Prefecture	88170	87856	81055		314	447
喀什地区	Kashgar [Kaxgar] Administrative Offices	599997	597594	549494		2403	1274
和田地区	Hotan Administrative Offices	301875	301755	286128		120	1840
石河子市	Shihezi City	723605	715796	667439		7809	2489
阿拉尔市	Aral City	163325	160503	147532		2822	20
图木舒克市	Tumxuk City	95724	90272	84583		5452	646
五家渠市	Wujiaqu City	93609	93608	86149		1	19

14-15 建筑企业亏损额及从业人数

Losses and Employed Persons of Construction Enterprises

(2011 年)

项　目	Item	企业数（个） Number of Enterprises (unit)	#亏损企业个数 Number of lossSuffering Enterprises	亏损企业亏损额（万元） Amount of Total loss (10000 yuan)	计算劳动生产率的平均人数（人） Average Number of Staff for Calculation of Labour Productivity (person)	期末从业人数（人） Employees at yearend (person)
总　计	**Total**	**1025**	**269**	**25579**	**585340**	**271071**
#一、二级企业	First, Second Enterprises	470	103	11544	491036	226266
#国有及国有控股	State-owned and State-holding	165	25	2885	291816	121555
按登记注册类型分组	**Grouped by Registration Status**					
内资企业	Domestic Funede	1021	267	25562	585327	271055
国有企业	State-owned Enterprises	66	14	1292	86594	41206
集体企业	Collective-owned Enterprises	22	5	4095	5944	4577
股份合作企业	Share-holding Cooperative					
有限责任公司	Limited Liability Corporations	371	73	8352	342058	146675
国有独资公司	Sole State -funded Company	23	2	193	29583	16812
其他有限责任公司	Other Limited Liability Companies	348	71	8159	312475	129863
股份有限公司	Share-holding Corporations Ltd	8			31662	15227
私营企业	Private Enterprises	551	175	11824	115816	60966
#私营有限责任公司	Private Limited Liability Companies	544	172	11558	113441	59687
私营股份有限公司	Private Stock Limited Companies	4	2	238	2231	1154
港、澳、台及外商企业	Enterprises With Funds from Hong Kong, Macao , Taiwan and Foreign	4	2	17	13	16
按国民经济行业分组	**Grouped by National Economic Sectors**					
房屋和土木工程建筑业	Buildings and Givil Engineering	635	147	18895	546756	241336
房屋工程建筑	Building	427	98	12047	444443	183336
土木工程建筑	Civil Engineering	208	49	6848	102313	58000
铁路、道路、隧道和桥梁	Railways, Roads, Tunnels and Bridges	72	13	1029	63364	35526
水利和港口建筑	Water Conservancy and Seaport	39	8	1892	24607	9304
工矿工程建筑	Mining Project	9	5	1010	2355	3067
架线和管道工程建筑	Cabling and Piping Project	31	10	1740	8819	8387
其他土木工程建筑	Other Civil Engineering	57	13	1177	3168	1716
建筑安装业	Construction and Installation	207	61	5398	31371	21853
建筑装饰业	Building Decoration	119	40	848	3882	3631
其他建筑业	Others	64	21	438	3331	4251
按隶属关系分组	**Grouped by Subordination**					
中 央	Central Government	64	3	303	196178	80148
地 方	Local	961	266	25276	389162	190923
按企业资质等级分组	**Grouped by Enterprise's Qualification**					
施工总承包	Undertaking Porjects	576	128	16977	550103	244199
特　级	Special Grade	1			8321	2853
一　级	First Grade	58	6	2201	215122	99107
二　级	Second Grade	250	40	4100	244380	107509
三　级及以下	Third Grade	267	82	10676	82280	34730
专业承包	Specialized Undertaking	336	106	8060	35237	22075
一　级	First Grade	20	6	304	7285	6441
二　级	Second Grade	90	33	4815	15928	6239
三级及以下	Third Grade	226	67	2941	12024	9395
劳务分包	Work Subcontractors	113	35	542	0	4797
三级及以下	Third Grade	113	35	542	0	4797

14-16 建筑企业工程施工情况

Condition of Building Works by Construction Enterprise

单位：万平方米 (10 000 sq.m)

年 份 Year	地 区 Region	房屋建筑施工面积 Floor Space of Buildings Under Construction	#本年新开工面积 New-opened Works for This Year	施工面积中实行投标承包面积 Space of Building and Contracting	#本年新开工面积 New-opened Works for This Year	房屋建筑竣工面积 Floor Space of Buildings Completed
	1995	1212.45	657.34	214.65	148.22	609.84
	1996	1207.45	673.17	397.83	272.22	645.89
	1997	1400.28	778.14	653.90	400.75	747.24
	1998	1662.36	1032.15	1023.88	678.42	879.67
	1999	1943.05	1068.05	1210.90	807.87	1042.51
	2000	2241.48	1448.34	1666.87	1110.04	1261.42
	2001	2659.69	1679.41	2056.30	1380.07	1467.54
	2002	2572.62	1489.38	2133.56	1274.07	1469.59
	2003	2719.22	1735.19	2411.27	1527.79	1450.80
	2004	2812.30	1791.50	2426.79	1613.19	1483.35
	2005	2767.64	1639.80	2512.79	1517.41	1429.36
	2006	2889.64	1854.91	2687.63	1751.99	1645.02
	2007	3552.36	2421.17	3299.73	2277.87	1849.64
	2008	4234.71	2862.31	3982.24	2784.92	2155.98
	2009	5151.60	3560.54	4812.84	3378.63	2517.79
	2010	6620.14	4449.78	6119.70	4235.58	2891.45
	2011	8947.71	5796.89	8318.62	5446.50	3465.49
乌鲁木齐市	Urumqi City	2371.23	1343.54	2309.52	1319.41	650.12
克拉玛依市	Karamay City	179.88	111.31	139.22	97.16	58.01
吐鲁番地区	Turpan Administrative Offices	113.96	87.43	103.56	78.36	68.64
哈密地区	Hami [Kumul] Administrative Offices	248.78	200.87	233.60	190.40	120.46
昌吉回族自治州	Changji Hui Autonomous Prefecture	632.66	436.65	565.54	407.21	326.95
伊犁哈萨克自治州	Ili Kazak Autonomous Prefecture	1337.06	933.32	1252.96	893.38	556.36
伊犁州直属县(市)	Counties (Cities) Direct Under Ili Prefecture	649.04	418.25	624.89	399.44	260.98
塔城地区	Tacheng [Tarbagatai] Administrative Offices	439.26	324.04	396.32	305.78	177.78
阿勒泰地区	Altay Administrative Offices	248.76	191.03	231.75	188.16	117.60
博尔塔拉蒙古自治州	Bortala Mongol Autonomous Prefecture	168.41	110.95	149.57	108.69	76.26
巴音郭楞蒙古自治州	Bayangol Mongol Autonomous Prefecture	1048.23	698.39	940.48	579.78	418.74
阿克苏地区	Aksu Administrative Offices	730.69	479.96	685.12	474.96	342.05
克孜勒苏柯尔克孜自治州	Kizilsu Kirgiz Autonomous Prefecture	102.27	62.32	82.92	59.64	69.48
喀什地区	Kashgar [Kaxgar] Administrative Offices	880.37	513.08	796.50	433.87	324.00
和田地区	Hotan Administrative Offices	296.09	232.13	290.09	227.42	123.74
石河子市	Shihezi City	598.72	388.91	555.26	378.20	201.45
阿拉尔市	Aral City	121.35	96.27	96.27	96.27	70.19
图木舒克市	Tumxuk City	55.24	52.64	55.24	52.64	34.06
五家渠市	Wujiaqu City	62.76	49.13	62.76	49.13	24.98

注：该表口径为总承包和专业承包企业，以下同。
Note: The data of the table refer to all general construction contractors and professional contractors. (the same as in the following)

14-17 按登记注册类型分建筑企业工程施工情况

Condition of Building Works by Construction Enterprise by Registration Status

单位：万平方米 (2011 年) (10 000 sq.m)

项　　目	Item	房屋建筑施工面积 Floor Space of Buildings Under Construction	#本年新开工面积 New-opened Works for This Year	施工面积中实行投标承包面积 Space of Buildings and Contracting	#本年新开工面积 New-opened Works for This Year	房屋建筑竣工面积 Floor Space of Buildings Completed
总　　计	**Total**	**8947.71**	**5796.89**	**8318.62**	**5446.50**	**3465.49**
#一、二级企业	First, Second Enterprises	7436.63	4700.97	7015.70	4502.52	2727.70
#国有及国有控股	State-owned and State-holding	3542.79	2216.67	3421.57	2166.30	1185.27
按登记注册类型分组	**Grouped by Registration Status**					
内资企业	Domestic Funede	8947.71	5796.89	8318.62	5446.50	3465.49
国有企业	State-owned Enterprises	882.71	561.97	809.33	520.92	304.69
集体企业	Collective-owned Enterprises	34.36	23.39	33.55	22.62	10.96
股份合作企业	Share-holding Cooperative					
有限责任公司	Limited Liability Corporations	5811.15	3821.71	5519.10	3642.58	2308.45
国有独资公司	Sole State -funded Company	326.09	201.01	320.46	199.15	95.19
其他有限责任公司	Other Limited Liability Companies	5485.07	3620.71	5198.64	3443.43	2213.26
股份有限公司	Share-holding Corporations Ltd	237.67	118.14	236.99	106.15	78.13
私营企业	Private Enterprises	1887.60	1224.95	1627.83	1107.49	731.70
#私营有限责任公司	Private Limited Liability Companies	1822.30	1201.93	1564.87	1087.01	722.03
私营股份有限公司	Private Stock Limited Companies	62.64	20.48	62.64	20.48	9.33
按国民经济行业分组	**Grouped by National Economic Sectors**					
房屋和土木工程建筑业	Buildings and Givil Engineering	8862.97	5754.30	8253.12	5409.57	3432.49
房屋工程建筑	Building	8554.68	5573.80	7995.72	5250.90	3304.35
土木工程建筑	Civil Engineering	308.28	180.50	257.40	158.67	128.14
铁路、道路、隧道和桥梁	Railways, Roads, Tunnels and Bridges	119.47	40.65	113.26	38.42	36.84
水利和港口建筑	Water Conservancy and Seaport	163.79	117.97	125.95	105.20	84.69
工矿工程建筑	Mine Project	16.73	13.58	11.77	8.63	4.38
建筑安装业	Construction and Installation	83.41	41.26	64.17	35.60	32.28
其他建筑业	Others	1.33	1.33	1.33	1.33	0.71
按隶属关系分组	**Grouped by Subordination**					
中 央	Central Government	2441.84	1500.54	2368.09	1488.39	813.23
地 方	Local	6505.87	4296.36	5950.52	3958.11	2652.25
按企业资质等级分组	**Grouped by Enterprise's Qualification**					
施工总承包	Undertaking Porjects	8755.74	5637.99	8138.15	5294.54	3419.87
特　级	Special Grade	204.52	103.16	204.52	103.16	72.80
一　级	First Grade	2679.59	1425.41	2577.62	1378.90	720.93
二　级	Second Grade	4369.92	3017.88	4054.50	2868.71	1890.21
三级及以下	Third Grade	1501.71	1091.53	1301.51	943.76	735.92
专业承包	Specialized Undertaking	191.97	158.90	180.47	151.97	45.62
一　级	First Grade	40.25	37.11	40.25	37.11	32.70
二　级	Second Grade	142.35	117.41	138.81	114.64	11.05
三级及以下	Third Grade	9.37	4.39	1.41	0.22	1.87

14-18 按登记注册类型分建筑企业竣工房屋建筑面积

Floor Space of Buildings Constructed of Construction Enterprises by Registration Status

单位：平方米 (2011 年) (sq.m)

项 目	Item	合 计 Total	住宅用房 Workshop	商业、居民服务业用 房 Residential Building	办公用房 Office Occupancy
总 计	**Total**	**34654857**	**24141317**	**1553228**	**1883487**
#一、二级企业	First, Second Enterprises	27277011	18639563	1375088	1588780
#国有及国有控股	State-owned and State-holding	11852718	8272039	561870	468871
按登记注册类型分组	**Grouped by Registration Status**				
内资企业	Domestic Funede	34654857	24141317	1553228	1883487
#国有企业	State-owned Enterprises	3046861	2046033	107446	87975
集体企业	Collective-owned Enterprises	109596	94821		3822
股份合作企业	Share-holding Cooperative				
有限责任公司	Limited Liability Corporations	23084458	16077010	1051236	1215964
国有独资公司	Sole State -funded Company	951884	639872	5937	41966
其他有限责任公司	Other Limited Liability Companies	22132574	15437138	1045299	1173998
股份有限公司	Share-holding Corporations Ltd	781317	557263	82145	6610
私营企业	Private Enterprises	7316987	5301268	284793	540694
私营有限责任公司	Private Limited Liability Companies	7220340	5214099	284793	539322
私营股份有限公司	Private Stock Limited Companies	93258	84000		1372
按国民经济行业分组	**Grouped by National Economic Sectors**				
房屋和土木工程建筑业	Buildings and Givil Engineering	34324907	24021150	1536877	1877744
房屋工程建筑	Building	33043508	23099527	1429878	1850855
土木工程建筑	Civil Engineering	1281399	921623	106999	26889
铁路、道路、隧道和乔梁工程建筑	Railways, Roads, Tunnels and Bridges	368446	228371	98611	12734
水利和港口工程建筑	Water Conservancy and Seaport	846926	646729	1252	5967
工矿工程建筑	Mine Project	43827	24323	7136	8188
架线和管道工程建筑	Stringing and Pipeline Constrnction Project				
其他土木工程建筑	Other Civil Engineering	22200	22200		
建筑安装业	Construction and Installation	322805	120167	16351	5743
建筑装饰业	Construction and Decoration				
其他建筑业	Others	7145			
按隶属关系分组	**Grouped by Subordination**	**34654857**	**24141317**	**1553228**	**1883487**
中央	Central Government	8132321	5624291	340130	361275
地方	Local	26522536	18517026	1213098	1522212
按企业资质等级分组	**Grouped by Enterprise's Qualification**	**34654857**	**24141317**	**1553228**	**1883487**
施工总承包	Undertaking Porjects	34198688	23783486	1514092	1878351
特级	Special Grade	727958	424378	183056	39079
一级	First Grade	7209287	4438512	494299	389560
二级	Second Grade	18902266	13424211	658597	1155005
三级及以下	Third Grade	7359177	5496385	178140	294707
专业承包	Specialized Undertaking	456169	357831	39136	5136
一级	First Grade	326961	264108	39136	
二级	Second Grade	110539	88354		5136
三级及以下	Third Grade	18669	5369		

14-18 续表 Continued

单位：平方米 (sq.m)

项　目	Item	科研、教育、医疗用房 House for Commerce and Residential Services	文化、体育、娱乐用房 House for Culture and Education	厂房及建筑物用房 House for Medical Care	仓库 House for Scientific Research	其他 Others
总　计	**Total**	**2733743**	**482145**	**2233359**	**169484**	**1458094**
#一、二级企业	First, Second Enterprises	2011856	388809	2002827	148842	1121246
#国有及国有控股	State-owned and State-holding	653787	212692	1148917	103514	431028
按登记注册类型分组	**Grouped by Registration Status**					
内资企业	Domestic Funede	2733743	482145	2233359	169484	1458094
#国有企业	State-owned Enterprises	166379	19780	446920	41542	130786
集体企业	Collective-owned Enterprises	5100	1600	4253		
股份合作企业	Share-holding Cooperative					
有限责任公司	Limited Liability Corporations	1931066	353896	1406696	89089	959501
国有独资公司	Sole State -funded Company	84648	18500	148243	5326	7392
其他有限责任公司	Other Limited Liability Companies	1846418	335396	1258453	83763	952109
股份有限公司	Share-holding Corporations Ltd	42490		45320	27778	19711
私营企业	Private Enterprises	470257	106869	320280	8505	284321
私营有限责任公司	Private Limited Liability Companies	462371	106869	320280	8505	284101
私营股份有限公司	Private Stock Limited Companies	7886				
按国民经济行业分组	**Grouped by National Economic Sectors**					
房屋和土木工程建筑业	Buildings and Givil Engineering	2724457	482145	2213847	169484	1299203
房屋工程建筑	Building	2644703	479662	2090113	165741	1283029
土木工程建筑	Civil Engineering	79754	2483	123734	3743	16174
铁路、道路、隧道和桥梁工程建筑	Railways, Roads, Tunnels and Bridges	27217		1513		
水利和港口工程建筑	Water Conservancy and Seaport	52537	2483	118041	3743	16174
工矿工程建筑	Mine Project			4180		
架线和管道工程建筑	Stringing and Pipeline Constrnction Project					
其他土木工程建筑	Other Civil Engineering					
建筑安装业	Construction and Installation	9286		12367		158891
建筑装饰业	Construction and Decoration					
其他建筑业	Others			7145		
按隶属关系分组	**Grouped by Subordination**	**2733743**	**482145**	**2233359**	**169484**	**1458094**
中央	Central Government	485409	105966	915047	27386	272817
地方	Local	2248334	376179	1318312	142098	1185277
按企业资质等级分组	**Grouped by Enterprise's Qualification**	**2733743**	**482145**	**2233359**	**169484**	**1458094**
施工总承包	Undertaking Porjects	2733105	481462	2214910	168684	1424598
特级	Special Grade	62495	4225	14725		
一级	First Grade	594304	208000	789235	113771	181606
二级	Second Grade	1354419	175901	1181818	35071	917244
三级及以下	Third Grade	721887	93336	229132	19842	325748
专业承包	Specialized Undertaking	638	683	18449	800	33496
一级	First Grade	638	683			22396
二级	Second Grade			17049		
三级及以下	Third Grade			1400	800	11100

主要统计指标解释

建筑业统计单位 指从事房屋、构筑物建造和设备安装活动的法人企业。建筑业法人企业应具有建筑业资质并能够独立核算，同时其应具备以下条件：①依法成立，有自己的名称、组织机构和场所，能够承担民事责任；②独立拥有和使用资产，承担负债，有权与其他单位签订合同；③独立核算盈亏，能够编制资产负债表。

建筑业总产值 是以货币表现的建筑安装企业在一定时期内生产的建筑业产品和提供的服务的总和。建筑业总产值包括：

(1)建筑工程产值：指列入建筑工程预算内的各种工程价值。

(2)安装工程产值：指设备安装工程价值，不包括被安装设备本身价值。

(3)其他产值：建筑业总产值中除建筑工程、安装工程以外的产值。包括房屋构筑物修理产值、非标准设备制造产值、总包企业向分包企业收取的管理费以及不能明确划分的施工活动所完成的产值。

a.房屋构筑物修理产值：指房屋和构筑物修理所完成的产值，但不包括被修理房屋、构筑物本身价值和生产设备的修理价值。

b.非标准设备制造产值：指加工制造没有定型的非标准生产设备的加工费和原材料价值(如化工厂、炼油厂用的各种罐、槽，矿井生产统一使用的各种漏斗、三角槽、阀门等)以及附属加工厂为本企业承建工程制作的非标准设备的价值。

建筑业增加值 指建筑业企业在报告期内以货币表现的建筑业生产经营活动的最终成果。

从2004年第一次全国经济普查开始，建筑业现价增加值按生产法和分配法(收入法)两种方法计算，以收入法的计算结果为准，即从收入的角度出发，根据生产要素在生产过程中应得的收入份额计算。具体计算方法：经济普查年度建筑业增加值按照《经济普查年度GDP核算方案》计算，非经济普查年度建筑业增加值按照《非经济普查年度GDP核算方案》计算

房屋建筑施工面积 指在报告期内施工的全部房屋建筑面积，包括本期新开工的房屋面积、上期施工跨入本期继续施工的房屋面积、上期停缓建在本期恢复施工的房屋面积、本期竣工的房屋面积及本期施工后又停缓建的房屋面积。

房屋建筑竣工面积 指在报告期内房屋建筑按照设计要求全部完工，达到了使用条件，经验收鉴定合格，正式移交使用单位的房屋建筑面积。

自有机械设备年末总台数 指归本企业所有，属于本企业固定资产的生产性机械设备年末总台数。包括施工机械、生产设备、运输设备以及其他设备。

自有机械设备年末总功率 指本企业自有施工机械、生产设备、运输设备以及其他设备等列为在册固定资产的生产性机械设备年末总功率，按设定能力或查定能力计算。包括机械本身的动力和为该机械服务的单独动力设备，如电动机等。计算单位用千瓦，动力换算可按1马力＝0.735千瓦折合成千瓦数。电焊机、变压器、锅炉不计算动力。

工程结算收入 指企业承包工程实现的工程价款结算收入，以及向发包单位收取的除工程价款以外的按规定列作营业收入的各种款项，如临时设施费、劳动保险费、施工机械调迁费等以及向发包单位收取的各种索赔款。

工程结算利润 指已结算工程实现的利润，如亏损以“—”号表示。计算公式为：

工程结算利润＝工程结算收入－工程结算成本－工程结算税金及附加

企业总收入 指与企业生产经营直接有关的各项收入，包括工程结算收入和其他业务收入。计算公式为：

企业总收入＝工程结算收入＋其他业务收入

Explanatory Notes on Main Statistical Indicators

Statistical Unit in the Construction Industry refers to a corporate enterprise engaged in the construction of buildings and structures and in the installation of equipment. A corporate construction enterprise should have qualification certificates with independent accounting system, and should meet the following 3 requirements: a) being set up in line with relevant legal basis, having its full name, organization and location, and capable of taking civil liabilities; b) independently possessing and using its assets and assuming its liabilities, and entitled to sign contracts with other institutions; and c) making independent accounts of its profits and losses, and capable of compiling its own balance sheet.

Gross Output Value of Construction refers to total of construction products and services, expressed in money terms, produced or rendered by construction and installation enterprises during a given period of time. It includes:

(1) Output value of construction projects: the value of projects covered by the project budgets;

(2) Output value of installation projects: the value of the installation of equipment, (excluding the value of the equipment to be installed);

(3) Other output values: the output value of construction industry apart from that of construction projects and installation projects. It includes: output value of repair of buildings and structures; output value of non-standard equipment manufacture-ing; overhead expenses received by contracted enterprises from the sub-contracted enterprises and the completed output value of construction activities for which there is no clear definition.

a. Output value of repair of buildings and structures: the value created through the repairs of buildings or structures. It does not include the value of buildings or structures being repaired and the value of the repair of production equipment;

b. Output value of manufactured non-standard equipment: the value of non-standard production equipment, including raw materials and manufacturing cost, made for the construction project (i.e., chemical plant; kettles or tanks used by refineries; various fillers, triangle tanks, valves used by mines). It also includes the output value of equipment manufactured by subsidiary workshops.

Value-added of Construction refers to the final result of the activities of production and operation of enterprises of the construction industry in monetary terms during the reference period.

Starting from the 2004 economic census, value-added of construction is calculated by both production approach and income approach, with the figures from the income approach as the final figures., Under the income approach,, calculation starts from the perspective of income and is based on the share of income derived from the production process by the relevant factors of production.. Specifically, value-added of construction for the Census years is calculated in accordance with the Programme of Compilation of GDP and National Accounts for the Year of Economic Census, and value-added of construction for other years is calculated in accordance with the Programme of Compilation of GDP and National Accounts for the Non Economic Census Years.

Floor Space of Buildings Under Construction refers to floor space of buildings under construction during the reference period, including the floor space of buildings for which construction has newly started; buildings for which construction has started earlier and is continuing during the reference period; and buildings for which construction has been suspended earlier but has restarted during the reference period; buildings completed during the reference period; and buildings under construction but construction has subsequently been during the reference period.

Floor Space of Buildings Completed refers to the floor space of buildings that are completed in the reference period in accordance with the requirements of the design, up to the standard for being put into use, and having been checked and accepted by departments concerned as qualified ones.

Total Number of Machinery and Equipment Owned by the End of Year refers to the number of machines and equipment owned by the enterprises, and listed as the fixed assets of the enterprises by the end of the year, including machinery and equipment for construction, production and transportation.

Total Power of Machinery and Equipment Owned by the End of Year refers to the total power of machinery and equipment owned by the enterprises,and listed as the fixed assets of the enterprises by the end of the year, including machinery and equipment for construction,production and transportation.The power of the machinery is calculated on basis of the designed or verified capacity,covering the power of the machinery/equipment and the separate power equipment serving the machinery/equipment (such as electric motors), but excluding welders, transformers and boilers.The unit used for the calculation of power is kilowatt, with horsepower converted to kilowatt by 1 horsepower=0.735 kilowatt.

Income from Settlement of Projects refers to the income received by the construction enterprise from the contracted project through settlement procedures, and other charges to the contractoree as operational costs in addition to the value of the project, such as temporary facility fee,labour insurance premium,moving cost of construction equipment,as well as various types of claims to the contractee.

Profit from Settlement of Projects refers to profit realized through settled projects. It is calculated with the following formula:

Profit from Settlement of Projects=Income from Settlement of Projects−Settled Cost−Settled Taxes and Other Cost

Total Revenue of Enterprises refers to the sum of income from production and operation of enterprises, including income from settlement of projects and other operational income, namely:

Total Revenue of Enterprises=Income from Settlement of Projects+Other Operational Incom

2012

新疆统计年鉴

XINJIANG STATISTICAL YEARBOOK

第十五篇
交通运输和邮电

CHAPTER 15
Transport, Postal and Telecommunication Services

简要说明
Brief Introduction

本篇资料的主要内容及来源

本篇资料反映新疆维吾尔自治区交通运输业和邮政、电信业发展的基本状况。

运输业资料主要包括：铁路、公路、民航、管道四种运输方式的线路条数、里程、总运量及周转量、货物运输平均运距、铁路运输主要技术经济指标；民用机动车辆情况。

邮政、电信业资料主要包括：邮政、电信业务完成情况，邮政、电信业务发展水平等资料。

铁路资料来自乌鲁木齐铁路局；公路资料来自新疆维吾尔自治区公路局；民航运输数据资料来自中国南方航空股份有限公司新疆分公司；电信资料来自新疆维吾尔自治区通信管理局；邮政数据来自新疆维吾尔自治区邮政公司。

本篇建筑业企业统计数据是根据国家统计局制定的《建筑业统计报表制度》整理汇总的。建筑业统计数据采取全面调查的方法。资料由新疆维吾尔自治区统计局固定资产投资统计处提供。

Main Content and Source of Data

Data in this chapter cover mainly the basic condition of the development of transportation, post and telecommunications in Xinjiang Uygur Autonomous Region.

Data on transport cover mainly the length of the routes of four means of railway, highways, civil aviation and pipeline. total fright traffic, total freight ton-kilometers, average transport distance of fright, principal economic and technical indicators of railway transport, possession of civil vehicles.

Data on post and telecommunication cover mainly the complete business volume of post and telecommunication services, and the development of the post and telecommunication service, etc.

Data on railways transportation come from the Urumqi Bureau of the Railway. Data on the highways come from the Bureau of Transportation. Data on the civil aviation transport come from the China Southwest Airlines, Xinjiang Branch. Data on telecommunication services come from telecommunication Bureau. Data on post are provided by the Post Bureau.

Data in this chapter are collected and compiled by the Division of Industry and Transport Statistics, Xinjiang Bureau of Statistics.

15-1 主要年份运输业基本情况
Basic Conditions of Transport in Main Years

指 标	Item	2000	2010	2011
运输线路长度(公里)	**Length of Transport Routes (km)**			
铁路营业里程	Railways in Operation	3010	4393	4480
公路里程	Highways	80875	152843	155150
民用航线里程	Total Civil Aviation Routes	152941	176992	175797
管道输油（气）里程	Petroleum and Gas Pipelines	2696	11464	11077
客运量(万人)	**Total Passenger Traffic (10 000 persons)**	**23191**	**46346**	**50461**
铁 路	Railways	1147	1523	2002
公 路	Highways	21877	44333	47927
民用航空	Civil Aviation	167	490	532
旅客周转量(亿人公里)	**Total Passenger-Kilometers (100 million passenger-km)**	**292.80**	**670.75**	**758.26**
铁 路	Railways	97.40	170.10	216.16
公 路	Highways	158.20	404.00	437.90
民用航空	Civil Aviation	37.20	96.65	104.16
货运量(万吨)	**Total Freight Traffic (10 000 tons)**	**33090.5**	**64596.7**	**70361.9**
铁 路	Railways	4199	6853	6904
公 路	Highways	27048	50448	55965
民用航空	Civil Aviation	3.5	3.7	3.9
输油(气)管道	Petroleum and Gas Pipelines	1840	7292	7489
货物周转量(亿吨公里)	**Total Freight Ton-kilometers (100 million ton-km)**	**660.88**	**2053.82**	**2199.52**
铁 路	Railways	355.00	814.03	857.01
公 路	Highways	272.90	767.14	852.17
民用航空	Civil Aviation	0.98	0.98	0.97
输油(气)管道	Petroleum and Gas Pipelines	32.00	471.67	488.38
民用汽车拥有量(万辆)	**Possession of Civil Motor Vehicles (10 000 units)**	**37.0**	**135.9**	**169.8**
#载客汽车辆数	Buses and Cars	18.0	87.6	114.8
载货汽车辆数	Trucks	17.5	37.0	43.8
#私人汽车拥有量	Privat Vehicles	13.9	85.8	113.2

注：1.2000 年以后公路里程包括兵团数据。2.2006 年起新疆公路通车里程包含村道里程(以下同)。
Note: a) Since 2000 the highway mileage cover the data of XJPCC. b) Length of highways include lenth of backroad since 2006.(the same as in the following table)

15-2 主要年份运输线路长度

Length of Transport Routes in Main Years

单位:公里 (km)

年份 Year	铁路营业里程 Length of Railways in Operation	#新疆境内 Inside Xinjiang	公路 Length of Highways	#高级次高级公路 High Grade & Seond High Grade Highways	民用航空 Length of the Civil Aviation	#新疆境内 Inside Xinjiang	管道输油(气)里程 Petrolurn and Gas Pipelines
1978	1031	796	23818	5810	4783	4783	443
1980	1103	868	21148	6390	4412	4412	443
1985	1579	1344	22232	8369	4527	4527	473
1990	1578	1343	25425	12566	36465	5159	740
1995	2038	1803	30298	19013	69789	6693	875
1996	2038	1803	31609	20461	122089	9183	928
1997	2038	1803	32053	21495	123664	9717	1373
1998	2038	1803	32762	22485	150473	9717	1955
1999	3008	2780	33484	23214	141872	9719	2496
2000	3010	2775	80875	31059	152941	9719	2696
2001	3010	2774	80947	31635	161814	9719	2965
2002	3010	2775	82929	32541	132483	9898	3153
2003	3009	2775	83633	33891	141456	9898	3008
2004	2999	2763	86824	40679	111768	8664	3003
2005	2925	2761	89531	43803	119481	8664	3003
2006	2925	2761	143736	50119	138564	9064	4631
2007	2925	2761	145219	55080	160354	11363	6793
2008	2925	2925	146652	60233	147753	10560	9455
2009	3837	3673	150683	67684	152392	10754	11235
2010	4393	4228	152843	72887	176992	9939	11464
2011	4480	4316	155150	80974	175797	9939	11077

15-3 主要年份运输线路质量

Quality of Transport Routes in Main Years

单位：公里 (km)

指标	Item	1995	2000	2010	2011
铁路营业里程	Length of National Railways in Operation	2038	3010	4393	4480
#复线里程	Double-Tracking Length		986	1324	1953
#自动闭塞里程	Automatic Blocking Length	273	685	1408	1424
公路线路里程	Length of Highways	30298	80875	152843	155150
#水泥沥青路面	Lenth of bituminous Pavement	27982	33035	72887	80974

注：铁路上述里程是新疆境内里程。
Note: Length of railways refers to length of railway inside in Xinjiang.

15-4 主要年份客运量及周转量

Passenger Traffic and Passenger kilometers in Main Years

年 份 Year	客运量(万人) Passenger Traffic (10 000 persons)				旅客周转量(亿人公里) Passenger-Kilometers (100 million passenger-km)			
	总 计 Total	铁 路 Railways	公 路 Highways	民用航空 Civil Aviation	总 计 Total	铁 路 Railways	公 路 Highways	民用航空 Civil Aviation
1978	941	148	786	7	25.23	13.72	10.96	0.55
1980	1356	193	1152	10	30.49	18.83	10.83	0.83
1985	3728	320	3399	9	63.16	33.16	29.13	0.87
1986	4058	362	3674	22	73.87	36.40	34.00	3.74
1987	4439	377	4327	34	83.67	37.14	39.44	7.09
1988	5205	459	4698	48	99.17	42.86	46.35	9.96
1989	8740	453	8240	47	120.69	44.52	66.37	9.80
1990	9602	388	9161	53	103.80	37.96	55.11	10.73
1991	14582	383	14142	56	122.08	41.94	68.05	12.09
1992	14997	425	14490	82	138.24	44.48	75.38	18.38
1993	16352	513	15749	90	174.23	50.04	103.51	20.73
1994	17181	670	16405	106	195.58	58.08	112.50	25.00
1995	17533	672	16739	122	204.89	58.00	117.17	29.68
1996	18858	610	18110	138	218.79	57.80	128.58	32.20
1997	20237	748	19360	129	233.39	64.70	139.00	29.69
1998	21747	878	20735	134	256.90	76.90	149.60	30.40
1999	22763	1000	21618	145	270.74	81.90	157.05	31.79
2000	23191	1147	21877	167	292.80	97.40	158.20	37.20
2001	24344	932	23255	157	309.70	104.10	170.30	35.30
2002	26016	950	24883	183	330.80	106.00	185.60	39.20
2003	26972	879	25878	215	342.00	106.10	195.00	40.90
2004	29782	1023	28473	286	423.80	121.90	249.00	52.90
2005	33220	1134	31747	339	457.42	125.20	271.20	61.02
2006	34471	1272	32835	364	498.30	138.90	292.10	67.30
2007	38434	1873	36159	402	548.10	144.46	326.70	76.94
2008	42111	1311	40392	408	594.60	149.89	363.60	81.11
2009	43410	1371	41604	435	614.66	152.90	376.30	85.46
2010	46346	1523	44333	490	670.75	170.10	404.00	96.65
2011	50461	2002	47927	532	758.26	216.16	437.90	104.16

注：2011 年民航旅客吞吐量为 1422.88 万人。
Note: Air passenger handling capacity is 14.2288 million persons in 2011.

15-5 主要年份货运量及货物周转量
Freight Traffic and Ton-kilometers in Main Years

年份 Year	货运量(万吨) Freight Traffic (10 000 tons)				
	总计 Total	铁路 Railways	公路 Highways	民用航空 Civil Aviation	输油(气)管道 Petroleum and Gas Pipelines
1978	6064.12	923	4843	0.12	298
1980	8422.16	884	7209	0.16	329
1985	10681.11	1278	8847	0.11	556
1990	13919.87	1691	11551	0.87	677
1995	25406.00	2733	21754	2.00	917
1996	26676.00	2951	22505	2.00	1218
1997	28790.00	3190	24125	3.00	1472
1998	30484.00	3324	25573	3.00	1584
1999	32076.17	3777	26596	3.17	1700
2000	33090.50	4199	27048	3.50	1840
2001	33589.00	3904	27751	2.00	1932
2002	34966.70	4121	28861	2.70	1982
2003	37485.20	4602	30881	2.20	2000
2004	38885.50	5083	31700	2.50	2100
2005	40600.20	5397	33000	3.20	2200
2006	43096.40	6001	34835	3.40	2256
2007	49009.62	7430	38427	3.62	3149
2008	57187.80	6120	44987	3.80	6077
2009	60162.80	6413	46787	3.80	6959
2010	64596.70	6853	50448	3.70	7292
2011	70361.90	6904	55965	3.90	7489

年份 Year	货物周转量(亿吨公里) Freight Ton-kilometers (100 million ton-km)				
	总计 Total	铁路 Railways	公路 Highways	民用航空(万吨公里) Civil Aviation (10 000 ton-km)	输油(气)管道 Petroleum and Gas Pipelines
1978	106.96	67.76	32.06	98.10	7.13
1980	121.14	67.27	45.89	137.80	7.97
1985	174.75	102.03	61.26	104.00	11.45
1990	262.29	141.16	108.09	2048.00	12.84
1995	474.39	240.88	219.72	5744.00	13.22
1996	507.15	260.96	229.55	6475.00	16.00
1997	541.40	269.70	247.00	7000.00	24.00
1998	553.60	264.20	262.80	7000.00	25.90
1999	602.94	303.60	270.46	8800.00	28.00
2000	660.88	355.00	272.90	9776.00	32.00
2001	714.43	403.90	275.90	6300.00	34.00
2002	759.62	425.30	298.00	8238.00	35.50
2003	837.04	475.00	325.00	6400.00	36.40
2004	947.24	548.50	361.00	7400.00	37.00
2005	1032.75	586.90	405.00	8500.00	40.00
2006	1143.31	647.10	425.68	8921.00	69.64
2007	1264.31	678.53	468.80	9085.78	116.07
2008	1656.88	758.74	672.30	9285.43	224.91
2009	1815.81	751.09	705.90	9700.00	357.85
2010	2053.82	814.03	767.14	9837.00	471.67
2011	2199.52	857.01	852.17	9700.00	488.38

15-6 主要年份货物运输平均运距
Average Transport Distance of Freight in Main Years

单位：公里 (km)

年份 Year	合计 Total	铁路 Railways	公路 Highways	民用航空 Civil Aviation	输油(气)管道 Petroleum and Gas Pipelines
1978	168	565	66	818	239
1980	139	566	64	861	242
1985	158	624	69	945	206
1990	188	835	94	2354	190
1995	187	881	101	2872	144
2000	200	845	101	2857	174
2001	211	1023	99	3150	176
2002	217	1032	103	3051	179
2003	224	865	105	2909	182
2004	244	904	114	2960	176
2005	254	901	122	2656	182
2006	265	894	122	2598	308
2007	257	913	122	2528	368
2008	289	926	149	2456	370
2009	301	873	151	2552	518
2010	317	934	152	2637	514
2011	312	935	152	2480	652

15-7 主要年份铁路运输主要财务指标
Main Financial Indicators of Railway Transport in Main Years

单位：万元 (10 000 yuan)

指标	Item	1990	1995	2000	2010	2011
运输总收入	**Total Transport Revenue**	**86686**	**192555**	**509480**	**1926749**	**2077692**
#客运收入	Revenue from Passenger Traffic	18763	33560	82121	234979	337091
货运收入	Revenue from Freight Traffic	62516	142168	318485	1197619	1398065
运输清算收入	**Transportation Claring Revenue**	**59765**		**467142**	**1311275**	**1493115**
运输总支出	**Toatl Transport Expenditure**	**51875**	**193693**	**418497**	**1552877**	**1803585**
#工资	Wages and Salaries	11163	38429	98293	238570	280706
材料	Materials	6702	23183	36210	79181	113957
燃料	Fuel	9308	32996	74487	340960	409340
电力	Electricity	666	2433	4701	8022	13654
折旧	Depreciation	17174	13137	60859	127368	146491
营业外收支净额	**Non-operating Net Revenue or Expenditure**	**6886**	**14503**	**23236**	**-21947**	**-15435**
实现利润	**Profits**	**6291**	**-12591**	**34130**	**-273121**	**-363834**
#运输利润	Transport Profits	5501	-11649	33195	-266910	-355338

注：运输总收入、旅客票价收入、货物运费收入是运送到全国范围的客、货运输收入。
Note: Revenue from transport,passenger traffic and freight traffic refer to revenue from transport to allover China.

15-8 铁路运输技术经济主要指标
Main Technical and Economic Indicators of Railway Transport

指　　标	Item	2010	2011
货运机车日产量(万吨公里)	Average Daily Ton-kilometers of Freight Locomotives (10 000 ton-km)	114.3	120.0
＃内燃机车	Diesel Locomotives	114.6	119.3
货运列车平均总重(吨)	Average Total Tonnage of Freight Locomotives (ton)	2724	2779
＃内燃机车	Diesel Locomotives	2729	2787
货运机车日车公里(公里)	Daily Distance per Freight Locomotive (km)	637	620
客运机车日车公里(公里)	Daily Distance per Passenger Locomotive (km)	638	973
内燃机车每万吨公里耗油(公斤)	Oil Consumption of Diesel Locomotives (kg/10 000 ton-km)	27.7	28.2
货物列车出发正点率(%)	Punctuality Rate of Freight Trains at Departure (%)	99.3	98.7
货物列车运行正点率(%)	Punctuality Rate of Freight Trains in Running (%)	96.3	98.4
旅客列车出发正点率(%)	Punctuality Rate of Passenger Trains at Departure (%)	98.6	99.5
旅客列车运行正点率(%)	Punctuality Rate of Passenger Trains in Running (%)	98.7	94.0
旅客列车技术速度(公里/小时)	Technical Speed of Passenger Trains (km/hr)	73.6	72.2
旅客列车旅行速度(公里/小时)	Travelling Speed of Passenger Trains (km/hr)	64.6	63.4
客运密度(万人公里/公里)	Density of Passenger Transport (10 000 passenger-km/km)	561.0	540.3
货物列车技术速度(公里/小时)	Technical Speed of Freight Trains (km/hr)	47.8	47.2
货物列车旅行速度(公里/小时)	Running Speed of Freight Trains (km/hr)	39.4	37.5
货运密度(万吨公里/公里)	Density of Freight Transport (10 000 ton-km/km)	2114.0	2325.7
货车周转时间(天)	Turning Around Time of Freight Cars (day)	4.2	4.2
一次货物作业时间(小时)	Handling Time of Freight (hour)	18.8	18.1
货车中转停留时间(小时)	Transfer Waiting Time per Car (hour)	3.3	3.2
货车静载重(准轨) (吨)	Static Load of Freight Cars (Standard Gauge)　(ton)	56.8	56.1

15-9 民用车辆拥有量
Number of Civil Vehicles

单位：辆　　(unit)

指　标	Item	2010		2011	
		总　计 Total	＃私　人 Private	总　计 Total	＃私　人 Private
民用汽车	**Civil Vehicles**	**1358466**	**857663**	**1697862**	**1131929**
载客汽车	Passenger Vehicles	875648	649793	1147873	896048
＃大　型	Large	27373	1212	29518	1377
中　型	Medium	28019	8360	31282	10123
小　型	Small	789887	615131	1054529	856243
微　型	Minicar	30369	25090	32544	28305
载货汽车	Trucks	369625	138638	437870	171797
＃重　型	Large	113464	12518	134918	13393
中　型	Medium	49361	12162	52061	12917
轻　型	Light	201295	110185	247015	142688
微　型	Mini	5505	3773	3876	2799
其它汽车	Others	113193	69232	112119	64084

15-10 主要年份邮电事业情况

Basic Conditions of Postal and Telecommunication Services in Main Years

指　　标	Item	2000	2010	2011
邮政局营业网点(处)	**Number of Post Offices (unit)**		**1276**	**1232**
邮路长度(单程)(公里)	**Length of Postal Routes (km)**	**134109**	**75571**	**68682**
#农 村	Rural	55852	18238	18960
邮政业务总量(万元)	Business Volume of Postal Services	59370	165794	138398
电信业务总量(万元)	Business Volume of Telecommunication Services	413630	5654665	2126602
函件(万件)	Number of Letters (10 000 pieces)	7148	2926	3202
包件(万件)	Number of Parcels (10 000 pieces)	163	174	224
特快专递(万件)	Pieces of Express Mail Services (10 000 pieces)	124	487	579
报刊期发数(万份)	Number of Newspapers and Magazines Circulation (10 000 copies)	535	307	296
长途电话(万分钟)	Number of Long-distance Calls (10 000 minutes)	34712	105001	91298
固定电话年末用户(万户)	Local Telephone Subscribers at Year-end (10 000 subscribers)	191.0	547.5	540.5
#城市电话年末数	Urban Telephone Subscribers at Year-end	136.3	395.8	390.8
乡村电话年末数	Number of Rural Telephones Subscribers at Year-end	54.7	132.1	127.5
#住宅电话年末数	Residential Telephone Subscribers	149.3	346.6	341.7
移动电话年末用户(万户)	Number of Mobile Telephones Subscribers at Year-end (10 000 subscribers)	78.0	1359.8	1670.9
长途电信线路	**Telecommunication Lines**			
光缆线路长度(公里)	Length of Long Distance Optical Cable Lines (km)	10828	259307	284353
邮电通信设备	**Telecommunication Facilities**			
固定长途交换机容量(路端)	Capacity of long-distance Telephone Exchanges (circuit)	102540	315982	301282
本地电话局用交换机容量(万门)	Capacity of Local Office Telephone Excharge (10 000 line)	241.7	928.2	915.1
邮电通信水平	**Level of Postal and Telecommunication Services**			
平均每百人每年发函件数(件)	Annual Arerage Number of Letters Mailed Per 100 persons (piece)	387.0	122.0	148.7
平均每百人每年订报刊数(份)	Annual Arerage Number of Newspaper Subscribed Per 100 Persons (piece)	28.9	12.6	13.7
平均每百人拥有电话机数(固定)(部)	Number of Telephone Sets Owned per 100 Persons(stable) (set)	15.0	25.4	25.0
平均每百人拥有电话机数(移动)(部)	Number of Telephone Sets Owned per 100 Persons (mobile) (set)		63.0	77.4
农村邮电通信水平	**Rural Level**			
通电话的乡(镇)比重(%)	Percentage of Townships with Telephone Communication (%)	100	100	100

注：2011 年电信邮政使用 2010 年不变价计算总量。
Note: The business volume of postal and telecommunication services in 2011 was caculated at 2010 constant prices.

15-11 主要年份邮电业务情况

Conditions of Postal and Telecommunication Services in Main Years

年 份 Year	邮政业务总量(万元) Business Volume of Postal Services (10000 yuan)	电信业务总量(万元) Business Volume of Telecommunication Services (10000 yuan)	函件(万件) Number of Letters (10 000 pieces)
1978			4842.7
1980			5890.8
1985			7032.6
1990	8203	8312	7380.5
1995	17322	71220	9041.8
2000	59370	413630	7148.0
2001	62265	572073	5601.0
2002	68032	878968	6814.0
2003	72007	1072831	5987.0
2004	74835	1457000	4756.7
2005	80500	1643259	4450.0
2006	94188	2195000	4129.8
2007	100498	2936000	3177.0
2008	113802	3673709	2900.0
2009	133535	4663000	2800.0
2010	165794	5654665	2926.0
2011	138398	2126602	3202.4

年 份 Year	特快专递(万件) Pieces of Express Mail Services (10 000 pieces)	报刊期发数(万份) Issue of Newspapers and Magazines (10 000 copies)	集邮业务(万枚) Stamps for Collection (10 000 pieces)	长途电话(万分钟) Length of Long-distance Calls (10 000 minutes)
1978		223.8		258.8
1980		329.6		276.5
1985		578.9		425.1
1990	…	805.7	1034.5	762.5
1995	93.6	478.1	3086.6	11705.9
2000	124.0	534.5	5766.0	34712.0
2001	147.0	358.0	5491.0	89844.0
2002	163.0	399.0	4620.0	45769.0
2003	199.0	587.3	3112.8	35554.2
2004	238.1	283.0	3141.3	62526.0
2005	266.0	293.0	2072.0	52482.0
2006	291.0	341.7	2205.1	46478.0
2007	324.0	305.0	2134.0	67660.0
2008	362.0	296.0	2335.0	42550.0
2009	412.0	296.0	2520.0	48816.0
2010	487.0	307.0	2672.0	105001.0
2011	579.0	296.4	2306.8	91298.0

注：从 1997 年起，市内电话户数统计口径有了较大调整，故农村电话户数增幅较大。

Note: Since 1997, greater adjustment has been made on the Statistic Method about the number of telephone subscribers and the number of rural subscribers has gone up by a bigger margin.

15-11 续表 Continued

年 份 Year	移动电话用户(万户) Number of Mobile Telephone Subscribers (10 000 subscribers)	国际互联网络用户(万户) Number of Subscribers of Internet Services (10 000 subscribers)	固定电话年末用户(万户) Number of Subscribers of Local Telephone at Year-end (10 000 subscribers)	#城市电话用户 Number of Urban Telephone Subscribers
1978			2.9	1.9
1980			3.2	2.1
1985			4.7	3.7
1990			8.9	7.9
1995	2.7		44.6	42.0
2000	78.0		191.0	136.3
2001	180.9	12.8	262.6	196.1
2002	297.0	17.3	337.5	238.3
2003	421.2	60.8	431.0	293.9
2004	489.7	78.0	516.7	387.0
2005	531.3	105.8	612.2	457.5
2006	671.1	123.7	706.9	533.6
2007	808.3	157.8	678.1	520.6
2008	1051.3	142.8	634.9	462.2
2009	1119.6	133.7	573.1	409.6
2010	1359.8	161.1	547.5	395.8
2011	1670.9	208.8	540.5	390.8

年 份 Year	#住宅电话 Household Fixed Telephone Subscribers	#乡村电话用户 Rural Fixed Telephone Subscribers	#住宅电话 Household Fixed Telephone Subscribers	公用电话(户) Public Telephone (subscriber)
1978		1.1		
1980		1.0		
1985		1.0		
1990	1.2	1.1		257
1995	26.0	2.6	1.2	5612
2000	101.1	54.7	48.2	70753
2001	124.3	66.5	57.8	84309
2002	179.9	79.5	73.4	166000
2003	180.0	93.5	88.6	281632
2004	194.0	108.2	103.4	432000
2005	318.9	135.2	115.4	570047
2006	369.9	154.5	131.7	668335
2007	359.6	157.5	136.1	675309
2008	310.6	150.0	126.3	597000
2009	234.6	140.8	117.2	570982
2010	237.4	132.1	109.2	529322
2011	236.8	127.5	104.9	476633

主要统计指标解释

铁路营业里程 又称营业长度(包括正式营业和临时营业里程)，指办理客货运输业务的铁路正线总长度。凡是全线或部分建成双线及以上的线路，以第一线的实际长度计算复线、站线、段管线、岔线和特殊用途线以及不计算运费的联络线都不计算营业里程。该指标可以反映铁路运输业基础设施的发展水平，也是计算客货周转量、运输密度和机车车辆运用效率等指标的基础资料。

铁路自动、半自动闭塞里程 为保证列车安全运行，在一个区间、同一时间内，一般只允许一列列车运行，这种保证列车在这个区间安全间隔运行的技术方法称为“闭塞”。自动和半自动闭塞里程指装有列车自动或人工完成闭塞状态的铁路设备里程。

公路里程 指在一定时期内实际达到《公路工程技术标准JTG B01-2003》规定的技术等级的公路，并经公路主管部门正式验收交付使用的公路里程数。包括大、中城市的郊区公路，以及公路通过小城镇（指县城、集镇）街道的公路里程和公路桥梁长度、隧道长度、渡口的宽度以及分期修建的公路已验收交付使用的里程，不包括大中城市的街道、厂矿、林区生产用道和农业生产用道的里程。两条或多条公路共同经由同一路段，只计算一次，不得重复计算里程长度。该指标可以反映公路建设的发展规模，也是计算运输网密度等指标的基础资料。

民用航空航线里程 指统计期间内全部民用航空航线的航线总长度。航线长度指民用航空航线的计费距离。计算航线里程可按重复和不重复两种方法，前者是指各航线长度相加的总和；后者则要扣除各航线之间相同航段重复计算的部分。

输油(气)管道长度 也称输油(气)里程，指油品(或天然气)的实际输送距离，一般按输油(气)管道的单线长度计算。若包括复线和备用线长度则称为输油(气)管道延展长度，是指管道铺设的实际长度。我们通常使用的是不包括复线的“输油(气)管道里程”，该指标可以反映管道运输的发展规模和水平。

货(客)运量 指在一定时期内，各种运输工具实际运送的货物(旅客)数量。该指标是反映运输业为国民经济和人民生活服务的数量指标，也是制定和检查运输生产计划、研究运输发展规模和速度的重要指标。货运按吨计算，客运按人计算。货物不论运输距离长短、货物类别，均按实际重量统计。旅客不论行程远近或票价多少，均按一人一次客运量统计；半价票、小孩票也按一人统计。

货物(旅客)周转量 指在一定时期内，由各种运输工具运送的货物(旅客)数量与其相应运输距离的乘积之总和。该指标可以反映运输业生产的总成果，也是编制和检查运输生产计划，计算运输效率、劳动生产率以及核算运输单位成本的主要基础资料。计算货物周转量通常按发出站与到达站之间的最短距离，也就是计费距离计算。计算公式为：

货物(旅客)周转量=∑（货物（旅客）运输量×运输距离）

铁路货车平均静载重 指铁路货车在始发站静止状态下平均每车装载的货物重量，用以分析货车完成装车时车辆载重力的利用情况。计算公式为：

货车平均静载重=货物发送吨数/装车数

静载重的多少取决于运送货物的性质、种类、车辆的类型和装载技术的高低。根据货车的平均标记载重与静载重进行对比，可以反映货车载重能力的利用程度。计算公式为：

货车载重力利用率(%)=货车平均静载重/货车平均标记载重×100%

铁路货运机车日产量 指在一定时期内，平均每台货运机车在一昼夜内所完成的总重吨公里数，包括载运货物的重量和车辆本身的自重。该指标从时间和牵引能力两方面反映了机车运用效率。计算公式为：

货运机车平均日产量=货运总重吨公里数/货运机车台日数

民用汽车拥有量 指报告期末，在公安交通管理部门按照《机动车注册登记工作规范》，已注册登记领有民用车辆牌照的全部汽车数量。汽车拥有量统计的主要分类：根据汽车结构分为载客汽车、载货汽车及其他汽车；根据汽车所有者不同分为个人(私人)汽车、单位汽车；根据汽车的使用性质分为营运汽车、非营运汽车和特种汽车；根据汽车大小规格不同载客汽车分为大型、中型、小型和微型，载货汽车分为重型、中型、轻型和微型。

邮电业务总量 指以货币形式表示的邮电通信企业为社会提供各类邮电通信服务的总数量，是用于观察邮电通信业务发展变化总趋势的综合性总量指标。分别按邮政业务总量和电信业务总量统计。邮电业务总量是以各类业务的实物量分别乘以相应的不变单价，得出各类业务的货币量再加总求得。

移动电话用户 指在电信运营企业营业网点办理开户登记手续，通过移动电话交换机进入移动电话网，占用移动电话号码的各类电话用户。包括GSM数字移动电话用户、CDMA数字移动电话用户和电信运营企业发行的报告期末已激活充值的能异地漫游的各种智能卡用户。

互联网上网人数 指平均每周使用互联网至少1小时的6周岁以上中国公民人数。

固定电话用户 指在电信运营企业营业网点办理开户登记手续并已接入固定电话网上的全部电话用户。包括普通电话用户、公用电话用户、窄带综合业务数字网（N—ISDN）用户、智能网专用接入终端用户等。按行政区划分为城市电话用户和农村电话用户。

住宅电话用户 指安装在居民住宅或农民家里并按照住宅电话用户登记注册和收费的各类电话用户。包括私人付费、单位付费和按规定免费安装的住宅电话用户。

长途电话交换机容量 指用于接入长途电话网的电话交换机的设备额定容量，包括国际电话交换机容量。

局用交换机容量 指安装在电信运营企业内用于接续本地固定电话的电话交换机容量，有倍增设备按倍增后的数量计数。包括现用和备用的人工或自动交换机的全部容量。不包括用户交换机容量。

Explanatory Notes on Main Statistical Indicators

Length of Railways in Operation refers to the total length of the trunk line for passenger and freight transportation (including both full operation and temporary operation). The calculation is based on the actual length of the first line if this line has a full or partial double (or more). Not included are double tracks, station sidings, tracks under the charge of stations, branch lines, special-purpose lines and non-payable connecting lines. The length of railways in operation is an important indicator to show the development of the infrastructure of railway transport. It is also essential data to calculate volume of passenger freight transport, traffic density and utilization efficiency of locomotives and carriages.

Length of Automatic-blocking and Semi-automatic-blocking Railways Blocking is a spacing technique by which a section of the railway only allows one train to pass at a time with the aim of ensuring traffic safety. Length of automatic-blocking and semi-automatic-blocking railways refers to length of railways installed with equipment to perform automatic or manual blocking of trains.

Length of Highways refers to the length of highways which are built in conformity with the grades specified by the highway engineering standard [Highways WTBZ-Technical Standard JTJB01-2003] in certain period, and have been formally checked and accepted by the departments of highways and put into use. The length of highways includes that of the suburb highways at large and medium-sized cities, highways passing through streets at small cities and towns, and also the length of bridges , width of ferry piers and phased construction of road that has been put into use. It does not include the length of streets in big and medium-sized cities and highways built for the production purpose at factories, mines, forest areas and agricultural areas. If two or more highways go the same section of the way, the length of the section is only calculated for once and no duplication is allowed. The length of highways is an indicator to show the development of the scale of highway construction and to provide essential information to calculate the transport network density.

Length of Civil Aviation Routes refers to the length of all routes for civil aviation flights, which is used to account the freight, during the period of statistics.. There are usually two ways to calculate the route length: duplicated calculation and non-duplicated calculateion, the former is the sum of length of all civil aviation routes, and the latter should deduct the duplication length of same route among all routes.

Length of Oil (Gas) Pipelines is used as an indicator to show the development, scale and leve! of the pipeline transportation. It refers to the actual transport distance of oil (or gas) products, and is in general calculated according to the length of single pipeline. If the length of the double pipelines and alternate pipeline are included, it is called the extension length of the oil (gas) pipelines, which indicates the actual length of the pipelines built. The commonly used indicator, the "length of "oil (gas)" pipelines, does not include the double pipelines. It can reflect the extent and level of development of pipeline transport.

Freight (Passenger) Traffic refers to the volume of freight (passenger) transported with various means within a specific period of time. This indicator reflects the service of the transport industry towards the national economy and people's living conditions, as well as an important indicator used in formulating and monitoring transport production plans and research into the scale and pace of transport development. Freight transport is calculated in tons and passenger traffic is calculated in terms of number of persons. Freight transport is calculated in terms of the actual weight of the goods and takes no account of the type of freight and distance of travel. Passenger traffic is calculated by the principle that one person can be counted only once in one trip and takes no account of the travelling distance and ticket price. The passengers who travel with a half price ticket or a child's ticket is also calculated as one person.

Freight Ton-kilometres (Passenger-kilometres) refers to the sum of the product of the volume of transported cargo (passengers) multiplied by the transport distance. It is an important indicator to reflect the achievement of the transportation industry. This is an important indicator to show the total results of the transport industry; to prepare and examine the transport plan; and to serve as the main basic data for calculating the efficiency, labour productivity and unit cost of transport. Normally, the shortest distance between the departure station and the destination station (i.e., the payable distance) is the basis in calculating the freight ton-kilometres. The formula is as follows:

$$\begin{matrix}\text{Freight ton-kilometres}\\ \text{(passenger-kilometres)}\end{matrix} = \sum \begin{matrix}\text{freight}\\ \text{(passenger)traffic}\end{matrix} \times \begin{matrix}\text{distance of}\\ \text{transportation}\end{matrix}$$

Average Static Load of Freight Cars refers to the average cargo weight as loaded by each freight car under the static condition at the departure station. It is used to show the utilization extent of the loading capacity of the freight cars. The formula is:

$$\begin{matrix}\text{Static load (ton)}\\ \text{of freight car}\end{matrix} = \frac{\text{tonnage of goods dispatched}}{\text{number of freight cars loaded}}$$

The static load of freight cars is determined by the nature and type of goods loaded the type of vehicles, and the technique of loading. Comparison of the average marked load with the static load of freight cars provides indication on the degree of utilization of loading capacity of freight cars. For its calculation the following formula is applied:

$$\begin{matrix}\text{Utilization rate of}\\ \text{capacity of freight cars (\%)}\end{matrix} = \frac{\text{Average static load}}{\text{Average marked load}} \times 100\ \%$$

Average Daily Haul of Freight Locomotives refers to the average total ton-kilometres accomplished by each freight transport locomotive over one day and night during a given period of time. It includes both the weight of the goods carried and the dead weight of the train itself. It is a comprehensive indicator reflecting the locomotive efficiency in terms of both time and the pulling force.

$$\text{Average daily haul of freight transport locomotive (ton} - \text{kilometre)} = \frac{\text{Total ton} - \text{kilometres of freight}}{\text{Daily number of freight transport locomotive}}$$

Possession of Civil Motor Vehicles refer to the total numbers of vehicles that are registered and received vehicles license tags according to the Work Standard for Motor Vehicles Registration formulated by the Transport Management Office under the department of public security at the end of the reference period. They are divided into categories. According to the structure of motor vehicles, they are divided into passenger vehicles, trucks and others; according to ownership into private vehicles and vehicles for the unit's use; according to kind of usage into working vehicles and non-working vehicles; and according to size of vehicles into large passenger vehicles, medium-sized passenger vehicles, small passenger vehicles and mini passenger vehicles, heavy trucks, light-heavy trucks, light trucks and mini-trucks.

Business Volume of Post and Telecommunications refers to the total amount of postal and telecommunication services, expressed in value terms, provided by the post and telecommunications departments for society. This indicator reflects the overall results of development of postal and telecommunication services. It can be classificated as postal services and and telecommunication services. Business volume of post and telecommunications is the sum of all services in kind multiplying with the unit price (constant price) to get the total business value.

Mobile Telephone Subscribers refer to persons who have gone through registration procedures in the operation points of enterprises engaged in telecommunications and are hence connected with the mobile telephone communication network through the mobile telephone switchboards and occupy mobile phone numbers. Included are GSM digital mobile phone subscribers, CDMA digital mobile phone subscribers and subscribers to intelligent phone cards with roaming facility issued by telecommunications enterprises and which have been subscribed to and activated at the end of the reference period.

Internet Users refer to the number of Chinese citizens aged 6 and over who use the Internet at least for one hour each week.

Local Telephone Subscribers refer to all subscribers who have gone through registration procedures in the operation points of enterprises engaged in telecommunications and are hence connected to the local telecommunications service provider through fixed line network. Included are general subscribers, public telephones subscribers, N-ISDN subscribers and intelligent network terminal subscribers. They are also classified in terms of administrative districts as urban telephone subscribers and rural telephone subscribers according to location.

Household Telephone Subscribers refer to telephone sets installed in the dwelling units of urban or rural residents, and registered as residence subscribers for payment, including three types of payment for the service: private payment, public payment and free service in accordance with relevant regulations.

Capacity of Long Distance Telephone Exchanges refers to the rated capacity of telephone exchanges to connect long distance telephone network, including capacity of international telephone exchanges.

Capacity of Office Telephone Exchanges refers to the capacity (measured in gate) of telephone exchanges installed in the offices of telecommunication service providers for communication between fixed telephones. It includes the capacity of both manual and automatic exchanges in use and for stand-by purpose. The capacity of subscriber exchanges is not included.

2012

新疆统计年鉴

XINJIANG STATISTICAL YEARBOOK

第十六篇 批发和零售业 住宿和餐饮业

CHAPTER 16 Wholesale & Retail Trades, Hotels and Catering Services

简要说明
Brief Introduction

本篇资料的主要内容及来源

本篇资料反映新疆维吾尔自治区商品流通市场发展及批发和零售业、住宿和餐饮业经营情况。主要内容有社会消费品零售额；限额以上批发和零售业、住宿和餐饮业情况；限额以上批发和零售业商品销售及商品分类销售情况；限额以上批发和零售贸易企业及住宿和餐饮企业主要财务情况；亿元商品交易市场成交情况；连锁经营情况等。

限额以上批发和零售业、住宿和餐饮业统计限额标准：批发业年销售额2000万元及以上；零售业年销售额500万元及以上；餐饮业年营业额200万元及以上；住宿业为年主营业务收入200万元以上企业。

本篇资料由新疆维吾尔自治区统计局贸易外经统计处编辑整理。

Main Content and Source of Data

Data in this chapter reflect the development of Xinjiang's circulation of domestic market and the management situation of wholesale and retail & hotels and catering services, etc.Main contents include the total retail sales,conditon of wholesales & retail trades and hotels and catering services above designated size;condition of sale value of enterprises above designated size of wholesales and retail trade;sale value of trade by category of main commodites ;basic statistics on commodity exchange markets of transaction value over 100 million yuan and basic conditions of chain retail enterprises by region ect.

Criteria for wholesale and retail sale trades, hotels and catering services above designated size is defined as follows: wholesale trade has annual sales over 20 million yuan; retail sale trade have annual sale over 5 million yuan; catering services have annual income over 2 million yuan. Enterprise above designated size in accommodation refers to star-rated unit.

Data in this chapter are provided by the Division of Trade Statistics, the Xinjiang Bureau of Statistics.

16-1 主要年份国内贸易基本情况

Basic Conditions of Domestic Trade in Main Years

指　标	Item	2000	2005	2010	2011
法人企业(个)	**Number of Corporation Enterprises (unit)**	**394**	**1097**	**1449**	**1554**
批发和零售业	Wholesale and Retail Trades	370	800	1175	1260
住宿和餐饮业	Hotels and Catering Servicess	24	297	274	294
＃餐饮业	Catering Services	24	65	53	59
产业活动单位(个)	**Number of Establishments (unit)**	**431**	**2396**	**4563**	**4405**
批发和零售业	Wholesale and Retail Trades	382	1998	4137	3922
住宿和餐饮业	Hotels and Catering Services	49	398	426	483
＃餐饮业	Catering Services	49	96	122	153
批发和零售业	**Wholesale and Retail Trades**				
商品销售总额（亿元）	Total Sales (100 million yuan)	478.3	1182.0	4230.9	6704.5
社会消费品零售总额(亿元)	**Total Retail Sales of Consumer Goods (100 million yuan)**	**374.5**	**640.2**	**1324.5**	**1557.1**
按销售单位所在地分	By Location of Establishments				
城　镇	City	233.7	443.9	1181.3	1411.0
＃城　区	County	65.2	95.6	945.0	1165.3
乡　村	Under County Level	75.6	100.7	143.2	146.1
按行业分	By Sector				
批发和零售业	Wholesale and Retail Trades	242.3	509.3	1156.6	1351.4
住宿和餐饮业	Hotels and Catering Services	38.2	92.8	167.9	205.7
其他行业	Others	94.0	38.1		

注：1.法人企业、产业活动单位统计范围为限额以上企业(单位)。2.商品销售总额、社会消费品零售总额为全口径数据。3.2008 年限额以上住宿业数据为年主营业务收入 200 万元以上企业。4.从 2010 年开始,按销售单位所在地分组由市、县、县以下调整为城镇、城区、乡村。5.从 2010 年开始,按行业分组取消其他行业。

Note: a) Scope of corporation enterprises,industrial activity units covers enterprises(units)above designated size. b) Data of total sales and total retail sales of consumer goods are those of full coverage. c) Data of hotels and catering services above designated size in 2008 are figures from enterprises of annual income over 2 million yuan. d) Since 2010,By the sales units of the group was adjusted,from city,county and under county level to town,city and country.e) Since 2010,by the sector of the group canceled oter sectors.

16-2 主要年份社会消费品零售总额
Total Retail Sales of Consumer Goods in Main Years

单位：亿元 (100 million yuan)

年 份 Year	社会消费品零售总额 Total Retail Sales of Consumer Goods	按销售单位所在地分 By Location 城 镇 City	#城 区 County	乡 村 Under County Level
1978	21.89	7.44	4.80	9.65
1980	29.36	11.06	6.05	12.25
1985	57.38	24.55	10.70	22.13
1990	104.30	57.17	24.27	22.86
1995	253.65	145.74	50.03	57.88
1996	295.36	171.51	55.38	68.47
1997	310.42	186.37	57.54	66.51
1998	327.52	197.89	59.89	69.74
1999	347.40	213.96	61.51	71.93
2000	374.50	233.66	65.15	75.69
2001	406.35	256.58	69.73	80.04
2002	442.88	284.74	74.32	83.82
2003	421.16	311.33	49.20	60.63
2004	563.41	385.81	85.79	91.81
2005	640.20	443.95	95.60	100.65
2006	733.20	513.12	107.68	112.40
2007	857.50	606.74	123.64	127.12
2008	1041.50	740.85	150.78	149.87
2009	1177.53	834.42	171.76	171.35
2010	1324.48	1181.27	945.03	143.21
2011	1557.09	1411.01	1165.29	146.08

年 份 Year	按行业分 By Sector 批发和零售业 Wholesale and Retail Trades	住宿和餐饮业 Hotels and Catering Services	其他行业 Others
1978	17.34	0.57	3.98
1980	22.95	0.94	5.47
1985	40.83	2.51	14.04
1990	72.68	6.06	25.56
1995	169.16	17.27	67.22
1996	191.14	19.44	84.78
1997	198.73	22.22	89.47
1998	206.92	27.84	92.76
1999	222.57	32.76	92.07
2000	242.29	38.21	94.00
2001	266.38	44.57	95.40
2002	296.13	53.04	93.71
2003	341.90	60.64	18.62
2004	450.65	76.22	36.54
2005	509.25	92.82	38.13
2006	582.28	111.55	39.37
2007	685.94	130.51	41.05
2008	841.65	156.49	43.36
2009	956.64	177.21	43.68
2010	1156.62	167.86	
2011	1351.36	205.73	

16-3 分类型、分地区限额以上批发和零售业、住宿和餐饮业基本情况

Basic Conditions of Enterprises above Designated Size in Wholesale and Retail Trades, Hotels and Catering Services by Category and Region

(2011 年)

指 标	Item	法 人 企业数 (个) Number of Corporation Enterprises (unit)	产业活动 单 位 数 (个) Number of Establishments (unit)	从 业 人员数 (人) Engaged Persons (person)
总 计	**Total**	**1554**	**4405**	**154781**
批发业	**Wholesale Trades**	**776**	**2187**	**63468**
内资企业	Domestic Funded Enterprises	772	2172	62337
国有企业	State-owned Enterprises	110	565	18241
集体企业	Collective-owned Enterprises	25	86	2201
股份合作企业	Cooperative Enterprises	2	2	87
有限责任公司	State Sole Funded Corporations	252	640	19796
国有独资公司	State Sole Funded Corporations	30	115	4610
其他有限责任公司	Other Limited Liability Corporations	222	525	15186
股份有限公司	Share-holding Corporations Ltd.	22	367	8458
私营企业	Private Enterprises	356	506	13056
私营独资企业	Private-funded Enterprises	6	6	182
私营合伙企业	Private Partnership Enterprises	2	2	7
私营有限责任公司	Private Limited Liability Corporations	342	491	12494
私营股份有限公司	Private Share-holding Corporation Ltd.	6	7	373
其他企业	Other Enterprises	5	6	498
港、澳、台商投资企业	Enterprises With Funds from Hong Kong, Macao and Taiwan	2	7	704
港、澳、台商独资经营企业	Enterprises with Sole Funds from Hong Kong, Macao and Taiwan	1	3	659
港、澳、台商投资股份有限公司	Enterprises with Share-holding Corporations Ltd. from HongKong,Macao and Taiwan	1	4	45
外商投资企业	Foreign Funded Enterprises	2	8	427
中外合资经营企业	Enterprises with Foreign Investment	2	5	125
外资企业	Enterprises with Sole Fund		3	302
零售业	**Retail Trades**	**484**	**1735**	**47868**
内资企业	Domestic Funded Enterprises	474	1721	45621
国有企业	State-owned Enterprises	43	368	5254
集体企业	Collective-owned Enterprises	3	9	174
股份合作企业	Share-holding Cooperative Enterprises	1	1	98
有限责任公司	Limited Liability Corporations	115	362	12420
国有独资公司	State Sole Funded Enterprises	5	5	368
其他有限责任公司	Other Limited Liability Corporations	110	357	12052
股份有限公司	Share-holding Corporations Ltd.	5	92	5406
私营企业	Private Enterprises	303	861	21855
私营独资企业	Private-funded Enterprises	10	11	577
私营合伙企业	Private Partnership Enterprises	2	2	65
私营有限责任公司	Private Limited Liability Corporations	287	844	21069
私营股份有限公司	Private Share-holding Corporation Ltd.	4	4	144
其他企业	Others	4	28	414
港、澳、台商投资企业	Enterprises With Funds from Hong Kong, Macao and Taiwan	4	4	487
港、澳、台商独资经营企业	Enterprises With Sole Funds from Hong Kong, Macao and Taiwan	4	4	487
外商投资企业	Foreign Funded Enterprises	6	10	1760
中外合资经营企业	Enterprises with Foreign Investment	5	5	764
外资企业	Enterprises with Sole Fund	1	5	996
住宿业	**Hotels**	**235**	**330**	**34062**
内资企业	Domestic-funded Enterprises	230	324	32999
国有企业	State-owned Enterprises	85	119	12255

16-3 续表 Continued

指 标	Item	法人企业数（个） Number of Corporate Enterprises (unit)	产业活动单位数（个） Number of Economic Active Unit (unit)	从业人员数（人） Engaged Persons (person)
集体企业	Collective-owned Enterprises	6	6	889
股份合作企业	Cooperative Enterprises		1	60
联营企业	Joint Ownership Enterprises	1	1	70
国有联营企业	State Joint Ownership Enterprises	1	1	70
有限责任公司	Limited Liability Corporations	61	91	10755
国有独资公司	State Sole Funded Corporations	7	7	736
其他有限责任公司	Other Limited Liability Corporations	54	84	10019
股份有限公司	Share-holding Corporations Ltd.	5	8	1040
私营企业	Private Enterprises	72	97	7840
私营独资企业	Private-funded Enterprises	14	21	720
私营合伙企业	Private Partnership Enterprises	2	2	148
私营有限责任公司	Private Limited Liability Corporations	56	73	6794
私营股份有限公司	Private Share-holding Corporation Ltd.		1	178
其他企业	Other Enterprises		1	90
港、澳、台商投资企业	Enterprises With Funds from Hong Kong, Macao and Taiwan	4	4	551
合资经营企业（港或澳、台资）	Joint-venture Enterprises (Funds from Hong Kong, Macao and Taiwan)	4	4	551
外商投资企业	Foreign Funded Enterprises	1	2	512
中外合资经营企业	Enterprises with Foreign Investment		1	492
外资企业	Enterprises with Sole Fund	1	1	20
餐饮业	**Catering Services**	**59**	**153**	**9383**
内资企业	Domestic Funded Enterprises	58	128	8515
国有企业	State-owned Enterprises	7	13	1400
有限责任公司	Limited Liability Corporations	8	10	841
其他有限责任公司	Other Limited Liability Corporations	8	10	841
股份有限公司	Share-holding Corporations Ltd.	1	39	1343
私营企业	Private Enterprises	39	62	4134
私营独资企业	Private-funded Enterprises	8	8	701
私营合伙企业	Private Partnership Enterprises	1	1	66
私营有限责任公司	Private limited Liability Corporations	30	53	3367
其他企业	Others	3	4	797
外商投资企业	Foreign Funded Enterprises	1	25	868
外资企业	Enterprises With Sole Fund	1	25	868
按地区分	**By Region**			
乌鲁木齐市	Urumqi City	530	1460	71978
克拉玛依市	Karamay City	64	137	8548
吐鲁番地区	Turpan Administrative Offices	22	64	2019
哈密地区	Hami [Kumul] Administrative Offices	81	187	4872
昌吉回族自治州	Changji Hui Autonomous Prefecture	66	195	5138
伊犁哈萨克自治州	Ili Kazak Autonomous Prefecture	225	439	13719
伊犁州直属县(市)	Counties (Cities) Direct Under Ili Prefecture	153	219	8868
塔城地区	Tacheng [Tarbagatai] Administrative Offices	47	119	2636
阿勒泰地区	Altay Administrative Offices	25	101	2215
博尔塔拉蒙古自治州	Bortala Mongol Autonomous Prefecture	21	56	1332
巴音郭楞蒙古自治州	Bayangol Mongol Autonomous Prefecture	129	296	8930
阿克苏地区	Aksu Administrative Offices	144	539	10423
克孜勒苏柯尔克孜自治州	Kizilsu Kirgiz Autonomous Prefecture	12	12	748
喀什地区	Kashgar [Kaxgar] Administrative Offices	73	226	7957
和田地区	Hotan Administrative Offices	18	156	1548
生产建设兵团	Production and Construction Corps	169	638	17569

16-4 分行业、分地区限额以上批发零售业商品销售额

Total Sales Values of Enterprises above Designated Size of Wholesale and Retail Trades by Sector and Region

单位：万元　　(2011 年)　　(10 000 yuan)

指　标	Item	销售总额 Total Sales Value	批　发 Wholesale Value	零　售 Retail Value
总　计	**Total**	**53005056**	**45347726**	**7657330**
批发业	**Wholesale Trade**	**46348919**	**44903072**	**1445847**
农畜产品批发业	Wholesale of Farm Produce and Livestock Products	6321201	6321188	13
谷物、豆及薯类批发业	Wholesale of Grain,Bean and Potato	452279	452279	
种子、饲料批发业	Wholesale of Seed and Fodder	218252	218252	
棉、麻批发业	Wholesale of Cotton and Liner	5617304	5617291	13
其他农畜产品批发业	Wholesale of Other Farm Produce and Livestock Products	33366	33366	
食品、饮料及烟草制品批发业	Wholesale of Food,Beverages and Tobaccos	1799070	1783037	16033
米、面制品及食用油批发业	Wholesale of Rice, Flour and Edible Oil	251332	250962	370
糕点、糖果及糖批发业	Wholesale of Pastry,Candy and Sugar	30227	28073	2154
果品、蔬菜批发业	Wholesale of Fruit and Vegetable	133420	128652	4768
肉、禽、蛋及水产品批发业	Wholesale of Meat,Birds and Equatic Products	5349	5349	
盐及调味品批发业	Wholesale of Salt and Condiment Flavoring Material	42738	42108	630
饮料及茶叶批发业	Wholesale of Soft Drink and Tea Leaf	88400	88379	21
烟草制品批发业	Wholesale of Tobaccos	1214529	1206439	8090
其他食品批发业	Wholesale of Other Food	33075	33075	
纺织、服装及日用品批发业	Wholesale of Textitle, Garments and Daily Consumer Articles	285567	284954	613
纺织品、针织品及原料批发	Wholesale of Textile,Hosiery and Raw Material	87816	87816	
服装批发业	Wholesale of Garment	122234	122234	
化妆品及卫生用品批发业	Wholesale of Cosmetics and Health Aids	36785	36172	613
其他日用品批发业	Wholesale of Other Covenience Goods	38732	38732	
文化、体育用品及器材批发业	Wholesale of Culture, Sports Appliances and Equipments	194201	176243	17958
图书批发业	Wholesale of Books	147143	137398	9745
其他文化用品批发业	Wholesale of Other Culture Products	47058	38845	8213
医药及医疗器械批发业	Wholesale of Medicines and Medical Appliances	548173	543564	4609
西药批发业	Wholesale of Western Medicine	490444	486282	4162
中药材及中成药批发业	Wholesale of Chinese Medicinal Plant and Chinese Patent Medicine	45563	45116	447
医疗用品及器材批发	Wholesale of Medicine and Medical Appliances	12166	12166	
矿产品、建材及化工产品批发业	Wholesale of Mineral Products, Building Material and Chemical Products	33960937	32753509	1207428
煤炭及制品批发业	Wholesale of Coal and Related Products	284930	284930	
石油及制品批发业	Wholesale of Petroleum and Related Products	27408505	26212796	1195709
金属及金属矿批发业	Wholesale of Metal and Metal Materials	3642286	3642277	9
建材批发业	Wholesale of Building Materials	520220	520220	
化肥批发业	Wholesale of Chemical Fertilizer	1466903	1463319	3584

16-4 续表 1 Continued

单位：万元 (10 000 yuan)

指标	Item	销售总额 Total Sales Value	批发 Wholesale Value	零售 Retail Value
农药批发业	Wholesale of Pesticides	8533	8533	
其他化工产品批发业	Wholesale of Other Chemical Product	629560	621434	8126
机械设备、五金交电及电子产品批发业	Wholesale of Machinery, Hardware and Electronic Equipments	2790700	2591553	199147
农业机械批发业	Wholesale of Agriculture Machinery	155898	155898	
汽车、摩托车及零配件批发业	Wholesale of Motor Vehicles, Motorcycles and Parts	821080	709229	111851
五金、交电批发业	Wholesale of Hardware and Electronic Equipment	507256	507256	
家用电器批发业	Wholesale of Household Electrical Appliances	155000	155000	
计算机、软件及辅助设备批发业	Wholesale of Computer, Software and Assistant Appliances	158878	135861	23017
通讯及广播电视设备批发业	Wholesale of Communicating and Broadcasting Television Device	285086	285086	
其他机械设备及电子产品批发业	Wholesale of Other Mechanical Equipment and Electronic Products	707502	643223	64279
贸易经纪与代理	Trades Broker and Agency	71650	71650	
其他批发业	Wholesales of Others	377420	377374	46
再生物资回收与批发业	Recovery and Wholesale of Regeneration Material	280402	280356	46
其他未列明的批发业	Wholesale of Un-listed	97018	97018	
零售业	**Retail Trades**	**6656137**	**444654**	**6211483**
综合零售业	Integrated Retail	1255703	11558	1244145
百货零售业	Retail of General Merchandise	907736	7039	900697
超级市场零售业	Retail of Supermarkets	347455	4519	342936
其他综合零售业	Retail of Other Integrate	512		512
食品、饮料及烟草制品专门零售业	Monopoly Retail of Foods, Beverages and Tobacco	20006	983	19023
粮油零售业	Retail of Grain and Oil	9431	492	8939
肉、禽、蛋及水产品零售	Retail of Meat,Poultry and Eggs	2331		2331
饮料及茶叶零售业	Retail of Soft Drink and Tea Leaf	2289	491	1798
烟草制品零售业	Retail of Tobaccos	5955		5955
纺织、服装及日用品专门零售业	Monopoly Retail of Textile, Garments and Daily Consumer Articles	344061	6224	337837
服装零售业	Retail of Garment	293803	6224	287579
钟表、眼镜零售业	Retail of Timelceeper and Spectacle	11265		11265
化妆品及卫生用品零售业	Retail of Cosmetics and Health Aids	6123		6123
其他日用品零售业	Retail of Other Covenience Goods	32870		32870
文化、体育用品及器材专门零售业	Monopoly Retail of Cultural, Sports Goods And Apparatus	180501	3745	176756
文具用品零售业	Retail of Stationery and Office Supplies	3946		3946
图书零售业	Retail of Books	140483	1299	139184
珠宝首饰零售业	Retail of Jewelry	33257	2284	30973
照相器材零售业	Retail of Photographic Materials	2815	162	2653

16-4 续表 2 Continued

单位：万元 (10 000 yuan)

指 标	Item	销售总额 Total Sales Value	批 发 Wholesale Value	零 售 Retail Value
医药及医疗器材专门零售	Monopoly Retail of Medicine and Medical-care Apparatus	660410	99745	560665
药品零售业	Retail of Medcine	656381	96824	559557
医疗用品及器材零售	Wholesale of Medical Treatment and Equipment	4029	2921	1108
汽车、摩托车、燃料及零配件专门零售业	Monopoly Retail of Car, Motor, Fuel and Parts as Well as Components	3483282	283444	3199838
汽车零售业	Retail of Automobiles	2326620	95521	2231099
汽车零配件零售业	Retail of Automobiles' Parts	24531		24531
摩托车及零配件零售业	Retail of Motorcycle and Fittings	18784	1255	17529
机动车燃料零售业	Retail of Auto Fuel	1113347	186668	926679
家用电器及电子产品专门零售业	Monopoly Retail of House Hold Electric Appliancesound Electronic Products	493433	30983	462450
家用电器零售业	Retail of Electric Appliances	395168	19359	375809
计算机、软件及辅助设备零售业	Retail of Cumputers,Software and Office Appliances	61464	4470	56994
通讯设备零售业	Retail of Telecommunication Equipments	36323	7119	29204
其他电子产品零售	Retail of other Electric Products	478	35	443
五金、家具及室内装修材料专门零售业	Monopoly Retail of Hardware, Furniture and Indoor Decorating Material	176782		176782
五金零售业	Retail of Hardware	4034		4034
家具零售业	Retail of Living Equipment	172748		172748
无店铺及其他零售业	Retail of Storeless and Others	41959	7972	33987
生活用燃料零售业	Retail of Life Fuels	31551	6439	25112
其他未列明的零售业	Retail of Un-listed	10408	1533	8875
按地区分	**By Region**			
乌鲁木齐市	Urumqi City	32858912	27989458	4869454
克拉玛依市	Karamay City	1085408	855547	229861
吐鲁番地区	Turpan Administrative Offices	382733	303388	79345
哈密地区	Hami [Kumul] Administrative Offices	1030026	837961	192065
昌吉回族自治州	Changji Hui Autonomous Prefecture	999157	716466	282691
伊犁哈萨克自治州	Ili Kazak Autonomous Prefecture	4087712	3735827	351885
伊犁州直属县(市)	Counties (Cities) Direct Under Ili Prefecture	3069497	2810464	259033
塔城地区	Tacheng [Tarbagatai] Administrative Offices	722116	670430	51686
阿勒泰地区	Altay Administrative Offices	296099	254933	41166
博尔塔拉蒙古自治州	Bortala Mongol Autonomous Prefecture	842564	811982	30582
巴音郭楞蒙古自治州	Bayangol Mongol Autonomous Prefecture	1451465	1156740	294725
阿克苏地区	Aksu Administrative Offices	2203186	1836348	366838
克孜勒苏柯尔克孜自治州	Kizilsu Kirgiz Autonomous Prefecture	39933	35168	4765
喀什地区	Kashgar [Kaxgar] Administrative Offices	1673991	1324550	349441
和田地区	Hotan Administrative Offices	223647	195641	28006
生产建设兵团	Production and Construction Group	6126322	5548650	577672

16-5 限额以上餐饮企业经营情况

Operations of Enterprises above Designated Size of Catering Services

单位：万元　　(2011 年)　　(10 000 yuan)

项　目	Item	法人企业数(个) Number of Corporation Enterprises (unit)	产业活动单位数(个) Number of Establishments (unit)	营业额 Business Revenue	#商品零售额 Retail Sales of Commodities
总　计	**Total**	**59**	**153**	**135578**	**123038**
正餐服务	Dinner	55	76	90592	78461
快餐服务	Snack	4	77	44986	44577
按地区分	**By Region**				
乌鲁木齐市	Urumqi City	27	101	99541	92366
克拉玛依市	Karamay City	1	13	7396	7149
吐鲁番地区	Turpan Administrative Offices	1	1	386	236
昌吉回族自治州	Changji Hui Autonomous Prefecture	3	5	1848	1303
伊犁哈萨克自治州	Ili Kazak Autonomous Prefecture	4	5	2932	2277
伊犁州直属县(市)	Counties (Cities) Direct Under Ili Prefecture	4	4	2718	2134
塔城地区	Tacheng [Tarbagatai] Administrative Offices		1	214	143
巴音郭楞蒙古自治州	Bayangol Mongol Autonomous Prefecture	15	16	15002	12777
阿克苏地区	Aksu Administrative Offices	3	4	3564	2973
喀什地区	Kashgar [Kaxgar] Administrative Offices	1	1	1024	731
生产建设兵团	Production and Construction Group	4	7	3885	3226

16-6 限额以上住宿企业经营情况
Operation of Enterprises above Designated Size in Hotels Services

单位：万元 (2011 年) (10 000 yuan)

项　目	Item	营业额 Business Revenue	客房收入 From Hotel Rooms	餐费收入 From Meals
总　计	**Total**	**471751**	**216339**	**200231**
按星级分	**By Stars**			
五　星	Five-Star	129446	46017	61546
四　星	Four-Star	124795	55992	51284
三　星	Three-Star	146531	74567	60852
二　星	Two-Star	21517	13978	6389
一　星	One-Star	1380	622	638
其　他	Others	48082	25163	19522
按行业分	**By Sector**			
旅游饭店	Tourist Hotel	425723	190079	183630
一般旅馆	Fonda	45229	25864	16213
其他住宿服务	Others	799	396	388
按地区分	**By Region**			
乌鲁木齐市	Urumqi City	260273	108733	108728
克拉玛依市	Karamay City	19852	7558	11071
吐鲁番地区	Turpan Administrative Offices	4594	2685	1673
哈密地区	Hami [Kumul] Administrative Offices	18713	7943	9788
昌吉回族自治州	Changji Hui Autonomous Prefecture	10650	4413	4971
伊犁哈萨克自治州	Ili Kazak Autonomous Prefecture	55829	27602	25911
伊犁州直属县(市)	Counties (Cities) Direct Under Ili Prefecture	34052	16215	16368
塔城地区	Tacheng [Tarbagatai] Administrative Offices	6352	2847	3175
阿勒泰地区	Altay Administrative Offices	15425	8540	6368
博尔塔拉蒙古自治州	Bortala Mongol Autonomous Prefecture	3087	1465	1450
巴音郭楞蒙古自治州	Bayangol Mongol Autonomous Prefecture	21161	10308	9682
阿克苏地区	Aksu Administrative Offices	11189	7128	3865
克孜勒苏柯尔克孜自治州	Kizilsu Kirgiz Autonomous Prefecture	1889	1031	790
喀什地区	Kashgar [Kaxgar] Administrative Offices	13280	7213	5056
和田地区	Hotan Administrative Offices	2883	2161	600
生产建设兵团	Production and Construction Group	48351	28099	16646

16-6 续表 Continued

单位：万元 (10 000 yuan)

项　　目	Item	商品销售收入 From Commodities	其他收入 Others	床位数（张） Number of beds (unit)
总　计	**Total**	**13198**	**41983**	**73984**
按星级分	**Classified by Star**			
五　星	Five-Star	8457	13426	7269
四　星	Four-Star	1524	15995	18282
三　星	Three-Star	2187	8925	33779
二　星	Two-Star	288	862	4613
一　星	One-Star	109	11	313
其　他	Others	633	2764	9728
按行业分	**By Sector**			
旅游饭店	Tourist Hotel	12461	39553	63594
一般旅馆	Fonda	722	2430	10254
其他住宿服务	Others	15		136
按地区分	**By Region**			
乌鲁木齐市	Urumqi City	10170	32642	26198
克拉玛依市	Karamay City	95	1128	2674
吐鲁番地区	Turpan Administrative Offices	8	228	1540
哈密地区	Hami [Kumul] Administrative Offices	273	709	2707
昌吉回族自治州	Changji Hui Autonomous Prefecture	47	1219	2007
伊犁哈萨克自治州	Ili Kazak Autonomous Prefecture	923	1393	14581
伊犁州直属县(市)	Counties (Cities) Direct Under Ili Prefecture	381	1088	7603
塔城地区	Tacheng [Tarbagatai] Administrative Offices	291	39	1746
阿勒泰地区	Altay Administrative Offices	251	266	5232
博尔塔拉蒙古自治州	Bortala Mongol Autonomous Prefecture	148	24	706
巴音郭楞蒙古自治州	Bayangol Mongol Autonomous Prefecture	543	628	4854
阿克苏地区	Aksu Administrative Offices	93	103	3049
克孜勒苏柯尔克孜自治州	Kizilsu Kirgiz Autonomous Prefecture		68	310
喀什地区	Kashgar [Kaxgar] Administrative Offices	99	912	3304
和田地区	Hotan Administrative Offices	66	56	1073
生产建设兵团	Production and Construction Group	733	2873	10981

16-7 各地、州、市、县(市)社会消费品零售总额

Total Retail Sales of Consumer Goods by Prefecture, Autonomous Prefecture, City and County

单位：万元　　(2011 年)　　(10 000 yuan)

地　区	Region	社会消费品零售总额 Total Retail Sales of Consumer Goods	城　镇 City	城　区 County	乡　村 Under County Level
总　计	**Total**	**15570925**	**14110155**	**11652949**	**1460770**
乌鲁木齐市	**Urumqi City**	**6497286**	**6493754**	**6493754**	**3532**
＃乌鲁木齐县	Urumqi County	85550	82034	82034	3516
克拉玛依市	**Karamay City**	**435790**	**434490**	**434490**	**1300**
吐鲁番地区	**TurpanAdministrative Offices**	**263280**	**192235**	**108892**	**71045**
吐鲁番市	Turpan City	133093	111363	106267	21730
鄯善县	Shanshan [piqan]County	88086	54385	2625	33701
托克逊县	Toksun County	42101	26487		15614
哈密地区	**Hami [kumul]Administrative Offices**	**465393**	**440805**	**400255**	**24588**
哈密市	Hami [kumul]City	415857	402484	400255	13373
巴里坤哈萨克自治县	Barkol KazakAutonomous County	37417	26518		10899
伊吾县	Yiwu [Araturuk]County	12119	11803		316
昌吉回族自治州	**Changji Hui Autonomous Prefecture**	**1330333**	**1218777**	**984998**	**111556**
昌吉市	Changji City	552568	537044	353136	15524
阜康市	Fukang City	183647	170947	121076	12700
呼图壁县	Hutubi County	156122	136538	136538	19584
玛纳斯县	Manas County	171635	143561	143561	28074
奇台县	Qitai County	150179	126285	126285	23894
吉木萨尔县	Jimsar County	72190	64921	64921	7269
木垒哈萨克自治县	Mori Kazak Autonomous County	43992	39481	39481	4511
伊犁哈萨克自治州	**Ili Kazak Autonomous Prefecture**	**1998735**	**1566198**	**879218**	**432537**
伊犁州直属县(市)	**Counties (Cities) Direct Under Ili Prefecture**	**1159316**	**902741**	**634827**	**256575**
伊宁市	Yining [Gulja]City	430038	409575	397476	20463
奎屯市	Kuytun City	156436	156436	155936	
伊宁县	Yining [Gulja]County	89467	48926	14036	40541
察布查尔锡伯自治县	Qapqal Xibe Autonomous County	19953	11986	6104	7967
霍城县	Huocheng [korgas]County	129307	76418	8689	52889
巩留县	Gongliu [Tokkuzlara]County	38823	24533	4366	14290
新源县	Xinyuan [kunes]County	152764	80624	19186	72140
昭苏县	Zhaosu [mongolkure]County	34241	21970	8691	12271
特克斯县	Tekes County	60000	34404	9762	25596
尼勒克县	Nilka County	48287	37869	10581	10418
塔城地区	**Tacheng [Tarbagatai] Administrative Offices**	**467027**	**332455**	**133884**	**134572**
塔城市	Tacheng [Qoqek] City	105081	68520	62312	36561
乌苏市	Usu City	99297	81577	48171	17720
额敏县	Emin [Dorbiljin] County	90986	53606	8212	37380
沙湾县	Shawan County	107320	82050	1484	25270
裕民县	Yumin [Qagantokay] County	17725	12493	2545	5232
和布克赛尔蒙古自治县	Hoboksar Mongol Autonomous County	20013	14592	5236	5421
托里县	Toli County	26605	19617	5924	6988
阿勒泰地区	**Altay Administrative Offices**	**372392**	**331002**	**110507**	**41390**
阿勒泰市	Altay City	156414	145377	110507	11037
布尔津县	Burqin County	78522	68843		9679
富蕴县	Fuyun [Koktokay] County	40817	33886		6931
福海县	Fuhai [Burultokay] County	39159	34582		4577
哈巴河县	Habahe [Kaba] County	30740	26906		3834
青河县	Qinghe [Qinggil] County	19186	15826		3360
吉木乃县	Jeminay County	7554	5582		1972

16-7 续表 Continued

单位：万元 (10 000 yuan)

地 区	Region	社会消费品零售总额 Total Retail Sales of Consumer Goods	城 镇 City	城 区 County	乡 村 Under County Level
博尔塔拉蒙古自治州	**Bortala Mongol Autonomous Prefecture**	**212161**	**181989**	**109557**	**30172**
博乐市	Bole [Bortala] City	156741	145873	109362	10868
精河县	Jinghe [Jing] County	38265	24045	195	14220
温泉县	Wenquan [Araxang] County	17155	12071		5084
巴音郭楞蒙古自治州	**Bayangol Mongol Autonomous Prefecture**	**674885**	**631306**	**424434**	**43579**
库尔勒市	Korla City	517285	498288	424434	18997
轮台县	Luntai [Bugur] County	29410	23644		5766
尉犁县	Yuli [Lopnur] County	13751	10872		2879
若羌县	Ruoqiang [Qarkilik] County	5627	4732		895
且末县	Qiemo [Qarqan] County	6673	5670		1003
焉耆回族自治县	Yanqi Hui Autonomous County	46096	42092		4004
和静县	Hejing County	24521	18939		5582
和硕县	Hoxud County	12687	10655		2032
博湖县	Bohu [Bagrax] County	18835	16414		2421
阿克苏地区	**Aksu Administrative Offices**	**722117**	**607585**	**348875**	**114532**
阿克苏市	Aksu City	405197	390226	334598	14971
温宿县	Wensu [Onsu] County	32403	19959		12444
库车县	Kuqa County	110034	78881	3949	31153
沙雅县	Xayar County	59329	45467	6794	13862
新和县	Xinhe [Toksu] County	24440	16574		7866
拜城县	Baicheng [Bay] County	46215	28871	3534	17344
乌什县	Wushi [Uxturpan] County	11174	4843		6331
阿瓦提县	Awat County	30117	21795		8322
柯坪县	Kalpin County	3208	969		2239
克孜勒苏柯尔克孜自治州	**Kizilsu Kirgiz Autonomous Prefecture**	**97924**	**89056**	**83603**	**8868**
阿图什市	Artux City	65343	62766	59927	2577
阿克陶县	Akto County	17400	13227	11629	4173
阿合奇县	Akqi County	6648	6294	6294	354
乌恰县	Wuqia [Ulugqat] County	8533	6769	5753	1764
喀什地区	**Kashgar [Kaxgar] Administrative Offices**	**894631**	**732133**	**393131**	**162498**
喀什市	Kashgar [Kaxgar] City	420174	401540	378765	18634
疏附县	Shufu County	9514	4925		4589
疏勒县	Shule County	43322	34711	12804	8611
英吉沙县	Yengisar County	27950	17260	911	10690
泽普县	Zepu [Poskam] County	29400	20561		8839
莎车县	Shache [Yarkant] County	86497	59189		27308
叶城县	Yecheng [Kagilik] County	71542	52252	651	19290
麦盖提县	Makit County	58901	40421		18480
岳普湖县	Yopurga County	21003	14387		6616
伽师县	Jiashi [Payzawat] County	40516	25208		15308
巴楚县	Bachu [Maralbexi] County	75816	53938		21878
塔什库尔干塔吉克自治县	Taxkorgan Tajik Autonomous County	9996	7741		2255
和田地区	**Hotan Administrative Offices**	**229120**	**167724**	**126509**	**61396**
和田市	Hotan City	111711	94526	78892	17185
和田县	Hotan County	14444	273		14171
墨玉县	Moyu [Karakax] County	31849	22952	18080	8897
皮山县	Pishan [Guma] County	15012	9468	3918	5544
洛浦县	Lop County	15118	11234	8278	3884
策勒县	Qira County	16470	10568	3266	5902
于田县	Yutian [Keriya] County	19316	14684	12539	4632
民丰县	Minfeng [Niya] County	5200	4019	1536	1181
生产建设兵团	**Xinjiang Production andConstruction Group**	**2427057**	**2185493**	**1374565**	**241564**

16-8 各地、州、市、县(市)社会消费品零售总额(按行业分)

Total Retail Sales of Consumer Goods by Sector and Prefecture, Autonomous Prefecture, City and County

单位：万元 (2011 年) (10 000 yuan)

地 区	Region	社会消费品零售总额 Total Retail Sales of Consumer Goods	批发和零售业 Wholesale And Retail Sale Trades	住宿和餐饮业 Hotels and Catering Services
总 计	**Total**	**15570925**	**13513578**	**2057347**
乌鲁木齐市	**Urumqi City**	**6497286**	**5751351**	**745935**
#乌鲁木齐县	Urumqi County	85550	64333	21217
克拉玛依市	**Karamay City**	**435790**	**377581**	**58209**
吐鲁番地区	**TurpanAdministrative Offices**	**263280**	**233267**	**30013**
吐鲁番市	Turpan City	133093	120557	12536
鄯善县	Shanshan [piqan]County	88086	76046	12040
托克逊县	Toksun County	42101	36664	5437
哈密地区	**Hami [kumul]Administrative Offices**	**465393**	**375202**	**90191**
哈密市	Hami [kumul]City	415857	339414	76443
巴里坤哈萨克自治县	Barkol KazakAutonomous County	37417	27874	9543
伊吾县	Yiwu [Araturuk]County	12119	7914	4205
昌吉回族自治州	**Changji Hui Autonomous Prefecture**	**1330333**	**1108088**	**222245**
昌吉市	Changji City	552568	460168	92400
阜康市	Fukang City	183647	151224	32423
呼图壁县	Hutubi County	156122	128588	27534
玛纳斯县	Manas County	171635	142981	28654
奇台县	Qitai County	150179	126251	23928
吉木萨尔县	Jimsar County	72190	61698	10492
木垒哈萨克自治县	Mori Kazak Autonomous County	43992	37178	6814
伊犁哈萨克自治州	**Ili Kazak Autonomous Prefecture**	**1998735**	**1687546**	**311189**
伊犁州直属县(市)	**Counties (Cities) Direct Under Ili Prefecture**	**1159316**	**992325**	**166991**
伊宁市	Yining [Gulja]City	430038	371996	58042
奎屯市	Kuytun City	156436	141195	15241
伊宁县	Yining [Gulja]County	89467	81298	8169
察布查尔锡伯自治县	Qapqal Xibe Autonomous County	19953	16750	3203
霍城县	Huocheng [korgas]County	129307	103374	25933
巩留县	Gongliu [Tokkuzlara]County	38823	33258	5565
新源县	Xinyuan [kunes]County	152764	126555	26209
昭苏县	Zhaosu [mongolkure]County	34241	30568	3673
特克斯县	Tekes County	60000	53506	6494
尼勒克县	Nilka County	48287	33825	14462
塔城地区	**Tacheng [Tarbagatai] Administrative Offices**	**467027**	**396289**	**70738**
塔城市	Tacheng [Qoqek] City	105081	87564	17517
乌苏市	Usu City	99297	81563	17734
额敏县	Emin [Dorbiljin] County	90986	83182	7804
沙湾县	Shawan County	107320	90485	16835
裕民县	Yumin [Qagantokay] County	17725	14887	2838
和布克赛尔蒙古自治县	Hoboksar Mongol Autonomous County	20013	15486	4527
托里县	Toli County	26605	23122	3483
阿勒泰地区	**Altay Administrative Offices**	**372392**	**298932**	**73460**
阿勒泰市	Altay City	156414	129743	26671
布尔津县	Burqin County	78522	51910	26612
富蕴县	Fuyun [Koktokay] County	40817	33929	6888
福海县	Fuhai [Burultokay] County	39159	33721	5438
哈巴河县	Habahe [Kaba] County	30740	26927	3813
青河县	Qinghe [Qinggil] County	19186	16552	2634
吉木乃县	Jeminay County	7554	6150	1404

16-8 续表 Continued

单位：万元 (10 000 yuan)

地　　区	Region	社会消费品零售总额 Total Retail Sales of Consumer Goods	批发和零售业 Wholesale And Retail Sale Trades	住宿和餐饮业 Hotels and Catering Services
博尔塔拉蒙古自治州	**Bortala Mongol Autonomous Prefecture**	**212161**	**180293**	**31868**
博乐市	Bole [Bortala] City	156741	139174	17567
精河县	Jinghe [Jing] County	38265	26477	11788
温泉县	Wenquan [Araxang] County	17155	14643	2512
巴音郭楞蒙古自治州	**Bayangol Mongol Autonomous Prefecture**	**674885**	**604592**	**70293**
库尔勒市	Korla City	517285	476691	40594
轮台县	Luntai [Bugur] County	29410	22652	6758
尉犁县	Yuli [Lopnur] County	13751	10147	3604
若羌县	Ruoqiang [Qarkilik] County	5627	3998	1629
且末县	Qiemo [Qarqan] County	6673	4748	1925
焉耆回族自治县	Yanqi Hui Autonomous County	46096	41816	4280
和静县	Hejing County	24521	20244	4277
和硕县	Hoxud County	12687	8111	4576
博湖县	Bohu [Bagrax] County	18835	16185	2650
阿克苏地区	**Aksu Administrative Offices**	**722117**	**646871**	**75246**
阿克苏市	Aksu City	405197	389262	15935
温宿县	Wensu [Onsu] County	32403	28942	3461
库车县	Kuqa County	110034	87149	22885
沙雅县	Xayar County	59329	46416	12913
新和县	Xinhe [Toksu] County	24440	19624	4816
拜城县	Baicheng [Bay] County	46215	40171	6044
乌什县	Wushi [Uxturpan] County	11174	9463	1711
阿瓦提县	Awat County	30117	23074	7043
柯坪县	Kalpin County	3208	2770	438
克孜勒苏柯尔克孜自治州	**Kizilsu Kirgiz Autonomous Prefecture**	**97924**	**86355**	**11569**
阿图什市	Artux City	65343	59961	5382
阿克陶县	Akto County	17400	14509	2891
阿合奇县	Akqi County	6648	5646	1002
乌恰县	Wuqia [Ulugqat] County	8533	6239	2294
喀什地区	**Kashgar [Kaxgar] Administrative Offices**	**894631**	**787122**	**107509**
喀什市	Kashgar [Kaxgar] City	420174	405333	14841
疏附县	Shufu County	9514	7554	1960
疏勒县	Shule County	43322	36963	6359
英吉沙县	Yengisar County	27950	20548	7402
泽普县	Zepu [Poskam] County	29400	24773	4627
莎车县	Shache [Yarkant] County	86497	73836	12661
叶城县	Yecheng [Kagilik] County	71542	55396	16146
麦盖提县	Makit County	58901	48276	10625
岳普湖县	Yopurga County	21003	14475	6528
伽师县	Jiashi [Payzawat] County	40516	33097	7419
巴楚县	Bachu [Maralbexi] County	75816	57086	18730
塔什库尔干塔吉克自治县	Taxkorgan Tajik Autonomous County	9996	9785	211
和田地区	**Hotan Administrative Offices**	**229120**	**200314**	**28806**
和田市	Hotan City	111711	99331	12380
和田县	Hotan County	14444	10678	3766
墨玉县	Moyu [Karakax] County	31849	29449	2400
皮山县	Pishan [Guma] County	15012	14359	653
洛浦县	Lop County	15118	13413	1705
策勒县	Qira County	16470	13111	3359
于田县	Yutian [Keriya] County	19316	15907	3409
民丰县	Minfeng [Niya] County	5200	4066	1134
生产建设兵团	**Production and Construction Group**	**2427057**	**2019571**	**407486**

16-9 限额以上批发企业资产及负债情况

Assets and Liabilities of Enterprises above Designated Size of Wholesale Trades

单位：万元　　(2011 年)　　(10 000 yuan)

指　　标	Item	资产合计 Total Assets	#流动资产 Working Capitals	#固定资产 Fixed Assets	负债合计 Total Liabilities
总　计	**Total**	**13727412**	**10955905**	**1151169**	**11114527**
按登记注册类型分	**By Type of Registration**				
内资企业	Domestic Funded Enterprises	13284572	10838340	1148371	11224056
国有企业	State-owned Enterprises	4159395	3409316	410486	3684658
集体企业	Collective-owned Enterprises	755907	645380	57881	636682
股份合作企业	Cooperative Enterprises	25424	22587	2648	22999
有限责任公司	Limited Liability Corporations	4707371	3963933	322255	3832877
国有独资公司	State Sole Funded Corporations	525423	436756	41297	455727
其他有限责任公司	Other Limited Liability Corporations	4181948	3527177	280958	3377150
股份有限公司	Share-holding Corporations Ltd.	1119056	735164	143086	1158411
私营企业	Private Enterprises	2419683	1970115	206512	1804109
私营独资企业	Private-funded Enterprises	8853	8143	653	6198
私营合伙企业	Private Partnership Enterprises	1280	1269	11	1020
私营有限责任公司	Private Limited Liability Corporations	2276030	1848660	195522	1690430
私营股份有限公司	Private Share-holding Corporation Ltd.	133520	112043	10326	106461
其他企业	Other Enterprises	97736	91845	5503	84320
港、澳、台商投资企业	Enterprises With Funds from Hong Kong, Macao and Taiwan	421412	98094	1420	-122718
港、澳、台商独资经营企业	Enterprises with Sole Funds from Hong Kong, Macao and Taiwan	6770	5623	1113	2055
港、澳、台商投资股份有限公司	Enterprises with Share-holding Corporations Ltd. from HongKong,Macao and Taiwan	414642	92471	307	-124773
外商投资企业	Foreign Funded Enterprises	21428	19471	1378	13189
中外合资经营企业	Enterprises with Foreign Investment	21428	19471	1378	13189
按批发行业小类分组	**By Sector of Wholesale**				
农畜产品批发业	Wholesale of Farm Produce and Livestock Products	5427448	4713271	437571	4666692
谷物、豆及薯类批发业	Wholesale of Grain,Bean and Potato	528004	435072	47879	495583
种子、饲料批发业	Wholesale of Seed and Fodder	305587	212925	44869	170475
棉、麻批发业	Wholesale of Cotton and Liner	4566857	4043248	342333	3978206
其他农畜产品批发业	Wholesale of Other Farm Produce and Livestoclc Products	27000	22026	2490	22428
食品、饮料及烟草制品批发业	Wholesale of Food,Beverages and Tobaccos	838105	605711	122439	599353
米、面制品及食用油批发业	Wholesale of Rice, Flour and Edible Oil	298804	253770	25879	265276
糕点、糖果及糖批发业	Wholesale of Pastry,Candy and Sugar	7874	5492	245	5291
果品、蔬菜批发业	Wholesale of Fruit and Vegetable	231410	139413	44606	168963
肉、禽、蛋及水产品批发业	Wholesale of Meat,Birds and Equatic Products	1294	1149	21	830
盐及调味品批发业	Wholesale of Salt and Condiment Flavoring Material	41695	17080	3560	16528
饮料及茶叶批发业	Wholesale of Soft Drink and Tea Leaf	36319	29446	1275	39152
烟草制品批发业	Wholesale of Tobaccos	161268	115148	37577	58644
其他食品批发业	Wholesale of Other Food	59441	44213	9276	44669
纺织、服装及日用品批发业	Wholesale of Textitle, Garments and Daily Consumer Articles	75455	63096	3601	61018
纺织品、针织品及原料批发业	Wholesale of Textile,Hosiery and Raw Material	13749	12389	42	9588
服装批发业	Wholesale of Garment	36181	28800	748	30286
化妆品及卫生用品批发业	Wholesale of Cosmetics and Health Aids	13977	11068	2647	11010
其他日用品批发业	Wholesale of Other Covenience Goods	11548	10839	164	10134

16-9 续表 Continued

单位：万元 (10 000 yuan)

指标	Item	资产合计 Total Assets	#流动资产 Working Capitals	#固定资产 Fixed Assets	负债合计 Total Liabilities
文化、体育用品及器材批发业	Wholesale of Culture, Sports Goods and Apparatus	106574	67934	20686	63837
图书批发业	Wholesale of Books	82628	47363	19119	42694
其他文化用品批发业	Wholesale of Other Culture Products	23946	20571	1567	21143
医药及医疗器械批发业	Wholesale of Medicines and Medical Appliances	304974	256125	28439	205875
西药批发业	Wholesale of Western Medicine	277043	230436	27361	183314
中药材及中成药批发业	Wholesale of Chinese Medicinal Plant and Chinese Patent Medicine	22666	20886	634	18796
医疗用品及器材批发	Wholesale of Medicine and Medical Appliances	5265	4803	444	3765
矿产品、建材及化工产品批发业	Wholesale of Mineral Products, Building Material and Chemical Products	5444645	3949373	449233	4316531
煤炭及制品批发业	Wholesale of Coal and Related Products	315581	190382	19473	90802
石油及制品批发业	Wholesale of Petroleum and Related Products	2504717	1739311	348592	2549032
金属及金属矿批发业	Wholesale of Metal and Metal Materials	1367110	926891	19806	627999
建材批发业	Wholesale of Building Materials	136506	116062	6335	106170
化肥批发业	Wholesale of Fertilizer	939138	816966	46002	800974
农药批发业	Wholesale of Pesticides	5358	3417	1329	3988
其他化工产品批发业	Wholesale of Other Chemical Product	176235	156344	7696	137566
机械设备、五金交电及电子产品批发业	Wholesale of Machinery, Hardware and Electronic Equipments	1374513	1179641	76570	1080374
农业机械批发业	Wholesale of Agriculture Machinery	138192	113275	19652	94454
汽车、摩托车及零配件批发业	Wholesale of Motor Vehicles, Motorcycles and Parts	510650	451569	21750	405544
五金、交电批发业	Wholesale of Hardware and Electromic Equipment	252626	241648	7861	237146
家用电器批发业	Wholesale of Household Electrical Appliances	27887	20305	6629	27458
计算机、软件及辅助设备批发业	Wholesale of Computer, Software and Accessory Equipment	38976	36509	1660	24477
通讯及广播电视设备批发业	Wholesale of Communicating and Broadcasting Television Device	23158	21046	1893	16350
其他机械设备及电子产品批发业	Wholesale of Other Mechanical Equipment and Electromic Products	383024	295289	17125	274945
贸易经纪与代理	Trades Broker and Agent	30595	19607	4043	21376
其他批发业	Wholesales of Others	125103	101147	8587	99471
再生物资回收与批发业	Recovery and Wholesale of Regeneration Material	71739	59405	4837	61289
其他未列明的批发业	Wholesale of Un-listed	53364	41742	3750	38182
按地区分	**By Region**				
乌鲁木齐市	Urumqi City	5465154	4359369	291238	3904543
克拉玛依市	Karamay City	304984	124610	58700	223094
吐鲁番地区	Turpan Administrative Offices	104519	83920	14378	78728
哈密地区	Hami [Kumul] Administrative Offices	251959	205501	33773	207173
昌吉回族自治州	Changji Hui Autonomous Prefecture	409884	311654	43933	448828
伊犁哈萨克自治州	Ili Kazak Autonomous Prefecture	1048377	835209	82688	1048229
伊犁州直属县(市)	Counties (Cities) Direct Under Ili Prefecture	552617	438096	52396	545511
塔城地区	Tacheng [Tarbagatai] Administrative Offices	447496	363090	18221	385835
阿勒泰地区	Altay Administrative Offices	48264	34023	12071	116883
博尔塔拉蒙古自治州	Bortala Mongol Autonomous Prefecture	186002	154087	11571	93024
巴音郭楞蒙古自治州	Bayangol Mongol Autonomous Prefecture	530881	379642	108572	404124
阿克苏地区	Aksu Administrative Offices	1021561	833459	113296	986206
克孜勒苏柯尔克孜自治州	Kizilsu Kirgiz Autonomous Prefecture	32316	28114	2730	24191
喀什地区	Kashgar [Kaxgar] Administrative Offices	588651	446434	102238	469923
和田地区	Hotan Administrative Offices	102250	28221	15633	89820
生产建设兵团	Production and Construction Group	3680874	3165685	272419	3136644

16-10 限额以上零售企业资产及负债情况
Assets and Liabilities of Enterprises above Designated Size of Retail Trades

单位：万元　　(2011 年)　　(10 000 yuan)

指　标	Item	资产合计 Total Asset	#流动资产 Working Capitals	#固定资产 Fixed Asset	负债合计 Total Liabilities
总　计	**Total**	**2914659**	**2005499**	**427970**	**2177269**
按登记注册类型分	**By Status of Registration**				
内资企业	Domestic funded Enterprises	2740958	1877962	401884	2062000
国有企业	State-owned Enterprises	272506	157745	64802	113839
集体企业	Collective-owned Enterprises	8045	5437	1778	6174
股份合作企业	Share-holding Cooperative Enterprises	1689	834	646	963
有限责任公司	Limited Liability Corporations	940623	728393	114432	617488
国有独资公司	State Sole Funded Corporations	8481	5727	2525	5947
其他有限责任公司	Other Limited Liability Corporations	932142	722666	111907	611541
股份有限公司	Share-holding Corporations Ltd.	448159	179394	95731	523291
私营企业	Private Enterprises	1042672	789664	122841	791784
私营独资企业	Private-funded Enterprises	27443	25108	1649	22722
私营合伙企业	Private Partnership Enterprises	165	117	49	150
私营有限责任公司	Private Limited Liability Corporations	1003302	755766	119378	760133
私营股份有限公司	Private Share-holding Corporation Ltd.	11762	8673	1765	8779
其他企业	Others	27264	16495	1654	8461
港、澳、台投资企业	Enterprises With Funds from Hong Kong, Macao and Taiwan	56472	43652	8176	40044
港、澳、台商独资经营企业	Enterprises with Sole Funds from Hong Kong, Macao and Taiwan	56472	43652	8176	40044
外商投资企业	Foreign Funded Enterprises	117229	83885	17910	75225
中外合资经营企业	Enterprises with Foreign Investment	89559	59465	15418	59478
外资企业	Enterprises with Sole Fund	27670	24420	2492	15747
按零售行业小类分组	**By Sector of Retail**				
综合零售业	Integrated Retail	753813	418011	124305	551774
百货零售业	Retail of Merchandile	601285	304109	103449	432041
超级市场零售业	Retail of Supermarket	152046	113490	20845	119351
其他综合零售业	Retail of other integrate	482	412	11	382
食品、饮料及烟草制品专门零售业	Monopoly Retail of Foods, Beverages and Tobacco	19544	10563	3181	13568
粮油零售业	Retail of Grain and Oil	8266	4657	1307	7143
肉、禽、蛋及水产品零售	Retail of Meat,Poultry and Eggs	4472	1820	1191	2795
饮料及茶叶零售业	Retail of Soft Drink and Tea Leaf	1907	1360	300	1874
烟草制品零售业	Retail of Tobauos	4899	2726	383	1756
纺织、服装及日用品专门零售业	Monopoly Retail of Textile, Garments and Daily Consumer Articles	146689	89134	32298	133159
服装零售业	Garment Retail	136271	80466	32182	123956
钟表、眼镜零售业	Retail of Timekeeper and Spectacle	9765	8072	58	8617
其他日用品零售业	Retail of Other Covenience Goods	653	596	58	586
文化、体育用品及器材专门零售业	Monopoly Retail of Cultural, Sports Appliances And Equipments	177979	110196	38542	82749
文具用品零售业	Retail of Stationery and Office Supplies	1511	1462	49	852
图书零售业	Retail of Books	135547	68830	38001	64795

16-10 续表 Continued

单位：万元 (10 000 yuan)

指标	Item	资产合计 Total Assets	#流动资产 Working Capitals	#固定资产 Fixed Assets	负债合计 Total Liabilities
珠宝首饰零售业	Retail of Jewelry	40211	39229	488	16574
照相器材零售业	Retail of Photographic Materials	710	675	4	528
医药及医疗器材专门零售业	Monopoly Retail of Medicine and Medical-care Apparatus	377669	333069	18565	275365
药品零售业	Retail of Medcine	375234	330747	18452	273560
医疗用品及器材零售	Wholesale of Medical Treatment and Equipment	2435	2322	113	1805
汽车、摩托车、燃料及零配件专门零售业	Monopoly Retail of Car, Motor, Fuel and Parts as Well as Components	1003136	711465	157891	910995
汽车零售业	Retail of Car	838681	640189	103427	602998
汽车零配件零售业	Retail of Automobiles' Accessories	7080	5763	749	4998
摩托车及零配件零售业	Retail of Motorcycle and Fittings	8701	7625	477	7399
机动车燃料零售业	Retail of Auto Fuel	148674	57888	53238	295600
家用电器及电子产品专门零售业	Monopoly Retail of House hold Electric Appliancesound Electronic Products	185202	164095	5853	104270
家用电器零售业	Retail of Electric Appliances	112730	101674	2737	73805
计算机、软件及辅助设备零售业	Retail of Cumputers,Software and Office Appliances	63875	54509	2802	25287
通讯设备零售业	Retail of Telecommunication Equipments	7010	6352	288	3659
其他电子产品零售	Retail of other Electric Products	1587	1560	26	1519
五金、家具及室内装修材料专门零售业	Monopoly Retail of Hardware, Furniture and Indoor Decorating Material	217763	153798	32773	92274
五金零售业	Retail of Hardware	1420	1362	29	1232
家具零售业	Retail of Living equipment	216343	152436	32744	91042
无店铺及其他零售业	Retail of Storeless and others	32864	15168	14562	13115
生活用燃料零售业	Retail of Life Fuels	28911	13705	13243	10974
其他未列明的零售业	Retail of Un-listed	3953	1463	1319	2141
按地区分	**By Region**				
乌鲁木齐市	Urumqi City	2101235	1455585	284375	1637007
克拉玛依市	Karamay City	68806	54022	8512	53822
吐鲁番地区	Turpan Administrative Offices	13190	6520	2210	11527
哈密地区	Hami [Kumul] Administrative Offices	67466	41661	10065	48194
昌吉回族自治州	Changji Hui Autonomous Prefecture	77353	52635	9696	59361
伊犁哈萨克自治州	Ili Kazak Autonomous Prefecture	152139	102494	17381	83000
伊犁州直属县(市)	Counties (Cities) Direct Under Ili Prefecture	132842	91722	10533	73420
塔城地区	Tacheng [Tarbagatai] Administrative Offices	14499	8721	5504	6960
阿勒泰地区	Altay Administrative Offices	4798	2051	1344	2620
博尔塔拉蒙古自治州	Bortala Mongol Autonomous Prefecture	5027	3184	1389	2348
巴音郭楞蒙古自治州	Bayangol Mongol Autonomous Prefecture	107152	82262	15924	83267
阿克苏地区	Aksu Administrative Offices	96843	60712	23469	73829
克孜勒苏柯尔克孜自治州	Kizilsu Kirgiz Autonomous Prefecture	3956	1480	2371	1917
喀什地区	Kashgar [Kaxgar] Administrative Offices	101165	73858	17453	76332
和田地区	Hotan Administrative Offices	9337	6385	2659	3826
生产建设兵团	Production and Construction Group	110990	64701	32466	42839

16-11 限额以上餐饮企业资产及负债情况

Assets and Liabilities of Enterprises above Designated Size of Catering Services

单位：万元 (2011 年) (10 000 yuan)

指 标	Item	资产合计 Total Asset	#流动资产 Working Capitals	#固定资产 Fixed Asset	负债合计 Total Liabilities
总 计	**Total**	**114195**	**36272**	**63512**	**53018**
按登记注册类型分	**By Status of Registration**				
内资企业	Domestic-funded Enterprises	104548	31092	62354	49365
国有企业	State – owned Enterprises	44227	5512	38706	1342
有限责任公司	Limited Liability Corporations	15475	9702	3551	12332
其他有限责任公司	Other Limited Liability Corporations	15475	9702	3551	12332
股份有限公司	Share-holding Corporations Ltd.	11709	5019	4250	3907
私营企业	Private Enterprises	31373	17536	7758	26079
私营独资企业	Private-funded Enterprises	2423	1197	1145	1391
私营合伙企业	Private Partnership Enterprises	2882	1951	346	84
私营有限责任公司	Private Limited Liability Corporations	26068	14388	6267	24604
其他企业	Others	1764	-6677	8089	5705
外商投资企业	Foreign Funded Enterprises	9647	5180	1158	3653
外资企业	Enterprises with Sole Fund	9647	5180	1158	3653
按餐饮行业小类分组	**By Sector of Catering**				
正餐服务	Dinner	91921	25405	57856	44912
快餐服务	Snack	22274	10867	5656	8106
按地区分	**By Region**				
乌鲁木齐市	Urumqi City	93021	24763	55615	40625
克拉玛依市	Karamay City	496	474	14	217
吐鲁番地区	Turpan Administrative Offices	69	62	7	53
昌吉回族自治州	Changji Hui Autonomous Prefecture	857	135	698	153
伊犁哈萨克自治州直属县(市)	Ili Kazak Autonomous Prefecture	1906	421	1453	367
巴音郭楞蒙古自治州	Bayangol Mongol Autonomous Prefecture	10420	5824	2903	7397
阿克苏地区	Aksu Administrative Offices	4345	2158	2179	1977
喀什地区	Kashgar [Kaxgar] Administrative Offices	1875	1712	163	1715
生产建设兵团	Production and Construction Group	1206	723	480	514

16-12 限额以上住宿企业资产及负债情况

Assets and Liabilities of Enterprises above Designated Size of Accommodation Services

单位：万元　　(2011 年)　　(10 000 yuan)

指　　标	Item	资产合计 Total Assets	#流动资产 Working Capitals	#固定资产 Fixed Assets	负债合计 Total Liabilities
总　计	**Total**	**875356**	**250853**	**489939**	**566390**
按登记注册类型分	**By Status of Registration**				
内资企业	Domestic-funded Enterprises	869658	248413	486727	555913
国有企业	State-owned Enterprises	297485	76547	195934	141440
集体企业	Collective-owned Enterprises	21455	6721	8254	20592
联营企业	Joint Ounership Enterprises	2502	1494	1008	1090
国有联营企业	State Ounership Enterprises	2502	1494	1008	1090
有限责任公司	Limited Liability Corporations	321826	103142	169954	213230
国有独资公司	State Sole Funded Corporations	17096	5481	10178	14915
其他有限责任公司	Other Limited Liability Corporations	304730	97661	159776	198315
股份有限公司	Share-holding Corporations Ltd.	22558	4575	14905	13722
私营企业	Private Enterprises	203832	55934	96672	165839
私营独资企业	Private-funded Enterprises	18658	5395	10320	13210
私营合伙企业	Private Partnership Enterprises	5732	2083	3378	5609
私营有限责任公司	Private Limited Liability Corporations	179442	48456	82974	147020
港、澳、台商投资企业	Enterprises With Funds from Hong Kong, Macao and Taiwan	5598	2356	3196	10455
合资经营企业（港或澳、台资）	Joint-venture Enterprises (Funds from Hong Kong, Macao and Taiwan)	5598	2356	3196	10455
外商投资企业	Foreign funded Enterprises	100	84	16	22
外资企业	Enterprises with Sole Fund	100	84	16	22
按住宿行业分组	**By Sector of**				
旅游饭店	Tourist Hotel	812317	234417	453011	529344
一般旅馆	Ordinary Hotel	63039	16436	36928	37046
按星级等级分	**Classified by Stars**				
五　星	Five-Star	241256	60520	170290	163439
四　星	Four-Star	200048	58716	124260	134518
三　星	Three-Star	342815	103930	153016	215825
二　星	Two-Star	36026	12418	16490	14567
一　星	One-Star	1473	383	709	1160
其　他	Other	53738	14886	25174	36881
按地区分	**By Region**				
乌鲁木齐市	Urumqi City	360925	130379	176127	221957
克拉玛依市	Karamay City	49653	2133	46197	53012
吐鲁番地区	Turpan Administrative Offices	11563	3208	5875	11281
哈密地区	Hami [Kumul] Administrative Offices	35589	9363	17118	23103
昌吉回族自治州	Changji Hui Autonomous Prefecture	9780	2844	5580	9939
伊犁哈萨克自治州	Ili Kazak Autonomous Prefecture	146907	30074	84460	75448
伊犁州直属县(市)	Counties (Cities) Direct Under Ili Prefecture	98781	18770	52806	52248
塔城地区	Tacheng [Tarbagatai] Administrative Offices	12523	3363	8312	6990
阿勒泰地区	Altay Administrative Offices	35603	7941	23342	16210
博尔塔拉蒙古自治州	Bortala Mongol Autonomous Prefecture	3075	2125	476	2764
巴音郭楞蒙古自治州	Bayangol Mongol Autonomous Prefecture	68014	11360	51535	62629
阿克苏地区	Aksu Administrative Offices	33676	7246	24421	20963
克孜勒苏柯尔克孜自治州	Kizilsu Kirgiz Autonomous Prefecture	7195	689	6313	3934
喀什地区	Kashgar [Kaxgar] Administrative Offices	62218	29775	21344	38973
和田地区	Hotan Administrative Offices	14162	3422	6913	6259
生产建设兵团	Production and Construction Group	72599	18235	43580	36128

16-13 限额以上批发企业主要财务指标

Main Financial Indicators of Wholesale Enterprises above Designated Size

单位：万元 (2011 年) (10 000 yuan)

指 标	Item	商品销售收入 Revenue of Product Sales	商品销售成本 Cost of Product Sales	商品销售税金及附加 Sales Tax and Extra Changes	商品销售利润 Profits of Product Sales
总 计	**Total**	**41131243**	**39749461**	**95415**	**1286367**
按登记注册类型分	**By Status of Registration**				
内资企业	Domesticfunded Enterprises	40941341	39567452	95274	1278615
国有企业	State-owned Enterprises	7381073	6994311	52194	334568
集体企业	Collective-owned Enterprises	689633	652071	350	37212
股份合作企业	Cooperative Enterprises	23458	22242		1216
有限责任公司	Limited Liability Corporations	17390900	16994134	27278	369488
国有独资公司	State Sole Funded Corporations	1231050	1101770	15572	113708
其他有限责任公司	Other Limited Liability Corporations	16159850	15892364	11706	255780
股份有限公司	Share-holding Corporations Ltd.	9880225	9668528	7784	203913
私营企业	Private Enterprises	5279621	4946449	7579	325593
私营独资企业	Private-funded Enterprises	24895	23486	23	1386
私营合伙企业	Private Partnership Enterprises	5503	5205	6	292
私营有限责任公司	Private Limited Liability Corporations	4943181	4628370	7381	307430
私营股份有限公司	Private Share-holding Corporation Ltd.	306042	289388	169	16485
其他企业	Other Enterprises	296431	289717	89	6625
港、澳、台商投资企业	Enterprises With Funds from Hong Kong, Macao and Taiwan	149295	144592	67	4636
港、澳、台商独资经营企业	Enterprises with Sole Funds from Hong Kong, Macao and Taiwan	12676	11336		1340
港、澳、台商投资股份有限公司	Enterprises with Share-holding Corporations Ltd. from HongKong,Macao and Taiwan	136619	133256	67	3296
外商投资企业	Foreign funded Enterprises	40607	37417	74	3116
中外合资经营企业	Enterprises with Foreign Investment	40607	37417	74	3116
按批发行业小类分组	**By Sector of Wholesale**				
农畜产品批发业	Wholesale of Farm Produce and Livestock Products	5919611	5633200	6422	279989
谷物、豆及薯类批发业	Wholesale of Grain,Bean and Potato	450360	420238	210	29912
种子、饲料批发业	Wholesale of Seed and Fodder	208850	167860	79	40911
棉、麻批发业	Wholesale of Cotton and Lliner	5236598	5023263	6121	207214
其他农畜产品批发业	Wholesale of Other Farm Produce and Livestoclc Products	23803	21839	12	1952
食品、饮料及烟草制品批发业	Wholesale of Food,Beverages and Tobaccos	1588940	1369056	61830	158054
米、面制品及食用油批发业	Wholesale of Rice, Flour and Edible Oil	238266	221503	145	16618
糕点、糖果及糖批发业	Wholesale of Pastry,Candy and Sugar	16402	14553	26	1823
果品、蔬菜批发业	Wholesale of Fruit and Vegetable	124433	106278	178	17977
肉、禽、蛋及水产品批发业	Wholesale of Meat,Birds and Equatic Products	4725	4249	3	473
盐及调味品批发业	Wholesale of Salt and Condiment Flavoring Material	36663	29518	108	7037
饮料及茶叶批发业	Wholesale of Soft Drink and Tea Leaf	81864	60541	469	20854
烟草制品批发业业	Wholesale of Tobaccos	1054241	903112	60802	90327
其他食品批发业	Wholesale of Other Food	32346	29302	99	2945
纺织、服装及日用品批发业	Wholesale of Textitle, Garments and Daily Consumer Articles	264864	246783	206	17875
纺织品、针织品及原料批发业	Wholesale of Textile,Hosiery and Raw Material	84879	83409	7	1463
服装批发业	Wholesale of Garment	114147	102830	137	11180
化妆品及卫生用品批发业	Wholesale of Cosmetics and Health Aids	31441	27889	53	3499
其他日用品批发业	Wholesale of Other Covenience Goods	34397	32655	9	1733

16-13 续表 Continued

单位：万元 (10 000 yuan)

指 标	Item	商品销售收入 Revenue of Product Sales	商品销售成本 Cost of Product Sales	商品销售税金及附加 Sales Tax and Extra Changes	商品销售利润 Product Sales Profits
文化、体育用品及器材批发业	Wholesale of Culture, Sports Goods and Apparatus	136325	121873	225	14227
图书批发业	Wholesale of Books	95729	83362	193	12174
其他文化用品批发业	Wholesale of Other Culture Products	40596	38511	32	2053
医药及医疗器械批发业	Wholesale of Medicines and Medical Appliances	476015	441044	1025	33946
西药批发业	Wholesale of Western Medicine	425041	393850	957	30234
中药材及中成药批发业	Wholesale of Chinese Medicinal Plant and Chinese Patent Medicine	39603	36801	56	2746
医疗用品及器材批发	Wholesale of Medicine and Medical Appliances	11371	10393	12	966
矿产品、建材及化工产品批发业	Wholesale of Mineral Products, Building Material and Chemical Products	30146670	29495995	21293	629382
煤炭及制品批发业	Wholesale of Coal and Related Products	265719	175018	3704	86997
石油及制品批发业	Wholesale of Petroleum and Related Products	24322860	23952180	15182	355498
金属及金属矿批发业	Wholesale of Metal and Metal Materials	3258542	3172970	1140	84432
建材批发业	Wholesale of Building Materials	415770	401560	199	14011
化肥批发业	Wholesale of Fertilizer	1315255	1259535	286	55434
农药批发业	Wholesale of Pesticides	8533	8763		-230
其他化工产品批发业	Wholesale of Other Chemical Product	559991	525969	782	33240
机械设备、五金交电及电子产品批发业	Wholesale of Machinery, Hardware and Electronic Equipments	2228577	2091068	2763	134746
农业机械批发业	Wholesale of Agriculture Machinery	153928	142774	77	11077
汽车、摩托车及零配件批发业	Wholesale of Motor Vehicles, Motorcycles and Parts	698001	641537	860	55604
五金、交电批发业	Wholesale of Hardware and Electromic Equipment	434126	426908	536	6682
家用电器批发业	Wholesale of Household Electrical Appliances	51816	46616	119	5081
计算机、软件及辅助设备批发业	Wholesale of Computer, Software and Accessory Equipment	110408	103788	310	6310
通讯及广播电视设备批发业	Wholesale of Communicating and Broadcasting Television Device	243406	242335	15	1056
其他机械设备及电子产品批发业	Wholesale of Other Mechanical Equipment and Electromic Products	536892	487110	846	48936
贸易经纪与代理	Trades Broker and Agent	68562	66469	70	2023
其他批发业	Wholesales of Others	301679	283973	1581	16125
再生物资回收与批发业	Recovery and Wholesale of Regeneration Material	239780	232903	1393	5484
其他未列明的批发业	Wholesale of Un-listed	61899	51070	188	10641
按地区分	**By Region**				
乌鲁木齐市	Urumqi City	25054291	24500552	34868	518871
克拉玛依市	Karamay City	724780	655552	3601	65627
吐鲁番地区	Turpan Administrative Offices	352627	331509	2264	18854
哈密地区	Hami [Kumul] Administrative Offices	766773	719852	3595	43326
昌吉回族自治州	Changji Hui Autonomous Prefecture	713082	657647	5875	49560
伊犁哈萨克自治州	Ili Kazak Autonomous Prefecture	3435883	3330527	12848	92508
伊犁州直属县(市)	Counties (Cities) Direct Under Ili Prefecture	2519887	2453291	6234	60362
塔城地区	Tacheng [Tarbagatai] Administrative Offices	664832	645678	4308	14846
阿勒泰地区	Altay Administrative Offices	251164	231558	2306	17300
博尔塔拉蒙古自治州	Bortala Mongol Autonomous Prefecture	742229	707011	1881	33337
巴音郭楞蒙古自治州	Bayangol Mongol Autonomous Prefecture	1061839	986771	8913	66155
阿克苏地区	Aksu Administrative Offices	1863789	1775109	6527	82153
克孜勒苏柯尔克孜自治州	Kizilsu Kirgiz Autonomous Prefecture	34870	31712	37	3121
喀什地区	Kashgar [Kaxgar] Administrative Offices	1357171	1307560	9270	40341
和田地区	Hotan Administrative Offices	183155	171043	1806	10306
生产建设兵团	Production and Construction Group	4840754	4574616	3930	262208

16-14 限额以上零售企业主要财务指标
Main Financial Indicators of Retail Enterprises above Designated Size

单位：万元　　(2011 年)　　(10 000 yuan)

指　标	Item	商品销售收入 Revenue of Product Sales	商品销售成本 Cost of Product Sales	商品销售税金及附加 Sales Tax and Extra Changes	商品销售利润 Product Sales Profits
总　计	**Total**	**5676440**	**5046885**	**20790**	**608765**
按登记注册类型分	**By Status of Registration**				
内资企业	Domestic Funded Enterprises	5277183	4702380	19038	555765
国有企业	State-owned Enterprises	591222	526340	1405	63477
集体企业	Collective-owned Enterprises	9163	7977	27	1159
股份合作企业	Share-holding Cooperative Enterprises	1744	1543	2	199
有限责任公司	Limited Liability Corporations	1575645	1376422	4987	194236
国有独资公司	State Sole Funded Corporations	14701	11391	62	3248
其他有限责任公司	Other Limited Liability Corporations	1560944	1365031	4925	190988
股份有限公司	Share-holding Corporations Ltd.	865664	777746	5828	82090
私营企业	Private Enterprises	2139504	1927236	6643	205625
私营独资企业	Private-funded Enterprises	74336	67419	438	6479
私营合伙企业	Private Partnership Enterprises	2015	1956	1	58
私营有限责任公司	Private Limited Liability Corporations	2023731	1823765	6149	193817
私营股份有限公司	Private Share-holding Corporation Ltd.	39422	34096	55	5271
其他企业	Others	94241	85116	146	8979
港、澳、台投资企业	Enterprises With Funds from Hong Kong, Macao and Taiwan	147086	127163	662	19261
港、澳、台商独资经营企业	Enterprises with Sole Funds from Hong Kong, Macao and Taiwan	147086	127163	662	19261
外商投资企业	Foreign funded Enterprises	252171	217342	1090	33739
中外合资经营企业	Enterprises with Foreign Investment	202196	175773	1090	25333
外资企业	Enterprises with Sole Fund	49975	41569		8406
按零售行业小类分组	**By Sector of Retail**				
综合零售业	Integrated Retail	1047166	884756	10090	152320
百货零售业	Retail of General Merchandise	746247	626002	8932	111313
超级市场零售业	Retail of Supermarket	300419	258344	1157	40918
其他综合零售业	Retail of Other Integrate	500	410	1	89
食品、饮料及烟草制品专门零售业	Monopoly Retail of Foods, Beverages and Tobacco	19152	17227	13	1912
粮油零售业	Retail of Grain and Oil	9462	8689		773
肉、禽、蛋及水产品零售	Retail of Meat,Poultry and Eggs	2331	2083		248
饮料及茶叶零售业	Retail of Soft Drink and Tea Leaf	1957	1678	4	275
烟草制品零售业	Retail of Tobaccos	5402	4777	9	616
纺织、服装及日用品专门零售业	Monopoly Retail of Textile, Garments and Daily Consumer Articles	253635	207439	2121	44075
服装零售业	Garment Retail	243095	198968	2115	42012
钟表、眼镜零售业	Retail of Timelceeper and Spectacle	9629	7716	5	1908
其他日用品零售业	Retail of other Covenience Goods	911	755	1	155
文化、体育用品及器材专门零售业	Monopoly Retail of Cultural, Sports Goods And Apparatus	154773	102646	1476	50651
文具用品零售业	Retail of Stationery and Office Supplies	3352	3131	4	217
图书零售业	Retail of Books	120591	88686	550	31355
珠宝首饰零售业	Retail of Bijouterie	28424	8560	918	18946
照相器材零售业	Retail of Photographic Materials	2406	2269	4	133

16-14 续表 Continued

单位：万元 (10 000 yuan)

指标	Item	商品销售收入 Revenue of Product Sales	商品销售成本 Cost of Product Sales	商品销售税金及附加 Sales Taxes and Extra Changes	商品销售利润 Product Sales Profits
医药及医疗器材专门零售业	Monopoly Retail of Medicine and Medical-care Apparatus	569384	514519	1183	53682
药品零售业	Retail of Medcine	565940	511824	1172	52944
医疗用品及器材零售	Wholesale of Medical Treatment and Equipment	3444	2695	11	738
汽车、摩托车、燃料及零配件专门零售业	Monopoly Retail of Car, Motor, Fuel and Parts as Well as Components	3045758	2853567	3855	188336
汽车零售业	Retail of Automobiles	2060113	1913572	2609	143932
汽车零配件零售业	Retail of Automobiles' Parts	21653	20156	20	1477
摩托车及零配件零售业	Retail of Motorcycle and Fittings	17514	16285	12	1217
机动车燃料零售业	Retail of Auto Fuel	946478	903554	1214	41710
家用电器及电子产品专门零售业	Monopoly Retail of House hold Electric Appliancesound Electronic Products	404128	364749	921	38458
家用电器零售业	Retail of Electric Appliances	315234	284298	689	30247
计算机、软件及辅助设备零售业	Retail of Cumputers,Software and Office Appliances	57512	52832	133	4547
通讯设备零售业	Retail of Telecommunication Equipments	30913	27197	98	3618
其他电子产品零售	Retail of Electric Products	469	422	1	46
五金、家具及室内装修材料专门零售业	Monopoly Retail of Hardware, Furniture and Indoor Decorating Material	150576	78646	859	71071
五金零售业	Retail of Hardware	2928	2744	19	165
家具零售业	Retail of Living Equipment	147648	75902	840	70906
无店铺及其他零售业	Retail of Storeless and Others	31868	23336	272	8260
生活用燃料零售业	Retail of Life Fuels	22454	16352	232	5870
其他未列明的零售业	Retail of Un-listed	9414	6984	40	2390
按地区分	**By Region**				
乌鲁木齐市	Urumqi City	3944367	3472504	15872	455991
克拉玛依市	Karamay City	155441	140876	609	13956
吐鲁番地区	Turpan Administrative Offices	14005	12115	36	1854
哈密地区	Hami [Kumul] Administrative Offices	121232	110900	222	10110
昌吉回族自治州	Changji Hui Autonomous Prefecture	153464	136620	630	16214
伊犁哈萨克自治州	Ili Kazak Autonomous Prefecture	196217	174893	1153	20171
伊犁州直属县(市)	Counties (Cities) Direct Under Ili Prefecture	159734	142725	451	16558
塔城地区	Tacheng [Tarbagatai] Administrative Offices	27035	23918	679	2438
阿勒泰地区	Altay Administrative Offices	9448	8250	23	1175
博尔塔拉蒙古自治州	Bortala Mongol Autonomous Prefecture	9123	7639	28	1456
巴音郭楞蒙古自治州	Bayangol Mongol Autonomous Prefecture	198964	181909	664	16391
阿克苏地区	Aksu Administrative Offices	152581	136225	270	16086
克孜勒苏柯尔克孜自治州	Kizilsu Kirgiz Autonomous Prefecture	4067	3310	10	747
喀什地区	Kashgar [Kaxgar] Administrative Offices	181406	163367	277	17762
和田地区	Hotan Administrative Offices	15613	13045	28	2540
生产建设兵团	Production and Construction Group	529960	493482	991	35487

16-15 限额以上餐饮企业主要财务指标

Main Financial Indicators of Catering Enterprises above Designated Size

单位：万元 (2011 年) (10 000 yuan)

指标	Item	主营业务收入 Revenue from Principal Business	主营业务成本 Cost of Principal Business	主营业务税金及附加 Tax and Addition of Major Business	主营业务利润 Profit From Principal Business
总计	**Total**	**113591**	**57033**	**6063**	**50495**
按登记注册类型分	**By Status of Registration**				
内资企业	Domestic-funded Enterprises	88526	45367	4661	38498
国有企业	State – owned Enterprises	8772	3149	281	5342
有限责任公司	Limited Liability Corporations	13019	6952	650	5417
其他有限责任公司	Other Limited Liability Corporations	13019	6952	650	5417
股份有限公司	Share-holding Corporations Ltd	11236	4311	629	6296
私营企业	Private Enterprises	47442	26397	2679	18366
私营独资企业	Private-funded Enterprises	5806	2921	291	2594
私营合伙企业	Private Partnership Enterprises	861	417	44	400
私营有限责任公司	Private Limited Liability Corporations	40775	23059	2344	15372
其他企业	Others	8057	4558	422	3077
外商投资企业	Foreign Funded Enterprises	25065	11666	1402	11997
外资企业	Enterprises with Sole Fund	25065	11666	1402	11997
按餐饮行业小类分组	**By Sector of Catering**				
正餐服务	Dinner	75096	39955	3958	31183
快餐服务	Snack	38495	17078	2105	19312
按地区分	**By Region**				
乌鲁木齐市	Urumqi City	87162	41254	4654	41254
克拉玛依市	Karamay City	3783	2935	212	636
吐鲁番地区	Turpan Administrative Offices	386	331	21	34
昌吉回族自治州	Changji Hui Autonomous Prefecture	1053	789	29	235
伊犁哈萨克自治州直属县(市)	Ili Kazak Autonomous Prefecture	2188	1400	128	660
巴音郭楞蒙古自治州	Bayangol Mongol Autonomous Prefecture	11960	6645	708	4607
阿克苏地区	Aksu Administrative Offices	3517	1821	223	1473
喀什地区	Kashgar [Kaxgan] Administratine Offices	1025	348		677
生产建设兵团	Production and Construction Group	2517	1510	88	919

16-16 限额以上住宿企业主要财务指标
Main Financial Indicators of Hotels Enterprises above Designated

单位：万元　　(2011 年)　　(10 000 yuan)

指　标	Item	主营业务收入 Revenue from Principal Business	主营业务成本 Cost of Principal Business	主营业务税金及附加 Tax and Addition of Major Business	主营业务利润 Profit From Principal Business
总　计	**Total**	**362646**	**158416**	**20549**	**183681**
按登记注册类型分	**By Status of Registration**				
内资企业	Domestic-funded Enterprises	353091	155959	20017	177115
国有企业	State-owned Enterprises	129471	57966	6883	64622
集体企业	Collective-owned Enterprises	11393	3309	580	7504
联营企业	Joint Ownership Enterprises	527	66	30	431
国有联营企业	State Joint Ownership Enterprises	527	66	30	431
有限责任公司	Limited Liability Corporations	120912	65349	7241	48322
国有独资公司	State Sole Funded Corporations	10880	3187	609	7084
其他有限责任公司	Other Limited Liability Corporations	110032	62162	6632	41238
股份有限公司	Share-holding Corporations Ltd.	6912	3461	389	3062
私营企业	Private Enterprises	83876	25808	4894	53174
私营独资企业	Private-funded Enterprises	13775	3162	760	9853
私营合伙企业	Private Partnership Enterprises	1834	356	100	1378
私营有限责任公司	Private Limited Liability Corporation	68267	22290	4034	41943
港、澳、台商投资企业	Enterprises With Funds from Hong Kong, Macao and Taiwan	9276	2457	516	6303
合资经营企业（港或澳、台资）	Joint-venture Enterprises (Funds from Hong Kong, Macao and Taiwan)	9276	2457	516	6303
外商投资企业	Foreign Funded Enterprises	279		16	263
外资企业	Enterprises with Sole Fund	279		16	263
按住宿行业小类分组	**By Sector of National Economic**				
旅游饭店	Tourist Hotel	325519	138643	18429	168447
一般旅馆	Ordinary Hotel	37127	19773	2120	15234
按星级等级分	**Classified by Stars**				
五　星	Five-Star	107968	62152	6426	39390
四　星	Four-Star	83257	33137	4703	45417
三　星	Three-Star	119164	44705	6678	67781
二　星	Two-Star	19157	7046	936	11175
一　星	One-Star	1436	569	88	779
其　他	Other	31664	10807	1718	19139
按地区分	**By Region**				
乌鲁木齐市	Urumqi City	193354	81216	11449	100689
克拉玛依市	Karamay City	9745	10493	490	-1238
吐鲁番地区	Turpan Administrative Offices	4598	1427	283	2888
哈密地区	Hami [Kumul] Administrative Offices	18658	9871	867	7920
昌吉回族自治州	Changji Hui Autonomous Prefecture	5418	1918	279	3221
伊犁哈萨克自治州	Ili Kazak Autonomous Prefecture	50641	23345	2859	24437
伊犁州直属县(市)	Counties (Cities) Direct Under Ili Prefecture	34316	14415	1926	17975
塔城地区	Tacheng [Tarbagatai] Administrative Offices	5827	3254	398	2175
阿勒泰地区	Altay Administrative Offices	10498	5676	535	4287
博尔塔拉蒙古自治州	Bortala Mongol Autonomous Prefecture	3088	1580	156	1352
巴音郭楞蒙古自治州	Bayangol Mongol Autonomous Prefecture	20437	7659	1124	11654
阿克苏地区	Aksu Administrative Offices	10011	2642	570	6799
克孜勒苏柯尔克孜自治州	Kizilsu Kirgiz Autonomous Prefecture	1889	737	95	1057
喀什地区	Kashgar [Kaxgar] Administrative Offices	9482	4272	469	4741
和田地区	Hotan Administrative Offices	2990	1408	163	1419
生产建设兵团	Production and Construction Group	32335	11848	1745	18742

16-17 限额以上批发和零售业商品销售类值

Total Sales of Enterprises above Designated Size in Wholesale and Retail Trades by Category of Commodities

单位：万元 (10 000 yuan)

项目	Item	销售总额 Value		批发 Wholesale Trades		零售 Retail Trades	
		2010	2011	2010	2011	2010	2011
总计	**Total**	**39909349**	**51087375**	**34674711**	**44152710**	**5234638**	**6934665**
食品、饮料、烟酒类	Foods, Beverages, Tobacco and Liquor	2952397	3814777	2589202	3339677	363195	475100
服装、鞋帽类、针纺织品类	Garments, Shoes and Hats, Knitted Goods and Textiles	594526	852503	101594	214780	492932	637723
化妆品类	Cosmetics	102757	135089	25162	31996	77595	103093
金银珠宝类	Gold and Silver Jewelry	109579	185515	2921	2539	106658	182976
日用品类	Commodity Categories	157096	218831	35105	56086	121991	162745
五金、电料类	Hardwares, Electrical Materials	20675	45557	14116	35068	6559	10489
体育、娱乐用品类	Sports and Recreational Articles	22845	24422	3170	1607	19675	22815
书报杂志类	Books and Newspapers	245418	281857	116152	136198	129266	145659
电子出版物及音像制品类	E-journal and Video Products	2797	19987	741	32	2056	19955
家用电器及音像器材类	Household Appliances and Video Equipments	311083	457559	86616	167511	224467	290048
中西药品类	Chinese Traditional Medicine and Western Medicines	920952	1169320	351821	390973	569131	778347
文化办公用品类	Office Articles	233395	256063	142555	149050	90840	107013
家具类	Furnitures	120761	158285	577	1417	120184	156868
通讯器材类	Communication Appliances	100169	99913	44624	44136	55545	55777
煤炭及制品类	Coal and Related Products	139307	203513	131293	199984	8014	3529
木材及制品类	Wood and Wooden Products		1		1		
石油及制品类	Petroleum and Related Products	21392892	26927041	20189641	25330826	1203251	1596215
化工材料及制品类	Raw Chemical Materials and Related Products	1434494	1946394	1434494	1946394		
金属材料类	Metal Materials	2959212	3954438	2959212	3954438		
建筑装潢材料类	Building and Decoration Materials	126953	87550	115370	85604	11583	1946
机电产品及设备类	Mechanical and Electrical Products and Accessories	1001030	1265313	987138	1248659	13892	16654
汽车类	Automobile	2196787	2925083	616475	808837	1580312	2116246
种子饲料类	Seed and Fddestuff	147463	192480	147463	192480		
棉麻类	Cotton and Hemp	4139974	5250189	4137739	5250183	2235	6
其他类	Others	476787	615695	441730	564234	35057	51461

16-18 亿元以上商品交易市场总体情况

Statistics on Commodity Exchange Markets of Transaction Value over 100 Million Yuan

项　　目	Item	市场数(个) Number of Markets (unit)		总摊位数(个) Number of Booths (unit)		年末出租摊位数(个) Number of Rental Booths at Year-end (unit)	
		2010	2011	2010	2011	2010	2011
总　计	**Total**	**68**	**68**	**56123**	**57514**	**49667**	**51665**
按市场类别分组	**By Market Categories**						
综合市场	**Integrated Markets**	**28**	**25**	**33730**	**31288**	**29730**	**27983**
生产资料综合市场	Production Comprehensive Market	4	3	5953	6062	5953	6062
工业消费品综合市场	Industrial Consumable Comprehensive Markets	8	8	12067	11238	11208	11015
农产品综合市场	Farm Produce Comprehensive Markets	7	7	5809	6513	5454	5972
其他综合市场	Other Comprehensive Markets	9	7	9901	7475	7115	4934
专业市场	**Special Markets**	**40**	**43**	**22393**	**26226**	**19937**	**23682**
生产资料市场	Production Markets	9	9	5880	6299	5543	5427
农用生产资料	Agricultural Production Markets	3	3	818	818	596	626
煤炭市场	Coal and Charcoal Markets	1	1	45	45	45	45
金属材料市场	Metal Materials Markets	2	2	853	654	810	654
机械设备市场	Mechanical Equipments Markets	1	1	1152	1100	1151	500
其他生产资料市场	Others	2	2	3012	3682	2941	3602
农产品市场	Farm Produce Markets	12	13	3429	3962	2543	2951
粮油市场	Grain and Oil Markets	1	1	181	181	110	96
肉禽蛋市场	Meat, Poultry and Eggs Markets	3	3	205	225	205	225
水产品市场	Aquatic Products Markets	1	1	400	400	400	400
蔬菜市场	Vegetables Markets	3	4	998	1514	750	1162
干鲜果市场	Dried and Fresh Melons and Fruits Markets	2	2	1212	1212	645	663
其他农产品市场	Others	2	2	433	430	433	405
食品、饮料及烟酒市场市场	Food, Beverages, Tobacco and Liquor Markets	2	3	1101	1263	780	717
食品饮料市场	Food and Beverages Markets	1	2	825	1025	548	479
其他食品饮料及烟酒市场	Others	1	1	276	238	232	238
纺织、服装、鞋帽市场	Textiles, Clothing, Shoes and Hats Markets	8	9	9075	11293	8308	11206
服装市场	Clothing Markets	5	6	4845	7045	4083	6958
其他纺织服装鞋帽市场	Others	3	3	4230	4248	4225	4248
电器、通讯器材、电子设备市场	Electrical Appliances, Communication Appliances and Electronical Appliances Markets	2	2	762	778	750	771
计算机及辅助设备市场	Computer and Auxillary Equipments Markets	2	2	762	778	750	771
家具、五金及装饰材料市场	Furniture, Hardware and Decoration Materials Markets	3	3	997	1429	990	1429
家具市场	Furniture Markets	1	1	416	416	409	416
装饰材料市场	Decoration Materials Markets	1	1	325	325	325	325
其他装饰市场	Others	1	1	256	688	256	688
汽车、摩托车及零配件市场	Cars, Motorcycles and Spare Parts Markets	3	3	827	702	701	681
汽车市场	Cars Markets	3	3	827	702	701	681
花、鸟、鱼、虫市场	Flower, Bird, Fish and Insects Markets	1	1	322	500	322	500
花卉市场	Flower Markets	1	1	322	500	322	500
按营业状态分组	**By Operating State**						
常年营业	Business Year	65	66	55472	54669	49049	48820
季节性营业	Seasonal Business	3	2	651	2845	618	2845
按经营方式分组	**By Mode of Operating**						
以批发为主	Mainly in the Wholesale	46	46	39839	38587	34428	33576
以零售为主	Mainly in the Retail	22	22	16284	18927	15239	18089
按经营环境分组	**By Operating Environment**						
露天式	Open Type	15	17	15599	12090	11825	9209
封闭式	Closed Type	45	46	36997	43289	34510	40391
其　他	Others	8	5	3527	2135	3332	2065

16-18 续表 Continued

项目	Item	营业面积(平方米) Operating Area (sq.m)		成交额(万元) Turnouer (100 million yuan)	
		2010	2011	2010	2011
总 计	**Total**	**5219629**	**5243876**	**6337074**	**7787385**
按市场类别分组	**By Market Categories**				
综合市场	**Integrated Markets**	**2599219**	**2386997**	**2268032**	**2556501**
生产资料综合市场	Production Comprehensive Market	838250	725348	576589	451772
工业消费品综合市场	Industrial Consumable Comprehensive Markets	522422	822892	345111	542081
农产品综合市场	Farm Produce Comprehensive Markets	343776	379776	983234	1224917
其他综合市场	Other Comprehensive Markets	894771	458981	363098	337731
专业市场	**Special Markets**	**2620410**	**2856879**	**4069042**	**5230884**
生产资料市场	Production Markets	1232716	777122	2050719	2840163
农用生产资料	Agricultural Production Markets	86090	86090	155847	142912
煤炭市场	Coal and Charcoal Markets	340	2000	156913	175120
金属材料市场	Metal Materials Markets	436283	320029	1137817	2289500
机械设备市场	Mechanical Equipments Markets	130000	100000	450000	30000
其他生产资料市场	Others	580003	269003	150142	202631
农产品市场	Farm Produce Markets	482680	985269	537851	825516
粮油市场	Grain and Oil Markets	10000	10000	30000	71820
肉禽蛋市场	Meat, Poultry and Eggs Markets	112742	708671	112612	188920
水产品市场	Aquatic Products Markets	5200	5200	92000	100000
蔬菜市场	Vegetables Markets	48998	78998	128783	271746
干鲜果市场	Dried and Fresh Melons and Fruits Markets	115000	115000	97802	114672
其他农产品市场	Others	190740	67400	76654	78358
食品、饮料及烟酒市场市场	Food, Beverages, Tobacco and Liquor Markets	49950	57450	54438	85112
食品饮料市场	Food and Beverages Markets	32946	39960	24849	52428
其他食品饮料及烟酒市场	Others	17004	17490	29589	32684
纺织、服装、鞋帽市场	Textiles, Clothing, Shoes and Hats Markets	221567	319534	877170	753825
服装市场	Clothing Markets	106296	203512	752925	569557
其他纺织服装鞋帽市场	Others	115271	116022	124245	184268
电器、通讯器材、电子设备市场	Electrical Appliances, Communication Appliances and Electronical Appliances Markets	11110	17098	45325	44040
计算机及辅助设备市场	Computer and Auxillary Equipments Markets	11110	17098	45325	44040
家具、五金及装饰材料市场	Furniture, Hardware and Decoration Materials Markets	189053	212653	53354	111560
家具市场	Furniture Markets	44053	44053	22777	31077
装饰材料市场	Decoration Materials Markets	70000	70000	13871	15477
其他装饰市场	Others	75000	98600	16706	65006
汽车、摩托车及零配件市场	Cars, Motorcycles and Spare Parts Markets	333334	387753	436925	538668
汽车市场	Cars Markets	333334	387753	436925	538668
花、鸟、鱼、虫市场	Flower, Bird, Fish and Insects Markets	100000	100000	13260	32000
花卉市场	Flower Markets	100000	100000	13260	32000
按营业状态分组	**By Operating State**				
常年营业	Business Year	5141289	5161876	6153109	7481473
季节性营业	Seasonal Business	78340	82000	183965	305912
按经营方式分组	**By Mode of Operating**				
以批发为主	Mainly in the Wholesale	4069070	3997593	5523017	6619651
以零售为主	Mainly in the Retail	1150559	1246283	814057	1167734
按经营环境分组	**By Operating Environment**				
露天式	Open Type	1107754	1550986	1176187	1471101
封闭式	Closed Type	3327792	3522224	4770577	5954996
其 他	Others	784083	170666	390310	361288

16-19 商品交易市场成交情况(按摊位分)

Basic Statistics on Commodity Exchange Markets (by Booths)

项目	Item	年末出租摊位数(个) Number of Booths at Year-end (unit)		成交额(万元) Turnover (100 million yuan)	
		2010	2011	2010	2011
总计	**Total**	**49850**	**51665**	**6337074**	**7787385**
食品、饮料、烟酒类	Food, Beverages, Tobacco and Liquor	11594	12108	1702618	2242385
粮油、食品类	Food,Grain and Oil	10622	11185	1617752	2147558
粮油类	Grain and Oil	898	912	83629	133453
肉禽蛋类	Meat, Poultry and Eggs	1131	1220	235355	348554
水产品类	Aquatic Products	784	765	193718	212328
蔬菜类	Vegetables	4030	4345	563421	609506
干鲜果品类	Dried and Fresh Melons and Fruits	2710	2847	475161	447654
饮料类	Beverages	467	510	42535	52591
烟酒类	Tobacco and Liquor	505	413	42331	42236
服装、鞋帽、针纺织品类	Clothing, Shoes, Hats and Textiles	14166	14396	905932	768499
服装类	Clothing	8725	9019	722637	510830
鞋帽类	Footwear and Hats	3250	3091	147147	211140
针纺织品类	Knitwear and Textiles	2191	2286	36148	46529
化妆品类	Cosmetics	797	734	34413	35933
金银珠宝类	Gold, Silver and Jewellery	175	185	10438	62122
日用品类	Articles for Daily Use	2779	2610	99460	131255
洗涤用品类	Washing Articles	1303	765	76568	60009
儿童玩具类	Children Toys	571	368	13774	8833
五金、电料类	Hardware & Electrical Materials	1621	2672	68507	135130
体育、娱乐用品类	Sports & Recreational Articles	214	379	10781	18849
书报杂志类	Newspapers and Magazines	77	262	1430	12974
电子出版物及音像制品类	E-journal and Video Products	201	329	12966	14946
家用电器和音像器材类	Household Appliances and Video Equipments	1205	1243	99048	102991
中西药品类	Traditional Chinese and Western Medicine	128	192	7743	9951
西药类	Western Medicine	43	79	4592	4242
中草药及中成药类	Traditional Chinese	29	61	998	4026
文化办公用品类	Cultural and Official Goods	1317	1550	86600	91453
家具类	Furniture	2891	2962	142061	148344
通讯器材类	Communication Appliances	294	292	16175	16313
煤炭及制品类	Coal and Related Products	211	259	168557	186916
木材及制品类	Wood and Wooden Products	769	689	28904	23360
石油及制品类	Petroleum and Related Products	156	176	10037	12044
化工材料及制品类	Raw Chemical Materials and Related Products	1199	1347	221251	228923
化肥类	Fertilizer	595	624	166816	172189
金属材料类	Metal Materials	1393	1284	1244348	2406791
建筑及装潢材料类	Building and Decoration Materials	2121	2034	205936	188105
机电产品及设备类	Mechanical & Electrical Products	2146	1306	508369	86721
农机类	Agricultural Machinery	74	125	9612	12040
汽车类	Automobile	888	877	535137	619942
种子饲料类	Seed and Feedstuff	309	336	34146	24546
棉麻类	Cotton and Hemp	28	18	444	346
其他类	Others	3171	3425	181773	218546

16-20 各地区商品交易市场总体情况

Basic Statistics on Commodity Exchange Markets by Region

项　　目	Item	市场数(个) Number of Markets (unit)		总摊位数(个) Number of Booths (unit)		年末出租摊位数(个) Number of Rental booths at Year-end (unit)	
		2010	2011	2010	2011	2010	2011
总　计	**Total**	**68**	**68**	**56123**	**57514**	**49667**	**51665**
乌鲁木齐市	Urumqi City	26	25	23307	23097	22102	21994
克拉玛依市	Karamay City	1	1	593	516	436	416
吐鲁番地区	Turpan Administrative Offices	1	1	650	650	620	650
哈密地区	Hami [Kumul] Administrative Offices	1	1	896	896	896	896
昌吉回族自治州	Changji Hui Autonomous Prefecture	2	2	3441	3998	3422	3521
伊犁哈萨克自治州直属县(市)	Ili Kazak Autonomous Prefecture	9	10	4838	5605	4702	5528
巴音郭楞蒙古自治州	Bayangol Mongol Autonomous Prefecture	9	9	7997	8031	4698	4744
阿克苏地区	Aksu Administrative Offices	3	3	1555	1555	1380	1322
喀什地区	Kashgar [Kaxgar] Administrative Offices	4	4	3495	6757	3447	6757
和田地区	Hotan Administrative Offices	2	2	4980	2187	4140	2117
生产建设兵团	Xinjiang Production and Construction Group	10	10	4371	4222	3824	3720

项　　目	Item	营业面积(平方米) Operating Area (sq.m)		成交额(万元) Turnover (100 million Yuan)	
		2010	2011	2010	2011
总　计	**Total**	**5219629**	**5243876**	**6337074**	**7787385**
乌鲁木齐市	Urumqi City	2583754	2235670	4631001	5538383
克拉玛依市	Karamay City	30000	30000	65000	64949
吐鲁番地区	Turpan Administrative Offices	15000	15000	72471	94230
哈密地区	Hami [Kumul] Administrative Offices	19249	20000	29583	25437
昌吉回族自治州	Changji Hui Autonomous Prefecture	320303	320303	107604	118523
伊犁哈萨克自治州直属县(市)	Ili Kazak Autonomous Prefecture	690894	756894	291503	493238
巴音郭楞蒙古自治州	Bayangol Mongol Autonomous Prefecture	734449	653164	374465	339443
阿克苏地区	Aksu Administrative Offices	355340	357000	317112	387138
喀什地区	Kashgar [Kaxgar] Administrative Offices	82250	513750	91718	289780
和田地区	Hotan Administrative Offices	153528	99859	66653	115111
生产建设兵团	Production and Construction Group	234862	242236	289964	321153

16-21 连锁零售企业总体情况
Total Conditions of Chain Retail Enterprises

项　　目　　Item	合　计 Total		直营店 Straight Camp Shop		加盟店 Join in Store	
	2010	2011	2010	2011	2010	2011
连锁总店数(个) Number of Head Stores (unit)		**95**				
连锁门店总数(个) Number of Stores (unit)	3409	3606	2871	3056	538	550
年末从业人员数(人) Engaged Persons at Year-end (person)	24875	29210	23626	28141	1249	1069
年末零售营业面积(平方米) Operating Area of Retail Enterprises at Year-end (sq.m)	3361951	3500086	3267032	3391332	94919	108754
连锁门店商品购进总额(万元) Total Purchases Value of Chain Stores (100 million yuan)	3531540	5378640	3459832	5289355	71709	89285
其中:统一配送商品购进额(万元) Centralized Purchase and Delivery (100 million yuan)	3049600	4342326	2982220	4257410	67380	84916
其中:自有配送中心配送商品购进额(万元) Own Purchase and Delivery (100 million yuan)	2844207	3985230	2833755	3969476	10452	15755
非自有配送中心配送商品购进额(万元) Public Puchase and Delivery (100 million yuan)	204735	356368	147807	287206	56928	69162
商品销售额(万元) Total Sales of Commodities (100 million yuan)	4033582	6031604	3961913	5813995	71669	217609
其中:零售额(万元) Of which:Retail of value	2053910	2706632	2018833	2649612	35077	57019

16-22 连锁零售企业基本情况
Basic Condition of Chain Retail Enterprises

项　目	Item	连锁总店数 Number of Chain Stores	门店数合计(个) Total Stores (unit)	
			2010	2011
总　计	**Total**	**95**	**3409**	**3606**
按登记注册类型分组	**by Status of Registration**			
内资企业	Domestic Funded Enterprises	94	3406	3603
国有企业	State-owned Enterprises	36	1906	2030
集体企业	Collective-owned Enterprises	1	8	8
有限责任公司	Limited Liability Corporations	19	397	417
国有独资公司	State Sole Funded Corporations	1	6	11
其他有限责任公司	Other Limited Liability Corporations	18	391	406
股份有限公司	Share-holding Corporations Ltd.	10	368	382
私营企业	Private Enterprises	27	642	721
私营有限责任公司	Private-funded Enterprises	27	642	721
其他企业	Other Enterprises	1	85	45
外商投资企业	Foreign Funded Enterprises	1	3	3
外资企业	Enterprises with Sole Fund	1	3	3
按行业分组	**By Sector**			
批发业	**Wholesale**	**29**	**2012**	**2165**
农畜产品批发	Wholesale of Farm Produce and Livestock Products	1	7	7
食品、饮料及烟草制品专门批发	Special Wholesale of Food, Beverages and Tobaccos	4	34	32
医药及医疗器材批发	Wholesale of Medicines and Medical Appliances	3	87	89
矿产品、建材及化工产品批发	Wholesale of Minerals、Building Materials and Chemical Materiac	21	1884	2037
零售业	**Wholesale**	**66**	**1397**	**1441**
综合零售	Wholesale of Farm Produce and Livestock Products	11	312	336
食品、饮料及烟草制品专门零售	Special Wholesale of Food, Beverages and Tobaccos	1	6	11
纺织、服装及日用品专门零售	Wholesale of Medicines and Medical Appliances	1	3	3
文化、体育用品及器材专门零售	Wholesale	14	112	114
医药及医疗器材专门零售	Wholesale of Farm Produce and Livestock Products	23	684	652
汽车、摩托车、燃料及零配件专门零售	Special Wholesale of Food, Beverages and Tobaccos	5	171	193
家用电器及电子产品专门零售	Wholesale of Medicines and Medical Appliances	9	73	88
五金、家具及室内装修材料专门零售	Wholesale	1	33	41
无店铺及其他零售	Wholesale of Farm Produce and Livestock Products	1	3	3
按业态分组	**By Business Categories**			
便利店	Convenience Store	1	52	80
超　市	Supermarket	5	41	49
大型超市	Hypermarket	2	6	6
百货店	Department Store	1	82	82
专业店	Specialty Store	58	2355	2462
加油站	Gas Station	19	766	815
专卖店	Franchised Store	8	78	84
其　他	Other Store	1	29	28

16-22 续表 1 Continued

项目	Item	年末从业人员数(人) Engaged Persons at Year-end (person)		年末零售营业面积(平方米) Operating Area of Retail Enterprises at Year-end (sq.m)	
		2010	2011	2010	2011
总　计	**Total**	**24875**	**29210**	**3361951**	**3500086**
按登记注册类型分组	**by Status of Registration**				
内资企业	Domestic Funded Enterprises	24335	28282	3210951	3471344
国有企业	State-owned Enterprises	8566	8945	1691530	1871780
集体企业	Collective-owned Enterprises	50	50	45000	45000
有限责任公司	Limited Liability Corporations	3939	5615	244903	257819
国有独资公司	State Sole Funded Corporations	40	181	690	690
其他有限责任公司	Other Limited Liability Corporations	3899	5434	244213	257129
股份有限公司	Share-holding Corporations Ltd.	5086	6165	944585	977399
私营企业	Private Enterprises	6513	7335	280561	315100
私营有限责任公司	Private-funded Enterprises	6513	7335	280561	315100
其他企业	Other Enterprises	181	172	4372	4246
外商投资企业	Foreign Funded Enterprises	540	928	151000	28742
外资企业	Enterprises with Sole Fund	540	928	151000	28742
按行业分组	**By Sector**				
批发业	**Wholesale**	**9999**	**10595**	**1932152**	**2127589**
农畜产品批发	Wholesale of Farm Produce and Livestock Products	67	67	1050	1050
食品、饮料及烟草制品专门批发	Special Wholesale of Food, Beverages and Tobaccos	673	717	337730	352080
医药及医疗器材批发	Wholesale of Medicines and Medical Appliances	278	280	6875	5961
矿产品、建材及化工产品批发	Wholesale of Minerals、Building Materials and Chemical Material	8981	9531	1586497	1768498
零售业	**Wholesale**	**14876**	**18615**	**1429799**	**1372497**
综合零售	Wholesale of Farm Produce and Livestock Products	3535	4196	318917	215010
食品、饮料及烟草制品专门零售	Special Wholesale of Food, Beverages and Tobaccos	40	181	690	690
纺织、服装及日用品专门零售	Wholesale of Medicines and Medical Appliances	12	9	300	150
文化、体育用品及器材专门零售	Wholesale	1610	1822	114309	100631
医药及医疗器材专门零售	Wholesale of Farm Produce and Livestock Products	3409	3751	78857	81926
汽车、摩托车、燃料及零配件专门零售	Special Wholesale of Food, Beverages and Tobaccos	2025	2707	713416	747089
家用电器及电子产品专门零售	Wholesale of Medicines and Medical Appliances	2150	2577	111219	148968
五金、家具及室内装修材料专门零售	Wholesale	1980	3257	89091	75033
无店铺及其他零售	Wholesale of Farm Produce and Livestock Products	115	115	3000	3000
按业态分组	**By Business Categories**				
便利店	Convenience Store	443	374	15800	26359
超　市	Supermarket	1174	1455	74520	104827
大型超市	Hypermarket	1373	1769	215672	71213
百货店	Department Store	96	96	3175	3175
专业店	Specialty Store	8523	9700	679654	708853
加油站	Gas Station	10344	11563	1936988	2149040
专卖店	Franchised Store	2887	4214	435087	435455
其　他	Other Store	35	39	1055	1164

16-22 续表 2 Continued

项　目	Item	直营店门店数(个) Straight Camp Shop (unit)		年末从业人员数(人) Engaged Persons at Year-end (person)	
		2010	2011	2010	2011
总　计	**Total**	**2871**	**3056**	**23626**	**28141**
按登记注册类型分组	**by Status of Registration**				
内资企业	Domestic Funded Enterprises	2868	3053	23086	27213
国有企业	State-owned Enterprises	1648	1716	8250	8635
集体企业	Collective-owned Enterprises	8	8	50	50
有限责任公司	Limited Liability Corporations	338	380	3829	5511
国有独资公司	State Sole Funded Corporations	6	11	40	181
其他有限责任公司	Other Limited Liability Corporations	332	369	3789	5330
股份有限公司	Share-holding Corporations Ltd.	368	382	5086	6165
私营企业	Private Enterprises	476	533	5790	6702
私营有限责任公司	Private-funded Enterprises	476	533	5790	6702
其他企业	Other Enterprises	30	34	81	150
外商投资企业	Foreign Funded Enterprises	3	3	540	928
外资企业	Enterprises with Sole Fund	3	3	540	928
按行业分组	**By Sector**				
批发业	**Wholesale**	**1820**	**1917**	**9762**	**10364**
农畜产品批发	Wholesale of Farm Produce and Livestock Products	7	7	67	67
食品、饮料及烟草制品专门批发	Special Wholesale of Food, Beverages and Tobaccos	34	32	673	717
医药及医疗器材批发	Wholesale of Medicines and Medical Appliances	87	89	278	280
矿产品、建材及化工产品批发	Wholesale of Minerals、Building Materials and Chemical Material	1692	1789	8744	9300
零售业	**Wholesale**	**1051**	**1139**	**13864**	**17777**
综合零售	Wholesale of Farm Produce and Livestock Products	163	168	2875	3604
食品、饮料及烟草制品专门零售	Special Wholesale of Food, Beverages and Tobaccos	6	11	40	181
纺织、服装及日用品专门零售	Wholesale of Medicines and Medical Appliances	3	3	12	9
文化、体育用品及器材专门零售	Wholesale	112	114	1610	1822
医药及医疗器材专门零售	Wholesale of Farm Produce and Livestock Products	487	518	3057	3505
汽车、摩托车、燃料及零配件专门零售	Special Wholesale of Food, Beverages and Tobaccos	171	193	2025	2707
家用电器及电子产品专门零售	Wholesale of Medicines and Medical Appliances	73	88	2150	2577
五金、家具及室内装修材料专门零售	Wholesale	33	41	1980	3257
无店铺及其他零售	Wholesale of Farm Produce and Livestock Products	3	3	115	115
按业态分组	**By Business Categories**				
便利店	Convenience Store	23	23	140	138
超　市	Supermarket	11	18	948	1206
大型超市	Hypermarket	6	6	1373	1769
百货店	Department Store	16	16	17	17
专业店	Specialty Store	1968	2093	8063	9376
加油站	Gas Station	740	788	10163	11382
专卖店	Franchised Store	78	84	2887	4214
其　他	Other Store	29	28	35	39

16-22 续表 3 Continued

项　目	Item	年末零售营业面积(平方米) Operating Area of Retail Enterprises at Year-end (sq.m)		加盟店门店数(个) Number of Join in Stores (unit)	
		2010	2011	2010	2011
总　计	**Total**	**3267032**	**3391332**	**538**	**550**
按登记注册类型分组	**by Status of Registration**				
内资企业	Domestic Funded Enterprises	3116032	3362590	538	550
国有企业	State-owned Enterprises	1653379	1843429	258	314
集体企业	Collective-owned Enterprises	45000	45000		
有限责任公司	Limited Liability Corporations	230253	235749	59	37
国有独资公司	State Sole Funded Corporations	690	690		
其他有限责任公司	Other Limited Liability Corporations	229563	235059	59	37
股份有限公司	Share-holding Corporations Ltd.	944585	977399		
私营企业	Private Enterprises	240335	257499	166	188
私营有限责任公司	Private-funded Enterprises	240335	257499	166	188
其他企业	Other Enterprises	2480	3514	55	11
外商投资企业	Foreign Funded Enterprises	151000	28742		
外资企业	Enterprises with Sole Fund	151000	28742		
按行业分组	**By Sector**				
批发业	**Wholesale**	**1896169**	**2101406**	**192**	**248**
农畜产品批发	Wholesale of Farm Produce and Livestock Products	1050	1050		
食品、饮料及烟草制品专门批发	Special Wholesale of Food, Beverages and Tobaccos	337730	352080		
医药及医疗器材批发	Wholesale of Medicines and Medical Appliances	6875	5961		
矿产品、建材及化工产品批发	Wholesale of Minerals、Building Materials and Chemical Material	1550514	1742315	192	248
零售业	**Wholesale**	**1370863**	**1289926**	**346**	**302**
综合零售	Wholesale of Farm Produce and Livestock Products	270899	141027	149	168
食品、饮料及烟草制品专门零售	Special Wholesale of Food, Beverages and Tobaccos	690	690		
纺织、服装及日用品专门零售	Wholesale of Medicines and Medical Appliances	300	150		
文化、体育用品及器材专门零售	Wholesale	114309	100631		
医药及医疗器材专门零售	Wholesale of Farm Produce and Livestock Products	67939	73338	197	134
汽车、摩托车、燃料及零配件专门零售	Special Wholesale of Food, Beverages and Tobaccos	713416	747089		
家用电器及电子产品专门零售	Wholesale of Medicines and Medical Appliances	111219	148968		
五金、家具及室内装修材料专门零售	Wholesale	89091	75033		
无店铺及其他零售	Wholesale of Farm Produce and Livestock Products	3000	3000		
按业态分组	**By Business Categories**				
便利店	Convenience Store	8000	7681	29	57
超　市	Supermarket	37570	52190	30	31
大型超市	Hypermarket	215672	71213		
百货店	Department Store	1007	1007	66	66
专业店	Specialty Store	654653	696782	387	369
加油站	Gas Station	1913988	2125840	26	27
专卖店	Franchised Store	435087	435455		
其　他	Other Store	1055	1164		

16-22 续表 4 Continued

项　　目	Item	年末从业人员数(人) Engaged Persons at Year-end (person)		年末零售营业面积(平方米) Operating Area of Retail Enterprises at Year-end (sq.m)	
		2010	2011	2010	2011
总　计	**Total**	**1249**	**1069**	**94919**	**108754**
按登记注册类型分组	**by Status of Registration**				
内资企业	Domestic Funded Enterprises	1249	1069	94919	108754
国有企业	State-owned Enterprises	316	310	38151	28351
集体企业	Collective-owned Enterprises				
有限责任公司	Limited Liability Corporations	110	104	14650	22070
国有独资公司	State Sole Funded Corporations				
其他有限责任公司	Other Limited Liability Corporations	110	104	14650	22070
股份有限公司	Share-holding Corporations Ltd.				
私营企业	Private Enterprises	723	633	40226	57601
私营有限责任公司	Private-funded Enterprises	723	633	40226	57601
其他企业	Other Enterprises	100	22	1892	732
外商投资企业	Foreign Funded Enterprises				
外资企业	Enterprises with Sole Fund				
按行业分组	**By Sector**				
批发业	**Wholesale**	**237**	**231**	**35983**	**26183**
农畜产品批发	Wholesale of Farm Produce and Livestock Products				
食品、饮料及烟草制品专门批发	Special Wholesale of Food, Beverages and Tobaccos				
医药及医疗器材批发	Wholesale of Medicines and Medical Appliances				
矿产品、建材及化工产品批发	Wholesale of Minerals、Building Materials and Chemical Materiac	237	231	35983	26183
零售业	**Wholesale**	**1012**	**838**	**58936**	**82571**
综合零售	Wholesale of Farm Produce and Livestock Products	660	592	48018	73983
食品、饮料及烟草制品专门零售	Special Wholesale of Food, Beverages and Tobaccos				
纺织、服装及日用品专门零售	Wholesale of Medicines and Medical Appliances				
文化、体育用品及器材专门零售	Wholesale				
医药及医疗器材专门零售	Wholesale of Farm Produce and Livestock Products	352	246	10918	8588
汽车、摩托车、燃料及零配件专门零售	Special Wholesale of Food, Beverages and Tobaccos				
家用电器及电子产品专门零售	Wholesale of Medicines and Medical Appliances				
五金、家具及室内装修材料专门零售	Wholesale				
无店铺及其他零售	Wholesale of Farm Produce and Livestock Products				
按业态分组	**By Business Categories**				
便利店	Convenience Store	303	236	7800	18678
超　市	Supermarket	226	249	36950	52637
大型超市	Hypermarket				
百货店	Department Store	79	79	2168	2168
专业店	Specialty Store	460	324	25001	12071
加油站	Gas Station	181	181	23000	23200
专卖店	Franchised Store				
其　他	Other Store				

16-23 连锁餐饮企业总体情况
Total Conditions of Chain Catering Enterprises

项目	Item	合计 Total 2010	合计 Total 2011	直营店 Straight Camp Shop 2010	直营店 Straight Camp Shop 2011
连锁总店数(个)	Number of Chain Stores (unit)		8		
门店总数(个)	Number of Stores (unit)	117	146	74	100
年末从业人员数(人)	Engaged Persons at Year-end (person)	2858	3873	2526	3517
年末餐饮营业面积(平方米)	Operating Area of Catering Enterprises at Year-end (sq.m)	27002	34040	24002	30940
客房数(间)	Number of Hotel Rooms (unit)	350	348	350	348
床位数(个)	Number of Beds (unit)	674	665	674	665
餐位数(位)	Number of Dining-seats (unit)	9894	13344	8334	11784
连锁门店商品购进（采购）额(万元)	Total Purchases Value of Chain Stores (100 million yuan)	11718	13764	11382	13399
其中:统一配送商品购进（采购）额(万元)	of which:Centralized Purchase and Delivery (100 million yuan)	11689	13735	11369	13387
其中:自有配送中心配送商品购进（采购）额(万元)	Purchases Value of Its Own Distribution Center	8832	10470	8512	10122
非自有配送中心配送商品购进（采购）额(万元)	Purchases Value of Non Its Own Distribution Center	2857	3265	2857	3265
连锁门店营业额(万元)	Business Revenue of Chain Store (100 million yuan)	35250	48806	33140	46534
其中:餐费收入(万元)	of which:From Meals (100 million yuan)	33541	46898	31629	44967

项目	Item	加盟店 Join in Store 2010	加盟店 Join in Store 2011
连锁总店数(个)	Number of Chain Stores (unit)		
门店总数(个)	Number of Stores (unit)	43	46
年末从业人员数(人)	Engaged Persons at Year-end (person)	332	356
年末餐饮营业面积(平方米)	Operating Area of Catering Enterprises at Year-end (sq.m)	3000	3100
客房数(间)	Number of Hotel Rooms (unit)		
床位数(个)	Number of Beds (unit)		
餐位数(位)	Number of Dining-seats (unit)	1560	1560
连锁门店商品购进（采购）额(万元)	Total Purchases Value of Chain Stores (100 million yuan)	337	365
其中:统一配送商品购进（采购）额(万元)	of which:Centralized Purchase and Delivery (100 million yuan)	320	348
其中:自有配送中心配送商品购进（采购）额(万元)	Purchases Value of Its Own Distribution Center	320	348
非自有配送中心配送商品购进（采购）额(万元)	Purchases Value of Non Its Own Distribution Center		
连锁门店营业额(万元)	Business Revenue of Chain Store (100 million yuan)	2110	2272
其中:餐费收入(万元)	of which:From Meals (100 million yuan)	1912	1931

16-24 连锁餐饮企业基本情况
Basic Condition of Chain Catering Enterprises

项　　目	Item	连锁总店数 Number of Head Stores (unit)	门店数合计(个) Total Stores (unit)		年末从业人员数(人) Engaged Persons at Year-end (person)	
			2010	2011	2010	2011
总　计	**Total**	**8**	**117**	**146**	**2858**	**3873**
按登记注册类型分组	**By Status of Registration**					
内资企业	Domestic Funded Enterprises	7	96	124	1783	2544
有限责任公司	Limited Liability Corporations	1	3	3	254	181
其他有限责任公司	Other Limited Liability Corporations	1	3	3	254	181
股份有限公司	Share-holding Corporations Ltd.	1	18	39	579	1343
私营企业	Private Enterprises	5	75	82	950	1020
私营有限责任公司	Private-funded Enterprises	5	75	82	950	1020
外商投资企业	Foreign Funded Enterprises	1	21	22	1075	1329
外资企业	Enterprises with Sole Fund	1	21	22	1075	1329
按行业分组	**By Sector**					
正餐服务	Restaurant Services	3	13	15	477	406
快餐服务	Fast Food Services	5	104	131	2381	3467

项　　目	Item	年末餐饮营业面积(平方米) Operating Area of Catering Enterprises at Year-end (sq.m)		#直营店门店数(个) Number of Straight Camp Shop (unit)	
		2010	2011	2010	2011
总　计	**Total**	**27002**	**34040**	**74**	**100**
按登记注册类型分组	**By Status of Registration**				
内资企业	Domestic Funded Enterprises	18721	24897	53	78
有限责任公司	Limited Liability Corporations	3824	3824	3	3
其他有限责任公司	Other Limited Liability Corporations	3824	3824	3	3
股份有限公司	Share-holding Corporations Ltd.	5239	11385	18	39
私营企业	Private Enterprises	9658	9688	32	36
私营有限责任公司	Private-funded Enterprises	9658	9688	32	36
外商投资企业	Foreign Funded Enterprises	8281	9143	21	22
外资企业	Enterprises with Sole Fund	8281	9143	21	22
按行业分组	**By Sector**				
正餐服务	Restaurant Services	6182	6212	13	15
快餐服务	Fast Food Services	20820	27828	61	85

16-24 续表 1 Continued

项　　目	Item	年末从业人员数(人) Engaged Persons at Year-end (person)		年末餐饮营业面积(平方米) Operating Area of Catering Enterprises at Year-end (sq.m)		#加盟店门店数(个) Number of Join in Store (unit)	
		2010	2011	2010	2011	2010	2011
总　计	**Total**	**2526**	**3517**	**24002**	**30940**	**43**	**46**
按登记注册类型分组	**By Status of Registration**						
内资企业	Domestic Funded Enterprises	1451	2188	15721	21797	43	46
有限责任公司	Limited Liability Corporations	254	181	3824	3824		
其他有限责任公司	Other Limited Liability Corporations	254	181	3824	3824		
股份有限公司	Share-holding Corporations Ltd.	579	1343	5239	11385		
私营企业	Private Enterprises	618	664	6658	6588	43	46
私营有限责任公司	Private-funded Enterprises	618	664	6658	6588	43	46
外商投资企业	Foreign Funded Enterprises	1075	1329	8281	9143		
外资企业	Enterprises with Sole Fund	1075	1329	8281	9143		
按行业分组	**By Sector**						
正餐服务	Restaurant Services	477	406	6182	6212		
快餐服务	Fast Food Services	2049	3111	17820	24728	43	46

项　　目	Item	年末从业人员数(人) Engaged Persons at Year-end (person)		年末餐饮营业面积(平方米) Operating Area of Catering Enterprises at Year-end (sq.m)	
		2010	2011	2010	2011
总　计	**Total**	**332**	**356**	**3000**	**3100**
按登记注册类型分组	**By Status of Registration**				
内资企业	Domestic Funded Enterprises	332	356	3000	3100
有限责任公司	Limited Liability Corporations				
其他有限责任公司	Other Limited Liability Corporations				
股份有限公司	Share-holding Corporations Ltd.				
私营企业	Private Enterprises	332	356	3000	3100
私营有限责任公司	Private-funded Enterprises	332	356	3000	3100
外商投资企业	Foreign Funded Enterprises				
外资企业	Enterprises with Sole Fund				
按行业分组	**By Sector**				
正餐服务	Restaurant Services				
快餐服务	Fast Food Services	332	356	3000	3100

主要统计指标解释

社会消费品零售总额　指批发和零售业、餐饮业、新闻出版业、邮政业和其他服务业等，售予城乡居民用于生活消费的商品和社会集团用于公共消费的商品之总量。社会消费品零售总额包括：

一、批发和零售业企业（单位）售予城乡居民用于生活消费和社会集团用于公共消费的商品。包括：

1.售予城乡居民的各种生活消费品；

2.售予入境旅游的外国人、华侨、港澳台同胞的各类商品；

3.售予行政事业单位、社会团体、军队和武警等机构的商品，以及以零售方式售予各类企业的商品。具体包括：用于非生产和社会交往的办公用品，如通讯设备、计算器具和设备、电讯网络设备、文印设备、音像视听器材和设备、纸张、本册、文具及装订文印材料、家具、日用电器、针纺织品、清洁卫生用品、文体用品、奖品、纪念品、礼品等；供内部人员乘坐的交通工具和燃料；用于办公设施修缮的各类配件、材料、工具等；用于取暖和防暑降温的设备、燃料、材料及食品等；专用于教学的用品和设备；非营利医疗机构的中、西药品、中药材和医疗设备器材；非专用的劳动保护用品；不对外营业的内部食堂用的餐具、炊具、设备、清洁卫生工具和食品、燃料等；军队、武警用于其人员生活的衣着品和个人用品；其他各类非生产性设备和用品。

二、餐饮业出售的主食、菜肴、烟酒饮料和其他商品。

三、新闻出版业、邮政业售予城乡居民、企事业单位、军队和武警等机构的书报杂志、音像制品、邮品等。

四、其他服务业出售的食品、烟酒饮料、服装鞋帽、日常生活用品、医药保健用品、艺术品、工艺美术品、玩具、殡葬用品以及其他消费品。

批发和零售业商品购进、销售、库存额　指各种登记注册类型的批发和零售业企业(单位)以本企业(单位)为总体的，从国内、国外市场购进的商品总量，销售和出口的商品总量、库存商品总量等情况。该指标可以反映商品流转过程中商品的购进、销售、库存之间的比例关系和存在的问题。

商品购进额　指从本企业(单位)以外的单位和个人购进(包括从境外直接进口)作为转卖或加工后转卖的商品金额（含增值税）。商品购进包括：：(1)从工农业生产者、批企业、出版社或报社的出版发和零售业企业、住宿和餐饮业发行部门和其他服务业企业购进的商品；(2)从机关团体、事业单位购进的商品；(3)从海关、市场管理部门购进的缉私和没收的商品；(4)从居民收购的废旧商品等，不包括：(1)企业为本单位自身经营用，不是作为转卖而购进的商品，如材料物资、包装物、低值易耗品、办公用品等；(2)未通过买卖行为而收入的商品，如接受其他部门移交的商品、借入的商品、收入代其他单位保管的商品、其他单位赠送的样品、加工回收的成品等；(3)经本单位介绍，由买卖双方直接结算，本单位只收取手续费的业务；(4)销售退回和买方拒付货款的商品；(5)商品溢余。

商品销售额　指对本单位以外的单位和个人出售的商品金额（包括售给本单位消费用的商品，含增值税）。商品销售包括(1)售给城乡居民和社会集团消费用的商品；(2)售给农业、工业、建筑业、运输邮电业、服务业、公用事业等国民经济各行业用于生产、经营用的商品，包括售予批发和零售业作为转卖或加工后转卖的商品；(3)对国(境)外直接出口的商品，不包括：(1)未通过买卖行为付出的商品，如随机构变动移交给其他企业单位的商品、借出的商品、归还受其他单位委托代保管的商品、付出的加工原料和赠送给其他单位的样品等；(2)经本单位介绍，由买卖双方直接结算，本单位只收取手续费的业务；(3)购货退回的商品；(4)商品损耗和损失；(5)出售本单位自用的废旧物资。

商品库存额　指报告期末各种登记注册类型的批发零售贸易企业(单位)已取得所有权的商品。它反映批发和零售贸易企业(单位)的商品库存情况和对市场商品供应的保证程度。商品库存包括：(1)存放在批发和零售业经营单位(如门市部、批发站、经营处)仓库、货场、货柜和货架中的商品；(2)挑选、整理、包装中的商品；(3)已记入购进而尚未运到本单位的商品，即发货单或银行承兑凭证已到而货未到的部分；(4)寄放他处的商品，如因购货方拒绝承付而暂时存放在购货方的商品和已办完加工成品收回手续而未提回的商品；(5)委托其他单位代销(未作销售或调出)尚未售出的商品；(6)代其他单位购进尚未交付的商品。不包括所有权不属于本单位的商品、拨付除批发零售贸易业以外的其他行业所属独立核算加工厂等加工生产尚未收回成品的商品、代国家物资储备部门保管的商品等。

住宿业　指有偿为顾客提供临时住宿的服务活动。不包括提供长期住宿场所的活动，如出租房屋、公寓等（列入房地产开发经营）。

餐饮业 指在一定场所，对食物进行现场烹饪、调制，并出售给顾客主要供现场消费的服务活动。

住宿和餐饮业营业额 指住宿和餐饮业法人企业（单位）在经营活动中因提供服务或销售商品等取得的收入。包括：客房收入、餐费收入、商品销售额和其他收入。客房收入指住宿和餐饮业法人企业（单位）在经营活动中因提供住宿服务取得的收入。餐费收入指住宿和餐饮业法人企业、（单位）因为顾客提供就餐服务取得的收入，包括经烹饪、调制加工后出售的各种食品，如主食、炒菜、凉拌菜等的收入。

Explanatory Notes on Main Statistical Indicators

Total Retail Sales of Consumer Goods refer to the sum of retail sales of commodities sold by wholesale and retail trades, catering services, publishing, post and telecommunications and other service industries to urban and rural households for household consumption and to social institutions for public consumption. Retail sales of consumer goods include:

1) Sales sold by wholesale and retail trades to urban and rural households for household consumption and to social institutions for public consumption.

a) of commodities to urban and rural households;

b) of commodities to foreigners, overseas Chinese and Chinese compatriots from Hong Kong, Macao and Taiwan visiting China;

c) of commodities to government agencies, institutions, social organizations, military and armed police units, and commodities to enterprises in the form of retail sales. More specifically, they include: office facilities and articles for non-production purposes such as communications equipment, computing equipment and instruments, TV and network equipment, printing and copying equipment, audio-visual equipment and instruments, paper, notebooks, stationeries, furniture, electric appliances, knitwear, sanitation and cleaning articles, cultural and sport articles, articles for prizes, souvenirs, etc.; transport vehicles and fuels for employees; materials, spare parts and tools for the maintenance of office facilities; equipment, fuels, materials and food for winter heating or summer cooling purposes; articles and equipment for teaching purpose; Chinese and western medicines and medical equipment and facilities purchased by non profit-making medical institutes; non-specialized work safety articles; cooking utensils, tableware, equipment, cleaning articles, food and fuels purchased by in-house cafeterias, clothes and personal articles purchased by military or armed police units for their officials and soldiers; and other equipment and articles for non-production purposes.

2) Sales of stable food, cooked dishes, beverages, tobaccos and other articles by catering units.

3) Sales of books, newspapers, magazines, audio-visual products and post products by publishing, post and telecommunications departments to urban and rural households and to enterprises, institutions, military and armed police units.

4) Sales of food, beverages, tobaccos, clothing, hats, footwear, articles for daily use, medicines, medical and health articles, work of art, handicrafts, toys, funeral articles and other articles by other service industries.

Purchase, Sales and Stock of Commodities by Wholesale and Retail Trades refer to the total volume of commodities purchased, total volume of sales and exports, and the stock of commodities by wholesale and retail enterprises (establishments) of different status of registration from domestic and overseas markets. This indicator reflects the relationship among purchase, sales and stock of commodities in the circulation of goods and reveals the existing problems.

Total Purchases of Commodities refer to the total value of purchases of commodities by enterprises (establishments) from other establishments or individuals (including direct import from abroad) for the purpose of re-selling, either with or without further processing of the commodities purchased. The commodities include: (1) commodities purchased from agricultural and industrial producer, wholesaler, retailer, publishing house and other service business; (2) commodities purchased from institutions and government departments; (3) confiscated goods purchased from the customs authorities or market management agencies; (4) second-hand goods and wastes purchased from residents; The commodities exclude (1) commodities purchased by enterprises (establishments) for use in their own business operation, commodities obtained without buying or selling procedures such as materials, consumable goods of low value, office appliance,etc. (2) received goods without trading, such as goods handed over from others, borrowed goods, preserved goods for others, donated goods from others, processed and retrieved goods, etc. (3) goods of direct settlement between buyer and seller with handling fees introduced by others, (4) goods returned or refused to pay by the buyer, (5) excessive goods.

Total Sales of Commodities refer to value of commodities sold by the establishments to other establishments and individuals (including goods sold for self consumption, including the value-added tax). The commodities include: (1) commodities sold to urban and rural residents and social groups for their consumption; (2) commodities sold to establishments in all industries for their production and operation, including agriculture, industry, construction, transportation, post and telecommunications, catering services, and public utility including commodities sold to wholesale and retail establishments for re-selling, with or without further processing; and (3) commodities for direct export to abroad. Excluded are (1) extended commodities without trading, such as goods handed over to other enterprises and institutions because of the change of organizations, lent goods, returned goods preserved for others, extended processing materials and samples donated to others, (2) goods of direct settlement between buyer and seller with handling fees introduced by others, (3) goods returned after purchase, (4) damaged and spoiled goods, (5) waste and used goods of self use,

Total Stock of Commodities refers to total commodities possessed by wholesaler and retailer of various types of registration status at the end of the reference period, reflecting the commodity stock level of various wholesaler and retailer and the potential for market supply. It includes: (1) commodities located in storage, garages, counters, and shelves of operating places (such as sale stores, wholesale centres, and operating offices); (2) commodities in the process of being selected, sorted, and packed; (3) commodities not arrived but recorded as purchase in the account, i.e. commodities not arrived but payment receipts for the commodities from the sellers or the banks arrived; (4) commodities deposited in other places rather than places mentioned above, for instance: commodities in the hold of purchasers temporarily due to the refusal of payment and commodities not taken back after going through the formalities; (5) commodities entrusted to other units to sell but not sold yet; (6) commodities purchased for other units but not delivered yet. Commodities not included as stock are those not owned by the enterprises (units), commodities on commission for processing but not yet delivered, imported commodities of agency of foreign trade enterprise but not yet delivered to ordering units and finally those put in stock on behalf of the state material reserves units.

Hotel Services refer to the charged accommodation services provided to customers, excluding the long term accommodation service activities such as rental housing and apartments(it is under real estate development and management).

Catering Services refer to the activities of enterprises providing on-the-spot services of selling food cooked and prepared to the customer in certain sites

Business Revenue of Hotels and Catering Services refers to revenue received from providing services or selling commodities by corporate enterprises and establishments engaged in hotels and catering services, including income from hotels, from catering services, from selling of commodities and from other services. Income from hotels refers to income of corporate enterprises and establishments engaged in hotels and catering services by providing lodging services. Income from catering services refers to income of corporate enterprises and establishments engaged in hotels and catering services by providing catering services, including selling of cooked or prepared foods such as staple food, cooked dishes or cold dishes. Income from selling of commodities refers to income of corporate enterprises and establishments engaged in hotels and catering services by selling commodities (including value-added tax) that accompany the services they provide. Income from other activities refers to income received other than income from hotels, catering services or selling of commodities, such as income from providing recreation, fitness or business services.

2012

新疆统计年鉴

XINJIANG STATISTICAL YEARBOOK

第十七篇 教育、科技和文化

CHAPTER 17 Education,Science & Technology and Culture

简要说明
Brief Introduction

本篇资料的主要内容及来源

教育统计资料包括研究生教育（高等学校研究生教育、科研机构研究生教育）；普通高等学校本专科教育；普通中等教育（中等专业教育、技工学校、普通中学、职业高中、工读学校）；初等教育（小学）、学前教育、特殊教育（盲聋哑和弱智儿童学校等）以及教育经费等资料。

教育部分资料由新疆维吾尔自治区教育厅依据年报资料整理提供。

科技统计资料包括科技活动基本情况、县级以上政府部门属研究与开发机构及科技信息与文献机构人员数、重大科学技术研究成果及奖励、专利申请和批准情况、高等学校科技活动情况、企事业单位专业技术人员情况、大中型工业企业科技活动情况、各类技术合同鉴定及执行情况、技术经济合同成交情况、技术流向地域情况等。

科技统计范围包括新疆地区有科技活动的企事业单位，具体涵盖规模以上工业企业（标准见工业篇）、各级各部门所属国有独立核算的科学研究与技术开发机构及科技情报与文献机构、普通高等学校等。

科技部分资料由新疆维吾尔自治区统计局社会科技统计处根据科技年报和新疆维吾尔自治区科技厅提供资料整理。

文化部分主要包括艺术表演团体、艺术表演场所、公共图书馆、博物馆、文化馆、档案馆、文化站、广播、电影、电视以及文物等文化单位的机构、人员、经费和业务活动情况。

文化部分资料是由新疆维吾尔自治区统计局社会科技统计处根据部门统计报表制度加工整理而成。艺术事业、图书馆事业、群众文化事业的资料主要来自新疆维吾尔自治区文化厅；文物资料来自新疆维吾尔自治区文物局；广播、电影、电视资料来自新疆维吾尔自治区广播电视局。

Main Content and Source of Data

The data on education cover the situation on postgraduate (regular institutions of higher education,research institutions), regular institution of higher education(universities and colleges), regular secondary education, (professional secondary schools,technical schools,regular secondary school,vocational senior secondary schools,schools for juvenile delinquents);primary education (primary schools), preschool education, special education(schools for the blind, deaf-mutes and the retarded) and expenditure on education.

Statistical data on education compiled by the Statistics Bureau of Xinjiang in accordance with the data from the Bureau of Education.

Data on technology mainly include: condition of scientific and technological activities, state-owned research and development institutions and information and literature institutions at and above county level and persons engaged; the situation of science and technological achievements & prizes and patent applications, basic statistics on scientific and technological activities of high education, condition of professional scientific and technological personnel of enterprises and institutions, statistics on signing and implementing technical contracts, statistics on transaction in technical and economic contract, statistics on location of technical contract.

Statistical scope on technology include scientific and technical activities in enterprises and institution, they are mainly: industrial enterprises above designated size, state-owned research and development institutions and information and literature institutions at and above county level and persons engaged, regular institutions of high education, etc.

Data on technology compiled by the Statistics Bureau of Xinjiang in accordance with the data from the Bureau of Science &Technology.

Data on culture cover mainly the situations on institutions, personal and business activities of arts (performing groups and venues), libraries, museums, cultural centers, archives, cultural stations, broadcasting, films, televisions, news and publication.

Data on culture are collected and tabulated in accordance with the statistical reporting schemes stipulated by the Statistical Bureau of Xinjiang. Data on the causes of arts, libraries, mass culture are provided by the Xinjiang Bureau of Culture; Data on archives are from Xinjiang Bureau of Archives; Data on broadcasting, film and television are mainly from Xinjiang Bureau of Broadcasting.

17-1 主要年份各级各类学校数
Number of Schools by Level and Type in Main Years

单位：所 (unit)

年份 Year	普通高等学校 Regular Institutions of Higher Education	中等学校 Secondary Schools	普通中等专业学校 Specialized Secondary Schools	普通中学 Regular Secondary Schools	#高中 Senior Secondary Schools	职业高中 Vocational Secondary Schools	技工学校 Technical Schools	小学 Primary Schools	特殊教育学校 Special Schools
1978	10	2078	78	1997	673		10	9891	1
1980	12	2197	96	2032	720	21	48	9006	2
1985	14	2360	97	2147	794	65	51	8104	3
1990	21	2274	112	1958	766	134	70	7247	6
1995	21	2121	115	1792	554	145	69	7086	6
2000	20	2000	112	1711	484	112	65	6718	7
2001	21	2179	99	1929	472	89	62	6221	7
2002	24	2173	87	1945	507	83	58	6043	7
2003	26	2154	78	1932	500	86	58	5832	8
2004	28	2186	78	1965	498	84	59	5451	8
2005	31	2185	79	1961	503	87	58	5209	10
2006	31	2101	67	1891	486	84	59	4815	9
2007	32	2040	74	1830	454	75	61	4589	9
2008	32	1973	75	1759	444	82	57	4159	10
2009	32	1832	80	1610	413	82	60	3651	10
2010	32	1772	81	1545	385	83	63	3598	13
2011	32	1766	96	1525	368	71	74	3536	15

注：从 2006 年起，职业初中并入普通中学统计。(以下同)
Note: Number of regular secondary schools include the number of junion vocational secondary schools from 2006.(The same follows)

17-2 主要年份各级各类学校教师数
Number of Teachers by Level and Type of School in Main Years

单位：人 (person)

年份 Year	普通高等学校 Regular Institutions of Higher Education	中等学校 Secondary Schools	普通中等专业学校 Specialized Secondary Schools	普通中学 Regular Secondary Schools	#高中 Senior Secondary Schools	职业高中 Vocational Secondary Schools	技工学校 Technical Schools	小学 Primary Schools	特殊教育学校 Special Schools
1978	2458	44417	2543	41661	8064		213	82616	28
1980	3149	50056	3459	45232	9292	77	1288	98027	54
1985	5473	69185	4554	60942	15059	1567	2122	98294	67
1990	7002	78596	6158	65814	19318	3117	3507	95060	139
1995	7687	76584	6540	62934	14434	3494	3616	106001	162
2000	7924	89211	6786	75895	16069	3104	3426	131259	183
2001	9123	93126	6842	79419	17025	2546	4319	132137	187
2002	10369	96469	6031	84714	19031	2399	3325	132435	200
2003	11237	103156	5157	89332	20976	2440	6227	132284	237
2004	12239	106839	5494	94381	22809	3079	3885	134915	257
2005	12733	112941	4993	102168	25153	1696	4084	134768	262
2006	13783	120777	4339	106975	26815	2832	6631	134718	286
2007	15096	123246	5553	108232	27970	2295	7166	133626	298
2008	15755	121898	5381	108729	28735	2586	5202	132797	313
2009	16234	125152	6086	110842	29402	2464	5760	134263	319
2010	16506	128306	6232	113990	30231	2708	5706	133963	347
2011	17256	132748	7210	116501	31258	2255	6782	135182	316

17-3 主要年份各级各类学校在校学生数

Number of Students Enrollment by Level and Type of School in Main Years

单位：人 (person)

年 份 Year	普通高等学校 Regular Institutions of Higher Education	中等学校 Secondary Schools	普通中等专业学校 Specialized Secondary Schools	普通中学 Regular Secondary Schools	#高 中 Senior Secondary Schools	职业高中 Vocational Secondary Schools	技工学校 Technical Schools	小 学 Primary Schools	特殊教育学校 Special Schools
1978	10229	838560	23696	806386	128376		8478	2028771	270
1980	14308	886740	42362	823161	147446	1416	19801	2055513	371
1985	26500	1054293	33251	955356	223405	41825	23861	1966306	706
1990	31271	1015214	45985	863118	251067	65862	40249	1857246	610
1995	44918	912597	68586	749788	141330	54122	40101	2301274	643
2000	74063	1311845	105255	1132912	198639	51270	22408	2477413	674
2001	109815	1390360	97321	1228566	225411	47673	16800	2435667	922
2002	134831	1493580	83902	1338836	272381	50787	20055	2359788	3876
2003	151256	1584700	71499	1448531	315178	45330	19340	2289066	1863
2004	168247	1676971	71324	1517948	359147	61502	26197	2218109	2549
2005	188752	1717403	86744	1587850	387763	63158	26219	2143833	4961
2006	207672	1739422	108131	1572502	402321	23488	35301	2097975	4843
2007	226012	1742947	141162	1529092	413452	31741	40952	2058884	6396
2008	241288	1722667	150715	1483550	418701	41611	46791	2012004	5574
2009	253272	1695984	147439	1444836	417139	54777	48932	1973890	5991
2010	263835	1684027	152227	1422419	419141	59593	49788	1935798	5974
2011	272818	1675169	161657	1409293	432724	60734	43485	1919457	4733

注：1.17-3、17-4、17-5 表中高等学校含研究生数。2.特殊教育学校 2002 年新增随班就读。(以下同)

Note: a) Institntions of higher education include the number of postgraduates with table 17-3,17-4,17-5.

b) In Special Schools for the blind,deaf, mute, new comers may follow the classes accordingly from the year 2002 (The same as follows).

17-4 主要年份各级各类学校招生数

Number of New Students Enrollment by Level and Type of School in Main Years

单位：人 (person)

年 份 Year	普通高等学校 Regular Institutions of Higher Education	中等学校 Secondary Schools	普通中等专业学校 Specialized Secondary Schools	普通中学 Regular Secondary Schools	#高 中 Senior Secondary Schools	职业高中 Vocational Secondary Schools	技工学校 Technical Schools	小 学 Primary Schools	特殊教育学校 Special Schools
1980	3767	336402	14688	310931	73959	792	10531	433089	90
1985	9298	386074	13919	341123	93692	20429	10603	374643	91
1990	8034	356615	15586	297641	84567	27968	15420	335552	103
1995	12307	356814	25260	286318	58203	25643	19593	419717	165
2000	30689	486763	38866	418790	76744	20027	9080	364193	175
2001	42253	510469	26763	459878	93519	16621	7207	352975	135
2002	42808	551353	22241	501824	113366	16746	10442	346386	874
2003	44733	583033	24016	532987	126163	15378	10652	347619	369
2004	53204	606666	27990	536405	138315	27585	14686	347364	390
2005	58653	602335	34882	539922	145044	12416	15115	338539	847
2006	62395	599748	45536	522425	142853	13017	18770	337994	780
2007	68999	619218	65290	510080	146449	19201	24647	340108	1158
2008	74670	603352	62098	497579	147914	21610	22065	328647	840
2009	73904	593290	53692	489838	148869	28243	21517	318488	869
2010	79216	597621	60418	489356	153238	28767	19080	311861	1055
2011	79337	581939	60669	482450	156497	21777	17043	322436	939

17-5 主要年份各级各类学校毕业生数

Number of Graduates by Level and Type of School in Main Years

单位：人 (person)

年 份 Year	普通高等学校 Regular Institutions of Higher Education	中等学校 Secondary Schools	普通中等专业学校 Specialized Secondary Schools	普通中学 Regular Secondary Schools	#高 中 Senior Secondary Schools	职业高中 Vocational Secondary Schools	技工学校 Technical Schools	小 学 Primary Schools	特殊教育学校 Special Schools
1978	1509	205862	8801	195542	53970		1519	388359	195
1980	814	264626	11946	246382	60370	341	5957	292515	37
1981	779	280171	17039	257478	67114	367	5287	397524	37
1982	4108	269927	17201	244853	69504	385	7488	310025	32
1983	4823	283120	11584	260906	77546	1144	9486	317227	27
1984	3426	275788	8130	257833	72191	2764	7061	295993	48
1985	3511	290077	8097	267302	68096	7424	7254	289045	73
1986	4797	296360	11551	268402	58585	8543	7864	307047	52
1987	8001	321981	10623	289556	73947	12280	9522	317820	101
1988	7792	346072	12026	311224	85718	12758	10064	288594	68
1989	6900	347719	12441	308467	86489	14650	12161	249888	57
1990	8603	343313	14260	297235	81062	17938	13880	259301	98
1991	7919	324031	15571	274913	79664	17505	16042	183350	159
1992	8402	310076	14950	260953	84518	18999	15174	268074	157
1993	7741	312284	16760	261502	78675	18558	15464	259468	104
1994	7734	250909	16206	198839	57090	18100	17764	262215	55
1995	10505	271992	18981	215756	44589	16490	20765	271227	57
1996	12272	271267	21701	215295	43478	15424	18847	279866	39
1997	10908	284580	21936	228287	37966	17181	17176	294420	71
1998	11401	313807	23090	259910	49702	18038	12769	321044	100
1999	11886	341434	25118	282486	52403	18826	15004	357801	84
2000	11220	363503	25879	308225	54985	17341	12058	371758	70
2001	16121	380946	26403	329801	59251	13881	10861	395010	104
2002	16380	410299	31598	356203	61932	15087	7411	411626	848
2003	25785	434523	31304	379269	70824	15685	8265	421443	264
2004	31013	468849	24758	420583	84418	15475	8033	417588	382
2005	37920	520798	19559	474621	103928	19492	7126	397592	714
2006	45810	541729	22515	501697	115422	5510	12007	373862	684
2007	48372	557512	25735	515494	127129	5943	10340	361921	716
2008	57076	557655	32537	507098	135240	6454	11566	349300	859
2009	60092	554905	41866	492259	137290	8883	11897	339836	935
2010	66903	547288	44478	473216	135706	14442	15152	334362	728
2011	67219	526007	47371	457944	129478	10256	10436	327704	652

17-6 主要年份研究生数
Number of Postgraduates in Main Years

单位：人 (person)

年 份 Year	招生数 New Enrollment	在校学生数 Total Enrollment	攻读博士学位 Working for Doctor's Degree	攻读硕士学位 Working for Master's Degree	毕业生数 Graduates	攻读博士学位 Working for Doctor's Degree	攻读硕士学位 Working for Master's Degree
1978	16	16		16			
1980	15	66		66			
1985	120	179		174	21		21
1990	73	256	3	253	112		112
1995	180	509	14	295	91		91
2000	544	1196	48	1148	235	5	230
2001	827	1749	80	1669	277	8	269
2002	1104	2495	112	2383	355	11	344
2003	1664	3629	186	3443	521	18	503
2004	2336	5120	283	4837	832	30	802
2005	2902	6938	415	6523	1066	35	1031
2006	3147	8421	489	7932	1628	90	1538
2007	3491	9623	549	9074	2244	110	2134
2008	3523	10317	595	9722	2786	132	2654
2009	4189	11635	653	10982	3021	121	2900
2010	4595	12675	713	11962	3360	158	3202
2011	4972	14099	840	13259	3421	133	3288

17-7 高等学校基本情况
Basic Statistics on Institutions of Higher Education

单位：人 (2011 年) (person)

项 目	Item	学校数(所) Schools (unit)	毕业生数 Graduates	招生数 New Enrollment	在校学生数 Total Enrollment	教职工数 Staff and Teachers	#专任教师 Full-time Teachers
总 计	**Total**		**63798**	**74365**	**258719**	**32935**	**20416**
普通高等学校	Regular Institutionsof Higher Education	32	62644	72949	254373	27629	17256
综合大学	Multiversity	6	16395	17978	67342	8395	4951
理工院校	Science Engineering	11	15629	20550	58149	5319	3619
农业院校	Agriculture	4	10519	12143	42976	3793	2445
医药院校	Medicine	3	4359	4998	20558	2908	1858
师范院校	Normal Institutions	4	9839	11017	42405	4374	2718
财经学院	Economics and Finance	1	3609	3851	15093	1678	1039
政法院校	Politics & Law	2	1595	1556	4516	712	375
艺术院校	Art	1	699	856	3334	450	251
总计中：高职学院	In total: Vocational Training	16	21139	27177	77378	7521	5154
成人高等学校	Ordinary Class for Adult Higher Education		1154	1416	4346	5306	3160

17-8 中等专业学校基本情况
Basic Statistics on Specialized Secondary Schools

单位: 人 (2011 年) (person)

项　目	Item	毕业生数 Graduates	招生数 New Student Enrollment	在校学生数 Student Enrollment	专业课教师 Teachers of Various Subjects
总　计	**Total**	**64508**	**90177**	**243039**	**5741**
农林牧渔类	Agriculture	8665	16207	39448	697
资源环境类	Resource and Environment	714	831	2179	30
能源与新能源类	Energy	2105	2634	7407	150
土木水利类	Civil and Hydraulic Engineering	3294	5717	13871	189
加工制造类	Processing and Manufacturing	8417	8991	22023	500
石油化工类	Petroleum and Chemical	4449	3922	9467	202
轻纺食品类	Textile and Food	1653	2651	8723	93
交通运输类	Transportation and Communication	3192	8003	17918	227
信息技术类	Information Technologies	4822	4842	12768	451
医药卫生类	Medcine and Health	10138	11235	38004	575
休闲保健类	Recreation and Health Care	238	861	2508	9
财经商贸类	Economics and Finance	3987	3922	10693	408
旅游服务类	Trades and Tourism	2229	3693	10410	177
文化艺术类	Culture Arts and Physical Education	3319	6035	19025	571
体育与健身类	Sports and Fitness	1023	1603	4311	183
教育类	Teacher Training	4728	7405	19175	822
司法服务类	Justice and Services	715	716	2127	67
公共管理与服务类	Scoial and Public Affairs	369	305	1114	50
其　他	Others	451	604	1868	340

17-9 普通中学和其他学校基本情况
Basic Statistics on Regular Secondary Schools and Other Schools

单位: 人 (2011 年) (person)

项　目	Item	学校数(所) Schools (unit)	毕业生数 Graduates	招生数 New Enrollment	在校学生数 Total Enrollment	教职工数 Staff and Teachers	#专任教师 Full-time Teachers
普通中学	Regular Secondary Schools	1525	457944	482450	1409293	133032	116501
高　中	Senior Secondary Schools	368	129478	156497	432724		31258
初　中	Junior Secondary Schools	1157	328466	325953	976569		85243
职业高中	Vocational Secondary Schools	71	10256	21777	60734	3137	2255
技工学校	Technical Shools	74	10436	17043	43485	8825	6782
小　学	Primary Schools	3536	327704	322436	1919457	149223	135182
特殊教育学校	Special Schools	15	652	939	4733	431	316

17-10 各类成人教育情况

Basic Statistics on Adult Education by Type

单位: 人 (2011 年) (person)

项目	Item	学校数(所) Schools (unit)	毕业生数 Graduates	在校学生数 Total Enrollment	教职工数 Staff and Teachers	#专任教师 Full-time Teachers
成人高等教育	Adult Education Schools	8	15634	59609	5306	3160
广播电视大学	Radio and TV Universities	2	881	2862	3671	2071
职工大学	Schools of Higher Education for Staff Workers	1	71	209	1533	1014
教育学院	Pedagogical Colleges	5	1209	2773	102	75
普通高校办的成人班	Adult Classes run by Ordinary Colleges and Universities		13473	53765		
成人中等教育	Secondary Schools for Adults	17	6881	20648	1140	917
成人中学	Secondary Schools for Adults	10	563	1768	185	49
成人技术培训学校	Technical adult college	1808	1511589	1724811	4981	1964
成人初等学校	Primary Schools for Adults	495	56044	71251	1395	538
#扫盲班	Literacy Courses		45756	61301	1366	468

17-11 主要年份教育发展水平

Development Level of Education in Main Years

年份 Year	各类学校在校生占全区人口比重(%) Students as Percentage of Total Population (%)	平均每万人口中(人) Number of Students per 10 000 Population (person)			大中小学生各占普通学校学生总数的比重(%) Students of Different Level as Percentage of Total Students(%)		
		大学生 University and College Students	中学生 Secondary School students	小学生 Primary School Students	大学生 University and College Students	中学生 Secondary School Students	小学生 Primary School Students
1978	23.34	8.30	654.00	1645.38	0.36	28.02	70.50
1980	23.04	11.15	641.47	1601.82	0.48	27.80	69.52
1985	22.39	19.47	701.88	1444.60	0.87	31.35	64.52
1990	18.99	20.45	564.44	1208.01	1.08	29.72	63.94
1995	19.61	26.84	453.23	1330.61	1.38	23.00	70.60
2000	22.84	41.05	638.26	1395.72	1.82	27.93	61.09
2001	20.98	58.53	654.84	1298.22	2.79	31.21	61.87
2002	23.14	70.04	702.72	1238.61	3.21	31.87	56.18
2003	22.53	76.33	749.00	1183.62	3.39	33.25	52.54
2004	21.91	83.09	773.23	1129.89	4.18	38.92	56.90
2005	21.96	90.44	766.67	1066.40	4.70	39.86	55.44
2006	21.78	97.20	767.07	1023.40	5.10	40.64	54.26
2007	21.21	103.20	729.77	982.65	5.69	40.19	54.12
2008	20.68	108.44	696.24	911.60	6.20	39.81	54.00
2009	20.57	111.94	669.33	914.42	6.60	39.47	53.93
2010	20.62	115.13	652.09	887.34	6.96	39.41	53.63
2011	20.65	117.14	638.06	869.04	7.21	39.28	53.51

17-12 主要年份各级学校教师负担学生数

Student-teacher Ratio by Level of School in Main Years

单位：人 (person)

年份 Year	高等学校 University and College		普通中学 Secondary Schools		小学 Primary Schools	
	教师数 Number of Teachers	平均每个教师负担学生数 Student-Teacher Ratio	教师数 Number of Teachers	平均每个教师负担学生数 Student-Teacher Ratio	教师数 Number of Teachers	平均每个教师负担学生数 Student-Teacher Ratio
1978	2458	4.16	41661	19.36	82616	24.56
1980	3149	4.54	45232	18.20	89027	23.09
1985	5473	4.84	60942	15.68	98294	20.00
1990	7002	4.47	65814	13.12	95060	19.54
1995	7687	5.78	62934	11.91	106001	20.77
2000	7924	9.34	75895	14.92	131259	18.87
2005	12733	14.82	101701	15.16	134768	15.91
2006	13783	15.07	106975	14.70	134718	15.57
2007	15096	14.33	108232	14.13	133626	15.41
2008	15755	14.66	108729	13.64	132797	15.15
2009	16234	14.88	110842	13.04	134263	14.70
2010	16506	15.22	113990	12.48	133963	14.45
2011	17256	14.99	116501	12.10	135182	14.20

17-13 主要年份各级学校女学生和女教师数

Number of Female Students and Teachers by Level of School in Main Years

单位：人 (person)

项目	Item	2000	2010	2011
女学生	**Number of Female Students**	**1889552**	**1911185**	**1908102**
高等学校	Institutions of Higher Education	38419	136071	142360
中等专业学校	Specialized Secondary Schools	49892	82554	87298
普通中学	Regular Secondary Schools	568060	718438	714429
职业高中	Vocational Secondary Schools	23670	26234	26138
技工学校	Technical Shools	8740	13228	11553
小 学	Primary Schools	1200513	932296	924510
特殊教育学校	Special Schools for the Blind, Mute and Deaf	258	2364	1814
女学生占学生总数的比重(%)	**Percentage of Female Students to Total Students (%)**	**48.9**	**49.3**	**49.5**
女教师	**Number of Female Teachers**	**134563**	**178259**	**183690**
高等学校	Institutions of Higher Education	3192	8362	8831
中等专业学校	Specialized Secondary Schools	3408	3421	3998
普通中学	Regular Secondary Schools	40030	67901	70273
职业高中	Vocational Secondary Schools	1601	1458	1239
技工学校	Technical Schools	1264	3937	4500
小 学	Primary Schools	84944	92917	94609
特殊教育学校	Special Schools for the Blind, Mute and Deaf	124	263	240
女教师占教师总数的比重(%)	**Percentage of Female Teachers to Total Teachers (%)**	**58.9**	**63.1**	**64.3**

17-14 主要年份初中毕业生和小学生升学率及小学学龄儿童入学率

Percentage of Graduates of Junior Secondary Schools and Primary Schools Entering Higher Level Schools, Enrollment Rate of School-age Children in Main Years

单位：人、%　　(person,%)

年份 Year	初中毕业生升高中情况 Student of Graduates of Junior Secondary Schools Entering Senior Secondary Schools			小学毕业生升初中情况 Student of Graduates of Primary Schools Entering Junior Secondary Schools			小学学龄儿童入学情况 Student of School-Age Children Enrolled		
	初中毕业生数 Graduates of Junior Secondary Schools	高中招生数 Students Entering Senior Secondary Schools	升学率 Percentage of Graduates of Primary Schools Entering Junior Secondary Schools	小学毕业生数 Graduates of Primary Schools	初中招生数 Students Entering Junior Secondary Schools	升学率 Percentage of Graduates of Primary Schools Entering Junior Secondary Schools	学龄儿童数 School-Age Children	已入学学龄儿童数 School-Age Children Enrolled in Schools	入学率 Enrollment Rate
1978	141572	68261	48.22	788359	255687	88.67	1541148	1480400	96.00
1980	186012	73989	39.76	292515	236432	80.83	1637610	1548653	94.57
1985	199206	93692	47.03	289045	247431	85.60	1645055	1569328	95.40
1990	216173	84567	39.12	259301	213074	82.17	1502163	1465325	97.50
1995	171167	58203	34.00	271227	228115	84.10	2036541	1976120	97.03
2000	253240	76744	30.30	371758	342046	92.01	2313890	2245190	97.03
2005	370693	145044	39.13	397592	394878	99.33	2007742	1981569	98.70
2006	386275	142853	36.98	373862	379572	101.53	1957604	1941068	99.15
2007	388365	146449	37.71	361921	363631	100.47	1930074	1916265	99.28
2008	371858	147914	39.78	349300	349665	100.10	1865105	1856800	99.55
2009	354969	148869	41.94	339836	340969	100.33	1839775	1829016	99.41
2010	337510	153238	45.40	334362	336118	100.53	1801872	1797853	99.78
2011	328466	156497	47.64	327704	325953	99.47	1785583	1780729	99.73

17-15 主要年份各级各类学校少数民族在校学生数

Number of Students Enrollment of Minority Nationalities by Level and Type of School in Main Years

单位：人　　(person)

年份 Year	高等学校 Institutions of Higher Education	中等学校 Secondary Schools	中等专业学校 Specialized Secondary Schools	职业高中 Vocational Secondary Schools	技工学校 Technical Schools	普通中学 Regular Secondary Schools	#高中 Senior Secondary Schools	#初中 Junior Secondary Schools	小学(万人) Primary Schools (10 000 persons)
1978	7890	310987	10807			300180	38837	261343	106.58
1980	6455	311213	22263	592	4514	283844	50340	233504	101.73
1985	13996	346833	17888	4915	7649	316381	71199	245182	116.43
1990	17542	439140	23897	13577	13685	387981	94579	293402	126.78
1995	24125	477379	33264	20013	16040	408012	52570	355492	157.84
2000	31989	834390	62572	34992	12260	724566	91843	632723	171.44
2005	75744	993338	32698	54773	13371	892501	152244	740257	136.94
2006	77627	975346	36393	13216	18002	907735	149963	757772	132.94
2007	81978	958643	55224	19181	20476	863762	156478	707284	131.32
2008	85942	935350	62337	28387	23396	821230	160238	660992	130.44
2009	91243	927939	66502	41666	24466	795305	160720	634585	130.31
2010	94708	933338	75924	49388	24894	783132	162687	620445	129.37
2011	102358	940729	82524	54357	21743	782105	173913	608192	129.25

17-16 各地、州、市各级各类学校数
Number of Schools by Level, Type and by Prefecture, Autonomous Prefecture and City

单位：所 (2011 年) (unit)

地　区	Region	普通高等学校 Regular Institutions of Higher Education	中等职业学校 Specialized Secondary Schools	#中等师范学校 Teacher Training Secondary Schools
总　计	**Total**	**32**	**184**	**13**
乌鲁木齐市	Urumqi City	17	36	2
克拉玛依市	Karamay City	1	3	1
吐鲁番地区	Turpan Administrative Offices		3	1
哈密地区	Hami [Kumul] Administrative Offices		5	
昌吉回族自治州	Changji Hui Autonomous Prefecture	3	8	
伊犁哈萨克自治州	Ili Kazak Autonomous Prefecture	2	37	3
伊犁州直属县(市)	Counties (Cities) Direct Under Ili Prefecture	2	17	1
塔城地区	Tacheng [Tarbagatai] Administrative Offices		10	1
阿勒泰地区	Altay Administrative Offices		10	1
博尔塔拉蒙古自治州	Bortala Mongol Autonomous Prefecture		4	1
巴音郭楞蒙古自治州	Bayangol Mongol Autonomous Prefecture	1	7	1
阿克苏地区	Aksu Administrative Offices	1	9	
克孜勒苏柯尔克孜自治州	Kizilsu Kirgiz Autonomous Prefecture		9	1
喀什地区	Kashgar [Kaxgar] Administrative Offices	1	27	1
和田地区	Hotan Administrative Offices	2	11	1
生产建设兵团	Production and Construction Group	3	23	
自治区直辖县级市	Municpality Country-LevelCity directly under the Central Govern-ment	1	2	1
石河子市	Shihezi City	1	2	1
阿拉尔市	Aral City			

地　区	Region	普通中学 Regular Secondary Schools	#高　中 Senior Secondary Schools	小　学 Primary Schools	特殊教育学　校 Special Schools
总　计	**Total**	**1525**	**368**	**3536**	**15**
乌鲁木齐市	Urumqi City	133	53	141	3
克拉玛依市	Karamay City	18	14	29	1
吐鲁番地区	Turpan Administrative Offices	49	14	84	1
哈密地区	Hami [Kumul] Administrative Offices	45	13	60	1
昌吉回族自治州	Changji Hui Autonomous Prefecture	49	19	97	1
伊犁哈萨克自治州	Ili Kazak Autonomous Prefecture	337	67	531	4
伊犁州直属县(市)	Counties (Cities) Direct Under Ili Prefecture	184	33	357	3
塔城地区	Tacheng [Tarbagatai] Administrative Offices	77	21	108	1
阿勒泰地区	Altay Administrative Offices	76	13	66	
博尔塔拉蒙古自治州	Bortala Mongol Autonomous Prefecture	28	9	30	1
巴音郭楞蒙古自治州	Bayangol Mongol Autonomous Prefecture	63	22	90	1
阿克苏地区	Aksu Administrative Offices	149	40	585	1
克孜勒苏柯尔克孜自治州	Kizilsu Kirgiz Autonomous Prefecture	36	10	160	
喀什地区	Kashgar [Kaxgar] Administrative Offices	211	44	982	1
和田地区	Hotan Administrative Offices	148	14	674	
生产建设兵团	Production and Construction Group	246	46	68	
自治区直辖县级市	Municpality Country-LevelCity directly under the Central Govern-ment	13	3	5	
石河子市	Shihezi City	12	3	5	
阿拉尔市	Aral City	1			

17-17 各地、州、市各级各类学校教职工数

Number of Teachers and Staff by Level and Type of School and by Prefecture, Autonomous Prefecture and City

单位：人 (2011 年) (person)

地区	Region	普通高等学校 Regular Institutions of Higher Education	中等职业学校 Specialized Secondary Schools
总计	**Total**	**27629**	**14936**
乌鲁木齐市	Urumqi City	16883	4737
克拉玛依市	Karamay City	510	621
吐鲁番地区	Turpan Administrative Offices		299
哈密地区	Hami [Kumul] Administrative Offices		601
昌吉回族自治州	Changji Hui Autonomous Prefecture	1644	703
伊犁哈萨克自治州	Ili Kazak Autonomous Prefecture	1785	2177
伊犁州直属县(市)	Counties (Cities) Direct Under Ili Prefecture	1785	1038
塔城地区	Tacheng [Tarbagatai] Administrative Offices		556
阿勒泰地区	Altay Administrative Offices		583
博尔塔拉蒙古自治州	Bortala Mongol Autonomous Prefecture		241
巴音郭楞蒙古自治州	Bayangol Mongol Autonomous Prefecture	573	483
阿克苏地区	Aksu Administrative Offices	434	344
克孜勒苏柯尔克孜自治州	Kizilsu Kirgiz Autonomous Prefecture		397
喀什地区	Kashgar [Kaxgar] Administrative Offices	935	1768
和田地区	Hotan Administrative Offices	645	586
生产建设兵团	Production and Construction Group	3846	1876
自治区直辖县级市	Municpality Country-LevelCity directly under the Central Govern-ment	374	103
石河子市	Shihezi City	374	103
阿拉尔市	Aral City		

地区	Region	普通中学 Regular Secondary Schools	小学 Primary Schools	特殊教育学校 Special Schools
总计	**Total**	**133032**	**149223**	**431**
乌鲁木齐市	Urumqi City	12219	10072	182
克拉玛依市	Karamay City	2710	2117	10
吐鲁番地区	Turpan Administrative Offices	3776	4644	
哈密地区	Hami [Kumul] Administrative Offices	3106	3269	37
昌吉回族自治州	Changji Hui Autonomous Prefecture	7531	7798	33
伊犁哈萨克自治州	Ili Kazak Autonomous Prefecture	24440	32720	50
伊犁州直属县(市)	Counties (Cities) Direct Under Ili Prefecture	13790	19391	16
塔城地区	Tacheng [Tarbagatai] Administrative Offices	6337	7867	34
阿勒泰地区	Altay Administrative Offices	4313	5462	
博尔塔拉蒙古自治州	Bortala Mongol Autonomous Prefecture	2556	3315	
巴音郭楞蒙古自治州	Bayangol Mongol Autonomous Prefecture	7263	9289	43
阿克苏地区	Aksu Administrative Offices	12435	13883	23
克孜勒苏柯尔克孜自治州	Kizilsu Kirgiz Autonomous Prefecture	4090	5960	
喀什地区	Kashgar [Kaxgar] Administrative Offices	23341	27397	53
和田地区	Hotan Administrative Offices	10691	12851	
生产建设兵团	Production and Construction Group	17648	15276	
自治区直辖县级市	Municpality Country-LevelCity directly under the Central Govern-ment	1226	632	
石河子市	Shihezi City	1214	594	
阿拉尔市	Aral City	12	38	

17-18 各地、州、市各级各类学校教师数

Number of Teachers by Level and Type of School and by Prefecture, Autonomous Prefecture and City

单位：人 (2011 年) (person)

地　区	Region	普通高等学校 Regular Institutions of Higher Education	中等职业学校 Specialized Secondary Schools
总　计	**Total**	**17256**	**10382**
乌鲁木齐市	Urumqi City	10030	3029
克拉玛依市	Karamay City	275	297
吐鲁番地区	Turpan Administrative Offices		229
哈密地区	Hami [Kumul] Administrative Offices		444
昌吉回族自治州	Changji Hui Autonomous Prefecture	1146	577
伊犁哈萨克自治州	Ili Kazak Autonomous Prefecture	1077	1565
伊犁州直属县(市)	Counties (Cities) Direct Under Ili Prefecture	1077	764
塔城地区	Tacheng [Tarbagatai] Administrative Offices		373
阿勒泰地区	Altay Administrative Offices		428
博尔塔拉蒙古自治州	Bortala Mongol Autonomous Prefecture		156
巴音郭楞蒙古自治州	Bayangol Mongol Autonomous Prefecture	526	371
阿克苏地区	Aksu Administrative Offices	334	289
克孜勒苏柯尔克孜自治州	Kizilsu Kirgiz Autonomous Prefecture		338
喀什地区	Kashgar [Kaxgar] Administrative Offices	711	1361
和田地区	Hotan Administrative Offices	360	485
生产建设兵团	Production and Construction Group	2502	1181
自治区直辖县级市	Municpality Country-LevelCity directly under the Central Govern-ment	295	60
石河子市	Shihezi City	295	60
阿拉尔市	Aral City		

地　区	Region	普通中学 Regular Secondary Schools	#高　中 Senior Secondary Schools	小　学 Primary Schools	特殊教育学　校 Special Schools
总　计	**Total**	**116501**	**31258**	**135182**	**316**
乌鲁木齐市	Urumqi City	9910	3692	9189	126
克拉玛依市	Karamay City	2264	868	1825	7
吐鲁番地区	Turpan Administrative Offices	3350	970	4354	
哈密地区	Hami [Kumul] Administrative Offices	2629	1095	3040	23
昌吉回族自治州	Changji Hui Autonomous Prefecture	6404	2455	7374	28
伊犁哈萨克自治州	Ili Kazak Autonomous Prefecture	21405	6233	29296	36
伊犁州直属县(市)	Counties (Cities) Direct Under Ili Prefecture	12149	3169	17544	9
塔城地区	Tacheng [Tarbagatai] Administrative Offices	5461	1976	6899	27
阿勒泰地区	Altay Administrative Offices	3795	1088	4853	
博尔塔拉蒙古自治州	Bortala Mongol Autonomous Prefecture	2195	707	2973	
巴音郭楞蒙古自治州	Bayangol Mongol Autonomous Prefecture	6282	2252	8367	39
阿克苏地区	Aksu Administrative Offices	11169	2652	12865	16
克孜勒苏柯尔克孜自治州	Kizilsu Kirgiz Autonomous Prefecture	3815	1033	5403	
喀什地区	Kashgar [Kaxgar] Administrative Offices	21621	3536	24998	41
和田地区	Hotan Administrative Offices	9786	901	11608	
生产建设兵团	Production and Construction Group	14589	4304	13318	
自治区直辖县级市	Municpality Country-LevelCity directly under the Central Govern-ment	1082	560	572	
石河子市	Shihezi City	1071	560	538	
阿拉尔市	Aral City	11		34	

17-19 各地、州、市各级各类学校在校学生数

Number of Students Enrollment by Level and Type of School and by Prefecture, Autonomous Prefecture and City

单位：人 (2011 年) (person)

地区	Region	普通高等学校 Regular Institutions of Higher Education	中等职业学校 Specialized Secondary Schools
总计	**Total**	**258719**	**243039**
乌鲁木齐市	Urumqi City	152314	79024
克拉玛依市	Karamay City	3851	1013
吐鲁番地区	Turpan Administrative Offices		3190
哈密地区	Hami [Kumul] Administrative Offices		2853
昌吉回族自治州	Changji Hui Autonomous Prefecture	21003	12611
伊犁哈萨克自治州	Ili Kazak Autonomous Prefecture	13618	20827
伊犁州直属县(市)	Counties (Cities) Direct Under Ili Prefecture	13618	11279
塔城地区	Tacheng [Tarbagatai] Administrative Offices		2806
阿勒泰地区	Altay Administrative Offices		6742
博尔塔拉蒙古自治州	Bortala Mongol Autonomous Prefecture		1598
巴音郭楞蒙古自治州	Bayangol Mongol Autonomous Prefecture	3727	13703
阿克苏地区	Aksu Administrative Offices	2817	15674
克孜勒苏柯尔克孜自治州	Kizilsu Kirgiz Autonomous Prefecture		2400
喀什地区	Kashgar [Kaxgar] Administrative Offices	11657	27637
和田地区	Hotan Administrative Offices	5386	24362
生产建设兵团	Production and Construction Group	38524	36361
自治区直辖县级市	Municpality Country-LevelCity directly under the Central Govern-ment	5822	1786
石河子市	Shihezi City	5822	1786
阿拉尔市	Aral City		

地区	Region	普通中学 Regular Secondary Schools	#高中 Senior Secondary Schools	小学 Primary Schools	特殊教育学校 Special Schools
总计	**Total**	**1409293**	**432724**	**1919457**	**4733**
乌鲁木齐市	Urumqi City	148896	57829	181702	680
克拉玛依市	Karamay City	25067	9276	23107	51
吐鲁番地区	Turpan Administrative Offices	33036	10701	50735	85
哈密地区	Hami [Kumul] Administrative Offices	32070	13426	32512	219
昌吉回族自治州	Changji Hui Autonomous Prefecture	81981	33689	80121	194
伊犁哈萨克自治州	Ili Kazak Autonomous Prefecture	245784	88746	334749	712
伊犁州直属县(市)	Counties (Cities) Direct Under Ili Prefecture	151429	50058	217846	423
塔城地区	Tacheng [Tarbagatai] Administrative Offices	62355	25789	70834	202
阿勒泰地区	Altay Administrative Offices	32000	12899	46069	87
博尔塔拉蒙古自治州	Bortala Mongol Autonomous Prefecture	23032	10118	26996	81
巴音郭楞蒙古自治州	Bayangol Mongol Autonomous Prefecture	70724	27662	92550	222
阿克苏地区	Aksu Administrative Offices	139393	35259	216428	305
克孜勒苏柯尔克孜自治州	Kizilsu Kirgiz Autonomous Prefecture	34659	11134	54280	26
喀什地区	Kashgar [Kaxgar] Administrative Offices	255222	51981	411081	948
和田地区	Hotan Administrative Offices	116033	13018	191985	864
生产建设兵团	Production and Construction Group	184582	59905	212154	324
自治区直辖县级市	Municpality Country-LevelCity directly under the Central Govern-ment	18814	9980	11057	22
石河子市	Shihezi City	18692	9980	10745	22
阿拉尔市	Aral City	122		312	

17-20 各地、州、市各级各类学校招生数

Number of New Students Enrollment by Level and Type of School and by Prefecture, Autonomous Prefecture and City

单位：人　(2011 年)　(person)

地　区	Region	普通高等学校 Regular Institutions of Higher Education	中等职业学校 Specialized Secondary Schools
总　计	**Total**	**74365**	**90177**
乌鲁木齐市	Urumqi City	43653	30362
克拉玛依市	Karamay City	1422	402
吐鲁番地区	Turpan Administrative Offices		948
哈密地区	Hami [Kumul] Administrative Offices		1046
昌吉回族自治州	Changji Hui Autonomous Prefecture	6988	4675
伊犁哈萨克自治州	Ili Kazak Autonomous Prefecture	3970	8099
伊犁州直属县(市)	Counties (Cities) Direct Under Ili Prefecture	3970	4291
塔城地区	Tacheng [Tarbagatai] Administrative Offices		1195
阿勒泰地区	Altay Administrative Offices		2613
博尔塔拉蒙古自治州	Bortala Mongol Autonomous Prefecture		312
巴音郭楞蒙古自治州	Bayangol Mongol Autonomous Prefecture	1316	4619
阿克苏地区	Aksu Administrative Offices	893	6037
克孜勒苏柯尔克孜自治州	Kizilsu Kirgiz Autonomous Prefecture		1056
喀什地区	Kashgar [Kaxgar] Administrative Offices	2775	9363
和田地区	Hotan Administrative Offices	1622	7156
生产建设兵团	Production and Construction Group	9748	15403
自治区直辖县级市	Municpality Country-LevelCity directly under the Central Govern-ment	1978	699
石河子市	Shihezi City	1978	699
阿拉尔市	Aral City		

地　区	Region	普通中学 Regular Secondary Schools	#高中 Senior Secondary Schools	小学 Primary Schools	特殊教育学校 Special Schools
总　计	**Total**	**482450**	**156497**	**322436**	**939**
乌鲁木齐市	Urumqi City	51606	20481	32536	155
克拉玛依市	Karamay City	8538	3136	3588	10
吐鲁番地区	Turpan Administrative Offices	11338	3840	8833	14
哈密地区	Hami [Kumul] Administrative Offices	11002	4765	5311	33
昌吉回族自治州	Changji Hui Autonomous Prefecture	26850	11079	12901	37
伊犁哈萨克自治州	IliKazak Autonomous Prefecture	83534	32119	59472	138
伊犁州直属县(市)	Counties (Cities) Direct Under Ili Prefecture	52444	18459	38925	100
塔城地区	Tacheng [Tarbagatai] Administrative Offices	20650	9063	11982	23
阿勒泰地区	Altay Administrative Offices	10440	4597	8565	15
博尔塔拉蒙古自治州	Bortala Mongol Autonomous Prefecture	7540	3398	4532	18
巴音郭楞蒙古自治州	Bayangol Mongol Autonomous Prefecture	24661	9829	17495	39
阿克苏地区	Aksu Administrative Offices	50523	14598	37431	39
克孜勒苏柯尔克孜自治州	Kizilsu Kirgiz Autonomous Prefecture	11959	3838	9528	6
喀什地区	Kashgar [Kaxgar] Administrative Offices	86272	20448	66291	214
和田地区	Hotan Administrative Offices	39256	5145	29631	192
生产建设兵团	Production and Construction Group	62718	20244	33147	42
自治区直辖县级市	Municpality Country-LevelCity directly under the Central Govern-ment	6653	3577	1740	2
石河子市	Shihezi City	6626	3577	1676	2
阿拉尔市	Aral City	27		64	

17-21 各地、州、市各级各类学校毕业生数

Number of Graduates by Level and Type of School and by Prefecture, Autonomous Prefecture and City

单位：人 (2011 年) (person)

地 区	Region	普通高等学校 Regular Institutions of Higher Education	中等职业学校 Specialized Secondary Schools
总 计	**Total**	**63798**	**64508**
乌鲁木齐市	Urumqi City	36726	26386
克拉玛依市	Karamay City	1257	347
吐鲁番地区	Turpan Administrative Offices		926
哈密地区	Hami [Kumul] Administrative Offices		537
昌吉回族自治州	Changji Hui Autonomous Prefecture	6005	3889
伊犁哈萨克自治州	Ili Kazak Autonomous Prefecture	3242	5567
伊犁州直属县(市)	Counties (Cities) Direct Under Ili Prefecture	3242	2749
塔城地区	Tacheng [Tarbagatai] Administrative Offices		814
阿勒泰地区	Altay Administrative Offices		2004
博尔塔拉蒙古自治州	Bortala Mongol Autonomous Prefecture		520
巴音郭楞蒙古自治州	Bayangol Mongol Autonomous Prefecture	710	4049
阿克苏地区	Aksu Administrative Offices	878	2519
克孜勒苏柯尔克孜自治州	Kizilsu Kirgiz Autonomous Prefecture		158
喀什地区	Kashgar [Kaxgar] Administrative Offices	2434	4557
和田地区	Hotan Administrative Offices	1503	2185
生产建设兵团	Production and Construction Group	9858	12558
自治区直辖县级市	Municpality Country-LevelCity directly under the Central Govern-ment	1185	310
石河子市	Shihezi City	1185	310
阿拉尔市	Aral City		

地 区	Region	普通中学 Regular Secondary Schools	#高 中 Senior Secondary Schools	小 学 Primary Schools	特殊教育学 校 Special Schools
总 计	**Total**	**457944**	**129478**	**327704**	**652**
乌鲁木齐市	Urumqi City	47614	18546	29473	141
克拉玛依市	Karamay City	7941	2994	4538	12
吐鲁番地区	Turpan Administrative Offices	11112	3328	8330	6
哈密地区	Hami [Kumul] Administrative Offices	9560	3708	5965	6
昌吉回族自治州	Changji Hui Autonomous Prefecture	26178	10617	14935	51
伊犁哈萨克自治州	Ili Kazak Autonomous Prefecture	79825	26340	53866	41
伊犁州直属县(市)	Counties (Cities) Direct Under Ili Prefecture	48121	14511	35077	31
塔城地区	Tacheng [Tarbagatai] Administrative Offices	20841	7812	12517	2
阿勒泰地区	Altay Administrative Offices	10863	4017	6272	8
博尔塔拉蒙古自治州	Bortala Mongol Autonomous Prefecture	7401	3197	4374	3
巴音郭楞蒙古自治州	Bayangol Mongol Autonomous Prefecture	22491	8320	15219	29
阿克苏地区	Aksu Administrative Offices	43923	10451	37098	28
克孜勒苏柯尔克孜自治州	Kizilsu Kirgiz Autonomous Prefecture	10810	3224	8528	1
喀什地区	Kashgar [Kaxgar] Administrative Offices	86098	13324	68061	172
和田地区	Hotan Administrative Offices	36783	3244	36399	92
生产建设兵团	Production and Construction Group	62275	19214	38807	70
自治区直辖县级市	Municpality Country-LevelCity directly under the Central Govern-ment	5933	2971	2111	
石河子市	Shihezi City	5912	2971	2074	
阿拉尔市	Aral City	21		37	

17-22 各类学校教育经费情况
Educational Funds in Various Schools

单位：万元　　(2011 年)　　(10 000 yuan)

指 标	Item	合 计 Total	国家财政性教育经费 Government Appropriation for Education	#预算内教育经费 Budgetary Education Expense	民办学校中举办者投入 Investor Derotion	社会捐资 Donations	事业收入 Income from Under-takings	其 他 Others
总 计	**Total**	**4628682.5**	**4202471.8**	**3890195.7**	**1610.9**	**7111.1**	**304949.3**	**112539.4**
高等教育	**Institutions of Higher Education**	**657017.5**	**477826.2**	**466211.8**		**468.8**	**132586.4**	**46136.1**
普通高等学校	Regular Institutions of Higher Education	610278.4	446618.5	435005.4		468.8	118999.0	44192.1
普通高等本科学校	Universities with Full Undergraduate Course	423519.1	317248.1	315028.6		258.2	73528.8	32484.0
普通高职高专学校	Regular Institutions of Specialized Course	186759.3	129370.4	119976.8		210.6	45470.2	11708.1
#高等职业学校	Universities With High Vocational Course	141707.9	94547.4	85153.8		207.2	36418.1	10535.2
成人高等学校	Institutions of Higher Education for Adults	46739.1	31207.7	31206.4			13587.4	1944.0
高中阶段教育	Senior Secondary Education	**788207.7**	**644853.1**	**598275.7**	**56.1**	**4608.4**	**111336.4**	**27353.7**
中等职业教育	Technical Schools	289847.0	230730.4	218150.7	43.6	4001.7	36751.5	18319.8
中等专业学校	Specialized Secondary Schools	180062.6	141105.0	138884.9	43.6	58.5	25236.4	13619.1
职业高中	Professional Senior High School	67251.3	58971.1	53306.5		3943.2	2416.2	1920.8
#农 村	Rural Areas	600.4	600.3	528.0				0.1
技工学校	Technical Schools	33363.0	23077.7	19717.8			7718.4	2566.9
成人中等专业学校	Specialized Secondary Schools for Adults	9170.1	7576.6	6241.5			1380.5	213.0
普通高中	Regular Senior Secondary Schools	498360.7	414122.7	380125.0	12.5	606.7	74584.9	9033.9
#农 村	Rural0 Areas	18828.2	17836.6	15447.6		1.9	547.8	441.9
义务教育	**Compulsory Education**	**2569806.6**	**2532786.1**	**2365311.2**	**318.4**	**1338.8**	**12887.4**	**22475.9**
#农 村	Rural Areas	1439628.9	1425891.5	1354764.5		684.7	2820.1	10232.6
普通初中	Regular Junior Secondary Schools	1067122.5	1049816.0	967794.4	109.1	508.2	7307.3	9381.9
#农 村	Rural Areas	550130.5	544801.1	513115.3		211.5	1178.5	3939.4
普通小学	Regular Primary Schools	1496028.3	1476692.8	1392162.8	209.3	824.6	5475.9	12825.7
#农 村	Rural Areas	889498.4	881090.4	841649.2		473.2	1641.6	6293.2
特殊教育	Special Education Schools	6655.8	6277.3	5354.0		6.0	104.2	268.3
学前教育	**Pre-school Education**	**190144.4**	**152345.0**	**140572.6**	**1236.4**	**186.3**	**33869.5**	**2507.2**
#农 村	Rural Areas	77311.3	73989.8	66971.6	25.9	83.3	3105.2	107.1
其 他	**Others**	**423506.3**	**394661.4**	**319824.4**		**508.8**	**14269.6**	**14066.5**

注：本表按隶属关系填列
Note: Data in The table according to the membership listed.

17-23 科技活动基本情况

Basic Statistics on Scientific and Technological Activities

指　　标	Item	2009	2010
研究与试验发展人员折合全时当量(人·年)	**Full-time Equivalent of Rearch and Development Personnel (person.year)**	**12655**	**21065**
研究与试验发展经费支出(万元)	**Funding for Scientific and Technological Activities (10 000 yuan)**	**218043**	**266545**
按活动类型分	Government Funds		
#基础研究	Self-raised Funds by Enterprises	10470	14325
应用研究	Bank Loans	77596	63005
试验发展	Experimental Development	129976	189215
按支出用途分	Service Fees		
日常性支出	Purchases or Construction of Fixed Assets	176974	233522
#劳务费	Expenditure on Research and Development	67607	73389
资产性支出	Basic Research	41069	33023
#仪器和设备	Applied Research	36372	30863
研究与试验发展经费支出相当于新疆生产总值比例(%)	**Proportion of Expenditure on Research and Development to GDP of Xinjiang (%)**	**0.52**	**0.49**

注：从 2009 年开始该表指标口径有所调整。
Note: Since 2009 Statistial coverage in this table have adjusted

17-24 县级以上政府部门属研究与开发机构及科技信息与文献机构数、人员数

State-owned Research and Development Institutions and Information and Literature Institutions at and above County Level and Persons Engaged

(2011 年)

指　　标	Item	合　计 Total	自然科学技术领域 Field of Natural Sciences and Technology	社会、人文科学技术领域 Field of Social Sciences and Humanities	科技信息和文献机构 Scientific-technical Information and Document Institutions
机构数(个)	**Institutions (unit)**	**108**	**94**	**6**	**8**
科技活动人员(人)	**Personal Engaged in Scientific and Technological Activities (person)**	**6322**	**5674**	**410**	**238**
#大学本科及以上学历	University Graduate or above	4037	3591	273	173
研究与试验发展全时人员(人·年)	**Full-time Equivalent of Rearch and Development Personnel (person.year)**	**3115**	**2767**	**305**	**43**
科技活动收入(万元)	**Sources of Funds for S&T(10 000 yuan)**	**134200.5**	**123959.6**	**5268.2**	**4972.7**
#政府拨款	Government Funds	107289.8	97890.7	4964.4	4434.7
科技经费内部支出额(万元)	**Internal Expenditures on Scientific and Technological Activities (10 000 yuan)**	**126310.4**	**116430.4**	**5511.6**	**4368.4**
#劳务费	Service Fees	41950.5	38163.8	1713.2	2073.5
固定资产购建费	Purchases or Construction of Fixed Assets	20769.5	19634.4	663.4	471.7
#研究与发展经费支出	Expenditure on Research and Development	57498.4	54520.1	1809.4	1168.9
#基础研究	Basic Research	9939.7	8511.7	1428.0	
应用研究	Applied Research	21776.9	20332.9	275.1	1168.9
试验发展	Experimental Development	25781.8	25675.5	106.3	

17-25 重大科学技术研究成果及奖励数
Number of Major Achievements in Scientific and Technological Research and Awarded Prizes

单位：项 (item)

年 份 Year	自治区级重大科技成果 Number of Major Achievements in Science and Technology of Autonomous Region	奖励情况 Awarded Prizes					
		国家级 National	自治区级 Autonomous Regional	一等奖 Frist Class Awards	二等奖 Second Class Awards	三等奖 Third Class Awards	四等奖 Fourth Class Awards
1978 年以前	1551	88	610				
1980-1985	1173	16	356	5	31	102	218
1990	444	3	129		18	56	55
1995	218	3	137	4	26	53	54
2000	250	2	90	5	18	67	
2001	285	6	92	4	23	65	
2002	207	5	99	5	30	64	
2003	232	3	111	8	34	69	
2004	218	4	108	4	33	71	
2005	225	3	101	6	27	68	
2006	212	3	107	8	37	62	
2007	220	8	118	10	42	66	
2008	69	8	108	9	40	59	
2009	166	12					
2010	228	9	130	15	47	68	
2011	205	6	121	14	46	61	

17-26 专利申请和批准数
Number of Patent Applications Examined and Approved

单位：件 (case)

年 份 Year	申 请 数 Number of Patent Applications Examined				批 准 数 Number of Patent Applications Granted				代理机构（个） Agency (unit)
	合 计 Total	发 明 Inventions	实用新型 Utility Models	外观设计 Designs	合 计 Total	发 明 Inventions	实用新型 Utility Models	外观设计 Designs	
1990	250	38	203	9	139	3	135	1	5
1995	609	92	467	50	312	11	285	16	6
2000	1088	179	699	210	717	66	475	176	7
2001	1088	189	683	216	755	90	522	143	5
2002	1239	216	779	244	627	61	407	159	4
2003	1472	253	940	279	751	75	520	156	5
2004	1492	272	870	350	792	75	530	187	5
2005	1851	320	1117	414	921	88	537	296	5
2006	2256	381	1166	709	1187	107	805	275	5
2007	2270	476	1255	539	1534	90	1035	409	5
2008	2412	482	1408	522	1493	82	1100	311	6
2009	2872	662	1865	345	1867	120	1261	486	6
2010	3560	914	2272	374	2562	189	2012	361	6
2011	4736	1273	2732	731	2642	302	1974	366	6

17-27 高等学校科技活动情况

Basic Statistics on Higher Education for Science and Technology Activities

指　标	Item	2010	2011
科技活动人员(人)	**Personnel Engaged in Scientific and Technological Activities (person)**	**12894**	**12712**
#科学家与工程师	Scientists and Engineers	9063	9803
研究与发展机构(个)	**Agencies of Research and Development (unit)**	**24**	**27**
研究与发展人员全时当量(人·年)	**Full-time Equivalent of R&D Personnel (person.year)**	**1765**	**2106**
#科学家与工程师	Scientists and Engineers	1534	1868
#基础研究	Basic Research	646	943
应用研究	Applied Research	942	1000
试验发展	Experimental Development	106	88
科技经费筹集额(万元)	**Funding for Scientific and Development Activities(10 000 yuan)**	**23628**	**36791**
#政府拨款	Government Funds	18411	33012
科技经费内部支出额(万元)	**Internal Expenditure on Scientific and Technological Activities (10 000 yuan)**	**19202**	**20598**
#劳务费	Service Fees	4412	5226
固定资产购建费	Purchases or Construction of Fixed Assets	3687	3058
#研究与发展经费支出	Expenditure on Research and Development	15644	18343
#基础研究	Basic Research	3990	7953
应用研究	Applied Research	9063	7909
试验发展	Experimental Development	1504	1637

17-28 主要年份企事业单位主要专业技术人员数
Number of Main Scientific and Technical Personnel in Enterprises and Institutions in Main Years

单位：人 (person)

年 份 Year	合 计 Total	工程技术人员 Engineering	农业技术人员 Agriculture	卫生技术人员 Health Care	科学研究人员 Scientific Researcn	教学人员 Teaching
1978. 6 月末	85063	22198	13141	31741	3042	14941
1985	158709	51636	20730	57559	3416	25368
1990	241524	92383	25089	71906	4326	47820
1995	437209	109463	28096	79014	4825	215811
2000	368262	58576	27764	62338	2409	217175
2001	385129	59913	30043	65585	2492	227096
2002	387726	58011	31867	65364	2337	230147
2003	385705	57506	30808	65622	2236	229533
2004	398318	55421	32831	68604	2928	238534
2005	402404	51915	32744	67945	2451	247349
2006	412977	52702	34131	68231	2460	255453
2007	411590	50680	33859	69101	2453	255497
2008	414277	49175	31799	71104	2261	259938
2009	411628	47525	30126	72827	2518	258632
2010	407651	47734	28433	77357	2071	252056
2011	421372	47357	27921	80290	6728	259076

注：1.1991 年起专业技术人员包括企事业单位(不含行政机关)人员数,教学人员包括社会和自然科技领域及小学教师人数。
2.1996 年后数据不包括中央单位的专业技术人员数，故人员减少较多。

Note: a) The Specialezed and technical personnel include those who work in enterprises and institutions (excluding administrative organs), teaching Staff, those work in social and nature scientific fields as well as elementary school teachers since 1991.
b) After 1996, the data exclude the figure of professionals with national establishments stationed to Xinjiang and thus the number of staff is reduced a lot.

17-29 主要年份企事业单位主要专业技术人员比重
Proportion of Scientific and Technical Personnel in Enterprises and Institutions in Main Years

单位：% (%)

年 份 Year	合 计 Total	工程技术 Engineering	农业技术 Agriculture	卫生技术 Health Care	科学研究 Scientific Research	教 学 Teaching
1978. 6 月末	100	26.10	15.45	37.31	3.58	17.56
1985	100	32.54	13.06	36.27	2.15	15.98
1990	100	38.25	10.39	29.77	1.79	19.80
1995	100	25.04	6.43	18.07	1.10	49.36
2000	100	15.91	7.54	16.93	0.65	58.97
2001	100	15.55	7.80	17.03	0.65	58.97
2002	100	14.96	8.22	16.86	0.60	59.36
2003	100	14.91	7.99	17.01	0.58	59.51
2004	100	13.91	8.24	17.22	0.74	59.89
2005	100	12.90	8.14	16.89	0.61	61.46
2006	100	12.76	8.26	16.52	0.60	61.86
2007	100	12.31	8.22	16.79	0.60	62.08
2008	100	11.87	7.68	17.16	0.55	62.74
2009	100	11.55	7.32	17.69	0.61	62.83
2010	100	11.71	6.97	18.98	0.51	61.83
2011	100	11.24	6.63	19.05	1.60	61.48

17-30 大中型工业企业科技活动情况

(2010 年)

项 目	Item	企业数(个) Nnmber of Industrial Enterprises (unit)	#有研究与试验发展活动的企业数 Number of Enterprises Having R & D Activities	科技机构(个) Number of Scientific Technological Agencies (unit)	研究与试验发展人员数(人) Number of R & D Persons	研究人员 Rese-arch perso-nal
总 计	**Total**	**325**	**50**	**64**	**6847**	**4280**
按登记注册类型分	**Grouped by Ownership**					
内资企业	Domestic-funded Enterprises	310	50	63	6847	4280
国有企业	State-owned	41	4	6	970	650
集体企业	Collective-owned Enterprises	3	1		17	7
有限责任公司	Limited Liability Corporations	167	20	31	1102	377
国有独资公司	Sole State-funded Corporations	23	2	2	41	39
其他有限责任公司	Limited Liability Corporations	144	18	29	1061	338
股份有限责任公司	Share-holding Corporations Ltd	44	18	18	4572	3165
私营企业	Private Enterprises	54	7	8	186	81
私营独资企业	Private-funded Enterprises	2				
私营有限责任公司	Private Limited Liability Corporations	45	3	5	119	56
私营股份有限公司	Private Stock Ltd. Co.	7	4	3	67	25
港澳台商投资企业	Enterprises With Funds from Hong Kong, Macao and Taiwan	7				
#合资经营企业(港或澳、台资)	Joint-ventures Enterprises	2				
港、澳、台商独资经营企业	Enterprises with Funds from Hong Kong, Macao and Taiwan	4				
外商投资企业	Foreign Funded Enterprises	8		1		
#中外合资经营企业	Joint-venture Enterprises	6		1		
按工业行业大类分	**Grouped by Sector**					
采矿业	Mining and Quarrying	63	9	15	4396	3288
煤炭开采和洗选业	Coal Extracting and Dressing	33	3	5	117	82
石油和天然气开采业	Petroleum and Natural Gas Extraction	12	6	8	4279	3206
黑色金属矿采选业	Processing of Ferrous Metals Ores	8				
有色金属矿采选业	Processing of Nonferrous Metals Ores	7		2		
非金属矿采选业	Processing of Nonmetal Ores	3				
制造业	Manufacturing	227	37	45	1966	810
农副食品加工业	Processing of Food from Agricultural Products	19	4	6	73	34
食品制造业	Food Manufacturing	15	1	2	76	19
饮料制造业	Beverage Manufacturing	8	1	1	27	5
烟草制品业	Tobacco Manufacturing	1				
纺织业	Textile Industry	38	4	4	239	80
纺织服装、鞋、帽制造业	Leather, Fur, Feather and Related Products Manufacturing	1				
家具制造业	Furniture Manufacturing	1				
造纸及纸制品业	Paper and Paper Products Manufacturing	3	2	2	161	19

Statistics on Technical Activities of Large and Medium-sized Industrial Enterprises

研究与试验发展人员折合全时当量(人.年) Full-time Equivalent of R & D personnel	研究人员 Research personal	研究与试验发展经费(万元) Expenditure on R & D	其中 Of which			其中 Of which		研究与试验发展项目数(项) Projects to R & D	新产品开发项目数(项) Number of New Produots
			基础研究 Basic Research	应用研究 Applied Research	试验发展 Experimental Development	政府资金 Government Appropriation Funds	企业资金 Self-raised Funds by Enterprises		
5970	**3714**	**167254**		**24261**	**142992**	**9292**	**157962**	**679**	**374**
5970	3714	167254		24261	142992	9292	157962	679	374
845	577	11659		1096	10564	166	11493	99	71
17	7	71			71	3	68	1	1
860	261	37680			37680	2621	35059	84	101
11	9	1190			1190	25	1165	4	9
850	252	36490			36490	2596	33894	80	92
4112	2804	112720		22596	90123	6271	106449	483	191
147	64	5124		569	4554	230	4894	12	10
113	50	897		6	891	230	667	3	3
34	14	4226		563	3663		4226	9	7
4050	3045	94069		22318	71752	5330	88740	432	96
36	28	2764			2764	23	2741	6	3
4013	3017	91305		22318	68987	5307	85998	426	91
									2
1568	613	65301		1399	63902	3732	61569	203	270
54	22	5297			5297	207	5090	5	9
58	14	1664			1664	280	1384	3	4
4	1	228		228			228	2	7
128	42	1977			1977	256	1721	8	13
161	19	697			697	48	649	52	52

17-30 续表

(2010 年)

项　　目	Item	企业数(个) Nnmber of Industrial Enterprises (unit)	#有研究与试验发展活动的企业数 Number of Enterprises Having R & D Activities	科技机构(个) Number of Scientific Technological Agencies (unit)	研究与试验发展人员数(人) Number of R & D Persons	研究人员 Research personal
印刷业和记录媒介的复制	Printing and Copying of Medium for Record	1				
石油加工、炼焦及核燃料加工业	Oil Processing, Coking and Nuclear Fuel Processing	18	5	4	267	201
化学原料及化学制品制造业	Raw Chemical Material and Chemical Products	31	6	7	539	273
医药制造业	Medicine Manufacturing	3	1	1	6	4
化学纤维制造业	Chemical Fiber Manufacturing	10		2		
橡胶制品业	Rubber Products Manufacturing	1	1		15	5
塑料制品业	Plastic Products Manufacturing	3	1		150	1
非金属矿物制品业	Nonmetal Mineral Products Manufacturing	31	4	6	97	60
黑色金属冶炼及压延加工业	Manufacture and Processing of Ferrous Metals	16	2	3	59	44
有色金属冶炼及压延加工业	Manufalture and Processing of Non-ferrous Metals	9				
金属制品业	Metal Products Manufacturing	5	1	2	15	5
通用设备制造业	General Purpose Machinery Manufacturing	2	1		50	24
专用设备制造业	Special Purpose Machinery Manufacturing	3		2		
交通运输设备制造业	Transport Equipment Manufacturing	2		1		
电气机械及器材制造业	Electric Equipment and Machinery Manufacturing	5	2	1	84	25
通信设备、计算机及其他电子设备制造业	Telecom Equipment, Computer and Other Electronic Equipment	1	1	1	108	13
电力、燃气及水的生产和供应业	Production and Suppoly of Electric Power,Gas and Water	35	4	4	485	182
电力、热力的生产和供应业	Electric Power and Thermal Production and Supply	33	4	4	485	182
燃气生产和供应业	Gas Production and Supply	1				
水的生产和供应业	Water Production and Supply	1				
按企业所在地区划分	**Grouped by Region**					
乌鲁木齐市	Urumqi City	74	15	20	610	278
克拉玛依市	Karamay City	21	10	10	3735	2684
吐鲁番地区	Turpan Administrative Offices	17	2	3	620	435
哈密地区	Hami [Kumul] Administrative Offices	15	2	1	61	61
昌吉回族自治州	Changji Hui Autonomous Prefecture	40	1	1	54	9
伊犁州直属县(市)	Counties (Cities) Direct Under Ili Prefecture	29	3	5	46	19
塔城地区	Tacheng [Tarbagatai] Administrative Offices	17	1	1	11	11
阿勒泰地区	Altay Administrative Offices	8		2		
博尔塔拉蒙古自治州	Bortala Mongol Autonomous Prefecture	8				
巴音郭楞蒙古自治州	Bayangol Mongol Autonomous Prefecture	23	5	5	789	518
阿克苏地区	Aksu Administrative Offices	26	3	7	60	23
克孜勒苏柯尔克孜自治州	Kizilsu Kirgiz Autonomous Prefecture	2				
喀什地区	Kashgar [Kaxgar] Administrative Offices	6	1	1	33	3
和田地区	Hotan Administrative Offices	3		1		
自治区直辖县级市	Municpality Country-LevelCity directly under the Central Govern-ment	36	7	7	828	239

Continued

研究与试验发展人员折合全时当量(人.年) Full-time Equivalent of R & D personnel	研究人员 Research personal	研究与试验发展经费(万元) Expenditure on R & D	其中 Of which			其中 Of which		研究与试验发展项目数(项) Projects to R & D	新产品开发项目数(项) Number of New Produots
			基础研究 Basic Research	应用研究 Applied Research	试验发展 Experimental Development	政府资金 Government Appropriation Funds	企业资金 Self-raised Funds by Enterprises		
226	160	8580			8580	873	7707	52	57
463	240	11014		20	10994	1774	9240	16	17
6	4	81			81	25	56	2	5
13	4	708			708		708	11	22
150	1	3671		601	3070	51	3620	15	6
61	43	2759		6	2753		2759	9	12
18	14	16208			16208	81	16127	15	16
									1
15	3	267			267	81	186	2	1
28	14	226			226	30	196	3	2
									8
									8
76	21	8304		543	7761	25	8279	6	25
108	13	3620			3620		3620	2	5
352	55	7884		545	7339	231	7653	44	8
352	55	7884		545	7339	231	7653	44	8
410	150	38173		957	37216	570	37603	64	100
3531	2565	67684		682	67002	2959	64725	376	134
543	383	20279		15938	4340	228	20050	66	3
31	31	1119			1119		1119	3	5
54	9	4685			4685	25	4660	4	17
10	7	279		234	45		279	4	8
1	1	249			249	95	154	1	
									2
719	459	20624		5718	14906	3745	16878	101	80
37	21	488			488		488	5	2
1		221			221		221	1	6
633	87	13454		732	12722	1669	11785	54	17

17-31 各类技术合同签定及执行情况

Statistics on Signing and Implementing Technical Contracts by Type

单位：项、万元 (item,10 000 yuan)

项　目	Item	合同数 Number of Contracts		合同金额 Contract Amount		#技术交易额 Transaction Value in Technical Market	
		2010	2011	2010	2011	2010	2011
总　计	**Total**	**1701**	**1473**	**46417.70**	**43778.69**	**43145.85**	**43045.15**
技术开发合同	Technology Development	276	305	14606.23	20955.88	14144.36	20843.54
技术转让合同	Technology Transfer	107	39	4949.42	1244.08	4100.13	1219.08
技术咨询合同	Technology Consultation	812	532	7762.90	8674.78	7729.30	8674.78
技术服务合同	Technology Service	506	597	19099.15	12903.95	17172.06	12307.75

17-32 各级技术计划项目进入技术市场情况

Statistics on Projects for Technical Plan Entering Technical Market by Level

单位：项、万元 (2011 年) (item,10 000 yuan)

项　目	Item	合　计 Total		国家计划 National Plans		部门计划 Department Plans	
		项　数 Number of Items	金　额 Values	项　数 Number of Items	金　额 Values	项　数 Number of Items	金　额 Values
总　计	**Total**	**1473**	**43778.69**	**6**	**411.65**	**19**	**208.92**
机关法人	Government Agency Legal Person						
事业法人	Institntion Legal Person	861	12134.05	1	19.50	2	49.30
社团法人	Corporation Aggregate	4	1253.00				
企业法人	Business Entity	607	30381.64	5	392.15	17	159.62
自然人	Person	1	10				

项　目	Item	省、自治区计划 单列市计划 Provinces, Municipality Plans		地、市、县计划 Area City and County Plans		计划外 Out of Plan	
		项　数 Number of Items	金　额 Values	项　数 Number of Items	金　额 Values	项　数 Number of Items	金　额 Values
总　计	**Total**	**11**	**389.25**	**40**	**430.09**	**1397**	**42338.78**
机关法人	Government Agency Legal Person						
事业法人	Institntion Legal Person	4	60.40	34	316.52	820	11688.33
社团法人	Corporation Aggregate					4	1253.00
企业法人	Business Entity	7	328.85	6	113.57	572	29387.45
自然人	Person					1	10.00

17-33 技术流向地域情况
Statistics on Location of Technical Contract

单位：项、万元 (2011 年) (item, 10 000 yuan)

地区 Region	合同类别合计 Contracts of Classification Total		技术开发 Technology Development		技术转让 Technology Transfer		技术咨询 Technology Consultation		技术服务 Technology Service	
	项数 Number of Items	金额 Values	项数 Number of Items	金额 Values	项数 Number of Items	金额 Values	项数 Number of Items	金额 Values	项数 Number of Items	金额 Values
总计 Total	**1473**	**43778.69**	**305**	**20955.88**	**39**	**1244.08**	**532**	**8674.78**	**597**	**12903.95**
北京 Beijing	16	663.12	5	378.52			1	29.80	10	254.80
天津 Tianjing	1	109.00	1	109.00						
河北 Hebei	2	29.00					2	29.00		
山西 Shanxi	3	120.98					3	120.98		
内蒙古 Inner Mongolia	9	474.00					9	474.00		
辽宁 Liaoning	5	150.80					4	140.50	1	10.30
黑龙江 Heilongjiang	2	120.00					2	120.00		
江苏 Jiangsu	6	117.00	4	72.00			1	40.00	1	5.00
浙江 Zhejiang	13	157.77	1	140.00			2	0.90	10	16.87
安徽 Aanhui	2	61.50	1	2.00	1	59.50				
福建 Fujian	1	5.00							1	5.00
江西 Jiangxi	14	56.60	2	15.00	12	41.60				
山东 Shandong	5	15.64	1	8.60			3	2.00	1	5.04
河南 Henan	3	31.00					3	31.00		
湖北 Hubei	1	46.00					1	46.00		
湖南 Hunan	3	128.90			3	128.90				
广东 Guangdong	2	153.25	1	133.25					1	20.00
四川 Sichuan	1	5.00					1	5.00		
贵州 Guizhou	1	3.60			1	3.60				
云南 Yunnan	1	6.00							1	6.00
陕西 Shaanxi	7	307.20	1	7.20			5	275.00	1	25.00
甘肃 Gansu	3	102.00					3	102.00		
青海 Qinghai	1	3.00							1	3.00
宁夏 Ningxia	4	240.00					4	240.00		
新疆 Xinjiang	1367	40672.33	288	20090.31	22	1010.48	488	7018.60	569	12552.94

17-34 技术经济合同成交情况
Statistics on Transaction in Technical and Economic Contract

单位：项、万元 (2011 年) (item, 10 000 yuan)

卖方类别 Classification of Sellers / 买方类别 Classification of Buyers		合计 Total		#事业法人 Institntion Legal Person		#社团法人 Corporation Aggregate		#企业法人 Business Entity		#自然人 Person	
		项数 Number of Items	金额 Values	项数 Number of Items	金额 Values	项数 Number of Items	金额 Values	项数 Number of Items	金额 Values	项数 Number of Items	金额 Values
总计	**Total**	**1473**	**43778.69**	**861**	**12134.05**	**4**	**1253.00**	**607**	**30381.64**	**1**	**10.00**
机关法人	Government Agency Legal Person	136	5974.54	73	1953.05	1	176.00	62	3845.49		
事业法人	Institntion Legal Person	164	2437.18	98	926.57			66	1510.61		
社团法人	Corporation Aggregate	6	801.40	4	11.40	2	790.00				
企业法人	Business Entity	1162	32810.66	684	7793.12			477	25007.54	1	10.00
自然人	Person	2	295.00			1	287.00	1	8.00		
其他组织	Others	3	1459.92	2	1449.92			1	10.00		

17-35 主要年份文化产业基本情况
Basic Statistics on Culture in Main Years

项目	Item	2005	2010	2011
文化产业机构数(个)	**Number of Culture Institutions (unit)**	**11777**	**9430**	**8879**
文化部门	Culture Departments	2404	1826	1911
其他部门	Other Departments	9373	7604	6968
文化产业人员数(人)	**Number of Person in Culture (person)**	**34001**	**37711**	**49222**
文化部门	Culture Departments	11515	13310	13697
其他部门	Other Departments	22486	24401	35525
各类文化艺术事业单位数(个)	**Number of Institutions on Various Culture and Art (unit)**			
文化馆	Cultural Centers	110	112	112
公共图书馆	Public Libraries	94	103	103
博物馆	Museums	28	71	73
艺术表演场所	Art Performance Places	47	15	13
艺术表演团体	Art Performance Troupes	89	132	133

17-36 文化艺术、文物事业机构和人员情况

Number of Institutions and Personnel in Culture, Art and Cultural Relics

(2011 年)

项　目	Item	机构数（个）Number of Institutions (unit)	从业人员数（人）Number of Persons Engaged (person)
艺术事业	**Art Institutions**	**151**	**5380**
艺术表演团体	Art Performance Troupes	133	5023
#话剧、儿童剧、滑稽剧团	Drama, Children Plays and Comedy Troupes	2	132
歌剧、舞剧、歌舞剧团	Opera, Ballet and Dance Troupes	4	283
歌舞团、轻音乐团	Song and Dance Troupe, Light Music Troupe	73	2596
文工团、文宣队、乌兰牧骑	Cultural and Performance Troupes and Ulanmuchi (equestrain art troupes)	36	1253
戏曲剧团	Local Opera Troupes	8	267
#京 剧	Local Beijing Opera Troupes	2	93
曲艺、杂技、木偶、皮影团	Recitation and Ballad Troupes, Acrobatics and Circus Troupes, Puppet Show Troupes and Shadow Play Troupes	5	142
艺术表演场所	Art Centers	13	308
#剧场、影剧院	Theaters and Music Halls	11	273
艺术创作机构	Art Creation Institutions	5	49
图书馆事业	**Libraries**	**103**	**981**
群众文化事业	**Mass Culture**	**1259**	**3803**
文化馆	Cultural Centers	112	1304
文化站	Cultural Stations	1147	2499
#乡镇文化站	Township Cultural Stations	1018	2267
艺术教育事业	**Culture and Education**	**2**	**132**
艺术科研机构	**Art Research Institutions**	**2**	**58**
文化市场经营单位	**Entertainment Operators**	**5032**	**21248**
文化娱乐业	Entertainment Operators	2544	13247
文化市场其他经营单位	Cultural Market Operators	2488	8001
其他文化事业	**Other Cultural Units**	**5**	**49**
文物事业合计	**Cultural Relics**	**250**	**2203**
文物机构	Historical Relics Agency	176	1476
文物保护管理机构	Agency of Historical Relics Preservation	50	608
文物科研机构	Scientific and Research Historical Relics Agency	2	104
其他文物机构	Other Historical Relics Agency	1	40
博物馆	Museums	73	696
#历史类	History Museum	30	258
文物商店	Cultural Relics Store	1	31

17-37 电影、电视、广播事业基本情况
Basic Statistics on Feature Film, Television and Broadcasting

项　　目	Item	2010	2011
电影制片厂(个)	**Number of Film Studios (unit)**	**1**	**1**
广播电台(座)	**Number of Broadcasting Stations (unit)**	**6**	**6**
中短波发射台及转播台(座)	Transmission and Relaying Stations of MW&SW (unit)	54	53
中短波广播发射功率(千瓦)	Power of MW & SW Transmitters (kw)	2820	2819
调频发射台及转播台(座)	FM Transmission and Relaying Stations (unit)	984	976
调频发射功率(千瓦)	Power of FM Transmitters (kw)	476.29	495.43
节目(套)	Program (set)	155	159
制作广播节目(小时)	Production of Broadcasting (hour)	260510	270895
#新闻资讯类节目	News Programs	52594	57718
专题服务类节目	Feature Programs	79677	83144
综艺类节目	Variety Show	85358	78111
广播剧类节目	Radio Play	6016	9494
广告类节目	Advertisement Programs	15221	21262
其他类节目	Other Programs	21644	21163
广播人口覆盖率((%)	Listener Rate (%)	94.90	94.90
电视台(座)	**Number of Television Stations (unit)**	**8**	**8**
广播电视台(座)	**Radio and TV Stations (unit)**	**88**	**88**
#县级广播电视台(座)	Radio and TV Station at County-Level (unit)	80	80
电视发射台及转播台(座)	TV Transmission Stations and Relaying Stations (unit)	914	911
电视发射机功率(千瓦)	Power of TV Transmitters (kw)	903.73	909.89
节目(套)	Program (set)	196	198
制作电视节目(小时)	Production of TV Programs (hour)	76467	85002
#新闻资讯类节目	News Programs	28256	30949
专题服务类节目	Feature Programs	18599	18391
综艺类节目	Variety Show	8811	9975
影视剧类节目	Film and TV Play Programs	2151	4238
广告类节目	Advertisement Programs	12740	14125
其他类节目	Other Programs	5910	7323
电视人口覆盖率(%)	Viewer Rate (%)	95.28	95.29
有线电视用户(万户)	Numbe of Users of CATV (10 000 households)	192.00	208.02
#数字电视用户	Number of users Digital TV	131.00	188.45
卫星收转站(座)	Satellite Receiving Stations (unit)	189902	554317

注：影视剧类节目不包括译制节目。
Note: Number of film and television programs exclude film dubbing program .

主要统计指标解释

普通高等学校 指按照国家规定的设置标准和审批程序批准举办的，通过全国普通高等学校统一招生考试，招收高中毕业生为主要培养对象，实施高等教育的全日制大学、独立设置的学院和高等专科学校、高等职业学校和其他机构(独立学院和分校、大专班)。

大学、独立设置的学院主要实施本科层次以上教育。高等专科学校、高等职业学校实施专科层次教育。其他机构是承担国家普通招生计划任务不计校数的机构，包括独立学院、普通高等学校分校、大专班和批准筹建的普通高等学校等。独立学院指由普通本科高校按新机制、新模式举办的本科层次的二级学院，一些普通本科高校按公办机制和模式建立的二级学院，"分校"或其他类似的二级办学机构不属此范畴。

小学学龄儿童净入学率 指调查范围内已入小学学习的学龄儿童占校内外学龄儿童总数(包括弱智儿童，不包括盲聋哑儿童)的比重。计算公式为：

小学学龄儿童净入学率=已入学的小学学龄儿童数/校内外小学学龄儿童总数×100%

科技活动 指在自然科学、农业科学、医药科学、工程与技术科学、人文与社会科学领域(简称科学技术领域)中，与科技知识的产生、发展、传播和应用密切相关的有组织的活动。可分为研究与试验发展(R&D)、研究与试验发展成果应用及相关的科技服务三类活动。该定义是联合国教科文组织考虑成员国特别是发展中国家开展科技统计工作的需要，而对科技活动所作的统计界定。

科技活动人员 指直接从事科技活动、以及专门从事科技活动管理和为科技活动提供直接服务，累计的实际工作时间占全年制度工作时间10%及以上的人员。(1)直接从事科技活动的人员包括：在独立核算的科学研究与技术开发机构、高等学校、各类企业及其他事业单位内设的研究室、实验室、技术开发中心及中试车间(基地)等机构中从事科技活动的研究人员、工程技术人员、技术工人及其它人员；虽不在上述机构工作，但编入科技活动项目(课题)组的人员；科技信息与文献机构中的专业技术人员；从事论文设计的研究生等。(2)专门从事科技活动管理和为科技活动提供直接服务的人员，包括：独立核算的科学研究与技术开发机构、科技信息与文献机构、高等学校、各类企业及其他事业单位主管科技工作的负责人，专门从事科技活动的计划、行政、人事、财务、物资供应、设备维护、图书资料管理等工作的各类人员，但不包括保卫、医疗保健人员、司机、食堂人员、茶炉工、水暖工、清洁工等为科技活动提供间接服务的人员。该指标用来反映投入科技活动人力的规模。

科学家与工程师 指科技活动人员中具有高、中级技术职称(职务)的人员和不具有高、中级技术职称(职务)的大学本科及以上学历人员。该指标用来反映投入科技活动人力的素质。

研究与试验发展(R&D) 指在科学技术领域，为增加知识总量、以及运用这些知识去创造新的应用进行的系统的创造性的活动，包括基础研究、应用研究、试验发展三类活动。国际上通常采用R&D 活动的规模和强度指标反映一国的科技实力和核心竞争力。

基础研究 指为了获得关于现象和可观察事实的基本原理的新知识(揭示客观事物的本质、运动规律，获得新发现、新学说)而进行的实验性或理论性研究，它不以任何专门或特定的应用或使用为目的。其成果以科学论文和科学著作为主要形式。用来反映知识的原始创新能力。

应用研究 指为获得新知识而进行的创造性研究，主要针对某一特定的目的或目标。应用研究是为了确定基础研究成果可能的用途，或是为达到预定的目标探索应采取的新方法(原理性)或新途径。其成果形式以科学论文、专著、原理性模型或发明专利为主。用来反映对基础研究成果应用途径的探索。

研究与试验发展人员 指参与研究与试验发展项目研究、管理和辅助工作的人员，包括项目(课题)组人员，企业科技行政管理人员和直接为项目(课题)活动提供服务的辅助人员。反映投入从事拥有自主知识产权的研究开发活动的人力规模。

研究与试验发展人员全时当量 指全时人员数加非全时人员按工作量折算为全时人员数的总和。例如：有两个全时人员和三个非全时人员(工作时间分别为2 0 %、3 0 % 和70%)，则全时当量为2+0.2+0.3+0.7=3.2 人年。为国际上比较科技人力投入而制定的可比指标。

专业技术人员 指从事专业技术工作和专业技术管理工作的人员，即企事业单位中已经聘任专业技术职务从事专业技术工作和专业技术管理工作的人员，以及未聘任专业技术职务，现在专业技术岗位上工作的人员。包括工程技术人员，农业技术人员，科学研究人员，卫生技术人员，教学人×100%员，经济人员，会计人员，统计人员，翻译人员，图书资料、档案、文博人员，新闻出版人员，律师、公证人员，广播电视播音人员，工艺美术人员，体育人员，艺术人员及企业政治思想工作人员，共十七个专业技术职务类别。用来反映科技人力资源情况。

科技活动经费筹集 指从各种渠道筹集到的计划用于科技活动的经费，包括政府资金、企业资金、事业单位资金、金融机构贷款、国外资金和其他资金等。反映各社会经济主体对促进科技进步所做的努力。

政府资金 指从各级政府部门获得的计划用于科技活动的经费，包括科学事业费、科技三项费、科研基建费、科学基金、教育等部门事业费中计划用于科技活动的经费以及政府部门预算外资金中计划用于科技活动的经费等。

企业资金 指从自有资金中提取或接受其他企业委托的、科研院所和高校等事业单位接受企业委托获得的，计划用于科研和技术开发的经费。不包括来自政府、金融机构及国外的计划用于科技活动的资金。

科技活动经费内部支出 指报告年内用于科技活动的实际支出，包括劳务费、科研业务费、科研管理费，非基建投资购建的固定资产、科研基建支出以及其他用于科技活动的支出。不包括生产性活动支出、归还贷款支出及转拨外单位支出。反映科技投入实际完成情况。

劳务费 指以货币或实物形式直接或间接支付给从事科技活动人员的劳动报酬及各种费用。包括各种形式的工资、津贴、奖金、福利、离退休人员费用、人民助学金等。反映改善科技人员待遇情况。

固定资产购建费 指报告年内使用非基建投资购建的固定资产和用于科研基建投资的实际支出额，即固定资产实际支出和科研基建投资实际完成额之和。固定资产是指长期使用而不改变原有实物形态的主要物资设备、图书资料、实验材料和标本以及其他设备和家具、房屋、建筑物。反映用于改善科研条件和科研手段方面的投入情况。

新产品 指采用新技术原理、新设计构思研制、生产的全新产品，或在结构、材质、工艺等某一方面比原有产品有明显改进，从而显著提高了产品性能或扩大了使用功能的产品。既包括政府有关部门认定并在有效期内的新产品，也包括企业自行研制开发，未经政府有关部门认定，从投产之日起一年之内的新产品。用来反映科技产出及对经济增长的直接贡献。

专利 是专利权的简称，是对发明人的发明创造经审查合格后，由专利局依据专利法授予发明人和设计人对该项发明创造享有的专有权。包括发明、实用新型和外观设计。反映拥有自主知识产权的科技和设计成果情况。

发明(专利) 指对产品、方法或者其改进所提出的新的技术方案。是国际通行的反映拥有自主知识产权技术的核心指标。

实用新型(专利) 指对产品的形状、构造或者其结合所提出的适于实用的新的技术方案。反映具有一定技术含量的技术成果情况。

外观设计(专利) 指对产品的形状、图案、色彩或者其结合所作出的富有美感并适于工业上应用的新设计。反映拥有自主知识产权的外观设计成果情况。

文化及相关产业 指为社会公众提供文化、娱乐产品和服务的活动以及与这些活动有关联的活动的集合。根据提供文化、娱乐产品和服务活动的属性特点，划分为公益性文化活动和经营性文化活动两大类。

文化及相关产业是第三产业的重要组成部分。是在我国《国民经济行业分类》基础上的派生分类，有文化服务和相关文化服务两大类：

文化服务 主要指新闻服务，出版发行和版权服务，广播、电视、电影服务，文化艺术服务，网络文化服务，文化休闲娱乐服务，其他文化服务。

艺术表演团体 由文化部门主办或实行行业管理（经文化市场行政部门审批或已申报登记并领取相关许可证），专门从事表演艺术等活动的各类专业艺术表演团体，含民间职业剧团。如话剧团、方言话剧团、滑稽剧团、儿童剧团、歌剧团、木偶团、皮影团等以及由若干剧种组成的综合性专业艺术表演团体。不包括半工半艺、半农半艺的剧团。

艺术表演场馆 指由文化部门主办或实行行业管理（经文化市场行政部门审批或已申报登记并领取相关许可证），有观众席、舞台、灯光设备，公开售票、专供文艺团体演出的文化活动场所。包括剧院（场）、音乐厅、歌剧院（场）、舞剧院（场）、话剧院(场)、戏院、马戏场、影剧院等进行文艺表演的场所。不包括电影院、礼堂、体育场馆、美术馆及绘画、雕塑等艺术馆。

文化市场经营机构 经文化市场行政部门审批或已申报登记并领取相关许可证的、从事文化经营和文化服务活动的机构。

广播节目综合人口覆盖率 指根据国家广电总局制定的《广播电视人口覆盖率统计技术标准和方法》进行统计调查的，在对象区内采用无线、有线、卫星等技术手段能够收听到包括中央、省、地市、县广播节目其中任意一套的人口数占全国总人口数的百分比。

电视节目综合人口覆盖率 指根据国家广电总局制定的《广播电视人口覆盖率统计技术标准和方法》进行统计调查的，在对象区内采用无线、有线、卫星等技术手段能够收看到包括中央、省、地市、县级电视节目中任意一套的人口数占全国总人口数的百分比。

Explanatory Notes on Main Statistical Indicators

Regular Institutions of Higher Education refer to educational establishments set up according to the government evaluation and approval procedures, recruiting graduates from senior secondary schools as the main target by National Matriculation TEST. They include full-time universities, colleges, institutions of higher professional education, institutions of higher vocational education, institutions of higher vocational education and others (non-university tertiary, branch schools and undergraduate classes).

Universities and colleges primarily provide undergraduate courses; institutions of higher professional education and institutions of higher vocational education primarily provide professional trainings; and others refer to educational establishments, which are responsible for enrolling higher education students under the State Plan but not enumerated in the total number of schools, including: branch schools of universities and colleges, and universities and colleges that have been approved and under plan for construction. Non-university tertiary refers to the regular undergraduate branch college which is running in new mechanism and mode, excluding the branch schools and other similar branches of educational institutions.

Net Enrolment Ratio of Primary Schools refers to the proportion of school age children enrolled at schools to the total number of school age children both in and outside schools (including retarded children, but excluding blind, deaf and mute children). The formula is:

$$\text{Net Enrolment Ratio of Primary Schools} = \frac{\text{Total Primary School}-\text{age Children at Schools}}{\text{Total Primary School}-\text{age Children Whether or Not Attending School}} \times 100\ \%$$

Scientific and Technological Activities (S&T Activities) refer to organized activities which are closely related with the creation, development, dissemination and application of the scientific and technical knowledge in the fields of natural sciences, agricultural science, medical science, engineering and technological science, humanities and social sciences (referred to as scientific and technological fields). S&T activities can be classified into 3 categories: research and development (R&D) activities, application of R&D results, and related S&T services. This statistical definition is made by UNICHIEF for scientific and technological activities to meet the need of carrying out statistical work in this field for its member countries particularly the developing countries.

Personnel Engaged in S&T Activities refer to personnel directly engaged in S&T activities, in the management of S&T activities, and in providing direct service to S&T activities, with over 10% of the total working hours in a year spent on S&T activities. (1) Personnel directly engaged in S&T activities include researchers, engineers, technicians and other related personnel engaged in S&T activities in independent-accounting R&D institutions, institutions of higher learning, and in research institutes, laboratories, technology development centres and central experiment workshops under enterprises and institutions. Also included are people working in S&T research project teams, professional and technical personnel working in S&T information archiving institutes, and graduate students working on the design of their thesis. (2) Personnel engaged in the management of S&T activities and in providing direct service to S&T activities include senior management people responsible for S&T activities in independent-accounting R&D institutions, S&T information archiving institutes, institutions of higher learning and in enterprises and institutions where S&T activities are undertaken. Also included are people responsible for the planning, administration, personnel management, financial management, logistics supply, equipment maintenance, information and library management that are related with S&T activities. People providing indirect services are excluded, such as security, medical service, drivers, plumbers, cleaners and those providing catering and related service. This indicator reflects the size of personnel engaged in S&T activities.

Scientists and Engineers refer to persons engaged in S&T activities either having obtained titles of senior and middle level professional positions, or those without such positions but have completed university or higher education. This indicator reflects the quality of personnel engaged in S&T activities.

Research and Development (R&D) refers to systematic and creative activities in the field of science and technology aiming at increasing the knowledge and using the knowledge for new application. R&D includes 3 categories of activities: basic research, applied research and experimentation for development. The scale and intensity of R&D are widely used internationally to reflect the strength of S&T and the core competitiveness of a country in the world.

Basic Research refers to empirical or theoretical research aiming at obtaining new knowledge on the fundamental principles regarding phenomena or observable facts to reveal the intrinsic nature and underlying laws and to acquire new discoveries or new theories. Basic research takes no specific or designated application as the aim of the research. Results of basic research are mainly released or disseminated in the form of scientific papers or monographs. This indicator reflects the innovation capacity for original knowledge.

Applied Research refers to creative research aiming at obtaining new knowledge on a specific objective or target. Purpose of the applied research is to identify the possible uses of results from basic research, or to explore new (fundamental) methods or new approaches. Results of applied research are expressed in the form of scientific papers, monographs, fundamental models or invention patents. This indicator reflects the exploration of ways to apply the results of basic research.

R&D Personnel refer to persons engaged in research, management and supporting activities of R&D, including persons in the project teams, persons engaged in the management of S&T activities of enterprises and supporting staff providing direct service to the research projects. This indicator reflects the size of personnel engaged in R&D activities with independent intellectual property.

Full-time Equivalent of R&D Personnel refers to the sum of the full-time persons and the full-time equivalent of part-time persons converted by workload. For instance, if there are 2 full-time persons and 3 part-time workers (20%, 30% and 70% of working hours respectively on R&D activities), the full-time equivalent are 2+0.2+0.3+0.7=3.2 person-years. This is an internationally comparable indicator of S&T manpower input.

Professional and Technical Personnel refer to persons engaged in professional and technical work or in the management of professional and technical activities, i.e., people with professional or technical positions who are engaged in professional and technical work or in the management of professional and technical activities, and people without professional or technical positions but are working on professional or technical posts. They include professionals and technicians working in 17 categories of technical occupations including engineering, agriculture, scientific researches, medical service, teaching, economic research and application, accounting, statistics, translation, libraries, archives, cultural and museum service, journalism and publication, lawyers, notarization service, radio and television broadcasting, handicraft and fine arts, sports, performing art, and political workers in enterprises. This indicator reflects the condition of human resources in S&T.

Funding for S&T Activities refers to funds obtained from various sources for S&T activities, including government funds, self-raised funds by enterprises, self-raised funds by institutions, loans from financial institutions, foreign funds and other funds. This indicator reflects the efforts made by various social economic entities in promoting the development of S&T.

Government Funds refer to funds obtained from government agencies at all levels to be used for S&T activities, including fund for scientific undertakings, 3 kinds of fund for S&T activities, fund for capital construction for scientific researches, science fund, funds from education expenditures by education departments for S&T activities, and extra-budget fund from government agencies for S&T activities.

Funds of Enterprises refers to funds of enterprises from their own budget; funds from other enterprises; or funds received by universities or research institutions from enterprises for scientific research or technical development projects. Excluded from this category are funds from government agencies, financial institutions or from foreign institutions.

Internal Expenditure on S&T activities refer to the actual expenditure on S&T activities during the reference year, including service fees, expenditure on research activities, expenditure on research management, purchase or construction of fixed assets not included in the investment for capital construction, expenditure on capital construction for scientific researches, and other expenditure on S&T activities. Not included are expenditure on production activities, repayment of loans and transfer expenditure. This indicator reflects the net investment in S&T more accurately.

Service Fees refer to direct or indirect payment, in cash or in kind, made to personnel engaged in S&T activities as remuneration and other fees. They include, in various forms, salaries, subsidies, bonus, benefits, retirement pension, stipend, etc. This indicator reflects the improvement of the remuneration package for S&T personnel.

Purchase or Construction of Fixed Assets refers to the fixed assets purchased or constructed using funds other than the investment in capital construction, and the actual expenditure on capital construction for scientific researches. In other words, it is the sum of the actual expenditure on fixed assets and the accomplished investment in capital construction for scientific researches. Fixed assets refer to main materials and equipment, literatures and documents in libraries, materials for experiments, specimen, instruments, furniture, buildings and constructions that can be used for a long time without changing the form and shape of those articles or constructions. This indicator reflects the input in improving the condition of S&T and the means of scientific research.

New Products refer to brand new products produced with new technology and new design, or products that represent noticeable improvement in terms of structure, material, or production process for improving significantly the character or function of the older versions. They include new products certified by relevant government agencies within the period of certification, as well as new products designed and produced by enterprises within a year without certification by government agencies. This indicator reflects the direct contribution of S&T output to economic growth.

Patent is an abbreviation for the patent right and refers to the exclusive right of ownership by the inventors or designers for the creation or inventions, given from the patent offices after due process of assessment and approval in accordance with the Patent Law. Patents are granted for inventions, utility models and designs. This indicator reflects the achievements of S&T and design with independent intellectual property.

Patented Inventions refer to new technical proposals to the products or methods or their modifications. This is universal core indicator reflecting the technologies with independent intellectual property.

Patented Utility Models refer to the practical and new technical proposals on the shape and structure of the product or the combination of both. This indicator reflects the condition of technological results with certain technical content.

Designs refer to the aesthetics and industrially applicable new designs for the shape, pattern and colour of the product, or their combinations. This indicator reflects the appearance design achievements with independent intellectual property.

Culture and Related Industries refer to the aggregate of activities, providing the mass with culture goods, amusement goods and services. According to the characteristics of culture goods, amusement goods and services, they can be classified into two categories, or nonprofit cultural activities and profit cultural activities.

Culture and related industries is the important component of the tertiary industry. These are the derivative sector from the Industrial Classification of the National Economy and are composed of two categories of culture services and related cultural services.

Culture services mainly include news services, publishing and copyright services, radio, television, film, arts, network, recreation, and other cultural services

Arts Performance Troupes refer to the various professional performing arts groups, which sponsored by the cultural sectors or guided by the cultural society (approved by the cultural market administration, or registered and permitted with the relative certificate), including non-governmental troupes, such as drama troupes, dialect troupes, comedy troupes, children troupes, Opera troupes, puppetry troupes, Shadowgraph troupes, etc., comprehensive professional arts performance troupes. The semi-working and semi-farming arts troupes are not included.

Arts Performance Places refer to the various sites for cultural activities, which sponsored by the cultural sectors or guided by the cultural society (approved by the cultural market administration, or registered and permitted with the relative certificate), with the facility of auditorium, stage, and lighting, and selling tickets in public, specially performed by arts troupes, including theatre, concert halls, opera halls, dance halls, drama halls, cinemas, circus fields, and other showplaces for the performing arts. The cinemas, auditoriums, stadiums, and arts museums, such as art galleries, painting houses, sculpture houses, are not included.

Cultural Market Operating Units refer to the units dealing in culture and cultural services, which registered and permitted with the relative certificate by cultural market administration.

Radio Coverage of Population refers to the percentage of population, which can listen to one of central, provincial, city, prefecture, and county radio programs by wireless, cable, satellite and other technical means, in the surveying area, to national total population, according to Statistical Standard and Method on Television and Radio Coverage of Population established by the State Administration of Broadcasting, Film and Television.

Television Coverage of Population refers to the percentage of population, which can watch one of central, provincial, city, prefecture, and county television programs by wireless, cable, satellite and other technical means, in the surveying area, to national total population, according to Statistical Standard and Method on Television and Radio Coverage of Population established by the State Administration of Broadcasting, Film and Television.

2012

新疆统计年鉴

XINJIANG STATISTICAL YEARBOOK

第十八篇
体育、卫生及其他

CHAPTER 18
Sports, Public Health and Others

简要说明
Brief Introduction

本篇资料的主要内容及来源

本篇资料主要包括卫生事业、体育事业、民政事业、公安机关案件受理处治情况、安全生产情况、道路交通事故和火灾事故等内容，除卫生、体育事业外其他部门数据由新疆维吾尔自治区统计局社会科技处与综合处根据有关部门资料整理。

卫生部门资料是由新疆维吾尔自治区卫生厅依据年报资料整理提供。体育资料是由新疆维吾尔自治区体育局提供。民政部分资料由新疆维吾尔自治区民政厅提供，治安、刑事案件资料由新疆维吾尔自治区公安厅提供，安全生产情况来自新疆维吾尔自治区安全生产监督管理局，道路交通事故和火灾事故分别由新疆维吾尔自治区公安交通管理局和新疆维吾尔自治区消防总队提供。

Main Content and Source of Data

Data in this chapter mainly include the development of public health, sports, civil affairs, labor and society protection, offense cases against public order handled by public Security organs, traffic accidents and fires. These statistics are provided by Department of Population and Social Science &Technology in Statistics Bureau of Xinjiang according to the data from the related Department of Statistics Bureau.

Data on public health are from the Bureau of Public Health,these statistics are according to the data of yearly statistics; increased the data of condition of villige clinic and basic condition of institution on new cooperative health care of agricultural and pastoral areas.

Data on sports are from the Bureau of Sports; Data on civil affairs and labor protection are provided respectively by the Bureau of Civil Affairs and the Bureau of Labor and Social Security. Data on public security, statistics on procuratorial, legal and judicial affairs are provided by the Bureau of Public Security. Data on production safety are come from Xinjiang Administration of Work Safety. Data on traffic accident and fire are respectively provided by the Xinjiang Traffic Management Bureau and the Xinjiang Fire Department.

18-1 体育局系统从业人员情况
Statistics on Staff and Workers in Physical Education System

单位：人 (2011 年) (person)

项　目	Item	合　计 Total	公务员 Civil Servants	教练员 Coaches	运动员 Athletes	科研人员 Scientific and Technical Personnel
总　计	**Total**	**3074**	**466**	**634**	**536**	**35**
体育行政机关	Administrative of Physical Culture and Sports	622	466	16		
运动项目管理部门	Sports Events Mangement	836		78	535	1
体育运动学校	Physical Education and Sports Schools	566		133	1	4
业余体校	Spare-time Sports Schools	596		392		
体育场馆	Stadium and Gymnasium	181				
体育科研机构	Sport Scientific Research Institutions	37				30
其　他	Others	236		15		

项　目	Item	医务人员 Medical Personnel	文化教师 Culture Teachers	管理人员 Administrative Personnel	工勤人员 Logistics Workers	其他人员 Others
总　计	**Total**	**28**	**275**	**437**	**357**	**306**
体育行政机关	Administrative of Physical Culture and Sports			58	58	24
运动项目管理部门	Sports Events Mangement	19		92	63	48
体育运动学校	Physical Education and Sports Schools	7	258	73	52	38
业余体校	Spare-time Sports Schools	2	17	58	63	66
体育场馆	Stadium and Gymnasium			60	97	22
体育科研机构	Sport Scientific Research Institutions			6	1	
其　他	Others			90	23	108

18-2 按项目分等级裁判员发展人数
Number of Referees in Levels by Type of Sports

单位：人 (2011 年) (person)

项目	Item	合计 Total	国家级裁判员 National Referee 小计 Sub-total	#男 Male	一级裁判员 First Level Referee 小计 Sub-total	#男 Male	二级裁判员 Second Level Referee 小计 Sub-total	#男 Male
总　计	**Total**	**912**	**8**	**4**	**349**	**232**	**555**	**421**
田　径	Track and Field	222	3	1	32	18	187	124
举　重	Weightlifting	13			13	10		
拳　击	Boxing	17			15	12	2	2
柔　道	Judo	31			21	14	10	10
跆拳道	Taekwondo	40					40	33
射　箭	Shooting	1					1	1
足　球	Football	27			24	20	3	3
篮　球	Basketball	165			46	39	119	103
排　球	Volleyball	21			21	16		
羽毛球	Badminton	134					134	90
网　球	Tennis	21			21	14		
手　球	Handball	2	2					
自行车	Bicycle	9					9	8
马　术	Equestrian	8					8	8
国际象棋	Chess	23			23	21		
中国象棋	Chinese Chess	18					18	18
武　术	Martial Art	45	2	2	33	26	10	7
桥　牌	Bridge	14					14	14
健美操	Aerobics	65			65	24		
体育舞蹈	Dance Sports	35			35	18		
信　鸽	Carrier Pigeon	1	1	1				

18-3 按项目分等级运动员发展人数
Number of Athletes at Levels by Type of Sports

单位：人 (2011 年) (person)

项　目	Item	合 计 Total	国际、国家级运动健将 International and National Level		一级运动员 First Grade		二级运动员 Second Grade	
			小 计 Sub-total	#男 Male	小 计 Sub-total	#男 Male	小 计 Sub-total	#男 Male
总　计	**Total**	**267**	**17**	**15**	**26**	**13**	**223**	**129**
田　径	Track and Field	8					8	5
游　泳	Swimming	7			1	1	6	1
拳　击	Boxing	9	4	4			5	2
举　重	Weightlifting	3	1				2	2
国际式摔跤	InternationalWrestling	10			2	2	8	8
中国式摔跤	Chinese-style Wrestling	9			2	2	7	1
柔　道	Judo	4					4	1
跆拳道	Taekwondo	39	6	5	4	2	29	17
射　击	Shooting	8	1	1	3		4	
射　箭	Archery	17			2	1	15	9
足　球	Football	32					32	21
篮　球	Basketball	6	1	1			5	5
排　球	Volleyball	7					7	5
沙滩排球	Beach Volleyball	11			1		10	4
乒乓球	Table Tennis	37			2	1	35	13
网　球	Tennis	15					15	12
手　球	Handball	4			4			
速度滑冰	Speed Skating	16	5	4	3	2	8	5
短道速滑	Short-track Speeding Skating	2			2	2		
健美操	Aerobics	3					3	1
武　术	Martial Art	18					18	15
围　棋	Weiqi	2					2	2

18-4 各地、州、市体育局系统机构数

Number of Institutions in Sports Committees by Prefecture,Autonomous Prefecture and City

单位：个　　　　(2011 年)　　　　(unit)

地　区	Region	合　计 Total	行政机关 Administrative Agencies	运动项目管理部门 Sports Events Mangement	体育运动学校 Physical Education and Sports Schools
总　计	**Total**	**221**	**110**	**6**	**5**
自治区直属	Under Autonomous Region	19	1	6	1
乌鲁木齐市	Urumqi City	19	9		1
克拉玛依市	Karamay City	6	5		
石河子市	Shihezi City	2	1		
吐鲁番地区	Turpan Administrative Offices	8	4		
哈密地区	Hami [Kumul] Administrative Offices	9	4		
昌吉回族自治州	Changji Hui Autonomous Prefecture	10	8		
伊犁哈萨克自治州	Ili Kazak Autonomous Prefecture	44	27		1
伊犁州直属县(市)	Counties (Cities) Direct Under Ili Prefecture	17	11		1
塔城地区	Tacheng [Tarbagatai] Administrative Offices	10	8		
阿勒泰地区	Altay Administrative Offices	17	8		
博尔塔拉蒙古自治州	Bortala Mongol Autonomous Prefecture	8	4		
巴音郭楞蒙古自治州	Bayangol Mongol Autonomous Prefecture	16	10		
阿克苏地区	Aksu Administrative Offices	22	10		1
克孜勒苏柯尔克孜自治州	Kizilsu Kirgiz Autonomous Prefecture	12	5		
喀什地区	Kashgar [Kaxgar] Administrative Offices	28	13		1
和田地区	Hotan Administrative Offices	18	9		

地　区	Region	业余体校 Spare-time Sports Schools	体育场馆 Stadium and Gymnasium	体育科研机构 Sport Scientific Research Institutions	其　他 Others
总　计	**Total**	**72**	**11**	**2**	**15**
自治区直属	Under Autonomous Region		1	1	9
乌鲁木齐市	Urumqi City	5	2	1	1
克拉玛依市	Karamay City	1			
石河子市	Shihezi City	1			
吐鲁番地区	Turpan Administrative Offices	4			
哈密地区	Hami [Kumul] Administrative Offices	3			2
昌吉回族自治州	Changji Hui Autonomous Prefecture	1	1		
伊犁哈萨克自治州	Ili Kazak Autonomous Prefecture	12	2		2
伊犁州直属县(市)	Counties (Cities) Direct Under Ili Prefecture	4	1		
塔城地区	Tacheng [Tarbagatai] Administrative Offices	1			1
阿勒泰地区	Altay Administrative Offices	7	1		1
博尔塔拉蒙古自治州	Bortala Mongol Autonomous Prefecture	4			
巴音郭楞蒙古自治州	Bayangol Mongol Autonomous Prefecture	5	1		
阿克苏地区	Aksu Administrative Offices	9	2		
克孜勒苏柯尔克孜自治州	Kizilsu Kirgiz Autonomous Prefecture	5	1		1
喀什地区	Kashgar [Kaxgar] Administrative Offices	13	1		
和田地区	Hotan Administrative Offices	9			

18-5 各地、州、市体育局系统机构从业人员数
Number of Staff and Workers in Sports Bureau by Region

单位：人 (2011 年) (person)

地　　区	Region	合　计 Total	行政机关 Administrative Agencies	运动项目管理部门 Sports Events Mangement	体育运动学　校 Physical Education and Sports Schools
总　计	**Total**	**3074**	**614**	**836**	**566**
自治区直属	Under Autonomous Region	1275	47	819	145
乌鲁木齐市	Urumqi City	433	37		227
克拉玛依市	Karamay City	46	37		
石河子市	Shihezi City	53	23		
吐鲁番地区	Turpan Administrative Offices	36	19		
哈密地区	Hami [Kumul] Administrative Offices	87	28		
昌吉回族自治州	Changji Hui Autonomous Prefecture	40	29		
伊犁哈萨克自治州	Ili Kazak Autonomous Prefecture	370	134	17	54
伊犁州直属县(市)	Counties (Cities) Direct Under Ili Prefecture	201	76	17	54
塔城地区	Tacheng [Tarbagatai] Administrative Offices	51	35		
阿勒泰地区	Altay Administrative Offices	118	23		
博尔塔拉蒙古自治州	Bortala Mongol Autonomous Prefecture	41	11		
巴音郭楞蒙古自治州	Bayangol Mongol Autonomous Prefecture	94	42		
阿克苏地区	Aksu Administrative Offices	171	59		57
克孜勒苏柯尔克孜自治州	Kizilsu Kirgiz Autonomous Prefecture	75	28		
喀什地区	Kashgar [Kaxgar] Administrative Offices	266	73		83
和田地区	Hotan Administrative Offices	87	47		

地　　区	Region	业余体校 Spare-time Sports Schools	体育场馆 Stadium and Gymnasium	体育科研机构 Sport Scientific Research Institutions	其　他 Others
总　计	**Total**	**563**	**181**	**37**	**238**
自治区直属	Under Autonomous Region		33	30	201
乌鲁木齐市	Urumqi City	83	74	7	5
克拉玛依市	Karamay City	9			
石河子市	Shihezi City	30			
吐鲁番地区	Turpan Administrative Offices				
哈密地区	Hami [Kumul] Administrative Offices	46			13
昌吉回族自治州	Changji Hui Autonomous Prefecture	9	2		
伊犁哈萨克自治州	Ili Kazak Autonomous Prefecture	96	34		19
伊犁州直属县(市)	Counties (Cities) Direct Under Ili Prefecture	43	11		
塔城地区	Tacheng [Tarbagatai] Administrative Offices				
阿勒泰地区	Altay Administrative Offices	53	23		19
博尔塔拉蒙古自治州	Bortala Mongol Autonomous Prefecture	30			
巴音郭楞蒙古自治州	Bayangol Mongol Autonomous Prefecture	39	13		
阿克苏地区	Aksu Administrative Offices	53	2		
克孜勒苏柯尔克孜自治州	Kizilsu Kirgiz Autonomous Prefecture	30	11		
喀什地区	Kashgar [Kaxgar] Administrative Offices	98	12		
和田地区	Hotan Administrative Offices	40			

18-6 卫生机构、床位、人员数

(2011 年)

项　目	Item	机构数(个) Number of Institutions (unit)	床位数(张) Beds (unit)	卫生人员合计(人) Total Number of Medical Personnel (person)	卫生技术人员 Medical Technical Personnel
总　计	**Total**	**17412**	**125391**	**167828**	**130604**
按经济类型分	**Grouped by Economic Type**				
公　立	Public	11415	111461	142525	110258
非公立	Non-public	5997	13930	25303	20346
按设置主办单位分	**Grouped By sponsors**				
政府办	Run by Government	7568	105543	128866	101552
社会办	Run by Society	4739	7951	17171	10729
个人办	Run by Private	5105	11897	21791	18323
按城乡分	**Grouped By City and County**				
城　市	City	2058	33822	49860	40040
农　村	County	15354	91569	117968	90564
按机构分	**Grouped By Organizations**				
医院合计	**Total Number of Hospitals**	**820**	**97436**	**102829**	**84202**
综合医院	Comprehensive Hospitals	641	75164	84524	69761
中医医院	Hospitals of Traditional Chinese Medicine	46	6142	6013	4879
中西医综合医院	TCM and Western Medicine Hospital	4	569	554	489
民族医院	Hospitals for Nationalities	46	6068	4491	3634
专科医院	Specialist Hospitals	83	9493	7247	5439
口腔医院	Nonnasality Hospitals	4	52	252	205
眼科医院	Ophthalmology Hospitals	6	170	251	145
耳鼻喉科医院	Otolaryngology Hospitals	2	70	191	141
肿瘤医院	Tumour Hospital	2	2104	1772	1396
心血管病医院	Cardiovascular Hospitals	1	252	529	312
胸科医院	Chest Hospital	1	516	432	353
妇产(科)医院	Hospitals for Gynaecology and Obsterics	16	495	583	464
儿童医院	Children Hospital	1	30	54	35
精神病医院	Mental Hospitals	12	3791	1545	1139
传染病医院	Infectous Diseases Hospitals	4	600	464	328
结核病医院	Tubercuiosis Hospitals	1	366	174	153

注：1.本表人员合计中包括乡村医生 9834 人和卫生员 1043 人；
2.不含乡镇卫生院在村卫生室工作的执业（助理）医师、注册护士数。

Number of Health Institutions, Beds and Persons Engaged by Type of Institutons

执业医师 Lecensed Doctors	执业助理医师 Lecensed Assistant Doctor	注册护士 Registered Nurses	药剂人员 Pharmacist	技师(士) Technician (artificer)	检验人员 Laboratory Technicians	其他 Others	其他技术人员 Other Technicians	管理人员 Administrative Personnel	工勤人员 Logistics Workers
40265	**9265**	**48760**	**6483**	**7726**	**5391**	**18105**	**6904**	**6837**	**12606**
32117	7922	42061	5451	6718	4790	15989	6187	5782	10938
8148	1343	6699	1032	1008	601	2116	717	1055	1668
28825	7255	38817	5006	6251	4450	15398	5873	5251	10136
3908	755	4101	577	598	427	790	465	700	1050
7532	1255	5842	900	877	514	1917	566	886	1420
14697	1045	16278	1964	2190	1514	3866	2733	2284	4803
25568	8220	32482	4519	5536	3877	14239	4171	4553	7803
25532	**3830**	**35523**	**4724**	**5018**	**3211**	**9575**	**4901**	**4692**	**9034**
20936	3213	29949	3554	4182	2672	7927	3747	3878	7138
1811	97	1839	385	303	200	444	426	290	418
102	29	194	27	20	14	117	11	40	14
1009	355	1039	522	215	130	494	275	159	423
1674	136	2502	236	298	195	593	442	325	1041
115	9	62	4	4	1	11	6	16	25
37	7	70	11	6	6	14	19	20	67
58	6	57	9	6	4	5	20	3	27
394	3	768	40	50	23	141	82	37	257
88	5	176	11	14	9	18	63	18	136
107		164	17	14	13	51	29	5	45
130	24	179	23	40	25	68	26	51	42
6	6	14	4	5	4		4	11	4
299	22	581	49	57	39	131	109	55	242
118	13	122	16	26	16	33	28	31	77
59	6	67	7	11	9	3	6	6	9

Note: a).Total data in this table included 9834 doctors and 1043 medical personnel.
b).Total data in this table didn't include licensed doctors and registered nurses in tounship in county health Centers.

18-6 续表 Continued

(2011 年)

项　目	Item	机构数(个) Number of Institutions (unit)	床位数(张) Beds (unit)	卫生人员合计(人) Total Number of Medical Personnel (person)	卫生技术人员 Medical Technical Personnel
骨科医院	Hospital of Orthopedics	4	135	108	90
康复医院	Recovery Hospitals	3	119	99	72
整形外科医院	Plastic surgical holpital	1	20	43	24
其他专科医院	Other Specialist Hospitals	25	773	750	582
基层医疗卫生机构	**Basic Medical Institutions**	**16120**	**25315**	**51882**	**36125**
社区卫生服务中心(站)	Community Health Service Center	683	3691	7700	6577
社区卫生服务中心	Community Health Service Center	145	2615	4353	3665
社区卫生服务站	Community Health Service Station	538	1076	3347	2912
卫生院	Total Number of　Public Health Center	922	21345	20585	17325
街道卫生院	Public Health Center in Neighbourhood	9	60	193	150
乡、镇卫生院	Public Health Center in Township and Towns	913	21285	20392	17175
中心卫生院	Public Health Center in Rural Area	132	4567	3803	3224
乡卫生院	Public Health Center in Township	781	16718	16589	13951
村卫生室	Village Clinics	9825		12127	1250
门诊部	Outpatients Department	247	279	1767	1526
诊所、卫生所、医务室	Clinics, Health Centers	4443		9703	9447
专业公共卫生机构	**Special Public Medical Institutions**	**464**	**2127**	**12772**	**10095**
疾病预防控制中心(防疫站)	Diseases Preventing & Controlling Center (Epidemic Prevention Station)	216		6419	4947
专科疾病防治院(所、站)	Specialized Stations	4	40	84	36
妇幼保健院(所、站)	Hospitals for Maternity and Child Care	90	2037	3729	3079
急救中心(站)	First-Aid-Stations(Center)	4	50	171	134
采供血机构	Blood Collection & Supply Organs	20		485	339
卫生监督所(中心)	Health Inspection Institution	128		1866	1547
计划生育技术服务机构	Institution for Family Planning Technical Services	2		18	13
其他卫生机构	**Other Medical Institution**	**8**	**513**	**345**	**182**
疗养院	Sanatorium	4	513	280	152
卫生监督检验(监测、检测)所(站)	Health Inspection Institution (center)	1		7	7
其　他	Others	3		58	23

Continued

执业医师 Lecensed Doctors	执业助理医师 Lecensed Assistant Doctor	注册护士 Registered Nurses	药剂人员 Pharmacist	技师(士) Technician (artificer)	检验人员 Laboratory Technicians	其他 Others	其他技术人员 Other Technicians	管理人员 Administrative Personnel	工勤人员 Logistics Workers
24	2	21	6	8	2	29		5	13
38	3	19	3	4	3	5	10	7	10
11	4	7	1	1	1		10	6	3
190	26	195	35	52	40	84	30	54	84
11530	**4494**	**11510**	**1546**	**1486**	**1065**	**5559**	**1274**	**1194**	**2412**
2418	372	2430	410	396	268	551	313	373	437
1231	201	1356	248	261	166	368	177	232	279
1187	171	1074	162	135	102	183	136	141	158
2867	3005	5292	773	929	689	4459	884	715	1661
39	16	49	13	14	11	19	20	10	13
2828	2989	5243	760	915	678	4440	864	705	1648
539	530	1001	129	181	130	844	117	129	333
2289	2459	4242	631	734	548	3596	747	576	1315
502	410	338							
667	107	414	115	111	69	112	77	106	58
5076	600	3036	248	50	39	437			256
3147	**930**	**1657**	**199**	**1210**	**1107**	**2952**	**706**	**903**	**1068**
1890	619	469	74	834	781	1061	386	444	642
16	8	6	2	3	1	1		45	3
1120	295	1018	116	238	191	292	227	220	203
62	1	60	1	1	1	9	13	6	18
52	6	101	6	132	131	42	46	33	67
						1547	32	152	135
7	1	3		2	2		2	3	
56	**11**	**70**	**14**	**12**	**8**	**19**	**23**	**48**	**92**
47	9	62	11	10	7	13	9	36	83
2		1		2	1	2			
7	2	7	3			4	14	12	9

18-7 主要年份卫生机构数(不含村卫生室)

Number of Health Institutions in Main Years(Excluding Village Clinics)

单位：个 (unit)

年 份 Year	合 计 Total	医院、卫生院 Hospitals And Township Hospitals	#医院 Hospitals	疗养院 Sanitarium	门诊部 Clinics	专科防治所、站 Specialized Prevention & Treatment Centers or Stations	疾病防控中心 Sanitation and Antiepidemic Agencies	妇幼保健所、站 Maternity and Child Care Centers	社区卫生服务中心(站) Health Service Center for Community	卫生监督所(中心) Research Institutes of Medical Science	其他卫生机构 Other Institutions	诊所、医务保健室、医务室 Clinics Health Care Room Infirmary	#私营、个体机构 Institutions of Privately Owned & Individual
1978	2581	806	204	2	1609	1	104	12			47		
1980	2818	884	270	4	1756	4	102	12			56		
1985	3320	947	389	5	2125	2	139	27			75		
1990	3945	1049	435	6	2536	13	191	59			91		
1995	3932	1292	507	8	2247	16	216	69			84		
2000	7314	1352	522	8	154	16	210	74			96	5404	3653
2005	8087	1516	685	6	224	8	197	88	46	30	113	5859	4183
2006	8175	1560	699	6	220	7	211	92	62	49	83	5885	4227
2007	7465	1629	756	7	240	7	214	87	250	112	30	4889	4093
2008	6739	1629	741	4	217	6	213	89	264	121	31	4165	3756
2009	7288	1669	763	5	221	5	214	90	405	128	30	4521	3678
2010	7650	1712	802	4	259	4	221	90	641	133	31	4555	3796
2011	7587	1742	820	4	247	4	216	90	683	128	30	4443	3745

注：1.2002 年起卫生部新制度规定持有"医疗执业许可证"所有卫生机构算为一个机构,兵团连队卫生室统计到卫生所中,所以卫生机构总数增加。2.从 2007 年开始卫生部门实行网络直报。

Note: a) From 2002, in line with new regulations of ministry of public health,all the health institutions that have medical service permit shall be counted as one and health care rooms shall be counted in health clinics,therefore the total number of health institutions increased.

b) Since 2007, health care institution have carried out direct network report.

18-8 主要年份卫生人员数(不含村卫生室)

Number of Persons Engaged in Health Institutions in Main Years(Excluding Village Clinics)

单位：人 (person)

年 份 Year	合 计 Total	#卫生技术人员 Medical Technical Personnel	#医 生 Doctors	执业医师 Lecensed Doctors	执业助理医师 Lecensed Assistant Doctor	#注 册 护 士 Registered Nurses	平均每万人医生数 Number of Doctors per 10 000 Population	在合计中私人个体开业人员 Persons of Privately Owned & Individual
1978	66252	51050	16898	7368	9530	10765	13.70	
1980	74627	57949	20614	10092	10522	12077	16.06	
1985	88460	68961	25721	13330	12391	17136	18.90	188
1990	102053	79853	33683	24967	8716	23386	22.03	2034
1995	116856	92028	39636	30038	9598	26350	23.86	4252
2000	122064	98093	45402	34892	10510	30850	24.55	5835
2005	117165	96266	41426	32563	8863	30657	20.61	13562
2006	121400	99839	42775	33988	8787	32119	20.87	13256
2007	127621	104671	43551	34838	8713	34662	20.79	14689
2008	130174	106853	43456	35320	8136	36084	20.39	14560
2009	138344	114521	45616	37223	8393	40425	21.13	16616
2010	149069	122860	48166	39301	8865	44238	22.25	19330
2011	155701	129354	48618	39763	8855	48422	22.49	19947

注：2002 年以前执业医师为中医师、西医师、中西医结合医师，执业助理医师为中医士、西医士、中西医结合医士，注册护士为护师、护士。(以下同)

Note: Prior to 2002,doctors with license were doctors trained in western medicine,assistant doctors are practioners with secondary western medical education,and registered nurses are master nurses and nurses (The following is the same as below) .

18-9 主要年份卫生机构床位数
Number of Sick-Beds in Health Institutions in Main Years

单位：张 (unit)

年 份 Year	合 计 Total	医 院 卫生院 Hospitals And Health Centers	#医 院 Hospitals	社区服务中心(站) Sanitarium	其他卫生机构 Other Health Institutions	每万人医院、卫生院床位数 Number of Hospital Beds per 10 000 Population
1978	57647	39179	25514		18468	31.78
1980	61075	47236	32944		13839	36.81
1985	60930	55298	42486		5632	40.63
1990	67414	60707	47924		6707	39.70
1995	72955	66696	53336		6259	40.15
2000	70542	65916	52438		4626	35.64
2005	79753	76002	63013	209	3542	37.81
2006	83722	80090	65589	445	3187	39.07
2007	90329	87131	71496	343	2855	41.59
2008	96852	93253	76321	843	2756	43.76
2009	107193	102620	83776	1851	2722	47.54
2010	116230	109851	89871	3588	2791	50.36
2011	125391	118781	97436	3691	2919	53.93

18-10 医疗机构病床使用情况
Utilization of Beds in Medical Institutions

(2011 年)

项 目	Item	实有床位(张) Number of Beds (bed)	实际开放总床日数(日) Beds Open to Patients (day)	实际占用总床日数(床日) Turnover of Beds (times)	平均开放病床(张) Number of Days per Bed in Use in a Year (day)
总 计	**Total**	**125391**	**43527571**	**37558797**	**119254**
医 院	Total Number of Hospitals	97436	34161138	31598131	93592
综合医院	General Hospital	75164	26575298	24592068	72809
中医医院	Hospital Specialized in Traditional Chinese Medicine	6142	2150760	2380611	5892
中西医结合医院	Hospital Specialized in Combination Of Traditional Chinese and Western Medicine	569	163885	145041	449
民族医院	National Hospital	6068	2143201	1913838	5872
专科医院	Specialized Hospital	9493	3127994	2566573	8570
基层医疗卫生机构	**Basic Medical Institutions**	**25315**	**8544188**	**5486834**	**23409**
社区卫生服务中心(站)	Health Service Center for Community	3691	1217359	601892	3335
社区卫生服务中心	Health Service Center for Community	2615	893449	478048	2448
社区卫生服务站	Health Service Center for Community	1076	323910	123844	887
卫生院	Total Number of Public Health Center	21345	7246819	4864768	19854
#乡镇卫生院	Township Health Center	21285	7229289	4864768	19806
门诊部	Out-patients Department	279	80010	20174	219
专业公共卫生机构	**Specialized Public Health Institution**	**2127**	**720150**	**446347**	**1973**
专科疾病防治院(所、站)	Specialized Disease Prevention & Treatment Institute	40	14600	10542	40
妇幼保健院(所、站)	Hospitals for Maternity and Child Care	2037	705550	435805	1933
#妇幼保健院	Women and Children Care Agencies	1458	499410	339223	1368
其他机构	**Other Institutions**	**513**	**102095**	**27485**	**280**
疗养院	Sanatorium	513	102095	27485	280

18-10 续表 Continued

项　目	Item	病床周转次数(次) Utilization Rate of Beds (%)	病床工作日(日) Number of Days per Bed in Use in a Year (day)	病床使用率(%) Utilization Rate of Beds (%)	出院者平均住院日(日) Average Stay Days in Hospital (day)
总　计	**Total**	**33.4**	**314.9**	**86.29**	**9.1**
医　院	Total Number of Hospitals	33.1	337.6	92.50	10.0
综合医院	General Hospital	35.8	337.8	92.54	9.2
中医医院	Hospital Specialized in Traditional Chinese Medicine	34.4	404.0	110.69	11.3
中西医结合医院	Hospital Specialized in Combination Of Traditional Chinese and Western Medicine Medicine	21.9	323.0	88.50	14.0
民族医院	National Hospital	25.6	325.9	89.30	13.2
专科医院	Specialized Hospital	15.3	299.5	82.05	18.1
基层医疗卫生机构	**Basic Medical Institutions**	**34.7**	**234.4**	**64.22**	**6.0**
社区卫生服务中心(站)	Health Service Center for Community	19.2	180.5	49.44	8.3
社区卫生服务中心	Health Service Center for Community	17.9	195.3	53.51	9.8
社区卫生服务站	Health Service Center for Community	22.8	139.6	38.23	5.0
卫生院	Total Number of Public Health Center	37.6	245.0	67.13	5.8
#乡镇卫生院	Township Health Center	37.7	245.6	67.29	5.8
门诊部	Out-patients Department	8.8	92.0	25.21	11.1
专业公共卫生机构	**Specialized Public Health Institution**	**35.0**	**226.2**	**61.98**	**6.1**
专科疾病防治院(所、站)	Specialized Disease Prevention & Treatment Institute	14.5	263.6	72.21	17.1
妇幼保健院(所、站)	Hospitals for Maternity and Child Care	35.4	225.5	61.77	6.0
#妇幼保健院	Women and Children Care Agencies	37.8	247.9	67.92	6.5
其他机构	**Other Institutions**	**2.5**	**98.3**	**26.92**	**31.1**
疗养院	Sanatorium	2.5	98.3	26.92	31.1

18-11 各地、州、市卫生机构、床位和人员数

年 份 Year	地 区 Region	机构数 (个) Number of Institutions (unit)	床位数 (张) Beds (unit)	卫生人员合计 (人) Total Number of Medical Personnel (person)
	2005	8087	79753	117165
	2006	8175	83722	121400
	2007	7465	90329	127621
	2008	6739	96852	130174
	2009	7288	107193	138344
	2010	7650	116230	149069
	2011	17412	125391	167828
乌鲁木齐市	Urumqi City	1772	26530	39986
克拉玛依市	Karamay City	93	1838	3464
吐鲁番地区	Turpan Administrative Offices	365	2262	3922
哈密地区	Hami [Kumul] Administrative Offices	467	3471	5449
昌吉回族自治州	Changji Hui Autonomous Prefecture	1392	9224	12730
伊犁哈萨克自治州	Ili Kazak Autonomous Prefecture	3956	21491	32008
伊犁州直属县(市)	Counties (Cities) Direct Under Ili Prefecture	1976	13886	19428
塔城地区	Tacheng [Tarbagatai] Administrative Offices	1210	4493	7416
阿勒泰地区	Altay Administrative Offices	770	3112	5164
博尔塔拉蒙古自治州	Bortala Mongol Autonomous Prefecture	639	2643	4233
巴音郭楞蒙古自治州	Bayangol Mongol Autonomous Prefecture	1212	8136	10779
阿克苏地区	Aksu Administrative Offices	1308	11771	11852
克孜勒苏柯尔克孜自治州	Kizilsu Kirgiz Autonomous Prefecture	300	3140	3848
喀什地区	Kashgar [Kaxgar] Administrative Offices	3463	18282	21448
和田地区	Hotan Administrative Offices	1503	10875	10473
自治区直辖县级市	Municpality Country-LevelCity directly under the Central Govern-ment	942	5728	7636
石河子市	Shihezi City	723	5023	6378
阿拉尔市	Aral City	132	496	750
图木舒克市	Tumxuk City	2	69	125
五家渠市	Wujiaqu City	85	140	383

注：1.本表 2011 年数据含村卫生室，人员合计中包括乡村医生 9834 人和卫生员 1043 人。
2.不含乡镇卫生院在村卫生室工作的执业（助理）医师、注册护士数。

Number of Health Institutions, Beds and Personnel by Prefecture, Autonomous Prefecture and City

卫生技术人员 Medical Technical Personnel	其他技术人员 Other Technicians	管理人员 Administrative Personnel	工勤人员 Logistics Workers	平均每万人床位数(张) Number of Beds per 10 000 Population (unit)
96266	4626	6330	9943	39.71
99839	5168	6258	10135	39.07
104671	5276	7143	10531	43.11
106853	5694	6419	11208	45.45
114521	6111	6453	11259	49.66
122860	6979	7089	12141	53.28
130604	6904	6837	12606	56.93
31762	2237	1778	4022	106.40
2695	201	218	348	65.11
3087	130	169	275	35.80
4625	178	228	287	59.45
10390	564	389	744	66.14
25217	1236	1241	1975	46.74
15459	800	821	1278	48.14
5739	239	231	453	43.00
4019	197	189	244	46.52
3341	104	245	310	54.24
9125	435	361	472	59.56
8835	523	424	771	49.26
3047	136	101	182	56.65
15607	348	1129	1406	44.57
6657	501	254	1346	52.39
6216	311	300	468	53.69
5274	261	246	421	80.44
573	13	34	31	25.97
108	9	5	3	4.30
261	28	15	13	15.38

Note: a).Total data in this table included 9834 doctors and 1043 medical personnel.
b).Total data in this table didn't include licensed doctors and registered nurses in tounship in county health Centers.

18-12 各地、州、市卫生技术人员数

单位:人

年 份 Year	地 区 Region	卫生技术人员合计 Number of Medical Technical Personnel	执业医师 Doctors with Licence	执业助理医师 Lecensed Assistant Doctor
	2005	96266	32563	8863
	2006	99839	33988	8787
	2007	104671	34838	8713
	2008	106853	35320	8136
	2009	114521	37223	8393
	2010	122860	39301	8865
	2011	130604	40265	9265
乌鲁木齐市	Urumqi City	31762	11879	660
克拉玛依市	Karamay City	2695	1030	39
吐鲁番地区	Turpan Administrative Offices	3087	1000	257
哈密地区	Hami [Kumul] Administrative Offices	4625	1508	314
昌吉回族自治州	Changji Hui Autonomous Prefecture	10390	3237	659
伊犁哈萨克自治州	Ili Kazak Autonomous Prefecture	25217	7772	2264
伊犁州直属县(市)	Counties (Cities) Direct Under Ili Prefecture	15459	4744	1238
塔城地区	Tacheng [Tarbagatai] Administrative Offices	5739	1664	651
阿勒泰地区	Altay Administrative Offices	4019	1364	375
博尔塔拉蒙古自治州	Bortala Mongol Autonomous Prefecture	3341	1079	286
巴音郭楞蒙古自治州	Bayangol Mongol Autonomous Prefecture	9125	2760	704
阿克苏地区	Aksu Administrative Offices	8835	2192	1111
克孜勒苏柯尔克孜自治州	Kizilsu Kirgiz Autonomous Prefecture	3047	666	319
喀什地区	Kashgar [Kaxgar] Administrative Offices	15607	3603	1492
和田地区	Hotan Administrative Offices	6657	1503	737
自治区直辖县级市	Municpality Country-LevelCity directly under the Central Govern-ment	6216	2036	423
石河子市	Shihezi City	5274	1796	326
阿拉尔市	Aral City	573	110	54
图木舒克市	Tumxuk City	108	19	13
五家渠市	Wujiaqu City	261	111	30

Number of Medical Technical Personnel by Prefecture, Autonomous Prefecture and City

(person)

注册护士 Registered Nurses	药剂人员 Pharmacist	技师(士) Technician (artificer)	检验人员 Laboratory Technicians	其他 Others	平均每万人医生数 Number of Doctors per 10 000 Population
30657	5848	4773		13562	20.61
32119	5948	4980		14017	20.87
34662	5647	6701	4746	14110	20.79
36084	5721	6876	4803	14716	20.39
40425	5989	7164	4977	15327	21.13
44238	6364	7742	5301	16350	22.25
48760	6483	7726	5391	18105	22.49
12918	1535	1662	1147	3108	50.29
1126	173	180	119	147	37.87
1139	173	207	154	311	19.89
1865	256	236	192	446	31.20
3902	587	581	400	1424	27.94
9119	1123	1737	1237	3202	21.82
5661	728	1140	825	1948	20.74
1982	227	376	241	839	22.16
1476	168	221	171	415	26.00
1219	191	190	136	376	28.01
3404	406	522	362	1329	25.36
3304	381	512	353	1335	13.82
1008	146	148	101	760	17.77
5262	780	988	687	3482	12.42
2081	451	399	242	1486	10.79
2413	281	364	261	699	23.05
2023	242	299	217	588	33.98
266	24	38	22	81	8.59
40	5	11	8	20	1.99
84	10	16	14	10	15.49

18-13 医疗机构、诊疗人次及入院出院人数

Number of Visits and Inpatients in Medical Institutions

(2011 年)

项　目	Item	机构数（个） Number of Institutions (unit)	诊疗人次（万人次） Total Number of Patients Treated (10 000 patient-times)	#门、急诊人次 Out-patients and Emergency Patients	#急诊人次 Emergency Patients
总　计	**Total**	**17042**	**7680.39**	**7401.15**	**280.37**
医　院	**Total Number of Hospitals**	**820**	**3738.33**	**3632.85**	**245.61**
综合医院	General Hospital	641	3100.24	3006.57	227.95
中医医院	Hospital Specialized in Traditional Chinese Medicine	46	336.36	332.94	12.36
中西医结合医院	Hospital Specialized in Combination ofTraditional Chinese and Western Medicine	4	23.21	23.07	0.15
民族医院	National Hospital	46	128.73	123.26	2.96
专科医院	Specialized Hospital	83	149.79	147.00	2.19
基层医疗卫生机构	**Sanitarium**	**16120**	**3696.13**	**3535.33**	**27.16**
社区卫生服务中心(站)	Health Service Center for Community	683	675.21	647.32	8.32
卫生院	Total Number of Public Health Center	922	1066.39	1025.34	18.17
村门卫室	Village Clinics	9825	764.61	715.64	
门诊部	Outpatients Department	247	109.70	109.19	0.68
诊所.卫生所.医务室	Clinic	4443	1080.22	1037.84	
专业公共卫生机构	**pecial Public Medical Institutions**	**98**	**243.78**	**230.89**	**7.60**
专科疾病防治院(所、站)	Urgent Care Center	4	2.44	2.44	0.46
妇幼保健院(所、站)	Hospitals for Maternity and Child Care	90	235.01	222.12	0.81
急救中心(站)	First-Aid-Stations(Center)	4	6.33	6.33	6.33
其他机构	**Hospitals for Maternity and Child Care**	**4**	**2.15**	**2.08**	
疗养院	Specialized Stations	4	2.15	2.08	

项　目	Item	门、急诊诊次占总诊次的比重（%） Percentage of Clinic Case and Emergence Case Among the Total Cases (%)	入院人数（万人） Hospital Admissions (10 000 patients)	出院人数（万人） Patients Discharged (10 000 patients)	治愈率（%） Cure Rate (%)
总　计	**Total**	**96.36**	**398.53**	**398.14**	**56.01**
医　院	**Total Number of Hospitals**	**97.18**	**311.54**	**309.85**	**52.78**
综合医院	General Hospital	96.98	261.80	260.38	54.52
中医医院	Hospital Specialized in Traditional Chinese Medicine	98.98	20.41	20.30	36.03
中西医结合医院	Hospital Specialized in Combination ofTraditional Chinese and Western Medicine	99.40	0.98	0.98	8.67
民族医院	National Hospital	95.75	15.20	15.06	48.81
专科医院	Specialized Hospital	98.14	13.14	13.12	51.95
基层医疗卫生机构	**Sanitarium**	**95.65**	**79.93**	**81.32**	**65.41**
社区卫生服务中心(站)	Health Service Center for Community	95.87	5.59	6.40	59.23
卫生院	Total Number of Public Health Center	96.15	74.15	74.72	66.02
村门卫室	Village Clinics	93.60			
门诊部	Outpatients Department	99.54	0.19	0.19	31.97
诊所.卫生所.医务室	Clinic	96.08			
专业公共卫生机构	**Special Public Medical Institutions**	**94.71**	**6.99**	**6.91**	**90.46**
专科疾病防治院(所、站)	Urgent Care Center	100.00		0.06	73.53
妇幼保健院(所、站)	Hospitals for Maternity and Child Care	94.52	6.99	6.85	90.60
急救中心(站)	First-Aid-Stations(Center)	100.00			
其他机构	**Hospitals for Maternity and Child Care**	**96.74**	**0.07**	**0.07**	**18.23**
疗养院	Specialized Stations	96.74	0.07	0.07	18.23

18-14 2000-2011 年历年分市县医院床位和专业卫生技术人员数
Hospital Beds and Medical Technical Personnel by City and County Areas(2000-2011)

年 份 Year	医院床位(张) Number of Hospital Beds (unit)		专业卫生技术人员(人) Number of Medical Technical Personnel (person)		#执业医师、执业助理医师 Lecensed Doctors & Assistant Doctors		#注册护士 Registered Nurses	
	市 City	县 County	市 City	县 County	市 City	县 County	市 City	县 County
2000	38398	27518	44115	31138	18408	13225	16805	9918
2001	38323	27685	44113	31055	18811	13271	16714	10105
2002	38700	26178	41850	27932	16689	10578	15965	8840
2003	42880	26915	44678	28228	17883	10916	17015	9087
2004	46300	27722	46956	28552	19207	10583	17185	9054
2005	50238	29515	54188	31132	23191	12323	18240	9289
2006	52275	31125	56701	32178	24033	13049	19365	9538
2007	54595	32536	68546	36125	28896	14655	24174	10488
2008	57242	36011	69292	37561	28215	15241	24976	11108
2009	58373	25403	54356	19490	20044	7242	22453	6979
2010	61157	28714	56706	21500	20953	7637	23777	8037
2011	65905	31531	61309	22893	21481	7881	26559	8964

18-15 2000-2011 年历年分市县卫生院床位和专业卫生技术人员数
Hospital Beds and Medical Technical Personnel by City and County Areas(2000-2011)

年 份 Year	卫生院床位(张) Number of Hospital Beds (unit)		专业卫生技术人员(人) Number of Medical Technical Personnel (person)		#执业医师、执业助理医师 Lecensed Doctors & Assistant Doctors		#注册护士 Registered Nurses	
	市 City	县 County	市 City	县 County	市 City	县 County	市 City	县 County
2000	2138	11119	3442	13131	1622	6299	1021	3756
2001	2141	11247	3602	13129	1782	6300	1095	3808
2002	2180	9991	4021	11215	1611	4370	970	2829
2003	2471	10147	3645	10901	1364	4227	946	2950
2004	2351	10479	3703	10936	1429	3963	992	2746
2005	5061	11679	10345	13646	5004	5704	2056	3024
2006	4732	13079	10930	14105	5370	6048	2207	3213
2007	2832	12803	18725	18220	9548	8000	4771	4182
2008	3037	13895	17745	19239	8888	8446	4710	4626
2009	3313	15531	3684	12578	1595	4435	1161	3527
2010	3383	16597	3641	13240	1536	4381	1180	3741
2011	3674	17671	3672	13653	1538	4334	1195	4097

18-16 社区卫生服务中心(站)工作量
Medical Services in Health Service Centers for Community

年 份 Year	社区卫生服务中心 Health Service Centers for Community				社区卫生服务站诊疗人次(万人) Health Service Stations for Community (10 000 patients)
	诊疗人次（万人次）Visits (10 000 patient-times)	入院人数(万人) Inpatients (10 000 patients)	病床使用率(%) Utilization Rate (%)	平均住院日(日) Average Stay Days (day)	
2002	76.84	0.16	53.86	10.16	34.41
2003	88.10	0.60	89.51	16.13	33.75
2004	85.62	0.03	36.42	10.00	82.67
2005	67.04	0.03	16.71	11.08	152.68
2006	107.49	0.35	11.71	6.94	179.32
2007	105.73	0.24	59.77	11.70	109.22
2008	156.05	0.94	51.68	11.30	121.92
2009	232.95	2.36	49.93	9.90	207.23
2010	298.47	4.24	61.07	10.40	355.78
2011	323.93	4.37	53.51	9.80	351.28

18-17 乡村卫生室基本情况
Basic Conditions of Country Health Room

(2011 年)

项 目	Item	合 计 Total	中 医 Traditional Chinese Medicine	西 医 Western Medicine	中西医结合 Combination Traditional and Western Medicine
机构数(个)	Number of Institutions(unit)	9825	85	8575	1165
执业(助理)医师(人)	Lecensed (Assistant) Doctors (person)	912	27	762	123
注册护士(人)	Registered Nurses(person)	338	5	312	21
乡村医生和卫生员(人)	Country Doctor and Assistant Nurse(person)	10877	92	9329	1456
乡村医生	Country Doctor	9834	82	8362	1390
卫生员	Assistant Nurse	1043	10	967	66
诊疗人次数(万人次)	Number of Patients Treated(10 000 patient-times)	764.61	12.16	698.01	54.44
#出 诊	Out-call	48.97	1.15	42.80	5.02

18-18 新型农牧区合作医疗基本情况

Basic Statistics on New Cooperative Health Care in Agricultural and Pastoral Areas

项　　目	Item	2010	2011
开展县(市)数(个)	Number of Counties(citys) to Carry Out(unit)	89	89
覆盖农牧业人口数(万人)	Population Coverage of Agriculture and Animal Husbandry(10 000 persons)	1033.70	1054.18
参合农牧业人口数(万人)	Livestok Population Parameters(10 000 persons)	1019.03	1050.93
参合率(%)	Ratio of Participation(%)	98.58	99.70
当年筹集基金(万元)	Paise Funds This Year(10 000 yuan)	161270.26	250295.47
#中央补助	Central Subsidy	61140.00	130308.00
自治区补助	Autonpmous Region Subsidy	51245.00	66294.18
地方补助	Local Subsidy	18365.91	20516.50
个人缴费	Individual Pay	29970.99	31636.49
当年人均筹集资金(元/人·年)	Annual per Capita Raise Funds(yuan/persons.year)	157.72	236.70
当年基金支出(万元)	Expenditure of Fund This Yesr(10 000 yuan)	147033.69	210775.48
当年基金使用率(%)	Ratio of Fund Utilization This Yesr(%)	91.17	84.21
当年补偿受益人次(万人次)	Benefit of Compensation Population this Year(10 000 person-times)	830.62	1140.04
住　院	Inpatients	145.38	168.48
门　诊	Out-patient Services	654.06	719.37
体　检	Physical Examination	30.78	27.59
其　他	Others	0.40	224.60
当年总体受益率(%)	Ratio of Total Benefit(%)	81.51	108.48
住院受益率	Benefit Ratio of be in Hospital	14.27	16.03
门诊受益率	Benefit Ratio of out-patient Services	64.19	68.45
当年总补偿比(%)	Total Compensation Ratio(%)	49.03	50.01
#住院平均补偿比	Average Compensation Ratio of be in Hospital	48.48	50.00
新农合管理机构实有人数(人)	Number of Employed Persons in Institution on New Cooperative Health Care of Agriculturial and Pastoral Areas(person)	1146.00	1275.00
新农合管理机构经费收入(万元)	Income of Institution on New Cooperative Health Care of Agriculturial and Pastoral Areas(10 000 yuan)	3767.45	5393.61
新农合管理机构经费支出(万元)	Expenditure of Institution on New Cooperative Health Care of Agriculturial and Pastoral Areas(10 000 yuan)	3719.78	5532.31
每实有人员管理参合人数(人)	Number of Participated Persons by per Practical Employed Persons(person)	14800	15100

18-19 法定报告传染病发病及死亡情况
Confirmed Incidence and Death from Infectious Diseases

项 目	Item	发病率 (1/10 万) Disease Incidence (1/100 000)		死亡率 (1/10 万) Death Rate (1/100 000)	
		2010	2011	2010	2011
总 计	**Total**	**682.195**	**754.058**	**2.608**	**2.865**
霍 乱	Cholera	0.014			
病毒性肝炎	Viral Hepatitis	253.813	276.331	0.093	0.092
细菌性和阿米巴性痢疾	Bacterial and Amebic Dysentery	43.625	41.277	0.009	
伤寒副伤寒	Typhoid and Paratyphoid Fever	3.335	1.159		
艾滋病	AIDS	2.497	3.177	1.649	2.054
淋 病	Gonorrhea	9.358	9.754		
梅 毒	Syphilis	50.175	70.284	0.019	
麻 疹	Measles	1.427	8.686		
百日咳	Pertussis	0.774	2.663		0.005
流行性脑脊髓膜炎	Epidemic Cerebrospinal Meningitis	0.130	0.110	0.014	0.003
猩红热	Scarlet Fever	4.846	11.821		
流行性出血热	Hemorrhage Fever		0.005		
布鲁氏菌病	Brucellosis	3.692	6.023		
炭 疽	Anthrax	0.255	0.206	0.005	
流行性乙型脑炎	Encephalitis B	0.005			
黑热病	Kala-Azar	0.686	0.293		
疟 疾	Malaria	0.028	0.023		
新生儿破伤风	Newborn Baby Tetanus	0.198	0.138	0.006	0.003
肺结核	Pulmonary Tuberculosis	164.461	157.830	0.783	0.651
甲型流感	H1N1 Influenza A	0.561	1.256		0.005

注：新生儿破伤风死亡率单位为千分率。
Note: The unit of incidence disease rate and death rate of newborn baby tetanus is 1‰.

18-20 城市前十位疾病死亡原因及构成
Death Causes and Percentage of 10 Major Diseases in Urban Areas

(2011 年)

疾病死亡原因	Cause of Death	死亡总人数 (人) Total Deaths (person)	占死亡总人数的比重 (%) Percentage to Total Deaths (%)
十种死因合计	**Total**	**7225**	**97.04**
循环系统	Circulatory system	2588	35.82
肿　瘤	Malignant Tumour	2101	29.08
呼吸系统	Diseases of the Respiratory System	839	11.61
损伤和中毒外部原因	Trauma and Toxicosis	414	5.73
传染病	Infections Disease	278	3.85
内分泌	Internal secretion	226	3.13
消化系统	Disease of the Digestive System	223	3.09
诊断不明	Diagnosis in nubibus	155	2.15
泌尿生殖系统	Disease of the Genifourinary system	105	1.45
起源于围生期的某些情况	Diseases of the Nervous system	82	1.13

注: 统计范围包括乌鲁木齐市及辖区资料。
Note: Statistics in data covers Urumqi and its Districts.

18-21 安全生产情况
Basic Statistics on Work Safety

单位：人 (person)

项　　目	Item	2010	2011
亿元新疆生产总值生产安全事故死亡人数	Mortality Rate of Work Safety Accident Average 100 Billion Yuan GDP	0.50	0.36
工矿商贸企业就业人员生产安全事故十万人死亡人数	Mortality Rate of Work Safety Accident of Employment in Industrial & Mining and Commercial & Tradal Enterprises Average 100 000 Persons	8.10	7.10
煤矿百万吨死亡人数	Mortality Rate of Coal Procuction Average 1 Million Tons	1.02	0.77
道路交通万车死亡人数	Mortality Rate of Highway Traffic Accident Average 10 000 Vehicles	7.58	6.47

18-22 社会福利事业单位基本情况
Basic Statistics on Social Welfare Institutions

(2011 年)

指　标	Item	院　数 (个) Number of Homes (unit)	工作人员数 (人) Number of Persons Engaged (person)	床位数 (张) Number of Beds (unit)	年末收养人数(人) Number of Persons Housed (person)	#女　性 Female
总　计	**Total**	**548**	**4094**	**37838**	**29081**	**7437**
社会福利院	Social Welfare Homes	49	656	7391	4911	886
儿童福利院	Children Welfare Homes	42	554	5496	4360	1438
光荣院	Homes for Disabled Veterans	9	66	492	356	53
社会福利医院	Psychopathy Welfare Homes	8	537	2213	2038	770
城镇老年性福利机构	Urban Elderly Welfare Units	67	995	6565	5034	1626
农村老年性福利机构	Rural Elderly Welfare Units	367	1236	15511	12309	2630
荣誉军人康复医院	Recuperative Hospital for Soldiers with Honour	1	35	80	9	
其他收养性机构	Other Residential Institutions	5	15	90	64	34

18-23 社会福利事业、企业单位数和工作人员数
Number of Social Welfare Institutions and Enterprises and Persons Engaged

(2011 年)

项　目	Item	机构数 (个) Number of Institutions or Enterprises (unit)	工作人员数(人) Number of Persons Engaged (person)
收养性福利事业单位	Adopting Social Welfare Institutions	548	4094
编制部门	Organization Department	357	2814
民政部门	Civil Administration Department	179	1209
社会福利企业	Social Welfare Enterprises	154	13862
优抚安置事业单位	Administration Agencies for Martyrs	31	374
救助类单位	Salvaged Deparement	51	384
殡葬服务事业单位	Funeral and Interment Institutions	151	843
福利彩票发行单位	Welfare Lottery-Ticked Issuance Unit	24	214
社区服务中心	Community Service Institutions	239	1221

18-24 社会救济情况
Basic Statistics on Social Relief Funds

指　　标	Item	2011
城镇居民最低生活保障人数(人)	**Number of Persons Receiving Lowest Cost-of-living in Urban Area (person)**	**848170**
老年人	Old Folks	109826
成年人	Adult	440275
在职人员	Full Employed Staff and Workers	9362
灵活就业人员	Flexible Employed Persons	125727
登记失业人员	Registered Employed Persons	122466
未登记失业人员	Unregistered Employed Persons	182720
未成年人	Minors	298069
在校生	Enrollment	192804
其　他	Others	105265
城镇居民最低生活保障家庭数(户)	**Number of Family Receiving Lowest Cost-of-living in Urban Area (household)**	**360870**
农村最低生活保障人数(人)	**Number of Persons Receiving Lowest Cost-of-living in Rural Area (person)**	**1348974**
农村最低生活保障家庭数(户)	**Number of Family Receiving Lowest Cost-of-living in Rural Area (household)**	**522606**

18-25 主要年份工会组织情况
Basic Statistics on Trades Unions in Main Years

年　份 Year	工会基层组织个数(个) Number of Grassroots Unions (unit)	全区已建工会组织的基本单位职工与会员人数(万人) Membership and Number of Staff and Workers in Grassroots Unions (10 000 persons)				专职工会干　部(万人) Number of Full-time Personnel of Unions (10 000 persons)
		职工人数 Number of Staff and Workers	#女 Female	会员人数 Number of Membership	#女 Female	
1980	3255	84.20	30.25	67.13	20.42	0.48
1985	6165	189.48	73.84	151.93	59.03	0.50
1990	10685	231.48	90.64	196.58	76.97	0.79
1995	14457	271.43	114.13	254.49	104.97	1.19
2000	13016	211.73	90.80	200.80	84.93	0.59
2001	18219	234.84	100.71	215.31	91.07	0.73
2002	20806	236.58	99.65	220.85	93.11	0.49
2003	11263	230.24	93.43	220.55	87.05	0.45
2004	11979	224.52	94.49	219.35	90.62	0.48
2005	11721	232.78	97.50	232.03	97.20	0.41
2006	13163	302.05	130.12	263.80	115.64	0.69
2007	15040	323.37	139.45	289.65	124.23	0.60
2008	16880	337.80	147.31	308.81	134.71	0.55
2009	17849	351.69	146.56	326.91	136.48	0.70
2010	19668	371.23	153.55	342.07	147.54	0.60
2011	21023	386.47	159.54	355.78	150.67	0.72

18-26 残疾人事业基本情况
Basic Information of People with Disabilities

项　目	Item	2010	2011
康　复	**Rehabilitation**		
白内障复明	Sight-restoring of Cataract Surgery		
白内障复明手术(万例)	Sight-restoring of Cataract Surgeries (10 000 cases)	0.54	0.69
低视力配用助视器(人)	Vision-aids Provided for Individuds with Low-vision (person)	1722	807
聋儿康复	Rehabilitation of Children With Hearing Disability		
年收训聋儿(人)	Hearing and Speech Training (person)	236	198
聋儿入普幼普小率(%)	Enrollment Rate to General Infant School or Elementary School (%)	32	18.7
培训家长(人)	Parents Trained (person)	362	1152
精神病防治康复	Prevention and Treatment of Psychiatric Diseases		
开展精神病防治康复工作市县数(个)	Number of Counties Carried on the Works (unit)	39	68
综合防治康复精神病人数(万人)	Number of Psychosis Sicks Synthetically Prevented, Cured and Rehabilitated (10 000 persons)	2.50	1.52
监护率(%)	Guardianship Rate (%)	74.18	69.00
显好率(%)	Rate of Getting Better (%)	35.03	35.30
社会参与率(%)	Social Participation Rate (%)	25.99	23.80
肇事率(%)	Violent Everds Rate (%)	0.26	0.05
救济贫困患者数(人)	Number of Poor Sufferer Relieved (person)	3220	3441
用品用具供应件数(万件)	Number of Appliances Supplied (10 000 units)	1.73	1.42
康复训练与服务	Rehabilitation Training and Service		
肢体残疾康复训练数(人)	Rehabilitation Training of Body Disabilities (person)	1641	2360
智力残疾儿童康复训练数(人)	Rehabilitation Training of Mental Disabilities Children (person)	337	217
教　育	**Education**		
未入学适龄残疾儿童(万人)	Number of Uneducated Children (10 000 persons)	0.5	0.42
残疾人中等职业学校(班)	Secondary Vocational Schools for PWDS		
残联系统办	Run by Institution of Disabled Person's	2	1
教育部门办	Run by Education	1	1
在校学生(万人)	Number of Enrollments	0.0626	0.0586

18-26 续表 Continued

项　目	Item	2010	2011
就　业	**Employment**		
城镇残疾人就业状况(万人)	Employment of Urban Handicappeds (10 000 persons)		
当年安排就业	Persons Employed in the Year	0.54	0.48
按比例就业	Employment by Quota Scheme	0.21	0.16
集中就业	Employment at Welfare Enterprises	0.13	0.14
个体就业	Individual Employment	0.20	0.14
未安排就业	Unemployment	1.88	1.62
农村残疾人就业状况(万人)	Employment of Rural Handicapped (10 000 persons)		
就　业	Employed	17.54	21.04
未就业	Unemployed	4.87	4.93
残疾人就业服务机构(个)	Number of Institutions Engaging in Handicappeds Employment (unit)		
省	Provinces	1	1
地	Prefectures	14	14
市(含县级市)	Cities (Cities at County Level)	16	16
县	County	68	68
市辖区	Districts under the Jurisdiction of Cities	11	11
实施分散按比例就业的地区数(个)	Number of Regions Implemented the Policy of the Disperse Employment by Proportion (unit)		
省	Provinces	1	1
地	Prefectures	14	14
市(含县级市)	Cities (Cities at County Level)	16	16
县	County	68	68
市辖区	Districts under the Jurisdiction of Cities	11	11
残联组织建设	**Organization of Association for the Handicapped**		
残疾人工作者(万人)	Number of Workers for the Handicappeds (10 000 persons)	0.23	0.28

18-27 历届全区人民代表大会代表人数

Number of Deputies to all the Previous People's Congresses of Xinjiang

项目 Item	第一届 (1954) First Congress	第二届 (1959) Second Congress	第三届 (1964) Third Congress	第四届 (1975) Fourth Congress	第五届 (1978) Fifth Congress	第六届 (1983) Sixth Congress	第七届 (1988) Seventh Congress	第八届 (1993) Eighth Congress	第九届 (1998) Ninth Congress	第十届 (2003) Tenth Congress	第十一届 (2008) Eleventh Congress
代表总数(人) Total Number of All Deputies (person)	**376**	**386**	**453**	**809**	**672**	**550**	**550**	**542**	**550**	**550**	**550**
#中国共产党党员 Deputies from the Communist Party of China	178		240			374	357	381	396	396	352
占总数比重(%) Percentage to Total (%)	47.3		53.0			68.0	64.9	70.3	72.0	72.0	64.0
#少数民族 Deputies from National Minorities	331		383	510	430	357	363	355	363	363	363
占总数比重(%) Percentage to Total(%)	88.0		84.5	63.8	64.0	64.9	66.0	65.5	66.0	66.0	66.0
#妇 女 Female Deputies	52	61	89	200	146	17	126	123	135	135	143
占总数比重(%) Percentage to Total(%)	13.8	15.8	19.6	24.7	21.7	21.3	22.9	22.7	24.5	24.5	26.0

18-28 历届全区政治协商会议委员人数

Number of Deputies to all the Previous People's Political Consultative Conferences of Xinjiang

项目 Item	第一届 (1954) First Congress	第二届 (1959) Second Congress	第三届 (1964) Third Congress	第四届 (1978) Fourth Congress	第五届 (1983) Fifth Congress	第六届 (1988) Sixth Congress	第七届 (1993) Seventh Congress	第八届 (1998) Eighth Congress	第九届 (2003) Ninth Congress	第十届 (2008) Tenth Congress
委员总数(人) Total Number of All Deputies (person)	**141**	**275**	**303**	**407**	**441**	**429**	**416**	**444**	**470**	**515**
#中国共产党党员 Deputies from the Communist Party of China	28	57	65	149	158	157	161	183	196	225
占总数比重(%) Percentage to Total(%)	19.9	20.7	21.5	36.6	35.8	36.6	38.7	41.2	41.7	43.7
#少数民族 Deputies from National Minorities	121	196	205	221	253	245	204	246	246	263
占总数比重(%) Percentage to Total(%)	85.8	71.3	67.7	54.3	57.4	57.0	49.0	55.4	52.3	51.1
#妇 女 Female Deputies	10	28	28	40	49	63	66	82	95	125
占总数比重(%) Percentage to Total(%)	7.1	10.2	9.2	9.8	11.1	14.7	15.9	18.5	20.2	24.3

18-29 主要年份律师、公证、调解工作基本情况
Basic Statistics on Lawyers, Notarization and Mediation in Main Years

项目	Item	1995	2000	2005	2010	2011
律师工作	**Lawyers**					
律师事务所(个)	Number of Law Offices (unit)	169	227	243	318	336
律师(人)	Number of Lawyers (person)	1705	2414	2088	2900	3035
#专职律师(人)	Full-time Lawyers (person)	1209	1508	1987	2704	2828
兼职和特邀律师(人)	Part-time Lawyers (person)	336	418	101	114	110
聘请担任常年法律顾问的单位(处)	Number of Units with Permanent Legal Advisors (unit)	2560	2613	2663	3858	4095
民事诉讼代理(件)	Agent of Civil Cases (case)	6380	16165	23389	38822	36437
刑事辩护及代理(件)	Defender and Agent of Criminal Cases (case)	5850	5826	7716	8510	7862
非诉讼法律事务(件)	Agent of Non-Litigious Legal Affairs (case)	5357	4810	7066	2450	1015
解答法律咨询(万件)	Agent of Legal Advisory Services (10 000 cases)	4.21	7.45	8.14	10.13	7.94
代写法律事务文书(万件)	Agent of Legal Documents Written on Behalf of Clients (10 000 cases)	1.06	1.94	3.00	2.16	2.00
公证工作	**Notarization**					
公证处(个)	Number of Notary Offices (unit)	126	131	126	125	125
公证员(人)	Notaries (person)	266	332	457	416	407
公证员助理(人)	Assistant Notaries (person)	49	43	61	144	245
办理公证文书(万件)	Number of Notarized Document (10 000 cases)	10.11	18.85	18.05	30.93	34.38
人民调解工作	**Number of People's Mediation**					
专职司法助理员(人)	Number of Full-time Judicial Assistants (person)	1515	1750	1706	1662	2458
人民调解委员会(个)	Number of People's Mediation Committees (unit)	19045	22294	15852	14157	13657
调解人员(万人)	Number of Mediators (10 000 persons)	12.04	10.04	7.86	7.62	7.08
调解民间纠纷(万件)	Number of Civil Disputes Mediated (10 000 cases)	9.18	8.09	6.83	17.21	22.47

18-30 调解民间纠纷分类
Number of Civil Disputes Mediated by Type

(2011 年)

项　目	Item	调解纠纷(件) Civil Disputes (case)	各类纠纷所占比重(%) Percentage (%)
总　计	**Total**	**224657**	**100**
婚姻家庭	Marriage and Family	57778	25.72
合　同	Contract	12912	5.75
劳　动	Labor	8617	3.83
村务管理	Village-affair Management	1856	0.83
土　地	Land	19416	8.64
征地拆迁	Requisitioned Land Demolition	2845	1.27
房屋宅基地	Housing and Housing Sites	7118	3.17
计划生育	Family Planning	358	0.16
邻　里	Neighbour	49089	21.85
损害赔偿	Compensation for Damages	16748	7.45
环境保护	Environment Protection	481	0.21
道路交通事故	Road Traffic Accidents	5454	2.43
物　业	Property Management	1841	0.82
医　疗	Medical Treatment	445	0.20
生产经营	Production and Operation	4945	2.20
其　他	Others	34754	15.47

18-31 火灾事故发生情况
Basic Statistics on Fire Accidents

(2011 年)

指　标	Item	合　计 Total	按事故发生程度分 By Serious Dgree of Fires			
			特　大 Extraordinarily Serious	重　大 Serious	较　大 Comparatively Serious	一　般 Ordinary
发生起数(起)	Fires (case)	5093			1	5092
死亡(人)	Death (person)	33			3	30
受伤(人)	Injuries (person)	21				21
损失折款(万元)	Losses Converted into Cash (10 000 yuan)	5178.54			0.24	5178.30
平均每起事故损失(元)	Average Loss per Fire (yuan)	12529.49			2360	10169.49

18-32 2009-2011 年历年交通事故发生情况
Basic Statistics on Traffic Accidents(2009-2011)

指　标	Item	2009	2010	2011
发生起数(起)	Traffic Accidents (case)	5041	4949	5182
死亡(人)	Death (person)	1870	1851	1992
受伤(人)	Injuries (person)	5656	5859	5903
损失折款(万元)	Losses Converted into Cash (10 000 yuan)	897	864	1036
平均每起事故损失(元)	Average Loss per Fire (yuan)	1779	1746	2000

18-33 公安机关受理查处治安案件情况
Offense Cases Against Public Order Handled by Public Security Organs

单位：起　　(2011 年)　　(case)

案件类别	Category of Cases	受理 Number of Cases Accepted to be Treated	查处 Number of Cases Investigated and Treated
总　计	**Total**	**104163**	**96822**
扰乱公共秩序	Disturbing Work or Public Order	2159	2115
扰乱单位秩序	Disturbing Business Orders	464	461
扰乱公共场所秩序	Disturbing the Orders in Public Places	301	298
寻衅滋事	Causing Quarrels and Making Troubles	889	860
其　他	Others	505	496
妨害公共安全	Disorderly Cordnct	598	580
非法携带枪支、弹药、管制刀具	Violation of Firearms Control Regulations	233	229
盗窃、损毁公共设施	Stealing and Damaging Public Facilities	79	67
其　他	Others	286	284
侵犯他人人身权利、财产权利	Offences Against, Citizens'Personal and Property Rights	79375	72286
侮辱、诽谤、诬告陷害	Insult, Slander and Circumvention	796	691
殴打他人	Beating Other Body	57312	53698
故意伤害	Wilfully Injuring Others	3267	2946
盗　窃	Stealing Property	10787	8471
诈　骗	Swindling, Seizing and Extorting Property	756	540
抢　夺	Robbery and Snatch	195	160
敲诈勒索	Extertion and Blackmail	84	75
其　他	Others	6178	5705
妨害社会管理	Disorderly Social Management	22031	21841
阻碍执行职务	Obstructing Government Workers in Performing Their Duties	685	671
违反旅馆业管理	Violating the Hotel Management Regulations	2080	2074
违反房屋出租管理	Violating the Rent Control Regulations	3533	3533
卖淫、嫖娼	Prostitution or Going Whoring	1161	1159
赌博或为赌博提供条件	Gambling	1865	1822
毒品违法活动	Illegal Drug Related Action	9421	9360
其　他	Others	3286	3222

18-34 2007-2011 年历年刑事案件中青少年犯罪情况
Juvenile Delinquency Among Criminal Cases(2007-2011)

单位：人　　(person)

年份 Year	刑事罪犯总数 Offenders	#青少年罪犯 Young Offenders	不满 18 岁 Less than 18	18 岁至 25 岁 Between 18 to 25	青少年罪犯占刑事罪犯 (%) Percentage to Total (%)
2007	38878	19838	7142	12696	51.03
2008	37222	18317	5899	12418	49.20
2009	33121	15989	4538	11451	48.27
2010	29257	13299	4012	9287	45.45
2011	29690	12627	3697	8930	42.53

主要统计指标解释

等级运动员人数 指经考核正式批准授予等级运动员称号的人数。运动员等级分为国际级运动健将、运动健将、一级运动员、二级运动员、三级运动员、少年级运动员。该指标主要反映运动员队伍的技术质量水平。

等级裁判员人数 指经考核正式批准授予等级裁判员称号的人数。裁判员等级分为国际裁判、国家级裁判、一级裁判、二级裁判。该指标主要反映裁判员队伍的技术质量水平。

体育场 指有400米跑道(中心含足球场),有固定道牙,跑道6条以上,并有固定看台的室外田径场地。体育场按看台容纳观众人数分为: 甲级25000人以上,乙级15000-25000人,丙级5000-15000人,丁级5000人以下。该指标主要反映大中型体育场数量水平。

体育馆 指有固定看台,可供篮球、排球、羽毛球、乒乓球、体操等项目训练比赛活动用的室内运动场地。体育馆按看台容纳观众人数分为: 甲级6000人以上,乙级4000-6000人,丙级2000-4000人,丁级2000人以下。该指标主要反映大中型体育馆数量水平。

卫生机构 指从卫生行政部门取得《医疗机构执业许可证》,或从民政、工商行政、机构编制管理部门取得法人单位登记证书,为社会提供医疗保健、疾病控制、卫生监督服务或从事医学科研和教育等工作的单位。卫生机构包括医院、疗养院、社区卫生服务中心(站)、卫生院、门诊部、诊所(卫生所、医务室)、急救中心(站)、采供血机构、妇幼保健院(所、站)、专科疾病防治院(所、站)、疾病预防控制中心(防疫站)、卫生监督所、卫生监督监测机构、医学科研机构、医学在职培训机构、健康教育所(站)等其他卫生机构。

医疗机构 指从卫生行政部门取得《医疗机构执业许可证》的机构,包括医院、疗养院、社区卫生服务中心(站)、卫生院、门诊部、诊所(卫生所、医务室)、妇幼保健院(所、站)、专科疾病防治院(所、站) 、急救中心(站)和临床检验中心。

社区卫生服务中心(站) 指为本社区居民提供预防、医疗、保健、康复、健康教育、计划生育技术服务等的基层卫生机构。包括社区卫生服务中心和社区卫生服务站。

卫生人员 指在医疗、预防保健、医学科研和在职教育等卫生机构工作的职工,包括卫生技术人员、其他技术人员、管理人员和工勤人员。

卫生技术人员 包括执业(助理)医师、注册护士、药剂人员、检验和影像人员等卫生专业人员。不包括从事管理工作的卫生技术人员。

执业医师 指具有《医师执业证》及其"级别"为"执业医师"且实际从事医疗、预防保健工作的人员,不包括实际从事管理工作的执业医师。执业医师类别分为临床、中医、口腔和公共卫生四类。

执业助理医师 指《医师执业证》"级别"为"执业助理医师"且实际从事医疗、预防保健工作的人员,不包括实际从事管理工作的执业助理医师。执业助理医师类别同样分为临床、中医、口腔和公共卫生四类。

每万人口执业(助理)医师 每万人口执业(助理)医师=(执业医师数+执业助理医师数)/人口数×10000。人口数系公安部户籍人口。

每万人口医院、卫生院床位数 每万人口医院卫生院床位数=(医院床位数+卫生院床位数)/人口数×10000。人口数系公安部户籍人口。

每万人口卫生技术人员 每万人口卫生技术人员=卫生技术人员数/人口数×10000。人口数系公安部户籍人口。

甲乙类法定报告传染病发病率 是指某年某地区每10万人口中甲、乙类法定报告传染病发病情况。即法定报告传染病发病率=甲、乙类法定报告传染病发病数/人口数×100000。

甲乙类法定报告传染病死亡率 是指某年某地区每10万人口中甲、乙类法定报告传染病死亡情况。即法定报告传染病死亡率=甲、乙类法定报告传染病死亡数/人口数×100000。

甲乙类法定报告传染病病死率 是指某年某地区甲、乙类法定报告传染病死亡数与发病数之比。即法定报告传染病病死率=甲、乙类法定报告传染病死亡数/发病数×100%。

参加新农合人数 指根据本地新农合实施方案到年内新农合筹资截止时已缴纳新农合资金的人口数。

新农合当年基金支出 指本年度实际从新农合基金帐户中支出用于新农合补偿的资金。

新农合补偿支出受益人次 指年内新农合参合人员因病就医获得补偿的人次数,包括住院、家庭帐户形式、门诊、特殊病种大额门诊、住院正常分娩、体检和其他补偿人次之和。

新农合本年度筹资总额 指为本年度筹集的、实际进入新农合专用帐户的基金数额。包括本年度中央及地方财政配套资金、农民个人交纳资金(含民政部门及其他相关部门代缴的救助资金)、新农合基金本年度产生的全部利息收入及其他渠道实际筹集到的新农合基金额。筹资数额以进入新农合专用帐户的基金数额为准,不含上年结转额资金。

卫生总费用 指一个国家或地区在一定时期内为开展卫生服务活动,从全社会筹集的卫生资源的货币总额。按来源法计算。它反映一定经济条件下,政府、社会和居民个人对卫生保健的重视程度和费用负担水平,以及卫生筹资模式的主要特征和卫生筹资的公平性、合理性。

政府预算卫生支出 指各级政府用于医疗卫生服务、医疗保障补助、卫生和医疗保险行政管理事务、人口与计划生育事务支出等各项事业的经费。

社会卫生支出 指政府支出外的社会各界对卫生事业的资金投入。包括社会医疗保障支出、商业健康保险费、社会办医支出、社会捐赠援助、行政事业性收费收入等。

个人现金卫生支出 指城乡居民在接受各类医疗卫生服务时的现金支付,包括享受多种医疗保险制度的居民就医时自付的费用。

人均卫生费用 即某年卫生总费用与同期平均人口数之比。

社会福利事业单位 指集中收养社会孤老、残、幼的机构，包括由民政部门管理的社会福利院、儿童福利院、精神病人福利院和城镇集体举办的福利院及农村集体举办的敬老院以及优抚医院和具有收养能力的社区服务中心等。该指标主要反映我国在社会福利性单位投入的水平。

社会福利事业单位收养人数 包括民政部门管理和城镇、农村集体举办的社会福利事业单位中收养的老人、少年儿童、缺乏生活自理能力的残疾人员和精神病人。该指标主要反映收养性社会福利单位的收养能力。

社会福利企业 指以集中安置有一定劳动能力的残疾人员就业为目（残疾职工占生产人员10%以上）、带有社会福利性质的企业总称。主要包括福利工厂、假肢厂和其他福利企业。

城市居民最低生活保障人数 指在报告期末家庭平均收入在当地规定的最低生活保障线以下的城镇居民数。包括“三无”对象，失业人员和在职、下岗、退休人员等。

农村居民最低生活保障人数 指报告期末在建立农村最低生活保障制度的地区，得到当地政府或集体给予最低生活保障的农业人口家庭人数。

五保户 指无法定抚养义务人，或者虽有法定抚养义务人，但是抚养人无抚养能力的；无劳动能力的；无生活年人来源的老年人、残疾人和未成年人。

聋儿入普幼普小率 指本年度内经康复训练后进入普通幼儿园、普通小学的聋儿数与在训聋儿数(不含当年新收训聋儿数)之比。

综合防治康复精神病人数 指在开展精神病防治康复工作地区，采取不同形式，接受综合性防治康复措施、开放式管理的精神病人数。该指标主要反映精神病患者接受治疗康复情况。

监护率 指通过监护小组、家庭病床、工疗站、社会就业以及精神卫生机构，接受社会化、综合性、开放式治疗与康复的精神病人占经调查摸底、登记在册的精神病人数的百分比。该指标主要反映对精神病患者落实治疗康复措施的情况。

社会参与率 指生活能自理，并参加生产劳动和社会生活的精神病人数占监护精神病人数的百分比。该指标主要反映精神病人康复状况和参与社会的情况。

未入学学龄残疾儿童少年总人数 指截止到本年度12月31日，在省级人民政府依照《义务教育法》规定的入学年龄段内的，因各种原因未能入学的各类残疾儿童少年人数。

律师 指依法取得律师执业证书，担任法律顾问，民事(刑事、行政)案件代理人、刑事案件辩护人、办理非诉讼业务，解答法律询问，代写法律事务文书等，为社会提供法律服务的人员。

公证人员 指在公证处工作的人员总称，包括公证处主任、副主任、公证员、公证员助理(助理公证员)和其他从事辅助性工作的人员。

公证文书 指公证处根据当事人申请，依照事实和法律，按照法定程序制作的，具有法律效力的司法证明文书。

调解员 指在人民调解委员会担负调解民间纠纷工作的人员，包括调解委员会的委员和调解小组的调解员。该指标主要反映从事人民调解工作的人员数量。

调解民间纠纷 指调解委员会按照法律规定，根据自愿原则，用说服教育的方法调解民间发生的有关民事权利和义务争执的件数，包括调解成功数和调解未成功数。该指标主要反映人民调解委员会的工作量。

特大交通事故 指一次造成死亡3人以上，或者重伤11人以上，或者死亡1人，同时重伤8人以上，或者死亡2人，同时重伤5人以上，或者财产损失6万元以上的交通事故。

重大交通事故 指一次造成死亡1至2人，或者重伤3人以上10人以下，或者财产损失3万元以上不足6万元的交通事故。

特大火灾 指造成30人以上死亡，或者100人以上重伤，或者1亿元以上直接财产损失的火灾。

重大火灾 指造成10人以上30人以下死亡，或者50人以上100人以下重伤，或者5000万元以上1亿元以下直接财产损失的火灾。

较大火灾 指造成3人以上10人以下死亡，或者10人以上50人以下重伤，或者1000万元以上5000万元以下直接财产损失的火灾。

一般火灾 指造成3人以下死亡，或者10人以下重伤，或者1000万元以下直接财产损失的火灾。

Explanatory Notes on Main Statistical Indicators

Number of Athletes in Grades refers to the number of athletes who have been given titles through examination. The titles of athletes include international masters of sports, masters of sports, first-grade, second- grade and third-grade sportsmen and young athletes. This indicator reflects skill of the athletes.

Number of Referees in Grades refers to the number of referees who have been given titles after examination. They are classified as international referees, national referees and referees of the first, second and third grades. This indicator reflects the skill of referees.

Stadiums refer to stadiums for track and field events with six lane 400-meter tracks around soccer fields, permanent track marks and permanent bleachers. Stadiums are classified according to seating capacity. They include: Class A stadiums have the capaCity of seating 25000 people each. Class B stadiums have the capaCity of seating 15000 to 25000 people each. Class C stadiums have the capaCity of s eating 5000 to 15000 people each, and Class D stadiums have the capaCity of seating fewer than 5000 people. This indicator reflects numbers of large and medium-sized stadiums.

Gymnasiums refer to indoor sports grounds with permanent seats in which basketball, volleyball. Badminton, table tennis and gymnastics competitions can be held. Gymnasiums are classified according to seating capaCity. They include: Class Agymnasiums with seating over 6000 people. Class B gymnasiums with seating 4000 to 6000 people. Class Cgymnasiums with seating 2000 to 4000 people, and Class D gymnasiums with eating fewer than 2000 people. This indicator reflects the total number of large and medium-sized gymnasiums Health Care Institutions include: medical institutions, disease prevent ion and control centers (epidemic prevention stations), blood gathering and supplying institutions, health supervision and inspection (checkup) institutions, medicinal scientific research and on-job training institutions, health education and son on.

Health Care Institutions include: medical institutions, disease prevention and control centers(epidemic prevention stations),blood gathering and supplying Institutions,health supervision and inspection(check up)institutions,medical scientific research and on-job training institutions,health education and so on.

Medical Organizations refer to the institutions which have been qualified the Certification of Health Care Institution by the administration of public health, including: hospitals, sanatoriums, community health service centers (stations), health centers, clinics (health stations and infirmaries), women and children care agencies (centres and stations), special disease prevention and curing agencies (centres and stations), first-aid centres (stations) and clinic inspection centers.

Community Health Service Centres (stations) refer to the primary units that provide the health care for community residents, such as disease prevention and control, medical treatment, health care, rehabilitation, health education, family planning technical services, including community health service centres and community health service stations.

Health Care Employee refer to all employee engaged in the health care institutions, such as medical organizations, disease prevention and control centres, health care agencies, medicinal scientific research and on-job training institutions, including medical technical personnel, other technical personnel, manager and labour.

Medical Technical Personnel refer to the professional staff engaged in health care, including licensed (assistant) doctors, registered nurse, pharmacists, laboratory technician, and imaging staff, excluding the medical technical personnel engaged in management job (included as the management staff).

Licensed Doctors refer to the medical workers who have obtained the licenses of qualified doctors and are employed in medical treatment, disease prevention or healthcare institutions, excluding the licensed doctors engaged in management job. The classification of licensed doctors is clinician, Chinese medicine, dentist and public health.

Licensed Assistant Doctors refer to the medical workers who have obtained the licenses of qualified assistant doctors and are employed in medical treatment, disease prevention or healthcare institutions, excluding the licensed assistant doctors engaged in management job. The classification of licensed assistant doctors is clinician, Chinese medicine, dentist and public health.

Number of Licensed (Assistant) Doctors per 10000 Population the formula is:

Number of Licensed Doctors per 10000 Population = (Number of Licensed Doctors + Number of Licensed Assistant Doctors) / Population ×10000

The population is the figure of household registration from the Ministry of Public Security.

Number of Beds of Hospitals and Health Care per 10000 Population the formula is:

Number of Beds of Hospitals and Health Care per 10000 Population = Number of Beds of Hospitals + Number of Beds of Health Care) / Population ×10000

The population is the figure of household registration from the Ministry of Public Security.

Number of Medical Technical Personnel per 10000 Population the formula is:

Number of Medical Technical Personnel per 10000 Population = Number of Medical Technical Personnel / Population ×10000

The population is the figure of household registration from the Ministry of Public Security.

Incidence Rate of A and B Type of Notifiable Infectious Diseases refer to the incidence cases notifiable class A and class B infectious diseases per 100 thousand population in the reference region in the reference year. The formula is:

Incidence Rate of Notifiable Infectious Diseases = Incidence Cases Notifiable Class A and Class B Infectious Diseases / Population *10000

Death Rate of A and B Type of Notifiable Infectious Diseases refer to the death cases notifiable class A and class B infectious diseases per 100 thousand population in the reference region in the reference year. The formula is:

Death Rate of Notifiable Infectious Diseases = Death Cases Notifiable Class A and Class B Infectious Diseases / Population×10000

Mortality Rate of A and B Type Notifiable Infectious Diseases refer to the ratio of death cases notifiable class A and class B infectious diseases to the incidence cases in the reference region in the reference year. The formula is:

Mortality Rate of Notifiable Infectious Diseases = Death Cases Notifiable Class A and Class B Infectious Diseases / Incidence Cases×100%

Standardized Mortality Rate refers to the mortality rate at reference age calculated according to the age structure of a group of population

Number of Persons Participated in the New Rural Cooperative Medical System refers to the number of persons who have given payment to the new cooperative medical system by the deadline of fundraising during the year according to the implementation plan of the new system.

Expenditure of Funds for the New Rural Cooperative Medical System This Year refers to expenditures on compensation funds for the new rural cooperative medical system from the fund account of new cooperative medical system this year.

Persons Benefited from the Compensation Expenditure of New Rural Cooperative Medical System refers to the number of persons participated in the new system who have been compensated for medical treatment in the year, including hospitalization, family account form, out-patient, large special diseases out-patient, normal childbirth in hospital, medical examination and other compensations

Funds Raised for the New Rural Cooperative Medical System this Year refers to the amount of funds raised this year and put into the special new rural cooperative medical account, including the matching funds of central and local governments, paid money by farmers (including relief funds paid by the civil affairs department and other relevant departments), all the interest income generated this year of the funds and funds actually raised from other channels this year. The amount of funding equals to the funds entering into the special new rural cooperative medical account, excluding the carry-over funds from the previous year.

Total Expenditure on Public Health refers to the monetary amount of health resources raised from the whole society that have been spent on health service activities. It is calculated by source. It reflects that under certain economic circumstance, the emphasis on health care from the government, society and individuals, the level of cost burden, the main features of the health financing pattern, the fairness and rationality of health financing.

Government Expenditure on Public Health refers to the expenditure of the governments at all levels on medical and health care services, health administration and health insurance management and undertakings of family planning.

Social Expenditure on Public Health refers to all inputs of society except the government in public health including the expenditures on social medical security, and commercial health insurance, private expenditure on operation of medical and health care, social donation and contribution, and income from administrative fees etc.

Individual Cash Expenditure on Health refers to expenditure in cash on various health services by rural and urban residents, including self payments of residents within the system of multi-medical insurance.

Average Expenditure on Health refers to the ratio of total expenditure on health in a year to the average population.

Social Welfare Institutions refer to institutions taking care of old pople without children, handicapped people and orphans. They include social welfare institutions run by civil affairs departments, children welfare institutions, social welfare institutions for mental patients, collective-owned old peoples homes in rural areas, convalescent homes and community service centers with the capaCity of receiving those people. This indicator reflects the input in social welfare institutions.

Number of People Taken in by Social Welfare Institutions refers to the number of old people, children, totally dependent handicapped people and mental patients taken in by social welfare institutions run by civil affairs departments and those run by collective units in urban and rural areas. This indicator reflects the cap a City of social welfare institutions.

Social Welfare Enterprises are collective owned enterprises which employ the blind, deaf-mute, and other handicapped people who are able to work in cities and towns and enjoy exemption from state taxes, including welfare plants, welfare commercial services, artificial limb plants and farms, etc. This indicator reflects the preferential policies toward disabled persons.

Number of Urban Residents Entitled to Minimum Living Allowances refers to the number of those whose average family income is below a minimum local standard by the end of the reporting period, including both the employed and unemployed, laid off and retired, and those jobless people without stable residence or valid IDs.

Number of Rural Residents Entitled to Minimum Living Allowances refers to the number of those receiving the minimum living allowances from the local government or community in the rural areas where this allowances system is in place as of the end of the reporting period.

Rural Households with Livelihood Guaranteed in Five Aspects refer to the households in which there are old people without child, orphans and handicapped people who are unable to work and without financial resources in rural areas. They are taken care of by the collective units and their food, clothing, housing, medical care, funeral expenses (or schooling for orphans) are guaranteed to be provided for. This indicator reflects the total number of disadvantageous groups of rural population.

Proportion of Deaf Children Enrolled in Ordinary Preschool and Primary Education refers to the proportion of deaf children who are enrolled in ordinary kindergartens or primary schools during the year in the total number of deaf children under rehabilitation programs (not including new comers into the rehabilitation programs during the year). This indicator mainly reflects number of rehabilitated deaf children entering ordinary kindergartens or primary schools.

Number of Mental Patients under Integrated Prevention and Rehabilitation Program refers to mental disease patients receiving integrated prevention and rehabilitation treatment of various forms under open environment in areas with mental disease rehabilitation programs. This indicator reflects the condition of metal patients receiving rehabilitation treatment.

Supervision Rate refers to the percentage of patients among the total number of registered mental disease patients, who participate in social integrated and open treatment and rehabilitation programs through various forms such as supervision groups, family treatment, employment or guidance from psychiatric institutions. This indicator reflects the implementation of various measures aimed at rehabilitating those metal patients.

Social Participation Rate of Mental Patients refers to proportion of mental disease patients who are able to manage their daily life and participate in economic activities to the total number of mental disease patients under supervision. This indicator reflects the condition of recovery of those metal patient sand their participation in social activities.

School-age Disabled Children not in Schools refer to children with disability in sight, listening, speaking, mentality, limbs or multi-disability who are obliged to compulsory education by law but have not been enrolled in schools due to various reasons. The definition of school age for disabled children is decided by the definition of school age as specified by provincial governments in line wit h the local laws on compulsory education. This indicator reflects the annual change of school-age disable children not entering schools by various reasons. It will provide foundation for the formulation of development plans of compulsory education for those disable children, and for related principles, policies and measures as well. It is also t he base for the job of funding t hose disabled children back to schools across the countries.

Lawyers are certified legal workers according to law, and who are employed by legal counseling firms to act as legal advisers, agents in criminal or civil lawsuits, or defenders in criminal lawsuits, or to handle non-litigious legal affairs, to advise on matters of law or t o write legal papers for others, and provide service to the public.

Notary Personnel refers to people working for notary offices including: directors, deputy direct or, notaries, assistant notaries, and other people providing assistance.

Notary Documents refer to the judicatory notary documents drawn up by the request of the party and are in accordance with facts and laws and following certain legal proceedings. According to usage and locality, the notary documents are divided into following 4 types: domestic notary documents, domestic economic notary documents, foreign-related civil notary documents and foreign-related economic notary documents.

Mediators refer to workers on peoples mediation committees responsible for mediating in civil disputes and cases of slight infraction of the law. They include members of the mediation committees and mediators of mediation groups. This indicator reflects the number of people engaged in meditation.

Mediation of Civil Disputes refers to number of cases made by mediation committees in mediating in civil disputes concerning civil rights and duties through persuasion and education in accordance witht he provisions of lawona voluntary basis, so as to solve disputes by helping the parties involved come to an agreement and understanding, including those unsuccessful ones. This indicator reflects the workload of the mediation committees.

Extraordinarily Serious Traffic Accident refers to an accident which has caused three or more deaths; or over 11 serious injuries; or one death and over 8 serious injuries; or two deaths and over 5 serious injuries; or a loss over 60 thousand yuan.

Serious Traffic Accident refers to an accident which has caused one or two deaths; or three to ten serious injuries; or a loss over 30 thousand yuan to 60 thousand yuan.

Extraordinarily Serious Fire Case refers to a case which has caused over 30 deaths; or over 100 serious injuries; or a direct property loss over 100 million yuan.

Serious Fire Case refers to a case which has caused over 10 to 30 deaths; or over 50 to 100 serious injuries; or a direct property loss over 50 million to 100 million yuan.

Comparatively Serious Fire Case refers to a case which has caused over three to ten deaths; or over 10 to 50 serious injuries; or a direct property loss over 10 million to 50 million yuan.

Ordinary Fire Case refers to a case which has caused less than three deaths; or less than 10 serious injuries; or a direct property loss less than 10 million yuan.

2012

新疆统计年鉴

XINJIANG STATISTICAL YEARBOOK

第十九篇
各地州市
主要经济指标排序

CHAPTER 19

Ranking of Main Economic Indicators by Region of Xinjiang

简要说明
Brief Introduction

本篇资料的主要内容及来源

本篇反映2011年新疆各地州（市）主要经济指标排序情况。

本篇资料由新疆维吾尔自治区统计局国民经济综合统计处根据新疆维吾尔自治区统计局各相关专业处提供资料整理。

Main Content and Source of Data

Data in this chapter mainly include main social economic statistics by prefecture, autonomous prefecture, city and county in 2011.

Data on this chapter are compiled by the Department of Comprehensive Statistic, XBS according to the data provided by the related department of Statistics Bureau of Xinjiang Uygur Autonomous Region.

19-1 各地、州、市生产总值

Gross Regional Product by Prefecture, Autonomous Prefecture and City

单位：万元　　　　(2011 年)　　　　(10 000 yuan)

地　区	Region	地区生产总值 Gross Regional Product	位次 Rank	第一产业增加值 Primary Industry	位次 Rank
乌鲁木齐市	Urumqi city	16900347	1	220550	12
克拉玛依市	Karamay city	8016856	2	41509	15
石河子市	Shihezi city	1705948	11	110015	13
吐鲁番地区	Turpan Administrative Offices	2214322	9	269967	11
哈密地区	Hami [Kumul] Administrative Offices	2209185	10	290925	10
昌吉回族自治州	Changji Hui Autonomous Prefecture	7029369	4	1903414	1
伊犁哈萨克自治州	Ili Kazak Autonomous Prefecture	10785471		2957942	
伊犁州直属县(市)	Counties (Cities) Direct Under Ili Prefecture	4951624	6	1155822	6
塔城地区	Tacheng [Tarbagatai] Administrative Offices	4196156	8	1473326	4
阿勒泰地区	Altay Administrative Offices	1637691	12	328794	9
博尔塔拉蒙古自治州	Bortala Mongol Autonomous Prefecture	1513225	13	524493	7
巴音郭楞蒙古自治州	Bayangol Mongol Autonomous Prefecture	7998671	3	1301123	5
阿克苏地区	Aksu Administrative Offices	5061427	5	1613602	2
克孜勒苏柯尔克孜自治州	Kizilsu Kirgiz Autonomous Prefecture	480250	15	90412	14
喀什地区	Kashgar [Kaxgar] Administrative Offices	4201512	7	1506655	3
和田地区	Hotan Administrative Offices	1269941	14	408264	8

地　区	Region	第二产业增加值 Secondary Industry	位次 Rank	第三产业增加值 Tertiary Industry	位次 Rank	人均地区生产总值（元） Per-capital GDP (yuan)	位次 Rank
乌鲁木齐市	Urumqi city	7590607	1	9089191	1	52649	4
克拉玛依市	Karamay city	7162011	2	813335	9	129105	1
石河子市	Shihezi city	943672	11	652261	11	54037	3
吐鲁番地区	Turpan Administrative Offices	1454538	8	489816	14	35629	7
哈密地区	Hami [Kumul] Administrative Offices	1088357	9	829903	8	38231	6
昌吉回族自治州	Changji Hui Autonomous Prefecture	3311095	4	1814859	3	44456	5
伊犁哈萨克自治州	Ili Kazak Autonomous Prefecture	4142546		3684983		23354	
伊犁州直属县(市)	Counties (Cities) Direct Under Ili Prefecture	1801656	5	1994146	2	18528	12
塔城地区	Tacheng [Tarbagatai] Administrative Offices	1557170	7	1165660	7	31373	8
阿勒泰地区	Altay Administrative Offices	783720	12	525177	13	26927	10
博尔塔拉蒙古自治州	Bortala Mongol Autonomous Prefecture	321491	13	667241	10	31204	9
巴音郭楞蒙古自治州	Bayangol Mongol Autonomous Prefecture	5279183	3	1418365	6	57636	2
阿克苏地区	Aksu Administrative Offices	1680934	6	1766891	4	20145	11
克孜勒苏柯尔克孜自治州	Kizilsu Kirgiz Autonomous Prefecture	121615	15	268223	15	8664	14
喀什地区	Kashgar [Kaxgar] Administrative Offices	1072198	10	1622659	5	10558	13
和田地区	Hotan Administrative Offices	245083	14	616594	12	6172	15

19-2 各地、州、市人口状况

Population Status by Prefecture, Autonomous Prefecture and City

单位：万人 (2011 年) (10 000 persons)

地　区	Region	总人口 Total Population	位 次 Rank	城镇人口 Urban Population	位 次 Rank
乌鲁木齐市	Urumqi City	249.35	3	242.24	1
克拉玛依市	Karamay City	28.23	15	28.23	15
石河子市	Shihezi City	62.44	11	62.44	9
吐鲁番地区	Turpan Administrative Offices	63.19	10	45.53	11
哈密地区	Hami [Kumul] Administrative Offices	58.39	12	51.58	10
昌吉回族自治州	Changji Hui Autonomous Prefecture	139.46	6	115.54	5
伊犁哈萨克自治州	Ili Kazak Autonomous Prefecture	459.84		269.89	
伊犁州直属县(市)	Counties (Cities) Direct Under Ili Prefecture	288.47	2	156.30	2
塔城地区	Tacheng [Tarbagatai] Administrative Offices	104.48	8	76.67	7
阿勒泰地区	Altay Administrative Offices	66.89	9	36.92	13
博尔塔拉蒙古自治州	Bortala Mongol Autonomous Prefecture	48.73	14	40.82	12
巴音郭楞蒙古自治州	Bayangol Mongol Autonomous Prefecture	136.60	7	108.07	6
阿克苏地区	Aksu Administrative Offices	238.97	4	150.62	3
克孜勒苏柯尔克孜自治州	Kizilsu Kirgiz Autonomous Prefecture	55.43	13	32.29	14
喀什地区	Kashgar [Kaxgar] Administrative Offices	410.20	1	145.20	4
和田地区	Hotan Administrative Offices	207.58	5	68.29	8

地　区	Region	乡村人口 Rural Population	位 次 Rank	人口自然增长率(‰) Natural Growth Rate (‰)	位 次 Rank
乌鲁木齐市	Urumqi City	7.11	12	5.88	12
克拉玛依市	Karamay City			5.14	14
石河子市	Shihezi City			-0.40	15
吐鲁番地区	Turpan Administrative Offices	17.66	10	14.92	4
哈密地区	Hami [Kumul] Administrative Offices	6.81	13	5.81	13
昌吉回族自治州	Changji Hui Autonomous Prefecture	23.92	8	6.84	11
伊犁哈萨克自治州	Ili Kazak Autonomous Prefecture	189.95		12.94	
伊犁州直属县(市)	Counties (Cities) Direct Under Ili Prefecture	132.17	3	15.44	3
塔城地区	Tacheng [Tarbagatai] Administrative Offices	27.81	7	8.16	9
阿勒泰地区	Altay Administrative Offices	29.97	5	9.65	7
博尔塔拉蒙古自治州	Bortala Mongol Autonomous Prefecture	7.91	11	7.69	10
巴音郭楞蒙古自治州	Bayangol Mongol Autonomous Prefecture	28.53	6	8.25	8
阿克苏地区	Aksu Administrative Offices	88.35	4	11.74	6
克孜勒苏柯尔克孜自治州	Kizilsu Kirgiz Autonomous Prefecture	23.14	9	20.18	1
喀什地区	Kashgar [Kaxgar] Administrative Offices	265.00	1	19.09	2
和田地区	Hotan Administrative Offices	139.29	2	13.47	5

注：城镇、乡村人口按公安年报口径计算。
Note: The urban and rural population in Prefecture, Autonomous Prefecture and City are calculated on the annals of public security.

19-3 各地、州、市全社会固定资产投资

Total Investment in Fixed Assets by Prefecture, Autonomous Prefecture and City

单位：万元 (2011 年) (10 000 yuan)

地区	Region	合计 Total	位次 Rank	建筑工程 Construction Works	位次 Rank
乌鲁木齐市	Urumqi City	6539156	1	3857740	1
克拉玛依市	Karamay City	2130936	9	1390529	8
石河子市	Shihezi City	1638136	10	694354	13
吐鲁番地区	Turpan Administrative Offices	1270996	12	701423	12
哈密地区	Hami [Kumul] Administrative Offices	2135256	8	978431	9
昌吉回族自治州	Changji Hui Autonomous Prefecture	5631443	2	3045920	2
伊犁哈萨克自治州	Ili Kazak Autonomous Prefecture	8331104		5422491	
伊犁州直属县(市)	Counties (Cities) Direct Under Ili Prefecture	4585258	3	2860085	4
塔城地区	Tacheng [Tarbagatai] Administrative Offices	2316119	7	1639711	6
阿勒泰地区	Altay Administrative Offices	1429727	11	922695	11
博尔塔拉蒙古自治州	Bortala Mongol Autonomous Prefecture	815624	14	509124	14
巴音郭楞蒙古自治州	Bayangol Mongol Autonomous Prefecture	3883539	5	2700825	5
阿克苏地区	Aksu Administrative Offices	2462047	6	1523099	7
克孜勒苏柯尔克孜自治州	Kizilsu Kirgiz Autonomous Prefecture	466943	15	347648	15
喀什地区	Kashgar [Kaxgar] Administrative Offices	3935437	4	3044507	3
和田地区	Hotan Administrative Offices	1208289	13	925173	10

地区	Region	安装工程 Installation Works	位次 Rank	设备工具器具购置 Purchase of Equipment and Instruments	位次 Rank	其他费用 Others	位次 Rank
乌鲁木齐市	Urumqi City	559844	1	1565527	2	556045	1
克拉玛依市	Karamay City	358495	2	264708	11	117204	10
石河子市	Shi Hezi City	178859	9	613832	5	151091	8
吐鲁番地区	Turpan Administrative Offices	103451	11	374683	10	91439	13
哈密地区	Hami [Kumul] Administrative Offices	234621	7	720331	4	201873	6
昌吉回族自治州	Changji Hui Autonomous Prefecture	320587	4	1880796	1	384140	3
伊犁哈萨克自治州	Ili Kazak Autonomous Prefecture	539151		1641429		728033	
伊犁州直属县(市)	Counties (Cities) Direct Under Ili Prefecture	354721	3	970004	3	400448	2
塔城地区	Tacheng [Tarbagatai] Administrative Offices	129002	10	437704	9	109702	11
阿勒泰地区	Altay Administrative Offices	55428	12	233721	12	217883	5
博尔塔拉蒙古自治州	Bortala Mongol Autonomous Prefecture	43061	13	182343	13	81096	14
巴音郭楞蒙古自治州	Bayangol Mongol Autonomous Prefecture	288402	5	607958	7	286354	4
阿克苏地区	Aksu Administrative Offices	228927	8	611211	6	98810	12
克孜勒苏柯尔克孜自治州	Kizilsu Kirgiz Autonomous Prefecture	12835	15	82244	15	24216	15
喀什地区	Kashgar [Kaxgar] Administrative Offices	254721	6	463117	8	173092	7
和田地区	Hotan Administrative Offices	29834	14	104519	14	148763	9

19-4 各地、州、市农林牧渔业总产值

Gross Output Value of Farming, Forestry, Animal Husbandry and Fishery by Prefecture, Autonomous Prefecture and City

单位：万元　　(2011 年)　　(10 000 yuan)

地区	Region	农林牧渔业总产值 Total	位次 Rank	农业 Farming	位次 Rank	林业 Forestry	位次 Rank
乌鲁木齐市	Urumqi City	302681	12	136767	12	5300	12
克拉玛依市	Karamay City	95011	14	33712	14	14885	7
吐鲁番地区	Turpan Administrative Offices	448620	10	355353	9	4038	13
哈密地区	Hami [Kumul] Administrative Offices	363691	11	188891	11	11570	10
昌吉回族自治州	Changji Hui Autonomous Prefecture	2409379	2	1079122	5	22107	6
伊犁哈萨克自治州	Ili Kazak Autonomous Prefecture	3706518		2160534		76998	
伊犁州直属县(市)	Counties (Cities) Direct Under Ili Prefecture	1577240	6	796691	6	52413	3
塔城地区	Tacheng [Tarbagatai] Administrative Offices	1619187	5	1115512	4	12122	9
阿勒泰地区	Altay Administrative Offices	510091	9	248331	10	12463	8
博尔塔拉蒙古自治州	Bortala Mongol Autonomous Prefecture	591080	8	457991	8	6163	11
巴音郭楞蒙古自治州	Bayangol Mongol Autonomous Prefecture	1891953	3	1442903	3	68307	2
阿克苏地区	Aksu Administrative Offices	1851959	4	1460786	2	31230	4
克孜勒苏柯尔克孜自治州	Kizilsu Kirgiz Autonomous Prefecture	180891	13	102015	13	3689	14
喀什地区	Kashgar [Kaxgar] Administrative Offices	3077305	1	2075708	1	76456	1
和田地区	Hotan Administrative Offices	839222	7	570630	7	30714	5

地区	Region	牧业 Animal Husbandry	位次 Rank	渔业 Fishery	位次 Rank	农林牧渔服务业 Farming, Forestry, Animal Husbandary and Fishery	位次 Rank
乌鲁木齐市	Urumqi City	152197	10	7064	6	1353	14
克拉玛依市	Karamay City	31650	14	668	12	14096	8
吐鲁番地区	Turpan Administrative Offices	81437	12	448	13	7344	12
哈密地区	Hami [Kumul] Administrative Offices	156795	9	2029	11	4406	13
昌吉回族自治州	Changji Hui Autonomous Prefecture	1266695	1	16813	1	24642	6
伊犁哈萨克自治州	Ili Kazak Autonomous Prefecture	1396879		18649		53458	
伊犁州直属县(市)	Counties (Cities) Direct Under Ili Prefecture	690441	3	10385	4	27310	4
塔城地区	Tacheng [Tarbagatai] Administrative Offices	472682	4	2606	10	16265	7
阿勒泰地区	Altay Administrative Offices	233756	7	5658	7	9883	11
博尔塔拉蒙古自治州	Bortala Mongol Autonomous Prefecture	98633	11	2705	8	25588	5
巴音郭楞蒙古自治州	Bayangol Mongol Autonomous Prefecture	315674	5	11264	2	53805	3
阿克苏地区	Aksu Administrative Offices	282147	6	9733	5	68063	1
克孜勒苏柯尔克孜自治州	Kizilsu Kirgiz Autonomous Prefecture	63367	13	211	14	11609	10
喀什地区	Kashgar [Kaxgar] Administrative Offices	846015	2	11241	3	67885	2
和田地区	Hotan Administrative Offices	221713	8	2672	9	13493	9

注：本表按当年价格计算。
Notes：The number in this table is computed at current price.

19-5 各地、州、市主要农产品产量

Yield of Major Farm Crops by Prefecture, Autonomous Prefecture and City

单位：吞 (2011 年) (ton)

地区	Region	粮食 Grain	位次 Rank	棉花 Cotton	位次 Rank
乌鲁木齐市	Urumqi City	168687	11	1669	13
克拉玛依市	Karamay City	3500	14	12674	11
吐鲁番地区	Turpan Administrative Offices	24066	13	29125	8
哈密地区	Hami [Kumul] Administrative Offices	132817	12	27800	9
昌吉回族自治州	Changji Hui Autonomous Prefecture	1802649	3	199219	5
伊犁哈萨克自治州	Ili Kazak Autonomous Prefecture	4348951		246176	
伊犁州直属县(市)	Counties (Cities) Direct Under Ili Prefecture	2367949	2	18006	10
塔城地区	Tacheng [Tarbagatai] Administrative Offices	1647212	4	228170	4
阿勒泰地区	Altay Administrative Offices	333790	9		
博尔塔拉蒙古自治州	Bortala Mongol Autonomous Prefecture	511178	7	135884	6
巴音郭楞蒙古自治州	Bayangol Mongol Autonomous Prefecture	353022	8	352013	2
阿克苏地区	Aksu Administrative Offices	1462257	5	534839	1
克孜勒苏柯尔克孜自治州	Kizilsu Kirgiz Autonomous Prefecture	263244	10	8956	12
喀什地区	Kashgar [Kaxgar] Administrative Offices	2575333	1	346846	3
和田地区	Hotan Administrative Offices	1061599	6	45413	7

地区	Region	油料 Oil Bearing Crops	位次 Rank	甜菜 Beetroots	位次 Rank
乌鲁木齐市	Urumqi City	8934	9	4960	8
克拉玛依市	Karamay City	264	14		
吐鲁番地区	Turpan Administrative Offices	479	13		
哈密地区	Hami [Kumul] Administrative Offices	1714	11		
昌吉回族自治州	Changji Hui Autonomous Prefecture	82309	3	563686	2
伊犁哈萨克自治州	Ili Kazak Autonomous Prefecture	331710		1723232	
伊犁州直属县(市)	Counties (Cities) Direct Under Ili Prefecture	139066	1	1384670	1
塔城地区	Tacheng [Tarbagatai] Administrative Offices	61392	4	314780	5
阿勒泰地区	Altay Administrative Offices	131252	2	23782	7
博尔塔拉蒙古自治州	Bortala Mongol Autonomous Prefecture	21037	5	146607	6
巴音郭楞蒙古自治州	Bayangol Mongol Autonomous Prefecture	7372	10	347186	3
阿克苏地区	Aksu Administrative Offices	9827	7	344614	4
克孜勒苏柯尔克孜自治州	Kizilsu Kirgiz Autonomous Prefecture	978	12		
喀什地区	Kashgar [Kaxgar] Administrative Offices	15091	6		
和田地区	Hotan Administrative Offices	9231	8		

19-6 各地、州、市规模以上工业企业主要经济指标

Main Indicators on Economic of Industrial Enterprises above Designated Size by Prefecture, Autonomous Prefecture and City

单位：%　　(2011 年)　　(%)

地　区	Region	工业总产值(万元) Gross Industrial Output Value (10 000 yuan)	位次 Rank	工业增加值(万元) Value-added Industry (10 000 yuan)	位次 Rank
乌鲁木齐市	Urumqi City	19925798.7	1	5647380.8	2
克拉玛依市	Karamay City	16390365.6	2	6962583.6	1
石河子市	Shihezi City	2893433.3	7	704017.8	9
吐鲁番地区	Turpan Administrative Offices	2220534.8	8	1136819.4	5
哈密地区	Hami [Kumul] Administrative Offices	1319855.1	10	560224.8	11
昌吉回族自治州	Changji Hui Autonomous Prefecture	4753317.6	4	1240406.5	4
伊犁哈萨克自治州	Ili Kazak Autonomous Prefecture	5679016.2		2424299.5	
伊犁州直属县(市)	Counties (Cities) Direct Under Ili Prefecture	2948603.2	6	1131675.1	6
塔城地区	Tacheng [Tarbagatai] Administrative Offices	1742036.1	9	708263.6	8
阿勒泰地区	Altay Administrative Offices	988376.9	11	584360.8	10
博尔塔拉蒙古自治州	Bortala Mongol Autonomous Prefecture	366244.0	13	114694.8	13
巴音郭楞蒙古自治州	Bayangol Mongol Autonomous Prefecture	7316459.2	3	5146033.8	3
阿克苏地区	Aksu Administrative Offices	3970304.1	5	1021426.6	7
克孜勒苏柯尔克孜自治州	Kizilsu Kirgiz Autonomous Prefecture	167746.2	14	55105.5	15
喀什地区	Kashgar [Kaxgar] Administrative Offices	796319.8	12	246480.4	12
和田地区	Hotan Administrative Offices	146736.4	15	59609.7	14

地　区	Region	总资产贡献率 Ratio of Total Assets to Industrial OutputValue	位次 Rank	资本保值增值率 Ratio of Capital Holding And Rise	位次 Rank
乌鲁木齐市	Urumqi City	13.7	6	109.1	13
克拉玛依市	Karamay City	27.8	3	110.8	12
石河子市	Shihezi City	11.1	9	119.3	8
吐鲁番地区	Turpan Administrative Offices	19.0	4	104.9	14
哈密地区	Hami [Kumul] Administrative Offices	9.7	10	156.0	2
昌吉回族自治州	Changji Hui Autonomous Prefecture	9.4	11	111.6	11
伊犁哈萨克自治州	Ili Kazak Autonomous Prefecture	14.7		131.4	
伊犁州直属县(市)	Counties (Cities) Direct Under Ili Prefecture	12.8	7	130.6	5
塔城地区	Tacheng [Tarbagatai] Administrative Offices	8.4	13	136.5	4
阿勒泰地区	Altay Administrative Offices	28.3	2	128.6	7
博尔塔拉蒙古自治州	Bortala Mongol Autonomous Prefecture	8.5	12	129.1	6
巴音郭楞蒙古自治州	Bayangol Mongol Autonomous Prefecture	37.7	1	113.4	10
阿克苏地区	Aksu Administrative Offices	16.9	5	116.5	9
克孜勒苏柯尔克孜自治州	Kizilsu Kirgiz Autonomous Prefecture	5.4	14	140.2	3
喀什地区	Kashgar [Kaxgar] Administrative Offices	11.2	8	157.8	1
和田地区	Hotan Administrative Offices	3.8	15	101.5	15

19-6 续表 Continued

单位：% (%)

地　　区	Region	资　产 负债率 Assets Liability Ratio	位 次 Rank	成本费用 利 润 率 Ratio of Profits to Industrial Cost	位 次 Rank
乌鲁木齐市	Urumqi City	52.6	12	9.9	8
克拉玛依市	Karamay City	38.4	15	17.9	4
石河子市	Shihezi City	61.9	5	13.9	6
吐鲁番地区	Turpan Administrative Offices	53.5	11	31.7	3
哈密地区	Hami [Kumul] Administrative Offices	59.2	8	15.7	5
昌吉回族自治州	Changji Hui Autonomous Prefecture	61.6	6	8.6	9
伊犁哈萨克自治州	Ili Kazak Autonomous Prefecture	60.4		16.1	
伊犁州直属县(市)	Counties (Cities) Direct Under Ili Prefecture	60.6	7	12.4	7
塔城地区	Tacheng [Tarbagatai] Administrative Offices	63.2	3	5.8	12
阿勒泰地区	Altay Administrative Offices	56.2	10	52.1	2
博尔塔拉蒙古自治州	Bortala Mongol Autonomous Prefecture	74.1	2	7.7	11
巴音郭楞蒙古自治州	Bayangol Mongol Autonomous Prefecture	51.4	13	78.3	1
阿克苏地区	Aksu Administrative Offices	58.6	9	7.8	10
克孜勒苏柯尔克孜自治州	Kizilsu Kirgiz Autonomous Prefecture	62.5	4	3.0	14
喀什地区	Kashgar [Kaxgar] Administrative Offices	75.6	1	5.5	13
和田地区	Hotan Administrative Offices	39.9	14	-1.1	15

地　　区	Region	产　值 利税率 Ratio of Profits and Taxes to Industrial Output Value	位 次 Rank	流动资产周转次数 (次/年) Number of Times of Annual TurnoverWorking Capitals (times/year)	位 次 Rank
乌鲁木齐市	Urumqi City	17.6	7	2.1	5
克拉玛依市	Karamay City	28.3	4	3.9	1
石河子市	Shihezi City	14.6	9	1.5	10
吐鲁番地区	Turpan Administrative Offices	32.6	3	1.6	9
哈密地区	Hami [Kumul] Administrative Offices	20.7	5	1.3	14
昌吉回族自治州	Changji Hui Autonomous Prefecture	11.6	11	1.5	10
伊犁哈萨克自治州	Ili Kazak Autonomous Prefecture	20.8		1.7	
伊犁州直属县(市)	Counties (Cities) Direct Under Ili Prefecture	20.7	5	1.5	10
塔城地区	Tacheng [Tarbagatai] Administrative Offices	7.6	14	2.1	5
阿勒泰地区	Altay Administrative Offices	44.5	2	2.0	7
博尔塔拉蒙古自治州	Bortala Mongol Autonomous Prefecture	12.4	10	1.4	13
巴音郭楞蒙古自治州	Bayangol Mongol Autonomous Prefecture	52.6	1	2.9	2
阿克苏地区	Aksu Administrative Offices	17.0	8	2.7	3
克孜勒苏柯尔克孜自治州	Kizilsu Kirgiz Autonomous Prefecture	9.5	13	1.2	15
喀什地区	Kashgar [Kaxgar] Administrative Offices	11.4	12	2.2	4
和田地区	Hotan Administrative Offices	6.5	15	2.0	7

19-7 各地、州、市主要工业产品产量

Output of Major Industrial Products by Prefecture, Autonomous Prefecture and City

(2011 年)

地 区	Region	纱(吨) Yarn (ton)	位次 Rank	布(万米) Cloth (10 000 m)	位次 Rank	呢绒(万米) Woolen Piece Goods (10 000 m)	位次 Rank
乌鲁木齐市	Urumqi City	25345	6	444	5		
克拉玛依市	Karamay City						
石河子市	Shihezi City	107565	1	3778	1	227	1
吐鲁番地区	Turpan Administrative Offices	3870	11				
哈密地区	Hami [Kumul] Administrative Offices	11979	10				
昌吉回族自治州	Changji Hui Autonomous Prefecture	76461	2	563	4	156	2
伊犁哈萨克自治州	Ili Kazak Autonomous Prefecture	36053		939			
伊犁州直属县(市)	Counties (Cities) Direct Under Ili Prefecture	18002	8	159	7		
塔城地区	Tacheng [Tarbagatai] Administrative Offices	18051	7	780	2		
阿勒泰地区	Altay Administrative Offices						
博尔塔拉蒙古自治州	Bortala Mongol Autonomous Prefecture	16004	9	115	8		
巴音郭楞蒙古自治州	Bayangol Mongol Autonomous Prefecture	30159	4	707	3		
阿克苏地区	Aksu Administrative Offices	41329	3	216	6		
克孜勒苏柯尔克孜自治州	Kizilsu Kirgiz Autonomous Prefecture						
喀什地区	Kashgar [Kaxgar] Administrative Offices	27422	5	89	9		
和田地区	Hotan Administrative Offices	877	12				

地 区	Region	成品糖(万吨) Sugar (10 000 tons)	位次 Rank	饮料酒(千升) Alcohol Beverage (kilo-liter)	位次 Rank	塑料制品(吨) Plastic Products (ton)	位次 Rank
乌鲁木齐市	Urumqi City			140667	1	263630	1
克拉玛依市	Karamay City			3599	11	23750	10
石河子市	Shihezi City			131333	2	139084	3
吐鲁番地区	Turpan Administrative Offices			6725	10		
哈密地区	Hami [Kumul] Administrative Offices			28102	9	12890	11
昌吉回族自治州	Changji Hui Autonomous Prefecture	5.00	4	63548	5	241733	2
伊犁哈萨克自治州	Ili Kazak Autonomous Prefecture	27.79		167738		144962	
伊犁州直属县(市)	Counties (Cities) Direct Under Ili Prefecture	18.16	1	85324	3	39651	7
塔城地区	Tacheng [Tarbagatai] Administrative Offices	8.90	2	81014	4	95433	4
阿勒泰地区	Altay Administrative Offices	0.73	7	1399	12	9878	12
博尔塔拉蒙古自治州	Bortala Mongol Autonomous Prefecture	2.55	5	1073	13	41210	6
巴音郭楞蒙古自治州	Bayangol Mongol Autonomous Prefecture	8.05	3	42456	6	34284	8
阿克苏地区	Aksu Administrative Offices	2.28	6	32093	7	48298	5
克孜勒苏柯尔克孜自治州	Kizilsu Kirgiz Autonomous Prefecture			2	15	223	14
喀什地区	Kashgar [Kaxgar] Administrative Offices	0.44	8	28292	8	30113	9
和田地区	Hotan Administrative Offices			185	14	1656	13

19-7 续表 Continued

地　区	Region	机制纸及纸板(吨) Machine-made Paper and Paper board (ton)	位次 Rank	原煤(万吨) Coal (10 000 tons)	位次 Rank	原油(万吨) Crude Oil (10 000 tons)	位次 Rank
乌鲁木齐市	Urumqi City	86283	3	1930.28	2	725.00	2
克拉玛依市	Karamay City			90.00	9	1090.01	1
石河子市	Shihezi City	31461	4	27.79	11		
吐鲁番地区	Turpan Administrative Offices			1302.05	5	155.00	4
哈密地区	Hami [Kumul] Administrative Offices	1912	8	1804.94	3		
昌吉回族自治州	Changji Hui Autonomous Prefecture	119126	1	3886.23	1		
伊犁哈萨克自治州	Ili Kazak Autonomous Prefecture	11525		1230.88		68.00	
伊犁州直属县(市)	Counties (Cities) Direct Under Ili Prefecture	5783	6	554.20	7		
塔城地区	Tacheng [Tarbagatai] Administrative Offices	5126	7	665.76	6	68.00	5
阿勒泰地区	Altay Administrative Offices	616	9	10.92	14		
博尔塔拉蒙古自治州	Bortala Mongol Autonomous Prefecture						
巴音郭楞蒙古自治州	Bayangol Mongol Autonomous Prefecture	104066	2	320.11	8	577.62	3
阿克苏地区	Aksu Administrative Offices			1308.62	4		
克孜勒苏柯尔克孜自治州	Kizilsu Kirgiz Autonomous Prefecture			12.82	13		
喀什地区	Kashgar [Kaxgar] Administrative Offices	15472	5	14.10	12		
和田地区	Hotan Administrative Offices			54.87	10		

地　区	Region	水泥(万吨) Cement (10 000 tons)	位次 Rank	发电量(亿千瓦小时) Electricity (100 million kwh)	位次 Rank	农用化肥(吨) Chemical Fertilizers (ton)	位次 Rank
乌鲁木齐市	Urumqi City	552.25	1	241.35	1	554202	2
克拉玛依市	Karamay City			43.36	7	34129	4
石河子市	Shihezi City	267.04	4	126.49	3		
吐鲁番地区	Turpan Administrative Offices	132.26	11	27.05	10		
哈密地区	Hami [Kumul] Administrative Offices	172.39	8	29.55	9	8684	6
昌吉回族自治州	Changji Hui Autonomous Prefecture	254.71	5	133.51	2	1660	7
伊犁哈萨克自治州	Ili Kazak Autonomous Prefecture	669.90		127.34		32827	
伊犁州直属县(市)	Counties (Cities) Direct Under Ili Prefecture	301.30	3	72.95	4	320	9
塔城地区	Tacheng [Tarbagatai] Administrative Offices	252.82	6	36.65	8	32507	5
阿勒泰地区	Altay Administrative Offices	115.78	12	17.73	12		
博尔塔拉蒙古自治州	Bortala Mongol Autonomous Prefecture	65.28	14	6.95	14	150	10
巴音郭楞蒙古自治州	Bayangol Mongol Autonomous Prefecture	195.76	7	49.49	5	1252132	1
阿克苏地区	Aksu Administrative Offices	477.41	2	44.94	6	379178	3
克孜勒苏柯尔克孜自治州	Kizilsu Kirgiz Autonomous Prefecture	70.30	13	0.51	15		
喀什地区	Kashgar [Kaxgar] Administrative Offices	154.18	9	22.62	11		
和田地区	Hotan Administrative Offices	144.09	10	10.28	13	656	8

19-8 各地、州、市社会消费品零售总额
Total Retail Sales of Consumer Goods by Prefecture, Autonomous Prefecture and City

单位：万元 (2011 年) (10 000 yuan)

地　区	Region	社会消费品零售总额 Total Retail Sales of Consumer Goods	位次 Rank	城镇 City	位次 Rank
乌鲁木齐市	Urumqi City	6497286	1	6493754	1
克拉玛依市	Karamay City	435790	9	434490	8
吐鲁番地区	Turpan Administrative Offices	263280	11	192235	11
哈密地区	Hami [Kumul] Administrative Offices	465393	8	440805	7
昌吉回族自治州	Changji Hui Autonomous Prefecture	1330333	2	1218777	2
伊犁哈萨克自治州	Ili Kazak Autonomous Prefecture	1998735		1566198	
伊犁州直属县(市)	Counties (Cities) Direct Under Ili Prefecture	1159316	3	902741	3
塔城地区	Tacheng [Tarbagatai] Administrative Offices	467027	7	332455	9
阿勒泰地区	Altay Administrative Offices	372392	10	331002	10
博尔塔拉蒙古自治州	Bortala Mongol Autonomous Prefecture	212161	13	181989	12
巴音郭楞蒙古自治州	Bayangol Mongol Autonomous Prefecture	674885	6	631306	5
阿克苏地区	Aksu Administrative Offices	722117	5	607585	6
克孜勒苏柯尔克孜自治州	Kizilsu Kirgiz Autonomous Prefecture	97924	14	89056	14
喀什地区	Kashgar [Kaxgar] Administrative Offices	894631	4	732133	4
和田地区	Hotan Administrative Offices	229120	12	167724	13

地　区	Region	城区 County	位次 Rank	乡村 Under County Level	位次 Rank
乌鲁木齐市	Urumqi City	6493754	1	3532	13
克拉玛依市	Karamay City	434490	4	1300	14
吐鲁番地区	Turpan Administrative Offices	108892	13	71045	6
哈密地区	Hami [Kumul] Administrative Offices	400255	6	24588	11
昌吉回族自治州	Changji Hui Autonomous Prefecture	984998	2	111556	5
伊犁哈萨克自治州	Ili Kazak Autonomous Prefecture	879218		432537	
伊犁州直属县(市)	Counties (Cities) Direct Under Ili Prefecture	634827	3	256575	1
塔城地区	Tacheng [Tarbagatai] Administrative Offices	133884	9	134572	3
阿勒泰地区	Altay Administrative Offices	110507	11	41390	9
博尔塔拉蒙古自治州	Bortala Mongol Autonomous Prefecture	109557	12	30172	10
巴音郭楞蒙古自治州	Bayangol Mongol Autonomous Prefecture	424434	5	43579	8
阿克苏地区	Aksu Administrative Offices	348875	8	114532	4
克孜勒苏柯尔克孜自治州	Kizilsu Kirgiz Autonomous Prefecture	83603	14	8868	12
喀什地区	Kashgar [Kaxgar] Administrative Offices	393131	7	162498	2
和田地区	Hotan Administrative Offices	126509	10	61396	7

19-9 各地、州、市海关进出口总额

Total Value of Imports and Exports by Prefecture, Autonomous Prefecture and City

单位：万美元 (2011 年) (USD 10 000)

地区	Region	进出口总额 Total Imports and Exports	位次 Rank	出口额 Exports	位次 Rank	进口额 Imports	位次 Rank
乌鲁木齐市	Urumqi City	902984	1	669589	1	233395	2
克拉玛依市	Karamay City	46888	9	42810	8	4078	7
石河子市	Shihezi City	90975	6	87854	6	3121	8
吐鲁番地区	Turpan Administrative Offices	3054	13	2410	13	644	11
哈密地区	Hami [Kumul] Administrative Offices	2615	14	1974	14	641	12
昌吉回族自治州	Changji Hui Autonomous Prefecture	211336	3	194570	3	16766	5
伊犁哈萨克自治州	Ili Administrative Offices	697825		423254		274571	
伊犁州直属县(市)	Counties (Cities) Direct Under Ili Prefecture	557956	2	306435	2	251521	1
塔城地区	Tacheng [Tarbagatai] Administrative Offices	53944	8	31224	9	22720	4
阿勒泰地区	Altay Administrative Offices	85925	7	85595	7	330	14
博尔塔拉蒙古自治州	Bortala Mongol Autonomous Prefecture	161098	4	102555	4	58543	3
巴音郭楞蒙古自治州	Bayangol Mongol Autonomous Prefecture	16492	11	14775	11	1717	9
阿克苏地区	Aksu Administrative Offices	32209	10	30966	10	1243	10
克孜勒苏柯尔克孜自治州	Kizilsu Kirgiz Autonomous Prefecture	15548	12	11435	12	4113	6
喀什地区	Kashgar [Kaxgar] Administrative Offices	100761	5	100269	5	492	13
和田地区	Hotan Administrative Offices	440	15	425	15	15	15

19-10 各地、州、市在岗职工工资总额和平均工资

Total Wages of Employed Staff and Workers and Average Wage by Prefecture, Autonomous Prefecture and City

(2011 年)

地区	Region	在岗职工工资总额(万元) Total Wages of Staff and Workers (10 000 yuan)	位次 Rank	在岗职工平均货币工资(元) Average of Staff and Workers Wage (yuan)	位次 Rank
乌鲁木齐市	Urumqi City	3205009	1	47747	2
克拉玛依市	Karamay City	950758	2	58657	1
石河子市	Shihezi City	448428	9	38909	4
吐鲁番地区	Turpan Administrative Offices	338235	11	45239	3
哈密地区	Hami [Kumul] Administrative Offices	324766	12	38202	5
昌吉回族自治州	Changji Hui Autonomous Prefecture	780941	5	36417	8
伊犁哈萨克自治州	Ili Kazak Autonomous Prefecture	1783066		29142	
伊犁州直属县(市)	Counties (Cities) Direct Under Ili Prefecture	853259	3	30802	12
塔城地区	Tacheng [Tarbagatai] Administrative Offices	611539	8	27825	14
阿勒泰地区	Altay Administrative Offices	318268	13	27662	15
博尔塔拉蒙古自治州	Bortala Mongol Autonomous Prefecture	268781	14	28391	13
巴音郭楞蒙古自治州	Bayangol Mongol Autonomous Prefecture	805282	4	37851	6
阿克苏地区	Aksu Administrative Offices	705113	6	34998	10
克孜勒苏柯尔克孜自治州	Kizilsu Kirgiz Autonomous Prefecture	134107	15	33131	11
喀什地区	Kashgar [Kaxgar] Administrative Offices	683397	7	36088	9
和田地区	Hotan Administrative Offices	347531	10	37664	7

19-11 各地、州、市地方财政一般预算收支

The General Budgetary Revenue and Expenditures of Local Finance by Prefecture, Autonomous Prefecture and City

单位：万元　　(2011 年)　　(10 000 yuan)

地　区	Region	地方财政一般预算收入 Local Financial Revenue	位 次 Rank	地方财政一般预算支出 Local Financial Expenditure	位 次 Rank
乌鲁木齐市	Urumqi City	2062035	1	2384851	2
克拉玛依市	Karamay City	509650	3	633033	10
石河子市	Shihezi City	192822	12	252565	15
吐鲁番地区	Turpan Administrative Offices	203580	10	452426	13
哈密地区	Hami [Kumul] Administrative Offices	235153	9	562908	11
昌吉回族自治州	Changji Hui Autonomous Prefecture	482221	5	1213830	7
伊犁哈萨克自治州	Ili Kazak Autonomous Prefecture	904482		3477638	
伊犁州直属县(市)	Counties (Cities) Direct Under Ili Prefecture	446529	6	1697966	3
塔城地区	Tacheng [Tarbagatai] Administrative Offices	257936	8	899382	8
阿勒泰地区	Altay Administrative Offices	200017	11	880290	9
博尔塔拉蒙古自治州	Bortala Mongol Autonomous Prefecture	82127	14	410284	14
巴音郭楞蒙古自治州	Bayangol Mongol Autonomous Prefecture	491289	4	1281237	5
阿克苏地区	Aksu Administrative Offices	621052	2	1576440	4
克孜勒苏柯尔克孜自治州	Kizilsu Kirgiz Autonomous Prefecture	55227	15	552425	12
喀什地区	Kashgar [Kaxgar] Administrative Offices	287506	7	2409603	1
和田地区	Hotan Administrative Offices	93231	13	1256735	6

19-12 分城镇居民消费价格指数和商品零售价格指数

General Retail Price and Consumer Price Index by City/County

(上年=100)　　(2011 年)(抽样调查) (Sampled Survey)　　(preceding year=100)

地　区	Region	商品零售价格指数 General Retail Price Index	位 次 Rank	居民消费价格指数 General Consumer Price Index	位 次 Rank
乌鲁木齐市	Urumqi City	104.1	20	104.5	20
喀什市	Kashgar [Kaxgar] City	106.0	9	106.0	7
伊宁市	Yining [Gulja] City	107.5	3	106.7	5
和田市	Hotan City	106.9	5	106.9	3
克拉玛依市	Karamay City	104.8	16	105.8	10
哈密市	Hami [Kumul] City	104.7	18	105.3	16
昌吉市	Changji City	105.8	10	105.3	16
库尔勒市	Korla City	105.3	14	105.6	13
阿克苏市	Aksu City	107.0	4	106.8	4
焉耆回族自治县	Yanqi Hui Autonomous County	107.7	1	108.0	1
塔城市	Tacheng [Qoqek] City	106.5	6	105.7	11
阿勒泰市	Altay City	106.1	8	105.5	14
乌苏市	Usu City	105.0	15	105.3	16
博乐市	Bole [Bortala] City	106.4	7	106.0	7
吐鲁番市	Turpan City	105.5	13	105.7	11
库车县	Kuqa County	104.4	19	106.1	6
阿图什市	Artux City	105.8	10	105.9	9
莎车县	Shache [Yarkant] County	107.7	1	107.3	2
奎屯市	Kuytun City	104.8	16	105.2	19
石河子市	Shihezi City	105.6	12	105.4	15

19-13 各地、州、市各类学校在校学生数

Number of Students Enrollment by Type of School and by Prefecture, Autonomous Prefecture and City

单位：人 (2011 年) (person)

地　区	Region	普通高等学校 Regular Institutions of Higher Education	位次 Rank	中等职业学校 Specialized Secondary Schools	位次 Rank
乌鲁木齐市	Urumqi City	152314	1	79024	1
克拉玛依市	Karamay City	3851	7	1013	15
石河子市	Shihezi City	5822	5	1786	13
吐鲁番地区	Turpan Administrative Offices			3190	9
哈密地区	Hami [Kumul] Administrative Offices			2853	10
昌吉回族自治州	Changji Hui Autonomous Prefecture	21003	2	12611	6
伊犁哈萨克自治州	Ili Kazak Autonomous Prefecture	13618		20827	
伊犁州直属县(市)	Counties (Cities) Direct Under Ili Prefecture	13618	3	11279	7
塔城地区	Tacheng [Tarbagatai] Administrative Offices			2806	11
阿勒泰地区	Altay Administrative Offices			6742	8
博尔塔拉蒙古自治州	Bortala Mongol Autonomous Prefecture			1598	14
巴音郭楞蒙古自治州	Bayangol Mongol Autonomous Prefecture	3727	8	13703	5
阿克苏地区	Aksu Administrative Offices	2817	9	15674	4
克孜勒苏柯尔克孜自治州	Kizilsu Kirgiz Autonomous Prefecture			2400	12
喀什地区	Kashgar [Kaxgar] Administrative Offices	11657	4	27637	2
和田地区	Hotan Administrative Offices	5386	6	24362	3

地　区	Region	普通中学 Regular Secondary Schools	位次 Rank	小学 Primary Schools	位次 Rank
乌鲁木齐市	Urumqi City	148896	3	181702	5
克拉玛依市	Karamay City	25067	13	23107	14
石河子市	Shihezi City	18692	15	10745	15
吐鲁番地区	Turpan Administrative Offices	33036	10	50735	10
哈密地区	Hami [Kumul] Administrative Offices	32070	11	32512	12
昌吉回族自治州	Changji Hui Autonomous Prefecture	81981	6	80121	7
伊犁哈萨克自治州	Ili Kazak Autonomous Prefecture	245784		334749	
伊犁州直属县(市)	Counties (Cities) Direct Under Ili Prefecture	151429	2	217846	2
塔城地区	Tacheng [Tarbagatai] Administrative Offices	62355	8	70834	8
阿勒泰地区	Altay Administrative Offices	32000	12	46069	11
博尔塔拉蒙古自治州	Bortala Mongol Autonomous Prefecture	23032	14	26996	13
巴音郭楞蒙古自治州	Bayangol Mongol Autonomous Prefecture	70724	7	92550	6
阿克苏地区	Aksu Administrative Offices	139393	4	216428	3
克孜勒苏柯尔克孜自治州	Kizilsu Kirgiz Autonomous Prefecture	34659	9	54280	9
喀什地区	Kashgar [Kaxgar] Administrative Offices	255222	1	411081	1
和田地区	Hotan Administrative Offices	116033	5	191985	4

19-14 各地、州、市每万人口医院床位数和医生数

Number of Doctors and Hospital Beds Per 10 000 Population by Prefecture, Autonomous Prefecture and City

(2011 年)

地 区	Region	每万人床位数(张) Number of Beds per 10 000 Population (unit)	位 次 Rank	平均每万人医生数(人) Number of Doctors Per 10 000 Population (person)	位 次 Rank
乌鲁木齐市	Urumqi City	106.40	1	50.29	1
克拉玛依市	Karamay City	65.11	4	37.87	2
石河子市	Shihezi City	80.44	2	33.98	3
吐鲁番地区	Turpan Administrative Offices	35.80	15	19.89	11
哈密地区	Hami [Kumul] Administrative Offices	59.45	6	31.20	4
昌吉回族自治州	Changji Hui Autonomous Prefecture	66.14	3	27.94	6
伊犁哈萨克自治州	Ili Kazak Autonomous Prefecture	46.74		21.82	
伊犁州直属县(市)	Counties (Cities) Direct Under Ili Prefecture	48.14	11	20.74	10
塔城地区	Tacheng [Tarbagatai] Administrative Offices	43.00	14	22.16	9
阿勒泰地区	Altay Administrative Offices	46.52	12	26.00	7
博尔塔拉蒙古自治州	Bortala Mongol Autonomous Prefecture	54.24	8	28.01	5
巴音郭楞蒙古自治州	Bayangol Mongol Autonomous Prefecture	59.56	5	25.36	8
阿克苏地区	Aksu Administrative Offices	49.26	10	13.82	13
克孜勒苏柯尔克孜自治州	Kizilsu Kirgiz Autonomous Prefecture	56.65	7	17.77	12
喀什地区	Kashgar [Kaxgar] Administrative Offices	44.57	13	12.42	14
和田地区	Hotan Administrative Offices	52.39	9	10.79	15

19-15 各地、州、市卫生技术人员和医生数

Medical Technical Personnel and Doctors by Prefecture, Autonomous Prefecture and City

单位：人 (2011 年) (person)

地 区	Region	卫生技术人员 Medical Technical Personnel	位 次 Rank	执业医师 Doctors with Licence	位 次 Rank	执业助理医师 Assistant Doctors with Licence	位 次 Rank
乌鲁木齐市	Urumqi City	31762	1	11879	1	660	6
克拉玛依市	Karamay City	2695	15	1030	13	39	15
石河子市	Shihezi City	5274	9	1796	7	326	10
吐鲁番地区	Turpan Administrative Offices	3087	13	1000	14	257	14
哈密地区	Hami [Kumul] Administrative Offices	4625	10	1508	9	314	12
昌吉回族自治州	Changji Hui Autonomous Prefecture	10390	4	3237	4	659	7
伊犁哈萨克自治州	Ili Kazak Autonomous Prefecture	25217		7772		2264	
伊犁州直属县(市)	Counties (Cities) Direct Under Ili Prefecture	15459	3	4744	2	1238	2
塔城地区	Tacheng [Tarbagatai] Administrative Offices	5739	8	1664	8	651	8
阿勒泰地区	Altay Administrative Offices	4019	11	1364	11	375	9
博尔塔拉蒙古自治州	Bortala Mongol Autonomous Prefecture	3341	12	1079	12	286	13
巴音郭楞蒙古自治州	Bayangol Mongol Autonomous Prefecture	9125	5	2760	5	704	5
阿克苏地区	Aksu Administrative Offices	8835	6	2192	6	1111	3
克孜勒苏柯尔克孜自治州	Kizilsu Kirgiz Autonomous Prefecture	3047	14	666	15	319	11
喀什地区	Kashgar [Kaxgar] Administrative Offices	15607	2	3603	3	1492	1
和田地区	Hotan Administrative Offices	6657	7	1503	10	737	4

2012

新疆统计年鉴

XINJIANG STATISTICAL YEARBOOK

附录:
各省市区
主要经济指标排序

APPENDIX:
Ranking of Main Econimic Indicators by Region

新疆统计年鉴

XINJIANG STATISTICAL YEARBOOK

2012

各省市区主要经济指标排序
Ranking of Main Economic Indicators by Region

(2011 年)

省市区	Region	地区生产总值(亿元) Gross Regional Product (100 million yuan)	位次 Rank	地区生产总值比上年增长(%) Increase Rate of Gross Region Production over the previous year(%)	位次 Rank
全国	**China**	**471563.7**		**9.2**	
北京	Beijing	16011.4	13	8.1	31
天津	Tianjin	11191.0	20	16.4	1
河北	Hebei	24228.2	6	11.3	25
山西	Shanxi	11100.2	21	13.0	12
内蒙古	Inner Mongolia	14246.1	15	14.3	5
辽宁	Liaoning	22025.9	7	12.1	20
吉林	Jilin	10530.7	22	13.7	8
黑龙江	Heilongjiang	12503.8	16	12.2	18
上海	Shanghai	19195.7	11	8.2	30
江苏	Jiangsu	48604.3	2	11.0	26
浙江	Zhejiang	32000.1	4	9.0	29
安徽	Anhui	15110.3	14	13.5	10
福建	Fujian	17410.2	12	12.2	18
江西	Jiangxi	11583.8	19	12.5	15
山东	Shandong	45429.2	3	10.9	27
河南	Henan	27232.0	5	11.6	24
湖北	Hubei	19594.2	10	13.8	7
湖南	Hunan	19635.2	9	12.8	13
广东	Guangdong	52673.6	1	10.0	28
广西	Guangxi	11714.4	18	12.3	17
海南	Hainan	2515.3	28	12.0	21
重庆	Chongqing	10011.1	23	16.4	1
四川	Sichuan	21026.7	8	15.0	3
贵州	Guizhou	5701.8	26	15.0	3
云南	Yunnan	8751.0	24	13.7	8
西藏	Tibet	605.8	31	12.7	14
陕西	Shaanxi	12391.3	17	13.9	6
甘肃	Gansu	5000.5	27	12.5	15
青海	Qinghai	1634.7	30	13.5	10
宁夏	Ningxia	2060.8	29	12.0	21
新疆	Xinjiang	6610.1	25	12.0	21

续表 1

省市区	Region	第一产业增加值(亿元) Value Added of the Primary Industry (100 million yuan)	位次 Rank	第二产业增加值(亿元) Value Added of the Secondary Industry (100 million yuan)	位次 Rank	第三产业增加值(亿元) Value Added of the Tertiary Industry (100 million yuan)	位次 Rank
全　国	**China**	**47712.0**		**220591.6**		**203260.1**	
北　京	Beijing	136.2	29	3744.4	24	12130.9	5
天　津	Tianjin	159.1	27	5878.0	19	5153.9	14
河　北	Hebei	2905.7	5	13098.1	6	8224.3	7
山　西	Shanxi	641.4	25	6577.8	17	3880.9	20
内蒙古	Inner Mongolia	1304.9	17	8092.1	13	4849.1	16
辽　宁	Liaoning	1915.6	11	12150.7	7	7959.6	8
吉　林	Jilin	1277.4	18	5601.2	21	3652.1	21
黑龙江	Heilongjiang	1705.6	12	6317.3	18	4481.0	17
上　海	Shanghai	124.9	30	7959.7	14	11111.1	6
江　苏	Jiangsu	3064.8	3	25023.8	2	20515.7	2
浙　江	Zhejiang	1580.6	14	16404.2	4	14015.4	4
安　徽	Anhui	2020.3	10	8226.4	12	4863.6	15
福　建	Fujian	1610.6	13	9167.5	11	6632.1	13
江　西	Jiangxi	1391.1	16	6592.2	16	3600.5	23
山　东	Shandong	3973.8	1	24037.4	3	17418.0	3
河　南	Henan	3512.1	2	15887.4	5	7832.6	9
湖　北	Hubei	2569.3	8	9818.8	9	7206.1	11
湖　南	Hunan	2733.7	6	9324.7	10	7576.8	10
广　东	Guangdong	2659.8	7	26205.3	1	23808.5	1
广　西	Guangxi	2047.3	9	5736.8	20	3930.3	19
海　南	Hainan	659.2	24	714.5	30	1141.6	28
重　庆	Chongqing	844.5	21	5542.8	22	3623.8	22
四　川	Sichuan	2983.5	4	11027.9	8	7015.3	12
贵　州	Guizhou	726.2	22	2334.0	27	2641.6	25
云　南	Yunnan	1407.8	15	3991.0	23	3352.2	24
西　藏	Tibet	74.4	31	209.5	31	321.9	31
陕　西	Shaanxi	1220.9	19	6836.3	15	4334.1	18
甘　肃	Gansu	678.2	23	2524.3	26	1798.0	27
青　海	Qinghai	155.4	28	939.1	29	540.2	30
宁　夏	Ningxia	184.1	26	1076.0	28	800.7	29
新　疆	Xinjiang	1139.0	20	3225.9	25	2245.1	26

Continued

第一产业占GDP比重(%) Composition of Primary Industry Product to GDP(%)	位次 Rank	第二产业占GDP比重(%) Composition of Secondary Industry Product to GDP(%)	位次 Rank	第三产业占GDP比重(%) Composition of Tertiary Industrial Product to GDP(%)	位次 Rank
10.1		**46.8**		**43.1**	
0.9	30	23.4	31	75.8	1
1.4	29	52.5	14	46.1	5
12.0	15	54.1	10	33.9	25
5.8	26	59.3	1	35.0	20
9.2	20	56.8	5	34.0	24
8.7	22	55.2	7	36.1	17
12.1	14	53.2	11	34.7	22
13.6	7	50.5	19	35.8	19
0.7	31	41.5	27	57.9	2
6.3	25	51.5	17	42.2	9
4.9	28	51.3	18	43.8	8
13.4	9	54.4	9	32.2	29
9.3	19	52.7	13	38.1	14
12.0	15	56.9	4	31.1	30
8.7	22	52.9	12	38.3	12
12.9	11	58.3	2	28.8	31
13.1	10	50.1	21	36.8	15
13.9	6	47.5	25	38.6	11
5.0	27	49.8	22	45.2	7
17.5	2	49.0	23	33.6	26
26.2	1	28.4	30	45.4	6
8.4	24	55.4	6	36.2	16
14.2	5	52.4	15	33.4	27
12.7	12	40.9	28	46.3	4
16.1	4	45.6	26	38.3	12
12.3	13	34.6	29	53.1	3
9.9	17	55.2	7	35.0	20
13.6	7	50.5	19	36.0	18
9.5	18	57.4	3	33.0	28
8.9	21	52.2	16	38.9	10
17.2	3	48.8	24	34.0	23

续表 2

省市区	Region	人均地区生产总值(元) Per Capita GDP (yuan)	位 次 Rank	总人口(万人) Total Population (10 000 persons)	位 次 Rank
全 国	**China**	**35083**		**134735**	
北 京	Beijing	80394	3	2019	26
天 津	Tianjin	84337	1	1355	27
河 北	Hebei	33571	14	7241	6
山 西	Shanxi	30974	18	3593	18
内蒙古	Inner Mongolia	57515	6	2482	23
辽 宁	Liaoning	50299	7	4383	14
吉 林	Jilin	38321	11	2749	21
黑龙江	Heilongjiang	32615	16	3834	15
上 海	Shanghai	82560	2	2347	24
江 苏	Jiangsu	61649	4	7899	5
浙 江	Zhejiang	58665	5	5463	10
安 徽	Anhui	25340	26	5968	8
福 建	Fujian	46972	10	3720	17
江 西	Jiangxi	25884	25	4488	13
山 东	Shandong	47260	9	9637	2
河 南	Henan	28981	21	9388	3
湖 北	Hubei	34131	13	5758	9
湖 南	Hunan	29828	20	6596	7
广 东	Guangdong	50295	8	10505	1
广 西	Guangxi	25315	27	4645	11
海 南	Hainan	28797	23	877	28
重 庆	Chongqing	34500	12	2919	20
四 川	Sichuan	26133	24	8050	4
贵 州	Guizhou	16413	31	3469	19
云 南	Yunnan	18957	30	4631	12
西 藏	Tibet	20077	28	303	31
陕 西	Shaanxi	33142	15	3743	16
甘 肃	Gansu	19517	29	2564	22
青 海	Qinghai	28891	22	568	30
宁 夏	Ningxia	32392	17	639	29
新 疆	Xinjiang	30087	19	2209	25

Continued

全社会固定资产投资（亿元） Total Investment in Fixed Assets in the Whole Country (100 million yuan)	位次 Rank	居民消费价格指数 Consumer Price Index	位次 Rank	城镇居民人均可支配收入(元) Per Capita Annual Disposable Income of Urban households (yuan)	位次 Rank	城镇居民人均消费性支出(元) Per Capita Annual Living Expenditures for Consumption (yuan)	位次 Rank
311021.9		**105.4**		**21809.8**		**15160.9**	
5578.9	23	105.6	11	32903.0	2	21984.4	2
7067.5	21	104.9	31	26920.9	4	18424.1	5
16404.3	6	105.7	10	18292.2	18	11609.3	26
7072.8	20	105.2	24	18123.9	21	11354.3	27
10403.9	12	105.6	13	20407.6	10	15878.1	8
17726.3	4	105.2	26	20466.8	9	14789.6	10
7436.7	19	105.2	23	17796.6	23	13010.6	17
7523.8	17	105.8	7	15696.2	28	12054.2	23
4879.2	24	105.2	25	36230.5	1	25102.1	1
26678.6	2	105.3	18	26340.7	6	16781.7	6
14185.1	8	105.4	16	30970.7	3	20437.5	3
12433.8	10	105.6	14	18606.1	14	13181.5	15
9926.4	13	105.3	21	24907.4	7	16661.1	7
9089.8	15	105.2	22	17494.9	25	11747.2	25
26770.7	1	105.0	28	22791.8	8	14560.7	11
17766.8	3	105.6	12	18194.8	20	12336.5	21
12585.7	9	105.8	8	18373.9	16	13163.8	16
11833.7	11	105.5	15	18844.1	13	13402.9	14
17158.5	5	105.3	19	26897.5	5	20251.8	4
7973.6	16	105.9	5	18854.1	12	12848.4	19
1669.5	28	106.1	3	18369.0	17	12642.8	20
7472.6	18	105.3	20	20249.7	11	14974.5	9
14239.8	7	105.3	17	17899.1	22	13696.3	13
3943.5	27	105.1	27	16495.0	26	11352.9	28
6185.3	22	104.9	30	18575.6	15	12248.0	22
516.3	31	105.0	29	16195.6	27	10398.9	31
9445.8	14	105.7	9	18245.2	19	13782.8	12
3961.7	26	105.9	6	14988.7	31	11188.6	29
1435.7	30	106.1	2	15603.3	29	10955.5	30
1639.1	29	106.3	1	17578.9	24	12896.0	18
4712.8	25	105.9	4	15513.6	30	11839.4	24

续表 3

省市区	Region	农民人均纯收入(元) Annual Per Capita Disposable Income of Rural Households (yuan)	位次 Rank	农民人均现金收入(元) Annual Per Capita Cash Income of Rural Households (yuan)	位次 Rank	农民人均生活消费支出(元) Annual Per Capita Living Expenditure of Rural Households (yuan)	位次 Rank
全　国	**China**	**6977.3**		**8638.5**		**5221.1**	
北　京	Beijing	14735.7	2	17157.9	1	11077.7	1
天　津	Tianjin	12321.2	4	15327.7	4	6725.4	6
河　北	Hebei	7119.7	12	8958.1	14	4711.2	17
山　西	Shanxi	5601.4	22	6396.6	25	4587.0	20
内蒙古	Inner Mongolia	6641.6	15	9750.9	13	5507.7	9
辽　宁	Liaoning	8296.5	9	12855.2	6	5406.4	10
吉　林	Jilin	7510.0	11	10792.7	9	5305.8	12
黑龙江	Heilongjiang	7590.7	10	11716.0	7	5333.6	11
上　海	Shanghai	16053.8	1	17079.4	2	11049.3	2
江　苏	Jiangsu	10805.0	5	13053.4	5	8094.6	4
浙　江	Zhejiang	13070.7	3	16916.8	3	9965.1	3
安　徽	Anhui	6232.2	20	7464.5	19	4957.3	15
福　建	Fujian	8778.6	7	9927.8	12	6540.9	7
江　西	Jiangxi	6891.6	14	7863.2	18	4659.9	19
山　东	Shandong	8342.1	8	11086.2	8	5900.6	8
河　南	Henan	6604.0	16	7318.1	20	4320.0	25
湖　北	Hubei	6897.9	13	8232.9	15	5010.7	14
湖　南	Hunan	6567.1	17	7887.1	17	5179.4	13
广　东	Guangdong	9371.7	6	10262.0	10	6725.6	5
广　西	Guangxi	5231.3	25	6448.8	24	4210.9	26
海　南	Hainan	6446.0	19	8085.6	16	4166.1	27
重　庆	Chongqing	6480.4	18	6963.3	23	4502.1	22
四　川	Sichuan	6128.6	21	7248.7	21	4675.5	18
贵　州	Guizhou	4145.4	30	4439.5	31	3455.8	30
云　南	Yunnan	4722.0	28	5951.3	27	3999.9	28
西　藏	Tibet	4904.3	27	4587.1	30	2741.6	31
陕　西	Shaanxi	5027.9	26	6323.9	26	4491.7	23
甘　肃	Gansu	3909.4	31	4914.0	29	3664.9	29
青　海	Qinghai	4608.5	29	5263.4	28	4536.8	21
宁　夏	Ningxia	5410.0	24	7034.3	22	4726.6	16
新　疆	Xinjiang	5442.2	23	10258.7	11	4397.8	24

注：现金收支为不含储蓄借贷后的现金收支。

Continued

农林牧渔业总产值(亿元) Gross Output Value of Farming, Forestry, Animal Husbandry and Fishery (100 million yuan)	位次 Rank	农林牧渔业总产值比上年增长(%) Output Value Increase Rate in 2011 over 2010 of Farming,Forestry, Animal Husbandry and Fishery(%)	位次 Rank	粮食产量(万吨) Grain (10 000 tons)	位次 Rank	棉花产量(万吨) Cotton (10 000 tons)	位次 Rank	油料产量(万吨) Oil bearing Crops (10 000 tons)	位次 Rank
81303.9		**4.5**		**57120.8**		**658.90**		**3306.8**	
363.1	26	0.9	30	121.8	29	0.05	22	1.4	30
349.5	28	4.2	18	161.8	27	7.23	11	0.7	31
4895.9	5	3.9	24	3172.6	6	65.34	3	141.8	8
1207.6	22	5.8	5	1193.0	19	6.34	13	18.7	25
2204.5	18	5.7	6	2387.5	11	0.23	18	133.9	9
3633.6	9	6.0	4	2035.5	13	0.07	21	119.8	10
2275.1	16	5.2	10	3171.0	7	1.21	16	69.6	14
3223.5	12	5.5	8	5570.6	1			23.3	24
314.6	29	-0.6	31	122.0	28	0.48	17	1.9	29
5237.4	3	4.2	20	3307.8	4	24.68	7	144.1	7
2534.9	14	3.1	28	781.6	23	3.24	14	39.9	21
3459.7	10	4.0	22	3135.5	8	37.80	6	213.8	6
2730.9	13	4.1	21	672.8	24	0.01	25	27.5	23
2207.3	17	4.2	19	2052.8	12	14.29	9	113.6	11
7409.7	1	3.8	25	4426.3	3	78.46	2	341.0	2
6218.6	2	3.8	26	5542.5	2	38.24	5	532.4	1
4252.9	8	4.4	16	2388.5	10	52.58	4	304.7	3
4508.2	6	4.3	17	2939.4	9	22.70	8	215.3	5
4384.4	7	3.9	23	1361.0	16			91.9	12
3323.4	11	4.8	14	1429.9	15	0.23	19	50.1	19
1002.4	25	6.6	2	188.0	26			9.9	27
1265.3	21	4.8	12	1126.9	20	0.01	24	46.5	20
4932.7	4	4.6	15	3291.6	5	1.46	15	278.4	4
1165.5	24	1.4	29	876.9	22	0.10	20	78.9	13
2306.5	15	6.1	3	1673.6	14	0.04	23	60.7	17
109.4	31	3.6	27	93.7	31			6.4	28
2058.6	19	5.6	7	1194.7	18	6.74	12	59.0	18
1187.8	23	5.4	9	1014.6	21	7.60	10	63.5	16
230.8	30	4.8	13	103.4	30			33.3	22
354.7	27	5.1	11	359.0	25			18.4	26
1955.4	20	6.9	1	1200.8	17	289.77	1	66.8	15

Note: The cash income and expenditure refer to the one abscent of deposit loan.

续表 4

省市区	Region	工业增加值(亿元) Value-added of Industry (100 million yuan)	位次 Rank	天然气(亿立方米) Natural Gas (100 million cu. m)	位次 Rank	原油(万吨) Crude Oil (10 000 tons)	位次 Rank
全国	**China**	**188571.7**		**1030.6**		**20287.6**	
北京	Beijing	3039.0	24				
天津	Tianjin	5380.5	19	18.4	7	3187.8	3
河北	Hebei	11741.9	6	12.2	9	586.1	9
山西	Shanxi	5903.9	15				
内蒙古	Inner Mongolia	7158.9	13				
辽宁	Liaoning	10696.5	7	7.2	10	1000.0	7
吉林	Jilin	4907.7	21	15.0	8	739.4	8
黑龙江	Heilongjiang	5583.2	18	31.0	6	4006.0	1
上海	Shanghai	7230.6	12	3.0	14	8.1	17
江苏	Jiangsu	22072.3	2	0.5	18	189.0	12
浙江	Zhejiang	14535.5	4				
安徽	Anhui	6979.6	14				
福建	Fujian	7775.1	11				
江西	Jiangxi	5611.9	17				
山东	Shandong	21290.3	3	5.2	11	2713.5	4
河南	Henan	14401.7	5	5.0	12	485.5	10
湖北	Hubei	8538.0	9	2.3	15	79.0	13
湖南	Hunan	8083.2	10				
广东	Guangdong	24408.1	1	83.3	4	1152.8	6
广西	Guangxi	4914.4	20			2.3	19
海南	Hainan	475.0	30	2.0	16	19.7	15
重庆	Chongqing	4690.5	22	1.7	17		
四川	Sichuan	9491.0	8	268.0	2	16.2	16
贵州	Guizhou	1969.7	27				
云南	Yunnan	3205.9	23	0.1	20		
西藏	Tibet	48.9	31				
陕西	Shaanxi	5727.8	16	272.2	1	3225.4	2
甘肃	Gansu	2071.3	26	0.2	19	62.6	14
青海	Qinghai	775.7	29	65.0	5	195.0	11
宁夏	Ningxia	836.9	28	3.0	13	3.6	18
新疆	Xinjiang	2700.2	25	234.1	3	2615.6	5

Continued

社会消费品零售总额(亿元) Total Retail Sales of Consumer Goods (100 million yuan)	位 次 Rank	社会消费品零售总额比上年增长(%) Increase Rate in 2011over 2010 of Total Retail Sales of Consumer Goods(%)	位 次 Rank	进出口总 额(亿美元) Total Value of Imports and Exports (USD 100 million)	位 次 Rank	#出口总额(亿美元) Total Exports (USD 100 million)	位 次 Rank
183918.6		**17.1**		**36420.6**		**18986.0**	
6900.3	10	10.8	31	3894.9	4	590.3	7
3395.1	23	18.7	2	1033.9	8	445.0	9
8035.5	9	17.8	19	536.0	10	285.8	11
3903.4	19	17.6	20	147.6	23	54.3	23
3991.7	17	18.0	16	119.4	26	46.9	25
8095.3	7	17.5	24	959.6	9	510.4	8
4119.8	16	17.5	23	220.5	20	50.0	24
4750.1	15	17.6	21	385.1	12	176.7	16
6814.8	12	12.3	30	4373.1	3	2096.9	4
15988.4	3	17.5	25	5397.6	2	3126.2	2
12028.0	4	17.4	26	3094.0	5	2163.6	3
4955.1	14	18.0	12	313.4	16	170.8	17
6276.2	13	18.2	6	1435.6	7	928.4	6
3485.1	22	17.9	18	315.6	15	218.8	12
17155.5	2	17.3	27	2359.9	6	1257.9	5
9453.6	5	18.1	11	326.4	14	192.4	15
8275.2	6	18.0	15	335.2	13	195.3	14
6884.7	11	17.9	17	190.0	21	99.0	20
20297.5	1	16.3	29	9134.8	1	5319.4	1
3908.2	18	18.0	14	233.5	18	124.6	19
759.5	28	18.8	1	127.6	25	25.4	27
3487.8	21	18.7	3	292.2	17	198.4	13
8044.6	8	18.1	10	477.8	11	290.5	10
1751.6	25	18.1	9	48.8	28	29.9	26
3000.1	24	18.0	13	160.5	22	94.7	21
219.0	31	18.2	8	13.6	30	11.8	30
3790.0	20	18.6	4	146.2	24	70.1	22
1648.0	26	18.2	7	87.4	27	21.6	28
410.5	30	17.0	28	9.2	31	6.6	31
477.6	29	18.3	5	22.9	29	16.0	29
1557.1	27	17.5	22	228.2	19	168.3	18

续表 5 Continued

省市区	Region	入境旅游人数(万人) Total Number of Overseas Visitor Arrivals (10 000 persons)	位次 Rank	#外国人 Foreigners	位次 Rank	旅游外汇收入(亿美元) Earnings from International Tourism (USD 100 million)	位次 Rank
全 国	**China**	**13542.4**		**2711.2**		**484.6**	
北 京	Beijing	520.4	5	447.4	5	54.16	4
天 津	Tianjin	73.1	26	63.6	24	17.56	9
河 北	Hebei	114.1	23	98.3	21	4.48	23
山 西	Shanxi	155.3	19	98.3	22	5.67	20
内蒙古	Inner Mongolia	151.5	20	147.6	14	6.71	18
辽 宁	Liaoning	405.3	8	339.4	6	27.13	7
吉 林	Jilin	99.3	24	85.5	23	3.85	25
黑龙江	Heilongjiang	206.5	15	197.8	9	9.18	17
上 海	Shanghai	668.6	4	555.0	2	57.51	2
江 苏	Jiangsu	737.3	3	537.9	3	56.53	3
浙 江	Zhejiang	773.7	2	515.0	4	45.42	5
安 徽	Anhui	262.9	12	151.7	13	11.79	12
福 建	Fujian	427.4	6	140.0	15	36.34	6
江 西	Jiangxi	135.8	21	44.0	26	4.15	24
山 东	Shandong	424.2	7	312.3	7	25.51	8
河 南	Henan	168.3	17	104.3	20	5.49	21
湖 北	Hubei	213.5	14	160.1	12	9.40	16
湖 南	Hunan	227.6	13	119.8	18	10.14	14
广 东	Guangdong	3331.6	1	749.3	1	139.06	1
广 西	Guangxi	302.8	10	171.5	11	10.52	13
海 南	Hainan	81.4	25	56.2	25	3.76	26
重 庆	Chongqing	186.4	16	132.6	16	9.68	15
四 川	Sichuan	164.0	18	113.7	19	5.94	19
贵 州	Guizhou	58.5	27	23.6	28	1.35	27
云 南	Yunnan	395.4	9	281.0	8	16.09	10
西 藏	Tibet	27.1	28	24.9	27	1.30	28
陕 西	Shaanxi	270.4	11	189.9	10	12.95	11
甘 肃	Gansu	9.1	29	5.5	29	0.17	30
青 海	Qinghai	5.2	30	4.1	30	0.27	29
宁 夏	Ningxia	1.9	31	1.4	31	0.06	31
新 疆	Xinjiang	132.5	22	124.9	17	4.65	22

中国统计出版社最新图书简目

(仅供参考,以最后出书为准)

统计资料

中国统计年鉴-2012
2012 中国发展报告
中国劳动统计年鉴-2012
中国建筑业统计年鉴-2012
中国商品交易市场统计年鉴-2012
中国民政统计年鉴-2012
中国科技统计年鉴-2012
中国高技术产业统计年鉴-2012
全国农产品成本收益资料汇编-2012
大中型批发零售和住宿餐饮企业统计年鉴-2012
中国县（市）社会经济统计年鉴-2012
第二次全国 R&D 资源清查资料汇编－综合卷

中国统计摘要-2012
中国第三产业统计年鉴-2012
中国社会统计年鉴-2012
中国人口和就业统计年鉴-2012
中国房地产统计年鉴-2012
中国贸易外经统计年鉴-2012
中国农村统计年鉴-2012
中国教育经费统计年鉴-2010
中国科学技术协会统计年鉴-2012
中国农村住户调查年鉴-2012(中、英文)
第二次全国 R&D 资源清查资料汇编－工业企业卷
中国民族统计年鉴 2012、2012

国际统计年鉴-2012
中国区域经济统计年鉴-2012
中国城市统计年鉴-2009
中国工业经济统计年鉴-2012
中国能源统计年鉴-2012
2012 中国地区经济监测报告
中国农产品价格调查年鉴-2012
中国农村贫困监测报告-2012
工业企业科技活动资料-2012
中国城市(镇)生活与价格年鉴-2012
中国农村全面建设小康监测报告-2012
中国零售和餐饮连锁企业统计年鉴-2012
2010 年中国第六次人口普查公报

2012 年省级综合统计年鉴系列

北京 天津 河北 山西 内蒙古
河南 湖北 湖南 广东 广西
新疆 新疆生产建设兵团
辽宁 吉林 黑龙江 上海 江苏
海南 重庆 四川 贵州 云南
浙江 安徽 福建 江西 山东
西藏 陕西 甘肃 青海 宁夏

2012 年市(县)级综合统计年鉴系列

天津滨海新区
运城 忻州 临汾 呼和浩特
上海浦东新区
杭州 宁波 绍兴 台州 温州
厦门经济特区 南昌 上饶
十堰 荆州 咸宁 长沙 广州
贵阳 昆明 庆阳 西安
石家庄 唐山 邯郸 太原 大同
包头 沈阳 大连 长春 吉林
苏州 无锡 常州 徐州 南通
金华 嘉兴 衢州
济南 青岛 潍坊 郑州
东莞 惠州 深圳 桂林 南宁
兰州 银川 乌鲁木齐
长治 阳泉 晋城 朔州 晋中
四平 哈尔滨 黑龙江垦区
盐城 镇江 江阴 丹阳
福州 福州经济技术开发区
洛阳 三门峡 南阳 武汉 宜昌
柳州 来宾 河池 海口 成都 绵阳

2010 年人口普查资料系列

中国 2010 年人口普查资料
浙江 安徽 福建 江西 山东
西藏 陕西 甘肃 青海 宁夏
中国分县 2010 年人口普查资料
北京 天津 河北 山西 内蒙古
河南 湖北 湖南 广东 广西
新疆 新疆生产建设兵团
中国分乡镇、街道 2010 年人口普查资料
辽宁 吉林 黑龙江 上海 江苏
海南 重庆 四川 贵州 云南
河南省各市 2010 年人口普查资料丛书
中国分民族 2010 年人口普查资料

"十一五"规划教材

非参数统计　医学统计学
多元统计分析　经济计量学教程
统计数据处理概论
企业经营管理统计
统计学:从数据到结论
概率论与数理统计　统计学
应用时间序列分析
质量管理统计方法　社会统计学
市场调查与预测
国民经济核算教程(国民经济统计学)
现代金融投资统计分析
统计指数理论及应用
多元统计分析实验
统计学原理（非统计专业使用）
概率论与数理统计(经济、管理类专业使用)

重点图书

挑大学选专业 2012—高考志愿填报指南　挑大学选专业 2012—考研择校指南

New Published Statistical Yearbook by China Statistics Press

Statisticses Data

China Statistical Yearbook -2012
China Development Report in 2012
China Labor Statistical Yearbook-2012
China Construction Statistical Yearbook-2012
China Statistical Yearbook-2012 of Commodities Market
China Civil Affair's Statistical Yearbook -2012
China Science and Technology Statistics Yearbook- 2012
China Statistics Yearbook on High Technology Industry-2012
China Agricultural Production Cost and 2012 Data
China Statistical Yearbook of Retail and Catering Service Corporation in Chain- 2012
China County(City) Social and Economic Statistical Yearbook-2010
China Statistical Abstract-2012
China Tertiary Industry Statistical Yearbook-2012
China Society Statistical Yearbook-2012
China Population and Employment Statistical Yearbook-2012
China Real Estate Statistical Yearbook-2012
China Foreign Economic Statistical Yearbook-2012
China Rural Statistical Yearbook-2012
China Education Finance Statistical Yearbook-2012
China Statistics on Science and Technology Activities of Industry Enterprises-2012
International Statistical Yearbook-2012
China Region Economic StatisticalYearbook-2012
China City Statistical Yearbook-2012
China Industrial Economic Statistical Yearbook-2012
China Energy Statistical Yearbook-2012
Poverty Monitoring Report of Rural China-2012
China Data Industrial Enterprises Activities-2012
China Country(Town) Life and Price Statistical Yearbook-2012
China Monitoring Report on Xiaokang-2012
China Chain Store and Catering Services Statistical Yearbook-2012
China No.6 Population Survey Report-2010

Series of Provinces Comprehensive Statistical Yearbook-2012

Beijing Tianjin Hebei Shanxi Inner Mongolia
Liaoning Jilin Heilongjiang Shanghai Jiangsu
Zhejiang Anhui Fujian Jiangxi Shandong
Henan Hubei Hunan Guangdong Guangxi
Hainan Chongqing Sichuan Guizhou
Yunnan Tibet Shaanxi Gansu Qinghai
Ningxia Xinjiang
Xinjiang Production & Construction Group

Series of City(Country) Comprehensive Statistical Yearbook-2012

Binhai New Region of Tianjing
Yuncheng Xinzhou Linfen Hohhot
Shanghai Pudong New Area
Hangzhou Ningbo Shaoxing Taizhou
Nanchang Shangrao Shiyan Jingzhou
Xianning Changsha Guangzhou
Guiyang Kunmin Qingyang Xi'an
Shijiazhuang Tangshan Handan
Taiyuan Datong Baotou Shenyang Dalian
Changchun Jilin Suzhou Wuxi Changzhou Xuzhou
Nantong Jinhua Jiaxing Quzhou
Jinan Qingdao Weifang Zhengzhou
Dongguan Huizhou Guiling Nanning
Lanzhou Yingchuan Urumqi
Changzhi Yangquan Jincheng Shuozhou Jinzhong
Siping Harbin Heilongjiang Assarting District
Yancheng Zhenjiang Jiangyin Danyang
Fuzhou Economic & Technical Development District
Luoyang Sanmenxia Nanyang Wuhan
Yichang Liuzhou
Laibin Hechi Haikou Chengdu Mianyang

Series of the 2010 Population Survey Data

Data of the 2010 Population Survey Data
Zhejiang Anhui Fujian Jiangxi Shandong
Tibet Shaanxi Gansu Qinghai Ningxia
Data of the 2010 Population Survey Data by Region
Liaoning Jilin Heilongjiang Shanghai Jiangsu
Hainan Sichuan Guizhou Yunnan
Series of Henan Data of the 2010 Population Survey Data by City
Beijiong Tianjin Hebei Shanxi
Inner Mongolia Henan Hubei
Hunan Guangdong Guangxi
Xinjiang Xinjiang Production and Construction Group
Data of the 2010 Population Survey Data by town and village
China Data of the 2010 Population Survey Data by Nationality

Planning program of the Eleventh five-year

Nonparametric Statistics Medical Statistcs
Mutiple Statistical Analysis
Economic Measure Learning Course
Statistical Data Processing Overview
Enterprise Management Statistics
Probability Theory and Math Statistics Statistics
Application Time Sequence of Analysis
Quality Management Statistical Methods
Society Statistics
Market Research and Forecasts
Modern Financial Investment Statistical Analysis
Multiple statistical analysis experiment Statistical Indicators Theory and Application
Statistical Principles
Statistics (From Practice to Theory)
National Accounts Tutorial
Probability Theory and Math Statistics Statistics (Economic and Management)

Emphases Books

For University Entrance Exam for Professional 2012
---- the Reporting Guidelines
For Postgraduate Entrance Exam for Professional 2012
---- the Reporting Guidelines

Tongjihang Bookstore: (010) 63376907 63376908 68783171 68783172
Address: No 57 Yuetan Nanjie, Sanlihe, Beijing P. R. China Statistics Press Zip code:100826

《新疆统计年鉴——2012》特邀编委

（排名不分先后）

充分发挥第一推动力作用　努力开创新型工业化和信息化建设新局面

新疆维吾尔自治区经济和信息化委员会

（新疆维吾尔自治区国防科学技术工业办公室）

工业和信息化部、自治区人民政府、新疆生产建设兵团主办，自治区经信委承办中国新疆 2011 产业转移系列对接活动

自治区政协副主席、经信委主任王永明与 7 个省市经信委签订产业转移合作协议

2011 年，全区经济和信息化系统贯彻落实中央和自治区的部署，充分发挥新型工业化第一推动力作用，深入推进“十项工程”，全区经济和信息化形势总体向好，实现了“十二五”的良好开局。

工业实力显著增强。全年完成工业增加值 2764 亿元，增长 11.4%，其中非油工业增长 17.9%；规模以上企业实现利润 910 亿元，增长 13.4%。

工业投资增势强劲。工业领域完成固定资产投资 2377 亿元，增长 46.2%，高出全国平均水平 18.9 个百分点。

中小企业发展步伐加快。规模以上中小工业企业达到 1529 家，完成增加值 879 亿元，增长 20.7%。

技术进步深入推进。新认定自治区级企业技术中心 18 家、产学研示范基地 20 个，新产品产值率提高到 4.75%。战略性新兴产业实现产值 700 亿元。

产业集聚水平进一步提高。6 家园区（开发区）升格为国家级园区，新设立自治区级园区 7 家，20 个对口援疆产业园区建设全面启动。园区规模以上工业完成增加值 693 亿元，增长 15%。

信息化水平进一步提升。“两化”融合示范企业扩大到 62 家。克拉玛依等 3 个“数字城市”建设率先推进，“两化”融合试验区加快发展。

信息产业发展取得新突破。全年实现主营业务收入 264 亿元，增长 27.3%。软件服务外包取得初步成效。“天山云”计划开始启动。

天然气利民工程取得新成效。提前一年完成全疆 75%城镇实现天然气入户的目标任务。

自治区经信委召开“新疆云计算产业发展战略研究及规划论证会”，新疆启动实施“天山云”计划

自治区经信委隆重举行“庆祝建党 90 周年老党员重温入党誓词、新党员入党宣誓仪式暨‘唱支新歌给党听’合唱比赛活动”

自治区常务副主席黄卫视察新疆乌鲁木齐北站国家粮食储备库

自治区副主席靳诺在科技活动周期间查看我区优质粮油产品

自治区粮食局

2011 年，全区新建粮食仓容 38.2 万吨，维修改造仓容 16.4 万吨。图为自治区粮食局党委书记雍其新（左三）在巴州调研粮食仓储设施建设情况。

2011 年，全区国有粮食购销企业收购小麦 300 万吨、稻谷 40 万吨，财政兑付农民粮食直补资金 6.84 亿元。图为自治区粮食局局长米尔扎依·杜斯买买提（左三）在阿克苏调研夏粮收购工作。

国以民为本，民以食为天。新疆远离内地，是一个相对独立的经济区，粮食问题不能依赖进口，也不能依赖区外市场，必须立足区内保证自给有余。长期以来，自治区坚持“区内平衡，略有结余”的粮食工作方针，实施了一系列扶持粮食生产的政策措施，有效调动了农民种粮和各地抓粮的积极性，全区粮食生产连续 4 年实现大丰收，总产突破千万吨，收购量超过 400 万吨，为确保我区粮食安全和农民增收奠定了坚实基础。

2011 年，全区粮食系统认真贯彻落实自治区党委、自治区人民政府的决策部署，紧紧围绕推进新疆跨越式发展和长治久安两大历史任务，解放思想、主动作为、真抓实干，以“稳市场、保安全、强产业、惠民生”为目标，认真贯彻执行自治区粮食敞开收购、敞开直补和最低保护价政策，不断深化粮食流通体制改革，完善粮食宏观调控体系，加快粮食仓储设施建设和产业化发展进程，不断提高军需民食保障能力和依法管粮、信息化水平，有力促进了我区粮食流通工作全面发展。

站在新的起点上，全区粮食系统将紧紧抓住新疆大建设、大开发、大发展的重大历史性机遇，坚持“夯实基础、强化创新、拓展领域、壮大实力”的发展思路，重点推进粮食仓储、现代物流、粮食市场、产业发展、军粮保障、质量监测、行政执法等“七大体系”建设，力争“十二五”末，初步建成涵盖粮食生产和粮食收购、储存、运输、加工、物流、贸易、消费等环节以及政府调控、监管、支持、引导和服务等方面的完整产业体系，实现粮食流通产业的跨越式发展，为确保新疆粮食安全和经济社会稳定发展做出新的更大贡献。

目前，全区地方国有粮食购销企业总仓容达到 465 万吨，有效仓容 366 万吨。图为现代化的粮库为我区储粮安全奠定基础。

目前，全区“放心粮油”销售店已达 582 个，不断满足城乡居民消费需求，保障粮油质量安全。图为放心粮油产品进万家。

新疆维吾尔自治区信息中心
新疆维吾尔自治区电子政务外网管理中心

国家信息中心常务副主任杜平检查指导工作

自治区电子政务外网三级网项目建设运行维护分析会

国家电子政务外网新疆 RA 系统认证审查会

自治区信息中心(自治区电子政务外网管理中心)成立于1988年,是隶属于自治区发展和改革委员会管理的副厅级事业单位,核定事业编制85名,专业技术人员占75%,其中高级、中级专业技术人才占50%以上。其主要职责是承担全区经济信息资源开发利用的规划和管理,为自治区党委、人民政府及经济综合管理部门宏观经济决策提供信息服务;承担全区电子政务外网规划、建设、运行、维护及相关管理工作;为党政机关、事业单位提供信息化技术支持与服务。

近年来,在自治区党委、人民政府和自治区发改委党组的正确领导下,我中心紧紧围绕“一个中心、两大任务、三大建设”的工作部署,按照以电子政务外网建设为主线,以实现信息化建设和信息服务两翼齐飞为目标,以效能促建设,强化管理、突出重点、探索创新、狠抓落实,各项工作都取得了显著的成绩。2010年获得自治区文明委授予“自治区级文明单位”荣誉称号,2011年又被自治区妇联授予“巾帼文明岗”和自治区总工会授予“自治区级模范职工之家”的荣誉称号。

自治区电子政务外网是我国电子政务重要基础设施的国家电子政务外网组成部分。其建设目标是整合现有网络资源,建成横连各级政务部门、纵连国家、省、地、县统一的政务外网网络,支持跨部门、跨地区信息交换、资源共享和业务系统的互联互通,满足各级政务部门社会管理和公共服务的需要,促进政府监管能力和服务水平的提高。

在自治区党委和自治区人民政府的高度重视和正确领导下,自治区电子政务外网一期建设项目于2009年正式启动,项目按照自治区人民政府新政办发【2010】229号文件要求,本着统一规划、统一建设、统一标准、统一管理、统一运维的“五统一”建设原则,科学规划,健全机构,强化管理,重视培训,积极推动建设工作朝深度和广度发展,项目整体建设工作稳步推进。通过不懈的努力,我区政务外网建设和应用工作得到国家肯定。在2011年全国政务外网工作会议上,我区作为在国家政务外网建设中抓落实、抓管理后发赶超的单位被指定做典型发言。

我中心在今后的发展中,将紧紧围绕自治区党委、人民政府和发改委的中心工作,以科学发展观为统领,按照《新疆维吾尔自治区电子政务外网“十二五”发展规划》确定的目标,抢抓机遇,攻坚克难,践行新疆效率,为自治区跨越式发展和长治久安做出新的贡献。

自治区电子政务外网管理培训班

信息专报

新疆维吾尔自治区奶业办公室

厅领导视察学生饮用奶推广宣传活动

奶业办领导班子观摩检查工作

奶业办领导下基层检查指导工作

一、主要职能

根据国家《乳品质量安全监督管理条例》和《新疆维吾尔自治区奶业条例》，我办承担自治区奶业行业管理、指导、协调、监督和服务工作；具体负责奶业生产和市场情况进行调查研究，为自治区党委、政府和主管部门提供制定奶业发展政策的依据；负责对奶牛养殖、原料奶生产、收购、运输等环节的质量安全监管；负责协调"学生饮用奶计划"推广工作，组织评定、审批学生饮用奶定点企业和奶源基地，会同有关部门对学生饮用奶质量安全实施监督管理和监测；建立奶业信息系统，开展奶业统计、奶价监测、生鲜乳第三方监测工作；承担全疆奶牛生产性能测定工作；组织开展奶业新技术推广、技术咨询、科普宣传，产品展示和行业宣传，开展国（区）内外奶业界科技交流与经济技术合作。

二、单位的基本情况

新疆维吾尔自治区奶业办公室成立于1994年，位于乌鲁木齐市南湖西路北一巷25号，是隶属于自治区畜牧厅的县处级事业单位，2001年以后，我办职能不断调整和增加，目前有五个牌子，一是自治区奶业办公室，二是自治区学生饮用奶计划协调办公室，三是自治区乳品质量监测中心（科级），四是自治区奶业协会，五是自治区奶牛生产性能测定中心。

地　　址：新疆乌鲁木齐市南湖西路北一巷25号

邮　　编：830063

联系电话：0991—4638304

传　　真：0991-4694233

自治区农机局

自治区副主席钱智参观第十二届新疆国际农业机械博览会

党组书记　贾立新

自治区农机局局长　巴拉提·阿斯木

2011 年，新疆主要作物农业综合机械化水平达到 80.5%，位居全国前列，为自治区农牧业现代化建设提供了有力的装备和技术支撑。2012 年，自治区农机系统全面贯彻落实自治区第八次党代会精神，不断创新工作机制，改进工作作风，打造“五型农机”（即学习型、务实型、服务型、创新型、廉洁型）。以农业增效、农民增收为核心，以依靠科技进步转变农机化发展方式为主线，以深入推进农业机械化提升工程为抓手，以调整优化农机装备结构、主攻薄弱领域和关键环节机械化、提高农机化服务能力建设为重要任务，积极推进农机、农艺、农业经营方式及信息化协调发展，不断强化安全监管，着力提高农业机械装备水平、作业水平、科技水平、服务水平、安全水平，全区农业机械总动力达到 1500 万千瓦，主要农作物耕种收综合机械化水平达到 81%，农林牧渔业综合机械化水平力争达到 60%。

新疆维吾尔自治区级农业机械专业研究机构新疆农业科学院农业机械化研究所，隶属于新疆农业科学院，先后增挂“农业部牧业机械化研究所”、“新疆乡镇企业机械装备研究所”。承担了国家及自治区的重大科研、推广项目，应用基础研究和公益性研究及服务工作。近年来，面向“三农”生产需要，从事农机装备与农艺相结合的新工艺、新装备和新技术的研究、引进、推广和技术服务。“十一五”期间完成科研项目 45 项，其中国家科技部项目 4 项，国家成果转化项目 1 项，自治区科技厅项目 21 项。

新疆本土的农机制造企业新疆中收农牧机械公司，直属中国农业机械化科学研究院，是国内收获机械行业中具备生产和研发能力为一体的重点国有生产企业。研制生产的新疆 -2.5 牵引式联合收割机曾获国家颁发的银质奖，新疆 -2 收割机代表农机行业参加建国 50 周年庆典成就展。公司拥有自治区级企业技术中心，各类机械加工设备 1200 多台，检测设备 250 台（套），通过了 ISO10012 计量确认，取得了 ISO09001、14001、28001，质量、环境、职业健康安全管理体系证书。经过多年的自主研发，小麦收获机械产品中有 5 项专利，玉米收获机械产品中有 2 项专利，棉花和辣椒的采摘、输送机械中有 3 项专利，在经济作物蓖麻、核桃的收获和加工方面有 3 项专利，其他农牧产品的储藏和输送方面有 3 项专利。

农机局领导到农机化所调研

党组书记贾立新到中收调研

1JSM-1800A1 型棉秸秆还田及残膜回收联合作业机

为推进棉花产业，促进生态环境可持续发展，新疆农业科学院农业机械化研究所研制出 1JSM-1800A1 型棉秸秆还田及残膜回收联合作业机，该机具有秸秆粉碎后输送还田（铺条）、松土、挑膜、脱膜、集膜等功能，工作效率高、清膜率高，使用方便可靠。

6HT-3000 型核桃破壳、壳仁分离加工成套设备

6HT-3000 型核桃破壳壳仁分离加工成套设备

为进一步延长核桃产业链，新疆农业科学院农业机械化研究所研制出 6HT-3000 型核桃破壳、壳仁分离加工成套设备，解决了国内核桃加工的技术瓶颈问题，该套设备申报国家专利 19 项，其中授权发明专利 2 项，实用新型专利 9 项。

新疆—3.6(4LZ-3.6)型自走式辣椒收获机

4LZJ-3 自走式谷物秸秆一体收获机

地委书记黄三平，地委副书记、行署专员麦尔丹·木盖提陪同自治区党委副书记、新疆生产建设兵团政委车俊在阿克苏纺织工业城调研

跨越奋进超千亿 两个率先铸辉煌

阿克苏位于天山南麓、塔里木盆地北缘，居南疆中心，邻五地州接两国，总面积13.13万平方公里，辖8县1市、10个街道办事处、85个乡（镇）、41个农林牧场，总人口257万，由36个民族构成，其中少数民族人口占比达75%。

阿克苏资源富集，水土光热条件得天独厚，是全国最大的优质商品棉基地、自治区重要的粮食生产基地和环塔里木盆地最大的特色林果基地，阿克苏红枣、核桃、苹果、葡萄为北京奥运会指定果品。油、气、煤炭及矿产资源量大质优，是“西气东输”的主气源地、国家油气资源重要接替区，铝土、岩盐及稀有金属铌、钽的储量居全国前位。文化资源特色鲜明，是龟兹文化、多浪文化的发祥地，旅游资源集南北疆之大成。

地委书记黄三平为浙江省对口支援新疆阿克苏地区指挥部落成揭牌

中央新疆工作座谈会以来，阿克苏地区深入贯彻落实科学发展观，抢抓新一轮援疆工作历史机遇，围绕“稳疆兴疆、富民固边”总战略，以现代文化为引领，以科技、教育为支撑，以改革开放为动力，以“黄牛精神加袋鼠步伐”和“三干两努力”为精神指引，大力实施“64122”工程，不断加快“三化”进程，地区经济社会步入快速发展轨道。新型工业化迈出强劲步伐，以钢铁基地和纺织工业城为代表的园区建设突飞猛进，六大产业初具规模，“日月星珠”企业集群活力初显；现代农牧业加快发展，粮食安全有效保障，棉花产量突破千万担，特色林果效益凸现，畜牧业提质增效，各项惠农政策全面落实，农村面貌发生显著变化，农牧民生产生活水平大幅度提高；新型城镇化稳步推进，打造宜居宜业南疆中心城市迈出新步伐，城镇化质量和水平不断提高，城镇化率提升到37.5%；民生保障力度空前，各族群众生产更加舒心、生活更加殷实、心绪更加顺畅，团结稳定、和谐发展的主旋律更加响亮；切实履行“当好中流砥柱、确保长治久安”的政治责任，各项维稳措施

地委副书记、行署专员麦尔丹·木盖提在拜城八钢南疆钢铁生产基地调研

天山神秘大峡谷

美丽的胡杨林

——阿克苏

有效落实，社会政治大局持续稳定。2011年，全地区实现生产总值789.13亿元，比上年增长15.8%，其中地方生产总值374.47亿元，增长24%，三次产业结构比调整为24.6:35.1:41.3；全口径财政收入达到195亿元，增长53%，其中地方财政一般预算收入62.1亿元，增长45.4%；全社会固定资产投资252.1亿元，增长48%；社会消费品零售总额72.2亿元，增长20%；农牧民人均纯收入达到6895元，增长15.1%；城镇居民人均可支配收入达到15820元，增长15.7%。

乘风破浪会有时，直挂云帆济沧海。近年来，在自治区党委、自治区人民政府的坚强领导下，阿克苏地区呈现经济发展、社会进步、团结稳定、边防巩固、各项事业蓬勃发展、各族人民安居乐业的大好局面。未来地区各族干部群众将继续以"黄牛精神加袋鼠步伐"，凝心集智聚力、跨越奋进超越，推动各项事业取得更大进步。规划到2015年，地区生产总值突破千亿元，地方财政收入突破百亿元，农牧民人均纯收入、城镇居民人均可支配收入比"十一五"末翻一番，公共保障和服务能力达到西部省区平均水平；2020年，地方生产总值在2015年的基础上再翻一番半，与全国同步进入小康社会。

工业园区夜景

红枣

核桃

蓬勃发展的棉纺工业

克孜尔尕哈烽燧

克孜尔千佛洞

地区四套班子领导在研究哈密发展规划

地区领导在地区福利园区新址实地调研

哈密地区

日新月异争跨越 瓜乡美名扬四海

哈密是新疆的东部门户，地处亚欧腹部、中西亚经济圈内。辖哈密市、巴里坤哈萨克自治县和伊吾县，总面积15.3万平方公里，总人口58.39万人。有汉、维、哈、回、蒙等36个民族，少数民族人口占31.9%，城镇人口占61.1%。

2011年，哈密地区全年实现地区生产总值220.92亿元，增长22.0%。其中：一产增长8.1%，二产增长31.0%（工业增加值增长29.0%），三产增长16.9%。完成全社会固定资产投资307.87亿元，增长40.8%。招商引资到位资金134亿元，增长40.4%。完成地方财政收入25.42亿元，增长57.2%（其中：财政一般预算收入23.52亿元，增长56.3%）。完成社会消费品零售总额46.54亿元，增长20.4%。城镇居民人均可支配收入达到15666元；农村居民人均纯收入达到7143元。

（一）大力实施“生态立区”战略，扎实推进节水型社会建设

供用水结构调整取得显著成果。万元GDP用水量由2005年的1518立方米减少为627立方米，农业用水量由2005年的88.1%减为81.5%，工业用水由2.6%增到5.3%，生态用水由3.9%增到7%。完成人工造林3.44万亩，累计面积达59万亩；狠抓东天山生态功能区保护，加大污染企业治理力度，严禁高污染企业和项目落地，严格执行“土地零开荒”制度。

（二）加快“三化”进程，着力推进经济科学跨越发展

加速新型工业化发展。做大做强优势产业和支柱产业，目前已有38家国内500强企业进驻哈密。坚持“五个优先”原则，由资源型招商向宽领域招商转变，全年地区招商引资项目125个，到位资金134亿元，增长40.4%。高起点、高标准规划建设特色鲜明、产业关联度高、辐射带动力强的工业园区，地、县（市）财政投入5351万元加强园区基础设施建设，入驻园区企业达到165家。重点规划新能源、节能环保、生物制药等战略性新兴产业，加快发展装备制造业。

加快农牧业现代化。以“调粮、退棉、增经、扩草”为重

点，大力调整农业产业结构。全年新建日光温室大棚2500座；新植红枣1.8万亩，完成酸枣嫁接49548亩；饲草料种植面积10.57万亩；牲畜出栏150.56万头（只）。完成农村劳动力培训1.2万人，新增转移就业1.62万人，组织化转移率70%以上，外出人员人均劳务收入8705元。投资8700万元在13个村实施73个财政扶贫项目，整合资金1.12亿元实施了“三乡一区”整村推进连片开发项目；地、县（市）财政继续投入1200万元，集中扶持12个少数民族贫困村加快发展。

疆电外送”750千伏

加快新型城镇化进程。按照建大建强中心城市、建精建优特色城市、加快发展各具特色的小城镇群的思路，编制一批体现现代文明、历史文化、地域特色于一体的城镇建设规划，加快“文化旅游名镇”、“特色农业镇”的规划建设。不断完善城市供排水、供电、供热、供气等基础设施，加快城市绿化、净化、硬化、亮化、美化进程，加大公共服务设施建设力度。目前，地区城镇化率已达61.1%，建成区绿地率38.71%。

着力提升第三产业发展水平。围绕建设东西双向开放的重要枢纽和现代化的商品物流集散地的目标，积极培育集交通运输、仓储物流、包装配送为一体的物流中心和综合物流园区。全力支持物流、电子商务等现代服务业发展，提高地区服务业的整体水平。围绕建设“新疆风光旅游盆景、文化旅游长廊、休闲度假旅游乐园”的目标，高起点做好旅游规划，加快基础设施和精品景区建设。2011年，接待国内游客223.65万人次，同比增长22.3%；实现旅游收入5.32亿元，同比增长28.4%。

㈢坚持民生优先、群众第一，加快推进社会事业发展

坚持把保障改善民生作为全部工作的落脚点和出发点，认真抓好民生建设年各项工作。2011年，新农合参合率达到99.77%，人均筹资标准均达到290元以上，实现新型农牧区合作医疗“一卡通”和定点医疗机构即时结报；建立国家基本药物制度，实现基层医疗机构全覆盖；地区人口出生率和自然增长率分别为10.16‰和5.81‰。加快推进公共文化基础设施建设；全面落实农牧民群众基本收视服务免费的政策；实现零就业家庭就业动态统计为零，大中专毕业生基本实现稳定就业；城镇登记失业率为3.1%。新建安居富民工程8700套、廉租房1826套、公共租赁房2141套、经济适用房500套、棚户区改造3834户。完善社会救助保障体系，进一步扩大基层干部补贴范围，提高补贴标准。2011年，全地区用于民生的财政支出占到财政一般预算支出的72.6%。

华能风电项目

哈密市五堡镇安居富民工程

戈壁明珠——石河子

八师石河子市地处天山北麓中段、古尔班通古特沙漠南缘，面积7762平方公里，耕地296万亩，人口62万人，其中少数民族占5.5%，人口和经济总量均占新疆兵团的四分之一左右。八师石河子市实行一个党委领导，领导班子分设，部门一套机构两块牌子的体制。

石河子垦区开发建设60年来，昔日人迹罕至的亘古荒原发生了沧桑巨变。石河子以天蓝、地绿、水清、夜明、人和的生态宜居环境，赢得了"戈壁明珠"的美誉，成为兵团屯垦戍边事业和对外开放的重要窗口。石河子市先后获得联合国"改善人类居住环境良好范例城市"迪拜奖、首届"中国人居环境奖"、"国家森林城市"、"全国科技进步示范市"、"中国优秀旅游城市"、"全国创新型试点城市"等17项国家级以上殊荣，

兵团党委常委、副政委、八师石河子市党委书记、八师政委卢晓峰（中）和八师石河子市党委副书记、八师师长、石河子市市长王平海（右一）在基层调研。

中央新疆工作座谈会召开以来，八师石河子市深入贯彻落实科学发展观，认真落实中央推进新疆跨越式发展和长治久安一系列重大决策部署，坚持以城镇化为载体、新型工业化为支撑、农业现代化为基础，着力转变经济发展方式、推进科学跨越发展。2011年，八师石河子市实现生产总值235亿元、增长15.4%，石河子市全口径财政收入41.8亿元、年均增长48.5%，地方财政收入26.8亿元、增长45.6%；城镇居民人均可支配收入17000元、年均增长13%，团场农牧工家庭人均纯收入11641元、年均增长14%，实现招商引资到位资金114亿元、增长61.9%，实现了"十二五"时期的良好开局。

面对新的形势和任务，八师石河子市坚持走城镇化、新型工业化、农业现代化发展道路，处理好屯垦与戍边、特殊体制与市场机制、兵团与地方"三个重大关系"，更好地发挥建设大军、中流砥柱、铜墙铁壁"三大作用"。到2015年，八师石河子市预计实现生产总值500亿元、年均增长21%，力争实现生产总值600亿元；石河子市实现全口径财政收入110亿元、年均增长33%，城镇居民人均可支配收入3万元以上，团场农牧工家庭人均纯收入达到2万元以上，当好兵团的排头兵和领头羊，率先在兵团实现全面建设小康社会目标。

新型工业化异军突起

农业现代化全国领先

荣获“中国纺织名城”称号

城镇化建设方兴未艾

阿克苏地区发展和改革委员会

阿克苏地区发展和改革委员会荣获自治区发改系统“四五”普法先进单位

地区发改委主任周春阳、党组书记卡米力·赛买提带领干部深入对口扶贫村开展慰问活动

地区发改系统庆祝建党90周年唱红歌暨党的知识竞赛

阿克苏地区发展和改革委员会是综合研究制订阿克苏地区经济和社会发展战略、规划和政策，进行总量平衡、结构调整，指导地区经济体制改革，主管重点项目和固定资产投资的宏观调控部门。内设机构8个，主要有：办公室、国民经济综合和社会发展科、农村经济科、产业交通能源发展科、固定资产投资科、外资经贸流通科、经济体制改革科（行政审批服务科）、价格收费管理科。

近年来，委党组领导班子认真贯彻落实党的十七届六中全会、中央新疆工作座谈会和自治区第八次党代会以及地委扩大会议精神，以构建学习型、创新型、服务型和谐文明机关为目标，深入贯彻落实科学发展观，带领发改系统各族干部共同营造勤政廉洁、奋发向上的工作环境，充分发挥工作职能，不断振奋精神，以实现“两个率先”为目标，全力推进“64122”工程和“日、月、星、珠”工程建设，积极开展“民生建设年”和“机关作风效能建设年”活动，重点项目建设、固定资产投资、“十二五”规划实施、对口援阿、价格管理、医疗体制改革等各项工作取得了较好成绩。先后获得“国家发改委收费统计工作先进集体”、“国家发改委先进集体”、“全国成本工作优秀集体”、“自治区发改委”十二五“规划先进集体”、“国民经济和社会发展先进单位”、“收费许可证审验工作先进集体”、“五五”普法依法治理先进集体、“地区第二次全国经济普查工作先进集体”、“地区政府系统信息工作先进单位”、“地区应急管理工作先进单位”、“地区纪检监察信访工作先进单位”、“地区人口和计划生育工作先进单位” 等荣誉，连续七年（2005年-2011年）被地委、行署授予“阿克苏地区目标管理考核优秀单位”荣誉称号，为实现地区经济跨越式发展和社会长治久安做出了突出贡献。

地区发改委领导班子

科学发展争跨越　全面进步谱新篇

特克斯县

县委书记　刘莉

县长　江尔森·努尔阿西

特克斯县地处天山北坡西部，著名乌孙山南麓，平均海拔800—1200米，风光秀丽，气候宜人。全县总面积8352平方公里，总人口17万人，县辖六乡两镇，由哈萨克、汉、回、维吾尔、柯尔克孜、蒙古等33个民族组成。境内有大小河流18条，地表水年径流量80亿立方米。矿产资源有铜、镍、金、石英矿、花岗岩等23种。特克斯县作为世界上唯一保存完整、建筑正规、规模最大的“八卦城”，继2001年被载入吉尼斯记录之后，2004年4月被自治区人民政府命名为“历史文化名城”，2007年5月被列为国家历史文化名城。

特克斯县旅游资源十分丰富、独具特色，有西北罕见、新疆唯一的天然钟乳石溶洞，有神奇广袤、驰名中外的喀拉峻大草原，有塞种人古墓、乌孙古墓、古代岩画、草原石人等人文景观，旖旎的自然风光，神奇的自然现象，浓郁的民族风情组合在一起，为特克斯县开发建设旅游支柱产业创造了极为有利的条件和无限商机。

改革开放30年来，通过全县干部群众齐心合力、艰苦卓绝的努力，今天的特克斯已成为通讯快捷、交通便利、基础设施和投资环境较为完善的名副其实的草原八卦名珠。

目前，全县上下以学习贯彻党的十七大、自治区党委会议、州党委工作会议和县委十一届一次全委(扩大)会议精神为契机，围绕“生态立县、科教兴县、优势资源转换”战略，圆满完成了既定的各项目标任务。2011年完成生产总值16.6亿元，比上年增长12.8%。全社会固定资产投资完成12.5亿元，增长22.9%；招商引资到位资金9.19亿元，增长53.17%；社会消费品零售总额完成6亿元，增长14.4%；财政一般预算收入完成9560万元，增长50.46%；城镇居民人均可支配收入达到12750元，增长15%；农牧民人均纯收入净增1006元，达到7166元。

万亩油葵生产基地

喜悦挂枝头

万亩设施农业生产基地内的草莓

人工生态林工程

千亩温室大棚外景

实行毛色分群改良的哈萨克羊

吉木萨尔县："聚宝盆"

县委书记　彭国春

代县长　王　燕

"十一五"时期，吉木萨尔县委、县人民政府团结带领全县各族人民，认真贯彻中央和区、州的各项方针政策，坚持以经济建设为中心，抢抓机遇、加快发展，县域经济综合实力稳步增强、产业结构继续优化、基础设施建设不断完善、精神文明建设和社会各项事业取得明显成效。

"十一五"以来，全县地区生产总值翻了 1.8 番，由 2005 年的 11.2 亿元增长到 2011 年的 39 亿元，年均增长（增长）17.8%；一二三产比重由 2005 年的 51:16:33 调整为 2011 年的 35:40:25；财政一般预算收入翻了 2.1 番，由 2005 年的 1.12 亿元增长到 2011 年的 4.75 亿元，年均递增 27.2%；固定资产投资翻了 5.5 番，由 2005 年的 2.66 亿元增长到 2011 年的 120 亿元；农牧民人均纯收入翻了 1.1 番，由 2005 年的 4212 元增长到 2011 年的 9232 元，年均增加 836 元。

农村经济结构进一步优化。2011 年，全县农业总产值达到 17.3 亿元，是 2005 年的 1.9 倍。其中：畜牧业产值 10.5 亿元，占农业总产的比重达到 60%。全县渠道防渗率由 2005 年的 26.5% 提高到 2011 年的 40%，森林覆盖率由 2005 年的 8.3% 提高到 2011 年的 10.6%。畜产品基地建设初见成效，东大龙口水库投入使用，东二畦水库、黄水槽子水库除险加固顺利竣工，水利基础设施进一步完善，天然林建设、天然草场保护、退耕还林工程进展顺利。

工业产业体系初具规模。工业发展步伐加快，县域个体、民营经济快速增长，多种所有制经济共同发展。2011 年，工业总产值达到 38.65 亿元，工业增加值完成 12.4 亿元，较 2005 年增长 39 倍，初步形成了以矿产开采、农副产品加工、新型建材、玻璃制品等产业为主导的工业体系。北庭工业园区被国家农业部授予"农产品加工创业就业基地"，被自治区乡镇企业局命名为"乡镇企业创业园区"。

固定资产投资规模不断加大。2011 年，地区全社会固定资产投资完成 120 亿元，是 2005 年的 45 倍。北庭园、天地园一期、文博中心、五彩湾展示服务中心、神新煤矿、神东天隆煤矿、天池能源煤矿、兖矿吉新煤矿、县乡农村公路、天然气入户工程、县城供排水工程、县三中、三小、中等职业技术学校、县医院综合病房楼等一批项目的顺利开工建设和投入使用，进一步加强和改善了县、乡基础设施建设。

项目和招商引资成效显著。"十一五"期间，全县上下始

的可持续发展梦

终将项目建设和招商引资工作做为拉动经济社会发展的重要抓手，健全机制，多措并举。先后有神华集团、庆化化工、湖北宜化、天池能源集团、新疆屯河等区内外大企业，建设了一批投资规模大、带动能力强的重点项目，极大增强了经济发展后劲。2011 年，全县争取各类国家项目资金 5.1 亿元，是 2005 年的 11 倍；招商引资到位资金 96 亿元，是 2005 年的 98 倍，为县域经济发展注入了活力，提供了动力。

商贸流通和旅游业快速发展。逐步建立起适应经济发展的商品流通渠道，商品交易市场快速发展，商贸流通企业竞争能力不断增强，市场主体日趋多元化。旅游业进一步发展，以构建区域旅游中心为契机，建设旅游景点 9 个，争创了自治区级旅游强县。成功举办了“吉木萨尔北庭民俗旅游文化节”、玫瑰花节，拍摄《话说北庭》、《天火传说》、《车师古道》、《狼来了》、《野马长啸》等影视作品，出版《北庭春秋》、《北庭历史文化研究》等书籍，提高了吉木萨尔在国内外的知名度。2011 年，全县接待游客 104.8 万人次，是 2005 年的 3.7 倍；实现旅游收入 5.57 亿元，是 2005 年的 7.2 倍。

交通、邮电、通讯业全面发展。2011 年，县域公路运输完成货运周转量 2.4 亿吨，完成客运周转量 3716.9 万人。2005 年至今，新建、改建农村公路 1158.35 公里，其中农村重要公路 380.6 公里，通村油路 444.89 公里，通达公路 332.86 公里。2011 年末固定电话用户达到 2.2 万户；移动电话用户达到 7 万部，乡镇宽带覆盖率达到 100%，行政村宽带覆盖率达到 98%。

社会保障体系逐渐完善。2011 年，全县参加失业保险人数达到 0.68 万人，参加基本养老保险人数达到 1.02 万人；农村基本养老保险试点工作全面启动，参加城镇基本医疗保险人数达到 1.68 万人；农村新型合作医疗覆盖率达到 98.5%。

社会各项事业取得新成就。教育事业不断进步，“两基”工作顺利通过国家验收，全县中小学适龄儿童、少年入学率达到 100%，中小学校布局调整进一步完善，教育体制改革不断深

自治区党委书记张春贤调研我县少数民族居住地区发展情况

自治区定居兴牧水利工程开工奠基

自治区副主席钱智调研我县经济社会发展情况

表彰创新争优优秀基层党组织

化，办学条件明显改善。卫生事业健康发展，初步建立了县、乡、村三级卫生服务体系，农村医疗卫生合作面不断扩大，地方病得到有效防治，妇女儿童健康程度进一步提高，继续稳定低生育水平，人口出生率控制在12.5‰以内，争创了全国计划生育优质服务先进县。文化、体育事业健康发展，县乡村文化体育设施不断完善。广播电视事业快速发展，2011年，全县广播人口覆盖率98.26%，电视人口覆盖率96.26%，数字电视用户达到1300万户，村村通入户率达69%。人民生活水平显著提高，城镇居民人均可支配收入逐年增加。2011年农民人均纯收入创历史新高，达到3232元，年均增加836元。

生态环保建设取得新进展。2005年至2011年，全县完成重点公益林面积72万亩，改造农村户用沼气池11194个；大力实施准噶尔盆地南缘防沙治沙、天山北坡谷地森林植被保护与恢复、防护林和湿地保护等工程，完成人工造林159458.3万亩，封育120205万亩，退耕还林4.8万亩，治理水土流失面积5.9平方公里；森林覆盖率达到10.6%，城镇绿化面积3648.3亩，绿化率由2005年的9.6%提高到2011年的35.3%。工业企业污染排放得到有效治理，大力实施“蓝天工程”，新增集中供热面积173万平方米，积极推广使用天然气、太阳能等新型清洁能源。

2011年安全生产工作会议

吉木萨尔县创建民族团结进步模范县动员大会

颁发2012年安居富民补助资金到群众手中

北庭故城国家考古遗址公园公路改建项目剪彩

中粮新疆屯河吉木萨尔县番茄制品分公司

万亩现代农业示范区

准东五彩湾煤化工采煤现场

北庭国际民间文化艺术节闭幕

参加解放军总后政治部援建的八一爱民小学剪彩

关心残疾人士勉励他们做对社会有用的人

县委书记　周立新

县委副书记、县长　努尔卡·卡那甫

尼勒克县

2011年，在州党委、州人民政府的坚强领导下，我县紧紧围绕推进跨越式发展和长治久安这一主题，团结和带领全县各族干部群众，开拓创新，扎实工作，战胜“11·1”地震等各类自然灾害，全县经济和社会事业掀开了和谐发展的新篇章。

主要经济指标大幅提升。全县实现生产总值28.68亿元，比上年增长16.3%；人均生产总值达到15698元，增长24.9%；三次产业结构由“十一五”末的28：50：22调整到28：52：20；地方财政一般预算收入达到2.71亿元，增长44.9%；全社会固定资产投资32.39亿元，增长50.9%；社会消费品零售总额4.83亿元，增长15.2%；城镇居民人均可支配收入12127元，增长16.8%；农牧民人均纯收入达到7023元，增加1190元，增长20%。

新型工业化建设实现新突破。全年实现工业增加值11.54亿元，比上年增长20.7%。工业占GDP的比重达40.2%。全年实施招商引资项目18个，到位资金25.6亿元。尼勒克矿区总体规划、能源化工园区总体规划、园区产业发展规划已通过上级相关部门评审。筹资2.05亿元加快工业园区基础设施建设。

农业农村工作取得新成效。全年投入支农惠农资金3.6亿元（县财政投入4206万元，增长24%）。畜牧业对农牧民人均增收的贡献率达到54.62%。新建、改建标准化养殖小区9个、定居小区5个。完成千元田9.6万亩、特色作物9.05万亩，新建和改造温室大棚324座。完成植树造林2.6万亩，建成万亩林果示范基地2个。转移富余劳动力4.79万人次，创收2.08亿元。

基础设施建设力度进一步加大。全年完成投资5.53亿元，一大批交通、水利、电力、城市建设等基础设施项目相继开工建设或建成投入使用。《尼勒克县总体规划》修编和《村镇体系规划》、《新农村建设规划》编制工作基本完成。新型城镇化步伐加快，城镇化率达到27%。

以旅游业为主的第三产业快速发展。全年接待游客35万人次，实现旅游收入4900万元，增长30%。完成《尼勒克县旅游发展总体规划》评审工作。旅游发展水平和服务功能进一步提升。商贸物流、餐饮娱乐、通讯等服务业实现较快发展。

民生建设成效显著。全年用于民生建设和社会事业发展的资金达7.03亿元，增长30.29%。完成安居富民、定居兴牧工程3970户，新建保障性住房1717套。实现就业4325人。学前双语教育普及率达96.9%。高龄补贴、城乡低保、大病医疗等补助标准普遍提高。农牧区新型合作医疗参合率、城镇居民基本医疗保险参保率均达到97%。实现822户3565人稳定脱贫。教育、文化、卫生、体育等社会事业加快发展。年初向群众承诺的15类22项民生实事全部如期兑现。

生态环境保护得到提升。坚持环保优先、生态立县。严格执行《环境影响评价法》和“三同时”制度，新开工建设项目、工业项目、各类开发利用规划、专项规划全部实行了环评。重点实施喀什河流域水电开发生态修复治理工程。水土保持方案已经全部优化。主要污染物排放总量严格控制在指标范围之内。

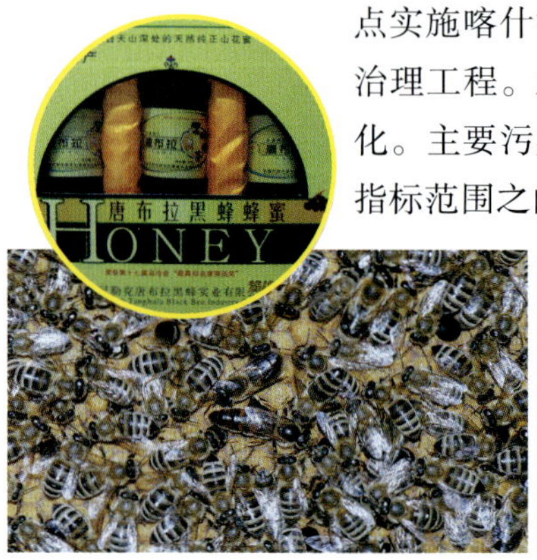

新疆黑蜂种蜂王

奶酪成品

中心幼儿园

尼勒克一年一度的草原民俗文化活动—姑娘追

庆祝建党90周年尼勒克百人红歌演唱

塞外明珠城 霍城县

伊犁州党委常委、县委书记王进健，县委副书记、代县长热夏提，县委常委、常务副县长孙志红一行在调研

霍城县地处伊犁河谷西北部的开阔地带，北依天山与博尔塔拉蒙古自治州温泉县为邻，南与察布查尔县隔河相望，东与伊宁市接壤，西以霍尔果斯与哈萨克斯坦国为界，国道312线、218线以及精—伊—霍铁路和清—伊、赛—果、果—霍高速公路贯穿全境，边界线长183公里，是祖国的西大门，是伊犁的门户，也是通往中西亚等国的“咽喉”。全县总面积5720平方公里，耕地面积60.15万亩。2011年，全县实现生产总值60.3亿元，比上年增长12.4%；完成固定资产投资19.84亿元，增长54.4%；完成工业增加值5.93亿元，增长16.4%；实现财政一般预算收入1.74亿元，增长6%；农牧民人均纯收入达到8171元。全县总人口40.4万人（含兵团10万人），聚居着维、汉、回、哈等30个民族，少数民族人口占54%。霍城县历史悠久、物产丰富，交通便利，人文荟萃，经济发展，社会稳定，素有“塞外明珠城”、“塞外小江南”之美誉。

安居富民工程

十分优越的自然条件。全县地势平坦、草原辽阔、河流纵横、田原平整、土地肥沃，有着良好的水、土、光、热、农林矿产和旅游等资源。境内可供开发利用的土地达800余万亩，四季草场400万亩，森林资源37.59万亩；有大小河流23条，年径流量12.74亿立方米，地下水储量为0.7-1亿立方米；全县矿产资源丰富，有煤、铁、铜、铅、金、银、磷、石灰石、大理石等33种，现已探明煤炭储量45亿吨；野生动物资源主要有马鹿、四爪陆龟、黄羊、野猪、狐狸、熊、狼、野兔、旱獭、野鸡、天鹅等，野生植物资源主要有野苹果、野樱桃李、野杏、野山楂、核桃等，其中四爪陆龟是世界珍奇动物，野生樱桃李属世界稀有树种。

霍城县江苏职业技术学校

独具特色的旅游资源。境内有高原平湖之美誉的的赛里木湖、山势雄奇险峻的果子沟、闻名遐迩的察合台汗国首府阿力麻里城遗址、风景秀丽的大西沟福寿山汉庙、风光旖旎的伊犁河、气势雄浑的惠远钟鼓楼、富丽堂皇的伊犁将军府、新疆唯一的绿洲沙漠—图开沙漠、火龙洞、万亩怪榆林、千亩野酸梅、中国薰衣草之乡、万亩葡萄长廊、世界著名东方小夜曲—《草原之夜》的诞生地可可达拉等名胜古迹和旅游景点。经国务院、国家旅游局批准，已能够与周边国家开展“二日游”，使游客轻松踏出霍尔果斯边境口岸，实现边境游。

不断扩大的对外开放。霍城是我国和中亚、西亚等46个国家和地区的商品集散地和中转站，是新疆各地区和祖国各地进入伊犁河谷和霍尔果斯口岸的必经之路。1989年国务院批准霍城县为对外开放县，1992年国务院有关部门先后批准霍城县享有边贸权、建立霍尔果斯边民互市、设置清水河经济技术开发区；2002年被中组部确定为援疆试点县，2010年国家将霍尔果斯定为经济开发区，对全面带动伊犁河谷外向型经济快速发展，实现向西开放的新突破起到了积极的作用。

惠远钟鼓楼

伊犁玉龙钢管有限公司

中国薰衣草之乡——霍城

塞外江南——伊宁市

伊犁州党委书记李学军在伊宁市调研

伊犁州党委常委、伊宁市委书记李宁平在企业调研

伊宁市市长阿不都沙拉木·沙德克陪同江苏省委常委、南京市委书记杨卫泽参观考察伊宁市城市规划建设工作

伊宁市是伊犁州的首府城市，是伊犁河谷的政治、经济、文化、交通中心。最早建城于清朝乾隆年间(1762 年)，1952 年 5 月 23 日经国务院批准设市，是新疆解放后最早设市的三个城市之一。全市总面积 645 平方公里，其中建成区面积 37 平方公里，现辖 10 个乡镇(场)、8 个街道，有驻市系统单位 100 多家。全市有 37 个民族、52 万人口，其中世居民族 13 个，维吾尔族占 49.4%，是一个多民族聚居城市。伊宁市气候宜人，水源充足，生态优势和自然优势独特，素有“花城”、“苹果城”、“白杨城”等诸多美誉。2010 年被南方人物周刊评选为中国十座宜居中小城市之一，并先后荣获“中国优秀旅游城市”、“国家园林城市”的称号。

伊宁市是东西陆路交通的要冲，地缘优势突出，对外开放的条件优越，距霍尔果斯口岸 88 公里，距中亚重镇哈萨克斯坦最大城市阿拉木图 460 公里，具备完整的公路、铁路、民航三位一体的立体交通体系，是新亚欧大陆桥西部桥头堡和连接中亚的重要枢纽，是新疆和全国向西开放的重要门户。早在汉代，就已形成了一条古丝绸通道，不仅沟通中亚各地和西亚，也有许多支线联接南亚和欧洲各地，历史上的伊宁是中国西部的一个繁华商埠。1989 年元月，伊宁市被国务院定为开放城市，1992 年又被确定为沿边进一步开放城市，并在市区内设立国家级边境经济合作区。2010 年 5 月，国家设立霍尔果斯经济开发区，在随后的经济开发区的划定中，伊宁市 35 平方公里被划入霍尔果斯经济开发区，2012 年将全面启动霍尔果斯经济开发区伊宁产业配套园区 35 平方公里的规划建设工作。

近年来，特别是自治区第八次党代会以来，伊宁市按照建设“天山北坡西部中心城市、对外开放门户城市和区域中心城市”要求，进一步发挥区位优势、比较优势和后发优势，加快推进新型工业化、新型城镇化、现代服务业和现代农牧业进程，以“伊犁河两岸”为重点的“一带、三心、六区”开发建设已拉开序幕，35 平方公里经济开发区建设已经进入开发建设阶段，庆华、国投、科伦等一批大企业大项目已落地建设，伊宁市已经进入了新型工业化和新型城镇化加速推进的新时期。

伊宁市夜景

喀赞其民俗旅游区

根据自治区、自治州和“十二五”发展的战略部署，伊宁市今后一个时期发展战略和奋斗目标是：以科学发展为主题，以转变经济发展方式为主线，以增加城乡居民收入和财政收入为核心，以改善民生为出发点和落脚点，坚持“资源开发可持续、生态环境可持续”的原则，大力实施文化立市、城建强市、产业富市、科教兴市战略，加快推进新型工业化、新型城镇化、现代服务业和现代农牧业进程，进一步统筹经济社会、城乡、区域、人与自然协调发展，努力打造天山北坡西部的重要增长极、中心城市和向西开放的桥头堡，把伊宁市建设成为充满生机的活力城市、民富市强的实力城市、环境优美的生态城市、安居乐业的幸福城市、团结稳定的和谐城市。到2015年生产总值达到300亿元，年均增长23.6%，人均生产总值达到5万元，在河谷率先超过全国平均水平；财政一般预算收入达到24亿元，年均增长20.3%；城镇居民人均可支配收入达到3.3万元以上，农牧民人均纯收入达到1.2万元，城镇居民收入和基本公共服务能力超过西部平均水平。

伊宁市城市新建道路

川宁生物有限公司在建项目

国投伊宁市热电联产在建项目

伊宁火车站

伊宁市达达木图乡富民安居项目

伊宁市巴彦岱镇举办农牧民使用技能培训班

察布查尔锡伯自治县

州党委常委、县委书记王奕文陪同州党委书记李学军视察社区建设情况

州党委常委、县委书记王奕文陪同州党委书记李学军视察榛子苗木基地

"察布查尔"锡伯语为"粮仓"之意,是全国唯一以锡伯族为主体多民族聚居的自治县,位于新疆西天山支脉乌孙山北麓,伊犁河以南辽阔的河谷盆地。全县东西长约 90 公里,南北宽约 70 公里,总面积约 4485 平方公里。2011 年末,全县境内总人口 19.30 万人,其中锡伯族 2.06 万人。县辖 13 个乡镇、1 个国营农场、1 个农村经济管理中心,县内驻有兵团农四师 67 团、68 团、69 团及核工业 737 矿等单位。

这里山青水秀、风景如画。"不到新疆不知中国之大,不到伊犁不知新疆之美",而察布查尔又是伊犁河谷一颗璀璨的明珠,向世人展示着她的雄奇与秀美。乌孙山山体气势如虹,其主峰 -- 白石峰,海拔 3480 米,登上峰顶,能真正体会到"不敢高声语,恐惊天上人"的美妙感觉。乌孙山下的琼博拉森林公园集林海、草场、高峡、奇峰、雪原、垂岩、小溪于一园,融传说与民俗为一体,既可与华山争险,又能同黄山媲美,令人神往。万亩河谷次生林环绕伊犁河绵延数十里,冬季冰雪覆盖,银装素裹,夏季林密树茂,郁郁葱葱。伊犁河的日落虽然没有海上日落壮观,但漫天的晚霞映照在波光粼粼的河面上,依然美不胜收。

这里历史厚重悠久、广为流传。公元前 60 年,察布查尔被正式纳入汉王朝版图,在西汉、东汉、晋、东晋时期是乌孙国故地。公元 1764 年,奉清朝乾隆皇帝诏命,4000 多名锡伯军民翻雪山、过草地、斗天险、战疾寒,饱经艰辛与磨难,从东北跋山涉水来到伊犁,屯垦戍边,创造了"西迁"壮举,留下了千古绝唱。二百多年来,一代又一代锡伯族人民平荒原、开阡陌,顽强拼搏,辛勤耕耘,用智慧和汗水谱写了保家卫国、屯垦戍边的新篇章,让这片钟灵毓秀的土地向世人散发出夺目的光辉,展现出无穷的魅力。

这里民俗文化浓郁独特、色彩纷呈。"世界唯一,唯我独有"的人文资源独具特色。凝聚锡伯族"西迁"悲壮史的图公祠及乌孙古墓群、海努克古城、银顶寺遗址等名胜古迹,文化底蕴深厚,民俗风情浓郁。锡伯民俗风情园和伊犁九大名寺之一的"靖远寺"融为一体,更加丰富了人们对锡伯族文化内涵的感受。

这里射手云集、射箭运动源远流长。锡伯族先辈早年生

州党委常委、县委书记王奕文在2012年半年经济观摩会现场

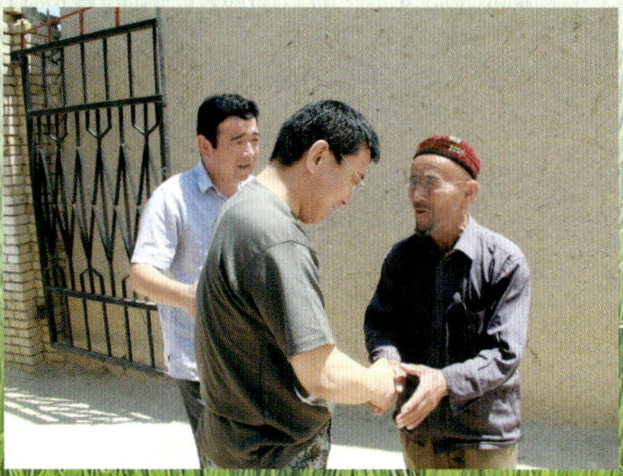

州党委常委、县委书记王奕文慰问四老人员

州党委常委、县委书记王奕文在定居兴牧工地参加劳动

2012 年 5 月 8 日,万人贝伦舞展示获大世界吉尼斯之最,县长王春光与工作人员共同展示证书

活在东北兴安岭地区时就以狩猎为生,把弓箭作为狩猎的主要工具和随身携带的战斗武器。随着时代的变迁,弓箭逐渐远离战争和渔猎生活的范畴,但锡伯族英勇善射的优良传统一直广为传承,射箭成为群众锻炼身体的体育项目,使察布查尔享有“箭乡”之美誉。汝光、巴永善、永富军、薛海峰等世界级优秀射箭运动员,均出自察布查尔,为我国射箭运动的发展做出了积极贡献。

这里物产丰富、资源得天独厚。县境内有大小河流 13 条,地表水资源年均径流量 9.301 亿立方米,人均拥有水资源 8348 立方米,年均降水量 230 毫米。2011 年末,全县耕地面积 92.5 万亩,牧草地面积 391.61 万亩,森林面积为 82.18 万亩,森林覆盖率为 11%。全年有效光照时数达 2810 小时,无霜期 168 天,积温 3600℃,适宜种植各种农作物。这里的大米色泽鲜亮、口感醇香,伊犁河鱼肉细味美、堪称一绝。野生药用植物有雪莲、贝母、党参、大黄、甘草、附子、防风、红花等;野生动物有马鹿、旱獭、黄羊、野羊、野猪、狼、豹、狐狸、野兔、野鸭、野鸡、雪鸡、獾等。这里矿产资源丰富,初步探明的有煤、铀、金、铜、铁、铅、锌、锰、重晶石、石灰石、冰洲石、花岗岩、建筑用砂、粘土等,其中,石灰石已探明储量 10 亿吨,煤炭已探明储量 52 亿吨,远景储量 1500 亿吨,占伊犁河谷盆地含煤区预测总资源量的 50%以上。

这里厚积薄发、潜力巨大。一是政策优势明显。作为多民族聚居的自治县、国家扶贫重点县、边境县、开放县,除享受国家西部大开发的优惠政策外,在土地、信贷、税收等方面有着更为灵活的政策;二是地缘优势突出。东邻巩留县,南以乌

锡伯民俗风情园

国家 AAA 级景区清水湖生态园景区

孙山分水岭为界与特克斯、昭苏两县毗连,北隔伊犁河与伊宁市、伊宁县、霍城县相望,西与哈萨克斯坦接壤,边境线长 70 公里,沿边有都拉塔、霍尔果斯两个国家一级陆路口岸,是国家向西开放的最前沿。三是交通便捷、电力充足。全县公路总里程 1119.16 公里,形成了以省道 313 线为轴线,县道 714、715、716、717、718、720 线和专用道 762 线等为主骨架的“三横三纵”的县域公路网布局。同时,精伊霍铁路为察布查尔县预留了接口。三是面临难得的发展机遇。国务院 32 号文件特别提出加快建设伊犁河南岸干渠、抓紧实施伊犁河拦河引水枢纽等重大工程,这些工程受益最大的是我县;横跨两国区域的中哈霍尔果斯国际边境合作中心建设工作已进入实施阶段,都拉塔口岸贸易突飞猛进,将极大推进区域经济一体化进程;国家将伊犁作为全国七大煤化工基地之一,确立了伊犁在全疆乃至全国重点煤产业区的地位,而我县又具有投资煤化工最大的资源优势;精伊霍铁路、赛里木湖 - 霍尔果斯、清水河 - 伊宁高速公路、恰甫其海、吉仁台水电站等重大项目已建成,制约伊犁河谷经济发展的瓶颈将彻底打破,我县的后发优势将很快转化为经济强势,一个前所未有的经济增长期即将到来。

这里思路明确、发展势头强劲。近年来,我县充分挖掘潜力,加快优势资源转换步伐,经济社会步入了较快发展的轨道。已经形成的特色产业有煤电产业、农畜产品加工业、水泥、建材制造业和旅游业等。与此同时,社会各项事业发展全面进步,先后被命名为“全国体育先进县”、“全国第一个民族语言环境建设示范县”、“自治区两基工作先进县”、“自治区科技进步先进县”、“自治区退耕还林先进县”、“自治区造林先进县”,靖远寺评为国家级重点文物保护单位,锡伯族“西迁节”列入首批国家级非物质文化遗产目录,锡伯族萨满舞蹈、贝伦舞、弓箭制作技艺等列入第一批自治区级非物质文化遗产名录等。

全疆最大的肉产品生产线——巴口香

伊犁天山水泥有限责任公司

察布查尔县万亩榛子基地

丝路古城 时代新港——奇台

奇台县城夜景

奇台县位于新疆维吾尔自治区东北部，昌吉回族自治州东部。县城西距乌鲁木齐市 195 公里，县域总面积 1.93 万平方公里。全县辖 6 镇 9 乡，总人口 29.4 万人，有 22 个民族，少数民族占总人口的 25%。有全国唯一的塔塔尔族乡。

奇台县历史悠久，清乾隆三十八年（公元 1773 年）建县，是古丝绸之路北道上的交通枢纽和重要商埠，曾与哈密、乌鲁木齐、伊犁并称新疆四大商业都会，有“金奇台”“旱码头”之美誉。

农业资源优势突出，有可耕地 200 万亩，是全国优质大麦、小麦之乡，国家级商品粮基地县和全国粮食生产先进县标兵。矿产开发前景广阔，有煤、金、铜、铁、石灰石、花岗岩等 20 多种矿产资源。预测煤炭资源量 3000 亿吨，是目前已探明全国最大的整装煤田，现已入驻煤炭煤电煤化工企业 40 多家；已建成自治区级石材产业园区，“卡拉麦里金”石材品牌享誉区内外。旅游资源独具特色，有国家森林公园、江布拉克国家 4A 级旅游景区、国家级工业旅游示范点——古城酒史馆和硅化木·恐龙国家地质公园，被誉为“恐龙之乡”。

全国最大的整装煤田

近年来，县委、县人民政府坚持以科学发展观统领经济社会发展全局，认真贯彻中央新疆工作座谈会和区、州党代会精神，抢抓区、州全力推动准东开发崛起的战略机遇，不断解放思想、变化变革，科学跨越、敢于担当，深入实施“大产业、大园区、大城区”三大战略，打响“中国五都·新疆奇台”（煤都、粮都、酒都、龙都、俪都）文化品牌，着力打造天山北坡东部区域中心城市，有力开创了奇台大建设、大开放、大发展的新局面。2011 年，全县实现地区生产总值 72.4 亿元，增长 22.6%；完成固定资产投资 69 亿元，增长 107.6%；实现地方财政收入 6.16 亿元，增长 54%；农牧民人均纯收入达到 9421 元。

现代化设施农业育苗中心

江布拉克国家 4A 级旅游景区

中国驰名商标——新疆第一窖

花岗岩板材加工生产线

发展中的区域经济强县

富蕴县

县委书记　祁崇江

县委书记祁崇江与县委副书记、县长沙比提·哈再孜调研新农村建设

新鑫矿业股份公司喀拉通克铜镍矿

2011年，富蕴县委、政府团结带领全县各族人民，以邓小平理论和"三个代表"重要思想为统领，牢固树立和落实科学发展观，以增加农牧民收入和财政收入为主线，以实现"两个率先"为目标，紧紧围绕"工业强县"的发展思路，努力克服金融危机带来的不利影响，大力实施优势资源转换战略，全县以经济建设为中心的社会各项事业取得了丰硕成果。

2011年完成生产总值41.12亿元，按可比价计算比上年增长8.8%。一、二、三产分别完成增加值5.79亿元、29.01亿元、6.32亿元，分别增减-1.9%、12.3%和6.3%。社会消费品零售总额4.96亿元，增长10.2%；固定资产投资30.09亿元，增长12.8%；财政一般预算收入达到6.74亿元，增长16.8%，地方财政支出达15.85亿元，增长27.6%；金融机构存款余额为26.65亿元，增长20.3%，贷款余额为3.84亿元，增长37.5%。农民人均纯收入达6236元，增长11.8%。全县播种面积达36.83万亩，增长5%；粮食产量达5.82万吨，增长17%；油料作物产量1.65万吨，增长13.7%；牲畜存栏60.99万头(只)，下降0.4%；牲畜出栏44.05万头（只），增长3.5%；肉产量达1.52万吨，下降5.6%；牛奶产量达4.02万吨，增长6.3%；主要工业产品产量：铁精粉372万吨，增长5.7%；高冰镍1.14万吨，增长55.1%；水泥26.84万吨，增长20.8%。

2012年，富蕴将开启新的发展篇章！以邓小平理论和"三个代表"重要思想为指导，深入落实科学发展观，全面贯彻中央新疆工作座谈会和自治区第八次党代会精神，坚决执行"保护生态、放大优势、突出民生、形成特色、创先争优"二十字方针，紧紧围绕地委扩大会议确定的目标任务和工作要求，更加注重提升产业发展水平，更加注重基础设施建设，更加注重资源开发可持续和生态环境可持续，更加注重民生改善和社会建设，更加注重现代文化引领和科技教育支撑，更加注重民族团结和社会和谐，更加注重党的建设和基层基础工作，全力推进经济社会跨越式发展和长治久安。

地质圣坑——可可托海3号坑

高冰镍冶炼

塞北渔乡——福海县

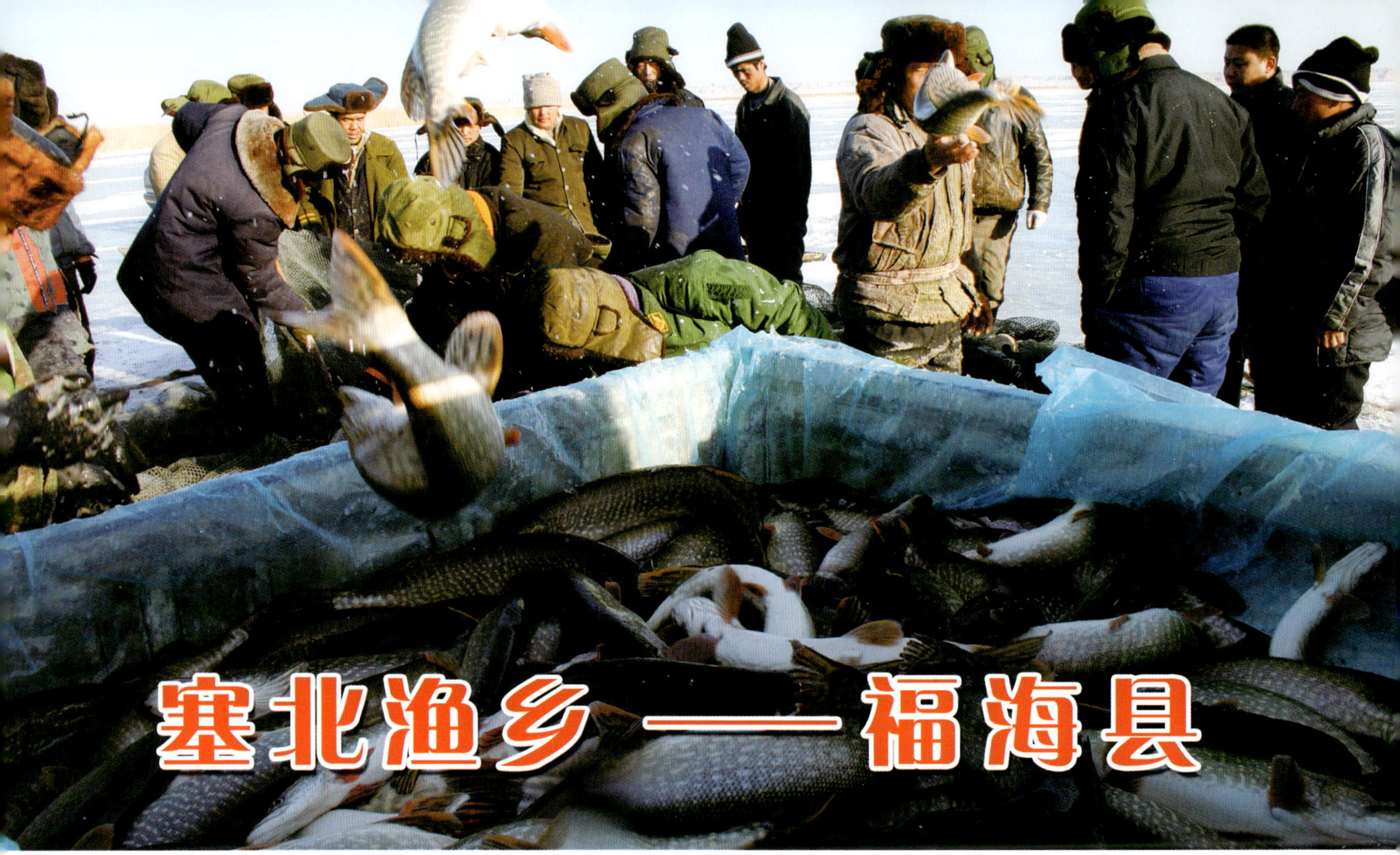

福海县地处新疆阿勒泰地区中部，素有“准噶尔明珠”、“塞北渔乡”、“大漠大海”之美誉。交通便利，县城南距首府乌鲁木齐市637公里，距克拉玛依市300公里，西南距伊宁市850公里，北距地区行署驻地阿勒泰市99公里，216国道、318省道和奎北铁路穿境而过，在准噶尔盆地和阿勒泰地区形成了环形旅游线路。随着克－阿高速开建，福海县区域交通枢纽优势愈发突出。全县辖域面积3.33万平方公里，辖区5乡1镇2场，62个行政村，辖区含驻县团场。2011年全县总人口10.08万人(含驻县兵团)，全县由汉族、哈萨克族等26个民族组成，以哈萨克族为主的少数民族占总人口的34.3%。全县资源丰富，风光独特，可概括为“草盛、畜壮，水丰、鱼香，山奇、湖秀，林茂、矿富”。

福海草肥鱼香，是全疆的畜牧业生产基地之一，全县草原总面积3535万亩，可利用草场2300万亩，是地方优良绵羊品种阿勒泰大尾羊的故乡，是全疆的阿勒大尾羊良种繁育基地；2008年，全县有10万只羊和2万头牛通过国家有机产品认证。全疆的渔业生产基地之一，境内“全国十大内陆淡水湖”之一的乌伦古湖，水域面积1035平方公里，尤其以盛产鲤鱼、东方欧鳊、白斑狗鱼、梭鲈等几十种冷水鱼，均通过国家有机产品认证，以天然、野生、无公害、无污染、风味独特而著称。

素有“准噶尔明珠”“塞外江南”之美誉的福海，具有美丽的海滨风光，神奇的大漠风情、悠久的草原文化、独特的民俗风情，是旅游度假的好去处。自然风光分乌伦古湖区和阿尔泰山区两大区域。湖区主要景点有国家4A级景区乌伦古湖海滨景

颂歌献给党

民俗文化节

文化惠民

区、神秘准噶尔海上魔鬼城、吉力湖万亩芦苇湿地、鸟岛、中海子天鹅湖；山区主要景点有国家级森林公园阿拉善森林公园、金塔斯草原自然保护区、阿拉善温泉群、蝴蝶沟、霍加雪夫岩画、卡拉额尔齐斯河、卓尔特河风光区、萨尔布拉克怪石沟、红山嘴边防口岸。森林资源丰富是福海的又一特色。有山地自然林7.42万公顷，河谷阔叶林0.55万公顷，荒漠灌木林1万公顷。兽类有5目11科34种，鸟类有18目41科97属173种，矿产富集，潜力巨大。有矿产资源34种，探明储量27种，矿床88个，锂、铍、砂金、蛋白土、硅石等较为丰富。福海县还是阿勒泰地区油气资源最为富集的县，境内的克拉美丽气田是准噶尔盆地首个千亿立方米的整装大气田，初步探明石油储量1100万吨，天然气储量1000亿方，预计天然气储量可达7500亿方。

水产养殖业

2011年福海县全年完成县域生产总值22.7亿元，比上年增长7.5%；地方财政收入1.82亿元，增长17%；地方全社会固定资产投资11.8亿元，增长17.6%；农牧民人均纯收入达到6389元，增收408元。

奎北铁路运营

龙源社区外景

民族手工刺绣

旅游业渐入佳境

阿勒泰羊赛畜会

乌伦古湖小海子——吉力湖风光

全国人大常委会副委员长司马义·铁力瓦尔地在新疆乌苏啤酒(乌苏)有限公司视察

塔城地委书记张博(前排中)深入我市棉花高产示范区实地查看棉苗长势

励精图治谱新篇 乌苏市

乌苏市委书记　梁　浩

乌苏市委副书记、市长　马依山·扎合帕尔

市委书记梁浩(前排右三),市委副书记、市长马依山·扎合帕尔(前排左三)调研新疆北方科技投资有限公司

乌苏市地处天山北麓、准噶尔盆地西南缘,居伊犁、塔城、阿勒泰三区之要津,是通往霍尔果斯、巴克图、阿拉山口口岸的重要门户,与国家石化基地独山子、新型商贸城奎屯市形成北疆“金三角”,国道312线、217线和欧亚第二大陆桥(铁路)横贯东西,奎—赛高等级公路从境内穿过,东距自治区首府乌鲁木齐市260公里。乌苏区域总面积2.07万平方公里,辖区总人口37万余人,全市辖10镇、7乡、3个牧场、1个林场和5个街道办事处。

乌苏市水土、光热、矿产、旅游等资源十分丰富,境内奎屯河、四棵树河、古尔图河三条主要河流年径流量达到12.5亿立方,地下水可开采量4.34亿立方,年均无霜期182天,充足的水土光热资源为棉花、玉米、番茄、瓜菜等作物提供了良好的生长条件,使乌苏成为国家和自治区优质棉基地、粮食基地和畜牧业基地。

乌苏境内初步探明的矿产有煤、铁、铜、砂金、石油、铅、石墨、石灰石、石膏、膨润土、花岗岩等,尤以煤资源最为丰富,已探明储量7亿吨,远景储量达21亿吨。依托丰富的大农业资源和矿产资源,规划并建设了49.2平方公里的乌苏石化工业园,其中一期规划19.2平方公里,建成区9平方公里,现有54家企业入驻园区,涉及石化上下游产业、能源、农产品、建筑、制造等领域近百种产品,已基本形成门类比较齐全、结构趋向合理的工业体系。

重庆云河年产 2 万辆汽车项目奠基仪式

新疆华巨化工奠基仪式

民生工程奠基仪式

乌苏市历史悠久，文化源远流长，文物古迹众多，风景秀丽，是中外游客旅游观光、休闲娱乐的理想选择。南部山区有连绵浩翰的天山原始森林、天山山脉的冰达板、南山温泉、乌兰萨德克高山湖泊；中部平原区有草场、湖泊、中国最大的泥火山群、夏尔苏木喇嘛庙、乌孙土墩墓葬群等；北部荒漠生态区有世界上保存最完好的 267 万亩原始白梭梭林。

2011 年全市实现生产总值 98.6 亿元，比上年增长 18.3%。其中：第一产业 21.9 亿元，增长 8.5%；第二产业 57.9 亿元，增长 24.6%；第三产业 18.8 亿元，增长 13.8%。全年完成工业增加值 42.6 亿元，增长 32.8%；实现农业增加值 21.9 亿元，增长 8.5%；农牧民人均纯收入达到 11620 元，比上年增加 1471 元。一般预算收入顺利突破年初制定的增长 50%的目标，达到 6.34 亿元。三次产业比重由 2010 年的 25∶54∶21 调整为 2011 年的 22∶59∶19。

乌苏啤酒生产车间

泥火山

枸杞

高起点 谋发展 创辉煌

霍尔果斯经济开发区

伊犁州党委常委、霍尔果斯经济开发区党工委书记 陆民

霍尔果斯经济开发区管委会主任 吴宏

中哈国际边境合作中心商业项目集中开工仪式

霍尔果斯，古“丝绸之路”新北道上的一个重要驿站，因其历史悠久、辐射中亚市场区位最优、自然条件最好、综合运量最大、基础设施最完善，近年来成为世人瞩目的焦点。

霍尔果斯口岸于1983年11月16日经国务院批准正式恢复开放。口岸地处国道312线、连霍高速公路、陇海——兰新铁路国际新通道的最西端，距新疆维吾尔自治区首府乌鲁木齐市670公里，距哈萨克斯坦原首都阿拉木图市378公里，果霍高等级公路、精伊霍铁路全线贯通，中亚天然气管道实现通气，常住人口1.5万人，流动人口每日近万人，道路、供排水、通讯、电力、金融、旅游等基础设施完备、机构齐全，能够满足近期10万人、远期20万人的生活需求。

党中央、国务院高度重视霍尔果斯的开发建设，近年来，胡锦涛、温家宝等党和国家领导相继来霍尔果斯视察指导工作；国内外多家知名企业前来参观、考察、洽谈、落户。

2010年5月，中央召开新疆工作座谈会，决定设立霍尔果斯经济开发区，实行特殊的政策。在自治区、自治州党委、政府高度重视和大力支持下，开发区党工委、管委会迅速开展调研工作，在深入分析研究的基础上，科学谋划“十二五”发展，提出了构建“开放的、奋进的、绿色的、和谐的霍尔果斯”的发展理念。以“环境立区、开放活区、质量兴区、人才强区、民生安区”五大战略为指导，高起点、高水平、高效益规划建设经济开发区，努力将霍尔果斯建设成为新疆新的经济增长点、全国向西开放的桥头堡、国际贸易中心城市的发展思路。

随着霍尔果斯经济开发区的进一步开发建设，霍尔果斯正在迅速形成人流、物流、资金流的高度集聚。未来的霍尔果斯经济开发区必将成为新疆加快发展的重要经济增长极和进出口贸易集散地、出口产品加工基地、边境商贸旅游基地；成为新疆乃至全国向西开放的重要窗口和推动新疆跨越式发展新的经济增长点；成为中国西部最璀璨的明珠。

合作中心联检厅

神山圣水 西域泉都 温泉县

温泉县地处祖国西北部，准噶尔盆地西缘，距自治区首府乌鲁木齐市630公里、亚欧大陆桥头堡阿拉山口口岸169公里，伊犁霍尔果斯口岸170公里。东连博乐市、南邻伊犁霍城县，西北与哈萨克斯坦共和国接壤，边境线长276公里。全县总面积5881平方公里，辖2镇，3乡，2场，境内驻有兵团农五师所属87、88团。温泉县被誉为“神山圣水 西域泉都”。从地图上看形状酷似一扇芭蕉叶，温泉河和鄂托克赛尔河形成了叶片的纹路，连绵起伏的阿拉套山为这扇叶片镶上了一道华丽的花边。高山雪水与山泉灌溉了47万亩绿色农产品基地，养育了汉、蒙、哈、维等24各民族7.48万群众。温泉县是西迁戍边察哈尔蒙古的故乡。西迁历史可以追溯到1762年。灿烂悠久的草原文明孕育了温泉丰富瑰丽的文化内涵，这里是“新疆蒙古族短调民歌之乡”。以察哈尔短调、阿肯强唱及蒙、哈、维等民族民间手工艺品为代表的民俗文化在这里传承和发展，乌兰牧骑演绎着近50年红色轻骑兵的传奇。“那达慕”草原节、环赛里木湖公路自行车赛、百日乡村文体竞赛等更是您观自然秀美风光，赏民俗文化艺术，听原生态歌谣，浴塞外养生温泉不容错过的精彩。

温泉县是中国唯一以温泉命名的县，境内以圣泉（博格达尔温泉）、天泉（鄂托克赛尔温泉）、仙泉（阿尔夏提温泉）为代表的147处泉眼和比县城大两倍的湿地氧吧为人们打造了延年益寿的“养生天堂”。100余种野生动物在这里繁衍生息，享受着生态自然的呵护。素有活化石之称的世界唯一的新疆北鲵在这里繁衍生息了三亿五千万年，是“中国新疆北鲵的故乡”。温泉县景色旖旎，空气中负氧离子浓度较高。春天，草原、山麓姹紫嫣红，生机盎然；盛夏，牧场郁郁葱葱、群山连绵起伏；秋天，麦浪滚滚，瓜果飘香；冬季，银装素裹的县城宛如身着圣洁礼服的少女，素洁、宁静的让人心醉。

温泉县农牧业资源富集，是自治区22个畜牧业县和41个粮食生产县之一，国家级绿色小麦生产基地，无公害、绿色、有机农产品已覆盖全县，已建成赛湖冷水鱼、天源花卉、猛进牌马铃薯三大出口基地。温泉县矿产资源较为丰富，目前已探明稀有金属、贵金属、黑色金属、有色金属及非金属矿产27种，发现矿床、矿点70余处，钨矿资源储量丰富。已开采铜、铁、石灰石、石英石等矿产品，正在勘探钨、锡、钼、铅、锌等矿产资源，待勘探的有钽铌、石墨、煤等矿产资源。

2009年温泉县成功创建为自治区“旅游强县”。2011年，全县地方生产总值达到11.57亿元，增长10.7%；人均生产总值17728元，增长9.58%。固定资产投资达7.2亿元，增长60%。实现地方财政收入4664万元，增长30%。农牧民人均纯收入6085元，比上年增加790元。2012年获批“国家级生态文明示范工程试点县”。这个独具魅力的宜居新城，正在发生着翻天覆地变化，一股加快发展的持久动力和强大的合力正在形成；一幅风正气顺、人和业兴的发展画卷正在这片热土上徐徐展开；一座现代、文明、生态的旅游新城正在世人聚焦的目光中崛起，腾飞。

新疆北鲵

察哈尔纪念塔

泉城新貌

神韵七彩湖

沙湾县

全国人大常委会副委员长司马义·铁力瓦尔地一行来沙湾县视察经济社会各项工作

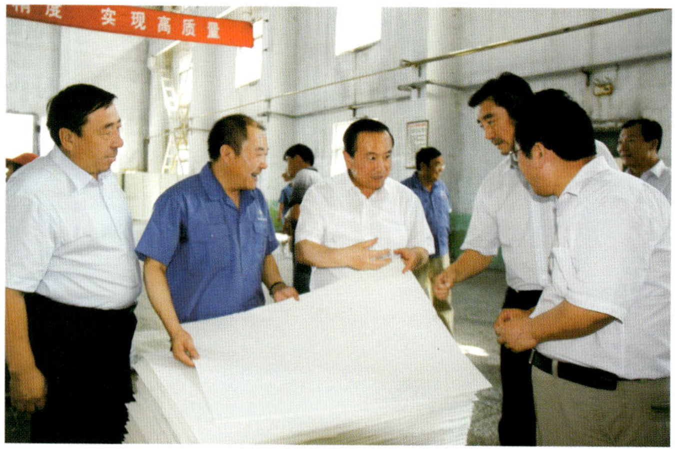

沙湾县委书记谢强与副书记、县长赛力克·乌拉孜别克陪同塔城地委书记张博在沙湾县调研

县委书记　谢强

县委副书记、县长　赛力克·乌拉孜别克

沙湾县位于天山中段北麓，准噶尔盆地南缘，312 国道、国防公路、北疆铁路、乌奎高速公路和克榆公路自东向西横穿县境，219、223、224 三条省道纵贯南北。辖区面积 1.31 万平方公里，全县地方人口 21 万人，由汉、哈萨克、回、维吾尔等 24 个民族组成，辖 9 镇、3 乡、5 个农林牧场和 2 个管理处，240 个村(队)。境内交通发达，水土、光热、矿产、旅游等资源丰富，区位优势明显，城乡基础设施完备，是自治区确定的西部大开发优先发展县市之一。

2011 年，沙湾县委、政府坚持以科学发展观为统领，全面贯彻上级党委、政府的各项决策部署，紧紧围绕“巩固提高抓一产，发展壮大强二产，突出特色活三产，统筹社会促和谐”的发展思路，把握重点，突破难点，大干快上，促进了县域经济社会健康、快速发展。全县完成生产总值 92.8 亿元，比上年增长 15.5%；三次产业结构调整为 33.2：35.4：31.4；完成地方财政一般预算收入 4.06 亿元，增长 21.7%；农牧民人均纯收入达到 13195 元，县域经济社会发展呈现出持续增长、结构优化、效益提高、后劲增强、民生改善的良好势头，实现了“十二五”发展良好开局。

县委书记谢强等领导分组慰问了部分老党员、退休党员、老八路、老干部和困难党员

浙江梦娜袜业股份有限公司扩建项目奠基仪式在沙湾县工业园区举行

“十二五”期间，沙湾县将深入贯彻落实科学发展观，以解放思想为先导，以现代文化为引领，以科技、教育为支撑，以改革创新为动力，大力实施工业强县、科教兴县、商旅活县、生态美县战略，坚持巩固提高抓一产、发展壮大强二产、突出特色抓三产、统筹社会促和谐，加速推进新型工业化、农业现代化、新型城镇化、旅游特色化，全面推进经济建设、政治建设、文化建设、社会建设以及生态文明建设和党的建设，走出一条具有沙湾特色、符合县域实际的科学跨越发展之路，不断开创沙湾县跨越式发展和长治久安的新局面。“十二五”期间，沙湾县将实现生产总值年均增长20%以上，工业增加值年均增长30%以上，地方财政收入年均增长20%以上，农牧民人均纯收入2万元以上，率先在全疆基本实现农牧业现代化、率先建成自治区经济社会协调发展先进县、率先实现全面建设小康社会。

新疆沙湾首届大盘美食文化节盛大开幕

鹿角湾旅游区

丝路明珠 杞都新韵——精河

县委书记　尤占军

县委副书记、县长　乌玛尔江·努合曼

精河县位于新疆西北部，天山支脉婆罗科努山北麓，准噶尔盆地西南边缘，隶属博尔塔拉蒙古自治州，是古“丝绸之路”北道重镇。它以“精河河”得名，是一个多民族聚居的地区，主要由汉、维吾尔、蒙古、哈萨克、回等26个民族组成，现有人口14万人（含兵团），总面积11187平方公里。现辖两镇、三乡、一场，境内驻有新疆生产建设兵团农五师所属的83、91两个团场。

精河县地处北疆交通要冲，312国道和第二亚欧大陆桥穿境而过，处在两个国家一类口岸——阿拉山口口岸和霍尔果斯口岸出境铁路、公路交汇处。经公路西至伊犁268公里，东至新疆首府乌鲁木齐423公里，距乌鲁木齐国际机场400公里，距博乐飞机场仅有70公里，至霍尔果斯250余公里；经铁路至阿拉山口口岸75公里，至霍尔果斯口岸286公里。独特的交通优势使精河成为新疆东联西出、西进东出的黄金枢纽。中哈石油管道、西气东输二线和即将建设的西气东输三线天然气管道自境内穿过，从而使精河成为国家能源大通道的重要枢纽。

精河县经济以农为主，农牧结合，工业门类齐全。拥有丰富的棉花、枸杞等农产品资源和石灰石、盐、硭硝等非金属矿产资源，是“全国优质棉基地县”和“自治区出口棉基地县”。精河枸杞素有“红玛瑙”之称，赢得了“精河枸杞甲天下”的美誉。1998年被国家农业部命名为“中国枸杞之乡”，2001年“精河枸杞”被认定为“新疆农业名牌产品”，2002年“寿国牌”枸杞被中国经济林协会认定为中国名优经济林产品，同年“精河枸杞”被国家工商局认定为“原产地证明商标”，成为精河枸杞产业发展史上的一个新的里程碑。2005年“精河枸杞”荣获“新疆著名商标”称号。目前全县枸杞种植面积已达10.7万亩，6500亩枸杞基地通过有机认证，成功研制了枸杞油、枸杞酒、枸杞红色素、枸杞胶

新疆精河“那达慕”草原节

首届枸杞交易会开幕式

囊、枸杞叶茶等系列产品，远销美国、东南亚、港澳台。

2011年精河地区生产总值完成38.03亿元，比2010年增长11.7%，其中：第一产业增加值20.13亿元，增长11.8%；第二产业增加值6.94亿元，增长17.2%；第三产业增加值10.96亿元，增长8.4%。2006年至2011年，精河地区生产总值总量在5年期间连续跨跃20亿元、30亿元2个新台阶，2011年精河地区生产总值比2006年增长79.28%，期间年均增长12.39%。从2006年至2011年，人均生产总值从9556元增长到26425元，增长68.98%，年均增长11.1%，2011年全县三次产业结构为56:16:28。

精河宛如一条蜿蜒腾飞的巨龙，发生着翻天覆地的喜人变化。按照县委的总体部署，紧紧抓住中央新疆工作座谈会和全国对口支援新疆加快发展的历史机遇，坚持资源开发可持续、生态环境可持续的原则，大力推进“城镇化带动”、“口岸强县”和“民生优先”战略，以新型城镇化为载体，以新型工业化和农牧业现代化为产业支撑，全面协调推进经济建设、政治建设、文化建设、社会建设和生态文明建设，努力实现经济社会跨越式发展和长治久安，为实现“十二五”规划各项目标任务开好头、起好步。精河已经步入经济社会发展的战略机遇期，面对新的形势、新的要求，全县各族干部群众，将深入贯彻科学发展观，进一步打牢全县各族人民的思想基础，凝聚全县各族人民的智慧力量，同心同德，团结奋进，努力把精河打造成为天山北坡经济带上一颗璀璨的明珠！

八家户中华寿桃长势喜人

设施农业花卉长势喜人

有机西瓜

新疆青少年足球赛北疆片区决赛

第五届环湖赛

枸杞产品

奋进发展的乌什县

县委书记　申海涛

县长　吐尔洪·阿不拉

乌什县位于塔里木盆地西北边缘的天山南麓，东西长约 139.5 千米，南北宽约 124.5 千米，行政区总面积 9082 平方千米，边境线长 153 千米。全县辖八乡一镇，下设 5 个社区居民委员会，108 个村民委员会。总人口 21.75 万人，其中农业人口 17.99 万人。县内居住有维吾尔、汉、回、柯尔克孜等 23 个少数民族，少数民族占 94.3%，汉族占 5.7%，是全疆 32 个少数民族边境县之一，也是国家扶贫重点县。

2011 年，在地委、行署的正确领导下，县委团结带领全县各族党员干部群众，坚持以科学发展观统领经济社会发展全局，深入推进“特色农业和劳务输出富民，矿产及优势资源开发转换强县，生态旅游及口岸开发兴边”经济发展战略，抓住自治区加大对贫困县扶持力度和浙江衢州对口支援的大好机遇，坚持把“富民”作为首要发展目标，不断壮大“林果、畜牧、劳务”三大富民支柱产业，坚持把加快发展“矿业、水电开发和农副产品加工”为三大强县主导产业，新型工业化水平快速跃升。全县招商引资工作富有成效，全年新签约招商引资项目 6 个，签约金额 23.02 亿元，到位资金 2.39 亿元。项目援疆工作成效显著，全年实施对口援疆项目 30 个，总投资 6.9 亿元，其中援疆资金 2.92 亿元，2011 年累计完成投资 6.66 亿元，城乡群众生产生活条件明显改善。

2011 年，全县完成地方生产总值 153590 万元，同比增长 18.1%，其中：第一产业增加值 59198 万元，同比增长 10%；第二产业增加值 19199 万元，同比增长 26.9%；第三产业增加值 75193 万元，同比增长 23.4%。完成全社会固定资产投资 9.83 亿元，同比增长 88.15%；完成社会消费品零售总额 11173.6 万元，同比增长 12.75%；完成财政一般预算收入 6745 万元，同比增长 64.3%；城镇居民可支配收入达到 14502 元，同比增长 39.2%；农牧民人均纯收入达到 4007 元，同比增长 14.4%。全县综合经济实力迈上新台阶，各项社会事业全面发展。

杏子

国庆中学

浙江省衢州市援建“衢州新村”

富民安居新村

玛尔江湖水上乐园

阿图什市

克州党委副书记、市委书记　刘军海

阿图什市委副书记、市长　亚力坤·吐尔地

阿图什市在阿扎克乡库木萨克设施农业产业区举行江苏昆山——阿图什戈壁产业科技示范园项目奠基仪式

阿图什市位于新疆维吾尔自治区西南部，天山南麓，塔里木盆地西缘，西与吉尔吉斯坦共和国交界，边境线长120多公里。市境东西长241公里，南北宽136公里，全市总面积约1.55万平方公里。

阿图什市于1986年经国务院批准撤县设市，辖7乡2个街道办事处，是克孜勒苏自治州的首府，为克州政治、经济、文化中心。全市总人口25.09万人，有维吾尔、柯尔克孜、汉等11个常住民族。其中：维吾尔族19.82万人，占78.99%；柯尔克孜族2.92万人，占11.64%，汉族2.27万人，占9.0%。

阿图什成矿条件好，矿藏资源十分丰富，已探明钒、钛、铜、锰、铁、铅、锌、磷、大理石、石灰石、冰洲石等32种矿产。已经探明的有皮羌钒钛磁铁矿、霍什布拉克铅锌矿、奇吉尔布拉克铜锌矿、艾西曼铜矿、塞斯布拉克金矿5大金属矿，此外还有皮羌含磷砂矿、销尔库勒与吐孜苏盖提湖盐矿、峡口石灰岩矿和皮羌大理石矿4大非金属矿。野生动植物分布区广，种类繁多，共有60余种列入国家重点保护，有棕熊、仙鹤、猞猁、雪豹、长尾雉、天鹅、青羊、盘羊等十多种。还有党参、掌参、独活、阿魏、野红花等珍贵的药用植物。

境内旅游资源丰富，人文景观独具特色，阿图什市辖区内有阿图什大峡谷、摩尔佛塔、哈拉峻巴格苏盖提古柳林、哈拉峻乡盐湖、阿图什天门、赛福鼎·艾则孜故居等等。阿图什特色瓜果四季飘香。这里是闻名遐迩的稀有果品——无花果之乡，是荣获中国农业博览会金奖的木纳格葡萄原产地，更有甜瓜骄子——卡拉库赛瓜，群杏之王——胡安纳杏，是名符其实的瓜果之乡。

2011年，阿图什市完成地区生产总值23.29亿元，比上年增长19.0%；完成固定资产投资14.21亿元，增长52.8%；地方财政收入1.62亿元，增长53.8%。其中：一般预算收入达到1.48亿元，增长48.5%；社会消费品零售总额达到5.76亿元，增长14.9%；农林牧渔业总产值7.62亿元，增长8.6%；工业总产值11.66亿元，增长84.9%；农牧民人均纯收入达到2690元，增长27.4%。

阿图什市是一片希望的热土，是一块尚待开发的宝地。随着西部大开发战略的全面实施和第三条亚欧大陆桥的即将开通，阿图什市以得天独厚的口岸、资源优势日益显示出广阔的发展前景。市委、市人民政府将以最优惠的政策、最优质的服务、最宽松的环境，热忱欢迎国内外各界有识之士来阿图什市大展宏图，创立伟业，共同开发、建设阿图什市。

天门风光

哈拉峻巴格苏盖提古柳林

无花果

木纳格葡萄

十二木卡姆的故乡　中国巴旦姆之乡

中央政治局委员、上海市委书记俞正声在自治区党委书记张春贤等领导的陪同下考察莎车教育工作

自治区党委常委、纪委书记宋爱荣等领导考察莎车县城市建设

莎车县位于新疆西南边陲，昆仑山北麓，帕米尔高原南缘，全县总面积8955.65平方公里，辖29个乡镇、491个行政村、25个社区，全县户籍人口84万。

莎车始建于西周初年，先后称为莎车国、渠沙国、叶尔羌汗王国，至今已有3000多年的历史，是人类口头和非物质文化遗产——十二木卡姆的故乡，中国巴旦姆之乡。

近年来，莎车县牢固树立只有努力才能改变，只要努力就能改变的理念，全力打造喀什南部中心城市和"双百"工程(工业产值100亿元、农业产值100亿元)，加速推进新型工业化、农业现代化和新型城镇化进程，深入实施招商引资"一号工程"，加快工业园区建设，着力打造"九大基地"；坚定不移加快发展"世界少有、中国唯一"的巴旦姆产业，推动了县域经济社会快速发展。2011年全县实现生产总值48.02亿元，全社会固定资产投资31.1亿元，地方一般财政预算收入2.4亿元。

今后，莎车县委、县人民政府将紧扣跨越式发展和长治久安两大历史任务，继续加快喀什南部中心城市建设，大力实施"双百"工程，加速推进"三化"进程，深入实施"农业稳县、工业强县、商贸富县、旅游活县、科教兴县、文化塑县"和"变人大县为人力资源强县"战略，力强现代农业新基础、力推新型工业化新突破、力保民生水平新提升、力促社会事业新进步、力创团结稳定新局面，力争2015年，实现全县生产总值136亿元，工业增加值30亿元，地方财政一般预算收入5.31亿元，奋力推进莎车跨越式发展和长治久安。

莎车县恒昌冶炼有限公司制酸系统

莎车县现代农业示范园

莎车县

喀什地委委员、县委书记何利民和县委副书记、县长艾海提沙依提查看巴旦姆管理

大力弘扬两姆(十二木卡姆、中国巴旦姆)文化;图为莎车首届巴旦姆采摘节

莎车县大力发展以色素辣椒、豇豆、万寿菊、甜瓜为主的特色农业

莎车县坚定不移打造世界少有、中国唯一的巴旦姆产业,十二五末将建成100万亩全国最大的巴旦姆生产基地

跨越发展的新和县

地区领导视察我县民族乐器制造作坊

自治区冬博会上，县委书记马国强参加屯田遗址(汉唐时期)最大规模县——新和县授牌”仪式。图为县委书记马国强接过上海大世界基尼斯之最证书

县委副书记、县长艾买尔江·依明在亚欧博览会上发放宣传册

新和县位于天山南麓，塔里木盆地北缘，东与库车相望，南与沙雅相连，西与温宿相交，北与拜城相邻，南疆铁路、314 国道横跨县城，距库车新飞机场 20 公里，交通非常便利。全县东西长 136 公里，5817.83 平方公里，辖 6 乡、2 镇、1 个国有农场，总人口 17.21 万人，有维吾尔、汉、回、哈萨克、满、土家等 22 个民族。其中，维吾尔族 15.92 万人，占总人口的 92.5%，汉族 1.24 万人，占总人口的 7.20%，是一个以维吾尔族为主体的多民族聚居县。

新和县地处古“丝绸之路”，享有“汉唐重镇”、“龟兹故里”、“班超府治”的美誉，境内有历史文化遗产 40 余处，其中通古孜巴什古城遗址和托乎拉克艾肯石窟是第六批全国重点文物保护单位，塔什艾日克乡被文化部授予“中国民间艺术之乡”称号，新和已成为龟兹旅游的理想目的地。

新和县水土光热条件得天独厚，是国家优质棉基地县，也是自治区粮食生产基地之一，盛产棉花、小麦、玉米、瓜果等。全县已形成年产 108 万担优质皮棉的生产能力，棉纺、种子产业发展潜力巨大；以红枣、核桃为主的特色林果面积达 30 万亩，红枣、核桃等产品远销国内外。矿产资源主要有石油、天然气，境内英买力、羊塔克、玉东三个区块为“西气东输”主气源地，已布探井 101 口，天然气地质储量 656.28 亿立方米、凝析油及原油地质储量 2600 万吨。位于境内的英买力油气群年产天然气 25 亿立方米、凝析油 50 万吨、液化气 4 万吨。

2011 年，完成地方生产总值 20.67 亿元，地方财政一般预算收入 4.19 亿元，全社会固定资产投资 12.1 亿元，城镇居民人均可支配收入 15230 元，农牧民人均纯收入 7270 元(不含农场)。

新和县是一块正在开发的宝地，勤劳朴实的新和各族人民热情欢迎四海宾朋、五湖客商及各界有识之士共同开发、共同建设、携手共绘新和经济发展的宏伟蓝图。

新和县境内的英买里油气田

新和县健鹰纺织有限责任公司生产车间

丰收的红枣——新疆天娇红农业科技发展有限公司红枣凉晒基地

中国民间艺术之乡——塔什艾日克乡维吾尔弹唱老人

新和县出土文物——汉归义羌长印

金果玉叶 铜铁之城——叶城

县委书记　李国平

县委书记李国平(左四),县委副书记、县长阿迪力·尤努斯（右一）为叶城县宗郎水库—城区引水工程竣工通水剪彩

叶城,地处祖国西北边陲,是古丝路南道重镇,位于喀喇昆仑山北麓,与克什米尔接壤,边境线长80多公里。县域总面积3.1万平方公里,辖26个乡镇(场区),总人口50万余人,素有中国核桃之乡、石榴之乡、玉石之乡、歌舞之乡美誉。

叶城系古西域三十六国之西夜、子合国,文化底蕴深厚,有棋盘千佛洞、锡提亚古城、宗朗灵泉等历史文化古迹;叶城风光雄奇,有万山之祖喀喇昆仑、探险天堂乔格里峰、一日历四季的新藏千里文明运输线和果萨斯原始森林公园等自然景观,是新疆"五区三线"旅游重点的必经之地;叶城资源秉赋,蕴藏着丰富的石油、天然气、铅、锌、铜、铁、玉石等30多种资源,现藏于北京故宫大型玉雕"大禹治水"玉料产自叶城密尔岱山;叶城区位优势明显,地处新疆喀什、和田、西藏阿里两区三地交汇处,是国家首批对外开放边境县,现建有"轻工业园、商贸物流园、化工园和重工业园"为特色的"一区四园";叶城农业优势独特,现已形成50多万亩薄皮核桃、20多万亩优质杏、10万亩大籽石榴的特色林果,2.1万座2.5万亩设施农业,22万亩多熟高效田,100万头牲畜1000万只家禽的农业产业格局;叶城安定和谐,在稳疆兴疆的历史进程中,党政军警民始终并肩携手,构筑起一道道坚不可摧的"钢铁长城"。

墨玉

铅、锌、铜矿

农副产品深加工——核桃麻糖和核桃油

县委书记　陈远华

县委副书记、县长　阿力甫·阿不都力米提

创新发展的洛浦县

洛浦县位于塔里木盆地南缘，喀喇昆仑山北麓，东接策勒县，南接和田县，西与和田市、和田县、墨玉县相邻，北入塔克拉玛干沙漠与阿拉尔市、阿瓦提县接壤。县人民政府驻地洛浦镇，全县总面积14104平方公里，其中山地占10.4 %，绿洲占5.6 %，沙漠占84 %，耕地面积33.99万亩。现辖1镇8乡，一个街道办事处，207个村委会，9个社区，全县62549户、总人口24.06万人，有维吾尔、汉、哈萨克、回、蒙古、锡伯、满、藏、土家、瑶、彝等12个民族，其中维吾尔族占98%。

2011年，是全面贯彻落实中央新疆工作座谈会精神、实施“十二五”规划的开局之年。一年来，洛浦县在地委、行署的坚强正确领导下，始终坚持以科学发展观为指导，认真贯彻落实党的十七届五中、六中全会和自治区党委七届九次、十次全委(扩大)会议及八次党代会精神，紧紧围绕“富民强县固边”战略，扎实推进政治、经济、文化、社会和党的建设，全力维护社会稳定，为实现洛浦跨越式发展和长治久安打下了良好的基础。

2011年，全县实现生产总值13.02亿元，按可比价计算比上年增长10.8%。其中，第一产业增加值4.18亿元，增长3.8%；第二产业增加值2.33亿元，增长43.2%；第三产业增加值6.51亿元，增长6.9%。三次产业比例为32.12：17.87：50.01。人均生产总值5410元。固定资产投资11.87亿元，增长69.6%。财政一般预算收入5938万元，增长26.7%。社会消费品零售总额1.25亿元，同比增长14.3%。农牧民人均纯收入3428元，增长16.4%。年末畜牧存栏头数51.11万头(只)，增长2.0%。

县城夜景

阿其克农家度假

富民安居房

新建天山水泥厂

自治区党委书记张春贤参观文化中心展览馆

自治区党委副书记、组织部长韩勇考察和静展览馆

聚焦和静发展 谱写辉煌篇章

50万吨矿微粉生产线竣工剪彩仪式

州富民安居富民兴牧现场会

和静县位于新疆中部，天山南麓，巴音郭楞蒙古自治州西北部，是巴州蒙古族的主要聚居地。县域总面积近4万平方公里。县辖5镇、7乡、7个国营农牧场。境内驻有农二师3个团场、4个团级以上部队等自治区、自治州直属单位40多个。全县总人口25万，由汉、蒙古、维吾尔、回等29个民族组成。基本县情可概括为：一是地理位置重要。和静是新疆的地理中心，是连接南北疆的交通要地，国道216、217、218线、南疆铁路横贯县境，周边有库尔勒、乌鲁木齐、那拉提、库车等机场，与乌鲁木齐、昌吉、伊犁等地15个县市相毗邻，是世界上接壤县市最多的县。二是自然资源富集。已探明的具有开采价值的矿产29种127处，优势矿产有铁、铜、金、铅锌、菱镁、石英石、大理岩等。全县地表水年径流量58亿立方米，规划建设的开都河梯级电站装机容量达220万千瓦。旅游资源及其类型十分丰富，主要景区（点）有国家级天鹅自然保护区、九曲十八弯、巩乃斯国家森林公园、巴伦台黄庙、天山石林、阿尔先温泉等。三是文化底蕴厚重。震惊中外的人类历史上最后一次大迁徙，东归英雄土尔扈特的后裔，就生活在这片富饶的土地上，他们有着"音乐民族"、"诗歌民族"之美誉。

近年来，在自治州党委、政府的坚强领导下，全面落实科学发展观，紧紧围绕打造自治州副中心城市目标，深入推进做大县城和文化产业改革试点工作，统筹城乡一体化发展，加速推进新型工业化、农

金特钢铁股份有限公司二期技改竣工投产仪式

新疆金特钢铁股份有限公司生产车间

城貌

牧业现代化和新型城镇化建设，经济社会各项事业取得长足发展。成功争创了国家卫生县城、全国“五五”普法先进县、全国老龄工作先进县、全国养老服务示范单位、自治区平安县、自治区旅游强县、自治区计划生育优质服务先进县、自治区创业型先进县、自治区生态园林县城等荣誉，和静工业园区升格为自治区级工业园区，巴音布鲁克景区创建为国家4A景区，国家科技进步先进县、自治区精神文明建设先进县、双拥模范县(城)通过复验。2010年完成生产总值43.9亿元，比上年增长11.6%；完成固定资产投资22.5亿元，增长27.1%；完成全口径财政收入4.88亿元，增长21%，其中地方财政收入3.16亿元，增长41.7%，财政支出10.6亿元，增长36%；城镇居民人均可支配收入达13607元，增长10%；农牧民人均纯收入达到8201元，增长23.9%。

中央新疆工作座谈会开启了和静县大开发、大建设、大发展的序幕。县委十一届七次全委(扩大)会议提出了“十二五”时期经济社会发展思路和奋斗目标，即：到“十二五”末，全县生产总值达到100亿元(现价)，力争突破110亿元；地方财政收入达到9亿元，力争突破10亿元；五年累计完成固定资产投资136亿元，力争突破150亿元；农牧民人均纯收入突破10000元；城镇化率达到57%，力争突破60%，努力把和静打造成为巴州经济强县、文化大县、旅游名县和南北疆交通枢纽。

立足新起点，抢抓新机遇，树立新标杆，促进新跨越是各族干部群众共同的期盼和愿望。和静这片投资的热土，真诚希望八方宾朋齐聚和静，共谋发展，谱写和静明天更加辉煌的篇章，创造天山脚下新的人间奇迹！

第二届中国天鹅湖国际马术耐力赛

和静县阳光之路滑雪场

察汗乌苏水电站——水库大坝

和静县天山金特矿微粉有限公司

凯宏矿业诺尔湖铁矿100万吨铁精粉厂剪彩仪式

且末县

且末塔中油田生产区

卡特里西铜锌矿开发

舒适的农村安居富民小区

且末县位于塔里木盆地东南缘，昆仑山、阿尔金山北麓，全县总面积14.025万平方公里，辖15个乡（镇）场，总人口8万余人。

县内石油、矿产、水土光热资源丰富。石油储量20亿吨。境内7条较大河流，地表水年径流量18亿立方米，地下水储量8亿立方米。有198万亩优质可垦荒地。有铜、锌、铁、镍、玉石、黄金、云母、石棉等40余种矿产。风能光热资源开发前景广阔。

“十二五”期间，且末县将加快建设“矿业且末、红枣且末、生态且末、美丽且末、幸福且末”。

矿业且末——把矿业作为跨越式发展的第一推动力。全面加快矿产资源勘探开发步伐。加快卡特里西铜锌矿60万吨、迪木那里克铁矿300万吨选矿厂和120万吨球团厂建设。

红枣且末——把红枣作为农民增收的支柱产业和重中之重加快发展。加快有机红枣基地建设，全力打造生态健康和高端有机品牌，力争到2015年全县红枣种植面积突破20万亩。

生态且末——把生态建设摆在更加突出的位置，牢固树立环保优先、生态立县的理念。坚持走“以生态产业养生态工程”的可持续发展路子，加快推进30万亩防沙治沙生态工程建设，2012年高标准完成治沙任务4万亩，建成南疆乃至全疆发展沙产业的示范点。

美丽且末——把县城建成宜业宜居、生态良好、充满活力的现代文明城市。到2015年全面完成县城10个规划区棚户区改造，使县城建成区面积达到10平方公里，使城乡面貌焕然一新，让且末既美又好。

幸福且末——把改善民生作为一切工作的出发点，加快定居兴牧工程建设，让定居牧民有“一套房、一座圈、一群畜、一块地、一个园”，到2013年全面完成农村危旧房改造和牧区1700户牧民定居任务，加快教育、卫生、医疗、文化事业发展，确保社会和谐稳定和长治久安。

通过努力，到“十二五”末，全县生产总值达25亿元，年均增长18.5%；财政收入达5亿元，年均增长21.6%；地方固定资产投资总额达15亿元，年均增长24.6%；城镇居民人均可支配收入达23600元，年均增长13.4%；农牧民人均纯收入达15760元，年均增长14.5%。

优美的昆仑广场

丰收的喜悦

河东肉苁蓉种植基地

塞外江南 博湖县

县委书记杨伟辉（右二）陪同自治区、州领导调研旅游工作

县委书记　杨伟辉

县委副书记、县长　那生巴图

博湖县位于新疆焉耆盆地东南部，开都河下游。县城博湖镇距乌鲁木齐市430公里，1971年建县，因境内有全国最大的内陆淡水湖——博斯腾湖而得县名。全县辖5乡2镇，驻县单位有巴州种畜场、农二师25团、27团种马场和河南油田塔里木石油勘探公司博湖基地等。县域总人口6.1万人，由汉、蒙、维、回等20个民族组成。总面积3808平方公里，其中水域面积1646平方公里。博斯腾湖水灌溉着孔雀河流域万顷良田，养育着巴州各族人民，被喻为巴州的"母亲湖"。

博湖县水草丰美，资源丰富，气候温和湿润，土地平坦肥沃，被誉为鱼肥、草茂、粮多的"塞外江南"。县域内拥有丰富的水产、芦苇、旅游、特色农副产品、石油天然气等自然资源。主要矿产有石油天然气、芒硝、泥炭、食盐等，石油储量占焉耆盆地储量的70%左右。博斯腾湖有32个鱼类品种，是新疆最大的渔业生产基地，有10个水产品种和150万亩水域通过国家有机水产品产地认证，是全国最大的有机鱼生产水面。环湖芦苇面积60余万亩，芦苇年储量20余万吨，是全国四大苇区之一。博斯腾湖有全国最大的野生睡莲群和种类数量众多的候鸟，自然风光秀丽，是国家级风景名胜区、国家4A级旅游景区、西部大开发新疆十大风景名胜旅游区、新疆旅游强县。2011年，县域地区生产总值14.8亿元，地方固定资产投资7.4亿元，地方财政收入8260万元，农牧民人均纯收入8568元。

绿色新生态　魅力新伊吾

自治区党委书记张春贤、地委书记郭连山在淖毛湖镇明光村视察安居富民工程

自治区主席努尔·白克力、地委书记郭连山到伊吾县四十天保卫战烈士陵园祭奠烈士

2011年是“十二五”的开局之年。一年来，我们在自治区党委、政府的亲切关怀下，在地委、行署的正确领导下，在河南省的无私援助下，深入贯彻落实中央新疆工作座谈会及自治区党委七届九次、十次全委（扩大）会议、自治区第八次党代会和地委委员（扩大）会议精神，围绕“五个率先”发展目标，坚持“六大战略”，着力打造“五大基地”，培育“八大产业”，坚持一手抓改革发展、一手抓团结稳定，狠抓落实，经济社会发展取得新成绩，社会各项事业取得新进步，人民生活得到新改善。

全年实现生产总值（GDP）15.18亿元，按可比价格计算，比上年增长16.9%。其中，第一产业增长10.9%，第二产业增长20.4%，第三产业增长16.1%。三次产业结构为22.4∶51.5∶26.1。人均生产总值67143元，增长15.3%。全社会固定资产投资完成47亿元，增长11.9%；地方财政收入15806万元，增长33.8%；城镇居民人均可支配收入17525元，增长16.3%；农牧民人均纯收入7238元，增长25.4%。先后荣获全国科普示范县、科技进步先进县、自治区文明县城、自治区旅游强县等荣誉。圆满承办了中国科协“科普富民兴边”工作推进会、国际沙漠休闲运动会、哈密地区“兴边富民行动”十年总结暨现场观摩交流会、地区人口计生系统大比武等大型活动。

2012年，我们会深入贯彻落实党的十七届六中全会、自治区第八次党代会、自治区党委经济工作会议和地委委员（扩大）会议精神，坚持以经济建设为中心、科学发展为主题、现代文化为引领、资源和生态可持续为前提，加快推进新型工业化、农牧业现代化和新型城镇化，不断开创伊吾跨越式发展和长治久安新局面，以经济社会发展的优异成绩向党的十八大献礼。

巴里坤哈萨克自治县

县委书记陈毅士检查海子沿乡定居兴牧工程建设情况

县委副书记、县长叶尔江在奎苏镇富民安居工程现场调研

三塘湖百万千瓦级风电基地

巴里坤哈萨克自治县成立于1954年9月30日，地处新疆东北部，东邻伊吾县，南接哈密市，西毗木垒哈萨克自治县，北与蒙古国接壤，是全国三个哈萨克自治县之一，也是国家扶贫开发工作重点县，是新疆典型的边境县、高寒县、易灾县，2006年被国家确定为五类地区。境内中蒙边界线长309公里，设有国家一类季节性开放口岸--老爷庙口岸，是新疆与蒙古国发展边贸的重要开放口岸之一。

巴里坤行政区划总面积3.84万平方公里，县域总人口10.24万人，由汉、哈萨克、维吾尔、蒙古等13个民族构成，其中哈萨克族占35%，其他少数民族占2%。县辖15个乡镇场区、46个行政村。境内驻有69330部队、兵团农十三师红山农场和哈密地区伊吾马场。

巴里坤地形特征为“三山夹两盆”，有“新疆缩影”之称。巴里坤地处亚欧大陆腹地，属温带大陆性冷凉干旱气候区，平均海拔1650米，冬季严寒，夏季凉爽，光照充足，四季不分明。极端最高气温35℃，极端最低气温-43.6℃，年均气温1℃。无霜期98-104天。年降水量220毫米左右，蒸发量1638毫米。

巴里坤可利用土地资源丰富，有可耕地50.4万亩，其中基本农田36.6万亩，主要农作物有马铃薯、大麦、饲用玉米、小麦、晚熟哈密瓜等。有天然草场2866万亩，可利用草场1998万亩，主要畜种有牛、羊、马、驴、骆驼等，是东疆地区重要的畜牧业生产基地，1996年被自治区确定为牧业县。有湿地134万亩；林地123万亩，森林覆盖率1.45%。

巴里坤矿产资源丰富，种类多、品位高、储量大，现已探明煤、石油、芒硝、黄金、膨润土等30余种。其中：煤炭探明千米以浅资源量614.8亿吨，主要分布在三塘湖煤田（探明千米以浅资源量585亿吨）和巴里坤西部煤田（预测千米以浅资源量312亿吨，探明资源量29.8亿吨），是“疆煤东运”、“疆电东输”的重要基地之一；芒硝资源净储量4893万吨，其主要产品硫化碱占全国市场份额的25%；石油资源预测油气资源当量9.3亿吨，被国土资源部油气储量评审办公室验收确认为亿吨级油田。

巴里坤古称蒲类，是古丝绸之路北新道进入新疆的第一重镇。人文景观有国家重点文物保护单位大河唐城，自治区重点文物保护单位兰州湾子古遗址群、汉满两城、烽火台和地藏寺、仙姑庙等8处，县级文物保护单位70余处；自然风光有全国四大鸣沙山之一的巴里坤鸣沙山、新疆三大草原之一的巴里坤草原以及新疆有名的怪石山和巴里坤湖等。现有国家AAAA级景区1处、AA级景区2处、A级景区1处。先后被自治区命名为历史文化名城、旅游强县。

“双语”幼儿园

城东新区保障性住房

海子沿乡定居兴牧

人间天堂那拉提

哈萨克舞

迎娶解忧公主

那拉提草原

在新疆浩瀚的大漠中，那拉提犹如一块镶嵌在黄绸缎上的翡翠，光彩夺目，她集草原、雪山、森林、河流、湖泊、瀑布、温泉等各种自然景观于一体，保持了天山雄浑、优美的原始风格。蓝天、白云、雪山、云杉、草原、银色河流、毡房，景观层次错落有致，组合丰富多彩，因自然生态景观和人文景观独具特色，而被誉为“天山深处的绿岛”、“绿色家园”、“人间天堂”。

那拉提景区地处天山腹地，伊犁河谷东端，规划总面积 960 平方公里，东北至 217 国道乔尔玛与尼勒克唐布拉风景区；东至和静县；东南至巴音布鲁克交界处；南到那拉提山南麓纵深处；西至那拉提镇塔亚苏村牧业大桥；北至阿吾热勒山。景区三面环山，巩乃斯河蜿蜒流过，可谓是“三面青山列翠屏，腰围玉带河纵横”。这里居住着占全国人口十分之一，以热情好客、能歌善舞而著称的天山儿女——哈萨克族，至今仍保留着古朴浓郁的民俗风情和丰富悠久的草原文化。景区平均海拔 1800 米，年降雨量平均 880 毫米，夏季平均气温 20 摄氏度。是一个集雪山、冰川、森林、沟谷、草甸、河流、瀑布及草原历史文化和哈萨克族民俗风情于一体的旅游休闲度假胜地。

那拉提景区属于典型的高山河谷草原，资源丰富，景观多变。景区内视野开阔，风景层次突出，随着海拔的升高，垂直景观带明显。可谓一山一景，一景一坡，车随景转，景景如画。同一景观站在不同角度会有不同的视觉感受，正所谓“千峰万峰同一峰，一峰去青一峰浓；千松万松同一松，一松稍墨一松红”。

那拉提风景区是伊犁旅游的龙头景区，也是新疆著名景区之一。2004 年被评为自治区级风景名胜区，2005 年 6 月，景区通过 ISO9001 国际质量体系、ISO14001 环境管理体系和 OSHMS18001 职业安全健康管理体系认证；同年 10 月，以那拉提草原为代表的伊犁草原被中国国家地理杂志社评为全国六大最美的草原之一，12 月被国家旅游局授予国家 AAAA 级风景区。2006 年 8 月，被中国保护消费者基金会评为“全国文明诚信(窗口)单位”；2007 年初被评为“中国最佳旅游目的地”；2008 年 12 月，被评为自治区级文明风景旅游区，2009 年 12 月，被评为自治区旅游行业优秀企业；2010 年，被评为“国际休闲度假旅游目的地”；2010 年 4 月，被评为“伊犁知名商标”；2010 年 4 月，被评为全国文明诚信窗口单位；2011 年 1 月，被评为国家 AAAAA 级景区。

中华联合财产保险股份有限公司
新疆分公司

财政部驻新疆专员办莅临公司检查

中华联合财产保险股份有限公司是经中国保监会批准，于 2006 年 12 月由中华联合保险控股股份有限公司发起设立的全国性财产保险公司。其前身是由国家财政部、农业部专项拨款，新疆生产建设兵团组建成立的新疆兵团保险公司，成立于 1986 年 7 月 15 日，是我国第二家具有独立法人资格的国有独资保险公司。2010 年 12 月，为了适应新的发展形势，公司总部从乌鲁木齐迁至北京。2012 年 3 月，经中国保监会核准同意，公司注册资本金增加至 75 亿元人民币。

截至 2011 年底，中华保险已在全国设立了 23 家省级分公司、1900 多家各级经营机构，共有员工近 3 万名。2011 年，公司实现保费收入 209 亿元，位居国内产险市场第四位，各项主要经营指标名列行业前茅。

公司总部从乌鲁木齐迁至北京后，于 2011 年 2 月 24 日成立了中华保险新疆分公司以管理原总公司直接管辖的新疆各地州分公司。2011 年，新疆分公司实现保费收入 18.38 亿元，市场规模位居全疆 15 家财险公司第 2 位，为新疆经济社会跨越式发展和长治久安做出了积极贡献。

中华财险新疆分公司与安华农险内蒙古分公司交流

公司的业务经营范围涵盖非寿险业务的各个领域，包括机动车辆保险、企业财产保险、家庭财产保险、工程保险、船舶保险、货物运输保险、责任保险、信用保证保险、种植业保险、养殖业保险以及短期健康保险和意外伤害保险等。近年又适时开发推出了电话营销专用车险等符合市场需求的新险种，还开发了一系列适合农村市场的涉农险种，目前经营的险种已达 400 多个。

公司始终践行“服务至上、信守承诺、回报社会”的服务宗旨，遵循“稳健、创新、持续、高效”的经营理念，勇于承担社会责任，通过诚信服务赢得市场，通过提供全方位的保险保障服务社会经济发展大局，得到了社会各界的广泛认可。公司曾连续四年入选“中国企业 500 强”和“中国服务业企业 500 强”；先后多次被授予“国家 A 级守信企业”、“诚信服务消费者满意单位”、“诚信经营示范单位”等称号；多次获得“亚洲品牌 500 强”、“亚洲品牌成长 100 强”、“中国 500 最具价值品牌”、“中国保险行业最具影响力品牌”、“中国最受信赖的财险公司”等荣誉。

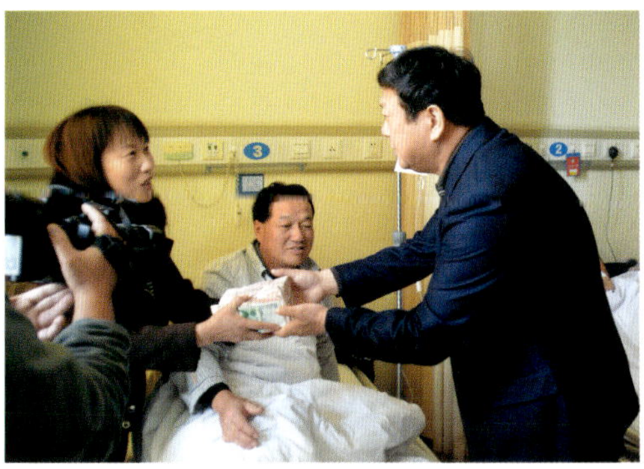

款款情深　爱心捐助

站在新的历史起点，公司将以市场为导向，以客户为中心，以改革创新为驱动，着力实施“二次创业”发展战略，开拓创新、勇担责任，为政府分忧，为企业、家庭解难，努力为新疆经济社会发展和长治久安做出更大的贡献。

车险集中拆检定损提升业务品质

文艺活动展示风姿

新疆大明矿业集团股份有限公司

XINJIANG DAMING MINING GROUP CO.,LTD

资源转化效率最佳的实践者

安全标准化启动仪式

机械化——3.5 米卷扬机控制室

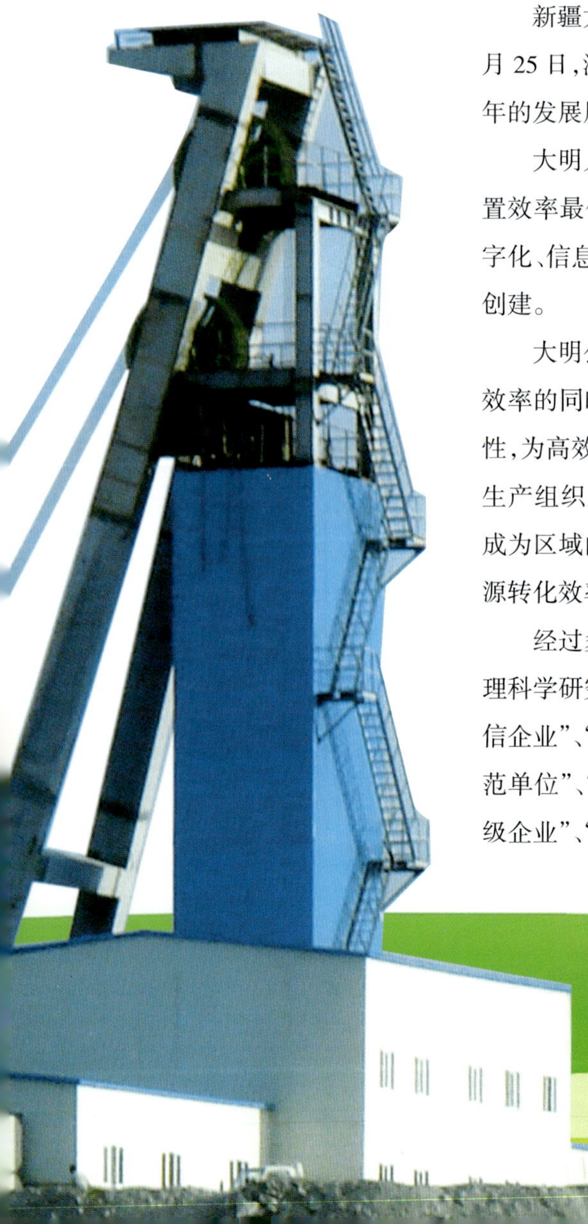

新疆大明矿业集团股份有限公司(以下简称“大明矿业”或“公司”)成立于1997年2月25日,注册股本15000万股,公司主要从事黑色金属矿产资源的采选业务。历经十余年的发展历程,公司已成为新疆区域铁矿石采选行业具影响力的中型矿山企业。

大明人始终以“推动行业技术进步,创建本质安全矿山”为指导思想,以矿山资源配置效率最优为经营原则,专注于采矿技术能力进步,在矿山生产中积极推进机械化、数字化、信息化技术的应用,实现了地下矿山生产组织模式的创新和本质安全的采掘环境创建。

大明公司天湖铁矿目前已实现井下关键生产环节的全机械化作业,大大提高生产效率的同时也保证了安全生产。数字化技术的应用提高了设计精度、生产计划的准确性,为高效的生产组织提供保障。辅以信息化手段,使矿山生产在工艺设计、计划安排、生产组织及职能管理等方面实现高效衔接,公司天湖铁矿初具现代化矿山的雏形并成为区域内矿产资源采掘行业的安全标准化、信息化建设的标杆企业。大明作为矿产资源转化效率最佳的探寻者和实践者,始终以引领行业生产方式变革、技术进步为己任。

经过多年的奋斗公司也获得了政府和社会的认可。近年先后获得自治区及中国管理科学研究院等单位授予的“安全生产先进单位”、“纳税先进企业”、“诚信纳税户”、“诚信企业”、“AAA”级诚信单位、“第一批两化融合示范单位”、“节水型企业”、“诚信中国示范单位”、“环境保护优秀企业”、“推动行业进步贡献企业”、“全国质量、服务、信用AAA级企业”、“中国优秀创新企业”、“成长型企业”、“信息化建设先进单位”等荣誉称号。

天湖环境规划效果图

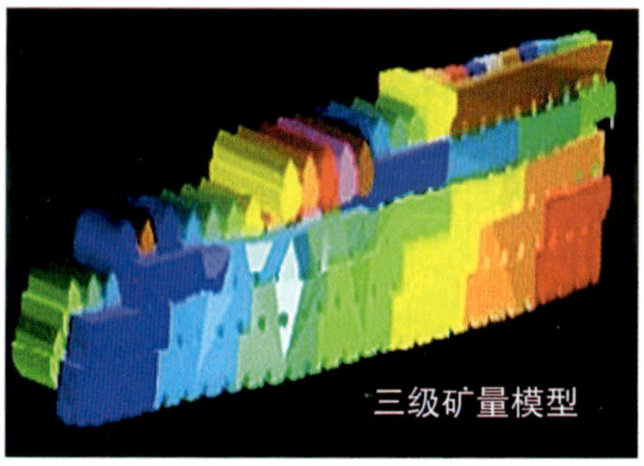
三级矿量模型

井下大巷

1254 钻机作业现场

凿岩台车作业现场

红云红河烟草(集团)有限责任公司新疆卷烟厂

自治区党委书记张春贤视察新烟易地技改项目

易地技改奠基仪式

红云红河烟草(集团)有限责任公司新疆卷烟厂始建于1960年,坐落于新疆伊犁哈萨克自治州奎屯市,是新疆唯一的卷烟生产企业。1986年上划国家烟草专卖局,1999年10月加入将军烟草集团有限责任公司,2005年12月加入红河卷烟总厂,2008年11月红云红河烟草(集团)有限责任公司成立,企业有幸成为集团一员。

企业建成花园式工厂,固定资产12.65亿元,技术装备已达国内烟草行业先进水平。2011年企业年产卷烟32万箱,实现税利首次突破20亿元大关,近10年,新疆卷烟厂已累计为国家创造税利71.9亿元。

新疆卷烟厂拥有"云烟"、"红河"、"雪莲"系列品牌卷烟。"雪莲"牌卷烟是新疆"名牌产品",深受广大消费者青睐,也是国家烟草专卖局百牌号之一。新疆卷烟厂是自治区30家重点扶优扶强工业企业之一,2001年通过ISO9000质量管理体系、2006年通过ISO14000环境管理体系、OHSAS18000职业健康安全管理体系"三标"管理体系认证。新疆卷烟厂是国家AAAA级标准化良好行为企业,员工住宅小区是国家物业管理示范小区。2005年、2009年、2012年企业三创全国文明单位,成为全国文明标兵单位。

2010年,企业经国家局批准投资15亿元在乌鲁木齐市启动50万箱易地技术改造项目,计划2012年年底投产。它的建设对企业长远发展具有重要战略意义,将为国家和新疆维吾尔自治区的经济建设与长治久安做出重要贡献。

制丝生产线

卷包生产线

红云红河集团新疆卷烟厂

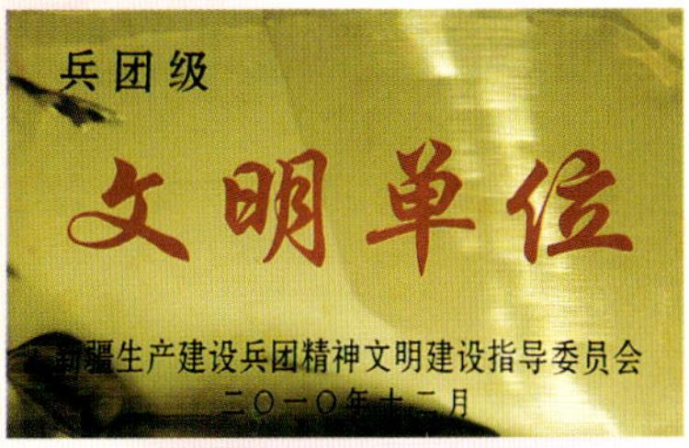

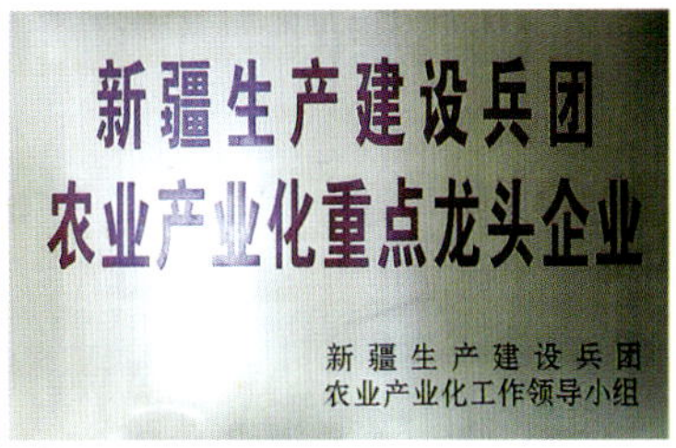

新疆昆仑神农股份有限公司

自治区党委书记张春贤视察昆神公司

中央政治局委员广东省委书记汪洋、自治区主席努尔·白克力在昆神公司视察指导工作

兵团政委车俊在昆神公司视察指导工作

公司党委领导班子

新疆昆仑神农股份有限公司是南疆喀什、克州、和田三地州首家拟上市公司，目前以甘草人工种植、野生甘草管护、甘草系列制品生产经营及沙生特色中草药资源科技开发为主业，兼营农用地膜的生产销售。是集农、科、工、商、贸为一体的新疆兵团新型工业化企业和农业产业化重点龙头企业。截至2011年末，公司资产总额达32140万元，净资产20729万元，年销售收入14608万元，年实现利税2779万元，年职均收入3.85万元。

公司主营业务甘草产业经过五年的发展，产品种类由2个扩增至9个系列23个品种，是行业内规模最大、品种最全、质量优良、装备先进、科技含量较高的甘草深加工企业。公司生产的甘草制品，以其独特的形、色、质、气、味等优良品质享誉畅销国内外市场，市场占有率30%以上。公司在做大规模的同时，不断增强甘草资源的管控能力，野生甘草管护面积已达36万亩，人工甘草种植保有面积已达3万亩；已全面掌握了列入国家药典的乌拉尔甘草、胀果甘草、光果甘草的人工种植管护及机械采挖技术，各项指标均居国内同行业先进水平。

公司以“卓越管理”模式提升核心竞争力，追求产品企业标准的国际化，实现跻身甘草行业内一流企业的目标。公司近年来荣获“新疆名牌产品”、“最具商业商品奖”、“新产品开发奖”、“新疆最具成长力三十强企业”、“中国行业领先十大品牌”、“中国食品安全示范单位”、“兵团级农业产业化重点龙头企业”及兵团级“文明单位”和兵团级“四好”领导班子称号。

“死亡之海”创造人间奇迹

SDIC 国投新疆罗布泊钾盐有限责任公司

党委书记、总经理　李浩

国投新疆罗布泊钾盐有限责任公司（以下简称国投罗钾）成立于2000年9月，2004年成为中国最大的投资控股公司——国家开发投资公司的控股企业，注册资金5.4亿元人民币，以开发罗布泊天然卤水资源制取硫酸钾为主业。

国投罗钾公司成立11年来，以总经理李浩为核心的经营班子带领和团结全体员工，以世人惊叹的速度，在环境极端恶劣的罗布泊腹地开发出了国内外独一无二的、拥有完全自主知识产权的“罗布泊硫酸镁亚型卤水制取硫酸钾”工艺技术，并建成了世界上最大的硫酸钾生产项目——年产120万吨硫酸钾项目。被列为国家“十一五”重点建设项目，总投资48亿元，2004年4月开工建设，2008年11月正式投产，2011年达产，达到年产130万吨硫酸钾的生产能力。新疆自治区党委张春贤书记评价罗钾公司“在死亡之海创造了人间奇迹”。

目前，国投罗钾公司硫酸钾产量已位居世界首列，成为名副其实的世界硫酸钾航母。公司年产300万吨钾肥项目二期工程2011年启动，计划2015年投产，建成后达到年产300万吨钾肥的能力，为保障我国钾肥供应，保证粮食生产安全，推进新疆经济社会发展做出更大贡献。

地理位置：罗布泊盐湖位于新疆维吾尔自治区巴音郭楞蒙古自治州境内，塔里木盆地东部，其行政区划属若羌县罗布泊镇管辖。盐湖南北长115公里，东西宽90公里，面积10350平方公里，是世界上最大的干盐湖之一。

年产300万吨钾肥项目二期开工仪式

公司篮球队获得京唐港杯国投集团第三届男子篮球赛冠军

《罗钾之魂》获得中组部优秀作品奖

盐田鸟瞰图

公司自主研发的采盐船

硫酸钾包装车间

自治区党委书记张春贤在公司视察

自治区党委书记、自治区人民政府主席努尔·白克力视察公司

国家开发公司董事长王会生视察公司

公司硫酸钾生产及基地位于罗布泊盐湖罗中区，东北距哈密市410公里，西距库尔勒542公里，东距敦煌市340公里，北距鄯善380公里，西距若羌县城330公里。公司的后勤办公基地、仓储基地设在哈密市。

气候特点：罗布泊地区属典型的大陆性干旱气候，降水量少，蒸发量大，昼夜温差大，冬季长达半年之久，日照时间长，太阳辐射强，风多风大，尤其3–5月，6级以上大风经常出现，沙尘暴天气时有发生。湖区年降水量38.5毫米，年蒸发量达3776.5毫米，属强烈蒸发区。年平均气温13.4，6–8月为高温季节，最高温度为48℃，11月至次年3月为寒冷季节。

2010年，国投罗钾公司共生产硫酸钾成品83.91万吨，销售硫酸钾80.92万吨，实现主营业务收入18.45亿元（不含税），国内硫酸钾的市场占有率从2009年的60%提升到70%。

2011年国投罗钾公司共生产硫酸钾成品132万吨，销售硫酸钾110万吨，实现主营业务收入32亿元（不含税）。

自罗钾公司发展伊始，共产党员就发挥模范带头和战斗堡垒作用，形成了一支敢打硬仗，勇于奉献、无私进取的党员先锋队伍，在亘古荒原罗布泊竖起党的旗帜。目前公司党员人数达到242人，积极向党组织靠拢的员工已达300多人。2005年，自治区党委任命李浩总经理为公司党委书记。李浩总经理先后当选为自治区第七、第八次党代表。

2011年国投王会生董事长为公司题词，并在各种场合多次宣扬"罗钾精神"，对公司给予高度评价。2011年，公司以迎接建党90周年为契机，组织各基层党支部开展了丰富多彩的纪念活动，并制作了创先争优活动专题片--《罗钾之魂》。该片获得2011年中组部优秀党员教育片"最佳作品"，成功入选《全国党员教育电视片观摩交流活动优秀作品集萃》，面向全国各级党组织发放观摩。国家开发投资公司王会生董事长亲笔批示，号召国投各级党组织、成员企业组织学习收看，以更加饱满的激情，为国投公司二次创业，为党的十八大贡献力量。

罗布泊环境极端恶劣，与世隔绝。公司成立以来，罗钾人战风沙、斗酷暑，克服重重难以想象的困难，终于在罗布泊腹地实现了路通、水通、电通，建成了世界最大的硫酸钾生产基地。

公司还举办各种文体活动，丰富员工业余文化生活。组建了合唱团，参加哈密地区建党90周年红歌赛获得优异成绩；公司篮球队获得了"京唐港杯"国投集团第三届男子篮球邀请赛冠军、哈密地区2010年、2011年"体彩杯"男子甲级联赛冠军。公司还组织了各类安全生产宣传活动，营造良好的安全生产环境，2010年国家安监总局授予公司全国非煤矿山强基固本"五个一百"示范单位；2011年公司荣获全国"安全生产月活动优秀单位"荣誉称号，企业安全标准化二级达标通过自治区安全协会现场验收。还积极组织员工参加哈密地区首届技能大赛，公司获得"优秀组织奖"，参赛员工全部获奖。

坚持创新是国投罗钾的优良传统，始终坚持"澎湃的研发动力是本公司的核心竞争力之一"这一理念。2001年国投罗钾公司成立了企业技术中心，并获得自治区级"企业技术中心"认定资格，聚集了一批国内从事钾盐开发的专家和技术人才、管理人才，中心还建有设施齐全的试验盐田和中间试车间，研发条件优越，学术氛围浓厚，具有雄厚的自主研发实力。

罗布泊硫酸钾生产基地全景

自治区党委书记张春贤（右）在乌鲁木齐亲切会见山东能源董事长、总经理卜昌森

自治区党委书记张春贤（右）在乌鲁木齐亲切会见山东能源副董事长、新矿集团董事长、党委书记李希勇

山东能源新汶矿业集团伊犁能源公司

新汶矿业集团副总经理、伊犁能源公司董事长　张开顺

新汶矿业集团总经理助理、伊犁能源公司党委书记　陈宝良

新汶矿业集团伊犁能源公司总经理（法定代表人）　王贯东

山东能源是省属特大型企业集团，由新矿集团等六家企业组成，横跨山东，新疆、内蒙、贵州、陕西、山西等12个省区。2011年，销售收入1560亿元，实现利润172亿元，成为全国煤炭亿吨俱乐部的重要成员，位列世界500强第460位。新矿集团伊犁能源是山东能源新矿集团的全资子公司，全面负责在疆煤炭资源开发、转化项目建设。

新矿集团伊犁矿区煤田分布在伊犁河南北两岸，由伊南、伊北两个煤田组成。伊南煤田位于察布查尔县南部，面积338km²；伊北煤田位于霍城县东南部，伊宁市北部及伊宁县境内，面积141km²。煤种以长焰煤、不粘煤为主，低灰、特低硫、中高发热量，挥发份高、化学活性强，是动力、气化、液化优质原料。

按照“力争用5-10年时间将伊犁打造成为世界一流、国内领先的煤化工基地，成为国内重要的能源供应基地，成为支撑区域跨越式发展的重要经济增长极”的战略定位，“十二五”时期是伊犁伊宁矿区快速建设、跨越发展的关键阶段。我们将以科学发展观为指导，以转变经济发展方式为总抓手，以优化调整产业结构为着力点，以“世界一流、国内领先”为总体目标，始终坚持“资源开发可持续、生态环境可持续”发展理念，2011——2015，分三步走，规划五年内完成投资1063.38亿元，到2015年煤炭产能达到4560万吨，煤制天然气产能达到40亿m³/年，建成伊南180万吨甲醇转60万吨烯烃项目，机械加工能力达到3000台件，商贸物流产值达到40亿元，产值收入1200亿元，实现利税260亿元。

建设“国际一流、国内领先”的伊犁煤化工基地是新矿集团伊犁能源的不懈追求。我们决心坚定目标，加快推进，全力把伊犁矿区打造成科技含量高、生态环境好、资源消耗低、核心竞争力强的经济体、拉动区域经济发展的重要增长极，成为国际能源化工产业发展的重要一翼，以实际行动和实绩回报国家、回报社会、回报伊犁各族人民，为打造天山北坡的经济强区、中心城市和向西开放的桥头堡，为伊犁跨越式发展和长治久安做出新的更大贡献！

伊犁能源60万吨煤基烯烃项目开工仪式

伊犁能源年产20亿立方米煤制天然气项目地面建设现场

矿井单轨吊运输

标准化的矿井大巷

自治区党委书记张春贤与公司董事长、全国劳动模范李延杰同志亲切握手

巴音郭楞蒙古自治州州委书记彭家瑞一行莅临公司

新疆泰昌实业有限责任公司

董事长　李延杰

丰富的职工文化生活

新疆泰昌实业有限责任公司位于新疆巴音郭楞蒙古自治州库尔勒经济技术开发区，始建于1994年，现有资产总额15亿元，拥有15万锭综合规模的棉纺厂、年产15万吨的棉浆粕厂、3.1万千瓦时的余热发电厂、15万吨/年加工能力的棉籽脱绒厂。其全资的巴州泰昌农业有限公司规模为10万亩棉花种植基地、年加工能力为5万吨的两座轧花厂及种业公司一个，控股的新疆新沛新材料科技有限公司，是集贸、工、农、科为一体的大型棉花产业化经营企业，既是自治区农业产业化重点龙头企业，也是自治区重点支持的“30户民营企业”之一，以泰昌公司为主导开发建设的西尼尔工业园区先后荣获国家农业部“全国乡镇企业东西合作示范区、全国乡镇企业科技园区”等称号。公司现有员工1750余人，其中管理员工252人；技术员工380人；普通员工1118人。

公司主营产品有“LOULAN(楼兰)牌”7支-200支精、普梳纯棉单纱、股线和10支-40支OE纱及棉浆粕，其中“LOULAN(楼兰)”牌纯棉纱曾多次荣获国家农业部和自治区授予的“名

产品荣誉证书

牌产品"称号。公司棉纱产品主要销往华东和华南、香港等地区的一些知名纺织企业和上市公司,并通过香港向韩国、日本、美国、东南亚等国家和地区做转口贸易,产品深受客户信赖。棉浆粕产品主要销往河南、河北、四川、浙江、江苏、湖北等地,产品质量信誉上乘,销售率100%。

多年来,泰昌公司始终坚持"棉花优势资源转换战略",致力于企业做大、做强、做优、做精,为振兴地方经济、带动农民增收致富、推进社会主义新农村建设以及构建和谐社会做出了应有的贡献。先后荣获国家农业部授予的"全国乡镇企业质量工作先进单位"、"全国新农村建设百强示范企业"、"全国壮大县域经济突出贡献乡镇企业""推进自治区新型工业化进程先进乡镇企业"、"自治区守合同、重信用企业"、"自治区节能减排先进单位"等荣誉称号。

秉承"求实、创新、诚信、高效"之经营理念,在未来发展的道路上泰昌公司一直坚持并努力着。

浆粕五万吨生产车间

热电厂主控室

棉纺厂生产车间

棉纺生产车间

新疆伊珠葡萄酒有限公司

新疆伊珠葡萄酒有限公司，原名新疆伊犁葡萄酒厂，国有独资企业，隶属新疆兵团农四师七十团。是新疆伊犁哈萨克自治州最早生产葡萄酒系列产品的厂家，也是自治区和兵团最早生产干葡萄酒、冰葡萄酒的重点企业之一。六十年代初开始种植各种酿酒葡萄，1964年建厂开始酿造葡萄酒，1984年扩建。

厂区北距伊宁市24公里，紧靠218国道，位于伊宁县境内，年有效积温3178℃-4100℃，日照2820小时，地理坐标：北纬43°49'-43°53'与世界生产葡萄酒的法国波尔多地区，生产冰酒的加拿大安大略省纬度基本相一致。这里光照充足，昼夜温差大，土壤有机含量高，是我国种植酿酒葡萄和冰葡萄的最佳产区。

20世纪六十年代末，企业先后引进十余种世界优质酿酒葡萄品种：雷司令、晚红蜜、赤霞珠、品丽珠、梅鹿辄、蛇龙珠、法国兰等，现已发展优质无污染葡萄基地6000余亩，近期计划将葡萄基地发展到一万亩。公司设有原料部，负责葡萄基地的管理和对种植户的技术指导，

经过四十多年的发展，现厂区占地4万平方米，年生产各种葡萄酒3500吨，现有员工83人。产品主要有“伊珠”冰酒、干酒、甜酒、饮料四大系列51个品种。目前，公司自主研发设计的伊珠15.5度、12度冰酒、伊珠2001、2003世纪干红、伊珠桃红、纯红葡萄酒，伊珠葡萄庄园酒7款瓶贴外观设计获得国家专利。

原兵团司令员华士飞来公司参观指导工作

澳大利亚旺马库钠瓦拉萄萄酒业总裁来厂参观考察

投资 600 多万元新建不锈钢发酵罐

欧亚博览会上，伊珠冰酒引起外国客商浓厚兴趣

采收冰葡萄

公司新一届领导班子检查生产现场

公司员工包装干葡萄酒生产现场

公司近几年投资引进了法国、意大利先进葡萄酒生产设备，加大科技投入和技术创新力度，不断提高产品品质。2004 年在厂技术人员的努力下，成功研发出了高档冰红、冰白葡萄酒，达到国内先进技术水平，填补了新疆自治区空白。

公司产品以其选料精良、浓香悦人、绵甜爽口、风味独特而畅销天山南北，并远销北京、上海、广州、福建、江苏、浙江、甘肃兰州、陕西西安、苏州、湖南、四川、深圳等十余个省市。多次获国家、自治区荣誉，2006 年 2 月新疆伊珠葡萄酒有限公司被中国特产之乡推荐暨宣传活动组织委员会定为“中国冰葡萄酒之乡”，2006 年 4 月“伊珠冰红、冰白葡萄酒”同获第二届亚洲葡萄酒质量大赛金奖，2006 年 9 月冰葡萄酒产业化开发被国家科学技术部星火计划办公室列入星火计划项目。2006 年 10 月荣获“新疆特色产品(上海)交易会最佳畅销产品奖”，2007 年 9 月，“伊珠”冰红、冰白葡萄酒被授予“新疆名牌产品”称号。2008 年 7 月“伊珠”品牌被自治区命名为“新疆著名商标”。为纪念改革开放 30 周年，公司被国家农业部乡镇企业局授予“全国优秀乡镇企业开拓创新奖”，2009 年“伊珠”干红葡萄酒荣获新疆名牌产品，同时干酒和冰酒通过了有机食品转换认证。2010 年，“伊珠”精制干红葡萄酒在烟台国际葡萄酒质量大赛上，从来自世界各地的 180 多款葡萄酒中脱颖而出，荣获银奖。2011 年伊珠冰酒获新疆名牌产品称号。

和田市给排水公司

地委书记闫汾新、市委书记钟伯利等地市领导了解生产经营情况

经理　张　嘹

办公楼落成典礼

城市供排水工作是城市的生命线，我们始终以抓安全供水、保稳定、促发展，促进城市工业化建设步伐，理念不动摇，两水厂运行人员一年 365 天，放弃节假日和亲人团聚的机会，带上冰凉的便餐，默默无闻地职守在工作一线。特别是在 6 月至 8 月份供水高峰期间，能合理调配出厂水压力，没有因为高峰期用水量增加而影响各族人民的生活和工作，在全体干部职工辛勤工作，部门之间相互协作和较好的配合下，如期完成了公司每年初制定的供水售水生产工作指标。2011 年实际完成供水量 1340 万立方米，售水量 1187 万立方米，与去年同期相比各增加 23%和 17%，漏损率为 10%，管网水压合格率保持在 98%，供水设备完好率为 98%，全年安装各类供水管网 4817 米，排水管网 9268 米，新增用户 300 户，实现总收入 1338 万元，比去年同期增长 169 万元，实现工业增加值 890 万元，上缴各项税金 100 多万元。

2011 年市政府 16 件惠民工程，都是民心工程，尽管十六件实事，直接没有分解给我公司，但我们深知十六件实事的 90%需要我们协助才能完成，这是我们义不容辞的责任。为了解决居民和北京棚户区、南苑小区，园区廉租房，四条道路改造，火车站等地生活生产供排水问题。一年来，在时间紧、任务重、资金紧张的情况下，公司主要领导经常身处工地现场，处理安装和维修工作中的技术难题和安全隐患，紧张时带领全公司干部职工参加劳动，有个别部门职工，战严寒、斗酷暑，迎风沙，风餐露宿，经常加班加点，配合相关单位按时保质保量完成了各项安装任务和和田市惠民工程的施工和工程建设进度。

供水工程：2009 年 9 月 28 日，经自治区发改委已(新发改项目【2009】238 号)批复了和田市供水管网改扩建工程项目初步设计和招标方案，批复总投资 965.14 万元，新建管网总长度 14100 米，公司周密组织，精心管理，有力地促进了施工进度和工程质量，全年已完成玫瑰大道和加买路 5700 米；北京路延伸 200 米，塔乃依路 1000 米，计划 2012 年 8 月建成并投入运行。和田市供水管网改扩建二期工程项目的建设，将极大的缓解和改善建城区部分路段水压不足的局面，给城区各族人民的生活和工作提供了极大的方便。

排水工程：2009 年 6 月 29 日，经自治区发改委以(新发改项目【2009】1371 号)批复了“和田市排水改扩建二期工程初步设计批复”，总投资 9374.44 万元。占地面积为 185 亩；新建二级污水处理厂一座(工艺采用旋流沉沙池和 A2/O SBR 法处理工艺)和配套建筑以及排水管道 12.7 公里。污水处理厂的建设分近期、远期两期进行，建设规模：近期(2012 年)5 万吨 / 日，远期(2025 年)达到 10 万吨 / 日的污水处理规模。工程建设于 2011 年 7 月开工，截止去年底已完成厂区临时设施建设，地基处理、打降水大口井 85 眼、1650 米围墙、配电房、风机房、二座污水池、污泥压滤房、警卫室等工建工程和厂区内道路基础等工作，计划到 2013 年建成并投入试运行。和田市排水改扩建二期工程项目的建设将极大的改善城区周边卫生环境，提高人民生活健康和水平，将对和田市的发展提供有利的外部环境，是造福子孙后代的民心工程。

慰问一线职工

水质分析

拔河比赛

哈密信合棉业有限公司
哈密双银棉业有限责任公司

中储棉领导在董事长陈淑静陪同下视察棉花储备仓库

董事长　陈淑静

哈密信合棉业有限公司成立于2003年，注册资金1513.6万元，2010年公司成功收购哈密双银棉业有限责任公司，哈密双银棉业有限责任公司注册资金7500万元，信合、双银棉业公司拥有纺纱厂一座、400型轧花厂三座、棉花收购站十座，农资经销站十座。现有员工300余人，公司主要经营：棉花收购、加工、纺织、农资销售、种子销售等，公司现已拥有注册商标"信合"牌棉花、"双银"牌棉花、"银信"牌棉花专用滴溉肥、"银信"牌水溶性二胺、"银信"牌水溶性钾肥。

公司成立以来牢固树立"小信诚，大信立"的理念，诚实守信，精诚合作，并形成一套行之有效的管理模式。在棉花种植环节：我公司大力支持农户，协助农户解决种植困难；在棉花收购环节：我公司遵循公平公正的原则与农户互惠互利；在产品加工环节：我公司严把质量关，棉花质量已被客户认可为免检产品，我公司棉花加工质量经纤检部门公检结果统计后居哈密地区首位，公司生产的毛巾纱和皮棉均申请了"信合牌"注册商标。我公司视信用为生命，棉花产品质量得到广大客户的认可，因此在经营过程中拥有固定的纺织企业客户。在企业诚信经营方面，我公司已建立了良好的信用体系，2010年我公司被自治区银行业协会评为"2008-2009年信贷诚信客户"；2011年我公司被农发行评为信用等级AA级企业；2011年被农十三师评为"规范农民管理先进单位"；2012年5月被自治区民宗委指定为"自治区民族贸易企业"。我公司以开拓创新，与时俱进为发展思路，主动迎合市场需求，以良好的信誉，热情的服务，不断提升企业的综合实力，开拓更为广阔的发展空间。

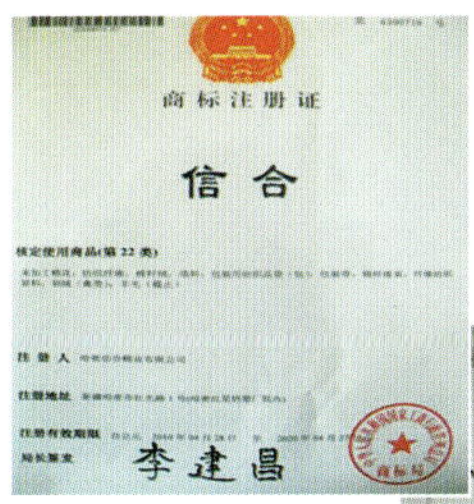

生产车间

原棉仓库

爱国主义教育活动

伊犁肖尔布拉克酒业有限责任公司

全国政协常委邱衍汉调研

国家环保局领导莅临检查

自治区副主席艾尔肯·吐尼亚孜参观指导

国家安监总局领导参观

伊犁州党委书记李学军前来参观指导

伊犁肖尔布拉克酒业有限责任公司坐落于著名的新疆酒乡——伊犁新源县肖尔布拉克镇。公司占地面积300多亩，建筑面积18万平方米，有固定资产7800万元，流动资产4800万元，总资产达2亿元。公司现拥有两个白酒生产基地，年产优质白酒1万吨。在兰州、西安、杭州、天津等地设有销售公司，在全国多个省设有办事处，产品远销内地十多个省市，2001年通过“ISO9001国际质量体系”认证，2010年8月通过国家AAA级标准化管理体系认证。目前已初步形成了品牌价值达亿元的集白酒生产、销售、生态工业旅游为一体的集团公司。

多年来，公司通过诚信经营，依法纳税，认真履行合同，维护合作商和消费者的合法利益，使企业得到了健康快速的发展，各项工作得到了各级领导的认可，相继荣获“新疆名牌产品”、“伊犁州纳税先进企业”、“伊犁州优秀基层党组织”、“自治区消费诚信单位”、“自治区农业产业化重点龙头企业”、“自治区守合同重信用企业”、“中国白酒工业百强企业”，“中国十大最具增长潜力品牌”、“国家级守合同重信用企业”、“国家级工业旅游示范点”、“国家AAA级旅游景区”等几十项荣誉。

从2003年起，肖尔布拉克酒业把生产开发“有机、绿色、生态、健康”的高端产品，作为企业的研究课题和发展方向。并于2004年引进贵州茅台酒酿造技术，投资上千万元，建成一座年产量200吨的酱香型白酒酿造车间。被中国酿酒工业协会白酒分会技术委员会认定为“新疆酱香第一坊”。产品经过五年的贮存，于2010年9月1日在乌洽会展出亮相，受到了社会各界的高度关注。肖尔布拉克酱香型白酒的成功研制，填补了新疆无酱香型白酒生产的历史空白。创建了新疆白酒工业史上第一个酿造酱香型白酒的企业，从此，新疆有了第一款能代表新疆酿酒新水平的高品质酱香型白酒。

2006年，投资1200万元建立了全疆乃至全国唯一一座综合反映西域酒文化的博物馆和全疆最大规模的产业文化博物馆。

2007年以酿酒、包装、制曲等生产车间及西域酒文化博物馆为核心的肖尔布拉克酒业工业旅游园区，被国家旅游局评选为“全国工业旅游示范点”，这也是迄今为止伊犁州唯一的一家。

世界唯一　古海温泉

五彩湾古海温泉旅游度假区

冬日泡温泉

客房休闲区

露天标准泳池

五彩湾古海温泉旅游度假区，地处浩瀚神秘的古尔班通古特沙漠，卡拉麦里自然保护区内，紧邻216国道，是通往喀纳斯景区的黄金线路及一个重要的游客集散地和中转站。国家AAA级景区，景区内设有三星级酒店，是在2001年由西域旅游开发有限公司投资兴建的，度假区有五栋豪华别墅、32间标准间、可同时容纳200人就餐的清真餐厅及可容纳100人的特色餐饮区，是集温泉疗养、住宿、用餐、沙漠旅游探险等旅游项目为一体的多功能旅游度假区。

景区周边有著名的神话般的五彩城雅丹地貌、恐龙沟、硅化木园、将军戈壁、石钱滩等自然景观，和唐代北庭都护府遗址、千佛洞、西大寺、车师古道等人文历史景观。距景区18公里处的玛瑙滩是探寻奇珍异石的宝地，让您在徒步拓展的途中发现意想不到的收获。3公里处还设有野生动物观赏点可近距离观赏到野驴、鹅喉羚、野狼等珍稀野生动物。在往返途中还可观赏到比大熊猫更为珍惜的普氏野马。

古海温泉是在1982年由新疆石油管理局在勘测石油时发现的，井深2200米；经中科院新疆水质鉴定分析确定，此水为7.7亿年前古海相沉积水，出水温度高达75度，具有高渗透、高温、自喷等特性，水中富含硫化氢、钙、溴、锂、锶、[illegible]等26种矿物质，是世界罕见全亚洲唯一的沙漠温泉和古海水温泉；经事实证明古海温泉浴疗能够扩张血管、促进血液循环、增进新陈代谢，对神经系统功能障碍、肌肉偏瘫、动脉硬化、半身不遂、关节炎、痛风、风湿、肩周炎、皮肤病有显著的疗效。

古海温泉景区是一个四季开放的经营性景区，是四季有着不同特色的景区。每当夏夜夜幕来临之际，满目繁星；景区内灯火阑珊，歌舞升平，恍如世外桃源；冬日时分，当大地掩裹在冰天雪地时，温泉泡池烟雾缭绕，温暖如春，让您在严寒的冬日享受到来自地心的温暖。

随着天池至喀纳斯(216)线的逐渐火热，以吉木萨尔县为首的昌吉东部旅游环线的兴起、准东经济技术开发区的崛起，游客量每年都以30%的速度递增，游客量由2005年不足1万人次，递增为2011年的8万人次的成熟景区。2009年，昌吉州人民政府直接关怀指导并明确提出：加快古海温泉景区的二期建设，努力打造成为"以亚洲唯一、世界罕见"的古海水为核心的集休闲、理疗、会议拓展、科普为一体的综合性旅游景区。

网　　址：http://www.wucaiwan.com.cn

服务热线：0994-6928222　0991-8887607

残疾人联谊会

冬泳节

歌舞晚会